The Person

An Introduction to Personality Psychology

Second Edition

Dan P. McAdams
Northwestern University

Harcourt Brace College Publishers

Fort Worth Philadelphia San Diego New York Orlando Austin
San Antonio Toronto Montreal London Sydney Tokyo

To the Memory of Henry A. Murray (1893–1988)

Publisher	Ted Buchholz
Acquisitions Editor	Eve Howard
Editorial Assistant	Betsy Cummings
Project Editor	Annelies Schlickenrieder
Production Manager	Cindy Young
Art Director	Jim Dodson
Cover Art	Pam-Ela Harrelson
Picture Editor	Sue Howard

ISBN: 0-15-501274-6

Library of Congress Catalog Card Number: 93-78992

Address for Editorial Correspondence:
Harcourt Brace College Publishers
301 Commerce Street, Suite 3700, Fort Worth, Texas 76102

Address for Orders:
Harcourt Brace & Company
6277 Sea Harbor Drive, Orlando, Florida 32887
1-800-782-4479, or 1-800-433-0001 (in Florida)

Printed in the United States of America

7 8 9 0 1 2   0 3 9   9 8 7 6

Preface

There is nothing more interesting to persons than persons. And there is nothing more important. Personality psychology is first and foremost the scientific study of the person. Over 50 years ago, both Gordon Allport and Henry Murray challenged psychologists to put the person at the center of their investigations—to take the individual human being as the scientific unit of analysis. Since then, personality psychology has developed in many directions and has extended through many phases. In the late 1960s and '70s, when many questioned the scientific need for a study of the person, the discipline lost some of its early favor. But today, in the middle of the 1990s, personality psychology is more vital than ever. My goal in this book is to impart some of that vitality, to talk to you about the best and the brightest in theory and research that personality psychology has to offer.

The success of this text's first edition was due largely to (1) its unswerving focus on *the person* as an integrative theme in personality psychology, (2) its innovative organization of classical and contemporary approaches to persons around four central metaphors or goals (intrapsychic mysteries, interaction episodes, interpretive structures, and interpersonal stories), and (3) its engaging, literary style. The second edition builds on these strengths. I have sharpened even more the focus on the person. With some clarifying modifications, I have retained the innovative organizational scheme. And I have continued to try to engage, as well as challenge, my reader by framing issues in the most humanly relevant terms and drawing frequently, as I did before, on literature, biography, mythology, folklore, and other social sciences to illustrate points and to elaborate perspectives.

When I began the second edition, I figured I would make some minor changes and updates and do a little reorganizing. I am amazed now at how wrong I was! Because I received some tremendously helpful feedback on the first edition and because my thinking and the field of personality psychology have both evolved in the past few years, I found myself undertaking a major revision—as exciting and involving as writing the book the first time, but more exhausting and time consuming than I ever imagined. The end result is a second edition that is clearer, more tightly organized, and easier to assimilate than its predecessor. Every chapter has been updated and rewritten, many extensively so. Theorists have been regrouped in ways that are more familiar to most readers. And each of the book's four major sections has been revamped to make a clearer and, I think, more convincing case for why I present material in the way I do.

Those familiar with the first edition will notice many significant changes. Under "Intrapsychic Mysteries," I have now grouped Freud and Jung together in a long opening chapter (Chapter 2) that also includes a host of other psychodynamically oriented theories (Horney, Fromm, object-relations, ego psychology, Kohut), each presented in historical context. I have brought together material on the psychoanalytic case study and psychoanalytic research, previously scattered throughout the book, into a single, integrative chapter on "discovery and proof " in psychoanalysis. I have expanded considerably my treatment of sociobiology and evolutionary personality psychology, in accord with the rising influence of these approaches, and I have highlighted Bowlby and Ainsworth's seminal work on mother–infant attachment, as an example of personality/developmental psychology from an evolutionary point of view. With the wide acceptance of the Big Five model of personality traits, trait psychology has never been stronger than it is today, warranting the expanded coverage I have given to traits in this second edition. In the domain of cognitive personality psychology, new approaches emphasizing life tasks and strivings, self-determination, and the situated nature of purposive human behavior have gained considerable currency in the past few years, and I now feature these more prominently.

In addition, the last few years have witnessed an upsurge of creative theorizing and discussion concerning the role of stories and story making in personality. My fourth large section on "Interpersonal Stories," therefore, has been completely revamped to describe a number of very new approaches focusing on life narratives and to make clearer why theorists such as Henry Murray, Erik Erikson, Alfred Adler, and Silvan Tomkins belong together as classic contributors to the psychology of interpersonal stories. The key to understanding this is to realize, as I do more clearly now than I did before, the way in which each of these theorists focuses on the human life *situated in time*. Lives over time are made sensible through stories, narratives that provide beginnings, middles, and endings to explain "what leads to what," where it all came from "in the beginning," and how it all will "turn out" in "the end."

At the end of this writing odyssey, I am happy with the way this second edition has turned out. I am also extremely thankful to those who have contributed to the second edition. In particular, I would like to thank Richard Ryan, Randy Larson, Laura King, and Elaine Donelson for their thoughtful, painstaking, and sometimes brutal critiques of the first edition and my prospectus for this one. I trust that they were paid well for their efforts. Todd Heatherton and Carolin Showers provided invaluable advice in their reviews of the first edition, published in *Contemporary Psychology*. I would like to thank Eve Howard, my editor, for encouraging me to stay with this project, even when it mushroomed beyond what I thought I could handle. And I am still indebted to the editor of my first edition, Marcus Boggs, for his guidance, support, and friendship. My wife, Rebecca Pallmeyer, has given me unconditional support from beginning to end. Over the past couple of years, I have had many conversations with many people about personality psychology, and many of those have influenced my writing of the second edition. I cannot remember everybody to thank. Those who stand out in my mind for their helpful suggestions, however, include Irv Alexander, Michael Apter, Jack Block, Rae Carlson, Paul Costa, Keith Davis, Rodney Day, Ed de St. Aubin, Bob Emmons, David Funder, Harrison Gough, Gunhild Hagestad, Ravenna Helson, Hubert Hermans, Oliver John, Jane Loevinger, Jeff McCrae, Dan Ogilvie, Bill Revelle, Mac Runyan, Jeff Singer, M. Brewster Smith, Abby Stewart, Avril Thorne, Joel Weinberger, Dave Winter, Barbara Woike, and Peter Zeldow.

—Dan P. McAdams

Table of Contents

Preface iii

Introduction   1

Chapter 1   Studying the Person   2

Introduction..3
Two Lives 4
    Yukio Mishima: Novelist 4
    Margaret Mead: Anthropologist 7
Four Perspectives on the Person 10
    Intrapsychic Mysteries: Mishima...10
    Interaction Episodes: Mead 13
    Interpretive Structures: Mishima 17
    Interpersonal Stories: Mead 19
    Creativity and the Four Approaches to the Person 22
Science and the Person 27
    Feature 1.A: Joseph Kidd: An Ordinary Guy 30
    Step 1: Unsystematic Observation 32
    Step 2: Building Theories 34
    Step 3: Evaluating Propositions 36
        Setting Up an Empirical Study 37
        The Correlational Design 39
        The Experimental Design 41
Personality Psychology 43
Summary 46

Part I   Intrapsychic Mysteries
Unconscious Determinants in the Person's Life   49

Chapter 2   Psychoanalytic Tradition
           An Overview   51

Introduction 52
Sigmund Freud and the Origins of Psychoanalysis: A Life Story 53
    The Setting 53
        The Romantic Struggle 54
        Science, Reason, and Morality 55
        The Great War 57
    The Characters 57
        The Mother: Amalie Freud 57
        The Father: Jakob Freud 58
        The Scientist: Ernst Brucke 59
        The Visionary: Jean Martin Charcot......................................60
        The Healer: Josef Breuer 60
        The Confidante: Wilhelm Fliess..61
        The Sons and Daughter 65
Three Main Tenets of Psychoanalysis 65
    Determinism 66
    Conflict...68
    The Unconscious 69
The Development of the Sexual Instinct 70
    The Oral Stage...71
    The Anal Stage 72
    The Phallic Stage...73
        Feature 2.A: Psychoanalysis and the Sociology of Gender........78
    Latency and Maturity...80
The Structural Model of the Mind 81
    The Id 81
    The Ego 82
    The Superego...85
Psychoanalysis After Freud..86
    Expansion of the Ego...87
    Karen Horney 89
    Erich Fromm 92
    Object Relations 96
    Heinz Kohut 99
Carl Jung's Analytical Psychology..101
    The Basic Nature of Human Beings...102

Personality Types and Personality Development.................................106

Goddesses and Heroes 109

Summary 113

Chapter 3   Discovery and Proof in Psychoanalysis   **115**

Introduction 116

The Context of Discovery: Psychoanalytic Interpretation 117

The Case of Dora...117

Two Traumatic Events 118

The Dream of the Jewel-Case..120

Dora Revisited 124

Feature 3.A: Understanding Transference 126

Methods of Interpretation...130

Text and Treaty 130

Manifest and Latent 131

Symptoms and Everyday Life 133

Myth and Symbol: Jungian Meanings...136

The Context of Justification: Testing Hypotheses 141

The Unconscious 141

Unconscious Information Processing 142

Studies in Repression...145

The Activation of the Unconscious...149

Mechanisms of Defense...152

Developmental Stages..156

Feature 3.B: The Authoritarian Personality................................162

Internalized Objects 165

Jung's Types..170

Feature 3.C: Falling in Love With the Self:
The Problem of Narcissism 172

Summary...176

Chapter 4   Evolution and Human Nature   **178**

Introduction..179

Instinct and Evolution..180

Instinctive Behavior in Animals 180

Human Evolution 182

Sociobiology and the Person 184

Evolutionary Personality Psychology 188

Mating 191

Feature 4.A: Some Women (and Men) Are Choosier Than
Others: Sociosexuality 194

Socioanalytic Theory and the Problem of Shyness 202

Aggression Versus Altruism 206

Hurting Others 206

Helping Others 212

The Evolution of Love: Attachment Theory 218

Attachment in Infancy 219

Secure and Insecure Attachments 223

Adult Attachments 235

Summary 238

Part II   Interaction Episodes
The Person, the Situation, and the Prediction of Behavior   241

Chapter 5   Personality Traits   244

Introduction 245

Measuring Traits 248

What Is a Trait? 248

Constructing a Trait Measure 249

Feature 5.A: Allport and Cattell: Trait Psychologists
Extraordinaire 250

Criteria of a Good Measure 255

Personality Inventories 258

The Basic Traits 263

The Big Five 264

E: Extraversion 265

Feeling Good 267

Arousal 269

Stability and Change 272

N: Neuroticism 274

Gray's Approach: Impulsivity and Anxiety 280

Feature 5.B: Feeling Really Good and Really Bad:
*   Affect Intensity* 282

O: Openness to Experience 284

C and *A*: Conscientiousness and Agreeableness............................288

The Interpersonal Circumplex..293

Trait Genetics...295

Infant Temperament 295

Feature 5.C: Cubness: The Most Dreaded Trait.............................298

Heritability Studies...300

Summary..307

Chapter 6   Social Learning and the Social Situation   309

Introduction..310

Behaviorism: A Brief Course 312

Observation 313

Environmentalism 314

Learning 315

Classical Conditioning..316

Instrumental Conditioning 319

Social-Learning Theories..323

Rotter's View: Expectancies and Values 323

Mischel's Approach: Cognitive/Social Learning/Person Variables 324

Feature 6.A: The Integration of Freud and the Behaviorists:
*   Miller and Dollard's Learning Theory*................................326

Bandura's Theory: The Role of Observational Learning 330

Observational Learning..330

Self-Efficacy 333

Reciprocal Determinism..335

Assessment and Research 336

Behavioral Assessment 336

Self-Regulation..340

Delay of Gratification..340

Individual Differences and a Personal Work Ethic....................343

Aggression and Altruism 345

Bandura and the Bobo Doll 346

Television Violence 347

Altruism, Prosocial Behavior............................352

Behaviorism, Social Learning, and Personality 353

Feature 6.B: How Should Parents Raise Their Children?........354

Summary..358

Chapter 7   The Interaction of Person and Environment   360

Introduction..361

Mischel's Critique..361

Behavior Is Complex..364

Predicting Some of the People Some of the Time...................366

Feature 7.A: Traits as Categories of Acts:
The Act-Frequency Approach 368

Aggregating Behaviors 372

Patterns of Traits Over Time....................................377

Behavior Is Contextual..385

Feature 7.B: The Type A Personality 386

What Is a Situation? 390

Modern Interactionism 395

Persons Versus Situations Versus Interactions..............396

An Interactional Model of Anxiety 398

Reciprocal Interactionism.......................................400

Macrocontexts..402

Families and Other Systems 402

Race and Social Class..404

Culture and History..408

Conclusion: Traits and Situations Revisited...................410

Summary..416

Part III   **Interpretive Structures**
The Person's Strategies for Understanding Behavior   419

Chapter 8   Humanistic Themes
Meaning and Self-Determination   422

Introduction..423

The Focus on Consciousness: Existentialism and Phenomenology.................424

    Consciousness Is Primary..424

    We Create Ourselves...425

        Feature 8.A: Finding Meaning in the Absurd:

        The Psychology of Ernest Becker..428

    We Alone Are Responsible for Who We Become 430

Freedom, Control, and Challenge in Human Affairs 431

    Who (or What) Is in Control?...433

        Personal Causation and Control..433

        Locus of Control...438

    Self-Determination Theory..440

    The Hardy Personality...445

    Reversal Theory...450

Humanistic Psychology..455

    Carl Rogers' Theory..456

    Abraham Maslow's Psychology of Being...459

    Examples of Humanistic Research 463

The Bridge to Cognitive Psychology: George Kelly..469

        Feature 8.B: A Rigorous Humanism: Joseph Rychlak 470

    The Psychology of Personal Constructs..473

    Exploring Personal Constructs: The REP Test...477

Summary...480

Chapter 9   Cognitive Approaches to the Person   482

Introduction..483

Cognition and Personality..488

    Social Intelligence...488

    Self-Schemata...494

    Gender Schemata 497

        Feature 9.A: Masculinity, Femininity, and Androgyny 500

    Depressive Schemata..504

        Feature 9.B: Thinking and Feeling...508

From Thought to Action 511

Middle-Level Units and Purposive Behavior..512

The Regulation of Behavior...516

Differentiation and Integration 522

Field Independence–Dependence 522

Integrative Complexity..528

Feature 9.C: Human Values..530

Summary...534

Chapter 10   The Self as Knower and Known   535

Introduction...536

The I..539

Characteristics of the I 539

Four Views on the Development of the I 540

Allport's Proprium...540

Sullivan's Self-System 541

Loevinger's Ego...542

Kegan's Evolving Self...545

The Infant I...548

Feature 10.A: Born With a Self: Daniel Stern's Infant 552

The Child I...554

The Adolescent I..557

The Adult I...558

Assessing the I: The WUSCTED...560

Conclusion...562

The Me...564

Self and Other 564

The Me on Stage..566

A Confederacy of Selves..570

Possible Selves 571

Discrepancies Among Selves..573

Self-With-Other 577

Feature 10.B: Feeling Good About the Me: Self-Esteem............580

Development of the Me 583

Summary..585

Part IV   Interpersonal Stories
Narrative Patterns in Human Lives   **587**

Chapter 11   Motivational Themes in Stories
The Legacy of Henry Murray   **590**

Introduction...591
Icarus...591
The Personology of Henry A. Murray...596
   Murray and the Harvard Psychological Clinic.....................................596
   Murray's System..601
      Feature 11.A: Rising, Falling, Fantasy, and Sex.......................602
   The Study of Lives...610
      Personology After World War II..610
      Science and the Single Case...615
Three Social Motives..620
   The Thematic Apperception Test...620
   Achievement Motivation..622
      Measuring the Achievement Motive.......................................622
      Careers in Business...625
      The Achieving Society..626
   Power Motivation...629
      Leadership...631
      Love and Health...633
   Intimacy Motivation...637
      Feature 11.B: A Movie Is Like a TAT: The Case of Alfred
       Hitchcock...638
   Motivation in Perspective...644
Summary...647

Chapter 12   Biography and the Life Course
Erikson, Adler, and the Seasons of Adulthood   **649**

Introduction...650
Luther's Biography...650
Erikson's Theory of Psychosocial Development..656
   Erikson and the Psychoanalytic Tradition...656

Stages as Chapters...660
The Early Stages..661
The Problem of Identity...663
  Adolescence and Young Adulthood...664
  Identity Statuses 668
  Identity and Intimacy...671
  Feature 12.A: The Feminine Social Clock Project 674
The Later Stages..678
  A Model of Generativity...678
  Stories of Generativity...685
  Integrity..687
Story Beginnings and Endings: Alfred Adler..688
  Alfred Adler and Individual Psychology...688
  Beginnings: The Earliest Memory...689
  Feature 12.B: Birth Order and the Family Saga 690
  Endings: Fictional Finalism..694
Biography, Narrative, and Lives..696
  Psychobiography...697
  Feature 12.C: Why Did van Gogh Cut Off His Ear?.....................................702
  Life Histories 706
  Seasons of Adult Life 708
Summary...713

Chapter 13   Life Scripts, Life Stories   716

Introduction...717
The Meaning of Stories...719
  The Narrating Mind 720
  What Is a Story?...723
  Healing and Integration...727
  Feature 13.A: Time and Story in Bali..728
Feeling and Story: Tomkins' Script Theory...736
  Affects 738
  Scenes and Scripts 740
  Basic Concepts...740
  Types of Scripts...742

A Life-Story Model of Identity 745

    Origins of the Story: Tone, Imagery, Theme 749

    Characters in Narrative: The Imago 754

    Storymaking in Midlife 760

        Feature 13.B: When Did Identity Become a Problem? 766

Lives as Texts 768

    Hermans' Dialogical Self 770

    Music and Story: Gregg's Approach 777

    The Postmodern Self 781

Summary 783

Epilogue   **785**

Chapter 14   Perspectives on the Person   786

Introduction 786

Four Conclusions About the Four Perspectives 789

    No Single Perspective Is "The Best" 789

    All Approaches Have Strengths and Weaknesses 794

    Mixing and Matching Makes for a Muddle 794

    Personologists Must Make a Choice 795

Ascendant Themes, Common Ground 796

    Cognition and the Self 797

    Affect 797

    Interactionism 797

    Biology 798

Glossary G-1

References R-0

Name Index NI-1

Subject Index SI-1

Photo Credits SI-11

Copyrights and Acknowledgments CR-0

Introduction

Chapter 1   Studying the Person

Studying the Person

Introduction

Two Lives
Yukio Mishima: Novelist
Margaret Mead: Anthropologist

Four Perspectives on the Person
Intrapsychic Mysteries: Mishima
Interaction Episodes: Mead
Interpretive Structures: Mishima
Interpersonal Stories: Mead
Creativity and the Four Approaches to the Person

Science and the Person
Feature 1.A: Joseph Kidd: An Ordinary Guy

Step 1: Unsystematic Observation
Step 2: Building Theories
Step 3: Evaluating Propositions

Setting up an Empirical Study
The Correlational Design
The Experimental Design

Personality Psychology

Summary

If you are reading this book, you are probably a **person.** Of course, there could be some debate about this, depending on what definition of person you might want to employ. We all qualify for person status according to the dictionary's first and least restrictive meaning of the term: "an individual human being" (*Webster's Third New International Dictionary of the English Language,* 1966, p. 1686). But other definitions are pickier, like *Webster's* eighth one: "a being characterized by conscious apprehension, rationality, and a moral sense" (p. 1686). Before we all consider disqualifying our parents and roommates on the basis of these new stricter criteria, we should acknowledge that most all persons are not always rational and do occasionally suffer significant lapses in morality. So most parents—and probably even professors and used car salesmen—qualify. But what about the psychopathic killer who appears to have no moral sensibility? What about the profoundly retarded adult whose powers of rationality appear very limited? What about the newborn baby?

Like many things that we take for granted, the concept of person gets fuzzier and more confusing the more we think about it. Whether or not we might agree on what and who is or is not a person in every individual case, we can probably agree on at least two propositions. The first of these is that a person is an *integrated totality:* a complex whole in which various parts or aspects are intricately related. Our experience of personal wholeness is so fundamental that deviations from wholeness appear bizarre and frightening. Some schizophrenics describe feelings of **depersonalization,** or the sense that one is somehow incomplete (Bleuler, 1950). The individual experiencing depersonalization may feel that he or she is profoundly empty or hollow, or that he or she is merely a piece or fragment of a person, or that he or she is inhabited by many persons, each split off from any kind of central organizing core. Most of us, most of the time, however, do not doubt that the various thoughts, feelings, and behaviors that we experience and display are in fact our *own* thoughts, feelings, and behaviors—that they "belong" to the same self. As persons, we are integrated wholes, for the most part, and we tend to regard our fellows—friends, neighbors, and enemies—in the same manner.

A second proposition on which most of us would probably agree is that *different persons are similar and different in many ways.* To paraphrase two prominent social scientists who spent much of their lives studying persons, every individual is in certain respects

1. like all other persons
2. like some other persons
3. like no other person. (Kluckhohn & Murray, 1953, p. 53)

As fellow members of the human race, we all share a host of basic similarities, many of which appear to be rooted in our common biologies (like all other persons). On the other hand, each of us believes ourself to be unique in some essential respect (like no other person). Most of us like to think that we do things in a way not quite like anybody else, that we have certain feelings that do not completely match those of our peers, that we have experienced life in a unique way. And we are right. Even identical twins—who are genetically exactly alike—do not experience the world in an identical manner.

Though each of us is unique in many ways, we would generally concede that some people are more similar to us than others (like some other persons). Different individuals can be compared and contrasted. For instance, your mother and your best friend may be similar in that they are both relatively shy and withdrawn. Yet they are almost certainly so different from each other in so many other ways that no person who knows them both would ever say that they are the same person, or even that they are highly similar persons in a *large number* of respects.

This book concerns the study of whole persons who are in certain respects like all other persons, like some other persons, and like no other persons. It is about **personality psychology.** Personality psychology is *the scientific study of the whole person.* Personality psychologists—sometimes called **personologists** (Murray, 1938)—seek to understand both the universal and the unique in persons. They focus both on those central psychological aspects of the person that may comprise a basic core to personality and on those distinguishing psychological features that render different persons different, even unique (Maddi, 1980). In the words of David Buss (1984), personality psychology concerns itself with both the most important **species-typical characteristics** (individual characteristics that appear throughout the human species) and the most important **individual differences** in persons (ways in which individual human beings differ from each other).

What personologists have in common and what distinguishes them from other social scientists is their consideration of the whole person in all of his or her complexity as the major unit of scientific analysis. So that we may begin to understand what this means, let us first look in some detail at two very complex and fascinating persons whose lives are a matter of public record.

Two Lives
Yukio Mishima: Novelist

The morning he killed himself, Yukio Mishima rose early, shaved slowly and carefully, showered, and put on a fresh, white cotton loincloth and a military uniform. On a table in the hall, he left the final installment of his last novel. The envelope was addressed to his publishers, who were to send a representative for it later that day. At the front gate of his home, Mishima met with four students, and the five of

Yukio Mishima

them drove to a Tokyo army base. According to a plan rehearsed for weeks, Mishima and the four fought off a group of army personnel with their swords, took hostage one General Mashita, and forced a temporary truce whereby a thousand men of the 32nd Infantry Regiment were to gather in front of the headquarters at noon to hear Mishima deliver a patriotic speech. Constant heckling cut the speech short. Mishima and the four then retreated to a back room and, as planned for weeks, performed the Japanese ceremonial rite of *seppuku,* in which he shouted a last salute to the Emperor of Japan and then plunged a samurai dagger deep into his stomach, forcing the cutting edge across his abdomen from left to right. One of the four students then chopped off his head. For years, Mishima had rehearsed this gory suicide in numerous plays and stories he wrote, and in his private fantasies.

Yukio Mishima was in the prime of his life when, on November 25, 1970, he enacted the suicide. He was healthy, successful, famous, rich, and, according to most who knew him, relatively happy. With over 100 full-length books to his credit, he was considered by many the single greatest novelist of modern Japan. And he was much more than a novelist. He was a playwright, a sportsman, a film actor, the founder of a private army, a family man, and a world traveler. Indeed, one biographer characterized Mishima as the "Leonardo da Vinci of modern Japan" (Scott-Stokes, 1974).

From the many notable elements in Mishima's life history, let us look quickly at seven, drawn from Mishima's autobiographical writings (Mishima, 1958, 1970) and the English biographies written by Scott-Stokes (1974) and Nathan (1974).

1.   On Mishima's fiftieth day of life (in 1925), his paternal grandmother took the infant away from his mother and moved him, crib and all, into her dark sickroom downstairs, where Mishima lived until he was 12. In the first few years, Mishima's mother was able to see her son only during times of feeding. Later in childhood, Mishima would meet her on an occasional secret rendezvous. For the most part, Mishima's grandmother strictly controlled the environment of his early years. Because of her neuralgia, she could tolerate little noise. Mishima was allowed to play quietly with three carefully chosen cousins, all girls. As a young boy, Mishima spent many of his waking hours nursing his sick grandmother, sponging her brow, massaging her back and hip, bringing her medicine, and leading her to the toilet.

2.   From the age of 4, Mishima was obsessed with bizarre fantasies of heroism that presaged his eventual suicide—fantasies "tormenting and frightening me all my life" (Mishima, 1958, p. 8). One of these fantasies was formed in response to seeing a handsome young laborer bearing buckets of animal excrement. The 4-year-old Mishima was fascinated with the figure of the "night-soil man," experiencing a confusing mixture of excitement, longing, and sadness in his presence. The night-soil man became, in Mishima's fantasy life, a model for the tragic hero whose body is in constant communion with death. As decaying matter, the feces symbolize death.

3.   Mishima's fantasies of heroism were suffused with homosexual longing. His feelings for the night-soil man were replayed again and again in subsequent fantasies in which he felt a powerful sexual attraction to muscular young men. One of the students who accompanied Mishima on the day of his death is thought to have been his homosexual lover.

4.   Though little solid information is available, Mishima's marriage of 13 years to Yoko Sugiyama appeared to most people to have been a happy one. In their many public appearances, Mishima and Yoko seemed to enjoy each other. Mishima often brought Yoko into his conversations with others, soliciting her opinions and apparently valuing her responses to a degree that was unusual for other male Japanese writers. The couple raised two children.

5.   In the late 1950s, Mishima began to express dissatisfaction with the process of writing fiction. Despite the critical acclaim of his work, he began to see

writing as a cowardly escape from reality. He began to contrast the *word* and the *act,* arguing that words were "corrosive" and that heroism in life could be attained only by the pure action of a strong and beautiful body.

6.   In order to make his own body strong and beautiful, Mishima began, at the age of 30, a rigorous weight-lifting program that he followed religiously to the week he died. A frail and sickly boy and youth, Mishima transformed himself in his 30s into the musclebound hero of his fantasies. In strange ways, weight lifting was connected, in Mishima's mind, to death. Attacking the barbell involved "ceaseless motion, ceaseless violent deaths, ceaseless escape from cold objectivity—by now, I could no longer live without such mysteries" (Mishima, 1970, p. 76). The "ceaseless violent deaths" of weight training prepared him for the glorious final death that would make him a tragic hero:

> I cherished a romantic impulse toward death, yet at the same time I required a strictly classical body as its vehicle. . . . A powerful, tragic frame and sculpturesque muscles are indispensible in a romantically noble death. Any confrontation between weak, flabby flesh and death seemed to me absurdly inappropriate. (Mishima, 1970, pp. 27–28)

7.   In the 1960s, Mishima created a private army, called the Shield Society. The army was dedicated to the revival of patriotism in modern Japan and to the ultimate defense of the Japanese emperor. Mishima said he wished to save Japan from both communism and Western capitalism. The army was composed of college students, for the most part, including the four who witnessed the *seppuku* on that November day in 1970.

Margaret Mead: Anthropologist

Whereas Mishima's life culminates in a single momentous event that we might guess holds the key secret of his personality, there is no such all-encompassing episode in the life of the American anthropologist, Margaret Mead. This is not to say that Mead's life was dull. Margaret Mead (1901–1978) traveled to the South Seas as a 23-year-old to study primitive cultures and returned years later having authored her first book, *Coming of Age in Samoa.* Her descriptions of adolescent sexuality and seemingly guilt-free love shocked many readers and made her famous, associating her name forever with sex and freedom. During the subsequent 50 years, Mead established herself as one of the preeminent social scientists of the twentieth century and probably the greatest popularizer of anthropology in the English language.

The following seven highlights from Mead's life history are drawn from her autobiography, *Blackberry Winter* (Mead, 1972), from the writings of her daughter (Bateson, 1984), and from a well-regarded biography of Mead authored by Howard (1984).

Margaret Mead

1.   A first child, Margaret Mead was "wanted and loved" (Mead, 1972, p. 17). Though her father's job for the university made it necessary that his wife and children repeatedly move from one home to another "like a family of refugees," Margaret recalled an essentially happy but restless childhood in which she delighted in being something of a favorite in the eyes of relatives, friends, and acquaintances. She was told again and again that "there's no one like Margaret," a foreshadowing of a felt "specialness" that Mead kept with her for life.

2.   After a miserable freshman year at DePauw College in Indiana, Mead transferred to Barnard College in New York City and fell in with a group of young women who came to be known on campus as the "Ash Can Cats." Housed first in Apartment 21 at 606 West 116th Street, the Ash Can Cats made up a unique, highly intelligent, and artistic group. Margaret remained close friends with many of these women after graduating from Barnard.

3.   Mead was married three times. Her first marriage was to a theology student named Luther Cressman. In her autobiography, Mead dismissed the relationship as a "student marriage." What attracted Margaret and Luther to each other remains a mystery. Howard (1984) speculates that as a child Mead cherished

an image of herself as a pastor's motherly wife, but there seems little evidence of this in Mead's own accounts of her childhood.

4.   Exhibited in her personal life and professional writings, Mead's views on love, marriage, sexuality, and the family were always controversial. During a time when divorce was much less prevalent and accepted than today, Mead married and divorced three different men. During a time when homosexuality was rarely discussed and hardly ever tolerated, rumors occasionally surfaced that Mead was sexually involved with other women. A long-time psychiatrist acquaintance, Rollo May, had no doubt she was bisexual (Howard, 1984). When a relative once asked Mead what she thought of homosexuals, Mead paused several seconds and then replied: "They make the best companions in the world" (Howard, 1984, p. 367). An ideal society, Mead declared in one of her last articles, would consist of people who were homosexual in their youth, heterosexual in the middle of their lives, and homosexual again in old age. Throughout all of her writing, Mead urged the acceptance of ways of living and loving, many of these observed in her visits to "primitive" cultures, that were outside the traditional norms of the Western middle class. Margaret Mead gave birth to and raised one child, Mary Catherine Bateson, daughter of her third husband, Gregory Bateson.

5.   Throughout her life, Mead was a woman on the move. Her anthropological studies took her all over the globe—from the South Pacific to collect field data, to London to report her findings, to New York City where she served as a museum curator. Howard (1984) writes, "She rushed across oceans and continents, time zones and networks and disciplines, knocking down barriers and redefining boundaries" (p. 13). Gregory Bateson described his marriage to Mead as "almost a principle of pure energy. . . . I couldn't keep up, and she couldn't stop. She was like a tugboat. She could sit down and write three thousand words by eleven o'clock in the morning, and spend the rest of the day working at the museum" (Howard, 1984, p. 253). One of Mead's life mottos in college was "Be lazy, go crazy."

6.   For an academic engaged in scholarly research and writing, Mead appears to have been remarkably unreflective. Mead was more the observer than the philosopher. She had little patience for leisurely speculation about anything, even about herself. Though always willing to try new experiences, Mead adamantly refused to enter psychoanalysis to examine in depth her own life. Such an adventure in self-reflection would have been too time-consuming and too intangible for a person in a hurry whose mind tended toward the more practical and concrete. After completing a field study in July of 1932, Mead found she had too much free time on her hands and complained, "I had too much time to think—too many empty spaces." Writes Howard (1984), "unstructured time, all the rest of her life, was a prospect that would fill Mead with dread" (p. 145).

7.   As one of the most successful women of the twentieth century, Mead was not comfortable with feminism. Indeed, as a self-proclaimed prophet of cross-cultural tolerance and the equality of different human societies, Mead was surprisingly quiet about women's rights, suggesting, according to one of her colleagues at Columbia University, that "wives, with very rare exceptions, should

defer to their husbands' careers" (Howard, 1984, p. 363). Mead saw the women's movement of the 1960s and 1970s as a passing and overrated invention of the media, claiming that the real pioneers for equal rights between the sexes were members of her great-grandmother's generation.

Four Perspectives on the Person

The preceding life-history data on Yukio Mishima and Margaret Mead are not meant to provide a comprehensive or even a representative sampling of the behavior, thought, or feelings of these two very complex persons. Rather, the seven biographical highlights for each person are examples of the kind of data or information that a personologist, interested in these two lives, might find useful for analysis. A serious investigation into either person's life would, however, require much more biographical material, more carefully selected and organized. But my purpose here is not to provide a definitive or even valid interpretation of Mishima and Mead. Nor am I concerned with comparing and contrasting the two as, say, representatives of two different types of persons, such as males *versus* females, Japanese writers *versus* American social scientists, narcissists *versus* humanists, or suicides *versus* nonsuicides. Instead, I simply suggest that both of these people present us with complex and intriguing lives that challenge our theories and methods for making sense of the person.

Yukio Mishima and Margaret Mead were, in varying respects, like all other persons, like some other persons, and like no other person. Their lives must be viewed as integrated totalities set in a particular time and place and subject to a particular but complex set of determining forces. As personologists, how are we to understand these whole persons? How are we to make sense of their lives? There are at least four very different ways to proceed. The personologist can focus on

1. intrapsychic mysteries
2. interaction episodes
3. interpretive structures
4. interpersonal stories.

Intrapsychic Mysteries: Mishima

A strong tradition in the study of persons maintains that to understand fully the whole person one must delve into the deep, dark secrets of the mind: the person is to be understood in terms of the mysteries that reside within. These mysteries take the form of unconscious and almost uncontrollable wishes and conflicts, long-forgotten memories of the past, and biological urges and inclinations concerning sexuality, aggression, and survival. These forces make for conflict in the individual's life; they derive from the biological nature of human beings and the universal task of adapting that nature to the demands of living in human societies. The workings of the forces and conflicts, however, remain largely outside the person's awareness, which is to say that the intrapsychic mysteries generally remain *unconscious.*

Included within this tradition are the classic psychoanalytic theories of Sigmund Freud and Carl Jung and the more modern derivatives of Anna Freud, Margaret Mahler, and groups of psychologists calling themselves "ego psychologists" and/or "object-relations theorists." Also included are approaches that emphasize the evolution and the inborn propensities of the human species.

Personologists who understand human lives in terms of intrapsychic mysteries tend to place a premium on the interpretation of the person's relatively spontaneous and open-ended speech and writing, especially if these verbal productions involve some kind of creative effort. Therefore, the interpretation of dreams and fantasies is a popular approach to analyzing data on persons in this perspective, though numerous other procedures are commonly employed, including the careful observation of behavior in real-life settings. Of the four different perspectives on the person, the intrapsychic-mysteries approach is probably the most speculative in that scientists must go well beyond what is observed to infer meanings about persons' lives that lie buried deep beneath the surface of what the casual observer might see.

Because of the rich display of his dreams and fantasies in his fiction and autobiography, because of his extensive discussion of the issues of sexuality and aggression in his own life, and perhaps most of all because of the great intrapsychic mystery of his own enigmatic suicide, Yukio Mishima presents a life and a death that invite an analysis from this first perspective on persons. Indeed, the invitation is so alluring that I was drawn to undertake just such an analysis a few years ago (McAdams, 1985a), employing some of the theories and methods described in Chapters 2–4 of this book. Here I highlight a few of the main points of my psychodynamic interpretation of Yukio Mishima to illustrate how the personologist might address a life from the perspective of intrapsychic mysteries.

The question I sought to answer was "What was the psychological meaning of Yukio Mishima's suicide?" Many answers could be offered. I saw mine as a viable alternative among a number of equally compelling explanations. The main point of my interpretation is that there existed in Yukio Mishima's life a fundamental and fatal confusion between "having" and "being." This confusion has been identified by Sigmund Freud (Chapter 2) as that between **object choice** and **identification.** It is a confusion that resides at the center of many intrapsychic mysteries, including why young children unconsciously hate and love their parents at the same time (the Oedipus Complex, as described in Chapter 2) and why the death of a loved one elicits grief and sometimes chronic depression in the person who is left behind.

According to Freud, the person tends, on an unconscious level, to relate to important other people in his or her life in one or both of two very primitive ways.

The person seeks either to *have the other in a powerful/sensual way* (object choice) or to *be the other* (identification). In object choice, the person unconsciously desires the other as an object of affection. He or she feels, unconsciously, a strong need to "own" the other person, to hold on to the other as the exclusive object of his or her sensual longings. This is, argued Freud, the basic unconscious way that preschool boys relate to their mothers (and/or mother figures in their environment) and preschool girls to their fathers (and/or father figures). Identification, on the other hand, involves the desire to be like the other, to take in all of the other's qualities and, quite literally at the unconscious level, to become the other. As we shall see in Chapter 2, the desire to be the other is sometimes commingled with a strong fear of or hatred for the same other, as in the case of what psychoanalysts have termed *identification with the aggressor.* Identification is, argued Freud, the basic unconscious way that preschool boys relate to their fathers (and/or father figures) and preschool girls to their mothers (and/or mother figures).

Object choice and identification appear to be related to each other in an extremely interesting way. Freud suggests that, in some sense, *object choice is generally preferred at the unconscious level* and that *identification arises often when object choice is thwarted.* In other words, we seek first to *have* the other, but when we cannot have the other we seek to *be* the other. This is why, said Freud (1917/1957), people often take on the personal characteristics of loved ones after those loved ones have died. With the death of the other, object choice is no longer a possibility, and the person thus comes to identify with the lost object. A symbol for the identification with the other in dreams, fantasy, and mythology is *eating* the other—the literal "taking in" of the lost object.

Because of a complex host of factors, including his 12-year stay in his grandmother's sickroom, Mishima was never able to sort out, on the unconscious level, object choice and identification. Rather than developing a typical sensual orientation to his mother and coming to identify with a father figure, Mishima came to project both object choice and identification onto the same alternative object: the tragic hero initially identified as the night-soil man. Mishima's life story can thus be understood in terms of transformations over time in the tragic hero, whom he longed both *to have* and *to be.* In Confessions of a Mask, Mishima (1958) traces how the tragic hero was transformed in his childhood and adolescent fantasies from the night-soil man to a picture of Joan of Arc, then to the figure of the Christian martyr Saint Sebastian, and finally to his first real-life love object—a strapping teenaged boy named Omi.

At the age of 14, Mishima fell in love with a boy whom he also wished to become. Omi was the real-life personification of the tragic hero that Mishima had first identified as the night-soil man. In addition, Omi was everything that, in reality, Mishima was not. Whereas the teenaged Mishima was weak and sickly, Omi was strong and robust—the adored best athlete in class. Whereas Mishima was constantly absorbed in thought and fantasy, Omi seemed to be an unselfconscious youth devoted to the pure action of the body. Whereas Mishima was sheltered and naive, Omi seemed, in Mishima's perception, to exude real-world confidence, maturity, and an intimate acquaintance with sex, death, and heroism.

Mishima's homosexual love for Omi, however, came to a grinding halt one day on the playground when he felt pangs of jealousy while observing Omi's flawless performance on the parallel bars. In this moment, Mishima realized that he wished to be like Omi as much as he wished to have Omi in a sensual way. The fact that he was too weak and sickly to be like his lover infuriated Mishima, forcing him to abandon his object choice and, as Freud would have it, to accelerate his mission to *become* Omi, the tragic hero. Remember that eating the object may symbolize, in fantasy, identification with the object. The loss of Omi and subsequent identification with him are symbolized in a startling dream that Mishima had shortly after the playground scene in which he literally ate a naked young boy served to him on a platter.

In adulthood, Mishima struggled to become Omi through his rigorous weight-training program. By changing weak and flabby flesh into muscle, Mishima fashioned himself into the tragic hero that he had loved from the age of 4. No longer was his love object confined to internal fantasy or the external world. By becoming Omi and the night-soil man, *he came unconsciously to be his own lover.* Therefore, if he was to become Omi (identification), he *must have himself* (object choice). One result of this unconscious dynamic may have been the intensified narcissism of his later years: his egotistical manner suggested that he had quite literally fallen in love with himself. Another result, I would argue, was his suicide.

For Mishima, the Japanese rite of *seppuku* had always had a profoundly sexual significance. Since the age of 4, Mishima had romanticized death, and his novels and stories are filled with erotic images of death and killing. *Seppuku* was, for Mishima, a macabre sexual union with himself. It enabled him to consummate symbolically both his desire to be and to have Omi. In thrusting the dagger into his own stomach, Mishima became both the lover and the beloved—symbolically, both the male phallus and the female vagina. At the moment of death, he was able, therefore, to become the tragic hero of his dreams and to have that same tragic hero simultaneously, in a deadly sexual union.

Interaction Episodes: Mead

A second tradition in the study of persons maintains that to understand the whole person one must be able to predict precisely what he or she will *do* in a particular situation. The focus here is on the observable *behavior* that a person displays, not on his or her fantasies, dreams, or unconscious desires. Personologists of this second persuasion argue that inner, generally unconscious phenomena cannot be studied in any reliable and objective manner by the scientist. What can be studied reliably, however, is behavior. Behavior is available for public scrutiny: it can be directly observed, reliably classified, and accurately measured.

Personologists who align themselves with this second general orientation tend to see the prediction of behavior as a matter of sorting out how the person and the environment interact to produce an observable behavioral response. Behavior is a function of the interaction of the person with the environment, and therefore personality is conceptualized in terms of a series of interaction episodes. Personologists who seek to understand interaction episodes so as to predict human behavior tend to fall within one of three overlapping categories. The first consists of those who place somewhat greater emphasis on the individual differences among persons rather than among environments in predicting behavior. These are sometimes called **trait psychologists** (Chapter 5) because of their relative emphasis on personality traits that can be measured in persons in order to predict behavior. The second group is made up of those who tend to emphasize individual differences among environments rather than among persons. These are sometimes called **situationists** (Chapter 6) because of their focus on situations as determinants of human behavior. A third group of personologists tends to place relatively equal emphasis on inner personality dimensions (like traits) and outer situational factors, and they are sometimes called **interactionists** (Chapter 7).

The interaction episodes approaches place a premium on precise quantification of data through self-report questionnaires, surveys, and careful observation of behavior in controlled settings, as in the laboratory experiment. Though we cannot administer trait questionnaires to Margaret Mead or observe her behavior in the laboratory, we can still speculate as to how Mead's life might be understood in terms of interaction episodes. For instance, I would argue that significant aspects of Margaret Mead's behavior can be understood in terms of the interaction between a very strong personality *trait* of extraversion and the *situational* influence of a generally liberal, intellectual, upper-middle class, American environment of the early part of this century, which instilled the values of social activism and doing "good works." Various aspects of this pervasive environment in Mead's life were personified in the important role models of her parents, paternal grandmother, and teachers.

One of the most obvious and observable personality differences is that some people are relatively more outgoing, sociable, and impulsive than are others. We say that those who are particularly outgoing are more *extraverted* than those who are more inwardly oriented, whom we may categorize as *introverts*. Most people seem to be somewhere in the middle, between extreme extraversion and extreme introversion. The trait psychologist, Hans Eysenck, has done some of the most valuable research on the concept of extraversion. He believes that extraversion is one of a small number of central dimensions of human personality (see Chapter 5). The relatively extraverted person is sociable, has many friends, craves excitement, takes chances, acts on the spur of the moment, and is generally easygoing and optimistic (Eysenck, 1973). The extravert exhibits *stimulus hunger*—a desire for greater and greater levels of stimulation from his or her social environment.

Table 1.1 reproduces a self-report questionnaire designed to measure extraversion. The person answering this questionnaire is to respond *yes* or *no* to each of the 20 questions. If her biography is a valid indication of the kind of person Margaret Mead was, I think that she would have answered most of the questions in the extraverted direction. Of course we can't be sure, but a great deal of biographical information suggests that Mead often longed for excitement (item #1),

Table 1.1

Questionnaire Measuring Extraversion

For each of the following 20 questions, answer either *yes* (if it is generally true for you) or *no* (if it is generally not true for you).

1. Do you often long for excitement?
2. Are you usually carefree?
3. Do you stop and think things over before doing anything?
4. Would you do almost anything for a dare?
5. Do you often do things on the spur of the moment?
6. Generally, do you prefer reading to meeting people?
7. Do you prefer to have few but special friends?
8. When people shout at you do you shout back?
9. Do other people think of you as very lively?
10. Are you mostly quiet when you are with people?
11. If there is something you want to know about, would you rather look it up in a book then talk to someone about it?
12. Do you like the kind of work that you need to pay close attention to?
13. Do you hate being with a crowd who play jokes on one another?
14. Do you like doing things in which you have to act quickly?
15. Are you slow and unhurried in the way you move?
16. Do you like talking to people so much that you never miss a chance of talking to a stranger?
17. Would you be unhappy if you could not see lots of people most of the time?
18. Do you find it hard to enjoy yourself at a lively party?
19. Would you say that you were fairly self-confident?
20. Do you like playing pranks on others?

To arrive at your score for extraversion, give one point for each of the following items answered *yes:* #1, 2, 4, 5, 8, 9, 14, 16, 17, 19, 20. Then, give yourself one point for each of the following items answered *no:* #3, 6, 7, 10, 11, 12, 15, 18. Add up all the points to arrive at a total score. Your total score should be between 0 and 20 inclusive. The higher your score, the higher your extraversion (and, of course, the lower your introversion). Therefore, high scores suggest extraversion and low scores suggest introversion.

From Wilson (1978, p. 219). Properly standardized self-scoring scales may be found in Eysenck and Wilson (1976) and in Eysenck and Eysenck (1964).

would do many things just for a dare (#4), often acted on the spur of the moment (#5), generally preferred meeting people to reading (#6), preferred having many friends to having only a few (#7), was seen by others as lively (#9), very much enjoyed talking to people, including strangers (#16), and was very self-confident (#19). Reports from virtually everybody who knew her agree that Mead was an extraordinarily energetic and outgoing person who made many friends quite easily. Mead once claimed that she made a new friend of importance "every two or three months, without ever losing any of her old ones" (Howard, 1984, p. 13).

Eysenck argues that extraversion is a personality dimension with a significant biological component. This means a number of things. First of all, Eysenck's theory claims that a certain part of the central nervous system is intimately involved in extraversion, and that differences in this personality trait are correlated with slight differences in the workings of this central physiological mechanism. Second, research on extraversion reveals that the trait tends to run in families and that the transmission of the trait from one generation to the next may be a matter of genetics. In other words, people may *inherit* a certain tendency to be extraverted or introverted. Though the environment surely plays a role in the development of this trait, Eysenck argues that biology may also be a strong determinant of how outgoing and sociable a person is. With this in mind, we can speculate that Mead may have inherited from her biological parents a certain tendency to develop along extraverted lines.

Mead's extraversion found suitable outlets for its expression in a series of childhood and adult environments that fostered creativity, individuality, and freedom to pursue one's life dreams unencumbered by economic hardship and strict stereotypic roles. Her parents remarked "There's no one like Margaret" as they sought to create a world for their precocious daughter that would encourage and appreciate her uniqueness. In *Blackberry Winter,* Mead implies that a substantial part of her personality was formed through the careful observation of other people's behavior, especially the behavior of a few key role models. Social learning theorists such as Albert Bandura (Chapter 6) term such a process in personality development *observational learning,* arguing that much of our behavior is learned by observing others and then doing what we see them do, even if we are not rewarded for doing so. In the life of Margaret Mead, much of the observational learning appears to have been rather subtle—Mead's watching the behavior of others, listening to words, and deducing the values that her environment presented her. Agents for the transmission of these values—role models whom Mead ultimately emulated—included her mother, father, and paternal grandmother. Concerning her mother's influence on her life, Mead wrote:

> In many ways she [my mother] shared the intellectual snobbishness of the tradition that was so characteristic of families of New England origins, Unitarian or once Unitarian, college-bred, readers of serious novels and deeply imbued with the attitudes and imagery of the nineteenth-century essayists and poets, especially Robert Browning. . . . fine people were highly literate and had

taste and sophistication. Even more important, they engaged actively in efforts to make this a better world. They fought for causes and organized community efforts. Mother believed strongly in the community, in knowing her neighbors and in treating servants as individuals with dignity and rights. (Mead, 1972, p. 27)

Summing up the childhood environments that preceded her trip to DePauw as a freshman, Mead concluded:

the overriding academic ethos shaped all our lives. This was tempered by my mother's sense of responsibility for society, by my father's greater interest in real processes than in theoretical abstractions, and by my grandmother's interest in real children, in chickens, and in how to season stewed tomatoes with toasted bread. But at the heart of their lives, the enjoyment of the intellect as mediated by words in books was central, and I was the child who could make the most of this—the child who was not asked to constrain or distort some other gift. (Mead, 1972, pp. 95–97)

Interpretive Structures: Mishima

A third approach to studying the person has as its central aim understanding how whole persons consciously understand themselves and the worlds in which they live. In this tradition in personality psychology, the scientist inquires into how people make sense of things, how they make meaning in their everyday lives. The general assumption is that the whole person imposes upon his or her subjective experience some kind of organization, pattern, framework, plan, or structure that manages to put things in order and enables him or her to predict, control, and interpret life's events. The focus, therefore, is on *cognition,* or thinking, and *consciousness,* rather than, say, on unconscious dynamics, biological instincts, traits, situations, or behavior.

A number of diverse approaches to the person fall within this third general orientation. Included, for instance, are George Kelly's *personal construct* psychology (Chapter 8), Abraham Maslow's *humanistic* theory of personality (Chapter 8), a number of social-cognitive approaches to the person emphasizing ideas like *schemas* and *scripts* (Chapter 9), and some theories and research on *the self* (Chapter 10). These many approaches to studying the person draw upon a host of disciplines and orientations outside of psychology proper, ranging from cognitive science to existential philosophy. Yet personologists who adopt these various approaches all attempt, in one way or another, to see the world through the eyes of their subjects. Be it through empathy in an individual interview, role playing in group discussion, or a special paper-and-pencil test that asks the subject to dissect his or her own interpretive structures, the personologist endeavors to understand how the subject understands, in the subject's own terms.

George Kelly (1955) argued that people make sense of their conscious experience by creating *personal constructs*. A personal construct is a *bipolar category* that a person uses to organize information. For instance, you may organize information about your romantic life into the category of "exciting moments *versus* dull routine." If I the personologist were to understand the meaning of this construct for you, however, you would need to describe in detail numerous examples from your romantic life of exciting moments and of dull routine, because my idea of exciting might seem quite dull to you, and vice versa. The point is that personal constructs are highly subjective, and therefore their meanings are not apparent to the observer without many examples provided by the subject. Kelly adds that each of us employs a number of favorite personal constructs to make sense of our experience, and that some people use more constructs than do others. People who employ a rich and diverse set of personal constructs to make meaning are said to have a more *differentiated* view of reality, which is to say that they are more *cognitively complex*. These people tend to see many subtleties, many shades of gray in construing events. People who employ relatively few constructs, however, have a simpler and more global view of reality. They tend to see complex issues in black-and-white terms. The more cognitively complex person might claim that such a black-and-white, all-or-none mentality *over*simplifies things and fails to do justice to the rich nuances of human behavior and experience.

Let us now consider Yukio Mishima's life from the perspective of personal constructs. To do so, we must try to see the world through Mishima's eyes. We must discern how Mishima attempted to make sense of his own conscious experience so as to predict and control events in his life. The task may seem difficult because Mishima appears so strange to us on first glance, but it is made easier by the fact that he explicitly described many of his views in his essays and some of his novels. Reading these suggests that Mishima lived according to a strange but relatively simple personal construct system. Despite his doubtlessly high intelligence and prodigious powers of creativity, Mishima appeared to manifest a surprisingly low level of cognitive complexity.

Mishima's essays are rife with examples of all-or-none and us-or-them kind of thinking. For Mishima, Japan was good; the rest of the world was bad. The man who made war was good; the woman who made peace was bad. The beautiful body was good; beautiful words were bad. Toward the end of his life, he seemed to believe that only *seppuku* was truth; writing was a lie. To be a hero one *had* to die in a glorious fashion: there were no exceptions. Mishima appeared to recognize that his own construct system required antagonism between two global ideas, leaving little room for shades of gray. In describing why he became, in his last years, a fanatical opponent of communism, he wrote:

> For every action there must be a reaction. And where does that reaction come from? It comes from your opponent. Without an opponent, there's no point to action. Well, I was very much in

need of an opponent and I settled on communism. It's not as if Communists had attacked my children or set my house on fire. I have very little reason really. I simply chose communism as an opponent, because I needed an opponent to provoke me to action. (Nathan, 1974, p. 241)

Personal constructs often reflect the culture within which they are formed. Mishima provides a good example. His overall *interpretive structure* for making sense of reality drew heavily on a fundamental dualism of traditional Japanese culture identified by anthropologist Ruth Benedict (1946) as "the chrysanthemum and the sword." The chrysanthemum theme refers to the traditional Japanese preoccupation with beauty, color, and aesthetics. Modern manifestations of this influence abound in the elegant Japanese flower gardens, the very delicate lines of Japanese architecture, and Japanese mores, which remain relatively courtly and refined even today. The emphasis is upon style, grace, propriety, charm, and gentility. The contrasting theme of the sword reflects Japan's rise to political power in the seventeenth through nineteenth centuries under the leadership of militaristic *shoguns*. Within this emerging feudal society, the aristocratic fighting man on horseback became an ideal; unequivocal loyalty to one lord above all served as his oath. The samurai ethic proclaimed the values of rigid discipline, the glory of death in righteous battle, and the honor of *seppuku*.

For Mishima, the chrysanthemum and the sword appeared to exist as a grand personal construct under which an incredible amount of subjective experience was classified. He identified his own writing as a daughter of the feminine chrysanthemum. The beauty of words was an illusion. Indeed, Mishima ultimately argued that writing separates the man from life, and words are by nature "corrosive." Like a cancer, words eat away the flesh of human existence, leaving but an emaciated skeleton that can at best merely dream of glory. Mishima ultimately rejected all that was associated with the chrysanthemum. Glory lay instead in the cut of the sword.

Interpersonal Stories: Mead

A fourth and final perspective in personality psychology maintains that to understand the whole person the scientist must discern or construct a coherent story that specifies how the person's life is embedded in significant interpersonal relationships and in the context of society and history. Stories are the key because stories make sense of human lives *over time*, as patterned wholes with beginnings, middles, and endings. Included within this view are a number of classic and contemporary theories of personality and the self, all of which are primarily concerned with lives situated in time. Henry Murray's personological system (Chapter 11), Erik Erikson's theory of psychosocial development (Chapter 12), Alfred Adler's individual psychology (Chapter 12), and a number of contemporary formulations focused on "life stories" and "life scripts" (Chapter 13) all concern themselves centrally with how lives are organized over time in the manner of integrative narratives, culturally shaped interpersonal stories that define who we are, who we were, and who we may become in the future.

We will again use the life of Margaret Mead to illustrate this fourth way of studying the person. Our brief analysis will concern what Erik Erikson (1958, 1959) has termed the development of *ego identity*. Recall that Margaret was an intellectually gifted child whom her family considered a little "different," a little more "special" than other children: "There's no one like Margaret." As a child, she was encouraged to develop this perceived specialness, to explore her self and her environment to a greater extent than is probably true for most American children, especially most little girls growing up in the early years of this century. Her family was constantly on the move, and in each new neighborhood Margaret found that there were more new people to meet and more new territory to explore. Recurrent themes of her childhood years are *learning through exploration* and *constant movement,* and in many instances the themes are merged:

> Looking back, my memories of learning precise skills, memorizing long stretches of poetry, and manipulating paper are interwoven with memories of running—running in the wind, running through meadows, and running along country roads—picking flowers, hunting for nuts, and weaving together old stories and new events into myths about a tree and a rock. (Mead, 1972, p. 74)

With her entrance into DePauw College as a freshman, Mead appeared to encounter the first environment in her life that stifled her movement and her exploration—the first environment not very tolerant of her specialness. In her mind, DePauw was provincial, oppressive, and too traditional for the likes of a free spirit like Margaret Mead. She found the social life—dominated by fraternities and sororities—dull and rejecting. Her friends and her classes seemed boring. There was no psychosocial place for Margaret Mead at this small Indiana college at this time in her life. In the terms of Erik Erikson's psychosocial theory of the person, Mead was able to find little at DePauw to help her in the crucial task of formulating her own adult identity. So she left after a year and enrolled at Barnard College, a decision that she would never regret:

> In the autumn of 1920, I came to Barnard, where I found—and in some measure created—the kind of student life that matched my earlier dreams. In the course of those three undergraduate years friendships were founded that have endured a lifetime of change, and by the end of those years I knew what I could do in life. (Mead, 1972, p. 109)

According to Erikson, the central psychosocial task of late adolescence and young adulthood is figuring out who you are. This is the task of identity formation. As we shall see in Chapters 12 and 13, developing an identity is not always an easy thing to do. It involves exploring many options in life and making commitments to a carefully considered belief system and occupational path. It involves tying together, as an adolescent or young adult, your childhood past and your expected adult future into a coherent narrative or story that defines who you were, who you are, and who you will become (McAdams, 1985b).

In Margaret Mead's life, Barnard College proved vastly superior to DePauw as a setting that could foster her developing identity. (For a different person embarking on a different kind of identity search, DePauw might have proven vastly superior to Barnard.) In the midst of some of the most intense friendships of her life, Mead arrived at a vision of who she was and who she might become, and she was able to tie this back, in a very satisfying manner, to her perception of who she had been in the past. By the time she graduated from Barnard, she knew that she wanted to devote her life to the study of human cultures so as to learn something of the various "homes" in which people around the world lived. Mead's newly fashioned identity as an anthropologist who, like the Margaret of her childhood, continually moved from one home to another was formulated according to a perceived special relationship between "travel" and "home":

> For many people moving is one kind of thing and travel is something very different. Travel means going away from home and staying away from home; it is an antidote to the humdrum activities of everyday life, a prelude to a holiday one is entitled to enjoy after months of dullness. Moving means breaking up a home, sadly or joyfully breaking with the past; a happy venture or a hardship, something to be endured with good or ill grace. For me moving and staying at home, traveling and arriving, are all of a piece. The world is full of homes in which I have lived for a day, a month, a year, or much longer. How much I care about a home is not measured by the length of time I lived there. One night in a room with a leaping fire may mean more to me than many months in a room without a fireplace, a room in which my life has been paced less excitingly. (Mead, 1972, p. 7)

At Barnard, Mead began to fashion a new life story in which the main character was an intrepid explorer who traveled from one home to another, observing, classifying, and spreading the news of her discoveries. Like the Greek god Hermes, Mead was to be the fleet messenger, always exploring, always communicating what she learned to an audience unable to keep up. This kind of identity enabled her to put into practice her mother's values of social activism and doing good works. Like her father, she could also become an intellectual. Like her grandmother, she could delight in children and the domestic rituals of everyday life, observing these practices and often taking part in them, in the different cultures she studied. And like the little Margaret who ran through the meadows, Margaret Mead the adult could stay on the move. The glee Mead felt with the development of her new identity as anthropologist-on-the-move stands in dramatic contrast to her discontent as a freshman who was "stuck." Just before leaving for her first anthropological expedition to Samoa, Mead celebrated her newfound identity in a poem she wrote about herself, entitled "Of So Great Glee":

> She used to skip when she was small
> Till all her frocks were tattered,
> But mother gently gathered up
> The dishes that she shattered.
>
> Her skipping rope got caught in trees
> And shook their blossoms down,
> But her step was so lighthearted
> That the dryads could not frown.
>
> And when at last she tore a star
> Out of the studded sky,
> God only smiled at one whose glee
> Could fling a rope so high.

(Mead, 1972, p. 143)

Creativity and the Four Approaches to the Person

Before we leave Yukio Mishima and Margaret Mead, let me illustrate again the general distinctions among the four perspectives on persons by drawing on these two lives in a different way. Virtually everybody who knew either of these two people would agree, as I suspect would you, that Mishima and Mead were very *creative* people. It is indeed primarily for their creative contributions to the arts and sciences that Mishima and Mead are recognized and celebrated by posterity. Creativity and the creative person are topics that have traditionally been of great interest to personality psychologists. Many different definitions of creativity have been offered, but in very simple terms we may see creativity as the ability to bring something new into existence (Barron, 1969). Especially creative people are more successful than most other people in creating products and outcomes that are particularly original, fresh, novel, clever, apt, and ingenious. Creativity is *adaptive;* creative products meet needs, solve problems, push knowledge forward, provide for a useful adaptation to the world (Barron, 1969). Let us briefly consider creativity as a topic about which personality psychologists may have interesting things to say. How might each of the four perspectives on persons approach the topic of creativity?

Following Sigmund Freud, one may look upon creativity as yet another *intrapsychic mystery* in human life. Freud believed that creativity originated in the person's unconscious conflicts concerning powerful instinctual drives (Arieti, 1976). In an analysis of the life of Italian artist Leonardo da Vinci, Freud

Leonardo da Vinci's painting of the virgin Mary and St. Anne with the infant Jesus. Freud argued that Leonardo included two mother figures in this painting as an expression of his conflictual feelings about his own mother.

(1916/1947) asked why the Virgin Mary and Saint Anne both appear with the infant Jesus in one of Leonardo's most famous paintings. (More typical in Italian paintings of the time was the appearance of Jesus with Mary only, or with Mary and Joseph.) Freud speculated that Leonardo had an unconscious need to reproduce a conflictual childhood experience. He was raised by two mothers—his real biological mother, who was a peasant woman, and his father's legal wife, in whose home he grew up. The painting portrays two maternal figures because Leonardo was struggling on a deep and unconscious level with the problem of duality in motherhood. The same kind of process may be seen in Mishima's creative writings. The characters and scenes often appear to symbolize personal conflicts rooted in traumas or preoccupations from childhood.

In Freud's view, the creative person's desire to explore the unknown may be traced back to a curiosity about sexual matters that begins in early childhood. Indeed, the psychological energy or force for creative activity comes from sexual and aggressive drives or instincts, Freud maintained. As we will see in Chapter 2, Freud believed that under the best of conditions human beings are capable of channelling their sexual and aggressive energy into productive and socially acceptable forms of behavior. The process is called **sublimation,** whereby raw instinctual energy is made more "sublime" as it is diverted into culturally useful products and outcomes. Psychoanalysts since Freud have emphasized how the creative person seems to be in close touch with the more primitive regions of the mind. People like Mishima, Mead, and Leonardo are able to draw deftly and repeatedly upon the mind's vast reservoir of irrational, dreamlike material, from which creative insights may spring. Some psychoanalysts describe this process as a "regression in service of the ego" (Kris, 1952). Creative adults are able to regress, or go back to, primitive forms of thinking, closely tied to the instinctual urges, and retrieve images and ideas that they then transform into paintings, stories, projects, songs, discoveries, and various other products and outcomes that come to be seen by others as especially "creative."

A second and very different way to approach creativity is to ask what personal dispositions and environmental influences go into the making of creative behavior. How might we predict creative behavior from assessing personality traits, situations, and their interactions? From the standpoint of *interaction episodes,* psychologists have identified such traits as "self-confidence," "openness to experience," and "aesthetic interests" and such environmental influences as "creative role models" and "warm, noncontrolling parenting styles" as significant predictors of creative behavior (Martindale, 1989). Studies of art students, for example, have shown that the most creative tend to be sensitive, open to new experiences and impulses, self-sufficient, and relatively uninterested in social norms and social acceptance (Csikszentmihalyi, 1990). Writes one author, "over the years the trait that most consistently differentiated the successful artist from those who gave up a creative career has been the trait of cyclothymia, or a cold and aloof disposition" (Csikszentmihalyi, 1990, p. 192). The tendency toward cyclothymia would appear to be quite prominent in the life of Mishima, but certainly not Mead. Traits of self-confidence, self-sufficiency, openness to experience, and disregard of social norms would appear to be strong in both Mishima and Mead. Mead's autobiography, furthermore, suggests that her childhood was blessed with creative role models and the warm, supportive, and noncontrolling influence of her parents. Mishima, however, shows a very different pattern of childhood influences.

A good example of creativity research from the standpoint of interaction episodes is Ravenna Helson's (1976, 1990) studies of creative behavior among women mathematicians. Helson found that the traits especially characteristic of the most creative female mathematicians were (1) "rebellious independence, narcissism, introversion, and a rejection of outside influence"; (2) "strong symbolic interests and a marked ability to find self-expression and self-gratification in directed research activity"; and (3) "flexibility" both in general attitudes and in mathematical work. But traits do not develop in a vacuum; situational influences can be extremely important. Helson (1976) found that "almost all of the women mathematicians grew up in homes with strong respect for learning and cultural values" (p. 247). Most of them, as little girls, were rewarded for intellectual successes. And many seemed to form strong identifications with their fathers.

Studies that seek to predict creative behavior from traits and situations, like all personological inquiries, must be understood in social and historical context. Helson examined creativity among women who attended graduate school and received their Ph.D.s in mathematics between the years of 1950 and 1960. It is now almost 40 years later, and Americans have witnessed a revolution of attitudes since the 1950s concerning professional achievement and gender. Do the same traits and situational influences predict creative accomplishment among women mathematicians today? We do not know. Traits and situational forces may change meaning and significance as times change and culture evolves. "Openness to experience" may mean something different today than it meant in the 1950s. As more and more women enter professional settings, young girls may begin to identify more with mothers rather than fathers as they aspire to achieve and to be creative in their adult years. This is just to say that interaction episodes unfold in the encompassing contexts of culture and history. We must always be alert to the possibility that what predicts behavior today may not predict the same behavior tomorrow (Gergen, 1973).

From the third approach of *interpretive structures,* the psychologist may consider the characteristic ways in which the creative person makes sense of reality. How do creative people think about themselves and their world? What is their conscious *experience* of everyday life and of the creative process? Humanistic psychologists Abraham Maslow and Carl Rogers (Chapter 9 in this text) suggest that especially creative people seem able to perceive the world in an unusually fresh and innocent way, much like a child. They exhibit a "special kind of perceptiveness that is exemplified by the child in the fable who saw that the emperor had no clothes on." This kind of perception is "spontaneous, effortless, easy, a kind of freedom from stereotypes and cliches" (Maslow, 1976, p. 88). Rogers says that to be creative, a person must have the ability "to play spontaneously with ideas, colors, shapes, relationships—to juggle elements into impossible juxtapositions, to shape wild hypotheses, to make the given problematic, to express the ridiculous, to translate from one form to another, to transform into improbable equivalents. It is from this spontaneous toying and exploration that there arises the hunch, the creative seeing of life in a new and significant way" (Rogers, 1976, p. 301).

In sharp contrast to Freud, Rogers and Maslow see creativity as springing from the loftiest inclinations of women and men. There is no need to "make sublime" (sublimation) the base instincts of sex and aggression in order to create an innovative and useful product. Rather, the mainspring of creativity is the human tendency to actualize the self, to become all that the single human being can become. To be creative is to exercise one's inherent capacities to the fullest. In contrast to the perspective of interpersonal stories, Maslow and Rogers focus on what is inside the individual rather than within the social world in explaining creativity. Especially creative people judge their own work according to internal standards. They are not swayed very much by social praise or criticism. As we might imagine in the life of Mishima, their subjective experience of creating may often involve feelings of separateness, of being cut off from other people and from the conventions of society:

> I do not believe that many significantly creative products are formed without the feeling, "I am alone." No one has ever done just this before. I have ventured into territory where no one has been. Perhaps I am foolish, or wrong, or lost, or abnormal. (Rogers, 1976, p. 302)

A fourth and final approach to creativity is to consider the narrative pattern of the creative person's life. What is the *interpersonal story* that provides the creative person's life with unity and purpose? A clear statement of this aim appears in the writings of Howard Gruber on "the evolving systems approach to creative work." Gruber insists that "the central problem for the study of creative work is to understand how one organizes and reconstructs a life to form a system of knowledge, purpose, and affect that can do creative work" (Gruber & Davis, 1988, p. 245). Gruber does not desire to explore the unconscious determinants of the creative process. He is not interested in predicting creative accomplishment from measures of traits and environments. Instead, Gruber examines detailed biographical data from the lives of a select few eminent writers and scientists (for example, William Wordsworth and Charles Darwin; Wallace & Gruber, 1989) in order to address questions such as these: How is creativity born? How does it grow over time? What is *the story* of its evolution in one woman's or man's life? How is that story situated in culture and history?

Gruber (1989) lists five principles of the evolving systems approach to creativity:

1. *Development:* Creative work evolves over long periods of time. It is purposeful work and there is a constant interplay among purpose, play, and chance.
2. *Pluralism:* The creative person enjoys and exploits not one but many insights, metaphors, social relationships, projects, heuristics, and so on.
3. *Interaction:* The creative person works within some historical, societal, and institutional framework. The work is always conducted in relation to the work of others.
4. *Constructionism:* The creator participates in choosing and shaping the surroundings within which the work proceeds, the skills needed for the work, and the definition of the ensemble of tasks. The creator must reconstruct and take possession of whatever he or she needs for the work.
5. *Awareness:* The creator is not considered simply as the doer of the work, but also as a person in the world. Such a person has emotions and aesthetic

feelings as well as social awareness of the relation of his or her work to the world's work, its needs, and feelings. (Adapted from Gruber, 1989, pp. 4–5.)

From the perspective of interpersonal stories, the evolution of a person's creative work cannot be separated from his or her evolving identity within a particular sociohistorical context. As one psychologist puts it, "creativeness and identity drive one another and are dependent on the other's development" (Albert, 1990, p. 18). Mishima wrote novels and plays in accord with his own personal and interpersonal quest to create a coherent set of meaningful roles for himself as a postwar novelist in Japan. He created a life script that made sense, as bizarre as it may seem, within the conventions of the Japanese literary world. Mead fashioned a meaningful narrative for her own life by finding and recreating roles for herself in the domain of American anthropology. For both Mishima and Mead, purpose, play, and chance combined to create careers of creativity that defined who they were.

In conclusion, we see that the four general approaches to studying persons can also be applied to particular topics with which personality psychologists have traditionally been interested, such as the topic of creativity. To sum up this introduction of the four orientations around which this textbook is organized, Table 1.2 outlines the major goals, points of emphasis, methods of measurement, and representative theories for intrapsychic mysteries, interaction episodes, interpretive structures, and interpersonal stories.

Science and the Person

Personality psychology is best learned and appreciated through the lives of real, flesh-and-blood persons, which is why we have spent so much time on Mishima and Mead. However, although both of them are interesting, especially in light of the four perspectives on personality psychology (Table 1.2), the choice to focus on them was actually rather arbitrary. Personality psychologists need not limit their studies to persons who are famous or whose lives, like Mishima's, seem strange and enigmatic. For instance, Robert White (1975) has shown that personality psychologists can find much to challenge and intrigue them in the careful case analysis of three very "normal" and "ordinary" American adults, whom he names Hartley Hale, Joseph Kidd, and Joyce Kingsley (See Feature 1.A). As we will see, most empirical research in personality psychology deals with everyday people, often college students like you.

Having introduced Mishima and Mead as a flesh-and-blood context for our discussion of persons, let us now shift gears. I stated at the outset of this chapter that personality psychology involves the *scientific* study of the whole person. It is time to examine the "science" part of this statement. What is science? How can we study persons scientifically?

 **Table 1.2**

Four Perspectives on the Person

	Intrapsychic Mysteries	Interaction Episodes
1. Major Goal of Inquiry	To uncover the hidden forces, factors, and conflicts within the person that serve as the ultimate determinants of personality.	To identify the variables in the person and in the environment that must be known in order to predict the person's overt behavior in a given situation.
2. Points of Emphasis	Unconscious wishes, urges, desires, conflicts; biological instincts concerning survival, reproduction/sexuality, aggression.	Personality traits; learning in the environment; characteristics of situations; interaction of traits and environmental factors.
3. Preferred Methods of Measuring Personality	Interpretation of spontaneous and creative productions, such as dreams, fantasies, responses to ambiguous stimulus (Rorschach inkblot test); examination of myth and folklore; also naturalistic observation.	Self-report questionnaires; direct observation of overt behavior in both experimental and natural situations; emphasis on precise quantification in measurement.
4. Representative Theorists and Theories	Sigmund Freud Carl Jung Ego psychology Object-relations theory Sociobiological/evolutionary approaches Hogan's socioanalytic theory Bowlby's theory of attachment	Trait theory: 　Hans Eysenck 　The Big 5 traits 　Temperament theory Social Learning theory: 　Albert Bandura 　Julian Rotter 　Walter Mischel behaviorism Interactionism Block's typologies

Science is a multifaceted human endeavor whereby we try to make the confusion of everyday experience more understandable. Through science, we formulate statements about reality and then assess their truth value through rigorous and replicable tests. We do this in order to create an orderly and predictable model of the universe and how it functions. Our motivations for doing this are many. They include the desire to control our environments in order to stave off threat and danger posed by the natural world (disease, natural catastrophe) or by

	Interpretive Structures	**Interpersonal Stories**
1. Major Goal of Inquiry	To determine the persons's own strategies, plans, and frameworks for understanding the self and the world.	To discern or construct a narrative that depicts the psychosocial pattern or form of the person's life, embedded in a world of other persons.
2. Points of Emphasis	Cognition and consciousness; meaning-making; the self as knower (subject) and known (object); values, beliefs, schemas, scripts, philosophies of life; subjective conscious experience.	Interpersonal relationships; emotions; identity; the storylike quality of persons' lives; beginnings and endings in narrative; goals and motives; general themes in biography.
3. Preferred Methods of Measuring Personality	Phenomenological methods in which person describes subjective experience; cognitive methods such as Kelly's REP test; value surveys.	Narrative and biographical approaches: autobiography, personal documents, the Thematic Apperception Test.
4. Representative Theorists and Theories	Existentialism/phenomenology Carl Rogers Abraham Maslow George Kelly Self-determination theory Social cognition theories Cognitive-developmental theories of self Loevinger's ego development	Henry Murray McClelland's research on motives Erik Erikson Alfred Adler Levinson's seasons of adulthood Tomkins' script theory Narratives of identity The Postmodern self

other humans whom we fear (enemies in times of war, people we do not like). Our motivations for doing science also include the wish to improve our lives and the lives of generations to come, through understanding more about the world and by making things (telephones, X-ray machines, jet planes, VCRs) that promise to enhance our lives in the world. Most basic, however, is the simple desire to understand—the fundamental motive of curiosity. Science depends on the human desire

Continued on p. 32

Joseph Kidd: An Ordinary Guy

Yukio Mishima and Margaret Mead were extraordinary persons whose works and lives are a matter of public record. Personality psychologists, however, do not limit their investigations to extraordinary and famous people. Personality theories are designed to illuminate the lives of the most ordinary among us, and most personality research conducted today takes as its subjects of study relatively normal and not-so-famous people, like college students, businessmen, nurses, store clerks, and homemakers.

A classic attempt to study in depth and over time the lives of three relatively normal, even ordinary, American adults is Robert White's (1952, 1966, 1975) *Lives in Progress.* White focused exclusively on the lives of two men and one woman in order to accomplish two goals: (1) "to understand them as fully as possible in light of existing ideas from biological research, psychology, psychoanalysis, and the social sciences" and (2) "to name some of the ideas that need to be added in order to account for natural growth" (1975, p. 3). Physician Hartley Hale, businessman Joseph Kidd, and social worker Joyce Kingsley (the names are pseudonyms) were each studied on several occasions, beginning in college and extending (in two of the cases) past the subject's fiftieth

birthday. The three were interviewed and administered a series of psychological measures, including questionnaires and open-ended tests of imagination at regular intervals. White's masterful case summaries illustrate the complexity of normal personality development while providing a great amount of interesting life data that can be interpreted in many different ways and on many different levels.

Raised as the second son in a close-knit Irish Catholic family, Joseph Kidd was a mentally precocious and physically beautiful child, who enjoyed high levels of self-esteem, until he was double-promoted from fourth to sixth grade in elementary school. As Kidd tells it, the double promotion marked the beginning of a difficult chapter in his life wherein he repeatedly behaved in a childish and silly manner in order to regain the praise and attention of his early years. Excessive masturbation in early adolescence exacerbated his painful self-consciousness and insecurity and left him with an image of himself as a "soft" and "sissylike" class clown. Kidd believed that he had reached the lowest point in his personality development a year or two before his first interview for the study. After a series of setbacks, including learning that his first girlfriend, Mildred, had deceived him, the high school junior came to feel that he had "no personality." In terms of Erikson's psychosocial theory, we might restate Kidd's concern as a profound feeling of identity confusion: of not knowing who he is and how he fits into an adult world.

In subsequent years, Kidd appears to find an identity, though the process is by no means smooth. Indeed, a careful reading of the case may raise serious doubts about the extent to which Kidd ever attains "maturity." Nonetheless, a 4-year stint in the military, successes in the family business, a venture into local politics, marriage and the establishment of a family, and a number of other key events and transformations in Kidd's life bring with them a significant increase in self-confidence and a feeling of personal control over his own destiny: "It dawned on me after a while that I was knowing what I wanted. I was able to make up my mind" (White, 1975, p. 130). The course of the development, however, is uneven, full of fits and starts. In a rather dramatic turn of events, Mildred resurfaces 30 years after the conclusion of their high school romance, now unhappily married in her late 40s. For the next 8 months, Joseph and Mildred have the sexual affair they both wish they had followed through on in high school, "making up for the chastity we had

sacrificed for in our six years of going together" (White, 1975, p. 204).

Now age 54 at the last interview White conducts, Kidd appears to be entering another extremely difficult period in his life. His political fortunes have ebbed, and he feels that he is unlikely to regain the prominence in public life he once enjoyed. Relationships with his wife and children are going fairly well despite occasional frustrations. But relationships with his brother and father have deteriorated badly, and he has not talked with either of them for 10 years, describing his relatives with such blunt words as "thief" and "drunk." Though his business continues to provide him with security and a decent income, new financial problems have emerged. At age 54, Kidd often feels discouraged and resentful, but he manages to cope moderately well with the many trials of everyday life as a middle-aged, middle-class American man. There is no return in Kidd's life to "the indiscriminate self-blame, conviction of inferiority, and disorganized behavior that were so conspicuous at eighteen" (p. 204). Concludes White (1975, p. 204), "the natural growth of personality does not necessarily go into reverse because conditions are hard. Sometimes it even works the other way."

Continued from p. 29
to know for the sake of knowing. Therefore, while the personality psychologist may study the person for a wide variety of reasons—to provide a diagnosis in the clinic, to help select a job candidate, to design an appropriate treatment strategy—the fundamental goal is to understand the person for the sake of understanding.

Science generally proceeds according to three steps: (1) unsystematic observation, (2) building theories, and (3) evaluating propositions. These three steps refer both to what the individual scientist does when exploring a new problem or issue and to what particular fields of science do or have done—fields such as organic chemistry, economics, botany, and personality psychology—as they evolve from "primitive" to more "mature" sciences. Because it is relatively new, personality psychology is still a fairly primitive science. Nonetheless, all three steps in the scientific process are clearly evident in what personality psychologists do today. Let us then examine each of these steps in some detail.

Step 1: Unsystematic Observation

The first step in developing a scientific understanding of anything is to look at, listen to, feel, smell, and/or taste the thing we want to understand. We may do this with the help of special instruments like telescopes and stethoscopes or we may rely solely on our unassisted five senses (most often seeing and hearing). But however we do it, we must carefully *observe* the phenomenon of interest over a long period of time. Early observation is relatively unsystematic. We explore the phenomenon with few expectations about what we will see (or hear). We look for patterns, regularities in the phenomenon, so that we can arrive at a tentative first ordering or classification of what we are observing. The process requires a playful and almost naive approach to reality on the part of the scientist. The great physicist, Sir Isaac Newton (1642–1727), captured the attitude perfectly in this passage written shortly before his death:

> I do not know what I may appear to the world, but to myself I seem to have been only like a boy playing on the sea shore, and diverting myself in now and then finding a smoother pebble or a prettier shell than ordinary, whilst the great ocean of truth lay all undiscovered before me. (Judson, 1980, p. 114)

Let us not be fooled into thinking, however, that the scientist's curiosity is slaked by collecting innocent sense impressions about the world. The right image of the scientist in Step 1 of the scientific process is that of a *creative observer* who perceives order or pattern where it has not been perceived before. Discussing the physical sciences, Hanson (1972) states that the keen observer is "not the man who sees and reports what all normal observers see and report, but the man who sees in familiar objects what no one else has seen before" (p. 30). Thus, unsystematic observation is not a passive and casual sort of thing but rather an active attempt to *discern* and then *describe* organization, pattern, design, or structure

The creative observer, like this blind-from birth physicist, discovers new ways of seeing "reality."

in a phenomenon that initially seems to be unorganized and without design. This highly descriptive exploratory phase of the scientific enterprise is crucial, for it provides the scientist and the scientific community with a set of articulately described patterns in the concrete world that can be synthesized into a more general or abstract theory about how that world works.

It may be surprising to learn that science as described in Step 1 is an inherently *subjective* endeavor. We tend to believe science to be a rational, objective, and dispassionate sort of thing. Whereas this view has a good deal of merit with respect to certain aspects of science (especially Step 3, as described below), it is misleading when it comes to Step 1. The creative observer of reality who sees things in a way different than does anybody else is not necessarily "objective" in his or her point of view. Rather, the creative observer interacts in a highly subjective way with the phenomenon of study, in some cases altering the phenomenon by virtue of observing it (Hanson, 1972; Zukav, 1979). The scientist in Step 1, operating in the **context of discovery** (Reichenbach, 1938), seeks to discover new ways of seeing reality, formulating in a highly subjective manner new categories, new terminologies, and new distinctions to describe the careful observations that he or she undertakes. As the scientist begins to organize observations into categories, he or she moves from the *concrete* and *particular* events that are discerned to the more *abstract* and *general* representation of those events, a process that philosophers call **induction.** The ultimate result of induction is the creation of the abstract and general theory of Step 2, which is ultimately grounded in the subjective observations of Step 1 (Glaser & Strauss, 1967).

There are numerous examples in psychology of highly subjective observation of human behavior resulting in new insights and theories. The Swiss developmental psychologist, Jean Piaget (1952, 1965), based many aspects of his theory of cognitive development on the careful observations he made of his own three children in their first few years of life. Many of the most influential ideas in the personality theory of Sigmund Freud (Chapters 2–3) are results of Freud's highly subjective observations of the dream reports, spontaneous utterances, and behavioral symptoms displayed by his neurotic patients, his colleagues, and (maybe most of all) himself. Both Piaget and Freud organized many of their initial observations within **case studies.** A case study is an in-depth investigation of a single individual, sometimes conducted over a substantial period of time. The case-study method gives the personologist a good deal of information about one human being. Though case studies can be used in a number of different ways (Hersen & Barlow, 1981; Yin, 1984), personality psychologists have traditionally used them as ways to organize complex observations about a single person so as to build a theory about some (or all) persons in general. In later chapters we will encounter numerous examples of case studies in personality psychology that serve as bridges between the unsystematic observation of single individuals in Step 1 and the building of more general theories in Step 2.

Step 2: Building Theories

The second step of the scientific enterprise involves making a theory. Scientists organize the various observations collected in Step 1 into a more or less coherent system that explains the phenomenon of interest. Precisely how scientists do this, however, is one of the great mysteries of science. Though theories arise out of observations, they are not always arrived at in a completely logical or systematic manner. Some highly creative scientists stress the seemingly irrational and unconscious manner in which a theoretical insight may have come to them.

In a famous story, Friedrich Kekule, a German chemist of the nineteenth century, described how a series of discoveries concerning the structure of organic molecules came to him in hypnagogic reveries, or waking dreams. In Kekule's day, chemists had discerned a number of different chemical compounds containing carbon, hydrogen, oxygen, and a few other elements, but they had found it especially difficult to link these observations together via an abstract theory specifying the rules of their structure. Kekule had dwelt on the compounds' behavior so intensely that, on occasion, the atoms would appear to dance before him in hallucinations. One summer evening, he fell into a reverie and (he later wrote) "Lo! The atoms were gamboling before my eyes. . . . I saw how, frequently, two atoms united to form a pair; how a larger one embraced two smaller ones; how still larger ones kept hold of three or even four of the smaller; whilst the whole kept whirling in a giddy dance. I saw how the larger ones formed a chain" (Judson, 1980, p. 115). Another time, when Kekule was nodding in his chair before the fire, the atoms danced again, "all twining and twisting in snakelike motion. But look! What was that? One of the snakes had seized hold of its own tail, and the form whirled mockingly before my eyes" (Judson, 1980, p. 115). The chains and rings that Kekule imagined came to comprise the fundamental models or pictures of organic molecules that underlie basic theories of organic chemistry even today.

I do not want to suggest that scientific theories are always, or even often, formulated through dreams and reverie, but they are sometimes developed in strange ways. How strange these ways are is not necessarily a reflection of how good the theory is. This is an important point in personality psychology, because (as we will see in the chapters to follow) the many theories of personality that have been offered have been created in a wide variety of ways, some stranger than others. There is no consensus in the scientific community about the *best* way of proceeding in Step 2 of the scientific process—the step in which the scientist builds a theory.

There is a lot of agreement, however, on what a theory is and what it should do. A **theory** is *a set of interrelated statements proposed to explain certain observations of reality.* A theory is always a tentative and somewhat speculative abstraction. A theory is generally accepted by a scientific community to the extent that it is consistent with observations of the phenomena it purports to explain. Theories are subject to change whenever new, inconsistent observations become available.

A theory provides at least four different tools that the scientist can use to increase understanding (Millon, 1973): (1) an abstract *model* or picture that serves as an easily envisioned representation for the structure of the theory, (2) a conceptual *terminology* or set of names for key ideas and major classes of observations in the theory, (3) a set of *correspondence rules* that describe the specific relationships to be expected between the various components, and (4) *hypotheses* or testable predictions that are logically derived from the correspondence rules.

In other words, a theory provides a particular picture of reality, well-defined terms that name the major components of that picture, specified relationships among the components, and specific predictions about how those relationships can be tested in empirical research. The four aspects of theory are used by scientists to explain a set of observations in a clear and precise manner. Many psychologists in general and personologists in particular lament that their theories do not explain as much as they would like. Nonetheless, virtually all agree that theories are at the heart of science. Furthermore, they agree that some theories are "better" than others, though they disagree wildly as to exactly *which* ones are better. What makes one theory better? What are the criteria of a good theory? Below are seven standards by which a scientific theory may be judged (from Epstein, 1973; Gergen, 1982).

1.   *Comprehensiveness.* The wider the scope of a theory's explanatory abilities the better. All other things being equal, a theory that explains more is preferred to one that explains less.

2. *Parsimony.* Science is a simplifying and economizing game. Theories attempt to explain the maximum number of observations with the minimum number of explanatory concepts. Thus, a simpler and more straightforward explanation is generally preferred to a more complex one.

3. *Coherence.* A theory should be logical and internally consistent. The various statements that make it up should hang together in a sensible manner.

4. *Testability.* From the theory, a scientist should be able to derive hypotheses that can be readily evaluated (tested) through empirical research.

5. *Empirical Validity.* Empirical tests of hypotheses derived from the theory should support the theory's major claims. In other words, the results of hypothesis-testing research should be in accord with what the theory says.

6. *Usefulness.* Theories that are able, in some way, to solve humanly significant problems are generally preferred to those that seem less relevant, all other things being equal.

7. *Generativity.* A good theory should generate new research and new theorizing. It should give birth to a wide variety of creative activity on the part of scientists and laypersons alike. In the social sciences, a generative theory may serve "to challenge guiding assumptions of the culture, to raise fundamental questions regarding contemporary social life, to foster reconsideration of that which is 'taken for granted,' and thereby to generate fresh alternatives for social action" (Gergen, 1982, p. 109).

Step 3: Evaluating Propositions

Science distinguishes itself from all other modes of understanding the world by virtue of its insistence on evaluating propositions in an empirical fashion. The theories of Step 2 that derive from the observations of Step 1 must be empirically *tested* in Step 3 as the scientist moves from the context of discovery to the **context of justification** (Reichenbach, 1938). In Step 3, the scientist attempts to evaluate or "justify" the truth of a given statement proposed by a given theory. The scientist seeks to subject a portion of a theory to a rigorous and objective test. This is where the image of the scientist as a no-nonsense, hard-headed, cool, and dispassionate examiner of the real world has its origin and its validity. The context of justification is no place for flights of fancy and wild speculation; it is no place for exploring phenomena in an unsystematic and subjective manner. Rather, the scientist carefully determines the truth and utility of theoretical propositions that were formulated in the more freewheeling Steps 1 and 2 of the scientific process.

However, although Steps 1 and 2 are *more* freewheeling than Step 3, they are not so freewheeling that virtually anything goes. Indeed, the scientist's *anticipation* of Step 3—his or her knowledge that theories must ultimately be subjected to empirical test—influences the way in which the scientist explores the phenomenon of interest (Step 1) and the kinds of theories he or she eventually produces (Step 2). In other words, the anticipation of Step 3 in the scientific process feeds back to influence what the scientist does in Steps 1 and 2. Therefore, scientists who are making theories are urged by the logic of scientific inquiry to make theories that present *testable hypotheses.* In the words of the philosopher of science, Karl Popper (1959), a theory should be stated in such a way as to render its propositions **falsifiable.** The theory *should specify what observations it would take to disprove its major propositions,* or such observations should at least be deducible from the theory's propositions.

Popper's standard of falsifiability is a real bugaboo for the more speculative and philosophical among us because it puts fairly substantial constraints on the kinds of theoretical statements we can make. For instance, a personality theory that proposes that all human beings are basically good is not, in and of itself, falsifiable, because any instance of bad behavior can be dismissed as merely superficial behavior that masks the *fundamental* goodness of people. We can design no set of observations that would enable us to prove the statement false, to prove that people are *not* good. Therefore, as a scientific proposition, the statement that all people are good (or that all people are bad, or neutral, or even intelligent) flunks the basic test of falsifiability. There are many statements like this, and some are included as basic assumptions in certain personality theories existing today. Nonetheless, personality theories also contain a number of propositions that *are* falsifiable, such as Adler's claim (Chapter 12) that firstborn children tend to be more conservative than other children, or Erikson's proposition (Chapter 12) that healthy psychosocial development involves the establishment of identity *before* one establishes intimacy with others. Statements such as these can be tested using standard personality research methods. Let us now consider in general terms how this is done. In later chapters, we will examine many specific examples of evaluating theoretical propositions through personality research.

Setting Up an Empirical Study   Let us imagine that we wish to evaluate Alfred Adler's proposition, embedded within his more general personality theory (Chapter 12), that firstborn children tend to be more conservative than later-born children. How might we begin? Well, chances are that we have already begun! By stating a testable hypothesis derived from Adler's theory, we are showing that we have some familiarity with Adler's theory. *Scientific hypotheses should be grounded in theories.* Immersing oneself, therefore, in the theoretical and empirical literature that bears on a given proposition is an essential early task of hypothesis-testing research. Thus, our initial responsibility in carrying out this empirical study is to go back to Adler's writings to review exactly what his theory suggests. In doing this, we come to realize that we cannot possibly submit all of Adler's ideas to empirical test at once. Rather, we can test one hypothesis at a time. We would continue our background reading to include various other theories of birth order and theories about conservatism. We would eventually move to the empirical literature, much of it found in scientific journals, on both birth order and conservatism to see (1) how these ideas have been examined empirically by others (what methods scientists have employed) and (2) what empirical findings or results have been obtained. Our background reading would supply us with invaluable ideas concerning how to think about our present study and how to design it to test the hypothesis in a fair and precise way.

Having reviewed the literature on the relationship between birth order and conservatism, we should next choose an appropriate sample of persons to examine. All hypothesis-testing research in personality psychology must confront the problem of sampling. No sample is perfect. One researcher may choose to investigate Adler's hypothesis in a sample of 100 sophomores attending the University of Illinois in the summer of 1993. Another researcher may prefer to look at a sample of 60 girls attending a preschool in Alabama. Another more ambitious researcher may select a nationwide sample of middle-aged men and women, the data for which exist in a national archive that was established 30 years ago.

It is very easy to criticize another person's research in terms of the sample he or she employs, claiming, for instance, that the sample does not represent all people, that the sample is *biased* in some way. The problem is that *all* samples are biased in some way, though some certainly more so than others. In general, we should strive to obtain a sample for our study that is appropriate for the proposition to be evaluated. Therefore, if we are testing a hypothesis about, say, clinically depressed adults, a random sample of college students will not do. If we are testing a hypothesis about changes in normal personality development that occur around age 40, then we need a sample of midlife men and women who have little history of serious psychiatric disturbance. To confirm or disconfirm a given hypothesis, different researchers employing different kinds of samples should, over time, produce similar results. Thus, no single study, no matter how representative or how large the sample, establishes "truth" in science.

With the choice of an appropriate sample of subjects within which to study our hypothesis, the next step is to operationalize the variables that we have chosen to investigate. A variable is *any quality that can assume two or more values.* In our example of testing Adler's hypothesis, both birth order and conservatism are variables because both can be given at least two different values or levels. For instance, a subject in our study can be a firstborn, a second-born, and so on. He or she can also be "extremely conservative," "mildly conservative," "not very conservative," and so on.

To operationalize a variable is *to decide how to measure it*—that is, to specify the "operation" through which it is to be assessed. In our example, birth order is relatively easy to measure. We would merely ask subjects to indicate what their birth order is. Conservatism is a trickier variable. We might wish to administer an established paper-and-pencil test of political values to assess conservatism. Or we might wish to interview subjects to determine the extent of their conservative orientation. Or we might wish to observe "conservative behavior" in a standard laboratory task. There are many possibilities. The important thing to note in all of this is that we would ultimately have to translate our observations about conservatism into *numbers* in order to assess our hypothesis. In other words, the operationalization of most variables in personality research requires us to quantify the data. Personality psychologists have devised a number of different procedures for quantifying variables. We will have numerous opportunities to see these methods in action when we examine particular research efforts in subsequent chapters.

As they operationalize variables in order to evaluate theoretical proposi-tions, personality psychologists tend to design studies according to one of two very simple, basic research designs, or combinations of the two. These two gen-eral formats for hypothesis-testing research are the *correlational* and the *experi-mental* design.

The Correlational Design   Empirical studies that assess the extent to which two different variables relate to each other are termed *correlational* ("co-related") studies. In a correlational study, the scientist asks a very simple question: When one variable changes in value, what happens to the other variable?

If an increase in the value of one variable tends to be associated with an increase in value of the other variable, the variables show a *positive correlation* to each other. An example of a positive correlation would be the relationship between the two variables of height and weight in a random sample of 200 Ameri-can adults. In general, as height goes up, weight goes up, though of course there are exceptions. A positive correlation between height and weight in this sample says that taller people, on the average, tend to be heavier than shorter people. Thus, having information about one of the variables for a given subject gives you a reliable hint about the value of the other variable for that subject: if you know that John is tall, you might guess—with a fair chance of being correct—that he is relatively heavy (compared to a short person).

A *negative correlation* is indicated when an increase in one variable is gen-erally associated with a *decrease* in the other variable. An example here might be the relationship between the variables of age and thumb sucking in a random sample of 500 American children between the ages 12 weeks and 12 years. In gen-eral, as age goes up, thumb sucking goes down: older children suck their thumbs less frequently, on the average, than younger children.

When two variables are not related to each other in any systematic manner, we say that there is little or no correlation between them. An example of this third possibility might be the relationship between the variables of weight and intelli-gence in a random sample of 1000 American adults. In general, heavier adults are neither consistently more intelligent nor consistently less intelligent than lighter adults. Therefore, weight and intelligence are uncorrelated with each other: merely knowing an adult's weight will give you no reliable hint concerning his or her intelligence.

A numerical way of expressing the degree of correlation between two vari-ables is the *correlation coefficient.* Readily calculated with a hand calculator or computer, correlation coefficients range from $+1.0$ (a perfect positive correla-tion) through 0.0 (no correlation between the two variables) to -1.0 (a perfect negative correlation). Figure 1.1 illustrates the distribution of scores on two vari-ables that would produce five different values for correlation coefficients. In per-sonality research, correlations generally fall within a "moderate" range. For instance, a moderately strong positive correlation between two personality vari-ables might be $+.50$ ($r = +.50$); a moderately strong negative correlation between two personality variables might be $-.50$ ($r = -.50$).

Like most statistics used by personality psychologists, individual correlation coefficients are often evaluated in terms of their statistical significance. Statistical

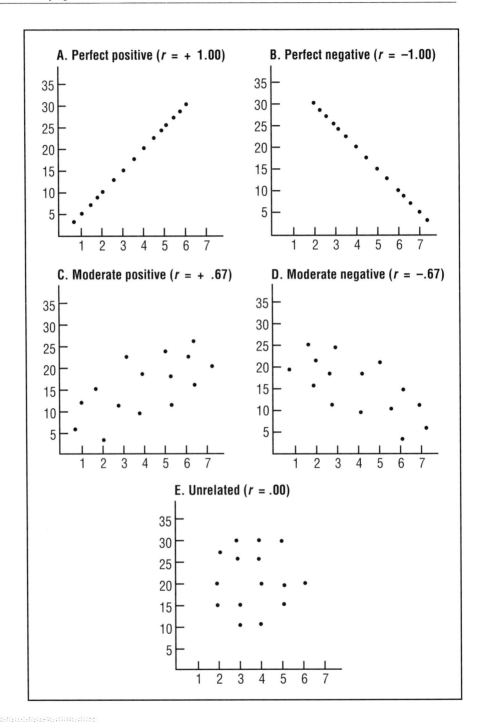

Figure 1.1

Scatter Diagrams Showing Various Degrees of Correlation Between Two Variables.

significance is a measure of the extent to which a given result can be attributed to chance. As a general convention, personality psychologists maintain that a given effect, relationship, or difference is statistically significant when the probability of obtaining that effect, relationship, or difference by chance is *less than 5%*. We say, in this case, that the finding is "significant at the .05 level," meaning that there is less than a 5% likelihood that the particular finding we have obtained is due to chance (or, saying it another way, there is more than a 95% likelihood that the finding is *not* due to chance). With respect to correlation coefficients, statistical significance is determined by the absolute value of the correlation coefficient and the number of subjects from which the correlation was obtained. Thus a relatively strong negative correlation of −.57 would be statistically significant in a sample of 100 subjects, but the same −.57 would not be strong enough to reach statistical significance in a sample of only 10 subjects.

Although a correlational study shows which different variables naturally relate to each other, *correlation does not imply causation.* Just because variables A and B are correlated in a statistically significant manner, we cannot legitimately conclude that A causes B or that B causes A. Thus, a statistically significant correlation coefficient of +.45 between two variables—say, number of silk blouses owned and the size of one's office in a sample of 50 female business executives— does not mean that owning silk blouses causes one to occupy large offices or that large offices cause one to own silk blouses. We might instead speculate that a third variable, such as executive status, is probably at work here, causally responsible for the other two variables. Female executives with higher statuses probably, because of their status, occupy larger offices and enjoy greater purchasing power (with which to buy silk blouses) than do low-status executives.

The Experimental Design   It is generally believed that personality psychologists *can* determine cause-and-effect relationships between different variables *in an experiment.* In an experiment, a scientist *manipulates or alters one variable of interest in order to observe its impact on another variable of interest.* The first variable—the one that is manipulated or altered—is termed the *independent variable.* The second variable is the *dependent variable.* The dependent variable is understood as the subject's response to the experimental alteration or manipulation of the independent variable. Thus, the dependent variable is a function of the independent variable: it is "dependent" on the independent variable. In cause-and-effect terms, experimentally controlled variations in the independent variable are seen as *causing* variations in the dependent variable.

If an experiment is to give valid information concerning cause and effect, the experimenter must make sure that the independent variable is the *only* variable that is systematically altered. Therefore, the experimenter designs the study to hold all variables constant except one—the independent variable—so that he or she can conclude that variations in the subject's responses (the dependent variable) are functions of variations in the independent variable, and *only* in the independent variable. Other extraneous variables threaten to confound the results; therefore, they must be controlled, to the greatest extent possible. This is why experiments are usually conducted in highly controlled environments, such as laboratory rooms. In these kinds of settings, the experimenter is able to control closely the kinds of stimuli to which the subjects are exposed and to observe carefully the subjects' responses.

Let us illustrate the basic principles of the experiment with a very simple example. Imagine that you wished to design an experiment testing the hypothesis that a person smiles more when interacting with another person who smiles than when interacting with a person who does not smile. You obtain a sample of 100 college students to participate as subjects in your study. Each subject is asked to come to a laboratory room to engage in a one-on-one interview, which is to be videotaped. Subjects are randomly assigned to one of two different groups: the experimental group and the control group. This means that 50 of your 100 subjects are chosen by chance (such as by flipping a coin or pulling names out of a hat) to participate in each of the two *conditions,* or groups. For the experimental group, the interviewer talks with the subject for about 20 minutes, emitting smiles at regular intervals determined ahead of time by the experimenter. Subjects in the control group experience the same interview except for one critical difference: the interviewer does not smile. *It is essential that the conditions of the experimental and control groups, therefore, be identical with the exception of one variable:* the interviewer's smiling. Thus, the independent variable in this experiment is whether or not the interviewer smiles. The dependent variable is the amount of smiling emitted by the subject being interviewed, which could be assessed by observing the videotapes. The hypothesis would receive experimental support if the subjects in the experimental group smile more than do subjects in the control group, at a level reaching statistical significance. A statistically significant difference between the two groups in this experiment would suggest that variations in the experimentally manipulated independent variable were responsible for, or *caused,* variations in the dependent variable. In other words, the level of smiling of the interviewer was responsible for determining the level of smiling of the interviewee.

Because of the experiment's ability to tease out cause and effect through the careful manipulation and control of variables under standardized conditions, some psychologists consider the experiment vastly superior to the correlational design as a basic method for doing hypothesis-testing research. For instance, one researcher terms the experiment "the basic method of science" (Mischel, 1986, p. 15), while others characterize it as the "preferred" (Byrne & Kelley, 1981) or the "most prestigious" (Singer, 1984) method. By contrast, other personality psychologists are highly critical of laboratory experimentation, arguing that experiments tend to be contrived, artificial, and trivial (Carlson, 1971, 1984; Gergen, 1982). Indeed, many empirical questions in personality psychology defy experimental investigation because the independent variables of concern cannot be systematically varied for individual subjects—variables such as sex, age, ethnic origin, birth order, and body size. In some cases in which independent variables can be systematically varied, such an experimental manipulation is unfeasible or unethical. For instance, a scientist wishing to study the effects of child abuse on personality development in humans cannot legally or ethically subject half of the children in a sample to abuse (the experimental group) and half to nonabusive conditions (the control group) and then observe the effects of the manipulation. Rather, child abuse must be studied in the real world through some modification of a general correlational design.

The study of the person is a broad and rich enough endeavor to encompass *both* experimental and correlational approaches to hypothesis-testing research (Duke, 1986). Therefore, later chapters in this book contain numerous examples of good personality research that is purely correlational in nature, many that are purely experimental, and some that are combinations of the two. Both correlational and experimental methods are alive and well, and both are extremely valuable in studying the person. When it comes to personality psychology, it is probably misleading to consider either of the two methods *the* basic method of science.

The three basic steps of scientific inquiry—unsystematic observation, building theories, and evaluating propositions—bring us full circle. We begin in Step 1 with observation; we move to abstractions in Step 2 in which our observations are organized within a theory; and then we move back to observation in Step 3—this time, a more systematic form of observation—as we attempt to test hypotheses empirically. The results of our experiments and correlational studies in Step 3 feed back to modify our theory. Therefore, the observations of Step 3 function in much the same way as their less systematic sisters of Step 1: they influence the making and remaking of theory. *Science progresses through a continuous dialogue between observation and theory.* Observations ultimately give rise to theories. Theories give rise to new observations designed to evaluate the theories' propositions. These new observations feed back to influence the theories from which they were derived, occasionally even giving birth to radically new theories. And so on. An underlying assumption of the whole procedure is that over the long course of observation followed by theory followed by observation, science formulates better and better ways of understanding the world, perhaps moving closer and closer, over a period of many years, to "truth."

Personality Psychology

How are we to understand the person? I mean any person: a friend, a lover, a parent, a daughter, a brother, a classmate, ourselves? What must we *know* to know a person well? What must we *do* in order to comprehend—to know in detail and as a whole—a person's life? How do we know when we know?

These are the kinds of questions with which personality psychologists have traditionally struggled. Their struggle with questions concerning *human individuality* distinguishes personologists from most other psychologists and social scientists. It takes a fair amount of hubris to place the individual human person at the center of all inquiry, to maintain that the person in his or her very individuality is important enough and cohesive enough to warrant special status as *the* main unit of analysis. Modern personality psychology is the heir to what psychological historian Daniel Robinson has called "Renaissance Humanism," the 16th-century worldview that celebrated "the dignity of man, the theme insisting that the world was made for man" (1981, p. 171). Robinson points out that modern science, in its dispassionate objectivity and urge towards reductionism, has generally rejected Renaissance Humanism. But personality psychology has moved against the tide. For the personologist, scientific investigation *is* made for man and for woman. In focusing unswervingly on the individual, personality psychology has come to occupy a unique and extraordinarily critical place in the world of science.

Personality psychology was born within psychology departments in American universities in the 1930s. Although personality theorists such as Freud, Jung, and Adler had been writing for over 30 years by then, it was during the 1930s that a number of separate lines of inquiry came together to generate a new academic discipline. The first issue of the journal *Character and Personality* (now the *Journal of Personality*) appeared in 1932. The journal aimed to join German studies of character with British and American studies of individual differences in persons, incorporating case studies, correlational surveys, experiments, and theoretical discussions. In 1937, Gordon Allport published the first major textbook in personality: *Personality: A Psychological Interpretation.* Although textbooks on mental hygiene, abnormal psychology, and character and personality had appeared in earlier years, Allport's was the first to articulate a grand vision for the field of personality and to place it within the context of historical and contemporary scholarship in the arts and sciences. Allport viewed personality psychology as the study of the individual person. He defined the personality as "the dynamic organization within the individual of those psychophysical systems that determine his unique adjustment to his environment" (Allport, 1937, p. 48).

From the beginning, personality psychology was a *dissident* field on the large scene of American psychology (Hall & Lindzey, 1957). In the 1930s, American psychology tended to focus minutely on such things as habits, reflexes, stimuli, and discrete responses—the basic molecular elements of organisms' behavior. By contrast, personality was holistic, taking the *whole person* as a primary unit of study, suggesting that unity, coherence, and wholeness are properties of human lives. In the 1930s, American psychology obsessed over the vicissitudes of animal learning, focusing on the relation between external stimuli and publicly observed responses in rats and pigeons. By contrast personality concerned itself with the problems of human *motivation,* understood in terms of unobservable urges and promptings from within. This orientation is evident even in textbooks written before Allport. Writes Garnett (1928), "It is surely in the springs of human action, if anywhere, that the key to personality is to be found" (p. 14). In the 1930s, American psychology searched for universal laws applicable to all organisms.

American psychology was a thoroughly **nomothetic** enterprise at this time, meaning that it aimed to discover and test general principles or laws of behavior. By contrast, personality emphasized how people were *different* from each other as well as how they were alike. Allport went so far as to suggest that the scientist should examine each individual personality as a unique entity. He argued for an **idiographic** approach to personality, which, in contrast to the nomothetic approach, would ignore general laws to discern the specific and individual patternings of particular lives. While Allport's insistence on the idiographic has always been controversial even within the field of personality psychology (e.g., Holt, 1962), personologists have traditionally been much more interested than most other psychologists in the complexities of the single case.

From its inception in the 1930s, then, personality psychology stood out from its neighbors for its emphases on (1) the whole person, (2) motivation, and (3) individual differences. Personality still stands out in these three ways. Most of the theories and research examples described in the pages to follow concern themselves with one or more of the three traditional emphases of personality studies. This book reflects the view that personality psychology has indeed developed its own identity as a field of inquiry, and that personality psychology cannot be reduced to other related disciplines. With its emphasis on the whole person, motivation, and individual differences, personality stands at the crossroads of a number of different disciplines within and outside psychology proper. As you will see in the pages to come, the study of the person draws on fields as diverse as human physiology, evolutionary biology, sociology, cultural anthropology, mythology, folklore, biography, and even literary studies. Within psychology proper, personality shares some affinities with developmental, social, abnormal, and clinical psychology. Yet important differences may also be identified.

Although personality psychologists are concerned with the development of human beings from birth to death, they differ from most developmental psychologists in tending to focus their inquiries on the *adult years*. Further, whereas developmental psychology concerns itself with meaningful change and transition over time, personality psychologists tend to focus on those aspects of the person that show some degree of *continuity* or *stability* over time. Although personality psychology and social psychology have many ties (Blass, 1984), personality psychologists traditionally emphasize *individual differences in persons*, whereas social psychologists tend to downplay individual differences and focus instead on how social situations influence persons *in general*. To oversimplify somewhat, personality psychologists are interested in how different people react differently to the same situation, whereas social psychologists emphasize how people in general react differently to different situations.

Certain approaches to personality psychology (such as psychoanalysis) have evolved from the study of abnormal or pathological individuals. Nonetheless, personality psychology differs from abnormal psychology in its emphasis on relatively *normal* functioning. Similarly, though certain personality theories prescribe specific techniques for changing abnormal behavior, personality psychology should not be confused with clinical treatment. As the scientific study of

A background in personality psychology can help a practicing psychologist become an effective counselor.

the whole person, personality psychology is *not centrally concerned with psychotherapy and other "treatment" aspects of clinical practice.* Nonetheless, a thorough grounding in theory and research in personality psychology is, I believe, a fundamental prerequisite for becoming an effective and knowledgeable psychotherapist. As I hope you will also see, such an understanding can enhance a person's own life, as well.

Summary for Chapter 1

1. Personality psychology is the scientific study of the whole person.

2. The person may be viewed from four different conceptual standpoints: intrapsychic mysteries, interaction episodes, interpretive structures, and interpersonal stories. The lives of Japanese novelist Yukio Mishima and American anthropologist Margaret Mead are examined from these four perspectives.

3. From the perspective of intrapsychic mysteries, the personologist searches for the hidden forces, factors, and conflicts within the person that function as the ultimate, unconscious, and biologically grounded determinants of behavior.

4. From the perspective of interaction episodes, the personologist seeks to predict exactly what a person will do in a given situation, either by assessing personality traits, examining the situation, or analyzing the interaction of the two.

5. From the perspective of interpretive structures, the personologist seeks to discern the organization, framework, or plan that the person employs to make sense of self and world.

6. From the perspective of interpersonal stories, the personologist seeks to discover or construct an integrating narrative that specifies how the person's life is embedded in significant interpersonal relationships and in culture.

7. Scientists formulate theoretical statements about reality and assess their truth values through rigorous and replicable tests.

8. The first two steps of scientific inquiry are unsystematic observation and building theories.

9. The third step of scientific inquiry involves deriving hypotheses from theories and testing their adequacy in research.

10. One general design of hypothesis-testing research is the correlational design, in which the psychologist determines the extent to which two or more variables covary.

11. A second general design is the experiment, in which the psychologist manipulates the independent variable in order to assess its impact on the dependent variable.

12. Personality psychology was born in university psychology departments in the 1930s. From the beginning, the field has emphasized the whole person, human motivation, and individual differences in persons.

13. Personality psychologists tend to focus on the enduring and stable characteristics of adults and on individual differences among relatively normal persons.

Part I

Intrapsychic Mysteries

Unconscious Determinants in the Person's Life

Chapter 2   Psychoanalytic Tradition: An Overview
Chapter 3   Discovery and Proof in Psychoanalysis
Chapter 4   Evolution and Human Nature

ntrapsychic mysteries are the deeply buried and instinctually ingrained determinants of human behavior over which we all have very little control. They are
the enigmatic forces within that motivate us to behave in ways that sometimes
seem senseless or irrational on the surface but that obey a hidden logic of survival, sexuality, aggression, or the fulfillment of the unconscious self. In Chapters 2–4, we consider the person from the standpoint of intrapsychic
mysteries. We examine a rich variety of theories, methods, and findings that
stem from a general appreciation of or fascination with the ways in which persons are beholden to an unconscious script for life that was written for them
millions of years ago—a script that ultimately exposes us for the instinctually
driven creatures we have always been.

Chapter 2 provides an historical overview of the psychoanalytic tradition,
beginning with the pioneering work of Sigmund Freud and moving through theories emphasizing ego psychology, object relations, and other important trends
in psychoanalysis. The chapter focuses exclusively on theory, as opposed to
research, and attempts to ground theoretical insights in the social and historical context within which they arose. In addition to Freud, the major theorists we
examine are Carl Jung, Anna Freud, Heinz Hartmann, Karen Horney, Erich
Fromm, W. R. D. Fairbairn, Margaret Mahler, and Heinz Kohut.

Chapter 3 shifts from theory to research by taking a close look at some of
the most interesting and illuminating efforts by psychologists to explore psychoanalytic concepts in an empirical manner. This research takes two very different forms. In the context of discovery, Freud and other psychoanalysts have
interpreted dreams, fantasies, symptoms, slips of the tongue, and other phenomena as if they were written texts, to derive insights and hypotheses for general scrutiny. In the context of justification, psychoanalytically informed
researchers have subjected these insights to careful empirical test to assess the
extent to which their value goes beyond the particular cases within which they
were derived. Chapter 3 presents the best in recent research into such phenomena as repression, nonconscious thinking, the dynamic unconscious, defense
mechanisms, psychosexual stages, object relations, and Jungian types.

In Chapter 4, we leave the psychoanalytic tradition to consider theory and
research in personality that are centrally concerned with evolution and human
nature. Like Freud, Jung, and the psychoanalytic tradition, the approaches we
examine in Chapter 4 share a general belief that behavior is motivated by
instinctual forces over which the individual has minimal control and about
which the individual may be unaware. But these forces are firmly rooted in
gene-driven, instinctive behavior patterns that have evolved over millions of
years as individuals have struggled to survive and reproduce under a wide variety of selection pressures. Chapter 4, therefore, considers what ethology and
sociobiology have to offer the study of persons and examines in detail contemporary evolutionary approaches to human mating, aggression, altruism, and
attachment. The major theories we will encounter include Robert Hogan's
socioanalytic theory of personality and John Bowlby and Mary Ainsworth's
attachment theory.

Chapter 2

Psychoanalytic Tradition
An Overview

Introduction

Sigmund Freud and the Origins of Psychoanalysis: A Life Story
The Setting
> The Romantic Struggle
> Science, Reason, and Morality
> The Great War

The Characters
> The Mother: Amalie Freud
> The Father: Jakob Freud
> The Scientist: Ernst Brucke
> The Visionary: Jean Martin Charcot
> The Healer: Josef Breuer
> The Confidante: Wilhelm Fliess
> The Sons and Daughter

Three Main Tenets of Psychoanalysis
Determinism
Conflict
The Unconscious

The Development of the Sexual Instinct
The Oral Stage
The Anal Stage
The Phallic Stage
> *Feature 2.A: Psychoanalysis and the Sociology of Gender*
Latency and Maturity

The Structural Model of the Mind
The Id
The Ego
The Superego

Psychoanalysis After Freud
Expansion of the Ego
Karen Horney
Erich Fromm
Object Relations
Heinz Kohut

Carl Jung's Analytical Psychology
The Basic Nature of Human Beings
Personality Types and Personality Development
Goddesses and Heroes

Summary

The person is a mystery, even to the self. All that we do, all that we think, all that we feel, all that we love and hate is meaningful, and yet hardly anybody knows what it means. Our ignorance is so pervasive that, in most cases, we are completely in the dark about the meanings and causes of some of our simplest acts and experiences—our silly mistakes, for instance, and our seemingly senseless dreams. Were we to know the meanings, furthermore, we would shudder in disbelief, for even the most innocent comment or gesture may betray a shameful secret of the soul, a secret rooted in our unknown desires to kill, to love, to live, and even to die. In general, we are the anxious protagonists of a tragic drama we call human life. Our anxieties are the inevitable products of relentless conflict—conflict within the self and conflict between the self and the society within which the self resides.

As you may have guessed by now, I am sketching, in very broad strokes, a psychoanalytic image of the person. Though parts of this image can be traced back to earlier times and sources, Sigmund Freud (1856–1939) produced the first vivid, comprehensive, and compelling version of it almost 100 years ago in Central Europe. According to Freud and the psychoanalytic tradition, the person is an intrapsychic mystery, and knowing the person involves exposing and unravelling the inner deceits of daily life. Over the past century, the implications and reverberations of this general viewpoint have irrevocably altered Western civilization. As the most influential psychologist of the twentieth century, Freud gave birth to a revolutionary theory of the person that has left a mark on virtually all domains within psychology—from cognitive and perceptual psychology to psychotherapy and the study of abnormal behavior. Outside psychology his influence has been just as great. Anthropology, political science, literature, literary criticism, art, and the cinema all acknowledge certain Freudian underpinnings and influences. Freud's theories, valid or not, have even crept into our everyday parlance, as we speak knowingly of "inhibitions," the "Oedipus complex," and "Freudian slips."

One cannot be a well-educated person in Western society without some understanding of Sigmund Freud and the psychoanalytic tradition. Freud's is the first and most dominant theory of personality to be developed within this tradition. But the tradition has also given birth to a number of other extraordinarily influential approaches to the study of persons. These include the theories of Carl Jung (1875–1961) and Alfred Adler (1870–1937), each of whom was a close associate of Freud before breaking away from the fold to establish his own theory and professional following. Toward the end of Freud's life and after his death, Anna Freud (Sigmund Freud's daughter), Heinz Hartmann, Karen Horney, Erich Fromm, Erik Erikson, Margaret Mahler, and Heinz Kohut developed influential theories of the person that stem, in part, from central Freudian precepts. With the seminal contributions of these and other theorists, the psychoanalytic tradition has evolved in substantial ways since the early days of Freud. (For example, see Westen, 1990.) Yet the tradition cannot be well understood outside the historical context within which its founder came to his initial insights. Therefore, we will begin our overview of the psychoanalytic tradition with a close examination of Freud's life and times.

Sigmund Freud and the Origins of Psychoanalysis: A Life Story

The Setting

Sigmund Freud came of age in a world very different from ours. It was a world of kings and queens and empires—a nineteenth-century, European "old world" that was still highly aristocratic and, by our standards, extremely oppressive. It was a world yet to experience a major global war or the threat of nuclear annihilation. It was a world that would have found unthinkable our contemporary beliefs that, for instance, women should be allowed to vote or that the child of a poor black mother might someday become a great leader, writer, or scientist. We cannot understand and appreciate Freud and his theories without knowing something of the time and the place in which he lived. We cannot undervalue the conclusion that our survey of his world will convey: that many of Freud's insights—even those that continue to be relevant and illuminating today—directly reflect a world that, in many respects, no longer exists.

The Romantic Struggle Freud was born in 1856, at the end of what historians have termed the Romantic Age in Europe. Flourishing between (approximately) 1790 and 1850, **Romanticism** represented a revolution in human thought whereby many of the intellectuals of the day rejected classical teachings emphasizing reason, order, and the common good in favor of a celebration of the vigorous and passionate life of the individual (Cantor, 1971; Russell, 1945). Heroes of the Romantic movement in Europe included English poets such as Wordsworth, Coleridge, and Lord Byron, German men of letters such as Goethe and Schiller, and, in the political/military sphere, Napoleon. Goethe and Napoleon were two of Freud's great personal heroes (Jones, 1961; Sulloway, 1979). Both Napoleon and Goethe rebelled against societal conventions to become renowned "conquistadors"—one of lands and peoples and the other of the mind.

Freud's Romantic heritage is reflected in at least three critical points. First, both the Romantics and Freud considered the individual to be in bitter and incessant conflict with his or her society. Society is inherently oppressive in that it demands conformity to ensure social order, but the Romantic self seeks freedom and transcendence, often through passionate pursuits such as art and love. Second, both the Romantics and Freud focused on the *uniqueness of the inner self* and its development over time. For the Romantics, the development of the inner self was virtually a moral duty (Jay, 1984; Langbaum, 1982). Goethe's Faust seeks self-fulfillment at all costs, going so far as to sell his soul to the devil (Mephistopheles) to guarantee the full experiencing of his inner, unique being. The process of exploring the inner self in Freudian psychoanalysis is, likewise, a Faustian sort of endeavor, likened by at least one observer to a risky pact with the devil: writes Brown (1959), "to experience Freud is to partake a second time of the forbidden fruit" (pp. xi–xii).

Third is the Romantic glorification of the *emotional and irrational aspects of human nature* over and against reason. Writes Cantor (1971), "the Romantics welcomed back into the universe ghosts, spirits, dreams, gods, and ineffable yearnings" (p. 524). Human beings are ruled by impulses and emotions that are both perverse and sublime. This Romantic idea became a cornerstone of Freudian psychology. But unlike the Romantics, Freud did not celebrate human irrationality. Unconscious wishes concerning sexuality and aggression are the most basic motivators of the person's behavior, according to Freud, but these wishes must be channeled into indirect and disguised expressions within an orderly society if the

The power and passion of Romanticism, as exemplified by J.M.W. Turner's *The "Fighting Temeraire" Tugged to Her Last Berth to Be Broken Up, 1838.*

human being is to adapt and if society is to survive. Despite popular misconceptions, Freud was too much of a rational scientist to endorse the free reign of sex and passion.

Science, Reason, and Morality Though Romanticism left a lasting effect on Freud's thinking, he was not a pure Romantic. Indeed, he was educated at a time when Romanticism had given way, in Europe, to a more scientific, rational, and moralistic world view, which came to be loosely associated with the Victorian Age. Named for the reign of Queen Victoria (queen of England from 1837 to 1901), the Victorian Age saw European society become much more industrialized, urbanized, and nationalistic. Certain cultural changes during this period profoundly shaped the life of Freud. Among these were (1) the dominance of science and technology, (2) the spirit of social reform, and (3) the emphasis on morality and duty.

Many intellectuals in the latter half of the nineteenth century believed that advances in science and technology coupled with hard work would eventually solve the problems—both material and societal—of modern life. The railroads, steel mills, and other mighty conquests of technology, as well as the momentous achievements of nineteenth-century chemistry and biology, impressed upon the Victorian mind a faith in progress through scientific theory and practice. Scientific research was to be precise like that performed in the natural sciences, and scientific theories were to be grand and encompassing. Writes Robinson (1981), the Victorians held "the confident belief that the world or the human enterprise or the heavens or everything can finally be encompassed by a grand vision validated by a faultless method. Scholarship, neither before nor since, is displayed with such certainty and finality" (p. 354). What the physicists, chemists, and biologists had formulated for the natural world, therefore, Freud would have the temerity to propose for the human mind: a grand scientific theory that knew little modesty.

With the evolution of numerous reform societies, the passage of major social bills stressing individual rights and privileges in England and elsewhere, and the emphasis on high standards of moral behavior and decorum in the Victorian court, the Victorian Age came to be characterized by an emphasis on moral reform and rectitude (Cantor, 1971). The second half of the nineteenth century was the heyday of missionary societies and temperance leagues. The positive aspect of the Victorians' preoccupation with behaving "appropriately" and doing good works included some major advances in the lives of the middle and working classes, initiated by the spirit of liberal social reform. But there was a darker side, too, as evidenced by a zealous repression of those aspects of human living that the Romantics had celebrated. Unlike the eighteenth or the twentieth centuries, the Victorian Age rendered sexuality a virtual taboo. Though heterosexual union could be idealized in the consecrated middle-class marriage (Gay, 1984), sex was still conceived as a mysterious and frightening aspect of human nature to be subjugated to the higher callings of rational duty. The repression of sex was a cultural symptom of the Victorian tendency to *split* the person into a respectable self exhibited to the public and a secret and sometimes unseemly private self (Baumeister, 1986), giving form and content to the neuroses of the day.

The Victorian ethos affected Freud in a number of ways. In exposing the central part played by sexuality in normal and abnormal human functioning, even in the lives of children, Freud shocked many Victorians and offended their moralistic sensibilities. On the other hand, Freud was a Victorian, too, and he never went so far as to advocate the overt freeing up of the sexual instinct. Freud was too much of a moralist (Rieff, 1959) to adopt a purely Romantic approach to the relationship between the individual and society. Victorian duty and a commitment to practical reform were strong themes in his life story, reinforced by Freud's Jewish heritage that emphasized the blending of passion and rational thought. The mature person, in Freud's view, should be able to love and to work. In his tireless devotion to his own work, Freud relentlessly pursued truth through science. He worked hard to better the world under the belief that science would eventually provide the answers to the most vexing of human woes.

The Great War Freud was born in Freiberg, Moravia—a small town in the Austro-Hungarian Empire. The Great War of 1914–1918 wiped out this Central European confederation as well as much of the old world of which it was a part—Freud's world for 60 years—and replaced it with a confusing hodgepodge of political states and ideologies. The unprecedented destruction of the war, furthermore, made for what many historians have seen as a "demoralization of the Western conscience" (Cantor, 1971, p. 916). Ten million people had been slaughtered to produce a dubious peace that, many correctly predicted, would ultimately generate even greater levels of killing. In general terms, European society experienced an unprecedented disillusionment at the end of World War I—a devastating loss of innocence and idealism that is poignantly described in the personal memoirs and public rhetoric of the day (for example, Brittain, 1933/1970).

The war affected Freud in a similar manner, blackening his overall outlook and reinforcing anxieties about death and destruction. The devaluation of European currencies at the end of the war wiped out Freud's life savings. Two of his sons fought in the war as soldiers for the Central Powers, and though neither was killed or maimed, Freud experienced his share of anxiety about their welfare (Jones, 1961). Even more troubling, however, must have been the daily reports in the newspapers of unprecedented carnage and Freud's own encounters with soldiers returning from the war exhibiting signs of "war neurosis." Shortly after the war's end, Freud published his new and extremely controversial ideas about death instincts, suggesting that humans unconsciously desire their own death and often project this desire outwards in aggressive, even murderous, behavior toward others. Freud's late theory about human aggressiveness is, on one level, an attempt to understand the barbarism of World War I. The increasingly pessimistic tone of his later writings, furthermore, reflects the war's legacy of disillusionment.

The Characters

A number of highly influential people play the roles of main characters in Freud's life story. We will focus here on a few whose contributions to the development of Freud and his theories were particularly strong and long-lasting. Each of these characters personifies, or puts into personal form, significant trends and themes in Freud's own personality. Thus, each becomes, in a sense, part of Freud himself.

The Mother: Amalie Freud Freud was the firstborn and the favorite of his mother Amalie, who subsequently bore six other children. Looking back on his special childhood status in the family, Freud later wrote, "A man who has been the indisputable favorite of his mother keeps for life the feeling of a conqueror, that confidence of success that often induces real success" (in Jones, 1961, p. 6). Because of his mother's love, Freud could become the conquistador of his dreams, like the Romantic heroes of Goethe and Napoleon before him.

World War I influenced Freud's theories of aggression and the death instinct.

Freud's feelings for his mother appear to be the purest and least ambivalent of all his reported emotional experiences. He showered her with positive accolades and saved any negative things he had to say about maternal figures for a hired nanny. Stolorow and Atwood (1979) argue that Freud displaced unconscious negative feelings towards his mother—such as resentments he may have felt about the birth of younger siblings—onto the scapegoat nanny in order to maintain a perfect image of a pure and all-loving mother. As we shall see, Freud's idealization of mother love is a key component of his theory of psychosexual development. The mother–infant bond is the most basic of all attachments, he suggests, forming the ideal model of every later sensual relationship.

The Father: Jakob Freud A Jewish wool merchant living among Catholics, Jakob Freud suffered a financial reversal in 1859 that necessitated the family's move to Vienna, the city where Sigmund was to live most of his life. Whereas Freud expressed an unalloyed affection for his mother, his memories of Jakob were both highly positive and negative. In his key relationship with his father, therefore, we see the classic Freudian pattern of profound emotional ambivalence, a troublesome mixture of love and hate. Freud was to elevate this pattern to a universal experience in the **Oedipus complex,** wherein he argued that all sons unconsciously desire to kill, even if they love, their fathers. Freud discovered his own unconscious wish to murder his father in his intensive self-analysis that he began in 1897, shortly after the death of his father.

The general theme of seeking to triumph over the father and then experiencing either fear (that one may fail) or guilt (after one succeeds) is one of the centerpieces of Freudian psychology. In his own life, Freud appears to have struggled with both the fear and the guilt (Schur, 1972; Steele, 1982). In a famous incident 8 years after the death of Jakob, Freud and his brother Alexander visited the Acropolis in Athens where Freud experienced an overwhelming sensation of unreality—a distressing apprehension that what he saw was not *really* there. Travel to fabled cities, like Athens and Rome, usually made Freud feel "like a hero who has performed deeds of improbable greatness" (Freud, 1936/1964, p. 247), but such travel was also associated with hidden aggressive impulses toward his father as well as feelings of fear and guilt. Freud traced the Acropolis incident back to unconscious feelings of guilt over having symbolically triumphed over his dead father:

> The very theme of Athens and the Acropolis in itself contained evidence of the son's superiority. Our father had been in business, he had had no secondary education, and Athens could not have meant much to him. Thus what interfered with our enjoyment of the journey to Athens was a feeling of *filial piety.* (Freud, 1936/1964, pp. 247–248)

The Scientist: Ernst Brucke At an early age, Freud believed that science would offer him the best opportunity to perform "deeds of improbable greatness." He later wrote, "In my youth I felt an overpowering need to understand something of the riddles of the world in which we live and perhaps even to contribute something to their solution" (Jones, 1961, p. 22).

In 1873, Freud enrolled in the University of Vienna to study natural science. There he met the eminent physiologist Ernst Brucke. Working under Brucke's tutelage for 3 years, Freud came to embrace the twin scientific tenets of materialism and mechanism. As a crusading materialist, Brucke argued that all natural phenomena must be explained in physical and chemical terms. No spiritual or other-worldly forces could be invoked to account for the real world; anybody appealing to nonmaterial explanations of physical reality could not be considered a legitimate scientist. As a mechanist, Brucke preferred scientific explanations that were based on machine models. A machine is a complex mechanical system that uses energy through work. Freud was to adopt this conventional view in his own theories, insisting that the human mind should be understood as an energy system—a machine that requires psychic energy. The energy is derived from biologically rooted **instincts,** such as sex and aggression. The system works according to the law of conservation of energy. The mind transforms energy derived from instincts into useful work, Freud eventually argued, transforming a fixed amount of raw psychic energy into various forms and expressions of human thought, feeling, desire, and behavior.

The Visionary: Jean Martin Charcot A counterpoint to the conventional Victorian scientist personified in Brucke was the flamboyant Charcot—a worthy descendant of the Romantic heroes Goethe and Napoleon. In 1885, Freud was awarded a travel grant to attend the lectures and demonstrations of this legendary neuropathologist in Paris. Charcot was investigating the symptoms and causes of **hysteria.** A more common psychological disturbance during Victorian times than today, hysteria manifested itself in bizarre bodily symptoms, such as paralysis of the limbs and visual disorders, which had no apparent *physical* cause. Through hypnosis, Charcot was able to remove many hysterical symptoms. Further, he was able to document that these symptoms were indeed not related to physical abnormalities but instead resulted from the patient's peculiar *ideas.* Freud's early clinical work with hysterics followed Charcot's lead as he sought to find the *meaning* of the hysterical symptom in the patient's unconscious thoughts and wishes.

Freud's four months in Paris with Charcot marked a turning point in his career. He wrote to his future wife: "Charcot . . . is simply wrecking all my aims and opinions"; "I sometimes come out of his lectures . . . with an entirely new idea of perfection"; "no other human being has ever affected me in this way" (in E. Freud, 1960, pp. 184–185). In Charcot, Freud admired the power of the scientific visionary who could "learn to see in new ways and dare to see something new" (Steele, 1982, p. 32).

The Healer: Josef Breuer About to marry Martha Bernays and soon to begin a family, Freud reluctantly took on the more financially rewarding position of private physician in Vienna, though his primary interest remained scientific research. In 1882, he befriended one of Vienna's most prominent physicians, Josef Breuer. Described as a gentle and compassionate healer, Breuer was something of a father-figure for the younger Freud (Monte, 1987; Steele, 1982). Breuer helped Freud get established in the medical community, and he loaned him money when Freud was short. Both physicians spent many of their clinical hours in therapy with patients who were hysterics, like the ones hypnotized by Charcot.

Breuer recognized that while hysterical symptoms may appear to be random and bizarre they are in fact meaningfully organized according to an intricate emotional logic that guides the neurotic's life. The symptoms symbolize an unresolved conflict or problem that may be traced back to intensely negative experiences from the past. Though no longer consciously remembered, an emotionally abrasive experience from childhood presses for release and goads the patient to find symptomatic expression of the discomfort within. In the famous case of Anna O. (see Chapter 3), Breuer discovered that hysterical symptoms could be removed through a "talking cure," through which the patient talked through daytime hallucinations, fantasies, symptoms, and so on. The talking unstrangled the archaic emotions that were producing the neurotic symptoms, releasing the trapped emotional energy and temporarily freeing the patient from debilitating symptoms and distress.

The psychoanalytic tradition was launched when Breuer and Freud collaborated to investigate the psychological underpinnings of hysteria. Their work culminated in the landmark publication of *Studies in Hysteria* (1893–1895/1955). In this book, the two founders of psychoanalysis state conclusively that "*hysterics suffer mainly from reminiscences*" (p. 7). In other words, the bodily symptoms of hysteria are caused by problems in the memory of traumatic childhood events.

The collaboration of Freud and Breuer ended in a bitter feud sometime in the 1890s. The reasons for the falling out are not altogether clear. Freud's official biographer, Ernest Jones (1961), underscores disagreements between Freud and Breuer about the proper role of sexuality in the etiology of hysteria and other mental disturbances, Freud claiming that all neuroses have a sexual component and Breuer disagreeing. Some have argued that Breuer functioned as "Freud's last father" (Steele, 1982) and was therefore destined to be "killed" (that is, overcome) in line with Freud's strong Oedipal inclinations. Others have emphasized differences in personal and professional style (Sulloway, 1979). For whatever reasons, Freud came to feel that Breuer had betrayed him, and once they parted as enemies the two were never again to meet as friends.

The Confidante: Wilhelm Fliess After Breuer, Freud entered the most creative and scientifically productive period of his life. The late 1890s and early 1900s saw the maturation of the majority of Freud's most important ideas. The immediate source for their discovery was Freud's pioneering self-analysis. During much of this period, Freud perceived that he lived and worked in virtual isolation. The time was later romanticized by Freud as a "glorious heroic age" and the years of "splendid isolation" (Freud, 1914/1957, p. 22). During this period, Freud developed an extraordinarily close friendship with Wilhelm Fliess, a Berlin nose-and-throat specialist. Before the two colleagues parted as embittered enemies, Freud and Fliess exchanged hundreds of letters that bear witness to their mutual admiration and Fliess's function in Freud's lonely life as a supreme confidante and confessor.

From his days with Breuer, Freud had come to the conclusion that the symptoms of hysteria were invariably the result of repressed reminiscences of childhood trauma. The trauma, furthermore, concerned sexuality, Freud believed, in that his patients repeatedly suggested the presence of erotic impulses from childhood that were frustrated or laden with guilt. As a result, Freud formulated what has come to be known as the **seduction hypothesis,** arguing that the origins of hysterical symptoms are in experiences of childhood sexual seduction. Early sexual experiences are later repressed, as the organism defends against the guilt and anxiety that come to be associated with them. The strangulated affect eventually bursts forth in disguised symptomatic form.

However, Freud eventually *abandoned* the seduction hypothesis. In a letter to Fliess written in 1897, he expressed doubt that sexual abuse of children could be so common as to pervade the lives of nearly all of the neurotic patients he saw, and he told of how the revelation of seduction in therapy often failed to effect a lasting psychoanalytic cure. More likely than actual seduction, he came to believe, was the possibility that in many cases neurotics merely *fantasized* that they had engaged in sexual relations of various sorts as children. Rather than passive victims of real sexual abuse, most hysterics were active participants in their own neuroses, spinning imaginary tales of seduction and intrigue that stem not so much from seduction per se but from the fact, Freud came to believe, that children are inherently sexual beings, with strong sexual longings for parents and others in their environment.

The abandonment of the seduction hypothesis turned Freud's thinking away from sexual abuse and in the direction of erotic fantasy. Freud's theoretical turnaround has been hailed as a monumental move forward in the development of psychoanalytic thinking, opening up explorations into fantasy and imagination, unconscious dynamics, and the psychosexuality of children. However, a few scholars have suggested that the move was an unfortunate one because it covered up the real problem of sexual abuse in Victorian families of the time.

The most vocal critic of Freud in this regard is Jeffrey Masson (1984a, 1984b) who has charged that Freud needed to abandon the seduction hypothesis in part to protect the professional image of Fliess. Working from the unedited correspondence between Freud and Fliess, Masson contends that Freud chose to interpret a particular patient's repeated nosebleeding as a neurotic symptom stemming from fantasy instead of the physical result of an actual surgical operation on her nose, performed and botched by Fliess. By denying the organic basis of the patient's symptom, Masson contends, Freud set the stage for his subsequent dismissal of the reality of sexual abuse in favor of sexual fantasy. In addition, Masson remarks, Fliess himself may have actually molested his own son, which may have motivated Freud further to cover up reality and change his theory of the origins of hysteria. Finally, Freud may have also been motivated to abandon his initial impressions by a mounting concern for his reputation in the scientific community. Masson believes that the seduction hypothesis was scorned by Freud's contemporaries, perhaps again as part of a cultural coverup. Suggesting that seduction was more fantasy than real gave Freud a message that the scientific community found less threatening.

It does seem plausible that Freud, like many of his contemporaries, may have ultimately underestimated the prevalence of sexual abuse of children. It has become clear that sexual abuse today is much more common than once believed. Some surveys have yielded estimates of rates as high as 35% (Carver & Scheier, 1992). But beyond this, Masson's overall argument about Freud's motivations for abandoning the seduction hypothesis, especially as it applies to his relationship with Fliess, has not proven very convincing. Much of the argument is based on very ambiguous circumstantial evidence and rather far-fetched interpretations. Furthermore, the theoretical move toward fantasy and imagination in the lives of both neurotics and well-functioning persons may have been inevitable, regardless of Freud's views on seduction. Writes Monte (1987):

> Reality counts, but if Freud had not focused on fantasy in 1895, latter-day analysts would certainly have had to invent the idea. Whether Freud assumed this focus to protect himself and Fliess

Table 2.1

Selected Writings of Sigmund Freud

Date	Title	Thesis
1895	*Studies in Hysteria* (with J. Breuer)	Neurotic symptoms are the result of "reminiscences" and can be relieved through a psychological talking cure. Neurotic disturbances are creative solutions to unconscious conflicts, usually concerning sexuality.
1900	*The Interpretation of Dreams*	Dreams are compromises in wish fulfillments and must be understood as creative products of unconscious processes such as condensation, displacement, and symbolism. All dreams can be interpreted by employing free association to trace the latent undercurrents of manifest content.
1901	*The Psychopathology of Everyday Life*	Like neurotic symptoms and dreams, many accidents and mistakes we make in daily life have important psychological meaning and can be traced back to unconscious conflicts and instinctual urges.
1905	*Three Essays on the Theory of Sexuality*	The sexual instinct develops through childhood stages designated as oral, anal, and phallic, before reaching maturity in adolescence. Children are overtly sexual beings whose pre-genital manifestations of sex are similar to what polite society calls "perversions" in adults.
1913	*Totem and Taboo*	The Oedipus complex in children involves unconscious desires to make love to the parent of the opposite sex while killing the parent of the same sex. Freud speculates that social institutions such as government and religion have their historical origins in a prehistoric real-life enactment of the Oedipal complex, whereby the patriarch of a primal horde was

Table 2.1 continued

Table 2.1 continued

Date	Title	Thesis
		overthrown by younger men and killed and eaten. The new younger leaders then prescribed laws and rules to inhibit sex and aggression and assuage their guilt.
1920	*Beyond the Pleasure Principle*	Two basic instinctual urges are the underlying motivators of all behavior and experience: life instincts, expressed directly in sexuality; and death instincts, expressed in aggression.
1923	*The Ego and the Id*	The human mind is structured into three compartments: the id, wherein reside unconscious impulses and thoughts; the ego, which serves the id by channeling the id's energy into realistic pursuits; and the superego, which is an internal representation of the parents, exerting a moral force. The id operates according to the pleasure principle and the ego operates according to the reality principle.
1930	*Civilization and Its Discontents*	Human beings and societies are in constant conflict. Whereas the individual is motivated by unconscious sexual and aggressive impulses, society is built on the repression of sex and aggression. As a result, humans are generally anxious, miserable, and often neurotic.

Note. There is no substitute for reading Freud in the original. Indeed, part of his power as a theorist is the beauty of his writing, captured wonderfully in James Strachey's authoritative English translations of the original German. Unfortunately, many secondary sources on Freud are rather dry and technical compared to the rich original work. An exception is C. Monte's *Beneath the mask: An introduction to theories of personality* (New York: Holt, Rinehart & Winston, 1987), which has two long and splendid chapters on the evolution of Freud's thinking.

is an issue that is not yet resolved by Masson's intriguing argument. The positive effect of Masson's thesis may be to alert the psychoanalytic community to the importance of the interaction between fantasy and reality. (p. 52)

The Sons and Daughter In the last 40 years of his life (1900–1939), Sigmund Freud established himself as the father of the psychoanalytic movement. A gifted writer who won the coveted Goethe Prize for literature in 1930, Freud filled 24 volumes on psychoanalysis, including wide-ranging essays and monographs on theory and clinical practice as well as special papers addressing religious, cultural, and artistic questions. Table 2.1 lists a few of his most important writings with capsule descriptions of their contents.

Attracting a large number of intellectual followers, Freud founded the Vienna Psychoanalytic Society. The group held regular meetings and published a journal. In 1909, American psychologist G. Stanley Hall invited Freud to Clark University in Worcester, Massachusetts, where he delivered a series of lectures. Freud's writings were eventually translated into English and other languages as psychoanalysis became an international movement.

During the latter half of his life, Freud searched in vain for an intellectual "son" who, after the father's death, would preserve the orthodox purity of the psychoanalytic tradition. The Swiss psychologist, Carl Jung, was an early choice, Freud referring to Jung early on as the "crown prince" of the psychoanalytic movement. But Jung and other followers of Freud, such as Alfred Adler and Otto Rank, eventually broke away from the father, in classic oedipal style, to establish their own theories and intellectual movements. Other potential successors, such as Karl Abraham and Sandor Ferenczi, invariably disappointed Freud. Ironically, Freud's wish for an intellectual son was probably most closely realized in the life and work of his own daughter, Anna Freud. An original theorist in her own right, Freud's youngest daughter was a staunch guardian of Freudian orthodoxy until her death in 1983.

Sigmund Freud suffered from cancer of the mouth and jaw during the last 16 years of his life, enduring chronic pain and 33 surgical operations. German Nazis burned many of his books in the 1930s, and as a Jew he found it necessary to emigrate from Vienna to London in 1938. He died in September of 1939, just weeks after the beginning of World War II.

Three Main Tenets of Psychoanalysis

This expanded treatment of Freud's life story is designed to serve as more than merely the biography of the man; it also introduces a number of key ideas in

Freud's theories in the context of his life and times. Let us now discuss in greater detail some of Freud's central theoretical concepts. Freudian theories are grounded on three basic assumptions, or tenets, about human nature: *determinism, conflict,* and the *unconscious.*

Determinism

According to Freud and the psychoanalytic tradition, all significant behavior and experience is determined by forces over which we have little control. Although those forces come both from within the person and from the outside world, psychoanalysts are typically most interested in the *internal* impulses that shape the person's life. The most significant internal forces are instincts, (sometimes called "drives," from the German *Trieb*) which exist as "the ultimate causes of all activity" (Freud, 1940/1964, p. 5). An instinct or drive is "a mental representation of a physical or bodily need" (Freud, 1915/1957, p. 122). Instincts, therefore, function as bridges linking the biology and the psychology of the person. They are the mechanisms by which the biological energy of the person is translated into psychological form. As such, instincts are the fundamental motivators of human action.

The legacy of Brucke and the scientific ethos of the Victorian Age are no more apparent in Freud's theories than here, in his view of instincts. As a materialist, Freud believed that the energy of the mind must derive from physical sources, such as the tissue needs of the body. As a mechanist, Freud believed that the mind was akin to a machine that uses a fixed amount of energy in work. An increase in the body's needs is reflected in the arousal of an instinct and experienced by the person as a wish or desire to perform a physical or mental action that will reduce the tension that has resulted from the increase in need. The build-up of tension is aversive, but the reduction of tension feels good. Instincts, therefore, set into motion a cycle of tension increase, followed by work that reduces the tension, bringing with it the experience of pleasure, followed again by gradual tension increase, and so on. Rarely, however, are the instincts gratified in a straightforward way. Instead, psychic energy is usually displaced onto objects and activities that make for an indirect satisfaction of the instinct. Freud suggested that the entire fabric of modern civilization is a product of displaced instinctual energy. Unable to obtain direct and immediate satisfaction, human beings have learned to channel their instinctual energy into elaborate religious, political, economic, and artistic activities.

Instincts fall within two general groups: (1) sexuality and all other **life instincts** and (2) aggression and all other **death instincts** (Freud, 1920/1955). Life instincts serve the purposes of individual survival and reproduction. The form of the energy by which life instincts perform their work is called **libido;** sexual desires are often termed "libidinous urges." The person typically invests the libido in various "objects" (including persons and activities) that promise

Freud at Clark University, 1908: (top) A. A. Brill, Ernest Jones, and Sandor Ferenczi; (bottom) Sigmund Freud, G. Stanley Hall, and Carl Jung.

satisfaction of the instinct. Investing the libido in the self—in a sense, "falling in love" with the self—is termed *narcissism*. Investing the libido in others—other persons and even other pursuits—is termed *object choice*. The libido works according to the law of conservation of energy. In other words, a person has only so much libido to go around. If he or she invests some of it in one object, there remains just that much less to invest in others. Thus, the narcissist finds it difficult to love others.

Death instincts aim to return the individual to the stability of the inorganic world. They aim towards the death (nonlife)—which, for all organisms, is what preceded life. Turned toward the self, death instincts can take the form of masochism. More commonly directed toward the outside world, however, death instincts surface as overt or covert aggression toward others. Among other factors, World War I convinced Freud that men (and to a lesser extent women) were by nature aggressive. He observed, "men are not gentle creatures who want [only] to be loved." Rather, a good deal of their instinctual endowment is aggressiveness:

> As a result their neighbor is for them not only a potential helper or sexual object, but also someone who tempts them to satisfy their aggressiveness on him, to exploit his capacity for work

without compensation, to use him sexually without his consent, to seize his possessions, to humiliate him, to cause him pain, to torture and kill him. (Freud, 1930/1961, p. 111)

Conflict

Not only is the person's behavior dictated by forces, many instinctual, over which he or she has little control. In addition, these forces are in constant conflict with each other and with the outside world. As we see in Freud's theory of life and death instincts, human beings are conflicted at their very biological core. We seek both to love and to kill, to live and to die. It is because of conflict that libidinal and aggressive urges often cannot be channeled into useful expressions. It is because of conflict that all of us are anxious and many of us become neurotic.

In the Freudian view of the person, there is no way to get around conflict. Freud's Romantic heritage impressed upon his mind the inevitability of profound conflict between the person and society. In *Civilization and Its Discontents* (1930/1961), Freud lamented the fate of all civilized persons: that contemporary men and women, driven by their ancient sexual and aggressive inclinations, must find ways of living in modern societies that are (and must be) designed to stifle the immediate expression of instinctual urges. In other words, persons are driven by instincts while societies are driven to suppress instincts. Beyond the conflict between the individual and society, however, are the related and equally vexing conflicts that rage *within* the person. The Freudian man or woman is a bundle of contradictions, living according to internal dictates that run counter to each other. I wish I could be honored as the greatest American president of all time, and I seek to be publicly humiliated as a fraud. I want to kill my father, and I want him to take me to a Yankees game. I want to commit the most egregious sins the world has ever known, and I would love to be a saint. Such are the conflicts by which we live and die, and by which we become anxiety-ridden.

Freud's later view of anxiety finds it intimately connected with conflict. In his early writings, Freud explained the anxiety experienced by many of his neurotic patients as a manifestation of pent-up and frustrated libido (Freud, 1898/1962). Later, Freud (1926/1959) came to understand anxiety as a signal of impending danger in the personality. Danger implies a conflict between part of the person and either another part of the person or part of the outside world. In *realistic anxiety,* the individual fears real dangers posed by the external environment, such as wild animals and final examinations. In *neurotic anxiety,* the individual fears conflict between his or her own raging instinctual urges and his or her best efforts to control them. In *moral anxiety,* the individual fears punishment from within, suggesting a conflict between one part of the self that seeks immediate instinctual gratification and another part of the self that says this gratification is wrong. To cope with incessant conflict, the person may resort to **repression,** that is, to casting the conflictual material out of consciousness.

The Unconscious

Not only are we motivated by forces over which we have little control, and not only are these forces in perpetual conflict, rendering us anxious, miserable, and discontented. It gets worse: we do not even know what these forces and conflicts are. The major determinants of our personality, the intrapsychic mysteries of the mind, are **unconscious,** outside of our awareness. Further, there isn't a whole lot we can do, short of the extraordinary process of psychoanalytic interpretation discussed in the next chapter, to render the unconscious conscious. Driven by internal urges and suffering from inexorable conflict, human beings are forever anxious. Yet they generally do not, and usually cannot, know why.

The idea that much of who we are is outside of our awareness, residing in a shadowy unconscious realm, is not original with Freud. The notion that behavior is shaped by unconscious determinants was clearly in evidence some 100 years prior to Freud's theorizing (Ellenberger, 1970). For instance, the philosophies of Arthur Schopenhauer (1788–1860) and Friedrich Nietzsche (1844–1900) emphasized aspects of human functioning that are outside of consciousness, typically emotional and irrational urges that are antagonistic to conscious reason.

Nineteenth-century Romantics generally placed the person's heroic and creative powers in an unconscious, though sometimes accessible, realm. Hypnotism was used to gain access to the unconscious mind as early as 1784, and of course one of Freud's teachers, Charcot, employed the method with legendary effectiveness. Baumeister (1986) and Gay (1986) argue that middle-class adults in nineteenth-century Europe accepted the general idea of an inner world unknowable to the conscious self. Baumeister even asserts that Victorian men and women were preoccupied with the involuntary revelation of this inner self to others. While you might not be able to attain conscious insight into the deep secrets of your own mind, the Victorians believed there was always the danger of inadvertently disclosing the nature of your own unconscious to others, who as objective outside observers might even come to know you better than you know yourself!

In his **topographical model** of human functioning, Freud distinguished among conscious, preconscious, and unconscious regions of the mind. The conscious region contains what a person is currently aware of. People typically can verbalize their conscious experience and can think about it in a logical way. The preconscious region contains material about which the person is not currently aware but which *could readily enter awareness* should the person decide to retrieve the material. Therefore, the preconscious region may be seen as corresponding to what most of us think of as ordinary memory. I may not currently be aware of the color of my daughter's bicycle but I can easily remember what the color is if I decide to move my thinking in that direction, thereby bringing up material from the preconscious to the conscious region. The preconscious contains a vast storehouse of important as well as trivial information that is reliably at our disposal. For the most part, the contents of the preconscious do not summon up negative emotional experiences. The information is affectively positive or neutral; it does not threaten our well-being; it is compatible with how we wish to see our lives.

By contrast, material residing in the unconscious region of the mind cannot be readily retrieved. Rather the unconscious contains elements of experience that have been actively repressed. In part, the unconscious is a repository for ideas, images, urges, and feelings that are associated with conflict, pain, fear, guilt, and so on. Therefore, unconscious material is unconscious *for a reason*. The mind is topographically organized such that material that is incompatible with the dominant self-protective mask of consciousness is cast into an unconscious abyss. We cannot bear to know certain things about ourselves. Therefore, we do not (consciously) know them. Yet what resides in the unconscious profoundly affects our behavior and experience, even though we do not know we are being affected. That which is repressed lies behind our every life move. Repressed unconscious material is expressed in disguised or symbolic form, as in neurotic symptoms or when unconscious instinctual urges are indirectly satisfied in dreams, fantasy, play, art, work, or virtually any other arena of meaningful human intercourse.

For Freud, then, the unconscious is a distinct realm of the mind wherein are buried thoughts and impulses that are not "acceptable" for conscious consideration. Such material has been forced out of consciousness through the process of repression. Top candidates for repression are thoughts, feelings, impulses, and experiences having to do with sexuality. The erotic nature of human life is a great mystery, Freud suggests, because sexual material is too emotionally threatening to be rationally processed in the conscious domain. Yet the sexual instinct is behind much of our behavior and experience, both normal and neurotic. Just how the sexual instinct develops is the subject of the next section.

The Development of the Sexual Instinct

Freud conceptualized sexuality in extremely broad and general terms. Working unconsciously to energize and direct many facets of our behavior and experience, the sexual instinct is a diffuse and deeply rooted desire for sensual, bodily pleasure (Freud, 1905/1953). The libido is not confined to seeking sexual intercourse between men and women but rather may express itself in a rich assortment of ways. Certain regions of the body, such as the mucous membranes of the mouth and anus, appear to be libidinally charged. In common sexual practices, such as kissing, petting, and oral/anal sexuality, the mouth and the anus "seem, as it were, to be claiming that they should themselves be regarded and treated as genitals" (Freud, 1905/1953, p. 153). Adds Freud, "the claim *is* justified by the history of the development of the sexual instinct" (p. 42). The mouth, anus, and genitals are all **erogenous zones,** functioning as favorite sites for the expression of the libido. To chart psychosexual development, therefore, is to follow the odyssey of the libido as it travels from one erogenous zone to another over the course of the person's life.

The Oral Stage

Sex begins with sucking:

> Sucking at the mother's breast is the starting-point of the whole of sexual life, the unmatched prototype of every later sexual satisfaction, to which phantasy often enough returns in times of need. This sucking involves making the mother's breast the first object of the sexual instinct. I can give you no idea of the important bearing of this first object upon the choice of every later object, of the profound effects it has in its transformations and substitutions in even the remotest regions of our sexual lives. (Freud, 1916/1961, p. 314)

We see in this marvelous quotation Freud's idealization of the mother–infant bond. In the first year of life, the baby obtains both nourishment and pleasure from sucking at the breast (or bottle). Sucking reduces the tension caused by the hunger drive, and the reduction of tension feels good. The mother is generally the source of these good feelings, the provider of food and pleasure. She becomes the infant's first human love object. From this oral expression of the libido develops a lasting image of an ideal sensual experience, a legacy of pleasure that we, as adults, are fortunate enough to reexperience only in the most rewarding of our intimate relationships.

The infant in the oral stage is completely dependent on caregivers for the satisfaction of basic bodily needs. When the tensions produced by needs are consistently and regularly satisfied (reduced), the infant comes to perceive the environment as a relatively predictable and soothing milieu, laying the groundwork for healthy psychosexual development. Excessive indulgence or restriction, however, can make for **fixations** at the oral stage. In a fixation, certain problematic characteristics of a given stage remain central issues for the person long after he or she has moved to subsequent stages. A fixation at the oral stage might result from too much oral stimulation in the first year of life, or from too much frustration of oral activity—either of which results in the development of an **oral personality** in adulthood. Fixation at a relatively early point in the oral stage makes for the **oral-passive** personality type. The oral-passive type is blithely cheerful and overly dependent and expects the world to mother him or her. Fixation later in the oral stage, after the infant has begun to bite with teeth, makes for the **oral-sadistic** type. The oral-sadistic type is cynical, pessimistic, and "bitingly" sarcastic.

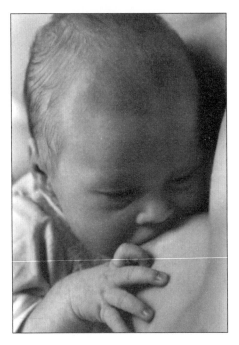

"Sucking at the mother's breast is the starting
point of the whole of sexual life." - Freud

The Anal Stage

The next stop for the libido is the anal stage. During the second and third years of life,
the toddler's sensual energy is expressed mainly in "holding in" and "letting go of"
feces. Retention and elimination involve regular cycles of tension build-up and
release, making again for the experience of bodily, sensual pleasure. As the child's
sphincter muscles mature, he or she becomes better able to determine when and
where the "letting go" will occur. Successful toilet training, therefore, signals a certain degree of mastery over the sexual instinct in that the libido comes under the control of socially prescribed schedules. Being able to control one's bowels is indeed one
of the first great accomplishments of the self, suggesting a sense of autonomy and
self-mastery that may be reexperienced in subsequent episodes of personal success.

The manner in which parents teach their children when and where to hold
on and let go may have long-term effects for personality. Parents who shower
praise upon their child's efforts at self-control foster a positive outlook concerning personal mastery and creativity. Parents who are excessively rigid and strict
about toilet training, on the other hand, may be sowing the seeds of the **anal-
retentive** personality, a fixation resulting in traits of stubbornness, stinginess, and
an overly regulated scheduling of one's life. The anal-retentive adult lacks spontaneity and flexibility in his or her compulsive efforts to "hold on." Another form

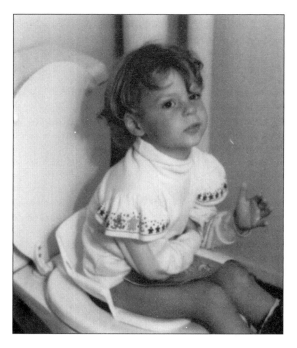

In the anal stage toilet training is one of the toddler's first great accomplishments of self.

of anal fixation is the **anal-expulsive** type, who persists in "letting go" in the most impulsive ways and inappropriate circumstances. The anal-expulsive person is extremely disorganized and disorderly, often cruel, and wantonly destructive.

The Phallic Stage

Between the ages of 3 and 5, the child enters the third stage of psychosexual development, the **phallic stage.** At this time, the libido is centered in the genital region. Children become fascinated with their own sex organs and become overtly curious about sexual practices among adults. During the phallic stage, children may begin masturbating. These manifest expressions of the libido's latest adventures are mirrored by a much more profound internal drama that plays itself out on an unconscious level. The drama is the ancient story of Oedipus, and its realization in the lives of young children is called the *Oedipus complex.*

One of the most famous tragic dramas in Western culture, Sophocles' *Oedipus Rex* was first performed in Athens between 430 and 426 B.C. The protagonist of the story is King Oedipus, a brilliant and courageous man in the prime of life who, at the outset of the play, has ruled the city of Thebes for many years. In the opening scene, a group of citizens, in despair over the recent famine and pestilence that have plagued Thebes, has gathered in front of the palace to ask the king for help. They have faith in the abilities of Oedipus to work wonders, for long ago he solved a great riddle and delivered the Thebans from the curse of the Sphinx. A monster with a woman's head and breasts and the body of a lion, the Sphinx had once sat on a rock outside Thebes and killed all travelers who could not answer her riddle: What animal walks on four feet in the morning, two at noon, and three at night? The clever Oedipus was the first to come up with the correct response: *man* (who crawls on fours when a child, walks erect in adulthood, and hobbles on a cane when he is old). Upon hearing the correct answer, the Sphinx killed herself. The Thebans, in gratitude, married the young Oedipus to their recently widowed queen, Jocasta, making him king of Thebes.

Oedipus learns that the city now faces a greater curse brought on by the evil deeds of one of its citizens. He pledges to find the villain and free Thebes a second time. A blind prophet, Tiresias, tells Oedipus the truth about the villain: that it is he, the king. But there is more. The nature of his villainy is an unspeakable horror: Oedipus has unknowingly killed his father (the former king of Thebes, Laius) and made love to his mother (the queen, his wife, Jocasta). Patricide and incest are his unforgivable and yet unwitting crimes, and for these Thebes now pays the price of the gods' curse. Incredulous and enraged, Oedipus listens as the blind Tiresias reveals the long-hidden truth that only he can see:

> And I tell you again:
> The man you have been looking for all this time,
> The damned man, the murderer of Laios,
> That man is in Thebes. To your mind he is foreign-born,
> But it will soon show that he is a Theban,
> A revelation that will fail to please.
>
> A blind man,
> Who has his eyes now; a penniless man, who is rich now;
> And he will go tapping the strange earth with his staff
> To the children with whom he lives now he will be
> Brother and father—the very same; to her
> Who bore him, son and husband—the very same
> Who came to his father's bed, wet with his father's blood.

(in O'Brien and Dukore, 1969, p. 21)

Oedipus, Jocasta, and all of Thebes eventually come to realize that Tiresias' vision is clear and true. Because of an oracle predicting that their son would kill his father and sleep with his mother, the king and queen of Thebes—Laius and Jocasta—long ago pierced the ankles of their newborn boy and left him to die on a lonely mountainside. A shepherd took pity on the boy, giving him to another shepherd, who gave him to the king and queen of another town, who named the boy "Oedipus" (meaning "swollen foot") and raised him as their own son, never telling him about his true origin. As a youth, Oedipus went to Delphi and learned of the oracle that he should grow up to murder his father and sleep with his

Oedipus and Jocasta

mother. So that he could not fulfill what the gods had destined to be his fate, Oedipus fled, eventually happening upon the Sphinx, solving the riddle, and becoming the glorious king of Thebes. As an impetuous man of the sword, he killed his share of men along the way. One of these was Laius, slaughtered in a forgettable skirmish at the intersection of three roads.

The price of Oedipus' crime is enormous. When she finally realizes that her husband is in fact her son, Jocasta hangs herself. Oedipus rips the golden brooches from his dead mother's gown and plunges them deep into his eyes. Blinded now like Tiresias, he finally sees the truth. At the end of the play, Oedipus banishes himself to a distant land. In later dramas (*Antigone, Oedipus at Colonnus*), he returns as something of a wise sage whose advice is greatly valued. In summary, then, *Oedipus Rex* is the story of a strong and clever young man who becomes an all-powerful king but eventually falls from glory and is maimed because of an unspeakable crime. The fall from power brings with it a kind of wisdom, in that Oedipus now knows "the truth" and eventually achieves a status, like that of Tiresias, of the blind sage. The crimes he commits are outside of Oedipus' own awareness. He kills his father and sleeps with his mother without knowing that he has done either—in other words, *unconsciously*.

So it goes with the young boy—and maybe the young girl. At an unconscious level, the young boy in the phallic stage of psychosexual development desires to have his mother as Oedipus had Jocasta. As we noted in the life of Yukio Mishima (Chapter 1), the desire to have the other in a powerful and sensual manner means investing the libido in that person—the process of object choice. In a vague, unspeakable, and mysterious way, claimed Freud, young boys seek to possess—to conquer in a powerful and an erotic manner—a primal feminine love object that exists in their fantasies and may correspond in reality to their own mothers. Equally vague and unspeakable is an unconsciously perceived threat—that from a powerful masculine force that stands in the way of the boy's conquests, represented by the father who threatens to castrate the boy. What Freud termed **castration anxiety** literally means the fear that one's penis will be cut off, but more profoundly it may symbolize the child's fear that he will, like Oedipus, lose his power (and his love object as well). Thus, the boy harbors an unconscious wish to kill the father, as Freud indeed discovered in the analysis of his own unconscious life.

The normal resolution of the Oedipus complex follows the ancient myth. The young boy eventually comes to identify with the aggressor of his fantasies, seeking to be like the father so to have the mother in a vicarious manner. The unconscious shift from object choice to identification marks both a major defeat and a victory for the boy. Like Oedipus, he can no longer be "king." On an unconscious level, the young boy at the close of the oedipal period understands that he is weaker, smaller, and more mortal than he (unconsciously) ever imagined. The loss of power is a kind of castration, symbolized in the Greek myth when Oedipus blinds himself. Omnipotence is replaced by a definite but painful sense of limitations. Yet, from the standpoint of healthy personality development, the oedipal defeat is ultimately a good thing. Like the blind Oedipus who knows the truth, the young boy who suffers the oedipal defeat eventually attains the rudiments of a certain kind of wisdom and maturity. Identification with the father (and to a lesser extent with the mother as well) at the end of the Oedipus complex leaves the boy with a basic moral attitude about life, encapsuled in what Freud termed the *superego*. Without the superego, the child would become a ruthless, though perhaps clever, tyrant—able to solve riddles, surely, but woefully deficient in the more challenging task of living in a moral society.

The little boy's resolution of the Oedipus complex is the prototype for the general tendency of all of civilized humankind to repress certain instinctual urges and establish in their place great institutions of social organization, such as government and religion. Freud's most powerful and controversial rendition of this argument is *Totem and Taboo* (1913/1958)—a wildly speculative account of human prehistory that can be interpreted in literal terms or as a Freudian allegory (Hogan, 1976). In *Totem and Taboo,* Freud followed Darwin in claiming that, long ago in the history of the human species, people lived in primal hordes, each ruled by an autocratic father. Acting on his unfettered instinctual urges, the patriarchal leader kept the women of the horde for his own sexual delight and prohibited the younger men (his sons) from sharing in the bounty. This form of social organization ended, speculated Freud, when young men rose up collectively to kill the ruthless father, subsequently devouring his flesh in a totem meal. Like Mishima in his dream of

Omi (Chapter 1), the young men symbolically accomplished an identification with the father by eating him. Collectively assuming his authority, the new rulers established fraternal social clans with strict taboos on free sexual expression, especially incest. From this first socially organized restriction of the sexual instinct evolved more elaborate restricting structures, such as bodies of laws and norms designed to quell the wild instinctual impulses of men.

But what about women? Freud attempted to adapt his oedipal theorizing to the unconscious lives of girls and women, but even he was forced to admit that his efforts were far from satisfactory. The young girl's unconscious dilemma begins with a positive attraction toward the mother, a mixture of object choice and identification. However, the fantasized mother figure disappoints the girl when the daughter realizes that both she and the mother lack a penis, which may symbolize a lack of power. The little girl may blame the mother for the perceived deficiency, resulting in what Freud termed **penis envy.** As a result, the girl shifts some of her unconscious affections to a "stronger" father figure. The girl eventually resolves her Oedipus complex by repressing her attraction to the father and completing an identification with the mother.

Whereas the boy resolves the Oedipus complex by identifying with the father who threatens him with castration, the little girl is, in a sense, already "castrated," suggested Freud, in that she has no penis. Therefore, she cannot fear castration. Because she lacks the fear, the little girl may feel less urgency to resolve the complex via identification. For many girls, Freud suggested, the Oedipus complex may last a very long time, and for some it is only partially resolved (Freud, 1933/1964). In addition, because the superego is the heir to the Oedipus complex, many women develop superegos that are weaker and less independent than those developed by men. This may be interpreted to suggest that women have less moral sensibility than men. Another interpretation is to suggest that the woman's superego is less dogmatic and harsh, perhaps freeing her up to make moral decisions in a more flexible manner. It is probably fair to say, however, that Freud's inclinations—steeped as they were in the patriarchal world in which he lived—tended in the direction of the first interpretation.

Freud's views on the Oedipus complex in women were very controversial, even at the time of their publication. Many felt it unwise to apply a male-dominated model of sexuality to women, arguing that the little girl's oedipal attachment develops out of her intrinsic femininity undergoing its own maturation processes. Clara Thompson, an influential analyst writing around the time of Freud's death, took issue with the claim that women literally envy the male penis. Rather, women wish to be men's equals; if such a desire for the penis exists, it is in fact a symbolic desire for power and privilege, qualities typically bestowed upon men in male-dominated societies (Thompson, 1942). As we shall see later in this chapter, other analysts, like Karen Horney (1939), argued that the Oedipus complex is a product of culture rather than instinct, and that its development for both men and women is strongly shaped by societal expectations, opportunities, and institutions. Some modern feminist reinterpretations of psychoanalysis have begun with a recasting of the Oedipus complex in feminine terms, as we see in Feature 2.A on the work of Nancy Chodorow.

Feature 2.A

Psychoanalysis and the Sociology of Gender

In her landmark book, *The Reproduction of Mothering: Psychoanalysis and the Sociology of Gender,* Nancy Chodorow (1978) reinterprets the Oedipus complex in order to explain gender differences in personality and the role of mothering in contemporary Western societies. Chodorow begins her argument with a stark, cross-cultural fact: *Women mother.* Biologically speaking, women bear children; sociologically speaking, women, in virtually all human societies, "take primary responsibility for infant care, spend more time with infants and children than do men, and sustain primary emotional ties with infants" (p. 3). Although the percentage of adult women employed in paid work outside the home has increased dramatically over the course of the twentieth century in the United States and Western Europe, mothering is still the province of women. Indeed, most babysitters, nannies, daycare workers, and nursery school teachers are women, and most boys and girls spend most of their early childhood in the company of women. Even in those two-career households in which fathers endeavor to engage in greater levels of childcare than the traditional masculine role has typically allowed, mothers still tend to do the lion's share of caregiving, especially with very young children, as recent empirical research has decisively shown (e.g., Biernat & Wortman, 1991).

Chodorow focuses on the different experiences of little girls and boys as they grow up in "a male dominant but father-absent family where women mother" (p. 40). She argues that by age 3 or 4, children have developed a basic sense of themselves as either female or male as a result, in part, of the different ways in which mothers relate to girls and boys. Even before the onset of the Oedipus complex, mothers tend to relate to girls with a greater sense of "openness and continuity" (p. 109). They identify more with their daughters than they do with their sons. Mothers and daughters experience greater levels of intimacy, merger, and a sense of oneness with each other. The relationship between mother and daughter becomes emotionally richer and more complex over time, a relationship of dependence, attachment, and symbiosis. By contrast, "mothers experience their sons as a male opposite" (p. 110). Sons are viewed as differentiated from their mothers, and maternal behavior is geared toward enabling sons to attain independence and autonomy. While mothers may cherish their sons and love them intensely, their attitude toward sons will always be one of opposition: He is male; he is not like me; he will grow up to be different, separate.

Over the course of his career, Freud became increasingly aware of the different experiences of girls and boys in the preoedipal period. Freud observed that the girl's preoedipal attachment to her mother tends to last longer than the boy's attachment to mother and that the relationship between mother and daughter can be much more dramatically intense and ambivalent than that between mother and son. Nevertheless, Freud felt compelled to describe the female Oedipus complex in terms that were parallel to the experience of boys. According to the orthodox Freudian position, the oedipal girl shifts her affection from mother to father when she realizes that father possesses the coveted penis. Chodorow concedes that the little girl may become disappointed in her mother, or see her as a rival, and the little girl may indeed form a new attachment to her father. But the relationship between father and daughter is rarely strong enough to erase the enduring mother/daughter bond:

> For a girl . . . there is no single oedipal mode or quick oedipal resolution, and there is no absolute "change of object." Psychoanalytic accounts make clear that a girl's libidinal turning to her father is not at the expense of, or a substitute for, her attachment to her mother. Nor does a girl give up the internal relationship to her mother which is a product of her earlier development. Instead, a girl develops important oedipal attachments to her mother *as well as* to her father. These attachments, and the way they are internalized, are built upon, and do not replace, her intense and exclusive preoedipal attachment to her mother. . . . (p. 127)

A girl's oedipal situation, therefore, is multilayered and complex, and it affords no simple resolution. As a result, the girl's basic gender identity is developed in the context of an ongoing and richly nuanced relationship with mother. The feminine self is defined *in relation.* For little boys, however, gender identity is a greater puzzle, a mysterious problem to be solved. Even though the boy may identify with the father, he is not likely to acquire the intimate familiarity with the father's traditional roles—as the man who works outside the house in order to bring home money and support the family—that little girls naturally develop with their mothers. In a sense, the boy must figure out how to be a man on his own, *through opposition.* According to Chodorow, the little boy experiences his own masculinity in opposition to the world of women. He knows that men are different from women, but he doesn't know exactly how. The little boy identifies with a disembodied "position" in the world—he renders a guess about what the position of men might be, and then he patterns himself after the guess. The masculine self is defined through separation and guesswork. By contrast, the feminine self develops from the connectedness of human relations.

What are the results of these two very different experiences of the oedipal period? Chodorow suggests that girls emerge from early childhood "with a stronger basis for experiencing another's needs and feelings as one's own." Girls come to experience themselves as "less differentiated than boys, as more continuous with and related to" other people (p. 167). Consciously and unconsciously, the girl experiences herself as continuous with her environment, connected in a web of intimacy (Gilligan, 1982). The boy, by contrast, must work to separate himself from the web, to identify the essential nature of maleness through separation, opposition, and individuation.

In addition, their differential experiences in the family prepare girls and boys for society's gender roles. Out of the mother/daughter bond emerge daughters with mothering capacities and the desire to mother, making for what Chodorow calls "the reproduction of mothering" from one generation to the next. By contrast, mothers (and fathers as nonmothers) produce sons whose nurturant capacities and needs are systematically curtailed and repressed, preparing the way for men's primary participation in the impersonal, nonfamily world of work and public life.

I have presented a simplified rendition of the Oedipus complex in both sexes. Given the essentially bisexual nature of humans, Freud suggested complicated variations on the standard script. For instance, early object choice of both boys and girls may be directed toward *both* mother and father; similarly, identifications that resolve the complex may incorporate both father and mother (Freud, 1923/1961). A given family's particular dynamics and constellation surely shape the oedipal scenario, but Freud also emphasized that the complex unfolds along certain biologically mandated lines. Exactly how it is played out in the unconscious, therefore, is a complex product of the interaction of biology and experience.

Latency and Maturity

With the resolution of the Oedipus complex, the libido is ready for an extended holiday. The child now enters **latency.** During latency, the libido is rarely expressed in an overt manner. Rather, children channel instinctual energy into play, schoolwork, and peer relations.

The onset of puberty marks the libido's return to center stage and its final, mature expression. In adolescence, the individual enters the **genital stage** of psychosexual development. Biologically capable now of full-fledged sexual intercourse, the young man or woman is finally at the point of attaining psychosexual maturity. He or she must now meet the challenges of expressing the libido in ways that benefit both self and society. This is very difficult. It involves channeling instinctual energy into genital *love* and productive *work* while simultaneously keeping at bay the anxiety that results from inevitable conflicts. Just how troublesome these conflicts can be in adulthood is best depicted in Freud's theory of how the adult mind is finally structured.

The Structural Model of the Mind

In one of his last theoretical innovations, Freud (1923/1961) proposed an integrative model of how the mind is organized. Figure 2.1 presents a picture of the model. Freud concluded that the mind can be broken down into three independent structures. Each of the three exists for a different purpose. The major conflicts that produce anxiety in adults' lives are often the result of disagreements among these three different agents of the mind. Resolving conflicts, therefore, involves forging creative agreements that enable the three to coexist with each other and with the outside world in relative, if short-lived, tranquility.

The Id

The most primitive structure is the **id** (German: *das Es,* or "the it"). Completely submerged in the unconscious, the id is the home of the instinctual impulses of sex and aggression and their derivative wishes, fantasies, and inclinations. The id is a chaotic, seething cauldron that provides all the instinctual energy for mental life. The id knows no inhibitions; it obeys no logical or moral constraints; it is completely out of touch with the outside world of reality, and will remain so always. The activity of the id is dictated solely by the **pleasure principle:** pleasure derives from the reduction of tension in the immediate gratification of impulses.

Developmentally, the id is the oldest structure of the mind. The baby is born "all id." As a bundle of primitive instinctual urges, the mind of the newborn is incapable of rational thought and displays instead **primary-process** thought, a very loose and irrational form of thought driven by instinctual demands. Primary-process thought is evidenced in nocturnal dreams and certain daytime fantasies. In dreams, for instance, impossible situations arise; opposites coexist without apparent contradiction; a thing can be "A" and "not-A" at the same time, and nobody seems to mind. In primary-process thought, the individual hallucinates the objects of instinctual urges, as when a desperately thirsty person experiences the hallucination of a cool, thirst-quenching waterfall. Unable to distinguish

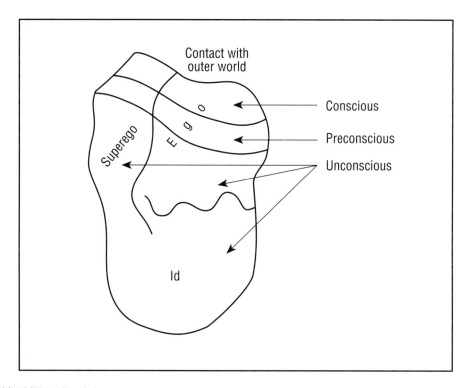

Figure 2.1

A Schematic Diagram of Freud's Model of the Mind.

between fantasy and reality, the id finds temporary gratification in such hallucinations, displaying what Freud termed hallucinatory wish fulfillment.

The Ego

If the mind remained "all id," the human being would quickly encounter very
serious trouble. Though the id finds satisfaction in hallucinatory wish fulfillment,
the organism cannot function for long on wish and fantasy alone. Beginning in
infancy, therefore, a second structure of the mind emerges out of the id. This is
the **ego** (German: *das Ich,* or "the I"). Borrowing its energy from the id instincts,
the ego exists as the "handmaiden" to the id, working tirelessly to mediate
between the blind demands of its master and the constraints imposed by logic and
the external world. The ego thus helps ensure the safety and self-preservation of
the organism by adopting the **reality principle** in conducting its affairs and by
relying on the power of **secondary-process** thought. The reality principle enables
the individual to suspend immediate instinctual gratification until either an
appropriate object or environmental condition arises that will satisfy the instinct.

Images of the unconscious: *Apparition of Face and Fruit Dish on a Beach,* by Salvador Dali (1938).

The ego is able to weigh the demands of the outside world and balance them with the needs and impulses expressed by the id, so to produce behaviors and modes of experience that best use the id's raw energy. In secondary-process thinking, furthermore, the ego can engage in rational cognitive activity in order to make measured and realistic decisions.

While the id is completely submerged within the unconscious, the ego manifests itself partly in certain conscious ways. When a person functions as a rational and self-reflective decision maker in the face of life's many challenges, he or she is displaying the ego's conscious powers. But significant aspects of the ego are unconscious, as well. A good deal of coping with the inevitable conflicts that arise in daily life is carried out unconsciously, by the ego through **defense mechanisms.** A defense mechanism is an unconscious strategy of the ego that distorts reality in order to lessen anxiety. In the defense mechanism of *projection,* for instance, the person unconsciously attributes to other people certain of his or her own characteristics whose existence within the self provokes unacceptable levels

Table 2.2

Some Defense Mechanisms of the Ego

Mechanism	Definition	Simple Example
Repression	A dangerous impulse is actively and totally excluded from consciousness.	An aging father fails to recognize his own feelings of hostility toward his strong, athletic son.
Projection	Attributing one's own unacceptable and disturbing thoughts and impulses to someone else.	A man preoccupied with doubts about his own heterosexuality frequently accuses others of being homosexual.
Reaction formation	Warding off an unacceptable impulse by overemphasizing its opposite in thought and behavior.	A man threatened by his desire to dominate others and to be aggressive thinks of himself as a passive and retiring sort of person and acts accordingly.
Rationalization	Devising an extremely "reasonable" explanation or excuse for an event or behavior that threatens the person's esteem.	A wife explains her husband's repeated infidelity as a product of his unfortunate upbringing or an overly seductive environment.
Regression	Retreating to an earlier and more primitive stage or mode of behavior in order to avoid pain, threat, or anxiety.	A mother lapses into diversionary "baby talk" with her daughter whenever she confronts a tough decision or threatening situation.
Displacement	Shifting an impulse from a threatening to a nonthreatening object.	Angry at his boss because of a demotion, the businessman goes home and argues with his wife.
Sublimation	Channeling socially unacceptable impulses into acceptable, even admirable, behavior.	The surgeon channels aggressive energy into constructive medical work; the artist employs the libido to produce a masterpiece.

Note: Defense mechanisms are always *unconscious*. They serve to distort reality while relieving anxiety.

of anxiety. Therefore, a man who harbors strong unconscious uncertainties about his own masculinity may be more likely than most people to accuse other men of being homosexual. This is not a conscious deceit but rather a subtle and unconscious strategy of the ego to ward off anxiety by distorting, to a certain extent, objective reality. Table 2.2 describes some other defense mechanisms commonly employed by the ego.

The Superego

As we have already noted, the **superego** emerges at the end of the Oedipus complex. The superego (German: *das Überich,* or "the over-I") is a primitive internalized representation of the norms and values of society as acquired through identification with the parents. As such, the superego is akin to an internalized authority that repeatedly tells the person what he or she should and should not be doing, as if the parents had quite literally been eaten and become now personified inside the self. The superego is typically a strict and inflexible agent who insists on the renunciation or repression of the id's instinctual demands. Whereas the id yells out, "Yes! Go for it—now!" the superego sternly replies, "No! Not in a million years!" Despite their opposing points of view, however, the id and superego share a number of characteristics. Both, for instance, are demanding and inflexible—both are blind to the constraints and demands of the outside world. Only the ego operates according to the reality principle.

Much of the superego is submerged within the unconscious. Operating for the most part, therefore, outside of awareness, the superego strives for three major goals: (1) to inhibit the impulses of the id, particularly sex and aggression, since these are the behaviors most seriously proscribed by society; (2) to persuade the ego to substitute moralistic goals for realistic ones; and (3) to accomplish perfection. Two subsystems of the superego involve themselves in these goals. The CONSCIENCE is governed by rules and norms concerning *bad* behavior—what the person should *not* do—and it is active in the pursuit of goals (1) and (2). The EGO IDEAL consists of idealized images and rules about *good* behavior—what the person *should* do—and it is actively involved in the pursuit of goals (2) and (3). In striving for the goals of instinctual repression, moralistic behavior, and self-perfection, the superego functions as the "vehicle of tradition and of all the time-resisting judgments of value which have propagated themselves in this manner from generation to generation" (Freud, 1933/1964, p. 67). A stern and unreasonable disciplinarian, the superego does not present an *objective* picture of the parents. Writes Freud (1933/1964), "a child's superego is in fact constructed on the model not of its parents but of its parents' superego" (Freud, 1933/1964, p. 67).

With the establishment of the superego, the ego now faces a third taskmaster and powerful source of conflict. The first, the reality of the outside world, poses objective dangers that produce realistic anxiety; the second, the id, threatens the ego with neurotic anxiety about the ever-present possibility of an uncontrollable release of instinctual energy; now the third source of conflict, the superego, adds the problem of moral anxiety, which may take the form of feelings of guilt over moral transgressions or regret in failing to live up to perfect ideals. The ego is a lonely agent of reasonableness amidst a host of uncompromising and relentless forces and factors. Dependent on the id for its energy, beholden to the superego as the lowly child to an ominipotent parent, and faced with almost impossible demands from the real world, the ego is perennially beleaguered and occasionally it may even break down, resulting in neurotic symptoms. No wonder that Freud was pessimistic about the possibilities of human happiness.

Psychoanalysis After Freud

The psychoanalytic tradition has grown and evolved in significant ways since the time of Freud, yielding a wide range of diverse theories and approaches to studying the person. The remainder of this chapter considers some of the more influential theoretical developments in the psychoanalytic tradition outside the writings of Freud. These theories share a number of points with Freud's original views, but they differ in significant ways such that they may be considered neo-Freudian, or *neoanalytic,* perspectives.

The first challenges to Freudian orthodoxy were posed by the early revisionists, Carl Jung and Alfred Adler. Both Jung and Adler were initially drawn to the psychoanalytic movement in their admiration of Freud's brilliant insights into human nature, neurosis, and psychotherapy. But both eventually took issue with Freud's unyielding emphasis on the sexual drive in explaining human behavior and experience. Both became disaffected with the Freudian orthodoxy and broke away to launch their own intellectual movements.

Centering his theory on the spiritual dimensions of human life and the deep meanings of myth and symbol, Jung developed a unique and highly complex theory of personality, which he called "analytical psychology." We will consider his contribution at the very end of this chapter. Adler developed a very different approach, emphasizing conscious, everyday motives such as striving for superiority and social interest, as well as the narrative quality of lives as *stories* with beginnings, middles, and endings. Adler's approach is sometimes called "individual psychology." Although Adler is traditionally viewed as a neo-Freudian theorist, his final theory has surprisingly little in common with Freud. Consequently, I believe that Adler's theory is a much better example of an approach to persons emphasizing "interpersonal stories" (Section IV in this textbook), rather than "intrapsychic mysteries" (the current Section I). Therefore, we will save an extended treatment of Adler's important contributions to personality psychology for Chapter 12.

Toward the very end of Freud's life and since his death, the psychoanalytic tradition has witnessed the growth of "ego psychology" in the writings of Anna Freud, Heinz Hartmann, Robert White, and others. Ego psychologists tend to underscore the adaptive qualities of the ego over and against the id's instinctual power. One of the most influential ego psychologists is Erik Erikson. But like Adler, Erikson's approach departs from Freud's in so many critical ways that it is not well described within the psychoanalytic tradition. I believe that Erikson's is also a "narrative theory" of personality at heart, fitting best under the rubric of "interpersonal stories." We will consider Erikson in depth in Chapter 12.

A second movement within the psychoanalytic tradition may be seen in the theories of Karen Horney and Erich Fromm, which tend to emphasize the cultural and historical determinants of human behavior over and against biological drives and instincts. Horney's and Fromm's theories are sometimes called "social-psychological" theories in the psychoanalytic tradition. Third are the "object-relations" theorists, such W. R. D. Fairbairn and Margaret Mahler. These theorists focus their attention on the earliest interpersonal relationships and the ways in which these relationships provide the self with an intrapsychic structure.

In sum, the three movements of ego psychology, social-psychological theories, and object-relations theories deemphasize Freud's concept of biological drives and replace it with either (1) a revitalized ego, (2) culture and history, or (3) interpersonal relationships, respectively. Finally, Heinz Kohut's increasingly influential "self psychology" merits examination as a post-Freudian movement that bears some similarity to object-relations approaches. We will, therefore, examine ego psychology, Horney and Fromm, object-relations theory, and Kohut's self psychology as important trends in the development of the psychoanalytic tradition since Freud. We will then end the chapter with a brief review of Jung's intriguing alternative to Freudian psychology.

Expansion of the Ego

Freud's structural model of the mind made the ego the *executive* of the personality, but by no means was it a very strong or confident executive. The Romantic legacy of conflict between the individual and society, the Victorian view of a dissociation between private and public selves, the pessimism engendered by the destruction of World War I, Freud's work with clinical patients, and Freud's own life experiences all converged to reinforce his rather pessimistic image of the ego. Besieged by instinctual demands and beleaguered by moral and societal constraints, the ego struggled to get by. "Getting by" meant reducing anxiety to tolerable levels by resolving conflicts.

Ego psychologists paint a more optimistic picture of the ego and its relationship to id, superego, and the outside world, anticipated in some of Freud's last writings (Freud, 1940/1964). They argue that the ego does more than merely cope with inevitable conflict. The ego promotes healthy adaptation to life through the ego functions of learning, memory, perception, and synthesis. More than a hapless defender, the ego is a master integrator. It organizes experience so that the organism can become an effective and competent member of society. According to ego psychologists, the ego is not the dependent handmaiden to the id. Rather, the ego may function as a more or less autonomous system in the personality (Hartmann, 1939, 1964; Kris, 1952; Rapaport, 1959).

Three years before her father's death, Anna Freud (1936) published *The Ego and the Mechanisms of Defense,* in which she gathered together scattered ideas in psychoanalytic writing and lore concerning the defense mechanisms as a way of demonstrating the substantial resources the ego may bring to bear in coping with conflict and anxiety. While Anna Freud remained faithful to Sigmund Freud's pronouncements concerning the determinant role of id drives in human behavior, her writing on ego defenses paved the way for the ego's empowerment in subsequent psychoanalytic theorizing. Anna Freud also articulated a broader view of human development than that proposed by her father, based largely on her clinical work with children and adolescents. Beyond the psychosexual sequence, Anna Freud (1965) observed **developmental lines** in childhood as the individual matured from complete dependency, passivity, and irrationality to rational independence and active mastery of the environment. She distinguished six developmental lines whose common theme is gradual mastery of oneself and one's world:

1. From dependency to emotional self-reliance
2. From sucking to rational eating
3. From wetting and soiling to bladder and bowel control
4. From irresponsibility to responsibility in body management
5. From body manipulation to toy play, from play to work
6. From egocentricity to companionship.

Called "the father of ego psychology," Heinz Hartmann (1939, 1964) moved beyond Anna Freud's attempts to strengthen the ego without diluting the id and argued that the ego and the id derive their energy from a common instinctual source and that the two agencies of the mind, therefore, are on equal footing, each regulating and affecting the other. With this seemingly small change in psychoanalytic thinking, Hartmann freed the ego up to take on the hitherto neglected functions of motility, organization of perception, reality testing, thinking and intelligence, anticipation of the future, synthesis of experience, and other high-level activities to which Freud seemed to pay little attention. In addition, Hartmann argued that the ego could potentially operate in a **conflict-free sphere** A significant portion of human behavior and experience, argued Hartmann, transpires outside the domain of conflict and tension reduction. Within this conflict-free sphere, the ego's primary role is to *adapt to the environment.* Where Freud underscored the ego's attempts to minimize anxiety associated with conflict, Hartmann and other ego psychologists celebrated the ego's successes in *adaptation.*

Robert White (1959, 1963) took ego psychology one step further with his argument that the ego has its own intrinsic energy and its own satisfactions which are completely independent of the id's instinctual gratifications. The ego's own fundamental energies find expression in the child's capacity to explore and manipulate the world. Exploration and manipulation are performed as intrinsically rewarding behaviors in and of themselves, *not* as indirect gratifications of sexual and aggressive instincts. White has reinterpreted Freud's stages of psychosexual development in terms of the ego's striving for **competence.** In each of these stages, the child is not only gratifying libidinal and aggressive urges, argues White, but is also expanding his or her sphere of interpersonal mastery in generating intentional effects in the world. In other words, a child's inborn tendencies toward curiosity and exploration of the environment express themselves in more and more mature ways over the course of development, as the person becomes more and more effective in carrying out "those transactions with the environment which result in [the organism's] maintaining itself, growing, and flourishing" (White, 1960, p. 275).

Karen Horney

In young adulthood, Karen Horney found in the psychoanalytic movement a religion, a role, and an identity. Gifted, energetic, and fiercely independent, Horney defied many of the cultural stereotypes for young German women in the years before World War I as she became one of the first women to graduate from a German medical school and embark upon a career in psychiatry. After marrying a businessman in 1909 and giving birth to her first of three daughters in 1911, Horney began her own personal psychoanalysis as a patient of Karl Abraham (a disciple of Freud). It does not appear that her analysis was especially successful in that she continued to suffer from serious bouts of depression throughout her early adult years. Nonetheless, Horney became enamored with the psychoanalytic view of human behavior and experience. Early on, she was a "true believer" in the psychoanalytic movement (Quinn, 1987), as the ideas of Freud and his followers filled an ideological void left by her adolescent rejection of religion. In the 1920s, however, Horney began to question some of the central Freudian dogmas, beginning with Freud's views on the female Oedipus complex. By the time of Freud's death, she had begun to sketch her own neoanalytic theory of personality, emphasizing social and cultural factors in personality over and against biological determinism. By the time of her own death in 1952, she was recognized as an original theorist and a pioneer in the psychoanalytic movement.

Horney's break with the Freudian orthodoxy began in her personal experience as a mother (McAdams, in press a; Quinn, 1987). Freud believed that the instinctual roots of childbirth reside in the mother's unconscious desire to have the penis she never received as a child. The baby symbolizes the desired penis, empowering the woman who bears the child with a delayed oedipal victory and providing a deeply satisfying experience of feminine completion. In Horney's view, such an interpretation bore no resemblance to the actual experience of motherhood. In her biography of Horney, Susan Quinn writes that with the birth of Brigitte, her first daughter, in 1911:

> Another fifteen years would go by before Karen Horney wrote her groundbreaking essay "The Flight from Womanhood." In the interim she gave birth to two more daughters and saw her world transformed by a world war. But it was the pleasure and pride she

Karen Horney

had felt in childbirth, first with Brigitte, and then twice more with Marianne and Renate, which became the touchstone of her argument for an alternative theory of female development. Childbirth, according to the Freudian view, was only a substitute and partial compensation for the lack of a penis. "I, as a woman," Horney wrote in 1926, "ask in amazement, and what about motherhood? And the blissful consciousness of bearing a new life within oneself? And the ineffable happiness of the increasing expectation of the appearance of a new being? And the joy when it finally makes its appearance and one holds it for the first time in one's arms? And the deep pleasurable feeling of satisfaction in suckling it and the happiness of the whole period when the infant needs her care?" Perhaps, she suggested, women's feeling of disadvantage had more to do with the social realities than with the lack of a penis. (Quinn, 1987, p. 171)

For Horney, the Oedipus complex had little to do with sexuality and biological drives. It is instead a culturally shaped family conflict involving hostility, jealousy, and **basic anxiety.** Basic anxiety is "the feeling a child has of being isolated and helpless in a potentially hostile world" (Horney, 1945, p. 41). Children who receive too little warmth and encouragement from their parents are especially prone to basic anxiety. Feeling more and more helpless and insecure as parents continue to neglect or intimidate them, anxious children begin to harbor deep feelings of resentment and anger toward parents. But the feelings cannot be expressed directly because the parents appear to be so big and powerful. Consequently, the child feels even greater levels of anxiety because of the surging hostile impulses within. Horney points out that the "resulting picture may look exactly like what Freud describes as the Oedipus complex; passionate clinging to one parent and jealousy toward the other or toward anyone interfering with the claim of exclusive possession" (Horney, 1939, p. 83). But the underlying meanings of these attachments are completely different from what Freud would propose. "They are early manifestations of neurotic conflicts rather than a primarily sexual phenomenon" (Horney, 1939, p. 84).

For Horney, neurotic conflicts are always rooted in faulty interpersonal relationships through which basic anxiety and hostility make for the *alienation of an individual from his or her real self.* The real self is the true core of one's being, containing the potential for growth, happiness, and power. The neurotic feels that he or she has lost touch with those aspects of the self that are good and authentic. In order to cope with this perceived alienation, the neurotic may adopt one of three different strategies for coping with inner conflict: *moving toward people, moving against people,* or *moving away from people.*

The first strategy is to express intense needs for approval and acceptance from others in a way that leads to superficial compliance and self-effacing dependency. Beneath the congenial surface, the neurotic who adopts the strategy of moving toward people may be masking underlying rage and resentment. The young man who wants to be everybody's friend may really want to excel and to dominate others, but he is cut off from his real wants (they are unconscious) and unable to summon up the confidence needed to confront his underlying ambitions. Horney (1950) describes him as:

> a stowaway without any rights. In accordance with this attitude, he also tends to suppress in himself anything that connotes ambition, vindictiveness, triumph, seeking his own advantage. In short he has solved his inner conflicts by suppressing all expansive attitudes and drives and making self-abnegating trends predominant. (p. 216)

The second strategy of dealing with inner conflicts is to adopt the expansive solution of moving against people. From this point of view, the world is a hostile and competitive place. One must, therefore, act aggressively, attack others before they attack you. The expansive individual may seem suave and sophisticated on the surface, but his urbane gestures of fellowship serve the rather crass underlying purpose of dominating others. "The expansive type glorifies and cultivates in him- or herself everything that leads to the mastery of others" (Horney, 1950, p. 214). Unlike the self-effacing type whose alienation from the real self keeps him from believing in his inherent worth and goodness, the expansive neurotic identifies with an idealized version of the self as all-powerful. The idealized self is a defense, however, against the basic anxiety of everyday life. The real self is gentler and more human, but it is locked away in the unconscious, and the expansive neurotic has lost the key.

The third strategy to neurotic conflict is moving away from people—the solution of resignation. In this case, neurotics withdraw from interpersonal relationships and seek to live in a self-sufficient and unassailable world. They hope never to be dependent on anyone. They desire no power over others. They strive for few instrumental or interpersonal goals. In the extreme, their lives seem stilted and joyless, self-contained spheres of triviality and ennui. Neurotics who adopt the solution of resignation may seem aloof and haughty to others. They stand apart, observe from afar. What is true in the interpersonal realm may also be true in the intrapsychic. These kinds of neurotic individuals adopt an aloof stance vis-à-vis their own inner lives, as well. They may become onlookers at themselves, always detached as they watch in amusement or disgust the workings of their own minds.

Each of Horney's three neurotic strategies is designed to minimize conflict in dealing with people. In their milder forms, each of the three may be adaptive strategies for healthy living. Indeed, all of us must learn how to move toward, against, and away from others as we seek to adapt to the challenges of our worlds. But in the case of neurosis, basic anxiety and hostility force the individual to use the styles in an inflexible and debilitating manner. Horney (1945) writes:

> As we have seen, each of the basic attitudes toward others has its positive value. In moving toward people the person tries to create for himself a friendly relation to his world. In moving against people he equips himself for survival in a competitive society. In moving away from people he hopes to attain a certain integrity and serenity. As a matter of fact, all three attitudes are not only desirable but necessary to our development as human beings. It is only when they appear and operate in a neurotic framework that they become compulsive, rigid, indiscriminate, and mutually exclusive. (p. 89)

Erich Fromm

Erich Fromm was a close associate of Karen Horney, and his theory of personality bears some resemblance to hers. Both theorists emphasized the social and cultural determinants of human behavior over and against biological drives. But

Erich Fromm

Fromm's thinking was more strongly influenced by sociology than was Horney's. Whereas Horney focused mostly on the family and other immediate social contexts within which behavior is embedded, Fromm took a more expansive view. As part of the contextual setting for the individual's behavior and experience, Fromm pointed to the distal dimensions of social structures, a society's economy and class system, and the ideological ethos of a particular culture at a particular point in history. Following Freud, Fromm believed that human actions are directed by forces over which we have little control. But following Karl Marx, Fromm identified some of those forces in the economic and ideological practices of society, as well as within the inner workings of the individual mind.

No personality theorist has taken more seriously the idea that the person is embedded in culture and history than has Erich Fromm. In Fromm's theory of **dialectical humanism,** the person's behavior is the complex and overdetermined product of internal needs manifesting themselves within the external social arrangements prescribed by a society at a particular moment in history. In Fromm's own life, the societal context that so influenced his view of persons was a heady European intelligentsia immersed in the writings of Freud and Marx. The decisive historical moment was World War I.

Fromm was born in Frankfurt, Germany, in 1900. A Jew raised among Christians, the 12-year-old Fromm was devastated by the suicide of an attractive young woman, an artist, who had been a close friend of the family (Fromm, 1962). This pivotal event from Fromm's childhood occurred shortly before the outbreak of World War I, during which the teenaged boy's abhorrence of and curiosity about human destructiveness and death grew to become a lifelong obsession. During the war, he asked himself a question that haunted many Europeans of his day, as we have already seen with Freud: "How is it possible that millions of men continue to stay in the trenches, to kill innocent men of other nations, and to be killed and thus to cause the deepest pain to parents, wives, and friends?" (Fromm, 1962, p. 8). Fromm ultimately committed himself to exploring the question. The answers he formulated were strongly shaped by his reading of Freud and Marx. From Freud, Fromm learned that human beings are not conscious of the most significant determinants of their behavior. From Marx, he adopted the conviction that humans are not free and that they cannot be free as long as they accept uncritically external control exerted by social custom and institutions.

In Fromm's view, men and women living in contemporary Western societies are overwhelmed by *too much freedom* and thus seek to escape freedom by submitting and conforming to authority or through wanton destructiveness (Fromm, 1941). Freedom began to pose serious problems for Westerners, argues Fromm, with the decline of the medieval world, the onset of the Protestant Reformation, and the rise of capitalism. As European society became more economically and religiously diverse in the sixteenth and seventeenth centuries, Europeans came to experience what was both an exhilarating and an uncomfortable surfeit of choice and opportunity. Over time, European middle-class society came to place greater emphasis on independence from the once all-powerful Catholic Church, on individual decision making, on personal achievement, and on fashioning one's own identity (Erikson, 1958; Fromm, 1941; McClelland, 1961). Industrialization, urbanization, and the rise of science and technology endowed Westerners with even greater freedom, but the freedom has bred greater separation from nature and alienation from other human beings.

Expressed against this cultural and historical background of freedom and isolation, six basic human needs motivate the person's behavior (Fromm, 1955, 1973). The need for *relatedness* is the desire to overcome isolation from nature and alienation from society through loving and caring for others. The need for *transcendence* moves men and women to master their environments and become effective creators. The need for *rootedness* is the desire for security, stability, and a permanent niche in the social order. The need for a *sense of identity* motivates people to make their own decisions, to reflect on them, and to feel that the life they are leading is truly their own. The need for *frame of orientation* directs human beings to search for meaning in their lives by formulating and adopting belief systems and ultimate goals that orient their life strivings. Finally, the need for *stimulation* is the desire to find ways of engaging with the world in stimulating activities.

Personal needs find expression within the rules of culture. Taking a page out of Freud, Jung, and Marx, Fromm argues that societies inculcate within their members a shared social unconscious, composed of thoughts and feelings that the society will not permit an individual to harbor in awareness. Through the categories of experience implied by a particular language, through social customs, prohibitions, and conventions, a society shapes how its members construe their life choices, subtly but powerfully molding the expression of needs. The interaction of personal needs and social context ultimately gives rise to specific character types, each of which represents a particular solution to the problem of adapting to social realities against a pervasive existential backdrop of freedom and aloneness. In contemporary capitalist societies, Fromm identifies five basic character types.

The **receptive** type fulfills personal needs by adopting a passive and dependent orientation, committed to the belief that all worthwhile comforts and values may be received from the outside. For the receptive type, the central task of life is to be loved, but not necessarily to love. Such an essentially unproductive individual may be described as submissive, unrealistic, cowardly, wishful, gullible, and sentimental. However, some basically receptive individuals show a more positive side of this character type, revealing an optimistic, idealistic, and accepting approach to life.

The **hoarding** type strives to accumulate possessions, power, and love, and to hold on to all that is accumulated. Objects, people, ideas, and most all of the world exist to be collected and stored away. The hoarding type is unimaginative, stingy, suspicious, obsessional, and possessive, reminiscent of Freud's description of the "anal retentive" personality type. The more positive version of the hoarding type may be practical, careful, reserved, methodical, and loyal.

The **exploitative** type is aggressive and self-centered. This type views the world as filled with objects, people, and ideas to be stolen, grabbed, or snatched away. This essentially Machiavellian and aggressive approach to life encourages a wanton individualism that masks a deep and troubling sense of isolation from humankind. In its less extreme versions, though, the exploitative type can appear self-confident, proud, and even captivating.

The **marketing** type is a peculiar product of modern industrial society. In the marketing orientation, one seeks to market oneself in the manner one might market a commodity to be sold. Such a person carefully manufactures him- or herself to attract "customers." Like a high-priced appliance, the well-marketed adult is very much in demand. Writes Fromm:

> Since modern man experiences himself both as the seller and as the commodity to be sold on the market, self-esteem depends on conditions beyond his control. If he is "successful," he is valuable; if he is not, he is worthless. (Fromm, 1947, p. 79)

The marketing type is described as opportunistic, aimless, tactless, and indifferent. In a more positive light, the marketing type has the potential to appear purposeful, curious, and open to change.

Although they each may show modestly positive characteristics, the receptive, hoarding, exploitative, and marketing types are essentially nonproductive solutions to the problem of finding a viable way to express human needs within contemporary Western societies. They, therefore, stand in marked contrast to the fifth character type: the **productive** type. This type fulfills his or her inner potential to become a creative worker and lover within a well-defined social identity. Such a person transcends superficial social roles to "use his powers and to realize the potentialities inherent in him" (Fromm, 1947, p. 91). The productive person is autonomous, spontaneous, loving, creative, and committed to the social good. As we will see in later chapters, Fromm's productive type has much in common with Erikson's (Chapter 12) *generative* and Maslow's (Chapter 8) *self-actualized* adult.

Object Relations

A very important contemporary trend in psychoanalytic theorizing is an increased emphasis on **object relations** in human functioning. The term object relations derives from Freud's idea that instinctual energy is invested in a particular "object," as in the case of object choice. Thus, the infant invests libido in the mental representation of mother—establishing the first object relation. Later objects may include father, friends, lovers, and so on. In each object relation, the person establishes a *gratifying involvement* (Behrends & Blatt, 1985) with another human being. Following his mechanistic instinct theory, Freud underscored the object's function as an outlet for the expression of the person's sexual and aggressive urges. Eagle (1984) accurately depicts Freud's somewhat limited understanding of the object: "Objects and object relations are important primarily as means and vehicles for discharge of libidinal and aggressive drives. In this regard, the former, indeed, have a secondary and derived status" (p. 10).

In the same way that ego psychology has given the ego new strength and dignity, modern object-relations approaches to personality seek to restore the dignity and primacy of interpersonal relationships. According to these views, the object relation is more than a mere outlet for the discharge of an instinct. Object relations are primary, *not* derived from instinctual discharge, and they function to provide structure to the self. For object-relations theorists such as W. R. D. Fairbairn (1952) and Donald Winnicott (1965), the person is, from birth and by nature, an object seeker. Much of human behavior is motivated by an inherent drive to establish object relations. The inevitable frustrations and losses that result from object relations leave behind **internalized** images of lost **objects,** and these images come to comprise the self. Once internalized, these objects live on in an unconscious, internal realm, tending to do battle with each other in fantasies while exerting real effects upon subsequent interpersonal relationships.

The roots of object-relations theory lie in Freud's (1917/1957) essay, "Mourning and Melancholia." In this study of human sadness, Freud sought to distinguish (1) the normal process of grieving that a person undergoes after the death of or separation from a loved one (mourning) from (2) the prolonged sadness experienced by the chronically depressed person (melancholia). Freud's clinical observations led him to conclude that both mourning and melancholia are the result of disruptions in object relations. In both cases, a loved object is lost, by death, separation, or some perceived parting, and the person reacts with sadness. In both cases, argued Freud, the bereaved person internalizes the lost object, establishing within the mind a fantasized representation of the object that acts as a substitute for the real object. Therefore, a person may unconsciously adopt the mannerisms, attitudes, or personality traits of the lost object, as if the lost object were now part of the self, living on in an internal world that knows no death or separation. In sum, when the object is lost, "object choice regresses, as it were, to identification" (Freud, 1933/1964, p. 63): If I cannot have the object, then I will become the object.

You may recall that object choice and identification—the unconscious desires to have and to be, respectively—played themselves out in a fatal way for the Japanese novelist Yukio Mishima (Chapter 1). You may also recognize the same process at work in the classic Oedipus complex. Note that the oedipal child seeks to have the parents in a powerful and sensual manner (object choice). When object choice fails, identification takes its place. The child seeks to be like the parents, opting for identification when the object of the libido is "lost," thereby resolving the Oedipus complex. The superego becomes the internalized parent objects.

The difference between mourning and melancholia, argued Freud, is *ambivalence*. Mourning is the result of any object loss, but when the lost object is strongly loved and strongly hated at the same time—an intensely ambivalent object relation—normal mourning can evolve into pathological melancholia. In melancholia, the anger felt toward the loved-and-hated object becomes directed toward the self, because the object has now been internalized to become part of the self. Melancholic sadness is anger turned inward.

Contemporary object-relations theorists argue that the general process of internalizing the lost object is much more common than Freud ever supposed. What happens in the Oedipus complex and in mourning and melancholia in fact happens almost every day: objects are lost and then internalized. The infant who forms its first object relation with a caregiver begins to internalize that caregiver, setting up an image of the caregiver in primitive fantasies, in the earliest experiences of temporary separation from the caregiver. Given that no mother spends 24 hours a day for her entire life with a single child, the child's internalization of the lost mother object is an inevitable fact of life.

The many object losses, separations, and frustrations we experience over the course of our lives leave behind internalized representations of those objects. These representations of the most important objects in our lives become internalized parts or structures of the self, split off from each other in the same way that Freud saw the superego as split off from the id and ego. Like Freud's superego, furthermore, internalized objects function as semiautonomous agents in the personality, making unconscious demands and influencing, in an unconscious manner, the ways in which we conduct interpersonal relationships in the real world. According to object-relations theorists, personality problems arise when old internalized objects cause deep splits in the structure of the ego, interfering with the ego's attempts to establish mature interpersonal relationships in the real world. For example, a young man may be unable to carry out a mature intimate relationship with a potential lover because he tends to replay an internalized standard script for relating to other women that is embodied in the deeply internalized object of a domineering-but-clinging mother. The fantasized internal object, thus, gets in the way of mature object relations in the real world. Psychological health and maturity, on the other hand, are functions of a well-integrated ego wherein different objects reside harmoniously.

The best-known developmental theory of object relations is that proposed by Margaret Mahler (1968; Mahler, Pine, & Bergman, 1975). According to Mahler, the first 3 years of life are crucial for establishing lifelong, mature object relations. In the first month or two of life, the infant is in an initial stage of *normal autism,* in which its biological needs and rhythms outweigh most object-seeking efforts. Withdrawn behind a *stimulus barrier,* the newborn spends most of its time sleeping and eating as various physiological mechanisms work to achieve homeostasis. In the second month of life, the infant enters *normal symbiosis,* behaving now as though it and the mother were a dual unity within a common boundary. The infant develops a dim recognition of the mother as an object but is unable to distinguish her from the self. Thus, in symbiosis the infant and mother merge into unity and boundaries between self and other are blurred.

At about the halfway point of the first year of life, the infant begins the critical process of **separation-individuation.** Emerging from the symbiotic bond of the early months, the infant enters the first subphase of separation-individuation, *differentiation of the body image* (5–9 months). Out of the unity of symbiosis, self and other become differentiated. As the infant moves and maneuvers, it may check back with the mother, making eye contact with her or exchanging sounds for assurance that, while she is no longer in perfect unity with the infant, she is still there. In the second subphase of *practicing* (10–14 months), the infant's expanded locomotor abilities enable it to explore the inanimate environment with much greater ease. The physical presence of the mother and other preferred caregivers promotes the infant's explorations, and when the mother is absent the infant may display low-keyed behavior, inhibiting exploration while focusing on an internal, imagined mother.

In the *rapprochement* subphase (14–24 months), the child develops an increased awareness of the separateness of the mother and may undergo a "crisis" wherein the conflict between the urge to reunite with her and the urge to separate completely becomes intense. The temporary result may be various forms of ambivalence and *approach–avoidance behavior,* as when the child follows the mother closely when she moves away but then darts away if she approaches. The resolution of the rapprochement crisis is reached in the last subphase, termed *consolidation of individuality* (2–3 years). At this time, the child establishes a stable sense of self and other and achieves emotional-object constancy, whereby he or she now accepts the fact that the mother and other caregivers remain loving and sustaining objects even when they are not present in a given situation. With the consolidation of individuality, the child has internalized a differentiated and complex image of the mother object and has integrated it successfully within the developing ego.

In conclusion, the many different approaches to personality that fall under the rubric of "object-relations theories" differ from each other in subtle and complex ways. Whereas some appear to be natural outgrowths of Freud's writings about object choice and identification (such as Kernberg, 1975; Mahler, 1968), others depart more radically from Freud's views (such as Fairbairn, 1952). They all have in common, however, a general view of the person as an *object seeker*. Personality structure and development are viewed in terms of the person's strivings to relate to other human beings in emotionally satisfying ways.

Heinz Kohut

One of the most influential developments in psychoanalytic theorizing in the last 15 years has been the rise of **self psychology,** championed by Heinz Kohut (1971, 1977, 1984). The origins of Kohut's ideas are readily traced to Freud and the object-relations theorists. But his theory also resembles a number of other approaches, including Erikson's theory of identity (Chapter 12) and the writings of humanistic psychologists such as Carl Rogers (Chapter 8).

As a therapist, Kohut worked with patients whose central disturbance involved feelings of emptiness and depression. Many of the patients suffered from problems of *narcissism*. It was only through empathy, through careful listening to what his patients told him and understanding what they said in their own terms (rather than in the traditional terms of ego, id, superego, libido, and so on), that Kohut came to view the self as the central construct and the central problem in personality:

> In trying, again and again, in analysis after analysis, to deter-mine the genetic roots of the selves of my analysands [patients], I obtained the impression that during early psychic development a process takes place in which some archaic mental contents that had been experienced as belonging to the self become obliterated or are assigned to the area of the nonself while others are retained within the self or are added to it. As a result of this process a core self—the "nuclear self"—is established. This structure is the basis for our sense of being an independent cen-ter of initiative and perception, integrated with our most central ambitions and ideals and with our experience that our body and mind form a unit in space and a continuum in time. (Kohut, 1977, p. 177)

At the center of personality is the **bipolar self.** Its two poles are (1) ambitions for power and success and (2) idealized goals and values. Linking the two poles in what Kohut describes as a "tension arc" are the person's basic talents and skills. In a sense, a person is driven by ambitions and guided by idealized goals and values in accord with talents and skills. The bipolar self is structured in the early years of life as the child interacts with important **self-objects** in the environment. Self-objects are people so central to our lives that we feel that they are, in some sense, parts of us. The bipolar self evolves through relationships with self-objects.

In most cases, the most salient self-object in the first year or two of life is the mother. With respect to the development of the self, one of the mother's main roles is to *mirror* the child's grandiosity. This means that she must confirm and admire the child's strength, health, greatness, and specialness. She must reflect and celebrate the child's budding agency and power. The mirroring relationship establishes, consolidates, and affirms the ambition pole of the bipolar self. Somewhat later in development, the mother or the father may serve as the *idealizing* self-object. The child admires and identifies with idealizing self-objects as sources of strength, care, and calmness. The idealizing relationship establishes, consolidates, and affirms the second pole of the bipolar self, wherein are located idealized goals and values.

Healthy mirroring and idealizing pave the way for the development of an *autonomous self,* the ideal personality type in Kohut's scheme. Persons with an autonomous self enjoy high self-esteem and self-confidence. They are not overly dependent on others but are able to engage people in intimate and fulfilling relationships. As children, their parents generally supported their grandiose strivings, while serving as models of responsibility, steadfastness, and calm security. For healthy development to occur, the child must also experience some degree of frustration. "Occasional failures are not destructive; on the contrary, they may well turn into the episodes of 'optimal frustration' that stimulate the youngster to stretch his resources to the limit and himself take over some of the functions that had been performed by the self-object" (Wolf, 1982, p. 32).

By contrast, faulty mirroring and/or idealizing can result in various kinds of "injured" selves. In the *understimulated self,* the person loses vitality and feels chronically numb and empty, grasping for "aliveness" in drug or alcohol abuse, sexual adventurism, gambling, and other desperate life-styles. The roots of the understimulated self reside in the actions of self-objects who repeatedly failed to mirror and to provide ideals. Another result of insufficient mirroring and idealizing is the *fragmenting self.* In this case, the person suffers from low self-esteem and feels chronically vulnerable, unbalanced, out of kilter, or lacking in cohesion and harmony.

The *overstimulated self* develops in the child whose self-objects are overly indulgent, excessively and inappropriately responding to the child's mirroring and idealizing needs. As adults, these people are flooded by unrealistic fantasies of greatness that produce tension and anxiety. The fear and anxiety prompt them to shy away from situations in which they might be the center of attention. Finally, people suffering from the *overburdened self* experience the world as a hostile and dangerous place, and they are likely to respond to minor setbacks with fits of rage. They "are deficient in self-soothing capacity, due to early deprivation of opportunities for merger with calming self-objects" (Wolf, 1982, p. 38). In these cases, the childhood failure lies in the idealizing relationship, as parents were deficient in providing models of values and goals to be idealized.

Carl Jung's Analytical Psychology

The last theory we will examine in the psychoanalytic tradition is Carl Jung's **analytical psychology.** Jung developed a highly original theory of personality that departs in significant ways from Freud. Like most of the neo-Freudian approaches we have reviewed thus far, Jung took issue with Freud on the topic of instinctual drives. But whereas the ego psychologists, the object-relations theorists, Horney, Fromm, and Kohut invoked social and cultural explanations for human motivation, Jung moved boldly in the opposite direction, toward even deeper recesses of the human psyche, wherein he discovered a subterranean sanctum of universal strivings projected through the ages in personal dreams and cultural myths. In many ways, Jungian psychology has evolved independently of the theories reviewed above, as a sharp alternative to Freud rather than a revision of psychoanalytic theory. Jung's ideas have proven especially influential in areas where psychology meets theology, mythology and folklore, and the arts. With his affirmation of the spiritual dimensions of human life, Jung offers what many people consider to be a compelling agenda for personality growth and human fulfillment.

Carl Gustav Jung was born in Kesswyl, a town on Lake Constance in the canton of Thurgau, Switzerland, July 26, 1875. He grew up in the Swiss city of Basel. His father, Dr. Paul Jung, was a frustrated pastor in the Swiss Reformed Church, chronically morose and plagued by religious doubts for most of his life. Jung's mother, Emilie, seemed on the surface to be the exact opposite of her husband: a strong-willed, pleasant, and plump housewife. According to Jung's autobiography, however, underneath lurked an "archaic and ruthless" prophetess, an "uncanny witch," a "strange animal" who evoked both terrible awe and fear in her overly sensitive son (Jung, 1961, p. 50). Obsessed with his own mythological dreams and fantasies from a very early age onward, Carl Jung grew up a solitary, introspective, and brilliant boy who was both troubled and fascinated by the secrets of his own soul—the intrapsychic mysteries revealed to him in childhood dreams and reveries about witches, monsters, devils, and gods.

After obtaining a medical degree and collaborating with noted psychiatrist Eugen Bleuler, Jung began a regular correspondence with Sigmund Freud (in 1906), which quickly escalated into an intense friendship. Freud saw Jung as the heir apparent of the psychoanalytic movement, his most promising intellectual "son." By 1913, however, the collaboration had dissolved in classic oedipal fashion, with Jung-the-son rejecting many of Freud-the-father's most cherished views about instincts and human sexuality. While Freud doubtlessly experienced disappointment and anger following the break with his protégé, Jung himself entered a period of profound disillusionment and personal examination, which, according to some scholars, resulted in several brushes with psychosis and even thoughts of suicide (Stern, 1976). Jung emerged from his period of self-scrutiny to create his own school of personality psychology. Until his death in 1961, Jung devoted himself to the study of the intrapsychic mysteries of human personality, fashioning a unique, influential, and controversial approach to the study of the person.

Like Freud's psychoanalysis, Jung's analytical approach seeks to unearth the deeply buried treasures of the unconscious in order to shed light on the mysteries of human behavior and experience. Unlike Freud, however, Jung saw much more in the recesses of the unconscious than merely instincts toward sex and aggression. According to analytical psychology, human beings are motivated by a spectacular pantheon of unconscious forces and factors—internal urges and images about unity, death, androgyny, wisdom, innocence, and yes, sex and aggression—which owe their existence less to the individual's own development and more to the rich heritage of human evolution. Whereas Freud believed that we spend our lives coping with the anxiety that results from incessant intrapsychic conflict, Jung viewed human life as a heroic struggle for psychic completion amidst paradox, mystery, and ambiguity. As Hall and Lindzey (1970) put it, "for Freud, there is only the endless repetition of instinctual themes until death intervenes. For Jung, there is constant and often creative development, the search for wholeness and completion, and the yearning for rebirth" (p. 80).

The Basic Nature of Human Beings

Jung agreed with Freud that human beings are motivated by innate, physiological urges, or instincts. Like Freud, he employed the term "libido" to refer to psychic energy. But whereas Freud's meaning for libido was restricted to the sexual domain, Jung viewed the libido in more general terms, as a creative life force. The libido obeys the **principle of equivalence.** This means that if the libido is dammed up or repressed, an equivalent or substitute expression must take place in consciousness. For example, a young girl who longed to be a ballerina may banish the wish from consciousness in light of her teachers' discouraging words and substitute a striving for popularity among her peers. Her "running" for student council president may symbolize the frustrated desire to move quickly and gracefully across the stage, a desire that she no longer remembers but that remains alive in dreams and unconscious fantasies. Transformations of the libido are guided by the symbolic powers of the human psyche. Human beings are an inherently symbol-making species, according to Jung. Throughout history, humans have transformed libido into the symbolic manifestations of myth, ritual, and magic.

On an individual level, the libido's psychic energy attracts constellations of related and emotionally charged ideas, giving birth to **complexes.** For example, a group of ideas and feelings concerning mother may cluster together in the mind to form a "mother complex." Another group of ideas and feelings about mastery, control, and domination may cluster together to form a "power complex." An individual for whom the mother complex is especially strong may find that much of his or her behavior is guided by concerns about what his or her own mother wants. A strong power complex may push a person to be ruthless and cruel in relationships with others. In general, the psyche (mind) expresses itself through complexes. Complexes may be wholly or partly conscious or they may be entirely submerged in the unconscious.

Jung split the unconscious region of the mind into two domains. He reserved the term **personal unconscious** for the realm containing buried conflicts, issues, and memories from one's own developmental past. The personal unconscious corresponds to Freud's concept of the unconscious. Breaking sharply from Freud and most other theorists in the psychoanalytic tradition, Jung posited a second realm, called the **collective unconscious.** The collective unconscious is a storehouse of archaic remnants from humankind's evolutionary past. It is our inherited racial memory, what all of us know by virtue of our membership in the human race, in the deepest and most inaccessible layer of the psyche. The collective unconscious is what human nature really is, in Jung's view. A result of our evolution as a species, it is the richly textured unconscious that each of us is born with and that each of us takes with us as we move across the human life cycle:

> The archetypal endowment with which each of us is born presupposes the natural life cycle of our species—being mothered, exploring the environment, playing in the peer group, adolescence, being initiated, establishing a place in the social hierarchy, courting, marrying, child-rearing, hunting, gathering, fighting, participating in religious rituals, assuming social responsibilities of advanced maturity, and preparation for death. (Stevens, 1983, p. 40)

The major structural components of the collective unconscious are **archetypes,** universal patterns or predispositions that structure how all humans consciously and unconsciously adapt to their world. As the major components of human nature, archetypes are inherited but somewhat flexible templates for human experience. They are not images or behaviors as such but rather are *predispositions* to develop universal images and to enact universal behavioral sequences (Jung, 1936/1969).

Table 2.3 describes some well-known Jungian archetypes, including the mother, the child, the wise old man, the trickster, and the hero.

Evidence for the existence of each of these, Jung argued, is pervasive in ancient myths, dreams, and universal symbols. For instance, the image of *mother*

 **Table 2.3**

Selected Jungian Archetypes

Archetype	Description	Projected Symbols (Ancient and Modern)
Mother	The embodiment of caregiving and fertility, which may be elicited in response to real mothers, grandmothers, spouses,and other nurturant figures; incorporates positive (warm, supportive) and negative (rejecting, threatening) characteristics.	Earth Mother in ancient mythologies, Virgin Mary, Alma Mater, the Church, fairy godmothers, witches, dragons.
Child-God	The embodiment of both innocence and future experience, representing "futurity" and potential for growth; often has divine or mystical powers.	Christ child, elves, dwarfs, the young Mozart, the child prodigy.
Hero	The protagonist of the classic and universal hero myth: miraculous but humble birth followed by early proof of superhuman power, rapid rise to prominence, triumphant struggle with evil, fallibility to the "sin" or pride, and eventual fall through betrayal or heroic sacrifice.	Christ, Oedipus, King Arthur, Achilles, Abraham Lincoln, Martin Luther King, Jr.
Trickster	An early form of the hero archetype, fond of sly jokes, malicious pranks; possesses magical powers.	Hermes, Biblical demons, Harry Houdini.
Wise Old Man	Embodiment of maturity and wisdom, able to foretell the future.	Oedipus in his later years, Tiresias, certain renditions of God-the-Father, prophets, Mahatma Gandhi.
Anima	The hidden feminine side of man.	Various idealized images of women worshipped by men, such as Cleopatra, Helen of Troy, Virgin Mary, Mona Lisa; woman as temptress, mother, friend, mediator; woman as witch and bitch; cars, ships.

Table 2.3 continued

Table 2.3 *continued*

Archetype	Description	Projected Symbols (Ancient and Modern)
Animus	The hidden masculine side of woman.	Various idealized images of men worshipped by women, such as Odysseus, Don Juan, Christ; man as seducer, hunter, statesman, mentor; man as pirate, rapist, outlaw.
Shadow	The embodiment of unacceptable, animalistic desires and impulses; the "dark half" of personality.	Satan, devils, aliens, enemies, wild beasts, Hitler, Mussolini.
Persona	The socially acceptable mask or front the person presents to the world. The persona is not a true archetypal form residing in the collective unconscious but rather an individual and highly conscious creation. Nonetheless, the individual's persona is built upon unconscious patterns concerning how a good "actor" presents an appropriate mask and plays an appropriate role for the world. The persona generally hides or disguises the true potential of the self.	Actors and actresses.

is a universal thought-form coded in stories, legends, art, ritual, customs, and fantasy around the world. Throughout history, mothers have behaved in certain instinctually bounded ways such that a template or pattern of who mothers are and what they do has come to exist as an archetype in the human collective unconscious. Thus, the human infant has within him or her an unconscious prototype of what mother is—a genetic predisposition to react to her and understand her in certain ways. The infant's perception of mother will, of course, be influenced by real-life experiences with her, but the internal and unconscious mother archetype will set limits on those experiences and help structure how they are understood. The mother archetype may be "released" and expressed in thought and image in response to one's real mother, mother-in-law, grandmother, stepmother, or any other person, place, or thing associated with maternity.

Three particularly prominent archetypes in the collective unconscious are the **anima, animus,** and **shadow.** Within all males exists an unconscious template of femininity, called the anima. Based on men's collective experiences with women throughout time, the anima resides deep within all men as a hidden feminine side of their personalities. Similarly, within all women exists an unconscious masculine aspect, called the animus. The anima and the animus constrain actual interactions between the sexes, each sex apprehending the nature of the other through an unconscious filter. The shadow archetype consists of a variety of unacceptable and socially reprehensible desires and impulses, inherited by virtue of our evolution from lower forms of life. The animalistic shadow is the "dark half" of our personality that most of us would prefer not to recognize. It is expressed in mythology via demons, devils, and evil ones, and it is partially responsible, argued Jung, for the Judeo-Christian belief in original sin.

Personality Types and Personality Development

In Jungian psychology, individual differences among persons are generally conceptualized as personality types. Types are determined by the intersection of **attitudes** and **functions.** Jung distinguished between two major attitudes about or orientations towards the environment: *extraversion* and *introversion* (discussed as central personality traits in Chapter 5). The extraverted attitude orients the person toward the external, objective world; the introverted attitude orients the person toward the internal, subjective world. Both attitudes are present in the personality, but for any given person one of the two is generally dominant and conscious while the other is subordinate and unconscious.

The four fundamental functions are used to understand events in life. Through *thinking,* a person analyzes an event in a rational and intellectual manner. Through *feeling,* a person experiences an event emotionally, through pleasure or pain, anger, fear, sorrow, joy, or love. *Sensing* yields concrete facts about an event, such as what it looks like and how it sounds. *Intuiting* goes beyond the facts, feelings, and ideas to apprehend the hidden or unconscious essence of an event. Usually, for a particular person, one of the four functions is most developed, dominant, and conscious, while one is least developed, subordinate, and most deeply buried in the unconscious. Therefore, the person whose superior function is thinking and whose inferior function is feeling may live a highly rational and dispassionate daily existence when the superior function holds sway. But when thinking gives way to the inferior function at night, he may dream as a "feeler" who apprehends the world primarily through emotion.

Crossing the two attitudes with the four functions yields eight possible personality types. For instance, the extravert–thinking type is the person who is primarily oriented towards the objective, outside world and who tends to understand that world as a thinker. The extravert–thinking type places a conscious premium on logical ideas about the world. His or her preoccupation with the intellect and the objective world may even appear cold and rigid. In contrast, the introvert–intuiting type of person is primarily oriented towards the subjective, internal world and tends to understand that world in terms of intuition. The introvert–intuiting type places a premium on mystical impressions about inner reality. The intuitive introvert may tend to be aloof and unconcerned with people and the outside world. Others may see this type as a peculiar artist, slightly mad genius, or wayward dreamer.

The various attitudes, functions, and archetypes in the personality are organized around the *self.* According to Jung, the self is the midpoint of personality around which all other systems are constellated. The self holds these systems together and provides the person with unity, equilibrium, and stability. The goal of human life is the development of the self, a process that Jung terms **individuation.** Individuation is a dynamic, complex, and lifelong balancing act whereby the person seeks to synthesize the various opposites in personality in order to become whole. Individuation, therefore, involves the full development of all aspects of the personality, both conscious and unconscious, and their ultimate integration within a grand unity. The extravert–feeling type must come to develop the attitude of introversion and the three functions of thinking, sensing, and intuiting. The man must explore and develop the anima; the woman, the animus. All must delve into the mysterious underground of the human psyche to make contact with the shadow, the wise old man, and a host of other lurking spirits.

In sharp contrast to Freud, Jung viewed personality development as a lifelong enterprise. Whereas a person's unique constellation of characteristics is established early in childhood for Freud, Jung saw possibilities for dramatic personality transformation across the human life-span. During childhood, Jung argued, various components of the personality become established as separate entities. Psychic energy is expended on learning how to walk, talk, and other skills necessary for survival. Sexuality is not a prominent theme in the early years but becomes a significant force with the arrival of puberty and adolescence. In young adulthood, the person directs psychic energy toward learning a vocation, getting married, raising children, and becoming integrated into community life. Ideally, the young adult should be energetic, outgoing, and passionate in his or her active engagement of social reality.

Around the age of 40, however, a profound shift may be experienced, as the individual begins to move away from a passionate engagement of the world to an inner and more philosophical exploration of the self. Jung viewed midlife as the most important developmental period in the life-span. Midlife is highlighted by a shift from materialism, sexuality, and propagation to more spiritual and cultural values. In addition, the adult may experience significant shifts in values, ideals, and interpersonal relationships at this time. Religion may become especially salient in the second half of the human life cycle, as the adult strives to find spiritual harmony, balance, and the full expression of the self through individuation.

The warrior archetype.

Jung used the term **transcendent function** to refer to the lifelong motive force behind the individual's desire to come to terms with all aspects of the self and to accept the content of the unconscious as "mine." Individuation, therefore, is the attainment of complete selfhood, the full development of all sides of the self within a unique configuration. The transcendent function is the guiding force in the achievement of this unique and self-defining wholeness.

Much of what may appeal to us in Jung stems from his characterization of human individuation. The development of the self is a romantic odyssey that each of us can and should undertake, a heroic adventure in self-discovery of truly mythic proportions. Like the Greek Odysseus exploring unknown lands, battling ferocious beasts, and communicating daily with the gods, each of us is challenged to do battle with and to explore all that hides and rages in the distant lands within

The mother archetype.

us. In the later years of one's life, individuation brings wholeness and completion. The mature self reconciles all opposites within a psychological circle of unity. The ancient symbol of this unity is the **mandala.** (*Mandala* is a Sanskrit word meaning "circle.") In various mythologies, religious rituals, and in dreams and fantasies, Jung observed an array of mandalalike figures. According to Jung, the mandala is the perfect symbol of the self's unity and integrity achieved through the lifelong adventure of individuation.

Goddesses and Heroes

In recent years, Jungian psychology has enjoyed increasing exposure and popularity among the American public as Jungian analysts and others have written books,

The Goddess Diana: one ancient model of femininity.

delivered lectures, and conducted workshops on the function of myths in human lives. A central message in this work is that personality development and human fulfillment are enhanced through a personal exploration of one's own mythic roots. Buried beneath consciousness or between the lines of our daily lives reside gods and goddesses, heroes and heroines, beauties and beasts with whom we need to become acquainted and through whom we may become better acquainted with our selves.

In *Goddesses in Everywoman,* Jean Bolen (1985) argues that women's lives are guided by powerful inner patterns, which she identifies as archetypes. The archetypes are captured in the goddesses of ancient Greece:

> The Greek goddesses are images of women that have lived in the human imagination for over three thousand years. The goddesses are patterns or representations of what women are like—with more power and diversity of behavior than women have historically been

allowed to exercise. They are beautiful and strong. They are motivated by what matters to them, and—as I maintain in this book—they represent inherent patterns or archetypes that can shape the course of a woman's life. (Bolen, 1985, p. 23)

Bolen identifies seven separate goddesses. Artemis is the goddess of the hunt and the moon who personifies independence and achievement. Athena is goddess of wisdom and craft, and she represents the logical and self-confident woman whose thinking is guided by reason rather than passion. Hestia is goddess of the hearth and home, embodied in the patient and steady woman who finds comfort in domestic rituals and the traditions of religion. Hera is the goddess of marriage, and she stands for the woman who considers the many roles in her life—such as student, professional, mother—secondary to her essential goal of marital happiness. The maternal archetype, Demeter, is also the goddess of grain and fertility. She embodies nurturance and the power of giving and sustaining life. Persephone is her beloved daughter, maiden and queen of the underworld, who personifies a tendency to be compliant, passive, and pleasing to others. Aphrodite is the goddess of love and beauty, sex and sensuality. She is creative and procreative, and she embodies the transformative power of love, in forms both erotic and platonic.

Bolen points out that patriarchal societies do not support all seven goddesses equally. Indeed, the only acceptable roles are often the maiden (Persephone), the wife (Hera), and the mother (Demeter). In some cultures, Aphrodite is condemned to be a whore, "which is a distortion and devaluation of the sensuality and sexuality of this archetype" (p. 28). Some cultures deny the expression of independence, intelligence, or sexuality in women, so that the signs of Artemis, Athena, and Aphrodite must be repressed. Contemporary American society would appear to offer a relative abundance of opportunities for the expression of each of the seven goddesses, but Bolen reminds the reader that negative stereotypes of women still abound and many cultural constraints may still stand in the way of the individuating woman.

Bolen sees myths as "insight tools," that "evoke feeling and imagination and touch on themes that are part of the human collective inheritance" (p. 6). By encouraging women to examine and explore their lives, their work, and their relationships in terms of the mythic patterns she describes, she hopes to "activate" the goddesses in the lives of her readers. In a second book on men's myths, Bolen (1989) aims for the same result, identifying eight male archetypes that guide men's lives: the all-powerful Zeus; emotional Poseidon; Hades, the god of the underworld; Apollo, god of the sun and lawgiver; Hermes, the messenger god; lame-footed Hephaestus; Dionysius, god of wine and ecstasy; and Ares, the god of war and passionate love.

In *The Hero Within,* Carol Pearson (1986) draws upon the writings of the great mythologist, Joseph Campbell (1949), who himself was influenced by Jung. Campbell identified an archetypal myth of *the hero,* appearing in countless tales and stories from a wide range of cultures. The hero myth is a story of separation,

The God Neptune: one ancient model of masculinity.

initiation, and return. Though there are many specific variations, the general form of the hero myth is this: "A hero ventures forth from the world of common day into a region of supernatural wonder: fabulous forces are there encountered and a decisive victory is won: the hero comes back from this mysterious adventure with the power to bestow boons on his fellow man" (Campbell, 1949, p. 30). Pearson draws loosely on the hero myth to identify six stages or incarnations of the hero's journey. The six may be arranged in a kind of developmental sequence.

According to Pearson, the six archetypes of the hero are the innocent, the orphan, the martyr, the wanderer, the warrior, and the magician. Each personifies human traits that are essential for the journey of individuation. The journey "begins with the complete trust of the Innocent, moves on to the longing for safety of the Orphan, the self-sacrifice of the Martyr, the exploring of the Wanderer, the competition and triumph of the Warrior, and then the authenticity and wholeness of the Magician" (p. xxvi). Personality development, in Pearson's view, involves the successive identification with each of the six archetypes over the life-span. Each person moves through the archetypes in his or her own way. Indeed, Pearson observes that men tend to dwell in the warrior stages whereas women are wont to be martyrs. The most advanced archetype for both men and women, though, is the magician. Pearson writes:

> The archetype of the Magician teaches us about creation, about our capacity to bring into being what never was there before, about claiming our role as cocreators of the universe. . . . When we enter the terrain of the Magician in our journey, after we have begun to take responsibility for our own lives and for our impact on the world, we discover that the Magician is not a shaman, witch, or wizard who sings a sacred song or concocts a sacred brew, whereupon a person is healed or killed, the war won or lost. . . . The magician is not other, we discover, but ourselves. At this point, heroes come to believe that the universe is not a static thing. It is in the process of being created all the time. All of us are involved in that creation. . . . (Pearson, 1989, p. 116).

Summary for Chapter 2

1. Freud's psychoanalysis is the prime example of an approach to persons that focuses on intrapsychic mysteries.

2. Three monumental historical phenomena had a major influence on Freud's thinking about the person: Romanticism, the strictures of nineteenth-century science and morality, and World War I.

3. A number of key people in Freud's life had major impacts on the development of his theory: his mother and father, Brucke, Charcot, Breuer, Fliess, Jung, Adler, and Freud's own daughter, Anna.

4. According to Freud's tenet of determinism, all significant behavior and experience are determined by forces over which the person has little control. The most important among these are the erotic and aggressive instincts.

5. According to Freud's tenet of conflict, virtually all human behavior is a product of compromise among conflicting forces. Conflict causes anxiety.

6. According to Freud's tenet of the unconscious, the person is generally not aware of the most important determining factors and conflicts in his or her life. People do not know why they do what they do; they do not know what their behavior means.

7. The development of the sexual instinct begins in infancy with the oral stage. Sucking at the mother's breast is the starting point of sexual development. The second stage of psychosexual development is the anal stage.

8. In the phallic stage of development, little boys and girls experience the unconscious Oedipus complex, the resolution of which establishes the superego.

9. The mind may be viewed as composed of three interrelated structures: the id, which obeys the pleasure principle; the ego, which obeys the reality principle; and the superego, which is a primitive moral agent representing the parents' dictates about good and bad behavior.

10. The ego aims to resolve conflict and reduce anxiety. To accomplish these ends, it frequently employs unconscious defense mechanisms, such as projection and reaction formation.

11. Since Freud's death, psychoanalytic theorizing has emphasized the adaptive and integrative capacities of the ego, as seen in the work of Anna Freud, Heinz Hartmann, and Robert White.

12. A second trend in psychoanalysis since the time of Freud is an increasing emphasis on social, cultural, and historical determinants of personality, as evidenced in the influential personality theories offered by Karen Horney and Erich Fromm.

13. A third trend is the emergence of object-relations theories, such as Margaret Mahler's model of separation/individuation.

14. A fourth trend is the focus on the self, as developed in the work of Heinz Kohut.

15. Carl Jung's analytical psychology represents a provocative alternative to Freudian and neo-Freudian theories, as it highlights the spiritual dimensions of personality and the salience of myth and symbol.

16. The main structures of the collective unconscious, Jungian archetypes are universal patterns or predispositions that structure how all humans adapt to the world. Important archetypes include the mother, the child, the hero, the trickster, the wise old man, the anima, the animus, the persona, and the shadow.

17. Individual differences among persons are understood by Jungians in terms of the intersection of two basic life attitudes (extraversion and introversion) and four functions (sensing, feeling, thinking, and intuiting).

18. Personality development, from Jung's point of view, involves lifelong individuation, as the person strives for wholeness and the full expression of all the contrasting aspects of the self.

Chapter 3

Discovery and Proof in Psychoanalysis

Introduction

The Context of Discovery: Psychoanalytic Interpretation
The Case of Dora
Two Traumatic Events
The Dream of the Jewel-Case
Dora Revisited
Feature 3.A: Understanding Transference
Methods of Interpretation
Text and Treaty
Manifest and Latent
Symptoms and Everyday Life
Myth and Symbol: Jungian Meanings

The Context of Justification: Testing Hypotheses
The Unconscious
Unconscious Information Processing
Studies in Repression
The Activation of the Unconscious
Mechanisms of Defense
Developmental Stages
Feature 3.B: The Authoritarian Personality
Internalized Objects
Feature 3.C: Falling in Love With the Self: The Problem of Narcissism
Jung's Types

Summary

From Freud and Jung to Kohut and the object-relations theorists, the psychoanalytic tradition has offered a rich assortment of personality theories and conceptions that have profoundly influenced the way in which we think about the person. Psychoanalytic ideas have spread to all corners of Western culture, permeating art and literature, mythology and anthropology, clinical practice and everyday speech. Among psychologists, the psychoanalytic tradition is most clearly manifest in clinical practice, as many therapists and counselors have incorporated theories and techniques originating in the early formulations from Freud's time or in later neoanalytic conceptions offered by Horney, Fromm, the ego psychologists, the object-relations theorists, and so on.

Outside the realm of psychotherapy, psychoanalysis has also had a strong impact on scientific research in personality. It is true that some critics have expressed deep skepticism about the scientific credibility of many psychoanalytic concepts (Grunbaum, 1984; Holt, 1985), and others have lamented the inability to test rigorously certain vague and ambiguous psychoanalytic propositions (Fisher & Greenberg, 1977; Kline, 1972). Nevertheless, the psychoanalytic tradition would appear to have generated very significant scientific work in personality psychology. In a recent comprehensive review, one scholar concludes that "when one considers not only research generated by psychoanalytic researchers but also the experimental evidence in other research traditions that corroborates, dovetails with, or refines basic psychoanalytic hypotheses, one finds that the empirical basis of psychoanalytic concepts is far better documented, and that psychoanalytic thinking is far more widely applicable, than is typically assumed" (Westen, 1990, p. 39). This chapter adopts just such a positive perspective in describing some of the best and brightest contributions to personality research that derive from the psychoanalytic tradition.

Scientific research always involves a complex interplay between theoretical ideas (the abstract) and particular data (the concrete). As we saw in Chapter 1, the relationship between theory and data in the scientific enterprise may be understood in at least two very different ways. In the *context of discovery,* the scientist builds theories inductively by moving from the concrete to the general. In other words, the scientist may derive, formulate, or construct a theory based on observations of particular events. This kind of observation may be rather unsystematic and exploratory in that the scientist is not especially sure as to what she or he will find at the outset of the inquiry. The purpose is to discover patterns in the data that will lead to the formulation of theory. By contrast, in the *context of justification,* the scientist evaluates particular aspects of existing theories by systematically observing events under either experimental or natural conditions. The purpose here is to test hypotheses. Such an hypothesis-testing strategy may ultimately lead to new discoveries, but it is not explicitly set up to do so, for the primary concern in the context of justification is to assess the viability or truth value of a clearly stated prior hypothesis.

In this chapter, we will examine selected topics that derive from the psychoanalytic tradition from the standpoint of both the context of discovery and the context of justification. With respect to the first, we will consider how psychoanalysts have traditionally *interpreted* various kinds of phenomena—such as dreams and symptoms—in order to generate ideas, derive hypotheses, and build theories. This interpretive activity is highly subjective and complex, and it is not usually understood as part of "science" per se. But such a narrow reading assumes that science is limited to the context of justification, and nothing else. It overlooks the fascinating (and admittedly subjective) enterprise of creating theory, of discovery. Scientific theories are human creations, formulated subjectively. Within the context of discovery, psychoanalytic interpretation is a valuable general tool for gaining insights. After examining psychoanalytic approaches to interpretation, we will then consider the second context for scientific inquiry. In the second half of the chapter, therefore, we will survey contemporary research testing psychoanalytic hypotheses as they apply to unconscious processes, defense mechanisms, developmental stages, object relations, and Jungian types.

The Context of Discovery: Psychoanalytic Interpretation

On October 14, 1900, Freud announced to his good friend, Wilhelm Fliess, that he was working on a case worth recording for history. "It has been a lively time," he wrote, "and I have a new patient, a girl of eighteen: the case has opened smoothly to my collection of picklocks" (Freud, 1954, p. 325). Three months later, the case was over. The "girl of eighteen" broke off therapy, putting an abrupt end to Freud's attempt to unlock the coffered treasures of her mind. Before the vaults were shut, however, Freud managed to escape with a few precious jewels. In January of the following year, Freud wrote the account of his short but exhilarating expedition: "Fragment of an Analysis of a Case of Hysteria" (1905/1963). He gave to the girl of 18 the name *Dora*.

The Case of Dora

Attractive, intelligent, articulate, and economically well-off, Dora was rarely happy with her life. She suffered from a number of symptoms that, Freud believed, were manifestations of the psychological disturbance termed *hysteria.* These included periodic difficulties in breathing, recurrent headaches, fainting spells, and violent attacks of nervous coughing often accompanied by a loss of voice. Though these symptoms took a physical form, they did not appear to have a physical cause. In addition, Dora was frequently depressed and irritable, argued incessantly with both her mother and her father, and had, on one recent occasion, hinted at suicide, leaving a note that said she could no longer endure life. Alarmed by her deteriorating condition, Dora's father insisted that she see his friend, Dr. Sigmund Freud, for therapy. Dora had seen many doctors during her troubled adolescent years, and she was very skeptical about Freud's ability to help her. During her regular visits with Freud over the next three months of therapy, Dora repeatedly disputed his interpretations and recommendations. At times the willful patient and her equally stubborn analyst seemed to spar like gladiators in a deadly game. When Freud felt he was on the brink of understanding more clearly the source of her problems, Dora suddenly quit therapy and deprived him of the interpretive victory he sought. Freud was shocked and hurt: "Her breaking off unexpectedly, just when my hopes of a successful termination of the treatment were at their highest, and her thus bringing those hopes to nothing—this was an unmistakable act of vengeance on her part" (p. 131).

Dora had good reason to take vengeance on the older generation, of which Freud was certainly a part. She had unwittingly become entangled in a web of deceit and infidelity that involved her father, mother, and a married couple who were their contemporaries—Herr and Frau K. Dora's father was a wealthy industrialist who had carried on a sexual affair with Frau K for many years. There is good reason to believe that Herr K knew of the affair and considered his friend's daughter—the teenaged Dora—to be a fair exchange for his wife, tacitly "handed over" to him as compensation for his tolerating the relationship between his wife and Dora's father. Herr K was extremely friendly to Dora, sending her frequent gifts and taking long walks with her. While Frau K nursed Dora's father back to health during his many illnesses, Dora worked as a babysitter for the K children and became a very good friend of her father's lover, discussing with Frau K a number of intimate topics, including sexuality. Unhappy in her marriage and repeatedly frustrated with her daughter, Dora's mother, on the other hand, spent most of her day cleaning house. All four adults attempted to conceal from Dora the truth about their tangled and pathetic lives. Dora, however, was well aware of the affair between her father and Frau K and suspected that her father, whom she claimed to love dearly, condoned Herr K's romantic interest in her. She may also have suspected that part of her father's reason for insisting on therapy was the hope that Freud would be able to convince Dora that no illicit affair was taking place. When he realized that Freud was more concerned about discerning the truth than lying to Dora, Dora's father lost interest in the therapy and apparently did not protest when his daughter terminated her sessions with Freud at the end of the year.

Two Traumatic Events   In her discussions with Freud, Dora revealed two incidents from her past in which Herr K had made sexual advances. Two years before, as they walked back to a vacation house from a visit to an Alpine lake, Herr K had proposed his love to Dora and, doubtlessly, intimated that the 16-year-old girl make love to him. Dora responded by slapping his face. Frightened and insulted, she told her mother of Herr K's proposition; her mother told her father; her father confronted Herr K about the report; and Herr K denied that any such event ever transpired and added that Dora was obsessed with sexual matters anyway—his wife had told him this—and doubtlessly fantasized the whole incident. Her father took Herr K's word over his daughter's. Two years before the incident, when Dora was 14, Herr K had suddenly embraced and kissed her at his place of business. Experiencing a "violent feeling of disgust" (p. 43), Dora broke loose from Herr K and ran into the street. Though neither of them ever mentioned this first incident (until Dora reported it to Freud in therapy), Dora continued to be friendly to Herr K afterward, meeting him for regular walks, accepting his gifts, and babysitting for the children. It was not until the scene at the lake, two years later, that she began to express extreme dislike for Herr K.

Freud saw these two incidents as the traumatic kernels around which Dora formed her hysterical symptoms. Freud believed that all neurotic symptoms have meaning. In content and form, *neurotic symptoms are symbolic manifestations of unconscious fears, desires, conflicts, and mysteries.* Trying to connect Dora's symptoms to the two incidents with Herr K, Freud asked Dora to engage in **free association** in response to her memories of the events. A standard procedure in psychoanalysis, free association involves the patient's letting his or her mind wander in response to a stimulus and reporting all thoughts (associations) aloud to the therapist as they occur. Freud believed that unconscious currents rise to the surface in free association and that the perceptive therapist can interpret the associations in order to make psychological sense of the case.

Based on Dora's associations to the two traumatic incidents, Freud arrived at a tentative and partial explanation for some of her symptoms, especially her troublesome bouts of coughing. Herr K was a handsome man towards whom the young Dora had obviously been attracted. Freud reasoned that the disgust Dora felt in response to Herr K's first kiss disguised her sexual interest. Her disgust took the place of excitement by the neurotic process of *reversal of affect*—a pleasurable emotion that is in some sense threatening (sexual excitement) is replaced by an unpleasurable one that is less threatening (disgust). In addition, Freud believed, disgust is a common, though neurotic, "means of affective expression in the sphere of sexual life" (p. 47), especially on the part of women in response to the male sexual organ because it supposedly serves as a reminder of urination (and, relatedly, defecation). Furthermore, *displacement* of sensation transferred the positive sensation of sexual arousal from the lower region of the body (Dora's genitals) to the upper region (her thorax and mouth). Since the incident, Dora had occasionally been troubled by a sensory hallucination in which she could feel the pressure of Herr K's embrace on the *upper* part of her body. Freud speculated that when Herr K embraced her on that first fateful day, he was highly sexually aroused and that Dora felt in the *lower* part of her body, through the layers of clothing they both wore, the pressure of his erect penis:

> In accordance with certain rules of symptom-formation which I
> have come to know, and at the same time taking into account cer-
> tain other of the patient's peculiarities, which were otherwise
> inexplicable—such as her unwillingness to walk past any man
> whom she saw engaged in eager or affectionate conversation with

a lady,—I have formed in my own mind the following reconstruction of the scene. I believe that during the man's passionate embrace she felt not merely his kiss upon her lips but also the pressure of his erect member against her body. The perception was revolting to her; it was dismissed from memory, repressed, and replaced by the innocent sensation of pressure upon her thorax, which in turn derived an excessive intensity from its repressed source. Once more, therefore, we find a displacement from the lower part of the body to the upper. On the other hand, the obsession which she exhibited in her behaviour was formed as though it were derived from the undistorted recollection of the scene. She did not like walking past any man who she thought was in a state of sexual excitement, because she wanted to avoid seeing for a second time the somatic sign which accompanies it. (pp. 45–46)

As we learned in Chapter 2, Freud believed that the mouth was the first erogenous zone. For the infant, the libido is centered in the oral zone, and sucking at the mother's breast is therefore the "starting point of the whole of sexual life, the unmatched prototype of every later sexual satisfaction," to which fantasy recurs in times of need (Freud, 1916/1961, p. 341). For Dora, the mouth retained an extraordinary sensual significance as she grew older. Compared to most other people, Freud argued, Dora had probably experienced excessive oral stimulation in childhood. She had been a thumbsucker for many years, continuing to derive sensual pleasure from sucking as she developed through her early and middle child years. A key childhood memory for Dora involved her sitting contentedly on the floor, sucking her thumb as she tugged at her brother's ear. Overlying this oral sensitivity was Dora's unconscious and highly charged personal symbolism for sucking. Again based on Dora's associations, Freud speculated that she unconsciously fantasized sexual relations between her father and Frau K in oral terms. Indeed, Dora consciously believed that her father was frequently impotent, and that he therefore often obtained sexual satisfaction and experienced orgasm with Frau K through oral stimulation. (She had read about such sexual practices while babysitting for the K children.) Dora's sexual fantasy about her father and Frau K, combined with other images and experiences centered on orality, produced an oral symptom of hysteria: her persistent cough. A short time after Dora "tacitly accepted" Freud's interpretation (p. 65), the cough disappeared.

The Dream of the Jewel-Case   During the course of therapy, Dora reported to Freud that she had again had a dream that she had dreamed in exactly the same way on a number of prior occasions. As one "royal road to the unconscious," a recurrent nighttime dream was a particularly rich piece of psychological data, in Freud's view, so he devoted a good deal of time and energy to interpreting it. Here is the dream as related by Dora:

A house was on fire. My father was standing beside my bed and woke me up. I dressed myself quickly. Mother wanted to stop and save her jewel-case; but father said: "I refuse to let myself and my

two children be burnt for the sake of your jewel-case." We hurried downstairs, and as soon as I was outside I woke up. (p. 81)

Dora reported that she had first had this dream two years ago, on the three
successive nights at the lake immediately following Herr K's proposition. Now it
had come back, in the wake of her recollection of the same incident. What was the
meaning of the dream? To find out, Freud asked Dora to associate freely to each
part of the dream, letting her mind wander in response to each element and symbol and reporting aloud the stream of thought and affect as it spontaneously
flowed. Freud tied the rich web of her dream associations together with the facts
and conjectures of the case, attempting to make sense of both the dream and
Dora's symptoms as alternative expressions of the same unconscious dynamics
(See Figure 3.1).

Dora's first association is to a recent argument between her father and
mother. For some reason that she does not understand, the dream reminds her of

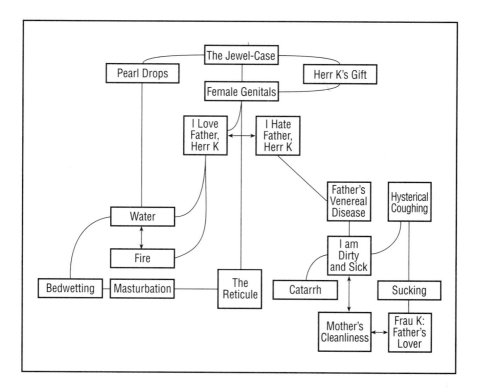

Figure 3.1

Some Associations From Dora's Dream of the Jewel-Case. The many connections
between and among these dream images, behavioral symptoms, and other
elements in the Dora case are explained in the text and in Freud (1905/1963).
Lines between boxes show associations; arrows show oppositions.

a parental dispute about locking her brother's bedroom door. Recently, Dora's mother wanted to lock the door at night, but her father objected, claiming that "something might happen in the night so that it might be necessary to leave the room" (p. 82). Something like a *fire*, Freud conjectures, and Dora agrees. Dora then remembers that, two years ago at the lake, her father had worried about a fire. The family and the K's were staying during this time at a small wooden house that her father feared might easily burn down. This was precisely the time that the dream first occurred and, of course, the time of Herr K's proposition. The fire in the dream is a natural outgrowth of these events.

Dora remembers that she returned from a walk with Herr K to the wooden house at noon and decided to take a nap on a sofa in one of the bedrooms. Shortly after lying down, she awoke, startled, to see Herr K standing beside her (as her father had awakened her and stood at the foot of her bed in the dream). She protested sharply, but Herr K responded that he was "not going to be prevented from coming into his own bedroom when he wanted" (p. 84). Determined to stay clear of Herr K for the rest of their time on the lake, Dora secured a key for the bedroom, but Herr K subsequently stole the key! After that, she always *dressed quickly* in the bedroom, as she did in the dream, in fear that Herr K would break in on her at any time. On one level, then, the dream brings to resolution Dora's problem with Herr K. In the dream, her father *saved* her from the fire by whisking her through the unlocked door of her bedroom so that she could escape. In so doing, her father symbolically saved her from the "fiery" sexual advances of Herr K.

The significance of sexuality in the dream is best seen, argues Freud, in the image of the *jewel-case*. Dora's associations to this particular element in the dream bring to mind an argument between her father and mother about jewelry. Mother had wanted pearl *drop* earrings, but father insisted instead on buying her a bracelet. Dora is also reminded that Herr K had once bought her a jewel-case— one of his many gifts to her. Freud points out that the word "jewel-case" (*Schmuckkästchen* in German) is a common slang word for a virgin girl's *genitals*. Dora quickly retorts, "I knew you would say that" (p. 87), a response that Freud remarks is "a very common way of putting aside a piece of knowledge that emerges from the repressed" (p. 87).

The dream concerns Herr K's attempt to make Dora's jewel-case his own— that is, to have sexual intercourse with her—and Dora's contradictory wishes (1) to escape his attempt and (2) to give in and thereby offer her jewel-case—her virginity, her genitals, her love—to him as a "gift." While her father functioned as a savior in the dream, he also represented, argues Freud, the object of Dora's own romantic/sexual longings, in accord with a young woman's Oedipus complex as described in Chapter 2. The image of her father in the dream represents, argues Freud, both her father and Herr K—both of whom Dora loves, fears, and occasionally resents. The image of her mother represents both her mother and Frau K—both of whom she also resents and yet wishes, on some level, to be. Though her mother spurned her father's gifts, Dora would be happy to accept the bracelet from her father (symbolically accepting her father's love) and would be happy to return the favor with the gift of her jewel-case to him. *All of this is deeply unconscious.* On a conscious level, however, Dora knows that her mother offers her father no sexual satisfaction; similarly, Frau K offers none to her husband. Unconsciously, Dora believes that she would prove a better wife to either of these men.

At this point in the interpretation, Dora's dream appears to be a cleverly disguised rendition of the standard Oedipus complex in young women. It is complicated somewhat by actual events in her life involving Herr K, making two older men, rather than just one, the objects of her unconscious sexual longing. Things become much more complicated, however, with Freud's further interpretations of the dream, revealing a number of highly peculiar meanings that link the dream content to Dora's neurotic symptomatology. Dora's associations to *fire* run in the opposite direction to *water,* hinted at in her mother's pearl *drops.* Freud reminds Dora of an old folk belief that children who play with matches (fire) tend to wet their beds (water). (Dora claims she is not familiar with the belief.) The father's fear that "something might happen in the night so that it might be necessary to leave the room" (in Dora's first association to the dream) may suggest both fire and bedwetting. Dora reports that both her brother and she had problems with bedwetting well into childhood. In her case, the problem was most serious when she was age 7 and 8, so serious that her parents brought in a doctor. As in the dream, her father may have occasionally woken her up in the middle of the night to take her to the toilet, so that she would not wet her bed. The problem of bedwetting subsided shortly before Dora developed her first neurotic symptom: periodic difficulties in breathing, described as "nervous asthma" (p. 90).

Bedwetting is an important association in the dream because of Freud's belief that bedwetting is intimately associated with *masturbation.*[1] Freud is never able to extract a conscious confession of childhood masturbation from Dora, although he believes that he has incontrovertible unconscious evidence one day in therapy when, after discussing at length the topic of masturbation in their previous session, Dora shows up wearing at her waist a small *reticule* (a small, purselike bag) that "she kept playing with," "opening it, putting a finger into it, shutting it again, and so on" (p. 94). This innocent behavior, argues Freud, in fact symbolizes masturbation, the reticule serving as a substitute for the female genitals.

Based on these circumstances, Freud surmises that Dora masturbated frequently as a child of age 7 and 8; that she was, at the same time, an inveterate bedwetter; and that she experienced a great deal of guilt about both behaviors. Dora came to see both of them as *dirty* actions associated with sexuality. Indeed, all sexuality acquired a dirty connotation after Dora learned, at an early age, that her father had contracted a *venereal disease* by leading a sexually loose life before

---

[1]Modern medical science has documented no link between childhood masturbation and enuresis. In 1901, however, many members of the medical establishment still held to the notion that masturbation was at the root of a number of personal illnesses and problems. Freud appears to have adhered to this view (Sulloway, 1979) and apparently believed that chronic bedwetting problems extending well into the elementary-school years were often by-products of excessive masturbation in children.

his marriage. In Dora's mind, Freud conjectures, her mother's obsession with *cleanliness* is a reaction to being dirtied by her husband's venereal disease. Freud is surprised that Dora is consciously aware of her father's disease, though Freud himself and many other people apparently were also aware of it. Dora's associations lead Freud to the conclusion that she blames her father for her illnesses in that, she believes, he has passed on his venereal disease to her. She unconsciously believes, asserts Freud, that she has a sexually transmitted disease simply by being born of a father afflicted with one. There was no medical evidence for Dora's hypothesis, Freud points out, but Dora nonetheless believes the connection to be true and cites as evidence her recurrent *catarrh*—an infectious secretion, manifested in periodic vaginal discharges, about which Dora felt great shame and disgust. On an unconscious level, the catarrh is one of Dora's psychological "proofs" that her many problems in life are her father's fault. Not only had he "handed her over" to Herr K, but he had also given her a dirty disease. The disease is a sexual disease. All sexual phenomena are dirty and bring about feelings of disgust, in Dora's private system of meaning. This is why, in part, Dora felt disgust, not sexual excitement, when Herr K kissed her in his office when she was 14 years old.

Many of Dora's symptoms affirm her unconscious convictions that (1) she is her father's daughter, (2) she, like him, is sick and dirty, and (3) this is because of sex. Though she is still drawn to sexuality and wishes unconsciously to consummate her love for her father and Herr K in typical oedipal fashion, venereal disease becomes her unconscious symbolic embodiment of sexual relations, and her neurotic symptoms all take on a sexual meaning. We have already seen how, for Freud, the cough symbolized oral sexuality and Dora's incestuous wishes concerning her father. Her difficulties in breathing, according to Freud, also express a sexual dynamic. Dora's father suffered from periodic shortness of breath, and doctors warned him that he should not exert himself too much. Thus, Dora's analogous symptom is another way of proving that she is her father's daughter and that her problems are due to his transgressions, not hers. Further, Freud submits that the difficulties in breathing may have stemmed from Dora's having heard, as a child of perhaps 7 or 8, her parents' heavy breathing while engaged in sexual intercourse. Her first asthmatic attacks occurred during a trip with her father to the mountains. Subsequently, Dora experienced difficulties in breathing when her father left home on trips. Thus, according to Freud, Dora was able to identify with her lost lover—her father—by acting in a way reminiscent of him. The dynamics behind her sympathetic imitation of her father's illnesses were, of course, completely unconscious.

Dora Revisited   Dora returned to Freud's office 15 months after terminating treatment to tell him that she had confronted Frau K and her father about their affair and Herr K about his inappropriate conduct. This brief interaction did not result in any further therapy, though Dora appeared to suffer still from hysterical symptoms. A year later she married and sometime afterwards bore her only child—a son. In an odd turn of events, Dora—whose real name turns out to have been Ida—visited another psychoanalyst—Dr. Felix Deutsch—in 1922 for treatment of an hysterical symptom, announcing that she indeed was the famous patient of Freud's Dora case. According to Deutsch (1957), Dora never recovered from her neurosis. Her cough and asthma still plagued her 20 years after her last meeting with Freud. As an adult, she repeatedly accused others—her husband, her son, her few acquaintances—of persecuting and betraying her. In Deutsch's view, her husband was "slighted and tortured by her almost paranoid behavior" (p. 57). Indeed, one of Deutsch's acquaintances claimed that Dora was "one of the most repulsive hysterics" he had ever met. From what we can tell, Dora lived an extremely unhappy life, and she managed to make those around her almost equally unhappy (Deutsch, 1957; Rogow, 1978). She died of colon cancer in New York City in 1945, at the age of 63.

Even in 1901, Freud realized that his case of Dora was both a great success and a great failure. From the standpoint of psychotherapy, Freud was unable to effect a satisfactory solution or cure for Dora's deeply ingrained neurotic symptoms. This failure was due in part to Dora's resistance to Freud's interpretations. Just when Freud felt he was gaining insights into the nature of her neurosis, Dora broke off the therapy relationship. Furthermore, Freud admitted that certain key realizations about Dora came to him too late in the course of her therapy. For example, Freud seems to have underestimated the problems of **transference** and **countertransference** in the case (Muslin & Gill, 1978). Belatedly, Freud came to see that Dora was unconsciously transferring dynamics from her interactions with Herr K and her father onto the therapeutic relationship, unconsciously relating to Freud as father/lover/enemy. Moreover, Freud may have been unwittingly doing something very similar—countertransferring some of his own unconscious feelings about young neurotic women onto Dora.

Consistent with the patriarchal sex roles of his time, Freud seems to have behaved toward Dora in a very domineering manner (Kahane, 1985; Moi, 1981). He was perhaps too quick to dismiss her protestations of innocence and betrayal, and he showed too little sympathy for Dora's plight as a young girl trapped in an intrigue that she did little to bring about (Blos, 1972; Rieff, 1959). Too young to be jaded and worn like her pathetic parents and the K's, Dora could not blithely accept their betrayal of her and of each other. More than for childish revenge, more than even for love and acceptance, Dora may have been searching for *fidelity* (Erikson, 1964), for honesty and truth in relationships, for sincere commitment to others as a way of defining the self.

While the Dora case, therefore, may reveal certain shortcomings in therapeutic technique and significant gender biases ingrained in Victorian society, Freud's analysis may also be considered a significant "success" with respect to its ability to illustrate psychoanalytic interpretation. Marcus (1977) marvels at the "over one hundred pages of dazzling originality, of creative genius performing with a compactness, complexity, daring, and splendor that seem close to incomparable in their order" (p. 407). In the scientific context of discovery, Dora's case generates a number of intriguing hypotheses about Dora herself and about neurosis and human personality more generally. From the standpoint of literature, the case has even been hailed as a harbinger of a new genre in modern writing (Marcus, 1977; Rieff, 1959; Steele, 1982). Organized along multiple analytic

Continued on p. 128

Feature 3.A

Understanding Transference

From the beginning of her association with Freud, Dora responded to her therapist in ways that recalled her relationships with her father and Herr K. By acting out in her meetings with Freud some of the dynamics in her conflicted relationships with other older men in her life, Dora exhibited classic features of what Freud called "transference." While Freud was aware early on that Dora was treating him as if he were her father/lover/enemy, he seemed to lose sight of the transference as the therapy progressed. By the time he put the possibility of transference back into the center of his thinking about the case, it was too late. Dora had taken her revenge on him (and older men in general) by breaking off the treatment meetings. In the last few pages of the case, Freud wrote:

> At the beginning it was clear that I was replacing her father in her imagination, which was not unlikely, in view of the difference between our ages. She was even constantly comparing me with him consciously, and kept anxiously trying to make sure whether I was being quite straightforward with her, for her father "always preferred secrecy and roundabout ways." But when the first dream came, in which she gave herself the warning that she had better leave my treatment just as she had formerly left Herr K's house, I ought to have listened to the warning myself. "Now," I ought to have said to her, "it is from Herr K that you have made a transference on to me. Have you noticed anything that leads you to suspect me of evil intentions similar (whether openly or in some sublimated form) to Herr K's? Or have you been struck by anything about me or got to know anything about me which has caught your fancy, as happened previously with Herr K?" Her attention would have been turned to some detail in our relations, or in my person or circumstances, behind which there lay concealed something analogous but immeasurably more important concerning Herr K. And when this transference had been cleared up, the analysis would have obtained access to new memories, dealing, probably, with actual events. (pp. 140–141)

In transference, patients "replace some earlier person by the person of the physician" [therapist], so that "a whole series of psychological experiences are revived, not as belonging to the past, but as applying to the person of the physician at the present moment" (Freud, 1905/1963, p. 138). Therefore, transference "refers to the patient's expression of attitudes and behavior derived from early conflictual relationships with significant parental figures in the current relationship with the therapist" (Luborsky, Crits-Christoph, & Mellon, 1986, p. 39). In Freud's view, transference is a powerful ally for the insightful therapist who can take advantage of the transference dynamics to make manifest psychologically significant memories and feelings that are associated with conflicted relationships from the past.

In an attempt to subject the concept of transference to empirical scrutiny, Lester Luborsky and his colleagues (Luborsky & Crits-Christoph, 1991; Luborsky et al., 1986) have developed a method of analyzing transcripts from psychotherapy sessions in terms of **core conflictual relationship themes** (CCRT). In the CCRT method, the researcher first identifies particular episodes in the transcripts of therapy accounts wherein the patient explicitly narrates experiences in relationships. Once identified, each episode is analyzed in terms of (1) the patient's main wishes, needs, or intentions toward the other person in the narrative; (2) the responses of the other person; and (3) the responses of

the self. Luborsky provides an example of one particular episode described by a male patient in psychotherapy:

> [A guy] came over to drink beer, and to have this conversation which was a little difficult. I pretended to be enjoying it, enjoying him, you know, in the spirit of good fellowship and shit and stuff, but I really wanted to be—well, I didn't want to be reading, but you know, I felt that this was the thing that was keeping me from reading and that hassled me. I really fucking resented it a lot. You know among my friends, they're respecting and always have really respected my wanting to do my own thing . . . But you know, with a guy like this (clears throat), he's just in another world totally from that. And, you know, he wouldn't understand if I said that, you know, he would be insulted and that kind of shit. You know it was kind of a hassle. (Luborsky et al., 1986, p. 41)

This verbatim account may be coded in the following way: (1) The subject's wish is "to be free of the unwanted visitor"; (2) the response from the other is "he wouldn't understand; he would be insulted"; and (3) the response from the self is "I feel hassled, resentful, compelled to suffer his presence" (Luborsky et al., 1986, p. 42). Luborsky goes on to code other episodes from this young man's therapy transcript, noting similarities and differences among the episodes with respect to wish, response from other, and response from self.

Collating CCRT results from eight different psychotherapy patients, Luborsky provides initial empirical support for a number of hypotheses about transference first articulated by Freud. For example, he finds that each patient tends to display one dominant and uniquely characteristic transference theme across the many different episodes in a therapy session; that patients tend to be highly consistent in patterns of transference over time, repeating the same kinds of core conflictual themes again and again; and that patients tend to reveal the same kinds of transference patterns both inside and outside of psychoanalysis.

The latter finding suggests that transference has implications that are broader than clinical treatment. Indeed, Singer and Singer (1990) suggest that the concept of transference may be one of Freud's greatest discoveries not just because of its importance in therapy but as "an intrinsic feature of human interaction." According to Singer and Singer, transferences are most broadly "the hidden agendas, based on childhood experience, which we all bring to each new social encounter" (p. 2). According to Thorne (1989), it is through such conditional and highly contextualized patterns of relating to important people in our lives that we reveal a core consistency and coherence in our personalities. As Dora related to Freud in ways reminiscent of her conflicted feelings for her father and Herr K, so does each of us relate to others in ways that are unconsciously shaped by the dynamics of our earliest and most salient interpersonal encounters.

Continued from p. 125

perspectives rather than in chronological sequence and employing a number of modernist literary devices, the Dora case has been compared to the twentieth-century novels of Marcel Proust, Henry James, and James Joyce, and to the plays of Henrik Ibsen. In his account of Dora, Freud moves effortlessly back and forth among a number of different kinds of writing—chronological reports, theoretical asides, dramatic flashbacks, warnings to the reader—as the narrative spontaneously follows an inner logic, often looping back around itself to convey multiple meanings at multiple levels.

For our purposes in this chapter, then, the case of Dora provides a vivid account of how Freud attempted to make psychological sense of one patient's troubled life. Although psychoanalysts vary widely in their characteristic methods of interpretation, certain basic principles and dominant emphases of psychoanalytic interpretation in general are still well exemplified in this particular case.

Table 3.1

Four Famous Case Studies in the History of Psychoanalysis

1. Anna O.	From 1880 to 1882, Josef Breuer treated this young hysteric, whose symptoms included paralysis of limbs, disturbed vision, and dual personality. The symptoms worsened with the death of her father in 1881. Breuer and Anna O. discovered the "talking cure," through which Anna O. experienced relief from the symptoms by talking about her daytime hallucinations and fantasies associated with the symptoms. The talking "unstrangled" the emotions that were producing neurotic symptoms. The therapy ended badly, however, after Anna O. experienced "phantom pregnancy" and "hysterical childbirth," unconsciously believing that Breuer had fathered a child within her.
2. Frau Emmy von N.	In 1889, Freud began treating Frau Emmy von N., employing the cathartic "talking cure" pioneered by Breuer. The patient suffered from facial ticks and speech disturbances. Freud attempted to trace each of her symptoms to its root by asking her under hypnosis to explain its meaning. Though the method met with some success early on, the patient's problems eventually escalated to include the refusal to eat. Freud came to realize that each of her symptoms was highly overdetermined: each overt symptom represented many emotional threads woven into a single pattern. For example, refusing to eat was the manifest culmination of many latent associations centered on the arousal of disgust for the act of eating, disgust over cold meat and fat, fear of contracting a disease by eating with shared implements, and revulsion at the act of spitting into a spittoon at dinner.
3. Little Hans	Little Hans was a 5-year-old boy who suffered from an intense fear of horses. Though Freud only saw the boy once, he was able to offer a psychoanalytic interpretation of his symptoms based largely on letters written to him by the father of Little Hans. Freud suggested that Little Hans was experiencing an especially severe Oedipus complex. Little Hans was fascinated with his own penis, calling it his "widdler." He liked to touch his penis and desired that his mother touch it, too. She warned him not to do this and even threatened to have it cut off. Little Hans' fear of horses was a manifestation of castration anxiety. Horses, with their large "widdlers," represented his father, whom Little Hans both loved and feared as the source of castration.

Table 3.1 continued

Table 3.1 continued

4. The Rat Man	This 29-year-old man suffered from severe obsession neurosis. He was tormented in his mind by a fantasy of rats nibbling at the backside of his girlfriend. He also had similar thoughts of rats feeding on his father's anus. Early childhood experiences relating to toilet training and erotic feelings were partial sources of the rat image. As a child, the patient had seen a rat near his father's grave and fantasized that it had been nibbling at the corpse. The neurosis was precipitated shortly after the man's army captain told him about an Asiatic punishment involving live burial of a prisoner who was then attacked from behind by rats. Freud was able to show that the symptoms provided a temporary escape from conflict by preventing him from finishing his education, marrying a socially acceptable woman, and thereby ending his current relationship with his beloved mistress.

Sources: Breuer & Freud (1893–1895); Freud (1909/1955; 1909/1963).

Methods of Interpretation

Text and Treaty   In thinking about psychoanalytic interpretation, it is helpful to keep the metaphor of the *text* on the top of your mind. Human behavior is like a text, for Freud. The great texts in our literary traditions are rich enough in *text*ure to be interpreted on many different levels. A great poem or novel suggests a multitude of meanings, some of which may even be outside the awareness of the poet or novelist who produced the text. Thus, a masterpiece like Herman Melville's *Moby Dick* or James Joyce's *Ulysses* captures many meanings, and indeed literary critics make it their livelihood to discover and critique these various "truths." You may have done the same thing yourself, perhaps in a class on English literature. When writing your analysis of, say, Nathaniel Hawthorne's *The Scarlet Letter,* you may have come to the realization that, while your particular interpretation may have been valid, no single interpretation could possibly be complete. And so it is with every aspect of human behavior and experience, suggests Freud. *There is no single and complete interpretation* of anything, no single answer. Rather, human behavior has multiple meanings, and like a text it can be interpreted on multiple levels. In Dora's dream, the jewel-case does not simply signify the female genitals. This may be one significance—perhaps a particularly important one, in Freud's view—but it is not the only one, nor is this meaning necessarily better than alternative meanings. In much of our behavior and experience, suggests Freud, we are each like the master novelist, unconsciously constructing literary masterpieces—such as our dreams, our symptoms, and our relationships with others—that can be interpreted on more than a single level.

Psychologists, therefore, should be skilled in the interpretation of multivalent texts (Bakan, 1958).

A second useful metaphor is that of the political *treaty*. A treaty is a compromise among conflicting forces. Two countries at war decide to end hostilities, and so they draw up a treaty that is designed to keep the peace. In a good treaty, all conflicting sides make peace by forging compromises. And so it is again with our behavior and experience, says Freud. Much of what we do, say, and experience is a product of compromise among internal conflicting forces. These internal forces assume an infinitude of forms—from deeply repressed wishes concerning sexuality and aggression to conscious interests and aversions. At any given moment, a thousand and one voices are clamoring within us—most of them unconscious—and making conflicting demands. *We behave and experience in such a way as to appease as many of these voices as we can,* and we do this, for the most part, unconsciously. Dora loved her father dearly, and yet she hated him for having made her sick and dirty. While overtly displacing her hatred for her father onto Herr K, she could continue to claim, consciously, that she loved her father while continuing to hate him through K. Of course, she had good reason to hate Herr K, too. Therefore, slapping Herr K and openly expressing her disgust with his behavior enabled Dora to kill many birds of the unconscious with the same behavioral stone, forging a tentative peace treaty among the wishes and desires at war within her.

Manifest and Latent   Psychoanalysts distinguish between the *manifest* level of behavior and experience, which is consciously known and seen, and the *latent* level, which is hidden in the unconscious and must be discovered. In reality, the latent is comprised of *many* levels, in that behavior is complexly determined, like a text. In the dream of the jewel-case, the manifest level is the actual dream as Dora remembered it and as Freud reproduced it for us in print. The manifest level of any behavior and experience is relatively straightforward and concise. Dora's dream seems, on the surface, simple enough, a short, clear scenario about a fire and a jewel-case. The latent levels of the dream, however, consist of the hidden forces, conflicts, impulses, wishes, and other determinants that went into the making of the dream. These are the unconscious building blocks of the dream. Whereas the manifest content of the dream is a simple, five-sentence story, the latent content could fill a volume, Freud suggests. *There is always much more material in the latent arena than in the manifest,* and much of what is hidden as latent never comes to be known consciously. In Freud's terminology, the manifest content of the dream is **overdetermined** by the latent content. What Dora remembers as the manifest dream is but the tip of a very large, mostly submerged, iceberg.

Figure 3.2 illustrates the relationship between manifest and latent content in dreams. The process of moving from the manifest to the latent content is what Freud (1900/1953) termed *dream analysis*. The movement involves, as we saw in Dora's dream, the dreamer's associating freely to the various dream elements. The psychoanalyst listens carefully to the spontaneous associations in order to discern patterns and recurrent themes. Dora's first association to her dream was

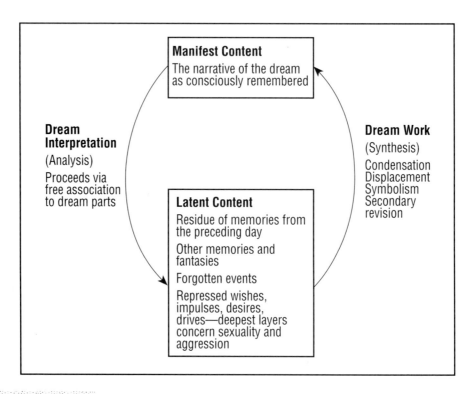

Figure 3.2

The Manifest and Latent Levels in Dreams.

to a seemingly unrelated argument her parents had recently had about her brother's bedroom door. This association eventually led to a host of latent images and meanings, having to do with fire, water, masturbation, jewelry, and sexuality. In dream analysis, the dreamer and the therapist break the dream apart and attempt to discover its hidden mechanisms.

The reverse process, of moving from the latent to the manifest, is what the dreamer has already done by dreaming. This spontaneous and unconscious process of synthesizing, rather than analyzing, is what Freud termed **dream work.** Freud suggests that each dreamer draws upon the various determinants that reside in the latent arena and fashions a full-blown manifest dream out of them. We synthesize our dreams, unconsciously, out of the latent material at hand. Dreaming is, therefore, a highly creative act, and each dreamer is like a poet who makes artful verse from a vast storehouse of images, ideas, experiences, and words. Writes Ricoeur (1970), "dreams attest that we constantly mean something other than what we say; in dreams the manifest endlessly refers to hidden meaning; that is what makes every dreamer a poet" (p. 15).

Dream work operates by "cunning distortion" (Ricoeur, 1970). In its attempt to construct a satisfactory compromise among all the warring factions in the personality, dream work disguises, cajoles, and cuts deals, thereby transforming an unwieldy bulk of latent material into a tidy manifest story. The text is written; the treaty is forged; the dream is made—all unconsciously. What emerges as the manifest story, therefore, is a masterpiece of deceit, for the dream is indeed not what it seems to be. Dora's innocent dream about a fire masks an unconscious story about sexual love, bitter hatred, sickness and filth, betrayal, and childhood bedwetting. We need not accept Freud's particular interpretations of Dora's dream to appreciate the psychoanalytic assumption that dreams mean much more than we might initially think and that these meanings are disguised.

What methods does dream work employ to disguise the meanings of dreams? Freud suggests that there are many, but he describes in some detail four dream-work strategies that are frequently used. In **condensation,** the dreamer compresses various latent elements into a single manifest image or theme. In Dora's dream, the manifest father standing at her bedside is a condensation of her real father, Herr K, and, perhaps, a few other authority figures in her life whom she both loves and resents. It is largely through condensation that a dream can say so much with so little. **Displacement** involves a shift of emphasis in a dream from an important but potentially threatening source to a trivial but safer one, as when one displaces a powerful emotion from its intended object to a substitute. Thus, Dora displaces hatred for her diseased and dishonest father onto Herr K, experiencing overwhelming disgust and resentment in his presence rather than in the presence of her father.

Symbolism is the third method of dream work. Through symbolism, the dreamer conjures up concrete images and actions that convey hidden but common meanings. According to Freud, hollow, boxlike objects into which things can be inserted—such as Dora's reticule and her mother's jewel-case—may symbolize, at the latent level, the female genitals. Though Freud tended to see symbolism as less important than condensation and displacement in the dream work (Freud, 1900/1953), psychoanalysts have catalogued many different kinds of Freudian symbols that can be discerned in dreams, myth, legends, and literature (Grinstein, 1983; Hall, 1953). Many, though not all, of these concern various aspects of human sexuality. Finally, through a fourth method of dream work termed **secondary revision,** the dreamer unconsciously smooths over the dream's rough spots, fills in gaps, clears up ambiguities, and edits the dream experience into a more-or-less coherent story with a setting, characters, and plot. It is this smooth narrative form that is recalled as the manifest content of the dream.

Symptoms and Everyday Life   The interpretation of dreams is the model for all psychoanalytic interpretation. Neurotic symptoms, artistic expressions, and certain everyday slips and mistakes are, like dreams, analogous to texts and treaties, with manifest and latent levels of meaning. To understand these phenomena, the psychoanalyst must piece together associations to manifest content as Freud pieced together Dora's associations to her dream. Similarly, symptom formation, artistic expression, and the "construction" of a mistake (a "Freudian slip") parallel dream work: all involve the creation of textlike and treatylike products through condensation, displacement, symbolism, and other unconscious methods that disguise the true meanings of the behaviors they create. Figure 3.3 shows how the psychoanalyst's interpretation of each of these phenomena (moving from manifest to latent) mirrors dream interpretation, while the person's construction of each phenomenon (moving from latent to manifest) mirrors dream work.

Dora's neurotic symptoms were ingenious products of complex unconscious dynamics, whereby internal conflicts were translated into physical infirmities. A good example is her hysterical coughing. Freud describes how Dora's most famous symptom was highly overdetermined and indicative of many different meanings at many different levels:

> We will now attempt to put together the various determinants that we have found for Dora's attacks of coughing and hoarseness. In the lowest stratum we must assume the presence of a real and organically determined irritation of the throat, which acted like the grain of sand around which an oyster forms its pearl. This irritation was susceptible to fixation, because it concerned a part of the body which in Dora had to a high degree

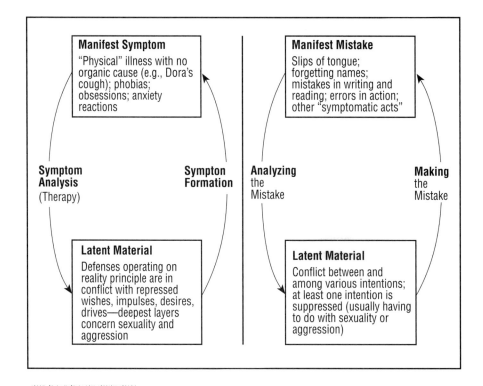

Figure 3.3

The Manifest and Latent Levels of Symptoms and Everyday Mistakes.

Sleep releases the monsters of the unconscious in this painting by Goya.

retained its significance as an erotogenic zone. And the irritation was consequently well fitted to give expression to excited states of the libido. It was brought to fixation by what was probably its first psychological wrapping—her sympathetic imitation of her father—and by her subsequent self-reproaches on account of her "catarrh." The same group of symptoms, moreover, showed itself capable of representing her relations with Herr K; it could express her regret at his absence and her wish to make him a better wife. After a part of her libido had once more turned towards her father, the symptom obtained what was perhaps its last meaning; it came to represent sexual intercourse with her father by means of Dora's identifying herself with Frau K. I can guarantee that this series is by no means complete. (Freud, 1905/1963, pp. 101–102)

All neurotic symptoms—phobias, obsessions, compulsions, anxiety reactions, and so on—can be interpreted as overdetermined texts or treaties with disguised unconscious meanings at several levels. Neurotic patients like Dora, therefore, are creative masters of symptom formation, though the profound meanings of their masterpieces are generally outside their own awareness. But such creativity is not limited to neurotics. All of us do much the same thing, argues Freud, in much of our everyday behavior and experience. We continuously create texts and forge compromises, and we display these masterpieces of overdetermination in the most unexpected and seemingly trivial ways. In *The Psychopathology of Everyday Life* (1901/1960), Freud gives many examples of slips of the tongue, forgetting names, mistakes in reading and writing, and everyday errors in simple actions that, like dreams and symptoms, can be interpreted as indicators of unconscious conflicts. Some of Freud's best examples, such as his forgetting a famous artist's name during a conversation on a train, are from his own life. In the case of Dora, her "symptomatic act" with the reticule is likewise an overdetermined example of the psychopathology of everyday life. A surprising amount of common behavior can be interpreted from a psychoanalytic framework, argues Freud, as each of us unconsciously betrays the secrets of the mind:

> He that has eyes to see and ears to hear may convince himself that no mortal can keep a secret. If his lips are silent, he chatters with his finger-tips; betrayal oozes out of him at every pore. And thus the task of making conscious the most hidden recesses of the mind is one which it is quite possible to accomplish. (Freud, 1905/1963, p. 96)

In what other ways do we forge unconscious treaties and compose overdetermined texts? In countless ways, suggests Freud. In our jokes (Freud, 1905/1960), our art (Freud, 1910/1957), our religious beliefs (Freud, 1927/1961), and our relationships with others (Freud, 1921/1955), to name a few. The psychoanalytic vision of human life is a profoundly radical portrait of *creative deceit.* Virtually all of our behavior is meaningful, but we unconsciously deceive ourselves and others so that we and they do not know what the behavior means. Our deceptions are the complex treaties and texts that we unconsciously and ingeniously weave. Psychoanalytic interpretation attempts to unravel our deceits and expose the truths that lie behind the creative cover-ups of everyday life.

Myth and Symbol: Jungian Meanings   In Chapter 2, I introduced Carl Jung's analytical psychology as a vigorous alternative to Freud and the neo-Freudian perspectives seen in the writings of Horney, Fromm, the ego psychologists, and the object-relations theorists. From its origins in Jung's break with Freud before the onset of World War I, Jungian psychology has shared with other strains in the psychoanalytic tradition a fascination with unconscious processes and the intrapsychic mysteries of the human soul. But in its emphasis on spirituality over sexuality and its portrayal of human development in terms of individuation across the life cycle, the Jungian alternative departs from Freud in a number of critical ways. Like Freud, Jung viewed dreams and symptoms as overdetermined manifest products replete with latent meanings. But whereas Freud viewed dreams as wish fulfillments originating in conflicts concerning sexual and aggressive urges, Jung portrayed dreams as *symbols* of the striving for *balance* in personality, as expressions of *universal myths,* and as *anticipations* of life problems for the *future.*

What makes the human species so fascinating and so unique, according to Jung, is its use of symbols. A symbol is "a term, a name, or even a picture that may be familiar in daily life yet that possesses specific connotations in addition to its conventional and obvious meaning. It implies something vague, unknown, or hidden from us" (Jung, von Franz, Henderson, Jacobi, & Jaffe, 1964, p. 20). Symbols are especially useful in the apprehension of concepts and phenomena that we cannot fully define or comprehend. This is one reason that all religions employ symbolic language or images. Individuals produce symbols consciously and spontaneously, in the form of dreams. The psychologist who seeks to interpret the symbols of dreams should be careful not to get led astray by the dreamer's free associations. Whereas Freud distrusted the manifest content of dreams and sought to find meanings in the dreamer's far-flung associations, Jung argued that one should pay closer attention to the form and content of the manifest dream itself. Associations to the dream itself are also important, but the interpretation should repeatedly come back to the dream itself, Jung maintained, for it is in the dream proper that the symbols reside.

Whereas Freud argued that dreams fulfill hidden wishes, Jung saw dreams as seeking to restore balance and harmony in the self. For example, one of Jung's male patients reported a dream in which his gentle and attractive wife appeared as a drunken and disheveled hag. Jung's interpretation of the dream rejected the possibility that the man was in fact dreaming about his wife per se and entertained instead the hypothesis that the vulgar woman symbolized the feminine side of his own personality—the anima. Whereas he behaved in a gentlemanly fashion in public, the man's inner anima was harsh and repulsive. Interestingly, Jung concluded that the dream should *not* be seen as urging the man to "change" or "make better" this inner reality. Instead the dream urges the man simply to see, to acknowledge, and to integrate what already exists, so that the self may be apprehended in more balanced and holistic terms:

> In the Middle Ages, long before the physiologists demonstrated that by reason of our glandular structure there were both male and female elements in all of us, it was said that "every man carries a woman within himself." It is this female element in every male that I have called the "anima." [In this particular man's case] this "feminine" aspect is essentially a certain inferior kind of relatedness to the surroundings, and particularly to women, which is kept carefully concealed from others as well as from oneself. In other words, though an individual's visible personality may seem quite normal, he may well be concealing from others—or even from himself—the deplorable condition of "the woman within."
>
> That was the case with this particular patient: His female side was not nice. His dream was actually saying to him: "You are in some respects behaving like a degenerate female," and thus gave him an appropriate shock. (An example of this kind, of course, must not be taken as evidence that the unconscious is

concerned with "moral" injunctions. The dream was not telling the patient to "behave better," but was simply trying to balance the lopsided nature of his conscious mind, which was maintaining the fiction that he was a perfect gentleman throughout.) (Jung and others, 1964, p. 31)

In the case of Dora, we see that Freud traced dream associations back to conflicts and issues rooted in Dora's adolescent and childhood past. The dream of the jewel-case connected to the masturbation and bedwetting of her early years and to her unconscious longings and fears about men, rooted in her early experiences with her father. By contrast, Jung's dream analyses sometimes focus on events yet to happen—on the future. Jung believed that "dreams may sometimes announce certain situations long before they actually happen" because they bring to consciousness a step-by-step movement toward danger of which the individual may not be previously aware (Jung et al, 1964, p. 50). For example, a man who had "developed almost a morbid passion for mountain climbing" (as a way of compensating, Jung argues, for his dissolute private life) began to dream of stepping off mountains into empty space (Jung et al, 1964, p. 50). The dream was a warning, in Jung's view, that the man was headed for disaster and that he should get his private life in order and cut back on his dangerous mountain ventures. The man did not heed the warning. Six months later he jumped off of a mountain and was killed.

The identification of archetypal themes and universal myths may be the most characteristic feature of Jungian dream analysis. This mode of interpretation is dramatically illustrated in Jung's interpretation of a series of dreams from the young daughter of a psychiatrist (Jung et al, 1964, pp. 69–82). At age 8, the girl recorded a series of her dreams in a notebook. Each dream account was fashioned like a fairy tale, beginning with the words, "Once upon a time. . . ." While the dreams were very childlike, they contained uncanny images that were totally incomprehensible to her father. Puzzled and troubled, he brought the notebook to Jung. Jung describes 12 of the dreams:

1. "The evil animal," a snakelike monster with many horns, kills and devours all other animals. But God comes from the four corners, being in fact four separate gods, and gives rebirth to all the dead animals.
2. An ascent into heaven, where pagan dances are being celebrated; and a descent into hell, where angels are doing good deeds.
3. A horde of small animals frightens the dreamer. The animals increase to a tremendous size, and one of them devours the little girl.
4. A small mouse is penetrated by worms, snakes, fishes, and human beings. Thus the mouse becomes human. This portrays the four stages of the origin of mankind.
5. A drop of water is seen, as it appears when looked at through a microscope. The girl sees the drop is full of tree branches. This portrays the origin of the world.

6. A bad boy has a clod of earth and throws bits of it at everyone who passes. In this way, all the passers-by become bad.

7. A drunken woman falls into the water and comes out renewed and sober.

8. The scene is in America, where many people are rolling on an ant heap, attacked by the ants. The dreamer, in a panic, falls into a river.

9. There is a desert on the moon where the dreamer sinks so deeply into the ground that she reaches hell.

10. In this dream the girl has a vision of a luminous ball. She touches it. Vapors emanate from it. A man comes and kills her.

11. The girl dreams she is dangerously ill. Suddenly birds come out of her skin and cover her completely.

12. Swarms of gnats obscure the sun, the moon, and all the stars, except one. That one star falls upon the dreamer. (Jung et al., 1964, p. 70)

The remarkable series of dream accounts contains startling similarities to certain classical myths and stories from ancient texts and other arcane sources with which the little girl could surely have had no familiarity. Some of the dreams play out motifs and images from sacred Jewish and Christian writings, Jung argued. For example, the first dream recalls the early Greek fathers of the Christian church who argued that at the end of time everything would be restored by a redeemer to its original and perfect state. Yet the little girl apparently had no religious instruction whatsoever, and her father was not familiar with the particular religious stories to which her dreams seemed to refer. Some of the other dreams seem to connect to primitive myths that predate Christianity, as in archetypal stories of creation, the flood, and the quest of the hero. The element of fourness—as in the four corners of the first dream—plays a great role in many religions and philosophies and was familiar to students of Hermetic philosophy in the Middle Ages before petering out in the eighteenth century. The horned serpent appears in sixteenth-century Latin alchemy as the *quadricornutus serpens* (four-horned serpent), a symbol of Mercury and an antagonist of the Christian trinity. Needless to say, this is an extraordinarily obscure reference.

Jung was familiar with many ancient and esoteric myths and writings, but the little girl simply could not have consciously known about these sources, he maintained. The dream images, he argued, arose from a *collective* unconscious, wherein are stored archaic images and symbols whose meanings have been elaborated by humankind since the dawn of human history. Rather than instinctual urges concerning sex and aggression, the girls dreams were driven and shaped by the same archetypal patterns that shaped ancient myth and folklore—symbols of creation, death, rebirth, and so on. But why should this particular girl dream these particular dreams? Why, for instance, should the dreams be so preoccupied with death and destruction? A year later the girl died of an infectious illness. Could her strange dreams have foreshadowed this turn of events? It may seem unlikely, but Jung entertains the possibility, in light of his belief that dreams may sometimes predict future happenings by projecting into the future from current

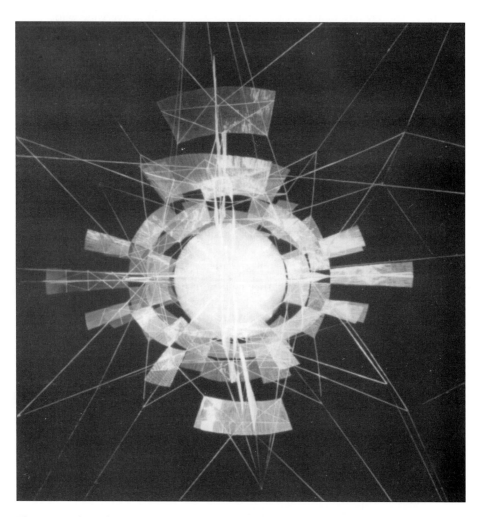

The Sun, a sculpture by Robert Lippold, as modern-day mandala: symbol of the unity of self.

unconscious trends. Although he comes to no firm conclusion on this issue for this particular case, Jung writes:

> These dreams open up a new and rather terrifying aspect of life and death. One would expect to find such images in an aging person who looks back upon life, rather than to be given them by a child who would normally be looking forward. Their atmosphere recalls the old Roman saying, "Life is a short dream," rather than the joy and exuberance of springtime. For this child's life was like a *ver sacrum vovendum* (vow of vernal sacrifice), as the Roman poet puts it. Experience shows that the unknown

approach of death casts an *adumbratio* (an anticipatory shadow) over the life and dreams of the victim. Even the altar in Christian churches represents, on the one hand, a tomb and, on the other, a place of resurrection—the transformation of death into eternal life. (Jung et al., 1964, p. 75)

The Context of Justification: Testing Hypotheses

Like Freud in the case of Dora and Jung in the analysis of a little girl's dreams, clinicians, scholars, and scientists in the psychoanalytic tradition have produced intriguing interpretations of dreams, symptoms, fantasies, associations, and many other behavioral expressions in an effort to unravel some of the intrapsychic mysteries of human lives. In the process, they have built highly influential theories of personality that, they propose, extend well beyond the lives of the particular cases from which they were derived. While every case study is a unique exploration, the discoveries made in any particular life may, in principle, be evaluated with respect to their applicability to other lives. There will never be another Dora, but principles of symptom formation and the working of the unconscious, derived from the Dora case and cases like it, may prove useful for other lives as well. The extent to which such principles are useful, however, must be evaluated in scientifically valid ways. To repeat a key point from Chapter 1, hypotheses derived in the scientific context of discovery must be subjected to appropriate test or evaluation in the scientific context of justification.

Let us consider five important content areas within the psychoanalytic tradition wherein central concepts and hypotheses have been derived from case studies and other nonsystematic observations and subsequently subjected to empirical test. These are the areas of (1) the dynamic unconscious, (2) mechanisms of defense, (3) stages of psychosexual development, (4) the development of object relations, and (5) Jungian typologies. In recent years, each of these five areas has been examined and articulated through vigorous and creative programs of hypothesis-testing research.

The Unconscious

A fundamental proposition of every psychoanalytic approach to personality is that much of what we know and feel is outside of our conscious awareness. Intrapsychic mysteries transpire at an unconscious level, buried deep beneath the manifest surface of everyday waking consciousness. In the psychoanalytic view, repression is an inescapable fact of daily life. "The essence of repression lies simply in the function of rejecting and keeping something out of consciousness," Freud wrote (1915/1957, p. 105). Within the scientific community, psychoanalytic ideas concerning repression and the unconscious have traditionally been viewed with a great deal of skepticism, as rather fanciful notions that cannot be supported by empirical proof (e.g., Holmes, 1976; Mischel, 1986). But in recent years a growing consensus has begun to emerge that, in somewhat qualified ways, Freud was right. There *is* an unconscious realm in human thought and feeling, and it exerts a significant influence in people's lives (Erdelyi, 1985; Kihlstrom, 1990; Maddi, 1980; Shevrin & Dickman, 1980; Westen, 1990).

Unconscious Information Processing   Outside the psychoanalytic tradition, cognitive psychologists of many different persuasions have begun to show that a great deal of human information processing occurs outside of awareness. In an informative review, Hill and Lewicki (1991) claim that "cognitive psychologists have accepted the view that most of our thoughts are nonconscious; or, to put it in the more technical terms of cognitive psychologists, most information processing follows algorithms (i.e., rules of procedure for solving problems) that are not accessible to conscious awareness" (p. 212). A number of experiments have demonstrated that people acquire a great deal of complex knowledge about their social environments without ever knowing that they are acquiring it, or how they are acquiring it (Lewicki, 1986). What Lewicki (1986) calls "nonconscious social information processing" occurs automatically and without volitional control in daily life, as we spontaneously apply ingrained algorithms to make sense of social information. According to Hill and Lewicki (1991), such processing may trigger emotional reactions, such as automatic liking or disliking for certain events and stimuli. Furthermore, these emotional reactions may be at odds with our conscious picture of what we consider reasonable, justified, and desirable when it comes to judging events and people. Yet we may be unable to change the reactions.

As an illustration of these points, I ask you to imagine the following scene. You are briefly introduced to an older man at a party, and you strike up a friendly conversation. From the second you see him, you begin to process, in an automatic fashion, a vast array of social information, including the way he speaks, the clothes he wears, the way he seems to start a new sentence before finishing the old one, his enthusiasm about politics, and the smell of his cologne. Most all of this is being processed outside your awareness, as you concentrate on the conversation you are having at the time. Fifteen minutes later, he leaves, and you say to yourself, "He seems like a very nice and reasonable person. I *should* like him." But you don't like him. There is something about him that bothers you a lot, but you cannot put your finger on it. The psychological truth of the matter is that his voice reminds you of an uncle whom you detested as a youth. Unconsciously, you immediately picked this information up, and it colored your subsequent perceptions, emotional reactions, and behaviors. Yet you were not aware of this happening at the time. And you may still not be aware of the processing algorithm you spontaneously employed. Write Hill and Lewicki (1991), "a person may find some of his or her 'automatic categorizations' of people or other stimuli unreasonable or even clearly wrong and still be unable to modify them or to stop their emotional consequences" (p. 218).

Modern theories of information processing typically assume that at least some aspects of human cognition are outside of awareness (Erdelyi, 1985; Kihlstrom, 1990). Classical "multistore" models, such as that proposed by Atkinson and Shiffrin (1968), conceive of the information processing system as a sequence of steps through which information in the environment passes, as it is first perceived, put into short-term memory, and then stored in long-term memory. In models like these, unconscious processes are implicated only in the early "pre-attentive" steps. In other words, these models contend that only what we consciously attend to or become aware of in the first place, before we consciously perceive and remember it, is influenced by automatic unconscious processes. The unconscious works as a kind of screen or filter, letting in certain kinds of information and blocking out other kinds.

More recent cognitive models, however, appear to give unconscious processes a larger role. A relatively new and very influential perspective in cognitive psychology, entitled the "parallel distributed processing" approach (PDP; McClelland, Rummelhart, & the PDP Research Group, 1986), argues that people process different kinds of information simultaneously, through a large number of interacting processing units or "modules." The modules work in a parallel fashion such that different units operate simultaneously on different types of information. Because there are so many parallel units and because they interact with each other in an extremely fast and efficient way, we are not consciously aware of most of the vast amount of information processing that is going on in our minds at any given point in time. Therefore, unconscious influences are not confined merely to what we notice or attend to. Rather, "PDP models seem to consider almost all information processing, including the higher mental functions involved in language, memory, and thought, to be unconscious" (Kihlstrom, 1990, p. 448).

John Kihlstrom (1990) conceives of "the psychological unconscious" as a set of *implicit* systems. Within the unconscious realm, Kihlstrom identifies four related processes whose existence is well supported by empirical research. **Implicit memory** is revealed when a person's behavior is modified by the apprehension of a past event, though the event itself is not consciously recollected. Evidence for **implicit perception** may be seen when the performance of a task changes as a result of some current event, but the current event is not consciously perceived. **Implicit thought** is reflected in problem-solving activity that occurs outside of awareness. Finally, **implicit learning** is the acquisition of knowledge in the absence of any reflective awareness of the knowledge itself. Table 3.2 provides examples of each of the four. In Kihlstrom's view, consciousness is a quality of experience that may be necessary for the voluntary control of certain cognitive functions, and for communicating one's mental states to others. But many forms of complex psychological functioning operate in an implicit or unconscious way.

Research and theory in cognitive psychology, therefore, are generally consistent with the psychoanalytic idea that a great deal of what the mind does, it

Table 3.2

Four Cognitive Aspects of the Psychological Unconscious

	Definition	Example
Implicit Memory	Unconscious recollection of past event that influences behavior	A grade school boy avoids dogs because he was terrorized by a German shepherd at a very young age. He does not consciously remember the incident with the German shepherd.
Implicit Perception	Current event that influences behavior, without being consciously perceived	A young woman lingers over coffee for a longer time than usual because the background music at the restaurant is especially appealing. But she is not consciously attending to the music, rather focusing her concentration on her plans for the next day.
Implicit Thought	Problem-solving activity that occurs outside of awareness	An executive dozes off at her desk and then awakens with an answer to a problem that has been bothering her for days.
Implicit Learning	Acquisition of knowledge in the absence of any reflective awareness of the knowledge itself	After weeks of overhearing her roommate's instructional tape recordings for a French class, a college student realizes one day that she knows how to speak a number of French phrases, even though she never tried to learn them.

does unconsciously. It is fair to point out, however, that Freud and the psychoanalysts are not the only kinds of psychologists who have traditionally argued for unconscious information processing. Kihlstrom identifies conceptions of unconscious processing in the writings of certain nineteenth-century scholars who were well outside of the psychoanalytic tradition, including the great pioneer in experimental psychology, Hermann Helmholtz. Kihlstrom (1990) writes that "most experimental work on nonconscious processing has followed Helmholtzian rather than Freudian lines, in employing neutral stimulus materials and sterile laboratory procedures that effectively limit the role played by personality factors, or the influence of the psychological unconscious on interpersonal relations" (p. 459). Therefore, while cognitive approaches to the unconscious are generally consistent with Freud, they do not specifically address features of the unconscious that are unique to Freud's view, like Freud's emphasis on the irrational, primary-process nature of unconscious processes and the dynamic roles of sexuality, aggression, and defense. Quips Westen, "one can read a thousand pages of social-cognitive theory and never know that people have genitals" (1990, p. 53). But Kihlstrom seems to suggest that, when it comes to the psychological unconscious, genitals may be irrelevant, as may be instinctual urges, inner conflicts, and other emotional and motivational dynamics of the Freudian unconscious. What emerges from cognitive research, he submits, is a conception of the unconscious that is "kinder, gentler, and more rational" than "the seething unconscious of Freud" (Kihlstrom, 1990, p. 460).

Studies in Repression   Like Freud, Fyodor Dostoyevsky saw little that was kind and gentle in the psychological unconscious. In *Notes from Underground*, the Russian novelist wrote:

> Every man has some reminiscences which he would not tell to everyone, but only to his friends. He has others he would not reveal even to his friends, but only to himself, and that in secret. But finally, there are others which a man is even afraid to tell himself, and every decent man has a considerable number of such things stored away. (1864/1960, p. 35)

For both Freud and Dostoyevsky, what makes certain memories unconscious is that they *threaten* the well-being of the rememberer. Repression is dynamic; it seeks to cast into the unconscious those aspects of life that bring anxiety and guilt; it works pro-actively to *protect* the individual from psychic harm. A long line of research on **perceptual defense** has evaluated this central psychoanalytic hypothesis (Erdelyi, 1974; Gur & Sackheim, 1979; Postman, Bruner, & McGinnies, 1948). Perceptual defense is *the unconscious monitoring of sensory perception by the censoring forces of repression* within the person. In a number of controversial experiments conducted in the late 1940s and 1950s, researchers showed that it often takes a person longer to recognize presumably traumatic or anxiety-producing stimuli (such as obscene words, or stimuli previously associated with pain) than to recognize neutral stimuli (Bruner & Postman, 1947; Cowen & Beier, 1954; Lazarus & McClearey, 1951; McGinnies, 1949). For instance, McGinnies (1949) found that students who were exposed to quick flashes of words on a screen required longer exposures before they could recognize such stimulus words as *penis* and *kotex* compared to such neutral words as *apple* and *river*. McGinnies argued that repression functions to keep such stimuli out of awareness, at least for a time.

In recent years, studies have examined the possibility that some people are generally more "repressive" than others. Weinberger, Schwartz, and Davidson (1979) describe **repressors** as persons who experience little anxiety on a conscious level and who adopt a highly defensive approach to life. The researchers were able to classify certain individuals as exhibiting an especially repressive coping style by virtue of their scores on two self-report, paper-and-pencil questionnaires—one measuring anxiety (the Manifest Anxiety Scale; Taylor, 1953) and the other defensiveness, or "social desirability" (Crowne & Marlowe, 1964), which indicates the extent to which a person will describe the self in socially acceptable and overly "nice" ways. In an experiment in which people were exposed to verbal phrases containing sexual and aggressive content, repressors reported very low levels of subjective distress compared to "low-anxious" (low anxiety, low defensiveness) and "defensive-high-anxious" (high anxiety, high defensiveness) individuals. At the same time, however, physiological measures indicated that the repressors experienced significantly higher levels of internal arousal than did the low-anxious and defensive-high-anxious subjects. In other words, whereas the repressors claimed that the sexual and aggressive content did not make them anxious, their bodily processes suggested otherwise. From a psychoanalytic perspective, the repressors did not *consciously* perceive the drive-related stimuli as threatening. Their heightened physiological arousal, however, indicated that the threat may have instead been perceived at an *unconscious* level.

Penelope Davis has conducted a series of influential studies examining how repressors recall emotional experiences in their lives. In one study, female college students were asked to recall six kinds of personal experiences from childhood—general memories, experiences of happiness, sadness, anger, fear, and wonder (Davis & Schwartz, 1987). As Figure 3.4 shows, repressors (low anxiety, high defensiveness) recalled significantly fewer negative memories than did low-anxious (low anxiety, low defensiveness) and high-anxious (high anxiety, low defensiveness) individuals. The results are consistent with the psychoanalytic hypothesis that repression involves an inaccessibility to negative emotional memories. However, the results also indicate, as can be seen in Figure 3.4, that repressors tended to report somewhat fewer *positive* memories as well, suggesting that repression may also involve a more general failure to retrieve emotional memories of various kinds.

In a second study, Davis (1987) found that repressors recalled fewer childhood experiences in which they felt happy, sad, angry, fearful, guilty, and self-conscious compared to other individuals. The inhibition was especially pronounced for fear and self-consciousness experiences. But she also showed that when recalling memories in which *someone else* felt happy, sad, angry, or fearful, repressors actually reported substantially *more* experiences. The findings suggest that repression is not simply a general memory deficit. Repressors actually report a greater number of memories involving emotional experiences of other people. But when it comes to recalling events in which the strong emotions experienced *are their own,* and especially when those emotions entail painful states of fear and self-consciousness, repressors seem to have difficulty summoning such memories into

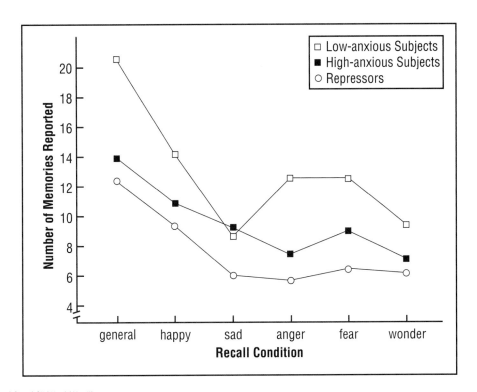

Figure 3.4

Mean Number of Memories in Each Recall Condition for Low-Anxious
Individuals, High-Anxious Individuals, and Repressors.

From Paris & Schwartz, 1987, p. 158.

awareness. Fear and self-consciousness occur in situations in which attention is
focused on the self in an evaluative and especially threatening way. What may
make these kinds of experiences the most suitable grist for the repression mill is
that they directly threaten the self with a negative evaluation, more so even than
experiences of sadness, anger, and other negative emotions. Repression may operate most powerfully in the domain of self-evaluation. We may be most prone to
repress those experiences in which the self is judged in a negative manner.

Why is it that some people have such a difficult time recalling and articulat-
ing negative emotional memories? What makes repressors different from other
people? Hansen and Hansen (1988) have explored what they call "the architecture
of repression," described as the mechanisms whereby emotionally tagged memories, especially unpleasant memories, are left inaccessible. They argue that repressors have an "associative network" for negative emotional experiences that is
substantially less complex and more discrete than that found for negative memories experienced by other people. For repressors, negative recollections have a

characteristically simple structure and these memories are split off from other memories, isolated outside the main network of interrelated autobiographical recollections. Repressors and nonrepressors organize their episodic memories in different ways. Repressors simplify negative memories to emphasize a single dominant feeling, as a way of keeping these memories from connecting in their minds to other autobiographical memories containing other feelings. By contrast, nonrepressors tend to describe their negative memories in more complex terms, emphasizing a number of different emotional states in the same memory and integrating the negative memory with the main lines of their autobiographical self.

Hansen and Hansen obtained evidence for their interpretation in a study of 433 undergraduate women and men, each of whom was assigned to recall, describe, and evaluate either an angering, embarrassing, sad, or fearful event from the past. For the particular event to be recalled, the subjects were told to picture the situation in their minds and to remember as vividly as they could how it felt to be (angry, embarrassed, sad, or fearful) at that particular moment. After writing a description of the experience on a sheet of paper, the subjects were asked to rate how they felt in the situation according to 10 different emotion dimensions—angry, embarrassed, sad, fearful, anxious, disgusted, ashamed, depressed, surprised, and happy. The results showed that each negative memory elicits a montage of different emotional reactions. For example, when subjects were asked to recall memories of sadness, they rated their feelings in these memories as very sad, but they also tended to rate highly feelings of depression, anger, and fear. By contrast, sad memories did not tend to elicit feelings of shame or embarrassment. For sad memories, then, the researchers determined that sadness was the dominant emotion but that other nondominant emotions of depression, anger, and fear could also be identified. Similarly, embarrassing memories showed the dominant emotion of embarrassment but were also tagged with the nondominant emotion of shame. Each category of emotional memory (angering, embarrassing, sad, and fearful), therefore, specified a corresponding dominant emotion and a set of nondominant emotions.

Differences between repressors and other individuals were revealed in the nondominant emotions, but not in the dominant ones. For any given negative event, repressors and nonrepressors reported comparable levels of dominant emotion intensity. For example, embarrassing memories were rated just as emotionally embarrassing by repressors as by nonrepressors. But repressors tended to rate the nondominant emotions associated with the given memory at less intense levels. Embarrassing memories, therefore, produced less shame for repressors than for nonrepressors. Sad memories produced less depression, anger, and fear for repressors than for nonrepressors. And so on. In purifying their particular memories to underscore a dominant emotional reaction rather than a host of related but nondominant emotions, repressors cordon off the negativity associated with any given memory, keeping it from spreading to other recollections of the past. Write Hansen and Hansen, "repression is fundamentally a phenomenon of the relatively impoverished structure of the repressor's memory linked to the less elaborate, more discrete emotional tags with which the repressor's memorial representations are associated" (p. 816). To protect the self from threat, repression works to keep negative memories from connecting to each other, rendering each a simple monad unto itself.

The Activation of the Unconscious According to psychoanalytic theories, the road to and from the unconscious is a two-way street, but the traffic in either direction is of a peculiar sort. Southbound from the land of manifest experience to the latent or implicit domain of the unconscious are headed those aspects of daily life that, like emotionally negative events in the lives of "repressors," will eventually find their destination outside the purview of everyday awareness. Northbound from latent to manifest travel conflicts and impulses that will eventually arrive on the scene of everyday behavior and experience in a disguised form, exerting an influence whose power and effect are not to be consciously known. Whereas the studies of repression we have discussed above examine the move from manifest to latent, the work of Lloyd Silverman and others adopting the **Psychodynamic Activation Method** clocks the traffic in the opposite direction—how unconscious impulses and conflicts make their way into daily life, how they may be *activated* to motivate human behavior in ways consistent with psychoanalytic theory (Silverman, 1976, 1985; Silverman & Fishel, 1981; Silverman, Lachmann, & Milich, 1982).

Silverman's method involves the subliminal presentation of Freudian messages. If you were to gaze at a blank screen upon which a *tachistoscope* flashed a picture or a word for *4 milliseconds* (4/1000 of a second), you would not see anything—or at least you would not *consciously* think that you have seen anything. The visual stimulus would flash so quickly that you would not register a perception of it. Yet, some psychologists would argue that you have in fact seen something *unconsciously*. Further, if the information concerned psychodynamic issues like sexuality, aggression, and guilt, then modest and temporary effects on your behavior and experience could result from such unconscious perception. Unconsciously "seeing" the written phrase MOMMY AND I ARE ONE, for instance, may make you feel happier, more competent, less depressed. This is because the stimulus MOMMY AND I ARE ONE can activate unconscious fantasies of union with the mother. On the other hand, if you are a male, unconsciously seeing the phrase BEATING DAD IS WRONG might decrease your performance on subsequent tasks and make you feel less secure and confident than usual, because fantasies of oedipal rivalry would have risen to the fore.

By presenting a subliminal Freudian message on a screen, Silverman aims to arouse a corresponding unconscious fantasy in the perceiver, and this unconscious fantasy is assumed to cause or motivate subsequent behavior for a short time afterwards, in subtle but measurable ways. The message must be subliminal; conscious recognition of the stimulus will *not* evoke the unconscious symbiotic fantasy (Bornstein, 1990). According to psychoanalytic theory, the early oral bond between mother and infant remains a source of sustenance for the entire life span: Freud wrote, "Sucking at the mother's breast is the starting point of the whole of sexual life, the unmatched prototype of every later sexual satisfaction, *to which fantasy often enough recurs in times of need*" (1916/1961, p. 314). Object-relations theorists speak of the early bond as a *symbiosis* between caregiver and infant from which will emerge a strengthened and autonomous infant self. MOMMY AND I ARE ONE, representing the Freudian oral bond, thus encapsulates the ideal psychodynamic essence of the first year of life. Apprehended unconsciously, this message should activate symbiotic fantasies in the adult, and these fantasies should provide the adult with temporary comfort and sustenance.

Silverman and his colleagues have conducted a large number of studies to show that the subliminal message of MOMMY AND I ARE ONE can reduce various forms of pathology and increase overall adaptation in both clinical and nonclinical populations. Many of the studies have been conducted with schizophrenic men, whose bizarre and debilitating symptoms include delusions, hallucinations, and chronic "thought disorder," manifested in illogical, loose, and unrealistic thinking. Psychoanalysts have long suggested that schizophrenia has its developmental origins in a faulty mother–infant bond, or "symbiotic failure," during the first year of life.

In one representative study (described in Silverman et al., 1982, pp. 72–76), the researchers saw each of 48 male schizophrenics on three different occasions. At the beginning of each meeting, the schizophrenic men responded to a number of standard psychological measures designed to assess pathological thinking and pathological behavior. One measure used was a story-recall test in which the man listened to a tape-recorded story and then retold the story to the experimenter. The degree of loose and illogical thinking and the amount of abnormal behavior (such as inappropriate laughter, peculiar mannerisms, and severe speech problems) were assessed on this test in order to provide a baseline measure of pathology. Each man then was exposed four times to one of three different subliminal messages: MOMMY AND I ARE ONE (symbiotic), DESTROY MOTHER (aggressive), or MEN TALKING (neutral). After the exposure to the subliminal message, the subject again responded to the measures designed to assess thought disorder and pathological behavior.

In this experiment, then, the independent variable was the kind of subliminal stimulus presented to the subject via the tachistoscope: either symbiotic, aggressive, or neutral. The dependent variable was the change in pathological thinking and behavior observed from before to after the subliminal stimulation. The experimenter predicted that the schizophrenic men would show a decrease in pathology when the subliminal stimulus was symbiotic. The subliminal MOMMY AND I ARE ONE should arouse positive symbiotic fantasies that temporarily relieve or lessen schizophrenic symptomatology. The aggressive DESTROY MOTHER, on the other hand, should arouse oral aggressive fantasies likely to temporarily increase pathology. The neutral stimulus should neither increase nor decrease pathological thinking and behavior.

Silverman's predictions were confirmed, though the positive effects of the symbiotic and the negative effects of the aggressive stimulus were moderate and very short-lived. At least 11 similar studies with schizophrenic men have subsequently been reported by Silverman and his colleagues that support the positive effects of MOMMY AND I ARE ONE (Silverman, 1983). In addition, two studies with schizophrenic *women* show similar positive effects for symbiotic fantasies, this time using the subliminal stimulus DADDY AND I ARE ONE (Cohen, 1977; Jackson, 1981). Other studies have found that symbiotic fantasies induced by the Psychodynamic Activation Method temporarily relieve sadness in depressives, help overweight people eat less, and lower anxiety in relatively normal college students (Silverman, 1983).

Silverman and Fishel (1981) describe a number of interesting studies on the male Oedipus complex. Using the subliminal message BEATING DAD IS WRONG, Silverman and his colleagues claim to have aroused unconscious fantasies of oedipal guilt—symbolically killing the father as did Oedipus in the ancient Greek myth—in college men who participated in a dart-throwing tournament. Subliminal exposure to BEATING DAD IS WRONG led to poorer accuracy in dart throwing, whereas a subliminal message designed to *lessen* oedipal guilt and therefore increase healthy competition—BEATING DAD IS OK—led to better performance in dart throwing. The neutral subliminal message PEOPLE ARE WALKING had no effect on performance. Whereas the "beating dad" messages tap into the "killing father" aspect of the male oedipal complex, messages like WINNING MOM IS OK and WINNING MOM IS WRONG tap into the oedipal desire to have mother in a sensual way. In subsequent studies, Silverman found that WINNING MOM IS OK resulted in significantly higher dart scores, whereas WINNING MOM IS WRONG resulted in lower scores. Failures to replicate Silverman's findings on competition among males, however, are reported by Haspel and Harris (1982) and Heilbrun (1980), who found no measurable effects of the two "beating dad" stimuli on dart-throwing performance.

As you might have guessed by now, Silverman's research is very controversial. Many psychologists find it difficult to believe that a simple subliminal exposure can have much of a psychodynamic effect. And many researchers report failures to replicate some of Silverman's results (e.g., Baley & Shevrin, 1988; Dauber, 1984; Oliver & Burkham, 1982; Porterfield & Golding, 1985). Recently, Hardaway (1990) conducted a careful quantitative meta-analysis of 56 empirical studies employing the Psychodynamic Activation Method to elicit symbiotic fantasies. Statistically accounting for differences among studies with respect to laboratory conditions, degree of exposure to subliminal cues, sex of subject, and other variables, Hardaway concludes: "The MOMMY AND I ARE ONE experimental effect is a real one" (1990, p. 182). The positive effect of this subliminal stimulus is small but significant, Hardaway maintains, and it is no longer necessary for researchers to churn out further replication attempts. Despite the criticisms of Silverman's work, therefore, it appears that the Psychodynamic Activation Method provides valid, though modest, results, at least with respect to the stimulus MOMMY AND I ARE ONE. Hardaway concludes that future research should attempt to determine under what kinds of conditions and for what kinds of people the activation of symbiotic fantasies is most effective.

In conclusion, recent research into unconscious processes provides growing but qualified support for fundamental psychoanalytic hypotheses. Researchers of many different theoretical persuasions agree that a good deal of human information processing occurs outside of conscious awareness, as in the cases of implicit thought, memory, learning, and perception. The distinction between the implicit and the explicit realms of information processing, however, does not perfectly match Freud's distinction between unconscious and conscious, in that the Freudian unconscious suggests a primary-process and drive-laden domain that has not been the subject of contemporary research into human cognition. Nonetheless, studies in repression continue to support the psychoanalytic idea that drive-related and threatening information may be cast out of consciousness in order to protect the ego. Repressors are especially adept at cordoning off negative memories in such a way as to keep threatening information isolated from their central self-conception. Research employing the Psychodynamic Activation Method suggests, furthermore, that Freud may have been right in viewing the unconscious in *dynamic* terms, as a psychic dynamo that energizes and directs what the person does, thinks, and feels, in ways that are implicit, subtle, and complex.

Mechanisms of Defense

In the Freudian view of the world, anxiety permeates all of human life. As we saw in Chapter 2, anxiety is the natural result of the inevitable conflicts we face in daily living—conflicts between self and others and conflict within the self. Coping with anxiety is the ego's most challenging job. According to Freud, the ego develops a set of unconscious strategies that help resolve conflict and thereby relieve anxiety. These *defense mechanisms* are viewed by most contemporary psychoanalysts as potentially adaptive and enhancing processes that strengthen the ego and facilitate its organization of experience (Schafer, 1968). Empirical psychologists have conducted a good deal of research on defense mechanisms (Cramer, 1988, 1991; Cramer & Carter, 1978; Gleser & Ihilevich, 1969; Haan, 1977). Though it is not clear that these methods for dealing with anxiety always function *unconsciously* (Holmes, 1978; Sherwood, 1981), research suggests that people do consistently employ effective defensive strategies in dealing with anxiety and stress.

There is considerable consensus among psychoanalysts that some defense mechanisms are relatively primitive and immature (such as denial) while others are more complex and mature (such as sublimation) (Anthony, 1970; A. Freud, 1946). The most significant empirical research on the development of defense mechanisms has been conducted by Phebe Cramer (1991). Cramer has tested the hypothesis that immature defense mechanisms should arise early in life and then taper off, while mature mechanisms should develop somewhat later. She has focused on three defense mechanisms. The most primitive of the three is **denial,** in which the person badly refuses to acknowledge an anxiety-provoking event. For instance, a young child visiting the doctor may insist that he is not afraid of a shot, or a recently widowed woman may claim she feels no grief. Denial may be employed by people of all ages, argue psychoanalysts, but it tends to be most common among the very young. Adults tend to use denial only in the most upsetting and threatening situations. More mature than denial is **projection,** in which the person attributes unacceptable internal states and qualities to external others. For instance, an adolescent girl who doubts her own religious values may accuse others of being "sinful," or a businessman insecure about his own marriage may suspect that many of his colleagues are having extramarital affairs. Projection requires that standards of "good" and "bad" be internalized such that the "bad" can be projected outward. Therefore, the use of projection should await the development of conscience (Freud's superego) in middle childhood. The most mature defense mechanism studied by Cramer was **identification,** whereby the person forms an enduring mental representation of significant others, that is, he or she internalizes and replicates the behavioral traits of others as a way of coping. Requiring the clear differentiation of self and others and a complex understanding of differences among various people, identification becomes an effective defense in adolescence and should remain so throughout life (Blos, 1979).

In one study Cramer studied the creative stories told or written by 320 children representing four age groups: young children (ages 4–7), intermediate (ages 8–11), early adolescent (ninth and tenth grades), and late adolescent (eleventh and twelfth grades). Each child was asked to look at two specially chosen pictures and make up an imaginative story about each. The stories were analyzed for examples of defense mechanisms according to the scoring categories shown in Table 3.3. As Figure 3.5 shows, the stories told by the youngest children contained a preponderance of denial themes, whereas those written or told by the children in the older three groups showed little denial. Projection and identification, on the other hand, were relatively low among the young children and increased markedly thereafter. The findings support the psychoanalytic hypothesis that these three defense mechanisms differ in relative maturity, with denial most prominent in the youngest children and projection and identification more evident in older children and adolescents.

The power of defense mechanisms is most apparent during times of great stress. Dollinger and Cramer (1990) describe an unusual study of the use of ego defenses among children who witnessed a traumatic event. Preadolescent boys from two rural Illinois towns were playing a league soccer game when a thunderstorm necessitated a delay in the action. The children retreated to their parents' cars to wait out the storm. Shortly after the game resumed, a lightning bolt struck the field and knocked down all participants and most of the children and adults on the sidelines. One boy was hit directly by the bolt. Never regaining consciousness, he died one week after the incident.

Clinical psychologists and counselors met regularly with the children who witnessed the tragedy and with their families. As part of their counseling efforts, the professionals took a number of measures of psychological variables during the course of the treatment. An especially useful index was an *upset rating* made by psychologists to gauge the overall level of emotional distress experienced by each child. The upset rating proved to be strongly related to parents' reports of

Table 3.3

Scoring Categories for Three Defense Mechanisms as Expressed in Imaginative Stories Written About Pictures

Denial

1. Statements of negation: A character in the story "does not . . ." an action, wish, or intention that, if acknowledged, would cause displeasure.
2. Denial of reality: The storyteller says that the story or situation is not "real," or characters do something that enables them to escape from something in reality that is unpleasant.
3. Reversal: A character takes on qualities that he or she had previously lacked.
4. Misperception: The storyteller perceives something in the picture in a distorted way or perceives a figure as being of the opposite sex from that usually perceived.
5. Omission of major characters or objects in the picture.
6. Overly maximizing the positive or minimizing the negative.
7. Unexpected goodness, optimism, positiveness, or gentleness.

Projection

1. Attribution of hostile feelings: The storyteller attributes aggressive or hostile feelings or intentions to a character in the story.
2. Ominous additions: The storyteller adds people, objects, animals, ghosts, and so on that are threatening.
3. Protection against threat: The storyteller expresses a need for protection against threat or assault, as in the use of disguises and the creation of protective barriers, suspiciousness, spying, anticipation of kidnap, and so on.
4. Themes of pursuit, entrapment, and escape.
5. Fear of death, injury, and attack.
6. The use of magic.
7. Bizarre or very unusual story or theme.

Identification

1. Emulation of skills: A character takes on the skill or talents of another.
2. Emulation of characteristics: A character takes on the attitudes or traits of another.
3. Regulation of motives or behavior: A character's behaviors or motives are controlled by external prohibitions, social demands, or self-criticism and self-reflection.
4. Self-esteem through affiliation: A character experiences satisfaction by associating with other people.
5. Work or delay of gratification.
6. Role differentiation: Characters assume specific adult roles, like teacher, lawyer, homemaker.
7. Moralism: The storyteller couches the story in moral terms—good versus bad, justice, fairness, and so on.

Adapted from Cramer (1987, pp. 610–612).

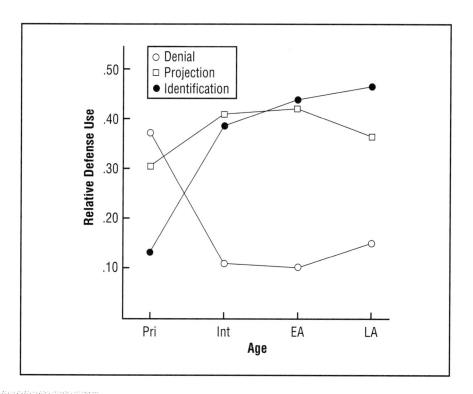

Figure 3.5

Relative Defense Scores of Primary (Pri), Intermediate (Int), Early Adolescent (EA), and Late Adolescent (LA) Groups as Expressed in Imaginative Stories.

From Cramer, 1987, p. 607.

children's sleep disturbances and somatic complaints after the event and to children's reports of fears (e.g., fears of storms, of dying, of bodily penetration, and of separation anxiety). In addition, children who scored high on emotional upset tended to avoid soccer in the subsequent two-year interval.

Children's imaginative stories told in response to pictures were also obtained. The pictures depicted scenes with lightning present. Examining the stories written by 27 10-to-13-year-old boys, Dollinger and Cramer found that denial was used as a defense at significantly higher levels in this sample than is typical in children of this age, probably because of the severity of the trauma. Psychoanalytic theory suggests that primitive defenses are more likely to appear during the most stressful points of a person's life. In addition, younger boys used significantly more denial than older boys, in keeping with previous research. Most interesting, however, was the relation between defense mechanisms and emotional upset. The stories written by those boys who showed the lowest levels of emotional upset tended to display the highest levels of *projection*. The authors point out that in boys of this age, projection is the most age-appropriate defense; denial is somewhat too primitive and identification too mature. It would appear that projection served these preadolescent boys quite well in their attempts to cope with the anxiety, fear, and sadness they experienced in the wake of the lightning incident. Those boys who showed low levels of projection exhibited high levels of emotional upset. For the most part, denial and identification were not effective defenses for coping with the upset. Only projection was negatively associated with upset. It would be expected, however, that denial would have been most effective among children at much younger ages than those in this sample and that identification would have proven most effective for adults. The lightning study underscores the psychoanalytic-developmental hypothesis that age-appropriate defense mechanisms may be most effective in warding off anxiety and helping people cope.

Like children, adults differ markedly with respect to the kinds of defense mechanisms they regularly employ. While some adults, like children, consistently use relatively immature mechanisms such as denial, others regularly adopt the more mature and complex strategies for dealing with anxiety and stress, such as identification, sublimation, and humor. George Vaillant (1971, 1977) has investigated the relationship between these characteristic defensive styles and overall adult adjustment. In a small sample of well-educated men studied over a 25-year period, Vaillant found that men's consistent use of mature defenses was positively associated with an overall index of adjustment, including physical health, career advancement, and marital enjoyment. Similarly, Vaillant and Drake (1985) found that the use of mature defenses predicted greater levels of interpersonal intimacy and meaningful and productive work in a large sample of working-class men.

In sum, empirical research suggests that defense mechanisms exist and are regularly used by children and adults to ward off anxiety and cope with stress. In keeping with hypotheses derived from Freud and the ego psychologists, defense mechanisms may be arranged in a developmental hierarchy, ranging from primitive defenses employed by young children to mature mechanisms shown by adults. Older children use more mature defenses than younger children, and defenses that are especially age-appropriate may be the most effective in dealing with stress. Among adults, the use of mature defense mechanisms has been associated with greater social adjustment and occupational achievement. With respect to the last finding, we do not know if defense mechanisms help promote adjustment or if adjustment helps promote the use of mature defense mechanisms. Most likely, both possibilities are true, as mature defenses and psychosocial adaptation work to reinforce each other.

Developmental Stages

The most well known developmental model in psychoanalysis is Freud's conception of psychosexual stages. As the libido is transformed from infancy to maturity, the individual passes through oral, anal, phallic (oedipal), latency, and genital stages. Particular character types in adulthood owe their existence to fixations at corresponding psychosexual stages. The oral-dependent type, for example, is passive, warm, and naive; and these character traits are thought to be a result of early oral experience. By contrast, the anal-retentive type is obstinate, compulsive, rigid, miserly, and obsessed with scheduling life into neat compartments; these character traits are thought to be a result of experiences associated with the anal stage. Empirical research supports the existence of a coherent cluster of personality traits corresponding to Freud's anal-retentive type (Fischer & Juni, 1982; Juni & Rubenstein, 1982; Pollack, 1979). However, there is no support in the research literature for a Freudian explanation for *why* these types come to be. In other words, anal traits in adulthood have not been shown to be a product of early childhood experiences associated with anality.

With respect to oral stages and oral types, Joseph Masling (1986) has developed a useful method for coding responses to the **Rorschach Inkblot Test** for images of orality. Probably the most famous personality test ever devised, the Rorschach Inkblot Test (Rorschach, 1921) consists of 10 symmetrical inkblots. The task presented to the subject or client is to examine each blot and tell what he or she "sees." In that the blots are accidental forms and not meant to look like anything in particular, people may see a myriad of things within them, as might a person gazing at the shapes of clouds on a warm summer day. The Rorschach is a classic **projective test.** Projective tests generally present ambiguous stimuli that the person perceives, interprets, or organizes in some fashion. The process of responding to the ambiguous cues is supposed to reveal signs of underlying personality structure. In the case of the Rorschach, it is assumed that the subject unknowingly projects unconscious conflicts, needs, and concerns onto the blots, unwittingly revealing aspects of personality that are usually hidden.

Table 3.4 describes Masling's system for detecting oral-dependent images in Rorschach responses. Oral categories include perceptions of food and drinks, passive food receivers, oral instruments, gifts and gift giving, passivity and helplessness, and references to babies and birth. Reflecting a preoccupation with drinking, eating, and other concerns of the mouth, alcoholics and overly obese adults tend to give more oral responses on the Rorschach than do other adults (Bertrand & Masling, 1969; Weiss & Masling, 1970). Cigarette smoking, however, does not appear to be related to orality on the Rorschach (Whitson, 1983). Illustrating their strong dependence on the authority of others, high-oral persons tend to comply with rules and regulations and to defer to the judgments of others more so than do low-oral persons (Feldman, 1978; Masling, O'Neill, & Jayne, 1981; Weiss, 1969).

The high-oral person is extremely concerned with establishing warm and supportive relationships with others, out of a presumed need to depend on strong others for support. Touching others can serve to promote such relationships. In a study in which college students led a blindfolded man or woman through a maze, orality on the students' Rorschachs was positively associated with touching the man's or woman's body (Juni, Masling, & Brannon, 1979). Asked to help a blindfolded person negotiate the way through a difficult maze, high-oral subjects spent more time touching the arm of the person they were helping than did subjects

Table 3.4

Categories of Oral-Dependent Rorschach Responses

Category	Sample Responses
1. Foods and drinks[a]	Milk, whiskey, boiled lobster
2. Food sources	Restaurant, saloon, breast
3. Food objects[b]	Kettle, silverware, drinking glass
4. Food providers	Waiter, cook, bartender
5. Passive food receivers	Bird in nest, fat/thin man
6. Begging and praying	Dogs begging, person saying prayers
7. Food organs	Mouth, stomach, lips, teeth
8. Oral instruments	Lipstick, cigarette, tuba
9. Nurturers	Jesus, mother, father, doctor, God
10. Gifts and gift givers	Christmas tree, cornucopia
11. Good-luck objects	Wishbone, four-leaf clover
12. Oral activity	Eating, talking, singing, kissing
13. Passivity and helplessness[c]	Looking confused, lost
14. Pregnancy and reproductive organs[d]	Placenta, womb, ovaries, embryo
15. "Baby talk" responses	Patty-cake, bunny rabbit, pussy cat
16. Negations of oral percepts	No mouth, not pregnant, woman with no breasts

[a]Score an animal only if it is invariably associated with being edible (that is, do not score *duck* or *turkey* unless food-descriptive phrases are used, such as *roast duck* or *turkey leg*).
[b]Score *pot* or *cauldron* only if the act of cooking is implied.
[c]Do not score *baby* unless there is some suggestion of passivity or frailness.
[d]Do not score *pelvis, penis, vagina,* or *sex organs.*
From Bornstein & Masling (1985, p. 307).

low in orality. In another study on helping, Peace Corps volunteers scoring high in orality showed a strong need to nurture others, effective helping behaviors, and accurate perceptions of other people, compared to those volunteers scoring low in orality (Masling, Johnson, & Saturansky, 1974).

The oral person's strong concern for supportive relationships is documented in another laboratory experiment by Masling, O'Neill, & Katkin (1982). College men interacted with either a warm (friendly) or a cold (unfriendly) male confederate while a physiological index of arousal—electrodermal activity or skin conductance—was monitored by a machine. For most of the men, physiological arousal increased over the course of the interaction with the confederate, suggesting an increase in anxiety as the interaction proceeded. The exception was the high-oral men interacting with the warm confederate, who showed no such increase in arousal. The researchers speculated that the high-oral men experienced the presence of a warm, interested other as especially soothing and supportive, so soothing that they did not show any increase in physiological activation over the course of the interaction.

A very different and innovative approach to psychosexual stages is evidenced in the research of Abigail Stewart (1982; Stewart & Healy, 1985; Stewart, Sokol, Healy, & Chester, 1986; Stewart, Sokol, Healy, Chester, & Weinstock-Savoy, 1982). Stewart sees Freud's four stages of the libido—oral, anal, phallic, and genital—as a general model for four different ways of adapting to the environment. Each of us develops through the four stages *many times over the course of life,* argues Stewart, continually circling back through the four-stage sequence with each major life turning point. Freud's four stages, therefore, are not merely psychosexual epochs through which we pass, once and for all, in childhood and adolescence. Rather, the oral, anal, phallic, and genital stages present a sequence of socioemotional *stances* that we assume in response to many kinds of significant life changes. With each major change in life, we reassume various stances.

Stewart's method of measuring the four stages involves careful content analysis of imaginative stories told or written by subjects in response to ambiguous pictures. This method—called the Thematic Apperception Test (TAT)—is the same one used by Cramer (1987) in her study of defense mechanisms earlier in this chapter. (See more about the TAT in Chapter 11.) Stewart developed her system by drawing on the orthodox Freudian descriptions of the four stages of the libido. She identified 24 college men whose behavior explicitly exemplified a preoccupation with one of Freud's four stages—six students for each of the four stages—and then she scrutinized the stories they wrote to detect Freudian themes.

To fit into one of the four types, a student had to meet all the criteria for that one type and none of the criteria from any of the other types. The six oral subjects reported unusually frequent and regular eating and smoking, suggesting an oral preoccupation. The six anal subjects reported highly ritualized and compulsive behaviors, an emphasis on cleanliness and order, and an excessively regulated lifestyle, in keeping with Freud's description of the anal-retentive type. The six phallic subjects reported high levels of sexual activity and a principal interest in sex and self-image, considered by Freudians to be phallic concerns. Finally, the six genital subjects personified Freud's formula for psychosexual maturity: they were preoccupied with issues related to love and work (*Lieben und Arbeiten*), involved in an intimate relationship with a woman while strongly committed to college studies.

One could argue that Stewart's behavioral criteria for psychosexual types are absurdly concrete. The results from her analysis of the imaginative stories written by these young men, however, strongly support the approach she uses. Table 3.5 summarizes the major differences among the stories. All were analyzed according to the characters' attitude toward authority, relations with other characters, emotions and feelings, and orientation to action. Oral men tended to write stories in which passive characters experiencing loss or confusion seek immediate gratification of their wishes in their relationships with others. The characters

Table 3.5

Thematic Concerns Defining Four Stances Toward the Environment as Scored in Imaginative Stories

Stance	Attitude Toward Authority	Relations With Others	Feelings	Orientation to Action
Receptive (oral)	View that authorities are benevolent; that they will help, advise, and praise one	View that others will fulfill one's wishes and meet one's needs	Expression of feelings of sadness (about losses) and/ or of global confusion (about the nature of things and how the world works)	Passivity and inaction
Autonomous (anal)	View that authorities are critical and punitive; that they are concerned not with persons but with rules	Views that others will *not* fulfill one's wishes or meet one's needs	Expression of anxiety about one's own competence to act or indecision about alternative actions	Actions taken to protect self from intrusions by others, or to cope in a limited way with problematic situations; all actions are reactive to existing situations
Assertive (phallic)	Oppositional stance toward authorities reflected in actions taken to oppose them or expression of view that authorities are corrupt	Orientation to others as objects to use for own benefit, reflected in direct exploitation or flight from mutual relationships	Expression of anger and hostility toward others	Individual initiative taken in confidence, but actions fail because of errors in judgment
Integrated (genital)	View that authorities are "human"; that they have limited power and are constrained in their actions	View of others as completely differentiated from the self and as full partners in mutually satisfying sharing relationships	Expression of complex, apparently incompatible feelings (ambivalence) toward single objects or people	Expression of commitment to and emotional involvement in work activities

From Stewart, Sokol, Healy, & Chester (1986, p. 146).

tend to regard powerful authorities, such as parents and teachers, as relatively kind and benevolent. In keeping with Freud's descriptions of the oral stage and the oral personality, therefore, Stewart's oral men wrote stories that were generally *receptive* (taking in, getting, incorporating) in tone and content. Paralleling Freud's descriptions of the other three stages, anal men wrote stories about *autonomy* (holding on, maintaining, hanging on); phallic men emphasized *assertiveness* (expanding, reaching out, intruding); and genital men wrote stories underscoring *integration* (relating, committing, connecting).

According to Stewart, a person adapts to change by cycling through the receptive—autonomous—assertive—integrative sequence of adaptive stances. For instance, in adjusting to marriage, divorce, a new job, or entering college, a person would be expected to adopt first a relatively receptive stance toward the environment (as does the dependent oral infant), gradually becoming more autonomous and then assertive (like the anal and phallic child), and finally taking on a mature integrative perspective (similar to Freud's genital stage) that signals mastery of the challenge and full adaptation.

Support for Stewart's view comes from a small number of studies employing her scoring system to analyze imaginative stories written by people who have gone through life transitions. New college students should be at a lower stage in adapting to college than more experienced students and should, therefore, show earlier adaptive stances; that is, they should show more receptive and autonomous orientations, and fewer assertive and integrative orientations, to the college environment. Supporting this prediction, Stewart (1982) found that freshmen scored at significantly lower stages than seniors in three different colleges.

Entering elementary school is certainly a major life transition for most children, and thus we would expect younger students to be at earlier adaptive stances than older ones. In a study of elementary school children who made up stories in response to pictures, kindergarten children tended to score in the receptive range, first graders scored autonomous, and second graders scored assertive (Stewart et al., 1982). The transition from elementary school to junior high school is also significant. Stewart and her colleagues (1982) found that, among middle-class students, those who had recently gone through this transition scored at lower stages than both those who had not yet gone through it and those who had gone through the transition longer ago. (Working-class students, however, did not show the predicted pattern of scores.) Looking at the transition of marriage, recently married women scored significantly lower than those not yet married but engaged. Also, new mothers scored lower than women who were expecting babies but who had not yet given birth.

Further support for Stewart's method and theory come from longitudinal studies that followed five groups of subjects over time: children beginning school, new junior and senior high school students, beginning college students, newlyweds, and new parents (Stewart et al., 1986). Each subject told or wrote an imaginative story in response to a picture at two different times: once immediately after the given transition (such as entering school or getting married) and again 1–2 years later. The results in Table 3.6 show that, in all of the groups except new

Continued on p. 165

Feature 3.B

The Authoritarian Personality

Deeply troubled by the rise of Nazi fascism in Germany during the 1930s and 1940s, the psychoanalyst and social critic Erich Fromm (1941) identified an **authoritarian** character type prevalent among Western Europeans of the day, especially among the lower-middle classes in Germany. Authoritarian men and women sought desperately to *escape from the freedom* that modern capitalist societies afforded them, by striving to idealize authority and by yearning to pledge unqualified allegiance to those in power above *and* to receive the same allegiance from those below. Fromm believed that the authoritarian character structure was partly responsible for Hitler's fateful domination of German politics. Historical and economic conditions had conspired to create in the minds of the German people a readiness and a willingness to be dominated by powerful authority. This partly explains, argued Fromm, how an otherwise intelligent and sensible German populace could rally around such a ruthless tyrant and passively acquiesce to the Nazi programs of persecution, enslavement, and genocide.

Following up on some of Fromm's ideas, a group of eminent social scientists launched an ambitious study of authoritarianism among Americans, resulting in the publication of a landmark book, *The Authoritarian Personality* (Adorno, Frenkel-Brunswik, Levinson, & Sanford, 1950). Conducting extensive interviews of groups of American adults who indicated that they were highly prejudiced against Jews and other ethnic and religious minorities, the researchers developed a questionnaire, the California F [for "Fascism"] Scale, to measure authoritarianism. Authoritarianism was identified as a cluster of nine attitudes and traits, each tapped by certain items on the F Scale. The nine characteristics comprised a coherent personality syndrome or type:

1. *Conventionalism:* Rigid adherence to conventional, middle-class values.
2. *Authoritarian submission:* Uncritical attitude toward authority.
3. *Authoritarian aggression:* Tendency to be on the lookout for and to condemn or punish people who violate conventional values.
4. *Anti-intraception:* Opposition to imaginative and subjective aspects of life, to such things as art, literature, and psychology.
5. *Superstition and stereotypy:* The belief in mystical determinants of the individual's fate, and the tendency to think in rigid categories.
6. *Power and toughness:* Preoccupation with dominance and strength.
7. *Destructiveness and cynicism:* Generalized hostility toward people.
8. *Projectivity:* The disposition to believe that wild and dangerous things go on in the world; the projection outwards of unconscious emotional impulses.
9. *Sex:* Exaggerated concern with sexual "goings on."

Heavily influenced by psychoanalytic theory, the authors of *The Authoritarian Personality* argued that authoritarianism had its roots in a complex web of family dynamics. In essence, a highly repressive family environment sows the seeds for the development of authoritarianism. The child represses strong biological impulses because of an overly punitive environment, ultimately projecting those impulses onto others in a defensive way. Parents who are emotionally distant and highly punitive fail to provide appropriate models for healthy identification, stunting ego development in the child and keeping the superego from being fully integrated into the personality. A pervasive sense of personal weakness and dependency on others, and perhaps a latent homosexuality in men, may further underlie the authoritarian syndrome.

Hundreds of empirical studies have been done on the authoritarian personality, most employing the original F Scale. A substantial body of research suggests positive relationships between authoritarianism, as assessed on the F Scale, and a number of attitudinal variables, such as rigidity in thinking, extremely conservative political values, anti-Semitism, distrust of outsiders, and highly punitive attitudes towards criminals and other deviants. Authoritarianism is negatively associated with intelligence, educational level, and socioeconomic status (Byrne & Kelley, 1981; Dillehay, 1978).

Criticisms, however, have been levied against the original conceptualization of the authoritarian personality and the questionnaire used to measure it (Christie & Jahoda, 1954). Many have taken issue with the authors' assumption that authoritarianism is associated with the American political right wing, arguing strongly that the same kind of attitudes and traits can be found among political leftists (Rothman & Lichter, 1982; Shils, 1954). Others have sharply criticized the F Scale as a poorly constructed test (Peabody, 1966). And some have doubted seriously the F Scale's ability to predict actual authoritarian behavior (Titus & Hollander, 1957). Recently, Heaven (1985) developed a new questionnaire designed to measure authoritarianism in more behavioral terms. Heaven's 35-item scale is written in much more contemporary language than is the original F Scale and embodies a number of good test-construction conventions that the F Scale neglected. Heaven's scale boils authoritarianism down into four basic behavioral characteristics: dominance/leadership, strong concern for achievement, interpersonal conflict, and verbal hostility.

Authoritarianism may also be viewed as a characteristic of a particular societal ethos. Sales (1973) has shown that authoritarian attitudes in society tend to rise during periods of threat. Reviewing statistics on personal incomes, crime rates, work stoppages, unemployment, bombing incidents,

Feature 3.B

and other indicators of economic, political, and social threat, Doty, Peterson, and Winter (1991) distinguished between two recent periods of U.S. history: 1978–82 as a "high-threat" period and 1983–87 as a "low-threat" period. They found that various societal indices of authoritarianism manifested themselves at much higher levels during the high-threat period. Especially notable in the study was the authors' survey of such intriguing indices of societal authoritarianism as increased activity on the part of the Ku Klux Klan, increased number of anti-Semitic incidents, increased interest in astrology (authoritarianism is linked to superstition and fantastical explanations for human conduct), increased number of boxing matches, increased support for capital punishment, increased sales of strong and powerful "attack" dogs (e.g., German shepherds), increases in aggressive imagery on television shows, and *decreasing* interest in psychology and psychotherapy (anti-intraception).

 Table 3.6

Mean Scores on Stages of Adaptation Following a Major Life Transition

Group	n	Time 1 (Immediately After Transition)	Time 2 (1–2 Years Later)	Statistically Significant Change
1. Children beginning school	26	2.08	2.85	Yes
2. Junior & Senior high school				
Males	34	2.59	3.00	No
Females	36	2.19	3.14	Yes
3. Adolescents beginning college				
Males	20	2.30	3.15	Yes
Females	56	2.46	2.50	No
4. Adults beginning marriage				
Males	19	1.95	2.58	Yes
Females	21	2.05	2.48	Yes
5. Adults becoming parents				
Males	23	2.35	2.35	No
Females	30	2.17	2.50	No

Note: Adaptation stage scores determined from analysis of imaginative stories.
From Stewart, Sokol, Healy, & Chester (1986, p. 148).

Continued from p. 161
parents, scores increased over time. In other words, the subjects made up stories indicative of lower or earlier adaptive themes immediately after the life transition, but showing higher or later adaptive themes a year or two later.

In sum, researchers have found Freud's conception of psychosexual stages to be useful in two ways. First, a modest amount of empirical support has been garnered for the existence of oral-dependent and anal-retentive personality types in adulthood, though they do not appear to be the adult outcomes of childhood oral and anal experiences. Second, Freud's psychosexual scheme may be viewed as a general model for adaptation to life changes. Research employing the Thematic Apperception Test suggests that when faced with major life transitions persons tend to cycle through a sequence of socio-emotional stances—from passive, to autonomous, assertive, and integrated—that bears thematic similarity to the psychosexual sequence of oral, anal, phallic, and genital stages.

Internalized Objects

A major development in the psychoanalytic tradition since the death of Freud has been the emergence of object-relations approaches to personality. The central propositions in object-relations theories came from the observations of clinicians who began to see that Freud's ideas concerning instinctual drives and neurotic symptoms were not sufficient to explain the problems their patients encountered. Drew Westen (1991a) provides a concise account of how this theoretical development began in clinical work:

> Interest in object relations grew as clinicians began confronting patients whose pathology was manifest interpersonally and appeared more pervasive and pernicious than simple neurotic symptoms such as phobias and compulsions. These patients have difficulty trusting other people and are often either disengaged socially or erratically engaged (e.g., jumping into relationships too quickly and then becoming enraged or suicidal when the other person is, inevitably, ungratifying or fails to meet overly idealized expectations). In addition, such patients have difficulty maintaining a cohesive sense of self and an investment in ideals and values over time. Clinically, these various interpersonal difficulties manifest in a tumultuous therapeutic relationship, in which patients may accuse the therapist of intending to abuse or destroy them, expect the therapist to be available at all hours of the day or night, withdraw suddenly from the relationship because of a peculiar or malevolent attribution, or alternate among such patterns. Whereas classical psychoanalytic theory understood neurotic symptoms as maladaptive compromises among conflicting motive systems, object-relations theorists hypothesized that these interpersonally troubled, character-disordered

patients manifested a "basic fault" in their experience of self and others that began in the first years of life in the relation between infant and primary caregiver. (pp. 430–431)

As we saw in Chapter 2, object-relations theories focus on the quality of early parent-child relations and the *internalized objects* or mental representations of significant others that result from early interaction, providing the maturing self with organization and structure. According to object-relations theories, we formulate unconscious representations of the most important people in our lives, and these representations influence how we carry on all of our interpersonal relationships. Most object-relations theories contend, furthermore, that as we mature, our mental representations of others become more articulated and differentiated (Blatt & Lerner, 1983; Urist, 1977; Westen, 1991a). With maturity, internalized objects should become richer, more detailed, and more individuated, as we continue to apprehend ourselves, our objects, and our relationships with our objects in more complex and sophisticated terms.

Empirical research on internalized objects has relied mainly on projective tests like the Rorschach and the TAT. Sydney Blatt (Blatt, Brenneis, Schimek, & Glick, 1976; Blatt & Lerner, 1983) has developed a method for analyzing responses to the Rorschach in terms of the maturity of object representations. The most mature object representations are highly *articulated* (having a great deal of detail), portray *active* persons who behave according to internalized *intentions,* and suggest a *benevolent* rather than malevolent orientation toward others. Assuming that persons project the qualities of their internalized objects onto the inkblots, Blatt scores "human" responses to the blots in terms of articulation, the quality of action, and malevolence-benevolence. In addition, the responses are scored for degree of differentiation revealed. The most differentiated (and mature) human response would be the perception of an entire, intact human being, as when the person sees in the blot a baby, an old man, two people dancing, or any other full human figure(s). Less differentiated and mature are quasi-human responses such as monsters, elves, ghosts, and other "almost human" figures. Lower still in differentiation are human detail responses, in which the person sees a human body part, such as a human hand or nose. At the bottom of the developmental scale (least differentiated, least mature) are quasi-human details, such as body parts of quasi-humans—a leprechaun's feet, the guts of a gargoyle, etc.

Blatt contends that the psychologically healthy and interpersonally secure person should perceive a greater preponderance of well-articulated human figures engaged in positive, benevolent actions on the Rorschach than should the neurotic and immature individual, whose stunted development in object relations is manifested in a greater number of human detail responses. Unable to apprehend others as independent and whole persons, the immature or disturbed person conceives of the most important people in his or her life in the same way that he or she sees the Rorschach inkblots: as threatening and dismembered parts, scattered one-dimensional pieces that cannot be put together into meaningful wholes.

Blatt's method for scoring the Rorschach has proven especially valuable in research into psychopathology. A number of studies have shown a significant relationship between maturity in object relations on the Rorschach and degree of severity in psychopathology (Blatt et al., 1976; Lerner & Peter, 1984; Ritzler, Zambianco, Harder, & Kaskey, 1980; Spear & Lapidus, 1981). In these studies, psychiatric patients with a greater level of impairment, such as hospitalized schizophrenics, show markedly lower levels of full human and quasi-human responses than less-impaired patients, such as neurotic outpatients. Blatt and his colleagues (1976) also examined longitudinal data provided by 37 normal subjects administered the Rorschach at ages 11–12, 13–14, 17–18, and 30. Over the 20-year period, the subjects showed a marked increase in the number of well-differentiated, highly articulated, and integrated human figures. The results suggest that object relations continue to develop and mature between early adolescence and adulthood.

Westen (1991b) has developed a measure of object relations for coding imaginative stories told or written in response to TAT pictures. Each story is evaluated in terms of four dimensions. The first dimension is *complexity of representations of people,* and it measures the extent to which the storywriter clearly differentiates the perspectives of self and other, sees the self and other as having stable and enduring dispositions, and sees the self and other as psychological beings with complex motives and subjective experience. The second dimension— *affect tone of relationship paradigms*—measures the emotional quality of people and relationships in the story, focusing on what the storywriter appears to expect of people in the world and the extent to which relationships may be viewed in benevolent or malevolent ways. *Capacity for emotional investment* measures the extent to which the storywriter portrays a world in which people are treated as ends rather than means, events are regarded in terms of others' needs rather than one's own, and moral standards are developed or considered. The fourth dimension is *understanding social causality,* and it measures the extent to which the storywriter's attributions about the causes of people's actions, thoughts, and feelings are logical, accurate, complex, and psychologically sophisticated. As shown in Table 3.7, each of the four dimensions may be scored in terms of five developmental levels, with Level 1 representing the most primitive and immature forms of object relations and Level 5 representing the most mature.

Westen's method for measuring object representations in imaginative stories would appear to be a very promising new tool for psychoanalytic, hypothesis-testing research. Recent studies support its validity when employed with clinical and nonclinical populations (Barrends, Westen, Leigh, Byers, & Silbert, 1990; Leigh, Westen, Barrends, & Mendel, in press; Westen, Klepfer, Ruffins, Silverman, Lifton, & Boekamp, in press; Westen, Lohr, Silk, Gold, & Gerber, 1990; Westen, Ludolph, Silk, Kellam, Gold, & Lohr, 1990). The object-relations scores obtained from the TAT stories tend to match fairly well ratings of object relations made from interview data on the same subjects. The TAT scales also correlate in predictable ways with measures of object relations taken from individuals' free descriptions of important people in their lives. Scores on three of the four scales

Table 3.7

Five Levels of Object Relations

Complexity of Representations of People	Affect Tone of Relationship Paradigms	Capacity for Emotional Investment	Understanding of Social Causality
Level 1			
People are not clearly differentiated; confusion of points of view.	Malevolent representations; gratuitous violence or gross negligence by significant others.	Need-gratifying orientation profound self-preoccupation.	Noncausal or grossly illogical depictions of psychological and interpersonal events.
Level 2			
Simple, unidimensional representations; focus on actions; traits are global and univalent.	Representation of relationships as hostile, empty, or capricious but not profoundly malevolent; profound loneliness or disappointment in relationships.	Limited investment in people, relationships, and moral standards; conflicting interests recognized, but gratification remains primary aim; moral standards immature and unintegrated or followed to avoid punishment.	Rudimentary understanding of social causality; minor logic errors or unexplained transitions; simple stimulus-response causality.
Level 3			
Minor elaboration of mental life or personality.	Mixed representations with mildly negative tone.	Conventional investment in people and moral standards;	Complex, accurate situational causality and rudimentary

Level 4	Expanded appreciation of complexity of subjective experience and personality dispositions; absence of representations integrating life history, complex subjectivity, and personality processes.	Mixed representations with neutral or balanced tone.	stereotypic compassion. mutuality, or helping orientation; guilt at moral transgressions.	understanding of the role of thoughts and feelings in mediating action. Expanded appreciation of the role of mental processes in generating thoughts, feelings, behaviors, and interpersonal interactions.
Level 5	Complex representations, indicating understanding of interaction of enduring and momentary psychological experience; understanding of personality as system of processes interacting with each other and the environment.	Predominantly positive representations; benign and enriching interactions.	Autonomous selfhood in the context of committed relationships; recognition of conventional nature of moral rules in the context of carefully considered standards or concern for concrete people or relationships.	Complex appreciation of the role of mental processes in generating thoughts, feelings, behaviors, and interpersonal interactions; understanding of unconscious motivational processes.

From Westen (1991a), p. 447.

(complexity, emotional investment, and social causality) have been shown to increase developmentally through late adolescence, whereas affective tone scores do not follow any predictable developmental pattern.

Finally, object-relations scores on the TAT differentiate among diagnostic groups in clinical settings. Compared to "normal" and "depressed" adolescents and adults, "borderline" patients reveal an especially aberrant quality of object relations on the TAT. The term "borderline" designates a particular diagnostic group characterized by serious impairment in interpersonal relationships, bordering on psychosis. In two studies employing Westen's system for coding object relations on the TAT, borderlines tended to represent people in highly malevolent and need-gratifying terms and in idiosyncratic ways that were sometimes too primitive and sometimes too advanced given the context of the story told. Of the three groups studied, borderlines showed the most seriously disturbed object representations in their TAT stories.

In sum, recent developments in coding Rorschach and TAT responses for the quality of object representations have paved the way for empirical research into the highly influential object-relations theories proposed since the time of Freud. Research supports the utility of viewing object relations in developmental terms, ranging from primitive and immature levels to mature stages in which internalized object representations are highly differentiated, articulated, and viewed in benevolent terms. It would appear that persons who develop mature object representations are advantaged as well in the areas of overall psychological adjustment and well-being.

Jung's Types

With its emphasis on myth, symbol, individuation, and the collective unconscious, Jung's theory of personality has been viewed by some as too esoteric and mystical to be subjected to rigorous hypothesis-testing research. In particular, the key Jungian concept of the *archetype* would appear to be an extremely difficult idea to operationalize in an experiment or correlational study. However, certain Jungian ideas have been examined in an empirical manner. Most significantly, a number of researchers have employed a popular self-report questionnaire, entitled the **Myers–Briggs Type Indicator** (MBTI: Myers, 1962; Myers & McCaulley, 1985), to study individual differences in Jungian types. The MBTI is widely used in industry, business, and education. An estimated two million people took the test in 1990 alone (Thorne & Gough, 1991).

The MBTI enables the researcher to classify the person into one of 16 possible personality types. The 16 represent all possible combinations of four bipolar scales: extraversion vs. introversion, thinking vs. feeling, sensing vs. intuiting, and perceiving vs. judging. As we saw in Chapter 2, Jung considered extraversion and introversion to be the two basic attitudes in personality and he considered thinking, feeling, sensing, and intuiting to be the four basic functions. The MBTI adds two more functions: perceiving (tending toward sensual and artistic experiences, preferring spontaneity, nonconforming) and judging (tending towards moral evaluations, preferring structure and organization, rule-governed).

Classifying adults with the MBTI, Carlson (1980) documented interesting relationships between Jungian personality types and personal memories. The participants in her study were asked to describe their most vivid personal experiences of several emotions, such as joy, excitement, and shame. Table 3.8 summarizes some of the memories recalled by introvert–thinking (IT) and extravert–feeling (EF) types. Carlson found that IT types tended to recall emotionally neutral, factual memories about private or nonsocial experiences, whereas EF types underscored personal feelings and the affective quality of highly interpersonal or social events. In addition, Carlson tested the validity of the sensing/intuiting dimension by asking the subjects to write a letter introducing themselves to an imaginary pen pal. Most sensing types (whether extravert or introvert) began their letters with detailed factual descriptions of themselves, in keeping with Jung's contention that sensing types focus on realistic and concrete facts. Intuiting types, on the other hand, often made reference to presumed common interests with the unknown correspondent, going beyond the known facts of the situation to speculate on possibilities in a relationship. The finding illustrates the "theoretically important difference between the intuitive's engagement in possibilities and the sensing type's command of realities" (p. 808).

Cann and Donderi (1986) examined the relationship between Jungian types assessed on the Myers–Briggs and the content of dreams. A sample of 30 volunteers (average age = 32 years) kept dream diaries over a period of 3 to 4 weeks. Each subject was asked to make a written record of all the dreams that he or she could remember on awakening each morning. The researchers analyzed each of the 384 dreams collected for the extent to which they expressed archetypal content. They decided that a highly archetypal dream should express heightened emotion, the presence of a mythological parallel, irrationality, or uniqueness. Nonarchetypal dreams, on the other hand, should have an everyday, mundane quality to them. Cann and Donderi found that approximately one-fourth of the dreams collected could be considered archetypal. Furthermore, individuals who scored high on the intuiting dimension of the Myers–Briggs reported a greater number of archetypal dreams than individuals scoring high on the opposite end, sensing. No differences between intuitive types and sensing types were observed, however, on the number of overall dreams recalled. Therefore, intuitive types do not appear to dream more often than do sensing types, but they do appear to draw more deeply from the collective unconscious in their dreams. The finding supports Jung's contention that intuitive types are in closer contact with the unconscious and subliminal aspects of life whereas sensing types focus on everyday facts observed through the senses.

In their recent book, *Portraits of Type,* Thorne and Gough (1991) summarize their analyses of MBTI data collected on 240 women and 374 men at the University of California's Institute for Personality Assessment and Research between the years 1956 and 1984. Ranging in age from 19 to 70 years, the participants were drawn from architects, members of an architectural firm, student writers,

Continued on p. 176

Feature 3.C

Falling in Love With the Self: The Problem of Narcissism

In the ancient Greek legend, the beautiful boy Narcissus falls so completely in love with the reflection of himself in a pool that he plunges into the pool and drowns. If we are to believe a number of contemporary journalists, psychologists, and social critics, something very much like the fate of Narcissus is happening all around us today. Contemporary American society is a "culture of narcissism," writes Christopher Lasch (1979). The ethic of the "me generation" encourages us all to love ourselves first and foremost, to seek, develop, perfect, and master *the self*. As a result, many of us are incapable of mature love for and commitment to others and are unwilling to devote ourselves to pursuits that transcend our own selfish concerns, to social institutions and communities that have traditionally integrated individuals within society (Bellah, Madsen, Sullivan, Swidler, & Tipton, 1985). In the eyes of the popular press, the modern-day American "Yuppie"—the young, upwardly mobile, urban professional—stands as the perfect example of the contemporary narcissist, obsessed with perfecting his body at the health club, desperately trying to "be all that she can be," "born to buy" and to accumulate both high-priced possessions and exotic personal experiences. Popular novels such as Jay McInerney's (1984) *Bright Lights, Big City* and Louis Auchincloss's (1986) *Diary of a Yuppie* dramatize what many observers believe to be a serious social problem among those between the ages of about 25 and 45 who are well-educated and well-off.

A number of prominent psychoanalysts consider **narcissism** to be the prototypical pathology of our time, rendering the "narcissistic personality disorder" one of the most popular and talked-about clinical syndromes of the 1980s and 90s. Psychoanalysts tend to regard pathological narcissism as a product of *faulty object relations* in the early years of life (Kernberg, 1976, 1980; Kohut, 1971). According to Kernberg, narcissism develops out of parental abandonment and rejection. Because of cold and rejecting parents, the child defensively withdraws from others and comes to believe that it is only him- or herself that can be trusted and relied on and therefore loved. According to Kohut, pathological narcissism results from the child's failure to idealize the parents due to their rejection or indifference. The high-tech, consumer society in which we live reinforces the narcissistic tendencies cultivated in early childhood, providing us with a thousand and one narcissistic delights—spectacular sound and video systems, luxurious vacation getaways, prime-time sex, recreational drugs—all at our fingertips, provided we have the money to pay for the delights.

Extreme narcissism includes (1) a grandiose sense of self-importance and uniqueness, (2) preoccupation with fantasies of unlimited success, power, beauty, or ideal love, (3) the need for constant attention and admiration, (4) expectation of special favors without reciprocation, and (5) interpersonal exploitiveness (American Psychiatric Association, 1980). Using this definition as their guideline, Raskin and Hall (1979, 1981) constructed a questionnaire designed to measure narcissism as a personality trait present in varying amounts in relatively normal people. The Narcissistic Personality Inventory (NPI) includes 54 pairs of items. For each pair, the subject chooses the one item that he or she agrees with more. Here are some examples of items that score for narcissism:

I really like to be the center of attention.
I have a natural talent for influencing people.
I like to look at my body.
I think I am a special person.
Everybody likes to hear my stories.
I insist on the respect that is due to me.
I will never be satisfied until I get all that I deserve.

The NPI taps four dimensions of narcissism: exploitiveness/entitlement, superiority, leadership, and self-absorption. It is the first of these four factors—exploitiveness/entitlement—that is believed to be associated with psychological maladjustment Exploitiveness/entitlement is associated with anxiety, depression, and lack of empathy for others (Emmons, 1984; Watson, Grisham, Trotter, & Biderman, 1984). In general, males score significantly higher on all four dimensions of narcissism than do females.

Raskin and Shaw (1988) found that students scoring high on narcissism tended to use significantly more first-person singular pronouns (*I, me, my*) in spontaneous speech. Emmons (1984) found that narcissism is positively associated with other measures of dominance, exhibitionism, and self-esteem, and negatively associated with deference towards others. Narcissism has also been linked to extreme mood swings and intensity of emotional experience in daily life (Emmons, 1987). With respect to this last finding, it is believed that the narcissist's superficial smugness masks a deeper insecurity and narcissistic vulnerability (Kernberg, 1980). Narcissists may be more sensitive to both success and failure experiences than are most other people, experiencing intense joy when the self is uplifted with success but devastating depression in the wake of even minor setbacks.

Recently, Wink (1991, 1992a, 1992b) has distinguished among three types of narcissism observable in *women* studied over time. The *hypersensitive* narcissists display a "covert" quality of narcissism that is linked to feelings of vulnerability, hostility, and depression. In Wink's longitudinal study, women who had high scores on hypersensitivity at age 43 were characterized by a downward spiral in their fortunes and resources during their 20s and 30s and by a lack of success either in a career or as a homemaker. The *willful* narcissists, by contrast, exhibit an "overt" quality of narcissism. From college days through midlife, they were consistently described as self-assured, grandiose, and exhibitionistic. Finally, the *autonomous* narcissists express a healthy form of narcissism. They were described at age 43 as creative, empathic, achievement-oriented, and individualistic. Following conflict in their 20s, the autonomous women experienced substantial personality growth into midlife. Hypersensitivity and willfulness, but not autonomy, were associated with evidence of troubled childhood relations with parents, particularly with mothers. In addition, willfulness was associated with early identification with a willful father.

 Table 3.8

Personal Memories Reported by Introvert–Thinking (IT) and Extravert–Feeling (EF) Types

	IT	EF
Experiences of joy	Receiving desirable part-time job. Graduating from junior college. Shooting his first rabbit.	Watching husband play with granddaughter. Meeting boyfriend in group attending Rose Parade. Chosen most popular counselor at church camp.
Experiences of excitement	Anticipating trip to San Francisco. Attending performance of *Die Meistersinger*. Beginning job in program for mentally retarded.	Cheering for friend at cross-country track meet. Helping cat have kittens, phoning husband on "progress." Attending Johnny Mathis concert with boyfriend.
Experiences of shame	Drinks too much, becomes "too candid" at a party. Steals a quarter, skips school; is reprimanded. Discovers he should have paid for coffee "refills."	Being punished, fights back and scratches mother. Unaware of dress code, wears wrong skirt to school. With friend, is arrested for shoplifting.

From Carlson (1980, pp. 804–805).

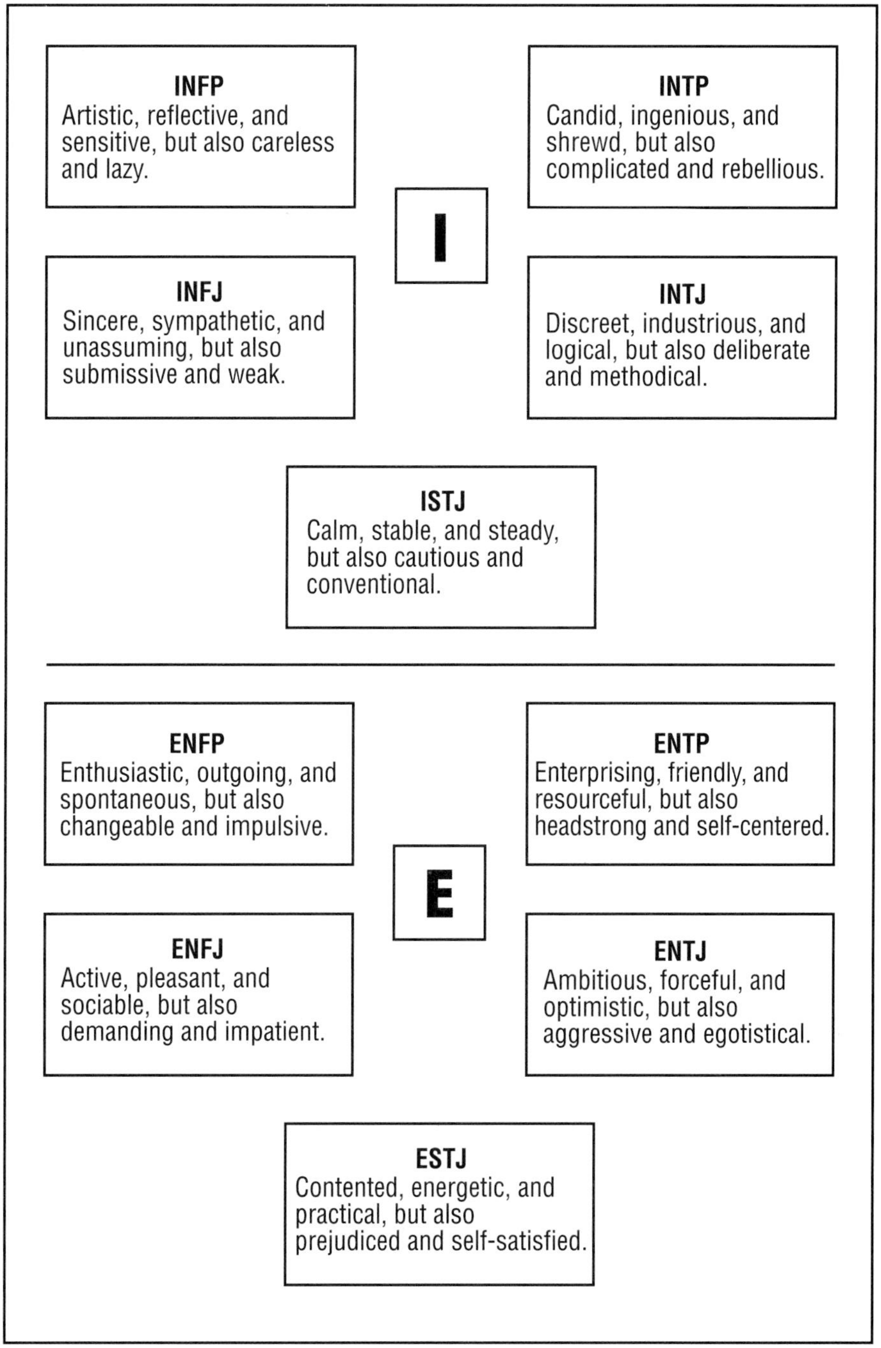

INFP
Artistic, reflective, and sensitive, but also careless and lazy.

INTP
Candid, ingenious, and shrewd, but also complicated and rebellious.

INFJ
Sincere, sympathetic, and unassuming, but also submissive and weak.

INTJ
Discreet, industrious, and logical, but also deliberate and methodical.

ISTJ
Calm, stable, and steady, but also cautious and conventional.

ENFP
Enthusiastic, outgoing, and spontaneous, but also changeable and impulsive.

ENTP
Enterprising, friendly, and resourceful, but also headstrong and self-centered.

ENFJ
Active, pleasant, and sociable, but also demanding and impatient.

ENTJ
Ambitious, forceful, and optimistic, but also aggressive and egotistical.

ESTJ
Contented, energetic, and practical, but also prejudiced and self-satisfied.

Figure 3.6

Summary of Observed Personality Features of 10 Types (modeled after Jung) Assessed on the Myers-Briggs Type Indicator.

From Thorne & Gough, 1991, p. 102.

Continued from p. 171
research scientists, mathematicians, engineering students, medical school students, law school students, college seniors and sophomores, Irish business executives, and selected residents of Marin County, California. Many of the participants were chosen for studies of creative potential. In addition to the MBTI, a wide range of tests and interviews was administered to the subjects in these studies, and psychologists made ratings of the subjects on many different personality dimensions.

Thorne and Gough show that many of the types that are derived from the MBTI provide valid and useful descriptions of how people behave and experience their worlds. For example, people who score relatively high on the dimensions of introversion (I), intuition (N), feeling (F), and perceiving (P) (the INFP type) are described by observers as especially artistic, reflective, and sensitive, but tending toward laziness and carelessness. By contrast, people high on extraversion (E), sensing (S), thinking (T), and judging (J) (the ESTJ type) are described by others as especially contented, energetic, and practical, but they also tend to be viewed as prejudiced and overly self-satisfied. Figure 3.6 summarizes findings on ten different Jungian types. As you can see, no single type is "ideal." All have their strengths and weaknesses.

Summary for Chapter 3

1. Scientific work on psychoanalytic concepts may be viewed from two complementary perspectives: the context of discovery, wherein psychoanalysts have employed unique frameworks of interpretation to make sense of dreams, symptoms, and so on in order to derive concepts and hypotheses, and the context of justification, through which psychoanalytically oriented researchers have tested the viability of hypotheses derived from Freudian, Jungian, and other psychoanalytic theories.

2. As an example of psychoanalytic interpretation in the context of discovery, Freud's case of Dora ties together themes of oedipal rivalry and revenge, fantasized incest, masturbation, bedwetting, and obsessive concerns about cleanliness.

3. Despite many flaws, the Dora case illustrates a number of basic principles of psychoanalytic interpretation. In the psychoanalytic view, every piece of significant behavior is like a text, which may be interpreted on many different levels, and like a treaty, which represents a compromise among conflicting forces.

4. Dreams, slips of the tongue, symptoms, and other aspects of behavior may be seen as manifest results of latent conflicts and issues, according to Freud. The psychoanalyst must look beyond the manifest to explore the latent domain.

5. The reverse process—moving from latent to manifest—is the spontaneous action of creating a dream, a slip of the tongue, symptom, or other piece of behavior—a synthetic process that must be taken apart carefully in psychoanalysis.

6. Jungian methods of interpreting dreams suggest that these experiences are symbolic expressions of universal myths, anticipations of life problems for the future, and indices of the striving for balance in personality.

7. In recent years, the concept of the unconscious has received a great deal of research attention among cognitive psychologists and personologists. Research suggests that a great deal of human information processing takes place outside the domain of conscious awareness, including nonconscious or "implicit" memory, perception, thought, and learning.

8. Research supports the notion that some people are more prone to repression than others. Repressors tend to have less access to emotionally negative memories than nonrepressors, perhaps because repressors cordon off negative memories in such a way as to keep threatening information isolated from their central self-conception.

9. Employing the Psychodynamic Activation Method, researchers have documented modest but interesting effects from eliciting unconscious fantasies associated with psychoanalytic themes through the presentation of subliminal stimuli. While controversial, the research tends to support Freud's conception of a *dynamic* unconscious.

10. Research on defense mechanisms supports the psychoanalytic claim that such ego strategies may be arranged on a developmental continuum. Among children, age-appropriate defenses are associated with more effective coping; among adults, more mature defenses are associated with psychosocial adaptation.

11. Modest empirical support exists for the oral-dependent and anal-retentive personality types as coherent clusters of personality characteristics among adults, though the developmental origins of such clusters remain unknown. Coding a person's imaginative stories for oral, anal, phallic, and genital themes provides empirical support for a four-step model of socio-emotional adaptation, through which individuals cycle when facing major life transitions.

12. Recent developments in coding Rorschach and TAT responses for the quality of object representations have paved the way for empirical research into object-relations theories. Research supports the utility of viewing object relations in developmental terms, ranging from primitive and immature levels to mature stages in which internalized object representations are highly differentiated, articulated, and viewed in benevolent terms.

13. Research employing the Myers–Briggs Type Indicator supports the validity of Jung's descriptions of various personality types, organized along the lines of extraversion vs. introversion, thinking vs. feeling, sensing vs. intuiting, and perceiving vs. judging.

Chapter 4

Evolution and Human Nature

Introduction

Instinct and Evolution
Instinctive Behavior in Animals
Human Evolution
Sociobiology and the Person
Evolutionary Personality Psychology
Mating
  Feature 4.A: Some Women (and Men) Are Choosier Than Others:
  Sociosexuality
Socioanalytic Theory and the Problem of Shyness

Aggression Versus Altruism
Hurting Others
Helping Others

The Evolution of Love: Attachment Theory
Attachment in Infancy
Secure and Insecure Attachments
Adult Attachments

Summary

Winner of the 1985 Nobel Prize for Literature, William Golding, painted a dark and frightening picture of human nature in his famous first novel, *Lord of the Flies* (Golding, 1962). In Golding's story, English schoolboys find themselves marooned on a deserted island after a plane crash during their evacuation from their homes in an atomic war. One of the older boys, Ralph, assembles all of the children and organizes a primitive society dedicated to securing their ultimate rescue. The boys establish rules and build a fire to signal passing ships and planes of their presence on the island. Ralph's society soon begins to fall apart, however, as many of the boys desert him to join Jack's rival group, dedicated to fun and feasting, to power and its ceremonies, to hunting pigs and sacrificing to the "beast," and to all of the pleasures and terrors of savagery. Jack rallies most of the children to his side, leading them on hunts in which they scream in unison, "Kill the pig! Bash his head! Run him in!" As the story progresses, the boys become increasingly intoxicated with aggression and cruelty. Killing pigs leads to killing each other, first in the spontaneous and unwitting slaughter of Simon, the kindest and gentlest of the boys, and then with ruthless premeditation in the murder of Piggy, a fat and rather intellectual boy who wears glasses. With the death of Piggy—the only boy who repeatedly insists that the children try to be "rational" and "civilized"—all vestiges of rational civilization disappear from the island. Ultimately, the children declare war on Ralph, who by now has become something of a beast himself as he realizes that "the desire to squeeze and hurt is overmastering" (p. 136). Under Jack's leadership, the children hunt Ralph down and set the island on fire. A nearby ship sights the smoke and fire and "rescues" the boys, whisking them back to England to face the reality of an adult war waged on a much grander scale.

Golding's innocent English schoolboys become frenzied murderers when transported to a natural setting and left to their own devices to survive. There is no beast stalking the island, concludes Simon, shortly before his death: *"It's only us"* (p. 103). The "beast" within each of the boys transforms him into a warmonger. Golding urges us to ask: Is there a "beast" within each of us? Many popular writings would suggest so. Books like *The Naked Ape* (Morris, 1967) and *The Social Contract* (Ardrey, 1970) made a large splash in the 1970s by arguing that human beings are explosive beasts by nature and that the psychological roots of human warfare lie within the aggressive souls of men. The arguments were consonant with Freud's concept of the death instinct (Chapter 2), which allegedly predisposes us to kill each other, to hurt and to maim, and to engage in aggressive fantasies and live out aggressive dreams. But whereas Freud based his speculations about human aggressiveness on clinical observation and his theory of human drives, other authors have more explicitly justified their conclusions in terms of human evolution. The violence inflicted by primitive hunters and gatherers over 10,000 years ago shares an origin with modern warfare today— both result from the chilling fact, some have argued, that it is part of human nature to kill. We are all potential warmongers by virtue of our evolutionary heritage.

The topic of aggression provides an entree into evolutionary personality psychology. In recent years, a growing number of personality psychologists have staked out new positions in understanding the person that emphasize instinctive behavior, human evolution, and the biological bases of social behavior. These new positions share with Freud and the psychoanalytic tradition a general belief that behavior is motivated by instinctual forces over which the individual may have but modest control. In addition, these forces may reside outside everyday consciousness in the sense that most people are not fully aware of the extent to which they behave in accord with the mandates of human evolution. In order to explore the intrapsychic mysteries that lie at the center of human nature, however, we must look not to dreams and unconscious fantasies but to social behavior in the animal kingdom and to certain features of human social behavior that appear in cultures around the world. What we will find is that human beings may indeed be warmongers. But evolution may have also prepared us well for cooperative social behavior, acts of altruism, and tender care. The beast may lie within, but he is joined by the altruist and the lover.

Instinct and Evolution

Instinctive Behavior in Animals

Much of what we know about instinctive behavior in the animal kingdom stems from the pioneering efforts of Konrad Lorenz and Niko Tinbergen who, in the 1930s, established the discipline of **ethology,** the study of the adaptive behavior of species in natural surroundings. Ethologists study animal behavior via **naturalistic observation,** carefully watching and cataloguing naturally occurring behavior patterns in the wild. Rather than bring animals into the laboratory for controlled experimentation, ethologists have traditionally observed animals in their natural habitats in order to compose **ethograms**—extensive and detailed descriptions of natural behavior observed over long periods of time. Comparing ethograms of different species, ethologists have identified a number of innate, or instinctive, behavior patterns in particular species.

Ethologists have traditionally agreed that a behavior pattern is innate if it is (1) observable in all or virtually all members of the species, (2) stereotyped in form across individuals of a species, (3) present without relevant previous experience that could have allowed it to be learned, and (4) relatively unchanged as a result of experience and learning after it is established (Cairns, 1979). One prominent form of instinctive behavior in many animals is the **fixed-action pattern (FAP),** which is defined as a biologically programmed sequence of coordinated

Social organization among mammals: a family of sprite monkeys.

behaviors. Examples of FAPs are courtship dances in some birds, web spinning in spiders, and attack rituals in certain fish. These behavior sequences appear to be carried out by the organism according to a relatively fixed biological program. A **sign stimulus** in the environment naturally sets into motion a series of actions that follows more or less the same form and course each time. Thus, the appearance of a rival male with a red belly triggers a stereotyped sequence of attack behaviors in the male stickleback fish. Indeed, FAPs may occasionally be acted out in the *absence* of a sign stimulus, a phenomenon termed *vacuum behavior*. For example, a starling raised in captivity will sometimes engage in complex sequences of mock hunting, killing, and even simulated eating of "prey." In a similar manner, caged female birds will sometimes go through the motions of building a nest, even though no material for making a nest is available in the cage.

FAPs are instinctive behavior patterns that are highly adaptive for the organism, often promoting successful feeding, mating, injury avoidance, or some other life-enhancing result (Eibl-Eibesfeldt, 1977). According to the traditional ethological explanation, FAPs are regulated by internal *drives* or *energy sources* (Lorenz, 1950; Tinbergen, 1951). Much like Freud's theory of libido, instinctual energy is thought to build up in the organism over time, to be released periodically in instinctive behavior.

Most modern-day ethologists, however, do not accept the traditional energy explanation for instinctive behavior. Given that nobody has been able to find or measure the hypothesized instinctual energy, most ethologists have abandoned Lorenz and Tinbergen's mechanical view of drives. In addition, modern ethologists tend to see certain instinctive behavior as highly flexible, suggesting that many "fixed" action patterns show great variability within the same organisms across different situations (Dewsbury, 1978). In addition to dictating precise behavior sequences in response to discrete sign stimuli, instincts may more generally "set boundaries or limits within which a good deal of variation may occur" (Breger, 1974, p. 24). Furthermore, instinctive behavior, especially in the higher mammals and primates, may be substantially modified and shaped by learning (Snowdon, 1983).

Modern instinct theories, therefore, suggest a complex biological picture for higher mammals, primates, and human beings. Rather than innate drives, blind urges, or inflexible blueprints, **instincts** are understood more generally as biologically rooted and adaptive *motivational tendencies,* giving rise to particular urges, emotions, and behavioral plans that can be influenced markedly by the environment (Breger, 1974; Feshbach & Weiner, 1986). Writes another ethological theorist, "the more complex forms of instinctive behaviour are regarded as resulting from the execution of plans that, depending on the species, are more or less flexible" (Bowlby, 1969, p. 18).

Classifying particular behaviors, therefore, as either "innate" or "learned" may be a mistake, argue some ethologists. Rather, animal and human behavior can more profitably be understood as ranging on a continuum from the most *environmentally stable* to the most *environmentally labile* behavior patterns. Behavior that falls toward the environmentally stable pole, such as certain of the most stereotyped FAPs in fish and birds, tends to be modified only minimally by changes in environment. Behavior falling toward the environmentally labile end, such as voting behavior in humans, tends to be easily influenced by the environment. Instincts set limits on environmental lability, restricting somewhat the environment's potential range of influence on a given behavior pattern and structuring the way in which a behavior pattern may be successfully enacted. In higher animals, and especially in human beings, instinctive behavior may be relatively flexible and responsive to environmental change—but biology still sets certain limits on just how flexible such behavior can be. The limits are mandated by the evolution of the particular species.

Human Evolution

It is difficult to overestimate the influence of evolutionary theory on the natural and social sciences. Presented to the world in its first systematic form in Charles Darwin's *On the Origin of Species* (1859), evolutionary theory has become a supreme framework or organizing view—what philosophers of science call a *paradigm* (Kuhn, 1962)—for understanding the nature of all life. Though specifics of the theory have changed over the years, the general principles set forth in

Darwin's classic manifesto have remained the same. Darwin argued that all existing living forms have evolved over time in response to their interactions with environments. Facing limited environmental resources for survival, organisms compete with each other, and ultimately the "fittest" survive.

The key to evolution over time is **natural selection,** a process whereby nature gradually selects those characteristics of organisms that promote survival. Darwin observed that organisms within a species manifest wide variation in physical and behavioral characteristics. Certain characteristics may promote the survival of the organism within the environment. Those organisms possessing the advantageous characteristic should live longer and produce more offspring than those organisms not possessing the characteristic. The offspring of those possessing the advantageous characteristic likewise should be more likely to possess the same advantageous characteristic, enabling them in turn to live longer and produce more offspring similarly equipped. In this way, nature selects, and causes to persist, the most adaptive characteristics in a species.

Darwin's vision of life on earth was and is a disquieting one, for it suggests that all organisms are ultimately beholden to the dispassionate whims of nature. Indeed, Darwin's vision is not unlike Freud's equally troubling view of human nature. Like Freud, Darwin implied that human behavior is ultimately determined by forces over which we have little control, identifying the forces as residing in the natural world and in our own deeply ingrained evolutionary heritage. Like Freud, Darwin underscored conflict in life, though he focused on the conflicts between different organisms (rather than within the single organism) and between organism and environment. And although Darwin did not address the issue of the unconscious, one would assume that he would be sympathetic to Freud's claim that human organisms are generally not aware of the ultimate forces controlling their destinies. There is ample evidence, furthermore, that Freud, writing after Darwin, was strongly influenced by evolutionary thought and admired Darwin's work greatly (Sulloway, 1979).

Although Darwin did not understand the precise mechanism for biological transmission of characteristics from parent to offspring, he did recognize that such transmission occurs. Today, we know that *genes* are responsible for the inheritance of characteristics. Genes are segments of chromosomes found in every cell in the body and are composed of deoxyribonucleic acid (DNA), a long threadlike molecule that is particularly well suited for passing on hereditary information.

Because sexual reproduction involves a mixing of parents' genes, an individual organism receives half of his or her genes from the biological mother and half from the biological father, thus inheriting characteristics from both. Through sexual reproduction, then, genes are passed down from one generation to the next. But in the transmission of genes, strange things occasionally occur. Genes may be transformed, generally by accident. Most changes make little or no difference in the organism's life, and what difference they do make may render the organism less fit. Sometimes, however, genetic mutations can make for accidental advantages, as when a transformation in the genes gives rise to a characteristic in the organism that promotes survival and success in adapting to the environment. Such naturally occurring alterations of genes over thousands of years can play a major role in the evolution of a given species.

Human evolution is a long saga of genetic recombination and alteration as individual organisms interact with their environments and struggle to survive. As Wilson (1978) puts it, "each living form can be viewed as an evolutionary experiment, a product of millions of years of interaction between genes and environment" (p. 17). One must, therefore, take "the long view" to understand the evolution of human beings. The long view tells us that for as much as 99% of our evolutionary history—indeed for at least 2 million years—we (our evolutionary ancestors) lived in small groups as hunters and gatherers (Kenrick, Montello, & McFarlane, 1985; Washburn & Lancaster, 1973). It has only been within the last 10,000 years that humans have taken up agriculture and within the last 4,000 years or so that they have built cities and become urbanites. Some human societies remain hunting-and-gathering societies to this day. Thus, human beings have evolved as successfully adapted to a nomadic way of life, moving in small groups from one domicile to another, hunting prey and gathering food in the wild. This does not mean that we are unable to adapt to other kinds of environments: obviously we have created and have adapted quite marvelously to a wide variety of agrarian, industrial, urban, and technological kinds of environments. But human evolution has selected genes that directly or indirectly promote adaptation to a way of life quite different from what most of us experience today.

Sociobiology and the Person

Return for a moment to the question with which we began this book: What is a person? Would your answer to the question be that *a person is only a gene's way of making another gene?* According to sociobiologists, this seemingly bizarre answer contains a precious kernel of truth, for the "movers and shakers" of human evolution, they claim, are not human organisms themselves but rather their genes. Genes are passed down from generation to generation; organisms serve as mere vehicles for the passing. To understand this claim, we need to know more about the controversial discipline of sociobiology.

Sociobiology is a relatively new field of scholarly inquiry that was launched in the 1970s with the publication of E. O. Wilson's *Sociobiology: A New Synthesis* (Wilson, 1975). Bringing together ethology, genetics, and ecology (the study of interactions between organisms and environments), sociobiology seeks to determine the biological bases of social behavior. The organizing framework is Darwinian evolution. Sociobiologists argue that much of animal behavior is strongly determined by the organism's genes, and that evolution selects out those genes that consistently confer upon their owners the greatest advantages in survival and reproduction. Human behavior, too, is strongly influenced by the individual's genetic endowment, although the greater complexity and flexibility of human life may mask these influences or render them more indirect and subtle.

A key concept in sociobiology is **genetic fitness.** A gene that increases genetic fitness enables the organism to do one or more of three things: (1) survive longer, (2) reproduce more, and (3) increase the survival and reproduction of biological relatives (such as parents, siblings, or children) who share some of the same genes (Wilson, 1978). A gene that decreases genetic fitness would do the reverse: shorten the organism's life, keep the organism from reproducing, and/or decrease the survival and reproduction of relatives.

If having a long neck enables a particular organism to survive longer in a given environment, to reproduce more, or to promote the survival and reproduction of its kin, then those genes implicated in the making of long necks are more likely to be passed down to the next generation. The passing down can occur not only through the organism's own sexual reproduction but also through the reproductive success of parents, children, siblings, or *others who share some of the same genes.* For example, I can pass my own genes down to the next generation either directly when I produce my own children or indirectly when my near relatives, who share many of my genes, produce their children. The sociobiological imperative is to pass down the genes, and whether I do it or my relatives do it is of little ultimate concern, since we have many genes in common. Therefore, I (like all other animals) am *biologically* programmed to engage in behaviors—whether of cooperation and sharing or of competition and conflict, depending on the situation—that maximize the likelihood that "my" genes will be passed down to the next generation either directly by me or indirectly by my near kin.

Although these claims about genes and persons may strike us as provocative, we generally do not find them too troubling when talking about long necks and other physical attributes. When it comes to human behavior, however, sociobiology is likely to bother and intrigue us more. Wilson claims that much of social behavior, indeed much of culture itself, is coded in the genes, existing as a complex and elaborate set of human symbols, products, institutions, and interactions designed ultimately to maximize the individual organism's genetic fitness. The evidence for this is circumstantial, consisting mostly of (1) observed similarities between human behavior and behavior in primates such as monkeys and apes (Wilson [1978, p. 31] calls chimpanzees our "little brother species") and (2) observed universals in human behavior across widely varying cultures. With respect to this second point, anthropologists have listed a large number of behavior patterns and societal customs that seem to be present in all known human societies. These include athletic sports, bodily adornment, cooperative labor, courtship, dancing, education systems, etiquette, family feasting, folklore, food taboos, funeral rites, games, gift giving, incest taboos, inheritance rites, law, marriage, medicine, penal sanctions, personal names, property rights, puberty customs, religious rituals, soul concepts, tool making, weaving, and attempts at weather control. Wilson argues that each of these universal patterns can be traced back to hunting-and-gathering societies, where they promoted individual survival and reproduction: "most and perhaps all of the . . . prevailing characteristics of modern societies can be identified as . . . modifications of the biologically meaningful institutions of hunter-gatherer bands and early tribal states" (1978, p. 92).

Given that these patterns proved adaptive for thousands, perhaps millions, of years, each has become part of human nature, coded in human genes.

As just one example of the sociobiological basis for complex human behavior, consider religion. Wilson (1978) states: "The predisposition to religious belief is the most complex and powerful force in the human mind and in all probability an ineradicable part of human nature" (p. 169). The power of religion today lies in the tremendous advantage it bestowed upon our evolutionary ancestors. Religion played a vital role in enabling hunters and gatherers to live together in bands and tribes. The shared beliefs and feelings of kinship engendered by religion helped persuade individuals to subordinate their immediate self-interests to the interests of the group. Such subordination promoted cooperative behavior in the acquisition of resources and defense against dangers, which increased the genetic fitness of tribe members, as they were better able to reproduce and care for their kin. In addition, religion has always provided human beings with transcendent assurances in the face of the chaos of everyday life, and this too may enhance genetic fitness. Wilson writes:

> The highest forms of religious practice, when examined more closely, can be seen to confer biological advantage. Above all they congeal identity. In the midst of the chaotic and potentially disorienting experiences each person undergoes daily, religion classifies him, provides him with unquestioned membership in a group claiming great powers, and by this means gives him a driving purpose in life compatible with his self-interest. His strength is the strength of the group, his guide the sacred covenant. (1978, p. 188)

Critics of sociobiology argue that Wilson and others have underestimated human diversity and the plasticity of human behavior and adaptation. Though certain universals in human adaptation may be observed, human societies are distinguished by the incredible variety of their adaptations to their environments (Kottak, 1979). Though genes may set certain limits on what people can do and learn, the limits are extremely broad and most significant human behaviors are strongly influenced by learning, culture, and the environment (Gould, 1981). Sociobiologists counter that they are not advocating a strict biological determinism but rather identifying behavioral tendencies that are both grounded in the genes and amenable to significant cultural shaping. Social behavior is always the result of the interaction between biological and cultural influences. Behavioral predispositions are like "whisperings within," writes the sociobiologist David Barash (1979). The whisperings provide a slight biological push to act in some general way as opposed to others. But cultural voices ring loud and clear, and they strongly determine the form behavior will take. Thus, there is a genetic tendency to learn language, but the kind of language learned is a product of culture. Similarly, there may be a genetic tendency to adorn one's body. But the manner in which it is adorned is culturally determined, a product of a culture's norms about fashion and hygiene. Religion may be part of human nature, but the

Modern customs may be built on a sociobiological base. A funeral.

particular kind of religion espoused is a result of what forms of belief a culture makes available to its members.

Critics have also identified a number of problematic political and ethical ramifications of sociobiology (Lewontin, Rose, & Kamin, 1985). For instance, sociobiology can be used to argue that current injustices and inequalities in human societies are not only acceptable but justified, because the fact that these kinds of societies and practices are the result of long-term evolution implies that they must therefore be adaptive and biologically "natural." One may see a subtle reactionary ideological streak running throughout sociobiology, intimating that the way things are is the way they ought to be—that human nature has made us and our institutions what they are and therefore we had better not try to change. In addition, arguments based loosely on genetic or biological determinism of human behavior have been used repeatedly to discriminate against, oppress, and even kill those people who are seen by some group as less biologically fit. In our century, examples range from U.S. immigration policies that discriminated against southern European and darker-skinned people to the Nazi massacre of 6 million Jews (Gould, 1981). Responsible and well-informed sociobiologists have tried to steer clear of politics and ideology. But even good science can become perverted and used for inappropriate ends. The potential for social abuse of socio-biological theory, especially when the theory is oversimplified by ideological extremists, is substantial and worthy of concern.

One might also suggest, however, that sociobiological insights can provide valuable tools for informed social policy debate. As an example, Barash (1986, 1987) has addressed such modern problems as the threat of nuclear war from a sociobiological standpoint. In *The Hare and the Tortoise,* Barash (1986) discusses the problems that result when cultural evolution (the hare) proceeds at a dramat-ically faster rate than the biological evolution (the tortoise). He writes: "This incongruity (literally: an inability to fit) between our biology, which has evolved by the laborious process of natural selection, and our culture, which has appeared with explosive speed through cultural evolution, is the root of nearly every human difficulty" (p. 60). Even though human beings have created complex mod-ern societies, the minds of humans are not well prepared by biological evolution to cope with the problems these societies produce. In fundamental ways, we still react to and think about things as did our hunting and gathering forebears. Yet we face a frightening new world of nuclear threat and diminishing global resources. We cannot wait for the tortoise to catch up with the hare. We must find ways, Barash says, to run faster, to resolve the daunting problems facing all of humankind, even if it is not in keeping with human nature to do so.

Evolutionary Personality Psychology

In recent years, personality psychologists have become increasingly interested in sociobiology, evolution, and instinct. Cunningham (1981) reviewed a number of studies appearing in social and personality psychology journals that, while not explicitly testing sociobiological hypotheses, produced results that were at least somewhat consistent with sociobiology as it might apply to human behavior. Leak and Christopher (1982) attempted to synthesize Freudian psychoanalysis and sociobiology, arguing that the two approaches are very similar and complement each other. Rushton (1990) has adopted an evolutionary perspective to explain individual and group differences in personality traits and reproductive strategies.

A major spokesman for the use of evolutionary theory in personality psy-chology is David M. Buss (1984, 1988, 1990, 1991a). In a recent review, he writes:

> A new discipline is emerging called "evolutionary psychology." Its central aim is to identify psychological mechanisms and behavioral strategies as evolved solutions to the adaptive prob-lems our species has faced over millions of years. Because per-sonality psychology is dedicated to studying human nature in all of its individually different manifestations, the field is uniquely positioned to contribute to, and become informed by, evolution-ary psychology. (Buss, 1991a, pp. 459–460)

David M. Buss

From this point of view, evolutionary theory provides the most compelling frame-work within which to understand human nature. Therefore, Buss submits that "personality theories inconsistent with evolutionary theory stand little chance of being correct" (1991a, p. 461).

The first thing to realize about evolutionary personality psychology, Buss argues, is that all human behavior, in one way or another, is biological. Environments shape behavior, but without an organism equipped in a certain anatomical and physiological manner there can be no behavior. The point is patently obvious, Buss concedes, but it is often overlooked by scientists and laypersons who seek to explain behavior in terms of learning, situations, environments, culture, social context, and the like. "There is no such thing as a purely environmental or situational cause of behavior," Buss (1991a, p. 461) insists. Everything that is done is done by a biological organism. Every response to a situation is a response of an organism biologically equipped to respond to certain cues in certain ways, and to ignore certain other cues in the environment to which it is not biologically designed to respond. Evolution by natural selection is the process that creates the physiological, anatomical, and psychological mechanisms that enable us to respond in the ways we do.

What is the nature of these mechanisms? From an evolutionary point of view, it makes little sense to posit a small set of general mechanisms like "tension reduction" (Freud) or "individuation" (Jung). These concepts are too global to be of much use in explaining behavior, argues Buss (1990, 1991a; Tooby & Cosmides, 1990), because human beings have evolved to do so many different things in order to adapt. The many different demands of human living call upon us to be specialists rather than generalists. Therefore, natural selection seems to have endowed human beings with a relatively large number of domain-specific mechanisms for solving particular adaptive problems. To make this point, Buss draws on an analogy of animal adaptations favoring physical survival:

> Most terrestrial mammals have evolved solutions to the survival problems of extreme heat (sweat glands or other evaporation mechanisms), cold (shivering), diseases and parasites (immune system), predators (specific evasive capacities), wounds (blood clotting), and what food objects to consume (taste preferences for sugar, salt, and fat). In the realm of reproduction, many primate species have had to solve the social problems of intrasexual competition, mate attraction, mate selection, hierarchy negotiation, coalition building, dyadic reciprocal alliance formation, and parental investment, to name just a few. Now, sweat glands do nothing to solve the problem of what foods to put in one's mouth or how to combat parasites. Solutions to the problem of attracting mates contribute little toward solving the problem of detecting nonreciprocators in social exchange. Different problems typically select for different adaptive solutions; natural selection results in a multiplicity of specific adaptations over time. (Buss, 1991a, p. 463)

What are the particular problems that human beings have faced over the course of evolution? There are two general kinds: those of individual survival and reproduction. Darwin (1859) identified many of the survival problems under the heading of "hostile forces of nature." These include food shortages, harsh climate, disease, parasites, predators, and natural hazards. Reproductive problems are typically more social in quality and, therefore, more centrally implicated in personality. Buss lists eight classes of reproductive problems:

1. *Successful intrasexual competition:* The individual must win out over competitors in gaining access to desirable members of the opposite sex, so that sexual reproduction can occur.

2. *Mate selection:* The individual must select those mates who have the greatest reproductive value to maximize the opportunity for passing his/her genes down to the next generation.

3.   *Successful conception:* The individual must engage in the necessary social and sexual behaviors to fertilize a mate or become fertilized by the mate.

4.   *Mate retention:* The individual must retain the mate, preventing the encroachment of intrasexual competitors as well as preventing the mate's defection or desertion. This problem is more acute among species and individuals who pursue "long-term mating strategies," and does not apply to what Buss (1991a, p. 465) calls "brief, opportunistic copulation."

5.   *Reciprocal dyadic alliance formation:* The individual must develop a relationship with the mate characterized by a certain degree of cooperation and reciprocity.

6.   *Coalition building and maintenance:* The individual must cooperate with others whose interests are aligned with his/her own, building coalitions that compete successfully with rival groups.

7.   *Parental care and socialization:* The individual must engage in actions that ensure the survival and reproductive success of his or her own offspring.

8.   *Extra-parental kin investment:* The individual must sacrifice his or her own self-interests to promote the survival and reproductive success of nondescendant genetic relatives. The reproductive success of genetic relatives is important because they share with the individual some of the same genes.

How do human beings deal with these problems? Drawing upon evolved internal mechanisms, we formulate goal-directed *tactics* and *strategies* that aim ultimately to assure our survival and reproductive success. Buss argues that the most important individual differences in human personality are characteristic differences in tactics and strategies. These kinds of individual differences are most clearly visible in research on human mate selection.

Mating

In terms of evolution, men and women mate for the prime reason of producing offspring, who will carry their genes into the next generation. The tactics and strategies whereby men and women seek to accomplish this end, however, differ markedly as a function of gender. For the male, it is to his "advantage" to impregnate as many females as possible, since this is the major way he can be assured of passing down his own genes. Theoretically, it is possible for a male to sire hundreds of offspring. (You may recall that, in a celebrated recent biography, the former professional basketball player Wilt Chamberlain claimed to have had sexual relations with 20,000 different women.) Hence, males may be biologically more inclined than females toward sexual promiscuity. The female, on the other hand, must invest a great deal of time and energy in each birth and can have only a very limited number of offspring. It is to her advantage to be "choosy" when it comes to sexual intercourse, securing a single mate for assistance in protecting and raising her offspring, thereby maximizing the likelihood of passing her own genes to the next generation. Barash (1979) describes the difference in terms of a rather crass evolutionary marketplace:

In virtually all species males are selected to be aggressive—sexual advertisers—while females are selected to be choosier—comparison shoppers. Again, these behaviors follow directly from the biology of what it means to be a male or female. For males, reproduction is easy, a small amount of time, a small amount of semen, and the potential evolutionary return is very great if offspring are produced. On the other hand, a female who makes a "bad" choice may be in real evolutionary trouble. If fertilization occurs, a baby is begun, and the ensuing process is not only inexorable but immensely demanding. . . . Small wonder that females in virtually every species are more discriminating than males in the choice of sexual partners . . . For males, a very different strategy applies. The maximum advantage goes to individuals with fewer inhibitions. A genetically influenced tendency to "play fast and loose"—"love 'em and leave 'em"—may well reflect more biological reality than most of us care to admit. (p. 48)

That males, in fact, are more promiscuous has been documented repeatedly. In most societies, men in general have sexual relations with more partners than do women, a difference that is most striking when comparing homosexual men to lesbian women (Cunningham, 1981). In addition, men appear to be much less discriminating in their choice of sexual partners. Kenrick (1989) asked college men and women to consider what personal qualities were required in a prospective sexual partner. Except on the dimension of physical attractiveness, women tended to be much choosier than men with respect to what attributes they insisted their partner should possess before they would consider sexual relations. In many cases, men reported that they were willing to have sexual relations with a woman who, by virtue of her low intelligence or obnoxious personality, they would not even consider dating! In other words, men held up stricter criteria for a casual date than they did for sex.

Cross-culturally, the widespread practice of polygyny—in which one man mates with more than one woman—also supports the sociobiological view. In a polygynous arrangement, men are able to mate with many different women (increasing their fitness) while many different women are assured of a mate and (because the practice is culturally sanctioned) an attendant social system supportive of their offspring (increasing their fitness, as well). By contrast, the cultural arrangement of polyandry, whereby one woman mates with many different men, is extremely rare. Wilson (1978) describes the stark differences:

[As a species, human beings are] moderately polygynous, with males initiating most of the changes in sexual partnership. About three-fourths of all human societies permit the taking of multiple wives, and most of them encourage the practice by law and custom. In contrast, marriage to multiple husbands is sanctioned

in less than one percent of societies. The remaining monoga-
mous societies usually fit that category in a legal sense only, with
concubinage and other extramarital stratagems being added to
allow *de facto* polygyny. (pp. 125–126)

If men and women have evolved to adopt markedly different reproductive
tactics and strategies, then we might expect that these differences would create a
good deal of conflict between the sexes, leading to anger and upset. From a sociobiological point of view, we might expect that men should become especially
angry and upset about women's refusal to engage them in sexual relations (sexually withholding behaviors). By contrast, women should experience anger and
upset as a result of men's excessive insistence on sexual relations (sexually
aggressive behaviors). Buss (1989b) presented college students and newlyweds
with a long list of behaviors that are likely to evoke anger and upset and asked
them to endorse those behaviors that their respective dating partners or spouses
had committed during the previous year. The study's results support the sociobiological prediction about sexually withholding behaviors (men report that women
do this more) but not the one about sexually aggressive behaviors (women do not
report higher levels than do men). As is evident in Table 4.1, the respondents in
the study endorsed a wide variety of partner behaviors eliciting anger and upset,
most of which do not seem to be associated with sexual relations per se. Compared to men's reports, women tended to complain most about condescending,
neglecting, and insulting behaviors on the part of their male partners. By contrast, men reported higher levels of moodiness and self-absorption on the part of
their female partners.

Beyond sex differences in evolved reproductive strategies, men and women
also look for different qualities in a prospective sexual partner. Sociobiological
theory suggests that the choosy female should prefer to mate with a male of high
social status and significant material resources, since he is most likely to promote
her genetic fitness. By contrast, the male should prefer to mate with the most fertile young women available, since they are most likely to bear offspring to carry
his genes. As a result, sociobiologists argue, older men (who have more necessary
resources) tend to marry younger women (who have many years of childbearing
ahead of them) (Snowdon, 1983).

Consistent with these predictions are the data from a number of studies.
For example, Buss and Barnes (1986) examined mate selection preferences
among 92 married couples and 100 unmarried college students. They found that
in choosing a sexual mate, men placed major emphasis on a woman's physical
beauty (generally associated with youth) while women placed major emphasis on
a man's earning potential. One might argue, however, that the inequality in earning potential for most men and women in contemporary American society renders mate selection one of the few viable means for securing adequate material
resources for some women. Such women's pragmatic approach to choosing a
mate, therefore, may have as much to do with present cultural constraints and
norms as it does with a biological mandate to maximize genetic fitness. However,

Continued on p. 199

Feature 4.A

Some Women (and Men) Are Choosier Than Others: Sociosexuality

Natural selection presents us with a stark question: How are we to maximize the possibility of passing our genes down to the next generation? The biology of sexual reproduction dictates two divergent answers: For men, it is best to impregnate as many females as possible, under the assumption that at least some of the resultant offspring will survive to maturity so that they, too, will reproduce and keep the genes moving down the line. For women, it is best to choose carefully, to select a mate who will provide reliable care and assistance and thus maximize the chance that the very limited number of offspring any particular woman can produce will indeed reach maturity, and eventually reproduce themselves. The divergent challenges natural selection poses for men and women may help explain general sex differences in mating strategies, for women do indeed seem to be choosier than men. But we all realize that there is wide variation among both women and men with respect to sexual attitudes and behaviors. Why, for example, are some women choosier than others? And why aren't all men trying to seduce nearly every woman they meet?

In a recent series of provocative articles, Jeffry Simpson and Steven Gangestad argue that, in terms of genetic fitness and human evolution, it is to some women's advantage to be especially *non*choosy. Similarly, some men may be naturally selected to adopt a more discriminating approach to

sexual relations (Gangestad, 1989; Gangestad & Simpson, 1990; Simpson & Gangestad, 1991, 1992). Simpson and Gangestad attempt to provide a sociobiological explanation for individual differences in **sociosexuality.** On one end of the continuum, individuals exhibiting a *restricted* sociosexuality insist on commitment and closeness in a relationship prior to engaging in sex with a romantic partner. Like the prototypical choosy female, both men and women with restricted sociosexuality require emotional closeness before they feel comfortable with sexual relations. They have few sexual partners, but their sexual relationships tend to endure for a long time. On the other end of the spectrum, individuals exhibiting an *unrestricted* sociosexuality tend to feel relatively comfortable engaging in sex without commitment or closeness. Like the prototypical dominant male, both women and men with unrestricted sociosexuality have several different sexual partners, and each sexual relationship is likely to endure for a relatively short period of time.

To assess individual differences in sociosexuality, Simpson and Gangestad have developed a questionnaire that asks respondents (usually college students) to report frequency of sexual relations in the past six months, number of lifetime sexual partners, number of partners in the past year, number of partners desired, number of different partners foreseen for the next five years, number of "one night stands," frequency of sexual thoughts, and frequency of fantasies about having sex with people who are currently not their partners (Simpson & Gangestad, 1991). The research shows that college students scoring toward the unrestricted end of the scale tend (1) to engage in sex at an earlier point in their relationships, (2) to engage in sex with more than one partner during a given period in time, and (3) to be involved in relationships characterized by less investment, commitment, love, and dependency (Simpson & Gangestad, 1991). The results also show that sociosexuality is independent of sex drive. In other words, being unrestricted with respect to sociosexuality is not the same thing as, nor can it be explained by, having a strong sex drive. Within sexually active couples, for example, the woman's score on sociosexuality is uncorrelated with the frequency with which she engages in sexual intercourse with her partner.

In a study of romantic partner choice, Simpson and Gangestad (1992) found that individuals with unrestricted sociosexuality tend to prefer romantic partners who are especially physically attractive and have high social visibility. The authors presented college students with two hypothetical romantic partners, Person A and Person B:

> Person A is considered physically attractive and "sexy." He/she has a sort of charisma that attracts the attention of those around him/her. Although some might consider him/her arrogant, A possesses a kind of self-confidence that others admire. A is not known, however, for living a responsible life-style. In the past, he/she has had a series of relatively short-term relationships. Some have ended because of questionable faithfulness on the part of A.
>
> Person B is an average looking person, someone most people wouldn't consider "sexy." He/she is sufficiently socially skilled but does not possess the kind of magnetic personality that draws the attention of others. Rather B has a stable and responsible personality. In a relationship, B is caring, dependable, and faithful. He/she would like very much to have a family, likes children, and would probably be good with them. (Simpson & Gangestad, 1992, pp. 39–40)

After reading both vignettes, the participants in the study determined which of the two persons they were attracted to, which they would prefer

Feature 4.A

as a romantic partner, and which was more similar to the person with whom they were currently involved. For both men and women, unrestricted individuals allotted a significantly larger number of their choices to the attractive and dominant Person A compared to restricted individuals. By contrast, restricted individuals tended to prefer the reliable and caring Person B. In a second study, the authors found that the actual partners of the respondents did indeed possess the qualities that the respondents tended to desire. For both men and women, the romantic partners of unrestricted individuals tended to score lower on measures of faithfulness/loyalty, kindness/understanding, and responsibility; higher on measures of social visibility; and were actually rated by observers as physically more attractive compared to romantic partners of respondents scoring toward the restricted end of the sociosexuality continuum.

So what does this have to do with evolution? Simpson and Gangestad argue that natural selection may have favored both restricted and unrestricted sociosexuality for both certain males and certain females. While it is easy to see the advantages of unrestricted sociosexuality for some dominant males, it is certainly true that every male cannot be a Don Juan. For one thing, there are not enough available women to go around, and in the exquisitely nonegalitarian world that Darwin has described, dominant males will usually attract the most mates, leaving many nondominant males with fewer options. The competitive powers of such nondominant males may be enhanced, however, by exhibiting traits of reliability and willingness to invest in relationships. Therefore, "males in evolutionary history who invested heavily in a mate's offspring should have desired long-term partners who demonstrated sexual exclusivity to the relationship, as revealed by resolute faithfulness and commitment" (Simpson & Gangestad, 1992, p. 34). Restricted sociosexuality can prove adaptive for some men in making them especially appealing to certain women who are most strongly concerned about relational investment.

For many females, the advantage of restricted sociosexuality is very clear. The choosy female enhances her genetic fitness by selecting the most reliable mate. She may indeed end up "settling down" with a mate whose sociosexual orientation is similarly restricted, as suggested in the above paragraph. But men have more to offer women than relational investment, Simpson and Gangestad point out. Men can also offer "good genes." For women, relatively unrestricted sociosexuality may have the advantage of enabling them to mate with the most attractive and most dominant men. (Recall that both college men and women with unrestricted sociosexuality show strong preferences for attractiveness and social visibility in their partners.) While some of these attractive men may not prove to be reliable mates in the long run, they still offer the prize of a genetic endowment tending toward dominance and attractiveness. If the ultimate goal is to pass one's own genes to succeeding generations, then the unrestricted female who mates with attractive and dominant men enjoys the potential advantage of seeing those traits of attractiveness and dominance replicated in her own offspring. Should these offspring survive to maturity, they themselves may be blessed with an advantage in the mating marketplace. This should be especially apparent in male offspring, or what Simpson and Gangestad refer to as "sexy sons." If a woman's son grows up to be especially attractive and dominant, then he is relatively well positioned to mate with many different women, potentially passing his own (and his mother's) genes down to the next generation.

If the above reasoning is correct, then the woman exhibiting unrestricted sociosexuality should maximize her genetic fitness in the production of sons, for the "sexy son" may potentially sire a greater number of offspring than the most fertile (and attractive) daughter could ever produce. One would predict, therefore, that natural selection should have arranged things such that unrestricted women should give birth to more sons than should women with a restricted sociosexual orientation. Gangestad and Simpson provide some

very limited but tantalizing support for this startling hypothesis, drawing upon data on sexual attitudes and behavior of Americans collected by Alfred Kinsey in the late 1940s and 50s (Gangestad, 1989; Gangestad & Simpson, 1990). Using reported number of premarital sexual partners as a rough index of sociosexuality in women, Simpson and Gangestad found a very modest but statistically significant correlation between number of premarital partners and the tendency to bear male children. Those women who scored in the top 5% of sociosexuality (greatest number of premarital sexual partners) had close to 60% boys, compared to 50% for those women at the bottom of the distribution (fewest number of premarital sexual partners).

Simpson and Gangestad conclude that "both unrestricted and restricted female strategies may, in our evolutionary past have been potentially viable: a restricted strategy enhancing parental investment; an unrestricted strategy enhancing the reproductive abilities of surviving male offspring" (Gangestad & Simpson, 1990, p. 81). Their work suggests that human nature allows for evolutionarily grounded individual differences in reproductive strategies. These differences may be associated with particular personality traits (such as dominance, nurturance, and reliability) that prove especially adaptive in certain kinds of environmental situations and undercertain kinds of selection pressures.

 **Table 4.1**

Average Levels of Upset Elicitors in Male and Female Partners

	Sex of Target of Complaint		
Upset Elicitor	**Male**	**Female**	***p***
Condescending	.14	.08	.000
Neglecting- Rejecting- Unreliable	.16	.11	.000
Inconsiderate	.23	.09	.000
Abuses Alcohol- Emotionally Constricted	.16	.13	.033
Insulting of Appearance	.04	.02	.021
Physically Self- absorbed	.07	.14	.000
Moody	.19	.30	.000
Sexually Withholding	.06	.14	.000
Possessive- Jealous- Dependent	.17	.19	*ns*
Abusive	.05	.06	*ns*
Unfaithful	.06	.07	*ns*
Sexualizes Others	.12	.15	*ns*
Disheveled	.07	.05	*ns*

Table 4.1 continued

Table 4.1 continued

	Sex of Target of Complaint		
Upset Elicitor	**Male**	**Female**	**p**
Sexually Aggressive	.03	.02	*ns*
Self-centered	.21	.18	*ns*
Total	.12	.11	*ns*

Note: N = 528. *"Ns"* means the difference between males and females is *not* statistically significant.
From Buss (1989b), p. 740.

Continued from p. 193

it is interesting to note that the differences Buss and Barnes found in the United States have also been found in a number of other cultures as well. In a study of 37 different cultures, Buss (1989a) found that men tend to prefer younger, physically attractive mates while women place greater value on slightly older mates possessing ambition, an industrious nature, and good financial prospects.

The sociobiology of human mate selection may even be evident in the way in which we judge the attractiveness of women's and men's faces (Cunningham, 1981; Cunningham, Barbee, & Pike, 1990). Both men and women prefer female faces with the childlike features of large eyes, small nose and small chin, the sexually mature features of high cheekbones and narrow cheeks, and the expressive features of a large smile and eyebrows set clearly above the eyes. A full, thick head of hair is also judged to be a significant female asset. Overall, the most attractive female face suggests youth, sexual maturity, good health, and friendliness. In our evolutionary past (long before people kept track of exactly how old they were—before indeed counting systems were invented), these features may have served as facial cues of fertility in females, suggests Buss (1989a). This is why we find them attractive today.

Surprisingly, attractive male faces share some of the same features. In three experiments, Cunningham, Barbee, and Pike (1990) demonstrated that American college women preferred faces of men who possessed large eyes, large cheekbones, and expressive smiles. In addition, prominent chins, thick eyebrows, and high-status clothing were judged to be especially attractive in men. The authors of the study argue that women judge men's faces with at least two implicit and somewhat contradictory criteria in mind. Women prefer men who are "cute" in an almost childlike way, as suggested by the big eyes and smiles. But in keeping with what sociobiology would predict, they also prefer men who exude maturity

Popular ads reflect the sociobiology of human mate selection: a wealthy man and a beautiful woman.

and social dominance, as indicated in the prominent chins, thick eyebrows, and high-status clothing. Women may see mature and socially dominant men as the best candidates for long-term relationships in that such men are best positioned in their society to provide the material resources that are required for the successful socialization of offspring.

A central tenet of Darwinian theory is that organisms compete with each other for limited reproductive resources. Darwin was intrigued by the existence in the animal kingdom of characteristics that seem to impair survival but nonetheless promote reproductive success by giving an organism a competitive edge. The elaborate plumage, heavy horns, and conspicuous displays of many species seem costly in the currency of survival. However, these characteristics increase success in mating and so evolve despite their cost. When it comes to humans, evolutionary theory predicts that men and women will compete for reproductive resources in contrasting ways. Given the evolutionary premium placed on feminine youth and beauty, women should strive to enhance their physical appearance in competing with each other to attract men. Given the evolutionary premium placed on masculine dominance and status, men should compete to attract women through displays of social dominance, employing tactics such as boasting of their accomplishments and future earning potential.

In order to test these hypotheses, Buss (1988) conducted a series of studies to identify the most common tactics of mate attraction employed by college men and women and by newlyweds. As predicted, women tended to use tactics aimed at enhancing their physical attractiveness, endorsing such behaviors as "wear makeup," "wear stylish clothes," "keep clean and groomed," and "wear jewelry." By contrast, men tended to use such tactics as "display resources" and "brag about resources." Men were more likely than women to display expensive possessions and to boast about accomplishments. However, the research is also noteworthy for the strong agreement that was found between men and women with respect to those behavioral tactics viewed to be most successful in obtaining reproductive resources. The acts frequently performed and considered most highly effective for *both sexes* involved displaying sympathy, kindness, good manners, helpfulness, and humor. Despite the sex differences obtained, therefore, men and women still show remarkable similarity in the tactics and strategies they employ to attract mates.

Of course the attraction of mates is only half of the story from the standpoint of sociobiology. Mating leads to reproduction. Here again marked sex differences are expected. The biology of sexual reproduction and child-rearing dictates that the female "invest" more in any given offspring than the male (Trivers, 1971). For example, in many mammals, the male invests a small amount of time and energy during courtship and copulation, whereas the female invests much more heavily during pregnancy and lactation. Since the female expends much more time and energy than the male in bearing and raising the offspring, argue sociobiologists, she is more inclined to form a closer emotional attachment to the offspring than is the male who happens to be the father. In addition, a male can rarely be 100% certain that he is in fact the father of any particular offspring, whereas maternity is never in doubt. According to sociobiology, therefore, the bond between males and their offspring is likely to be tenuous and ambivalent. Furthermore, biological relatives of the mother (maternal grandparents, maternal uncles and aunts) should form closer attachment bonds to the offspring than should the biological relatives of the father, partly because of the uncertainty of the "true" father.

Littlefield and Rushton (1986) tested sociobiological hypotheses about differential investment in offspring in a study of parents whose children had recently died. A sample of 263 bereaved parents filled out a lengthy questionnaire assessing the degree of their own grieving after the death of the child, their judgments of the grieving process in other family members, and a number of other factors and issues concerning the death of the child. Supporting predictions from sociobiological theory, the findings showed that mothers grieved more intensely than fathers, mothers' siblings grieved more intensely than fathers' siblings, and maternal grandparents grieved more intensely than paternal grandparents. With respect to the last finding, the maternal grandmother showed the highest level of grieving, followed by the maternal grandfather and paternal grandmother, who were about even, followed finally by the paternal grandfather, who showed the lowest level of grieving.

As intriguing as the results from Littlefield and Rushton's study are, there may be a danger in equating, as the researchers do, the intensity of grief with the degree of attachment. The implication is that, because they grieve more intensely when their children die, mothers have a stronger emotional bond with their children than do fathers. Grief, however, is a very complicated human experience, and its relationship to love and attachment is not clearly understood (Archer, 1988; Freud, 1917/1957). In addition, the sociobiological suggestion that the mother–infant bond is markedly stronger and more "natural" than the father–infant bond has not generally been supported by research. As we shall see later in this chapter, psychologists have documented both important similarities and differences between mother–infant and father–infant attachments.

In conclusion, sociobiology offers a number of provocative explanations for observed gender differences in human mating and reproduction. Though the explanations find some support in the animal kingdom, their value for understanding gender differences in humans remains somewhat controversial and open for debate. Mating and reproduction are emotionally and politically charged topics in contemporary American society. Even from a strictly scientific standpoint, these topics can be approached on many different levels. By focusing on the biological and evolutionary dimensions of these issues, sociobiology offers interesting explanations at a *distal* rather than *proximate* level of analysis (Archer, 1988). "Proximate levels emphasize the environmental, cognitive, and physiological mechanisms involved; distal explanations consider the significance of phenomena from perspectives further back in time, ultimately in evolutionary terms of reproductive fitness" (Littlefield & Rushton, 1988, p. 626). Therefore, the "whisperings within" harken back to a distant evolutionary legacy whose subtle influence today can be fully understood only in the proximate context of the pervasive social and cultural factors that shape human behavior and experience.

Socioanalytic Theory and the Problem of Shyness

Personality psychologist Robert Hogan has developed a general theory of the person, which neatly ties together strands of sociobiology, Freudian psychoanalysis, and sociological theories about "roles." Hogan calls his approach **socioanalytic theory** (Hogan, 1982, 1987; Hogan, Jones, & Cheek, 1985). Socioanalytic theory asserts that human beings are biologically predisposed to live in social groups that are variously organized into status hierarchies. Group living provided our evolutionary ancestors with advantages in cooperative ventures such as defense against predators. At the same time, having high status in one's group conferred decided advantages on the person who had it, providing first choice of food, romantic partners, living space, and whatever other desirable commodities and privileges the group afforded, ultimately promoting reproductive success. Therefore, human beings are genetically mandated to seek attention and status, to seek to be liked and to be powerful. As Hogan puts it, "getting along and getting ahead are the two great problems in life that each person must solve" (Hogan et al., 1985, p. 178).

These two great problems are always addressed and resolved, argues Hogan, in the context of ritualized social interaction. As sociologists such as George Herbert

Mead (1934) and Erving Goffman (1959) have long maintained, social behavior is an elaborate game, governed by rules and conventions, scripted into roles and routines, and mastered by the most skillful game-players among us (more on this in Chapter 10). This is true of the most informal aspects of living (morning coffee) and the most formal (a presidential inauguration), of the most trivial social interactions (passing strangers in the hallway) and the most personally meaningful (proposing marriage). Like actors on a stage, persons must play roles and follow scripts so that their "performances" in society can be affirmed and rewarded by their "audiences," who are also fellow "actors and actresses." Those human beings who adapt most successfully in a given society—those who are highly popular and powerful—know how and when to play the most effective roles and to engage in the most appropriate social rituals in the society. They are able to present themselves in ways that make positive and significant impressions on others. This is not to trivialize social behavior, nor to suggest that it is natural for people to be insincere. Rather, role playing and impression management are unconscious, central, genetic tendencies for all human beings. Hogan writes:

> Self-presentation and impression management are not trivial party games. They are fundamental processes, rooted in our history as group-living animals. They are archaic, powerful, compulsive tendencies that are closely tied to our chances for survival and reproductive success. (Hogan et al., 1985, p. 181)

Furthermore, role playing and impression management are the major mechanisms through which we define who we are as social beings. The sociobiological goal of life is to produce viable progeny, so that the individual's genes can be passed down to the next generation. To achieve this goal, however, the person must first find a part to play, a social identity that specifies a recognized niche in the community. Once such an identity is found, the person must employ role playing and impression management to sustain that identity.

Hogan argues that the expected audience for a person's self-presentational behaviors changes. In childhood, family members (especially parents) are the most important audience. Our ways of displaying the self to them come to comprise our **character structure.** In adulthood, the audience broadens to include colleagues, friends, peers, one's children, and even society at large. The characteristic ways in which we display ourselves to this larger audience become our **role structure.** But the earlier character structure does not go away. Rather, it lingers on in the unconscious, Hogan asserts. Identity conflicts in adulthood may turn on the discordance between unconscious character structure and conscious role structure, as when the blue-collar, working-class boy rises into the professional white-collar echelons of adult society. He may find it difficult to feel comfortable with an elite role structure that so contradicts the street-wise, tough-guy posture that carried him through his childhood years.

Some people are clearly better at adapting to society and mastering its roles and rituals than are others. Argues Hogan, these people are generally approved and accepted by others and attain high positions of influence. One personality variable that appears to have a significant effect on such adaptation is **shyness.** Jones, Briggs, and Smith (1986) define shyness as "discomfort and inhibition in the presence of others" (p. 629). As you might expect, shyness is quite common. One survey indicated that 73% of a large sample of American college students reported having experienced shyness and 42% claimed that they were chronically and characteristically shy (Zimbardo, 1977). Although virtually anyone may feel shy in certain highly unusual or threatening situations, shyness also appears to be a relatively stable personality disposition, with some people regularly and consistently experiencing more of it than others. As a personality disposition, shyness is "the propensity to respond with heightened anxiety, self-consciousness, and reticence in a variety of social contexts; a person high in the trait of shyness will experience greater arousal than a person low in shyness independent of the level of interpersonal threat in the situation" (Jones et al., 1986, p. 630).

Table 4.2 lists some of the items included in recent questionnaires for measuring individual differences in shyness. Persistent shyness brings with it discomfort and personal anguish. People scoring high in shyness tend to report greater fearfulness and self-consciousness and lower self-esteem than people scoring low in shyness (Cheek & Buss, 1981; Jones & Russell, 1982). Shy people tend to describe themselves as especially inhibited, awkward, unfriendly, and incompetent (DePaulo, Kenny, Hoover, Webb, & Oliver, 1987). When interacting with a member of the opposite sex, shy people report relatively more negative thoughts

 **Table 4.2**

Items From Questionnaires Measuring Shyness

1. I am often uncomfortable at parties and other social gatherings.
2. I often think up excuses in order to avoid social engagements.
3. I tend to withdraw from people.
4. I get nervous when I speak to someone in a position of authority.
5. I am socially somewhat awkward.
6. I usually feel relaxed when I am with a group of people.
7. I often find myself taking charge in group situations.
8. I have little difficulty being assertive, especially when it is appropriate or I need to be.
9. I make new friends easily.
10. It does not take me a long time to overcome my shyness in new situations.

Note: For each of these items, the person answers "yes" or "no." Answers of "yes" to items 1–5 and answers of "no" to items 6–10 indicate shyness.
From Jones, Briggs, & Smith (1986, p. 636).

about themselves and feelings of tenseness than do persons scoring low on measures of shyness (Bruch, Gorsky, Collins, & Berger, 1989; Hill, 1989). Shy persons report that they lack the confidence and skill necessary to perform effectively many of the roles and rituals necessary for social adaptation. (The popular radio humorist, Garrison Keillor, hits the mark squarely when he advertises "Powdermilk Biscuits"—the recipe that "gives shy people the strength to get up and do what needs to be done.") Other people tend to judge quite harshly the shy person's reticence and reluctance to interact. Shy persons are seen by others as untalented, unfriendly, aloof, snobbish, and lacking in leadership (Hogan et al., 1985). Objective ratings show that shy people actually do talk less, initiate fewer conversational sequences, avert their gaze more often, smile less, show less facial expressivity, and are more likely to engage in nervous self-touching, compared to nonshy people (Cheek & Buss, 1981; Mandel & Shrauger, 1980; Pilkonis, 1977). In Hogan's view, shyness is a common but highly unfortunate handicap in social interaction, and it renders the person less "fit." Shyness leads to personal distress, poor self-esteem, and a lower likelihood that the person will be able to attain the social approval and the status that all of us are biologically predisposed to want.

Caspi, Elder, and Bem (1988) followed the life course patterns of individuals born in the 1920s and who, as children, were described by their mothers as particularly shy and inhibited. Shy boys were more likely than their peers to delay entry into marriage, parenthood, and stable careers. They tended to attain less occupational achievement and stability. Those who were especially late in establishing stable careers were also likely to experience high levels of marital instability.

The costs of shyness among girls in this cohort, however, were much less pronounced. Shy girls were more likely than their peers to follow a conventional pattern of marriage, child-rearing, and homemaking. Although most women in this cohort placed marriage and children well above occupational concerns, the women with a history of childhood shyness were even less likely to engage in paid work outside the home than their nonshy peers. Interestingly, shy women tended to marry men who had *higher* occupational status at midlife than the husbands of other women. The authors of the study suggest that shy women in the 1950s and 60s may actually have aided their husbands' careers by fulfilling the traditional homemaker role. With respect to socioanalytic theory, the surprising finding suggests that under certain societal arrangements shyness may in fact enhance the adaptiveness of an individual by promoting the social standing of related others.

Finally, research on infants suggests that certain forms of shyness may have a physiological base. Jerome Kagan (1989) has shown that about 15% of Caucasian children in the second year of life are consistently shy and emotionally subdued in unfamiliar situations ("inhibited" children) whereas another 15% are consistently sociable and affectively spontaneous ("uninhibited children"). As 2-year-olds, inhibited children may be especially reluctant to play with an unfamiliar toy. In kindergarten they may shy away from new activities and people, showing a kind of "stage fright" in new situations. Compared to uninhibited children, inhibited children show intense physiological responses, such as more dilated pupils and higher heart rates, when confronted with mildly stressful social situations. In addition, inhibited children show higher levels of morning cortisol in the blood (indicating heightened arousal) compared to uninhibited children, a difference that is also apparent when comparing shy baby rhesus monkeys to their more sociable peers. Kagan argues that extremely shy and extremely sociable children constitute two separable genetic types whose striking behavioral differences are a function of different thresholds of reactivity in the brain's limbic system. Shy children have a lower threshold of reactivity. They are more easily aroused by social situations and respond by withdrawing.

Aggression Versus Altruism

Hurting Others

The myriad incidents of human violence and cruelty that you have read about, perceived, and maybe even experienced in your own life are all understandable manifestations of human nature, argue sociobiologists. We are, by nature, a *moderately aggressive* species, states Wilson (1978). An instinctual predisposition to aggression, coded in the genes, has proven adaptive in the course of human evolution, enabling the more aggressive among us to survive longer and reproduce with more success. However, human aggression is extremely flexible, Wilson concedes, and is subject to the limits and opportunities provided by society, learning, and context. The most dangerous form of human aggression is probably organized warfare. From the standpoint of sociobiology, war manifests itself as a violent rupture of the intricate and powerful fabric of the territorial taboos observed by social groups. Territoriality is reinforced by the feeling of kinship and affinity that one has toward relatives, fellow citizens, or those with whom one shares ideological beliefs. Thus, a major force behind most warlike policies is ethnocentrism (Wilson, 1978). In warfare, states, tribes, and other social groups marshal forces and organize aggressive actions to defend or expand their respective geographic, cultural, ethnic, or ideological turfs.

Table 4.3 shows how the term *aggression* can be used to designate a host of very different responses, from nagging one's roommate, to killing prey, to committing suicide. As you might imagine, defining the concept of aggression is a very difficult task. Psychologists have offered a number of formal definitions of aggression. Whereas some definitions focus on observable behavior patterns (such as hitting, biting, and killing), others underscore the *intent* of the behavior, suggesting that aggression is behavior *for the purpose of* hurting others (Parke & Slaby, 1983). Psychologists further distinguish between **instrumental aggression,** which involves hurting others in order to attain a nonaggressive aim, and **hostile aggression,** which has as its explicit aim or end hurting a victim (Hartup, 1974). Thus, a mugger who beats a middle-aged businessman in order to steal his wallet

Table 4.3

Some Examples of Aggression

1. A boy swats at a hornet and gets stung.
2. A cat kills a mouse, parades around with it, and then discards it.
3. A wolf kills and devours a stray sheep.
4. A farmer beheads a chicken and prepares it for Sunday dinner.
5. A hunter kills an animal and mounts it as a trophy.
6. A dog snarls at the mailman but never bites him.
7. A tennis player smashes his racket after missing a volley.
8. A boxer gives an opponent a bloody nose.
9. A small boy daydreams of beating up the neighborhood bully.
10. A woman nags and criticizes her husband, and he ignores her in return.
11. A firing squad executes a prisoner.
12. A bombardier presses a button and hundreds below are killed.
13. A bank robber is shot in the back while attempting to escape.
14. A politician evades legislation that might help clear up a crime-ridden slum.
15. A man commits suicide.
16. An assassin misses his target.
17. A man dislikes all blacks, Jews, and long-haired college students.
18. Two friends get in a heated quarrel after drinking too much.
19. A man rapes a woman.
20. A secretary insults the boss.

Items 1–18 are from Johnson (1972, pp. 4–5).

is displaying instrumental aggression—aggression as a means to another end. When the mugger, in a fit of rage, continues to beat and kick the businessman after he robs him, he is displaying hostile aggression—aggression as an end in itself, presumably motivated by a desire to hurt the other. Many aggressive actions appear to be combinations of both instrumental and hostile aggression.

Sociobiologists, instinct theorists, and a number of popular writers have made much of the comparison of human aggression to aggression in other species, especially among nonhuman primates. For a time, writings on the topic suggested that human beings were the most murderous of all animals, virtually unique in their propensity for systematically killing their own kind. Indirectly supporting this view were ethological observations suggesting that, while many primates and other mammals engage in a great deal of aggressive behavior, much of this ostensibly "violent" action has a benign quality, especially when exhibited towards members of the same species. For example, certain carnivores will kill members of *other* species in order to eat them (instrumental aggression), but they will rarely kill each other (hostile aggression).

Instead, much of intraspecies aggression may be ritualistic, involving only threats rather than real attacks. When fights do break out, the combatants often seem to be instinctively guided by inhibitory mechanisms that stop the fighting short of death and serious injury. For example, a dog who is the loser in a fight may present its unprotected neck to the mouth of the victorious dog or roll over on its back to expose its vulnerable underside (Lorenz, 1969). Such an appeasement gesture signals that the fight is over and that the victor emerges dominant. Some ethologists have argued that this kind of ritualistic fighting and mock aggression serves to establish stable dominance hierarchies in certain advanced animal societies. Dominance hierarchies, in turn, may promote the more efficient use of resources and space in a given group's habitat (Wynne-Edwards, 1963/1978). By establishing and affirming the status of dominant and submissive members of the group, instinctive ritualistic aggression may serve to decrease actual intraspecies violence.

While this view of benign aggression in the animal kindom has some merit, recent studies of hyenas, lions, monkeys, chimpanzees, and certain other species paint a much more menacing picture of intraspecies violence. Lethal fighting, cannibalism, and group warfare are observable in a number of nonhuman species. One of the most gruesome examples is *competitive infanticide,* documented in Indian monkeys known as Hanuman langurs (Konner, 1983). Langur social groups consist of a hierarchy of related females with their offspring and a small number of males attached to the group, often for a year or more. From time to time, new males appear on the scene, drive out the old males, and take over. Within a few days they may kill all infants under the age of 6 months and then reimpregnate the infants' mothers. Sociobiologists explain such brutality in terms of genetic fitness. By killing off the owners of competing genes (the children sired by their predecessors) and by producing new offspring to replace them, the new langur males are maximizing the chances of passing on their own genes.

Infanticide is by no means unknown to human societies (see Bakan, 1971), but one is hard pressed to find human examples as grotesque as the langur monkeys. Nonetheless, the sociobiological claim that human beings are innately aggressive can still be quite compelling. Konner (1983) suggests that singling out the most violent of human societies—such as the Yanomamo culture of highland Venezuela, the Plains Indians of the United States, the Zulu of southern Africa, the Germans of the Third Reich—is the easy way out in proving the argument that human beings are innately aggressive. More instructive and interesting, he maintains, is to examine the *least violent* societies. A case example is the Semai of Malaysia, a very simple society described as a paragon of peacefulness and tranquility. Dentan (1968) reports that before the 1950s, the Semai knew virtually nothing of war, murder, or violence. Almost all forms of instrumental and hostile aggression were nonexistent in Semai society. This all changed for a time in the early 1950s, when the British recruited troops among the Semai to fight a communist insurgency in the region. Initially lured into the military by high wages and pretty clothes, gentle Semai men proved to be amazing fighters:

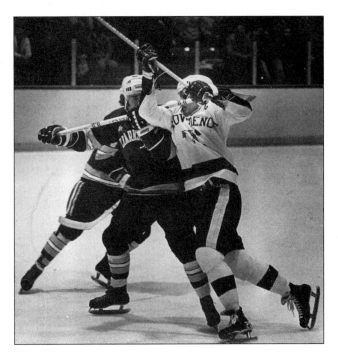

Human aggression: the beginning of a hockey fight.

Many people who knew the Semai insisted that such an unwarlike people could never make good soldiers. Interestingly enough, they were wrong. Communist terrorists had killed the kinsmen of some of the Semai counterinsurgency troops. Taken out of their nonviolent society and ordered to kill, they seem to have been swept up in a sort of insanity which they call "blood drunkenness." A typical veteran's story runs like this. "We killed, killed, killed. The Malays would stop and go through people's pockets and take their watches or money. We only thought of killing. Wah, truly we were drunk with blood." One man even told how he drunk the blood of a man he had killed. (Konner, 1983, p. 205)

Though one case study cannot prove any generalization, the case of the Semai is provocative and capable of bolstering a number of divergent views of human nature. Sociobiologists and others are likely to interpret the aggressive behavior of the Semai as a dramatic triumph of instinctual potential over environmental learning. Even this most peaceful group of men—trained from birth to eschew all violence—was capable of surprising acts of brutality in war. On the other hand, those who prefer to explain human aggression in terms of learning and cultural influences can argue that the inexperienced Semai were merely *conforming,* with shocking gusto, to the norms of warfare imposed upon them by an alien culture. That the Semai eventually returned to a peaceful way of life after the war, many seemingly baffled by their unorthodox behavior in battle, is a tribute to the power of culture to control aggression, but it still leaves open the question of the extent to which aggression can be considered a central component of human nature (Konner, 1983).

Unfortunately, we must leave the question open. In Chapter 6, we will return to the topic of human aggression from the very different perspective of social learning and environmental control. We will consider how human aggression is strongly influenced by one's learning history. Before we move on, however, let us consider a related question about aggression, of particular interest to personality psychologists who focus on individual differences in aggression level. Regardless of the nature of human aggression, are some people consistently more aggressive than others?

The answer to this question is "yes." A considerable body of research literature supports the idea that individual differences in aggressiveness, variously measured, are remarkably stable over time, for both males and females. This means that within a given group, those identified as relatively more aggressive than others at one point in time tend to be rated as relatively more aggressive than the same others at a later point in time. In other words, bullies remain bullies as they get older, though their particular ways of expressing aggression may undergo marked change. In addition, males tend to be more aggressive than females, a difference that shows up in most all cultures and across virtually the entire human life-span (Maccoby & Jacklin, 1974). That males are more likely than females to engage in behavior designed to hurt and to destroy is evident by the time boys and girls have reached the age of 2 or $2\frac{1}{2}$.

To assess consistency in aggression over time, Olweus (1977) conducted two short-term longitudinal studies of Swedish adolescent boys. In the first study, 85 boys were rated by their classmates at age 13 and again 1 year later. In the second study, 201 boys were rated at age 13 and again 3 years later. Table 4.4 shows the correlations between aggression scores at the two points in time for both studies. The results provide impressive evidence for the stability of aggressive behavior in boys over short periods of time, especially on such aggression indices as "starts fights" and "verbal protest." A review of 16 different longitudinal studies on male aggressiveness provides similar results (Olweus, 1979), though stability tends to decrease somewhat as the length of time between assessments increases. Early studies with girls and women showed little longitudinal stability in aggression scores (Kagan & Moss, 1962), but more recent research findings tend to parallel those from boys and men, suggesting relatively strong stability through the childhood years for girls in individual differences in aggression (Parke & Slaby, 1983).

A number of explanations have been offered for the marked longitudinal stability of individual aggression differences. Many focus on learning histories and other environmental factors (to be discussed in Chapter 6). Some, taking the biological view, have tried to relate individual differences in aggressiveness to

Table 4.4

Correlations Between Ratings of Boys' Aggressiveness[a]

Variable Rated	Study 1[b,c]	Study 2[b,d]
Starts fights[e]	.81	.65
Verbal protest[f]	.79	.70
Aggression target[g]	.59	.56

[a]Adapted from Olweus (1977).

[b]Pearson Product Moment correlations between ratings, made on same boys at two points in time. All correlation coefficients are statistically significant at the $p < .001$ level, indicating high longitudinal stability on all three indices of aggression in both studies.

[c]Sample: 85 boys rated at Time 1 in 6th grade and at Time 2 in 7th grade.

[d]Sample: 201 boys rated at Time 1 in 6th grade and at Time 2 in 9th grade.

[e]Boys were rated by chosen classmates on a 1–7 scale (1 = very seldom; 7 = very often) with respect to this item. "He starts fights with other boys at school."

[f]Boys were rated by chosen classmates on a 1–7 scale (1 = very seldom; 7 = very often) with respect to this item: "When a teacher criticizes him he tends to answer back and protest."

[g]Boys were rated by chosen classmates on a 1–7 scale (1 = very seldom; 7 = very often) with respect to this item: "Other boys at school start fights with and tease him."

hormone levels, especially levels of testosterone, a male sex hormone. These efforts have been intriguing, but somewhat inconclusive to date. The relationship between aggressive behavior and testosterone levels, in both men and women, appears to be exceedingly complex. Persky, Smith, and Basu (1971) found a positive correlation between levels of testosterone in the blood and a self-report measure of aggression in a sample of young men between the ages of 17 and 28. In a group of men over the age of 31, on the other hand, the positive relationship was not found. Kreuz and Rose (1972) examined testosterone levels in male prisoners. Those prisoners with a history of more aggressive crimes, such as armed robbery, assault, and murder, showed higher levels of testosterone than prisoners who had committed less violent offenses, such as burglary and larceny. Testosterone levels were unrelated to the amount of fighting and other aggressive behaviors exhibited in prison. However, a more recent study found that male prison inmates high in testosterone had violated prison rules more often and had been more dominant in prison than inmates lower in testosterone (Dabbs, Frady, Carr, & Besch, 1987). In addition, those higher in testosterone were more likely to have committed violent crimes. Of the 11 men in the sample whose testosterone levels were highest, 10 had committed a violent crime. By contrast, among the 11 men with lowest levels of testosterone, only 2 had committed a violent crime. Similar results were obtained in a study of female inmates (Dabbs, Ruback, Frady, Hopper, & Sgoutas, 1988).

In a study of military veterans who had served in the Vietnam War, Dabbs and Morris (1990) found that men high in testosterone were more likely to have engaged in a number of aggressive antisocial behaviors than those with low testosterone levels. For example, testosterone was associated with having gone AWOL while in the military, having assaulted other adults, and having abused alcohol and other drugs. Men with high testosterone levels also tended to report that, as children, they had repeatedly been in trouble with parents and teachers. Most of these associations were statistically significant, however, only among men from lower socio-economic classes. Among middle-class men, the only behavioral index that was significantly associated with testosterone level was marijuana usage. Therefore, it would appear that the socialization experiences of middle-class men function to overcome, or at least mitigate, the internal effects of testosterone as they apply to aggressive, antisocial behaviors.

Other studies have found modest positive association between testosterone levels and (1) aggressive response to threat among 16-year-old boys (Olweus, Mattson, Schalling, & Low, 1980) and (2) fighting during the game among male hockey players (Scaramella & Brown, 1978). Among 11-year-old boys and girls, those who were exposed, while in their mothers' wombs, to high levels of synthetic hormones (which act like male sex hormones) were more likely than other 11-year-old boys and girls to report that they would act in a physically aggressive manner in conflict situations (Reinisch, 1981). The finding is consistent with animal research showing that exposure to male sex hormones promotes aggressive displays in both males and females.

Finally, we should note that the connections obtained between hormone levels, which fluctuate markedly in a single person over time, and aggression are quite modest and subject to a number of other influences. In addition, levels of testosterone have been associated with other outcomes that, while related to aggression, do not directly involve hurting others or damaging property. These associated traits include social dominance, assertiveness, persistence, sex drive, and thrill seeking. A study of occupations among women found lawyers to be higher in testosterone than nurses, teachers, and athletes (Schindler, 1979). Another study found that women who were managerial and technical workers were higher in testosterone than those who were clerical workers or housewives (Purifoy & Koopmans, 1979). Recently, Dabbs, de LaRue, and Williams (1990) found that actors and football players exhibited higher testosterone concentrations than men who were religious ministers.

Helping Others

When it comes to altruism, sociobiology offers a surprising twist. Recall that genes exist to perpetuate themselves—genes are "selfish" (Dawkins, 1976).

Organisms, therefore, are biologically predisposed to engage in activities that ultimately perpetuate their own genes. However, such activities may not always appear to be selfish. Indeed, by acting sometimes in a seemingly selfless, altruistic way, an organism may increase its genetic fitness and promote the perpetuation of its own genes.

Because biologically related animals share some of the same genes, certain species are predisposed to engage in altruistic behavior *that benefits their relatives* (parents, children, siblings, and grandchildren, for the most part). Through **kin selection,** parents may sacrifice their own lives to save their children and thereby increase the likelihood of passing their own genes down, through their offspring, to subsequent generations. Siblings are inclined to help each other, even sacrifice themselves for each other, for to promote the survival and reproductive success of a sibling is to increase the chances of passing down the genes siblings have in common. In general, the closer the blood relationship, the greater the likelihood of altruism. Thus, we are biologically more strongly predisposed to help our children, brothers, or sisters than our cousins, uncles, or aunts. In general, altruism based on kin selection is most likely to occur (1) among closely related rather than distantly related individuals, (2) among individuals who live in close-knit and geographically limited societies wherein they are likely to share kinship ties, and (3) among species capable of recognizing relatives and distinguishing them from nonrelatives (Barash, 1977).

Even biologically unrelated members of the same species may be motivated to help each other if the helping is likely to result in selective advantages for both (Trivers, 1971). Individuals of certain species, therefore, may be instinctually predisposed to make implicit bargains with each other because such bargains ultimately increase their own reproductive success. For instance, rhesus monkeys, baboons, and anthropoid apes are known to form coalitions based on mutual assistance, while chimpanzees, gibbons, African wild dogs, and wolves beg for food from each other reciprocally (Wilson, 1975). Such **reciprocal altruism** is more likely to occur when the situation involves (1) low risk for the helper, (2) high benefit for the recipient, and (3) high likelihood that the situation will be reversed in the future (Barash, 1977).

From the sociobiological standpoint, therefore, altruistic behavior should occur either (1) among closely related individuals (kin selection) or (2) when the cost–benefit ratio for the helper is ultimately favorable (reciprocal altruism). Both forms exist among humans, Wilson argues, but the second is by far more important for the survival and success of human societies, because it is endlessly flexible and capable of producing strong emotional bonds between completely unrelated peoples. Human beings help each other in a variety of ways for many reasons, but behind much of the help, maintains Wilson, is the implicit expectation that the helper will, some day, be rewarded. This implicit expectation motivates us to surrender our own self-interests, on occasion, for the good of others. Writes Wilson (1978), "lives of the most towering heroism are paid out in the [conscious or unconscious] expectation of great reward, not the least of which is a belief in personal immortality" (p. 154).

In an article entitled "Is Altruism Part of Human Nature?" psychologist Martin Hoffman (1981) endorses Wilson's view that altruism has a biological base, but takes issue with the sociobiological image of the altruist as a cold calculator of ultimate "cost and benefit." Drawing from a wide range of psychological research, Hoffman argues for the existence of a general, biologically based human tendency to help others in distress. The basis for the tendency is **empathy,** which Hoffman defines as "a vicarious affective response to others: that is, an affective response appropriate to someone else's situation rather than one's own" (p. 128). To experience empathy is to feel what the other person feels. If I see a tattered old woman struggling to cross an icy city street as the wind and the traffic threaten to knock her to the ground, I may experience alarm and arousal, not for my sake but for hers. Clearly *she* is in distress, but *I* feel a corresponding emotion, and I may therefore try to help her. Argues Hoffman, my empathy is biologically rooted— developed out of a predisposition coded in the genes and mediated primarily, Hoffman speculates, by a primitive part of the human brain called the limbic system. My altruistic behavior is motivated, at least in part, by the experience of empathy.

Batson, Fultz, and Schoenrade (1987) distinguish feelings of personal distress from empathy—either or both of which may be experienced when we encounter a person in need. Personal distress (feeling alarmed, upset, worried, disturbed, troubled, and so on) seems to evoke *egoistic motivation* to reduce one's own arousal. Though we may help the person in need, we may do so in order to relieve our *own* distress. On the other hand, true empathy (feeling sympathetic, moved, compassionate, tender, warm, soft-hearted, and so on) evokes *altruistic motivation,* in which the ultimate goal is to reduce the other person's distress rather than one's own. Some psychologists, however, take issue with this distinction, suggesting that most helping is motivated by the attempt to reduce one's own personal distress, even if that distress is in the form of "sadness" about the plight of another (Cialdini, Schaller, Fultz, & Beaman, 1987). Nonetheless, an impressive array of recent findings seems to support the legitimacy of the altruism-empathy link. In five studies testing egoistic alternatives to the empathy hypothesis, Batson and his colleagues (Batson, Dyck, Brandt, Batson, Powell, McMaster, & Griffit, 1988) found consistent support for the proposition that people tend to offer assistance and help when moved to do so by feelings of empathy and concern for those in distress or need. In something of a compromise position, Smith, Keating, and Stotland (1989) provide evidence to suggest that altruism is motivated by both a general empathic concern for the victim's plight and a specific sensitivity to the prospect of vicarious joy at the resolution of the victim's needs.

In human development, the earliest forms of empathy may be traced all the way back to the newborn. There is evidence that 1- and 2-day-old infants will cry in response to the sound of another infant's crying (Sagi & Hoffman, 1976). Such crying is vigorous and intense and does not appear to be merely a response to an annoying physical stimulus, since infants do not cry as much in response to equally loud nonhuman sounds, including computer-simulated infant cries. The finding indicates that babies experience distress in response to cues of the distress of others, even though they are doubtlessly not conscious of the nature of the outside distress. With development, more mature empathic responses to the distress of others can be observed. Typically, such responses are measured as verbal reports, facial expressions, or physiological changes. Thus, most 4–8-year-old children give empathic verbal reports to slide sequences portraying other children in highly emotional situations (Feshbach & Feshbach, 1969; Levine & Hoffman, 1976). Adults spontaneously emit empathic facial expressions, such as frowns, when witnessing others in physically painful situations or failing at a task (Gaertner & Dovidio, 1977; Krebs, 1975).

Hoffman (1981) reviews a large number of studies supporting a connection between empathy and altruistic behavior. He argues that empathy provides a biologically rooted emotional base for many selfless and cooperative acts among humans. Of course, empathy is not the only ingredient in altruism. Helping behavior in humans is complexly determined by numerous environmental factors: family, peer, and cultural factors; characteristics of the recipient of help; characteristics of the helping situation; and the individual's levels of cognitive development, self-esteem, and even mood (Radke-Yarrow, Zahn-Waxler, & Chapman, 1983). Nonetheless, natural selection may have predisposed human beings to feel the distress of others, designating empathy as a biological undergirding for "an altruistic response system that is reliable and flexible" (Hoffman, 1981, p. 27). A comprehensive review of many different studies of empathy and helping behavior finds a moderate positive association between measures of empathy and various kinds of altruistic, cooperative, and prosocial behaviors (Eisenberg & Miller, 1987).

In recent years, some psychologists have suggested that a particular combination of traits constitutes the **altruistic personality** (Bierhoff, Klein, & Kramp, 1991; Carlo, Eisenberg, Troyer, Switzer, & Speer, 1991; Rushton, 1980). Included within the cluster of characteristics defining this personality type are sympathy, social responsibility, and mature perspective taking. Altruistic people tend to experience strong feelings for others in distress; they tend to assume a substantial level of responsibility to assist others and to make positive contributions to society; and they are able to see problems and situations from many different vantage points, rather than merely their own. While people scoring high on these personality dimensions are not necessarily more altruistic in every situation they encounter in life, they do tend on the average to engage in a greater number of altruistic behaviors than individuals scoring low on these characteristics.

A team of researchers in Germany examined the personality characteristics of men and women who volunteered to provide first aid to help victims of traffic accidents (Bierhoff et al., 1991). Working with ambulance teams, the researchers solicited the participation of 43 adults who had witnessed traffic accidents and volunteered first aid. The first-aiders completed a lengthy battery of personality questionnaires. Their questionnaire responses were compared to a group of 34 adults who had also witnessed traffic accidents but who had not volunteered to provide aid. Compared to the nonhelpers, the first-aiders scored significantly

Altruism: the late Audrey Hepburn working with the poor.

higher on measures of empathy and social responsibility. In addition, the first-aiders were much more inclined than the nonhelpers to believe in a "just world," endorsing the optimistic viewpoint that life is basically fair and that good people are eventually rewarded for their efforts. Finally, first-aiders expressed greater confidence than did the nonhelpers in their ability to produce positive outcomes and to control their own destinies.

Most of the research on altruism has focused on discrete altruistic acts, such as providing first aid or helping a victim in distress. But many forms of altruism involve long-term commitments to programs and causes that entail a complicated sequence of thoughts, intentions, actions, and consequences. People who work regularly with the mentally disabled, who volunteer time to distribute provisions at food pantries and soup kitchens, who take on roles as "big brothers" or "big sisters" for disadvantaged youth, who participate in such programs as the Peace Corps, and so on—these people have made commitments to programs of altruistic action. Altruism is not so much what they do on occasion; it is rather, in a sense, who they are.

In a superb example of how psychologists can address critical real-world issues, Mark Snyder and Allen Omoto have launched a series of studies on the psychology of AIDS volunteerism (Omoto & Snyder, 1990; Omoto, Snyder, & Berghuis, in press; Snyder & Omoto, 1992). The AIDS epidemic threatens to exhaust the world's health care resources. As societies struggle to care for the dramatically escalating number of people infected with the HIV virus, volunteer organizations have come to assume an increasingly important role in providing care. Capturing the spirit of the AIDS volunteer effort in the United States, the dean of the Harvard School of Public Health has recently observed:

> One of the most remarkable and heartening byproducts of the
> HIV epidemic in the U.S. has been the development of grass-roots

organizations dedicated to serving the needs of people with AIDS. . . . As nonprofit, community-based organizations, they have provided a way for thousands of volunteers to give countless hours of assistance and comfort to patients, their loved ones and families. These organizations developed AIDS telephone hotlines and created specific educational materials for various cultural groups at high risk of HIV infection. They have also been outspoken and effective advocates for all those touched by the epidemic. (Fineberg, 1989, p. 117)

Snyder and Omoto view AIDS volunteerism as a developmental process extended over time. The first step of the process includes the decision to become involved in volunteer work. At this point, the researchers examine the questions of "Who volunteers to do AIDS volunteer work and why do they volunteer?" The second step is the volunteer experience itself, and here the researchers focus on "Who remains in volunteer work for a long time, who quits, and why?" The third step in the process concerns the consequences of volunteerism and focuses on the changes in attitudes, knowledge, and behavior that occur as a result of volunteer work in volunteers themselves, in the members of their immediate social networks, and in society at large.

Snyder and Omoto have administered a series of questionnaires to many different men and women who have become involved in AIDS volunteer work. With respect to their reasons for becoming involved, AIDS volunteers identify five main motivations: (1) *community concern,* reflecting people's sense of obligation to or concern about a community or social grouping; (2) personal *values,* or beliefs that people should engage in helping or humanitarian behavior because it is good; (3) *understanding,* trying to learn more about the disease, about how people cope with it, or about how they themselves can deal with their own fears and anxieties about AIDS; (4) *personal development,* or growth and the desire to gain valuable experiences; and (5) *esteem enhancement,* or the desire to feel better about the self, to feel less lonely, and so on.

In the first step of the volunteer process, volunteers most often report motivations that are grouped under the values category, followed in descending order by community concern, understanding, personal development, and esteem enhancement. When it comes to maintaining a commitment to volunteer work over time, however, values and community concern assume somewhat less importance. Snyder and Omoto find that the people who focus their motivations on personal development and esteem enhancement are the ones who are *most* likely to continue their volunteer work over a relatively long period of time. In other words, those who provide self-oriented reasons for involvement, as opposed to more other-oriented reasons such as values and community concern, tend to stick with the volunteer work over the long haul. Also surprising is the finding that the extent to which a person remains actively involved in the volunteer work is *not* related to measures of overall empathy, social responsibility, and nurturance.

In sum, we should consider the work on volunteerism in the larger context of the study of empathy and the altruistic personality. It appears that empathy is an important ingredient in the making of altruism and that altruism is very much implicated in the kind of volunteer work that Omoto and Snyder are studying. But like most other complex behaviors involving commitments over time, the experience of volunteerism involves patterns of thought, feeling, and behavior that are determined by many different factors, both internal and external. To borrow a page out of Freud's book, altruism and volunteer work are *overdetermined*, shaped by a host of biological, attitudinal, societal, and cultural forces and factors.

The Evolution of Love: Attachment Theory

One of the most influential theories in psychology today is *attachment theory*, developed by John Bowlby and Mary Ainsworth. In his classic 3-volume set entitled *Attachment and Loss* (Bowlby, 1969, 1973, 1980) and in his last book entitled *A Secure Base* (Bowlby, 1988), John Bowlby articulated a grand theory of the dynamics of affectional bonds in human life. The theory draws liberally on psychoanalytic thought, ethology, cybernetics, and evolution. It couches the sublime experience of human love in the no-nonsense language of natural selection and shows how attachments between human beings have proven exquisitely adaptive over the long course of human evolution. Mary Ainsworth has pioneered the assessment and understanding of individual differences in attachment bonds, showing how the quality of early caregiver-infant interaction may have long-term effects on personality (Ainsworth, 1967, 1969, 1989; Ainsworth, Blehar, Waters, & Wall, 1978; Ainsworth & Bowlby, 1991). In recent years, attachment theory has generated a plethora of developmental research focused on infancy and childhood. The theory has also been extended in creative ways into the arenas of adult attachment histories (Main, Kaplan, & Cassidy, 1985), attachment styles in romantic love (Hazan & Shaver, 1987, 1990), and the psychology of religion (Kirkpatrick, 1992; Kirkpatrick & Shaver, 1992).

Like Freud, Bowlby believed that the bond of love formed between the infant and the caregiver in the first year of life is a general prototype of all subsequent love relationships. And like Freud, Bowlby argued that this bond is driven by instinctual demands of biology. But whereas Freud believed that the infant's love for the mother originates in the investment of oral libido in the mother's breast, Bowlby followed the object-relations theorists in rejecting Freud's model of drive reduction and suggesting instead that infants are object seekers by nature, predisposed to form affectional bonds with others for the primary benefits those bonds obtain. Unlike the object-relations theorists, however, Bowlby underscored the evolutionary significance of deep affectional bonds. He wrote:

It is . . . more than likely that a human being's powerful propensity to make these deep and long-term relationships is the result of a strong gene-determined bias to do so, a bias that has been selected during the course of evolution. Within this frame of reference a child's strong propensity to attach himself to his mother and his father, or to whomever else may be caring for him, can be understood as having the function of reducing the risk of his coming to harm. For to stay in close proximity to, or in easy communication with, someone likely to protect you is the best of all possible insurance policies. Similarly a parent's concern to care for his or her offspring plainly has the function of contributing to the child's survival. That success in the maintenance of these long-term relationships should usually bring satisfaction and contentment, and that failure should bring frustration, anxiety, and sometimes despair are, on this reading, the prizes and penalties selected during evolution to guide us in our activities. (Bowlby, 1988, p. 81)

Attachment in Infancy

Virtually no other human experience feels so "natural" as the love we feel for our babies. The **attachment** bond between caregiver (mother, father, or other who cares for the baby) and infant develops through a number of well-defined stages in the first years of the child's life. It begins with the newborn's vague and nondiscriminant orientation to social stimuli, develops through a phase of heightened sociality in which 2–7-month-olds smile and show various attachment behaviors towards people, and ends as an affectional partnership between the child and a select few clearly discriminated and preferred caregivers (Ainsworth, Blehar, Waters, & Wall, 1978; Bowlby, 1969). Although many cultural differences can be observed, the caregiver–infant attachment bond appears to develop in approximately the same manner in virtually all known human societies (Bowlby, 1969; Konner, 1983). The attachment experience may feel so natural because, many would say, it is an integral part of human nature.

In behavioral terms, attachment refers to seeking and maintaining proximity to another individual. Caregivers and infants seek to be physically close to each other and to engage in tender physical contact. Ethologists have regularly observed attachment behavior in nonhuman primates such as apes and rhesus monkeys. These behavioral patterns are generally considered to have a strong instinctual base. For instance, newborn rhesus monkeys, in the first few weeks of life, are in constant contact with their mothers, spending virtually all daytime hours gripping mother with their hands, feet, and mouth, and being held by her at nighttime. As they get older, the monkeys begin to venture away from mother, making tentative initial forays of a few feet and then checking back with mother

Mary D.S. Ainsworth

as if to see if all is still well. During most of the first year of life, the rhesus monkey uses its mother as a secure base from which to explore the world and as a source of comfort during times of fear and anxiety.

The mother rhesus monkey, in turn, appears to be instinctually predisposed to maintain almost constant contact with the infant during the first few weeks and then to encourage slowly thereafter the infant's independent exploration. Some ethologists have suggested that the mother's behavior in this regard is akin to a fixed-action pattern released by the natural sign stimulus of the baby's face (Eibl-Eibesfeldt, 1975). In many species including humans, babies have large heads (in proportion to their bodies), prominent foreheads, large eyes set below the midline of the face, and soft, protruding cheeks. These "cute" features may serve as natural releasers of instinctual caregiving behavior (Cunningham, 1985).

Some ethologists regard attachment in some species to be a form of **imprinting.** A few hours after birth, for instance, ducklings will learn to follow a large, moving stimulus and to prefer that stimulus to other stimuli for a long time afterwards. In a natural setting, this large stimulus is almost invariably the mother. Imprinting, therefore, is a form of rapid learning whereby the infant forms a lasting preference for a particular stimulus, usually the natural mother, during a *sensitive period* of development. The implication is that if the sensitive period is missed, imprinting may not occur or will occur in a less adaptive manner. In laboratory experiments and other artificial settings, ducks and geese have imprinted on, and thereby established strong and lasting preferences for, such objects as flashing lights, electric trains, moving milk bottles, and even a squatting and quacking Konrad Lorenz, when these objects were presented to the animals during the sensitive developmental period for imprinting.

Human attachment appears to be a much more complex and malleable phenomenon than imprinting or fixed-action patterns. Nonetheless, many psychologists believe that human attachment is an instinctually grounded behavioral system of profound evolutionary significance. Bowlby (1969, 1973, 1980) argues that the caregiver–infant attachment bond is a complex, instinctually guided behavioral system that has functioned throughout human evolution to protect the infant from predators. In the hunting-and-gathering way of life of our ancestors, attachment improved an organism's genetic fitness by increasing the likelihood that his or her genes would survive and be passed down. By ensuring that mothers and infants would seek contact and physical closeness with each other, the attachment system made it easier for older and stronger caregivers to protect their dependent and defenseless human infants from threats to their survival and ultimate reproductive success.

Bowlby conceives of attachment as a goal-directed system designed to ensure the overall end of caregiver–infant proximity. The system is comprised of a number of subsystems, called **attachment behaviors,** including sucking, clinging, following, vocalizing, and smiling. Infants emit attachment behaviors that beckon caregivers to seek or maintain physical closeness or contact. Although each attachment behavior follows its own independent developmental course in the first few months of human life, attachment behaviors become organized and integrated during the second half of the first year. Thus, newborn infants will cry and cling, but they do not show true smiles in response to social stimuli until about 2 months of age, and they are not able to follow mother until they are able to crawl, months after the first smile. Crying, clinging, smiling, following, and other discrete attachment behaviors, however, begin to work together, after 6 or 7 months, to achieve mother–infant proximity. During this time, infants begin to show clear preferences for mothers, fathers, and other *attachment objects* in their environments, engaging in a variety of behavioral combinations to promote proximity with attachment objects. These behavioral combinations are exquisitely subtle and flexible instinctual strategies for relating to others, markedly influenced by learning and experience but deeply ingrained in human biology.

With respect to emotional development, the attachment system organizes the earliest experiences of human love and fear (Bowlby, 1969, 1973; Sroufe & Waters, 1977). Toward the end of the first year of life, infants begin to experience *stranger anxiety* and *separation anxiety,* two benchmarks of normal psychological development. At this time, infants begin to express caution and fear in the face of novel events and objects and when confronted with strangers. Stranger fear makes evolutionary sense, Bowlby suggests, for unfamiliar objects and persons have been associated with threat and dangers throughout evolution. The presence of the attachment object, however, can go a long way to relieve the fear that infants experience when faced with strangers and novelty. The felt security experienced in the attachment bond makes new and strange things seem less threatening and dangerous, as indeed they usually are, and have usually been throughout our evolutionary past, when human infants are in the presence of their caregivers.

When separated from their main caregivers, even for a short period of time, 8-month and older infants may show considerable distress, manifested in extreme wariness or crying. Brief separations from the caregiver are relatively harmless inevitabilities of everyday life, but long separations may be problematic. Feelings of abandonment are the most emotionally painful experiences human beings can know, Bowlby suggests. The pain is deeply rooted in the evolutionary fact that parental abandonment of the infant usually means death. This is why parental threats of abandonment are especially frightening to children and, when issued repeatedly, especially detrimental to healthy personality development. This is also why the experience of prolonged separation from one's attachment object may initiate a process of "mourning," through which the infant or child adjusts, over the period of weeks and months, to the perceived loss of the caregiver. In mourning, the infant will move through stages of angry *protest, despair* and sadness, and finally *detachment* (Bowlby, 1973). Detachment marks a defensive severance of the attachment bond. As a tragic example of detachment, observations of infants who have been removed from their caregivers for long periods of time, as during times of war, show that many infants will appear not to recognize their caregivers when they are eventually reunited (Bowlby, 1973). In these cases, the attachment has been emotionally undone.

Over the normal course of the first 2–3 years of life, the child builds up a set of expectations about the nature of relationships with other people. The expectations come to comprise a **working model.** Writes Bowlby (1973), "in the working model of the world that anybody builds, a key feature is his notion of who his attachment figures are, where they may be found, and how they may be expected to respond" (p. 203). The working model serves as an internalized template of love (Shaver & Rubenstein, 1980). When the attachment bond is *secure,* the infant may experience a basic trust in its surroundings, which provides the self-confidence to explore the world with enthusiasm and aplomb (Erikson, 1963; Sroufe & Waters, 1977). In the best attachment relationships, the human infant, like the rhesus monkey discussed earlier, uses the attachment object as a *secure base* from which to explore the world. When the attachment bond is generally *insecure*, however, the infant may come to consider the world a threatening and dangerous place. Out of this early pessimism about life the child formulates a working model of the attachment object that underscores uncertainty and rejection. A working model of an inconsistent and rejecting attachment object may lead to subsequent deficits in self-esteem and a lasting vulnerability to loneliness (Bowlby, 1980; Shaver & Rubenstein, 1980).

Mother-infant attachment.

Secure and Insecure Attachments

Virtually all babies become attached to a caregiver in the first year of life. Yet, there are significant individual differences in the *quality* of that attachment relationship, and these differences can be measured. By the time the infant is 1 year old, individual differences in attachment quality are apparent. The most popular laboratory method for assessing these individual differences in 1-year-olds is the **Strange Situation** method, developed by Ainsworth and her colleagues (Ainsworth et al., 1978). The Strange Situation involves a series of short laboratory episodes through which the infant, the caregiver (usually mother, sometimes father), and a "stranger" (usually a woman who is working with the experimenter) interact in a comfortable setting and the behaviors of the infant are observed (Table 4.5). The infant and caregiver arrive and get comfortable; the stranger enters; the caregiver leaves for a short period of time; the caregiver returns, and the stranger leaves; the caregiver exits again, leaving the infant alone; the stranger reenters; and the caregiver finally returns again. Researchers analyze the behavior of the infant in all of the episodes of the Strange Situation, paying special attention to the two "reunion episodes" in which the caregiver returns after a brief separation.

Behavioral observations in the Strange Situation yield three different general patterns of attachment: what have been termed **A-babies, B-babies,**

 **Table 4.5**

Episodes in the "Strange Situation" Procedure for Assessing Individual Differences in Attachment

Episode	Who Is Involved	What Happens
1	Caregiver, Infant	After being introduced to the room and the many toys it contains, the caregiver (mother or father) sits and looks at a magazine while the infant explores the room and its contents.
2	Stranger, Caregiver, Infant	A woman whom the infant has never seen before enters, greets caregiver and sits silently for 1 minute. Then the woman engages caregiver in a conversation. Finally she initiates interaction with the infant.
3	Stranger, Infant	Caregiver quietly leaves room. If infant becomes too distressed, the episode is terminated.
4	Caregiver, Infant	Caregiver returns and stranger leaves. This is the first "reunion episode." Caregiver seeks to interest the infant in the toys.
5	Infant	After the infant appears comfortable again, caregiver leaves.
6	Stranger, Infant	The stranger enters again. She initiates interaction with the infant. If the infant prefers to play alone, the stranger retreats to a chair and reads a magazine.
7	Caregiver, Infant	Caregiver returns and stranger leaves. This is the second "reunion episode."

Some notes on method: Each of the episodes is approximately 3 minutes in length. All of the proceedings are observed by researchers behind a one-way mirror. Usually, the episodes are videotaped as well and later analyzed in various ways.

and **C-babies.** Approximately two-thirds of mother–baby pairs show *secure attachment.* The infants in these pairs are termed B-babies. Like most of the babies studied, securely attached infants find the brief separation from the caregiver and the entrance of strangers to be at least mildly upsetting. These are normal manifestations of mistrust shown by virtually all infants, regardless of their attachment classification, after about 8 months of age or so, at which time separation anxiety and stranger anxiety naturally emerge. However, when the caregiver is present, B-babies explore their environments with great ease and comfort, using the caregiver as a secure base. When the caregiver leaves, they show much less exploration, but when she returns again in the reunion episodes, they greet the caregiver with great enthusiasm and resume their exploration of the environment.

A-babies and C-babies show patterns of *insecure attachment*. The pattern for A-babies is termed *avoidant*. A-babies are most noted for their tendency to avoid the caregiver when she returns in the reunion episodes, as if to say, "Hey! You abandoned me; I'll do the same to you for a while." The pattern of insecure attachment for C-babies is termed *resistant*. C-babies show a mixture of approach and avoidance behavior in the reunion episodes of the Strange Situation. When the caregiver returns after the brief separations, the C-baby may approach the caregiver in a friendly manner but then angrily resist being picked up. C-babies are noted for their angry reactions to the caregiver, though they occasionally show passive reactions as well, reminiscent of the standard patterns shown by A-babies.

Developmental psychologists have undertaken investigations to determine what factors produce patterns of secure and insecure attachment in the first years. The quality of the early interaction between caregivers and the infant may play an important role. In this regard, Main (1981) has shown that mothers of securely attached infants tend to hold their babies more carefully and tenderly and for longer periods of time during early infancy than do mothers of insecurely attached babies. Others have suggested that maternal sensitivity is also a consistent predictor of attachment (Ainsworth et al., 1978; Egeland & Farber, 1984; Sroufe, 1985). A mother who is especially sensitive to her baby is "alert to perceive her baby's signals, interprets them accurately, and responds appropriately and promptly" (Ainsworth et al., 1978, p. 142). Observations of mothers and babies at home and in the laboratory during the infant's first 3 months suggest that mothers of infants who are later classified as securely attached respond more frequently to crying, show more affection when holding the baby, are more likely to acknowledge the baby with a smile or conversation when entering the baby's room, and are better at feeding the baby because of their attention to the baby's signals, compared to mothers of babies later deemed insecurely attached. A recent study of mothers and 12-month-old infants observed twice at home for two hours by two researchers shows a strong relation between secure attachment and maternal sensitivity (Pederson, Moran, Sitko, Campbell, Ghesquire, & Acton, 1990). Mothers of more secure infants were more frequently characterized as noticing their babies' signals and using the signals to guide their behavior; they also were more knowledgeable about their infants and appeared to enjoy them more than mothers of less secure infants.

In a small laboratory study of American children, Blehar, Lieberman, and Ainsworth (1977) found that the quality of early mother–infant play positively predicted attachment patterns at age 1 year. In this study, infants were first observed between the ages of 6 and 15 weeks as they played with their mothers. It is generally agreed that at this early point in development (during the first half-year of life) infants are not yet attached to their caregivers, but that the attachment bond is starting to form. Later, when the infants were around 1 year of age, the now-stable patterns of mother–infant attachment were assessed in the Strange Situation. Infants later identified as securely attached were more responsive in face-to-face play, and their mothers were more enthusiastic and encouraging, compared to infants later identified as insecurely attached. In general, the mother–infant pairs that were later classified as securely attached showed a high degree of *synchrony,* or interactive play. Isabella, Belsky, and von Eye (1989) found similar results in an intensive study of a wide variety of infant and mother behaviors, assessed at infant ages of 1, 3, and 9 months. The authors defined *interactional synchrony* as "the extent to which interaction appeared to be reciprocal and mutually rewarding, so that its frequent occurrence would presumably foster development of the infant's working model of mother as available, responsive, and trustworthy" (p. 13). Infants classified as securely attached at 9 months tended to show especially synchronous patterns of interaction with mothers at ages 1 and 3 months, compared to infants classified as insecure.

The importance of early caregiver–infant synchrony in the development of personality and interpersonal relationships has been underscored by a number of theorists (Brazelton, Koslowski, & Main, 1974; Stern, 1985). According to Stern (1985), early play between babies and caregivers resembles a synchronous "dance," with both partners continually adjusting the rhythm and tuning the exchange through a rich variety of verbal and nonverbal signals and signs. In Stern's view, the fundaments of a basic sense of self and one's relation to the outside world are established in early patterns of caregiver–infant play.

A growing body of research supports the general hypothesis that secure attachment in infancy leads to greater levels of mastery and competence in the preschool years and beyond. A representative study in this regard was conducted by Hazen and Durrett (1982). Children aged 30–34 months who had been assessed at 12 months for security of attachment were observed exploring with their mothers in a large laboratory playhouse. The researchers measured how much exploration the children showed according to the number of different movements the child made from one area of the playhouse to another, and they measured the extent to which the exploration was "active" (child leads mother) as opposed to "passive" (mother leads child). As Table 4.6 shows, children who 2 years before had been classified as securely attached (B-babies) explored more and engaged in a greater ratio of active to passive exploration compared to children who had been classified insecurely attached (A- and C-babies).

Other studies examining the relation between quality of attachment in the first year and indices of mastery and independence at ages 2 and 3 have found that secure attachment is positively associated with (1) higher quality of exploration (Main, 1983), (2) higher levels of pretend play (Slade, 1987), (3) greater competence in problem-solving tasks (Matas, Arend, & Sroufe, 1978), and (4) more rapid and smooth adjustments to strangers (Lutkenhaus, Grossmann, & Grossmann,

Table 4.6

Exploratory Behavior of 3-Year-Olds as a Function of Attachment at Age 1 Year

	Attachment Classfication		
Exploration Measure	**Avoidant (A-Baby)**	**Secure (B-Baby)**	**Ambivalent (C-Baby)**
Number of movements	31.2	35.7	31.7
Active movements (%)	73	88	65

Source: Hazen & Durrett (1982, p. 755).

1985). Sroufe (1988) reports that preschool children with histories of secure attachment neither victimized nor were they victimized by assigned play partners. In sharp contrast, children with avoidant histories were quite likely to victimize, and children with histories of resistant attachment were often victimized in their interactions with peers. In a recent study of 4-year-olds during free play, insecure boys tended to show more aggression, disruptiveness, and attention seeking compared to secure boys. Insecure girls were more dependent and less assertive than secure girls (Turner, 1991). The author suggests that gender differences in social behavior are exaggerated among children with histories of insecure attachments. The stereotypes of the aggressive boy and passive girl are *not* supported among preschool children with secure attachment histories, but the stereotypes *do* seem to characterize quite well the subgroup of insecure children examined in this study.

Following children into elementary school, research has shown that 5-year-olds who were securely attached as infants show more persistence and resourcefulness in challenging tasks than children who in infancy were rated less securely attached (Arend, Gove, & Sroufe, 1979; Sroufe, 1983). LaFreniere and Sroufe (1985) related attachment history to a broad array of assessments of peer competence in the preschool classroom. In this study, the researchers observed 40 children aged 4 and 5 years as they interacted with each other in class. They obtained the following five measurements of competence: (1) teacher ratings of social competence, (2) peer ratings of popularity, (3) observations of the quality of children's social participation, (4) the amount of attention each child received from other children based on analysis of who the children looked at while playing, and (5) ratings of social dominance. As Figure 4.1 shows, preschool children who were securely attached as infants scored higher on all

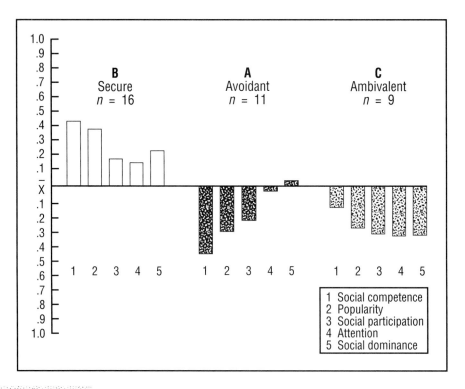

Figure 4.1

Profiles of Peer Competence as a Function of Attachment History.

From LaFreniere & Sroufe, 1985, p. 63.

five measures of social competence than their peers who as infants were classified as insecurely attached.

To date, longitudinal research on individual differences in attachment has not followed children beyond early elementary school. Therefore, we are unable to draw any informed conclusions concerning the long-term effects of attachment on personality development in adolescence and beyond. The picture we have for the first 6 years of life, however, reveals impressive continuity in attachment and in the organization of attachment-related behavior (Grossmann & Grossmann, 1991; Main & Cassidy, 1988; Sroufe, 1988). A growing number of researchers are viewing attachment as a key organizational construct for social, emotional, and personality development. A growing number are coming to endorse what Bowlby (1973) termed the "strong case for believing that an unthinking confidence in the unfailing accessibility and support of attachment figures is the bedrock on which stable and self-reliant personality is built" (p. 322).

As the results of attachment research have become disseminated in the public arena, informed citizens and policymakers have posed hard questions about the effects of contemporary economic, political, social, and cultural arrangements on the development of secure and insecure attachments (Silverstein, 1991). Are certain types of parents at great risk for having children who will become insecurely attached? Are working mothers more likely to have insecurely attached children? What is the relationship between infant day care and attachment? Can fathers substitute for mothers? Are father–infant attachments the same as mother–infant attachments?

Each of these questions is embedded in a complex and evolving matrix of cultural values, historical trends, and economic realities. While psychological research can help inform the debate around such questions, it cannot itself provide definitive answers to any of them. To a certain extent, research findings themselves are cultural constructions, products of the values and beliefs held dear by the researchers themselves. This is not to say that psychological researchers are unduly biased in their inquiries. Rather, social scientists, like all other people, make inquiries in a particular social and cultural context. Their questions and their methods are influenced by the evolving social world within which they live. Take for instance the quote from John Bowlby two paragraphs above. He suggests that secure attachment is the "bedrock" upon which is built a "self-reliant" and "stable" personality. In contemporary Western society, "self-reliance" and "stability" are strongly valued as desirable characteristics in persons. But different historical eras and different cultures value different attributes in persons. In some cultures, "self-reliance" may be synonymous with selfishness, perceived as a threat to the community good. Keeping these caveats in mind, therefore, we are better positioned to evaluate the different possible meanings of contemporary attachment research.

Are certain types of parents at risk for having children with insecure attachments? As we have seen, research suggests that mothers who are especially sensitive, responsive, and encouraging are more likely to raise children with secure attachments. But we should view these characteristics as relational attributes rather than personality traits per se. In other words, "responsiveness" and "sensitivity" refer to how a mother reacts to her infant and not necessarily to how she approaches the world overall. In general, research has not identified a set of global personality traits that predispose mothers to engage in interactions leading to a particular kind of attachment classification. There is one exception to this rule, however. Recent studies have suggested that mothers with chronic *negative affect*—such as chronically depressed mothers—tend to have infants who are less securely attached (Ainsworth & Eichberg, 1991; Spieker & Booth, 1988). In these cases, the mother is unable to summon up the enthusiasm to engage her infant in joyous and reciprocal exchange. Interactions lack energy and synchrony, leading to the development on the part of the infant of a working model of a neglecting and lethargic caregiver.

Surprisingly, socio-economic status per se does not appear to be significantly related to attachment classification (Spieker & Booth, 1988). Children from poor and working-class families are no less likely to establish secure attachments than middle-class and upper-class children, as long as cases of known abuse or neglect are eliminated from the samples. However, the stresses of poverty and unemployment may increase the likelihood of abuse and neglect, and therefore negative effects of disadvantaged social class may manifest themselves indirectly. Research suggests that children of abusive parents are indeed at risk for insecure attachment (Egeland & Sroufe, 1981). For example, Lyons-Ruth, Connell, Zoll, and Stahl (1987) found that maltreated infants were more avoidant of their mothers in the Strange Situation than nonmaltreated infants. Other studies suggest that chronic child abuse may promote the development of a "disorganized" attachment pattern—the **D-baby** (Carlson, Cicchetti, Barnett, & Braunwald, 1989). D-babies appear confused and disoriented in the presence of mother. Within this seriously disturbed pattern of attachment, the child appears to do little exploring in the mother's presence, and the mother appears unable to calm the child down during periods of distress. It is as if the infant perceives her to be as threatening as, or even more threatening than, the rest of the environment.

What about day care? In the 1990s, over half of American mothers of infants and approximately 75% of mothers with school-aged children participate in the paid workforce (Silverstein, 1991). As a result, paid child care has become an extremely important issue in contemporary American society. Unlike 75 other nations across the world, the United States has no comprehensive family policy that helps families cope with the competing demands of work and child care. Therefore, a growing number of families are dependent on the services of many different kinds of paid child-care providers.

A small number of studies have examined the development of attachment in infants who spend a considerable amount of time away from their mothers in day care. Data from the Netherlands, where government supports day-care programs, suggests that the day-care experience does not affect the quality of attachment in a negative manner (Goosens, 1987). Data from the United States, however, tend to show a slight tendency for infants in day care whose mothers work full time to manifest insecure attachment patterns (especially avoidant patterns of A-babies) in the Strange Situation, compared to infants raised solely by their mothers at home. In a comprehensive review, Clarke-Stewart (1989) reports: "Of the infants of full-time working mothers, 36% have been classified as insecure; of the infants of nonemployed or part-time working mothers, only 29% have been so classified" (p. 266). The meaning of the finding is ambiguous, however. Different day-care providers vary significantly with respect to cost and quality. In addition, the Strange Situation may hold different experiences for day-care and home-care children. The procedure depends on the infant's experiencing separation from the caregiver as a mildly stressful event. But the Strange Situation may not be equally stressful for infants of working and nonworking mothers. Those with significant day-care experience may have adjusted well to brief separations from mother. Their occasionally avoidant responses in reunion episodes of the Strange Situation procedure may be more indicative of the rather routine nature of brief separations in their lives than of insecure attachment per se.

Children playing at a daycare setting.

What about fathers? Studies suggest that infants may form intense attachment bonds with fathers, as well as other family members. Father–infant attachment resembles mother–infant attachment in many respects (Lamb, 1976, 1979). Infants may use fathers as secure bases for exploration; they may seek out fathers during periods of uncertainty or fear. Differences between mother–infant and father–infant attachments have been noted, too. Mothers spend more time with their infants and tend to be responsible for most of the caregiving. Fathers, in contrast, spend proportionally more of their interaction time in play. Moreover, fathers play in a more physical, idiosyncratic, and emotionally arousing way, whereas mothers tend to play in ways that are less arousing, more verbal, and more often involve toys and conventional games such as peek-a-boo. As a result, the father–infant relationship tends to be more concerned with affiliative needs (having fun) than attachment needs (felt security). The father as a socializer and playmate provides cognitive and social stimulation that is somewhat different from that provided by the mother (Bridges, Connell, & Belsky, 1988). It is not surprising to learn, therefore, that the level of security in an infant's attachment to mother may not be the same as that with father (Main & Weston, 1981). The two attachment relationships are relatively independent, though one recent study suggests a slight tendency for an infant's secure attachment with mother to be correlated with a corresponding secure attachment with father (Fox, Kimmerly, & Schafer, 1991).

Father-infant attachment.

Finally, we should consider the intriguing possibility that, in some cases, insecure attachment may be just as adaptive, in an evolutionary sense, as secure attachment. In their new "evolutionary theory of socialization," Jay Belsky, Laurence Steinberg, and Patricia Draper (1991) propose that evolution has provided for two divergent developmental pathways in the quest to pass one's genes to the next generation. For the securely attached infant growing up with adequate material resources and in the relative harmony of an intact, two-parent family, personality development is built on a working model of trust and reliability in interpersonal relationships. The relative lack of stress in such families may slightly delay the onset of puberty, the authors claim, which is associated with later sexual activity and may become connected with more commitment to long-term intimate relationships in adulthood (e.g., stable marriage) and greater investment in parenting. This would appear to be the developmental model favored by middle-class American society. With respect to genetic fitness, it works to maximize the *quality* of parent–child relationships to assure that the few progeny who are produced will survive and flourish, passing genes to subsequent generations.

A contrasting model emerges in unstable families, within which insecure attachment may be more likely. Children grow up in a stressful environment that is lacking in basic material and emotional resources. Their working models

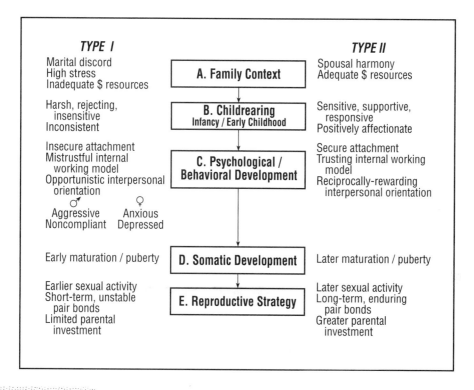

Figure 4.2

Two Divergent Development Pathways.

From Belsky, Steinberg, & Draper, 1991, p. 651.

emphasize the unpredictability of interpersonal relationships, leading them to adopt an "opportunistic" rather than reciprocal orientation toward others. Boys may tend to be more aggressive; girls may become somewhat depressed or anxious. The childhood stress may accelerate the onset of puberty, as some studies have suggested, leading to earlier sexual maturity, earlier sexual activity, promiscuity, and eventually limited parental investment. The emphasis is on the *quantity* of offspring produced, assuring that the maximum number of opportunities for passing one's genes down to the next generation are fulfilled. The authors concede that such a developmental pattern *seems* to have little going for it:

> To many readers it will no doubt seem counterintuitive to assert, as we and others do, that a developmental trajectory characterized by attachment insecurity, behavior problems, early maturation, precocious sexuality, unstable pair bonds, limited parental investment, and high total fertility makes "biological sense." In modern Western society, this reproductive strategy appears

clearly dysfunctional and disadvantageous. Why, then, would it have evolved? (Belsky, Steinberg, & Draper, 1991, p. 653)

The authors argue that within certain unfavorable environments, characterized by poverty and familial instability, early sexual activity and higher fertility may prove especially adaptive in removing the young boy or girl from the family of origin early on and positioning him or her for greater reproductive success than might be possible for those whose sexual maturation is delayed (Figure 4.2). They write:

> This strategy may be associated with higher offspring mortality, but from the point of view of fitness, individuals living in such adverse circumstances who *delay* reproducing may well be selected against (i.e., leave few or no offspring). In such an environment, a man who invests disproportionately in one woman and in children (who may not be his own) will leave relatively few of his own offspring behind. Likewise, a young woman who waits for the right man to help rear her children may lose valuable reproductive opportunities at a time when her health and physical capability are at their peak and when her mother and senior female kin are young enough to be effective surrogates. In such circumstances, nonbonded and relatively indiscriminate sexuality, as well as high fertility, can be positively selected. It is in this sense, then, we assert that both of the reproductive strategies that we detailed make "biological sense," in that they are optimal given the contexts in which they develop—and for which they were selected. (Belsky, Steinberg, & Draper, 1991, pp. 653–654)

In this theory, the relative security of attachment is one barometer of the prevailing relational context within which the child will grow up. As such, it will work with other indicators to influence the timing of puberty and the development of an appropriate reproductive strategy. According to the authors, "evolution has primed humans to learn particular lessons during the first 5–7 years of life that will shape their subsequent pair bonding and child-rearing behavior" (Belsky, Steinberg, & Draper, 1991, p. 648). Just how this influence works out at the physiological level is a matter of some speculation, and its overall importance in shaping pair-bonding and child-rearing strategies is open to considerable dispute (Maccoby, 1991). Still, the theory proposed by Belsky, Steinberg, and Draper is noteworthy for its serious attempt to understand important individual differences in human personality from the standpoint of modern evolutionary theory. Like the recent work of Buss on mating strategies and Gangestad and Simpson on sociosexuality, the evolutionary theory of socialization provokes us to think about both human nature and individual differences in persons from a sociobiological perspective emphasizing human adaptation within a wide variety of environments and under divergent selection pressures.

Adult Attachments

Attachment theory describes an affectional relationship between two persons through which one person provides support, protection, and a secure base for the other. The most obvious example of attachment, therefore, is the bond of love between the mature caregiver and the relatively defenseless infant. However, the dynamics of attachment may be played out in many other relationships as well, throughout the human life-span (Ainsworth, 1989; Bowlby, 1980). In recent years, psychologists have extended attachment theory into adulthood. To date their inquiries have focused on two ways in which attachments are influential in the adult years. First, they have examined adults' working models of their own childhood attachments, asking adults to tell the stories of their earliest relationships (Main, 1991). Second, they have entertained the possibility that romantic love in young adulthood and beyond may be understood in terms of secure and insecure attachment qualities (Hazan & Shaver, 1987).

Mary Main and her colleagues (George, Kaplan, & Main, 1985; Main, 1991; Main, Kaplan, & Cassidy, 1985) have developed an **Adult Attachment Interview** through which men and women respond to open-ended questions about their recollections of their own childhood attachment bonds with their parents or other caregivers. The adult is asked to choose five adjectives that best describe the relationship with each parent during childhood and then to provide an account of a particular episode from childhood illustrating each adjective. Later the adult is asked to describe what he or she did when upset as a child, to which parent he or she felt closer, whether he or she ever felt rejected as a child, why the parents may have acted the way they did, how the relationships with the parents have changed over time, and how the early experiences may have affected the adult's current functioning.

Based on the interview, Main classifies each adult into one of four categories: *Secure/autonomous, Dismissing* of attachments, *Preoccupied* by past attachments, and *Unresolved* with respect to traumatic attachment-related events. Her research suggests that mothers with Secure/autonomous attachments from childhood tend to raise securely attached infants themselves. Dismissing parents tend to have avoidant children (A-babies); Preoccupied parents tend to have resistant children (C-babies); and mothers with Unresolved attachments from childhood stemming from traumatic events such as abuse tend to have children with disorganized attachments (D-babies). In a recent prospective study, researchers administered the Adult Attachment Interview to pregnant women expecting their first child and then conducted the Strange Situation with their babies at age one year (Fonagy, Steele, & Steele, 1991). In keeping with Main's results, adult attachments of pregnant women in the interviews tended to match the subsequent attachment classifications of their infants at age 1.

Main (1991) describes the Adult Attachment Interviews typically produced by Secure/autonomous parents with securely attached children. Such parents "focused easily on the questions; showed few departures from usual forms of narrative or discourse; easily marked the principles or rationales behind their responses; and struck judges as both collaborative and truthful" (p. 142). An essential characteristic of their interviews appears to be the ease with which they are able to provide a *coherent* account of their childhood. Whether describing positive or negative experiences from childhood, Secure/autonomous adults are able to fashion a story from childhood that is consistent and convincing.

By sharp contrast, Dismissing and Preoccupied parents tend to be "relatively incoherent in their interview transcripts, exhibiting logical and factual contradictions; inability to stay with the interview topic; contradictions between general descriptors of their relationships with their parents and actual autobiographical episodes offered; apparent inability to access early memories; anomalous changes in wording or intrusions into topics; slips of the tongue; metaphor or rhetoric inappropriate to the discourse context; and inability to focus upon the interviews" (Main, 1991, p. 143). In particular, Dismissing parents of avoidant infants are usually distinguished for their insistence that they cannot remember much from their earlier years. Often they will idealize their parents in vague terms but be unable to provide behavioral proof for their claims. Preoccupied parents of resistant infants tend to provide lengthy but rambling responses about childhood that often contradict themselves.

Finally, Unresolved parents of infants displaying disorganized attachment tend to provide moderately coherent narratives of childhood, but they slip into magical and bizarre thought patterns when considering attachment-related events such as loss. "In these statements, the adult may indicate beliefs in 'magical' causality surrounding a death or other trauma, or subtly indicate a belief that a deceased attachment figure is simultaneously dead and alive" (Main, 1991, p. 145). Overall, these accounts lack *plausibility*. Just beneath the surface of a seemingly sensible narrative lie primitive and irrational thought processes linked up with unresolved trauma from childhood.

Research employing the Adult Attachment Interview suggests that working models of attachment laid down in childhood may continue to influence adult behavior in the realm of caregiving (Table 4.7). Cindy Hazan and Philip Shaver have extended this line of thought in a different direction by suggesting that working attachment models may also influence the ways in which adults engage each other in romantic love (Hazan & Shaver, 1987, 1990). Borrowing Ainsworth's original division among B-babies, A-babies, and C-babies, Hazan and Shaver have identified three corresponding **attachment styles** in adult love. Adults with a secure attachment style say they find it relatively easy to get close to others and are comfortable depending on others and having others depend on them. They don't worry too much about others' getting too close. They describe their most important love experiences as happy, friendly, and trusting. They emphasize being able to accept and support their partners despite their partners' faults. Adults with avoidant attachment styles (akin to Ainsworth's A-babies) report that they are somewhat uncomfortable being close to others and find it difficult to trust others completely. They are characterized by a "fear of intimacy," by emotional highs and lows, and by excessive jealousy. Adults with anxious/ambivalent styles (akin to Ainsworth's resistant C-babies) say they want to merge with others but that this desire sometimes scares other people away.

Table 4.7

Corresponding Attachment Types From Adult Interviews and Observations of Infants

Adult Attachment Interview	Infant Attachment Type
Secure/autonomous	Secure (B-baby)
Dismissing	Avoidant (A-baby)
Preoccupied	Resistant (C-baby)
Unresolved	Disorganized (D-baby)

They worry that their partners do not love them and will eventually abandon them. They experience love as involving obsession, desire for reciprocation and union, emotional highs and lows, and extreme sexual attraction and jealousy.

Employing a set of simple self-report questions concerning a person's general view of romantic love, Hazan and Shaver (1987) report that approximately 60% of their adult respondents are classified as securely attached, with the remainder falling within avoidant or anxious/ambivalent (resistant) categories. The breakdown is roughly comparable to the ratios of secure and insecure attachments obtained in research on infants. In addition, recent studies suggest a person's overall attachment style is predictive of love-related behavior. For example, Simpson (1990) found that secure attachment style was associated with greater relationship interdependence, commitment, trust, and satisfaction among dating college students. Mikulincer and Nachson (1991) found that students with secure and ambivalent styles exhibit greater levels of self-disclosure than avoidant students. Kobak and Hazan (1991) found that spouses with secure working models—that is, expectations that partners are psychologically available and ready to be relied upon—deal with their emotional conflicts in more constructive ways and report better marital adjustment. Recently, Hazan and Shaver (1990) have explored the possibility that love and work in adulthood—two key criteria of maturity, Freud is thought to have said—are functionally similar to Bowlby's conceptualization of attachment and exploration in infancy.

The crucial link between caregiver–infant attachment and adult attachment styles is the concept of inner working models. Hazan and Shaver propose that adult styles are the legacies of internalized models of relating that are laid down in infancy. Modest support for this idea comes from a study by Feeney and Noller (1990) showing that college students with secure attachment styles report relatively positive perceptions of early family relationships. By contrast, avoidant students tend to report childhood separations from their mothers, and anxious/ambivalent students describe fathers who are especially nonsupportive. For the most part, however, the precise linkage between infant attachment and adult love remains a mystery. Indeed, there are certain ways in which romantic love is *not* like attachment. Ideally, lovers are relative equals who share themselves with each other in an intimate and egalitarian manner. By contrast, attachment suggests a relation of relative nonequals—the infant attached to the stronger, wiser, more mature attachment object (McAdams, 1992a). Still, there is little doubt that lovers often function as attachment objects for each other, providing secure bases for each other's explorations in the world. The relationship between infant attachment and adult love, therefore, remains an exciting realm for future research.

Summary for Chapter 4

1. In recent years, a growing number of personality psychologists have emphasized instinctive behavior patterns, human evolution, and the biological bases of social behavior in their theories and research. These new positions share with Freud and the psychoanalytic tradition a general belief that behavior is motivated by instinctual forces over which the individual has minimal control and about which the individual may be unaware.

2. Ethology is the naturalistic study of adaptive behavior patterns. Recent ethological approaches suggest that instincts are biologically rooted and adaptive motivational tendencies that set boundaries or limits within which a good deal of behavioral variation may occur.

3. The human being's instinctual endowment has been forged through millions of years of evolution. Sociobiologists argue that a great deal of social behavior in animals and humans has an instinctual, evolutionary base and is strongly regulated and directed by genes.

4. Evolutionary approaches to understanding the person suggest that natural selection has endowed individuals with a relatively large number of domain-specific mechanisms for solving particular adaptive problems, such as problems of survival and reproduction.

5. Gender differences in mating and reproductive strategies have been documented in most human cultures and may be explained, in part, by considering the divergent strategies that males and females have typically adopted over the course of evolution to maximize their genetic fitness.

6. Robert Hogan's socioanalytic theory of personality argues that human beings have evolved to live in highly ritualized social groups wherein they seek status and approval from others. A major handicap in many such social contexts may be the trait of shyness.

7. According to some sociobiologists, human beings are by nature a moderately aggressive species. Individual differences among persons in aggressiveness appear to be relatively stable over time, and some recent studies suggest they may be linked to testosterone levels in both males and females.

8. Some sociobiologists argue that organisms may promote their own genetic fitness indirectly through altruism and self-sacrificial acts, as in kin selection and reciprocal altruism. Human altruism may be partly motivated by empathy, but it appears to be overdetermined by many other forces and factors as well.

9. One of the most influential theories in psychology today is attachment theory, formulated by John Bowlby and Mary Ainsworth. The theory suggests that the bond of love between infant and caregiver is a complex, instinctually grounded behavior system that has functioned throughout evolution to assure mother–infant proximity and thereby to protect the infant from predators.

10. As the caregiver–infant attachment relationship develops in the first few years of life, the infant builds up a set of expectations concerning human relationships, which come to comprise an internalized working model.

11. Utilizing the Strange Situation procedure, researchers have identified four patterns of attachment in 1-year-olds: secure (B-babies), avoidant (A-babies), resistant (C-babies), and disorganized (D-babies) attachment.

12. The antecedents of secure attachment include maternal sensitivity and synchrony in early mother–infant play.

13. Longitudinal studies have linked secure attachment in infancy to a number of positive indices of independence, mastery, and peer popularity in the preschool and early elementary school years.

14. In their evolutionary theory of socialization, Belsky, Steinberg, and Draper make a provocative argument for the evolutionary adaptiveness of insecure attachment and minimal parental investment under certain stressful situations and selection pressures.

15. Adult attachments have been examined in two ways: Through the Adult Attachment Interview, men and women tell the stories of their early relationships with parents, which are subsequently classified into categories of Secure/autonomous, Dismissing, Preoccupied, and Unresolved; and recent studies of romantic love yield three attachment styles that parallel the infant categories of secure, avoidant, and resistant attachment.

Part II

Interaction Episodes

The Person, the Situation, and the Prediction of Behavior

Chapter 5 Personality Traits
Chapter 6 Social Learning and the Social Situation
Chapter 7 The Interaction of Person and
 Environment

Human behavior is a function of the interaction between a person and the environment. Every human behavior, therefore, is embedded in an interaction episode. Indeed, the person's life may be viewed as a series of interaction episodes played out over time. How might we best account for what will occur in an interaction episode? What factors within the person and what factors in the person's environment must we measure in order to predict accurately a person's behavior within a given episode, across different episodes, and over time? Throughout the history of personality psychology, two very different schools of thought have battled over the issue of accurate prediction of human behavior. On one side, trait psychology has traditionally argued that behavior can be best predicted through the assessment of individual differences in internal and stable dispositions, or personality traits. On the other side, situationist approaches to personality have contended that the measurement of individual differences in environmental situations is the better strategy for predicting precisely what will occur in an interaction episode. In Chapters 5–7, we consider personality from the standpoint of traits, situations, and their interactions.

Chapter 5 provides an overview of modern trait psychology, beginning with a discussion of how to measure traits through self-report questionnaires and other rating procedures, with special emphasis on the concept of construct validation in personality research. While personality psychologists have developed many different trait theories and measurement techniques, factor-analytic studies in recent years have converged on a five-factor model of traits, called the Big Five. The Big Five is a comprehensive taxonomy of traits encompassing the broad domains of extraversion (E), neuroticism (N), openness to experience (O), conscientiousness (C), and agreeableness (A). Longitudinal studies suggest that individual differences in traits tend to be remarkably stable over the adult life span, and twin studies suggest a substantial genetic component for certain traits, especially extraversion and neuroticism. Individual differences in personality traits appear to have their first manifestation in dimensions of infant temperament.

Chapter 6 shifts to social-learning theories of personality, providing a situationist perspective on behavioral prediction. Modern social-learning theories have their origins in behaviorism, with its traditional emphasis on observation, learning, and the environment. Bandura's influential social-learning theory explains personality development in terms of observational learning, self-efficacy, and reciprocal determinism. Social-learning theory has been especially effective in explaining the development and proliferation of aggressive responses, through its emphasis on imitation of aggressive models, such as those we encounter in the media.

Which is more important in the prediction of behavior: traits or situations? In Chapter 7, we follow the controversy stimulated by Mischel's (1968) critique of trait psychology, in which he argued that behavior is more situationally specific than cross-situationally consistent and that traits probably exist more in the minds of observers than in the personalities of the persons whose behavior they observe. The person-situation debate dominated the field of personality psychology throughout the 1970s and early 1980s, though it appears to have died down in recent years. In the wake of the storm, the concept of trait has emerged with new strength and vitality, but personality psychologists have also developed a deeper understanding of how human behavior is situated within multiple and overlapping environmental contexts.

Chapter 5

Personality Traits

Introduction

Measuring Traits
What Is a Trait?
Constructing a Trait Measure
>   *Feature 5.A: Allport and Cattell: Trait Psychologists Extraordinaire*
Criteria of a Good Measure
Personality Inventories

The Basic Traits
The Big Five
E: Extraversion
>   Feeling Good
>   Arousal
>   Stability and Change
N: Neuroticism
Gray's Approach: Impulsivity and Anxiety
>   *Feature 5.B: Feeling Really Good and Really Bad: Affect Intensity*
O: Openness to Experience
C and *A:* Conscientiousness and Agreeableness
The Interpersonal Circumplex

Trait Genetics
Infant Temperament
>   *Feature 5.C: Cubness: The Most Dreaded Trait*
Heritability Studies

Summary

Born into the upper-middle-class comfort of a small town in northern England, Vera Brittain (1896/1970) appeared well on her way to becoming a respectable member of the English gentry. At the age of 18, she was, in her own words, a "provincial debutante," ready to enter the most "civilized" echelons of British society, two years before the outbreak of World War I. Vera's teenage diary recorded little more than tennis dates, dances, and happy family outings (Stewart, Franz, & Layton, 1988). She enjoyed "an unparalleled age of rich materialism and tranquil comfort"—a time and a way of life that "appeared to us to have gone on from time immemorial, and to be securely destined to continue for ever" (Brittain, 1933/1970, p. 50). Even her somewhat rebellious insistence that she be allowed to attend Somerville College at Oxford to study writing in 1914 might be seen as the relatively predictable striving of an intellectually gifted young woman of advanced social standing, surely to be married eventually, to raise children, perhaps to write, but most of all to assume her proper and prosperous role in the genteel world. Just before Oxford, she met and fell in love with a young poet named Roland Leighton. The future looked to be a rose garden.

Four years later, at the end of World War I, Roland was dead. Also killed were Vera's beloved brother, two dear friends, and millions of other young European men—soldiers and other victims of "The Great War" that, as we saw in Chapter 2, so blackened the spirits of Sigmund Freud and other men and women of the day. Early in the war, Vera abandoned her studies at Oxford to enlist as a nurse in the armed forces, ministering to the wounded and sick in London, Malta, and at the front in France. When she began her service, she was youthful, vibrant, patriotic, and idealistic. When the war ended in 1918, she emerged, along with many of her surviving peers, broken and disillusioned. Lovers, friends, and brothers were dead in the trenches, and very little moral or political justification could be dredged forth to make sense of the carnage. By the end of the war, Brittain had become a committed pacifist:

> Let him who thinks War is a glorious, golden thing, who loves to roll forth stirring words of exhortation, invoking Honour and Praise and Valour and Love of Country with as thoughtless and fervid a faith as inspired the priests of Baal to call on their own slumbering deity, let him look at a little pile of sodden grey rags that cover half a skull and a shinbone and what might have been its ribs, or at this skeleton lying on its side, resting half crouching as it fell, perfect but that it is headless, and with the tattered clothing still draped round it; and let him realise how grand and glorious a thing it is to have distilled all Youth and Joy and Life into a foetid heap of hideous putrescence! Who is there who has known and seen who can say that Victory is worth the death of even one of these? (Brittain, 1933/1970, p. 198)

In the 1920s, Brittain rejected the life-style she knew as a child and worked instead as an advocate for the fledgling League of Nations and the cause of international peace. She made speeches and led discussions throughout England, and eventually incorporated themes of peacemaking into her articles, novels, poetry, and other works. In the 1930s, she joined the Peace Pledge Union, thereby publicly promising never to support any war in any way (Stewart & Healy, 1986). During World War II, she continued to publish articles and books on pacifism, including her regular "Letter to Peace-Lovers," mailed out to 2000 subscribers during the war. Like the war of 1914, World War II exacted a significant cost to Brittain's life. Because the British government feared that her pacifist writings would be dangerous outside England, she was not allowed to travel to the United States to visit her two young children, whom she had sent to stay with relatives so that they might be far away from the German bombing. The children returned to England in 1943, but Brittain had already had to endure three painful years without them. Early in the separation, she wrote to her husband, George Catlin:

> Only this afternoon, walking through a country lane . . . I suddenly came to myself to find I was sobbing like a baby from sheer loneliness and unavailing grief. . . . At times, having lost the children, I feel I can't go on. (from Stewart & Healy, 1986, p. 26)

After World War II, Brittain continued her work for peace. In all, she wrote 29 books. The best-known is *Testament of Youth* (1933/1970), a moving and passionate autobiography chronicling the experiences of her adolescence and young adulthood. Throughout her adult years, Brittain was also well known as an ardent feminist.

How might the personologist approach the life of Vera Brittain? As we saw in Chapters 2–4, one approach might focus on "intrapsychic mysteries." A Freudian or Jungian perspective on Brittain, for example, might aim to unearth the unconscious determinants of Brittain's experience, highlighting such things as unconscious conflict, defense mechanisms, libidinal stages, superego structure, the Oedipus complex, internalized objects, archetypes, and so on. A second perspective might stick more closely to observable behavior, seeking to discern the readily measurable variables that need to be taken into account in order to predict the person's behavior. To account for Brittain's peacemaking behavior, for example, a personologist might seek to measure discrete *personality traits* within Brittain and *situations* in Brittain's environment, as well as the *interaction* of the two. From this perspective, Brittain might be understood in terms of interaction episodes: observable behavioral events (rather than, say, dreams, fantasies, or unconscious urgings) that are products of the interaction of internal personality traits and external situational demands. Chapters 5–7 adopt this general approach to the person.

It is easy enough to envision how a personologist might account for Brittain's peacemaking behavior in terms of the situations she encountered in her environment. Indeed, Brittain herself explicitly traces her peacemaking to her experiences in the war. In *Testament of Youth,* she writes of how the changing environments she encountered in early adulthood transformed her outlook on life and motivated her to change her behaviors toward working tirelessly for peace. Brittain's personality appears to have been shaped most by *social* situations, and key people in her environments stand out as major influences: Roland reinforced her prewar idealism and naiveté; from her brother Edward she learned fidelity and commitment to a family; through her later relationship with the author Winifred Holtby she consolidated her own vocation as a writer and lecturer. Her husband, George Catlin, was a perennial source of support. Even Brittain's prewar experiences as a provincial debutante appear to have left a lasting effect. Though she rejected much of what she perceived to be frivolous and uninspiring in her aristocratic past, Brittain retained an image of childhood joy and innocence and a faith in human ideals that seem to have kept her going during even the bleakest times. Thus, Vera Brittain would have been the first to admit that she was a product of her times and her environments— that much of what she did could be traced to what she learned to do in a variety of influential situations. We will examine this theme of social learning and the social situation in the prediction of behavior in Chapter 6.

The current chapter, however, looks at behavior from the standpoint of internal personality traits. While Brittain's peacemaking behavior was surely shaped by social experience, one might also argue that such behavior was a product of stable and internal personality dispositions. Though many young women had their hopes and dreams dashed by World War I, very few became actively involved in peace movements. Indeed, Brittain remarks that during the 1920s she felt completely isolated from her peers, most of whom seemed bent on forgetting the war and enjoying the razzle-dazzle and jazz of the "roaring twenties." To determine why Brittain took her own particular course, therefore, one might do well to look within, at personality traits.

Many of Brittain's biographers and Brittain herself frequently adopt trait explanations for her life. In general, Brittain has been consistently described as intelligent, rebellious and independent, driven by ambition, and idealistic. In her interpersonal relations, she has been described as somewhat shy and difficult to get along with on the one hand, and passionate, romantic, and enthusiastic on the other (Stewart & Healy, 1988). Her commitment to peace work appears to be a manifestation of a powerful lifelong conscientiousness (Cattell, 1965), a trait considered by many psychologists to be one of the five or so fundamental traits in personality (Goldberg, 1981; Norman, 1963). Individuals who have a strong conscientiousness are described as consistently responsible, scrupulous, and persevering. They behave in accord with strong personal convictions, are generally bound by duty, and suppress impulses in order to act for the "good." Argues one biographer, as Brittain developed from a provincial debutante to an internationally known writer and pacifist, "one thing that remained constant was her strong commitment to a Victorian ethical code that stressed duty, responsibility, self-sacrifice and courage" (Gorham, 1985, p. 22).

Let us, then, consider traits.

Measuring Traits

What Is a Trait?

The concept of a personality **trait** is rooted in common sense and everyday observation. As we watch, and try to make sense of, the behavior of other people, we notice consistencies within a given person and differences between different persons. For example, we notice that Rachel smiles at people and talks with them in a friendly manner in many different situations—in class, at the gym, eating lunch, studying in the library. Maria, on the other hand, seems rarely to smile or exchange friendly words with others. Whereas Rachel appears consistently warm and outgoing, Maria seems cool and detached. Of course, Rachel has her cool moments, and Maria may really warm up to people in certain situations, but Rachel seems *generally* friendlier than Maria.

Personologists consider a number of aspects of personality traits such as "friendliness" and "conscientiousness." First, they generally conceive of traits as *internal* dispositions that are relatively *stable* over time and across situations. If we are to conclude that Brittain had a strong trait of conscientiousness, we must find evidence that she was consistently conscientious in a variety of situations (such as in her work as a nurse, in her writing and lecturing, and in her family life) and over time (such as an adolescent, a young adult, and an older adult).

Second, traits are typically conceived in *bipolar* terms. Friendliness can be understood as a continuum ranging from one extreme of "high friendliness" to the other extreme of "high unfriendliness" (synonymous with "low friendliness"). Traits, therefore, are often couched in the language of opposites: friendliness *versus* unfriendliness, extraversion *versus* introversion, dominance *versus* submissiveness. People are seen as situated along any particular trait continuum in a relatively normal distribution, with many people residing toward the middle of the continuum (such as "moderately friendly" or "moderately unfriendly") and fewer lying at the extremes.

Third, different traits are generally seen as *additive* and *independent*. A trait approach to Vera Brittain might suggest that Brittain was "high" in the traits of conscientiousness and assertiveness, "medium" in the trait of emotional stability, and "low" in the trait of extraversion. The four traits thus combine as four independent "ingredients" in Vera Brittain's personality. Mix them together in the proper amounts and you have a recipe for predicting consistency in Brittain's behavior and for describing how Brittain is different from other people who have different recipes, that is, different trait profiles.

Finally, personality traits usually refer to *broad* individual differences in *socioemotional* functioning. Writes Conley (1985a), "personality traits constitute very generalized behavior patterns in response to emotional tendencies" (p. 94). Personality traits, therefore, may be distinguished from other variables that appear to be less socioemotional and more cognitive in nature, such as values, attitudes, world views, and schemas (Conley, 1985a; McClelland, 1951). Indeed, the distinction between socioemotional personality traits on the one hand and cognitive variables on the other goes back at least as far as the philosopher Immanuel Kant (1724–1804), who distinguished between "temperament" (traits) and "character" (schemas) (Conley, 1985a). We will consider cognitive personality dimensions in Chapters 8–10 as examples of "interpretive structures."

Constructing a Trait Measure

Most personologists who study traits assume that people can usually report their own traits accurately. In Freudian terms (Chapter 3), traits are presumed to reside in the realm of manifest experience; they are not latent, hidden, disguised, or mysterious, for the most part. The methods required to assess traits thus can and should be relatively straightforward (Burisch, 1984). *Self-report questionnaires* and *rating scales* are methods of choice in trait assessment. These objective measures of personality ask the person to report directly on his or her own behavior, typically by answering a series of questions with "yes" or "no" answers or by making a rating—for instance, on a 1–7 scale—concerning the extent to which the person "agrees with" or "disagrees with" a particular item.

Although a paper-and-pencil test designed to measure a personality trait may appear simple and straightforward from the standpoint of the person filling out the scale, constructing a reliable and valid trait measure is not easy. Psychologists have developed and evaluated a number of approaches to test construction (Burisch, 1984; Hase & Goldberg, 1967; Wiggins, 1973), but there is no single approach that everybody agrees is the best for all testing situations. Nevertheless, most personologists generally endorse a **construct approach** to test construction (Jackson, 1971; Jackson & Paunonen, 1980; Loevinger, 1957; Wiggins, 1973).

The construct approach begins with a clear conceptual definition of the trait of interest, usually embedded in a larger personality theory. Take, for instance, the trait of "conscientiousness" as we encountered it in the life of Vera Brittain. If we were to design a personality questionnaire to assess individual differences in conscientiousness, we might begin with the definition of and theory for this trait provided by Cattell (1965). One of Cattell's 16 basic "source traits" in human personality (see Feature 5.A), conscientiousness is defined as a general disposition "governing conscientious, perserving, unselfish behavior and

Continued on p. 252

Feature 5.A

Allport and Cattell
Trait Psychologists Extraordinaire

From about the time of World War II through the 1960s, the two generally acknowledged champions of trait psychology were Gordon W. Allport (1897–1967) and Raymond B. Cattell (1905–). Although Allport and Cattell approached the study of traits from different perspectives, they shared the conviction that the whole person should be conceptualized in terms of internal and stable personality dispositions, or *traits,* that exert a significant influence on behavior over time and across many different situations. They maintained, furthermore, that traits are generally available to consciousness and can be assessed through verbal self-report.

Allport was born in 1897 in a small town in Indiana, one of four sons of a physician and his wife. He grew up in Cleveland, attended Harvard University for his undergraduate and doctoral work, and studied extensively in Europe, through which he appears to have been influenced greatly by such German psychologists as William Stern and Edward Spranger. From 1930 to 1967, Allport taught at Harvard, where he helped establish the interdisciplinary Department of Social Relations. In 1937 he published what is generally considered to be the first major textbook on personality psychology, profoundly shaping the discipline for at least two generations to come. In *Personality: A Psychological Interpretation* (Allport, 1937) and in a number of other scholarly books and articles, Allport tried to lay the groundwork for a bona fide "psychology of the individual." In so doing, he sketched a number of far-reaching plans and principles that have found their way into contemporary personality psychology and that are discussed in later chapters of this book. Major contributions appear in the areas of biographical studies of the person, values and beliefs (Chapter 9), and the self (Chapter 10).

For Allport, the major structural unit of the personality was the trait, which he defined as a "neuropsychic structure having the capacity to render many stimuli functionally equivalent, and to initiate and guide equivalent (meaningfully consistent) forms of adaptive and expressive behavior" (Allport, 1961, p. 347). Note two important aspects of this definition. First, Allport insisted that trait labels were more than mere semantic conveniences. Traits really exist—they exist as unobservable neuropsychic structures. As real physiological entities, traits are among the more important causal factors in human behavior. We, therefore, may infer the existence of traits from observing behavior. Second, by rendering different stimuli "functionally equivalent," traits account for consistencies in human behavior. Behavior is more or less lawful and predictable because of the action of traits.

Allport's brand of trait psychology tended toward the literary in con-

Gordon Allport

Allport, 1965), in which Allport analyzed a series of personal letters written by one woman over a long period of time in order to delineate the key traits in her personality. According to Allport (1961), the existence of a particular trait in a person's life can be ascertained from at least three kinds of evidence: frequency, range of situations, and intensity. A particularly strong trait of "stubbornness," for instance, might be revealed in the person who is frequently stubborn over time and in many situations and who, when behaving stubbornly, does so with prodigious intensity.

Raymond B. Cattell was born in Devon, England, in 1905, into a comfortable middle-class family. Like Vera Brittain, Cattell was jolted out of his tranquility by the outbreak of World War I, reinforcing in him a realization of the "frailty and brevity of life and giving him the resolve to accomplish as much as he could in his own brief lifetime" (Gatchel & Mears, 1982, p. 178). At London University he cultivated interests in chemistry, physics, and social reform, ultimately envisioning his role in life as that of the creator of a truly scientific psychology that might promote social progress. After suffering poverty, joblessness, and the break-up of his marriage during the Depression in England, Cattell moved to the United States. He taught at Columbia, Clark, and Harvard Universities; at the latter, he met but did not get along well with

tent and style. While he encouraged nomothetic research on common traits, he tended to distrust statistical analyses of group data because, he argued, they tend to blot out the uniqueness of the single person. While large-scale trait studies could be useful for deducing general laws of behavior, Allport believed that these should be supplemented by the idiographic, in-depth examination of the unique and common traits manifested in the single case. The best example of this approach is his *Letters from Jenny*

Allport. Eventually he settled at the University of Illinois in 1945. For the next 40 years, Cattell published a great number of books, chapters, and articles reporting his own research into personality and laying out in great detail his articulate agenda for trait psychology. As of this writing, he is still actively working on and publishing in the topics of personality, social progress, and religion (e.g., Cattell, 1990).

Unlike Allport, Cattell advocates a rigorously quantitative science of traits. Cattell's own statistical analyses of various kinds of trait data have convinced him that the whole person can be well understood, and his or her behavior well predicted, by measuring at least 16 basic **source traits,** assessed on Cattell's 16PF (The Sixteen Personality Factor Questionnaire). Traits may also be divided into three general categories: *dynamic traits,* which set the individual into action to accomplish a goal; *ability traits,* which concern the effectiveness with which the individual reaches a goal; and *temperament traits,* which concern such stylistic aspects of response as speed, energy, and emotional reactivity. To predict a person's behavior in a given situation, says Cattell, the personologist must plug precise scores on trait measures into a **specification equation,** which differentially weights each trait according to its relevance to the situation. For example, Cattell (1990, p. 102) contends that he can predict well a salesperson's annual earnings from the following source trait equation: Earnings $= .21$ outgoingness $+ .10$ intelligence $+ .10$ emotional stability $+ .10$ dominance $+ .21$ easygoingness $+ .10$ conscientiousness $- .10$ suspiciousness $- .31$ imaginativeness $+ .21$ shrewdness. To increase predictive power, the specification equation may also includes nontrait variables pertaining to transient *states* (such as fatigue and temporary moods) and particular *roles* demanded by the situation. Therefore, to predict behavior with any degree of precision, the personologist must obtain precise measurements on a host of internal and external variables: personality traits, temporary states and roles, and situational factors.

Continued from p. 249

impelling the individual to duty as conceived by his [or her] culture" (p. 374). A highly conscientious person is "honest; knows what is right and generally does it, even if no one is watching him [her]; does not tell lies or attempt to deceive others; respects others' property." A highly unconscientious person is "somewhat unscrupulous; not too careful about standards of right and wrong where personal desires are concerned; tells lies and is given to little deceits; does not respect others' property" (p. 63). Most people fall somewhere between the two extremes.

Cattell emphasizes that conscientiousness is "not just a rational politeness or conformity but a somewhat fierce 'categorical imperative' (to use Kant's description) of the kind exemplified by the biblical saints" (p. 94).

After defining our trait, we would begin writing *items,* which are the test questions or statements. Here are three items that Cattell wrote for his scale for conscientiousness (1965, p. 94):

Do you usually keep emotions under control?

Are you a person who is scrupulously correct in manners and social obligations and likes others to be the same?

Are you cautious and considerate that you do not hurt people's feelings by unconsidered conversational remarks?

For each of these items, the respondent would answer "yes" or "no." In the case of these three items, "yes" answers indicate conscientiousness and "no" answers suggest unconscientiousness. Each item relates to the others in an additive way. Thus, a subject might receive one point for each "yes" answer on the scale. Adding up all the points would produce the total trait score for conscientiousness. Because some people, however, may answer "yes" to virtually any question ("yea-sayers") and others "no" to almost any question ("nay-sayers") regardless of content, we would do well to include items for which a "no" answer suggests conscientiousness and a "yes" answer suggests unconscientiousness (Jackson, 1971). Therefore, we might add such "reversed" items as these:

I frequently find that I must "cut corners" and "bend the rules" in order to achieve my goals.

Other people would *not* describe me as a dutiful and highly responsible person.

In writing test items, our goal would be to generate an item pool that completely covers the content domain of conscientiousness. Therefore, we should aim to include a large number of items initially, so that we might tap into the various manifestations of conscientiousness that our theory suggests might exist. In fact, it is a good idea, argue some test theorists, to include items that are hypothesized *not* to tap into the trait of interest—in other words, items that seem to have nothing to do with the trait of conscientiousness, such as these:

Other people regard me as a dominant person.

I enjoy parties and other opportunities to get together with large groups of people.

In covering a content domain that is larger than that envisioned for our trait, we decrease the chances of excluding unexpectedly relevant items while increasing the chances of learning precisely where the boundaries of our trait lie—that is, finding what content the particular trait does and does not include (Loevinger, 1957; Wiggins, 1973).

In the next step of test construction, we would administer the item pool to a large number of individuals and examine the results to determine which items should be retained in the final version. There are many statistical procedures available for examining the empirical results at this stage. For instance, we would probably perform an **item analysis,** through which we would determine the contribution that each item makes to the scale by correlating the scores on each item with the total score. Those items that make a negligible contribution (that is, those that produce low correlations) to the total would then be dropped. Presumably a number of the conceptually irrelevant items that we included by design would be dropped at this stage, though those correlating highly with the overall score would be retained. Further, a number of items that we initially thought were tapping the trait well might be deleted for lack of correlation with the total.

We might also perform a **factor analysis** on the data, through which each item is correlated with every other item to determine empirical clusterings. Let us imagine that our final scale has 30 items. We might administer the scale to 500 persons and then perform a factor analysis to determine which items "hang together" in clusters. The factor analysis might yield two relatively independent clusters of items—*factors*—that appear to tap into two somewhat different facets of conscientiousness. Perhaps 10 of our items appearing to tap into moral concerns hang together as a first factor, and another 12 items having more to do with conscientiousness in work hang together to form a second, independent factor. We might conclude that the overall scale in fact assesses two separate, though related, ideas—two facets of the trait "conscientiousness": "moral conscientiousness" and "task conscientiousness." Alternatively, we might decide that the two facets are in fact two separate traits, each having little to do with the other.

In the final step of test construction, we would examine the extent to which the trait measure predicts behavior. For instance, we might design a study in which people who fill out our conscientiousness measure participate in a laboratory experiment in which they are given various opportunities to choose between either responsible, conscientious behavior, or competing, nonconscientious behavior. Or we might examine the relationship between conscientiousness scores on our test and behaviors thought to be conscientious in daily life, such as church attendance, contributions to charities, and community involvement. Or we might correlate people's scores on our measure of conscientiousness and ratings of the same people made by their friends and acquaintances, our prediction being that those individuals scoring high on our measure would be rated by their friends and acquaintances as significantly more responsible and dutiful than low-scoring individuals.

As a trait measure develops, researchers learn not only what the particular scale measures but also what it does *not* measure. Therefore, we would expect that scores on our measure of conscientiousness would correlate positively with scores on *other* measures of conscientiousness. Evidence for positive associations between different measures of the same trait constitute **convergent validity:** the two measures are said to "converge" on the same trait (Campbell & Fiske, 1959). Further, scores on our measure of conscientiousness should *not* correlate with scores on measures of apparently unrelated traits. For instance, our theory of conscientiousness suggests that this trait should have little to do with such traits as "dominance," "extraversion," "intelligence," "friendliness," and so on. In other words, highly conscientious people should *not* be consistently high (or low) on dominance or on any other independent trait. If conscientiousness scores *were* highly positively (or negatively) correlated with dominance scores, we should suspect that our measure is in fact assessing something different from, or in addition to, "pure" conscientiousness. Evidence, therefore, that our trait measure does *not* correlate with measures of other, conceptually distinct traits would support the **discriminant validity** of our measure (Campbell & Fiske, 1959).

Criteria of a Good Measure

The construct approach to devising a personality trait measure follows logically from a crucial idea in personality psychology as a whole—the idea of **construct validity.** Construct validity is the process of simultaneously validating a test and the construct that the test is measuring. Cronbach and Meehl (1955) introduced the concept of construct validity in order to address a common and vexing problem in personality psychology: how do you know if a measure designed to assess something that you cannot observe directly is a good measure? Although we may be able to observe friendly behavior, we cannot directly observe "friendliness" per se. The trait of friendliness is an abstraction that cannot be directly seen, heard, touched, smelled, or tasted. The same could be said for all personality traits and, indeed, many other concepts in psychology overall—such as intelligence, prejudice, religious values, the superego. These ineffable abstractions are termed *constructs*. Trait scales measure such constructs.

   The process of construct validity begins with the construct itself, which is typically embedded in a larger theory of personality functioning. With an eye toward the theoretical meaning of the construct, the psychologist carefully designs a measure of the construct, and then observes the extent to which the measure itself produces empirical results—observable behaviors—that conform to the theory. For instance, I might conduct a study to test my prediction that persons scoring high on my new measure of "friendliness" will spend more time smiling in a friendly laboratory interview than persons scoring low on the measure, under the theoretical assumption that smiling is generally an index of friendly sentiment. Should my prediction be confirmed in my study, I will have obtained some small evidence for the construct validity of the new measure of friendliness. Should my prediction not be supported by the data, I might begin to question the adequacy of my measure, the adequacy of my construct "friendliness," or perhaps the adequacy of the particular study I conducted to test the hypothesis linking friendliness to smiling.

Each new empirical finding with a particular personality test contributes to the **nomological network** for the construct that the test measures. The nomological network is the interlocking system of propositions that constitute the theory of a given construct. The propositions specify how test performance should be related to particular nontest behaviors that can be directly assessed. Results from studies employing a particular trait measure may even feed back to change the nomological network, making for new propositions about the particular trait, thus redefining it and ultimately changing the theory in which it is embedded. There are numerous examples of this sort of thing in personality research—cases in which a particular trait assessed in a particular way starts out with one definition and theory, but over time (typically many years), and with extensive study, new empirical results change the trait's meaning and theory. For instance, early definitions of the "achievement motive" (Chapter 11) characterized it as a general desire to succeed, but subsequent research employing a particular measure of the need for achievement provided new evidence to suggest that its meaning was more closely tied to the "need to be efficient" and the "need to succeed at tasks of moderate challenge" (McClelland, 1985).

Construct validity, therefore, refers to the extent to which empirical support has been gathered for the propositions contained in the construct's nomological network. Constructs and their measures that have generated a large amount of empirical support for a rich variety of propositions in the nomological network can be said to have the greatest degree of construct validity. However, construct validity is never carved in stone: each new study employing a particular construct and its measure ultimately ties into the nomological network and thus contributes some kind of evidence—supportive or nonsupportive—for construct validity. A number of other forms of validity fall in the general category of construct validity (Table 5.1).

In addition to construct (and other forms of) validity, **reliability** is a cardinal criterion of a trait measure's worth. Reliability refers to the consistency of a particular personality measure. For self-report trait tests, two forms of reliability are especially important. In **test–retest reliability,** psychologists assess a test's *consistency over time.* Persons who score high on a particular trait on first taking the test should score high again on the same test a second time, say, a few months later. Similarly, those who score low at Time 1 should score low again at Time 2. Test–retest reliability is usually calculated by correlating the subjects' scores on a measure at Time 1 with their corresponding scores at Time 2. The most reliable trait measures exhibit test–retest correlation coefficients of +.85 and higher over relatively short periods of time (such as a few months). In **split-half reliability,** a test's *internal consistency* is assessed by correlating subjects' scores on one half of a particular test with their corresponding scores on the other half. If a test is internally consistent, each part of the test yields comparable results; indeed, each test item can be seen as contributing to a homogenous pool of information about a given trait.

Table 5.1

Forms of Validity in Personality Testing

Construct	The extent to which a test measures the construct that it is theoretically intended to measure. Construct validity increases as empirical support is garnered for the various propositions contained in the construct's nomological net. Construct validity is the most basic and encompassing form of validity, and other forms of validity can be seen as derivatives from it.
Content	The degree to which the items of a test cover the entire content domain of a construct and are not confounded with other content.
Convergent	The extent to which different measures of the same construct relate to each other.
Criterion	The extent to which a test is associated with external behaviors that it is designed to predict. When a test seeks to predict criterion behaviors that will occur in the future, we speak of "predictive validity." When the criterion behaviors are obtained at the current time, we speak of "concurrent validity."
Discriminant	The extent to which different measures of different constructs do *not* relate to each other.
Face	The extent to which test items seem, in the eyes of the respondent, to measure what they are supposed to measure. Face validity refers to the degree to which a respondent views the test as fair and appropriate under the given conditions of administration. (Jackson & Paunonen, 1980)

Beyond validity and reliability, personality psychologists have identified a number of other criteria of a test's worth. *Utility* is a criterion frequently raised— a test that provides practical information that can be used for specific purposes is preferred over one that cannot. Burisch (1984) suggests that *economy* and *communicability* should routinely be considered—all other things being equal, a short test is better than a long one (economy), and a test whose results are easily interpreted and communicated to others should be preferred to one whose results are more ambiguous. In addition, a number of personality psychologists argue that trait measures should be as free as possible of **social desirability** bias (Edwards, 1957; Jackson & Messick, 1958). This means that a good trait measure should not be influenced greatly by a person's desire to present a favorable or socially desirable facade. One common method of determining the extent to which social desirability plays into a particular trait measure is to correlate scores on the given measure with scores on a standardized social desirability scale. Low, nonsignificant correlations between this and another trait measure suggest that the latter is relatively free of social desirability bias.

Personality Inventories

It is often useful in personality research and in clinical work to assess many different traits at once. To do so, psychologists sometimes call upon omnibus **personality inventories,** which contain numerous trait scales, each scale comprised of a subset of items contained in the large item pool for the inventory. Although there is some indication that the use of these broad personality inventories has decreased in recent years (Lanyon, 1984), personality inventories are still extremely popular and valuable in research and clinical assessment.

The **Minnesota Multiphasic Personality Inventory (MMPI)** has been the most widely used and thoroughly researched personality measure in the last 40 years. Developed by a psychologist, Starke Hathaway, and a psychiatrist, J. C. McKinley, in the 1930s, the MMPI condenses questions that might be asked in a lengthy psychiatric interview into an efficient paper-and-pencil form. The test contains 550 statements such as "I have nightmares every few nights," "At times I feel like smashing things," "I would like to be a florist," and "I am sure I am being talked about." For each item, the respondent simply answers "true" or "false." The items are grouped into 10 different scales, named hypochondriasis, depression, hysteria, psychopathic-deviancy, masculinity–femininity, paranoia, psychasthenia, schizophrenia, hypomania, and social introversion. The inventory also contains scales designed to assess the extent to which the subject is lying, faking, or responding in a careless fashion.

The MMPI was originally designed to be a *clinical* diagnostic instrument. Scores on the various scales were designed to assist the psychologist or psychiatrist in distinguishing various psychopathologies. Indeed, the MMPI was constructed by administering various items to different diagnostic groups—such as schizophrenics, manic-depressives, anxiety neurotics—and determining which items they repeatedly endorsed. This general method of test construction, called the **criterion-key method,** assumes that a valid scale for, say, the "trait" of "depression" will consist of items that people whom clinicians have diagnosed as "depressives" frequently endorse, regardless of the content of those items and regardless of the theory of depression with which one is working. Therefore, if known depressives repeatedly answer "true" to the item "I am a Boston Red Sox fan," then this item becomes part of the scale for diagnosing depression, even though one is hard-pressed to come up with a cogent theoretical reason for its inclusion. The criterion-key method contrasts markedly with the theory-oriented construct method of test construction outlined earlier in this chapter.

Despite the fact that the MMPI scales were designed to assess *abnormality,* the test has been used to assess individual differences among normals as well, though with limited success (Kunce & Anderson, 1984). Even as a tool for clinical diagnosis, the MMPI has been resoundingly criticized for weak reliability and validity with respect to many of the scales, and for the fact that many of the test items seem out of date (Anastasi, 1976). Still, the test is used widely, for various purposes. Overall, the MMPI is probably most valuable in distinguishing in a general fashion between abnormal and normal populations, and thus determining the overall severity of a particular person's disturbance (Meehl & Dahlstrom, 1960). It is used much less successfully, however, for more fine-grained distinctions (Kleinmutz, 1982).

The **California Psychological Inventory (CPI)** was designed to assess a broad range of traits applicable to normal populations. Developed by Harrison Gough in the 1950s, the CPI was originally administered to thousands of normal individuals, resulting in a pool of 462 true/false items. The items are grouped into 20 scales, measuring such traits as dominance, sense of acceptance, self-control, and achievement via independence (Table 5.2). Compared to the MMPI, the individual scales on the CPI show relatively high reliabilities. Evidence for validity comes from many sources, including correlations between subjects' trait scores and ratings of the subjects made by friends and acquaintances. One major criticism of the CPI, however, is that the different scales tend to overlap, showing correlations with each other of .50 and higher. Apparently, each scale does not assess an independent and unique trait (Thorndike, 1959). Nonetheless, most experts agree that the CPI is one of the best personality inventories in use today (Anastasi, 1976; Kleinmutz, 1982).

Gough argues that the CPI's scales tap into common **folk concepts** of personality. Folk concepts are categories of personality that arise naturally out of human interactions in most, if not all, societies. For example, most all cultures signify a concept of social responsibility—a tendency to act in accord with the good of the group rather than out of pure self-interest. Within each culture, individuals vary widely in the extent to which they and their behavior implicitly endorse this folk concept. The two CPI scales of "socialization" and "responsibility" aim to assess this important individual difference. A substantial body of research supports the construct validity of these scales. For example, Gough and Bradley (1992) administered the CPI to hundreds of delinquent and criminal men and women as well as a comparable group of control subjects. Delinquent and criminal adults scored significantly lower than control subjects on a number of different CPI scales (such as empathy and achievement via conformance) but the two scales that showed the strongest difference were socialization and responsibility.

Recent work with the CPI has revealed three *vectors* or general dimensions that underlie the more specific folk-concept scales. Vector 1 pertains to an interpersonal orientation, which ranges from an involved, participatory approach to life on the one end to a detached, privacy-seeking orientation on the other. Vector 2 pertains to norms and values, ranging from a norm-accepting to a

Table 5.2

Scales on the California Psychological Inventory

Scale	Brief Description of a High Scorer
1. Dominance	Confident, assertive, dominant, task-oriented
2. Capacity for status	Ambitious, wants to be a success, independent
3. Sociability	Sociable, likes to be with people, friendly
4. Social presence	Self-assured, spontaneous; a good talker; not easily embarrassed
5. Self-acceptance	Has good opinion of self; sees self as talented and as personally attractive
6. Independence	Self-sufficient, resourceful, detached
7. Empathy	Comfortable with self and well-accepted by others; understands the feelings of others
8. Responsibility	Responsible, reasonable, takes duties seriously
9. Socialization	Comfortably accepts ordinary rules and regulations; finds it easy to conform
10. Self-control	Tries to control emotions and temper; takes pride in being self-disciplined
11. Good impression	Wants to make a good impression; tries to do what will please others
12. Communality	Fits in easily; sees self as a quite average person
13. Well-being	Feels in good physical and emotional health; optimistic about the future
14. Tolerance	Is tolerant of others' beliefs and values, even when different from or counter to own beliefs
15. Achievement via conformance	Has strong drive to do well; likes to work in settings where tasks and expectations are clearly defined

Table 5.2 continued

Scale	Brief Description of a High Scorer
16. Achievement via independence	Has strong drive to do well; likes to work in settings that encourage freedom and individual initiative
17. Intellectual efficiency	Efficient in use of intellectual abilities; can keep on at a task where others might get bored or discouraged
18. Psychological mindedness	More interested in why people do what they do than in what they do; good judge of how people feel and what they think about things
19. Flexibility	Flexible; likes change and variety; easily bored by routine life and everyday experience; may be impatient, and even erratic
20. Femininity/Masculinity	On this scale, a person scoring in the Femininity direction is seen as sympathetic, helpful, sensitive to criticism, and tending to interpret events from a personal point of view. A person scoring in the Masculinity direction is seen as decisive, action-oriented, not easily subdued, and rather unsentimental.

Adapted from Gough (1987), pp. 6–7.

norm-rejecting pole. Vector 3 pertains to what Gough calls "ego integration," which extends from self-defeating and interpersonally unacceptable behavior on one end to self-realization and superior ego functioning on the other.

The first two vectors may be crossed to produce four distinct life-styles, or ways of living. *Alphas* are high on Vectors 1 and 2; they are interpersonally involved and rule respecting. *Betas* are more detached and internalized (low on Vector 1) but still rule accepting. *Gammas* tend to enter into the interpersonal arena but remain dubious about its norms and conventions. They are interpersonally engaged but rebellious or dismissive of rules and regulations. Finally, *Deltas* seek escape from the interpersonal world and reject its norms and values. Ego integration from Vector 3 may be seen as modifying all four types. For example, alphas who are high in ego integration may show impressive leadership skills, but those low in ego integration may prove to be authoritarian and invasive. Deltas who are high in ego integration may be visionary and prescient in very personal ways, as in artistic or musical accomplishment. Deltas with low ego integration, however, may experience disintegrative conflict and may react with explosive violence or with disabling psychological disorders.

Harrison Gough

Another well-regarded personality inventory is the **Personality Research Form (PRF),** developed by Douglas Jackson in the 1960s. This instrument incorporates a number of sophisticated advances in test construction and format that were not available to the authors of the MMPI and CPI. In constructing and validating the PRF, Jackson closely followed the construct approach outlined earlier in this chapter. The resulting test contains 320 true/false items, making up 20 independent scales. Each of the scales purports to measure a basic personality "need," taken from a list delineated by Murray (1938). This list, described in Chapter 11 of this book, includes the needs for dominance, affiliation, achievement, aggression, and nurturance. The different PRF scales show much less overlap than occurs in the CPI, and a growing body of research supports the validity of many of the scales in predicting attitudes, values, and behavior. In addition, Paunonen, Jackson, and Keinonen (1990) have recently developed a nonverbal, pictorial version of the PRF in which each item is represented by a line drawing of a figure performing a need-relevant behavior. (See Figure 5.1.) For each item, the subject is asked to indicate the likelihood that he or she might engage in the

Figure 5.1

Two Sample Items From the Nonverbal Version of the Personality Research Form (Entitled the "Nonverbal Personality Questionnaire") Depicting Aggressive Behavior (A) and Thrill-Seeking Behavior (B).

From Paunonen, Jackson, & Keinonen, 1990, p. 485.

behavior represented in the drawing. The nonverbal PRF looks to be a promising research tool for cross-cultural personality research and for use with populations who are not linguistically adept.

The Basic Traits

You don't have to think about the concept of trait for very long to realize that there are probably hundreds of different traits that a person might invoke to explain and predict human behavior. You can doubtlessly imagine, furthermore, that different psychologists might disagree somewhat as to which of the possible traits that might be invoked are the most important traits in personality. How many traits are indeed needed to make for an adequate account of personality? It should come as no surprise that different psychologists have developed different lists of basic traits, and different measurement strategies have been standardized to assess individual differences in a wide variety of different trait taxonomies. For example, Raymond B. Cattell (1965) factor-analyzed countless scales and items to arrive at what he believed to be the essential 16 source traits of personality, assessed via the 16PF. Employing a different kind of factor analysis, J. P. Guilford (1959) argued for 10 basic trait dimensions, readily measured through the Guilford-Zimmerman Temperament Survey (GZTS: Guilford & Zimmerman, 1949).

In the development of the Adjective Check List (ACL), Harrison Gough (1952) put forth 300 different trait adjectives for describing individual differences in personality. Another popular measure, the California Q-Sort (see Chapter 7), sets forth 100 key descriptors (Block, 1961). By contrast, Hans Eysenck (1952, 1967, 1990) has insisted for years that three super traits, or "types," are all that is needed. Each of the three is really a collection of subordinate traits, and each is linked to a biological substrate of personality. For Eysenck, the three main types are extraversion/introversion, neuroticism, and psychoticism.

An important advance in personality psychology during the past 10 years has been the emergence of a consensus that the universe of personality traits may be divided into five or so large galaxies. The consensus is by no means unanimous, and significant disagreements exist as to how these galaxies might be best characterized and named. Nonetheless, there is growing acceptance of the usefulness of a five-factor model of personality traits (McCrae & John, 1992). On the current scene, the five-factor model is the most influential map of personality traits. While the future may produce better maps, it appears for the time being that most important personality traits can be located somewhere with respect to the "Big Five" galaxies.

The Big Five

How might you begin to determine what the basic personality traits in human functioning were? Following the early work of the German researchers Klages (1926) and Baumgarten (1933), Gordon Allport and his colleagues (Allport & Odbert, 1936) adopted a "lexical approach" and began with the English language. Plowing through an unabridged dictionary that contained about 550,000 separate entries, these intrepid researchers compiled a list of about 18,000 terms that referred to psychological traits, states, and evaluations. Of these about 4,500 reflected, in their judgment, relatively stable and enduring personality traits. Cattell (1943) reduced this list to 171 by grouping similar descriptors and eliminating rare and metaphorical usages. He then asked people to rate others on these 171 trait terms. On the basis of correlations among the ratings, Cattell developed a set of 35–40 clusters of related terms, and used them as the basis for constructing rating scales. While Cattell believed that the clusters reduced ultimately to 16 source traits, subsequent factor analyses of these and similar data consistently yielded five large, underlying factors (Fiske, 1949; Norman, 1963; Tupes & Christal, 1961).

Although the seminal research on the five factors was conducted by the early 1960s, it was not until 20 years later that personality psychologists came around to taking seriously what these early studies put forth. In the 1980s, psychologists such as Lewis Goldberg (1981, 1990), John Digman (1990; Digman & Takemoto-Chock, 1981), Dean Peabody (1987; Peabody & Goldberg, 1989), Oliver John (1989, 1990), and Robert McCrae and Paul Costa, Jr. (Costa & McCrae, 1985, 1988; McCrae & Costa, 1987, 1990) conducted extensive research with the five factors first identified by Fiske (1949) and Tupes and Christal (1961). Included among their studies were those suggesting that the same five factors can be found when different personality inventories originally developed without knowledge of the five factors were factor-analyzed. For example, Costa and McCrae (1988) factor-analyzed responses on Jackson's 20-scale PRF and obtained the predicted five-factor solution, and Paunonen, Jackson, Trzebinski, and Forsterling (1992) did the same with the pictorial, nonverbal form of the PRF, employing the measure in four countries (Canada, Finland, Poland, and Germany). A great deal of corroborative research has also been undertaken in Europe (Angleitner, Ostendorf, & John, 1990; DeRaad, Mulder, Kloosterman, & Hofstee, 1988), with comparable five-factor schemes proposed by German and Dutch psychologists (John, 1990). Cross-cultural personality studies have identified the five factors in trait inventories written in Japanese, Chinese, Tagalog (Filipino), and modern Hebrew (e.g., Church & Katigbak, 1989). The cross-cultural studies have moved one especially enthusiastic reviewer to ask, "Is this the way people everywhere construe personality, regardless of language or culture?" (Digman, 1990, pp. 443–444). In the wake of an avalanche of confirmatory research, the five factors have come to be called the **Big Five.**

There are a number of different names for each of the Big Five factors. There are also some significant disagreements about the meanings of some of these factors, especially with respect to the factor that has been termed "openness to experience" by some (McCrae & Costa, 1985b) and "intellectance" (Hogan, 1986) or "culture" (Norman, 1963) by others. Nonetheless, the degree of general agreement about the kind of content that makes up each of the five is quite impressive. Table 5.3 presents one popular version of the Big Five. Following the influential work of McCrae and Costa (1987), we will enumerate the Big Five as *extraversion, neuroticism, openness to experience, agreeableness,* and *conscientiousness.*

E: Extraversion

The first trait galaxy in the Big Five includes personality descriptors such as gregariousness, playfulness, expressiveness, spontaneity, assertiveness, dominance, amibitousness, humor, and optimism, as well as the opposites of these terms (Goldberg, 1990). Tupes and Christal (1961) gave the name of "surgency" to this domain, suggesting the quality of unrestrained force and vitality. We will adopt the well-known term **extraversion** (or simply, *E*), following the usage of Costa and McCrae and the seminal work of Hans Eysenck (1952, 1967), who contends that extraversion is one of the *three* basic traits of personality. As you may recall from Chapter 2, Carl Jung also employed the term extraversion in detailing psychological attitudes. *E* also summons up the words "energy" and "enthusiasm," which are central characteristics in this domain. Extraversion refers to one end of a general continuum, of which the other end is introversion. Individuals who score low on measures of traits within the extraversion domain are, by definition,

Table 5.3

The Big Five:
Adjective Items That Describe Each of the Five Basic Traits

Extraversion (*E*)
   Sociable–Retiring
   Fun loving–Sober
   Affectionate–Reserved
   Friendly–Aloof
   Spontaneous–Inhibited
   Talkative–Quiet

Neuroticism (*N*)
   Worrying–Calm
   Nervous–At ease
   High-strung–Relaxed
   Insecure–Secure
   Self-pitying–Self-satisfied
   Vulnerable–Hardy

Openness to Experience (*O*)
   Original–Conventional
   Imaginative–Down to earth
   Creative–Uncreative
   Broad interests–Narrow interests
   Complex–Simple
   Curious–Incurious

Agreeableness (*A*)
   Good natured–Irritable
   Soft hearted–Ruthless
   Courteous–Rude
   Forgiving–Vengeful
   Sympathetic–Callous
   Agreeable–Disagreeable

Conscientiousness (*C*)
   Conscientious–Negligent
   Careful–Careless
   Reliable–Undependable
   Well-organized–Disorganized
   Self-disciplined–Weak-willed
   Persevering–Quitting

Modified from McCrae and Costa (1987, p. 85)

introverted. They may be described as withdrawn, quiet, shy, inhibited, reserved, unaggressive, passive, and pessimistic (Goldberg, 1990).

You may remember that in Chapter 1 we introduced E as a major trait in the life of Margaret Mead. Table 1.1. reproduced a 20-item self-report questionnaire developed by Eysenck to measure individual-differences in extraversion/introversion. Over the years, Eysenck (1973) and his colleagues have correlated scores on that and similar self-report scales with a number of features of social behavior. The results have provided impressive evidence for the construct validity of E. For instance, extraverts talk more and sooner when they meet someone than do introverts (Carment, Miles, & Cervin, 1965) and engage in more eye contact when interacting with another (Rutter, Morley, & Graham, 1972). They tend to be drawn to and to excel in occupations that involve dealing directly with other people, such as sales and personnel work, nursing, and teaching (Wilson, 1978). Introverts, on the other hand, tend to prefer more solitary pursuits, sharing many interests with artists, research scientists, mathematicians, and engineers (Bendig, 1963). Extraverts tend to be more impulsive than introverts and are wont to take more risks. To nobody's surprise, extraverts do more gambling (Wilson, 1978). They also tend to be more sexually active than introverts (Giese and Schmidt, 1968). Wilson and Nias (1975) have shown that extraverts are more permissive in their sexual attitudes than introverts, confess to higher levels of sex drive, and are less prone to nervousness and inhibition in sexual relations.

Feeling Good   A significant body of recent research has found that E is positively associated with reports of feeling good about life. In other words, extraverts report greater levels of *positive affect* in everyday life than do introverts. Costa and McCrae (1980a, 1984) have conducted a number of studies in which they administered self-report measures of E and subjective well-being to large samples of adults. Measures of subjective well-being tap into two independent features: positive affect (reports of good feelings) and negative affect (reports of bad feelings). Costa and McCrae have consistently found that, for both men and women, E is positively associated with reports of good feelings but unrelated to reports of bad feelings. In other words, extraverts report more positive affect than introverts, but they do not necessarily report less negative affect. Similar results have been obtained by other researchers (e.g., Watson, Clark, McIntyre, & Hamaker, 1992). Indeed, the relations between E and positive affect seem so consistent across different studies that some psychologists have suggested that the E domain might more accurately be termed "Positive Emotionality" or "Positive Affectivity" (Tellegen, 1985; Watson & Tellegen, 1985).

Eysenck has argued that E is made up of at least two related components: sociability and impulsivity. To test the extent to which these two components are related to well-being, Emmons and Diener (1986a) administered an extraversion scale from the Eysenck Personality Inventory (Eysenck & Eysenck, 1964) to two samples of college undergraduates who each completed mood reports daily for 6–8 consecutive weeks. Each night before they went to bed, subjects filled out a form that asked them to rate their current mood on nine seven-point adjective scales. The nine mood adjectives were broken down into four positive terms—

"happy," "joyful," "pleased," and "enjoyment/fun"—and five negative ones—"unhappy," "depressed," "frustrated," "worried/anxious," and "angry/hostile." A student's total positive affect score on a given day, therefore, was the sum of his or her ratings on the four positive mood adjectives; the total negative affect score was the sum across the five negative mood items.

Table 5.4 shows correlations between E and its components "impulsivity" and "sociability" on the one hand, and positive and negative affect scores summed over the 6–8 week period on the other, for both samples in Emmons and Diener's study. While total positive affect was significantly correlated with total E, it was even more strongly associated with "sociability" and completely uncorrelated with "impulsivity." In other words, it is the sociability component of E—that having to do with friendliness, cheerfulness, warmth, and openness to people—that significantly predicts positive moods. The impulsivity component—having more to do with thrill seeking, risk taking, and seeking social stimulation in crowds—was unrelated to positive affect and even showed a positive, though weak, association with negative mood.

Why do extraverts report more positive feelings than introverts? One explanation is that extraverts may be less responsive to punishment than introverts. Introverts appear to dwell on the negative and punitive features of certain social situations (Graziano, Feldesman, & Rahe, 1985). Researchers report that intro-

 Table 5.4

Correlations Between Dimensions of Extraversion and Reports of Positive and Negative Affect

Trait	Positive Affect		Negative Affect	
	Sample 1[a]	Sample 2[b]	Sample 1	Sample 2
Impulsivity	.08	.04	.30**	.25**
Sociability	.49**	.44**	−.10	.11
Extraversion total	.32**	.34**	.01	.24*

Note: Impulsivity and Sociability are subscales of Extraversion total.
[a]$N = 68$
[b]$N = 72$
*$p < .05$
**$p < .01$
From Emmons and Diener (1986a, p. 1213).

verts recall less positive information and rate others less positively in social situations (Lishman, 1972), report interpersonal disagreements as being more aversive (Norman & Watson, 1976), and anticipate more disagreements between themselves and others than do extraverts (Cooper & Scalise, 1974).

Extraverts are more likely than introverts to continue responding in the face of punishment and frustration. Pearce-McCall and Newman (1986) exposed each of 50 introverted and 50 extraverted college men to one of two "pretreatment conditions" in a problem-solving experiment: either a "reward condition" in which the student received $2.50 for good performance or a "punishment condition" in which the student was told that his earnings had dwindled from $5.00 to $2.50 because of poor performance. (In reality, the students had been randomly assigned to the groups, and actual performance thus had nothing to do with whether they received rewards or punishments.) After the pretreatment, the students made bets on how well they might perform on a subsequent problem-solving task. In comparison to those introverts who had received pretreatment punishment, extraverts who had been punished placed larger wagers on their ability to succeed, reported higher levels of expecting to succeed, and expressed greater confidence that they could "control" the situation in the future. As Figure 5.2 shows, extraverts and introverts did *not* differ in their betting behavior following the reward pretreatment but *did* differ markedly following punishment, with extraverts making significantly higher wagers.

In another problem-solving experiment, Patterson, Kosson, and Newman (1987) showed that extraverts typically fail to pause following punishment, pushing ahead to the next trial before they can learn from their mistakes. Impulsively seeking out rewards, extraverts may actually be motivated by punishment to work even faster and more impulsively, failing to reflect on the reasons for punishment. In some situations, therefore, extraverts may show an overly impulsive approach to problem solving, continuing to produce errors even after they are punished for doing so (Nichols & Newman, 1986).

Arousal   Eysenck (1967) argues that E is rooted in human biology. Individual differences in E correspond to differences in the functioning of the brain's *reticular activating system (RAS)*. The RAS is a network of nerve fibers ascending from the spinal chord to the thalamus of the brain. The RAS is considered to be a relatively primitive part of the brain, uninvolved with thinking and other higher cortical functions. Rather, it is responsible for general arousal, regulating patterns of wakefulness and attention. Essentially, Eysenck argues that the RAS is "tuned" differently in introverts and extraverts. Given standard conditions of external stimulation, introverts are generally more highly aroused than extraverts: the RAS is set at a higher level. Both introverts and extraverts seek an optimal arousal in daily life, but because introverts are more aroused to begin with they can tolerate less increase in arousal than can extraverts. The introvert's cortex, therefore, must exercise more inhibition or control over the primitive lower brain centers. Consequently, the introvert exhibits more restrained and inhibited behavior than does the extravert. The introvert tends to avoid increases in arousal, whereas the extravert tends to seek them out.

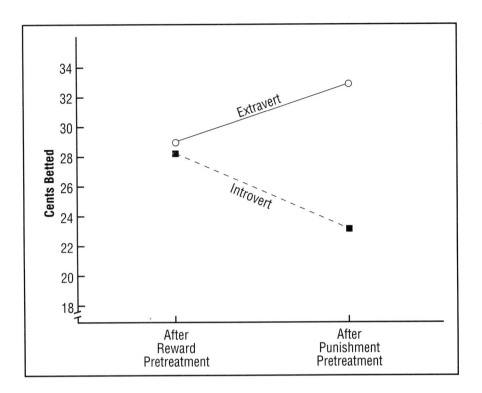

Figure 5.2

Betting Behavior of Introverts and Extraverts Following Reward and Punishment Pretreatments.

Adapted from Pearce-McCall and Newman, 1986, p. 442.

If introverts are chronically more aroused than extraverts, we would expect it to be more difficult to calm an introvert down. Some support for this proposition comes from studies with drugs. Employing depressant drugs ("downers") to reduce levels of arousal, psychopharmacologists have found that introverts are somewhat more difficult to sedate than extraverts, requiring a higher dosage of a drug such as sodium amatyl (Wilson, 1978). Sedation threshold—which may be measured by changes in electrical patterns in the brain, slurring of speech, or loss of facility on cognitive tasks such as adding numbers—is significantly higher in "dysthymics" (introverted neurotics) than hysterics (extraverted neurotics). There is also some evidence that depressant drugs (which decrease arousal) cause introverts to behave more like extraverts on certain laboratory tasks whereas stimulant drugs ("uppers," which increase arousal) may cause extraverts to act more like introverts (Wilson, 1978).

If introverts are chronically more aroused than extraverts, we would also expect them to be more sensitive to stimuli at all levels of intensity. Eysenck

(1990) has reported a number of studies indicating that, in general, introverts have greater sensitivity to barely detectable stimuli as well as lower pain thresholds, compared to extraverts. A rather amazing example of individual differences in stimulus sensitivity in introverts and extraverts is the lemon-drop test. Four drops of lemon juice are placed on an individual's tongue for 20 seconds. The person scores according to the amount of salivation produced under lemon-juice stimulating conditions as compared with the amount produced under neutral conditions (that is, when no lemon juice is present). Extreme extraverts show little or no salivation increase in response to the lemon juice, whereas extreme introverts show an increment of almost one gram of saliva. In other words, introverts respond vigorously to the lemon-juice stimulus, suggesting that they are more sensitive to stimulation. In a sample of 50 male and 50 female students, Eysenck (1973) obtained an extremely high correlation of +.71 between salivation increase on the lemon-drop test and introversion assessed on a questionnaire. In a review of nine subsequent studies on lemon drops and saliva, Deary, Ramsay, Wilson, and Raid (1988) find that Eysenck's original results are generally well replicated, especially when studies are done in the morning, during which time cortical arousal differences among introverts and extraverts seem to be at their peak. They write:

> The negative correlation between extraversion and acid-stimulation salivation holds: for both male and female Ss with different saliva collection procedures; whether fresh or synthetic lemon juice or citric acid is used as a stimulus (although fresh lemon juice appears to be the most reliable); whether the stimulation is dropped or swabbed on to the tongue and whether the saliva is collected for 10 sec. or 10 min. There is, however, some evidence that the correlation is more robust when testing is performed in the morning when arousal differences are at their greatest. Swallowing the stimulus also appears to reduce the correlation. (p. 906)

Similar results have been obtained in other laboratory situations. Weisen (1965) found that extraverts would expend considerable effort to obtain a reward of loud jazz music and bright lights whereas introverts would work hard to avoid these same stimuli. Geen (1984) found that extraverts chose higher levels of noise stimulation in a learning task than introverts and performed better in the presence of intense noise, whereas introverts performed better at lower levels of noise. Holmes (1967) looked at the pupillary response. When a person is exposed to bright lights, the pupils of his or her eyes automatically contract to ward off the sudden increase in stimulation. This is a natural, unlearned response. The rate at which such pupil contraction occurs, however, is a function of E, Holmes' study suggests. When a bright light was shone onto the eyes of an introvert, pupil contraction occurred significantly more quickly than when the light was shone onto the eyes of an extravert. Conversely, extraverts showed faster pupil dilation (opening up of the pupils to let light in) when they were exposed to dark conditions, compared to introverts. In other words, even at the level of the autonomic responding of the eye's pupil, introverts exhibit an avoidance of high levels of stimulation whereas extraverts manifest a kind of "stimulus hunger."

The hunger for increasing levels of stimulation is directly assessed on Zuckerman's (1978) Sensation Seeking Scale. **Sensation seeking** is the "need for varied, novel, and complex sensations and experiences and the willingness to take physical and social risks for the sake of such experiences" (Zuckerman, 1979, p. 10). Sensation seeking appears to incorporate four related factors: (1) thrill and adventure seeking (interest in activities involving physical risk), (2) experience seeking (desire for new experiences through music, art, travel, meeting unusual people, mood-altering drugs), (3) disinhibition (pursuit of pleasure through parties, social drinking, sex with various partners, gambling), and (4) boredom susceptibility (restlessness in unchanging environments and dislike for dull people). Although sensation seeking is *not* the same thing as Eysenck's concept of extraversion, it shares certain similarities and correlates positively, though only moderately, with *E*. A substantial body of empirical literature supports the construct validity of Zuckerman's sensation-seeking trait. Some important findings are summarized in Table 5.5.

Eysenck (1990) has recently reviewed a large number of studies investigating the relation between *E* and arousal. This research literature is very complex, involving many technical issues concerning physiological measurement. Cortical arousal has been indexed most often through assessments of brain wave patterns, through electroencephalography (EEG), and through electrodermal responses. Other studies have examined the role of the enzyme MAO in brain tissues, calcium ions, and cortisol. Some conflicting results have been obtained, and different researchers often disagree as to the meaning of the results they obtain. For example, researchers disagree as to the exact role of the reticular activating system and other particular areas of the brain in the production of arousal (Stelmack, 1990). Research also shows that at especially high levels of arousal, differences between extraverts and introverts sometimes do not appear. Nonetheless, Eysenck (1990) concludes that "when all is said and done, the data on the whole seem to support the general proposal that extraverts normally work at a lower level of arousal and are less easily aroused than introverts" (p. 262).

Stability and Change   Once an extravert (or introvert), is one forever an extravert (or introvert)? The answer, according to recent research, is a qualified "yes." In a number of longitudinal studies, *E* has shown remarkable stability over time, at least with respect to the adult years. Conley (1985b) analyzed data from a 50-year longitudinal study of several hundred adults. The subjects rated themselves and were rated by their spouses and acquaintances in 1935–1938, 1954–1955, and 1980–1981 on a number of personality traits. Individual differences in ratings comprising a general *E* dimension showed considerable longitudinal consistency, suggesting that *E* was a relatively stable disposition in this group.

Costa, McCrae, and Arenberg (1980) assessed a number of different traits, some of which comprise parts of *E,* at two different times for 460 male volunteers

Table 5.5

Some Behavioral Correlates of Sensation Seeking

Greater variety of sexual activities and greater number of sexual partners for both heterosexual and homosexual adults, males and females.

Greater use of recreational drugs, such as marijuana and amphetamines.

Smoke cigarettes.

Prefer spicy, sour, and crunchy foods.

More gambling and higher betting.

Engage in physically risky activities such as parachuting, motorcycling, scuba diving, and fire fighting.

Volunteer for unusual types of experiments such as sensory deprivation, hypnosis, and drug studies.

Volunteer for unusual types of activities such as encounter groups, alpha training, and transcendental meditation.

In leaderless, task-oriented groups, tend to begin conversations, speak more, and be selected by others as leaders of the group; tend to score high on measures of dominance.

Prefer complex artistic forms to simple ones.

Like the color blue.

With respect to the general trait of extraversion, are more likely to manifest characteristics of impulsivity rather than sociability.

Among delinquents, engage in more impulsive behavior such as fighting and defiance of rules.

Among psychiatric patients, score higher on scales reflecting elevated mood and sociopathy rather than schizophrenia.

Among heterosexual couples, tend to be romantically attracted to and marry people who are also high in sensation seeking, particularly on the subscales of experience-seeking, disinhibition, and boredom susceptbility. (Lesnik-Oberstein & Cohn, 1984)

These findings are reviewed in Zuckerman (1978).

in the Baltimore Longitudinal Study of Aging. At the time of the first testing, the subjects ranged in age from 17 to 85 years. Correlations between E scores at Time 1 and Time 2, separated by a 6–12-year period, were generally above .70, indicating substantial longitudinal consistency. Men in all age groups showed consistency in E scores over the 6–12-year span. In a large cross-sectional survey of 10,063 American men and women, E scores from various age groups were compared. In general, older men and women showed slightly lower scores than younger men and women, indicating a modest shift toward introversion among older adults (Costa, McCrae, Zonderman, Barbano, Lebowitz, & Larson, 1986). In sum, then, scores on extraversion/introversion appear to be stable over time: subjects' relative rankings on the E continuum appear to change little. With respect to overall level of E, however, older adults may obtain slightly lower scores than younger adults, though the difference is fairly small.

N: Neuroticism

The second superordinate personality trait domain is known by many names, but the most common label is probably **neuroticism,** (hereafter termed N). Measures of chronic anxiety, depression, emotionality, nervousness, moodiness, hostility, vulnerability, self-consciousness, and hypochondriasis all converge in this general factor, which is most generally described as a continuum from emotional instability to emotional stability. Watson and Clark (1984) point out that this general personality dimension is concerned with individual differences among people in their experience of negative emotions, such as sadness, anger, fear, anxiety, guilt, and the like. Consequently, they label the dimension "negative affectivity." People who score high on this general trait have a tendency to be distressed and upset in many realms of their lives. They are chronically worried, nervous, and insecure, and they hold a low opinion of themselves. People who score low on N, on the other hand, are generally calm, relaxed, hardy, secure, self-satisfied, and rather unemotional.

Eysenck's early factor-analytic studies at Maudsley Hospital in London identified N as the second major dimension of personality. Since then, Eysenck has developed a number of different self-report measures of N. (One example is reproduced in Table 5.6.) Eysenck (1967) argues that, like E, N is rooted in human biology. Individual differences in N correspond to differences in the functioning of the hypothalamus and limbic system—two structures in the brain that regulate the involuntary or autonomic nervous system and that are implicated in the experience of emotion. People whose hypothalamus and limbic system are set at a low threshold for activation are likely to be easily aroused emotionally. Events that would likely have little effect on many people may arouse in these persons a vigorous affective response. Such individuals are emotionally "labile" and thus likely to exhibit neurotic tendencies. Persons whose hypothalamus and limbic system are set at a relatively high threshold of activation, on the other hand, are less likely to experience intense and chronic emotional upheaval and

Table 5.6

Questionnaire Items Assessing Neuroticism (*N*)

1. Do you sometimes feel happy, sometimes depressed, without any apparent reason?
2. Does your mind often wander while you are trying to concentrate?
3. Are you inclined to be moody?
4. Are you frequently "lost in thought" even when you are supposed to be taking part in a conversation?
5. Are you sometimes bubbling over with energy and sometimes very sluggish?
6. Are your feelings rather easily hurt?
7. Do you get attacks of shaking or trembling?
8. Are you an irritable person?
9. Are you troubled with feelings of inferiority?
10. Do you suffer from sleeplessness?

All the items are drawn from Eysenck (1973, pp. 33, 43–45).

thus are less likely to exhibit characteristics associated with high levels of *N*. Emotional stability and instability, therefore, are largely a function of biological differences beyond the individual's control. Though experience and learning surely influence the extent to which a person manifests neurotic tendencies, Eysenck insists that inborn differences in the functioning of the brain predispose some people to develop in the direction of neuroticism and others in the direction of emotional stability. Psychophysiological research on *N*, however, has not been especially consistent, and in a recent review Eysenck (1990) concludes that we really know very little about the biological underpinnings of neuroticism. Nonetheless, some recent research implicates asymmetry in brain activity. Davidson and Tomarken (1989) review a series of studies suggesting that increased activation of the right hemisphere of the brain in anterior sites is linked to heightened negative affect (associated with *N*), decreased positive affect, or both. Similarly, increased activation of the left hemisphere anterior regions is associated with heightened positive affect, reduced negative affect, or both.

In his trait theory of personality, Eysenck has integrated the dimensions of extraversion/introversion and neuroticism in a manner that recaptures the ancient typology of personality presented by the Roman physician Galen. Both *N* and *E* are conceived as independent personality dimensions that together form a 2-dimensional coordinate space. As we can see in Figure 5.3 persons may be classified in this space according to their relative positions on the two basic traits. The extraverted and emotionally stable person (high *E*, low *N*) is cheerful, outgoing, and dependable, corresponding to what the ancients saw as the *sanguine* type of person. The introverted and emotionally stable person (low *E*, low *N*) is quiet, steady, and somewhat stoic, reminiscent of Galen's *phlegmatic* person.

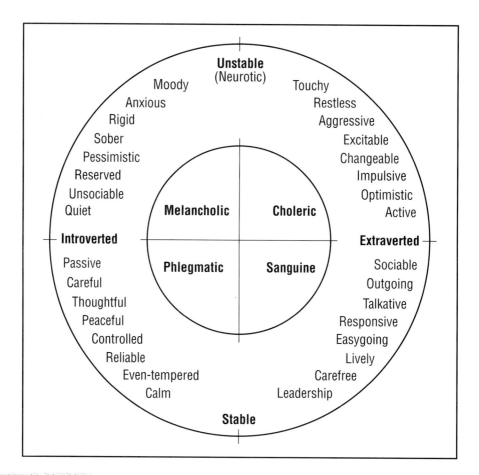

Figure 5.3

The Relations Among Extraversion/Introversion, Neuroticism, and the Four Ancient Personality Types.

From Eysenck, 1973, p.18.

Corresponding to the *choleric* type, extraverted neurotic persons (high *E,* high *N*) are outgoing and unstable, easily irritated, restless, and excitable. Clinically, such persons may develop symptoms of hysteria. Finally, the *melancholic* type is introverted and neurotic (low *E,* high *N*), chronically sad, anxious, moody, pessimistic, and brooding. Clinically, the introverted neurotic may exhibit symptoms of depression and anxiety disorders. These four characterizations refer to hypothetical types; most people, however, cannot be typed in such a simple manner because they score at intermediate levels on either *N, E,* or both.

Like *E, N* has shown substantial longitudinal consistency as a personality trait. A few recent longitudinal studies with adult samples suggest that *N* is highly stable over the adult life-span. Conley (1985b) found that adults' relative positions on an emotionally stable/unstable continuum changed remarkably little over the course of 50 years. Costa and others (1980) likewise found high stability correlations on N over a 6–12-year span in their longitudinal study. In their large cross-sectional survey of American men and women, Costa and others (1986) found that scores on N were slightly lower in older than in younger adults. No consistent sex differences have been observed.

While E has been consistently related to positive affect in daily life, N appears to be associated with *negative* affect. As we saw above, extraverts tend to report greater levels of good feeling about themselves than do introverts, though extraverts and introverts do not appear to differ with respect to bad feelings. Persons scoring high on N, on the other hand, report more bad feelings than do persons scoring low in N, though they do not necessarily report lower levels of good feelings. Good feelings and bad feelings appear to be quite independent. Thus, to oversimplify somewhat: extraverts report high levels of good feeling, introverts report low levels of good feeling, persons high in neuroticism report high levels of bad feeling, and persons low in neuroticism report low levels of bad feeling (Costa & McCrae, 1980a, 1984; Emmons & Diener, 1985; Meyer & Shack, 1989; Watson & Clark, 1984).

Beyond the realm of bad feelings, N has been shown to predict a number of important behavioral and attitudinal trends. For example, N has been associated with complaints about poor health among men (Costa & McCrae, 1980b). In a study following the daily life of 43 undergraduate students over the course of a semester, Larsen and Kasimatis (1991) found that students high in N tended to report a greater number of illnesses. Ormel and Wohlfarth (1991) found that high levels of N were a significantly stronger predictor of psychological distress than were environmental factors such as negative changes in one's life situation. Individuals high in N are likely to see the problems of middle age as a "crisis" according to Costa and McCrae (1978). In a 50-year longitudinal study of 300 married couples, neuroticism scores of both husbands and wives were a major predictor of divorce (Kelly & Conley, 1987).

Why is N so strongly associated with so many bad things? Bolger and Schilling (1991) conducted a study of daily stressors that provides insight into this question. The researchers recruited 339 adults who provided daily reports of minor stressful events and mood for 42 consecutive days. Each day the respondents indicated how strongly they had felt each of 18 emotions over the previous 24 hours. Emotion items included indices of anxiety, depression, and hostility, such as "nervous," "tense," "irritable," "worthless," and "angry." In addition, each respondent indicated whether or not he or she experienced any of nine different kinds of stressors during the day, including "overload at work," "argument with spouse," "argument with child," and "transportation problem." Scores on N were determined from an 11-item neuroticism scale that was administered before the daily reporting began.

The results indicated that on average high-N adults were more distressed than low-N adults over the six-week period, as indexed by the daily mood reports. The sources of their distress were three. First, high-N adults tended to report a greater number of daily stressors than did low-N adults. Now one could argue that this is because high-N individuals complain more; perhaps, they are overly sensitive and tend to report minor events that most other people would overlook. The results show, however, that the difference was *not* due to oversensitivity on the part of high-N adults, for reports from their spouses tended to support the accuracy of their own accounts of stressful events. In essence, then, high neuroticism appears to *expose* individuals to a greater number of stressful daily events. Especially significant in this regard were stressful events having to do with interpersonal conflict. Of the nine stressor categories, "argument with spouse" and "argument with other" were the two areas that showed the largest distinction between high-N and low-N adults.

A second source of distress was the respondents' *reactivity* to stressful events. Not only did the high-N subjects report a greater number of stressful events, but their negative emotional reactions to stressful events were significantly stronger than the negative emotional reactions to stressful events shown by low-N respondents. In fact, reactivity to stressful events was *twice as important* as exposure to stressful events as an explanation for the link between N and distress. The authors argue that this reactivity in high-N adults is a result of ineffective coping strategies such as self-blame and wishful thinking. Rather than taking constructive steps to deal with stressful situations, high-N individuals rely on self-defeating strategies that do not relieve their anxiety, depression, and hostility in the face of daily setbacks.

A third source of distress among high-N individuals was *unrelated to stressful events*. The authors show that as much as 60% of the relationship between neuroticism and distress had nothing to do with either the bad things that happened to the high-N individuals or their overly negative reactions to these bad things. It appears that on top of a greater exposure to stressful situations and a greater negative reaction to such stressors when they occur is a general negativity about life among high-N adults that cannot be explained by what happens on a daily basis. Even when bad things aren't happening, neuroticism brings with it bad feelings.

Other studies suggest that N is associated with inappropriate and awkward behavior in a number of different social situations. In one experiment, college men scoring either high or low on N were randomly assigned to one of two experimental conditions: a "low-intimacy" or a "high-intimacy" condition (Chaikin, Derlega, Bayma, & Shaw, 1975). In the low-intimacy condition, the participant spoke over the phone with a stranger who was a fellow student and who had been previously trained to talk about topics that were superficial and nonintimate, such as his house or apartment, how his family got together, and so on. In the high-intimacy condition, the person spoke over the phone with a fellow student who had been previously trained to talk about topics that were highly intimate, such as the birth-control methods he would prefer to use in marriage, the number of times he had cried as an adult, the frequency of his sexual behavior, and how he had felt when he saw his father hit his mother. The subjects were each given a list of topics to discuss over the phone. The topics varied with respect to their intimacy level, and thus the study's dependent variable was the amount of intimacy content that the participant introduced into the conversation.

Figure 5.4 presents the major finding of the study—subjects scoring low in N adjusted their level of intimacy to correspond to the level introduced by the experimental condition. In other words, when the fellow student disclosed intimate information (the high-intimacy condition) the participant reciprocated, offering intimate information about himself. Similarly, when the fellow student kept the conversation light and nonintimate, the participant reciprocated with less intimate information about himself. Men high in N, on the other hand, did *not* adjust their intimacy disclosure to the condition, disclosing at moderate levels of intimacy regardless of what the fellow student said. The results suggest that persons high in N find it difficult to adjust their social behavior to meet situational demands. Neurotic individuals appear to be oblivious to social cues, perhaps too self-preoccupied to note what their environments are saying to them.

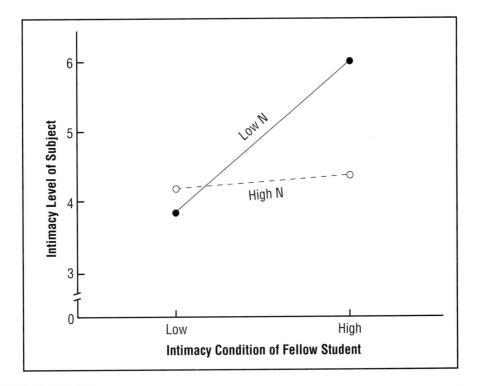

Figure 5.4

Level of Intimacy Expressed by Subjects High and Subjects Low in Neuroticism *(N)*, as a Function of Intimacy Level Expressed by Fellow Student.

Modified from Chaikin, Derlega, Bayma, and Shaw, 1975, p. 16.

Gray's Approach: Impulsivity and Anxiety

As we have seen, the general dimensions of E and N are centrally concerned with human emotionality. Extraverted people tend to report higher levels of positive emotion, such as joy, excitement, and happiness, compared to introverted people. Neurotic (high-N) people tend to report higher levels of negative emotion, such as sadness and anxiety, compared to stable people (low-N). In an important modification of Eysenck's views on E and N, Jeffrey Gray (1982, 1987) suggests that emotional experience is regulated by two different systems in the brain, one dealing with positive and one with negative emotionality. The **behavioral approach system (BAS)** arouses a person to move toward desired incentives that promise positive emotional reward. The **behavioral inhibition system (BIS)** causes a person to draw back from goals in the anticipation of a negative emotional punishment. My BAS may motivate me to walk confidently into a room of good friends to enjoy the night's party, but my BIS may keep me standing on the perimeter should I find myself in a very different sort of gathering in which, say, I know very few people, and they all look intimidating. In the first situation, I act spontaneously and on *impulse;* I am comfortable and ready for fun. In the second situation, I feel *anxious* and vigilant; I scan the room warily; I look for opportunities to escape.

While most all of us have had some experiences in which we approached joyfully and others in which we withdrew in fear, Gray argues that people differ substantially on the extent to which positive approach or negative withdrawal is their modus operandi. Approach-oriented individuals consistently seek out rewards and show a strong sensitivity to the incentive values of rewards. They manifest generally high levels of the trait *impulsivity*. Avoidance-oriented individuals, by contrast, are strongly motivated to inhibit their behavior in the face of perceived punishments. They manifest generally high levels of the trait *anxiety*. Individual differences in impulsivity are biologically rooted in the BAS. Anxiety stems from the BIS.

According to Gray, impulsivity and anxiety—*not E and N*—are the two basic personality dimensions associated with emotional life. Like E and N, impulsivity and anxiety are relatively independent of each other. One's position on one dimension does not predict one's position on the other. (A person can score high on one dimension and not the other; high on both; high on neither; and so on.) But the placement of impulsivity and anxiety in a two-dimensional map of personality differs from that of E and N in that impulsivity and anxiety form a coordinate system that is at a 45-degree tilt vis-à-vis extraversion and neuroticism. Figure 5.5 shows the relation between Gray's and Eysenck's dimensions. In Gray's terms, the extravert is high on impulsiveness and low on anxiety. The pure reward-seeker, the extravert's behavior is strongly guided by the BAS. By contrast, the introvert is inhibited by virtue of high anxiety (BIS) and low impulsiveness. The neurotic (high N, in Eysenck's scheme) is high on both impulsiveness and anxiety, revealing strong tendencies toward reward approach and punishment avoidance and a great deal of emotional *conflict*. By contrast, the person occupying the stable end of the N continuum tends to be low on both impulsiveness and anxiety.

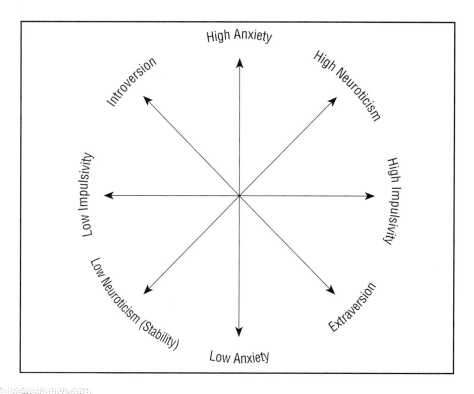

Figure 5.5

The Relation Between Eysenck's Dimensions of Extraversion and Neuroticism and Gray's Dimensions of Impulsivity and Anxiety

Eysenck's and Gray's theories make different predictions with respect to how people learn in the context of rewards and punishments (what we will call, in Chapter 6, "instrumental conditioning"). In Eysenck's view, because introverts are more highly aroused than extraverts and because arousal enhances certain kinds of learning, introverts should learn certain simple tasks more easily than extraverts. In essence, in most situations introverts are more "conditionable" than extraverts. By contrast, Gray suggests that conditioning differences split according to the BAS and BIS. Highly impulsive individuals should learn better (be more conditionable) in the context of rewards, compared to low-impulsive individuals. Highly anxious persons should learn better (be more conditionable) in the context of punishments. If you think about this for a minute and look at Figure 5.5, you should see how Eysenck and Gray would make very different predictions about Eysenck's introverts and extraverts. In essence, Esyenck should predict that introverts are more conditionable than extraverts in general whereas Gray should predict that introverts should be more conditionable only in punishment situations whereas extraverts should prove more conditionable in reward

Feature 5.B

Feeling Really Good and Really Bad
Affect Intensity

A central message of the research on E and N is that positive affect and negative affect are relatively independent. Compared to introverts, extraverts tend to experience life with a greater degree of positive affect (joy, excitement, happiness) but no less negative affect. Compared to stable (low N) individuals, neurotic people tend to experience life with a greater degree of negative affect (anxiety, fear, sadness) but no less positive affect.

There may be one sense, however, in which positive and negative affect are strongly related. Personality psychologists Randy Larsen and Ed Diener (1987) have conducted extensive research on the dimension of *affect intensity,* which refers to how strongly a person tends to experience both positive and negative emotions. Their studies support the commonly held notion that people who tend to experience strong emotional highs are the same people who also feel the intense lows. In four separate studies of daily mood involving 204 participants, the correlations between posi-

tive affect intensity and negative affect intensity ranged from +.70 to +.77. These results strongly suggest that, over time, people who experience intense positive affect will also experience intense negative affect. That is, intensity of emotional response appears to be a characteristic that generalizes to both positive and negative emotion domains (Diener, Colvin, Pavot, & Allman, 1991).

Larsen and Diener view affect intensity as a stable individual difference variable in behavioral style. This traitlike characteristic may have its origins in early infant temperament. Indeed, studies of infants show that emotional intensity is a readily observable dimension upon which newborns differ markedly from each other. Like the traits of E and N, individual differences in affect intensity appear to be quite stable over time. The relative stability of individual differences masks a general tendency, however, for affect intensity to decrease with age. As people move from young adulthood into middle adulthood, they tend to report

situations. Zinbarg and Revelle (1989) present data that is somewhat more consistent with Gray's predictions than with Eysenck's. Research in the area is hampered, however, by the difficulty in finding pure measures of these four dimensions. Measures of extraversion and impulsivity are often highly correlated. It is equally difficult to sort from each other measures of neuroticism and anxiety.

In conclusion, Gray provides us with an alternative "take" on the dimensions of E and N. For Gray, extraversion-introversion and neuroticism-stability are secondary products (blends) of the more fundamental, brain-based dimensions of less intense emotional reactions, both positive and negative. Why this occurs is not known. One possibility is that age differences reflect biological changes. Another is that life activities vary markedly by age. Young persons may be exposed to more positively stimulating as well as stressful experiences than their older counterparts. Yet another possibility is that as people grow older they become habituated to various emotional experiences. Ecstatic moments of youth may give way to more peaceful positive experiences in the middle-adult years and beyond. Intense angst and despair may shade gradually into melancholy as people grow older.

Research also suggests that overall women experience more intense positive as well as negative affects compared to men. This sex difference in affect intensity helps explain the common finding in survey research that whereas women report greater levels of depression than do men, there is no general difference between the sexes in overall life satisfaction. Fujita, Diener, and Sandvik (1991) reason that

women's greater depression is a direct result of greater affect intensity but that their greater affect intensity also produces higher levels of positive affect, which counterbalance the negative and provide them with life satisfaction and happiness scores that are comparable to men.

Still, there appear to be some negative ramifications of high levels of affect intensity. For example, strong affect intensity is predictive of tendencies to develop cyclothymia, a mild form of bipolar affective disorder (manic-depressive disorder). In addition, affect intensity is positively associated with such somatic symptoms as headaches, nervousness, nausea, and heart-pounding. Certainly the regular experience of strong emotion exacts a price to be paid in terms of wear and tear on the body. But it seems to be a price that some people are willing to pay. For some, life lacks vividness, vitality, and taste when they are not fully emotionally engaged. The crying and the laughing are all of a piece—you can't have one without the other.

impulsivity and anxiety. Eysenck contends, by contrast, that E and N are primary and rooted in the biology of the central nervous system, as well. It is interesting to note here that for both Gray and Eysenck, personality traits have their ultimate legitimacy in human physiology. This is not a view shared by all trait theorists. Indeed, the general rationale in support of the Big Five traits is statistical rather than biological. From the standpoint of the five-factor model of personality traits (but not from the standpoint of Eysenck and Gray), E and N represent two of the five big trait domains because factor analysis of personality scales and items consistently supports the existence of these domains in personality description.

O: Openness to Experience

Early factor-analytic studies of English-language traits identified one of the five basic dimensions of personality as "culture." Norman (1963) conceived of culture as a cluster of smaller traits having to do with how reflective, imaginative, artistic, and refined a person is. More than the other four trait domains, culture appeared to incorporate an intellectual dimension. High scorers were thought to be intellectually well rounded, broad, and insightful; low scorers were narrow, unimaginative, and even crude and boorish. Recently, McCrae and Costa (1980, 1985a, 1985b, 1987) have reconceptualized culture as the dimension of **openness to experience** (hereafter termed *O*). Persons high in *O* are described by themselves and by others who know them as especially original, imaginative, creative, complex, curious, daring, independent, analytical, untraditional, artistic, liberal, and having broad interests. Persons iow in *O* are described as conventional, down-to-earth, uncreative, simple, incurious, nonadventurous, conforming, nonanalytical, unartistic, traditional, conservative, and having narrow interests. Sample items from a self-report measure of *O* are presented in Table 5.7.

In one of the earliest investigations of *O*, McCrae and Costa (1980) administered a number of trait scales and a sentence-completion exercise to 240 adults between the ages of 35 and 80 years. On the sentence-completion exercise, the subjects were presented with sentence fragments such as "A good father/" and "Rules are/" and were asked to complete the sentences in any way they wished. Table 5.8 provides examples of how persons high and low on *O* responded to this task. Persons scoring high on *O* on the trait scales provided richer and more complex responses on the sentence-completion test, compared to persons scoring low in *O*. Their responses reveal a more differentiated fantasy life, more psychological

 Table 5.7

Questionnaire Items Assessing Openness to Experience (*O*)

1. I enjoy concentrating on a fantasy or daydream and exploring all its possibilities, letting it grow and develop.
2. I am sometimes completely absorbed in music I am listening to.
3. Without strong emotions, life would be uninteresting.
4. I enjoy trying new and foreign foods.
5. I find philosophical arguments boring. (reversed)
6. The different ideas of right and wrong that people in other societies have may be valid for them.

From McCrae and Costa (1985b). These items come from the NEO Openness Scales.

Table 5.8

Sentence-Completion Responses of Men Scoring High and Low on Openness to Experience (*O*)

Low

Sentence Stem	Response
Rules are	there to obey. laws to be governed by for the best interests of all concerned.
My main problem	is financial.
When they avoided me	I wondered why.
If my mother	gave a command, it was done.
A husband has a right to	come home and find his wife looking nice.

High

Sentence Stem	Response
Rules are	things that should be flexible enough to fit the real world. necessary, but civil disobedience is one way to change them for "progress."
My main problem	is I am too emotional or sensitive sometimes.
When I am criticized	I try to remain open-minded and not get defensive. It doesn't always work, however.
A good father	remembers the anxieties of childhood.
The worst thing about being a man	is the false image built for us by society.

Adapted from McCrae and Costa (1980, p. 1186).

insight, and a greater variety of experience. Whereas persons low in *O* held to rather rigid and traditional views of authority and society (Rules are/ "there to obey"), persons high in *O* tended to reject, or at least question, these stereotypical attitudes, revealing more flexible and personalized understandings of rules, authority, the family, and sex roles (Rules are/ "necessary, but civil disobedience is one way to change them for 'progress'"). The study suggests that openness to experience is associated with a more complex, nonconforming, and individualized understanding of the world.

Persons high in *O* are thought to have broad intellectual and aesthetic interests. This does not mean, however, that these people are necessarily highly intelligent. McCrae and Costa (1985a) argue that intelligence and *O* are very different constructs. To support this claim of the discriminant validity of trait scales assessing *O*, McCrae and Costa report a correlation of +.32 between vocabulary score on a standard adult intelligence (IQ) test and openness to experience in a sample of 253 men. Remember that, to show discriminant validity, one must prove that a particular trait scale does *not* measure the same thing that scales of *other* traits measure. In this case, the correlation of .32 suggests a statistically significant but rather weak relationship between intelligence and *O*, meaning that the two measures—intelligence (via vocabulary) and openness to experience— seem to be measuring different dimensions of human functioning.

People high in *O* appear to welcome challenge and change. For example, in one study of career changes in adults under the age of 55, 64% of the men and 71% of the women who changed jobs over a particular time period scored above the midpoint on *O* (McCrae and Costa, 1985b). Whitbourne (1986) interviewed 34 women and 23 men (average age 41 years) about anticipated work and family changes. Such changes might include seeking different work, finding employment outside the house, adding another child to the family, or retiring. Openness to experience, assessed via a questionnaire, was positively associated with anticipated change in life, as was age. In other words, older adults and adults scoring high in *O* anticipated more changes in their lives in the future. (In a 12-month follow-up of the same adults, however, *O* was not significantly associated with the number of *actual* changes that had occurred.)

Within the general domain of *O* resides an interesting trait that goes by the name of **absorption.** Absorption is formally defined as a predisposition to "experience emotional and cognitive alterations across a variety of situations" (Roche & McConkey, 1990, p. 92). The concept of absorption has its origins in Auke Tellegen's research into why some people seem especially susceptible to hypnotism and some do not. Tellegen and Atkinson (1974) found that hypnotizable individuals were more open to and more likely to have subjective experiences in which their attention was fully engaged by some object or event, resulting in an altered sense of reality. To assess individual differences in a predisposition to show such experience, they designed the Tellegen Absorption Scale (TAS), which later became part of Tellegen's (1982) Multidimensional Personality Questionnaire (MPQ).

Table 5.9

Coping Strategies Associated With *E*, *N*, and *O*

Extraversion (*E*)

Positive thinking:	thought about the good side, the positive aspects of the situation.
Rational action:	took some direct action to change the circumstances that were giving you a problem.
Restraint:	resisted making snap judgments or hasty decisions.
Substitution:	found satisfaction somewhere else in life.

Neuroticism (*N*)

Escapist fantasy:	spent time daydreaming to forget your troubles.
Hostile reaction:	became irritable and took it out on others.
Indecisiveness:	thought about the problem over and over without really reaching a decision.
Passivity:	procrastinated and delayed while others were waiting for you.
Sedation:	used tranquilizers, alcohol, meditation, or relaxation exercises to calm yourself down.
Self-blame:	blamed yourself, felt guilty, or became apologetic.
Wishful thinking:	just wished that the problem would be gone or that help would come.
Withdrawal:	withdrew from others and attempted to cope with the problem by yourself.

Openness to Experience (*O*)

Faith (*negatively* correlated with *O*):	just put your faith in God, or other people, or institutions.
Humor:	saw humor in the situation.

Adapted from McCrae and Costa (1986, pp. 393, 404–405).

Absorption is associated with an intense and vivid fantasy life. Persons who score high on absorption may become so immersed in their imaginative experiences that they lose all track of time, place, and identity (Pekala, Wenger, & Levine, 1985). Research shows that absorption is positively related to reports of parapsychological phenomena, such as out-of-body experiences, as well as reports of naturally occurring altered states of consciousness. According to a recent factor-analytic study, absorption connects closely to those aspects of O that invoke aesthetic sensitivity, unusual perceptions and associations, fantasy and dreams, unconventional views of reality, and awareness of inner feelings. By contrast, it does not appear to be related to O concepts such as intellectual curiosity, openness to unusual ideas, need for variety in actions, and liberal values (Glisky, Tataryn, Tobias, Kihlstrom, & McConkey, 1991). Research on absorption, therefore, underscores just how broad and varied is the galaxy of O.

Our final study in this section integrates O with E and N. Employing a standardized questionnaire designed to measure all three of these primary traits (the Neuroticism–Extraversion–Openness Inventory, or NEO), McCrae and Costa (1986) examined the relationship between traits and coping with stress in two large adult samples. Men and women who had reported a recent stressful life event participated in the study. Stressful events included losses (such as a death of a parent), threats (such as an illness in the family), and challenges (such as marriage). The participants completed a questionnaire that asked them to recall the particular stressful event and to indicate which of a series of 27 coping strategies they had ever used in dealing with it.

Table 5.9 shows that E, N, and O were significantly associated with use of particular coping strategies. Neuroticism, for example, was correlated with the coping strategies of hostile reaction, escapist fantasy, self-blame, sedation, withdrawal, wishful thinking, passivity, and indecisiveness. Virtually all of these coping strategies were rated by the participants as extremely *in*effective in dealing with stress. Extraversion and openness to experience, on the other hand, were associated with a number of effective coping strategies. E was correlated with rational action, positive thinking, substitution, and restraint. Adults high in O were more likely to use humor in dealing with stress; those low in O relied heavily on faith. McCrae and Costa argue that basic personality traits manifest themselves in times of stress by predisposing people to adopt certain corresponding coping strategies. While the choice of a coping strategy is likely partly determined by the nature of the stressful event and other situational factors, stable and internal personality traits like E, N, and O also play an important determining role.

C and *A*: Conscientiousness and Agreeableness

You may recall that Freud (Chapter 2) was thought to have said that the two major signs of maturity and mental health in the adult years were *Lieben und Arbeiten*—to love and to work. The fourth and fifth factors that we will examine in the Big Five model of traits concern issues of love and work, as well as certain

The traits of Agreeableness and Conscientiousness are involved in love and work. Here a school teacher works in what seems to be a loving way with her students.

other interpersonal and instrumental dimensions of personality (McCrae & Costa, 1991). **Conscientiousness *(C)*** encompasses a diversity of descriptors pertaining to a person's proclivities and dispositions in the instrumental worlds of work, achievement, accomplishment, and so forth. **Agreeableness *(A)*** incorporates expressive qualities of love and empathy, friendliness, cooperation, and the like. Compared to *E, N,* and *O,* conscientiousness and agreeableness have received relatively little empirical scrutiny in the Big Five scheme. Nonetheless, they are concepts that have been addressed in some detail by theorists and researchers outside the Big-Five tradition, and they possess a great deal of intuitive appeal. It is likely that they will be popular trait domains for future research.

At the high end of the *C* continuum, people may be described as well-organized, efficient, and dependable (Goldberg, 1990). They approach tasks in a systematic and orderly fashion. They analyze problems logically. They provide concise answers to questions and perform according to exacting standards in their work and their play. You can depend on conscientious people. Self-disciplined and duty-bound, they are reliable and responsible in their dealings with other people. They are rarely late for meetings; they don't miss class. Conscientious people plan their lives carefully, according to principles and goals. While they may seem overly cautious at times, they are nonetheless able to make hard decisions and stick by them when things get rough. They are persistent, steady, predictable, conventional, and thrifty. At the other end of the continuum, people low on the C dimension tend to be disorganized, haphazard, inefficient, careless, negligent, and undependable. It is difficult to predict what they will do from one situation to the next, so erratic and inconsistent is their behavior. Life lacks plan and purpose. Low-C people may be lazy and slothful, indecisive and wishy-washy, extravagant and impractical. Unconscientious people have little regard for serious standards of work or morality. While their spontaneity may seem like a breath of fresh air in the face of stale social conventions, their irresponsibility and utter inability to stand *by others* or stand *for anything* in the long run make them very poor risks in friendship and in love.

Many different personality scales tap into the C domain. On the CPI, for example, different aspects of C are revealed on scales assessing responsibility, socialization, self-control, achievement via conformance, and achievement via independence. Conscientiousness appears to be an important determinant of school achievement. The best predictor of educational achievement may be a person's overall intellectual aptitude, as assessed via intelligence tests and other aptitude measures. Beyond these, however, C may play an important part. Renaming C the "will to achieve," Digman (1989) reviews many studies to suggest that this dimension of personality is responsible for much of the variance in achievement left unexplained by aptitude measures. In a similar vein, Graziano and Ward (1992) examined adjustment to junior high school in a sample of 91 adolescents. Classroom teacher ratings of how well the students had adjusted to the challenges of school were positively related to the students' self-ratings on C.

The term "agreeableness" may be a bit too meek for the A domain in traits, a domain that includes such concepts as altruism, affection, and many of the most admirably humane aspects of human personality (Digman, 1990; John, 1990). Individuals at the high end of the A continuum are described as interpersonally warm, cooperative, accommodating, helpful, patient, cordial, empathic, kind, understanding, courteous, natural, and sincere (Goldberg, 1990). They are more than just nice people. They are also described as especially honest, ethical, and selfless—peace-loving humanists, committed to their friends and their family, and to the social good. Their counterparts on the other end of the A continuum, however, get some of the worst press in the entire Big Five dictionary. They are antagonistic, belligerent, harsh, unsympathetic, manipulative, disingenuous, scornful, crude, and cruel. While the low-C's may be unreliable, the low-A's are untrustworthy and malicious. They operate with wanton disregard of other's feelings. They get in fights. They hurt people.

A number of personality scales tap into dimensions of A. The CPI, for example, presents scales assessing sociability, empathy, tolerance, and femininity. Measures of the "need for affiliation" tap into the general warmth assumed to lie at the heart of A whereas measures of the "need for nurturance" assess individual differences in an empathic and caring attitude toward others (Jackson, 1974). Dimensions coming out of other theories reviewed later in this book, such as

McAdams' narrative measure of intimacy motivation (Chapter 11) and Adler's concept of social interest (Chapter 12) appear to cover some of the same ground covered by *A*.

McCrae and Costa (1991) show that self-report measures of both *C* and *A* are positively correlated with psychological well-being. In a sample of 429 adults, both conscientiousness and agreeableness were positively related to reports of positive affect, negatively related to reports of negative affect, and positively related to total well-being. McCrae and Costa suggest that high levels of conscientiousness and agreeableness create life conditions that promote well-being. They write:

> Although personality traits may directly affect the tendencies to experience positive or negative emotions, they may also have indirect effects on well-being: Certain traits may be instrumental in creating conditions that promote happiness or unhappiness. In particular, the dimensions of A and C might be hypothesized to have instrumental effects on well-being. Agreeable individuals are warm, generous, and loving; conscientious people are efficient, competent, and hard-working. The interpersonal bonds that A fosters and the achievements and accomplishments that C promotes may contribute to greater quality of life and higher life satisfaction. This is perhaps what Freud meant when he suggested that *Liebe und Arbeit,* love and work, were the keys to psychological health and happiness. (McCrae and Costa, 1991, p. 228)

While it is interesting to link up *C* with work and *A* with love, you should realize that the quality of people's work lives and their love lives is influenced by a great many variables, including many different traits. For example, we would probably expect that scoring high on traits in the *N* domain should have a negative influence on both love and work. For *O,* it would seem to depend on the situation. We could imagine that scoring high on measures of openness to experience might predict success in occupations where intellectual curiosity and aesthetic sensitivity are highly valued, as in the cases, say, of novelist and college professor. In other occupations requiring a more convergent mind—say, business or accounting—it might be better to score low on *O. E,* too, is likely to relate to work and love in a variety of ways.

A recent study by Shaver and Brennan (1992) focuses directly on the ways in which the Big Five traits relate to aspects of love. The researchers adopted an attachment perspective on heterosexual adult love. As we saw in Chapter 4, Bowlby and Ainsworth's theory of caregiver–infant attachment has recently been expanded to incorporate individual differences in adult attachment styles. Adults with a "secure" attachment style find it relatively easy to get close to others. They seem especially comfortable with intimacy, friendship, and love. Adults with an "anxious-ambivalent" style, by contrast, desire closeness but either draw back from others or feel that they drive others away when they attempt to establish intimate relationships. Adults with an "avoidant" attachment style feel that they cannot trust other people and therefore withdraw from close relationships.

Shaver and Brennan administered a measure of attachment styles and Costa and McCrae's (1985) standard questionnaire for assessing the Big Five Traits (the NEO-PI) to 242 college students. Table 5.10 shows the mean trait scores for the three groups of attachment styles. Students showing the secure attachment style scored significantly higher on agreeableness compared to those with the avoidant styles. Anxious-ambivalent students scored in between—not significantly higher nor lower than the other two groups. Extraversion and neuroticism also showed significant differences. Students with secure attachment scored significantly higher on E and lower on N than avoidant and anxious-ambivalent students. Conscientiousness and openness were unrelated to attachment. The results suggest that a secure attachment style in early adulthood is linked with traits denoting energy and positive affect (E), interpersonal warmth (A), and low levels of negative affectivity or neuroticism (N). Correlational studies such as this one cannot

 Table 5.10

Mean Scores on the Big Five Traits as a Function of Adult Attachment Style

	Attachment Style Types		
Trait	**Secure**	**Anxious**	**Avoidant**
Neuroticism	2.84[a]	3.28[b]	3.15[b]
Extraversion	3.58[a]	3.41[b]	3.37[b]
Openness	3.48	3.48	3.46
Agreeableness	3.63[a]	3.51[ab]	3.39[b]
Conscientiousness	3.57	3.47	3.43

Note: Items were answered on a 1–5 continuum with higher scores indicating higher ratings on the given trait dimension. Means with different superscripts differ significantly from each other at the .05 level. A total of 226 subjects participated in the study.
(From Shaver & Brennan, 1992, p. 539)

tell us about the causal relations between traits and attachment styles—whether, that is, trait levels precede or lead to certain attachment styles, attachment styles lead to traits, or the two are caused by some third factor, such as early caregiving experiences or genetic effects. But the research is still instructive as to how traits and relational styles line up with each other. And it is further noteworthy for its attempt to bring together two lines of personality theory and research—attachment and traits—that are usually thought to be quite separate.

The Interpersonal Circumplex

Going back to the 1950s and the work of Leary (1957), psychologists have found it useful to arrange interpersonally oriented traits and behaviors within a circle, called the interpersonal circumplex. As Gurtman (1992) describes it, "the interpersonal circumplex is a comprehensive model of interpersonal tendencies (e.g., motives, needs, orientations, problems, and traits) depicting an interpersonal space as a circular array of variables organized around the two principal axes of Dominance and Love" (p. 105). Figure 5.6 shows a version of the circumplex from Gurtman (1991). Characteristics are arranged on the circle such that those at 180 degrees from each other (on the opposite sides of the circle) are opposite in meaning (e.g., dominant vs. submissive, friendly vs. hostile, exhibitionistic vs. inhibited, trusting vs. mistrusting), whereas those at 90 degrees from each other are conceptually unrelated (e.g., dominant vs. friendly, hostile vs. submissive, inhibited vs. trusting, exhibitionistic vs. mistrusting). A considerable body of research in psychology and social relations supports the power of the circumplex for organizing and making sense of interpersonal phenomena (Kiesler, 1983; Wiggins, 1982).

Jerry Wiggins (1979; Wiggins & Broughton, 1985) has analyzed self-report data from a large number of personality measures and found a good deal of statistical evidence to support the utility of organizing interpersonally oriented traits in a circular manner. In his **circumplex model of traits,** Wiggins bisects the circular space with the independent axes of *agency* and *communion,* which roughly correspond to dominance/power and love/warmth, respectively. Following Bakan (1966), Wiggins argues that primacy of these two dimensions goes beyond their statistical salience on the circumplex. Throughout folklore, myth, and history, these two general themes—agency and communion—are the principle organizers of human interpersonal behavior. Indeed, many theories of personality outside the trait tradition present interpersonal dichotomies that capture the basic distinction between agency and communion. Examples in this book include Freud's (Chapter 2) motivational distinction between the aggressive death instincts (agency) and the erotic life instincts (communion), Kegan's (Chapter 10) distinction between independence and inclusion, Adler's (Chapter 12) distinction between striving for superiority and social interest, and McAdams' (Chapter 13) distinction between the thematic lines of agency/power and communion/intimacy in life narratives.

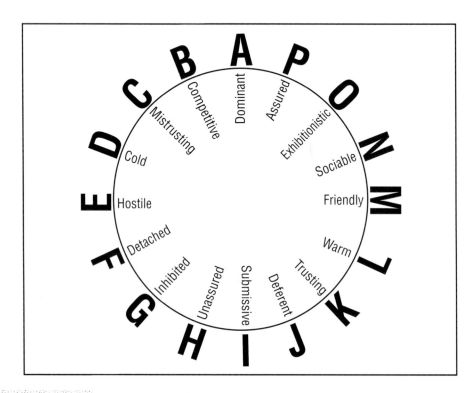

Figure 5.6

The Interpersonal Circumplex

From Gurtman, 1991, p. 670.

On first blush, the circumplex model of traits would appear to be a competing alternative to the Big Five scheme. However, Wiggins and others have recently suggested that the interpersonal circumplex gives definition and articulation to the intersection of E and A (McCrae & Costa, 1989; Trapnell & Wiggins, 1990; Wiggins, 1992). It is indeed easy to see how the agreeableness domain (A) corresponds neatly to Bakan's notion of communion, incorporating dimensions of love, care, warmth, and so on. The match between extraversion and dominance is a bit more problematic, but it would appear that the general E domain, with its emphasis on energy and surgency, may overlap considerably with the notion of dominance.

But what about the other three Big Five trait domains? Can they be arranged on the interpersonal circle? The answer is no: They cover concepts that are primarily outside the interpersonal circumplex. But any of the Big Five domains can be paired with any of the others to produce their own circumplex. We have already seen the usefulness of pitting E against N in a circumplex, to capture a conceptual space of positive and negative affectivity and to recapture, as in the work of Eysenck, the ancient Greek taxonomy of sanguine, choleric, melancholic, and phlegmatic types. Recently, Hofstee, deRaad, and Goldberg (1992) constructed 10 different circumplexes from statistical analyses of hundreds of ratings on hundreds of different trait adjectives, pitting each of the Big Five factors against each of the others. Future research should reveal the conceptual usefulness of various circumplex strategies and clarify how the different trait domains may interact to produce meaningful behavioral profiles.

Trait Genetics

One of the most controversial questions in trait psychology is one of the simplest: Where do traits come from? Most trait psychologists profess that traits develop out of some interaction between biology and society—that traits are a product of *both* nature and nurture. But there are, nonetheless, significant differences in emphasis. Some psychologists emphasize the environmental shaping of traits. According to this line of reasoning, an adult who scores high on a measure of extraversion "learned" to become outgoing, sociable, and impulsive as a child and adolescent. Numerous environmental opportunities for effective extraverted action presented themselves as the child grew. Other psychologists propose that traits may develop from inherited biological underpinnings. The extravert may be born with a biological predisposition toward extraversion, nudging behavior in the direction of the outgoing, sociable, and impulsive throughout life.

In recent years, two lines of research and theory have supported the idea that individual differences in traits may be at least *partially* grounded in biology. The study of *infant temperament* suggests that important individual differences in personality may be present at birth. Research on the *heritability* of traits suggests that biologically related people tend to show similar trait levels. Neither line of research makes a definitive case for biological determinism in the development of traits, yet each presents data that bear on the question of the origins of personality traits.

Infant Temperament

Many personologists, from Freud to trait theorists, trace the origins of personality all the way back to the first year of life. Freud, for instance, believed that excessive dependency in adulthood was ultimately rooted in the dynamics of the infant's oral libido (Chapters 2 and 3). Likewise, some personologists suspect that the origins of many personality traits may be found, quite literally, at the very beginning—that is, at birth. According to this view, each baby emerges from the womb with a certain set of biologically rooted predispositions to act in certain ways. Each baby comes into the world with a unique **temperament** distinguishing him or her from all other babies (with the possible exception of identical twins, who are biologically the same). According to Allport (1961):

> Temperament refers to the characteristic phenomena of an individual's nature, including his susceptibility to emotional stimulation, his customary strength and speed of response, the quality of his prevailing mood, and all the peculiarities of fluctuation and intensity of mood, these being phenomena regarded as dependent on constitutional make-up, and therefore largely hereditary in origin. (p. 34)

In short, temperament refers to individual differences in basic behavior style, assumed to be present in some form at birth and thus, to a large degree, biologically determined (Willerman, 1979).

Developmental psychologists have devised a number of methods for measuring temperament, and a number of conceptual schemes for understanding what they measure. The simplest and best-known scheme was delineated by Thomas, Chess, and Birch (1970), based on their interviews of mothers of babies. They distinguished among three different types of temperament patterns. **Easy** babies show consistently positive mood, low-to-moderate intensity of emotional reactions, and regular sleeping and eating cycles. **Difficult** babies show consistently negative moods, intense emotional reactions, and irregular sleeping and eating cycles. **Slow-to-warm-up** babies reveal a combination of the previous two forms, with relatively negative moods, low intensity of emotional reactions, and the tendency to withdraw from new events at first but then approach them later. Other researchers have adopted more fine-grained schemes for categorizing temperament. For instance, Rothbart (1986) enumerates six temperament dimensions reliably observed in infants in the first year of life: activity level, smiling and laughter, fearfulness, distress to limitations, "soothability," and vocal activity.

Another temperament dimension that has received a great deal of attention is what Jerome Kagan (1989) calls *behavioral inhibition*. In Chapter 4, we briefly considered Kagan's work under the rubric of "shyness." Extremely inhibited young children show great timidity in the face of new events and people. Their shyness, furthermore, is linked with a series of physiological responses suggestive of high levels of arousal. Recall that Eysenck, too, suggests that introverts operate under high levels of arousal than extraverts. Will Kagan's excessively shy, behaviorally inhibited children grow up to be introverted adults?

Kagan believes that some will. Out of every 100 Caucasian newborns, he maintains, approximately 20 will show extreme irritability and excitability shortly after birth. By the age of two years about 75% of these (say, 15 or so) will be very shy, timid, and fearful when they meet unfamiliar people, are put in unfamiliar rooms, or encounter unfamiliar objects. By adolescence, 10 will still be very shy, and by adulthood you are likely to find that 6 or 7 of the original 20 are extremely
Continued on p. 300

Table 5.11

The EASI Temperament Survey

Emotionality

Child gets upset easily.
Child tends to cry easily.
Child is easily frightened.
Child is easygoing or happy-go-lucky. (reverse)
Child has a quick temper.

Activity

Child is always on the go.
Child likes to be off and running immediately on awakening.
Child cannot sit still long.
Child prefers quiet games such as block play or coloring to more active games. (reverse)
Child fidgets at meals and similar occasions.

Sociability

Child likes to be with others.
Child makes friends easily.
Child tends to be shy. (reverse)
Child tends to be independent. (reverse)
Child prefers to play by himself rather than with others. (reverse)

Impulsivity

Child tends to be impulsive.
Child has difficulty learning self-control.
Child gets bored easily.
Child learns to resist temptation easily. (reverse)
Child goes from toy to toy quickly.

Modified from Buss and Plomin (1975).

Cubness
The Most Dreaded Trait

Whenever I try to trace back my occasional dark moods and deep-seated doubts about the world, I find myself reflecting on my father and an incident that occurred when I was in the second grade. I had just started collecting baseball cards and was gradually becoming interested in the game when I made the mistake of turning on the television to watch the Chicago White Sox play a few innings. My father came home, saw what I was doing, and quickly shut the television off. With great fervor and seriousness, he told me: "You don't watch the ——— White Sox; you're a Cubs fan." I did not know who the Cubs were, for I had not as yet obtained a baseball card portraying a Cubs player. But I figured that this was a pretty big deal, so I endeavored to learn about the Cubs and what it meant to be a fan.

My current membership card in the Chicago Cubs Die Hard Fan Club (# 0-275-99) is embossed with the date 1962—designating the year of my conversion and the beginning of the curse. As most baseball fans know, the Cubs are the perennial losers of the National League. Though virtually all fans of other teams claim that they have suffered great misery, Chicago fans who root for the Cubs have the saddest stories to tell. This can be documented. The last time the Cubs made it to the World Series was 1945—no other current team has a longer Seriesless streak. The last time the Cubs *won* the World Series was *1908:* William Taft was president and Sigmund Freud was still 12 years away from developing his idea of a "death instinct" (an idea to which Cubs fans have always resonated). Yet Cubs fans are the most devoted in sports. (This can also be documented.) And every year the Cubs break their hearts.

A Chicago writer has recently discovered that the Cubs manage to make nonCubs fans miserable, too, through an insidious personality trait called *Cubness.* Ron Berler did extensive research on the composition of World Series teams since 1946. He discovered a simple and frightening truth: when a team has at least three players who *used* to be Cubs, they lose. Since 1946, a dozen teams with three or more ex-Cubs have been in the World Series. Many of these teams were extremely good. But only one of these 12 teams was able to win. Chicago *Tribune* columnist Mike Royko (1986) describes recent evidence:

> We've seen the Cubs factor at work in recent years. In 1984, when the hated [San Diego] Padres beat out our Cubs [in the National League Playoff],

the laugh turned out to be on them. They had three ex-Cubs, the fools, while the Tigers [their opponents in the World Series] had only one and, of course, the Tigers won.

The year before it was the same story. The Phillies had three ex-Cubs. The winning Orioles prudently had kept their roster free of Cubs.

It is Berler's theory that having been a Cub infects a player with something called "Cubness," which seems to spread to other members of their new team.

As Jim Brosnan, a former Cubs pitcher, once said: "You have to have a certain dullness of mind and spirit to play here. I went through psychoanalysis and that helped me deal with my Cubness."

Royko has devised a corollary to Berler's theory. You don't really need three ex-Cubs to lose the World Series, he maintains. All you need is to have more ex-Cubs than the other team has. For the 1986 World Series, Royko bet on the Mets (who had no ex-Cubs) over the Red Sox (who had one—Bill Buckner). Red Sox fans are still plagued with nightmares about the 1986 World Series—how the Red Sox lost it in seven exciting games and how Bill Buckner played a pivotal last-inning role in the defeat.

It is interesting to speculate on the nature of this trait. It clearly seems to be due to environment over heredity. A person is not born with Cubness. But if he is unfortunate enough ever to don a Cubs uniform, he seems to be cursed for life with the trait. Yet the trait only manifests itself in certain critical situations. An ex-Cub can have a distinguished career with another team, showing few behavioral signs of the inner flaw. But, if that team gets into the World Series. . . .

Is Cubness a component of one of the Big Five traits—like neuroticism? Is Cubness a linear and continuous trait? Or is it an "all-or-none" sort of thing? Are there degrees of Cubness? Does the length of time a player spends with the Cubs increase the trait's severity? Does the trait manifest itself in other realms? Do ex-Cubs have smaller checking accounts? More traffic accidents? Should a woman marry an ex-Cub? Or even date him?

Perhaps future research will provide the answers.

Continued from p. 296
introverted in their behavior. The two–thirds who lost their excessive shyness by adulthood may have been strongly influenced by environmental experiences encouraging them to be more outgoing. Indeed, American society tends to favor outgoing and sociable people. Like the 6 or 7 resultant introverts, however, the former inhibited children who grew up to be somewhat less introverted than we might have originally expected retain what Kagan believes to be a "shyness physiology." Further research is needed to assess the validity of Kagan's interpretation.

Personality psychologists Arnold Buss and Robert Plomin (1975, 1984) believe that enduring personality traits develop out of temperament endowments. In their *temperament theory of personality,* they argue for the existence of four basic temperament dimensions upon which people may differ from birth onwards: emotionality, activity, sociability, and impulsivity. In the view of Buss and Plomin, all four of these dimensions are (1) inherited, (2) stable during development, (3) present across the life-span, (4) generally adaptive, and (5) present as meaningful behavioral dimensions in animals biologically similar to humans. People are born with predispositions to develop these four temperaments to different levels. The social environment reacts to these dispositions, modifying and shaping them in certain ways, but only within the limits established by heredity. Table 5.11 displays items from the EASI Temperament Survey, used to assess these four dimensions in children.

Heritability Studies

It is a common observation that genetically identical twins—that is, *monozygotic* (MZ) twins—tend to be remarkably similar. Not only do they look very much alike, but it seems that their interests, tastes, styles, and behavior patterns are often strikingly concordant. By contrast, *dizygotic* (DZ), or fraternal twins, tend to look no more similar to each other than any other set of biological siblings, and their behaviors often seem to be equally discordant as well. In that they developed out of the same zygote, monozygotic twins have the same genetic makeup; dizygotic twins have only about half of their genes in common. In the 1980s, a group of researchers at the University of Minnesota undertook a large study of about 350 sets of MZ and DZ twins, a number of whom, from infancy onward, *had been raised apart* (Bouchard, Lykken, McGue, Segal, & Tellegen, 1990). In most of these cases, the twins had been given up for adoption, and each of the two members of the twin pair was adopted by a different family. Thus, each grew up not knowing his or her twin. Bringing the twin pairs back together for the study, the researchers were struck by some of the amazing similarities in personality revealed in the MZA (monozygotic, raised apart) twin pairs:

> While videotaping an interview with one [MZA] twin, we discovered he was an accomplished raconteur with a fund of amusing anecdotes, so, while interviewing the co-twin, we asked him if he knew any funny stories. "Why sure," he said, leaning back with a

practiced air. "I'll tell you a story" and proceeded to demonstrate his concordance. A pair of British MZAs, who had met for the first time as adults just a month previously, both firmly refused in their separate interviews to express opinions on controversial topics; since long before they discovered each other's existence, each had resolutely avoided controversy. Another pair were both habitual gigglers, although each had been raised by adoptive parents whom they described as undemonstrative and dour, and neither had known anyone who laughed as freely as she did until finally she met her twin. Both members of another pair independently reported that they refrained from voting in political elections on the principle that they did not feel themselves well enough informed to make wise choices. A pair of male MZAs, at their first adult reunion, discovered that they both used Vadmecum toothpaste, Canoe shaving lotion, Vitalis hair tonic, and Lucky Strike cigarettes. After that meeting, they exchanged birthday presents in the mail that proved to be identical choices, made independently in separate cities.

There were two "dog people," among the MZA individuals; one showed her dogs, and the other taught obedience classes— they were an MZA pair. Only two of the more than 200 individual twins reared apart were afraid to enter the acoustically shielded chamber used in our psychophysiology laboratory, but both separately agreed to continue if the door was wired open—they were a pair of MZA twins. When at the beach, both women had always insisted on entering the water backwards and then only up to their knees; they were thus concordant, not only in their phobic tendencies, but also in the specific manifestations of their timidity. There were two gunsmith hobbyists among the group of twins; two women who habitually wore seven rings; two men who offered a (correct) diagnosis of a faulty wheel bearing on Bouchard's [one of the researcher's] car; two who obsessively counted things; two who had been married five times; two captains of volunteer fire departments; two fashion designers; two who left little love notes around the house for their wives . . . in each case, an MZA pair. (Lykken, McGue, Tellegen, & Bouchard, 1992, pp. 1565–1566)

The authors of this account concede that a few of the similarities they observed may have been coincidences. Nonetheless, these memorable examples illustrate a general trend in the quantitative data that these researchers collected with respect to personality traits. In this study, and in a number of others in which researchers compared MZ and DZ twins with respect to their standing on self-report personality scales, the evidence suggests that for most traits measured,

MZ twins are much more similar to each other than are DZ twins (Loehlin, 1992; Plomin, Chipuer, & Loehlin, 1990). In simple terms, correlations between MZ trait scores are significantly higher than correlations between DZ trait scores. If one MZ twin is high in, say, extraversion, it is a relatively good bet that the other MZ twin also scores pretty high on *E*. By contrast, if one DZ twin is high in extraversion, it is still difficult to predict the extraversion rating of the other DZ twin. Whether the twins are raised together or apart seems to make little difference.

According to the standard logic of twin studies, evidence for the genetic determination of a given trait emerges when trait scores for MZ twins are highly correlated to each other *and* scores for DZ twins on the same trait are *not* highly correlated. The logic hinges on the notion of heritability. A **heritability quotient** estimates the proportion of variability in a given characteristic that can be attributed to genetic differences between people. A common method for estimating heritability of a given trait in a study of twins is to substract the correlation coefficient for fraternal twins from the correlation coefficient for identical twins and then multiply the difference by 2. Thus, if test scores on Trait A for identical twins correlate $+.60$ and for fraternal twins $+.30$, then heritability would be 60%, that is, $2(.60 - .30) = .60$. This would mean that approximately 60% of the variability in Trait A may be attributed to genetic differences among subjects in this sample; the remaining 40% of variability is assumed to be a complex function of various environmental effects and of error in measurement.

Heritability is a tricky concept. Its correct interpretation requires an understanding of three essential points. First, heritability is a *group* statistic; it does not apply to the individual. If the characteristic of height has a heritability of .80 in a particular population, then we can assume that approximately 80% of the variation in height among the members of that population at the time of measurement is a function of genetic factors (Plomin, DeFries, & McClearn, 1980). A heritability of .80, however, obviously does *not* mean that a woman who is 5 feet tall attained 4 feet of her structure from her genes and an additional foot from the environment!

Second, heritability estimates may vary over time, by environment, or across populations: the variability manifested in a given characteristic may shrink or expand with changing circumstances. And as variability changes, so may heritability, since heritability is the *proportion* of variability accounted for by genetic differences. Heritability is thus akin to a simple fraction with variability as the denominator. When the denominator changes, the value of the fraction changes along with it.

Third, genes influence behavior in highly indirect and not-well-understood ways, assumably through a complex set of chemical and biological interactions. Even if a particular personality trait shows a high heritability quotient, no particular gene or even a combination of genes is likely to be discovered as the "cause" of that particular trait.

Most twin studies show *substantial* heritability quotients for many traits. Evidence is probably strongest for two of the Big Five traits discussed in this chapter: *E* and *N*. A huge study of 13,000 adult twins in Sweden obtained heritability estimates of slightly over 50% for both *E* and *N* (Floderus-Myrhed,

Identical twins (age 12 years).

Pedersen, & Rasmuson, 1980). Other twin studies have yielded moderately high heritability quotients (between .30 and .60) for a range of personality traits measured on a number of scales and personality inventories (Loehlin & Nichols, 1976; Rushton, Neale, Nias, & Eysenck, 1986). In the University of Minnesota study, broad heritabilities (over 40%) were obtained for the traits of leadership/mastery, traditionalism (tendency to follow rules and respect authority), stress reaction (similar to neuroticism), absorption (the tendency to become engrossed in sensory experiences), alienation, well-being, avoidance of harm, and aggressiveness (Tellegen, Lykken, Bouchard, Wilcox, Segal, & Rich, 1988).

In an authoritative review of behavioral genetic studies in personality, Robert Plomin and colleagues (1990) conclude that

> genetic influence on self-report measures of personality is nearly ubiquitous. Much of this evidence relies on comparisons between correlations for identical, or monozygotic (MZ), and fraternal, or dizygotic (DZ), twins. On average across diverse personality dimensions, MZ correlations are about .50 and DZ correlations are about .30. These twin correlations suggest that genetic influence on personality is not only significant but substantial. Doubling the difference between the two correlations results in an estimate that heritability, the proportion of phenotypic variance explained by genetic variance, is 40%. (Plomin, Chipuer, & Loehlin, 1990. p. 226)

The plot of this simple story has thickened in recent years, however, as two puzzling findings continue to emerge. The first is that some recent studies employing very large samples of twins and highly reliable trait measures have shown that MZ correlations are sometimes *more than twice as high* as DZ correlations. For example, in four large twin studies of extraversion and neuroticism totalling over 23,000 pairs of twins, the weighted average MZ and DZ correlations were about .51 and .18 respectively. For neuroticism, the corresponding MZ and DZ correlations were .48 and .20, respectively (Loehlin, 1989). The conventional wisdom on twin studies is that, because MZ twins share 100% common genes and DZ twins share 50% common genes, MZ twins should be no more than twice as similar to each other as DZ twins. In other words, genetic variance should be *additive*. A second puzzling finding is that studies of adoption yield *very low heritability estimates*. If heredity is a major factor in determining traits, then we would expect that biological siblings (50% common genes) should be significantly more similar to each other than adoptive siblings (0% common genes). But this does not seem to be the case. A number of adoption studies suggest surprisingly small differences between correlations, yielding heritability estimates no greater than 20% (Loehlin, Willerman, & Horn, 1987; Scarr, Webber, & Wittig, 1981).

Let us put these two puzzling findings in the simplest possible language: First, for some traits (like extraversion) *identical twins seem to be even more similar to each other* (over twice as similar to each other as fraternal twins) than expected. Second, adoption studies suggest that *biological siblings are less similar to each other* (only barely more similar to each other than are adoptive siblings) than expected. Your relative standing on personality traits bears only modest similarity to that of your biological siblings (including fraternal twins), your parents, your cousins, or anybody else to whom you are biologically related, unless of course you have an identical twin, in which case the two of you are likely to be remarkably similar (Dunn & Plomin, 1990). When it comes to personality traits measured on self-report questionnaires, why are you likely to be so remarkably similar to an identical twin and so remarkably dissimilar to anybody else with whom you share common genes?

One possible explanation is **nonadditive genetic variance.** Genes may not influence traits in a linear, additive way, but rather combine and interact in a "configural" pattern in which all components are essential and "the absence of, or a change in any one (i.e., any gene) can produce qualitative or a large quantitative change in the result" (Lykken et al., 1992). Thus, if two individuals (DZ twins or any biological siblings) share only 50% common genes, they may be *less than half* as similar to each other as are two individuals (MZ twins) who share 100% common genes: Because genes influence traits in a nonadditive fashion, 100% is, in a sense, *more than twice* as large as 50%. I am not likely to be concordant with my brother (we are not MZ twins) on, say, extraversion because the nonadditive genetic configurations that may be required to give us a similar extraversion makeup cannot occur (unless we share 100% of our genes). There is a threshold in trait genetics. Either your genotype is the same as another person's (MZ twins) or it isn't (everybody else). If it is the first, then your trait ratings are likely to be very similar to those of your MZ twin. If it is the second, you are probably not especially similar (in traits) to anybody in your family, although there is likely to be some modest similarity. Merely sharing 50% common genes with another (a sibling) does not make much of a bang in making the two of you all that similar. In this sense, 50% *is not much more than* 0%. Thus, biological siblings (non-MZs) are not very much more similar to each other than are adoptive siblings. This may be one of the answers, write Dunn and Plomin (1990), to the question of "why siblings are so different."

But what about the environment? What about the influences of growing up in the same family? After all, if a trait heritability is around 40% for a given population, then that leaves 60% of phenotypic variance (the amount of observed variability) unaccounted for. Is this where the effects of family environment come in? The answer to this last question appears to be "yes, but in a very surprising way." Recent trait genetic studies suggest that after genetic effects are taken into consideration, growing up in the same family appears to contribute *very little* to making siblings similar to each other. As Figure 5.7 suggests, *shared environment* accounts for no more than about 5% of the variance in personality trait scores. There appear to be a few exceptions to this. For example, agreeableness

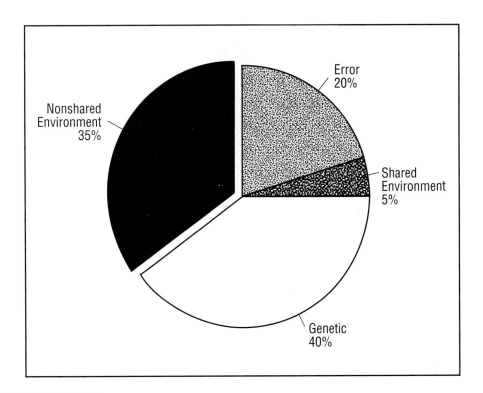

Figure 5.7

Components of Variance in Personality Traits

From Dunn & Plomin, 1990, p. 50.

appears to show a larger effect for shared environment (around 21%) (Plomin, Chipuer, & Loehlin, 1990). In general, though, unless they are MZ twins, siblings are remarkably different from each other on most personality traits, as we have already seen, and being raised in the same family does not appear to lessen the differences very much. Sandra Scarr, a leading researcher in the field, makes this point forcefully:

> Lest the reader slip over these results, let us make explicit the implications of these findings: Upper-middle-class brothers who attend the same school and whose parents take them to the same plays, sporting events, music lessons, and therapists, and use similar child-rearing practices on them are little more similar in personality measures than they are to working class or farm boys, whose lives are totally different. (Scarr & Grajek, 1982, p. 361)

How is this possible? Nobody knows for sure, but many authorities have recently suggested that children (and adults) experience the same environments in very different ways. While one girl may find her middle-class suburban family to be comfortable and supportive, her sister may see it as stifling and oppressive. The two may react to what seems to be a shared environment in markedly different ways. To a certain degree, in fact, the two may create their own environments. The first girl makes friends with the most popular students in her school; her sister hangs out with a more rebellious crowd; their lives take different paths as the environments they create help create them, as well (Scarr & McCartney, 1983). A major determinant of trait standing, therefore, may be the effects of *nonshared environments*. According to Plomin, Chipuer, and Loehlin (1990), "the message is not that family experiences are unimportant; rather the argument is that environmental influences in individual development are specific to each child, rather than general to an entire family." Dunn and Plomin (1990) estimate that nonshared environment accounts for about 35% of the variance in personality trait ratings. Summing up Figure 5.7, then, Dunn and Plomin argue that genetics accounts for under half of the variance in phenotypic trait ratings (around 40%); nonshared environment accounts for a little over a third (around 35%); shared environment accounts for very little (about 5%); and the rest (20%) is a result of a certain amount of error that is inherent in the measurement of personality traits through self-report questionnaires.

This is not the last word on traits, genetics, and environment. Equipped with improved measures and sophisticated mathematical designs, researchers in this field are proceeding apace. They are exploring such issues as the extent of genetic influence on traits across the life-span, the relative influence of genetics and environment on personality change, and the effects of genetics on environments. In a very recent report, McGue, Bacon, and Lykken (1993) present longitudinal twin data to suggest that (1) genetic effects on traits appear to decrease as people get older, (2) personality trait stability is due largely to genetic factors, and (3) personality change is determined largely by environmental influences. Other research suggests that certain environmental measures (such as perception of parental warmth) are themselves influenced by genetics. MZ twins raised together report their environments to be more highly similar than do DZ twins raised together. Even reports of life events seem to be influenced genetically, especially controllable life events (Plomin, Lichtenstein, Pederson, McClearn, & Nesselroade, 1990). Nature and nurture are especially difficult to disentangle in the measurement of personality and its determinants. To a certain extent, people interpret, select, and construct their own environments in accord with their genetic make-ups. And those environments influence the development of traits. In the next chapter, we will examine how environments exert their important influences.

Summary for Chapter 5

1. Vera Brittain's peacemaking behaviors can be understood in terms of internal personality traits, like conscientiousness, interacting with a variety of social environments, such as her experiences in World War I. To predict behavior, the personality psychologist must examine both traits and environments.

2. Traits refer to broad individual differences in social and/or emotional functioning. Traits are usually measured through self-report questionnaires.

3. To construct a self-report scale to measure a trait, a psychologist must follow a series of steps that ultimately aim at construct validity for the measure. Construct validity is the process of simultaneously validating a test and the construct it is designed to measure, and involves the gradual articulation of a nomological network of research findings.

4. Beyond validity, other important criteria of a trait measure's worth are reliability, utility, economy, and communicability.

5. Psychologists have developed a number of omnibus personality inventories that assess many different traits at once. The most popular among these are the MMPI, the CPI, and the PRF.

6. Factor-analytic studies of trait ratings and personality descriptions in the English language have recently converged on a five-factor model of personality traits called the Big Five. The Big Five serves as a useful model for the organization of many different traits in personality.

7. The first Big Five trait domain is extraversion (E). Extraverted people tend to be relatively outgoing, energetic, and sociable; introverts tend to be quiet, withdrawn, and introspective.

8. Eysenck argues that E is rooted in individual differences in arousal level, which may be linked to the reticular activating system of the brain.

9. A second Big Five trait domain is neuroticism (N), which taps into chronic anxiety, depression, emotionality, moodiness, hostility, and hypochondriasis. Whereas high levels of E are associated with positive affect, high levels of N are associated with negative affect.

10. In an important modification of Eysenck's approach to E and N, Gray substitutes the traits of impulsiveness and anxiety, respectively, and argues that impulsiveness stems from a behavioral approach system and anxiety from a behavioral inhibition system. Eysenck's and Gray's theories make different predictions about individual differences in learning.

11. A third trait domain is openness to experience (O), which incorporates a number of smaller traits, such as absorption, having to do with how artistic, reflective, imaginative, and nontraditional a person is.

12. Conscientiousness (C) and agreeableness (A) round out the Big Five scheme. People high in C are described as well-organized, efficient, self-disciplined, and achievement-oriented. People high in A are loving, cooperative, warm, empathic, and altruistic.

13. The interpersonal circumplex organizes trait descriptors on a circle bisected by the dimensions of dominance and love. In the context of the Big Five, dominance and love correspond roughly to E and A, respectively.

14. The roots of certain personality traits may lie in individual differences in infant temperament.

15. Twin studies show rather substantial heritability quotients for many traits, especially E and N. Recent work in trait genetics argues that as much as 40% of the observed variance in traits may be accounted for by genetics. By contrast, shared family environment appears to have very little influence on traits, but non-shared environmental effects appear to be relatively strong.

Chapter 6

Social Learning and the Social Situation

Introduction

Behaviorism: A Brief Course
Observation
Environmentalism
Learning
Classical Conditioning
Instrumental Conditioning

Social-Learning Theories
Rotter's View: Expectancies and Values
Mischel's Approach: Cognitive/Social Learning/Person Variables
Feature 6.A: The Integration of Freud and the Behaviorists: Miller and Dollard's Learning Theory
Bandura's Theory: The Role of Observational Learning
Observational Learning
Self-Efficacy
Reciprocal Determinism

Assessment and Research
Behavioral Assessment
Self-Regulation
Delay of Gratification
Individual Differences and a Personal Work Ethic
Aggression and Altruism
Bandura and the Bobo Doll

Television Violence

Altruism, Prosocial Behavior

Behaviorism, Social Learning, and Personality

Feature 6.B: How Should Parents Raise Their Children?

Summary

In the climactic scene of B. F. Skinner's novel *Walden Two,* Frazier, the founder of a scientifically engineered utopia, gazes down on his creation from a hilltop, concludes that "it is good," and falls back onto the ground in a pose of crucifixion. His companion, a visiting college professor named Burris, fears that, in assuming this Christlike pose, Frazier now believes that he has become God. Hoping against hope that he will renounce any divine powers, Burris half-jokingly asks Frazier if he thinks he is God:

"There's a curious similarity," he [Frazier] said. I [Burris] suf-fered a moment of panic.

"Rather considerably less control in your case, I should imagine," I said, attempting to adopt a casual tone.

"Not at all," he said, looking up. "At least, if we can believe the theologians. On the contrary, it's the other way around. You may remember that God's children are always disappointing Him."

"While you are in complete command. Well, I congratulate you."

"I don't say I'm never disappointed, but I imagine I'm rather less frequently so than God. After all, look at the world He made." (Skinner, 1948/1962, p. 296)

Frazier has made a different kind of world—a community of about 1000 people who live in near-perfect peace and happiness. His world rarely disappoints him, for it is carefully engineered to provide its inhabitants with the Good Life—good health, a minimum of undesirable labor, the opportunity to exercise talents and abilities, intimate relationships with others, and a maximum of relaxation and rest. Most of the citizens of Frazier's community work no more than four hours a day, leaving a prodigious amount of time for leisure, art, music, and conversation. The citizens are generally happy and satisfied with life, highly productive and creative, and emotionally tied to each other in bonds of tender friendship. They appear to experience little jealousy, rage, depression, or guilt. They are prosperous and well educated. Divorce and family violence are rare. Crime is virtually nonexistent.

Following after Henry David Thoreau, the nineteenth-century author and visionary who created his own ideal world of solitude on Walden Pond, Frazier names his community "Walden Two." Like Thoreau's Walden, Walden Two provides refuge from the grasping materialism, petty frustrations, and ceaseless violence of modern life. Like Thoreau, the citizens of Walden Two learn how to simplify their lives and to get by with few personal possessions. Unlike Thoreau's isolated existence, however, Walden Two builds a life "in which people live *together* without quarreling, in a social climate of trust rather than suspicion, of love rather than jealousy, of cooperation rather than competition" (Skinner, 1979, p. 346). The Good Life is not the life of the isolated and self-sufficient hermit, according to Frazier. It is rather a thoroughly *communal* existence that, at the same time, provides ample opportunities for individual expression and personal fulfillment. We learn to be good and happy people in *social* situations, argues Frazier. The person is shaped by the social environment. The better and happier the environment, the better and happier the person.

Walden Two is designed according to scientific principles of "behavioral engineering." The principles are simple, but their potential application is vast. The basic principle is **positive reinforcement.** Essentially, this means that people act to obtain positive consequences, or rewards. When a positive consequence follows a behavior, the behavior is strengthened, or reinforced, and its subsequent occurrence is made more likely. Whether in "God's world" or Frazier's, the behavior of persons is shaped, influenced, indeed controlled by the reinforcement that societies provide. Walden Two, therefore, provides a social environment that, like all social environments, controls the behavior of its inhabitants. But the control is more consistent and effective than that exerted in the real world. And it is benevolently aimed to engender peace, happiness, and creativity for all.

From birth onward, the citizens of Walden Two are enrolled in an elaborate educational program that systematically reinforces positive behaviors. Infants and children are trained to restrain negative emotions, practice self-control, and care for themselves and for each other by eschewing jealousy, rivalry, fighting, and pride. The training is accomplished without punishment: by rewarding socially desirable behavior, rather than by punishing socially undesirable behavior, the educational system of Walden Two gently and gradually instills behaviors compatible with the Good Life in all citizens.

Walden Two's use of positive reinforcement to shape beneficial behaviors is a grand experiment in the shaping of social behavior. Frazier tells Burris:

"I'll let you in on a secret," he [Frazier] continued, lowering his voice dramatically. "You have just described the *only* side of Walden Two that really interests me. To make men happy, yes. To make them productive in order to assure the continuation of that happiness, yes. But what else? Why, *to make possible a genuine science of human behavior!*

"These things aren't for the laboratory, Burris. They're not 'academic questions.' What an apt expression! They concern our very lives! We can study them only in living culture, and yet a culture which is under experimental control. Nothing short of Walden Two will suffice. It must be a real world, this laboratory of ours, and no foundation can buy a slice of it." (pp. 291–292)

Has Frazier indeed organized an ideal world? Might a society based on systematic positive reinforcement truly make men and women happy? Like Burris in the early chapters of the novel, many readers of *Walden Two* are likely to be extremely skeptical, or to conclude, as did one reviewer, that Frazier's utopia is "alluring in a sinister way, and appalling, too." Like every utopia since Plato's *Republic,* somebody must make the key decisions and hold power over the many. In the case of *Walden Two,* the elected planners and managers of the community make momentous decisions about what behaviors are to be reinforced, and how. Furthermore, one wonders if all people can be shaped to behave in accord with the public good, or even if such behavior is always beneficial. Though Frazier can be very convincing, the reader may fear that blind conformity and ultimate oppression are the likely results of a social system explicitly designed to program people for good behavior. Frazier's utopia raises as many questions as it answers. Yet, at the end of the novel, Burris is won over. After leaving *Walden Two,* he turns back and makes the 3-day, 60-mile pilgrimage back to the little community on foot, ready to take his place in this brave new world of social engineering. Thirty years later, in one of Skinner's last writings, Burris is still there—serving as a "historian" for *Walden Two,* happy with his life at last (Skinner, 1987).

Behaviorism: A Brief Course

Walden Two is a fictional manifesto of a very real and influential approach to psychology termed **behaviorism.** And B. F. Skinner (1904–1990), the author of the account, was behaviorism's most eloquent and influential spokesman. Like Freudian psychoanalysis, behaviorism cuts an extremely broad path in psychology, seeking to explain all human behavior (as well as the behavior of animals) in terms of a comprehensive and general scheme. Unlike psychoanalysis, however, behaviorism does not provide an explicit theory of the person—a personality theory per se. Indeed, Skinner would argue that such a theory is not needed, and that terms like *the person* and *personality* are scientifically superfluous. Yet behaviorism has influenced personality psychology by undergirding approaches to the person that tend to emphasize social learning and the social situation in the shaping of persons. In contrast, therefore, to the approaches surveyed in the last chapter that focused on internal personality traits, we will concern ourselves in Chapter 6 with approaches to the person that predict behavior based on external, situational factors.

John B. Watson launched the behaviorist movement in the United States in 1913 with the publication of "Psychology as the Behaviorist Views It." Behaviorism was *the* dominant force in American academic psychology from about 1920 through the 1950s. During this period, a number of very different behaviorist theories were developed, such as Clark Hull's (1943) biological-drive theory and Edwin Tolman's (1948) cognitively oriented "purposive behaviorism." Despite their diversity, all the approaches share three central tenets or themes that characterize behaviorism as a whole: observation, environmentalism, and learning.

Observation

Behaviorism has traditionally concerned itself with directly *observable* behavior. A person's private thoughts and feelings cannot be directly observed by others, and therefore thinking, feeling, mind, and consciousness are outside the realm of scientific psychology, according to the behaviorist view. While some behaviorists have almost gone so far as to suggest that subjective thinking and feeling do not even exist (Watson, 1924), most behaviorists acknowledge the existence of such phenomena but insist that internal states (1) cannot be directly observed and therefore cannot be studied scientifically and (2) do not need to be taken into consideration anyway because behavior can be predicted well enough through careful observation and measurement of public behavior and the environment in which it occurs.

More than any other approach to psychology, behaviorism has been reluctant to make inferences that go much beyond what can be observed. Therefore, behaviorists have had little need for such hypothetical constructs as "ego" (Freud), "trait" (Eysenck), "archetype" (Jung), or "internalized object" (Mahler). Nobody has ever seen an "ego" or a "trait," and therefore such constructs cannot be of much direct scientific use, argue the behaviorists. Behaviorists tend to invoke the minimum number of theoretical concepts to account for the maximum amount of behavior. In the terms of Chapter 1, they tend to distrust inductive approaches to science as well as elaborate theories containing many hypothetical constructs, while they favor careful experimentation under controlled conditions to test empirically precise hypotheses about how changes in a directly observable environment can produce changes in directly observable behavior. All behaviorist approaches, therefore, place a premium on objectivity in observation, experimental rigor, and precision of measurement.

B.F. Skinner

Environmentalism

In 1690, the British philosopher John Locke penned these famous words:

> Let us then suppose the Mind to be, as we say, white Paper, void of all Characters, without any *Ideas;* How comes it to be furnished? Whence comes it by that vast store, which the busie and boundless Fancy of Man has painted on it, with an almost endless variety? Whence has it all the materials of Reason and Knowledge: To this I answer in one word, from *Experience:* In that all our Knowledge is founded; and from that it ultimately derives itself. (From *An essay concerning human understanding,* reprinted in Herrnstein & Boring, 1965, p. 584)

Locke is speaking here of his doctrine of the *tabula rasa,* or "blank slate." For the newborn, the mind is like a blank slate or white piece of paper. Nothing is written on the slate; it is completely clean and empty. Over time, "experience" "writes" upon the slate, giving the mind its characteristic content. Locke rejected the notion of innate ideas and argued instead that the *environment* shapes the person. If the human mind is originally a blank slate, then all humans are born psychologically equal. In sharp contrast to temperament theories reviewed in the last chapter, individual differences in personality are a function of different environmental exposures. Personality is made (by the environment), not inborn. As Skinner (1971) puts it, "a person does not act upon the world, the world acts upon him" (p. 211). Therefore, if the environment shapes the person, then a just and happy society should produce just and happy citizens.

All brands of behaviorism emphasize the environment as the key determinant of the person's behavior. To predict precisely what a person will do, therefore, the psychologist is only wasting time looking "within" the person. Instead, the psychologist should scrutinize the person's external environment and analyze the subtle behavior—environment interactions shown over time. Environments are generally understood as providing *stimuli* that shape the person's behavior, which is seen in terms of a *response* to the stimuli. Environmental situations, rather than personality traits, are the prime movers of behavior. Thus, behaviorists have traditionally deemphasized and on occasion even denied the validity of genetic and inborn differences between persons. The most dramatic statement to this effect was made by John B. Watson, who in this much-quoted passage sounds much like Skinner's Frazier in *Walden Two*:

> Give me a dozen healthy infants, well-formed, and my own specified world to bring them up in and I'll guarantee to take any one at random and train him to become any type of specialist I might select—doctor, lawyer, artist, merchant, chief and, yes, even beggerman and thief, regardless of his talents, penchants, tendencies, abilities, vocations, and race of his ancestors. There is no such thing as an inheritance of capacity, talent, temperament, mental constitution, and behavioral characteristics. (Watson, 1924, p. 104)

Learning

How does the environment shape behavior? Through learning, answer the behaviorists. Each of us is who we are because of what we have learned. According to the behaviorists, our environments teach us to be who we are; we are what we learn to be. But why do we learn to be anything at all? What *motivates* us to learn? The behaviorist answer is that we learn in order to obtain pleasure and avoid pain.

That the ultimate determinants of behavior reside in pleasure and pain is an idea at least as old as Aristotle, but it found its earliest flowering in the ancient school of thought called Epicureanism. Epicurus (341–270 B.C.) was a Greek philosopher who preached that freedom from pain and the pursuit of gentle pleasures and peace of mind were the hallmarks of the Good Life. Not only do optimal pleasure and minimal pain make men and women happy, they also serve as the foundations for ethical action, according to Epicurus. In an ethical or moral sense, the world is constructed so that, in general, what is good is what eventually brings pleasure and peace of mind; what is ethically or morally bad is what ultimately brings displeasure or pain. Through the ages, this doctrine has been adapted to play a central role in many different philosophical systems, including that of Locke.

In the eighteenth and nineteenth centuries, the philosophy of **utilitarianism** put forth the idea that the "good" society should make for the greatest happiness or pleasure for the greatest number of people. Utilitarians such as Jeremy Bentham (1748–1832) and John Stuart Mill (1806–1873) argued that this could be accomplished if societies were structured in a more egalitarian fashion. Thus, the utilitarians advocated equality for all, women's suffrage, the abolition of discrimination on the basis of religion and race, and redistribution of society's wealth (Russell, 1945). They tended to distrust the authority of king and church and to glorify democratic education as the answer to many of life's problems. In ethics, the utilitarians were pragmatic and nondogmatic, insisting that principles need to be flexible to accommodate changing ethical circumstances. Behaviorism, in all its forms, is steeped in a utilitarian ideology. Like its philosophical forerunner, behaviorism has always been egalitarian, pragmatic, and supremely optimistic about the possibility of changing the person's life for the better through education—that is, through learning or training in social contexts. Ultimately, learning is shaped by pleasure and pain. And learning should, in turn, make for the greatest amount of pleasure and the least amount of pain.

Classical Conditioning   Why do you like soft music and candlelight? According to Mill and other utilitarians, it is because these stimuli have been associated in your environment with positive events, perhaps in this case with sensual experiences. The doctrine of **associationism** has it that various objects and ideas that are contiguous in time or space come to be connected, or associated, with each other into meaningful units. Simple forms of learning proceed by associations.

Classical conditioning represents one such form of simple learning. In Pavlov's well-known examples of classical conditioning, a hungry dog *learns* to salivate in response to a neutral stimulus (a tone) because that neutral stimulus has become associated with a stimulus (meat) that typically elicits salivation naturally. In the terminology of classical conditioning, the meat is an *unconditioned stimulus* that naturally gives rise to salivation, which is the *unconditioned response*. When on a number of experimental trials, however, the dog hears the neutral stimulus of the tone immediately *preceding* the presentation of meat, the dog learns to salivate (*conditioned response*) to the tone, now called a *conditioned stimulus,* even when no meat is present. The tone (conditioned stimulus) and meat (unconditioned stimulus) therefore become associated with each other because of their contiguity in time. Figure 6.1 illustrates the process.

Watson believed that classical conditioning was a cornerstone of human learning. In the legendary case study of Little Albert, Watson and Raynor (1920) showed how an 11-month-old infant could be conditioned to fear white rats by

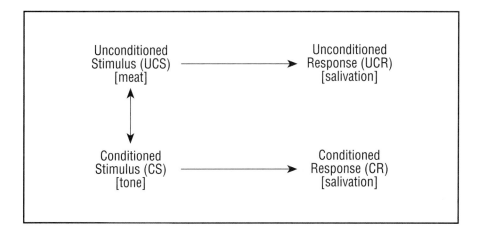

Figure 6.1

Classical Conditioning (Pavlov's Dog).

being repeatedly exposed to a white rat (a presumably neutral conditioned stimulus) and a loud, frightening noise (unconditioned stimulus) at about the same time. The loud noise naturally gave rise to an unconditioned fear response (Albert would cry and avoid the stimulus), but the previously neutral stimulus of the rat also came to elicit fear (conditioned response) by virtue of its repeated association with the unconditioned stimulus. Although the results of this study are murky, there is some evidence that little Albert's fear of rats may have naturally expanded over time to include other white, furry objects, an example of what behaviorists have called **stimulus generalization.**

Classical conditioning may be implicated in the development of certain neurotic symptoms, especially phobias, and in the ontogeny of more complex attitudes and behavior systems. In some cases, such complex associations are achieved through **higher-order conditioning.** In higher-order conditioning, conditioned stimuli, which have obtained their eliciting power through associations with unconditioned stimuli, come to be associated with other neutral stimuli, which themselves become conditioned stimuli by virtue of the association (Figure 6.2). Therefore, a young man may develop an aversion to a particular brand of women's cologne because that was the cologne his mother wore the summer he broke up with his girlfriend. In other words, the aversion is a higher-order conditioned response to the conditioned stimulus of the previously neutral cologne, now associated with "mother that summer," which is itself a conditioned stimulus by virtue of its association with the aversive unconditioned stimulus of the end of a love affair. Higher-order conditioning could also produce emotionally positive associations, as might be the case if the young man's sister wore the cologne on the day he found out that he had been named his high school's outstanding student.

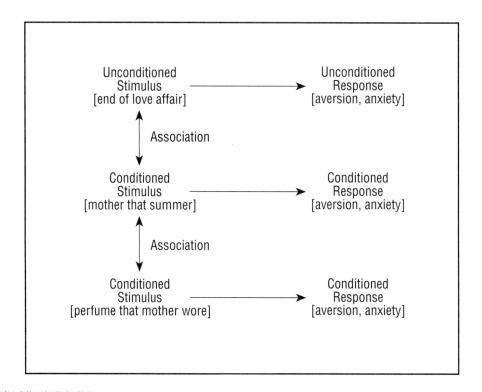

Figure 6.2

Hypothetical Example of Higher-Order Conditioning.

Traditionally, classical conditioning has been viewed as an extremely simple, low-level form of learning whereby two stimuli become associated because of their appearing together at the same time. Recent thinking about the phenomenon, however, suggests a more complicated and high-level process. Rescorla (1988) argues that contiguity in time and place is not what makes conditioning work. Instead, classical conditioning enables the organism to form an accurate representation of the world. In the standard Pavlovian example, the tone becomes associated with the bell not because the two arrive on the scene at about the same time but rather because one stimulus (the tone) *provides information* about another (the meat). Rescorla summarizes his cognitive interpretation of classical conditioning by saying:

> Pavlovian conditioning is not a stupid process by which the organism willy-nilly forms associations between any two stimuli that happen to co-occur. Rather, the organism is better seen as an information seeker using logical and perceptual relations among events, along with its own preconceptions, to form a sophisticated representation of the world. (1988, p. 154)

Instrumental Conditioning.   A second form of learning is **instrumental conditioning,** termed by Skinner **operant conditioning.** (The basic principles of operant conditioning are outlined in Table 6.1.) In operant conditioning, behavior is modified by its consequences. Positive consequences for a behavior increase the likelihood of its recurrence, thus reinforcing the association between the behavior and the various stimuli in the environment present at the time the behavior occurred. Negative consequences decrease the likelihood the behavior will recur, thus weakening stimulus–response connections.

Skinner has conducted the best-known experiments in operant conditioning. In these laboratory studies, he employed the basic principles of reinforcement and punishment to teach animals, such as rats and pigeons, to perform complex behaviors. Typically, the animal is placed in a tightly controlled laboratory setting and allowed to do whatever it pleases. When, in its random activity, the animal happens to behave approximately as the experimenter wants it to, the animal is rewarded—often with a small amount of food. The experimenter thus selectively reinforces the desired behavior, and over time the animal emits the reinforced behavior with increasing frequency. The process of reinforcing closer and closer approximations to a desired behavior in an attempt to elicit that behavior is called *shaping*. Shaping was a central practice in the educational regimen of Frazier's *Walden Two*.

Operant conditioning is more than merely a matter of increasing certain behaviors through reinforcement and decreasing others through punishment or lack of reinforcement. Organisms must also learn when and where to perform or refrain from certain behaviors. Quiet activity, therefore, may be reinforced in the classroom but not on the playground. The school child may learn to discriminate between these two environmental settings and to perform the appropriate behaviors for each. Thus, the classroom desks and the teacher may serve as *discriminant stimuli* for the child: when these stimuli are present in the environment, certain behaviors (reading, writing, being quiet) are likely to be reinforced, while others (running and playing ball) are likely not to be reinforced and may even be punished. Certain response patterns, however, may be reinforced in a great variety of environmental settings. In this case, *generalization* occurs. For example, the child may be rewarded for telling the truth at home, in school, *and* on the playground. Ideally, he or she would learn that such behavior is virtually always appropriate and that it should therefore be shown in the presence of a great variety of stimuli.

Concepts of reinforcement and punishment are both intuitively obvious and paradoxical. Most people know that behavior can be shaped through the judicious use of rewards and punishments. Indeed, parents employ basic principles of operant conditioning routinely in daily child care and discipline. However, they employ them wrongly in many cases, Skinner would argue. For instance, many parents rely much too heavily on punishment. Because punishing a response merely alerts the person to what should *not* be done while providing no example of a constructive alternative, punishment is generally a rather weak form of behavioral control, Skinner maintains. Overt punishment played virtually no role in the educational program in *Walden Two*.

Table 6.1

Key Concepts of Operant Conditioning

Concept	Definition	Example
Positive Reinforcer	Any stimulus that, because of its *presentation* after a response, *strengthens* (increases the probability of) the response. In effect, the organism is rewarded for the response.	A first grade teacher's praise for a child's obedient behavior leads to increased obedience in the future.
Negative Reinforcer	Any stimulus that, because of its *removal* after a response, *strengthens* (increases the probability of) the response. In effect, the organism experiences relief (a kind of reward) after the response.	Criticism from one's mother-in-law about smoking cigarettes ceases when the individual quits smoking. Removal of criticism is reinforcing, serving as a reward for giving up cigarettes.
Positive Punishment	Any stimulus that, because of its *presentation* after a response, *weakens* (decreases the probability of) the response. Positive punishments are aversive or painful stimuli that reduce the behavior they follow.	A speeding motorist on his way to the Indianapolis 500 is pulled aside by a state patrolman and given a $100 citation. The traffic ticket serves as a punishment, which leads to less speeding by the motorist in the future.
Negative Punishment	Any stimulus that, because of its *removal* after a response, *weakens* (decreases the probability of) the response. Negative punishments remove pleasurable stimuli.	A teenager who repeatedly breaks curfew is "grounded" by her parents for a week. A positive reinforcer (going out with her friends) is therefore removed. In subsequent weeks the teenager comes home at the correct time.
Extinction	A previously reinforced behavior is no longer reinforced; eventually the behavior decreases and drops to baseline levels.	A child no longer says "please" and "thank you" at the dinner table because the parents no longer reinforce the behavior with smiles and compliments.

Table 6.1 continued

Concept	Definition	Example
Shaping	Getting the organism to emit a complex response by reinforcing successive approximations to the response. A complex, final response may be shaped by rewarding the organism for the simple component responses that make it up.	A Little League coach teaches a child to hit a ball by praising a number of simple behaviors that comprise the complex behavior of batting. Early on, the child is reinforced for standing in the appropriate way, then for level swinging of the bat. Then the child is praised when bat actually strikes ball. Finally, praise is delivered only when the child shows the entire proper batting stance and swing and hits the ball solidly.
Continuous Reinforcement	Delivering reinforcement after every instance of a particular response. Behavior submitted to a continuous reinforcement schedule is learned rapidly.	Every time a man tells his girlfriend he loves her, she kisses him.
Partial Reinforcement	Not reinforcing every instance of the behavior, but rather delivering reinforcement intermittently according to a particular schedule. *Interval* reinforcement schedules administer reinforcement after a particular period of time. *Ratio* reinforcement schedules administer reinforcement after a particular number of responses. Behavior submitted to partial reinforcement schedules, either interval or ratio, is more resistant to extinction than behavior that is reinforced continually.	*Interval* schedule: A factory worker receives a paycheck once every two weeks. *Ratio* schedule: A vacuum cleaner salesman receives a bonus after he sells 25 vacuum cleaners.

Parents also routinely *under*estimate the power of **partial reinforcement.** In partial reinforcement a particular response is reinforced intermittently, whereas in **continuous reinforcement** the response is reinforced every time it occurs. When behavior is no longer reinforced, *extinction* might eventually occur: the behavior decreases in frequency and eventually dies out. However, behavior that

Table 6.2

Types of Social Reward

Stimulation Rewards		
Reward	**Absence**	**Excess**
Presence of others	Isolation	Crowding
Attention from others	Shunning	Conspicuousness
Responsivity	Boredom	Overarousal
Initiation	No Interaction	Intrusion

Affective Rewards	
Reward	**Opposite**
Respect	Insolence
Praise	Criticism
Sympathy	Disdain
Affection	Hostility

From A. Buss (1986, pp. 14, 27).

has been partially reinforced is much more difficult to extinguish than continuously reinforced behavior. Therefore, a parent who only occasionally rewards a child's temper tantrums may unwittingly be establishing a partial reinforcement schedule for the tantrums, making it difficult to eliminate this undesirable behavior. Particularly thorny problems can arise when the same undesirable behavior—such as a temper tantrum, physical aggression, or immature dependency—is occasionally reinforced, occasionally punished, and occasionally ignored.

Reinforcement comes in many different forms. Although experiments with animals routinely employ such basic reinforcers as food and drink, human beings are typically subject to a multitude of positive consequences that subtly shape behavior. Some of the most powerful reinforcers are called **conditioned generalized reinforcers**—reinforcers that acquire their power because of their association with a large variety of other reinforcers. The best example of a conditioned generalized reinforcer is money, which enables one to purchase a great variety of other reinforcers. Many human reinforcers, moreover, are highly social in nature. Arnold Buss (1986) divides social reinforcers into two general classes: *stimulation rewards* and *affective rewards*. Stimulation rewards include receiving attention from others; affective rewards include receiving respect, praise, and affection. Affective rewards constitute an *emotional* response from others; stimulation rewards merely indicate that others are responding in some way to the self. Table 6.2 lists the basic social rewards in Buss' scheme and the consequences of receiving too much or too little of each of these fundamental reinforcers.

Social-Learning Theories

Although American psychology is no longer dominated by the behaviorist perspective, the radical science of behavior launched by Watson in 1913 has left a powerful legacy. Some of the strongest features of behaviorism have been incorporated into the mainstream of American psychology, such as its pragmatic and functional spirit and its emphasis on experimental rigor and quantification. Behaviorism has also had a major impact on clinical practice and has led to a wide variety of practical techniques for changing problematic behavior, loosely grouped under the rubric of "behavior modification" or "behavior therapy." With respect to theory, behaviorism has spawned a number of more modern approaches that fall under the name of **social-learning theories.** These theories retain some of behaviorism's emphasis on the observables, environmentalism, and learning, while adopting a broader view of human behavior that incorporates important *cognitive* variables that cannot be directly observed. Leading proponents of social-learning theories as applied to personality psychology include Julian Rotter, Walter Mischel, and Albert Bandura.

Rotter's View: Expectancies and Values

One of the first psychologists to introduce cognition into behaviorist accounts of human personality was Julian Rotter. A practicing psychotherapist who helped build a clinical psychology program of national renown at Ohio State University in the late 1940s and early 1950s, Rotter is generally credited with developing the first social-learning theory (Phares, 1988). His eclectic viewpoint broadened the traditional boundaries of behaviorism to account for certain aspects of learning that appeared to be unique to human beings. Rotter (1954, 1972) views the person as actively constructing his or her own reality, rather than merely passively responding to it. In this sense, Rotter's approach bears striking resemblance to existential and cognitive views of the person, discussed in Chapters 8 and 9. Most human learning, furthermore, occurs in a social context, as people learn to anticipate what others will do and then act on those anticipations.

A key concept in Rotter's theory is the **expectancy,** a subjectively held probability that a particular reinforcement will occur as the outcome of a specific behavior. Over time and across different situations, each of us learns to expect that we will probably be reinforced for certain behaviors in certain situations but not in others. For instance, a college student may expect that working hard in her psychology class will earn her a high grade. On the other hand, she may also expect that working hard at improving her relationship with her boyfriend is not likely to earn her much satisfaction. In this case, the woman holds very different subjective expectancies as to the probability that "hard work" will pay off in two very different situations. Over time, furthermore, people develop *generalized expectancies* about the nature of reinforcement in the world at large. In Chapter 8, we will examine some of the empirical research that has come out of Rotter's view of generalized expectancies, under the topic of "locus of control."

A second key concept is **reinforcement value.** Reinforcement value refers to the subjective attractiveness of a particular reinforcement. For the college student, the reinforcement value of improving her relationship may be much higher than the reinforcement value of obtaining a high grade in her psychology course. Therefore, she may work hard at mending the relationship anyway, and she may even neglect her psychology course, even though her expectancies dictate that she will be more "successful" if she acts in an opposite manner. To predict how a person will behave, the psychologist must take into account that person's particular combination of expectancy and reinforcement value for a particular goal-directed action in a given situation. In Rotter's terminology, behavioral potential (BP), that is, the likelihood that a particular person will perform a given behavior, equals the combination of the expectancy (E) and the reinforcement value (RV) that the behavior holds for that person: $BP = E + RV$. People are most likely to act to obtain goals for which (1) they expect to be reinforced (high E), and (2) the expected reinforcements are highly valued (high RV). They are least likely to act to obtain goals for which (1) they do not expect to be reinforced (low E), and (2) the reinforcements they might obtain are not especially valued (low RV).

Mischel's Approach: Cognitive/Social Learning/Person Variables

An influential spokesman for the social learning view of personality has been Walter Mischel. An associate of Rotter's at Ohio State University in the 1950s, Mischel

Walter Mischel

stunned the field of personality psychology in 1968 with his vigorous attack on trait psychology. As we will see in Chapter 7, Mischel argued for the supremacy of situational factors in the prediction of behavior over and against the use of personality-trait measures, like those surveyed in Chapter 5. In arguing that behavior is primarily a function of the situation rather than of internal personality traits, Mischel aligned himself philosophically with the behaviorist tradition of Watson and Skinner. In recent years, however, Mischel (1973, 1979) has put forth a list of **cognitive/social learning/person variables** to suggest that people invest situations with particular *meanings*, which are directly implicated in producing behavior. These meanings can be seen as characteristic strategies or styles of approaching situations, and are thought to grow out of the individual's previous experiences with both situations and rewards. Like Rotter, therefore, Mischel has developed a brand of social-learning theory with a distinctively cognitive flavor.

Mischel delineates five basic cognitive/social learning/person variables. The first, *competencies,* refers to what a person knows and can do. Each person approaches a situation with his or her own set of skills or competencies. One person may be particularly adept at showing empathy for other people; another person is extremely skillful in analyzing social problems in a cool and dispassionate

Continued on p. 329

Feature 6.A

The Integration of Freud and the Behaviorists
Miller and Dollard's Learning Theory

In the 1940s and 1950s, sociologist John Dollard and experimental psychologist Neal E. Miller, along with such eminent colleagues at Yale University as Robert Sears and O. H. Mowrer, brought together the opposing beasts of psychoanalysis and behaviorism. The resultant offspring was an extremely influential learning theory of personality that blended some of the best of both parents. Dollard and Miller were more than just intellectual midwives; their creative synthesis of two traditions in psychology went beyond the traditions themselves and introduced a social and cultural perspective on human personality that had been missing up to then.

In their early writings on the **frustration-aggression hypothesis,** Dollard and Miller proposed that animal and human aggression was not a simple turning outwards of the Freudian death instinct but rather a socially molded behavior aimed at injuring another organism *as a consequence of frustration* (Dollard, Doob, Miller, Mowrer, & Sears, 1939). According to the frustration-aggression hypothesis, the greater the extent to which an organism's goals are blocked, the greater the frustration and, in turn, the greater the resultant aggression. Frustrations can mount over time, minor frustrations adding up to produce major aggressive reactions. The threat of punishment may inhibit aggressive responding, but as

frustrations increase and aggression remains inhibited, the build-up is likely to lead to an *indirect* expression of the aggression: kicking a chair instead of one's frustrating boss; making sarcastic jokes instead of hitting one's father. Freud's notion of the displacement of the aggressive instinct, therefore, was explained as the inhibition of an aggressive response in the face of anticipated punishment and the substitution of a socially dictated "safer" response that serves to relieve pent-up frustration.

According to Miller and Dollard, all significant human behavior is *learned* in a particular social, cultural, and historical context. Learning involves four fundamental factors. First, learning is motivated by *drives,* a proposition that brings together Freud's idea of instincts and Hull's (1943) idea of a generalized drive. A drive is a strong internal stimulus that propels behavior. Examples include such primary or physiological drives as hunger and thirst and such secondary or learned drives as dependency and autonomy. Learned drives are social needs that derive ultimately from primary drives. Second, learning is given direction and guidance by *cues,* which are stimuli in the environment that provide information concerning what the organism should attend to and how it should respond. Third, learning involves a *response:* propelled by drive and guided by cue, the organism *acts.*

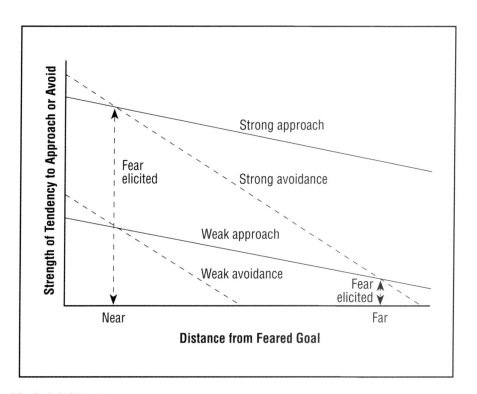

Figure 6.A.1

Approach and Avoidance Tendencies in Conflict Situations.

Adapted from Dollard & Miller, 1950, p. 361.

This response leads to a *reduction of drive,* which in itself is rewarding and thus constitutes *reinforcement,* the fourth and final component of learning. *There can be no reinforcement without some kind of drive reduction,* maintained Miller and Dollard. In sum, then, learning is generally a matter of "wanting something" (drive), "noticing something" (cue), "doing something" (response), and, as a result, "getting something" (reinforcement) (Miller & Dollard, 1941, p. 2).

Miller and Dollard translated a number of classic Freudian ideas into the more objective and operational language of drive, cue, response, and reinforcement. For instance, they substituted for Freud's "pleasure principle" the "principle of reinforcement," understood as the reduction of a primary or secondary drive. The psychoanalytic concept of "transference" was seen as a special case of "stimulus generalization." "Repression" became "inhibition." "Anxiety" was a learned, secondary drive, acquired through repeated experiences of pain (a primary drive itself) and threatened pain. Psychosexual development was explained according to basic principles of learning applied to the realms of feeding and weaning, cleanliness training, sex training, and the socialization of a child's anger (Dollard & Miller, 1950).

One of the most enduring contributions of Miller and Dollard is their theory of conflict. According to this view, conflicts are socially anchored goal-dilemmas that possess *approach* and *avoidance* characteristics. Laboratory studies with rats have shown that the tendency to approach a desired goal becomes stronger as the organism nears the goal (approach gradient), just as the tendency to avoid a negative or feared stimulus becomes stronger as the organism nears the stimulus (avoidance gradient). However, avoidance gradients are generally *steeper* than approach gradients (Figure 6.A.1). An increase in the drive behind either an approach or avoidance raises the general level of that gradient. When two response tendencies compete in any given situation, the conflict is resolved when the stronger tendency prevails over the weaker.

The dynamics of approach and avoidance produce four different kinds of conflict. In an *approach–approach* conflict, the individual finds him- or herself between two equally attractive goals. If some random activity points in the direction of one of the two goals, he or she is likely to resolve the conflict quite easily by proceeding toward that goal, given that the strength of the tendency to approach the goal has increased with closer proximity. In an *avoidance–avoidance* conflict, on the other hand, the individual is stuck between two equally unappealing or feared stimuli. Such a conflict is more difficult to resolve because movement in the direction of either stimulus is likely to increase the tendency to avoid or retreat from that same stimulus and to push the individual back to the middle between the two.

In an *approach–avoidance* conflict, the individual perceives the same goal as having both approach and avoidance characteristics—what Freud would term "ambivalence." As the individual gets closer to the goal, both approach and avoidance tendencies increase, but avoidance tendencies increase at a faster rate. If the avoidance tendencies finally outstrip the approach tendencies, the individual retreats from the goal. Finally, many complex human dilemmas may take the form of *double approach–avoidance* conflicts, in which the individual is caught between two goals, both of which are both desired and feared. Double and even multiple approach–avoidance conflicts may be the experiential stuff of which human neuroses are made.

Continued from p. 325
manner; and a third person has a gift for making small talk. Each skill is likely to influence what each person in fact does in a particular situation.

A second person variable, *encoding strategies,* deals with the manner in which people interpret information. Each person sees a particular situation from a different point of view. Imagine, for a moment, that two weeks into the semester a professor explodes at his students, chastising them all in class for their poor performance on a written assignment. He tells them that he has been too easy on them for the first two weeks and that the class is now going to be a lot tougher. For one student, this professor's "no more Mr. Nice Guy" lecture is interpreted as a legitimate threat that may motivate the student to work harder (or perhaps to drop the course and find a more mild-mannered professor). Another student may interpret the outburst as a carefully orchestrated bluff designed to scare students: underneath it all, the professor didn't really mean what he said. A third student may conclude that the professor did mean it at the time, but that he was simply having a very bad day and that, therefore, there is no need to worry. People clearly behave according to their own characteristic ways of interpreting, or "encoding," information—a theme we return to in some detail in Chapters 8–10.

Following Rotter (1954), Mischel's third person variable is *expectancies.* Three different kinds of expectancies are identified: expectancies concerning (1) the outcome of behaviors in a particular situation; (2) the meaning of particular stimuli in a given situation; and (3) a person's confidence that he or she will be able to perform a specific behavior in a particular situation.

Again following Rotter, Mischel's fourth person variable is *subjective values,* which refers to what we like, dislike, and fear with respect to specific outcomes of behavior in certain situations. Subjective values are often closely tied to particular situations. Therefore, not only may two people differ radically from each other with respect to what they value within a given situation, but each person may hold different values across situations. John may revel in the fact that he is considered a leader in his small group of friends, but he has no interest in obtaining fame in the population at large. Roger, on the other hand, shuns a high profile with his close friends, preferring comfortable sharing and intimacy. In a larger setting, however, he values and strives for fame—so much so that Roger has recently decided to run for public office.

Mischel's fifth person variable is *self-regulatory systems and plans.* These refer to the ways we regulate and guide our own behavior through self-imposed goals and standards. Wanda's plans to attend law school and eventually work for a large law firm in New York City clearly influence the way she approaches situations. Such a plan dictates that she spend a good deal of her time studying to obtain high grades, that she take certain courses as an undergraduate that best prepare her for law school, and that she discuss with her fiancé, who thinks he might like to be a psychology professor, how the two of them hope ultimately to merge their careers and their lives. Plans provide our lives with guidelines and agendas. They specify how we might achieve important goals, and they help us determine what is worth doing and what is not worth doing at particular times and in particular situations.

Albert Bandura

Bandura's Theory: The Role of Observational Learning

The most wide-ranging and influential social-learning theorist today is probably Albert Bandura. As a graduate student at the University of Iowa, Bandura came under the influence of the prominent behaviorist Kenneth Spence. He received training as a clinical psychologist at Wichita Guidance Center in Kansas and then assumed a faculty position at Stanford University, where he has remained to the present. Bandura provides an especially inclusive social-learning perspective, which greatly expands the domain of learning to encompass observational learning and cognitive processes and which pays close attention to the complex and recursive ways in which person variables, environmental variables, and behavior itself influence each other.

Observational Learning   The social-learning approaches of Rotter and Mischel are mainly concerned with predicting what a person will do in a particular situation. This is to say, these theories concern themselves with *performance*. They tend not, on the other hand, to focus on the *acquisition* of behavior per se. Bandura's theory complements Rotter's and Mischel's in that it emphasizes how people acquire or learn particular behaviors—behaviors that they may or may not perform (Phares, 1988). The distinction between acquisition (learning) and performance is a crucial one. Bandura has argued that some of the traditional principles of learning that derive from behaviorism—such as the laws of reinforcement and punishment—have more to do with performance than with acquisition or learning per se. Rewards and punishments directly shape what people will *do,* concedes Bandura, but they may not always be implicated in what people *learn.*

The behaviorist theories of Skinner, Hull, and Miller and Dollard cannot explain why people learn in the absence of reinforcement and/or the satisfaction of biological needs. Taking issue with the legacy of Epicurus, Bandura argues that certain learning occurs *outside* the bounds of pleasure and pain. We do not need to be rewarded in order to learn. Rather, argues Bandura, human beings learn a great deal simply by watching other people behave, reading about what other people do, and generally *observing* the world. This deceptively simple process is called **observational learning.** People routinely learn by observing, and they often perform (behave) by imitating what they see.

Figure 6.3 presents Bandura's (1971, 1977) conceptual scheme for observational learning and imitation. Bandura views the sequence as four sequential component steps through which a person observes another person's behavior (the

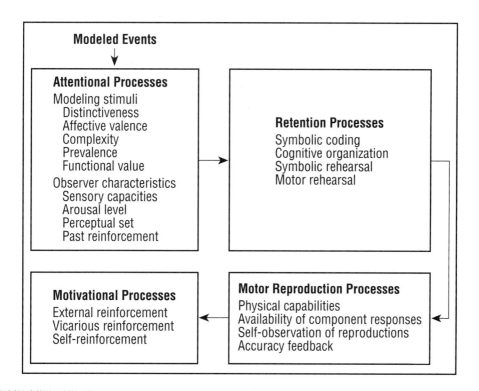

Figure 6.3

Four Steps in Observational Learning and Imitation.

From Bandura, 1977, p. 23.

model) and eventually imitates what the model does. Step 1 specifies the *attentional processes* involved in observing the model. Certain features of the model may increase the likelihood that the person will notice or pay attention to what the model is doing. For instance, a highly distinctive model, or one who is especially attractive, familiar, or even strange, may capture the observer's attention better than a less distinctive model. Conversely, attentional processes can also refer to characteristics of the observer. A person must have the capacity to observe the model. (A blind person cannot imitate what he or she cannot see, but can rely on other sensory modalities in observational learning.) A person must also be motivated to observe. It may not matter how distinctive or attractive a particular model is, for if the observer is too tired to notice the model, no observational learning will occur.

The second step in observational learning is *retention processes.* The person must be able to encode, remember, and make sense of what he or she observes if learning is to occur. However much you present addition and subtraction flashcards to a newborn infant, the infant will not learn basic arithmetic, because newborns cannot encode this kind of symbolic information.

Bandura's third step—*motor reproduction processes*—concerns the capabilities of performing what is observed and the availability of such performance in the observer's repertoire of behavior. My brother and I spent hours—years, in fact—of our youth carefully observing Ernie Banks hit baseballs for the Chicago Cubs. In his glorious career, Ernie hit 512 home runs, and I think we saw most of them on TV. My brother and I obsessively and repeatedly attended to the model (Bandura's Step 1), and both of us can remember Banks' beautiful swing with perfect clarity (Step 2). Yet between the two of us, we hit all of two home runs in our many years of playing Little League.

Finally, Step 4 in Bandura's scheme is *motivational processes.* An observer must *want* to imitate behavior if imitation is to occur. It is at this point in Bandura's scheme that rewards and punishments play their strongest roles. Assuming the person has attended to the model's behavior, has encoded the behavior, and is capable of reproducing the behavior, the person is now most likely to imitate the model if reinforced for doing so. Reinforcement in this case might come directly from the external environment, from the individual observer him- or herself (what is called "self-reinforcement"), or by seeing or imagining someone else being reinforced for the behavior ("vicarious reinforcement").

Bandura's views on observational learning underscore the profoundly social quality of human learning and performance. Observational learning occurs within a particular interpersonal context. Observer and model are involved in a complex personal relationship, the nature of which can profoundly influence how learning occurs and the extent to which imitation will be shown. Empirical literature on imitation in children, for instance, shows that a number of characteristics of the model and of the relationship between the model and the child may promote or hinder imitation. In general, children are more likely to imitate models of their own sex (Bandura, Ross, & Ross, 1961), models who are perceived as powerful (Bandura, Ross, & Ross, 1963), and models whose behavior is observed to be reinforced by others (Bandura, 1965; Parke & Walters, 1967).

Self-Efficacy   A central concept in Bandura's social-learning theory is **self-efficacy.** Self-efficacy is a person's belief that he or she can successfully carry out "courses of action required to deal with prospective situations containing many ambiguous, unpredictable, and often stressful elements" (Bandura & Schunk, 1981, p. 587). In other words, self-efficacy is our belief in our own behavioral competence in a particular situation. High self-efficacy is reflected in a strong belief that I can perform a particular behavior; low self-efficacy is reflected in the belief that I cannot perform the behavior (Table 6.3).

Self-efficacy should be distinguished from outcome expectancies, which refer to a person's beliefs about what the outcome of a particular action is likely to be in a given situation. A positive outcome expectancy means that I believe that a behavior will produce a desired result; a negative outcome expectancy means that I suspect the behavior will not produce a desired result. It is theoretically possible, therefore, that I might have a high self-efficacy expectation in a given situation but a low outcome expectancy: for example, I might be certain that I can explain logically and forcefully to my good friend why I think that he should not divorce his wife (high self-efficacy) but I might also be sure that any explanation of this sort will nonetheless do very little good (low outcome expectancy).

Research has suggested that self-efficacy judgments help determine whether we undertake particular goal-directed activities, the amount of effort we

Table 6.3

Four Sources of Self-Efficacy

Performance Accomplishments. Past experiences of success and failure in attempts to accomplish goals are the most important regulators of self-efficacy.

Vicarious Experience. Witnessing other people's successes and failures provides one with a basis of comparison by which to estimate one's own personal competence in similar situations.

Verbal Persuasion. Being told by others that one can or cannot master a task may also increase or decrease self-efficacy, though the effect of such persuasion is usually weak.

Emotional Arousal. A person's feelings of self-efficacy are influenced by the degree and quality of emotional arousal he or she feels in a given performance situation. The degree of anxiety felt provides important information about the perceived degree of difficulty, stress, and persistence that a task represents. Very high levels of anxiety signal to the person that he or she is not feeling very masterful.

put into them, and the length of time we persist in striving for goals in particular situations. A representative empirical study of the relation between self-efficacy judgments and behavior was conducted by Manning and Wright (1983). These researchers studied 52 pregnant women who were attending childbirth classes designed to teach them how to master the pain of labor and delivery without medication. The women completed self-efficacy questionnaires before and during labor. The questionnaires asked them to assess how well they thought they would be able to handle the pain of childbirth without medication. Outcome expectancy was also assessed before and during labor through a questionnaire that asked the women to rate the extent to which they believed that the pain-control techniques they learned in their childbirth classes were generally effective in enabling a woman to go through labor and delivery without medication. After their babies were born, the women were interviewed to assess the timing and amount of medication used in labor and delivery. The results of the study showed that women who manifested high self-efficacy judgments were ultimately able to cope with pain better during labor and delivery and to resist the use of medication, compared to women scoring low in self-efficacy.

In recent writings, Bandura (1988, 1989) couches the concept of self-efficacy in the cognitive and humanistic language of human "agency" and "control." As such, Bandura's concept has evolved to resemble a number of other ideas in different theoretical traditions, including Robert White's (Chapter 2) concept of "competence" and notions of "locus of control," "personal causation," "self-determination," and "hardiness," among others, whose roots lie partly in existential and humanistic approaches to personality (Chapter 8). By believing in their capabilities to mobilize the motivation and cognitive resources needed to carry out a difficult task, people exercise control over given events. Whereas Skinner suggested that personal agency is an illusion in the face of strict environmental control of human behavior, Bandura tells us that, at minimum, a *belief* in one's agency may enable a person to exert significant control over the environment. Judgments of self-efficacy affect choice of activities and selection of environments. Thus, people tend to avoid activities and situations they believe exceed their coping capabilities, but they readily undertake activities and select environments they judge themselves capable of handling. As they move into activities and situations wherein they feel high levels of self-efficacy, they meet new people and develop new skills and interests that expand their domain of expertise and competence.

The development of self-efficacy is a key mechanism whereby people are able to exercise control over threatening events. Bandura conceives of "threat" as a "relational property concerning the match between perceived coping capabilities and potentially hurtful aspects of the environment" (Ozer & Bandura, 1990, p. 473). A person experiences a situation as threatening when he or she perceives that the personal resources at hand are not adequate to meet the strong demands of the environment. In these situations, the person feels highly anxious and is likely to experience a flood of negative thoughts about the extreme hazards of the situation and his or her personal inadequacies in dealing with the hazards. Heightened self-efficacy reduces anxiety and moves the person's thinking processes in the direction of effective interactions with the environment. In this way, self-efficacy exerts "empowering effects" (Ozer & Bandura, 1990).

Recent research on self-efficacy has highlighted its clinical applications and possible health benefits. Bandura and his colleagues have designed intervention strategies for promoting self-efficacy among people facing various kinds of environmental threats. For example, Ozer and Bandura (1990) documented increases in self-efficacy among women who participated in a program in which they mastered the physical skills to defend themselves successfully against unarmed sexual assaults. The "mastery modeling" program enhanced self-efficacy, decreased perceived vulnerability to assault, and reduced the incidence of intrusive negative thinking and anxiety arousal in encounters with men.

Another group of researchers focusing on self-efficacy implemented a program to reduce anxiety about snakes among 20 individuals whose snake phobias were so severe that they were unable to engage in camping, biking, gardening, swimming in lakes, or traveling to rustic areas (Wiedenfeld, O'Leary, Bandura, Brown, Levine, & Raska, 1990). In this study, increases in self-efficacy were associated with enhanced functioning of the body's immunological system, as measured by the concentration of lymphocytes and "helper" and "suppressor" T cells in the blood. When the subjects participated in the "guided mastery" program, which involved gradual mastery of progressively more threatening forms of interactions with snakes, they initially experienced a great deal of anxiety. But this stress activated in the process of gaining coping mastery, and thus increasing self-efficacy, proved to immunoenhancing rather than immunosuppressing. In other words, whereas stress often weakens the body's powers to fight off illness and disease, stress experienced *in the process of building up mastery and self-efficacy* may actually strengthen the body's immune system. Put simply, heightened immune system functioning, and thus better health, is associated with high levels of self-efficacy, but the benefits of self-efficacy training begin to show up even before self-efficacy has had a chance to improve. The sometimes stressful process of *building up* one's self-efficacy in the face of threat may enhance the body's defenses. This kind of stress—stress in the service of promoting self-efficacy—is a good kind of stress to have.

Reciprocal Determinism   As Bandura's social-learning theory has adopted a more cognitive flavor in recent years, it has also distanced itself somewhat from the standard behaviorist assumption of environmentalism. Though behaviorists have traditionally argued that behavior is largely determined by the environment, recent editions of Bandura's theory have acknowledged important determinants of behavior within the person as well. Bandura's (1978, 1983) concept of **reciprocal determinism** maintains that behavior is determined by multiple factors in the environment and within the person. According to Bandura, external determinants such as rewards and punishments and internal determinants such as beliefs and expectancies are all part of a complex system, and all parts of the system—external determinants in the environment, internal determinants within the person, and the person's behavior—interact in a complex and intricate manner (Figure 6.4). Change in one part of the system, therefore, potentially influences all other parts, and none is more important than any other.

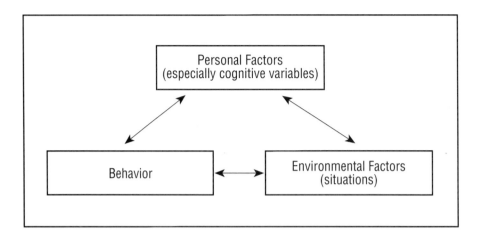

Figure 6.4

Bandura's Model of Reciprocal Determinism.

Assessment and Research

Behavioral Assessment

Every theoretical approach to the study of persons has its favorite methods of measuring or assessing personality. The psychoanalytic approaches tend to favor open-ended and highly interpretive procedures and devices, such as dream analysis and the Rorschach Inkblot Test (Chapter 3). Trait approaches have relied heavily on self-report questionnaires (Chapter 5). The behaviorist and social-learning perspectives have likewise developed their own preferred methodologies of assessing persons. Reflecting the behaviorist tradition, these techniques of collecting and interpreting data focus on (1) objective and observable behavior, rather than on subjective mental states, (2) learning in a social context, and (3) the particular environmental stimuli and rewards associated with a behavior. In keeping with the spirit of behaviorism, furthermore, behavioral assessment tends to be pragmatic and functional. Behavioral approaches to assessment are, therefore, less closely tied to elaborate theories of human functioning than other approaches and are more concerned with "what works" for a particular person in a particular environment.

Behavioral assessment is as much a general attitude about assessment as it is a group of assessment procedures (Goldfried & Kent, 1972). The attitude is well exemplified in the distinction between signs and samples. As Evans (1983) puts it, "traditional assessment interprets test responses as signs of something else; whereas in behavioral assessment, the test response is interpreted as a sample of the way the individual might respond in other, nontesting situations" (p. 392). Take, for example, a person's responses on the Rorschach Inkblot Test, which, as we saw in Chapter 3, asks the subject to report what he or she "sees" in ambiguous

Self-efficacy: women engaged in self-defense.

blots of ink. Let us imagine that a person sees a "mouth," a "peach," and "two peo-ple eating dinner" on one of the Rorschach blots. A Freudian might interpret these manifest responses as *signs* of a latent "oral character" formation. In this case, the responses are theoretically important in that they signify a deeper and hidden meaning. The behaviorist or social-learning theorist, on the other hand, is likely to view these responses as *samples* of "verbal behavior," indicative of no particular "inner meaning"; they signify nothing beyond the behavior itself but, at most, pro-vide hints as to how a person might behave in a similar situation in the future.

Table 6.4 lists different approaches to behavioral assessment and brief examples. These methodologies are built on the assumption that general motives and traits assumed by psychoanalysts and trait theorists to underlie and cut across many different situations are *not* especially relevant in the prediction of behavior. Given that human action is largely a function of the situation, behavior is *not* expected to be especially consistent across different situations. Therefore, behavioral assessment focuses on specific behavior in its specific situational con-text, effectively assessing the behavior and the situation simultaneously.

 **Table 6.4**

Some Behavioral Assessment Techniques

Technique	Examples
Problem checklists	*Fear Survey Schedule* (Curran & Gilbert, 1975). 75 fears are rated on a 5-point scale.
	Moody Problem Checklist. Covers many possible problems young adults bring to college counseling centers or health clinics.
	Assertion Inventory (Gambrill & Richey, 1975). Persons list situations and degree of discomfort they would probably experience by being assertive in each.
Self-monitoring	Persons keep daily records of various problem behaviors, such as smoking, arguments, drinking. For each instance of behavior, the subject may record information about situational factors involved, associated thoughts and feelings, events immediately preceding the behavior, and so on (Mahoney & Arnkoff, 1979; Wolpe & Lazarus, 1966).
Naturalistic observation	Behavior is directly recorded by outside observers as it occurs in a natural setting. The observers are usually trained with an explicit and objective coding system which specifies precisely what behaviors are to be coded. Patterson and his colleagues have developed coding systems for observing family interactions of conduct-disordered children (Jones, Reid, & Patterson, 1975; Reid, 1978).
Laboratory observation	*Behavioral Avoidance Test* (Borkovec & Craighead, 1971). Avoidance responses to feared objects such as dogs or snakes are directly measured by exposing fearful persons to these stimuli at various degrees of distance.
Psychophysiological measures	Mechanical monitoring of heart rate, blood pressure, electrodermal response, and muscle activity provides precise measurements that can be used for a wide variety of purposes. Other similar, useful measures to appear in recent years are genital-response indices for assessing sexual responsiveness. These include mercury-in-rubber strain gauges for measuring penile circumference (Farkas, Evans, Sine, Eifert, Wittlieb, & Vogelmann-Sine, 1979) and photoplethys- mography for measuring vaginal blood flow (Wincze & Lange, 1981).

A number of behavioral measures have adopted the format of the self-report questionnaire. For instance, the *Fear Survey Schedule* (Curran & Gilbert, 1975) lists 108 events that may induce fear in some persons (such as the sound of vacuum cleaners, open wounds, flying insects, and taking written examinations), for each of which the person rates the extent to which he or she is likely to experience fear. The purpose of the test is not to assess overall fearfulness but rather to determine in what situations a person may experience fear. On a more emotionally positive note, MacPhillamy and Lewinsohn (1974) developed the *Pleasant Events Schedule,* which lists 320 events likely to be seen as highly reinforcing. For this questionnaire, the respondent indicates how often the event occurred in the last month and how enjoyable or pleasant (how reinforcing) it was. (See Table 6.5 for sample items).

The bulk of behavioral assessment is conducted in clinical settings as part of behavioral treatment programs (Evans, 1983; Sundberg, 1977). These programs—often called "behavioral modification" or "behavior therapy"—are usually

Table 6.5

A Few Items From the Pleasant Events Schedule

Instructions: First, rate the frequency of occurrence of each of the following events during the last 30 days on a 1–3 scale: a rating of "1" = has not happened; "2" = happened a few (1–6) times; 3 = happened often (7 or more times) during the last 30 days. Second, rate the subjective enjoyability of each event on a 1–3 scale: a "1" = not pleasant; "2" = somewhat pleasant; "3" = very pleasant.

1. Being with happy people
2. Being relaxed
3. Having spare time
4. Having people show interest in what you have said
5. Looking at the sky or clouds
6. Talking about philosophy or religion
7. Meeting someone new
8. Watching attractive women or men
9. Reading stories or novels
10. Seeing beautiful scenery
11. Having coffee or a coke with friends
12. Having someone agree with you
13. Being with someone you love
14. Breathing clear air
15. Amusing people

Adapted from Lewinsohn & Libet (1972, p. 294) and MacPhillamy & Lewinsohn (1974, p. 652).

tailored to change problem behaviors for particular clients. Problem behaviors generally fall into one of three categories: excesses (such as overeating, smoking too much, compulsive handwashing), deficits (such as poor study habits, too few friendly interactions), and inappropriate behaviors (such as enuresis, talking to imaginary people) (Kanfer & Saslow, 1969). The problem behavior is objectively measured over the course of a particular treatment, so as to evaluate the success of treatment. Behavioral assessment aims at what Skinner has termed a full **functional analysis** of a problem behavior, in which the psychologist attempts to measure the environmental causes and effects of behavior in precise and objective terms. The assessment would seek to answer such questions as these: Under what conditions and in what kinds of environments (situations) does the problem behavior occur and not occur? In what ways is the behavior being reinforced or not reinforced? How was the behavior acquired (learned) in the first place? How might the environments be changed, or how might the person change the environments, in order to change the behavior?

Self-Regulation

A major theme in social-learning theory is that the environment exerts control over behavior in subtler ways as the person matures. Although young children's behavior may be directly determined by explicit environmental rewards and punishments, older children and adults regulate their own behavior because they have learned expectations, rules, and standards by virtue of repeated interactions in their environments. Therefore, while the ultimate source of internalized rules is a person's environmental or social-learning history, the individual eventually learns to exert marked control over his or her own behavior, even to the extent that people can reinforce and punish themselves. This process, called **self-regulation,** is defined as

> the ability to comply with a request, to initiate and cease activities according to situational demands, to modulate the intensity, frequency, and duration of verbal and motor acts in social and educational settings, to postpone acting upon a desired object or goal, and to generate socially approved behavior in the absence of external monitors. (Kopp, 1982, pp. 199–200)

Behavior that is self-regulated is guided by internalized standards and expectations, which are the products of past social learning, rather than by the vicissitudes of the immediate situation.

Delay of Gratification   Early forms of self-regulation can be seen in children's attempts to "delay gratification," a phenomenon studied in detail by Mischel (1966, 1974, 1983). Figure 6.5 shows Mischel's "clown box" apparatus used to assess young children's ability to delay their gratification by waiting for a reward in the face of an immediate temptation. The clown box presents the child with a choice between two windows: the window in front of the smaller reward can be opened at once, but the window displaying the larger reward remains sealed for a

Figure 6.5

Mischel's Clown Box.

predetermined time. By depositing a token in the appropriate slot in either of the clown's two hands, the child indicates whether he or she wants the immediate but smaller reward or is willing to wait for the larger reward. Mischel's research has shown that a child's willingness to defer gratification depends on the outcomes *expected* from the choice and the *value* of these outcomes. Children who trust that the waiting will actually lead to the larger reward and who believe that this reward is worth waiting for are likely to postpone immediate gratification and wait for the big prize. Such expectations of trust, in turn, appear to depend on the child's history of keeping promises, of observing other people wait for rewards, and of being reinforced for waiting.

What strategies do children use to delay their gratification in the face of an immediate temptation? Studies suggest that an effective waiting strategy is to divert oneself. In a classic study by Mischel and Ebbesen (1970), preschool children waited by themselves in a room in order to receive various rewards. After becoming comfortable with the laboratory setting and the experimenter, the children were told that they would have to wait alone in the room until the experimenter returned. If they were able to wait the entire time, they would receive a favorite food treat. While waiting, however, the children were free to signal that they wanted the experimenter to return immediately, in which case they would receive a different but less preferred food treat. Each child was exposed to one of four different experimental conditions: either (1) both food rewards were present in the room while the child waited, (2) the preferred food (delayed reward) was present, (3) the less preferred food (immediate reward) was present, or (4) neither food was present in the room while the child waited.

Figure 6.6 shows that those children who waited in the room in which neither food reward was actually present were able to wait the longest. Those in the
room with both rewards, on the other hand, showed the least delay of
gratification. The presence of one or both rewards seemed to interfere with waiting, doubtlessly making the temptation too salient for successful delay. More
interesting, however, were Mischel and Ebbesen's observations of the children's
behavior while waiting. Essentially, the children engaged themselves busily in
distractions. Some sang to themselves; others invented games with their hands
and feet; some covered their eyes so that they couldn't see the rewards; and some
even tried to put themselves to sleep—one child, in fact, successfully did so! By
diverting themselves, these children were able to transform, *in a cognitive manner,* a potentially frustrating situation into a pleasant one. Not surprisingly, this
principle of self-regulation was anticipated by Skinner (1948) in *Walden Two:*

> "Take the principle of 'Get thee behind me, Satan,' for example,"
> Frazier continued. "It's a special case of self-control by altering
> the environment. Subclass A 3, I believe. We give each child a

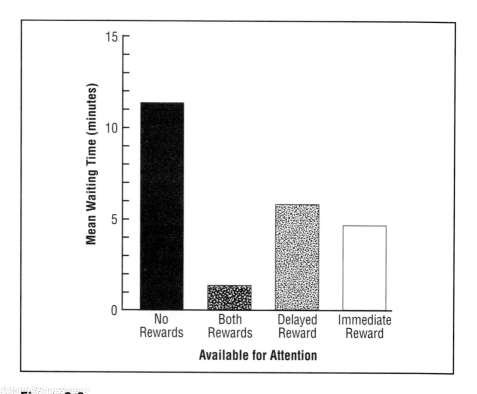

Figure 6.6

Delay of Gratification in Four Different Conditions.

From Mischel, 1986, p. 420.

lollipop which has been dipped in powdered sugar so that a single touch of the tongue can be detected. We tell him he may eat the lollipop later in the day, provided it hasn't already been licked. Since the child is only three or four, it is a fairly diff—" "Three or four!" Castle exclaimed. "All our ethical training is completed by the age of six," said Frazier quietly. "A simple principle like putting temptation out of sight would be acquired before four. But at such an early age the problem of not licking the lollipop isn't easy. Now, what would you do, Mr. Castle, in a similar situation?" "Put the lollipop out of sight as quickly as possible."

"Exactly. I can see you've been well trained." (Skinner, 1948, pp. 107–108)

Mischel and his colleagues have recently examined delay of gratification in older children at risk for adjustment problems (Rodriguez, Mischel, & Shoda, 1989). The researchers studied a group of 59 boys between the ages of 6 and 12 years who were attending a summer residential program for children who were having behavioral problems in school or home. Many of the boys in the study had exhibited a great deal of impulsive behavior, suggesting that delay of gratification was an especially salient problem in their lives. In an experimental procedure that resembled Mischel's earlier studies with younger children, the boys were given an opportunity to earn a large reward if they were able to sit in their seats and resist the temptation of sampling the goodies (M&Ms or marshmallows) for a full 25-minute period. If they were unable to wait, they earned a smaller reward. In one condition, the candy was covered up; in the other it was exposed in full view. Measures were also taken of verbal intelligence (before the experiment), attention deployment (during the experiment), and knowledge of effective strategies for delay (after the experiment).

The results showed that among older boys whether or not the candy was covered had little effect on their ability to delay gratification. However, intelligence, age, deployment of attention, and delay knowledge were all implicated in affecting the length of time they were able to wait. Older boys and those with higher levels of intelligence were able to distract themselves from the reward by focusing their attention away from the candy and onto other aspects of their environment. This shift in focus was correlated with longer delay times. Even when the researchers statistically controlled for individual differences in age and intelligence, furthermore, the ability to deploy attention onto non-reward stimuli significantly predicted delay of gratification. In addition, boys who showed greater knowledge of how to handle problems in delaying gratification also showed longer delay times, even when individual differences in age, intelligence, and attention deployment were controlled.

Individual Differences and a Personal Work Ethic   As we see in the preceding study, some children are consistently more adept at gratification delay than are others. Social-learning theorists tend to explain these differences in terms of different learning histories, suggesting that those children with greater self-control have been regularly reinforced by their parents for delaying gratification and for

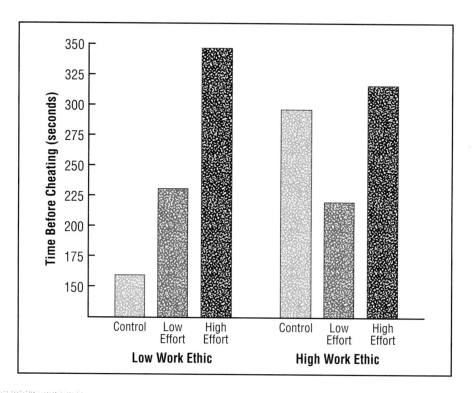

Figure 6.7

Mean Number of Seconds Spent Working on Unsolvable Anagrams Before Cheating, as a Function of Personal Work Ethic (Low Versus High) and Three Pretest Conditions (Absence of Effort Training, Low-Effort Training, or High-Effort Training).

From Eisenberger & Shank, p. 525.

expending considerable effort to obtain long-term rewards (Eisenberger & Andornetto, 1986). A longitudinal study following 116 4-year-old children into preadolescence supports the conclusion that these early differences among children have long-range predictive consequences (Funder, Block, & Block, 1983). Various personality ratings were obtained from the children at ages 4, 7, and 11 years. Boys who performed well on delay-of-gratification tasks at age 4 were rated by their school teachers and a group of psychologists at ages 7 and 11 as significantly more deliberative, attentive, reasonable, reserved, and cooperative compared to boys who did not do well on delay of gratification. Boys low on delay of gratification were seen as aggressive, restless, and not well controlled. Girls scoring high on delay of gratification at age 4 were later rated as more intelligent, resourceful, and competent compared to girls low on delay of gratification, who in contrast tended to "go to pieces under stress," feel victimized, and appear sulky and whiny.

Early training in delay of gratification may establish the groundwork for a life-long **personal work ethic,** manifested as a "general interest and satisfaction in performing tasks industriously" (Eisenberger & Shank, 1985, p. 520). In one study, 357 college students assessed for individual differences in personal work ethic were then subjected to different training procedures that consistently rewarded them for expending either low effort or high effort (Eisenberger & Shank, 1985). Later the students were given an unsolvable task to complete and were provided the opportunity to "cheat" on the task by falsely stating they had solved it. Probably because the task strongly encouraged the students to report falsely, over 75% of them did eventually cheat. However, the students with a high personal work ethic persisted almost twice as long on the task before cheating as did students with a low work ethic.

As you can see in Figure 6.7 the study's training procedures produced different results for high- and low-work-ethic students. Being trained to expend high effort or low effort did not appear to influence the performance of students who were already high in work ethic, but, among those students low in work ethic, high-effort training greatly improved their subsequent performance, causing them to be more persistent in the task. The authors surmised that students who have a high personal work ethic have previously been trained by their parents, teachers, and others to delay immediate gratification and to expend considerable effort to obtain rewards, whereas those who have a low personal work ethic have generally not been so trained. For the students with a low personal work ethic, the study's high-effort training procedures may have helped compensate for insufficient past training in delaying gratification and working hard for long-term rewards.

Aggression and Altruism

In Chapter 4, we examined the phenomena of people *hurting* each other (aggression) and *helping* each other (altruism) from the standpoint of evolutionary theory and sociobiology. We saw that aggression and altruism can be understood as instinctually grounded behavioral patterns that have proven adaptive in various ways throughout human evolution. In a very general sense, the tendencies to hurt or help others may be viewed as central aspects of human nature, ultimately encoded in human genotypes. While such views of aggression and altruism provide provocative frameworks for understanding the nature of *all* people, they are not very helpful in explaining the different aggressive and altruistic natures of *individual* people—that is, why some people are more aggressive (or altruistic) than others. On the other hand, the behaviorist theory of Miller and Dollard considers individual differences in aggression from the perspective of the "frustration-aggression hypothesis," as we saw in Feature 6.A. Social-learning theories provide us with even more powerful explanations for these individual differences, especially with respect to aggression. A large body of research has investigated individual differences in aggression from a social-learning point of view, while a

A child strikes the bobo doll as researchers look on.

smaller but informative literature has looked at altruism. Let us then consider these two fundamental qualities of personality from the perspective of modern social-learning theory.

Bandura and the Bobo Doll   That children acquire aggressive responses through observational learning was documented most memorably in Bandura's famous experiments with the bobo doll (Bandura, 1965; Bandura, Ross, & Ross, 1961, 1963). A bobo doll is a large, plastic, inflated doll that is weighted at the bottom. It is fun to punch a bobo doll because each time you hit it, it pops back into an upright position by virtue of its weighted bottom. Children (or adults) are not likely to punch the doll ferociously—unless they observe somebody else, especially a role model or authority figure, "punch out" the doll. Once such behavior is observed, it may be repeated with great enthusiasm, especially if the observer finds him- or herself frustrated in some way.

In Bandura's original study, 72 preschool children were randomly assigned to one of three experimental conditions. One group observed an adult repeatedly hit and kick the bobo doll and scream such things as "sock him in the nose, hit him down, boom, boom!" A second group observed an adult behave tranquilly and ignore the doll. A third (control) group did not see a doll. Following the observations, the children were taken to a room containing a bobo doll and a number of attractive toys, such as a fire engine, a colorful spinning top, and a doll set complete with wardrobe. They were told they could play with the toys. After two minutes, however, the experimenter returned to tell them that she had changed her mind and decided they could *not* play with these toys. The children expressed their disappointment in various ways. Those who had seen the adult pummel the bobo doll tended to aggress against the doll with fury, often mimicking the identical behaviors and uttering the same expressions they had observed in the adult model. The children in the nonaggressive condition and in the control condition, on the other hand, showed much lower levels of aggression (Bandura, Ross, & Ross, 1961).

Research has identified a number of other factors that influence the extent to which children and adults will imitate the aggressive behavior they observe. For instance, children are more likely to imitate the aggressive behavior of a model who is *rewarded* for aggression than one who is punished. In a study of first and second graders, Slife and Rychlak (1982) found that children are most likely to imitate aggressive behaviors that they like to perform and that are performed with toys they like. College students are more likely to imitate the aggressive behavior of "teachers" in a learning experiment when the aggression is seen as leading to successful teaching (Lando & Donnerstein, 1978). Other studies have shown that aggression tends to be imitated when it appears to the observer that the aggression is justified (Berkowitz & Powers, 1979; Geen, 1981). Children are more likely to imitate the aggressive behavior of a superhero who hits or kills a bad guy for the good of society than the less justified aggression of a villain.

Television Violence   If people can learn aggressive responses by simply observing them in others, what might be the effect of the relentless drumbeat of violence and aggression on American television, in movies, and in the media? The question is quite alarming, in that it has been estimated that the average American 10-year-old watches over 40 hours of television per week and that by the time that child reaches college age he or she is likely to have observed some 18,000 murders on television, many of these on weekend cartoon and adventure programs produced especially for children (National Institute of Mental Health, 1982).

A great deal of empirical research in the past 20 years has examined this. The bulk of the findings strongly suggests a positive link between viewing television violence and engaging in aggressive behaviors, in both boys and girls (Eron, 1987; Friedrich-Cofer & Huston, 1986; Huesmann & Malamuth, 1986).

Laboratory studies have consistently documented short-term increases in aggressive behavior following the viewing of violent films and television shows (Geen & Thomas, 1986). After viewing segments of such violent shows as "The Untouchables," children were more willing to hurt others than after viewing a neutral program about a track race (Liebert & Baron, 1972). Similarly, after watching cartoon characters clobber each other for some time, children engaged in greater levels of aggressive behavior compared to their peers who viewed nonviolent cartoons (Steuer, Applefield, & Smith, 1971). Viewing erotic films laced with themes of aggression—such as sadomasochism and rape—is especially likely to stimulate aggression in males and to result in greater acceptance of sexual violence directed against females (Donnerstein, 1980; Malamuth & Briere, 1986). Viewing erotic films that do *not* portray violence, however, has not consistently been shown to have an effect on subsequent aggressive behavior.

The most impressive longitudinal study of aggression and television viewing has been in progress for over 30 years now, originally conceived by Leonard D. Eron and his colleagues (Eron, 1987; Eron & Huesmann, 1984; Eron, Huesmann, Lefkowitz, & Walder, 1972). In the spring of 1960, the researchers began interviewing and testing 870 children between the ages of 7 and 9 years—the entire third-grade population of Columbia County, a semirural area in New York State. Most of these children's parents were also interviewed. The focus of the testing and interviews was aggressive behavior in schools and the presumed psychological and social antecedents and correlates of aggressive behavior. Individual differences in aggressiveness were determined by peer ratings. Third-grade children were asked to rate their classmates with respect to how aggressive they were: to what extent their classmates "were bullies," "hit other kids," and so on. Early results centered on parental behaviors associated with high levels of aggression in children. For instance, it was found that parents who were less nurturant and accepting of their children and (contrary to initial expectation) parents who physically punished their children severely for aggression at home were particularly likely to have aggressive children (Eron, Laulicht, Walder, Farber, & Spiegel, 1961).

In three follow-up assessments—at ages 8, 19, and 30 years—the amount of television violence regularly viewed was strongly and significantly related to aggressiveness. One of the best predictors of how aggressive a young man would be at age 19 was the violence of the television programs he preferred to watch when he was 8 years old. Television-viewing habits in third grade also predicted criminal activity at age 30 (Figure 6.8). Essentially, the more frequently children watched violent television at age 8, the more serious were the crimes for which they were convicted by age 30. The relationship between viewing violence on television and crime holds up for both men and women, though men show much higher levels of criminal activity overall.

Eron and his colleagues have conducted other longitudinal studies of aggression among elementary school children living in Finland, Poland, and Australia (Eron, 1982). The results are consistent with those found in the United States: in first, second, and third grade, viewing violent television and peer-nominated aggressiveness are strongly related. These studies have also implicated a number of other social and psychological factors that predict aggressiveness. Aggressive children are less popular with their peers, they score lower on tests of intellectual ability and achievement, and they are likely to engage in aggressive fantasy. In addition, the parents of aggressive children are likely to reject them and to use excessive physical punishment, and they are likely to endorse antisocial attitudes and values.

Many of these factors can coalesce in a tragic manner in the single life. Consider the case of Ronald, one of the third graders who participated in Eron's origi-

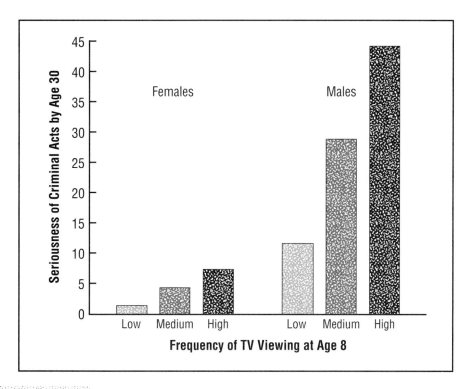

Figure 6.8

Seriousness of Criminal Acts by Age 30 as a Function of Frequency of TV Viewing at Age 8. *Note: Seriousness of crime* refers to a score assigned to each crime by the New York State Criminal Justice Division in which each type of offense is assigned a specific seriousness score.

From Eron, 1987, p. 440.

nal study in New York. Here we see a number of factors converge into the making of a highly aggressive young man. Among these are overly punitive and rejecting parents, chronic academic problems, unruly behavior at an early age, low popularity among his peers, excessive viewing of violent television programs, and a belief that the violence depicted on the television screen accurately represents the real world:

> Ronald was first seen by me when he was eight years old and in the second grade. His teacher, who described him as "a likeable and happy-go-lucky child," had referred him because of immature behavior and poor work habits. He had repeated the first grade, but the teacher felt he was brighter than group tests indicated. Ronald was the youngest of three children. His brother,

age 11, was out of the home at a special school for emotionally disturbed youngsters and his sister, age 12, was progressing normally in school. Ronald had been sickly since infancy, having suffered from severe attacks of asthma until the previous year. . . .

Ronald was next seen by another psychologist when he was 12 years old and in the sixth grade. At this time he was failing in school, reading at a second-grade level, and a management problem in class. He talked back to the teacher, provoked fights, and was constantly making noise. He was not allowed to go to the lavatory with his classmates because he would get into fights with them. . . . The parents did not seem to be concerned about the boy's behavior. . . .

By coincidence Ronald was a subject in the longitudinal study of aggression. It was possible to retrieve the parent interviews conducted when Ronald was nine years old and his own interview, when he was 19. In the third grade, Ronald was already seen by his peers as one of the most aggressive boys in his class, doing things that bothered others, starting a fight over nothing, saying mean things, not obeying the teacher, and pushing other children. At the same time the father and mother indicated that Ronald was disobedient at home, that he annoyed and pestered them, had a bad temper, and used foul language. They did not approve of a number of things that he did, giving many indications of a rejecting attitude toward Ronald and little indication that they understood him or were concerned about him. They related having had many arguments between themselves that did not settle anything; they moved around a lot, so Ronald continually had to find new friends. These behaviors and occurrences must have created a very frustrating situation at home that probably instigated Ronald to be aggressive both there and at school. The father related using many physical punishments when Ronald was aggressive, including spanking him severely and washing out his mouth with soap, thus adding to the youngster's frustration and providing a model of an aggressive adult. Other aggressive models were furnished on Ronald's favorite TV programs, "Maverick," "Have Gun Will Travel," and "The Three Stooges." The parents indicated that Ronald showed few signs of internalized standards of behavior, such as feeling sorry after he disobeyed, worrying about telling a fib or a lie, or confessing when he had done something naughty. Thus according to information furnished by his parents at that time, Ronald at age nine was experiencing many instigations to aggression at home, had a physically punitive father as well as other aggressive models, and showed little indication of having developed a conscience.

When Ronald was interviewed at age 19, he was on probation for three years for petty larceny. A few weeks after the interview, he was picked up by the police and charged with "criminal mischief in the third degree," and one week later with "criminal possession of drugs, fourth degree." During the interview it was revealed that he had dropped out of high school in the 10th grade, but he insisted that he expected to go to graduate school so that he could eventually do research in "brain biology." He admitted that he engaged in many aggressive behaviors. On the MMPI he had high scores on a pattern of scales characteristic of recalcitrant delinquents (Scales 4, 8, and 9—psychopathic deviate, schizophrenia, and mania, respectively). He continued to prefer violent television programs and thought that "Mod Squad," "Mannix," and "Dragnet" were very realistic in showing what police work was really like.

Unfortunately, Ronald is no longer a subject in our 21-year longitudinal study. He was killed in a violent accident within a year of the second interview. (Eron, 1982, pp. 207–208)

Violent television shows provide *models* for observational learning. Children and adults observe the aggressive behavior of these models and then imitate them in their daily lives. Violent television also provides the viewer with aggressive *cues*. Berkowitz (1974) has argued that certain stimuli such as guns and blood, repeatedly paired with violence on television, may become conditioned stimuli that are likely to arouse aggressive behavior in some people. Repeated exposure to television violence may also serve a *disinhibiting* function. In this case, television violence sends to the viewer the implicit message that aggression is acceptable and that one need not inhibit violent responses. Finally, repeated exposure to violence on television may serve to *desensitize* the viewer. Whereas excessive violence may have at one time elicited feelings of disgust, horror, or revulsion, it may no longer have the power to stimulate strong emotional responses after, for instance, a child has witnessed 18,000 murders on TV. People get used to aggression and, in this subtle way, come to accept it and to condone its continued proliferation.

But does television viewing actually *cause* aggressive behavior? The results of empirical studies like Eron's, as well as the case of Ronald, suggest that a simple cause-and-effect interpretation *cannot* be justifiably made. A number of other factors appear to be involved as determinants and correlates of aggressive behavior. Furthermore, studies have suggested that, while viewing television violence may lead to higher levels of aggressiveness, higher levels of aggressiveness may also lead to increased viewing of television violence (Eron, 1982, 1987). Individuals who are more aggressive to begin with tend to watch more television violence, which in turn may increase their characteristic aggressiveness, and so on. In other words, television viewing and aggression appear to be related to each other in a reciprocal or circular manner. Each is the cause and the effect of the other.

Altruism, Prosocial Behavior A consistent finding in Eron's longitudinal studies of aggression is a negative relationship between aggression and such prosocial behaviors as helping people and showing kindness. Writes Eron, "it appears that aggression and prosocial behavior represent opposite kinds of interpersonal problem-solving strategies that are learned early in life." He adds, "if a child learns one mode well, he or she does not tend to learn the other well" (1987, p. 440). Highly aggressive children are rarely altruistic and show little altruism in adulthood as well. Highly altruistic children are rarely excessively aggressive and rarely become aggressive adults (Eron & Huesmann, 1984).

Social-learning theories emphasize the role of observational learning and imitation in the development of altruism and prosocial behavior. While altruism, like aggression, appears to be influenced by a large number of overlapping factors at a number of different levels, a significant body of research supports the general notion that children and adults can and do learn to behave in altruistic ways through observing others, especially by observing parents.

London (1970) interviewed Christian men and women who had rescued Jews from the Nazis during World War II. The retrospective accounts indicated that this altruistic behavior in the face of great danger was partly motivated by a strong identification, on the part of the Christians, with moralistic and principled parents. One might assume that such parents modeled altruistic behaviors for their children, who in turn exhibited high levels of altruism as adults. Rosenhahn (1969) examined students involved in the American Civil Rights movement. He classified the youths as either "committed altruists," who had sustained a long-term involvement in work with the underprivileged, or "partially committed," who were only casually involved in the movement. From detailed life-history interviews, Rosenhahn learned that most of the parents of committed altruists had themselves been involved in altruistic social causes of considerable magnitude. They had given their children many opportunities to observe and participate in these causes. These parents were also likely to hold strong humanitarian values. While many of the parents of the partially committed youth held the same values, they were less often actively involved in altruistic behavior—behavior that could potentially put into social practice what they perennially preached.

Numerous laboratory studies reveal that when children are exposed to the helping and cooperative behavior of an adult model, they often increase their own prosocial responding. In many studies, experimenters have employed games in which children can win tokens to be redeemed for prizes. The children first observe adults play the game, win tokens, and then either donate some of their winnings to a hypothetical charity or keep it all. After the adult model departs, the children are able to play the game and are then asked to donate some of their winnings to needy causes. Generally, the results of these studies support what our knowledge of observational learning would lead us to expect. Those children who observe the charitable giving are more likely to donate their winnings, compared to children who observe the model keep all the tokens (Radke-Yarrow, Zahn-Waxler, & Chapman, 1983). Similarly, studies of gift giving among adults have shown that observing a coworker make a sizable contribution to a needy cause is likely to lead to increased giving on the part of the observer (Blake, Rosenbaum, & Duryea, 1955).

As in the case of aggression, children and adults will not imitate altruistic behavior indiscriminately. Certain characteristics of the observed model appear to mediate the relation between observation and imitation. For instance, people are more likely to imitate the altruistic responding of a model when the model (1) is perceived to be similar to them in some way and (2) expresses altruistic behavior in a positive and cheerful, rather than a negative and complaining, manner (Hornstein, Fisch, & Holmes, 1968).

Behaviorism, Social Learning, and Personality

It is ironic that a tradition of scholarship that began by rejecting *the person* as a significant agent in human behavior should be seen as making a contribution to our understanding of persons and personality. The leading lights in the behaviorist movement never saw themselves as personality theorists. Watson, Hull, and Skinner fashioned theories of behavior, not personality. They saw little scientific use for the term personality. At best, the study of persons might be an amusing distraction from the serious business of accounting for the behavior of organisms. In accounting for behavior, the scientist need not look within the person (or the rat) to imagine inner thoughts, feelings, and desires. The scientist need not invoke such ineffable concepts as ego and trait to explain the lawfulness of human behavior. One need not focus on the person at all. Behavior is where it's at. Observable, measurable, predictable behavior. Behavior in the environment. Response in the context of stimulus.

Like freedom and dignity, personality is an illusion, Skinner might say. Psychologists such as Gordon Allport might wish to account for the consistency and coherence of human behavior over time and across situations by summoning forth traits. Recall that Allport defined the trait as a "neuropsychic structure having the capacity to render many stimuli functionally equivalent, and to initiate and guide equivalent (meaningfully consistent) forms of adaptive and expressive behavior" (Chapter 5 in this text; Allport, 1961, p. 347). According to Skinner, it is superfluous to talk about such unobservable, hypothetical neuropsychic structures. If you want to account for the lawfulness of human behavior, you don't need these kinds of ideas. Sure, human behavior may sometimes seem consistent and coherent, Skinner concedes. But this stems from the fact that the contingencies of reinforcement in the environment are highly organized, and it is this external organization that gives rise to the appearance of coherence, organization, and stability. Human behavior seems organized according to a "personality" because the organization of the environment often produces consistent and coherent responses on the part of persons. At most, personality exists merely as a

Continued on p. 357

Feature 6.B

How Should Parents Raise Their Children?

Because all of us have been children and many of us will have children, we tend to formulate our own pet theories about how parents should raise them—how to enforce rules and carry out discipline, how and when to show affection, how to deal with conflicts between children, and what mistakes not to make. As generally optimistic Americans in the great empiricist tradition of John Locke, we tend to hold highly environmentalistic views of child development: we sincerely believe that what we do to, and for, our children really matters, that patterns of child-rearing actually make a difference in the child's ultimate adjustment to the world. Like the behaviorists and social-learning theorists, we believe that parents create environments for their children within which crucial learning takes place and personalities are formed. Therefore, we read with great interest the many child-training manuals written by child psychologists, pediatricians, and others whose expertise we consider to be even greater than our own.

Over the past 50 years, child psychologists and other researchers have amassed a huge literature on patterns of child-rearing and their effects on personality development. It is impossible to summarize this body of study with any hope of being accurate, comprehensive, and detailed—even textbooks in developmental psychology only skim the surface. Nonetheless, there are three extremely general conclusions that we *can* draw from this body with some degree of assurance.

The first conclusion is that we really don't know much. Many of the rules, norms, tips, and guidelines offered by popular books on child-training have virtually no basis in scientific research (Kagan, 1984). This does not mean that these books and manuals are necessarily bad or useless. Rather, it means that many of the conclusions stated with such assurance by experts in child care are based on common sense, intuition, informed speculation, or ideology. In the absence of scientific knowledge, this is probably the best we can do— but readers should adopt an open-minded and critical approach to reading and evaluating child-rearing advice, perhaps comparing many different views and integrating what they read with what they feel and think, based on their own personal experience.

A second general conclusion is that most of the informed advice offered by experts in child-rearing— whether or not such advice is based on scientific evidence—reflects a *cultural ideal* about what it means to be a good (healthy, happy) child and a good (healthy, happy) adult. This cultural ideal in America and in a number of other Western industrialized nations emphasizes individualism, freedom, and the autonomous self. To be healthy, happy, and well-adjusted, we believe, the child and the adult should be self-sufficient and able to cope with challenge on their own. Thus, we idealize such personality traits as "competence," "mastery," and "independence," and we seek to nurture such characteristics in our children.

Keeping in mind, therefore, our very limited scientific understanding of child-rearing and our cultural bias toward individualism, we can draw a third general conclusion about child-rearing and personality. A broad and coherent literature on family patterns points to four basic styles of parenting: the authoritative–reciprocal, authoritarian, indulgent–permissive, and neglecting styles. The four types can be organized according to the two basic dimensions of "demanding/undemanding" and "accepting/rejecting" (Maccoby & Martin, 1983). Figure 6.B.1 illustrates the four types and the two dimensions.

A consistent body of research favors the authoritative–reciprocal pattern as the style most likely to promote competence and mastery in children.

The *authoritative–reciprocal* pattern of child-rearing is one in which "children are required to be responsible to parental demands, and parents accept a reciprocal responsibility to be as responsive as possible to their children's reasonable demands and points of view" (Maccoby & Martin, 1983, p. 46). In the authoritative–reciprocal pattern, parents establish clear standards for appropriate behavior in the family, but they are open to and accepting of the points of views of the children. Thus, parents are both highly controlling and highly responsive in their relations with their children. A

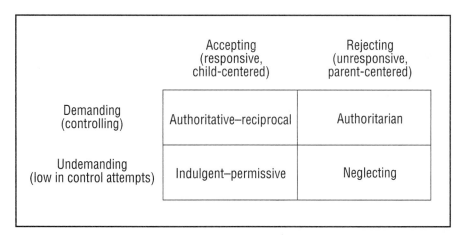

	Accepting (responsive, child-centered)	Rejecting (unresponsive, parent-centered)
Demanding (controlling)	Authoritative–reciprocal	Authoritarian
Undemanding (low in control attempts)	Indulgent–permissive	Neglecting

Figure 6.B.1

A Two-Dimensional Classification of Parenting Patterns.

From Maccoby & Martin, 1983, p. 39.

number of studies have shown that the authoritative–reciprocal pattern of child-rearing is positively associated, though at generally moderate statistical levels, with children's independence and autonomy in both cognitive and social realms, with ability to control aggression, with social responsibility, and with self-esteem.

The *authoritarian* pattern of child-rearing, on the other hand, is high on demands but low on responsiveness. Authoritarian parents may be autocratic and rigid. Strict rules are enforced as if they were divine edicts; the reasons behind rules are rarely explained and virtually never discussed. These parents strongly value obedience and discourage spontaneous give-and-take between children and their elders. Research has shown that children of authoritarian parents tend to lack social competence with their peers; they are somewhat withdrawn and lacking in spontaneity; they tend to show relatively low levels of self-esteem. Some studies also suggest that authoritarian styles may retard the development of an internalized conscience in children. Children of authoritarian parents are more likely to make moral decisions based on what external authorities tell them to do; other children may rely more on internalized standards.

The *indulgent–permissive* parenting style is the opposite of the authoritarian. In this case, parents fail to set high standards for behavior but tend to be highly responsive to the demands of children. Indulgent parents take a tolerant and accepting attitude toward the child's impulses, including sexual and aggressive impulses. They use little punishment and avoid, whenever possible, asserting authority or imposing control and restrictions, making few demands for mature behavior. Children raised in these highly egalitarian and freewheeling families tend to be relatively impulsive, aggressive, and lacking in independence or the ability to take responsibility for their behaviors. While certain benefits of highly permissive parenting have also been identified, the indulgent–permissive pattern appears "on the whole to have more negative than positive effects" (Maccoby & Martin, 1983, pp. 45–46).

Finally, the most seriously flawed parenting style is the *neglecting* and uninvolved pattern shown by parents who are unresponsive to their children and who place few demands on them. The neglecting pattern comes in different forms, ranging from passive neglect and emotional indifference to active child abuse. Children growing up in these families may show a variety of negative characteristics—from low self-esteem to poor impulse control to high levels of aggression (Baumrind, 1971; Block, 1971; Egeland & Sroufe, 1981; Martin, 1981).

Continued from p. 353

locus of environmental input. At most, it exists as a redundant internal factor in the prediction of behavior. It is redundant because it, like behavior, is simply a function of the environmental context. If the goal is to predict behavior, why not skip the middleman? Go directly from stimulus (environment) to response (behavior). Leave personality to the poets.

Writers of textbooks in personality have perennially faced an interesting conundrum when it comes to behaviorism. Almost invariably, they have decided to include behaviorism as an important tradition in personality psychology, even though it denies the importance of personality. A similar point may be made about social-learning theories, the humbler and more ecumenical grandchildren of early behaviorism. For all their attention to cognitive processes, social-learning person variables, self-efficacy, and the like, theories in the social-learning tradition have generally been perceived as deemphasizing the importance of the person in the prediction of behavior. Personality concepts such as ego (Chapter 2), instinct (Chapter 4), trait (Chapter 5), motive (Chapter 11), and even self (Chapter 10) do not find comfortable homes in these theoretical frameworks. Indeed, social-learning theorists have sometimes denied the usefulness, if not the existence, of many concepts in personalty studies, and even the concept of personalty itself (Mischel, 1968). Social-learning theories have provided the conceptual grounding for the *situationist critique* in personality psychology. Situationists argue that behavior is mostly a function of the environmental situation within which a person finds him- or herself. Behavior has much more to do with situations than with persons.

There are, nonetheless, two reasons that historical behaviorism and contemporary social-learning theories have important implications for the study of persons and personality. First, these frameworks provide the most influential *environmentalist* account of how personality dispositions and characteristics come to be. Personality characteristics such as traits and motives may be (at least partly) the product of learning. Behaviorists and social-learning theorists tell us about how organisms learn. Dominance or achievement motivation or ineffective defense mechanisms in an adult personality may be the result of a particular developmental history of classical conditioning, instrumental conditioning, or observational learning. As in the extensive work on child-rearing patterns and personality dispositions (Feature 6.B), one may see personality in terms of a patterning of relatively stable or evolving dispositions that are shaped by learning. You can be a trait psychologist who believes that the development of traits is well explained by the kind of learning principles spelled out by the behaviorists (e.g., Sears, Maccoby, & Levin, 1957). You can incorporate Freudian defense mechanisms to account for individual differences in coping behavior and explain the development of those mechanisms in terms of Bandura's theory of observational learning. Many ideas in the behaviorist and social-learning theory tradition can be usefully employed to augment theories of personality from other traditions.

A second source of implications for personality theory and research lies precisely in the conceptual tension that has always existed between behaviorism and social-learning theory on the one hand and various streams in personality psychology on the other. The tension has played itself out in many incarnations over the past 80 years. On one side you have Thorndike, Pavlov, Watson, Hull, Skinner, and the social-learning theorists. On the other you have Freud, Jung, Allport, Murray, Eysenck, and many others. Most broadly, the distinction has to do with where one looks when one looks at a psychological phenomenon. Does one look outside or inside? The behaviorists and social-learning theorists have traditionally looked outside the person, in the environment. By contrast, most personality theories (from Freud to the Big Five) look primarily inside the person. When it comes to the *prediction of behavior,* the tension has revealed itself most clearly in the controversy between the situationists, who are aligned with the points of view described in this chapter, and the trait psychologists, whose conceptual underpinnings lie in Chapter 5.

We now turn to the recent controversy in personality psychology that has pitted the trait against the situation in the prediction of human behavior. Chapter 7 pits Chapter 5 against Chapter 6. What is more important for the accurate and useful prediction of human behavior? Is it traits? Or is it situations?

Summary for Chapter 6

1. In his utopian novel, *Walden Two,* B. F. Skinner describes how a society based on fundamental behaviorist principles of learning might effectively ensure the greatest happiness for the greatest number of citizens.

2. Behaviorism has traditionally focused on observable behavior, rather than on internal mental states, and has tended to emphasize the environmental or situational determinants of behavior.

3. According to behaviorists, the environment shapes behavior through learning. Two simple forms of learning are classical and instrumental conditioning.

4. Behaviorism has spawned a number of modern social-learning theories that tend to adopt a broader and more cognitive perspective on behavior. One of the first of these is Rotter's value-expectancy theory, which attempts to predict what a person will do when confronted with choices for goal-oriented behavior in a particular situation.

5. Mischel's social-learning approach identifies five cognitive social-learning person variables which need to be taken into consideration when attempting to predict what a person will do in a particular situation: competencies, encoding strategies, expectancies, subjective values, and self-regulatory systems and plans.

6. Bandura's social-learning theory emphasizes the roles of observational learning, self-efficacy, and reciprocal determinism in human behavior. While reinforcement and need satisfaction may be instrumental in behavioral performance, Bandura argues that learning does not necessarily require reinforcement and may proceed instead through simple observation and imitation.

7. Methods of behavioral assessment tend to view test behavior as a sample of situationally specific behaviors rather than a sign of some deeper or internal trait, motive, or complex.

8. A major interest of researchers influenced by social-learning theory has been self-regulation, especially as manifested by children facing situations in which they must postpone immediate gratification.

9. Longitudinal studies have shown that preschool children who perform well on delay-of-gratification tasks are rated by their teachers and psychologists in preadolescence as especially competent, attentive, and cooperative.

10. A large body of research has investigated observational learning of aggression. One especially important line of research suggests that excessive viewing of television violence increases aggressive behavior, which increases the viewing of television violence, and so on.

11. Altruism and prosocial behavior are also learned through observation and imitation.

12. The tradition of behaviorism and social-learning theories provides two main implications for personality psychology in general: First, this tradition provides learning explanations for the origins of individual differences in personality characteristics. Second, behaviorism and social-learning theories set up a central conflict in the field between trait theories and situationism.

Chapter 7

The Interaction of Person and Environment

Introduction

Mischel's Critique

Behavior Is Complex
Predicting Some of the People Some of the Time
Feature 7.A: Traits as Categories of Acts: The Act-Frequency Approach
Aggregating Behaviors
Patterns of Traits Over Time

Behavior Is Contextual
Feature 7.B: The Type A Personality
What Is a Situation?
Modern Interactionism
Persons Versus Situations Versus Interactions
An Interactional Model of Anxiety
Reciprocal Interactionism
Macrocontexts
Families and Other Systems
Race and Social Class
Culture and History

Conclusion: Traits and Situations Revisited

Summary

When I arrived at Harvard in the fall of 1976 as a first-year graduate student in psychology, I was looking for a hero. I searched for someone to believe in—someone whose work and life might give me clues as to what I could become and thus help me define my future. I eventually *did* find some heroes, both in my reading about psychology and psychologists and in my personal and professional relationships with faculty and peers. But before I found these, I encountered a "villain." As we will see in Chapter 13, the discovery of heroes and villains can be an important part of a search for one's own identity (Erikson, 1959, 1963). We figure out who we are, in part, by figuring out who we would want to become and who we should never wish to become.

In my case, I never met the villain face to face. But I read a lot about him, and I listened with strong emotions, ranging from outrage to despair, as my professors in personality psychology discussed, often with strong emotions of their own, the villain's controversial claims. The man about whom my professors spoke was a personality psychologist at Stanford University named Walter Mischel. In my mind, he was a villain because he claimed, as I saw it then, that *there is no such thing as personality.* If Mischel was right, personality psychologists had joined the ranks of those misguided many throughout the world who believed in Santa Claus, the tooth fairy, and ghosts.

Walter Mischel is the same psychologist whose work on "cognitive/social learning/person variables" and "delay of gratification" was highlighted in Chapter 6. I now respect Mischel's approach to psychology, and I have learned how to be a psychologist without relying on heroes and villains. Nevertheless, why *was* he a villain for me? The answer tells us much about how personality psychologists have thought about persons and about the discipline of personality psychology during the last 25 years.

Mischel's Critique

Walter Mischel never *literally* said that "there is no such thing as personality." Rather, this is the conclusion that many readers, myself included, believed was implied in his controversial book *Personality and Assessment* (1968). What Mischel in fact *did* say was that personality traits—as conventionally measured—are not particularly useful in the prediction of behavior. One of the reasons that they are not useful, he argued, is that human behavior is not especially consistent from one situation to the next.

The concept of "trait," as we saw in Chapter 5, implies that behavior is cross-situationally consistent: an extraverted person, for instance, is supposed to act in an extraverted, outgoing manner in many different settings, as a general trend across various situations. Mischel argued instead that human behavior is much more situationally specific than the concept of trait would suggest. In the traditions of behaviorism and modern social-learning theory (Chapter 6), Mischel maintained that behavior is shaped largely by the exigencies of a given situation. That people act in consistent ways across different situations, reflecting an underlying consistency of personality traits, is a myth.

Mischel's argument was not new. Behaviorists had made many of the same points, though usually in a different context, since the early days of John Watson (1924). Mischel's thesis, however, was extremely powerful because of the wealth of empirical data he presented. Reviewing scientific literature on such personality variables as honesty, dependency, aggression, rigidity, and attitudes toward authority, Mischel showed that the correlations between (1) personality-trait scores, as determined by personality tests and rating procedures and (2) actual behavior in a particular situation were generally low, rarely exceeding the modest level of +.30. Furthermore, the correlation between indices of the same kind of behavior (such as "honest behavior," "friendly behavior," or "aggressive behavior") emitted by the same persons across different situations was also low.

For example, a classic study of moral behavior in over 8000 school children (Hartshorne & May, 1928) found that copying from the answer key on one classroom test showed only the modest correlation of +.29 with another form of cheating whereby students inflated their own scores on a different test. The major lesson from this study, argued Mischel, is that individual differences in moral behavior are not consistent across different situations: children who cheat on one particular test don't necessarily cheat on another. If one wishes to predict the extent to which different children will actually cheat in a particular situation, it makes little sense to invoke a general trait of "honesty" upon which children can be said to differ. As Skinner might have put it in *Walden Two,* there is no such thing as an "honest" or a "dishonest" child, only honest or dishonest behavior displayed in a given situation.

Mischel (1968, 1973) suggested the disturbing possibility that personality traits exist nowhere but in the mind of the observer. The same argument has been forcefully made by social psychologists such as Jones and Nisbett (1972) and Ross (1977) who speak of the **fundamental attribution error**—a general tendency for people to overemphasize traits and underemphasize situations when explaining the causes for *other* people's behaviors. According to this view, when people are asked to explain why another person does what he or she does, they are likely to invoke a general *personality* trait: "Randy punched another basketball player because Randy is an aggressive person" or "Martha got 100% on the mathematics exam because she is brilliant." When asked to explain their own behavior, on the other hand, people are more likely to invoke the specific *situation:* "I punched another basketball player because I was provoked to do so" or "I scored 100% on the mathematics exam because I studied hard." The implication here is that personality psychologists, in attempting to predict and explain the behavior of other people, repeatedly commit the same fundamental attribution error. Personality traits, therefore, are no more than convenient but misleading labels about other people. They exist in the mind of the observing psychologist, not in the personality of the person being observed.

If personality traits exist in the minds of observers rather than in the behavior of those they observe, then traits may tell us more about how people think about other people's behavior than they tell us about behavior itself. In one of the more acerbic critiques of trait conceptualizations, Shweder (1975; Shweder & D'Andrade, 1979) insists that when trait researchers do indeed demonstrate empirical correlations among different traits (e.g., between, say, "dominance" and "aggressiveness"), their findings simply reflect the semantic similarity of the constructs involved. For example, Passini and Norman (1966) asked students to rate people *whom they had never met* on a number of personality scales. The raters were instructed to base these ratings on what they imagined these people might be like. Factor analysis of the ratings yielded a structure of correlations among the different scales that was almost identical to those structures obtained in other studies employing the same scales—studies in which the raters *were* acquainted with the subjects they were to rate or in which they directly observed subjects' behavior.

Shweder interprets results like these to suggest that our ratings of personality traits are probably based more on our knowledge of how words (trait descriptors) go together than on our observation of real behavioral associations. If the traits of dominance and aggressiveness, for instance, seem to be similar in meaning, then we assume that behavioral manifestations of these traits are similarly correlated. In this view, people develop a set of assumptions about how certain trait words go together and then they apply these assumptions uncritically in judging the behavior of others. Each person, therefore, develops his or her own **implicit personality theory** (Bruner & Tagiuri, 1954)—the set of associations among trait words that resides in the person's mind. Some have suggested that once people have formed an initial impression about where another person stands on a given trait continuum, then they use their implicit personality theories to infer the person's relative standing on other traits as well (Berman & Kenny, 1976). Thus, traits are convenient categories for our perceptions rather than real characteristics of the persons we perceive.

Mischel's critique of personality traits and other highly critical reviews of personality psychology as a whole (for example, Fiske, 1974) launched what has been termed the *person–situation debate* in personality psychology. Defenders of traits (such as Alker, 1972; Block, 1977; Hogan, DeSoto, & Solano, 1977) argued that Mischel had (1) misrepresented many trait theories and trait theorists, (2) selectively reviewed the empirical literature in an unfair way, and (3) overlooked many methodologically sophisticated studies that supported cross-situational consistency of behavior and the inner coherence of personality. Supporters of the Mischel position (such as Argyle & Little, 1972; Mischel, 1977; Shweder, 1975) marshalled more data to buttress their "situationist" claims, often invoking findings from social psychology documenting the influence of situations on behavior.

Throughout the 1970s, a doctrine of **situationism** seemed to threaten the viability of the trait concept in particular and, according to some views, the very enterprise of personality psychology *in toto*. The doctrine may be summarized in four points:

1. Behavior is highly situation-specific, not cross-situationally consistent.
2. Individual differences within a situation are attributed primarily to measurement error rather than broad internal dispositions.
3. Observed response patterns can be causally linked to the stimuli present in the situation.
4. The experiment is the most appropriate method for discovering such stimulus-response links. (Krahe, 1992, p. 29)

In other words, situations rather than traits drive and shape human behavior, a fact that is clearest to see under well-controlled conditions of the laboratory experiment. Observed behavioral differences among persons in the same situation are small, unimportant, or the result of errors or biases on the part of observers and/or methods of measurement. With its conceptual emphasis on the external environment (situation) and methodological preference for controlled laboratory experimentation, situationism came to be associated with certain aspects of the behaviorist legacy—that is, with social-learning theories such as Bandura's and Mischel's (Chapter 6) and with the kind of research conducted by experimental social psychologists.

The person–situation debate seemed to die down in the mid 1980s (Krahe, 1992; Maddi, 1984; West, 1983) as most advocates appeared to settle on something they claimed they were advocating all along: a compromise position of **interactionism.** As the eminent psychologist Kurt Lewin said almost 60 years ago, behavior is a function of the person (and his or her traits) in interaction with the environment (Lewin, 1935). Yet this seemingly simple, even obvious, statement is more complex than might first appear, and there still exists considerable controversy as to how it is to be interpreted. There are many ways to conceive of and study the interaction of the person and the environment in the prediction of human behavior. Mischel's critique and the subsequent person–situation debate have stimulated considerable thought and research in the field of personality psychology. In the remainder of this chapter, we will sample the most influential results of the controversy, and we will end with an evaluation of where the concepts of trait, situation, and interaction stand today.

Behavior Is Complex

Over the past 25 years, many personality psychologists have responded to the Mischel critique and the subsequent person–situation debate by underscoring the *complexity* of human behavior and of human personality itself. Behavior is complexly determined—indeed, Freud said "overdetermined"—by many factors that reside both in the environment and in the person. To assume that a single trait score should predict accurately a single behavior in a single situation, therefore, is to simplify an interaction episode to absurdity (Houts, Cook, & Shadish, 1986). At minimum, many different traits of many different kinds (e.g., motivational, stylistic, and ability traits) are probably involved in determining any single behavior (Cattell, 1965). McClelland (1951, 1981), for example, has consistently argued that, to predict a person's behavior accurately, the personologist must obtain reliable measurements on at least three different kinds of personality variables: (1) *traits* (which McClelland limits to basic stylistic variables, such as extraversion, which are typically assessed via self-report questionnaires, as in Chapter 5), (2) *schemas* (conscious cognitive variables such as values, attitudes, and beliefs, which we will examine in Chapter 9), and (3) *motives* (unconscious goal states that are assessed via open-ended fantasy measures, which we will examine in Chapter 11).

According to McClelland, then, the accurate prediction of behavior requires the assessment of personality dispositions at three different *levels*—the levels of trait, schema, and motive. The problem of levels is a thorny one in personality psychology. It applies not only to the typical predic*tors* of behavior (e.g., traits and other personality dispositions themselves) but also to those behaviors to be predic*ted*. Psychologists may employ different *levels of analysis* in their observations of behavior. Imagine a study in which psychologists observe people as they discuss a controversial social issue (Funder & Colvin, 1991). In search of behavioral consistencies, the psychologist may operate at a very concrete level and record each time a subject laughs, smiles, or makes a joke. Or the psychologist may work at a more abstract and psychologically meaningful level and rate reliably the extent to which the subject "behaves in a cheerful manner." Similarly, observation may focus on the concrete instances of "asking dumb questions" or "mumbling responses," or it may focus on the more abstract level of "exhibiting an awkward interpersonal style." It is certainly true that the observer must engage in a greater degree of interpretation at abstract as opposed to concrete levels of behavioral observation. But if it can be done with high levels of reliability, the coding of more abstract and psychologically meaningful categories of behavior often tends to reveal a greater degree of behavioral consistency than is the case when observations are done at the more concrete levels (Block, 1971, 1977; Funder & Colvin, 1991).

The issue of levels is but one example of how the prediction of behavior through traits, situations, and their interactions is a very complex affair. The problem of complexity in human behavior is a major theme in three influential responses in the 1970s and 1980s to the person–situation debate. These three involve (1) the role of *moderator variables* in personality prediction, (2) the power of *aggregation* in showing consistency across situations, and (3) the efficacy of personality *typologies* in revealing the coherent organization and evolution of personality traits and their links to behavior.

Predicting Some of the People Some of the Time

The heart of Mischel's critique is that people are not consistent in their behavior across different situations. Is it possible, however, that this conclusion is true for only some people? Are some people relatively consistent in their behavior across different situations while certain other people are highly inconsistent? If this is true, then lumping the two types of people together may fool us into concluding that *everybody* is inconsistent.

This intuitively appealing response to the Mischel critique was offered by Darryl Bem (Bem & Allen, 1974) in an influential article, "On Predicting Some of the People Some of the Time." In traditional trait research, argued Bem, the investigator assumes that the trait scored for each subject is equally relevant to all subjects. In other words, while some people may score high and some low on a measure of the trait "friendliness," we generally assume that all people in the study recognize friendliness to be a trait that is germane to their lives. Bem suggests that this assumption may be wrong. For some people (regardless of how they score), friendliness may not be a relevant dimension and may, therefore, not be linked in a consistent fashion to friendly behavior. Significant correlations between behavior and traits are likely only among people for whom a trait is especially relevant: these people are the "some of the people" whose behavior we can predict "some of the time." The other people are less predictable.

Some studies support Bem's position (Bem & Allen, 1974; Cheek, 1982; Kenrick & Stringfield, 1980; Underwood & Moore, 1981). In investigations of this kind, the researchers typically administer a conventional measure of personality traits and a second measure asking subjects to judge how consistent their behavior is with respect to each of the traits assessed. Those who report that their behavior is consistent with a particular trait (regardless of their score on the trait) are identified as the people for whom the trait is especially relevant. It is for these people only that the actual trait score is assumed to be a good predictor of behavior. Employing this strategy, Bem and Allen (1974) found that consistency between self-reports and peer ratings on the traits of "friendliness" and "conscientiousness" was much higher for individuals who reported consistent behavior compared to individuals who reported low consistency. Kenrick and Stringfield (1980) obtained similar results employing Cattell's 16 source traits. For this study, Table 7.1 shows the intercorrelations of the subjects' personality ratings made by the subjects themselves, by their parents, and by peers for those traits deemed by the subjects to be "most consistent" and "least consistent" in their lives. The correlations between self-ratings and the parent/peer-ratings on traits deemed by the subject to be especially consistent are generally quite high, around +.61. For traits considered by the subjects to be inconsistent, on the other hand, the correlations are much lower.

Research that fits under the heading of "predicting some of the people some of the time" makes use of what psychologists call **moderator variables** (Ghiselli, 1956). In a nutshell, studies employing moderator variables are based on the idea that a relation between two variables is moderated or influenced by a third. For example, the relation between Variable A (a self-report measure of friendliness)

Table 7.1

Intercorrelations of Personality Ratings[a]

	Trait[b]	
Raters	**Most Consistent**	**Least Consistent**
1. Self × Parent	.62 (75)	.16 (76)
2. Self × Peer	.61 (77)	.12 (70)
3. Parent × Peer	.61 (64)	.39 (62)

[a]Ratings made by self, parents, and peers for self-chosen most- and least-consistent traits.
[b]Numbers in parentheses are numbers of subjects.
Modified from Kenrick & Stringfield (1980, p. 95).

and Variable B (friendly behavior observed by others) is moderated by Variable C (the "relevance" of the trait friendliness for the individual's life, as judged by the individual). Variable C is the moderator. In the simplest case, we might divide subjects on the Variable C distribution into two groups: those for whom the trait friendliness is relevant (say, above the median or middle score in the distribution of scores on self-reported trait relevance) and those for whom the trait friendliness is irrelevant (below the median). For the first group (relatively high relevance on friendliness), the relation between Variable A and Variable B may be strong: one can predict accurately friendly behavior (Variable B) from the level of friendliness trait (Variable A). For the second group (relatively low relevance on friendliness), the relation between Variable A and Variable B may be weak: one cannot predict accurately friendly behavior (Variable B) from scores on friendliness trait (Variable A). In this way, then, the score on Variable C determines the extent to which the behavior is predictable from the trait score.

The same logic can be used in a study in which Variable A is a self-rating on friendliness (or any other personality trait) and Variable B is a peer-rating on friendliness (or any other corresponding personality trait). Again, Variable C (trait relevance) may moderate the relation between A and B, such that self-ratings and peer-ratings on friendliness are highly correlated among those individuals for whom the trait is relevant (Variable C) and only weakly correlated or noncorrelated among those individuals for whom the trait is not relevant, as we saw in the study by Kenrick and Stringfield (1980). The same logic can also be used with other kinds of moderator variables, that is, other kinds of Variable C. For example, Wymer and Penner (1985) have shown that the consistency between self-ratings (Variable A) and peer-ratings (Variable B) of traits is significantly moderated by

Continued on p. 371

Traits as Categories of Acts
The Act–Frequency Approach

As we saw in Chapter 5, Gordon Allport (1937, 1961) believed that traits were "neuropsychic structures" that accounted for the consistency of human behavior over time and from one situation to the next. While the psychologist could not directly observe the physiological reality of the trait as manifested in the central nervous system, he or she could still make inferences about the functional effects of that reality from observing the person's behavior, Allport thought. While not all trait theorists have agreed with Allport (and Eysenck, as well) that traits must have a neuropsychic substrate, most have held to the idea that traits are internal *dispositions* that, in one way or another, have a real influence on behavior. It was indeed the dispositional view of traits toward which Mischel's critique was squarely aimed. As Mischel saw it, trait scores indicating the relative strength of a person's internal disposition of friendliness, for example, are of little use in predicting the extent to which he or she will engage in friendly behavior in any given situation.

David Buss and Kenneth Craik (1983, 1984) have fashioned an interesting response to the Mischel critique of traits that begins with a repudiation of the idea that traits are indeed internal dispositions. According to the **act-frequency** approach to personality, traits are merely convenient language categories for the organization of discrete behavioral acts. As such, traits do not influence behavior per se. Rather, traits *are the behaviors*. Essentially, a trait consists of the acts that make it up. In

the case of extraversion, for example, the trait refers to a set of acts—such as, "I danced in front of a crowd" and "I entered into a conversation with a group I didn't know"—that are grouped together as members of a family. Some acts are more central members than others. And different trait families may overlap, sharing the same acts.

How do we know which acts belong to which families? Buss and Craik begin by asking people to generate lists of acts for numerous trait categories—such as, gregariousness, submissiveness, quarrelsomeness, agreeableness, and dominance. Thus, for the category of dominance, someone might be asked to "think of the three most dominant females [or males] you know" and "write down five acts or behaviors they have performed that reflect or exemplify their dominance" (Buss & Craik, 1984, p. 251).

After a composite list of about 100 discrete acts is generated, raters then judge the prototypicality of each act with respect to that category. A highly prototypical act is a "best example," the "clearest case," an "ideal instance" of the category (Rosch, 1975). Taking an example from the natural world, an "apple" is seen by virtually everybody as a highly prototypical fruit, whereas a tomato is less prototypical, even though it is still technically a fruit. An apple seems to embody more of the essence of "fruitness" than does a tomato. Other highly prototypical fruits probably include oranges and grapefruits; pumpkins are less prototypical. According to Buss and Craik, traits like "dominance" and "extraversion" are like fruits in that we can understand them as *fuzzy sets* that are not discrete and separate but rather fade into one another, as fruits may fade into vegetables in our minds. The most prototypical member of a fuzzy set seems to reside at the center of the set whereas less prototypical ones exist on the periphery, sometimes overlapping into other fuzzy sets. Similarly, certain acts are highly prototypical of extraversion (such as, talking to strangers on a subway car) whereas other acts are more peripheral and may even shade into other dispositions. (Is arguing with a professor an example of extraversion or dominance?)

Viewing personality traits as families of acts, the personologist may be able to perform certain kinds of analyses that have typically eluded trait approaches, suggest Buss and Craik. For example, one may examine the absolute *change* in a personality trait over time within a particular person's life *without making reference to how that person compares to others* (Lamiell, 1981). If Sylvia performs an average of 8.4 dominance acts per day as a freshman in college and 16.4 dominance acts per day as a senior, then we can conclude that she has shown an almost twofold increase in dominance over a four-year span of her life. In that a traditional trait measure provides a relative rather than absolute reading on a trait dimension, traditional measures cannot make for conclusions like these. Similarly, one might imagine how the act-frequency approach could be employed in cross-cultural research. Are Italians more gregarious than Norwegians? For Buss and Craik, the

answer would lie in comparing the average number of gregarious acts performed by native-born citizens of Italy and Norway, respectively.

Act-frequencies may also be used in conjunction with traditional trait measures. For example, Table 7.A1 shows the results of a study utilizing traditional trait measures and reports of act frequencies to test the *prototypicality gradient hypothesis*. This hypothesis essentially states that a trait measure should be more successful in predicting behaviors that are highly prototypical of the corresponding dimension than behaviors that are less prototypical. In this study, 186 married people (1) completed standard measures of "traits" and (2) reported how many times they had shown each of 100 acts previously selected as indicators of those traits during the previous 3 months. The 100 acts were broken down into four groups, ranging from the "most prototypical" (Group I) to the "least prototypical" (Group IV) acts. In addition, the subjects' spouses also reported the frequency of each of the 100 acts displayed by their partners. The strongest correlations are between traditional trait measures and the frequency of the most prototypical acts (under Column I). As acts within a trait category become less prototypical, they are predicted less well by the trait score.

In conclusion, by stripping traits of their status as causal dispositions, the act-frequency approach would seem at first to agree with Mischel that traits are not especially influential in the prediction of behavior. But in redefining traits as summary

 Table 7.A.1

Correlations Between Trait Scores and Frequency of Prototypical Acts

Scale	Act Data Source	Prototypicality of Acts[a]			
		I	II	III	IV
Extraversion					
Eysenck Personality Questionnaire	Self	.57***	.54***	.27***	.28***
	Observer (spouse)	.45***	.40***	.22***	.16*
Sociability					
(California Psychological Inventory)	Self	.47***	.50***	.28***	.24***
	Observer (spouse)	.39***	.42***	.14	.16
Affiliation					
(Personality Research Form)	Self	.45***	.42***	.27***	.21**
	Observer	.36***	.27***	.16*	.18*

[a]Acts range from "most prototypical" (I) to "least prototypical" (IV).
$N = 180; -*p < .05; **p < .01; ***p < .001$.
Adapted from Buss & Craik (1984, p. 273).

categories of discrete acts, Buss and Craik seem to be taking the situation out of the equation as well, a result that flies in the face of Mischel's situationist view. According to the act-frequency approach, counting acts in different trait categories over time gives the clearest reading on personality and enables the researcher to predict what people will do in the future. In general, a person who exhibits a large number of dominance acts, for example, is likely to continue to do so, enabling the psychologist to predict his behavior with some degree of accuracy, even without information about situations.

Taking acts out of situations and assigning them to simple trait categories, however, may also exact a price. Critics of the act-frequency approach question the wisdom of disregarding the *meanings* of particular acts in particular *contexts* (Block, 1989; Moser, 1989). They question whether the retrospective methods used to measure act frequencies are as psychometrically sound as traditional trait-scale items. And they wonder whether a purely descriptive account of traits—as mere summaries of discrete acts—can further our *understanding* of what makes behavior relatively consistent or inconsistent from one situation to the next, and over time.

Continued from p. 367

the variable of *communication skill* (Variable C, the moderator variable). People with good communication skills rate themselves on traits (Variable A) in ways similar to the way they are rated by others (Variable B). Wymer and Penner have also shown that *inner-directedness* can be an important moderator variable. People who value their "inner selves"—their own beliefs and attitudes, thus showing more inner-directedness than other-directedness—behave in ways that are highly consistent with their trait scores. They are more predictable (Variable A is highly correlated with Variable B) than subjects who are other-directed. Wymer and Penner conclude that inner-directed people are generally "unwilling, unable, or both to change their behavior in response to situational demands" (1985, p. 1002).

A key distinction in research with moderator variables is that between *person-specific* and *trait-specific* moderators (Chaplin, 1991; Koestner, Bernieri, & Zuckerman, 1989). Person-specific moderators are assumed to influence the relation between Variable A and Variable B *for all traits* in a given person. The logic is that some people (those "high" on Variable C) are more predictable overall than are other people (those "low" on Variable C). Moderator variables such as "communication skills" and "inner-directedness" are examples of person-specific moderators. Other person-specific moderators include "self-consciousness" and "self-monitoring" (see Chapter 10). By contrast, trait-specific moderators are based on the logic that some people are more predictable than other people *for some traits*. For example, John may be especially predictable (his trait score predicts his corresponding behavior) for the trait of friendliness, but he may not be especially predictable for the trait of conscientiousness (his trait score does not predict well his behavior).

Roy Baumeister and Dianne Tice have coined the term **metatraits** to refer to trait-specific moderators (Baumeister & Tice, 1988; Tice, 1989). A metatrait is "the trait of having vs. not having a particular trait" (Baumeister & Tice, 1988, p. 573). People who are *traited* "have" the trait in question, and thus their behavior should be predictable from their trait score. People who are *untraited* "do not have" the trait in question, and thus their behavior should not be predictable from their trait score. Baumeister and Tice suggest that one index of traitedness is the degree of variability that a person exhibits in responding to individual items on a particular trait scale. As an example, imagine two people—Jennifer and Rebecca—who both score "moderately high" (say, about a 7 on a scale ranging from 1 to 10) on the trait conscientiousness. In Jennifer's case, her responses to the individual items on the measure are consistently in the moderately high range, around a 7 throughout. By contrast, Rebecca arrives at the total score of 7 by giving some extremely high responses on some items (scores of 9 and 10) and some relatively low-to-medium responses on some other items (scores of 4 and 5). Rebecca's total score averages ought to be the same as Jennifer's, but Rebecca shows much more variability in her responding on the trait test. According to Baumeister and Tice, Rebecca's high variability suggests that she is relatively "untraited" on conscientiousness: she does not "have" this trait to the extent that Jennifer does. By virtue of her consistent responding from one item to the next, Jennifer is "traited" on conscientiousness. Therefore, even though Rebecca and

Jennifer have the same conscientiousness scores (they both score 7 on the average), Jennifer's conscientious behavior should be more predictable from her trait score than should Rebecca's conscientious behavior. For the traited Jennifer the link between the trait and behavior is closer, suggesting greater consistency in the domain of conscientiousness. For the untraited Rebecca, the link is not so close; she shows less consistency in this domain. However, it is entirely possible that for a different trait—say, extraversion—Rebecca is traited and Jennifer untraited.

Personality psychologists have proposed a number of trait-specific moderator variables. They include the aforementioned concept of "trait relevance" (How relevant is the trait in your life? Amelang & Borkenau, 1986) and the similar idea of self-reported "trait consistency" (How consistent are you on this trait? Bem & Allen, 1974), as well as "uniqueness" (How similar to other people are you on this trait? Zuckerman, Miyake, Koestner, Baldwin, & Osborne, 1991), and "observability" (How observable are the manifestations of this trait for you? Kenrick & Stringfield, 1980; Zuckerman, Bernieri, Koestner, & Rosenthal, 1989). Some research supports the notion that persons for whom the trait is especially relevant and observable and who see themselves as relatively consistent and unique with respect to the trait do indeed show more correspondence between their self-report trait scores and other indices of the trait (e.g., peer ratings, behavior).

Despite the success that some researchers have reported with trait-specific moderator variables, recent reviews of the empirical literature have tempered the early enthusiasm about the moderator approach (Chaplin, 1991; Chaplin & Goldberg, 1984). In general, research has shown that moderator effects are usually quite small, though often statistically significant. For example, Chaplin (1991) concludes that moderator effects in personality are rarely larger than the equivalent of a +.10 correlation. While even small moderator effects can be important and interesting, "moderator variables generally will not serve to transform weak relations among personalty variables into strong ones," Chaplin (1991) concludes (p. 143). Other researchers, by contrast, see more promise in the moderator approach (Zuckerman et al., 1989). In the overall, nonetheless, the concept of moderator variables suggests that behavior is more complexly determined than the Mischel critique might lead us initially to believe. Taking some of this complexity into consideration can improve, though perhaps only modestly, the ability of personality psychologists to predict behavior from traits.

Aggregating Behaviors

According to Mischel, traits do not work well in the prediction of behavior because behavior itself is not very consistent from one situation to the next. The lack of cross-situational consistency in behavior poses a formidable problem for trait theories. However, personality psychologist Seymour Epstein suggests a solution to the problem that is quite old and familiar, making that perennial observation that "sometimes the obvious escapes us." For Epstein and a number

Seymour Epstein

of personologists, the answer to the problem of cross-situational consistency in human behavior is quite simple and has been around for a long time. The answer is **aggregation** (Epstein, 1979, 1984, 1986).

To understand Epstein's argument, we have to recall from Chapter 5 how a psychologist might construct a questionnaire designed to measure a particular personality trait. That procedure involves generating a large pool of "items," which is then reduced through a number of different methods to an economical scale with maximum reliability and validity. Each item on the test is seen as contributing something to the test as a whole: each item "zeroes in on" the trait from a slightly different angle. Such "zeroing in" is necessary because a trait is a complex construct that might be manifested in a large number of ways, and no single item can successfully capture all the complexity. Therefore, psychologists get as close as they can to a "pure" measure of a trait, minimizing measurement error by constructing tests with multiple items—that is by aggregating test items. Even the simplest trait test, therefore, requires more than 1 or 2 items if it is to be

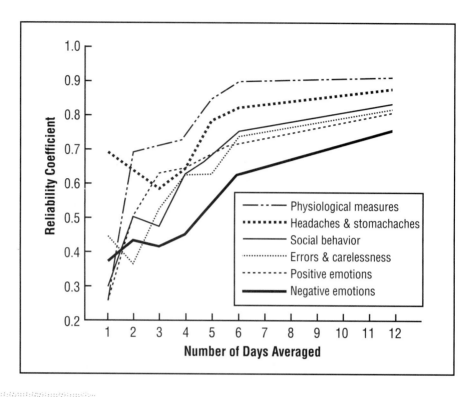

Figure 7.1

Stability Coefficients as a Function of the Number of Occasions Aggregated. (The correlations were obtained by correlating the mean of odd days with the mean of an equal number of even days. The values plotted are the means of the correlations for the variables in a category.)

Source: Epstein (1979).

considered reliable. Within reason and all other things being equal, the more items a test has, the more reliable it will be.

With this in mind, then, consider a typical personality study in which an investigator administers a questionnaire containing many items designed to assess a particular trait and correlates scores on that measure with a single instance of behavior, perhaps emitted under laboratory conditions, shown by the subject. While the trait measure itself may be highly reliable by virtue of aggregation of test items, the single measure of behavior is likely to be highly unreliable, unrepresentative, and saturated with error. It is no wonder, states Epstein, that Mischel's review of the personality literature finds so much inconsistency between trait measures and behavior. According to Epstein, Mischel has clearly identified a problem, but he has completely misinterpreted its primary cause. *Overall, the trait measures are sound; it is the single measures of behavior that are at fault.* Substantial consistency between trait scores and behavior across different situations should appear, Epstein maintains, when single instances of behavior are aggregated across many different situations. Trait scores, therefore, should predict consistent trends in behavior across different situations and over time.

Recent research suggests that Epstein is right. Figure 7.1 presents data from Epstein (1979) that show that the reliability of a number of different measures—ranging from headaches and stomachaches to social behavior—increases as the number of occasions upon which the measures are taken increases. Therefore, if we wish to obtain a reliable estimate of a person's blood pressure, positive mood, verbal eloquence, food consumption, smile frequency, or whatever, we will do better to sample the phenomenon in question on numerous occasions. As Figure 7.1 shows, the greater the degree of aggregation over time, the higher the reliability of the measure and the closer we get to a pure, stable, and representative estimate of behavior. Table 7.2 presents similar findings from a study by Moskowitz (1982).

In an impressive review, Rushton, Brainerd, and Presley (1983) illustrate the usefulness of aggregation in 12 different areas of psychological research. Especially interesting is their discussion of the famous Hartshorne and May (1928) study of moral behavior—a study that Mischel (1968) cited forcefully as an example of failure to find cross-situational consistency in behavior. Suggesting that the findings in this study have perennially been misinterpreted, Rushton argues that children's moral behavior manifested considerable consistency when appropriate behaviors were aggregated across different tests and situations. Although any single behavioral test of "honesty" correlated, on the average, only .20 with any other single test of honesty, much higher relationships were found when the measures were aggregated into meaningful groups and correlated with other combined behavioral measures, with teachers' ratings of the children, or with children's moral-knowledge scores. Often these correlations were on the order of .50 or .60. For example, a battery of tests measuring cheating by copying correlated +.52 with another battery of tests measuring other types of classroom cheating. Contrary to Mischel's conclusion, aggregation reveals that the children in the Hartshorne and May (1928) study showed consistent individual differences in cheating behavior. Thus, some children may indeed be consistently more honest than others.

Like any good research procedure, aggregation can be used wisely or foolishly (Epstein, 1986). For instance, merely lumping together different instances of behavior will not necessarily increase reliability in measurement. Aggregated items must "hang together" conceptually and/or empirically. In determining how to aggregate data, the personologist must keep clearly in mind what he or she wishes to learn from a particular study. Therefore, if a child's aggressive behavior towards her sister is a topic of interest, the researcher should not aggregate aggression across different targets (such as aggression towards father, mother,

 **Table 7.2**

Coefficients of Generalizability Dominance and Dependency Behaviors of Preschool Children

	Number of Weeks	
Broad Construct and Referents	**1**	**8**
Dominance	.34	.76***
Displace	.23	.70***
Command	.24	.71***
Suggest	.08	.40**
Direct	.10	.47***
Threat	.00	.00
Dependency	.07	.38*
Proximity	.16	.60***
Touch	.14	.23
Seek help	.07	.36*
Seek recognition	.06	.36*
Seek supervision	.02	.14

$N = 47$ children (9 children omitted because they were absent for 1 complete week); *$p < .05$; **$p < .01$; ***$p < .001$.
From Moskowitz (1982, p. 759).

brother, or pets) but should nevertheless aggregate across occasions with the sister. Similarly, if a researcher wishes to know how three different situations differentially influence altruistic behavior in college students, it would be useless to aggregate data across the different situations. In this case, the data should be aggregated across students—the researcher would seek to cancel out individual differences in students in order to see more clearly situational effects for all students in general.

Critics of aggregation argue that it bypasses rather than resolves the problem of cross-situational consistency in behavior (Mischel & Peake, 1982). When researchers aggregate behaviors across many different situations, they fail to show how a particular trait score predicts particular behavior in a particular situation. In settling for predicting general trends across a wide variety of situations, they sacrifice a great deal of precision with respect to any particular situation—precision that may come from a careful analysis of the exigencies in the situation itself. Recent research, however, has examined more precisely the extent to which different kinds of situations and different traits can be successfully examined through aggregation. The results of these studies suggest that aggregation works better across certain kinds of situations than across others.

For example, Moskowitz (1990) examined behavioral manifestations of dominance and friendliness in six different laboratory situations—two involving a same-sex friend, two involving a male stranger, and two involving a female stranger. Friendly and dominant behaviors were rated by observers and by the subjects themselves. As in other studies of aggregation, behavioral self- and observer-ratings pooled across the six situations were more strongly correlated with each other than were ratings made within any particular situation itself. But cross-situational consistency was stronger across certain situations than across others. In particular, the greatest degree of convergence between self-ratings and observer ratings on dominance and friendliness occurred *in the two situations with friends.* Less consistency was revealed across the four situations with strangers. Moskowitz concludes that "validity varies as a function of the situation" (p. 1105). Aggregating across different situations in which one is interacting with close friends reveals especially strong levels of cross-situational consistency in behavior. Aggregating across different situations in which one is interacting with strangers reveals less consistency. In the former case, behavior appears to be more strongly shaped by traits. In the latter, situational influences appear to be stronger.

Patterns of Traits Over Time

Throughout the person–situation debate, one of the staunchest advocates of personality consistency across situations has been Jack Block (1971, 1977, 1981). Consistency in personality is largely a function, Block argues, of the kind of data employed by personality researchers. Drawing from Cattell, Block presents a three-part classification of personality data, as can be seen in Table 7.3. **R data** are ratings of a person's behavior made by outside observers; **S data** are self-reports, as on well-validated personality inventories; **T data** are observations and other information obtained from controlled laboratory settings and other contrived situations in which the person is maneuvered into behaving in a certain way. According to Block, Mischel's critique of trait psychology is relevant only to T data, where evidence for consistency is spotty and uneven. However, well-designed personality research employing observer's ratings (R data) and self-reports (S data) shows marked cross-situational consistency and longitudinal stability. Because behavior is often measured with T data, however, many studies that attempt to relate R data or S data to behavior in standardized settings fail to show impressive consistency.

Much of Block's own work on personality has employed R data. An example of a powerful method of obtaining R data is the **California Q-sort.** This test consists of 100 statements about personality (such as "Is a genuinely dependable and responsible person," "Has a wide range of interests," "Is critical, skeptical, not

Table 7.3

Three-Part Classification of Personality Data

Type of Data	Description	Examples
R data	Information derived from observers' ratings and evaluation of individuals leading more or less natural lives.	Teacher ratings of children in nursery school; parent ratings of children's temperament; peer ratings of personality; psychologists' ratings of family interaction in natural settings.
S data	Information derived from self-observations and evaluation of one's own behavior, feelings, and personality characteristics.	Various self-report scales and standard personality inventories; the Adjective Check List, the MMPI, trait measures of Extraversion, Neuroticism, and Openness to Experience.
T data	Information derived from observations of behavior under structured and controlled conditions, as in the laboratory.	Experiments in which observations are made of aggressive, altruistic, or conforming behavior under a variety of controlled conditions.

easily impressed") that a rater sorts into nine different piles, ranging from those statements deemed by the rater to be most characteristic of the individual being rated to those being least characteristic.

Block trained 36 psychologists to compose Q-sorts for 70 men and 76 women at four different points in the subjects' lives. For the four different points in time, Block assembled four separate files, one each for information obtained about the subject when he or she was in early adolescence (age 13–14), late adolescence (15–17), his or her 30s, and his or her 40s. For each of the files, then, a trained psychologist composed a Q-sort for each subject, arranging the 100 personality descriptors into nine groups based on the wide variety of information on the subject contained in the file.

One reason the Q-sort is an appealing method for collecting R data is that each of the 100 items is grouped into one of the nine stacks with other items that are relatively equally characteristic of the same individual. Such a procedure enables the researcher to examine *patterns* of personality traits within the person. Comparing Q-sorts of the same individual over time, furthermore, allows the researcher to examine the longitudinal stability of these patterns. In his study,

Jack Block

Block (1981) also identified clusters of individuals manifesting similar patterns of traits over time, some of which are listed in Table 7.4. Each cluster represents a personality type, specified in terms of individuals displaying a particular pattern of personality traits that evolves in a particular fashion over time.

Underlying the personality types identified by Block are two central dimensions of personality that organize many different aspects of human functioning. The first is what Block calls **ego control** (Block & Block, 1980). Ego control is the extent to which a person typically modifies the expression of impulses. At one extreme of the ego control continuum are undercontrolled people who cannot inhibit their desires and impulses, cannot delay gratification for longer-term rewards. Such people may become enthusiastic about many different things in their lives, but their involvements are fleeting and frustrating. They are distractible and exploratory and seem to live a relatively impromptu rather than planned life. At the other extreme are overcontrolled people who are especially conforming and restrained. Their lives may be well scripted, but their inhibitions sometimes keep them from spontaneous joy and creativity. In general, it would

Continued on p. 382

Table 7.4

Eight Personality Types for Men and Women

Men	
Ego Resilients	Men who showed long-standing characterological integrity and resourcefulness. In junior high school, they were seen as dependable, productive, ambitious, bright, likable, philosophically inclined, and satisfied with self. In their 40s, they continued to exhibit many of these characteristics. As adults, they valued independence and objectivity, and they tended to evaluate situations in motivational terms. On the California Psychological Inventory (CPI), they scored high on dominance, self-acceptance, intellectual efficiency, and psychological mindedness.
Unsettled Under-controllers	Men who showed a pervasive impulsivity and changeableness. In junior high school they were seen as rebellious, talkative, hostile, unconventional, verbally fluent, irritable, and self-dramatizing. In their 40s, they continued to exhibit undercontrol, and were rated especially rebellious, hostile, deceitful, and unpredictable. On the CPI, they scored high on dominance and social presence, while scoring low on socialization, self-control, achievement via conformance and femininity. Over a 10-year span, they changed jobs more than other men.
Vulnerable Over-controllers	Men who showed consistently excessive restriction. In junior high they were seen as aloof, thin-skinned, ruminative, distrustful, submissive, and introspective. In their 40s, they were withdrawn, self-pitying, fearful, bothered by demands, and despondent. On the CPI, they scored high on over-control and good impression; they scored low on social presence and sense of well-being. They tended to remain bachelors.
Belated Adjusters	Men who showed a delayed but impressive adjustment. In junior high they were generally belligerent and negativistic. By contrast, however, as adults they were seen as dependable and sympathetic, though lower in achievement orientation than other men. These men often came from lower socioeconomic classes and showed improvement in their socioeconomic standing in adulthood.

Table 7.4 continued

Women

Female Prototypes

Women who personified many of the qualities and values prescribed by American society as ideal for women in the 1940s and 1950s. In junior high they were poised, likable, gregarious, cheerful, dependable, warm, productive, giving, sympathetic, and socially perceptive. In their 40s, they continued to show many of these qualities. On the CPI, they scored high on dominance, sociability, social presence, responsibility, and achievement via conformance. They tended to have more children than other women.

Vulnerable Under-controllers

Women who were "homogeneous in their unmodulated impulsivity of action and reaction coupled with a plaintive submissiveness that leaves them open to exploitation by others" (Block, 1981, p. 39). In junior high they were seen as undercontrolled, self-indulgent, changeable, limit-testing, irritable, hostile, brittle, and affected. In their 40s, they were undercontrolled, self-defeating, self-indulgent, socially obtuse, unconventional, and lacking in fastidiousness. On the CPI, they scored low on responsibility, socialization, femininity, and ego control. They married early, more often, and less satisfactorily compared to other women. They tended to smoke too much and be somewhat overweight.

Hyperfeminine Repressives

Women who showed a repressive and emotionally fitful adaptation and an ambivalent expression of sexuality. In junior high they were seen as feminine, repressive, submissive, dependable, dependent, and concerned with physical appearance. In their 40s, they continued to be highly concerned with their bodies and physical well-being; they were withdrawing, fearful, brittle, distrustful, self-pitying, moralistic, negativistic, and overcontrolled. On the CPI, they scored high on psychoneurosis and neurotic over-control; lower on dominance, social presence, tolerance, flexibility, and achievement via independence. They have had significantly more menopausal surgery.

Cognitive Copers

Women who showed gradual improvement in adjustment over the years. In junior high they were seen as thin-skinned, uncomfortable with uncertainty, and ruminative. In adulthood, by contrast, they were viewed as introspective, aesthetically sensitive, warm, talkative, straightforward, and valuing independence. These women tended to pursue intellectual interests.

From Block (1971, 1981).

Continued from p. 379
seem that a rating somewhere in the middle of the ego control continuum is one that best fits contemporary American views concerning appropriate adaptation to life and mental health.

The second major dimension underlying Block's types is **ego resiliency.** This is the capacity to *modify* one's typical level of ego control—in either direction—to adapt to the demands of a given situation. In contrast to ego control, ego resiliency would appear to be a characteristic for which "more is better." People who are high on ego resiliency are resourceful and flexible and able to adapt to a wide range of life challenges. In a recent study of the extent to which adolescents are able to delay immediate gratification to obtain longer-term benefits, Funder and Block (1989) found that ego resiliency, ego control, and intelligence all contributed to the significant prediction of delay behavior. Teenagers who scored high on Q-sort ratings suggestive of high ego resiliency and strong (less impulsive) ego control, as well as those who scored high on measures of IQ, tended to reveal the highest levels of adaptive delay behavior.

Taking a somewhat different tack, Norma Haan (1981) has analyzed longitudinal data obtained from 136 adults, some of whom were included in Block's (1981) analysis, for developmental trends in six basic personality factors: *cognitively invested* (verbally fluent, intellectual, philosophically inclined, achievement-oriented), *emotionally under/overcontrolled* (highly volatile and dramatic *versus* calm and restricted), *open/closed self* (self-aware and insightful *versus* conventional and repressive), *nurturant/hostile* (warm and responsive *versus* cold and suspicious), *under/overcontrolled heterosexual* (uninhibited *versus* inhibited in the realm of sexual expression), and *self-confident.* Haan's statistical analyses showed that Q-sort scores on these six dimensions were relatively stable for both men and women over time but more stable for women. Men were more likely than women to show significant change on these dimensions, especially between late adolescence and adulthood. Over time, both men and women, furthermore, appeared to become more cognitively invested, more open to self, more nurturant, and more self-confident. Sexual expressiveness, on the other hand, appeared to reach high levels in late adolescence, drop to lower levels when the subjects were in their 30s, and then rise again to surprisingly strong levels when the subjects reached their 40s.

Integrating the work of Block and Haan with a number of other approaches to personality structure, including the Big Five personality traits, York and John (1992) have developed a new typology of women's personality at midlife—what they call "the four faces of Eve." York and John argue that personality types should be defined as prototypes rather than discrete categories of traits. As such, types lack clear boundaries but rather shade into each other. While some persons exemplify the central features of a given type, other people appear to reside on the fuzzy boundaries between types, as mixtures or blends that are especially difficult to characterize in a clear-cut fashion.

York and John analyzed longitudinal data on 103 graduates (from the years 1958 and 1960) of an exclusive women's college. Included in the data were followup questionnaires administered in 1981, when the women were in their early-to-mid-40s. York and John employed a statistical procedure called "inverse factor analysis," whereby subjects rather than variables are intercorrelated across a wide range of personality characteristics. In the current study, the procedure provided a numerical estimate of the extent to which each of the 103 women was well represented on each of four "person factors": *Individuated, Traditional, Conflicted,* and *Assured.* In this person-centered rather than variable-centered approach, therefore, each woman in the study could be viewed in terms of "how much" of her personality was well captured by each of the four factors. Some women proved to be "exemplars" of particular factors—"pure" Individuated, Traditional, Conflicted, or Assured types. Other women, by contrast, expressed characteristics that were spread across a number of factors. For example, one woman might appear on the border between Individuated and Traditional; another might show equal elements of three types.

Table 7.5 lists the items from the California Q-set that were most and least characteristic of each of the four person factors. The "factor scores" indicate how strongly a descriptor is associated with the type. A high positive number suggests a strong positive association; a "high" (in terms of absolute value) negative number suggests a strong negative association. Exemplars of the Individuated type combined strong ambitions in life with interpersonal warmth and sensitivity. They tended to manifest the highest levels of ego resiliency of all four types and relatively low levels of ego control, suggesting that they were spontaneous and uninhibited in their expression of impulses but that they knew well when to hold themselves back and when to let go. Of all the types, they were the most flexible and adaptive in the expression of their feelings, needs, and desires. With respect to the Big Five traits, they tended to score high on measures of extraversion (*E*), agreeableness (*A*), and openness to experience (*O*). By contrast, the women who exemplified best the Traditional person factor expressed characteristics indicative of high levels of ego control, as well as high scores on the Big Five trait conscientiousness (*C*). Like the Individuated women, the Traditionals were rated as especially agreeable (*A*), but unlike the Individuated women they expressed very conservative values about the proper role of women in contemporary society. While they were described as especially giving and sympathetic, the Traditionals were also more prone to feelings of guilt than were women exemplifying the other types.

Exemplars of the Conflicted person factor consistently showed the lowest levels of ego resiliency and highest levels of neuroticism (*N*). They appeared less satisfied with themselves than the other types; they were described as anxious, hostile, and aloof. Finally, the Assured women appeared to be the most emotionally stable of the four groups, though their stability hinted at narcissism and an interpersonally detached approach to life. They were the most confident, rational, productive, and skeptical women in the group. They showed relatively high levels of ego resiliency and conscientiousness (*C*) and the lowest levels of neuroticism (*N*). They were the least likely to suffer from guilt and doubt. But they were also the least likely of all the types to engage in fantasy and introspection.

Table 7.5

Factor Scores of the California Q-Set Items Most and Least Characteristic of Each of Four Person Factors

Item Number/ Factor	Factor Score	Item Number/ Factor	Factor Score
Factor 1: Individuated		**Factor 2: Traditional**	
Characteristic		**Characteristic**	
71. Has high aspirations	2.2	11. Is protective	2.2
96. Values independence	2.1	2. Is dependable	2.1
16. Is introspective	1.8	5. Is giving	2.1
8. Has high intellectual capacity	1.7	25. Overcontrols needs	2.0
		7. Has conservative values	1.9
52. Behaves assertively	1.5	17. Is sympathetic	1.7
35. Has warmth	1.5	93. Has a feminine style	1.7
3. Has wide interests	1.5	47. Is guilt prone	1.6
66. Has aesthetic sensitivity	1.3		
Uncharacteristic		**Uncharacteristic**	
30. Gives up, withdraws	−2.3	62. Is nonconforming	−2.5
14. Is genuinely submissive	−2.1	65. Pushes limits	−2.3
97. Is affectively bland	−2.0	53. Undercontrols needs	−2.2
42. Avoids action	−2.0	99. Is histrionic	−2.2
7. Has conservative values	−1.9	94. Expresses hostility directly	−1.9
55. Is self-defeating	−1.6	37. Is guileful, deceitfull	−1.9
78. Is self-pitying	−1.6	67. Is self-indulgent	−1.8
37. Is guileful, deceitful	−1.6	50. Is unpredictable	−1.7

In the wake of the person-situation debate, a growing number of personality psychologists are focusing their empirical efforts on personality typologies—patterns of traits organized over time (e.g., Mumford, Stokes, & Owens, 1990; Ozer & Gjerde, 1989). Behavior would appear to be too complex to be viewed as the straightforward function of a single trait in interaction with an immediate environment. And personality itself would appear to be too complex to be well captured by either single traits or situational histories. It is in the patternings of traits, argue Block and others, that the complexity of personality organized over time and across situations can best be perceived and appreciated.

Item Number/ Factor	Factor Score	Item Number/ Factor	Factor Score
Factor 3: Conflicted		**Factor 4: Assured**	

Characteristic		**Characteristic**	
72. Questions self-adequacy	2.6	24. Is rational, objective	2.2
68. Is basically anxious	2.3	52. Behaves assertively	2.2
38. Is hostile	2.0	74. Is satisfied with self	2.0
12. Is defensive	1.8	48. Is distant, aloof	2.0
74. Is satisfied with self	2.0	91. Is power oriented	2.0
40. Is generally fearful	1.8	1. Is critical, skeptical	1.7
48. Is distant, aloof	2.0	26. Is productive	1.6
22. Lacks personal meaning	1.4	96. Values independence	1.5
Uncharacteristic		**Uncharacteristic**	
75. Has clear-cut personality	−2.4	90. Is philosophical	−2.3
54. Is gregarious	−2.1	47. Is guilt prone	−1.8
74. Is satisfied with self	−2.1	16. Is introspective	−1.8
84. Is cheerful	−1.8	21. Arouses nurturance	−1.5
33. Is calm, relaxed	−1.8	46. Daydreams, fantasizes	−1.5
77. Is straightforward	−1.5	40. Is generally fearful	−1.4
29. Gives advice, reassurance	−1.4	45. Has a brittle ego	−1.4
83. Is insightful	−1.4	19. Seek reassurance	−1.3
50. Is unpredictable	−1.7		

From York & John (1992, p. 499).

Behavior Is Contextual

A central message of Mischel's critique of personality psychology was that behavior is contextual. To put it simply, if the major predictors of a person's behavior are traits and situations, and if traits do a poor job of predicting behavior, then we are left with situations—that is, we are left with the environmental contexts that

Continued on p. 388

The Type A Personality

Block's (1971, 1981) analyses of personality-trait clusters that develop over time resulted ultimately in a taxonomy of personality **types.** Personality psychologists have traditionally employed types to describe persons who share similarities on a *group* of related traits. The use of types in personality theorizing has both advantages and drawbacks. One advantage, as we see in Block's work, is that a type approach allows the researcher to discern patterns among *many* traits in a person's life, thus enabling the personologist to study "more of" the whole person at once. On the other hand, types can lead to gross oversimplification as the personologist attempts to pigeonhole each individual into one type of person or another. Therefore, the use of types has always been somewhat controversial in personality psychology.

Despite the controversy, recent years have witnessed an increasing interest in conceptualizing persons in terms of personality types (Block, 1981; Carlson, 1980; Loevinger, 1976). One extremely popular approach, whose origins lie outside the field of personality psychology proper, is the classification of people as either Type A or Type B. The **Type A** personality refers to a constellation of overlapping characteristics including high ambitiousness, hostility, time-urgency, competitiveness, impatience, and irritability. The Type A person adopts a hard-driving and fast-paced style of life, reflected even in characteristically rapid and emphatic speech styles.

The Type A person strives to accomplish as much as possible in a short period of time.

Though we all know that our time on earth is limited, the Type A person seems to experience this truism more acutely and appears, therefore, driven to achieve more and more in what little time remains. The Type B person, on the other hand, is relatively easygoing and relaxed. The distinction between Type A and Type B is most significant for its documented linkage to coronary heart disease: Type As are viewed as being at higher risk for heart attacks than Type Bs.

The Type A syndrome was originally identified and described by two cardiologists, Meyer Friedman and Ray Rosenman, who observed that many of their heart patients seemed especially impatient, hurried, and tense. They proposed that a constellation of personality traits, labelled "Type A," may indeed predispose individuals to be at risk for heart disease. Subsequent epidemiological studies bore out their suspicions. In one eight-year longitudinal study of 3000 men, Type As had over twice the incidence of heart disease compared to Type Bs, even after other risk factors concerning diet and health were taken into consideration (Rosenman, Brand, Jenkins, Friedman, Straus, & Wurm, 1975). Another investigation (Jenkins, Zyanski, & Rosenman, 1976) found that Type A was a better predictor of heart attacks than were cholesterol level or cigarette smoking. It is generally believed that the link to heart disease comes from the Type A person's enhanced cardiovascular and neuroendocrine responsiveness to certain kinds of stressors in daily life, especially those concerning challenge and demands for achievement. Indeed, Type A men show markedly faster heart rate (Ortega & Pipal, 1984) and higher systolic blood pressure (Holmes, McGiley, & Houston, 1984) when working on especially challenging laboratory tasks, compared to Type Bs. Further, some believe that Type As actively seek such challenge: "Type A persons do not simply respond to challenges and demands; they seek and create them through their cognitions and actions" (Smith & Anderson, 1986, p. 1166).

Psychologists and medical researchers have conducted hundreds of studies on Type A. Most of them employ a standard questionnaire called the Jenkins Activity Survey (JAS) or a structured interview to measure the Type A syndrome (Matthews, 1982). One central theme in the literature is that Type A persons seem to manifest an inordinately strong need for control (Glass, 1977; Strube & Werner, 1985). Many studies show that, when faced with a difficult but nonetheless solvable task, Type A persons will strive with great persistence to master it; when such efforts fail, they tend to take defeat very hard (Brunson & Matthews, 1981; Schwartz, Burish, O'Rourke, & Holmes, 1986). Type As tend to take more credit for their own successes than do Type Bs (Strube, 1985; Strube & Boland, 1986), and they tend to be seen by others as generally in control and masterful (Strube, Lott, Heilizer, & Gregg, 1986). The desire to master and to control the world is evident in Type As' approach to academic demands and the challenges of their profession. Ovcharchyn, Johnson, and Petzel (1981) found that Type A college freshmen saw class grades as more important, took more credit hours in their first semester, and actually received higher grades at the end of the semester, compared to Type B students. Surveying a number of professions, Mettlin (1976) found that Type A was a significant predictor of higher aspirations and rapidly achieved status in one's field. Type A psychologists publish more scientific articles (quantity) and are cited more frequently by other psychologists (a rough index of quality of scientific work), compared to Type B psychologists. Kelly and Houston

(1985) found that Type A among women was associated with higher occupational achievement but also with greater reported stress and tension. Similarly, Howard, Cunningham, and Rechnitzer (1977) found that Type A managers of large companies made more money than Type B managers but also reported less satisfaction with their jobs. The relation between Type A on the one hand and happiness and life satisfaction on the other is, however, unclear. For instance, it is difficult to reconcile results indicating greater stress and lower job satisfaction among Type As with a recent study by Strube, Berry, Goza, and Fennimore (1985).These researchers found that Type A is associated with overall greater well-being among *younger* adults, perhaps because it leads to an active and successful life, but less well-being among *older* adults, who face greater limitations in the range and level of activities.

What are the developmental origins of Type A? Strube and Ota (1982) found that Type As tend to be first-borns, especially in large families. Other researchers implicate child-rearing practices emphasizing extremely high performance standards and punitive or hostile control of the child's behavior (Matthews, 1978; Price, 1982). In one study, 186 college men completed the JAS and the Parent Behavior Form, an instrument designed to assess perceptions of a variety of parental child-rearing attitudes and practices (McCranie & Simpson, 1986). Type A men were significantly more likely than Type Bs to indicate that their parents placed high emphasis on achievement, expecting competence in a wide variety of areas and continually demanding higher performance. They were also more likely to describe one or both parents as strict, as using frequent physical punishment, and as frequently communicating disapproval when the child failed.

Continued from p. 385
shape and give expression to behavior and within which behaviors are observed. If behavior is more situationally specific than cross-situationally consistent, then the personologist who desires to predict behavior as it is exhibited in interaction episodes should focus on the external, environmental aspects of the interaction. As we have seen, some personologists have responded to the Mischel critique and the subsequent person–situation debate by underscoring the complexity and multiplicity of the person's behavior. However, a second general response has been to redouble efforts to understand the contextuality of human action (Gergen, 1982; Veroff, 1983). If behavior is complexly determined, it is likewise highly contextual. But what does this mean?

At any given moment in a person's life, his or her behavior is "situated" in a number of overlapping contexts. Another way of saying this is that *the person is in more than one situation at a time.* Thus, if any single episode of behavior is

As provocative and compelling as many of the findings on Type A seem, certain limitations to and problems with the concept have recently been identified. First, as a personality typology, the Type A/Type B distinction leaves much to be desired. Exactly what traits make up the core of Type A is unclear (Matthews, 1984), with some researchers pointing to the need for control as central and others suggesting that hostility or time-urgency is really what Type A is all about (Heilbrun, Palchanis, & Friedberg, 1986). Furthermore, Type B is also extremely vague and does not seem to represent a coherent grouping of characteristics. Friedman, Hall, and Harris (1985) even suggest the possibility of two distinct "types" of Type A—one repressed and tense and the other dynamic and charismatic—and two types of Type B—one healthy and easy-going and the other submissive and prone to illness.

Second, measurement of Type A is controversial, with some researchers preferring the JAS and others insisting that interviews are paramount. The two assessment methods, however, often do not agree and thus should not be used interchangeably (Matthews, Krantz, Dembroski, & MacDougall, 1982).

Finally, there is mounting evidence that the link between Type A and coronary disease is not as robust as previously believed. In a recent longitudinal study incorporating measures of blood pressure, cholesterol levels, smoking habits, and other risk factors in 12,000 men, no direct relation between Type A and heart disease was found (Fischman, 1987)—though critics of this study point to fundamental flaws in its methodology. In any case, we still do not know exactly what the Type A syndrome is and precisely how it relates or does not relate to heart disease.

multiply determined by numerous traits, motives, skills, values, and beliefs within the person, it is also influenced by an equally large and complex variety of situations coexisting simultaneously outside the person. The person's behavior is embedded in a *social ecology* (Bronfenbrenner, 1979). The social ecology for a person's behavior consists of the many simultaneous contexts within which the behavior must be understood. These contexts include the proximal or immediate setting in which the behavior is displayed and larger, more distal contexts that provide behavior with a variety of meanings.

For the most part, personality psychologists have focused on the proximal settings, whether they be the immediate situational factors that can be measured in the laboratory or the concrete and contemporaneous features of specific everyday events—classrooms, parties, dinners, sporting events—that can be described by participants in or observers of the situation. Research guided by theories of modern interactionism (Krahe, 1992) tends to examine how personal dispositions interact with proximal features of situations to produce behavior. A few psychologists—along with sociologists and anthropologists—have sought to examine more encompassing and distal contexts for human behavior, contexts such as the family system, race and social class, culture and ideology, and history.

What Is a Situation?

Rudolph Moos (1973, 1974, 1976) provides a useful starting point for considering the surprisingly difficult question of "What is a situation?" Moos formulated a six-part taxonomy of human environments, identifying the various features that can be taken into consideration in conceptualizing a particular situation: (1) dimensions of the physical ecology, (2) behavior settings or episodes, (3) organizational structure, (4) characteristics of persons in the situation, (5) organizational climate, and (6) functional and reinforcement properties. Table 7.6 summarizes the scheme and provides examples.

Barbara Krahe (1992) offers an alternative outline that arranges situational characteristics into a nested hierarchy. At the lowest level of the hierarchy are the *situational stimuli,* such as single objects or acts inherent in a situation that are meaningful in their own right. For example, in the situation "taking an examination at the end of the term," situational stimuli would include a specific array of tables and chairs, pens and paper, fellow students sitting in the room, and so on. At the next level, we may view *situational events* or episodes. In the examination example, these might be "being told to begin the exam" and "answering the essay questions at the end of the exam." At the third level, events combine into an overall picture, or *total situation.* What is characteristic of the total situation is its unique occurrence in time and space. The examination might be the first one a student takes in her college career, or, say, the only examination she has ever taken in a psychology course. At the next level up, situations are defined in generalized terms, such as "exams in general." While each exam may be unique, most may share certain features defining the essence of "examness." Finally, at the fifth and most encompassing level, we may talk about *life situations.* According to Krahe (1992) these are "the totality of social and physical factors which affect the person and are affected by his or her actions at a certain stage of development" (p. 196). The life situation pertaining to our example of the college examination might be defined as "being an undergraduate in her first year at college," involving all the particular circumstances associated with this point in life.

Moos and Krahe provide useful generic schemes for organizing situations in the abstract. But they are not equipped to provide the kind of specific information about situations that most psychologists believe is required to predict human behavior. In recent years, therefore, a growing number of psychologists have taken up the task of classifying situations with a greater degree of specificity (Krahe, 1992; Magnusson & Endler, 1977). Recent efforts have shown that classifying situations is an extremely difficult thing to do. One might initially think

Table 7.6

Six General Categories of Human Environments

Category	Examples
Ecological	Climate, geography, type of building one lives in, physical characteristics of the setting.
Behavior settings	Church, football game, kitchen, classroom.
Organizational structure	Population density in an organization, site of organization, degree of hierarchic structure, student–teacher ratio in a school.
Characteristics of inhabitants	Age, sex, abilities, status, talents, and so on of people in the environment.
Organizational climate	Social morale, nature and intensity of personal relations.
Functional properties	Reinforcement consequences for particular behaviors in the situation, such as whether aggressive acts are rewarded or encouraged.

From Moos (1973).

that since traits are "inside" and situations are "outside," that situations should be defined in terms of external, physical, and objective criteria, such as "air temperature," "room size," and "number of persons present." This appears, however, to be wrong, or at least not especially useful. Psychologists have found instead that people's *perceptions* of situations matter more than the objective features of the situations themselves, and that people tend to perceive situations in terms of *psychological,* rather than physical, qualities (Krahe, 1992). As such, situations reside as much in the minds of the observers as in the external environment itself. Writes Ball (1972), "the definition of the situation may be conceived as the *sum of all recognized information, from the point of view of the actor, which is relevant to his locating himself and others, so that he can engage in self-determined lines of action and interaction*" (p. 63).

People often characterize particular situations in terms of their psychological *affordances*—what opportunities for behavior and experience the situations afford or offer for the participant (Dworkin & Goldfinger, 1985). For example, Magnusson (1971) asked persons to evaluate 36 heterogeneous situations and found that the key dimensions upon which the situations could be ordered included how rewarding the situation was, the extent to which the situation induced negative feelings, how passive a person might be in the situation, the amount of social interaction afforded in the situation, and level of activity. Forgas (1978) identified four dimensions that organize 15 different kinds of interpersonal environments: the amount of anxiety the situation elicits, the extent to which a person feels involved in the situation, overall goodness versus badness of the situation, and the extent to which the situation involves accomplishing tasks versus socioemotional interaction. Table 7.7 provides examples of other schemes offered in recent studies. As you can see, there turn out to be a dauntingly large number of dimensions upon which immediate situations can be compared and contrasted and little agreement about which dimensions are the most important.

If situations are best defined in terms of people's subjective psychological affordances, then it becomes extremely difficult to separate what's "really" in the situation from what's "really" in the person. Furthermore, if a person's personality shapes his or her perceptions, then it would seem to be equally difficult to separate traits from situations, for traits may determine how a person interprets the environment. In support of this idea, Forgas (1983) found that introverted subjects tended to organize information about situations in terms of a self-confidence dimension. Extraverts, by contrast, categorized situations in terms of how pleasant the situations were and how strongly they afforded interpersonal involvement. Put simply, introverts and extraverts are usually in different situations, even when it appears from the outside that they are in the same.

Whether introvert or extravert, however, the average person appears to possess a "vast and varied expertise about situations" that can be tapped and translated into behavioral guidelines (Cantor, Mischel, & Schwarz, 1982, p. 70). According to one recent approach to the understanding of situations, people may routinely formulate elaborate personal taxonomies specifying **situational prototypes** (Cantor et al., 1982; Schutte, Kenrick, & Sadalla, 1985). A situational prototype is an abstract set of features about a given class of situations. It serves as a working model for the person, telling him or her what to expect and how to behave in situations of a particular type. A situational prototype may include information about the physical setting, the physical features of the people involved, and common behaviors exhibited by the people in the situation.

For example, the situation of "party" may suggest a large number of features typically associated with parties. Perhaps the prototypical party generally occurs in the evening and involves a large number of people congregating in a circumscribed space, informal dress, eating and drinking, lively conversation, laughing, music and dancing, and lots of noise. Of course, parties vary, and each party contains its own constellation of defining features. Nonetheless, we extract from our experience a core of "partyness" that represents for each of us the "best example" or "ideal case" for defining the situation we call "party." Subsequently, each party we encounter may be evaluated in terms of this implicit categorization. A large dance party at a sorority house may, therefore, appear to us to be a highly prototypical party, embodying many of the features that parties tend to have in common. In the context of our earlier example of "fruits" as a natural

Table 7.7   Studies Exploring the Major Perceptual Dimensions of Situations

	Magnusson (1971)	Wish et al. (1976)	Forgas (1978)	Battistich and Thompson (1980)	Forgas et al. (1980)	Amato and Pearce (1983)	King and Sorrentino (1983)
Type of situation	Heterogeneous	Interpersonal relations	Interaction episodes	Heterogeneous	Aggressive episodes	Helping episodes	Interpersonal goal-oriented situations
Number of raters	3	87	15	216	137	45	200
Number of situations	36	45	17	30	22	62	20
Dimensions	1 positive/ rewarding 2 negative 3 passiveness 4 social interaction 5 activity	1 cooperative/ friendly vs. competitive/ hostile 2 equal vs. unequal 3 intense vs. superficial 4 socioemotional/ informal vs. task-oriented/ formal	1 anxiety 2 involvement 3 evaluative 4 socioemotional vs. task -oriented	1 emotional involvement 2 group vs. individual activity 3 social isolation 4 behavioral conformity	1 probability of occurrence 2 justifiability 3 provocation 4 control	1 spontaneous/ informal vs. planned/formal help 2 serious vs. non-serious 3 direct vs. indirect help	1 pleasant vs. unpleasant 2 accidentally vs. intentionally caused 3 physically vs. socially oriented 4 sensitive vs. insensitive 5 intimate vs. nonintimate 6 nonintimate/ uninvolved vs. intimate/ involved 7 work-vs.- relaxation-oriented

From Krahe (1992, p. 209)

A situational prototype: Grandmother's birthday.

category, such a party may be like an apple. On the other hand, a poetry-reading party at the home of a college English professor may seem less prototypical, further away from what we typically think of when we think of the party situation.

Bem and Funder (1978) describe a similar way of classifying situations in their **template-matching** approach. This approach draws on the Q-sort methodology employed by Block (1971) and others, which, as we have already seen, has been used successfully in assessing patterns of personality traits over time. In template matching, a person sorts the 100 personality statements that make up the California Q-sort into nine piles, ranging from those characteristics deemed to be "most like" to those "least like" an "idealized 'type' of person expected to behave in a specified way in that setting" (Bem & Funder, 1978, p. 486). For example, the rater might sort items according to the idealized type of "person most likely to achieve success as an attorney in a small law firm." This distribution is the *template* (model, pattern, portrait) for the situation. Therefore, situations are classified according to the personality traits of the idealized person who "fits" the situation in a particular way. Two different situations would be functionally similar if they produce similar templates, that is, if similar types of people were deemed likely to behave in a certain way in each of the situations. Likewise, two situations that might seem similar to some observers would be functionally dissimilar if they produce markedly different templates.

In the wake of the person–situation debate, the template-matching approach suggests two important implications about behavioral consistency across situations. First, the probability that a person will behave in a certain way in a certain situation should be a direct function of the match or similarity between the person's characteristics and the template associated with the corresponding behavior. For instance, the likelihood that John (person) will become a successful car salesman (behavior) in a rural Chrysler dealership (situation) should be positively correlated with the extent to which John's personality profile matches the template of the idealized salesman judged to do well in this setting.

A second implication of the template-matching approach concerns the match among different situations. Mischel's (1968) review of the personality literature highlighted numerous examples in which people's behavior was inconsistent across situations that were assumed to be similar. According to Bem and Funder, however, these "similar" situations may have been very different from one another—which is to say, they may have involved markedly different templates. For instance, an experimenter who finds that subjects are inconsistent in their helping behavior across three situations may conclude that altruism lacks cross-situational consistency. Bem and Funder point out, however, that the three situations may involve three very different templates. Template analyses might indicate that the idealized altruist in Situation A should be "outgoing" and "strong;" in Situation B, "gentle" and "nurturant;" and in Situation C, "unconventional" and "self-assured." One should not expect behavioral consistency across functionally different situations.

Modern Interactionism

As personality psychologists have become more concerned in recent years with identifying and defining the situational contexts for human behavior, they have come to develop ways of understanding behavior that are clearly *interactional.* One positive result of the person–situation debate, therefore, is that some personologists have broadened their emphases (Kenrick & Funder, 1988). In so doing they have reexamined old theories to discern their interactional concepts, sought to frame new theories that are more explicitly interactional, and attempted to formulate more sophisticated methods of research that assess interactions.

Many personality psychologists today endorse some variation of what Krahe (1992) calls the doctrine of *modern interactionism.* The core of the modern interactionist approach is captured in four basic postulates:

1. Actual behavior is a function of a continuous process of multidirectional interaction or feedback between the individual and the situation he or she encounters.

2.   The individual is an intentional, active agent in this interactional process.

3.   On the person side of the interaction, cognitive and motivational factors are essential determinants of behavior.

4.   On the situation side, the psychological meaning of situations for the individual is the important determining factor. (pp. 70–71)

From the standpoint of modern interactionism, personality is "a person's coherent manner of interacting with himself or herself and with his or her environment" (Endler, 1983, p. 179).

Persons Versus Situations Versus Interactions   There are many different ways of thinking about interactionism (Ozer, 1986). One approach, termed **mechanistic interactionism** (Endler, 1981), derives from the concept of an interaction effect as it appears in certain statistical procedures. In mechanistic interactionism, a person's trait constitutes one independent predictor, the situation constitutes a second independent predictor, and the interaction between trait and situation constitutes a third predictor. The dependent variable, or outcome to be predicted, is some form of measurable behavior. In such a study, a significant effect for the trait–situation interaction indicates (1) that there exists a statistical tendency for the trait to be associated with the behavior *when a particular level of the situation* is involved, or, similarly, (2) that there exists a tendency for the situation to be associated with the behavior *when a particular level of the trait* is involved.

Many studies in personality and social psychology draw implicitly upon a mechanistic model of interactionism (Blass, 1984). A good example of this approach is a study of altruism by Romer, Gruder, and Lizzadro (1986). The researchers administered questionnaires designed to identify two types of college students enrolled in a psychology class, likely to show helping behavior. One type, scoring high on the need for nurturance (need to care for others) but low on the need for succorence (need to be cared for by others), was called "altruist." The other type, scoring high on both needs for nurturance and succorance, was called "receptive–giving." Helping behavior was operationalized as the student's volunteering to help a distressed experimenter complete a research project by participating in a psychological experiment. The experimenter appealed for the student's help over the phone. In one scenario (the "no-compensation" situation), the student was told that his or her help was desperately needed but that the experimenter could not offer any course credit for the help. The "compensation situation" involved the same plea but in this situation the student was promised that course credit would be received as compensation.

The researchers believed that helping behavior was likely to be a function of the interaction of personality and situation. Specifically, they predicted that altruists would show high levels of helping behavior in situations in which they were *not likely to be compensated for helping,* given that their need for succorance was low. Receptive-giving persons, on the other hand, should show high levels of helping behavior in situations in which they *were likely to be compensated,* since their need for succorance was high. As Figure 7.2 shows, the percentage of students agreeing to help is well predicted as an interaction of person and

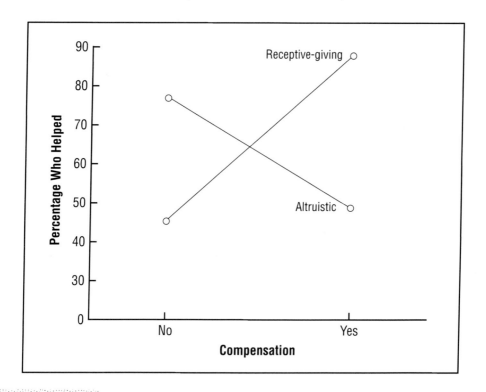

Figure 7.2

Percentage of Subjects Who Helped as a Function of Helping-Orientation Type and Compensation.

From Romer, Gruder, and Lizzadro, 1986, p. 1006.

environment, supporting the interactional hypothesis. Altruists helped more in the no-compensation condition than in the compensation condition. Receptive-giving students showed the reverse pattern, exhibiting higher levels of helping when compensated.

In an influential review of 11 studies on persons, situations, and interactions, Bowers (1973) found that person–situation interactions accounted for more variance than either persons alone or situations alone in 14 out of 18 comparisons. Similarly, Magnusson and Endler (1977) summarized a number of studies carefully designed to tease out effects of personality variables, situations, and interactions of the two, concluding that personality variables account for about 12% of the variance in behavior, situations for about 10%, and interactions for about 20%. This leaves well over 50% of the variance unaccounted for, considered to be a function of other factors and "error." Sarason, Smith, and Diener (1975)

Anxiety of social evaluation: a cocktail party.

conclude that none of the three general predictors in the mechanistic interaction model consistently account for an impressive amount of variance, leaving most of the variance in behavior unexplained. As Mischel (1986) points out, the extent to which each of the three—traits, situations, interactions—accounts for a large proportion of behavior in any given study depends on many factors, including the kinds of traits and situations chosen, the type of behavior assessed, and the purpose of the assessment.

An Interactional Model of Anxiety   Endler (1975, 1981) has formulated an interactional model of anxiety that has stimulated a good deal of recent research (e.g., Endler, Parker, Bagby, & Cox, 1991). Following Zuckerman (1960) and

Physical danger is a major source of anxiety.

Spielberger (1966), Endler views anxiety as having both trait and state dimensions. **Trait anxiety** (A-trait) is a relatively stable personality disposition—a general tendency to be fearful and nervous. **State anxiety** (A-state) is the transitory emotional experience of anxiety at a given moment in time. If I say that I am now anxious, I am referring to A-state; if I say that I tend to be anxious a lot, I am referring to A-trait. Endler views A-trait as a multidimensional construct, manifesting itself in five separate arenas in which the person may be threatened: physical danger, ego/interpersonal threat, novelty ambiguity, daily routine, and social evaluation. According to the interactional model of anxiety, people scoring high on A-trait for a specific kind of threat, say physical danger, will respond to a specific situation with A-state only if the situation presents that particular kind of threat.

A number of studies support the interactional model of anxiety. Most of these employ Endler's paper-and-pencil measure of A-trait, called the "S–R Inventory of General Trait Anxiousness" (S–R GTA; Endler & Okada, 1975). Endler and Magnusson (1976) administered the S–R GTA to Swedish college students and then assessed their A-state through a questionnaire and pulse rate measure administered just prior to an important college examination (presumably an ego/interpersonal threat) and again two weeks later. Data on pulse rate supported the interactional model. Students scoring high on A-trait for ego/interpersonal threat showed higher levels of pulse rate just prior to the examination (but not two weeks after) than students scoring low on A-trait for ego/interpersonal threat.

Similarly, Endler and Okada (1975) administered the S–R GTA and a self-report measure of A-state to students who thought they were about to be exposed to electric shock, a physical-danger threat. The results supported the interactional model for females, though not males. Females high on A-trait for physical-danger threat showed higher levels of A-state prior to the shock threat than females low on A-trait for physical danger. Consistent with the interactional model, moreover, A-trait for ego/interpersonal threat did *not* predict increased A-state in the physical-danger situation.

Reciprocal Interactionism   While mechanistic interactionism partitions the variance in behavior into that accounted for by persons, situations, and their interactions, **reciprocal interactionism** conceives of a more fluid and complex pattern in which person, situation, and behavior continually and reciprocally influence each other (Endler, 1981). This general way of seeing interactions is similar to Bandura's notion of "reciprocal determinism" (Chapter 6) and bears resemblance, as well, to systems theory. Person, situation, and behavior are parts of an interdependent system of causes and effects. Another way of understanding reciprocal interactionism is in terms of two multidimensional systems—the person and the environment—repeatedly "coming to terms" with each other via mutual and dynamic transactions (Brunswik, 1957):

> Both organism and environment will have to be seen as systems, each with properties of its own, yet both hewn from the same block. Each has surface and depth, or overt and covert regions . . . the interrelationship between the two systems has the essential characteristic of a "coming-to-terms." And this coming-to-terms is not merely a matter of the mutual boundary or surface areas. It concerns equally as much, or perhaps even more, the rapport between the central, covert layers of the two systems. It follows that, much as psychology must be concerned with the texture of the organism or of its nervous processes and must investigate them in depth, it also must be concerned with the texture of the environment as it extends in depth away from the common boundary. (p. 5)

It is probably some form of reciprocal interactionism that is regularly implied by most personologists when they say that behavior is a function of the interaction of person and environment. It has, however, proven extremely difficult to design studies that can measure dynamic, reciprocal interactions in a meaningful way (Ozer, 1986). One successful effort however, is the work of Emmons, Diener, and Larsen (1986) and Emmons and Diener (1986b), who have offered two alternative models of reciprocal interactionism. The "choice of situations" model suggests that people select situations and avoid others on the basis of certain personality traits and needs. The "affect congruence" model suggests that people experience greater positive affect and less negative affect in situations congruent with their personality characteristics. While it is not clear that these models fully capture the sense of Brunswik's "coming to terms" of systems, they have the advantage of being amenable to scientific study. Studies of the daily lives of college students provide modest support for both the choice and the congruence model. The authors conclude that while "some meaningful interactions do occur, they are not necessarily strong or easily predictable" (Diener, Larsen, & Emmons, 1984, p. 580).

Avshalom Caspi has recently developed a conception of personality that is grounded in reciprocal interactionism (Caspi, Bem, & Elder, 1989; Caspi & Moffitt, in press). Drawing upon archival data from a long-term project started in 1928, Caspi and his colleagues have followed the life courses of different cohorts, living under different historical conditions. Analyses of these data suggest that interactional styles developed in childhood influence subsequent development through two distinct but complementary processes. The first is termed *cumulative continuity* and refers to the notion that "an individual's interactional style channels him or her into environments that themselves reinforce that style, thereby sustaining the behavior pattern across the life course through the progressive accumulation of its own consequences" (Caspi et al., 1989, p. 375). For example, an ill-tempered adolescent may be expelled from school for vandalism. His leaving high school renders him fit for only the lowest-paying jobs. The frustration he experiences in these jobs further promotes an ill-tempered style of interacting with the environment.

The second process whereby continuity is created in individual development is called *interactional continuity*. This process operates as the person evokes "reciprocal, sustaining responses from others in ongoing social interaction, thereby reinstating the behavioral pattern across the individual's life whenever the relevant interactive situation is replicated" (Caspi et al., 1989, p. 375). As an example of this process, imagine how a cheerful little girl evokes pleasant and cooperative responses from people in her environment. Such responses reinforce her own cheerfulness and make it more likely that she will continue to evoke pleasant responses in the future.

From Caspi's point of view, reciprocal interactionism can work to build continuity in personality characteristics from one situation to the next and over time. Rather than pitting traits versus situations, Caspi sees personality as profoundly "situated" from the beginning. Personality coherence results from the relentless march of reciprocal interactions. Over time persons and their environments seem to come to terms, to use Brunswik's felicitous phrase. The personality may become more coherently organized as traits and situations match themselves up.

An interesting twist in Caspi's interactional approach concerns the role of traits during periods of rapid transition in people's lives (Caspi & Moffitt, in press). What happens to people's personality traits when they encounter periods of significant environmental change? What happens when, for example, students enter college, young people get married, people change residences or jobs, a woman becomes a widow? Common sense might tell us that it is during these kinds of transitional periods that personality is most likely to change. But Caspi argues that common sense may be wrong. Many transitional experiences may be characterized as novel, ambiguous, and uncertain. When a person enters this kind of life situation, he or she seeks to transform it into something that is familiar, clear, and expectable. In order to do so, a person is most likely to adopt those patterns of behavior that are most characteristic of his or her personality. In other words, during *situations of uncertainty* people often behave in ways that are especially congruent with their traits. They act in the ways they have always acted, only more so. In Caspi's view, traits are not likely to change very much during periods of uncertainty and change. On the contrary, traits become *accentuated* during transitions, and trait-consistent behaviors are given some of their best opportunities to shine forth.

Macrocontexts

Beyond the immediate situations within which behavior is contextualized, beyond the situational prototypes of "party" and "examination," beyond the transitional periods within which a person may find her- or himself, entering college, getting married, living on one's own in that first apartment, beyond the exigencies of the here-and-now reality that is bounded in time and space are the more encompassing contexts, the "macrocontexts" whose influences on behavior are more subtle, but sometimes more profound. At any given time, behavior is situated in a hierarchy of environments, contexts encompassing contexts. As we move to the higher and more distal contexts for human behavior, we move beyond the direct purview of modern interactionism and into the sociohistorical realms of family, race, class, and culture. Personality psychologists have been somewhat reluctant to examine macrocontexts like these. Yet a thorough understanding of the contextual nature of human behavior requires an historical and societal perspective. As Gadlin and Rubin (1979) put it: "People do not act in situations; they act in specific historical circumstances that they interpret in certain ways and that constrain and compel them in certain ways; and it is the particular features of those circumstances we must understand to understand why they act as they do" (p. 225).

Families and Other Systems A large and enduring situational context for a person's behavior consists of the interpersonal **systems** within which the person spends a large portion of his or her waking life. The best example of such an organized system is the family; others include certain clearly structured peer groups and occupational milieus. These groups and organizations are composed of separate parts, roles, and functions that work together according to an implicit plan or goal. A system is a highly differentiated and integrated totality, within which various components relate to and communicate with each other, *each part* *affecting every other part and the whole* (Bateson, 1972). At a more global level of analysis than the particular behavior setting, organized social systems, like the family, are generally believed to be significant shapers of long-term behavior patterns. They help determine how a person will behave and what the meaning of that behavior will be.

During the past 25 years, a growing number of psychotherapists have adopted a *family-systems* perspective (Minuchin, 1974; Parkison, 1982; Weakland, 1976). These clinicians seek to understand their clients' pathological behavior within a particular family system. Both healthy and pathological behaviors have their origins and their ultimate contextual meanings within the family system.

Minuchin (1974) identifies four cardinal features of a family system. First, a family is an *open* system that may be influenced by a wide variety of outside forces and factors. Second, a family system is perennially evolving, passing through *developmental stages* that can create disturbances or stresses of various intensities. As Haley (1980) notes, the time of most stress in a system is when a member enters or leaves that system. Such occurrences as the birth of a second child, the first child's entering school, or the last child's leaving home may mark major transformations of the system. A third aspect of the family system is a *power hierarchy*. Within the family, certain members (such as parents) wield more power than do others (such as children), and each member develops his or her own roles or niches within the family to accommodate the power differential. When the power hierarchy becomes confused or disorganized, the family structure is threatened. Finally, families share with other open systems the *tendency to maintain themselves*. This means that a family system develops toward stability and equilibrium. Habitual patterns of interaction are established that perpetuate a balanced structure—a system status quo. Yet, in many instances, such patterns may prove problematic for certain members of the family. In other words, what works best for the family, in the sense of maintaining the system equilibrium, may not be in the best interests of every member of the family.

Within a family-systems perspective, the person's behavior is embedded in a complex web of patterned relationships, complete with feedback loops, vicious cycles, and bidirectional patterns of causality. For example, a father may be unhappy and withdraw from other family members. Partially in response to the father's withdrawal, a child misbehaves. The mother reprimands the child for the misbehavior, but her attempt is ineffective, and the child persists in misbehaving. In response to the mother's failure, the father gets involved in disciplining the child, which ultimately proves effective, decreasing the mother's confidence in her own child-rearing expertise so that she relies even more heavily on the father's intervention in disciplining the child. The higher expectations place additional pressures on the father, who becomes more unhappy and withdraws even further. In response to this, the child misbehaves. And so the cycle repeats.

Families vary on a number of important systemic dimensions. Two dimensions that have received considerable attention are *adaptability* and *cohesion*

(Olson, 1985). Adaptability refers to a system's ability to change in response to circumstance. Families vary in this dimension from the most rigid systems, which cannot change, to those that change so much as to be chaotic. A healthy system, therefore, manifests moderate adaptability, somewhere between rigidity and chaos. Cohesion, on the other hand, refers to the extent to which family members are emotionally involved with each other, ranging from the emotionally enmeshed to the emotionally uninvolved or disengaged family. Again, a healthy system is probably in the middle of this dimension, promoting close emotional bonds while encouraging a certain degree of individual autonomy. The important thing to note with respect to the behavior of a single person in a family system is that the degree of adaptability and cohesion is likely to frame the meaning of his or her individual actions. Thus, a father who withdraws in a cohesive family is manifesting a behavior pattern that is likely to mean something different from that shown by a father who withdraws in a disengaged family. Though both fathers seem to be doing the same thing, the different contexts signal that their actions are indeed quite different from each other.

While adaptability and cohesion may be crucial dimensions in families, other social systems may be characterized in other ways. Schools, clubs, churches, corporations, and other organized systems vary with respect to such structural dimensions as size, density, number of supervisors, the degree of hierarchical order, degree of centralization, and turnover rate (Moos, 1974). The person's behavior within the system is likely to be a function of the system's properties and the person's role or niche within the system. In addition, the person's overall happiness and well-being may be powerfully influenced by the perceived quality of the system. In a study of employees at 37 different bank branches, Repetti (1987) found that the quality of the social environment at work was positively related to the employees' mental health. Those bank employees who perceived a positive organizational climate in the workplace reported less depression and anxiety in their lives as a whole, compared to bank employees who viewed their work environments more negatively.

Race and Social Class   Race and class are examples of what Bronfenbrenner (1979) terms **macrosystems** in human development. Broader and more pervasive than the family or organizational system, race and class exist as "super contexts" for behavior, subtly but powerfully shaping the person's development and providing the person's behavior with yet another layer of meaning.

Developmental psychologists have identified a number of social-class differences in child-rearing patterns. With respect to lower- and working-class families, Kagan (1984) writes:

> Parents who have not attended college, who see themselves and their children as part of the working class, and who live with chronic financial insecurity, often attribute their personal *angst* to economic stress, which they view as being not completely under their control. These families award a high priority to job security; and a central goal in socializing their child is to ensure

that he or she will develop the qualities that guarantee a secure job. Two key qualities are acceptance by peers and the ability to resist being exploited by those with more power. (p. 249)

In contrast, middle-class families are likely to be better educated and better off financially. The parents are likely to have professional positions, and the children are likely to be socialized within a much different macrosystem of values, beliefs, and world views:

> College-educated parents, especially those with professional vocations, regard freedom of choice, intellectual challenge, and the status of one's work as more important than job security. They believe that anxiety over peer rejection or disapproval obstructs the attainment of these goals, and they try to inoculate their youngsters against the anxiety that accompanies peer rejection, while emphasizing autonomous choice and competition. (Kagan, 1984, p. 249)

Studies carried out in the United States and in England have shown that middle-class adolescents and adults use more complex and less stereotyped language than do lower-class people, even when their intelligence test scores are similar (Hess & Shipman, 1965). Bernstein (1970) has argued that lower-class parents adopt a restricted linguistic code in communicating with their children, which means that they limit their verbal exchanges to direct expressions of concrete statements and commands. Middle-class parents, on the other hand, tend to use an elaborated linguistic code consisting of complex syntax, conditional statements, and the expression of abstract ideas. Critical of this characterization, Labov (1972) argues that middle-class psychologists are not sensitive to the nuance and range of meaning in lower-class speech. Both Bernstein and Labov would agree, however, that language reflects context, and that differences in verbal behavior between lower- and middle-class people reflect different systems for making meaning in the world and thus different contexts within which behavior can be understood.

In the United States, race may be an even more powerful context for behavior than social class. Because blacks and Hispanics are disproportionately represented in the lower economic classes, race and class are not completely independent phenomena. Yet, many anthropologists and sociologists insist that one's racial background, regardless of social class, exerts a marked influence on the person's development and relationships with others. In a provocative and rueful analysis of psychological research comparing American blacks and American whites, Jones (1983) remarks:

> Over the past few decades, psychological analysis of race has identified an unending stream of dysfunctions, maladaptations, deficient social organization, poor intellectual performance,

Social class as a context for behavior: American factory workers . . .

inadequate motivation, restricted ego domains, doubts, stresses, and fears. One wonders, on the basis of this extensive literature, how black Americans have managed to survive. The genetic versions of these negativistic analyses are based on the assumption that deficient genes explain the poor adaptation to American society; the environmental versions instead point the finger at poverty and racist oppression. While the environmentalists often accuse the geneticists of racism, black psychologists cannot help noticing that neither position recognizes a single attribute, capacity, or contribution of black people that could be considered positive, desirable, or worth preserving. An essential goal of black psychology, then, is to go beyond the reactive conception of black Americans' history to develop a cultural-evolutionary perspective that recognizes African origins, and more recent developments in the United States (and other countries), and the effects of prolonged oppression. The new perspective should include what is distinctively good and useful in the Afro- or African-American experience. (p. 142)

. . . and Japanese factory workers.

Jones indicts American social scientists for failing to understand the macrosystem of black culture. Cole (1976) identifies three principal components of black culture: (1) an "American mainstream" component shared with white Americans and espousing such values as individualism and materialism, (2) a "minority sense" component shared with other disadvantaged minorities in American society, reinforcing the sense that being black is likely to make one the subject of discrimination, and (3) a unique "blackness" component that incorporates certain African and African-American values, mannerisms, and styles. The blackness component includes what Cole terms "soul"—a sense of people facing hardship together as a spirited and vital community—and "style," which refers to characteristic ways of talking, walking, dressing, and thinking.

Many black scholars draw sharp contrasts between Euro-American philosophical orientations (which provide a foundation for the American white macrosystem) and African philosophical orientations (which are more instrumental in the black macrosystem) (e.g., Akbar, 1991; Dixon, 1976; White & Parham, 1990). The differences suggest that black heritage is highly social rather than individualistic, oriented toward the present rather than the future, and focused on subjective emotional experience over and against objective rationality. These are *cultural* rather than personal differences. They represent contrasts in the implicit philosophical contexts behind behavior rather than differences in behavior per se. Again, we see that different contexts imbue a person's behavior with different meanings.

Culture and History Culture and history are the most encompassing contexts for human behavior. Every interaction episode—every meeting of person and situation—takes place within a particular culture and at a particular moment in the history of that culture. A **culture** is a tradition of rules embraced by a particular society of people. As Robert LeVine puts it, culture is

> an organized body of rules concerning the ways in which individuals in a population should communicate with one another, think about themselves and their environments, and behave toward one another and toward objects in their environments. The rules are not universally or constantly obeyed, but they are recognized by all and they ordinarily operate to limit the range of variation in patterns of communication, belief, value, and social behavior in the population. (LeVine, 1982, p. 4)

The "rules" of which a particular culture is made generate two fundamental features of that culture: (1) its maintenance system and (2) its projective system (Whiting & Child, 1953). A culture's **maintenance system** is its ecological, economic, and sociopolitical structure and the child-training or socialization practices accepted by the society as appropriate. The maintenance system exists to ensure the survival of the group in its relation to its external physical environment. Thus, external environments give birth to maintenance systems and their corresponding patterns of socialization. For example, harsh physical climates with relatively little rainfall, such as desert and arctic tundra, have traditionally called for cultural maintenance systems centered around hunting and fishing. Human societies living in such regions, such as the Eskimo, have traditionally moved from one place to another, across the terrain in search of food and temporary shelter. Within this nomadic lifestyle, the individual must rely on wits and expertise to survive, and therefore socialization practices in these societies tend to encourage the values of autonomy and self-reliance. In contrast, temperate climates have traditionally been associated with agricultural maintenance systems calling for large-scale accumulation of food and a more sedentary settlement pattern. In these societies, socialization practices tend to emphasize the values of obedience and social responsibility (Berry, 1976).

The **projective system** of a culture refers to a society's art, religion, folklore, and other expressive media. Whereas the maintenance system is seen as *shaping* the personality of the society's members, the projective system is generally considered to be *an expression of* personality. Anthropologists have documented fascinating connections between maintenance and projective systems within cultures. For instance, Whiting and Child (1953) used available ethnographic records to examine child-rearing methods (maintenance system) and beliefs about disease (projective system) in 75 preliterate societies. They found that societies that tended to punish children severely for aggressive behavior tended also to view disease as caused by hostile sorcerers who invaded the people's bodies. Societies in which mothers weaned their infants early tended to see disease as caused by consuming bad food or poison.

A consistent theme in the literature on culture and personality is that Western industrialized societies tend to encourage the values of independence and competition, at the expense of interdependence and cooperation, more than do most non-Western societies. In many traditional, nonindustrialized societies, infants are weaned later and children are isolated less often than in contemporary Western life. Parental values stress the interdependence of persons, and children are encouraged to be part of the functioning community rather than to excel over others (Damon, 1983). Research by Edwards and Whiting (1980) suggests that such cultural differences may even be sharper for girls than boys. In several African and Asian communities, Edwards and Whiting found that parents frequently ask their daughters to help care for the younger children. According to the researchers, this practice strengthens traits and values of nurturance in girls. In contemporary Western societies, daughters typically spend their free time with peers, except for those specially rewarded occasions of babysitting. This difference in parental expectations for the behavior of daughters may help to explain two things: (1) why many traditional societies appear to value cooperation to a greater extent than do Western societies and (2) why the differences between girls and boys on personality traits associated with nurturance and caregiving tend to be greater in traditional societies than in their modern Western counterparts.

The emphasis on competition, autonomy, individualism, and the self is generally considered to be a hallmark of modern Western culture. The emphasis is complexly determined and has historical roots in Western religion, philosophy, economy, and government (Bellah et al., 1985, 1991; Bloom, 1987). This pervasive ideological context for behavior suggests that we as Westerners tend to see people as potentially self-sufficient agents endowed with fundamental and even inalienable individual rights—such as the rights to "life, liberty, and the pursuit of happiness," the right of free speech, and the right of assembly. We view society as comprised of autonomous agents who freely choose to behave as they do. This position contrasts starkly with the view of persons espoused in, say, a traditional Hindu village in India. Miller (1984) has shown that children in American society tend to explain everyday social events in terms of the personal dispositions of individual persons. Hindu children, on the other hand, tend to explain everyday events in terms of the pressures of the environment and the influences of society on persons.

The promise and the problems of American individualism are described in this passage from Bellah's critique of American society (Bellah et al., 1985):

> Clearly the meaning of one's life for most Americans is to become one's own person, almost to give birth to oneself. Much

of this process, as we have seen, is negative. It involves breaking free from family, community, and inherited ideas. Our culture does not give us much guidance as to how to fill the contours of this autonomous, self-responsible self, but it does point to two important areas. One of these is work, the realm, par excellence, of utilitarian individualism. Traditionally, men, and today women as well, are supposed to show that in the occupational world they can stand on their own two feet and be self-supporting. The other is the lifestyle enclave, the realm, par excellence, of expressive individualism. We are supposed to be able to find a group of sympathetic people, or at least one such person, with whom we can spend our leisure time in an atmosphere of acceptance, happiness, and love. (p. 83)

As Bellah sees it, contemporary American culture offers few clear guidelines concerning how the individual is to make commitments to something larger and more important than the self. Americans manifest a *utilitarian* individualism in their work, expanding and defining the self by what they do for a living. And they manifest an *expressive* individualism in their play, getting together during leisure time—evenings, weekends, vacations—with other like-minded persons, what Bellah calls "life-style enclaves," who enjoy the same kinds of fun. Yet, neither realm of activity—work or play—fosters commitment to others and to community. Indeed, it is often not clear who those others and communities are. Many Americans, therefore, may be free to choose their commitments, but the choices that exist are often vague and unfulfilling.

Bellah's analysis of contemporary American society alerts us to the fact that a person's behavior—in America or elsewhere—cannot be understood outside the culture and its history enveloping that person's life. In a small way, indeed, the social scientist who seeks to understand a culture changes that culture by virtue of what he or she learns and tells others and their reactions to it. As such, he or she contributes to the history of that culture and changes the broadest context for behavior.

Conclusion: Traits and Situations Revisited

When Walter Mischel (1968) launched his attack on traits, many believed that the entire discipline of personality psychology had come under siege. Since the days of Gordon Allport (1937), the concept of trait has been closely identified with personality. Allport employed the trait concept to account for the consistency of an individual's behavior over time and across situations. But if the individual's behavior is not consistent, if behavior instead is primarily driven by the exigencies of the situation, then the concept of trait would appear to be useless. As traits go, so goes personality, some have argued. Indeed, some have suggested that the definition of personality *is* traits—plain and simple (A. Buss, 1989). Therefore, to undermine traits is to deny the existence of personality itself. And if there is no such thing as personality, then what indeed are personality psychologists to do?

A major premise of this text is that there is more to personality than traits. Many strong traditions in the study of persons do not emphasize the concept of trait at all, including most of those theories and outlooks discussed in this book under the headings of "Intrapsychic Mysteries" (Chapters 2–4), "Interpretive Structures" (Chapters 8–10), and "Interpersonal Stories" (Chapters 11–13). It would seem that Mischel's critique, therefore, posed only a minor threat to psychoanalytic, sociobiological, humanistic, and cognitive approaches to personality, for example. Nonetheless, these approaches share with trait theories a penchant for looking inside the person to formulate explanations for human behavior and experience. To the extent, then, that situationism suggests that internal processes are relatively unimportant, then we can imagine how a wide range of personality theories might find the Mischel critique somewhat bothersome. Still, it is important to note that the Mischel critique and the subsequent person–situation debate in the field of personality psychology applied most directly to traits and trait theory. And many viable theories of personality are not primarily concerned with traits.

So, what has happened to traits? How well have they fared in the wake of the Mischel critique? It would seem that they have fared amazingly well. The concept of trait made a strong comeback in the 1980s and early 1990s. Today, personality psychologists appear more confident about the usefulness of the trait concept than perhaps ever before. At the same time, there appears to be a greater appreciation today than ever before for the many different ways in which human behavior may be situated in multiple contexts. Recent developments in personality psychology suggest that a strong trait psychology can coexist with an enlightened doctrine of situationism. How can we explain these developments?

Looking over the past 20 years of research on traits, one can see at least five reasons that the concept of trait has emerged from the Mischel critique and the person–situation debate in a strengthened position:

1.   *Traits are more than mere linguistic conveniences.* Standard situationist rhetoric of the 1970s had it that traits are in the minds of observers rather than in the behavior of the people they observe. Social psychologists such as Richard Nisbett argued that when people (and trait psychologists) observe the behavior of others, they make simplistic attributions about cross-situational consistency—fundamental attributional errors—that are, in fact, not supported by empirical evidence (Nisbett & Ross, 1980). Similarly, Richard Shweder and others (Bourne, 1974; Shweder, 1975; Shweder & D'Andrade, 1979) argued that trait ratings simply reflect observers' biases about how different words in language "go together." A significant body of research, however, shows that these critiques were probably more clever than true (Block, Weiss, & Thorne, 1979; Funder & Colvin, 1991;

Kenrick & Funder, 1988; Moskowitz, 1991). While there is no doubt that trait ratings reflect in part the subjective cognitive processes of the raters themselves, research shows rather conclusively that when raters are given sufficient opportunity to observe the behavior of those persons whom they are to rate, their ratings are generally both reliable and valid. In other words, trait attributions made by subjective raters are *not* illusions—residing merely in the eyes of the beholder. Rather they reflect real differences in behavior and personality of the people being rated.

2.   *Many traits show remarkable longitudinal consistency.* There are at least two simple ways to think about the consistency of individual differences in personality traits—consistency *across situations* and consistency *over time.* Mischel's critique of traits mostly concerned the first way. He argued that behavior was not consistent enough from one situation to the next to warrant the use of the trait concept. Mischel said much less, however, about the extent to which individual differences in traits were consistent over time. But at the time of Mischel's critique there was relatively little empirical data collected to support longitudinal consistency (or "stability") in traits. Since then, things have changed dramatically. Longitudinal studies of the 1980s demonstrate that individual differences in many traits, such as extraversion and neuroticism, are quite stable over long periods of time (Conley, 1985b; McCrae & Costa, 1990). Stability has been demonstrated when trait scores come from self-ratings, spouse ratings, or peer ratings. Even though, therefore, the person–situation debate was not directly concerned with the longitudinal stability of trait ratings, findings such as these tend to increase psychologists' faith in the concept of trait. You can easily see why. If, for example, Bill's high school teachers rate him as "highly extraverted" relative to other teenagers in 1940, his wife rates him "highly extraverted" on their 20th wedding anniversary in 1965, and his coworkers rate him as "highly extraverted" in 1990 when he retires from his company, and if Bill rates himself as "highly extraverted" compared to most other people he knows at ages 18, 43, and 68, then we might start to think that Bill really *is* highly extraverted! It makes sense to use the trait concept here, we might conclude.

3.   *Aggregation shows that traits often predict behavior fairly well.* As we have seen in this chapter, personality psychologists have sought to increase the predictive power of trait scores by employing moderator variables and aggregation strategies in their research. Aggregation has proven to be an especially powerful tool. Beginning with Epstein (1979), studies consistently show that individual differences in personality traits are often strongly correlated with individual differences in theoretically related behavior when behavior is aggregated across situations. Individual differences in traits can often account for a substantial amount of variance in aggregated behaviors (Kenrick & Funder, 1988).

4.   *Situational effects are often no stronger than trait effects.* The person–situation debate centered on the question of what accounts for the greatest degree of variance in behavior: Is it traits? Or is it situations? According to the situationist views of the 1970s, if traits are weak predictors, then situations must be strong predictors. Mischel and others tried to show that traits were weak

predictors. But they neglected to demonstrate that situational variables were especially strong predictors. Funder and Ozer (1983) reexamined some of the most well known laboratory studies of the 1960s and 1970s demonstrating significant effects for *situational variables* in predicting behavior. They found that the statistical effects obtained in these studies were typically no higher than those obtained in many studies employing personality traits. Funder and Ozer argued that while trait scores may sometimes account for only modest amounts of variance in behavior, it appears that carefully measured situational variables often account for no more. The simple message: When it comes to predicting behavior, traits may not be so hot; but often situations ain't much better.

5.   *Trait psychologists have rallied around the Big Five.* The most important development in trait psychology of the 1980s was the emergence of the Big Five model. As we saw in Chapter 5, findings from many recent studies converge on a five-factor model of personality traits. The five broad factors have been labeled extraversion (*E*), neuroticism (*N*), openness to experience (*O*), conscientiousness (*C*), and agreeableness (*A*). Only 20 years ago, many personality psychologists seemed to be despairing over the possibility that traits may not exist. Today, there appears to be little doubt about the existence of traits. And there is growing consensus about how all the many different kinds of traits that might be invoked can be organized into a five-factor scheme. The emergence of a sensible and empirically grounded taxonomy for personality traits represents a tremendous boost for the trait concept. As we saw in Chapter 1, an important first step in science is an adequately comprehensive *description* of a phenomenon. The Big Five scheme appears to be the first truly comprehensive and consensual description of the trait domain to appear in the history of personality psychology. This is not to say that the Big Five is the last word on traits (Briggs, 1989; McAdams, 1992b). But the model is an impressive achievement, and it has substantially enhanced the position of trait psychology in the eyes of the scientific community.

This said, the ascent of the Big Five model of traits has begun to reveal some important limitations of trait psychology. Some of the limitations have to do with the model itself. For example, the five factors of *E, N, O, A,* and *C* operate at such a general and abstract level of analysis that they may not always be useful in the prediction of specific behaviors. More narrowly defined traits sometimes show stronger predictive power, especially when the behavior to be predicted is narrowly defined (Briggs, 1989; A. Buss, 1989). In addition, the Big Five model tells us very little about (1) personality development and (2) personality organization. How do traits develop and change? How are they linked to particular stages of the life cycle? How are they organized within the individual? How do they make for personality coherence and wholeness? It does not appear that the Big Five model of traits is conceptually well positioned to answer questions like these (McAdams, 1992b).

Other limitations point to problems with the concept of trait itself—problems that have still not been resolved, even as the concept has regained prominence in recent years. To what extent are traits able to *explain* behavior? With the possible exception of such biologically grounded trait theories as Eysenck's and Gray's, trait approaches to personality have never offered especially compelling explanations for why people do what they do. To say that a person engages in warm and friendly behavior because he or she has a strong trait of agreeableness may represent a first step in explanation, but only a first step. We want to know precisely how this trait of agreeableness makes for the behavior. We want to know what the *causal mechanisms* are, the linkages between the trait label we invoke and the behavior we observe.

Beyond the problem of explanation is the problem of *context*. In their search for trait universals, proponents of the five-factor model of personality traits have disregarded the roles of situational, cultural, and historical contexts. McCrae and Costa (1984) claim that the Big Five model is "transcontextual." Life conditions and contexts may change over time, but traits remain the same. McCrae and Costa (1984) write: "The life course, then, can profitably be studied as the interplay of enduring dispositions and changing contexts" (p. 178). According to this view, extraversion is extraversion is extraversion. The meaning of the trait is the same, whether we're talking about extraversion in childhood or among adults, whether extraversion is measured among African-American men or German women, in nineteenth-century London or among Australian aborigines last week. Yet as we have seen in this chapter, a major lesson of the Mischel critique and the subsequent person–situation debate is that personality needs to be seen in contextual terms. Context appears to be necessary for accurate prediction, detailed description, and comprehensive understanding. But as Mischel rightly saw, the concept of trait has not traditionally encompassed context.

In one way or another, the Big Five traits point to a good deal of information one might expect to gather in order to describe an individual's personality. Indeed, the five factors are ultimately derived from and appear to be ingrained within the common language we use to describe persons. As such the five factors cover the fundamental questions we seek to answer about persons. Goldberg (1981) writes:

> They [the five factors] suggest that those who have contributed to the English lexicon as it has evolved over time wished to know the answers to at least five types of questions about a stranger they were soon to meet: (1) Is X *active and dominant* [E] or passive and submissive (Can I bully X or will X bully me)? (2) Is X *agreeable* [A] (warm and pleasant) or disagreeable (cold and distant)? (3) Can I count on X [C] (Is X *responsible and conscientious* or undependable and negligent)? (4) Is X crazy [N] (unpredictable) or sane (stable)? (5) Is X *smart* [O] or dumb (How easy will it be for me to teach X)?
> Are these universal questions? (p. 161)

Notice the language in this revealing passage. Goldberg suggests that the Big Five traits apply to fundamental questions about personality that we would be likely to ask *when meeting a stranger*. In an initial encounter with a person, we are likely to want to obtain information about *E, N, O, C,* and *A*. Such information provides us with a "first read" of another person. It provides us with important guidelines concerning how we should interact with this person in the future. But as we get to know the person better, as we learn more about a person's *life,* we tend to move beyond the dimensional realm of the Big Five and develop conclusions about the person that are more nuanced and contextualized. We see the person in many different situations, noting both cross-situational consistencies (traits) and interesting situational variations on general behavioral trends. We begin to see the person in terms of the person's developmental past and life goals for the future. We begin to appreciate the texture of the person's life in a way that goes well beyond the Big Five traits, indeed goes well beyond traits in general. It would appear that the Big Five scheme represents a comprehensive *psychology of the stranger.* The five factors encapsule those most general and encompassing attributions that we might wish to make *when we know virtually nothing else about a person.*

As we saw in Chapter 5, psychologists employ the trait concept to refer to linear dimensions of behavioral functioning upon which individuals can be observed to differ. Traits are inherently comparative. If I score "high" on agreeableness, it means that I score high *relative* to other people. As I rate myself on items making up a scale measuring agreeableness, I am implicitly comparing myself to others, to provide the psychologist with a first and very general read on just how "warm and friendly" (agreeable) I am relative to other people. When other people rate me on trait items, they, too, are implicitly comparing me to others. As we saw in Chapter 5, if such ratings are to be reliable and valid, the items to be rated must be simple, clear, and straightforward. Such is the nature—the necessary nature, it would seem—of trait ratings and trait psychology. The greatest strength of the trait concept is also its greatest weakness: Traits provide us with simple and noncontextualized generalizations about how people differ from each other.

If behavior is to be viewed in contextual terms, however, then information on a person's traits must be supplemented by information on the person's situations, including how a *person's life* is currently situated, how it has been situated in the past, how it might be situated in the future. In and of themselves, dispositional traits are *nonconditional* constructs. For example, a "high" trait score on extraversion suggests that a person will tend to show relatively high levels of outgoing and impulsive behavior over time and across situations, but it does not specify *under what conditions* such behavior will appear. By contrast, *conditional* constructs are more interactional than traits in that they provide information about how a person will behave under particular conditions. Thorne (1989) describes the distinction:

> By nonconditional attributes, I mean traits such as dominance and extraversion, moods such as happiness, and behaviors such as talking and smiling. These kinds of concepts can be contrasted

with explicitly conditional categories such as: My dominance shows when my competence is threatened; I fall apart when people try to comfort me; I talk the most when I am nervous. (p. 149)

Trait scores provide us with nonconditional information about a person. From scores on the dimension of agreeableness, we learn about the extent to which a person will tend to show warm and friendly behavior over time and across situations. We are given no information, however, about the conditions under which we are likely to see especially high levels or low levels of warm and friendly behavior. We are told only about trends. Conditional statements, by contrast, provide information about the conditions under which particular kinds of behavior might occur. As we get to know a person better, we are likely to become better informed about the conditions under which particular patterns of behavior should occur in the person's life. We should be able to move beyond nonconditional trait statements—the initial read on personality—to more conditional personality attributions made in context. We should be able to move beyond traits to explore the goals, tasks, challenges, conflicts, and situational and developmental demands that characterize a person's life. Think about a person whom you know very well. What is it that you know about him or her that you don't know about other people? Is it traits? Probably not. It is likely that you know a person well by virtue of knowing what the person's *life* is like, what it has been like in the past, and what it may be like in the future. As part of this knowledge, you may have access to the person's desires, needs, wishes, wants, goals, challenges, conflicts, values, and the unique way in which the person him- or herself puts this all together, puts it together into a narrative pattern to make sense of who he or she is. This kind of knowledge about a person is exquisitely conditional and contextualized.

As the concept of the nonconditional trait has regained prominence, a countermovement in personality psychology has also gained momentum in recent years, toward examination of the conditional and contextualized patterns of behavior and experience that characterize the individual life (Cantor, 1990; Emmons, 1986; Norem, 1989; Palys & Little, 1983; Runyan, 1990; Wright & Mischel, 1987; Zuroff, 1986). We will review some of these approaches in the pages to come, under the headings of "Interpretive Structures" and "Interpersonal Stories." The strong interest in conditional patterns and life context suggests that while it is foolish to deny the existence and validity of personality traits, human behavior remains profoundly situated in multiple contexts. To move beyond a psychology of the stranger, you may have to move beyond traits.

Summary for Chapter 7

1. Mischel's (1968) critique of personality traits argued that behavior is more situationally specific than cross-situationally consistent and that traits probably exist more in the mind of the observer than in the actual personality of the person

whose behavior is observed. Mischel's critique launched the person–situation debate in personality psychology.

2. In response to the Mischel critique, some psychologists have utilized moderator variables to show that behavior for some people is easier to predict from trait scores than is behavior for other people.

3. A number of studies have shown that substantial consistency in persons across situations and over time can be observed when behaviors are aggregated rather than analyzed as single events.

4. Some personologists have argued that the coherence and consistency of the person's behavior is evident only when the researcher carefully examines patterns of traits over time, resulting in personality typologies such as those developed by Block.

5. An especially useful instrument for the development of personality typologies is the California Q-sort, which consists of 100 statements about personality that a rater sorts into nine piles, ranging from those statements most like to those least like the person being rated. Studies employing the Q-sort have identified two central dimensions of personality functioning: ego control and ego resiliency.

6. In response to the person–situation debate, psychologists have tried to define and classify situations. Recent efforts suggest that situations are best characterized in terms of their subjective psychological affordances, making it very difficult to separate the concepts of "internal" traits and "external" situations.

7. The template-matching approach classifies situations in terms of the personality traits of a hypothetical person deemed to fit the situation in a particular way.

8. Modern interactionism views behavior as a continuous process of multidirectional interaction between the individual and the situation he or she encounters.

9. Behavior is always embedded in overlapping situational systems, such as those represented by family and social organizations. The behavior of the individual member of the system must be seen in terms of the system's characteristic dynamics.

10. Broader and more pervasive than families and other such systems are race and social class, which exist as macrosystems for the person's behavior. Culture and history are the most encompassing contexts for behavior.

11. As the person–situation debate has died down in recent years, the concept of trait has enjoyed an upsurge in popularity because of significant advances in research and the emergence of the Big Five model as an organizational framework for traits. Yet an exclusive reliance on traits in studying the person may produce a "psychology of the stranger."

12. The resurgence of interest in traits is coupled with a parallel emphasis, in recent years, on the ways in which behavior is situated in multiple contexts.

Part III

Interpretive Structures

The Person's Strategies for Understanding Experience

Chapter 8 Humanistic Themes: Meaning and
    Self-Determination
Chapter 9 Cognitive Approaches to the Person
Chapter 10 The Self as Knower and Known

We are forever trying to make sense of ourselves and of the world in which we live. And we are forever aware of ourselves as creatures who are trying to make sense, trying to understand, trying to find meaning in our existence. By virtue of both biology and culture, human beings self-consciously seek to make conscious meaning, as they act and interact, struggle and cope in a world that does not always appear to be especially meaningful. To understand experience, human beings must impose upon it some kind of interpretive structure. To understand another person, we must comprehend the nature of the interpretive structures employed by the person to make sense of his or her experience. To know another person well is to know how a person knows. Chapters 8–10 address perspectives on the person that center on human meaning making, on consciousness and cognition, on how people make sense of themselves and their worlds.

We begin in Chapter 8 by considering a wide variety of approaches to the person that come out of existentialism, phenomenology, and humanistic psychology. Existentialism provides a philosophical portrait of the modern man or woman as a highly self-conscious agent faced with the responsibility of creating personal meaning out of the nothingness that threatens authentic human existence. Ideally, the modern adult should confront the challenge in good faith by freeing the self from banal societal conventions in order to understand life's meanings and control life's destiny. In recent years, psychologists have empirically examined these themes of freedom, control, and challenge in human affairs and generated fascinating findings and theories about human nature and about individual differences in persons. Humanistic psychologists such as Carl Rogers and Abraham Maslow offer grand personality theories that are premised on the idea that people are self-conscious meaning-makers, seeking to determine their own lives and fulfill their own potentials. Finally, George Kelly provides an influential psychology of personal constructs that recasts some of the central motifs of this chapter within the model of a person-as-scientist, seeking to predict, control, and understand the world.

Kelly's theory is a bridge to the many cognitive approaches to the person described in Chapter 9. Modern cognitive theories emphasize the ways in which human beings process information about themselves and about their worlds. The central metaphors of these approaches come from computers and robotics. People take in, organize, and store semantic and episodic social information through the use of schemas, scripts, plans, and other cognitive vehicles and formats. Purposive human behavior is regulated by informational feedback systems organized hierarchically, through which values, self-schemata, and expectations serve as reference points against which current behavior is constantly compared. While much of social information processing is domain specific, certain general differences in processing style may be observed, as shown in research on field-independence and integrative complexity.

Moving from the social-cognitive and cognitive-motivational perspectives of Chapter 9, Chapter 10 examines cognitive-developmental perspectives on persons, focusing on the development of self. From the time of William James, the self has been construed as both subject and object—the "I" and the "Me." The I is commonly viewed as the agent, trend, or process in personality responsible for intentionality and wholeness. Loevinger's theory of ego development charts how the I changes over time, moving from globality and egocentricity to increasing differentiation, integration, and tolerance. As the object of the I's conscious observation, the Me develops in tandem with the I. A person may have many different Me's; multiple selves may exist in a self-concept confederacy, made up of possible selves, ideal selves, actual selves, ought selves, dreaded selves, selves-with-others, and so on. If the I is the agent of meaning making, then the Me is probably the most important meaning that the I ever makes.

Chapter 8

Humanistic Themes

Meaning and Self-Determination

Introduction

The Focus on Consciousness: Existentialism and Phenomenology

Consciousness Is Primary
We Create Ourselves
Feature 8.A: Finding Meaning in the Absurd: The Psychology of Ernest Becker
We Alone Are Responsible for Who We Become

Freedom, Control, and Challenge in Human Affairs

Who (or What) Is in Control?
Personal Causation and Control
Locus of Control
Self-Determination Theory
The Hardy Personality
Reversal Theory

Humanistic Psychology

Carl Rogers' Theory
Abraham Maslow's Psychology of Being
Examples of Humanistic Research

The Bridge to Cognitive Psychology: George Kelly

Feature 8.B: A Rigorous Humanism: Joseph Rychlak

The Psychology of Personal Constructs
Exploring Personal Constructs: The Rep Test

[handwritten: Human experience is subjective]

Summary

Consider this line from the Talmud: "We do not see things as they are. We see them as *we* are" (from Rowe, 1982, p. 1). Or as the Greek Stoic philosopher Epictetus said almost 2000 years ago, "It is not things in themselves that trouble us, but our opinions of things." The point is that all human experience is subjective. The world in and of itself is not meaningful; rather, each of us must *make* meaning out of it. To understand another person, we must inquire into his or her characteristic ways of making meaning in the world; we must see the world clearly from the other's point of view.

To see the world from the other's point of view—this is essentially the main goal of a broad group of approaches to personality psychology that seek to discern the interpretive structures that people employ to make sense of their conscious subjective experience. From these points of view, the personologist is most concerned with discovering precisely how a particular person consciously comprehends his or her own happiness and misery, what meaning he or she ascribes to the problems and possibilities encountered in life. The goal is not to expose the hidden unconscious truths, as it is for Freud and Jung. Rather, for these approaches, truths reside in consciousness. And unlike the behaviorist perspective, these approaches are not primarily concerned with discerning patterns of learning in the immediate environment in order to predict behavioral responses. In fact, the "objective" environment is of little interest here. The focus instead is on how the person subjectively views that environment—what the environment *means* to the person. Meanings are self-determined. People actively engage their environments in meaningful ways. And meanings guide behavior.

To begin our consideration of the person from the standpoint of interpretive structures, we will consider theory and research stemming from the traditions of existentialism, phenomenology, and humanism in personality psychology, each of which centers on how persons make conscious meaning of their worlds and their lives.

[handwritten margin notes: truth resides in consciousness; Freud hidden unconscious; Behaviorist concern w/ discern patterns of learning in the environment]

[handwritten at bottom: What the environment means to the person]

The Focus on Consciousness: Existentialism and Phenomenology

The broad intellectual movement known as **existentialism** began in Europe in the mid-1800s with the writings of the Danish theologian Søren Kierkegaard (1813–1855). The movement was advanced through the philosophical contributions of Friedrich Nietzsche (1844–1900), Karl Jaspers (1883–1969), and Martin Heidegger (1889–1976), and reached probably its most influential form in the work of the French philosopher Jean-Paul Sartre (1905–1980). Other significant figures in existentialism include the philosopher Gabriel Marcel (1889–1973) and the Jewish theologian Martin Buber (1878–1965). In the last 50 years, a number of psychiatrists and psychologists—mainly of a Freudian or Jungian persuasion—have incorporated major ideas from existentialism into their theories of personality and psychotherapy. The best known among these include Ludwig Binswanger (1881–1966), Medard Boss, Rollo May, and Victor Frankl.

Existentialism began as a protest against European rationalism, science, and some of the negative aftermath of the Industrial Revolution. Existentialists repudiated the philosophies of Kant and Hegel, which had glorified human reason and abstract thought, and argued instead for a general view of human existence emphasizing passionate feelings, human irrationality, and concrete individual consciousness. They rejected the tenets of an objective, mechanistic, hypothesis-testing science in favor of the study of subjective consciousness and human intentionality. They observed widespread discontent and alienation in modern industrial life, and they urged modern men and women to explore their own consciousness to fashion new meanings for life that transcend social norms and traditional religion. In psychology, existentialists rebelled against the Freudian emphasis on biological drives and instincts and various other trends in the social sciences that, in their view, dehumanized human beings and stripped them of their will and integrity. But existentialism is an uneven and very diverse movement in Western thought that offers no single, coherent theory of the person. Instead, it presents us with a number of intriguing concepts and emphases that may be gleaned from a wide variety of sources. The most significant existentialist themes for the study of persons are consciousness, becoming, and individual responsibility.

Consciousness Is Primary

An existentialist perspective on the person begins with the concrete and specific consciousness of a single human being existing at a particular moment in time and space. In the words of Sartre (1965), what all existentialists "have in common is that they think that existence precedes essence, or if you prefer, that subjectivity must be the starting point" (p. 34).

Sartre views consciousness as whole and unitary. In principle, the person is capable of becoming aware of any and all contents of consciousness. It makes no sense, argues Sartre, to posit a repressed unconscious domain. Sartre rejects Freud's division of the mind into conscious and unconscious and into ego, id, and superego. Asks Sartre, how can the ego repress thoughts that originate in the id without knowing that it is doing it? How can the ego repress from consciousness the act of repressing from consciousness?

Existentialists suggest that human consciousness cannot be examined according to standard scientific methods of objective observation and hypothesis testing. What is required, instead, is the method of **phenomenology.** In phenomenology, the person describes his or her own immediate conscious experience. Edmund Husserl (1859–1938) is generally considered to be the father of phenomenology. Around the turn of the century, he proposed phenomenology as a positive alternative to the experimental and naturalistic methods of scientific psychology. In Husserl's view, the phenomenologist should seek to purge him- or herself of all biasing preconceptions in order to describe the unique conscious experience as it exists in its raw and pure form. Such a purging is not easy to accomplish. Among other things, it entails overcoming the *natural attitude* (Jennings, 1986), which is our tendency to accept the surrounding environment as something that really exists "out there" as a fixed reality shared by others. Husserl does not suggest that the natural attitude is wrong. Rather, these commonsense assumptions must be temporarily suspended if the phenomenologist is to "purify" consciousness.

The existentialists' phenomenological investigations of consciousness reveal that a person's existence is that of **Dasein,** translated as "being-in-the-world." The concept of Dasein underscores the idea that human beings have no existence apart from the world and that the world has no meaning apart from the people in it. There are essentially three modes of Dasein, three ways of being in the world (Heidegger). The **Umwelt** is the physiological base of human life and the natural environment within which it is embedded. The **Mitwelt** is the world of interpersonal relationships. The **Eigenwelt** is the self-world of inner feelings and affections. The person is simultaneously in three worlds at once. Existence is simultaneously natural, social, and personal. And thus, a person's conscious experience incorporates the three overlapping realms of Dasein.

We Create Ourselves

As the existentialists see it, each of us is thrown into the world at a given moment in time and space, with certain inborn capabilities and limitations, and we are challenged to make something meaningful out of our lives. The condition of our "**thrownness**" determines certain aspects of our lives. If, for instance, I am thrown into the world of the American South in the early 1800s as a black baby born of slaves, the chances are good that I will become a slave. If I am thrown into a contemporary rural Indian village as a woman, I am likely to follow the Hindu precepts for feminine identity, marrying at an appropriate age and remaining forever deferential to my husband. By contrast, if I am thrown as a male into a wealthy and white American family in the early 1950s, my prospects are much different.

Jean-Paul Sartre

Throwness is the "luck of the draw"—completely arbitrary and beyond anybody's control.

In the twentieth century, Westerners are thrown into a world that appears to embody no overarching meaning or purpose. There is no essential meaning to life, suggest the existentialists. Organized religion has ceased to provide a framework of meaning for most Westerners. Science, art, and philosophy have also failed to provide a worldview that tells us clearly why we are here on this planet and what we should be doing while we are here. In the wake of life's perceived randomness and ambiguity, modern men and women may experience **Angst,** or anxiety about being and about the prospects of nothingness (Sartre, 1965). In other words, a conscientious assessment of life and consciousness alerts the man or woman to the possibility of *nonbeing*—of leading a life that is nothing, meaningless, void. To live an authentic life, one must seek meaning in the void.

To make one's own meaning in life is to create the self. Existentialists believe that authentic men and women create themselves anew with each new moment of existence. Ideally, we are continually *becoming* a new person. Writes Sartre (1965), "man is nothing else but what he makes of himself" (p. 36). The lifelong process of creating the self is what Sartre called the *fundamental project.* Through the fundamental project, the person continually questions who he or she is and searches for more authentic ways of being in the world. In Sartre's

Creative fidelity: A nun provides home care for an elderly American Indian.

view, each person ultimately seeks to be God, which is to say that each person aims to become the architect of his or her own life—the ultimate maker or creator of the self. This is not blasphemy or ridiculous pride, according to Sartre. Rather, such a desire is the only legitimate existential response to a thrown world that, in and of itself, has no meaning.

While Sartre finds authenticity in the human being's project to become God, other existentialists find it elsewhere. Buber (1947, 1970) finds authenticity in the meeting of two persons via the "I–Thou" encounter (Chapter 11). Buber's conception of the I–Thou is an especially intimate moment in two people's lives in which each fills the other's consciousness. In a similarly interpersonal vein, Marcel (1964) finds authenticity in what he calls **creative fidelity.** People find meaning in life when they commit themselves to each other in bonds of faithfulness. Such fidelity is creative in that the partners define themselves anew through relation. Marcel believes that creative fidelity opens the door to spontaneity and growth in human relations. Yet too many people misunderstand such faithfulness. They view it as a begrudging duty that ties them down and limits life's possibilities. In such instances, fidelity degenerates into mere *constancy,* or the unexamined commitment to a stale routine.

Feature 8.A

Finding Meaning in the Absurd
The Psychology of Ernest Becker

The hero of one of Jonathan Swift's poems describes the absurd paradox of human life. Swift's hero is tormented by the realization that his beautiful and idealized lover, Caelia, must, like all other animals on earth, occasionally relieve herself on the toilet. It's enough to drive him to the brink of madness:

> Nor wonder how I lost my wits;
> Oh! Caelia, Caelia, Caelia shits!

Swift's hero is troubled by more than a mere neurotic peccadillo, argues Ernest Becker in the book for which he was awarded, posthumously, the Pulitzer Prize. In *The Denial of Death*, Becker (1973) asserts that Swift's poor hero has articulated *the* essential paradox of human existence. The fact that his lover, Caelia, must obey her creaturely urges is but one example of the fact that the human being is both a transcendent god, as Sartre might contend, and a defecating animal. As such, human beings exist both outside and inside nature. On the one hand, humans are symbolic creatures who soar above the natural world, who can place themselves "imaginatively at a point in space and contemplate bemusedly" their own planet. "This immense expansion, this dexterity, this ethereality, this self-consciousness gives to man literally the status of a small god in nature, as the Renaissance thinkers knew" (Becker, 1973, p. 26). Yet at the same time:

as the Eastern sages also knew, man is a worm, and food for worms. This is the paradox: he is out of nature and hopelessly in it; he is dual, up in the stars and yet housed in a heart-pumping, breath-gasping body that once belonged to a fish and still carries the gill marks to prove it. His body is a material fleshy casing that is alien to him in many ways—the strangest and most repugnant way being that it aches and bleeds and will decay and die. Man is literally split in two: he has an awareness of his own splendid uniqueness in that he sticks out of nature with a towering majesty, and yet he goes back into the ground a few feet in order blindly and dumbly to rot and disappear forever. It is a terrifying dilemma to be in and to have to live with. (Becker, 1973, p. 26)

Becker views the ancient duality of mind and body from a psychoanalytic and existential perspective, blending ideas from Freud, Kierkegaard, and the psychoanalyst Otto Rank. In the unconscious, writes Becker, mind is associated with the immortality of the spirit, with soaring above nature, and with escaping clean away from the earth. By contrast, the body connects to the mortality of the flesh, being bound to the earth and encased within our dirty corporeality. The mind is reason and the body is emotion. The mind is abstract and the body is concrete. The mind is represented by the Sky God; the body is represented by the Earth Mother (deReincourt, 1974). These associations are evident in myths and dreams, writes Becker.

The human being is the only animal who anticipates and dreads its own mortality. Indeed, the fear of death is the fundamental motive for all living, argues Becker. As transcendent and mindful beings who long to soar above our bodily entrapments, we all know that we are not long for this world, that worms will eventually eat our flesh. Our fundamental response to the paradox is to deny death, to engage in "activity designed largely to avoid the fatality of death, to overcome it by denying in some way that it is the final destiny for man" (p. ix). Through heroism, writes Becker, the adult seeks to transcend death by giving birth to products, people, and ideas that may outlive the self. The hero creates a legacy of the self and then offers it to others as a gift. Yet Becker is not glib about the gift giving. It is with great terror and confusion that people generate their legacies of the self:

Who knows what form the forward momentum of life will take in the time ahead or what use it will make of our anguished searching? The most that any one of us can seem to do is to fashion something—an object or ourselves—and drop it into the confusion, make an offering of it, so to speak, to the life force. (p. 285)

In Becker's view, people differ in their characteristic approach to generating a death-denying legacy—an "offering" or gift—and in the quality of these gifts. Here Becker follows closely the writings of Rank (1936, 1968). The man or woman who is unable to offer any kind of gift at all is the *neurotic.* As a defense against the fear of death, the neurotic erects an impenetrable character shield that keeps him or her from engaging the world in a heroic manner. On one level at least, neurosis is a failure in courage, or "will" (Rank, 1936). The *average* man or woman offers "the gift that society specifies in advance" (Becker, 1973, p. 173). Conforming and dependable, the average person finds a conventional niche in the social world and performs the heroic behaviors—builds a home, raises children, contributes to society, and so on—that society deems appropriate. The average person does not seek heroism beyond the dictates of the social order.

The man or woman who offers the most authentic and influential gift is the *artist* (Becker, 1973; Rank, 1968). The artist expresses ideal development in which the fear of death is most successfully transformed into creative activity. The artist understands the world in complex terms and experiences life in all of its emotional richness. The gift that the artist offers has a lasting value, transcending society to speak to the "highest powers":

> If you are an artist you fashion a peculiarly personal gift, the justification of your own heroic identity, which means that it is always aimed at least partly over the heads of your fellow men. After all, they can't grant the immortality of your personal soul. As Rank argued in the breath-taking closing chapters of *Art and Artist,* there is no way for the artist to be at peace with his work or with society that accepts it. The artist's gift is always to creation itself, to the ultimate meaning of life, to God. We should not be surprised that Rank was brought to exactly the same conclusion as Kierkegaard: that the only way out of human conflict is full renunciation, to give one's life as a gift to the highest powers. (Becker, 1973, p. 173)

We Alone Are Responsible for Who We Become

The search for meaning and authenticity is not a hobby that we can pursue in our idle time, when we are free to introspect and make sense of things. It is not something we pursue to enhance our enjoyment in life or to broaden our interests, like taking a course in ballroom dancing or learning how to meditate. The search for meaning is not something we do to find greater success in life or to improve our job performance. It is rather an integral part of all living, suggest the existentialists. Rather than an idle pastime, the search for meaning is a *moral imperative* in human life. Men and women who do not struggle with meaning shirk their existential responsibility. In simple terms, it is downright *wrong* to deny the Angst of existence, to accept uncritically the hackneyed meanings provided by society and its institutions. This is an example of what the existentialists call **bad faith.**

In bad faith, the person denies the unity of consciousness, thereby splitting off from conscious experience some important truth about the self. The person refuses to reflect on the possible meanings of significant aspects of his or her experience, effectively deceiving the self. For instance, a rich stockbroker may fail to consider the negative ramifications of his materialistic lifestyle for the well-being of society. Or a college sophomore may fail to consider carefully why she is going to bed with that popular young man whom she hardly knows. In bad faith, people deny responsibility for their own behavior, suggesting instead that what they do is sanctioned or encouraged by friends, family, teachers, the church, tradition, social customs, or society at large. In the extreme, bad faith makes for blind conformity and grand self-deception. Those who perpetually live in bad faith avoid the Angst of meaninglessness by adopting the unexamined meanings of others. Their lives are cowardly lies, according to existentialists. Relatedly, bad faith can lead to intense feelings of **existential guilt,** or guilt over failing to fulfill the many possibilities of life. While everybody is susceptible to existential guilt, it is the person who fails to make the hard choices about defying conventions and leading an authentic human existence who in the long run is most vulnerable in this regard. In its strongest form, existential guilt, therefore, is the deep regret a person may feel in realizing that he or she has been unable to take advantage of the many opportunities for growth and commitment that life has offered.

According to the existentialist views of Kierkegaard and Sartre, the man or woman who rejects bad faith and lives an authentic existence is still likely to experience the pain of loneliness. The loneliness is part of Angst, in the existentialist view, for a careful examination of consciousness tells us the awful truth: each of us is forever alone in the world—forever alone and forever responsible. (Existentialism is not for the faint-hearted.) Life frightens us and causes us to tremble. In his mysterious and lyrical essay, *Fear and Trembling,* Kierkegaard (1843/1941) suggests that there are three basic ways for Western men and women to respond to the lonely challenge of human existence. The first, and perhaps most popular, is to live the life of the aesthetic, seeking the pleasure and fulfillment of the senses in daily life. In its most enlightened form, aestheticism strives for physical, sensory *beauty.* The ethical person seeks *truth* and *goodness* by fashioning a life guided by rational, objective, and abstract ethical principles.

The third and highest form of existence is exhibited by the religious person, epitomized in Kierkegaard's description of the "knight of faith." Kierkegaard's existential brand of Christianity exhorts men and women to go beyond rational moral principles and live by faith, even though life seems absurd. Many forms of existentialism do not adopt Kierkegaard's religious emphasis. Yet all tend to share his riveting conviction that the individual person is essentially alone in the world, solely responsible for his or her own unique project of consciousness. Like the knight of faith, the authentic existential man or woman goes beyond social conventions, even ethical norms, to grapple with ultimate issues of meaning in a world that appears absurd.

Freedom, Control, and Challenge in Human Affairs

The direct effects of existentialism on psychology can most clearly be seen in clinical work, where existential psychiatrists like Binswanger, Boss, and Frankl have developed innovative approaches to therapy (see especially Frankl, 1965). For instance, the main goal of Frankl's *logotherapy* is to help clients find meaning in

Freedom.

their own lives. With respect to scientific research on the person, however, the influence of existentialism has been more subtle. Existentialism and phenomenology have combined with a number of other developments in psychology, especially with what has been called the "cognitive revolution" in psychology (described in Chapter 9) to promote research into how people make meaning in their daily lives, how they seek to predict and control events, and how they deal with freedom and challenge.

In this section, we survey four vigorous lines of research into personality processes that are of central interest to the existentialist/phenomenological traditions. Though none of these approaches employs the strict phenomenological methods advocated by existentialists (Jennings, 1986), and only two pay explicit homage to existentialism, they all focus on the quality of subjective conscious experience in human lives. And all four begin with an image of the person more or less commensurate with existentialist approaches—an image of the person as a responsible decision maker who seeks meaning and coherence and who is more or less free to control the fate of his or her own existence.

Who (or What) Is in Control?

Personal Causation and Control   Different approaches to the person vary markedly in their views concerning who or what controls human behavior. As we saw in Chapter 2, psychoanalysts suggest that human behavior is controlled by forces within the person but outside of the person's awareness, such as unconscious wishes, conflicts, and instinctual dynamics. By contrast, the behaviorists and social-learning theorists of Chapter 6 point to forces outside the person, residing in the environment, as the main shapers of human destiny. Yet both psychoanalysts and behaviorists agree that the person is not the master of his or her own fate—that forces beyond the person's control (in the unconscious or in the environment) are the main controlling agents in human behavior and experience. Existentialists, on the other hand, insist that people control their own behavior. They believe that human beings are essentially free to create themselves within the context established by the thrownness of their existence. Because of this freedom, human beings are ultimately responsible for what they do.

The debate between determinism (as represented by traditional psychoanalysis and behaviorism) and free will (as represented by the existentialists) is one of the oldest debates in Western scholarship. In that philosophers, theologians, and scientists have struggled with it for over 2000 years, we are not likely to resolve the debate right here. However, it is important to recognize that some people function in such a way as to suggest that they *perceive* that they have control over their lives, whereas other people tend to function under the implicit assumption that they have very little control. In the words of psychologist Richard deCharms (1968) some people experience life as if they were *origins;* others feel that they are *pawns.* An origin is a person who feels that he or she causes things to happen, that he or she is the determining source in his or her own life. Origins feel that they are free to choose. Pawns, on the other hand, do not feel free. A pawn feels that what he or she does is determined by external forces. Like the expendable chess pieces, pawns perceive that they are "moved around" by larger forces over which they have very little control. Origins and pawns differ in their fundamental understanding of what deCharms calls **personal causation.** The origin is the prime causal agent in his or her life; by contrast, the pawn feels that he or she is "caused."

Ryan and Grolnick (1986) examined individual differences in elementary school students' perceptions of the "origin climate" of their classrooms. A total of 140 students in nine classes in the fourth through sixth grades completed a questionnaire assessing their perception of the origin/pawn orientation of their teacher and classroom environment. In origin classrooms, teachers were perceived as warm and accepting and as encouraging the children to accept personal responsibility for their behavior. In pawn classrooms, teachers were more controlling and directing. About 2 months later, the children completed questionnaires designed to measure feelings of self-worth, competence, and mastery. They also wrote imaginative stories in response to a picture of a teacher and a classroom. The stories were rated on dimensions of technical goodness, creativity, effort, aggression, the "origin character" of the students in the story, and the degree of autonomy of the teacher in the story.

Table 8.1 displays some of the main results from the study. Students who perceived that their classroom encouraged personal responsibility (high origin climate) reported greater levels of self-worth, perceived competence, and mastery, compared to students who perceived their classroom as less encouraging of personal responsibility. In addition, high-origin-climate children wrote stories that showed greater technical skill, greater effort, and more creativity, and the content of their stories emphasized teacher autonomy and student responsibility, compared to the students reporting low origin climate. Ryan and Grolnick's results underscore that it is the subjective impressions of children—their phenomenological experience of the classroom—that is the important determinant. When children perceive that they are encouraged to be free origins rather than controlled pawns they feel better about themselves and their abilities, and they project an image of a positive classroom onto the imaginative stories they compose.

 Table 8.1

Correlations Between Students' Perceptions of Classroom Origin Climate and Measures of Self-Worth, Competence, and Mastery

	Perceived Origin Climate		
Self-Report Measures	**Boys**	**Girls**	**Total**
General self-worth	.41**	.26*	.32**
Cognitive perceived competence	.40**	.35**	.35**
Mastery motivation	.24**	.27*	.27**

*p < .05
**p < .01
Note: Perceived Origin Climate scores were modified in order to remove variance due to different classrooms.
From Ryan & Grolnick (1986, p. 553).

Psychologist Ellen Langer (1981) has worked at the other end of the age spectrum—examining the elderly in nursing homes. She argues that what is sometimes regarded as senility in old people is really a response to an environment that treats the elderly as pawns rather than as origins. Langer and Rodin (1976) studied two groups of elderly residents in a New England nursing home. In one group, the residents were encouraged to show personal responsibility in their daily lives. They could decide on their own room arrangement, where they wished to meet visitors, and what activities they might pursue in their free time. They were also given a living plant to care for. Residents in the other group were provided with the same opportunities but were left with the clear impression that the staff would take responsibility for most of the important daily decisions, even to the point of caring for the plants. Three weeks later the residents in the first group, encouraged to take personal responsibility and perceive themselves as origins rather than pawns, reported greater levels of happiness and independence than residents in the comparison group. Ratings of the residents by the attending nurses showed the same differences, even though the two groups were well matched in health and well-being before the study began. The positive effects of encouraging personal control and responsibility were still evident in a follow-up assessment taken 18 months later (Rodin & Langer, 1977).

The perception that one is in control of events can have positive consequences even in life situations in which personal control seems unlikely. Langer (1975) suggests that people sometimes operate under an **illusion of control.** For example a man playing a lottery may (erroneously) believe that if he chooses his own number he stands a better chance of winning the jackpot than if somebody else chooses the number for him, even though lottery winnings are determined by pure chance and his belief in personal control in this regard is a pure illusion. Illusions of control, however, may promote psychological well-being, mental health, and recovery from illness (Alloy & Abramson, 1979; Taylor & Brown, 1988). People who feel that they are the masters of their fate—even if they really aren't—tend to be less depressed and anxious and tend to cope better with major setbacks in life, such as serious illness. In contrast, those who feel helpless in the face of life's challenges—even if their perceived helplessness makes rational sense—tend to be depressed, as we shall see in Chapter 9.

Social psychologist Shelly Taylor (1983) has examined illusions of control in women who have undergone surgery for breast cancer. Based on intensive interviews of 78 women and their family members, Taylor suggests that healthy adjustment to threatening life events, like cancer, involves three interrelated themes: the search for meaning, gaining a sense of mastery, and self-enhancement. The search for meaning involves the need to understand why a crisis occurred and what its impact has been. Breast cancer is a complicated disease with many possible causes, most of which probably remain unknown. Physicians find it virtually impossible to pinpoint the exact cause of the cancer in any particular individual. Therefore, a patient's efforts to pinpoint the cause would seem a futile endeavor. Yet Taylor's research shows that virtually all women with breast cancer eventually develop a theory about the origins of their own disease. Many attribute the illness to stress, hereditary factors, or poor diet. Some point to a particular carcinogen to which they may have been exposed. Some suggest a particular event or accident—such as a blow to the breast. (One of Taylor's subjects said her breast cancer resulted from being hit by a flying Frisbee.) All of these interpretations have an illusory quality, for the patient cannot possibly know the origins. But the illusions are positive. They illustrate the human yearning to make sense of subjective experience, what existentialists call the *will to meaning.*

Taylor writes that successful adaptation to threatening life events involves gaining a feeling of mastery or control over the event in order to manage it or to keep it from occurring a second time. Again illusion prevails. Two-thirds of the breast cancer patients believed that they had at least some control over the course of or recurrence of their cancer. Table 8.2 displays some of their stated beliefs concerning their ability to control the cancer. Once they had rendered the cancer meaningful and controllable, the best-adapted women continued to bolster their self-esteem by concentrating on positive thoughts and images about themselves, some of which also had an illusory quality. A favorite method for accomplishing this was to compare oneself positively to others who seemed less fortunate, a process that Taylor calls *downward social comparison.* This process enables the individual to sustain the illusion that he or she is doing better than most other people in similar situations:

> The point, of course, is that everyone is better off than someone as long as one picks the right dimension. In our study, several women with lumpectomies [surgery that removes only the malignant lump] compared themselves favorably to women with mastectomies [removal of the entire breast]; no woman with a mastectomy ever evaluated herself against a woman with a lumpectomy. Older women considered themselves better off than younger women; no younger woman expressed the wish that she had been older. Married women pitied the single women; no single woman pointed out that it would have been easier if she'd been married. The women who were the worst off consoled themselves with the fact that they were not dying or were not in pain. The amount of self-enhancement in these dimensional comparisons is striking. Not only choice of comparison target, then, but also choice of comparison dimension is important for restoring self-enhancement in the face of threat. (Taylor, 1983, p. 1166)

Taylor's research is in line with a growing body of findings from personality, social, and clinical psychology that suggests that illusions of personal control promote psychological health and well-being (Suls & Rittenhouse, 1987; Taylor & Brown, 1988). As we shall see in Chapter 9, people prone to depression are less apt to harbor these illusions than are "normal" people. People who are *not* depressed overestimate how much control they exert over positive events in their lives (while underestimating their responsibility for negative ones). They tend to reward themselves more than their objective performance warrants, and they show a sometimes unrealistic optimism about life (Scheier & Carver, 1987). In

Table 8.2

Sense of Mastery Over Disease: Women's Stated Beliefs About Their Cancers

"I believe that if you're a positive person, your attitude has a lot to do with it. I definitely feel I will never get it again."

"My mental attitude, I think, is the biggest control over it I have. I want to feel there is something I can do, that there is some way I can control it."

"I think that if you feel you are in control of it, you can control it up to a point. I absolutely refuse to have any more cancer."

[Where the cancer came from] "was an important question to me at first. The doctor's answer was that it was a multifaceted illness. I looked over the known causes of cancer, like viruses, radiation, genetic mutation, environmental carcinogens, and the one I focused on very strongly was diet. I know now why I focused on it. It was the only one that was simple enough for me to understand and change. You eat something that's bad for you, you get sick."

"I felt that I had lost control of my body somehow, and the way for me to get back some control was to find out as much as I could. It really became almost an obsession."

One spouse described his wife: "She got books, she got pamphlets, she studied, she talked to cancer patients, she found out everything that was happening to her, and she fought it. She went to war with it. She calls it taking in her covered wagons and surrounding it."

Attempting to control the side effects of one's treatments represents another effort at mastery. For example, 92% of the patients who received chemotherapy did something to control its side effects. For slightly under half, this involved simple medications or sleep, but the remaining half used a combination of mental efforts at control. These included imaging, self-hypnosis, distraction, and meditation. Similar efforts were made to control the less debilitating but still unpleasant side effects of radiation therapy. For example, one woman who was undergoing radiation therapy would imagine that there was a protective shield keeping her body from being burned by the radiation. Another woman imaged her chemotherapy as powerful cannons which blasted away pieces of the dragon, cancer. One 61-year-old woman simply focused her attention on healing with the instruction to her body, "Body, cut this shit out."

Quoted from Taylor (1983, pp. 1163–1164).

Table 8.3

Selected Items From Rotter's Locus of Control (I–E) Scale

I more strongly believe that:

1. a. Many of the unhappy things in people's lives are partly due to bad luck. (E)
   b. People's misfortunes result from the mistakes they make. (I)
2. a. In my case, getting what I want has little or nothing to do with luck. (I)
   b. Many times we might just as well decide what to do by flipping a coin. (E)
3. a. As far as world affairs are concerned, most of us are the victims of forces we can neither understand nor control. (E)
   b. By taking an active part in political and social affairs, people can control world events. (I)
4. a. Sometimes I can't understand how teachers arrive at the grades they give. (E)
   b. There is a direct connection between how hard I study and the grades I get. (I)
5. a. What happens to me is my own doing. (I)
   b. Sometimes I feel that I don't have enough control over the direction my life is taking. (E)
6. a. When I make plans, I am almost certain that I can make them work. (I)
   b. It is not always wise to plan too far ahead because many things turn out to be a matter of good or bad fortune anyhow. (E)

Source: Rotter (1966).

addition, they may compensate for lack of control in certain domains of life by increasing their sense of control in others. For example, a recent study of 71 cancer patients showed that even when patients felt they could not control the course of the disease itself, their adjustment was positively related to their ability to compensate for their lack of control by increasing their efforts to control their daily emotional reactions to and physical symptoms of the disease (Thompson, Sobolew-Shubin, Galbraith, Schwankovsky, & Cruzen, 1993).

Locus of Control The pioneering research in the psychology of personal control was undertaken by E. Jerry Phares (1957) and Julian Rotter (1966) within the context of Rotter's social-learning theory (Chapter 6). You may recall that a key concept in Rotter's theory is *expectancy,* which he defines as the subjectively held probability that a particular reinforcement will occur as the outcome of specific behavior. **Locus of control** refers to individual differences in expectancy. People with an *internal* locus of control expect reinforcements to follow their own actions. In other words, they believe that their own behavior controls the consequences that subsequently follow—subsequent reinforcing events are contingent on the person's behavior. The person with an *external* locus of control expects that his or her behavior will not lead to predictable reinforcement. Rather, reinforcements are

Table 8.4

Selected Findings on Locus of Control

Having a relatively internal (as opposed to external) locus of control has been associated with all of the following:

Showing less compliance and conformity.

Greater perceived competence and independence.

Greater efforts to acquire information from the environment.

Greater knowledge of one's own health and sickness.

More positive attitudes about physical exercise.

Lower levels of cigarette smoking.

Lessened susceptibility to essential hypertension and heart attack.

Better prognosis once heart attack occurs.

Greater academic achievement, especially among male adolescents.

Greater levels of overall psychological adjustment.

Demographics and childhood origins of locus of control:

Minority groups and those from low socioeconomic strata tend to score more external than middle-class whites.

Child-rearing practices characterized as warm, protective, positive, and nurturant seem to be related to subsequent development of an internal locus of control in the child.

Externals tend to report that their parents were inconsistent in their discipline.

Few age differences in general I–E scores have been shown. However, when specific I–E measures that relate to beliefs about intelligence and health are used, older individuals are found to be more external than younger ones.

Sources: Lachman (1986); Phares (1977, 1988).

dispensed by external sources of control, such as powerful others, chance, luck, and so forth. Reinforcing events do not appear to be contingent on his or her behavior.

Many self-report scales have been developed to measure locus of control (Phares, 1978). The most popular measure is the **I–E Scale** (Rotter, 1966), which contains 29 forced-choice items like those reproduced in Table 8.3. Rotter's scale assumes that locus of control is a broad, generalized factor that cuts across many different domains in which expectancies might reveal themselves. Recent years have witnessed a proliferation of more specialized scales, designed to assess beliefs about control in specific domains. These include scales to assess locus of control as it pertains to one's understanding of marriage (Miller, Lefcourt, Holmes, Ware, & Saleh, 1986), affiliation situations (Lefcourt, Martin, Fick, & Saleh, 1985), intellectual functioning (Lachman, 1986), and health (Wallston & Wallston, 1981).

The I–E Scale has been used in literally thousands of research studies, and the massive literature suggests that locus of control is an extremely important and influential personality factor (Phares, 1977, 1988). Some of the best-established findings are summarized in Table 8.4. In general, having an internal locus of control has been associated with many positive outcomes in life, from better academic achievement to better adjustment in interpersonal relationships. In keeping with much of the literature on personal control and causation, people who believe that their own behavior is responsible for the reinforcements they receive (internal locus of control) tend to be healthy and independent information-seekers who adapt well to many life challenges. However, internal locus of control is not always an asset. In *nonresponsive* environments, wherein efforts to exert personal control are repeatedly thwarted, the person with an internal locus of control may encounter many difficulties and report lower levels of satisfaction, compared to people with external loci of control (Janoff-Bulman & Brickman, 1980; Rotter, 1975).

Self-Determination Theory

A major theme in most existential approaches to the person, and in the related humanistic approaches discussed later in this chapter, is that people seek to control their environments and determine their fates. Therefore, human beings should actively resist those forces that threaten to rob them of their freedom of choice. According to this view, people seek to be origins rather than pawns.

A related line of research focuses on **intrinsic motivation.** Research on intrinsic motivation began in the early 1970s with the observation that in certain situations material rewards produce surprising *decreases* in human performance (Deci, 1971, 1972; Lepper & Greene, 1978). While traditional theories of reinforcement, like Skinner's behaviorism (Chapter 6), tell us that people learn and perform best when they are rewarded for what they do, numerous studies show that receiving an extrinsic reward has its *costs* in certain situations. Extrinsic rewards may undermine the intrinsic value of certain behaviors and reduce the person's perceived freedom to do what he or she wants to do.

Consider these simple experiments conducted by Deci (1971). College students were typically asked to solve a series of interesting mechanical puzzles. In the experimental condition, the students were told that they would be paid $1 for each puzzle solved during a specified period of time. In the control condition, the students were given no information about monetary rewards. After the time period had elapsed, the students were given an opportunity to choose from a number of different activities available to them. Their behavior during this free-choice period was observed through a one-way mirror. Deci found that those students who had been promised payment for their puzzle performance (the experimental group) spent significantly less time playing with the puzzle during the free-choice period than did the students who were not promised payment (control group). Furthermore, the students who were paid for their performance reported that they enjoyed the puzzle task less and found it less interesting than did the students who were not paid.

What do these differences mean? Deci concluded that the students who received an extrinsic reward for their performance experienced a decrease in intrinsic motivation. The reward undermined their interest in the puzzles. Now that they were no longer being paid for their performance, they saw little reason to continue playing with the puzzles. Similar studies have produced parallel results. For instance, Lepper, Greene, and Nisbett (1973) found a decrease in children's intrinsic motivation when they were rewarded for their artwork. Children who had received rewards for using certain highly desirable materials in their artwork were less motivated to use those same art materials days later than were those children whose use of the materials had not been rewarded before. College students working on interesting word games became less intrinsically motivated when external deadlines were imposed on their finishing than when none was applied (Amabile, DeJong, & Lepper, 1976). The external contingency of a deadline, like an external reward, shifts the person's perceived reason for undertaking a task from the intrinsic qualities of the task itself to extrinsic factors. The person loses interest in the task when he or she comes to see the motivation for doing the task as prompted from the outside.

Rewards, however, do not always undermine intrinsic motivation. First, a task must be intrinsically interesting if the costs of reward are to be seen. In boring routine tasks, the introduction of a reward may increase a person's interest in the task and improve performance (Calder & Staw, 1975). Second, not all rewards in all situations are equal. While money, grades, and other more or less material rewards that are clearly contingent on performance may undermine intrinsic motivation in certain situations, such social reinforcers as verbal praise and encouragement are likely to increase intrinsic motivation. Furthermore, it depends on exactly what aspect of behavior is being rewarded. Rewards for *effort* (trying hard) are perceived differently than rewards for *ability* (doing well).

A study by Koestner, Zuckerman, and Koestner (1987) illustrates the complexity of intrinsic motivation. In this laboratory study, the experimenters used verbal praise to reinforce college students' performance on an interesting hidden-figures puzzle. In one condition, the students were told that their performance was a test of creative intelligence, inducing an "ego-involvement" attitude. In another condition, the task was introduced as a neutral game, inducing a "task-involvement" attitude. After working with the puzzles, the students received either (1) ability praise ("That's very good; I see you really have a knack for these"), (2) effort praise ("That's very good; I can see you've really applied yourself on these"), or (3) no praise. Then, the students were left alone in a free-choice period during which they were secretly observed in order to determine how much time they spent playing with the hidden-figures puzzles—the behavioral measure of intrinsic motivation. Finally, they were given questionnaires measuring their interest in and enjoyment of the puzzle task.

Table 8.5 is shows some of the results from this experiment. First, task-involved students showed more intrinsic motivation (measured as the amount of time spent playing with the puzzles during the free-choice period) than did students in the ego-involved group. In other words, when the students were told that their performance measured creative intelligence, they showed less intrinsic interest in the puzzles later on. The ego-involving instructions diverted their attention away from the intrinsic enjoyment of the task. Second, students who were praised for their ability showed greater intrinsic motivation than those praised for effort and those who were not praised. Providing positive feedback about how well they were doing increased the students' interest in the task.

A third important finding, not apparent in Table 8.5 is that ability praise was relatively more effective in promoting intrinsic motivation in the ego-involving condition, whereas effort praise worked especially well in the task-involving condition. In other words, if you are performing a task that you enjoy mainly for the sake of enjoyment, then being praised for your effort is likely to increase your intrinsic motivation more than being praised for your ability. But when you perform the task in a context that tests your ability (in this case, a test of "creative intelligence"), receiving praise for your ability is likely to be especially reinforcing and to promote intrinsic motivation.

In an important theoretical development, Edward Deci and Richard Ryan have recently integrated research on intrinsic motivation into the broader framework of what they call **self-determination theory** (Deci & Ryan, 1980, 1985, 1991; Ryan, 1991). According to their view, intrinsic motivation is "the energizing basis for nat-

 Table 8.5

Free-Choice Time (in Seconds) for Type of Involvement and Style of Praise

Type of Involvement	Style of Praise			
	Ability	**Effort**	**Control**	*M*
Ego	270	52	120	147
Task	295	229	120	215
M	283	141	120	181

Note: M = "mean" or "average" score
From Koestner, Zuckerman & Koestner (1987, p. 386).

ural organismic activity" (Deci & Ryan, 1991, p. 244). Human beings are endowed with a natural tendency to encounter new challenges that will promote their self-development. Intrinsically motivated behaviors are experienced with "a full sense of choice, with the experience of doing what one wants, and without the feeling of coercion or compulsion" (Deci & Ryan, 1991, p. 253), such that the person spontaneously engages in activity that appears inherently interesting and enjoyable. Such activity "emanates from oneself, and is thus *self*-determined" (p. 253).

Intrinsically motivated behavior, therefore, is self-determined. By contrast, behavior that is not self-determined may be perceived by the actor as *controlled* or *amotivated*. Controlled behavior occurs when a person acts to meet the demands of some internal or external force; even though controlled behaviors may be "intentional," they feel as if they are things that the person does not truly want to do. Amotivated behaviors are unintentional and often disorganized because the person cannot regulate his or her own actions. For example, under the stress of an imminent writing deadline, a newspaper reporter may wander around her office in a daze. She cannot bring herself to do what she wants to do. She feels that she cannot possibly complete her project in the short time period allotted, so her behavior becomes random and amotivated.

Self-determination begins at birth. Deci and Ryan write:

> According to our perspective, a central feature of human nature is an active agency and a synthetic tendency that we ascribe to the self. From the time of birth, human beings are oriented toward the active exercise of their capacities and interests. They seek out optimal challenges, and they attempt to master and integrate new experiences. In other words, they are engaged in a developmental process that is intrinsic to their nature and is characterized by the tendency toward a more elaborate and extensive organization. (1991, pp. 238–239)

The infant is endowed with a nascent self—a vital core of personality that contains the potential for tremendous expansion. As Deci and Ryan (1991) put it, "the nature of life is to overtake itself" (p. 239). The self seeks to overtake its initial boundaries and limitations, to grow, to master its surround, to appropriate things, people, ideas, and environments, to make that which is nonself part of the self. As the infant masters and synthesizes new experiences, the self becomes more encompassing (it takes in more things) and more integrated (it organizes its contents into meaningful systems). Over time, self-determined behavior enhances the development of self, and as the self develops, more and more of the person's behavior may become self-determined. This means that in healthy development, the person's behavior becomes less like that of a pawn and more like that of an origin. An expanded self makes for a greater degree of *self-involvement* in behavior. The person's experience of life becomes akin to that of the "author" or "owner" of his or her own behavior. Behavior becomes less controlled and amotivated. Action becomes incorporated within and guided by the self.

Deci and Ryan argue that self-determined behavior stems from three basic psychological needs. First, the need for *competence* encompasses the person's strivings to control the outcomes of events and to experience a sense of mastery and effectiveness in dealing with the environment. (Remember that similar ideas are featured in White's [Chapter 2] neoanalytic theory of competence and Bandura's [Chapter 6] notion of self-efficacy.) Second, the need for *autonomy* involves the desire to feel that one is independent of external pressures and able to relate to the world as an origin rather than a pawn. Third, the need for *relatedness* encompasses a person's strivings to care for others, to feel that others are relating to the self in authentic and mutually supportive ways, and to feel a satisfying and coherent involvement with the social world more generally. The three needs generate self-determined behavior, and self-determined behavior promotes development, or what Deci and Ryan call *organismic integration*. Organismic integration has two facets—unity of the self and integration into the social order. Over time, self-determined behavior helps the person experience his or her inner life in a more cohesive and unified manner, and it helps involve the person in coherent and meaningful interactions with other people.

The development of the self is a product of an intricate dialectic between the person and the social world. Deci and Ryan view the social world in terms of the opportunities and constraints it may provide for self-determined behavior. Three social dimensions are particularly important. First, the social environment may offer *autonomy support*. In other words, it may be encouraging of choice and innovation in behavior. Environments that discourage choice function to control a person's behavior. Second, the social environment may provide *structure* for behavior. Highly structured environments provide clear guidelines about what kinds of behaviors lead to what kinds of outcomes, and they give the actor explicit feedback concerning how "well" he or she is doing in the environment. Third, the social environment may offer interpersonal *involvement*. Involvement describes the degree to which significant others (e.g., parents, teachers, friends, spouse) are interested in and devote time and energy to a relationship. All in all, social contexts that provide high levels of autonomy support, *moderate* structure, and that contain involved others are optimal for encouraging self-determined behavior and organismic integration.

In sum, intrinsically motivated behavior is inherently interesting and enjoyable, involves optimally challenging tasks and activities, and is often performed in the absence of external rewards. Such behavior is self-determined. Self-determined behavior serves the basic needs of competence, autonomy, and relatedness. Self-determined behavior flourishes in environments that support autonomy, provide moderate structure, and involve people who care about the person and are invested in the person's life. Self-determined behavior makes for organismic integration, by promoting unity of one's inner life and integration into a social order. Deci and Ryan argue that self-determination ultimately enables the person to experience the "true self," so that he or she may lead what the existentialists call an "authentic" life:

Authenticity, we suggest, is a descriptor for behavior that is an expression of the true self and for which one accepts full responsibility. When an action is endorsed by its "author," the experience is that of integrity and cohesion—the experience is one of being true to one's *self*. Authenticity is thus self-determination. (1991, p. 277)

The Hardy Personality

In her provocative research on **hardiness,** psychologist Suzanne Kobasa draws explicitly from existential psychology. Existentialism paints a picture of the authentic person as an active and responsible creator who thrives on challenge and change and is willing to make courageous commitments. Likewise, Kobasa's hardy men and women seek meaning in life through *commitment* to the activities of their lives, *control* over the events of their experience, and anticipation of change as an exciting *challenge* to further development. The hardy personality thrives on challenging events and significant life changes that other people are likely to find especially distressing.

A substantial body of research suggests that high levels of stress in daily life tend to lead to physical illness (Dohrenwend & Dohrenwend, 1974; Kobasa, 1985). Many of these studies conceptualize a "stressful event" as a change in an average person's normal routine. These changes may be negative (loss of job, illness of family member) or positive (marriage, promotion). A popular and extremely useful instrument for assessing the extent of life changes in a person's life is the **Social Readjustment Rating Scale** (Holmes & Rahe, 1967). As shown in Table 8.6, this scale lists life events likely to induce stress, from the most stressful events (death of spouse) to the least stressful (minor traffic violations). Many studies suggest that people who score high on this test during a particular period of their lives—indicating that many of these events or especially severe events have occurred—tend to become sick. The direct positive correlation between stress and illness, however, is modest in strength, averaging around +.30 (Kobasa, 1985).

Kobasa asks a simple question: Given this modest relation between stress and illness, what can we say about the many people who experience high levels of stress but do not get sick? Kobasa hypothesizes that hardiness buffers people from the ill effects of stress. It is the hardy people among us who thrive in the face of stress.

In an initial study of middle- and upper-level executives of a public utility company, Kobasa (1979) found that those who experienced high stress and low levels of illness scored significantly higher on indices of hardiness than did those with high stress and high levels of illness (Table 8.7). Two years after the original assessment, the men were separated into two levels of interim stress (high versus low) and two levels of hardiness (high versus low), and self-reports of new

Continued on p. 449

 **Table 8.6**

The Social Readjustment Rating Scale

Rank	Life Event	Mean Value[a]
1	Death of spouse	100
2	Divorce	73
3	Marital separation	65
4	Jail term	63
5	Death of close family member	63
6	Personal injury or illness	53
7	Marriage	50
8	Fired at work	47
9	Marital reconciliation	45
10	Retirement	45
11	Change in health of family member	44
12	Pregnancy	40
13	Sex difficulties	39
14	Gain of new family member	39
15	Business readjustment	39
16	Change in financial state	38
17	Death of close friend	37
18	Change to different line of work	36
19	Change in number of arguments with spouse	35
20	Large Mortgage	31
21	Foreclosure of mortage or loan	30
22	Change in responsibilities at work	29

Rank	Life Event	Mean Value[a]
23	Son or daughter leaving home	29
24	Trouble with in-laws	29
25	Outstanding personal achievement	28
26	Spouse begin or stop work	26
27	Begin or end school	26
28	Change in living conditions	25
29	Revision of personal habits	24
30	Trouble with boss	23
31	Change in work hours or conditions	20
32	Change in residence	20
33	Change in schools	20
34	Change in recreation	19
35	Change in church activities	19
36	Change in social activities	18
37	Small mortgage or loan	17
38	Change in sleeping habits	16
39	Change in number of family get-togethers	15
40	Change in eating habits	15
41	Vacation	13
42	Christmas	12
43	Minor violations of the law	11

[a]A weighted value. A higher weight indicates a more seriously stressful event.
From Holmes & Rahe (1967, pp. 456–457).

Table 8.7

Differences Between High Stress/Low Illness and High Stress/High Illness Executives

Variable	High Stress/ Low Illness	High Stress/ High Illness	*t* Value
Control			
Nihilism	196.05	281.02	2.49**
External locus of control	5.92	7.90	2.03**
Powerlessness	301.15	388.47	2.11**
Achievement	16.50	15.12	−1.20
Dominance	14.60	13.85	.86
Leadership	33.47	34.63	.73
Commitment			
Alienation from self	102.35	219.15	3.36**
Alienation from work	181.67	223.73	1.22
Alienation from interpersonal	256.02	316.10	1.64
Alienation from family	158.47	198.72	1.27
Alienation from social	202.15	226.95	.94
Role consistency	29.22	29.50	.19
Challenge			
Vegetativeness	155.50	216.27	1.98*
Security	21.11	22.19	.34
Cognitive structure	13.55	14.10	1.10
Adventurousness	269.00	337.54	1.78*
Endurance	15.97	14.37	−.96
Interesting experiences	34.97	32.52	−.92
Perception of personal stress	**3.00**	**3.83**	**2.46****

*$p < .05$
**$p < .01$

Note: In this study there were 40 executives in the high stress/low illness group and 40 in the high stress/high illness group. Also, "*t* value" refers to a statistical procedure (the *t*-test) that determines the extent to which the means from two different groups are significantly different from each other.

From Kobasa (1979, p. 7).

Continued from p. 445
symptoms were compared (controlling for old symptom levels). Once again, hardiness was an important predictor of symptom reports among men exposed to high levels of stressful events (Kobasa, Maddi, & Kahn, 1982). In the following passage, Kobasa describes the positive ways in which the hardy male executive might cope with the stress of a job transfer:

> The hardy executive does more than passively acquiesce to the job transfer. Rather, he throws himself actively into the new situation, utilizing his inner resources to make it his own. . . . For him, the job transfer means a chance that can be transformed into a potential step in the right direction in his overarching career plan and also provide his family with a developmentally stimulating change. An *internal* (rather than an *external*) locus of control allows the hardy executive to greet the transfer with the recognition that although it may have been initiated in an office above him, the actual course it takes is dependent on how he handles it. For all these reasons, he is not just a victim of a threatening life change but an active determinant of the consequences it brings about. In contrast, the executive low in hardiness will react to the transfer with less sense of personal resource, more acquiescence, more encroachments of meaninglessness, and a conviction that the change has been externally determined with no possibility of control on his part. In this context, it is understandable that the hardy executive will also tend to perceive the transfer as less personally stressful than his less hardy counterpart. (Kobasa, 1979, p. 9)

Other studies have found that (1) hardy college students report lower levels of illness than their more alienated peers, regardless of stress level (Wiebe & McCallum, 1986); (2) lawyers who score high on commitment scales report lower levels of physiological strain than those scoring low in commitment (Kobasa, 1982); and (3) hardiness is positively associated with higher levels of social support, both of which help people stay healthy during times of stress (Ganellen & Blaney, 1984). Kobasa and Puccetti (1983) have explored the relations among hardiness, social support, coping strategies, strain, and illness. Figure 8.1 illustrates their proposed model of these relations. According to the model, stressful life events tend to increase physiological strain, which in turn increases the likelihood of illness. Indices of strain include heartburn, headaches, insomnia, nervousness, and other physiological symptoms indicating that the body is suffering from stress. Hardiness serves to buffer or lessen the direct effect of stressful life events on strain by promoting successful coping with problems and by increasing the likelihood that the person will draw on appropriate social resources (friends, family, coworkers) to help cope with stress. Thus, hardiness exerts an indirect effect on strain by promoting (1) coping and (2) social support, which in turn promotes coping.

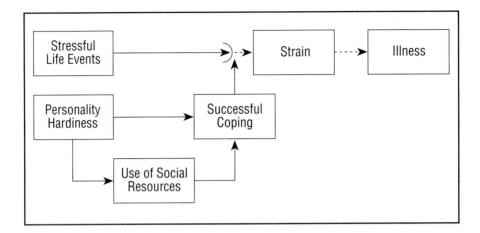

Figure 8.1

Hardiness, Social Resources, and the Stress-Resistance Process.

From Kobasa & Puccetti, 1983, p. 844.

Not all studies, however, support Kobasa's model of hardiness. Schmied and Lawler (1986) found that hardiness did not modify the relation between stress and illness in a sample of 82 working women. Hardy women were no healthier than nonhardy women, and high hardiness did not mitigate the generally positive relation between stress and physical illness. In that most of Kobasa's research has dealt exclusively with men, Schmied and Lawler call into question the validity of hardiness theory for women. Hull, Van Treuren, and Virnelli (1987) argue that hardiness should not be considered a unitary personality type but rather three separate phenomena—control, commitment, and challenge. They indict the challenge dimension as poorly measured and relatively weak in predicting health outcomes. And they suggest that if commitment and control do exert a positive influence on health, they do it directly rather than by moderating stressful events. Essentially, these critics suggest that low levels of control and commitment are themselves inherently stressful. Lack of control and lack of commitment are stressors, they maintain, adding to the overall stress in a person's life and leading to greater physiological strain and eventual physical illness.

Reversal Theory

We have seen how research and theory on personal causation, self-determination theory, and hardiness seem to converge on a common picture of human functioning that reflects the existentialist motifs of freedom, control, and challenge in human affairs. People who perceive that they are in control of their lives, whose behavior is self-determined and intrinsically motivated, and who greet challenges as opportunities for growth and fulfillment lead authentic and meaningful lives in the modern world. Authors of their own existence, they eschew the bad faith of societal conventions and external rewards and focus their efforts instead on self-determined life goals and commitments.

This picture becomes somewhat more complex, however, when we consider Michael Apter's (1982, 1989) **reversal theory** of motivation, emotion, and personality. Like the existentialists, Apter begins his inquiry into human functioning by examining subjective human experience. Adopting an approach he terms "structural phenomenology," Apter seeks to discover the organizing principles of subjective consciousness. According to his view, consciousness is a "complex surface phenomenon below which organizing structures are to be fathomed" (Apter, 1989, p. 4). But Apter's exploration of consciousness yields a number of contradictory qualities that seem to characterize human experience from one moment to the next. Even under the best of conditions, human experience is not always driven by self-determined goals, life commitments, and a sense of personal causation. Instead, experience seems to shift back and forth between sharply contrasting qualities or states. In Apter's view, consciousness is organized according to contrasting pairs of *metamotivational modes,* or ways of being. "Reversals" from one mode or way of being to the other are central features of human consciousness.

Two especially familiar ways of being are the **telic mode** and the **paratelic mode.** Figure 8.2 illustrates the two modes. The Greek word "telos" means "end"

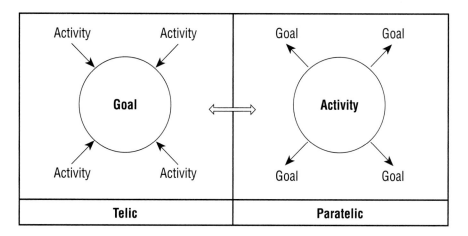

Figure 8.2

The Telic and the Paratelic Modes.

From Apter, 1989, p. 34.

or "goal," and thus in the telic mode, the goal exists as the center of all activity. Consciousness is goal-directed. "In the telic mode, pleasure comes primarily from the feeling of movement towards the goal, of progress and improvement, as well as from the attainment of the goal itself," Apter writes (1989, p. 33). Telic activities are typically oriented toward the future. One strives in the present to attain a desired future end. By contrast, the paratelic mode places the activity itself at the center of consciousness; the activity is an end in itself. "In the paratelic mode, pleasure comes primarily from the activity—from the immediate sensual gratification, from the satisfaction of skilled performance and kinesthetic sensations which go with it, from the continuing interest in seeing what will happen next," Apter writes (1989, p. 33). The paratelic mode appears to be oriented toward the present rather than the future. The here-and-now activity takes precedent over future goals.

The sharp distinction between telic and paratelic modes can be well illustrated when considering the psychological phenomenon of *arousal*. By arousal, Apter simply means "the degree to which one feels oneself to be 'worked up' or emotionally intense about what one is doing" (1989, p. 9). Four arousal-related emotions with which everybody is familiar are relaxation, boredom, excitement, and anxiety. When arousal is low, a person may feel relaxation or boredom. Relaxation feels good; it is hedonically positive. Boredom feels bad; it is hedonically negative. Similarly, under conditions of high arousal, one may feel excitement (hedonically positive) or anxiety (negative). The key point here is that a given level of arousal may be experienced as either positive or negative. I may experience a calm autumn day as relaxing or boring. I may find that a lively party brings me excitement or anxiety.

Part of what determines the hedonic tone of my experience at a given level of arousal is my momentary metamotivational mode. In essence, the telic is an *arousal-avoidance* mode; the paratelic is an *arousal-seeking* mode. Therefore, when my consciousness is focused on goals to be achieved in the future, anything that makes those goals more difficult to achieve, such as obstacles or challenges of some sort, is likely to increase my arousal and lead to the negative experience of anxiety. But when I make progress toward the goal and when I eventually achieve the goal, then arousal tapers off and I experience the pleasant emotions of relaxation and gentle enjoyment—that good feeling of a job well done, progress made, goals achieved or soon to be achieved. When I am in the paratelic mode, by contrast, I adopt a more activity-oriented, rather than goal-oriented, approach to existence. I move from work to play. In the paratelic mode, I may find high levels of arousal to be especially exciting, and I may therefore seek them out. At high levels of arousal, I may experience passion, fascination, thrill, exhilaration, elation, euphoria, and so on. But low levels of arousal may be viewed as understimulating. I become bored in the absence of emotional involvement. There seems to be nothing to do; no activity seems involving enough to provide my conscious experience with the stimulation jolt I need to feel good.

Figure 8.3 illustrates the relations among levels of arousal (low vs. high), hedonic tone (positive vs. negative), and the four emotional states we have dis-

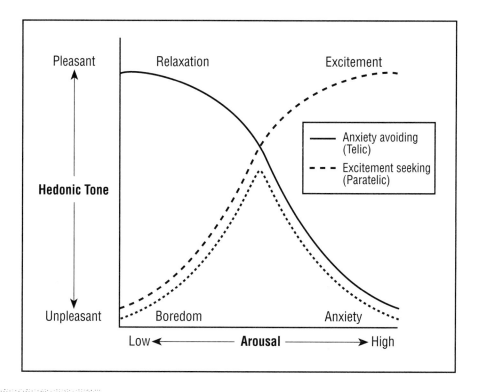

Figure 8.3

The Relationship Between Arousal and Hedonic Tone in Reversal Theory.

From Apter, 1989, p. 18.

cussed (relaxation, boredom, excitement, and anxiety). According to Apter, the telic mode incorporates the emotional dimension of relaxation-anxiety, moving from the upper left to the lower right corner of Figure 8.3. The paratelic mode moves in the opposite direction, from the lower left emotion of boredom to the upper right emotion of excitement.

According to reversal theory, daily experience frequently reverses itself, sometimes from one moment to the next. John may start the day out in the telic mode, moving in a goal-directed fashion through his shower, shave, breakfast, and first class—focusing more on getting things done, accomplishing the goals of the day, rather than on the activities themselves. He may switch into the paratelic mode at lunch, as he sits with his good friends and talks about last night's basketball game. Switching to the telic mode for his class in personality psychology, he may find himself drifting into the paratelic as the professor drones on and on about existentialism. His doodling on a sketch pad evolves into an opportunity to draw humorous caricatures of the teaching assistant. The activity becomes fun in and of itself; the goal of obtaining information from the lecture no longer takes center stage in consciousness. John loses track of time, is startled when class is suddenly dismissed. The bell jolts him out of the paratelic into the telic. He's got to get to the gym for soccer practice. Dinner that evening represents a failed attempt in the paratelic. He cannot keep his mind on the conversation with his friends; he does not even taste his food. He keeps thinking about all of the homework he has. In the grip of the telic mode, he goes up to his room and works hard to prepare for tomorrow's examination in his history class. But one of the books for the course proves more interesting than he expected. He finds himself immersed in a chapter that wasn't even assigned by the professor. As the paratelic takes hold, he comes to enjoy the material for its own sake, forgets about the test for a few minutes. He calls his girlfriend; excitement mounts as the two of them engage in a witty conversation about people they know and about their own soaring relationship. But excitement shifts quickly to anxiety as he remembers the examination again, reversing modes suddenly from paratelic to telic. As he works through the material for the history exam, he begins to feel better, more relaxed. It looks as if it is going to be a pretty easy examination. He is well prepared. Savoring the low arousal of a telic mode, he decides it's time to go to sleep.

For a given individual, metamotivational modes shift frequently over the course of a day. But people differ significantly with respect to how dominant one or the other mode is in daily consciousness. Some people appear to be telic-dominant, some are paratelic-dominant, and some fall in the middle between the two modes. Apter assesses individual differences in mode dominance through a self-report **Telic Dominance Scale.** The scale incorporates three aspects of telic-dominance: seriousmindedness, planning-orientation, and arousal-avoidance.

Research employing the Telic Dominance Scale has identified telic and paratelic "life-styles." Telic-dominant individuals carry out more carefully planned activities, continually monitor themselves while doing so, and appear to spend more of their lives accomplishing tasks or moving toward long-term goals. When asked to talk about themselves, they tend to describe their lives in detailed and objective terms, sometimes providing specific names, dates, and times for important experiences in their past. Paratelic-dominant individuals (those scoring low on the Telic Dominance Scale) appear to indulge in a greater variety of activities, to have a more exciting time, and to be less well organized and more spontaneous than telic-dominant people. Their life stories are more impressionistic, dramatic, and sometimes exaggerated.

While there are important individual differences in dominant modes, Apter emphasizes that both ways of being are natural and adaptive in daily life. It would seem, furthermore, that existential authenticity and self-fulfillment would require a creative balance between the telic and the paratelic. The existentialist emphasis on finding meaning through life goals and commitments appears to resonate better with the telic than the paratelic mode. Feeling that one is in control and actively mastering the environment can result from concerted telic activity, as self-determined goals guide behavior and give meaning to human strivings.

By contrast, existential authenticity also involves defying external conventions in finding one's true self, rejecting the goals set forth by others to savor the process of becoming in and of itself. Self-determined behavior can be spontaneous and exciting; in the paratelic mode, one seeks challenge and stimulation, one finds interest and fulfillment in the activities themselves rather than the goals to which they may be aimed. Intrinsic motivation appears to resonate with the paratelic more than the telic.

In conclusion, Apter's reversal theory illustrates some of the complexities of subjective human experience and the search for meaning, freedom, control, and challenge in human affairs. Meaningful and authentic human experiences may be focused on goals or activities. Consciousness may be dominated by the telic or paratelic modes. And experience shifts dramatically over time, as consciousness reverses itself from one mode to the other. Life's meanings must be formed and reformed through the shifting qualities of experience, our opposing ways of being. The fundamental project of creating an authentic existence, living a self-determined life, evolves over time and across consciousness in a way that is unique and self-defining for each person in the world.

Humanistic Psychology

The term **humanistic psychology** became popular in the 1960s and 1970s in the United States to refer to a diverse group of theoretical approaches to personality and clinical psychology comprising what was sometimes called the "human potential movement" or the "third force." Reacting to the dominant first two forces of the time—behaviorism and psychoanalysis—these approaches offered an optimistic alternative to what they viewed as the mechanistic and dehumanizing models of human nature presented by mainstream psychology. The movement was also heavily influenced by social and cultural factors of the 1960s, such as the civil rights and women's movements in the United States, the growing interest in Eastern religions and philosophies (such as Zen Buddhism and transcendental meditation), the disillusionment with the Vietnam War, and the widespread disaffection of many American youth who questioned many accepted truths of the older establishment. The fervor of humanistic psychology has died down since then, but its influence is still important in personality psychology, clinical practice, social work, counselling, and religious and literary studies.

The most representative approaches to humanistic psychology are those of Carl Rogers (1902–1987) and Abraham Maslow (1908–1970). But many other approaches to personality share significant humanistic emphases, such as those of Robert White (Chapter 2), Erich Fromm (Chapter 2), Alfred Adler (Chapter 12), George Kelly (this chapter), and Gordon Allport (Chapters 5 and 10), as well as virtually all approaches deriving from existentialism (this chapter) and cognitive psychology (Chapter 9). In general, humanistic approaches share with existentialism a strong emphasis on human consciousness, becoming, and responsibility. Indeed, the terms *existential, phenomenological,* and *humanistic* are often used interchangeably. For instance, existential psychologists Rollo May and Victor Frankl are frequently called "humanistic psychologists." Some differences in connotation, however, can be observed. The term *humanistic* is most often used for approaches that emphasize the idea that human beings have virtually unlimited potential to develop in positive, self-fulfilling ways. While one can read this into the existential approaches of, say, Sartre and Binswanger, the thrust of humanistic psychology is decidedly more optimistic. In general, humanistic approaches deemphasize the Angst and the thrownness of human existence. While Kierkegaard and Sartre are likely to jolt us into the realization of life's ultimate and even harsh significance, humanistic approaches like Rogers' and Maslow's are more likely to make us feel a warm, soft glow.

Carl Rogers' Theory

Born in Oak Park, Illinois, in 1902, Carl Rogers grew up in a deeply religious and financially secure family. After receiving a degree in history and attending the Union Theological Seminary in New York, Rogers moved to clinical psychology and earned a Ph.D. in 1931. He worked as a staff psychologist in a child-guidance center before moving to Ohio State University and then the University of Chicago, where he directed the Counselling Center. It was at Chicago in the 1950s that his point of view became a major force in psychological theory and practice, following the publication of his major work, *Client-Centered Therapy: Its Current Practice, Implications, and Theory* (Rogers, 1951). Rogers' developing humanistic perspective contrasted markedly with the prevalent psychoanalytic approaches to therapy and with popular behavioral approaches, such as behavior modification. Many of the hallmarks of Rogers' **client-centered therapy**—his emphasis on the therapist's warmth and sincerity, empathy, acceptance, role-playing, and the dignity of the client—have become mainstays of a wide variety of therapeutic and educational approaches employed by clinicians, social workers, teachers, child-care workers, and other helping professionals today. It is difficult to overestimate Rogers' profound influence on clinical practice and in education.

Rogers offers a simple and elegant theory of the person. In Rogers' view, the person must be understood from the perspective of his or her **phenomenal field.** The phenomenal field is the entire panorama of a person's experience, the person's subjective apprehension of reality. It is the individual's overall frame of reference—the most encompassing interpretive structure for the person, which can be fully known only to the person him- or herself. To learn about another person's phenomenal field, the psychologist must listen carefully to the person's subjective report of experience, thereby achieving empathy with the other. The roots of behavior are in the phenomenal field, says Rogers. Unconscious conflicts, biological needs, environmental influences, and all other forces impinging on the

Carl Rogers

experiencing person are rendered meaningful or irrelevant through and only through the phenomenal field.

Human behavior and experience are guided by one basic striving in life. Writes Rogers, "The organism has one basic tendency and striving—to actualize, maintain, and enhance the experiencing organism" (1951, p. 487). There is "an inherent tendency of the organism to develop all its capacities in ways which serve to maintain or enhance the person" (1959, p. 196). While Freud viewed human motivation in terms of two classes of instinctual demands (death and life instincts) and Murray (Chapter 11) identified some 20 basic psychogenic needs, Rogers insists on a simple, monistic theory of human motivation. All urges, desires, wants, goals, values, and motives may be subsumed under the general umbrella of *organismic enhancement*. Each person's fundamental mandate in life is to become all that he or she can become, to fulfill one's inner potential. In so doing, the person advances toward greater differentiation, independence, and social responsibility over the life-span. People change through conscious, goal-directed choices, as the existentialists would have it. Choices must be clearly perceived if the person is to continue *becoming*, to continue moving toward full actualization of inner potential.

The person who is able to fulfill his or her potential is described as the **fully functioning person.** For the fully functioning person, the self has expanded to encompass the lion's share of the phenomenal field. The person is, therefore, consciously aware of the many different facets of his or her life, is able to integrate seemingly inconsistent aspects of experience into a coherent whole. Such a person leads a life that is rich in emotional experience and self-discovery. He or she is reflective, spontaneous, flexible, adaptable, confident, trusting, creative, and self-reliant. The fully functioning person experiences a subjective sense of free will; he or she is always an origin, not a pawn. The fully functioning person operates according to the **organismic valuing process.** This means that those experiences in accord with the basic organismic-actualizing tendency are viewed as satisfying and therefore are approached and maintained. Those that are contrary to actualization—those experiences that do not promote growth and fulfillment—are avoided or minimized. Unlike many theorists, Rogers does not delineate a series of developmental stages as stepping stones to full functioning. But he does identify important environmental conditions that promote the fulfillment of the organism. All people experience a need for *positive regard,* or the desire to be loved and accepted by others. The fully functioning person is likely to have experienced a great deal of **unconditional positive regard.** This means that he or she has been loved and accepted by others in an uncritical and noncontingent manner. People need to be loved for their very existence as persons, through the kind of unconditional love that the ancient Greeks and the Christian church have called *agape.* Regard from others promotes basic *self-regard.* Every person needs to be regarded positively both by others and by him- or herself.

But love and acceptance are often conditional: we are praised, rewarded, liked, admired, and blessed for particular things that we do, say, think, and feel. Such conditional positive regard from others leads to the apprehension of **conditions of worth.** We come to believe that certain aspects of our experience are worthy and others are not worthy. A young boy who is repeatedly praised for good school performance may introject this condition of worth and make it a positive part of the self-structure. The person builds a self-image commensurate with what other important people, who provide the person with positive regard, urge him or her to adopt.

Those aspects of self that are viewed by others as not worthy may ultimately be denied or distorted, for they engender no positive regard and may, instead, be the harbingers of punishment. For instance, a young girl who enjoys vigorous sports may be criticized by her parents or peers for playing basketball with the boys. Their regard for her becomes conditional: dependent on her adherence to appropriate feminine roles. As a result, she may revise her self-image to deny that she enjoys playing vigorous sports. Her conscious denial hides an inner truth, which results in inner conflict and distress.

Like Freud, Rogers believes that people suffer from important conflicts, many of which involve unconscious issues in their lives. But the conflicts derive from conflicts between the self and apprehended conditions of worth rather than between instinctual forces and superego demands. Rogers is much more optimistic than Freud about the possibility of living without conflict, of transcending conditions of worth to accept the self unconditionally. If we attain the fully functioning status, Rogers argues, we no longer impose conditions of worth on our experience but accept our entire organismic experience as good and fulfilling.

The road to full functioning, however, is not a smooth one. Along the way, the person is sure to experience disappointment and anxiety. Anxiety results when a person unconsciously perceives—"subceives"—an experience as incompatible with the self-structure and the introjected conditions of worth. **Subception** is the detection of an experience before it enters awareness. When faced with an event that threatens the self, the person quickly and unconsciously recognizes the threatening nature of the event and endeavors to protect the self from harm, typically by distorting or denying the event's reality. In this case, the event is unconsciously evaluated with regard to internal conditions of worth rather than with regard to the organism's general tendency toward growth and actualization. We see here that the directional tendencies of the self may come into conflict with the organism's general actualizing tendency. A person may consciously desire one thing to enhance the conscious self but unconsciously desires another thing to fulfill the spontaneous and growth-promoting tendencies of the entire organism.

But for the fully functioning person, no denial or distortion need take place, for he or she need not evaluate experience according to conditions of worth. The fully functioning person is keenly aware of those subtle feelings and impressions in life signalling opportunities for growth and enhancement. Therefore, the fully functioning person has less anxiety in life. Free from conditions of worth and willing to risk the conscious self in order to fulfill deeper yearnings, the fully functioning person embraces unconditionally the entire panoply of subjective experience. In a very real sense, the fully functioning person feels unconditional positive regard for all aspects of his or her subjective human experience.

Abraham Maslow's Psychology of Being

Abraham Maslow was born in Brooklyn, New York, in 1908, the son of Jewish parents who had emigrated from Russia. In contrast to Rogers, Maslow grew up isolated and very unhappy in a socially and economically deprived family. He earned his Ph.D. in psychology from the University of Wisconsin in 1934 under the tutelage of Harry Harlow, completing a dissertation on the sexual behavior of monkeys. At first an ardent behaviorist, Maslow's firsthand experience with his own children convinced him that this mechanistic approach to the person was not for him. Sometime around the beginning of World War II, Maslow experienced a profound personal conversion that eventually led to his formulation of a humanistic alternative in psychology. According to his own reports, he witnessed a pathetic and beggarly civilian parade designed to drum up support for the war, shortly after the bombing of Pearl Harbor. In Maslow's eyes, the parade only underscored the futility and tragic waste of war. With tears streaming down his face, he made a firm vow: to prove that human beings were capable of achievements grander than hate and destructiveness, and to do so by studying the people in the world who seemed to be the psychologically *healthiest* (Hall, 1968). In 1951, Maslow became a professor at Brandeis University where he gained international fame as the foremost spokesman for humanistic personality theory.

Maslow shares Rogers' view that human beings strive to actualize their inner potential. His term for this fundamental human striving is **self-actualization.** But Maslow (1954, 1968) suggests that the need for self-actualization is undergirded by at least four other kinds of needs, forming a **need hierarchy** (Figure 8.4). At the base of the hierarchy are *physiological* needs, such as the needs for food, water, and sleep. Above them are *safety* needs: the needs for structure, security, order, avoidance of pain, and protection. *Belongingness and love* needs comprise the third level. People desire to be accepted and loved by others and to form affiliative, loving, and intimate unions. Next are the *esteem* needs, which refer to needs for self-respect and esteem from others, the desire to be seen by others and by the self as a competent and effective organism. Finally, there are the needs for *self-actualization,* which motivate the person to fulfill his or her own potential above and beyond the lower needs.

The key notion in Maslow's need hierarchy is that higher needs cannot generally be addressed until the lower needs are satisfied. For instance, a starving man will not act in accord with his needs for belongingness until he has secured food (physiological needs) and a safe position in life (security needs). A lonely woman will not be able to fulfill her needs for esteem until she finds belongingness and love. Self-actualization sits at the pinnacle of the hierarchy. We cannot expect people to fulfill their innate potential, says Maslow, until they have taken care of business at the lower and more basic levels of the hierarchy.

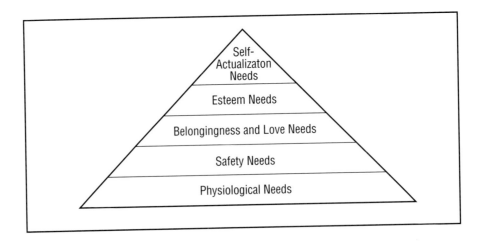

Figure 8.4

Maslow's Need Hierarchy.

Abraham Maslow

While many theories of personality derive from clinicians' work with neurotics and other people suffering psychological pain, Maslow is especially refreshing for his opposite point of view. Though he was a clinician, Maslow's theory of personality is most heavily influenced by his understanding of the healthiest subjects, the most mature and actualized people among us. From interviewing friends and clients, reading biographies, and conducting structured research, Maslow sketched a personological portrait of the "self-actualizing" person, or "self-actualizer" (SA). Table 8.8 lists some of the characteristics Maslow identified as common in SAs.

The SA is motivated primarily by **being values (B-values).** Some of Maslow's B-values are listed in Table 8.9. B-values encourage growth and the enrichment of experience. The person who structures his or her life in accord with the B-values has transcended the **deficiency motives,** which exist in lower parts of the need hierarchy. Deficiency motives are based on lacks, absences, and tensions: eating out of hunger is motivated by a lack of food; exploitative sexual behavior may be motivated by a build-up of libidinal tension or by sadistic aggressive urges. Behavior dominated by deficiency motives operates to return the organism to a steady state of equilibrium—to fill the lack or reduce the tension.

Table 8.8

Some Characteristics of Self-Actualizing Persons

Superior perception of reality.
Increased acceptance of self, of others, and of nature.
Increased spontaneity.
Increased detachment and desire for privacy.
Greater freshness of appreciation and richness of emotional reaction.
Increased autonomy and resistance to conformity.
Higher frequency of peak experiences.
Increased identification with the human species.
Improved interpersonal relationships.
More democratic character structure.
High levels of creativity.

Modified after Maslow (1968, p. 26).

Thus, people quit eating when they are full. Behavior motivated by B-values, on the other hand, grows and becomes richer over time. The woman who acts out of an appreciation for "beauty," for instance, does not quit once she has experienced something beautiful but seeks yet other beautiful experiences.

Another important characteristic of the SA is his or her proclivity for **peak experiences.** Peak experiences are just what they sound like: wonderful moments

 Table 8.9

The B-Values

Wholeness	Richness	Effortlessness
Perfection	Simplicity	Playfulness
Completion	Beauty	Truth
Justice	Goodness	Self-sufficiency
Aliveness	Uniqueness	

Adapted from Maslow (1968, p. 83).

of happiness, ecstasy, transcendence. Put simply, SAs have more of these than do the rest of humankind. Yet virtually anyone can have a peak experience. Maslow sampled peak experiences among his friends and some of his college students by asking them to respond to this request:

> I would like you to think of the most wonderful experience or experiences in your life; happiest moments, ecstatic moments, moments of rapture, perhaps from being in love, or from listening to music or suddenly "being hit" by a book or a painting, or from some great creative moment. First list these. And then try to tell me how you feel in such acute moments, how you feel *differently* from the way you feel at other times, how you are at the moment a different person in some ways. (Maslow, 1968, p. 71)

Maslow's admittedly impressionistic analysis of the responses to his request suggested that in peak experiences people perceive and understand their world from the standpoint of **being cognition (B-cognition).** B-cognition sounds a bit like Husserl's pure phenomenological experience (discussed earlier in this chapter) or the total concentration on the other described by Buber in the I–Thou encounter (Chapter 11). In B-cognition, the "experience or the object tends to be seen as a whole, as a complete unit, detached from relations from possible usefulness, from expediency and from purpose" (Maslow, 1968, p. 74). The "percept is exclusively and fully attended to" (p. 74), and "perception can be relatively ego-transcending, self-forgetful, egoless" (p. 79). There may even be a "disorientation in time and space" (p. 80), through which the person loses the subjective sense of time passing or of existing in a particular place. Most of all, though, B-cognition makes for a *unity* of consciousness:

> In some reports, particularly of the mystic experience or the religious experience or philosophical experience, the whole of the world is seen as unity, as a single rich live entity. In other of the peak experiences, most particularly the love experience and the aesthetic experience, one small part of the world is perceived as if it were for the moment all of the world. In both cases the perception is of unity. Probably the fact that the B-cognition of a painting or a person or a theory retains all the attributes of the whole of Being, i.e., the B-values, derives from this fact of perceiving it as if it were all that existed at the moment. (Maslow, 1968, p. 88)

Examples of Humanistic Research

The humanistic approaches of Rogers and Maslow have had their greatest influence in the realms of clinical treatment, counseling, and education. Researchers, too, have drawn extensively from Rogers' theory in studies of psychotherapy process and outcome and in applied research in clinical and educational settings. Rogers' theory has also been a prime stimulus for research on the self (Chapter 10). Beyond these important contributions, personality researchers have found two humanistic concepts especially worthy of empirical scrutiny: self-actualization and peak experiences.

Starting from Maslow's theory, Shostrom (1965, 1966) developed the **Personal Orientation Inventory (POI),** a 150-item questionnaire designed to assess various dimensions of self-actualization. The test yields two summary scores for "inner-directedness" and "time competence." In addition, 10 subscales provide scores on such characteristics of SAs as "spontaneity," "capacity for intimate contact," and "self-acceptance." The POI appears to have adequate reliability, and validity studies are generally positive (Maddi, 1980). Studies have shown that scores on all of the POI scales are negatively correlated with Eysenck's trait of neuroticism (Chapter 5) and positively correlated with self-report tests of autonomy and creativity. POI scales correlate negatively with alcoholism, felony, and hospitalization for psychopathological symptoms, and they correlate positively with teaching and therapist effectiveness (Maddi, 1980).

Jones and Crandall (1986) developed a short index of self-actualization. Their 15-item scale is reproduced in Table 8.10. In a study of over 500 college stu-

 ## Table 8.10

A Short Scale Measuring Self-Actualization

I do not feel ashamed of any of my emotions.
I feel I must do what others expect me to do. (N)
I believe that people are essentially good and can be trusted.
I feel free to be angry to those I love.
It is always necessary that others approve of what I do. (N)
I don't accept my own weaknesses. (N)
I can like people without having to approve of them.
I fear failure. (N)
I avoid attempts to analyze and simplify complex domains. (N)
It is better to be yourself than to be popular.
I have no mission in life to which I feel especially dedicated. (N)
I can express my feelings even when they may result in undesirable consequences.
I do not feel responsible to help anybody. (N)
I am bothered by fears of being inadequate. (N)
I am loved because I give love.

Note: Respondents answer each item on a 4-point scale: "agree," "somewhat agree," "somewhat disagree," "disagree." Items followed by an "N" are coded in the negative direction, meaning that *dis*agreement with them suggests greater self-actualization.
From Jones & Crandall (1986, p. 67).

dents, Jones and Crandall found that scores on this short scale correlated highly with the overall self-actualization scores from the much-longer POI ($r = +.67$). The scale shows good reliability and in general does not seem to be susceptible to "social desirability" response sets (see Chapter 5). Self-actualization on the scale was positively associated with measures of self-esteem and "rational behavior and beliefs" and was negatively associated with neuroticism.

A few empirical studies have supported Maslow's claim that people who are self-actualized should report a greater number of peak experiences (Klavetter & Mogar, 1967; Rizzo & Vinacke, 1970). Other studies have examined qualitative differences among peak experiences (Hallaq, 1977). For example, McAdams (1982b) found that college students scoring high in intimacy motivation (Chapter 11) described peak experiences laden with themes of love and friendship, reciprocal communication and sharing, helping others and being helped, and tender interpersonal touch. Students high in power motivation, on the other hand, underscored themes of perceived strength, powerful inspiration, having impact, vigorous activity, and increased fame or recognition. Underlying personality dispositions, such as intimacy and power motivation, may shape and be shaped by the quality of a person's peak experiences. Interestingly, McAdams found no relation between (1) power and intimacy motivation and (2) corresponding themes of power and intimacy in students' descriptions of "nonpeak" experiences, such as everyday neutral experiences. The finding suggests that the content of peak experiences is an especially revealing piece of personological data, much more informative of a person's fundamental strivings and orientations than a random slice of subjective experience.

In his books *Beyond Boredom and Anxiety* (1977) and *Flow* (1990), Mihalyi Csikszentmihalyi has argued for a psychology of *optimal experience.* Taking a lead from Maslow, Rogers, and other humanistic and existential approaches, Csikszentmihalyi has explored the phenomenology of artists, athletes, creative professionals, and other active people when they are involved in the life activities they enjoy most. Csikszentmihalyi terms these **autotelic** activities—behaviors deeply enjoyable in and of themselves, functioning as their own ("auto") ends ("telos"). The subjective experience that a person feels when engaged in an autotelic activity is best described as **flow.** Rock climbers describe the flow experience:

> When I start on a climb, it's as if my memory input had been cut off. All I can remember is the last thirty seconds, and all I can think ahead is the next five minutes. . . . With tremendous concentration the normal world is forgotten.

> You're moving in harmony with something else, you're part of it. It's one of the few sorts of activities in which you don't feel you have all sorts of different kinds of conflicting demands on you.

> It's the Zen feeling, like meditation or concentration. One thing you're after is the one-pointedness of mind. You can get your ego

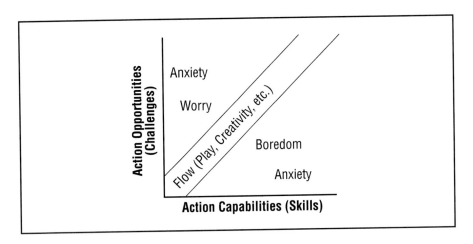

From Csikszentmihalyi, 1977, p. 17.

Figure 8.5

Model of the Flow State.

mixed up with climbing in all sorts of ways and it isn't necessarily enlightening. But when things become automatic, it's like an egoless thing, in a way. Somehow the right thing is done without you ever thinking about it or doing anything at all. . . . It just happens. And yet you're more concentrated. (Csikszentmihalyi, 1977, pp. 81, 87)

Dancers report flow experiences in dance; surgeons report flow when operating on patients; chess players report flow in the middle of an especially intense match. All flow experiences are not the same, but they do appear to share a common structural dimension, suggests Csikszentmihalyi. First, flow involves a *focused and ordered state of consciousness,* described by one of the rock climbers as the "one-pointedness of mind." The person focuses complete attention on the event or activity, not unlike Buber's description of how two people ideally interact with each other in the I–Thou encounter (Chapter 11). Consciousness is highly structured and organized as the information that the mind deals with appears at an optimal level for comprehension. Second, flow involves an *equivalent ratio of skills to challenges.* If the challenge vastly exceeds the person's skill (for example, if the mountain is too rough), the person may experience worry or anxiety and a fragmentation of consciousness. If, on the other hand, the person's skill vastly exceeds the task challenge (if the mountain is extremely easy to climb), the person may subside into boredom. Figure 8.5 shows how flow goes beyond (or is it between?) boredom and anxiety.

Flow may be experienced in all sorts of activities and situations. Although intense forms of play and recreation (such as rock climbing and dancing) often yield flow experiences, many people also report flow when they are optimally engaged in their work, as Table 8.11 shows. In a study of 82 adult workers, 87% reported that they had had flow experiences. Of these, 30% reported that they experienced flow less than once a week, 40% reported that they experienced it about once a week, and 30% said they experienced flow daily. Those adults who reported more flow experiences also spent more time on the job actually working and less time "goofing off." They also reported many fewer instances in daily life in which they "wished they were doing something else" (Csikszentmihalyi, 1982).

Csikszentmihalyi's description of flow resembles Maslow's peak experiences. Privette and Landsman (1983) identify yet a third form of optimal functioning,

Table 8.11

Frequency of Activities Mentioned as Producing Flow Experiences

	Percentage of Subjects Mentioning
Social Activities (Vacationing with family; being with children, wife, or lover; parties; traveling)	16
Passive Attending Activities (Watching TV, going to the theatre, listening to music, reading)	13
Work Activities (Working, electrical work, challenging problems at work)	31
Hobbies and Home Activities (Cooking, sewing, photography, singing, etc.)	22
Sports and Outdoor Activities (Bowling, golf, dancing, swimming, etc.)	18
	100

Note: For each subject ($N = 71$), the one activity mentioned most often in response to the three quotes was selected.
From Csikszentmihalyi (1982, p. 24).

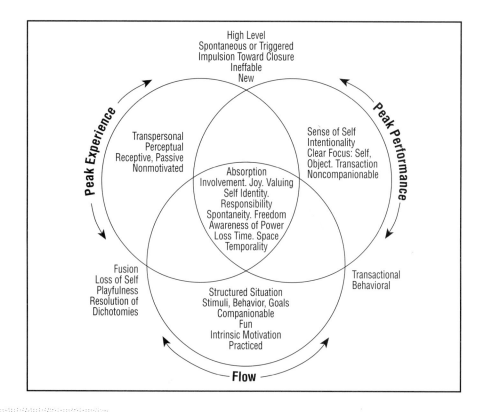

High Level
Spontaneous or Triggered
Impulsion Toward Closure
Ineffable
New

Peak Experience

Peak Performance

Transpersonal
Perceptual
Receptive, Passive
Nonmotivated

Sense of Self
Intentionality
Clear Focus: Self,
Object. Transaction
Noncompanionable

Absorption
Involvement. Joy. Valuing
Self Identity.
Responsibility
Spontaneity. Freedom
Awareness of Power
Loss Time. Space
Temporality

Fusion
Loss of Self
Playfulness
Resolution of
Dichotomies

Transactional
Behavioral

Structured Situation
Stimuli, Behavior, Goals
Companionable
Fun
Intrinsic Motivation
Practiced

Flow

Figure 8.6

Peak Experience, Peak Performance, and Flow.

From Privette, 1983, p. 1366.

which they call **peak performance.** In peak performance, a person performs above and beyond expectations, as in breaking an athletic record or putting on a truly exceptional performance in the arts.

Peak experience, flow, and peak performance all share certain basic features. Yet they have different emphases. Peak experience nearly always involves intense joy whereas peak performance always involves superior functioning. Flow may involve either joy or superior functioning, but it is more centrally defined as an intrinsically rewarding experience. Privette (1983) has examined the similarities and differences among the three forms of optimal functioning. Her interesting characterization of the three, shown in Figure 8.6, is an attempt to discern the phenomenology of three different ways in which human beings engage their worlds in authentic ways suggestive of full functioning and self-actualization.

Experiencing flow: mountain climbing.

The Bridge to Cognitive Psychology: George Kelly

One of the most idiosyncratic figures in the history of personality psychology is George A. Kelly (1905–1966). Kelly labored in relative obscurity as a school teacher, aeronautical engineer, and clinical psychologist until he wrote and published his two-volume *The Psychology of Personal Constructs* in 1955. The book took the field of personality psychology by storm. It presented a boldly original theory of the person that seemed to bear little if any resemblance to the classic theories of the day, such as those proposed by Freud, Jung, Adler, Murray, Allport,

Continued on p. 472

A Rigorous Humanism

Joseph Rychlak

According to Joseph Rychlak, "humanistic" psychology often gets a bad name. When some psychologists and educated laypersons hear the term *humanistic,* they think of something soft and cozy—a brand of psychology too mushy to be taken seriously from a hard-headed scientific point of view. For some, *humanistic* summons up the many avant-garde approaches to therapy and counseling that came out of the "human potential movement" of the 1960s and 1970s, including "gestalt psychotherapy," "rolfing," "est," "primal scream," "transcendental meditation," "encounter groups," "transactional analysis," and the like. While some of these have faded away over the years, others have made valuable contributions to the helping professions. Still, many psychologists look upon them with great skepticism. Even Rogers and (especially) Maslow are viewed in many scientific circles as too "soft" and "nonscientific" in their approaches to personality.

In contrast, Joseph Rychlak has proposed a thoroughly humanistic framework for personality that, he maintains, is as rigorous as any approach that scientific psychology can offer. For Rychlak, a theory is humanistic to the extent that it grants the human being *intentionality.* Human beings are potentially free agents, Rychlak maintains, whose actions are not necessarily determined by antecedent events. Personality is not simply the product of heredity interacting with environment over time. In existentialist terms, heredity and environment are part of the "thrownness" of existence, but the person defines him- or herself above and beyond these. Though their behavior is influenced by genetic and environmental forces, human beings typically act for the sake of envisioned goals, ends, and outcomes. The Greek word for "end" or "goal" is *telos,* from which we get the English word *teleology.* As intentional agents who determine their own fates, human beings are *teleological* organisms.

Rychlak (1977, 1981, 1986) calls his humanistic approach to psychology **logical learning theory.** The central concept of logical learning theory is the **telosponse.** A telosponse is "the affirmation of a meaningful premise (e.g., as a visual image, language term, statement, or judgmental comparison) relating to a referent (point, end, goal, etc.) that acts as a purpose for the sake of which behavior is then intended (performed, enacted, etc.)" (Rychlak, 1981, p. 733). Contrary to the learning theories we reviewed in Chapter 6, logical learning theory proposes that people do not respond as passive mechanisms to stimuli in their environment, producing output in response to input. Rather, they *telospond* with respect to ends and goals. They act *for the sake of* a telos.

What enables human beings to act teleologically as free agents is their natural capacity for **dialectical**

Joseph Rychlak

reasoning. Dialectical thought is most apparent in the apprehension of opposites. In order to know "hot," a person must also know "cold." Hot implies cold, in a dialectical sense. Noisy implies quiet. Good implies bad. When I know that something is good, I also know that that same something is *not* bad, though it *might* have been. When I walk down the east side of the street,

I know that I *could* have walked down the west side. *Human beings always know that they could have done otherwise,* for they continually frame life's possibilities in dialectical opposites. In dialectical reasoning, the person freely chooses among alternatives, functioning as an active, self-defining, and intentional agent. Rychlak (1981) writes, "In place of Descartes' classic 'I think, therefore I am,' logical learning theory advances 'I think, and realize that I could be (dialectically) thinking otherwise, therefore *I* exist'" (p. 735).

Once the dialectical thinker selects a meaning from alternatives, he or she then *predicates* the stimuli in the environment in accord with the meaning selected. Predication is the "act of affirming, denying, or qualifying certain patterns of meaning in relation to others" (Rychlak, 1986, p. 736). I predicate when I say "my wife is beautiful" or "ice cream is cold." In these two statements, the words *beautiful* and *cold* are the predicates, following the linking verb *is; my wife* and *ice cream* are the subjects of the sentences. The predicates are more general categories than the subjects. I extend the meaning of the subjects— my wife and ice cream—by identifying them with the broader categories. Therefore, meaning flows from right to left in each sentence: from beautiful or cold (the broad, encompassing class) to my wife or ice cream (the narrower subject who is predicated in terms of the larger class). Predication is a basic cognitive operation in everyday life, a fundamental way of making meaning as an active, telosponding agent in the environment.

Telosponsivity begins at birth. Before they develop language, infants behave for the sake of *affective assessments*. An affective assessment is a simple determination of "I like it" *versus* "I don't like it." According to Rychlak, from birth onwards human beings engage their environments through continual affective assessment. When confronted with a stimulus, they immediately form an affective impression that then shapes the way in which they behave (telospond). Affective assessment is the most primitive form of dialectical reasoning, as the person chooses among alternative affective reactions—like *versus* dislike—to a stimulus.

Rychlak and his colleagues have examined the dialectical nature of affective assessments in a large number of laboratory studies. In these learning studies, people typically rate various to-be-learned materials for "likability" on a 4-point scale (like much, like slightly, dislike slightly, dislike much). Then they engage in different kinds of learning and performance tasks. One common finding in research of this sort is that people learn those materials they like better than those they dislike. From a dialectical standpoint, material with opposite meanings to presented stimuli is learned better than material that is conceptually unrelated to presented stimuli. Moving from these simple findings, Rychlak and his colleagues have delineated a large number of more elaborate hypotheses that have been tested in carefully designed laboratory studies. The results generally support and extend Rychlak's rigorous humanistic framework for personality.

Continued from p. 469

Cattel, and the behaviorists. The unusual terms Kelly proposed became part of the standard lexicon of personality psychology—terms such as *personal construct, range of convenience, fixed-role therapy,* and *Rep Test.* Indeed, Kelly became something of an overnight celebrity in the field. Unfortunately, however, Kelly's one major book is the only comprehensive statement of the theory he ever produced. An early death prevented his developing and refining the theory further, though selected papers from his last years have been edited into a valuable collection (Maher, 1969). Since Kelly's death, his theory has remained popular and influential. Yet it is difficult to classify for, like Kelly himself, the theory stubbornly refuses to fit into the mainstream. Because it rejects such time-honored personality concepts as "motivation," "the unconscious," "needs," "instincts," "traits," "reinforcement," and "developmental stages," Kelly's theory seems an oddity in the field of personality psychology. Yet linkages and relations between

Kelly and other approaches can be discerned. For instance, two of the major spokesmen for social-learning theory—Julian Rotter and Walter Mischel (Chapters 6 and 7)—worked closely with Kelly at Ohio State University, as did Joseph Rychlak (Feature 8B). Kelly's focus on subjective experience aligns him with phenomenologists, existentialists, and humanists, like those discussed in this chapter. And the cognitive flavor of Kelly's theory is obvious in Rotter and Mischel and in many contemporary cognitive and information-processing approaches to personality (Chapter 9), though, more than most modern cognitive approaches, Kelly emphasizes the radically subjective quality of human information-processing. Every person sees the world differently, he asserts.

The Psychology of Personal Constructs

In a striking departure from common practice in personality psychology, Kelly (1955) asserts that the "problem" of human motivation is not a problem at all. The search for underlying principles to explain *why* people do what they do is futile, he asserts. We need not posit life and death instincts (Freud), unconscious archetypes (Jung), drives (Miller & Dollard), principles of reinforcement (behaviorists), traits (Eysenck, Cattell, Allport), needs and motives (Murray, McClelland), affects (Tomkins), strivings (Adler), or the urge toward self-actualization (Rogers, Maslow) to explain what motivates people to act. People are alive. They act by virtue of being alive. It's really quite simple.

Well, not that simple. Kelly's radical dismissal of the concept of motivation is really only partial, for his theory implies a fundamental principle of motivation itself (Hogan, 1976; Shotter, 1970): *a person is motivated to predict or anticipate what will happen to him or her.* What moves people to act is their desire to know what the world has in store for them. Fundamentally, the person is like a scientist, seeking to predict and control events:

> Mankind, whose progress in search of prediction and control of surrounding events stands out so clearly in light of the centuries, comprises the men we see around us every day. The aspirations of the scientist are essentially the aspirations of all men. (Kelly, 1955, p. 43)

Table 8.12 summarizes the main points of Kelly's theory in terms of the postulates and corollaries he presented in *The Psychology of Personal Constructs.* Kelly's model for human life is a commonsense brand of science. As we saw in Chapter 1, the first step of scientific inquiry is the classification of experience. Science begins when the observer seeks to make initial sense of the world by imposing some kind of organization upon it. What William James called the "blooming, buzzing confusion" of subjective human experience must be ordered, classified, and divided into categories if the scientist is to know anything at all. From these initial classifications are built synthesizing theories, from which are

Table 8.12

Kelly's Fundamental Postulate and Eleven Corollaries

Fundamental Postulate: A person's processes are psychologically channelized by the ways in which he or she anticipates events.

Construction Corollary: A person anticipates events by construing their replications.

Individuality Corollary: Persons differ from each other in their construction of events.

Organization Corollary: Each person characteristically evolves, for his or her convenience in anticipating events, a construction system embracing ordinal relationships between constructs.

Dichotomy Corollary: A person's construction system is composed of a finite number of dichotomous constructs.

Choice Corollary: A person chooses for himself or herself that alternative in a dichotomized construct through which he or she anticipates the greater possibility for extension and definition of his or her system.

Range Corollary: A construct is convenient for the anticipation of a finite range of events only.

Experience Corollary: A person's construction system varies as he or she successively construes the replications of events.

Modulation Corollary: The variation in a person's construction system is limited by the permeability of the constructs within whose range of convenience the variants lie.

Fragmentation Corollary: A person may successively employ a variety of construction subsystems which are inferentially incompatible with each other.

Communality Corollary: To the extent that one person employs a construction of experience which is similar to that employed by another, his or her psychological processes are similar to those of the other person.

Sociality Corollary: To the extent that one person construes the construction process of another, he or she plays a role in a social process involving the other person.

Slightly modified from Kelly (1955).

subsequently deduced discrete hypotheses to be tested through experimentation and other systematic procedures.

According to Kelly, each of us classifies his or her world by developing **personal constructs,** which are characteristic ways of construing how some things are alike and some things are different from each other. Every construct is *bipolar* (the "dichotomy corollary"), specifying how two things are similar to each other (lying on the same pole) and different from a third thing (lying at the opposite pole). For example, I may routinely classify my friends in terms of the personal construct "serious/funny." Grant and Jack are relatively serious; Dean differs from them both in that he is relatively "funny." All three friends are, in fact, similar to and different from each other in a great many ways. Despite the blooming, buzzing complexity of my experiences with these friends, I nevertheless anticipate my interactions with them, in part, by virtue of the construct "serious/funny." The construct helps me predict and control my interpersonal world. I know from past experiences with these friends (the "experience corollary") that when I am with Jack or Grant we will usually talk seriously about professional issues or current events; getting Dean to talk seriously about anything at all, on the other hand, requires a lot of extra effort.

People are best understood in terms of their own construct systems. Each person develops his or her own construct system that contains a number of constructs organized into a hierarchy ("organization corollary"). This means that within any construct system certain constructs are *superordinal* (encompassing many other constructs) and others are *subordinal* (being encompassed by larger constructs). Thus, the subordinal construct of "helpful/unhelpful" may be encompassed by the more general superordinal construct of "friendly/unfriendly." Every person's construct system is unique ("individuality corollary"), which means that everybody divides up subjective experience in a slightly different way. To know another person's construct system is to see the world through his or her eyes ("sociality corollary").

Within a given person's construct system, particular constructs differ from each other with respect to their **range of convenience** ("range corollary"). Thus, the construct "friendly/unfriendly" may have a wide range of convenience: it is likely to guide the person's anticipations of events in a large number of situations. By contrast, the construct "liberal/conservative" is likely to have a narrower range of convenience for most people. For most people, "friendly/unfriendly" is a more salient and determining dimension in their interactions with other people than is "liberal/conservative." Of course, there are marked individual differences across persons with respect to range. For instance, a politically astute woman who is especially sensitive to political issues may utilize the construct "liberal/conservative" in a wide range of situations. She may be tuned in to information in her environment suggestive of political meaning. Therefore, one of the first dimensions upon which she judges people may be their perceived political persuasion. At a cocktail party, she is introduced to a middle-aged man who looks like a banker, dressed in a three-piece suit. His hair is impeccably groomed; his wristwatch, expensive. She immediately says to herself, "I think this guy is a political conservative; I bet he usually votes Republican." Of course, she may be wrong. She may learn that he is an activist lawyer for the American Civil Liberties Union, and that he always votes for liberal candidates. The woman need not be wedded to her initial hunch; constructs are more like hypotheses to be tested than like assumed facts. But the hunch provides her with an important starting point in her interaction, a way of anticipating what may or may not happen next. Anticipations guide behavior and experience. In the words of Kelly's "fundamental postulate," "a person's processes are psychologically channelized by the ways in which he [or she] anticipates events" (Kelly, 1955, p. 46).

Constructs differ in other ways, too. Some constructs are highly *permeable* whereas others are not ("modulation corollary"). A permeable construct is open to modification and the introduction of new elements. A person with an especially permeable construct system is likely to be seen by others as very open-minded. By contrast, a person who is unable to modify his or her constructs in light of new information and expanding experiences is likely to be viewed by others as relatively rigid and inflexible. Complete permeability, however, is not altogether good. If a construct is so permeable that it changes with virtually every relevant happening, it does not function well as an aid in anticipating events. Another problem can arise when different constructs within a person contradict each other. When a person's constructs are mutually incompatible and contradictory ("fragmented"), then he or she is likely to have a difficult time making consistent sense of the world and anticipating events in an adaptive way ("fragmentation corollary").

Kelly's personal-construct theory provides an interesting perspective from which to view a number of traditional concepts in personality psychology. Take, for instance, the concept of "the unconscious." Kelly sees no need to posit a mysterious unconscious domain to which have been consigned repressed wishes and conflicts. In Kelly's cognitive view, "the unconscious" is merely those constructs that are nonverbal, submerged, or suspended. For certain constructs, we are unable to assign a verbal name; thus, we may not be aware of them. Other constructs are submerged beneath other constructs or suspended from the construct system because they do not seem to fit. A highly fragmented construct system, therefore, is likely to contain submerged or suspended constructs of which the person is not aware. Yet these unconscious constructs continue to "channelize" behavior and experience.

Kelly views "anxiety" as "the recognition that the events with which one is confronted lie outside the range of convenience of one's construct system" (Kelly, 1955, p. 482). In other words, when we confront inexplicable events in the world for which our construct system does not seem to be prepared, we experience anxiety. Ultimately, then, anxiety is a fear of the unknown—the fear that the blooming, buzzing confusion cannot be understood. "Guilt" is a "perception of one's apparent dislodgment from his core role structure" (Kelly, 1955, p. 502). "Core role structure" is the construction a person has of who he or she is in relation to significant people, like parents. It is embedded within the person's general construct system. In essence, then, guilt follows the perception that one is no longer living according to an especially valued aspect of one's personal-construct system.

Exploring Personal Constructs: The Rep Test

Despite the formal postulates and corollaries, Kelly's theory of personal constructs has an appealing commonsense quality that fits well with most people's daily experience. One of the best ways to get a feel for Kelly's approach is to participate in the **Role Construct Repertory Test (Rep Test),** a personality assessment procedure designed by Kelly to explore personal constructs in people's lives. The Rep Test is a very flexible procedure that can be used in clinical work and in research. It is also easy to administer to yourself, and it is fun to take.

One version of the Rep Test asks you to make a series of comparisons among those people who play important roles in your life. Kelly defined a role as an understanding or expectation of what particular people in a person's life do. The role of "mother," therefore, consists of a person's understanding of how mothers behave in various situations. The first step in the Rep Test is to compile a Role Title List. Let us consider 15 different roles in your life. For each of the 15 roles listed in Table 8.13, write the name of the person who fits the description presented. Do not repeat names. If any role title appears to call for a duplicate name, substitute the name of another person whom the second role suggests to you.

When you have listed 15 people who play important roles in your life, compare and contrast them in a way to discern some of the important personal constructs you employ to make sense of your interactions with these people. Table 8.14 lists 15 sets of numbers. Each set contains three numbers, referring to the role titles you have listed above. Thus, the number "14" refers to "the most successful person whom you know personally." For each set of three numbers, think of how the people corresponding to the *first two* numbers are *similar* to each other and at the same time *different from* the person corresponding to the *third* number. Write a word or phrase in the blank under "Similar" to denote how the two are similar and then a contrasting word under "Contrast" to denote how the two people differ from the third. For example, the first set presents the numbers "9, 11, 14" (corresponding to "Boss," "Sought Person," and "Successful Person," respectively). Imagine that the Boss you have in mind is similar to your Sought Person in that they are both "easygoing" and that they both differ from the Successful Person who seems, by contrast, "hard-driving." You would write "easygoing" in the "Similar" blank and "hard-driving" under "Contrast."

Each of the 15 pairings of "Similar" and "Contrast" represents a single construct. At this point, the analysis of your responses can take many different paths. You may wish to look carefully at the ways in which you characterize certain critical contrasts in your life, such as those between Ex-Flame and current Boy (Girl) Friend. Or you may wish to look at the overall pattern of constructs you have delineated. How do the various constructs relate to each other? Are some constructs subordinal or superordinal to other constructs? Do you use many different constructs? Do you tend to use certain constructs again and again? If you tend to view many of the similar–contrast characterizations in terms of, say, the construct "honest/dishonest," or some variation on this idea, then you may conclude that this is an especially robust and meaningful construct in your life.

 **Table 8.13**

Role Title List

1. Your mother or the person who has played the part of _____
   mother in your life.

2. Your father or the person who has played the part of _____
   father in your life.

3. Your brother nearest your age. If you have no brother, _____
   the person who is most like one.

4. Your sister nearest your age. If you have no sister, the _____
   person who is most like one.

5. A teacher you liked or the teacher of a subject you liked. _____

6. A teacher you disliked or the teacher of a subject you _____
   disliked.

7. Your closest girl (boy) friend immediately before you _____
   started going with your wife (husband) or present closest
   girl (boy) friend [Ex-Flame].

8. Your wife (husband) or closest present girl (boy) _____
   friend.

9. An employer, supervisor, or officer under whom you _____
   served during a period of great stress [Boss].

10. A person with whom you have been closely associated _____
    who, for some unexplainable reason, appears to
    dislike you [Rejecting Person].

11. The person whom you have met within the past six _____
    months whom you would most like to know better
    [Sought Person].

12. The person whom you would most like to be of help _____
    to, or the one whom you feel most sorry for [Pitied
    Person].

13. The most intelligent person whom you know personally. _____

14. The most successful person whom you know personally. _____

15. The most interesting person whom you know personally. _____

Table 8.14

Personal Constructs, Represented by "Similar" and "Contrast" Pairings

	Similar	Contrast
1. 9, 11, 14	_____	_____
2. 10, 12, 13	_____	_____
3. 2, 5, 12	_____	_____
4. 1, 4, 8	_____	_____
5. 7, 8, 12	_____	_____
6. 3, 13, 6	_____	_____
7. 1, 2, 9	_____	_____
8. 3, 4, 10	_____	_____
9. 6, 7, 10	_____	_____
10. 5, 11, 14	_____	_____
11. 1, 7, 8	_____	_____
12. 2, 7, 8	_____	_____
13. 3, 6, 9	_____	_____
14. 4, 5, 10	_____	_____
15. 11, 13, 14	_____	_____

Based on Kelly (1955).

Procedures have been developed for quantifying results from the Rep Test for personality research. One line of research has examined individual differences in *cognitive complexity* as revealed by the Rep Test (Crockett, 1965). People who use many different kinds of constructs are said to manifest higher levels of cognitive complexity. They tend to view the world in a highly differentiated manner.

People who use few different kinds of constructs are viewed as having a simpler, more global construct system.

Another line of research has examined *construct similarity* among friends and acquaintances (Duck, 1973, 1979). Researchers have administered various forms of the Rep Test to college students and then examined their patterns of peer interaction and friendship formation. In general, those students who have similar construct systems tend to become close friends and to remain friends for longer periods of times. For example, Duck and Spencer (1972) obtained personal-construct measures for female college freshmen at the beginning of the school year. The women in the study had all been assigned to the same residence hall. Though they were unacquainted at the beginning of the study, those women who shared similar constructs were most likely to become friends over the course of the school year. In another study, similarity of constructs was a more significant predictor of friendship formation than was similarity on self-report measures of traits (Duck & Craig, 1978). In other words, friends may be drawn together not so much by a perception that they behave in the same kinds of ways (that they are both extraverted or achievement-oriented, for instance) but rather by the perception that they see the world in the same way. People look to match their subjective experience with that of others. People look for affirmation of their own conscious meanings in the meanings of others. In relating to fellow men and women, *sharing meanings* may be more important than *doing* the same thing.

Summary for Chapter 8

1. The interpretive-structures approach to personality assumes that the person imposes some kind of pattern, organization, framework, or plan on subjective experience in order to predict, control, and interpret life's events. The emphasis is on cognition, consciousness, subjective experience, and the responsibility each person has to make life meaningful.

2. Existentialism provides one philosophical foundation for a psychology of subjective conscious experience. Such experience may be examined through the phenomenological method.

3. The fundamental project of human life, in the existentialist view, is to create the self by creating meaning in life.

4. One vigorous line of empirical research examines the extent to which people perceive that they have control in their lives. People who perceive they are in control are called origins; those who feel they exert little control are called pawns.

5. People with an internal locus of control expect reinforcements to follow their own actions; those with an external locus of control expect that their behavior will not consistently lead to reinforcement.

6. Research on intrinsic motivation shows that, in certain conditions, material rewards may undermine a person's desire to perform an intrinsically enjoyable task, by suggesting to the person that his or her behavior is controlled by extrinsic sources.

7. Stemming from research on intrinsic motivation, self-determination theory suggests that human beings act in self-determined ways, stemming from a natural tendency to encounter new challenges that will promote their self-development and in accord with fundamental needs for competence, autonomy, and relatedness.

8. Research on hardiness draws explicitly from existential theory in suggesting that the hardy person seeks control, commitment, and challenge in life. High levels of hardiness may buffer people from the ill effects of stress.

9. Reversal theory employs the method of structural phenomenology to discern opposing metamotivational modes, or ways of being, in human experience. A telic, goal-directed mode organizes the emotional dimension of relaxation-anxiety; a paratelic, activity-directed mode organizes the emotional dimension of boredom-excitement.

10. Carl Rogers' humanistic theory of personality urges the personologist (and the therapist) to explore the person's phenomenal field through empathy and, ideally, unconditional positive regard. The basic motive in living is the urge toward organismic fulfillment, achieved by the fully functioning adult.

11. Abraham Maslow's humanistic theory posits a hierarchy of needs, with self-actualization needs at the top. Self-actualized people tend to have many peak experiences.

12. A small body of empirical research has focused on self-actualization and phenomena like peak experiences, peak performance, and flow.

13. George Kelly's theory of personal constructs is a bridge between the existential/humanistic theories of this chapter and the modern cognitive approaches of Chapter 9. Kelly's theory begins with an image of the person as a scientist, seeking to predict and control events in the world.

14. By construing regularities in the events in the world, a person develops a system of personal constructs, which serve as more-or-less flexible categories for interpreting subjective conscious experience. The nature of a person's construct system may be examined through the Rep Test.

Chapter 9

Cognitive Approaches to the Person

Introduction

Cognition and Personality
Social Intelligence
Self-Schemata
Gender Schemata
Feature 9.A: Masculinity, Femininity, and Androgyny
Depressive Schemata
Feature 9.B: Thinking and Feeling

From Thought to Action
Middle-Level Units and Purposive Behavior
The Regulation of Behavior

Differentiation and Integration
Field Independence–Dependence
Integrative Complexity
Feature 9.C: Human Values

Summary

Most people in my generation will never forget the afternoon of November 22, 1963. For the fourth graders attending Pittman Square Elementary School in Gary, Indiana, the day began as might any grey and chilly weekday in late autumn. The morning was uneventful, as far as I can remember. We said the Pledge of Allegiance and sang "My Country, 'Tis of Thee." Sometime around noon, we started our artwork with Miss Porter. In the middle of our lesson, the school principal walked into the classroom and turned on a radio. Class stopped, and we all listened to the report from Dallas that President John F. Kennedy had been shot. We sat in silence, knowing that something big was happening, something unprecedented, for the principal had never before interrupted class in such a sudden fashion. Of course, this was not the first time that we had witnessed a major national event in the classroom. In second grade, we had all watched the coverage of John Glenn's three orbits of the earth on a classroom television. But Glenn's historic space flight had been advertised for weeks in advance. We knew exactly when it was coming and what was supposed to happen. November 22nd, on the other hand, was completely unexpected.

Now that class was effectively suspended, we were free to sit in our seats and talk with our neighbors. We chattered excitedly about who might have shot the president. We wondered aloud what the term "critical condition" meant, though surely it did not sound good. A couple of kids were certain the president would die and had asked the teacher who would succeed him as the next president. She told us that the vice-president would assume office. We did not know who the vice-president was, though some kids thought it was probably Richard Nixon, since he had finished second in the 1960 election. Failing to understand the gravity of the situation, most of us were mildly confused and excited. Only later were most of us to feel pain, anger, and the despair of loss. But a few children seemed genuinely sad at the time, even before we learned that John Kennedy had indeed died. Mary Lee Watkins sat two rows to my left. She put her head down on her desk and cried bitterly. She kept saying that she wished she had been shot instead.

In the mid-1970s, cognitive psychologists Roger Brown and James Kulik asked 80 American men and women ranging in age from 20 to 54 to describe their memories of certain key events in recent American history (Brown & Kulik, 1977). All but one of the respondents reported a **flashbulb memory** of the moment they learned of the assassination of John F. Kennedy. Brown and Kulik defined a flashbulb memory as an especially vivid and detailed recollection of a particular event in one's life. Like a photograph, the memory captures forever the concrete experience of the happening, where the person was, what he or she was doing, thinking, and feeling at the moment the flash went off. Unlike a photograph, however, the flashbulb memory is selective. I remember Miss Porter, the principal, and Mary Lee Watkins most clearly; I cannot recall who was sitting right next to me in class, what I was wearing, or how much time elapsed between learning of the shooting and the death.

A flashbulb memory for many people over the age of 35: John F. Kennedy's motorcade in Dallas, shortly before the assassination, November 22, 1963.

According to Brown and Kulik (1977), when the principal turned on the radio and I heard the news, certain parts of my central nervous system immediately "recognized" the novelty and consequentiality of the information I was receiving and, figuratively speaking, "took a picture" of the experience, a flashbulb illumination to be stored in memory forever. Cognitive psychologist Ulric Neisser (1982) offers a different interpretation. He argues that my memory of Kennedy's assassination is not akin to a flashbulb picture at all but is rather a life-history "benchmark." Over the years, I and others in my generation have come to understand the truly momentous nature of November 22, 1963. We have rehearsed and replayed the event in our minds. Over time, the event has become indelibly etched in memory as one of "the places where we line up our own lives with the course of history itself and say, 'I was there'" (Neisser, 1982, p. 48).

The remembrance of things past is more than an idle curiosity, argue psychologists who stress the cognitive dimensions of human experience and the person's abilities to process information in daily life. Remembrance ties us to the past and orients us to the future. Cognitive approaches to the person therefore address a basic question about human life: How do people take

Cognitive approaches to the person emphasize human thought and information processing.

in information from the environment, process and store that information in memory, and later recall what they have stored in order to use the information in an adaptive way? A flashbulb memory is one vivid example of how the past endures in the mind's vast storehouse of information. In the last 30 years, cognitive psychologists have systematically explored the storehouse to understand what it contains, how it is organized, and how it is utilized in daily information processing. Their explorations have generated some of the approaches to personality featured in this chapter, approaches that emphasize human memory, cognition, and the cognitive control of purposive human behavior. A classic text in cognitive psychology concludes: "Information-processing psychology is fundamentally committed to the concept of representation: Everything you know is considered to be represented in your memory" (Lachman, Lachman, & Butterfield, 1979, p. 8).

Perhaps the greatest conceptual change in psychology in the last 35 years has been the rise of *cognitive psychology* as the systematic study of "perception, memory, attention, pattern recognition, problem solving, the psychology of language, cognitive development, and a host of other problems that had lain dormant for half a century" (Neisser, 1976, p. 5). Although psychologists had examined these problems in numerous ways before the 1950s, their various investigations were quite limited and unintegrated, and they were not generally viewed as part of a common enterprise focused on human cognition, which is "the activity of knowing: the acquisition, organization, and use of knowledge" (Neisser, 1976, p. 1). The basic mental processes involved in human knowing include "attention, perception, abstraction, problem solving, learning, memory, and language" (Lachman et al., 1979, p. 128).

The historical roots of cognitive psychology lie in the study of verbal learning, human engineering, communications, computer science, linguistics, and the rigorous experimental methods of laboratory science (Lachman et al., 1979). But the single most important reason for the emergence of cognitive psychology as a viable scientific area is probably the development of the computer. The computer provides a new and powerful *metaphor* for human cognition. Like computers, human beings appear to accept information from the environment, manipulate symbols, store events in "memory," retrieve memories, classify inputs, recognize patterns, and engage in a number of other cognitive operations by which they organize and utilize information:

> Computers take symbolic input, recode it, make decisions about the recoded input, make new expressions of it, store some or all of the input, and give back symbolic output. By analogy, that is most of what cognitive psychology is about. It is about how people take in information, how they recode and remember it, how they make decisions, how they transform their internal knowledge states, and how they translate these states into behavioral outputs. (Lachman et al., 1979, p. 99)

Some of the basic concepts of cognitive psychology are introduced in Table 9.1. In recent years, personality psychologists have appropriated many of these concepts in their efforts to provide more adequate frameworks for understanding the whole person, human motivation, and individual differences in personality structure and functioning (e.g., Cantor, 1990; Cantor & Zirkel, 1990; Carver & Scheier, 1992; Wyer & Srull, 1989). Going back at least to the 1950s, however, many personality psychologists of many different persuasions have incorporated cognitive perspectives into their theorizing. As we saw in the last chapter, George Kelly (1955) developed an influential psychology of personal constructs that focused on how the individual consciously construes the world and the self. Similarly, Julian Rotter's (1954) social-learning theory placed prime emphasis on the cognitive phenomena of expectancies and values (Chapter 6). Even psychoanalytic

Table 9.1

Basic Concepts of Cognitive Psychology

Concept	Definition
Information	Anything that reduces uncertainty (Brody, 1970).
Encoding	The process of taking in information from the environment.
Episodic memory	Information for specific events stored in memory (Tulving, 1972).
Semantic memory	Information for concepts and meanings stored in memory (Tulving, 1972).
Short-term memory	Information held in memory for a few seconds. Without rehearsal or some other memory strategy, the information will quickly decay.
Long-term memory	Information held in memory on a more-or-less permanent basis.
Feedback loop	A system in which output is regulated by comparison of input to a reference point.
Plan	Hierarchical arrangement of goals with embedded subgoals and specific behaviors at base. Human behavior is partially regulated by plans, which specify the sequential processing of information in order to accomplish a particular goal (Miller, Galanter, & Pribram, 1960).
Script	Encoded knowledge of a stereotypic event sequence (Abelson, 1981).
Schema	An abstract knowledge structure.
Prototype	A highly representative example of a particular phenomenon. Prototypes may play a major role in human information processing in that they provide natural and readily retrieved category types according to which a person is able to organize perceptions, cognitions, interpretations, and judgments (Cantor & Mischel, 1979).

conceptions of "ego psychology" and "object relations" underscore the cognitive activities of persons. For example, the "ego" may be viewed as a master cognizer or information-processing system designed to make sense of the world as well as to enhance adaption; "internalized objects" may be seen as mental representations—cognitive schemas or patterns—that develop out of important interpersonal relationships (Chapter 2). It is virtually impossible today to consider personality functioning without examining some aspect of human cognition. Nonetheless, certain frameworks for understanding persons appear more closely linked to cognitive psychology than do others. Certain approaches are built explicitly around models of the person as a computerlike, goal-directed information processor. In the field of personality psychology, the 1980s have witnessed the emergence of a new *cognitive personology* (Cantor & Zirkel, 1990). It is to the approaches that are at the center of this movement that we now turn.

Cognition and Personality

Social Intelligence

Nancy Cantor and John Kihlstrom argue that a cognitive approach to the person should center on the concept of social intelligence (Cantor & Kihlstrom, 1985, 1987, 1989). Each person brings a set of skills, abilities, and knowledge to every social situation. Such "lawful intraindividual variability, especially across situations, is precisely the characteristic we ascribe to intelligence" (Cantor & Kihlstrom, 1985, p. 16). They write, "intelligent action, as contrasted with the instinctual or the reflexive, is flexible rather than rigidly stereotyped, discriminative rather than indiscriminate, and optional rather than obligatory" (p. 16). The implication is that people differ in social intelligence. Some people appear to have more than others. More important, however, people use their social intelligence in different ways to interpret and solve current tasks and problems in life.

In Cantor and Kihlstrom's view, social interaction involves problem solving. The social world confronts each of us with a series of mundane and momentous problems that call for socially intelligent behavior. We must interpret each problem we encounter and devise a strategy for mastering it, or at least for coping with it. For each social situation, the person asks such questions as "What do I want here?" "What are the likely consequences of my actions?" "How can I get what I want?" In working through the various facets of a social problem (situation), the person draws extensively on a repertoire of social intelligence, which "is stored in memory as organized knowledge" and which "forms the structural basis for personality" (p. 18). This organized knowledge consists of *concepts, episodes,* and *rules,* as shown in Table 9.2.

Nancy Cantor

Table 9.2

A Taxonomy of Social Intelligence

Declarative-Semantic (Concepts)	Declarative-Episodic (Episodes)	Procedural (Rules)
Implicit Personality Theory	Person Memory	Causal Attribution
Social Categories	Autobiographical Memory	Judgmental Heuristics
Self		Hypothesis Testing
Other persons		Encoding–Retrieval
Social behaviors		
Situations		
Scripts		

The major *concepts* existing within the structure of social intelligence are aspects of what Cantor and Kihlstrom called **declarative-semantic knowledge.** This is the abstract and categorical information that the person has gleaned over time concerning various social events and phenomena. Included here are **scripts** (Abelson, 1981; Schank & Abelson, 1977), the encoded knowledge of stereotypic event sequences. A good example is the script for eating at a restaurant. When we enter a restaurant, we expect to involve ourselves in a certain behavioral routine. We walk in and wait to be seated. Once seated, we expect to meet a waiter or waitress, to have our water glass filled, to receive and read the menu, to order what we want to eat, to spend a certain amount of time eating the food, to enjoy the conversation while eating, to receive the bill at the end of the meal, and so on. When we enter a restaurant, therefore, we activate a restaurant script, which then guides our behavior and our experience in the situation. We expect other people to do the same thing. The script provides general guidelines within which a good deal of behavioral flexibility may be manifest. Thus, I may order anything on the menu; I may discuss the upcoming presidential election over dessert; I may choose to pay with a credit card or cash. But I am not likely to stand on the table and juggle the plates. Violations of the script may be seen as odd and even troubling, for they undermine our well-established assumptions about how the world is supposed to work.

Conceptions of the *self* also assume a prominent position in declarative-semantic knowledge. Self-conceptions record likes and dislikes, goals and aspirations, and various assumptions about the self that the person has built up from past experience. Also included are abstract understandings and expectations concerning other people: what people will generally do in various social situations, what people are generally like, what kinds of people one prefers, and so on.

In Chapter 7 we encountered the concept of *implicit personality theories* (Rosenberg, 1977). Every person develops a "theory" of human functioning, made up of intuitive knowledge concerning the causes of human behavior, norms for various attributes of personality, and the relation of various personality attributes to each other. For example, my mother's implicit personality theory holds that, for the most part, smart people are morally good. In other words, she tends to believe that intelligence and morality are highly correlated. Another relative of mine seems to hold the opposite view. According to her implicit personality theory, highly intelligent people tend to be crafty and devious, and for the most part they should not be trusted. Like scripts, implicit personality theories are embedded in a person's repertoire of declarative-semantic knowledge.

The major *episodes* existing within the structure of social intelligence comprise **declarative-episodic knowledge.** This kind of knowledge comes in two forms: (1) knowledge of the experiences, thoughts, and actions of other people and (2) one's personal autobiographical record. The first of these is sometimes called *person memory* (Hastie, Park, & Weber, 1984; Wyer & Martin, 1986), and the second is called *autobiographical memory* (Kihlstrom, 1981; Robinson, 1976). My remembrance of the Kennedy assassination is a highlighted episode from my autobiographical memory. It also encodes important information about certain

John Kihlstrom

persons, such as Mary Lee Watkins and Miss Porter. Cantor and Kihlstrom (1989) write: "Personal recollections tend to be hot and wet rather than cold and dry: They often involve vivid images and feelings that are lacking in the raw factual material drawn up from semantic memory" (p. 25). Because declarative-episodic knowledge is encapsuled in recollections of concrete events, it provides a richness of texture and pattern to social intelligence that more abstract knowledge (declarative-semantic knowledge) can rarely provide. In addition, "there seems to be a sense of narrative integrity to autobiographical memory, with people able to reflect on the beginning, middle, and potential end of their life stories," write Cantor and Kihlstrom (1989, p. 26). In Chapter 13, we will discuss how autobiographical memory may indeed be organized in terms of a life narrative that integrates past, present, and anticipated future to provide life with unity and purpose.

The third component of social intelligence—that comprised of *rules*—is called **procedural knowledge.** This consists of various competencies, strategies, and rules "that enable us to form impressions of others, make causal attributions, encode and retrieve social memories, and predict social behaviors" (Cantor &

Kihlstrom, 1985; p. 20). Of special interest here are **causal attributions,** the perceived causes of events. A huge body of research in social psychology has examined how people understand causation in social events (Jones, Kanouse, Kelley, Nisbett, Valins, & Weiner, 1971; Kelley, 1972; Kelley & Michela, 1980). In Chapter 7, we briefly discussed the "fundamental attribution error," whereby people tend to view their own behavior as caused by situational factors and the behavior of others as caused by internal traits. The general principle is that people tend to make different causal interpretations for events in which they're personally involved (as actors) than they do for events that they witness or hear about (as observers). Observers tend to say that the behavior of other people is caused by intentions or dispositions residing within the other people. By contrast, the actors themselves tend to say that their behavior is caused by various factors in the situation. Actors offer a more contextualized account of their own behavior. Their intimate knowledge of their own role as a participant in a behavior sequence provides important information for their causal attributions. In that observers may not be privy to the same kind of information about the actors, observers tend to attribute cause in a rather noncontextual manner, by making global attributions about the actor's traits, motives, intentions, and so on.

Bernard Weiner (1979, 1990) offers another well-known scheme for understanding causal attributions, especially as they apply to outcomes of success and failure. To explain why a person succeeded or failed in a given task, we often resort to one or more of four basic attributions: ability, effort, task difficulty, and luck. Why, for example, did Maria receive a low grade on her term paper for American Literature 101? Her failure to do well on this assignment might be explained in terms of ability: Maria is simply not a very good writer. Or it may be explained in terms of effort: Maria did not put much time into the paper; she didn't try hard enough. Both ability and effort are *internal* attributions. They suggest that the cause of Maria's failure is in factors within Maria—her poor ability or her weak effort. By contrast, we may explain Maria's failure in terms of task difficulty: The assignment was too hard, too ambiguous; perhaps, the professor expected too much or failed to give the students enough time to write a good paper. Or we may say that Maria was just plain unlucky on this assignment. During the same week that her paper was due, Maria's boyfriend broke up with her and her mother called to say that she did not have enough money to pay the recent tuition bill. Because of her bad luck, Maria was distracted and failed to write the kind of paper she would normally write. Task difficulty and luck are *external* attributions: The causes of her failure are in the environment, not in Maria herself. The four attributions may also be organized along the lines of *stability.* Ability and task difficulty refer to stable factors; effort and luck are unstable. Maria's luck may change or she may try harder next time.

In general, people tend to make internal and stable attributions when accounting for successes in their lives. Had Maria received an "A" on the assignment, she might attribute her good fortune to her strong writing ability. By contrast, people tend to make unstable attributions when accounting for failure—not trying hard enough, or bad luck. In the wake of a failure, an unstable attribution has the advantage of suggesting that things are likely to change in the future. It would seem, therefore, that explaining failure in terms of momentary causes such as effort or luck helps protect one's self-esteem. Things will be better next time. I'm still okay. Nonetheless, people differ markedly in their characteristic attributional patterns. As we will see later in this chapter, some empirical evidence suggests that chronically depressed people tend to make causal sense of their successes and failures in ways that go against the norms. They may tend to explain their own successes in terms of unstable factors (e.g., "I got lucky") but their failures in terms of causes that are internal and stable (e.g., "I failed because I'm stupid.").

Summing up the concept of social intelligence, Cantor and Kihlstrom argue that people employ concepts (declarative-semantic knowledge such as scripts and implicit personality theories), episodes (declarative-episodic knowledge such as autobiographical recollections), and rules (procedural knowledge such as attributional patterns) to solve social problems they encounter in everyday life. Problem solving is most effective when people are able to act in flexible and discriminating ways, when they can enact creative solutions to the social problems they confront, enabling them to move forward in life with efficacy and aplomb. Especially significant for personality are those social problems that take the form of **life tasks.** According to Cantor and Zirkel (1990), life tasks are "self-articulated problems that individuals are motivated to try to solve, to which they devote energy and time, and that they see as organizing their daily life activity" *during a particular life period or life transition* (p. 150). Therefore, life tasks may arise from developmental demands—challenges and opportunities that we confront by virtue of the particular period or stage in the life cycle in which we are currently placed. For instance, a recent college graduate may see her main life task as that of "becoming established in a line of work" or "beginning a family" or "making new friendships." College freshmen may be most concerned with "adjusting to leaving home," "getting good grades in school," and "finding an academic area in which to major."

Cantor, Norem, Niedenthal, Langston, and Brower (1987) conducted a longitudinal study of life tasks and cognitive strategies among honors students in college. As freshmen, the students completed a life-tasks questionnaire. They were asked to list life tasks on which they were currently working and to categorize each task (if possible) into one of six groups: three achievement categories (doing well academically, establishing future goals, managing time) and three interpersonal categories (making friends, being on one's own, establishing an identity). The researchers detected two very different cognitive strategies for dealing effectively with the relatively stressful academic life tasks confronting the students. One group of students exhibited consistent optimism in their approach to academic life tasks. They viewed academic tasks as challenging but not especially overwhelming, and they tended to predict accurately their own academic performance, as evidenced by later grades in classes. A second group of students showed defensive pessimism (Norem & Cantor, 1986). The defensive pessimists rated their academic tasks (such as "getting good grades") in much more negative

So half empty does not effect.

half

Half full

terms than did the optimists, though they did not differ from the optimists in their ratings of interpersonal tasks (such as "making friends"). Defensive pessimists did not accurately predict the grades they eventually received. They tended instead to underestimate their own performance, setting defensively low expectations in spite of good past performance. Interestingly, these students were not debilitated by their pessimistic outlooks. In fact, the reverse seemed to be true. For pessimists, the higher the anxiety surrounding academic tasks, the higher their first semester GPA! Overall, the optimists and the defensive pessimists achieved comparable grades in their first semester of college.

Self-Schemata

A central concept in cognitive approaches to personality is the **schema.** A schema (plural: *schemata*) is any abstract knowledge structure. Fiske and Taylor (1984) write that a schema is a "cognitive structure that represents one's general knowledge about a given concept or concept domain" (p. 13). There are many ways to think about schemata. You may view them as "filters" or "templates" that we use to perceive, organize, and understand information, much like Kelly's (Chapter 8) concept of a "personal construct." Neisser (1976) writes that a schema is like a "format" in a computer-programming language. Formats specify that information must be of a certain sort if it is to be interpreted coherently. The format allows the program to deal effectively with a particular kind of information while ignoring or downplaying the rest. A person's schemata go beyond the information given by (1) simplifying information when there is too much for the person to handle efficiently and (2) filling in gaps when information is missing.

Every person employs a vast and complex set of schemata to make sense of the world. The cognitive approaches to personality contend that human adaptation is accomplished through the schematic processing of social information. Furthermore, schemata are applied to the self. Each person builds up a view of the self, a **self-schema** or series of self-schemata that structure the processing of self-relevant information and guide behavior. A self-schema is like all other schemata in that it simplifies incoming information and fills in gaps when information is missing. For example, if an important part of a young man's self-schema is the idea that he is especially attractive to women, he is likely to pick up information from the social environment that confirms his view and ignore or fail to process information that seems irrelevant. Seeing the puzzled facial expression of a woman sitting next to him in class, he may assume that she is thinking of him and wondering if he might ask her out. But self-schemata differ from other schemata, too. Self-schemata are generally (1) larger and more complex than other schemata, (2) richer in their network of associations and relationships among components, (3) more frequently activated in daily information processing, and (4) loaded with emotion (Markus & Sentis, 1982). One's own self-schema contains a vast and complex array of emotionally laden information. For each of us, it is probably our most popular, most frequently used schema.

The self-schema does not contain all information about the person. Rather, it emphasizes personally significant information about the self. We tend to place at the center of the self-schema those self-defining properties such as our name, representative aspects of physical appearance, significant personal relationships, and perceived traits, motives, values, and goals that we view as most representative of who we are. Figure 9.1 illustrates a small portion of a hypothetical person's self-schema. Many concepts may be linked with the self-schema, because we experience most things with reference to the self. In Figure 9.1, the self is linked to food and graduate school. Other concepts in memory that are not self-relevant, such as "ladders" and "gorillas," are not shown as connected to the self. Repeated associations of the self with other concepts and structures will lead to stronger and more certain links. Eventually, there may be some overlap between the self and another concept, as when a person takes up jogging and comes to see himself or herself as possessing many of the characteristics of other joggers.

A major finding in research on self-schemata is that people process information that is especially relevant to their self-schemata in highly efficient ways (Lewicki, 1984; Markus, 1977, 1983; Markus & Smith, 1981). In a classic study, Hazel Markus (1977) investigated the dimension of "independence–dependence" in self-schemata. Depending on how college students presented themselves in an initial phase of her research, Markus classified each as having a strong independence schema, a strong dependence schema, or as aschematic (having neither). Three to four weeks later, the students participated in an experiment in which adjectives were presented on a screen one at a time. The adjectives were either

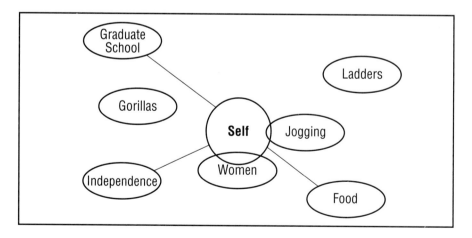

Figure 9.1

Portion of a Hypothetical Self-Schema.

From Markus & Smith, 1981, p. 244.

schema-relevant (related to independence or dependence) or *schema-irrelevant* (a set of adjectives related to the dimension of "creativity"). The student's task was to press one of two buttons, labeled either ME or NOT ME, to indicate whether the adjective described him or her.

Those students whose self-schemata underscored dependence showed faster reaction times in response to dependent adjectives than they did to schema-inconsistent (independent) adjectives and schema-irrelevant adjectives. Markus concluded that the dependent schematics were accustomed to thinking of themselves as "conforming," "obliging," and so on and could, therefore, make these judgments more quickly. The independent schematics showed a similar pattern of results, with faster reaction times to independent adjectives. The aschematics, on the other hand, did not differ at all in their processing times for dependent and independent words. Aschematics appeared not to have defined themselves with respect to independence and to be equally at ease labelling their behavior in these terms. They apparently did not have a structure for independence–dependence to guide their information processing about the self.

Studies similar to Markus' have shown that people with self-schemata emphasizing particular areas are readily able to (1) evaluate new information with respect to its relevance for the particular area, (2) make judgments and decisions in the domain with relative ease and certainty, (3) retrieve episodes and other behavioral evidence from their past that illustrates the particular area, (4) predict future behavior in the area, and (5) resist information that is counter to the prevailing schema (Markus & Smith, 1981).

Markus (1983) hypothesizes that a self-schema emerges as a person begins to experience feelings of personal responsibility in a particular domain of behavior. "Acquiring a self-schema becomes equivalent to staking out a personal claim in a given behavioral arena," writes Markus (1983, p. 561). "It is as if one is saying 'I have control over my actions here' (or 'I would like to have control over my actions here' or 'I am both the cause and the consequence of actions in this domain')." As a self-schema develops, the person becomes more concerned with his or her own behavior in the particular domain and seeks to exert control over the causes and consequences of that behavior.

Take for example a dominant self-schema from my own life—one that has sadly passed into oblivion to be replaced by others. I began to develop a self-schema related to baseball and athletics in the second grade. Before this time, I knew virtually nothing about baseball and had no interest in learning. If someone had told me in first grade that I was a poor baseball player, I would have reacted as I might now should someone tell me that I'm a poor mechanic: "Who cares?!" However, in the second grade, I started watching the Chicago Cubs on television (as related previously in Feature 5.C) and began to entertain the idea of playing the game. As I cautiously joined in the neighborhood sandlot baseball games, I began to see myself as a pretty good hitter and a very good fielder and pitcher. I worked hard to improve my performance. I fantasized about playing in the big leagues as an adult, going so far as to calculate my statistics for an envisioned 20-year career as a star pitcher for the Chicago Cubs, even down to my lifetime earned-run average and number of batters I would strike out. By the time I was in fifth grade, I was especially sensitive to compliments and criticisms about my baseball playing. My "good baseball player" self-schema expanded and became probably the largest part of my self-understanding in grade school. It served to organize information about myself and it functioned to regulate my behavior—I spent countless hours in the sun throwing, hitting, and catching balls.

Individuals develop very different self-schemata. Differences in the *content* of self-schemata—the self-relevant material contained within a schema—are virtually infinite in that no two people see themselves in identical ways. Differences in the *structure* of self-schemata can also be observed. For instance, some people present highly articulated and complex self-schemata, whereas other people see themselves in simpler terms (Linville, 1987). Some people have many different self-aspects, which are kept relatively separate from each other. Each aspect of their self-schema may be connected to a particular role they play in life, but the different roles may be relatively unconnected. Therefore, should they experience failure or trouble with respect to one area in their self-schema, other areas may remain relatively unscathed. In a sense, these people with high levels of *self-complexity* manage to compartmentalize the many different aspects of the self-schema, such that what happens in one aspect has little effect on the others. By contrast, people low in self-complexity present a less differentiated self-schema. For people low in self-complexity, feelings associated with a bad event in one aspect of life tend to spill over into other aspects as well. In the wake of failure in one domain, misery may spread quickly across the entire self-schema (Dixon & Baumeister, 1991; Linville, 1987).

Differences in the complexity of self-schemata have also been linked to differences in the focus of one's consciousness. Whereas some people tend to focus their attention on the outside, public world, others are more taken with their own inner lives, their private world of thought, feeling, and fantasy. Research by Nasby (1985) and others suggests that people who score high on scales measuring **private self-consciousness**—a tendency to introspect about the self (Fenigstein, Scheier, & Buss, 1975)—develop more elaborate and extensive self-schemata than do people who score low on self-consciousness. Not surprisingly, people who dwell on and ponder over the meanings of their own behaviors tend to develop self-schemata that are rich in detail and nuance.

Gender Schemata

When I took German in high school, I was amazed to discover that each German noun must be classified as either masculine, feminine, or neuter. English, of course, does not make these distinctions. Thus, it seemed strange to me that *toilet* should be feminine (*die Toilette*) and *toothpick* should be masculine (*der Zahnstocher*). Odd pairings of nouns and their gender were the source of many adolescent jokes in our class, which our German teacher found very tiresome, since he had heard them all before. Yet the German designation of gender in the naming of persons, places, and things points to an important fact about human life—that gender can be a great organizing principle. In her **gender schema theory,** Sandra Bem (1981, 1987) suggests that people differ in the extent to which they understand their lives and contexts in gender-related terms. Some people repeatedly process social information along the lines of gender, showing strong gender schemata. Other people are relatively "aschematic" with respect to gender, less inclined to interpret social life in terms of masculinity and femininity.

Feature 9.A discusses the extensive body of research that psychologists have generated on the sex-role orientations of masculinity, femininity, and androgyny. Men and women who see themselves as relatively masculine report that they are assertive, self-reliant, dominant, ambitious, and so on. Those who see themselves as relatively feminine report that they are affectionate, sympathetic, soft-spoken, gentle, and so on. Some people are psychologically androgynous, describing themselves in highly masculine and highly feminine terms. Undifferentiated people use few masculine and few feminine terms to describe themselves.

Bem argues that individual differences in sex-role orientations are best understood in terms of different gender schemata. A man who scores high on masculinity or a woman who scores high on femininity exhibits a strong gender schema, or generalized tendency to process information on the basis of sex-linked associations. These people should be especially sensitive to gender differences in daily information processing. Androgynous and undifferentiated men and women show weaker gender schemata. They are less likely to see and interpret the world in terms of gender.

In a famous experiment that has been repeated many times, Bem (1981) administered a sex-role inventory (the BSRI) to college students and then engaged the students in a memory task. She first presented a list of 61 words in random order consisting of proper names (such as *Henry, Deborah*), animal names, (*gorilla, butterfly*), verbs (*hurling, blushing*), and articles of clothing (*trousers, bikini*). Within each of the four categories, some of the words were masculine oriented (*Henry, gorilla, hurling, trousers*) and some were feminine oriented (*Deborah, butterfly, blushing, bikini*).

After the words were presented, the students were given 8 minutes to write down as many of the words that they could remember in any order. The important finding in the study concerns the *order* in which words were remembered. As Figure 9.2 shows, college students with strong gender schemata (masculine men and feminine women) tended to show higher levels of *clustering* in their recall of words. This means that they tended to string together words of the same gender designation. For instance, if the first word they remembered and wrote down was *Henry* (a masculine word), their second word remembered was likely to be masculine as well (for example, *hurling*). Thus, sex-typed men and women (those with strong gender schemata) tended to group together masculine and feminine words in recall. In Bem's words, they "spontaneously imposed a gender-based classification system on the stimulus array" (1987, p. 267). Non-sex-typed men and women—those with presumably weaker gender schemata—showed lower levels of clustering. These students tended not to use gender as an organizing principle for recalling the words (see Figure 9.2, p. 502).

Frable and Bem (1985) obtained intriguing findings in a study of memory for conversations that show, in their words, "if you are gender schematic, all members of the opposite sex look alike" (p. 459). Sex-typed, cross-sex-typed (feminine men and masculine women), androgynous, and undifferentiated men and women participated in either a "gender study" or a "race study." Each participant listened to a 5-minute taped conversation among three men and three women (gender study) or among three blacks and three whites (race study). During the conversation, a photograph of each speaker was projected onto a screen as he or she spoke. After the taped conversation and slide show, each participant was presented with a list of verbatim excerpts from the conversation along with photographs of the six speakers and was asked to match each excerpt with the appropriate speaker.

Some of the results are shown in Figure 9.3. Frable and Bem found that, for the gender study, sex-typed people (masculine men and feminine women) and cross-sex-typed people (feminine men and masculine women) made more "opposite-sex errors" in the matching task than did androgynous or undifferentiated participants. For a male participant, an "opposite-sex-error" would be when he correctly identified the speaker as a woman but incorrectly identified the *particular* woman speaking. Similarly, an opposite-sex-error for a female participant in the study would occur when she correctly stated that a man was speaking but misidentified which particular man it was. By contrast, no significant differences in opposite-sex-errors as a function of gender schemata were obtained in the race study (see Figure 9.3, p. 503).

The findings suggest that both sex-typed and cross-sex-typed men and women are relatively more gender-schematic (have stronger gender schemata) than androgynous and undifferentiated men and women. According to Frable and Bem, the sex-typed and the cross-sex-typed persons employ a relatively strong gender schema to group gender-relevant social events in memory. They "confuse opposite-sex speakers with one another more, implying that they are more likely to encode the sex of opposite-sex speakers and also to use that information to treat them as similar to one another" (Frable & Bem, 1985, p. 466). Such sex-typed individuals appear to have much more knowledge, enabling them to make finer distinctions, about their own sex than about the opposite sex. Interestingly, cross-sex-typed men and women *do the same thing:* feminine men fail to differentiate among women; masculine women fail to differentiate among men. Frable and Bem speculate that feminine men and masculine women may have gender schemata that are just as strong as those of sex-typed men and women. Like their sex-typed counterparts, they too appear to know much more about their own sex than about the opposite sex, even though they describe themselves in opposite sex terms. Frable and Bem offer three possible explanations:

The first possibility is that parents and other socializing agents may have tried to "correct" the cross-sex-typed individual's deviance by constantly pointing out and discussing culturally appropriate examples of behavior (or hairstyle or clothing or body movement or whatever) in other same-sex individuals.

Continued on p. 502

Feature 9.A

Masculinity, Femininity, and Androgyny

According to common social lore, men are strong, assertive, independent, and instrumental—that is, *masculine.* Women are gentle, caring, dependent, and expressive—that is, *feminine.* These are *sex-role stereotypes* familiar to all of us. While many of us (for good reason) may take issue with the "truth" of these stereotypes as they apply to real men and women, virtually none of us would deny that the stereotypes themselves exist—that is, that many people have traditionally *believed* that these conceptions of sex roles are (or should be) true. Furthermore, masculinity and femininity are typically viewed as opposite ends of a single continuum. Thus, if you are not especially masculine, then you must be feminine, and vice versa.

You might expect that simplistic stereotypes like these would be seen as "the enemy" by personologists who pride themselves on studying that which is unique or especially characteristic in the single person. However, in recent years personality psychologists have turned these stereotypes to their research advantage. They have developed numerous self-report questionnaires and rating scales designed to assess the extent to which people see themselves in sex-role stereotypic terms—measures such as the Bem Sex-Role Inventory (BSRI: Bem, 1974) and the Personal Attributes Questionnaire (PAQ: Spence, Helmreich, & Stapp, 1975). Taking issue with the common assumption that masculinity and femininity are opposites (Constantinople, 1973), they have argued that the two may be seen as separate dimensions within individuals. Accordingly, sex-role conceptions for both men and women are generally understood as follows: people who are high on masculinity (describing themselves as "strong," "assertive," and so on) and low on femininity are *masculine;* those who are high on femininity (describing themselves as "gentle," "compassionate," and so on) and low on masculinity are *feminine;* those who are high on both dimensions are *androgynous;* and those who are low on both are *undifferentiated.*

Early research by Sandra Bem (1975) and others suggested that **psychological androgyny** was the "best" of the four sex-role orientations. People who described themselves in both highly masculine and highly feminine terms tended to show a more flexible style of relating to other people, adjusting their behavior to the demands of the situation. Thus, when they needed to be strong, they were strong; when compassion was the rule, they expressed love and good cheer. Androgyny was positively associated with higher levels of psychosocial adjustment, greater levels of reported happiness (Shaw, 1982), and higher self-esteem (Heilbrun, 1981).

While some more recent studies still support this view (for example, Roos & Cohen, 1987; Selva & Dusek, 1984), the tide of recent research seems to suggest that many of the positive effects of androgyny on adjustment and well-being are *due to the high masculinity component* of androgyny (Marsh, Antill, & Cunningham, 1987; Orlofsky & O'Heron, 1987; Taylor & Hall, 1985; Whitley, 1983). In other words, for both men and women, being high in self-ascribed masculine traits tends to be associated with greater well-being and adjustment. Explanations for these findings sometimes underscore Western society's glorification of traditional masculine values such as independence and its comparative underappreciation of such traditional feminine values as compassion. High femininity tends *not* to contribute significantly to positive outcomes in many studies. However, one interesting exception is the longitudinal research on medical students conducted by Peter Zeldow and his associates, which shows that high femininity scores predict satisfaction with interpersonal relationships, capacity for experiencing pleasure, and low levels of alcohol abuse (Zeldow, Clark, & Daugherty, 1985; Zeldow, Daugherty, & Clark, 1987). Femininity has also been associated with higher levels of commitment in personal relationships (Rusbult, 1987) and higher "relationship quality" among married and cohabitating couples (Kurdek & Schmitt, 1986).

From its inception, research on masculinity, femininity, and androgyny has stirred controversy. Some personality psychologists have claimed that masculinity and femininity are simply stale old traits with trendy new names, virtually the same as "dominance" and "friendliness," respectively. Some have argued that androgyny—when understood as scoring high on both masculine and feminine stereotypes—is a poor model for psychological adaptation, reflecting an assumption that a single person can be totally self-sufficient, completely masculine and feminine at the same time (Sampson, 1985). Writes Morawski (1986), "the androgynous image is a mirror of the ideals of contemporary professional life, reflecting a historical moment when women professionals, in particular, required a model that promoted conventional masculine (instrumental) actions without compromising the feminine self" (p. 53). Similarly, Bem (1981) suggests that, politically and socially speaking, "androgyny was a concept whose time had come" (p. 362).

Suggesting that androgyny's time may now have passed, Bem (1983) now maintains that, rather than encourage androgyny in men and women, society should instead "temper its insistence upon the ubiquitous functional importance of gender dichotomy. In short, human behavior and personality attributes should cease to have gender, and society should stop projecting gender into situations irrelevant to genitalia" (p. 363).

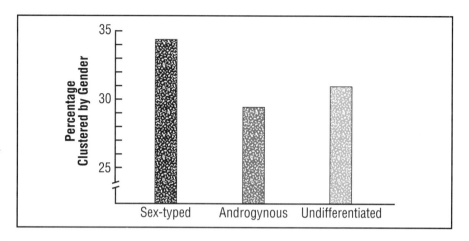

Figure 9.2

Mean Percentage of Clustered Word Pairs.

From Bem, 1981, p. 357.

Continued from p. 499

Second, if cross-sex-typed individuals tend to be rejected by their same-sex agemates as a result of their being gender deviant, that rejection may itself have caused same-sex others to hold a special fascination for the cross-sex-typed individual. Finally, whether rejected or not, cross-sex-typed individuals may have felt ambivalent or even negative about their gender deviance, and those feelings, in turn, may have led them to pay especially close attention to the group with respect to whom they feel deviant. Any or all of these processes would clearly lead the cross-sex-typed individual to have much more knowledge about same-sex others than about cross-sex others. (Frable & Bem, 1985, p. 468)

MacKenzie-Mohr and Zanna (1990) examined the role of men's gender schemata and their tendency to treat women as sexual objects in a nonsexual or professional setting. Gender-schematic (high on masculinity, low on femininity) and gender-aschematic college males watched either a pornographic or neutral video and were then interviewed by a female research assistant. The researchers reasoned that viewing a pornographic video would likely "prime" or make salient thoughts about heterosexual relations among the men and that, as a result, gender-schematic men would be more likely than gender-aschematic men to adopt a "heterosexuality schema" in subsequent interaction with a woman in a professional setting, thinking and acting in a relatively sexist manner. The results of the experiment supported the researchers' prediction. Even though she did not know

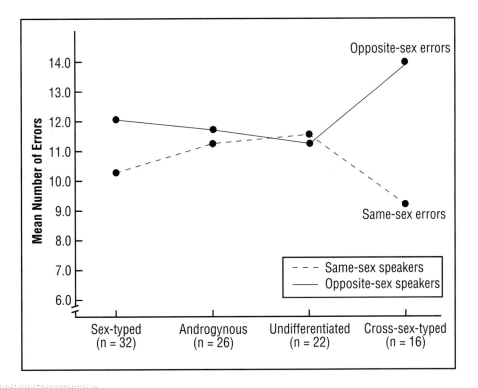

Figure 9.3

Mean Number of Same-Sex and Opposite-Sex Errors.

Adapted from Frable & Bem, 1985, p. 464.

anything about the men she interviewed, the female research assistant experienced her interaction with the gender-schematic men who had viewed the pornographic video as more sexually provocative than interaction with subjects in the other three conditions (schematic/neutral, aschematic/pornography, aschematic/neutral). For example, she reported that gender-schematic men who had viewed the pornographic video were more likely than the other men to look at her body while she was interviewing them. In addition, these men tended to sit closer to her than men in the other conditions. Finally, all the men were asked to describe their interaction with the female assistant immediately after the interview. In the first minute of this free-recall task, 72% of the information recalled by the gender-schematic men who had viewed the pornographic video centered on the interviewer's physical characteristics, compared to 49% of the information recalled by men in the other three conditions. Summing up their results, the authors write:

For gender-schematic males, exposure to nonviolent pornography seems to influence the way they view and act toward a woman in a task-oriented (or "professional") situation. These males were seen by the female experimenter as more sexually motivated, they positioned themselves closer to her, and they had faster reaction times and greater recall for information about her physical appearance. Importantly, these males also recalled less about the survey the female experimenter was conducting. These variables all triangulate on the conclusion that this group of males treated our female experimenter, who was interacting with them in a professional setting, in a manner that was both cognitively and behaviorally sexist. (MacKenzie-Mohr & Zanna, 1990, p. 305)

Bem's gender schema theory has aroused considerable controversy in the scientific literature (Payne, Conner, & Colletti, 1987). Some researchers have been unable to replicate Bem's original findings that sex-typed individuals should show strong gender schemata through high levels of gender clustering in recall (Deaux, Kite, & Lewis, 1985; Edwards & Spence, 1987). Other theorists have offered alternative gender schema theories. According to Markus (Markus, Crane, Bernstein, & Saladi, 1982), for example, androgynous individuals may also show strong gender schemata as they impose well-defined categories of what it means to be both masculine and feminine on social information processing. According to Markus, sex-role orientations signify gender schemata regardless of the person's gender. Thus, a masculine man or woman is schematic for masculinity but not femininity. A feminine man or woman is schematic for femininity but not masculinity. Androgynous persons are schematic for both, and undifferentiated persons are schematic for neither.

Depressive Schemata

In the past 20 years, there has been a veritable explosion of scientific research on the ways in which people who are chronically depressed process information in daily life. Scores of books and hundreds of scientific articles have addressed the topic. A number of major theories have been developed. While these theories differ from each other in important ways and while scientific research does not consistently support all of their tenets, a general theme cuts across all cognitive approaches to human depression: *depressed people perceive, understand, and interpret their worlds and themselves in a peculiar and dysfunctional way.* Cognitive theories of depression do not deny that other noncognitive factors may be implicated in the experience of depression, especially biological factors that may predispose some people to chronic depression. But they do assert that at the center of the depressive experience are depressive cognitions—depressive thoughts, beliefs, values, attributions, schemata. Some theories suggest that these cogni-

The experience of depression.

tions *cause* the emotional feelings of sadness and despair; others suggest that the depressive cognitions are a *result* of depression.

Psychotherapist Aaron Beck was one of the first to offer a cognitive theory of depression (Beck, 1967, 1976). Beck observed that depressed people typically hold a negative view of themselves, are pessimistic about the future, and have a tendency to interpret ongoing experience in a negative manner. These negative interpretations lead to feelings of sadness and despair. During an episode of depression, the depressed person is caught in a downward spiral, as bad thoughts lead to bad feelings which lead to more bad thoughts and more bad feelings. Therefore, depressed people tend to see the world through **depressive schemata.** Depressive schemata *distort* reality by casting information in a negative light. For instance, depressives tend to recall more negative and unpleasant adjectives (such as *bleak, dismal, helpless*) in memory tasks than do nondepressed people (Derry & Kuiper, 1981; McDowall, 1984). They tend to have a difficult time recalling positive themes from stories (Breslow, Kocis, & Belkin, 1981). Depressives tend to recall unpleasant memories more rapidly than pleasant ones (Lloyd & Lishman,

1975). They tend to remember failures and forget successes (Johnson, Petzel, Hartney, & Morgan, 1983). In describing various positive and negative autobiographical memories, depressed college students tend to recall more *different kinds* of negative episodes from their pasts and fewer different kinds of positive episodes than do nondepressed students (McAdams, Lensky, Daple, & Allen, 1988).

Inspired by Beck's schema theory, a good deal of the cognitive research on depression has assumed that depressives *negatively distort* reality. In the last 5 years, however, some studies suggest that "distortion" is, in fact, more characteristic of nondepressives than depressives. Rather than assuming that depressives process information in an overly negative fashion, we may wish to consider the possibility that "normal" or nondepressed people process information in an overly positive manner! The staving-off of depression may be a function of seeing the world through rose-colored glasses. Like Freud's defense mechanisms (Chapter 3) and the illusions of control and invulnerability discussed by Taylor and Langer (Chapter 8), these glasses distort our view but keep us happy. While the idea that distorted perceptions and judgments promote health and happiness is controversial, some evidence has been obtained to suggest that *mildly* depressed people tend to be especially accurate and nonbiased in processing various kinds of social information, while nondepressed people tend to be less accurate because of a positivistic bias (Ruehlman, West, & Pasahow, 1985). *Severely* depressed people, on the other hand, show the negativistic bias in information processing that Beck first identified.

Ingram (1984) has argued that depressed people have a difficult time summoning up positive self-schemata, even in the wake of positive events in their lives. In one laboratory experiment, depressed and nondepressed college students were provided with either positive ("success" condition) or negative ("failure" condition) feedback concerning their performance on a multiple-choice test (Ingram, Smith, & Brehm, 1983). (The bogus feedback was not related to their actual performance on the test, though the students thought that it was at the time.) The students then listened to a prerecorded set of 48 adjectives. After each adjective was presented, the student answered either "yes" or "no" to one of four different questions about the adjective:

1. Was the adjective read by a male? (structural question)
2. Does the adjective rhyme with _____? (phonemic)
3. Does the adjective mean the same as _____? (semantic)
4. Does the word describe you? (self-referent)

According to Ingram, the four different questions call for four different levels of information processing. At the "deepest" level of processing is the self-referent question, for it asks the student to make a very personal judgment about the applicability of the adjective to his or her personality. At the most superficial levels are the structural and phonemic questions, which simply ask the student to make a judgment about the acoustical sound of the adjective as it was heard on the tape.

Following the tape and associated questions, each student was asked to recall as many of the adjectives as possible. The results are shown in Table 9.3. Nondepressed students tended to recall more positive self-references in the success condition (5.13) than in the failure condition (3.06). Depressed students, on the other hand, recalled about the same number of positive self-referents in both conditions (3.04 vs. 3.33). The authors argued that the success feedback preceding the recall task activated a positive self-schema for the nondepressed students, sensitizing them to positive adjectives about themselves. Therefore, they recalled a large number of positive adjectives about themselves in the success condition. By contrast, the success feedback was *not* effective in activating a positive self-schema in the minds of the depressed students, who remembered about the same low number of positive self-referent adjectives in both conditions.

Another influential cognitive approach to depression is Seligman and Abramson's **reformulated learned-helplessness theory.** In his early research with animals, Martin Seligman (1975; Seligman & Maier, 1967) discovered that dogs subjected to uncontrollable aversive stimulation, like random electric shocks, eventually become helpless and do not act to avoid the shocks even when they have a clear opportunity to do so. Analogously, Seligman reasoned, human beings subjected to uncontrollable negative events in life will eventually learn to be helpless and will become chronically depressed. In their reformulated interpretation of learned helplessness, Seligman and Abramson (Abramson, Seligman, & Teasdale, 1978; Peterson & Seligman, 1984) link helplessness and depression to cognitive attributions, or what they have most recently called an *explanatory style.* They argue that depressed people experience the world in a helpless fashion by virtue of their characteristic patterns of assigning causality and explaining events.

According to the reformulated learned-helplessness model, depressives tend to explain *negative* events in their lives as stemming from *internal, global,* and *stable* causes. For example, they may attribute their low grade on an examination to their own general "stupidity"—"I am generally stupid" (stupidity is *internal* to

Continued on p. 510

Table 9.3

Self-Reference Scores for Recalled Words

	Success	Failure
Depressed	3.04	3.33
Nondepressed	5.13	3.06

From Ingram, Smith, & Brehm (1983, p. 417).

Thinking and Feeling

Many people believe that thinking (cognition) and feeling (emotion) are opposing processes in human functioning. While our thinking seems cool and rational, our feelings seem to come from primitive levels of the mind that are deep, "hot," and irrational. Indeed, Freud (Chapter 2) argued that much of what we consider rational thought is a conscious gloss over a submerged and irrational realm of feelings, drives, and repressed conflicts. But the separation of thinking and feeling goes back thousands of years in Western scholarship, at least to Plato, who contrasted the cool light of reason to the hot impulses, appetites, and affects surging upward from the deeper recesses of the soul.

By contrast, in recent years some cognitively oriented psychologists have maintained that, in one way or another, feeling can be understood in terms of thinking. They have examined the relation between cognition and emotion in at least two general ways. First, they have explored how feelings influence thoughts and thoughts influence feelings (Blaney, 1986; Bower, 1981). Second, they have reinterpreted feelings in cognitive terms (Averill, 1984; Lazarus, 1982, 1984).

To understand depression, for example, different cognitive approaches agree that what we feel is influenced by what we think, and (to a somewhat lesser extent, perhaps) vice versa. While these approaches concern themselves with relatively consistent individual differences in depression, other experimental research examines how moods and feelings influence and are influenced by cognitive processes. Some of the best-known work in this regard has been conducted by cognitive psychologist Gordon Bower (1981). In a number of different experiments, Bower has induced temporary happy or sad moods in laboratory subjects—sometimes through hypnosis— and then observed how the moods influence their memory and thinking.

The results of Bower's (1981) experiments can be summarized in three points. First, people exhibit what Bower calls **mood-state-dependent memory** in recall of words lists, in personal experiences recorded in daily diaries, and in recall of childhood experiences. This means that people who are in a happy mood tend to recall material that is relatively happy in nature; people in sad moods recall sad material. Second, emotion influences such cognitive processes as free associations, imaginative fantasies, social perceptions, and judgments about other people's personalities. For example, people who are in an angry mood generate angry associations, tell hostile stories, and are likely to find fault in others. Third, when people listen to stories, they recall best those narratives whose affective tone matches their own.

Bower proposes an **associative network theory** to account for these results, illustrated in Figure 9.B.1.

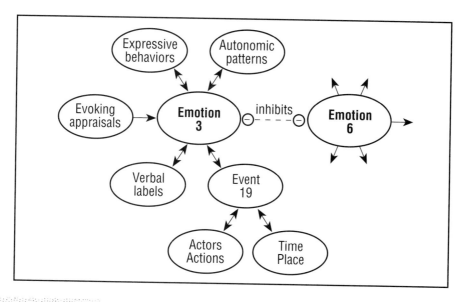

Figure 9.B.1

Small Section of an Associative Network Surrounding an Emotion.

From Bower, 1981, p. 135.

Essentially, Bower views a person's emotional state as an informational unit that is stored in memory in the same manner as any other unit of information. When a person experiences a particular mood, that particular emotion unit may be activated in memory. The activation then spreads to related units. Thus, when you are happy, you will have an easier time remembering happy moments from your past because they are linked to or associated with happy emotion units in your long-term memory storehouse.

Other cognitively oriented theorists have reconceptualized emotions in cognitive terms. For instance, James Averill (1984) states, "in cognitive terms, emotions may be conceived of as belief systems or schemas that guide the appraisal of situations, the organization of responses, and the self-monitoring (interpretation) of behavior" (p. 25). Richard Lazarus (1982) adds, "thought is a necessary condition of emotion" (p. 1019). According to Lazarus, emotional responses in humans are elicited by a "complex cognitive appraisal of the significance of events for one's well-being" (1982, p. 1019). Human beings are "meaning-oriented, meaning-creating creatures who constantly evaluate events from the perspectives of their well-being and react emotionally to some of these evaluations" (p. 1020). A man is likely to experience fear when he appraises a situation as a threat to his well-being. A woman feels joy when she appraises a situation as highly beneficial to her well-being. A boy feels shame when his cognitive appraisal tells him that he has disgraced himself in front of others. According to Lazarus, cognition and emotion are intertwined and simultaneous.

Critics of cognitive theories of emotion counter that emotions should not be reduced to cognitions nor viewed as mere by-products of cognitive appraisal. Robert Zajonc (1980, 1984) asserts that emotions are relatively independent of and prior to cognitions. In Zajonc's view, emotions are too "quick" for cognition—an immediate "hot" affective response may occur in a given situation, followed by a slower "cold" cognition that exists as something of a rationalization for what has already occurred emotionally. In Zajonc's (1980) words, "preferences [emotions] need no inferences [cognitions]" (p. 151). The poet e. e. cummings expresses the same sentiment:

> since feeling is first
> who pays any attention
> to the syntax of things
> will never wholly kiss you.
> (1973, p. 160)

Continued from p. 507

the person, rather than a feature of the external situation); "I am stupid in many things" (*global*); and "I will always be stupid" (*stable*). On the other hand, depressives tend to explain *positive* events in their lives as stemming from *external, specific,* and *unstable* causes. Therefore, they may view a high grade on an examination as a lucky break. The high grade might be due to an easy test (*external*) in a particular area (*specific*) that is not likely to occur again in the future (*unstable*). In essence, the depressive person's explanatory style accentuates the importance of negative events by suggesting that they are due to broad and uncontrollable forces. At the same time, it minimizes the importance of positive events by suggesting that they are specific flukes that are not likely to recur.

Seligman's attributional approach to learned helplessness has stimulated much empirical research. Overall, the findings provide modest but inconsistent support for the model (Coyne & Gotlib, 1983; Peterson & Seligman, 1984; Peterson, Villanova, & Raps, 1985; Robins, 1988). A number of studies have shown that depressed people tend to attribute failures to internal, global, and stable factors, though the obtained relationships between these attributional patterns and depression are weak (Robins, 1988). Further, other sorts of nonattributional dimensions of information processing, such as the person's expectations about the extent to which particular negative events are "intended" or "likely to happen again," appear to be associated with depression, too (Gong-Guy & Hammen, 1980; Hammen & Cochran, 1981). In addition, many researchers appear to be skeptical about Seligman's claim that attributional patterns precede or cause depression. Teasing out such a causal relation requires a longitudinal study in which cognitions and depressive symptomology are monitored over time. Data from an intensive longitudinal case study collected by Peterson, Luborsky, and Seligman (1983) offer interesting support for the causal role of attributions. Other studies, however, are less supportive. For instance, Cochran and Hammen (1985) undertook a 2-month longitudinal study of college students and depressed outpatients and concluded that "in terms of the direction of causality, the data were more consistent in indicating that depression causes cognitions than in indicating the reverse" (p. 1562).

While the findings are sometimes conflicting and the different theories do not agree on a number of noteworthy points, the application of cognitive perspectives to the phenomenon of depression has proven to be especially fruitful. Depressed people do indeed employ different kinds of schemata for making sense of life than do nondepressed people. Whether these schemata are causally implicated in depression, or alternatively the results of depression, cannot be determined at this time. Indeed, the truth probably lies with a little bit of both possibilities—cognition as both a cause and result of the personality constellation we call depression, personality and cognition influencing each other, linked in an intricate web of mutual causation. As in the studies of self-schemata and gender schemata, adapting categories from cognitive psychology to the problem of depression illustrates the value of viewing personality from the standpoint of human cognition.

From Thought to Action

From cognitive psychology, personality psychologists have fashioned an image of the human being as an information-processing system, a computer who takes in information, organizes and stores the input into meaningful categories or schemata (interpretive structures), and retrieves the organized information in order to make decisions or solve problems. But human beings do more than process information. They also act upon the information that they process. And their actions feed back to influence subsequent information processing. As Charles Carver and Michael Scheier suggest, people are as much like robots as they are like computers. Indeed, "robots are a combination of computer and something else" (Carver & Scheier, 1992, p. 496). "Rather than just process and store information, robots engage in actions directed towards goals" (p. 496). From the new field of robotics, therefore, cognitive personality psychologists have drawn metaphors and models for human functioning that enable them to explain how people move from computation to performance, from thought to action. A central assumption in this regard is that *people act according to goals*. Goal-directed action, furthermore, is exquisitely regulated by complex feedback and control mechanisms, mechanisms that function for people in ways that may be modelled in complex performance machines, such as robots.

Middle-Level Units and Purposive Behavior

One of the more startling claims in George Kelly's psychology of personal constructs is that the concept of human *motivation* is redundant (Chapter 8). Since the time of Freud, many personality psychologists have concerned themselves with the problem of motivation, the problem of identifying the underlying forces and factors that *move* behavior, that set it into *motion,* that provide the springs of human action. Freud, for example, argued that human beings are motivated by sexual and aggressive urges over which they have little control. These urges were understood to be grounded in human biology, as derivatives of drives or instincts. Personality theorists such as Carl Jung (Chapter 2), Carl Rogers (Chapter 8), and Abraham Maslow (Chapter 8) appealed to loftier motivations, like strivings for individuation and self-actualization. Kelly, by contrast, saw no need to posit particular motivational forces. Human beings act because that is what human beings do. Of course, their actions must be understood in terms of their attempts, as naive scientists, to understand, predict, and control their worlds. Kelly's focus on cognition over motivation, his reluctance to explain why people do what they do in terms of motivating factors, his unswerving focus on how people make sense of things, their interpretive structures rather than their behavior per se—all these distinguished Kelly as an early cognitive theorist in personality. Until quite recently, cognitive approaches to personality seemed relatively uninterested, like Kelly, in the problem of motivation, of why people do what they do.

But this all seems to have changed in recent years. Today, cognitive approaches to the person are often labelled as "social-cognitive" or "cognitive-motivational," suggesting that how people process social information and how they act upon that information in the service of goals, plans, and anticipated outcomes are intricately related to each other (Cantor & Zirkel, 1990; Pervin, 1989). People are as much like robots as they are like computers because people, like robots, are designed to be motivated to act according to goals. A growing body of research in recent years has examined the different kinds of goals people set for themselves and the ways in which goals motivate behavior. Some psychologists have found it useful to conceive of goal concepts in personality psychology as *middle-level units* (Buss & Cantor, 1989; Cantor & Zirkel, 1990). Midway between general dispositions (like traits and needs) and specific behaviors lie such phenomena as life tasks, strivings, plans, projects, and concerns. These middle-level units are both cognitive and motivational. They are cognitive in that they specify particular ways in which people make sense of their worlds and their lives. They capture thoughts, beliefs, values, and schemata of various sorts. They are motivational because they energize people to act along certain lines and to pursue certain desired ends. In that people act to achieve their life tasks, strivings, plans, projects, and concerns, human behavior is inherently *purposive*—guided by purpose, directed by the anticipation of attaining desired end states in the future.

As we have already seen, Cantor and Kihlstrom designate the "life task" as a central goal concept in their theory of social intelligence. In their view, the life course essentially involves the person's confronting a series of social and developmental tasks, each of which requires that the person successfully draw upon semantic, episodic, and procedural knowledge to meet the demands of the task. These tasks "are always importantly embedded in and responsive to the 'agenda' set by cultures and social groups for particular ages or life periods" (Cantor & Zirkel, 1990, p. 150). In contemporary Western society, college students typically face such life tasks as separating from parents, establishing new friendships, meeting academic demands, choosing an academic major, embarking on a career path, and establishing intimacy with a special other person. The pursuit of intimacy may become an increasingly salient life task as the college student moves through his or her early 20s. Yet each young person appears to meet the social and developmental demands of this task in a different way, expressing and experiencing a unique set of satisfactions, difficulties, and conflicts in the arena of intimate relationships (Cantor, Acker, & Cook-Flannagan, 1992).

Similar to the concept of life task is Brian Little's idea of a **personal project** (Little, 1989; Palys & Little, 1983). Little conceives of a personal project as a series of activities coordinated to achieve a specific personal goal. Projects vary in their difficulty, pleasantness, and intended duration. A project oriented toward a short-term aim might be "planting a garden" (in order to reap the harvest of tomatoes and zucchini in the fall). A long-term project might be "writing a book" or "saving enough money to buy a business." In one study, Palys and Little (1983) found that individuals who reported involvement in *enjoyable* and *moderately* difficult projects oriented toward relatively *short-term* goals tended to be happier and more satisfied with their lives. Adults with less enjoyable and highly difficult projects oriented to the long-term tended to score low on happiness and life satisfaction. In addition, relatively happy adults reported that they shared project involvement with a supportive network of friends, family, and acquaintances.

In constructing and living out our personal projects, Little finds, we need to strike a balance between "meaning" and "manageability." In some cases such long-term and abstract projects as "making myself into a better human being" may prove highly meaningful but too hard to manage effectively. On the other hand, short-term and concrete projects such as "cooking delicious dinners for my spouse" may be fairly manageable but may not provide a satisfactory level of meaning in one's life. The challenge is to organize one's purposive behavior according to personal projects that are grand enough and humble enough to be both meaningful and manageable. The organization of purposive behavior is always accomplished in an interpersonal context. Personal projects are constantly negotiated and renegotiated with important people in one's life and within the opportunities and constraints offered by one's family, community, profession, and society at large. Within a complex social context, it is essential that people find effective ways to *communicate* their personal projects to others. Other people need to know clearly what goals you have in mind for your life if they are to facilitate the accomplishment of those goals and find creative ways to integrate their goals with yours.

Robert Emmons has launched a successful research program on the meaning and function of **personal strivings** (Emmons, 1986, 1989, 1992; Emmons & King, 1988; Emmons & McAdams, 1991). Emmons defines personal strivings as "characteristic, recurring goals that a person is trying to accomplish" (1992, p. 292). In that such goals are "recurring," personal strivings tend to reflect relatively stable dimensions and demands in personality. Compared to life tasks, for example, personal strivings are somewhat less connected to the developmental challenges facing an individual in a given period of life and more indicative of recurrent goal states, or what we will call in Chapter 11, "motives."

Emmons finds that the content of personal strivings may be classified into such motivational categories as "achievement," "power," "affiliation," "intimacy," and "self-maintenance." As we will see in Chapter 11, human motives are general goal preferences that people express across a wide variety of life domains. On one level, then, personal strivings represent specific ways in which people translate their general motives into daily life (Emmons & McAdams, 1991). Thus, a woman with a strong power motive (Chapter 11) may report that the most important personal strivings in her life are "getting to the top of my company," "persuading my daughter that she should stay away from drugs," "becoming president of the local school council," and "freeing myself from my abusive husband." Each of these four strivings displays a strong concern for having an impact over others, a strong need for power. However, the strivings tell us much more, as well. They specify the particular ways in which this woman's motives are enacted and understood in the context of her own life. They provide as much information about the situation as they do about the person herself. Personal strivings provide a great deal of idiographic description—concrete details about the particular life, in context. As such, the psychologist may employ a personal-strivings analysis to obtain a more richly textured portrait of the individual than a nomothetic study of traits or motives would typically allow.

In a given individual's life, different strivings may conflict with each other. For instance, your striving to "improve my relationship with my mother" may conflict with your striving to "gain independence." Emmons (1986) administered various personal strivings measures to 40 undergraduate students who then reported their daily moods and thoughts for three weeks. Positive emotional experiences during that period were positively associated with reports of strivings that were highly valued and for which the person had experienced success in the past. Negative emotional experiences were associated with striving ambivalence and with greater levels of conflict between different strivings. In a similar study,

Emmons and King (1988) found that conflict and ambivalence in strivings were associated with higher levels of negative affect, depression, neuroticism, and psychosomatic complaints, and with a greater number of illnesses and visits to the campus health center. In examining the connections between strivings and behavior, the researchers also found that when people reported conflicting strivings they often were unable to act upon those strivings but instead spent an inordinate amount of time thinking about the conflict itself. To sum up, high levels of conflict among strivings lead to poor health, low levels of happiness, high levels of depression and anxiety, and a tendency to ponder obsessively about conflictual strivings rather than acting upon them.

Strivings also differ from each other with respect to their level of abstractness. Consider these two strivings: (1) "going to church more often" and (2) "getting closer to God." Both strivings concern a person's religion, but the first one is framed in concrete behavioral terms whereas the second is more abstract or general. People differ on how abstract vs. concrete their strivings are. Those who frame their goals in primarily broad, abstract, expansive, introspective, and self-reflective ways may be termed *high-level strivers*. Those who frame their goals in more concrete, specific, and superficial terms are *low-level strivers*. Table 9.4 provides strivings from two different people—code names "Gandhi" and "Coffee Bean." "Gandhi" is a high-level striver, and Coffee Bean is a low-level striver.

Gandhi and Coffee Bean were two subjects in a study by Emmons (1992) that examined the relation between abstractness of strivings on the one hand and physical and mental health on the other. Emmons administered strivings measures and various assessments of mood, well-being, and symptomatology to two samples of college students and a sample of young married couples. He found that high-level strivers tended to be more depressed and *psychologically* distressed than low-level strivers. However, low-level strivers reported more *physical* illness. In Emmons' words, the results illustrate a "depression vs. sickness tradeoff." Basing his interpretation on the work of Pennebaker (1989), Semmer and Frese (1985), and others, Emmons suggests that high-level strivers are more likely to confront directly the stresses and disappointments in their lives and experience negative affect as a result. In addition, the highly abstract nature of their strivings makes it difficult for them to obtain satisfying feedback from their environment concerning progress toward their goals. For example, it is much more difficult to tell at the end of the week if you are "closer to God" (abstract striving) than you were at the beginning of the week, but it is quite easy to determine whether or not you "attended church" (concrete striving).

Psychological distress, therefore, may be a function of the complexity and ambiguity of high-level goals. In sharp contrast, the low-level strivers may be more susceptible to physical illness as a result of failing to confront stress directly. In focusing on excessively concrete goals, low-level strivers may avoid the psychological distress that accompanies a more introspective and probing attitude toward the self. They may manifest a *repressive personality style* (Chapter 3), characterized by a denial of distress but a correspondingly more highly aroused sympathetic nervous system, making them more vulnerable to

Table 9.4

Examples of High-Level and Low-Level Strivings

High-Level Striving ("Ghandi")	Low-Level Striving ("Coffee Bean")
Treat others with dignity	Look well-groomed and clean cut
Increase my understanding of the Bible	Stand out when engaging in physical/
Deepen my relationship with God	recreational activities
Be totally honest	Be funny and make others laugh
Express my feelings to close friends and	Speak clearly and straightforward to
family openly and honestly	strangers
Be humble	Look physically conditioned and
Discern and follow God's will for my life	physically fit
Expose my faith to others without	Act physically aggressive around those
offending them or pushing it on them	folks I dislike
Keep positive thoughts in my mind	Keep good posture/walk straight
Make new friends	Look attentive and not bored in class
Be a fun person to be around	Avoid being stereotyped
Make others feel good about themselves	Use proper language and manners around
Express to people that I love them	adults and attractive girls
Compete against myself rather than	Make myself noticeable
others	Work hard (or at least make it look like it)
Increase my knowledge of the world	Keep quiet and not go talking about
	myself freely with others
	Be organized and neat, always have a
	clean room and a made bed

(From Emmons, 1992, p. 295).

psychosomatic illness. Keeping their goals simple and concrete enables low-level strivers to avoid a direct confrontation with difficult and more abstract problems in life, but such a strategy may exact the cost of poorer physical health.

The Regulation of Behavior

Emmons' study of abstractness in personal strivings provides one illustration of an important principle of cognitive-motivational approaches to personality. It is the principle of *hierarchical control of behavior* (Carver & Scheier, 1988; Hyland, 1988; Vallacher & Wegner, 1987). Purposive behavior is controlled or regulated by strivings, plans, tasks, and so on that exist in a nested hierarchy. Concrete goals are nested (contained within) more abstract goals, which themselves are nested in even more abstract goals. There exists for every person a hierarchy of levels of control, with various levels of standards or goals arranged from the most concrete and narrow to the most abstract and broad organizing principles. The lower levels indicate how the action is to be carried out, whereas the higher levels provide information on the purposes or implications of the action. Goals or standards can be characterized at different levels within this hierarchy, and people may be said to differ as to the level at which they characterize their goals within the hierarchy, as we see when we compare Emmons' high-level and low-level strivers.

Carver and Scheier have developed a representative hierarchical model of how cognition regulates purposive behavior (Carver & Scheier, 1981, 1988, 1992; Scheier & Carver, 1981). The model draws heavily on the concept of **feedback.** In a feedback loop, a system regulates itself around a set point, as in a thermostat. Deviations from the set point stimulate adjustment activities, which are terminated when the set point is once again achieved. In the case of a thermostat, the set point might be 65° Fahrenheit. When the temperature in the room dips below 65°, the thermostat turns on the furnace, which will shut off when the air temperature reaches or exceeds the set point. In the case of human behavior, the set point might be any goal, standard, or reference value against which behavior is compared. These comparison points for behavior, however, come in almost an infinitude of forms, and include such things as values, self-schemata, situational expectancies, and conscious intentions.

Figure 9.4 illustrates the feedback relation between comparison points and behavior. According to the model, a person is constantly monitoring his or her own behavior and the behavior of others. Sometimes people literally watch what they are doing (as in weight-lifting rooms with mirrored walls), but, more often, "monitoring your behavior is a matter of sensing in a vague, general way the qualities you've been displaying in your actions" (Carver & Scheier, 1988, p. 476). When the perception of your behavior matches well the goal or standard to which you are comparing the perception, then you do not alter your behavior. This is analogous to the thermostat's sensing that the air temperature is still above 65°—the furnace is not switched on. When, however, the person perceives a *discrepancy* between the current behavior and some goal, standard, or reference value to which the behavior is compared, he or she changes behaviors in order to move closer to the comparison point. Therefore, if in the middle of a conversation in which you desire to be friendly, you feel that you are beginning to offend the person to whom you are speaking, you will probably change your behavior in some way. You may begin to compliment the person, or you may change the topic to something lighter and friendlier in order to move the interaction toward the goal. Once the goal is achieved, you may change goals and alter your behavior accordingly. According to Carver and Scheier (1988), "behavior is inherently purposive (even if the purposes underlying some acts are pretty trivial)." As they put it, "human life is viewed as a continual process of establishing goals and intentions, and adjusting current patterns of behavior so as to match them more closely, using informational feedback as a guide to progress" (Carver & Scheier, 1988, p. 476).

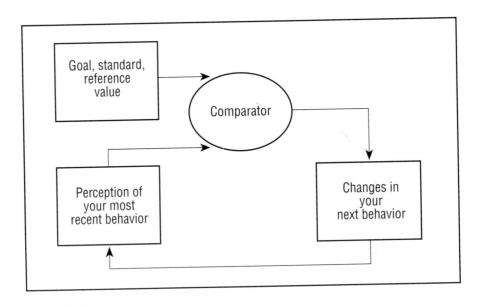

Goal, standard, reference value

Comparator

Perception of your most recent behavior

Changes in your next behavior

Figure 9.4

A Simple Self-Regulation System.

From Carver & Scheier, 1988, p. 476.

The goals and intentions that regulate human behavior are dynamic; they shift from one situation to the next and over time. Thus, the process of self-regulation is continuous and neverending. Every change in output (behavior) creates a change in the perceived present condition. This new input, then, must be checked against the reference value, which itself will change over time. There is a continuous interplay between making adjustments to action and evaluating the effects of those adjustments. Better regulation, furthermore, is accomplished by closer self-scrutiny. Therefore, any environmental condition that promotes a person's self-examination is likely to promote the smooth and effective regulation of behavior, as numerous experimental studies have shown.

In these studies, a person's self-focus is accentuated in some way, as when the person must observe his or her own behavior in a mirror (Wicklund & Duvall, 1971). The result of the self-focus is increased goal matching in behavior. In one study, Carver (1975) chose students who either opposed or favored the use of punishment in teaching. Several weeks after the students' attitudes on punishment were assessed, they participated in a laboratory task in which they administered punishments for errors committed by a person they thought (erroneously) was another subject in the study. In the self-focus condition, the students observed their own administration of punishments in a mirror. In the control

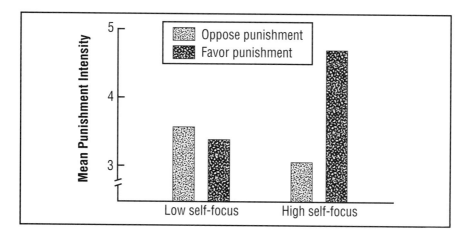

Figure 9.5

Level of Punishment Administered, as a Function of Self-Directed Attention and Attitude Toward Use of Punishment.

From Carver & Scheier, 1988, p. 480.

condition, no mirror was present. As Figure 9.5 shows, the students in the self-focus condition tended to act in close accord with their values. Those who said they opposed punishment delivered only low levels of punishment; those in favor of punishment administered high levels. In the low self-focus (control) condition, however, the students did not differ on the punishments they administered as a function of their values. In other words, when they were not explicitly monitoring their own behavior, they tended not to regulate what they were doing in accord with their stated beliefs about punishment.

The feedback loops that regulate human behavior are much more complex than the simple illustration portrayed in Figure 9.4. To deal with this complexity, Carver and Scheier propose a **feedback hierarchy** made up of subordinate and superordinate goals. According to this view, illustrated in Figure 9.6, the output of one feedback loop becomes the reference value for the feedback loop subordinate to it (Powers, 1973). Higher-order or superordinate levels in the hierarchy provide reference values for lower levels. There are many possible levels, but the three highest ones in the hierarchy are *program, principles,* and *system concept.*

At the program level, behavior is guided by scripts (Abelson, 1981) and other general guidelines for courses of action. Many of our daily intentions operate at the program level, from taking out the garbage to preparing for an examination. At the principles level, behavior is regulated by overriding qualities that might be realized through various scripts or programs. For example, a woman

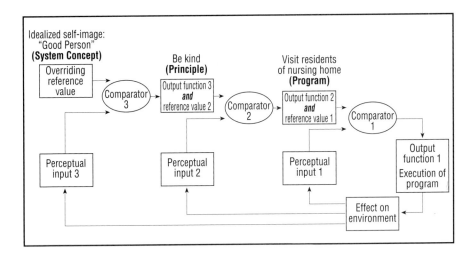

Figure 9.6

Schematic Diagram of a Three-Tiered Hierarchy of Feedback Systems.

From Carver & Scheier, 1988, p. 482.

may see herself as a generally "friendly" person. This self-ascription serves as a principle for behavior, providing the reference value of "being as friendly as I can be" for various scripts or programs she may enact. Finally, her principle of friendliness may itself be regulated and organized by the highest level in the hierarchy, the level of system concept. Here reside the highest abstractions for behavioral analysis, such as the "generalized sense of self that people try to maintain over time and place" (Carver & Scheier, 1988, p. 483). One's general sense of self, sometimes called *identity* (Chapters 12, 13), is an overarching regulator for behavior. It provides reference values for the principles level in the hierarchy, which in turn provides reference values for the program level, and so on.

A similar point of view is expressed in Vallacher and Wegner's (1987) *action identification theory*. According to Vallacher and Wegner, an action can be identified in a wide variety of ways, ranging from the most concrete to the most abstract. For example, the same behavior can be identified as "moving wooden pieces on a board," "playing a game of chess," or "improving my mind through intellectual stimulation." Lower-order identifications frame action in simple behavioral terms: writing a term paper is reduced to "making marks on a sheet of paper." Higher-order identifications frame action in broad conceptual terms: writing a term paper may be elevated to "striving for excellence in academics." Research on action identifications suggests that when both a low-level and high-level identification are available, people tend to adopt the higher one, as long as they can do so comfortably. In other words, people tend to view (and regulate) their activities *in as abstract a way as they can without difficulty.* When faced with difficulty, however, they will retreat from higher-order to lower-order identifications. Such a move may make it easier to master the challenges of a given act. Once the problem is resolved, movement toward a higher-level identification may ensue.

A fascinating application of this point of view may be found in Baumeister's (1990) theory of suicide as an "escape from self." Baumeister suggests that suicide may result from a relentless cognitive movement from higher-order to lower-order identifications in response to tremendous pain and suffering. According to this view, a person first experiences a series of painful setbacks in a number of different life domains, such as romantic involvements and work life. These failures are attributed to the self. The person may come to believe that he is at fault for the bad things that have happened, or he may believe that he is a helpless victim of forces he cannot control. In either case, what results is a painful state of self-awareness.

To escape this excruciating self-awareness, the person launches into a process that Baumeister calls *cognitive deconstruction.* Cognitive deconstruction involves a dramatic slide from relatively adaptive, higher-order thinking into a narrowly focused and concrete frame of mind that blocks out emotion and erases concerns for meaning. The person comes to adopt a narrower and narrower time perspective, as concerns for the future give way to an obsessive focus on the here-and-now. The person comes to focus on progressively more concrete events, as well. For example, eating a meal may be cognitively reduced to moving the food from plate to mouth. The person obsessively focuses on the molecular action of moving the knife and fork in order to blot out any awareness of the larger contexts for action, for those larger contexts are painful. To think of the act as "eating" might lead to thoughts about "having meals," which might remind the person of the people with whom he has shared meals in the past, who indeed may be the sources of his current pain. Better, then, to focus consciousness on the fork.

As life becomes reduced in time and space, the person abandons higher-level meanings (as in "What is my life about?") for the relatively meaningless minutiae of simple acts (as in "Will I move the food to my mouth again?"). This intense focus on only the most immediate, concrete, and meaningless things works to divest life of its characteristic emotional tone. Operating at the lowest possible level of action identification, the person has retreated from time, thought, feeling, and significance. The retreat has not enabled him, however, to master the challenges of a simpler order of life. There is still too much pain and suffering awaiting him, should he seek to reverse the tide of deconstruction. Thus, the suicide act may follow as a final retreat from the complexity of life to the simplicity of death, a tragic result of a progressively more nihilistic narrowing of one's cognitive focus, the ultimate escape from self.

Differentiation and Integration

As we have seen, a major theme in the vast literature on personality, cognition, and the regulation of purposive behavior is that people differ with respect to the overall level of complexity that characterizes their thought (Emmons, 1992; Linville, 1987; Vallacher & Wegner, 1987). Two features of cognitive complexity that psychologists often employ in their work are differentiation and integration. *Differentiation* refers to the number of differences or distinctions that exist in a given phenomenon. Something highly differentiated contains many parts. A person who sees the world in a highly differentiated way perceives many distinctions and "shades of grey." That which is relatively undifferentiated contains few parts, and the person who sees things in an undifferentiated manner sees few distinctions and differences. *Integration,* on the other hand, refers to the connections between the parts, the perception of similarities. To integrate is to bring things together. A person who sees things as highly integrated sees many connections between various parts—how discrete things relate to each other as larger wholes. Therefore, to a certain extent, integration builds on differentiation. Put simply, one cannot see the connections among different parts until one sees the different parts.

Certain theories of cognitive development propose that higher levels of functioning involve greater levels of cognitive differentiation and integration (for example, Kohlberg, 1969; Piaget, 1954). In Chapter 10, we will survey certain views of the self that are based on this same assumption. Outside of an explicitly developmental framework, however, are two additional cognitive approaches to differentiation and integration that have important implications for personality functioning. These are seen in the theory and research on (1) field independence–dependence and (2) integrative complexity.

Field Independence–Dependence

In the 1940s, Solomon Asch and Herman A. Witkin began studying how people decide whether an object is perpendicular to the ground or tilted to some degree. They asked people sitting in tilted chairs placed in custom-built tilted rooms to adjust their chairs until they felt that they were in an upright position—objectively perpendicular to the ground (Witkin, 1949). The task is tricky because the tilted room provides visual information that conflicts with the body's inner cues concerning what is upright. Some people tilt their chairs to become perpendicular to the (tilted) room; others ignore the tilt of the room and adjust their chairs according to inner cues. The people who use the room as the reference for their adjustment exhibit a **field-dependent** style for solving the problem. Their perception and judgment of perpendicularity depend on the "field," or environment. The people who bypass the field and make their perception and judgment according to inner cues show a **field-independent** style.

Over the past 40 years Witkin and his colleagues have come to understand field independence–dependence as a broad and pervasive cognitive style that underlies many important personality differences (Bertini, Pizzamiglio, & Wapner, 1986; Goodenough, 1978; Lewis, 1985; Witkin, Goodenough, & Oltmann, 1979). The dimension has two poles. At one extreme, highly field-independent people process information in an especially analytical and differentiated style. They rely on internal frames of reference that enable them to act upon information in a highly autonomous fashion. At the other extreme, highly field-dependent people employ external frames of reference available in the field. They tend to base their perceptions on the external context within which they occur. Each pole has certain benefits and liabilities, depending on specific conditions. Therefore, neither end of the continuum is "better" than the other. Most people fall somewhere in the middle of the field independence–dependence continuum.

Field independence–dependence is one of the most thoroughly researched personality dimensions in the world. It ranks with extraversion (Chapter 5) and locus of control (Chapter 8) in terms of its perennial popularity with researchers, having generated over 3000 experimental studies. One textbook author writes that field independence–dependence "constitutes perhaps the strongest body of evidence available for any trait or style in personality psychology" (Singer, 1984, p. 217). A few of the many research findings employing the construct are summarized in Table 9.5.

Field-independent people are adept at pulling information out of an embedding context. A good example of this is identifying camouflaged figures, as assessed on the **Embedded Figures Test** (Witkin, 1950). In Figure 9.7, the problem is to locate a square, like the one shown in A, that is hidden in the picture of the coffeepot shown in B. (The solution is shaded in C.) As you may discover for yourself, the several parts of the square in B are difficult to imagine as belonging to the same (square) figure. Instead, the right half of the square is immediately seen as part of the coffeepot while the left is seen as part of the background. To find the camouflaged square, it is necessary to *restructure the perceptual field*. People who are field-independent restructure the perceptual field so that they perform quite well in camouflage tasks.

In general, field independence is associated with greater levels of perceptual and cognitive restructuring. Field-independent people tend to reshape information from the environment according to internalized plans, rules, and goals to a greater extent than do people who are field dependent. They tend to view information in the nonsocial world in a highly differentiated manner. In one study, 32 field-dependent and 32 field-independent college women solved a series of anagrams (scrambled words) under various conditions (Frank & Noble, 1985). The results showed that field-independent students solved the anagrams more quickly and found the task easier than did field-dependent students. The field-independent students found it easier to provide a disorganized field with organization.

Like Kelly's model of the scientist (Chapter 8), the field-independent person approaches the world as a hypothesis-tester, systematically differentiating causes and effects and analyzing the world in terms of its separate parts. Not

Table 9.5

Selected Research Findings on Field Independence–Dependence

Correlates of Field Independence
  Greater accuracy in estimating what confused or distorted images "should" look like.
  Better problem solving in tasks requiring unconventional use of common objects and tools.
  Hypothesis-testing approach to complex problems.
  Experiences of guilt rather than shame.
  Tendency to describe other people in negative terms.
  Preference for solitary games in childhood.
  Careers in mathematics and science, such as physics, architecture, and engineering; in health professions such as medicine and dentistry; and in certain practical occupations such as carpentry, farming, and mechanics.
  Socialization patterns emphasizing independence and autonomy.
  Predominant in hunting societies.
  Unrelated to overall academic achievement.

Correlates of Field Dependence
  Tendency to rely on other people for guidance.
  Greater sensitivity to nuances of interpersonal relationships.
  Higher levels of eye contact.
  Better memory for names and faces.
  Knowing more people and being known by more people.
  Greater levels of self-disclosure with other people.
  Experiences of shame rather than guilt.
  Tendency to describe other people in relatively positive terms.
  Preference for social play in childhood.
  Careers in helping humanitarian occupations such as social worker, minister, and rehabilitation counselor; in certain teaching areas such as elementary school and social sciences; and in certain business occupations such as selling, advertising, and personnel.
  Socialization patterns emphasizing conformity and dependence on authority.
  Predominant in agricultural societies.

Sources: Goodenough (1978), Singer (1984), Witkin et al. (1979).

surprisingly, people who are field-independent are drawn to careers that require cognitive restructuring and objective analysis of information, such as careers in science, mathematics, management, and mechanics. By contrast, field-dependent people are more global and intuitive in processing information about the world. They tend to engage in less cognitive restructuring, accepting information from

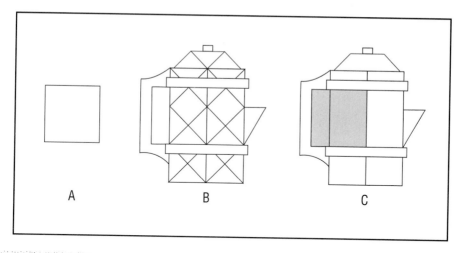

Figure 9.7

An Embedded Square. Find the square shown in A camouflaged in the coffeepot shown in B. (The solution is shaded in C.)

From Goodenough, 1978, p. 175.

the environment in its own contextual terms, rather than employing internal plans and guidelines for information processing. Interestingly, field-dependent people tend to be more interested in humanitarian and social-welfare professions, such as careers in the ministry, social work, teaching young children, the social sciences, and selling and advertising (Goodenough, 1978).

Cognitive style appears to have significant influences on interpersonal functioning. Numerous studies suggest that the field-dependent person is more sensitive to social context than the field-independent person. Field-dependent people pay closer attention to interpersonal cues and social information. They tend to spend more time looking at people than at inanimate objects and to make more sustained eye contact when talking with others. Field-dependent people prefer being physically closer to others than do field-independent persons. In one study, for example, participants were required to give prepared talks on several topics to the experimenter, and the physical distance between the speaker and the experimenter was measured during the presentations (Justice, 1969). Field-dependent speakers chose to stand closer to their listeners than did field-independent speakers. In another study of interpersonal distance, field-dependent people showed more speech disturbances when seated 5 feet away from their conversational partners than when seated only 2 feet away. In contrast, the interpersonal distance had less of an effect on field-independent speakers (Greene, 1973).

Chinese farm laborers: Field-dependence may be adaptive in agrarian societies.

Helen Block Lewis (1971, 1985) has revealed interesting emotional differences between field-dependent and field-independent people. Field dependence is associated with experiences of *shame* whereas field independence is associated with experiences of *guilt*. The experience of shame or humiliation requires a social context within which the emotion is experienced. The field-dependent person is especially sensitive to social context and is likely, therefore, to be susceptible to real or imagined mockery, derision, or contempt expressed by other people. In contrast, people usually feel guilt when they sense that they have violated some internal standard of their own. Guilt does not require an explicit social context. Field-independent people are less likely to feel humiliated in the presence of others, since they are not especially sensitive to other people's opinions. But they *are* susceptible to condemnation from within as they evaluate their own actions according to internalized standards that are independent of the particular interpersonal field within which their behavior is displayed. The result is that they are more likely to experience guilt than shame.

In general, women score toward the field-dependent end of the continuum whereas men score toward the field-independent end. This gender difference is not huge, but it is relatively consistent. From childhood to adulthood, people develop in the direction of field independence. Thus, children are generally more field dependent than adults. Nonetheless, individual differences in elementary school are predictive of adult differences. Thus, a boy who is relatively field independent compared to his male peers at age 10 is likely to remain somewhat more field independent than his peers 20 years later. Certain socialization practices have been associated with differences in cognitive style. In general, evidence supports the commonsense conclusion that development proceeds toward greater field independence when socialization encourages separation from parental control. A more tightly organized and controlling milieu, on the other hand, is likely to encourage field dependence. In general, field-independent people report that their parents were relatively permissive, whereas field-dependent persons often report an emphasis on parental authority in their families.

Some of the most interesting findings on field independence–dependence come from cross-cultural studies. Witkin and Berry (1975) provide evidence that migratory hunting-and-gathering tribes tend to be field independent, whereas societies organized around subsistence-level agriculture tend to be more field dependent. Hunting-and-gathering societies are constantly on the move from one geographical setting to the next. Field-independence would appear to be an adaptive cognitive style for this migratory and predatory lifestyle. Witkin and Berry (1975) write:

> The ecological demands placed upon persons pursuing a hunting and gathering subsistence economic life style require the ability to extract key information from the surrounding context for the location of game and the ability to integrate these bits of information into a continuously fluctuating awareness of the hunter's location in space for the eventual safe return home. (p. 16)

On the other hand, agrarian societies are much more sedentary. Because agrarian societies stay put for long periods of time, their members build up elaborate systems of social interaction. Adherence to group norms may become more valuable to group survival than autonomous individual functioning.

Integrative Complexity

Witkin maintains that individual differences in field independence–dependence are differences in *style,* and that neither style is generally better than the other. Some researchers dispute this claim, arguing that field independence is a *skill* reflecting a particular cognitive ability (McKenna, 1984). According to this view, field-dependent people are deficient in a general cognitive skill associated with organizing and differentiating information. Nonetheless, the major thrust of the research on cognitive style is that neither style is better in all situations. Cognitive restructuring may be useful in certain nonsocial, task-oriented situations, whereas the field-dependent person's sensitivity to context may promote certain forms of interpersonal functioning. The same nonevaluative position cannot be taken, however, in the area of **integrative complexity.** Here, complexity is superior to simplicity. The person who is integratively complex sees the world in more sophisticated terms, making more distinctions between various things and ideas (differentiation) and seeing more connections (integration):

> Increasing levels of complexity are marked by clearer recognition that more than one point of view or evaluation on an issue can exist and may be legitimate; the identification of larger numbers of relevant dimensions and points along these dimensions; the acceptance and eventual integration of conflicting positions; and the combinatorial use of ideas, attitudes, and approaches in the development of plans to reach some generally desired goal. (Porter & Suedfeld, 1981, p. 325)

Individual differences in integrative complexity are assessed through content analysis of written material (Schroder, Driver, & Streufert, 1967). For example, a person's account of a particular experience, a speech or diary entry, an essay, an argument, or a letter written to a friend can all be scored for integrative complexity. The researcher rates particular passages in the text with respect to the degree of differentiation and integration shown. Passages that rely on simplistic explanations and isolated single judgments receive relatively low scores. Those that bring in many different perspectives and that balance different explanations and considerations receive relatively high scores for integrative complexity. While people differ with respect to their characteristic levels of integrative complexity, the same person may also show many different levels depending on the situation. For example, when a college student writes a love letter to her boyfriend, she may show a rather low level of integrative complexity. But in composing a history essay to explain economic changes in Europe during the 1800s, her expressed integrative complexity may be higher.

Some of the most creative research on integrative complexity has been conducted by Philip Tetlock on political reasoning, and Peter Suedfeld on literary correspondence. In one especially provocative study, Tetlock (1981a) analyzed selected speeches of twentieth-century American presidents before and after their elections to office. He found that integrative complexity was generally low while the man was campaigning for the presidency but rose markedly after he was elected. Tetlock interpreted the finding to mean that presidential candidates tend to present issues in simplistic black-and-white terms in order to get elected but, once elected, adopt more complex reasoning patterns. Interestingly, when incumbent presidents begin campaigning for a second term, the integrative complexity levels of their rhetoric drop again, as they again seek to sway the voters by simplifying the issues.

Coding Supreme Court decisions (Tetlock, Bernzweig, & Gallant, 1985) and the political rhetoric of American senators (Tetlock, 1981b; Tetlock, Hannum, & Micheletti, 1984) and of members of the British House of Commons (Tetlock, 1984), Tetlock has made a compelling case for a connection between political ideology and integrative complexity. Politicians with relatively liberal voting records (for the most part, liberal Democrats in the United States Senate and moderate socialists in the British House of Commons) tend to exhibit higher levels of integrative complexity in their speeches than do those with relatively conservative voting records. Also low in integrative complexity are politicians with extremely liberal (such as extreme socialists in the Britain) or extremely conservative views. The data for the British House of Commons are displayed in Figure 9.8.

Tetlock explains his controversial findings in terms of *value plurality.* Adopting Rokeach's 2-factor view of political values (see Feature 9.C), Tetlock

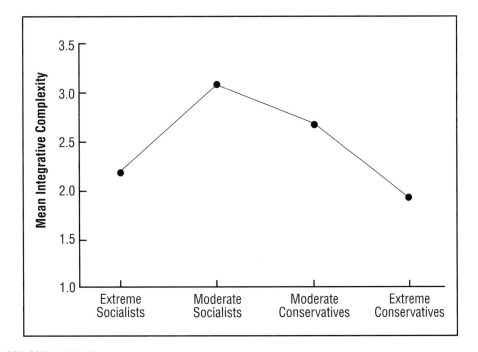

Figure 9.8

Mean Integrative Complexity of Members of the British House of Commons.

From Tetlock, 1984, p. 370.

Feature 9.C

Human Values

The cognitive revolution has rekindled psychologists' interest in human values. Many cognitive approaches to personality routinely nominate "values" as important dimensions of information processing. A value may be seen as a special kind of schema or knowledge structure. Values are distinguished by their prescriptive dimension (Feather, 1975; Rokeach, 1973), which is to say that a value is a belief about what is good or bad, right or wrong, worthy or unworthy, desirable or undesirable, and so forth. Like other kinds of schemata, values help us make sense of ourselves and the world in which we live.

One of the first psychologists to subject values to systematic study was Gordon Allport. Allport and his colleagues designed the Study of Values, a questionnaire assessing individual differences on six value types (Allport & Vernon, 1931). The six types were the "theoretical," "economic," "social," "religious," "political," and "artistic." The theoretical person values truth and knowledge, the artistic person values beauty, and the political person values power and influence. Another early measure was developed by Morris (1956), who specified 13 different "ways of living" or philosophies of life. Here are four of them: to "preserve the best that man has attained," to "experience festivity and solitude in alternation," to "control the self stoically," and to "meditate on the inner life."

Today the most popular conception of human values is Rokeach's (1973) theory. Rokeach delineates 36 basic human values. Half of them are *instrumental* values, referring to means and modes of human conduct. These include "ambitious," "clean," "courageous," "honest," "logical," and "obedient." The other half are *terminal* values, referring to desired end states. These include "a comfortable life," "a world at peace," "equality," "freedom," "national security," and "wisdom." On the Rokeach Value Survey, the person rank-orders the 18 instrumental values from most important to least important and then rank-orders the terminal values in a similar manner.

The Rokeach Value Survey has been used in a large number of studies. It has proven especially sensitive in distinguishing between value hierarchies held by different social groups. For instance, American college students in the 1970s ranked "freedom" as their most cherished terminal value, followed in order by "happiness," "wisdom," and "self-respect." "A world of beauty" attained their lowest rank.

argues that *freedom* and *equality* are the two fundamental dimensions upon which political rhetoric can be evaluated. Conservatives tend to value freedom over equality. Extreme liberals (extreme socialists, communists) value equality over freedom. Moderate liberals, however, value both. Therefore, a moderate liberal is likely to fashion a more complex political ideology in order to

With respect to instrumental values, American students ranked "honest" highest and "obedient" lowest. By contrast, Israeli students ranked "a world at peace" as their top terminal value, followed by "national security," "happiness," and "freedom." Their lowest terminal value was "salvation." They shared with the Americans the designation of "honest" as their top instrumental value, but they placed at thebottom of their instrumental list the value of "forgiving" (Feather, 1980). Values have also been related to personality traits. For instance, Feather (1984) found that masculinity is positively associated with the values of "ambitious," "independent," and "an exciting life" and negatively associated with "loving," "inner harmony," and "a world of beauty." Femininity is positively associated with "loving" and "true friendship" and negatively associated with "a comfortable life" and "pleasure."

Other value schemes deal with broader value systems or personal ideologies. For instance, Forsyth (1980, 1985) distinguishes among four different ethical ideologies: (1) *situationism,* which says that each situation must be evaluated in its own ethical terms; (2) *absolutism,* which argues for the reliance on inviolate and universal ethical principles; (3) *subjectivism,* which emphasizes one's own personal values as central determinants in moral decision making; and (4) *exceptionalism,* which admits that exceptions should be made to moral absolutes. Hogan (1973) highlights the sociologist Max Weber's distinction between an *ethic of conscience* and an *ethic of responsibility,* both assessed via a questionnaire called the Survey of Ethical Attitudes. According to Hogan, the ethic of conscience is oriented to a "higher law," as we find in the German idealism of Immanuel Kant, which advocates universal prescriptions articulated through one's own private moral vision—for example, internalized absolutes such as the New Testament's "golden rule." The ethic of responsibility, on the other hand, can be represented by British utilitarianism as we find it in the philosophies of Jeremy Bentham and John Stuart Mill, and it emphasizes one's commitment to implicit social contracts bound to particular societies. Hogan argues that mature value systems should incorporate both the ethic of conscience and the ethic of responsibility.

accommodate his or her allegiance to both freedom and equality—two values that often conflict. While a traditionally conservative politician in Great Britain or the United States is likely to oppose increases in taxes for welfare spending because of the belief that citizens should be free to spend their hard-earned money on what they want, the liberal may find the issue more difficult in that he or she places a premium on equality, as well as freedom. According to the value of equality, tax dollars should support those who are less well-off. Yet, freedom dictates low taxes and laissez faire capitalism. As a result, the liberal is likely to bring in more considerations and find more shades of grey in political rhetoric about such issues as taxation and social programs. In Tetlock's view, the liberal is more complex and conflicted. From the standpoint of the conservative, on the other hand, the liberal may seem "wishy-washy" or "afraid to take a stand."

A very different approach to integrative complexity is apparent in the research of Suedfeld on the relation between social events and literary correspondence (Porter & Suedfeld, 1981; Suedfeld, 1985). Porter and Suedfeld (1981) analyzed the personal correspondence of five eminent British novelists of the nineteenth and twentieth centuries: Charles Dickens, George Eliot, George Meredith, Arnold Bennett, and Virginia Woolf. Each novelist's life was divided into 5-year periods and the investigators randomly sampled between 10 and 20 paragraphs from the novelist's personal correspondence for each period. Each paragraph was scored on a 7-point scale, ranging from very low to very high integrative complexity. Table 9.6 provides an example of a verbatim paragraph scoring relatively low and another scoring relatively high in integrative complexity.

Porter and Suedfeld correlated integrative complexity scores with various historical events and personal changes in the novelists' lives. They found that integrative complexity scores *decreased* during times of war but *increased* during periods of civil unrest. War appeared to exert a simplifying effect on literary correspondence. During periods in which their countries were involved in international combat, the novelists tended to present issues in relatively undifferentiated terms, failing to take into consideration multiple and complex points of view. Porter and Suedfeld speculate that war has the general effect of restricting the "information flow" in the environment. By contrast, civil unrest (such as major political changes) appeared to evoke a more flexible and integrative outlook, perhaps by stimulating new ideas and possibilities in the environment's information flow.

With respect to personal changes, Porter and Suedfeld found that integrative complexity decreased during times of illness, was unrelated to other stressful events, increased with age, and decreased shortly before death. The last finding is especially intriguing in that research on life-span developmental psychology has suggested that just before people die they experience a marked decrease in cognitive functioning, called a *terminal drop.* In another study, Suedfeld and Piedrahita (1982) examined the correspondence of 18 eminent individuals during the last 10 years of their lives. Supporting the hypothesis of terminal drop, they found that integrative complexity scores fell markedly in the last 5 years before death for those who died of a protracted illness and during the year immediately prior to death for those who died suddenly.

Table 9.6

Verbatim Passages From the Correspondence of Eminent Novelists Scored for Integrative Complexity

Low on integrative complexity (score = 2)

> Tonight I finished *First Principles*. I suppose that I can never have again the same thrills of admiration as this book has given me. If any book could be called the greatest book in the world, I suppose this can. I have never read anything a tenth part so comprehensive. And it makes its effects by sheer honest argumentative force. There are no ornaments of brilliance, wit, ingenuity, or even eloquence. Yet the closing pages of Part I, and the closing pages of Part II, are equally overwhelming in their effect. Faults there, of course, are in it but it is surely the greatest achievement of any human mind. This I do think. And Spencer has not yet come into his own, in England. As a *philosopher,* in the real sense—not as a discoverer, or a man of science—but as a philosopher, he is supreme in the history of intelligence. I say this, not because I have read all the other great ones, but because I cannot imagine the possibility of anyone having produced anything else as great as *First Principles*. [Note that in this passage the author elaborates on an absolute rule or declaration. There is little by way of alternative perspectives discussed.]

High on integrative complexity (score = 6)

> The professor says you do not consort with Germans at all. I am grieved at this. I am sure you do not altogether underrate the fine qualities of German youth; but perhaps your immediate sympathies, and a somewhat exaggerated sensitiveness, stand in your way. It will be a pity, if this is so, and for more reasons than one. If you do not cultivate the people you are living amongst in your youth, you will fail in having pleasant places to look back at—landmarks of your young days. And besides, the Germans are your hosts, and you owe them at least a guest's thankfulness. I esteem them deeply for their fine moral qualities. Just now they are abusing us roundly, but that will pass away. I know they have the capacity for friendship, and that as a rule English friendships are not so lasting. Look around you, and try to be accessible to your German associates. Consider whether you are not yielding to luxurious pre-dispositions in your marked preference for English ones. You will see enough of the latter when you return here. [This passage shows simultaneous operation of alternatives and consideration of the functional relations between them.]

From Porter and Suedfeld (1981, pp. 325–326).

Summary for Chapter 9

1. Cognitive approaches to personality emphasize the ways in which human beings process information about themselves and about their worlds.

2. Social intelligence is stored in memory as organized knowledge, forming the structural base of personality, according to one prominent cognitive viewpoint. This organized knowledge consists of concepts (such as scripts and self-conceptions), episodes (autobiographical memory and person memory), and rules (competencies and strategies such as attribution).

3 People use their social intelligence to master the life tasks that they face during particular developmental periods in their lives.

4. A schema is an organized knowledge structure. Self-schemata are generalizations about the self derived from repeated categorizations and evaluations of one's own behavior by self and others. People process information that is especially relevant to their self-schemata in highly efficient ways.

5. People with strong gender schemata (highly masculine men and highly feminine women) tend to process information along the lines of gender to a greater extent than do men and women who are relatively aschematic with respect to gender categories.

6. One cognitive view of depression suggests that depressives distort reality by imposing overly negativistic schemata on social information. Another cognitive approach argues that depressives suffer from a faulty explanatory or attributional style.

7. Cognitive approaches to the person suggest that purposive human behavior is guided by such middle-level motivational constructs as personal projects and strivings. Conflicts among strivings tend to be associated with psychological distress.

8. Behavior may be regulated by informational feedback systems, organized hierarchically, whereby values, self-schemata, and expectations serve as reference points against which current behavior is compared. Deviations from the reference point stimulate change in behavior.

9. People who are field-independent process information in an autonomous, differentiated, and analytical fashion. Those who are field-dependent pay closer attention to context and tend to process information in a more intuitive and synthetic way.

10. Field independence is associated with stronger skills in cognitive restructuring. Field dependence is associated with greater social sensitivity.

11. Integrative complexity refers to the extent to which a person's reasoning is differentiated and integrated. Coding various public documents such as speeches and correspondence for integrative complexity, psychologists have investigated relations between complexity and (1) political ideology, (2) historical events, (3) personal stress and illness, and (4) impending death.

Chapter 10

The Self as Knower and Known

Introduction

The I
Characteristics of the I
Four Views on the Development of the I
Allport's Proprium
Sullivan's Self-System
Loevinger's Ego
Kegan's Evolving Self
The Infant I
Feature 10.A: Born With a Self: Daniel Stern's Infant
The Child I
The Adolescent I
The Adult I
Assessing the I: The WUSCTED
Conclusion

The Me
Self and Other
The Me on Stage
A Confederacy of Selves
Possible Selves
Discrepancies Among Selves
Self-With-Other
Feature 10.B: Feeling Good About the Me: Self-Esteem
Development of the Me

Summary

The most famous chapter ever written on "the self" begins:

> The Me and the I—Whatever I may be thinking of, I am always at the same time more or less aware of *myself*, of my *personal existence*. At the same time it is *I* who am aware; so that the total self of me, being as it were duplex, partly known and partly knower, partly object and partly subject, must have two aspects discriminated in it, of which for shortness we may call one the *Me* and the other the *I*. I call these "discriminated aspects" and not separate things, because the identity of *I* with *me*, even in the very act of their discrimination, is perhaps the most ineradicable dictum of commonsense, and must not be undermined by our terminology here at the outset, whatever we may come to think of its validity at our inquiry's end. (James, 1892/1963, p. 166)

The quote is from the first comprehensive textbook ever written in psychology, published before the turn of the twentieth century. Its author is William James (1842–1910). James begins with a distinction that, on the surface at least, seems simple enough. The **self as I** and the **self as Me.** The self, according to James, is "duplex." Within its apparent unity are two discriminable aspects. First, there is the self as *subject:* the I who knows, feels, and acts. Second, there is the self as *object:* the Me who is known, felt, and observed in action. The I and the Me are fundamentally the same in that they both refer to the self. And yet they are fundamentally different, too. The difference is both subtle and profound, and it stems from a basic phenomenological characteristic of human experience: the person may be both the *subject and the object of consciousness at the same time. I* observe, know, and experience *myself.* The self is both knower and known.

It is easier to talk about the Me—the self as known. James suggests that the Me consists of all that a person considers to be his or her own. Not surprisingly, your body, your feelings, your values and beliefs are all aspects of your Me. In addition, however, your clothing, your boyfriend or girlfriend, your parents, the posters on your dormitory walls, your favorite sports team, and a host of other "possessions" may also be, more or less, subsumed within the Me, to the extent that they are experienced as belonging to you. Indeed, some of these external aspects of the Me may be more important components of the self than certain internal ones. For example, a very important part of my sense of self—my Me—are my books, papers, and notes collected in my office. Beyond their value to me in my everyday work, these things symbolize and affirm my sense of self as a professor of psychology who has spent much of the last 15 years studying personality. Now compare these external things to the little toe on my left foot. The toe is clearly (literally) part of me. I suppose I cherish my toe as much as most people. But, what if I ran over my toe with a lawnmower? The loss of my toe

William James

would affect my life in important ways (my basketball playing would probably be compromised; I'd be embarrassed about going to the beach), but I
honestly think that such a loss would be less of a jolt to my sense of self
than the permanent loss of the contents of my office—losing the toe would
have less of an effect on my understanding of who I am. Of course, I might
feel different about this if I were, say, a professional athlete or a model, a
person for whom the perfection of one's body is a more salient self-concern.
Therefore, every person's total Me is unique. The intricate arrangement of
its constituents differentiates the self from all other selves.

   According to James, the Me can be roughly divided into three regions.
The *material Me* is made up of one's body, clothing, certain possessions,
and family members. The *social Me* consists of the recognition a person
gets from other people. In fact, each person has many social Me's. In an

influential passage, James writes, "a man has as many social selves as there are individuals who recognize him and carry an image of him in their minds" (p. 169). Social Me's can be arranged in a hierarchy. Paramount is an ultimate and ideal social Me, reflected in a person's apprehension of God or "fate" or some ultimate force, being, or power. Most human beings desire to fashion an ideal social self to be recognized by an ultimate "spectator" or ideal social "tribunal." Writes James, "all progress in the social Self is the substitution of higher tribunals for lower; this ideal tribunal is the highest; and most men, either continually or occasionally, carry a reference to it in their breast" (p. 179). The third aspect of the self-as-object is the *spiritual Me,* described by James as "the entire collection of my states of consciousness, my psychic faculties and dispositions taken concretely" (p. 170). The spiritual Me consists of our own understandings of ourselves as persons who think, feel, act, and experience life. Here are located most of the psychological attributions we make about the self—our understandings of our own traits, motives, values, beliefs, desires, fears, and so on.

As you can see by now, James' view of the Me is very broad. This contrasts starkly with his view of the I. The I is the knower at a given moment of knowing. James saw no need to posit a continuous and stable knower—a broad and pervasive I that remains the same over time. Rather, the knower changes from one moment to the next. The I is "that which at any given moment is conscious, whereas the Me is only one of the things which it is conscious *of*" (p. 182). Put simply, *the I is a moment in consciousness.* Moments follow moments in a stream of consciousness, each successive moment incorporating information from the moments preceding. Usually we experience the stream as a continuous flow, suggesting a continuity, even a permanence, of the I. Theologians have deemed this underlying, ineffable self the "soul." Some philosophers have called it the "transcendental ego." But scientific psychologists, James maintains, need not make such an assumption. To sum up:

> The consciousness of Self involves a stream of thought, each part of which as "I" can remember those which went before, know the things they knew, and care paramountly for certain ones among them as *"Me,"* and *appropriate to these* the rest. This Me is an empirical aggregate of things objectively known. The *I* which knows them cannot itself be an aggregate; neither for psychological purposes need it be an unchanging metaphysical entity like the Soul, or a principle like the transcendental Ego, viewed as "out of time." It is a *thought,* at each moment different from that of the last moment, but *appropriative* of the latter, together with all that the latter called its own. All the experiential facts find their place in this description, unencumbered with any hypothesis save that of the existence of passing thoughts or states of mind. (p. 197)

The I

In the wake of psychology's cognitive revolution (Chapters 8 and 9), the "self" has emerged as one of the hottest topics in personality psychology today (Lapsley & Power, 1988; Scheibe, 1985). Whereas American psychology had little use for the concept of a self during the heyday of behaviorism (Chapter 6), the past 15 years have witnessed an explosion of interest in the topic, and the proliferation of a great many "self" theories (e.g., Epstein, 1973; Greenwald, 1980a; Markus and Cross, 1990). A number of the theoretical approaches already discussed in this textbook make reference to the self. Freud (Chapter 2) viewed the self as the ego, which in German was termed *das Ich* ("the I"). Object-relations theorists such as Mahler (Chapter 2) argue that the self develops out of key interpersonal relationships, a process described as separation-individuation. Jung's (Chapter 2) view of the self is especially broad, encompassing all of the properties of the psyche in a unifying constellation. Similarly, Maslow and Rogers (Chapter 8) speak of the self as the general unity of personality. Heinz Kohut (Chapter 2) has developed a psychoanalytic self-psychology. Certain cognitive theorists view the self as a schema (Chapter 9). Even social-learning theorists have recently left room for the self, as we saw in Bandura's concept of self-efficacy (Chapter 6).

In keeping with the general theme of "interpretive structures," this chapter considers theories about and research on the self that emphasize *conscious cognitive dimensions* of the I and the Me, with special emphasis on those theories that describe how the self *develops* over time. Like William James, the various approaches to be discussed agree that the self is both knower and known. The I interprets and structures experience; the Me is interpreted and structured. The self is dual, yet it is also whole. James' distinction between the I and the Me is a useful organizational frame, for some theories seem to focus more on the I and others on the Me. But we must also remember that the I and the Me are two aspects of the same thing—two different perspectives on the self. As James would have it, any theory of the I is also a theory of the Me, and vice versa.

Characteristics of the I

In considering the I, or the self-as-subject, developmental psychologist Augusto Blasi (1988) begins by disputing William James. Blasi argues that the I is more than a momentary state of consciousness. Instead, a durable and pervasive sense of the I can be experienced and even known, albeit indirectly and not through thinking or introspection. According to Blasi, the I is tacitly and immediately grasped in and through *intentional action*. Writes Blasi, "in every intentional action that we perform, in fact in every experience that we undergo, we experience ourselves, *in the process of acting and experiencing,* as related to our actions and experiences" (1988, p. 228). In the heat of intentional action, we experience ourselves as distinct, whole agents and possessors of our own actions. Within this experience, we may isolate four dimensions of the I: agency, identity with oneself, unity, and otherness.

Agency refers to "the degree to which an action is unreflectively grasped as one's own and oneself is grasped as its source" (Blasi, 1988, p. 229). When I pick up my 2-year-old niece and give her a kiss, I never doubt the fact that I am the person who is kissing her. My sense that I am the sole agent of this action—that the kiss is mine and originates with me—is immediately and unreflectively grasped. In an intentional act, a person experiences an *identity with oneself.* In kissing my niece, I immediately understand that the person kissing her is the same person who is aware of himself kissing her. Such an identity is the foundation for self-reflection. The third dimension of the I is the experience of *unity* among the various components of an intentional action. I know that the entire sequence of picking up and kissing my niece is accomplished by the same person—that I am performing the complete sequence. It never occurs to me to suppose that the I who picked her up is different from the I who kissed her. Finally, the I is experienced in complete *otherness.* I am I; others are others. I do not confuse myself with the niece I am kissing, nor with other uncles who have kissed their nieces in identical situations.

In Blasi's view, the I is a *stance* with respect to which the person regards an object. He writes, "the subject's stance—his believing, desiring, controlling, or hoping—is not one component among others, but permeates every aspect of the action and gives unity to it" (p. 232). Similarly, a number of self theorists view the I as a *process* and the Me as a *product* of the process. The I is the *process of knowing, thinking, synthesizing, adapting, unifying, willing,* and so on. The I is understood as a grand function responsible for human intentionality and wholeness. For example, Hart (1988) writes that the self-as-subject functions to provide the person with a sense of (1) self-continuity, (2) distinctness from others, and (3) volition. The I functions to ensure that the person feels that he or she is a continuous entity across time and space, that he or she is essentially distinct from others, and that he or she is the agent of action that is willed or intended. If I feel that I am literally not the same person from one moment to the next, if I feel that I am somebody else or somebody else is me, or if I feel that my actions are not my own, then I am suffering from disorientations and disturbances of the subjective self. Such disturbances are commonly reported in schizophrenic episodes and in certain drug-induced states of consciousness.

Four Views on the Development of the I

Allport's Proprium   Gordon Allport's term for the self, in both its I and Me aspects, is the **proprium.** According to Allport (1955), "the proprium includes all aspects of personality that make for inward unity" (p. 40). Eight different aspects of the proprium can be identified, each arising at a particular period of development. The most basic aspect is the sense of a *bodily self,* which develops in the first year of life as infants experience the regularities of interaction with the world. With the development of language in the second year and the maturing understanding of time and causality, a toddler's sense of self expands beyond the body to encompass *self-identity*. In self-identity, children know that they are the same Me as time passes, affirmed verbally as boys and girls learn their own names. The third aspect of the proprium—*self-esteem*—develops in early childhood when boys and girls come to feel good about mastering tasks in the world.

Around the age of 4 or 5, children experience *self-extension* as they come to see their own likes and dislikes as integral parts of the self. Next develops *self-image,* through which children distinguish their own good behavior (good Me) from bad behavior (naughty Me). Because adolescents are able to engage in abstract thinking and systematic decision making, they may view the self as a *rational coper* who is able to make important judgments in life. In adolescence, the sense of self expands to include *propriate strivings* through which people sense ownership and responsibility for feelings, needs, and life-governing goals. As we will see in Chapter 12, the realization of propriate strivings seems to correspond to Erikson's idea of establishing an identity in adolescence and young adulthood.

The culmination of the development of the proprium is the unifying sense of the *self-as-knower,* consolidated in adulthood. Allport (1961) argued that the self-as-knower is the totality of the person as a process that is continually changing and becoming. While the first seven aspects of the proprium focus on the Me, this last aspect alludes to the self-as-subject. But Allport, like James, was not comfortable suggesting that a transcendent I actually exists within the person as a separate "homunculus," or "little person within the person." Thus, the I is an ineffable process, not a thing, that reaches a mature manifestation in adulthood when the proprium is fully developed. Before adulthood, we can assume that it is still functioning as a unifying and clarifying trend or tendency in personality.

Sullivan's Self-System   We witness a more limited and less affirmative conception of the self in the interpersonal theory of personality developed by the American psychiatrist Harry Stack Sullivan (1892–1949). Sullivan is like Freud, Sartre, and Binswanger in his emphasis on life's tragedies rather than its comedies, and stands in marked contrast to the relatively optimistic theorists like Rogers, Maslow, Allport, and many of the self theorists discussed in this chapter. Indeed, Sullivan's (1953) conception of the **self-system** bears resemblance to certain aspects of Freud's ego. Like the ego's defense mechanisms (Chapter 3), the self-system's main function is to minimize the experience of *anxiety*. Sullivan's self-system is a set of protective measures developed in infancy and early childhood to ward off anxiety. Unlike Freud, however, Sullivan believed that anxiety stems primarily from external social forces rather than from unconscious conflicts within.

In Sullivan's view, all of life is negotiated within an interpersonal field. According to Sullivan, it makes no sense to speak of the development of the individual on his or her own; *person*ality is always *inter*personal. In the first few months of life, the interpersonal field is limited, consisting for the most part of the infant and the primary caregiver, usually the mother. While there is much that is good and wonderful in this earliest of human relationships, Sullivan emphasized instead the infant's tensions. An especially diffuse form of tension is anxiety, which Sullivan believed is empathically transmitted from the mother to the baby. When she feels anxious, the baby feels anxious. In that all adults feel some form of anxiety, Sullivan maintained, there is no way to shield the baby from this ubiquitous interpersonal condition. Rather, the baby learns to shield itself by developing the psychological armor of a self-system. Throughout childhood, the favored strategies of the self-system vary widely, from turning back the taunts of schoolchildren with a smile to escaping into a fantasy when parents fight.

As the person deals with anxiety by employing strategies of the self-system (Sullivan's version of the I), various conceptions of the Me and of others crystallize within the personality. These are called **personifications.** A personification is an image that an individual has of him- or herself or of another person. Personifications of the "good me" and the "bad me" are major constituents of the self-as-object. These develop and become more complex over time. With respect to the I, on the other hand, the development of the self-system follows a negative course, according to Sullivan's (1953) theory: He suggests that repeated experiences with anxiety lead to greater growth of the self-system, in that the primary function of the self-system is to reduce anxiety. But as the self-system grows, it becomes less connected to the rest of the personality.

In preadolescence, the person experiences strong desires for *intimacy* with a close friend or **chum,** argues Sullivan. In adolescence and adulthood, the person must integrate intimacy and *sexuality* (or what Sullivan called "lust") while continuing to ward off experiences of anxiety. Yet, the self-system is not prepared to help the person attain intimacy and sexual fulfillment. Indeed, the cautious and conservative nature of a person's self-system works to thwart intimacy and sexual fulfillment by discouraging the person from reaching out to others and taking chances in life. Thus, while the self-system still plays a major role in the adult's adjustment by minimizing the experience of anxiety, it can interfere with constructive living in other ways. A person whose life is dominated by the self-system is likely to feel relatively secure in the world. But he or she is also likely to be lonely and feel sexually unfulfilled.

Loevinger's Ego   Like the ego psychologists encountered in Chapter 2, Jane Loevinger views the **ego** (Freud's "the I") in a much more positive light than did Freud (and than did Sullivan in his view of the self-system). For Loevinger, the ego is the *master synthesizing I* that adapts to the world by making sense of it. She writes, "the organization or the synthetic function is not just another thing the ego does, it is what the ego is" (Loevinger, 1976, p. 5). And, "the striving to master, to integrate, to make sense of experience is not one ego function among many but the essence of the ego" (Loevinger, 1969, p. 85). In Loevinger's view, the I is a *synthesizing process* that can be understood in terms of stages of ego development.

Loevinger's model of ego development is theoretically grounded in what she terms the *cognitive developmental paradigm* in personality psychology (Loevinger, 1987). Epitomized in the monumental work of Jean Piaget on cogni-

Jane Loevinger

tive development, this broad approach to psychology views the individual as an active knower who structures experience in ever more adequate and complex ways. Development is viewed as progression through hierarchical stages. Earlier stages must be mastered before subsequent stages can be approached. Each stage builds on its predecessor and ultimately encompasses all that comes before it. Movement from one stage to the next is a complex product of both internal maturation and external forces, which are in constant reciprocal interaction. Higher stages of development are "better" than lower ones, providing interpretive structures for the world that are more differentiated, integrated, and adequate. These and other basic tenets of cognitive developmentalism are spelled out in great detail in the huge corpus of Piaget's work (for example, Piaget, 1952, 1965, 1970; Inhelder & Piaget, 1958); in the influential writings of Kohlberg (1969, 1981) on moral development; Perry (1970) on intellectual and ethical development; Selman (1980) on interpersonal understanding; and in Baldwin (1897), Werner (1957), and many college textbooks in developmental psychology.

Loevinger's stages of ego development are summarized in Table 10.1. Each stage is designated by a name (for example, the "impulsive" stage) and an "I" label (for example, "I-2"). Each stage provides an overall framework of meaning that the person employs to make sense of the world. The framework of meaning can be understood in many specific areas. Table 10.1 specifies three areas: impulse con-

 Table 10.1

Loevinger's Stages of Ego Development

Stage		Typical Manifestations		
Label	Name	Impulse Control	Interpersonal Mode	Conscious Preoccupations
I-2	Impulsive	Impulsive	Egocentric, dependent	Bodily feelings
Delta	Self-protective	Opportunistic	Manipulative, wary	"Trouble," control
I-3	Conformist	Respect for rules	Cooperative, loyal	Appearances, behavior
I-3/4	Conscientious-Conformist	Exceptions allowable	Helpful, self-aware	Feelings, problems, adjustment
I-4	Conscientious	Self-evaluated standards, self-critical	Intense, responsible	Motives, traits, achievements
I-4/5	Individualistic	Tolerant	Mutual	Individuality, development, roles
I-5	Autonomous	Coping with conflict	Interdependent	Self-fulfillment, psychological causation
I-6	Integrated		Cherishing individuality	Identity

Note: The first stage (I-1) is hypothesized to be nonverbal and therefore not readily measurable.
From Loevinger (1987, p. 226).

trol, interpersonal mode, and conscious preoccupations. In general, as one moves from lower to higher stages, the I becomes less the slave of immediate impulses and more a flexible agent that operates according to internalized standards of conduct. Interpersonally, the person moves from egocentrism through conformity to relative autonomy and mutual interdependence. With increased maturity, the issues that preoccupy the person's consciousness become less concerned with body and appearance, and more centered on the internal life of feelings and fantasies as well as internalized goals and plans. With development, the person becomes more cognitively complex, adopting more sophisticated frames of reference for understanding the world. Simplistic black-and-white thinking gives way to more subtle analyses and, ultimately, to a tolerance for ambiguity and paradox.

Loevinger's model of the self is a developmental typology. While people are expected to progress through the stages in the order in which they appear, people differ with respect to their terminal level of development. In other words, people reach a particular stage and then quit moving upward, and different people quit at different stages. Individual differences in a given group are understood in terms of stages. An adult who is at the "conformist" stage of ego development (I-3) is a different "type" of person than an adult who is at the higher "autonomous" stage (I-5). Given that ego development seems to taper off after early adulthood (Lee & Snarey, 1988), it is not likely that the conformist adult will ever "catch up" with peers scoring at the autonomous level. This is a very different understanding of "stage" than we see in, say, Freud, who assumes that normal human development involves the movement through *all* stages of psychosexual development.

Kegan's Evolving Self   Robert Kegan (1982) provides an elegant model of the development of self that bears some resemblance to Loevinger's scheme. Like Piaget, Kohlberg, Loevinger, Kelly, the existentialists (Chapter 8), and many of the cognitive psychologists (Chapter 9), Kegan views the person as actively constructing his or her own reality through constant interaction with the physical and social environment. With the evolution of the self across the human life-span, the I constructs reality and makes meaning in the world in ever more complex and adequate ways. Kegan also incorporates a number of themes and viewpoints from psychoanalytically oriented and humanistic theories of personality development, including object-relations theories, Erikson's psychosocial view (Chapter 12), and Maslow's hierarchy of needs (Chapter 8).

The key idea in Kegan's theory is *subject-object balance*. Each stage of the self's development involves the negotiation of a new balance between that which "I am" (subject) and that which "I have" (object). The essential movement in development is from subject to object—from being something (subject) to having that same thing that one previously was (object). The newborn self is structured such that the baby "is" her reflexes. Therefore, the subject of this first self-balance is the baby's reflexes; there is no object. The newborn has yet to emerge from the embeddedness of her reflexes; she is not yet able to distance self from reflexes in order to consider them as objects. This initial position of the self is what Kegan calls the *incorporative balance* (Stage 0).

The movement to the next position (Stage 1) involves negotiating an *impulsive* balance. This begins to happen toward the end of the first year of life, argues Kegan, with the natural appearance of separation and stranger anxiety. Through the second and third year, the child gradually comes to understand that she is not her reflexes but that she, instead, *has* reflexes. What was subject becomes object. The "lost" subject is replaced by a new one. In the case of the impulsive balance, the child *becomes* (subject) her current impulses, desires, and perceptions:

> Rather than being my reflexes, I now have them, and "I" am something other. "I" am that which coordinates or mediates the reflexes, what we mean by "impulses" and "perceptions." This is the new subjectivity. For the very first time, this creates a world separate from me. (Kegan, 1982, p. 79)

Each stage in the evolution of the self involves the loss of an old subject that in turn becomes a new object and the replacement of the lost subject with a new subject. (Table 10.2). In the *imperial* balance of later childhood (Stage 2), the person's impulses and perceptions become the object of attention, and the new subject is one's longer-term interests, needs, and wishes. These become the object of one's attention in the *interpersonal* balance of early adolescence (Stage 3),

 **Table 10.2**

Kegan's Stages of the Self

Stage	Subject	Object
0 Incorporative	Reflexes (sensing, moving)	None
1 Impulsive	Impulses, perceptions	Reflexes (sensing, moving)
2 Imperial	Needs, interests, wishes	Impulses, perceptions
3 Interpersonal	The interpersonal mutuality	Needs, interests, wishes
4 Institutional	Authorship, identity, psychic administration, ideology	The interpersonal mutuality
5 Interindividual	Interindividuality, interpenetrability of self systems	Authorship, identity, psychic administration, ideology

Adapted from Kegan (1982, p. 86).

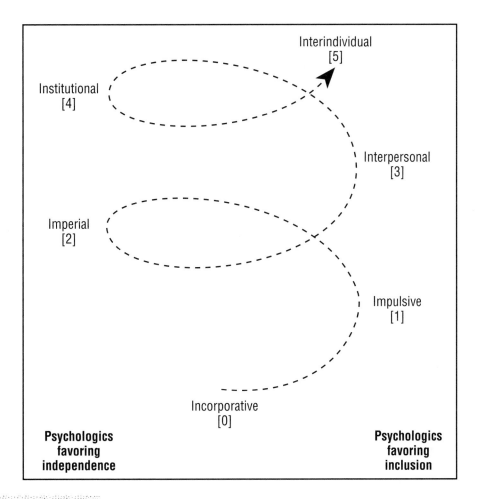

Figure 10.1

The Relation Between Kegan's Stages and the Poles of Independence and Inclusion.

From Kegan, 1982, p. 109.

wherein the new subject becomes "interpersonal mutuality." At this point, teenagers define themselves by their interpersonal associations. Their identification with "the group" relegates their personal interests, needs, and wishes to the status of objects—aspects of the Me that the I now "has." The I becomes more sociocentric.

The *institutional* balance of late adolescence and young adulthood (Stage 4) moves the I away from the group and towards a complex view of identity and ideology. One's friends and social relationships no longer dominate the I—they are seen, instead, as parts of the Me. The I becomes synonymous with the person's ideological values about right and wrong, good and bad, and other ultimate concerns and with the person's envisioned destiny. In the words of Erik Erikson (Chapter 12), the I becomes embedded in *identity;* from Allport's standpoint, propriate strivings become the determinants of I. Finally, in later adulthood, argues Kegan, the I transcends personal identity and ideology—which now, in turn, become objects—to negotiate a complex *interindividual* balance (Stage 5). At this highest stage in the evolution of the self, the person sees him- or herself as a unique and integral part of an encompassing system of interrelated human beings developing over time. Identity becomes something that I now have, and something that I can share with others.

There is a back-and-forth rhythm to Kegan's evolutionary stages. The I evolves dialectically between the poles of *independence* and *inclusion.* The imperial and institutional balances of the self favor independence. During these periods, the self tends to be defined as separate from others. The impulsive, interpersonal, and interindividual balances, on the other hand, are tipped in the direction of inclusion. During these periods, the self is viewed as intricately connected to others. Notice that the highest stage emphasizes connection, inclusion, and communion between selves. The relation between the poles of independence and inclusion on the one hand and the stages of the I on the other is illustrated in Figure 10.1.

The Infant I

Most theories of self assume that an infant is born without a sense of self-as-subject—without a sense of the I. (But for a counterview, see Feature 10.A.) Allport implies that such a sense develops out of basic bodily experiences, whereas Sullivan underscores early experiences of anxiety as stimulating the development of a self-system. In Freud's view, the ego emerges out of the id in order to meet the demands of the outside world. In addition, the infant comes to understand its separateness from mother with the realization that mother does not meet its every need. According to Mahler, the self emerges out of interpersonal relationships via a gradual process of separation-individuation. In general, various theories affirm the view of developmental psychologist Susan Harter (1983), who writes:

> The infant's first task is the development of a sense of self as subject. Thus, the infant must come to appreciate that he or she exists as an active causal agent, a source and controller of actions, separate from other persons and objects in the world. Once this "existential" self . . . has been differentiated from others, the infant must learn to recognize those particular features, characteristics, and categories that define the self as object. A representation of self that the infant can identify must be developed. (p. 279)

The precise sequence whereby the infant first develops a sense of the I as an active causal agent and then begins to formulate a vision of the Me has been outlined by developmental researchers such as Michael Lewis and Jeanne Brooks-Gunn in their studies of visual **self-recognition** (Amsterdam, 1972; Bertenthal & Fischer, 1978; Lewis, 1990; Lewis & Brooks-Gunn, 1979). In these studies, infants are observed as they behave in front of mirrors or as they watch themselves on videotape or in photographs. Lewis and Brooks-Gunn (1979) studied infants between the ages of 5 and 24 months, employing a wide variety of measures such as attention, emotional displays, play, use of the mirror to locate objects, pointing at the self, and labelling the self. The overall results of their studies and the implications of these results for the developing I and Me are summarized in Table 10.3.

Between 5 and 8 months, infants show a wide variety of self-directed behaviors in front of mirrors. For example, they smile at their images and watch their bodies intently. However, they do not recognize distinctive features of their own bodies, and they do not appear to differentiate themselves from others. There is no evidence that they understand that what they see in the mirror is a reflection of themselves. Between 9 and 12 months, infants begin to understand the reflecting quality of mirrors. They will use mirrors to reach for actual objects attached to their bodies. Between 12 and 15 months, infants consolidate an initial sense of self as an independent causal agent. They will now use the mirror to locate other people and objects in space. When a person or object is spotted in the mirror, the infants will reach toward the actual person or object rather than toward the mirror. On videotape, infants are able to distinguish between their own movements and the movements of others.

Now that the basic sense of I is established, an infant is ready to build an initial conception of the Me. This can be seen in mirror studies using infants between the ages of 15 and 18 months. In one version of this research, the mother applies rouge to the nose of her baby, leaving a large red spot that the baby can readily see when placed in front of the mirror. Infants younger than about 15 months of age will see the spots but not recognize them as alterations of their own faces. They may point at the spots in the mirror, but they are not likely to point directly at their own noses. After 15–18 months of age, most infants will touch their own noses when they see the rouge, showing that they have internalized an image of what their own faces should look like, that they recognize the image in the mirror as their own, and that they understand that the mark on the nose observed in the mirror signals that their own faces have been altered. As Table 10.3 shows, the Me continues to develop with the advent of language and the infant's increasingly sophisticated self-recognition behavior between the ages of 18 and 24 months.

Research and theory agree that by 2 years of age, the relatively normal and healthy infant has consolidated a basic sense of the I as an active agent clearly differentiated from the environment and others (Lewis & Brooks-Gunn, 1979; Mahler et al., 1975; Sander, 1975; Stern, 1985). The beginnings of what James called the material Me are also clearly evidenced. The four cardinal aspects of the self-as-subject—agency, identity with self, unity, and otherness (Blasi, 1988)— seem already to be manifesting themselves in the toddler's intentional acts.

Table 10.3

Emergence of Self as Subject and Object, Based on Studies of Visual Recognition

Behaviors	Age in Months	Interpretation
Self as Subject		
Interest in mirror image; regards, approaches, touches, smiles, vocalizes. Does not differentially respond to self *vs.* other in mirror, videotape, or pictorial representation.	5–8	No evidence that self is perceived as a causal agent, independent of others. No featural differentiation between self and other.
Understands nature of reflective surface: contingency play, imitation, rhythmic movements, bouncing, waving; can locate objects in space, attached to body.	9–12	Active agent in space emerges, awareness of cause-effect relationship between own body movements and moving visual image.
Uses mirror to locate people/objects in space. Reaches toward person, not image, and reaches toward object not attached to body. Distinguishes between self movement and movement of others on videotape.	12–15	Self-other differentiation with regard to agency. Appreciates self as an active, independent, agent separate from others, who can also cause own movements in space.
Self as Object		
In mirror and videotape, demonstrates mark-directed behavior, sees image and touches rouge on nose. Points to self. Distinguishes between self and other in pictorial representation and videotape.	15–18	Featural recognition of self; internal schema for own face that can be compared to external visual image.
Verbal labelling: infant can state name, attach appropriate personal pronoun to own image in mirror. Can distinguish self from same-gender infant in pictures and can label self.	18–24	Appreciation that one has unique featural attributes that can be verbally labelled as the self.

From Harter (1983, p. 283).

Self-recognition.

Feature 10.A

Born With a Self
Daniel Stern's Infant

Are infants born with a sense of self? Probably not, say many developmental theories. Or at best, the newborn's sense of self is extremely vague, primitive, and shadowy. In an especially influential proposal, Margaret Mahler (Chapter 2) contends that a sense of the self-as-subject emerges only gradually in the first year of life, out of an early period of *symbiosis,* or oneness with the environment. During the symbiotic period, the infant experiences the world in a very global and undifferentiated manner, with little sense of boundary between self and other. Around the middle of the first year of life, the infant begins to differentiate its own body from the rest of the environment, begins to understand where the body ends and the rest of the world begins. From this initial sense of physical boundary, the infant will eventually move through well-demarcated stages of separation and individuation, a journey in self-awareness that requires between two and three years to complete.

Psychiatrist Daniel Stern, however, disagrees. Stern (1985) argues that infants begin to experience a sense of an emergent self from birth. Newborns are biologically predisposed, he argues, to organize their experience in terms of a separate self's relating with a separate environment. They never experience a total self/other symbiosis. There is no confusion between self and other in the beginning or at any point during infancy. Babies are more precocious than we think. The I is there from the outset, ready to experience the social world in terms of self-other relations.

Basing his argument on his own observational studies and a review of the wide literature on infant social development, Stern contends that four different senses of self develop in the first two years of life, and each sense corresponds to a form of relating to the world. Between birth and age 2 months, the sense of an *emergent self* takes hold. Newborn infants show innate preferences for certain kinds of social stimuli, such as human voices and the smell of their mother's breast milk. They are able to process complex sensory experiences in surprisingly sophisticated and even abstract ways. For example, they seem to comprehend sights, sounds, and touches in terms of the abstract properties of intensity, shape, tempo, and rhythm. They are especially adept at getting a feel for the contours of social experience. The "feel" of experience is represented by such elusive qualities as "surging, fading away, fleeting, explosive, crescendo, decrescendo, bursting, drawn out, and so on" (Stern, 1985, p. 54). From the beginning, therefore, infants are processing experience in surprisingly sophisticated ways, as separate knowers who are predisposed to make sense of the social world, a world with which they are actively engaged.

Between the ages of 2 and 6 months, infants consolidate a sense of *core self,* as "a separate, cohesive, bounded, physical unit, with a sense of their own agency, affectivity, and continuity in time" (p. 10). During this period, infants understand themselves to be the authors of their own actions and the observers of the actions of others. They have a sense of being a non-fragmented, physical whole, with boundaries and a locus of integrated action, both while moving (or behaving) and when still. They experience themselves as "having" their own feelings and inner states. And they begin to develop a sense of "enduring, of a continuity with one's own past so that one 'goes on being' and can even change while remaining the same" (p. 71). As they interact more vigorously with the salient people in their lives, infants begin to represent those interactions in their minds in terms of generalized expectancies for self-other relating. Stern calls these "Representations of Interactions that have been Generalized" or *RIGS*. A RIG might be "the feeling of bursting excitement followed by soothing calm that I experience when my mother picks me up, smiles, rubs her face against my belly, and then gently sets me back in my crib." Of course, the infant does not have the words for this experience. But the RIG is established nonetheless, nonverbally. The sense of a core self, then, becomes further articulated and

elaborated as the infant constructs, modifies, and organizes within the mind the different RIGS that come out of social interaction.

The *subjective self* forms between 7 and 15 months. During this period, infants begin to share their subjective feeling states with others, especially primary caregivers. And they seem to expect others to do the same thing. This "state-sharing" occurs without words, for the most part. For example, the baby may become very excited when he reaches for a toy, and express this excitement with an exuberant "aaaah!" Then he will look at mother to see how she will react. Mother may respond by scrunching up her shoulders and performing a shimmy with her upper body. The shimmy lasts about as long as the baby's "aaaah!" and is equally exciting, joyful, and intense. The mother's dance mirrors the baby's "aaaah!" The form or contour is the same for both expressions, even though one is revealed through movement (the mother's shimmy) and the other through sound (the baby's "aaaah!"). When mothers and babies respond to each other like this, they are sharing what is inside them at the moment and attempting to match up or attune their emotional states. With subtle artistry, they are adjusting their reactions to each other and affirming each other's experience. In a preverbal way, they are "saying" to each other, "I know what

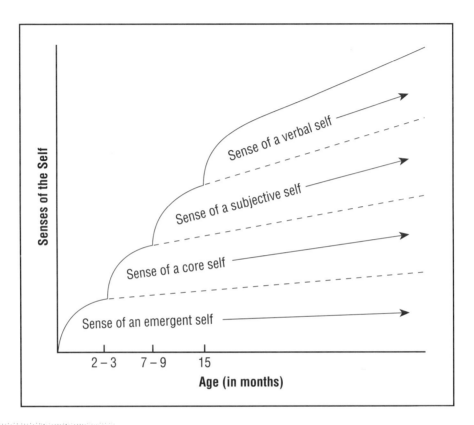

Figure 10.A.1

The Development of Four Senses of Self.

From Stern, 1985, p. 32.

The Child I

A major theme in many theories about the childhood self is the progressive movement from egocentric *impulsivity* to sociocentric *conventionality*. The synthesizing framework of meaning whereby the younger child makes sense of the world is generally viewed to be simple, concrete, one-dimensional, and rather "selfish." By the time the child has reached the age of 9 or 10 years, however, the I has become a more sophisticated and socialized structure for interpreting the world.

you are going through. I'm experiencing the same thing!" Stern calls this process *affective attunement*. Through affective attunement, the infant comes to understand better his own and other people's inner feeling states.

Finally, after about 16 months of age, the *verbal self* begins to take form. The advent of language provides the powerful mechanism for representing self and other through words. The possible ways of "being with" another increase enormously. Language permits us to share certain aspects of our experience in a more precise and elaborated manner. "It permits two people to create mutual experiences of meaning that had been unknown before and could never have existed until fashioned by words," writes Stern (p. 162). But language is also a double-edged sword, for it makes parts of our experience less shareable with ourselves and with others. Language "drives a wedge between two simultaneous forms of interpersonal experience: as it is lived and as it is verbally represented. Experiences in the domain of emergent, core, and intersubjective relatedness, which continue irrespective of language, can be embraced only very partially in the domain of verbal relatedness" (pp. 162–163). In other words, our verbal selves cannot capture the essence of our emergent, core, and subjective selves. Rather, over the course of childhood and probably beyond, the four senses of self develop in parallel, as shown in Figure 10.A.1. Born, then, with an emergent "I," the person eventually comes to experience the world by simultaneously employing different lenses—the different interpretive structures provided by emergent, core, subjective, and verbal selfhood—that together make up a complexly evolving and multilayered sense of self.

Both Loevinger (1976) and Kegan (1982) argue that the self of early childhood is locked in an *impulsive* (I–2) stage. According to Kegan, the subject of the impulsive balance is the person's own impulses and momentary desires: I am what I feel like being and doing at this particular moment of time. The young child is unable to distance him- or herself from these momentary wants, unable to view them as objects that "I have." Similarly, Loevinger argues that the child acts on impulse as a way of expressing the self. In general, the orientation of the impulsive stage is egocentric. The world is seen as a concrete setting for the satisfaction of personal wants and needs. The child is demanding and dependent in interpersonal relationships. Morality is primitive—what Kohlberg (1969) viewed as "preconventional morality," wherein the child understands good behavior to be that simply and only which is rewarded and bad to be that which is punished.

The impulsive stage as a general frame of reference is structurally quite simple. The child's classification of people into general categories of good *versus* bad is a global value judgment rather than an articulated moral judgment per se. Good and bad may be confounded with "nice to me" and "mean to me" or with "clean" and "dirty." Though emotional experiences may be intense during this time, the child's verbal descriptions of these experiences are relatively crude and global. The impulsive individual's orientation is primarily toward the present rather than toward the past or future. Loevinger states that the child who remains too long at this stage may be seen by others as "uncontrollable" or "incorrigible" (1976, p. 16).

Gradually the impulsive stage gives way to what Loevinger calls the *self-protective (delta)* stage of ego development, parallel to Kegan's concept of the imperial balance. According to Kegan, the imperial child is embedded in his or her long-term needs and wishes, as impulses become objects of attention rather than the sole defining features of the self. In Loevinger's view, self-protective individuals have "an appreciation of the world's rules, however wide their world may be, and know that it is to their advantage to play by the rules most of the time" (1987, p. 227). The self is a short-term hedonist at this stage, striving for the fulfillment of needs. The good life is the easy, happy life. Friendships may be viewed as nice things, to be collected, much like money. An older child or adult who stagnates at this stage may become opportunistic and deceptive in relations with others. As Loevinger (1976) puts it, "for such a person, life is a zero-sum game; what one person gains, someone else has to lose" (p. 17).

In late childhood and early adolescence, many people move from an egocentric frame of reference to an identification of one's own welfare with that of a group. This marks the developmental leap into what Loevinger calls the *conformist* (I–3) stage. Similarly, Kegan suggests that the older child is able to relegate his or her own needs and interests to the status of objects, opening the door to the emergence of "interpersonal mutuality" as the new subject of self. Morality becomes what Kohlberg (1969) termed "conventional," defined strictly by the rules and norms of social groups or even society as a whole. People, as well, are essentially defined according to their group allegiances. The conformist values cooperation, niceness, and loyalty to the group.

From the standpoint of Sullivan's theory, the conformist child or early adolescent is pressed by the emerging need for interpersonal intimacy to move beyond the safe maneuvers of the self-system and connect with others in collaborative and intimate ways. Interpersonal harmony, closeness, sharing, and identification with the other become the self's most cherished goals. The person seeks to find a special friend, or chum, who is as much like the self as possible. The welfare of the chum becomes a prime consideration, as important as one's own welfare. Through intimacy experienced with the chum, the self is able to affirm its fundamental *sameness* with another human being.

The Adolescent I

If the self of late childhood and early adolescence develops in the direction of Kegan's pole of inclusion and celebrates its sameness with other selves, the self's movement through adolescence and into young adulthood is generally believed to be in the opposite direction. Many theories of self and identity suggest that the teenaged years are marked by a search for individuality and uniqueness (Blos, 1979; Erikson, 1968). From Kegan's point of view, the adolescent and young adult progress toward the institutional self, seeking to consolidate an identity and an accompanying ideology that specify how they are independent and autonomous persons in a complex society. In Loevinger's model, conformity gives way to higher stages that emphasize how the person is no longer bound to social convention. From many different perspectives, adolescence in Western societies is often viewed as an extended *rite of passage* through which the person transforms him- or herself into an individuated adult (Conger & Petersen, 1984; Lapsley & Rice, 1988). In seeking individuality, the adolescent strives to integrate the various aspects of Me. Damon and Hart (1982) write:

> Virtually all researchers have found that, with development, adolescent self-understanding shows an increasing use of psychological and social relational concepts for describing the "Me," more prominent belief in the "I's" agency and volitional power, and a tendency toward integration of the disparate aspects of the self into an internally consistent construct system. (p. 855)

As we will see in Chapter 12 "the integration of the disparate aspects of the self" is Erikson's concept of identity. Such integration also resembles Allport's propriate strivings. In formulating an identity, the adolescent and young adult must fashion satisfying answers to the questions "Who am I?" and "How do I fit into the adult world?" The search for identity is the search for unity and purpose in life. To experience unity and purpose, a person must construct a new image of self—a new Me—that incorporates the self into the world of work and love while providing opportunities for expressing unique talents, dispositions, and inclinations. The I of adolescence and early adulthood, therefore, is an ever-discerning identity-maker. In terms of the "narrative" models of personality to be viewed in Chapter 13, the I of late adolescence and early adulthood is essentially the *life-story-making process,* working to fashion a personal narrative that integrates past, present, and envisioned future into a coherent and self-defining whole.

According to Loevinger's theory, adolescence may usher in the transitional *conscientious/conformist* (I-3/4) stage, as the young person realizes that it is impossible to live up to all of the standards of his or her self-defining group. The break with the group and conventional thinking begins slowly with an increasing self-awareness and an appreciation for a situation's multiple possibilities. The

A rite of passage of a Jewish adolescent girl: the Bas Mitzvah.

person becomes increasingly aware of his or her inner life. In the subsequent *conscientious* (I–4) stage of ego development, the adolescent or adult has moved considerably away from conventional standards and has substituted internalized personal standards. The major elements of adult conscience are now present: long-term, self-evaluated goals and ideals, differentiated self-criticism, and a sense of responsibility. Human behavior is understood in terms of internal determinants such as traits and motives. The person experiences a rich and differentiated inner life.

The Adult I

In realizing its full potential, the adult I can become a prodigiously complex and sophisticated framework for making sense of the world. Loevinger's highest stages of ego development, Kegan's interindividual balance of subject and object, Allport's pronouncements about the fullest expression of the proprium, and a host of other theories about the stages and phases of self celebrate the synthesizing power of the adult I. At the same time, many of these theories suggest that many adults fall well short of the I's highest levels. Research employing Loevinger's model of ego development suggests that most American adults score around the conscientious/conformist transition stage. Very few reach the highest echelons of her ego hierarchy. Writings on the adult self from Jung to Maslow to

Sartre consistently reveal that many people are unable, due to a host of internal and external circumstances, to realize the full potential of selfhood. Somewhere along the line, the knower stagnates, and the process of synthesizing experience—the self-as-subject—settles into a routine that may be adequate for daily functioning but that is less than inspiring for further growth.

Let us, however, follow the ideal and unencumbered scenario as set forth in Loevinger's scheme. At the *individualistic* (I-4/5) stage of ego development, the I develops a greater tolerance for the individuality of others and a greater awareness of the conflict between heightened individuality and increased emotional dependence. Though the realization that conflict is an inherent part of the human condition has not yet emerged, the person at the individualistic stage manifests an increased ability to tolerate paradox and contradiction—a sign of greater cognitive complexity. Distinctions are made between inner reality and outward appearances; between psychological and psysiological responses; between process and outcome. Psychological causality and psychological development, "which are notions that do not occur spontaneously below the Conscientious Stage, are natural modes of thought" to people at the individualistic level (Loevinger, 1976, p.23).

The *autonomous* (I–5) stage of ego development emerges with the capacity to cope adequately with the conflicts of the individualistic level. The individual at this level reveals tolerance for ambiguity and high cognitive complexity. He or she has acquired a respect for the autonomy of others while realizing that emotional interdependence is inevitable. Self-fulfillment partly replaces personal achievement as a central preoccupation in consciousness. The person at this stage expresses feelings vividly and convincingly, including sensual experiences, poignant sorrows, and existential humor intrinsic to the paradoxes of life. He or she formulates broad and abstract social ideals and makes decisions accordingly (Kohlberg's "post-conventional" morality). This developmental position is rare among adolescents and adults.

Rarer still is the fully *integrated* (I–6) individual. This is the most difficult stage to achieve. In general, most of what is true for the autonomous stage is also true at this level with the added elements of "cherishing individuality" and the full "consolidation of identity" (Loevinger, 1976, p. 26). At the two highest stages of ego development, the person transcends the polarities of earlier stages, seeing reality as complex and multifaceted. Opposites, from the vantage points of earlier stages, may be reconciled at the highest levels of ego development. Some of Maslow's "self-actualized" individuals (Chapter 8) may be examples of people who have attained the integrated stage of ego development.

Most Western formulations of the self's maturation in adulthood may be critiqued for their overemphasis on themes of independence, autonomy, and self-sufficiency (Broughton & Zahaykevich, 1988; Josselson, 1988). In Kegan's terms, we tend to glorify the "psychologics of independence" at the expense of the "psychologics of inclusion." Yet themes of inclusion, connection, and interdependence can be seen in many recent formulations of self-development, as well as in Erikson's (Chapter 12) conceptions of intimacy, generativity, and integrity in adulthood. Kegan's own theory is a good example, in that the highest stage of interindividuality involves the self's integration into an encompassing social system. Harter (1983) suggests that the highest level of the adult self may involve "the coordination of one's own identities over a lifetime, with those of others and with cultural values, so as to form a meaningful whole" (p. 317).

In a somewhat similar vein, certain Eastern conceptions as well as humanistic theories like those of Maslow (Chapter 8) suggest that ultimate selfhood entails a *transcendence* of the individual I and a *unity* with the cosmos. Such an "egoless" state is characterized by a total loss of self-consciousness and self-observation. Certain forms of Buddhism urge the adult to destroy the "illusion" of a separate I or ego. Enlightenment awaits the renunciation of self and the realization that one is subsumed by a larger whole. The same idea is expressed in other religious traditions. For example, the Christian concept of *grace* flies in the face of Western notions of the I as an active and intentional agent. According to this theological view, Christian salvation cannot be willed. Instead, the person must surrender the self to the power of Christ's gift of love and redemption.

Assessing the I: The WUSCTED

Loevinger's model of ego development has been especially influential in personality psychology because the ego stages can be measured via a standardized sentence-completion test, the **Washington University Sentence Completion Test for Ego Development (WUSCTED)** (Loevinger & Wessler, 1970). The WUSCTED is composed of a series of sentence stems, such as "The thing I like about myself is . . . ." and "At times she worried about . . . ." For each stem, the person writes an ending to the sentence. Each response is classified into one of Loevinger's stages, ranging from impulsive (I–2) to integrated (I–6), according to carefully designed scoring manuals (Loevinger, Wessler, & Redmore, 1970; Redmore, Loevinger, & Tamashiro, 1978). The scores are then tabulated and a final ego-stage score is derived according to a numerical formula. The WUSCTED is an especially useful instrument for examining individual differences in ego development among adolescents or adults. Because the test relies solely on verbal expression, all subjects must be able to read and write.

Table 10.4 presents sample responses scored for ego development to the especially self-relevant sentence stem of "I am. . . ." Loevinger's measure of ego development tends to be moderately correlated with intelligence test scores, with correlations ranging from +.10 to +.50 (Hauser, 1976; Loevinger, 1979). But Loevinger maintains that ego development is not synonymous with intellectual ability. The WUSCTED appears to have adequate test-retest reliability and internal consistency (Redmore & Waldman, 1975). Scorers trained with Loevinger's extensive scoring manuals show very high reliability in their scoring of sentence stems.

A growing body of research attests to the construct validity (Chapter 5) of Loevinger's model of ego development and its measurement via the WUSCTED (Hauser, 1976; Lee & Snarey, 1988; Loevinger, 1979, 1983, 1984, 1987). Cross-sectional studies of people from different age groups show that, in general, adults score slightly higher than adolescents and that older adolescents score higher

 **Table 10.4**

Sample Responses of Women to the Sentence Stem "I am. . . ."

Stage	Sample Responses
(I-2) Impulsive	a good girl. always good and respectful. a very pretty child when I want to be; I am *(age deleted)* and have been told to be good, so I try.
(Delta) Self-protective	easily hurt, ugly, nosy and not very tactful. crazy and in love. completely frustrated with selfish people.
(I-3) Conformist	a student. lucky to have such a wonderful husband. happy, and in a good mood, so please forgive my foolishness.
(I-3/4) Conscientious/Conformist	content most of the time. worried about my love affair. hoping for a successful future.
(I-4) Conscientious	lucky, because I love life. no better than anybody else. sorry for causing mother to worry about me.
(I-4/5) Individualistic	a rather complex person—as we all are, I think. a woman, a wife, a student, an individual person. hopeful that the state of man will become universally better.
(I-5) Autonomous	an introvert, shy, with a desire to be friendly and outgoing. too much in love with everything, and, I imagine, too unrealistic! woman living and creating life.
(I-6) Integrated	aware of human frailty and weakness, yet I believe that man can, through his own efforts, improve his own lot.

Excerpted from Loevinger, Wessler & Redmore (1970, pp. 275–286).

than younger adolescents, supporting the developmental assumptions of Loevinger's measure (Avery & Ryan, in press; Loevinger, 1984). In junior high and high school, girls tend to score slightly higher than boys, but boys may catch up in college (Loevinger, Cohn, Bonneville, Redmore, Streich, & Sargent, 1985). Overall, the most common (modal) stage score for American youth between the ages of 16 and 26 is I-3/4, the conscientious/conformist transition stage (Holt, 1980).

Ego development is positively associated with moral development as assessed according to Kohlberg's stage model (Lee & Snarey, 1988). With respect to personality traits, McCrae and Costa (1980) found no relationship between ego level and objective measures of extraversion and neuroticism. However, openness to experience (Chapter 5) was strongly associated with ego development. People at higher (post-conformist) stages of ego development tend to score relatively high on openness to experience, reflecting an openness toward and tolerance for alternative points of view and strong aesthetic and intellectual interests. Rootes, Moras, and Gordon (1980) investigated sociometrically evaluated maturity in 60 college women. After completing the WUSCTED, each woman evaluated all the others with respect to their potential for mature functioning in four adult social roles: career, marriage, parenthood, and community involvement. Ego development was positively related to peer ratings of maturity in careers and community involvement. However, it was unrelated to maturity in the two more interpersonally oriented social roles—marriage and parenthood.

Ego development is negatively associated with indices of deviance on the MMPI among adolescents (Gold, 1980) and measures of delinquency among inner-city girls (Frank & Quinlain, 1976). As one might expect, social conformity tends to peak at the middle conformist and conscientious/conformist levels of ego development and to decrease thereafter (Hoppe, 1972). Rosznafszky (1981) looked at ego development and individual differences in personality traits theoretically associated with particular ego stages. Employing the Q-sort personality ratings (Chapter 7) of 91 hospitalized male veterans made by nurses, therapists, and the patients, Rosznafszky found strong connections between stages and ratings. Impulsive (1–2) veterans manifested significantly higher levels of confused thinking, poor socialization, and limited self-awareness. Conformist (I–3) and conscientious/conformist (I–3/4) veterans placed great value on rules, accepted social conventions, material possessions, and physical appearance, and they appeared highly stable. Veterans at higher levels (I–4 and I–4/5) revealed greater insight into their own personality traits and motivations behind behavior, and expressed concern over interpersonal communication.

Conclusion

The I may be understood as a subjective stance, process, or framework that is responsible for synthesizing human experience. It is the self-as-knower, the subjective sense of self as an intentional agent in the world who is able to act upon and make sense of reality. For the most part, we take our "I-ness" for granted. We rarely question the nature of our subjective stance in the world. For most of us most of the time, therefore, the I is not a psychological problem. Instead, we seem to follow along blithely after Descartes, the French philosopher who asserted, "I think; therefore, I am." The fact that each of us comprehends the world from his or her own cognitive point of view, the fact that we experience ourselves as thinkers and knowers in the world and that we almost always take for granted that our thoughts are indeed *our own* thoughts gives us a deep confidence that we exist as selves—that the I *is*.

But even though the I is, the I does not remain the same I over the course of the life-span. Rather the I appears to develop through a series of well-documented stages, as we see in the writings of Loevinger and Kegan. The subjective stance from which the 4 year-old makes sense of the world is a very different I than what we see among adolescents and adults. Early and developmentally immature manifestations of the I are variously described as egocentric, preconventional, and impulsive. As the child grows up, the I takes on the perspectives of the social world; the I becomes conventional or conformist. This is an important and positive step in the development of the self, for it marks the person's emergence as a socialized being, a working member of the social context, able to take on the values, norms, and standards of the context, able to defer immediate gratification for long-term, socially sanctioned rewards, able to see reality from the collective point of view.

But conformity is not the end, suggest Loevinger and Kegan. The most mature manifestations of the I move beyond social conventions and appeal to higher, post-conventional truths. If the person is to reach the highest stages of ego development, the I must come to synthesize experience in increasingly complex ways, adopting multiple perspectives, cultivating a rich inner life, and fashioning a personal code of conduct—a working conscience—that transcends the conventional do's and don't's offered by parents, peers, religion, government, and even society at large (Loevinger, 1992). Ironically, as the I moves away from society's norms to adopt higher perspectives that are more complex and personalized, becoming more independent of social norms, it becomes more cognizant of the fact that no person is indeed fully independent and autonomous. Instead, I's are linked in bonds of interdependence. By maturing beyond the dictates of society, the I seems to move closer to people, both in the particular and in the abstract. At the highest level of ego development, people sometimes report a perceived kinship with their fellow human beings. And they may experience ever-more meaningful and fully reciprocal relationships with the most important particular people—spouse, lover, children, parents, friends—in their own lives. As the I comes to cherish its own individuality, therefore, it becomes better able to cherish the individuality of others.

The Me

Self and Other

For William James, the self-as-object was essentially an individual's concept of self, a self-concept containing certain social aspects (Scheibe, 1985). The social selves embedded in the total Me consisted of the individual's understandings of his or her reputation in the minds of others. The social world had less direct bearing on the development of the material and the spiritual components of the Me. The social nature of the Me, however, was expanded greatly in the writings of three social scientists strongly influenced by James: James Mark Baldwin (1861–1934), Charles Horton Cooley (1864–1929), and George Herbert Mead (1863–1931). Baldwin, Cooley, and Mead developed a sociological tradition in the study of the self (Hogan, 1976), focusing exclusively on how the Me is formulated out of social relationships.

In Baldwin's (1897) view, the Me develops as a function of the interaction of the child and the social world. The process involves mutual *imitation* of self and other. Person A's self grows by imitating Person B. As a result, Person A's understanding of B also grows, paralleling the development of the self. For Cooley (1902), the other is analogous to a social mirror. The self is formed as the person comes to imagine how other people observe and understand him or her. Cooley coined the term **looking glass self** to designate the way in which the Me is reflected in the other. He emphasized his point with a verse:

> Each to each a looking glass
> Reflects the other that doth pass.

Mead (1934) elaborated on the themes introduced by Baldwin and Cooley, emphasizing how the development of the Me involves the ability to *take the role of the other*. He writes, "the individual experiences himself as such, not directly, but only indirectly, from the particular standpoints of other individual members of the same social group, or from the generalized standpoint of the social group as a whole to which he belongs" (1934, p. 140). Young children invent imaginary companions, particularly while playing with dolls. During this play, the child talks to him- or herself with different voices for different characters. Eventually, children play at different *roles*, such as the roles of mother, policeman, teacher, and so on. This sort of play represents the child's first experience in adopting alternative perspectives from which to view the self, seeing the self from the viewpoint of other roles. Later, in organized games, the child must adopt several different roles simultaneously in order to play by the rules.

Experience in games and other complex social interactions leads to the formulation of the concept of a **generalized other.** This is a personal conception of the general "audience" or "observer" of one's behavior. To adopt the perspective of the generalized other is *to imagine how others in general see the Me*. Through such imaginative activity, the person builds and further refines a sense of self. The

Table 10.5

Selman's Five Stages in the Development of Perspective-Taking

Stage	Age Range[a]	Child's Understanding
Stage 0 Egocentric Viewpoint	3–6 years	Child has a sense of differentiation of self and other but fails to distinguish between the social perspective (thoughts, feelings) of other and self. Child can label other's overt feelings but does not see the cause and effect relation of reasons to social actions.
Stage 1 Social-Informational Role-Taking	6–8 years	Child is aware that other has a social perspective based on other's own reasoning, which may or may not be similar to child's. However, child tends to focus on one perspective rather than coordinating viewpoints.
Stage 2 Self-reflective Role-Taking	8–10 years	Child is conscious that each individual is aware of the other's perspective and that this awareness influences self and other's view of each other. Putting self in other's place is a way of judging his intentions, purposes, and actions. Child can form a coordinated chain of perspectives, but cannot yet abstract from this process to the level of simultaneous mutuality.
Stage 3 Mutual Role-Taking	10–12 years	Child realizes that both self and other can view each other mutually and simultaneously as subjects. Child can step outside the two-person dyad and view the interaction from a third-person perspective.
Stage 4 Social- and Conventional-System Role-Taking	12–15+ years	Person realizes mutual perspective taking does not always lead to complete understanding. Social conventions are seen as necessary because they are understood by all members of the group (the generalized other) regardless of their position, role, or experience.

[a]Age ranges for all stages represent only an average approximation.
From Selman (1976, p. 309).

Me consists of the reflected appraisals of others. It is inherently social in origin, developing out of play, games, and social action. The general movement in the development of the Me is toward a more objective and general perspective from which the Me may be observed and through which it is given form and meaning.

Developmental psychologist Robert Selman (1980) proposes that the perspective-taking ability through which a person formulates conceptions of self and other develops through specific stages over time. Table 10.5 outlines his developmental model. On the basis of intensive interviews of children and adolescents, Selman delineates five stages of perspective-taking. At the first level (Stage 0), the child is unable to differentiate between the social perspectives of self and other. At Stage 1, the young child comes to understand that others feel differently, but does not yet understand that others also know how the self feels. Thus, the I can observe others, but it does not yet understand that others have a corresponding perspective on the self that may be coordinated with the I's own. At Stage 2, the older child comes to appreciate that others may also know how the self is feeling. Thus, the I not only observes the Me but also observes others observing the Me. The child is able to see that the other is both an actor and an observer of the self's action, and the child is able to adopt that perspective and coordinate it with his or her own.

It is not until Stage 3, argues Selman, that the person can adopt the perspective of a generalized other. At this time, the older child or adolescent realizes that both self and other can view each other and view themselves *simultaneously*. The child can step outside the two-person process and adopt the role of an objective third party observing the interaction of the self and other. At the highest level, Stage 4, the person comes to understand some of the limitations of mutual perspective-taking. At this point, the person is able to take a "systems perspective" on self–other interaction. Social conventions are seen as necessary in that they may be understood by all members of a group regardless of their personal perspectives.

In sum, then, the social aspects of a person's self-concept have their origins in interpersonal encounters of various kinds. In each interpersonal encounter, a person adopts a characteristic perspective. Perspective-taking develops over time. Young children have very limited perspective-taking abilities. Their viewpoints are mainly egocentric. As they mature, however, children move through stages of simple role-taking, self-reflective role-taking, and mutual role-taking. In optimal development, the person eventually reaches the highest level of perspective-taking, in which he or she is able to view others and the self from the standpoint of an encompassing system of relationships. The development of the self-concept (the Me) parallels the development of perspective-taking.

The Me on Stage

From the keen perspective of sociologist Erving Goffman (1922–1982), the social nature of the Me is so pervasive that one may wonder if the Me in fact exists as a unified object of consciousness. While most of us acknowledge that we "play" various roles in our interactions with others, Goffman goes so far as to suggest that we *are* the roles we play—and nothing else. The thesis of Goffman's radical *dramaturgical* perspective on the self is that each of us is an actor or actress performing for a wide variety of social audiences. Our dramatic performances are enactments of socially anchored roles. The self is nothing more than a collection of observable roles. The implication is that there is no real Me (nor I) beneath it all—no unifying product or process that defines who we are beyond our social displays.

In *The Presentation of Self in Everyday Life,* Goffman (1959) compiles a wide variety of observations of social behavior in different cultures to buttress his claim, made famous by Shakespeare, that all the world's a stage and all the men and women merely players. The ultimate goal in play-acting is *impression management.* Each person must convey an appropriate impression to an audience in a given social situation. In impression management, appearance is everything; the "reality" beneath the mask is irrelevant for successful play-acting. Indeed, Goffman questions if such inner or deeper reality in social life even exists. People manage impressions with each **performance** they enact. A performance is "all the activity of a given participant on a given occasion which serves to influence in any way any of the other participants" (Goffman, 1959, p. 1). During a performance, an "actor" may enact a *routine*—"a pre-established pattern of action which is unfolded during a performance and which may be presented or played through on other occasions" (p. 16). That part of the individual's performance "which regularly functions in a general and fixed fashion to define the situation for those who observe the performance" is called the *front* (p. 22). The front can be broken down into the physical setting or layout for the performance and the actor's "personal" front, which consists of clothing, age, posture, speech patterns, facial expressions, and other cues that signify the actor's appropriate status or position in the performance.

In Goffman's view, most social behavior is highly ritualized. While many of us would probably agree with him when we think of such social encounters as getting a haircut, buying a used car, making the rounds at a cocktail party, or participating in a class discussion, we are less likely to see our behavior as mere role playing in other more "spontaneous" situations, like playing with our children, making love, engaging in a good conversation, going camping, or creating art. Yet, even spontaneity can be scripted, Goffman maintains, and many situations that seem improvised and sincere are, in his analysis, ritualized performances designed to manage the impressions of others. As one author puts it:

> We are forever on stage, even when we may believe that we are most spontaneous and sincere in our responses to others. Ego's conduct is always molded through dramaturgical encounters with various alters. We may play the role of deferential students in encounters with professors, ardent suitors with our beloved, dutiful sons and daughters with our parents, or ambitious young

executives impressing our superiors in bureaucratic structures. What we can never be, so Goffman argues, is men and women *tout court*. We are what we pretend to be. (Coser, 1977, p. 576)

Although Goffman's examples of impression management in social behavior are compelling and although a large empirical literature on impression management has been produced by social psychologists, many personologists find Goffman's view of the self too extreme. The dramaturgical approach has been criticized for focusing exclusively on the surface manifestations of everyday social behavior—what Goffman himself once called "the slop of social life"—and neglecting deeper realities concerning personal wholeness and integrity. Nonetheless, many personologists would agree that people show marked individual differences in the extent to which they function like Goffmanian performers. This individual difference has been explored by personality psychologist Mark Snyder (1974, 1983) in studies of **self-monitoring.**

Snyder assesses self-monitoring via a simple questionnaire, reproduced in Table 10.6. The items on the scale concern the extent to which a person monitors his or her own behavior in various situations. People who score high on self-monitoring strive to display the specific kind of behavior ideal for the situation in which they are operating at a given time. People scoring low on self-monitoring are less concerned with enacting the "correct" performance in a given situation. They are less vigilant in monitoring their own and others' behavior. Their social behavior tends to be guided by consistent internal standards rather than by the contingencies of the situation.

The self-monitoring scale has been used in a large number of research studies. Overall, the results show that people high in self-monitoring approach social situations in a highly observant and pragmatic fashion. They are quick to assess the demands of the situation and to respond accordingly. They prefer relatively structured social encounters in which roles are well understood. In terms of Chapter 7's controversy over whether behavior is determined by traits or situations, people high in self-monitoring appear to be guided by situations, more so than people low in self-monitoring, whose behavior appears to be guided more by internal dispositions (Snyder, 1983). Therefore, high self-monitors tend to show minimal consistency between their trait scores on standard personality measures and their display of trait-related behavior. For instance, an extravert who is high in self-monitoring will be outgoing and sociable *only* in situations that call for such a performance. If the situation suggests that an introverted display is more in order, he or she will readily alter the behavioral display. Not only will people high in self-monitoring astutely judge what the actor should do in a situation, but they are also likely to be better actors. For instance, they are especially adept at expressing emotions through facial movements, at deceiving others, and at reading others' facial expressions (Snyder, 1979).

By contrast, people scoring low in self-monitoring tend to be less sensitive to the nuances of situations and less likely to modify their behavior according to

Table 10.6

A Scale to Measure Self-Monitoring

1. I find it hard to imitate the behavior of other people.
2. At parties and social gatherings, I do not attempt to do or say things that others will like.
3. I can only argue for ideas which I already believe.
4. I can make impromptu speeches even on topics about which I have almost no information.
5. I guess I put on a show to impress or entertain others.
6. I would probably make a good actor.
7. In a group of people I am rarely the center of attention.
8. In different situations and with different people, I often act like very different people.
9. I am not particularly good at making other people like me.
10. I'm not always the person I appear to be.
11. I would not change my opinions (or the way I do things) in order to please someone or win their favor.
12. I have considered being an entertainer.
13. I have never been good at games like charades or improvisational acting.
14. I have trouble changing my behavior to suit different people and different situations.
15. At a party I let others keep the jokes and stories going.
16. I feel a bit awkward in public and do not show up quite as well as I should.
17. I can look anyone in the eye and tell a lie with a straight face (if for a right end).
18. I may deceive people by being friendly when I really dislike them.

Note: Score 1 point each for "Yes" answers to items #4, 5, 6, 8, 10, 12, 17, and 18. Score 1 point each for "No" answers to items #1, 2, 3, 7, 9, 11, 13, 14, 15, and 16. Add up the points. Higher scores mean higher self-monitoring.
From Snyder & Gangestad (1986, p. 137).

situational demands. More introspective than people high in self-monitoring, they show marked consistency between their personality-trait scores and the behavior they display in various situations. Of course, nobody is completely oblivious to situational information. But the extravert low in self-monitoring is more likely than his or her counterpart scoring high on Snyder's scale to behave in an outgoing and sociable fashion in many *different* situations, even when such behavior is not exactly what the situation demands. People low in self-monitoring tend to have fewer friends than those high in self-monitoring, but they engage in more different kinds of behavior with any or all of them. Less concerned with keeping roles clear and structured, they encourage social contact among their friends, even when the friends are very different from each other.

For Erving Goffman, social life is a series of scripted performances, and people are always, in a sense, on stage.

A Confederacy of Selves

Goffman reduces the Me to the many different roles that people play on the stage of everyday life. There are as many Me's, Goffman claims, as there are roles to play. Critics of his approach claim that Goffman fails to allow for people's own efforts to find unity and consistency among the different roles they play. People may strive to organize their various roles, performances, and self-attributed characteristics into a single, coherent self-concept—a unitary and consistent Me that transcends the particular situations within which the self is called upon to perform. Or perhaps there are multiple Me's, but not an infinite number of them. Roles and performances may be grouped into clusters of selves. While a single, all-encompassing Me may not exist in most people's lives, each person may have a small number of different Me's. We are thus faced with a perennial controversy in the study of self: Is the Me a single, organized entity? Or is it multiple? William James's chapter can be read to support either position, though most often it is used to buttress the latter. James made many references to the multiplicity of Me's, especially in the realm of the social Me. Yet certain Me's are much more important than others, and in one passage James implies that a person should seek to find the single Me upon which "to stake his salvation":

I am often confronted by the necessity of standing by one of my empirical selves and relinquishing the rest. Not that I would not, if I could, be both handsome and fat and well dressed, and a great athlete, and make a million a year, be a wit, a *bon-vivant,* and a lady-killer, as well as a philosopher; a philanthropist, statesman, warrior, and African explorer, as well as a "tone-poet" and saint. But the thing is simply impossible. The millionaire's work would run counter to the saint's; the *bon-vivant* and the philanthropist would trip each other up; the philosopher and the lady-killer could not well keep house in the same tenement of clay. Such different characters may conceivably at the outset of life be alike *possible* to a man. But to make any one of them actual, the rest must more or less be suppressed. So the seeker of his truest, strongest, deepest self must review the list carefully, and pick out the one on which to stake his salvation. All other selves thereupon become unreal, but the fortunes of this self are real. Its failures are real failures, its triumphs real triumphs, carrying shame and gladness with them. (James, 1892/1963, p. 174)

A number of recent views of the self emphasize the multiplicity of the Me, pointing to a wide variety of "possible selves," "ideal selves," "ought selves," and "undesired selves," that together make up a family of Me's (Markus and Cross, 1990). Yet, these views also tend to endorse James's suggestion in the passage above that some selves are more significant, more "real," than are others. Borrowing a felicitous phrase from Hart (1988), there may exist a "confederacy of self-concepts" in a single individual (p. 75). But certain members of the confederacy hold more prestige than do others.

Possible Selves   A significant portion of our behavior may be guided as much by who we *might* be as by who we are. A young man trains for years to be an Olympic swimmer. A struggling author labors over what she hopes will become "the great American novel." A married couple save all their extra money so that they will never sink into poverty. In each of these cases, the person strives to become something, or to avoid becoming something, that he or she is (currently) not. In these and countless other instances, people behave according to what Markus and Nurius (1986) call **possible selves.** Possible selves "represent individuals' ideas of what they might become, what they would like to become, and what they are afraid of becoming." They are "the cognitive components of hopes, fears, goals, and threats and they give the specific self-relevant form, meaning, organization, and direction to these dynamics" (Markus & Nurius, 1986, p. 954).

In the view of Markus and Nurius, the Me is an organized knowledge structure—what we called in Chapter 9 a *schema*—within which are contained many generalizations about the current and past self as well as prominent possible selves that link the self-concept to the future. The possible selves that we wish to become in the future might be "the successful self, the creative self, the rich self, the thin self, or the loved and admired self." On the other hand, "the dreaded possible selves could be the alone self, the depressed self, the incompetent self, the alcoholic self, the unemployed self, or the bag lady self" (Markus & Nurius, 1986, p. 954).

Each possible self is a *personalized* construction that has been articulated in rich detail. Therefore, if one of my dreaded possible selves is "the unemployed self," then I am likely to have developed a painfully clear picture of what this self would be like. I might imagine myself losing confidence in my ability to support my family, having to mortgage the house, struggling to get by on food stamps, living in an overpriced and undersized apartment in a "bad section" of the city, spending long hours with nothing to do, applying for menial jobs for which I feel overqualified, being humiliated in the presence of my parents, resenting my peers who have profitable jobs, gradually sinking into despair and hopelessness. Although many people may fear unemployment, my unemployed self is personally crafted to be unique to my personality. If this is an important possible self within my general self-concept, then I am likely to go to great lengths to avoid its realization.

Markus and Nurius view possible selves as the crucial link between motivation and cognition in self-understanding. Markus and Nurius contend that people are motivated by strong internal needs, desires, and inclinations. But these motivational dynamics are not activated in personality functioning until they are transformed into self-relevant form. Therefore, my fear of being unemployed may be a personalized translation of a strong "power motive" (Chapter 11) combined with certain fears rooted in my past history. Motives, fears, desires, hopes, and dreams are given expression through possible selves. In this sense, then, possible selves function first as *incentives* for future behavior—they are selves to be approached or avoided.

A second function of possible selves is *self-evaluation.* Possible selves provide frameworks by which the person can evaluate how well or poorly his or her life is going. Possible selves are therefore powerful structures for determining the meaning of personal events. For example, a junior in college who desires to become a physician will evaluate her current standing with regard to that possible self in very negative terms should she be carrying an extremely low grade-point average. Her boyfriend, whose most cherished possible self involves his future career as a professional athlete, will feel good about his prospects after being drafted for a professional team. His equally low grade-point average has less impact on his self-evaluation in that it is not linked to a dominant possible self.

In sum, the concept of possible selves leads to two interesting implications for understanding the Me. First, the Me may be viewed as a complex schema or knowledge structure within which is contained a finite number of personified characters. Each possible self personifies specific and highly personal information connected to the person's basic needs, wants, and fears. Second, an important aspect of the social Me is information about who the person *might be* in the future. Expanding on James, Markus and Nurius view the Me as encompassing not only what "is mine" now but also what "might be mine" in the future, whether I like it or not.

Discrepancies Among Selves   E. Tory Higgins (1987) suggests that the self-as-object encompasses three major domains: the *actual self,* the *ideal self,* and the *ought self.* The actual self consists of your representation of the attributes that someone (yourself or another) believes you actually possess. The ideal self consists of your representation of the attributes that someone (yourself or another) would like you, ideally, to possess—that is, a representation of hopes, aspirations, or wishes. The ought self consists of your representation of the attributes that someone (yourself or another) believes you should or ought to possess—that is, a representation of duties, obligations, or responsibilities. Each of the three domains, furthermore, may be seen from either the person's *own* standpoint or the standpoint of a significant *other* in the person's life, such as a parent, spouse, or friend. Therefore, the "actual/own self" consists of the characteristics that the person believes he or she actually possesses. The "actual/other self" consists of the characteristics that the person believes that a significant other believes he or she (the person) actually possesses. Similarly, Higgins distinguishes between "ideal/own self" and "ideal/other self" and between "ought/own self" and "ought/other self."

According to Higgins' (1987) **self-discrepancy theory,** problems occur when various selves in different domains or from different standpoints are inconsistent, or discrepant, with each other. Two kinds of discrepancies are especially salient, and each leads to a corresponding emotional reaction. Discrepancies between the *actual/own* self and *ideal* (either own or other) selves lead to the experience of *dejection-related emotions,* such as sadness, disappointment, and shame. In these cases, the person believes that he or she has been unable to attain hopes, dreams, or aspirations that either the person him- or herself or a significant other has set for him or her. When my own baseball performance failed to live up to my father's (and my own) hopes and dreams, I felt dejected and downcast. A huge discrepancy between actual and ideal was revealed. On the other hand, discrepancies between the *actual/own* self and *ought* (either own or other) selves lead to the experience of *agitation-related emotions,* such as fear, anxiety, guilt. In these cases, the person believes that he or she has failed to live up to standards (established by self or other) for good, dutiful, or responsible behavior. The agitated emotions stem from the experience of feeling that one is being punished (by self or other) for not doing what one ought to do.

A number of research studies support Higgins' characterization of the linkages between self-discrepancies and negative emotional experiences (Higgins, 1987). In most of these studies, college students list traits or attributes that describe the various selves that Higgins has identified. The researchers code matches and mismatches in traits across the various self domains. For instance, a person might describe his actual/own self as "ambitious," "honest," "sincere," "friendly," and "hot-tempered" and his ought/own self as "honest," "friendly," "easygoing," "forgiving," and "helpful." In this example, we can identify two clear matches—both lists contain "honest" and "friendly"—and one clear mismatch—

A man living out one of his "multiple selves" as journalist. . .

"hot-tempered" and "easygoing" seem to be discrepant. The greater the number of mismatches, the greater the discrepancy and corresponding negative emotional reaction. The link between discrepancy and negative emotion is strongest, Higgins maintains, for self domains that the person judges to be the most relevant in his or her life.

. . . as father

In one study, Higgins administered these kinds of self-description measures and (1 month later) various assessments of *depression* (involving dejection-related emotions) and *anxiety* (involving agitation-related emotions) to under-graduate students. Figure 10.2 displays the results. As predicted, actual/ought discrepancies predicted anxiety (but not depression) whereas actual/ideal

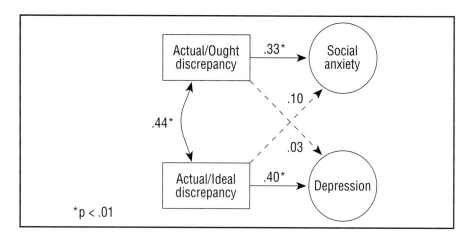

Figure 10.2

Empirical Relations Between Self-Discrepancies and Negative Emotional States.
(The numbers on the arrows are akin to correlation coefficients: the higher their
values, the stronger the association. p < .01.)

discrepancies predicted depression (but not anxiety). Students who felt that they
were not living up to their ideal selves reported high levels of sadness and depression. Those who felt that they were not living up to their ought selves reported
high levels of fear and anxiety.

Research conducted by Daniel Ogilvie (1987) has examined a different kind
of discrepancy in the Me. Whereas Higgins focuses on the extent to which the
actual self *differs* from other positive selves (ideal and ought), Ogilvie turns things
around to discern the extent to which the actual self is *similar* to *undesired*
selves. Undesired selves contain attributes that the person fears, dreads, hates,
and actively seeks to exclude from experience. Ogilvie suggests that we may be in
closer touch with our undesired selves than with our ideal and ought selves. Our
undesired selves are likely to be rooted in concrete past experiences in which we
felt humiliation, despair, fear, anger, and so on. Our ideal and ought selves, on the
other hand, are more hypothetical. They are abstractions towards which we strive
but which we rarely attain.

Ogilvie (1987) obtained students' characterizations of their actual, ideal,
and undesired selves and measured the "distance" between each student's selves
through a complicated statistical procedure that positions selves in a hypothetical
space. Questionnaire measures of life satisfaction were also obtained. The results
showed that the distance between a person's ideal and actual selves was negatively
associated with life satisfaction. In other words, the greater the discrepancy
between ideal and actual, the lower the life satisfaction. The distance between a
person's undesired and actual self was positively associated with life satisfaction.

People whose actual selves were "far away from" their undesired selves were happier with their lives. Most important, however, the second result was much stronger than the first. This is to say that the distance between undesired and actual selves was a much stronger predictor of life satisfaction than was the distance between ideal and actual selves. The implication of Ogilvie's findings is straightforward and intriguing: if we want to be happy, we will do better to avoid being the way we dread being rather than striving to be the way we wish to be. Future research should examine the validity of this claim.

Self-With-Other   Ogilvie and Ashmore (1991; Ashmore & Ogilvie, 1992) examine the multiplicity of the Me from the standpoint of what they call **self-with-other** representations. Drawing their inspiration from James's statement that there may be as many social selves as there are persons with whom the self is socially engaged, Ogilvie and Ashmore give special scrutiny to the person's cognitive representations of interactions with specific people. As we interact with a particular person again and again, we begin to form an *impression of ourselves in interaction with that particular person.* For example, I may come to realize that when I am with my best friend, I feel relaxed, extraverted, and creative. By contrast, when I am with my sister, I perceive myself to be tense, domineering, serious, and responsible. Each of these two self-perceptions is a representation of self-with-other. The Me is different with different people. From the perspective of Ogilvie and Ashmore, an important aspect of the social Me consists of the many different self-with-other units that we might identify in the most important relationships in our lives. Ogilvie and Ashmore summarize their conception of self-with-other in seven points:

1.   The self-concept comprises multiple components.
2.   One particularly important constituent is the social or interpersonal self.
3.   A crucial, yet to date neglected, unit of analysis in investigating the social self is "self-with-other." The "self-with-other" variable is a hypothetical construct. It is provisionally defined as a mental representation that includes the set of personal qualities (traits, feelings, and the like) that an individual believes characterizes his or her self when with a particular other person.
4.   Although each self-with-important-other internal representation is unique, the individual develops groupings of similar self-with-other representations. As an individual experiences self similarly in relationships with multiple specific others, a self-with-other family or constellation develops; for example, a preschool boy experiences himself as competent and comfortable with Mom, with Judy (a teenage babysitter), and with Grandpa.
5.   Constellations of self-with-others are, in turn, mentally organized into an overall self-with-others structure. The exact nature of this structure is impossible to specify at this time, and it is likely to vary considerably from person to person. At the same time, however, it is useful as a starting point to construe self-with-other groupings to be hierarchically arranged. This assumption is congruent with most current models of long-term memory and allows for the identification of self-with-others that vary in specificity versus generality.

6.   Individually, and as an overall structure, the mental representations of self-with-others are assumed to serve a variety of important functions for the individual. These include (a) summarizing past experience; (b) guiding present actions, especially interpersonal behavior; and (c) interpreting own and others' (especially interaction partners') behavior.

7.   Although self-with-other representations are dynamic rather than static, they are, for most adults most of the time, sufficiently stable to allow for reliable measurement. (Ogilvie & Ashmore, 1991, pp. 290–291)

Ogilvie and Ashmore have developed a sophisticated method of measuring self-with-other representations. In the first step of the method, a person is asked to list 25 important people (called "targets") in his or her life (e.g., parents, friends, children, lovers, bosses, coworkers, teachers, and so on) and to generate a lengthy set of adjectives (called "features") that describe how the person feels when he or she is with each of these various people. The researchers then reduce the lengthy list of features to a manageable set of descriptors. In a second session, the person is asked to envision a specific and representative scene in which he or she interacted with each of the 25 targets listed in the previous session. For example, if one of the targets is "my sister," I might think of a recent argument I had with my sister about her children's behavior at Christmas dinner. Then, the person rates each of the features, derived from the first session, as they apply to how he or she felt in the particular scene with the target person. In my example, therefore, I would think about how I perceived myself in the recent argument with my sister and I might rate highly the descriptors of "argumentative" and "angry," and I might rate as low the descriptors "easygoing" and "intellectual." Remember that these are ratings of me—how I perceive myself with this particular target person.

The person responds to the target/feature matrix by pushing keys on a computer. In addition, the person is asked to rate such items as "How I usually am," "Me at my best," and "Me at my worst" for each of the features. Also, targets may be split into two. For example, I might have one target that represents "my mother before she got divorced." A second target would be "my mother after she got divorced." The splitting may be necessary because I see myself as having behaved very differently with the earlier version of my mother compared to the later one. When all of the ratings have been made, a computer program generates a self-with-other portrait for that person. Each configuration is unique, reflecting the unique structure of a person's self-with-other representations. Figure 10.3 displays a self-with-other configuration for a subject named Sarah. The top half of the figure contains targets (written in capital letters). The bottom half of the figure contains features (in lowercase letters).

Notice the second row of the figure. This contains three clusters of targets: Cluster A (current boyfriend, past boyfriend, and so on), Cluster B (past boyfriend, past female high school enemy), and Cluster C (mother, me as I usually am, and so on). These three clusters are linked to three corresponding feature lists (in the next row down). Cluster A targets link up with Cluster 1 features—peaceful,

Continued on p. 582

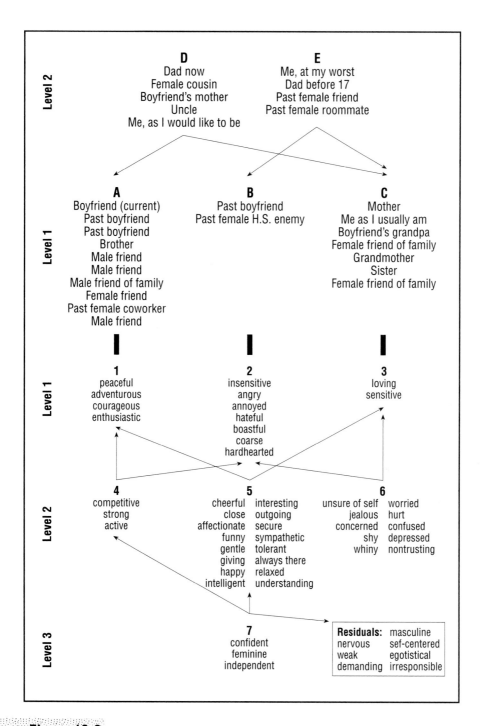

Figure 10.3

Sarah's Self-With-Other Representations.

From Ogilvie & Ashmore, 1991, p. 300.

Feature 10.B

Feeling Good About the Me: Self-Esteem

When we consider what makes us what we are, it is difficult to be cool and dispassionate. Like most any object of our reflection, the self-as-object—what James called the Me—can be seen as having a certain content and structure. But we are not likely to gaze upon that content and structure with the same objectivity with which we consider the listed contents of a cereal box or the structure of a new skyscraper. We *care* about the self more than we care about virtually anything else, and we are likely to *evaluate* the self accordingly, to adopt an affective perspective on the self, to feel good or bad about the Me. We may call this highly subjective and affective judgment of the Me *self-esteem*.

William James provided a simple definition of self-esteem:

$$\text{Self-esteem} = \frac{\text{Success}}{\text{Pretensions}}$$

In James's view, self-esteem equals one's successes divided by one's pretensions. In other words, how well you evaluate yourself depends on the amount of success you have relative to your aspirations for success. When successes are very low and pretensions high, the person is likely to suffer from low self-esteem. Similarly, relatively high self-esteem becomes more likely as successes increase or as pretensions decrease. You can feel better about the self either by being more successful and accomplished or by establishing more modest criteria for success.

Since the time of James, psychologists have offered many definitions of self-esteem. Coopersmith (1967) provides a representative example:

> By self-esteem we refer to the evaluation which the individual makes and customarily maintains with regard to himself; it expresses an attitude of approval or disapproval, and indicates the extent to which the individual believes himself to be capable, significant, successful, and worthy. In short, self-esteem is a *personal* judgment of worthiness that is expressed in attitudes the individual holds toward himself. (p. 5)

Many of the definitions are general and rather vague (Wylie, 1979). Nonetheless, a large number of instruments have been devised to measure self-esteem. Virtually all of them are self-report questionnaires in which the subject responds "yes" or "no" or makes ratings for each self-descriptive item.

Some psychologists argue that self-esteem is a global construct referring to a general evaluation of the self. Others counter that self-esteem can only be viewed as it pertains to separate life domains. According to this later view, a person may evaluate him-

or herself very differently in different content areas. Harter (1983) has identified three such areas in children's assessment of self-esteem: physical, cognitive, and social skills. A boy may see himself as a superb athlete in the physical domain but believe that he is only average in his school work and that he is an interpersonal klutz. Rosenberg (1979) suggests that self-esteem must be viewed both as a general and as a domain-specific evaluation and that the two may not always be related. A person can feel generally very good (or bad) about the self but show a great deal of dissatisfaction (or satisfaction) with different domains. In the example above, the boy who evaluates himself positively only in the physical domain may still see himself overall in highly positive terms if he believes that the physical domain is the most important domain for self-assessment. "Sure I'm not good at other things," he may say, "but all I really care about is sports!"

Because self-esteem has been measured in so many different ways, it is difficult to draw many firm conclusions from the voluminous research literature on the topic (Harter, 1983; Wylie, 1979). Self-esteem appears to be relatively stable during late childhood but may change more markedly in the adolescent years. Specific research in the adult years is sparse, though longitudinal studies of personality traits that appear to be related to self-esteem show a good deal of stability over time (Chapter 5). Despite popular misconceptions, self-esteem does not appear to be consistently related to either gender or race: males score no higher or lower on the average than females; blacks do not consistently differ from whites (Wylie, 1979). Self-esteem in children *does* appear to be positively related to achievement in school. Though the findings are not completely clear, it appears that increases in school achievement may precede, and likely cause, rises in self-esteem, rather than the reverse (Harter, 1983). Self-esteem is positively associated with an internal locus of control and other indices of personal causation (Chapter 8).

Coopersmith (1967) investigated the developmental antecedents of general self-esteem in 10–12-year-old sons. Parents of sons with high self-esteem tended to be affectionate and accepting while providing clear guidelines for appropriate behavior. They tended to prefer noncoercive types of discipline such as denial of privileges and isolation, rather than physical punishment. And they were democratic in the sense that they considered the child's opinions and viewpoints in making family decisions. Hales (1979) has obtained similar findings with parents of daughters.

Continued from p. 578
adventurous, courageous, and enthusiastic. This means that Sarah tends to see herself as being highly peaceful, adventurous, courageous, and enthusiastic when she is with the various people who make up Cluster A. Almost all of the people in this cluster are in her age cohort. By contrast, she feels insensitive, angry, annoyed, and so on (Cluster 2) when she is with one particular past boyfriend and with a particular female high school enemy. She feels loving and sensitive with mother and other members of Cluster C, most of whom are considerably older than Sarah.

The complexity of Sarah's configuration becomes apparent as you move away from the middle and toward the top and the bottom of Figure 10.3. Looking at the top row ("Level 2" of Targets), you see that Cluster E (which contains me at my worst, dad before I was age 17, past female friend, and past female roommate) connects to the negative images she has in Cluster B and the mostly positive ones she has in Cluster C. The targets in Cluster E refer to people who elicit in Sarah highly contradictory or ambivalent feelings and self-perceptions. In reflecting on her relationship with her father before she was 17 years of age, she reports feeling both loving and hateful, both sensitive and insensitive. Clusters 4, 5, and 6—which make up "Level 2" of Features—group descriptors according to their relations with each other. Following the arrows, you see that "competitive" (Cluster 4) links to Clusters 1 and 2, which themselves link directly to Clusters A and B, respectively. This means that Sarah feels herself to be competitive when she is with people who are in Cluster A and Cluster B. The descriptor "competitive," therefore, distinguishes between her self-with-other representations for brother (Cluster A) and past female high school enemy (Cluster B) on the one hand and mother (Cluster C) on the other. In simple terms, Sarah feels herself to be competitive when she is with her brother and with her past enemy from high school, but *not* when she is with her mother.

Finally, the bottom row ("Level 3" of Features) of Figure 10.3 refers to characteristics of Sarah's self-with-other configuration that apply either universally or not at all. Cluster 7 is made up of the features confident, feminine, and independent. This cluster connects to all other clusters in the configuration. This means that no matter whom she is with, Sarah consistently perceives herself to be confident, feminine, and independent. You might view these as cardinal or core traits of her social self-concept. By contrast, the box called "residuals" refers to descriptors that Sarah rarely, if ever, uses to describe herself when she is with other people. Regardless of which particular other she finds herself with, Sarah tends not to perceive herself as nervous, weak, demanding, masculine, self-centered, egotistical, or irresponsible.

One appealing virtue of the self-with-other approach to research is that it provides a detailed and precise idiographic account of an important aspect of the social Me. In addition, different configurations from different persons may be compared and contrasted in terms of such dimensions as the overall complexity of the self-with-other structure, enabling researchers to launch nomothetic investigations. Recent research in this regard hints at an interesting gender difference in self-with-other structures. Ashmore and Ogilvie (1992) report a tendency for men to isolate their negative self-with-other representations, separating them neatly from their positive clusters. By contrast, women tend to produce patterns with greater connections between negative and positive self-with-other representations. In other words, men more than women may tend to cordon off the negative elements of the social me, to keep the negative safely distanced from the positive aspects of the social self. For women, there appears to be a greater degree of fluidity in the self-with-other configuration. Negative elements may shade into positive ones. A woman may report that she feels a mixture of happiness and dread when she is with her boss or her sister. By contrast, a man may be more likely to report one or the other of these conflicting emotions, but not both for the relations with the same person. He may feel energetic with his sister, father, best friend from college, and next-door neighbor, but feel nervous with his older brother. The self-with-older-brother representation may be split off from all of the others, tucked away in a lonesome corner of the self-with-other configuration. Further research, however, is needed to determine if this possible gender difference really exists and, if it does exist, what it might mean.

Development of the Me

The I and the Me develop in tandem—different perspectives on an organized, developing self. At the beginning of his chapter on the self, James stressed the fact that I and Me are "discriminated aspects" of the same thing. Their unity "is perhaps the ineradicable dictum of commonsense." As the I—the synthesizing agent—matures, so matures the I's conception of the Me. Process (I) and product (Me) go hand in hand. Therefore, it should not be surprising to learn that various models of the development of self-conceptions—the Me, or self-as-object—recall similar themes and parallel movements from our earlier discussion of the development of the I.

In general, developmental models of the Me argue that self-conceptions become more complex, differentiated, and integrated as the person matures (Damon & Hart, 1982; Greenwald, 1988; Harter, 1983; Selman, 1980). This truism is obvious to you if you have ever compared how, say, children and adults describe themselves. Ask my 4-year-old daughter to tell you who she is, and she will probably talk about her blond hair, her Barbie dolls, her sister, and other simple, concrete, and external features of the self. My 30-year-old sister-in-law, on the other hand, is likely to tell you that she is a political liberal, that she believes deeply in social justice, that she is happy being a mother, and so on. Her self-descriptions are infinitely more complex, abstract, and internal.

Between my daughter and my sister-in-law are a number of stages in the developing Me—different numbers for different theories. For instance, Harter (1983) suggests that self-conceptions develop through four stages from early childhood to adulthood. At the lowest stage, the child uses *simple descriptions:* "I'm good at playing ball"; "I know my alphabet." From here, the child moves to the second level of *trait labels:* "I'm a friendly person"; "I'm smart in mathematics." Next comes *single abstractions,* usually reached in early

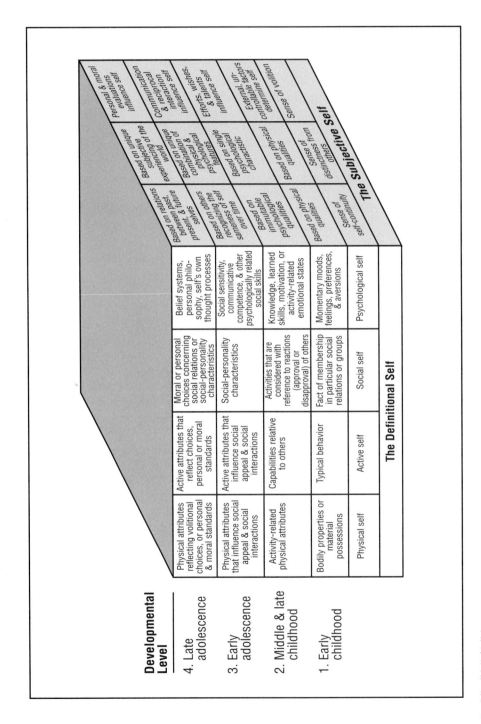

Figure 10.4

Developmental Model of Self-Understanding.

From Hart, 1988, p. 73.

adolescence: "I'm talented in art, music, and literature"; "I love people who are spontaneous." Finally, in later adolescence and adulthood the self becomes couched in *higher-order abstractions:* "I'm a bohemian who rejects conventional values of society"; "I'm a Freudian who believes that people are eternally conflicted and controlled by forces from within."

A related model of **self-understanding** has been developed by Damon and Hart (1982). These theorists distinguish four aspects of the "definitional self," or Me: the physical (similar to James's "material"), active, social, and psychological (James's "spiritual") selves (Figure 10.4). Each of the four develops through four stages of early childhood, middle and late childhood, early adolescence, and late adolescence. Focusing on what Damon and Hart call the psychological self, the young child will describe this aspect of the Me in terms of momentary mood states ("I'm sad") and preferences or aversions ("I like ice cream"). In middle and late childhood, descriptions emphasize such phenomena as knowledge and learned skills ("I can throw a curve ball"; "I'm the smartest kid in the class"). The early adolescent speaks of psychologically related social skills ("I'm a good listener"; "I care for people who are less fortunate than I"). Finally, at the highest stage, the late adolescent employs complex descriptions of his or her own values, belief systems, and thought processes ("I'm a devout Catholic"; "I worry a lot about nuclear war").

In addition to stages of the Me, furthermore, Damon and Hart delineate parallel stages for three self-functions traditionally associated with the I, or what they term "the subjective self." These appear as the right three columns of Figure 10.4. In this regard, Damon and Hart's model brings us full circle. In our initial consideration of the I, we emphasized such essential aspects of the subjective self as a sense of volition, separateness, and continuity over time. Damon and Hart suggest that we experience these subjective elements of the I in different ways at different developmental stages. As the I develops, subjective experience broadens—consciousness itself is transformed. And with these transformations follow the corresponding changes in how we understand ourselves—transformations in the Me. The knower and the known travel together. As personologists, however, we still have more to learn about their journey.

Summary for Chapter 10

1. William James distinguished two fundamental aspects of the self—the subjective I and the objective Me.

2. The I is commonly viewed as the agent or trend in the personality responsible for intentionality and wholeness.

3. Allport's term for self was *proprium.* The culmination of the proprium's development was the establishment of propriate strivings, such as life goals and values, and the consolidation of a unifying sense of the self-as-knower.

4. Sullivan viewed the self-system as a set of strategies developed in childhood to ward off anxiety.

5. Loevinger uses the term *ego* to refer to the I, which she views as an overall framework for making meaning in the world. Stages of ego development follow a structural developmental sequence, loosely tied to cognitive developmental shifts as described by Piaget.

6. Kegan understands the evolving self in terms of subject–object balances. Subjects become objects—what I "was" becomes what I now "have"—as the person develops.

7. Studies of self-recognition behavior show that human infants develop a sense of self-as-subject—an active, causal I—by the time they are about 18 months old.

8. Through later childhood, adolescence, and adulthood, the sense of self moves through egocentric and impulsive stages to more socialized stages of conformity and conventionality. Even higher stages suggest more individuated perspectives on life, emphasizing internalized standards of morality, a rich inner life, and tolerance for ambiguity and paradox.

9. Stages of the development of the I—ego development—may be assessed via a sentence-completion test, refined by Loevinger.

10. Baldwin, Cooley, and Mead launched a sociological tradition in the study of the self as Me, focusing on the social nature of self. A central concept in this tradition is perspective-taking, or the developing ability to assume the role of another.

11. The sociological extreme in the conception of the Me is Goffman's dramaturgical theory. According to Goffman, the Me is merely a succession of ritualized roles. Individual differences in the extent to which persons monitor their social behavior in accord with roles and situational demands are measured on the self-monitoring scale.

12. Many recent theories of self emphasize the multiplicity of the Me. Discrepancies among various selves—such as actual, ideal, and ought selves—lead to different kinds of negative emotional reactions, depending on the nature of the discrepancy.

13. The social self may be viewed as a collection of self-with-other units, each containing a set of descriptors referring to how the I perceives the Me in a particular relationship with a particular other person.

14. The development of the Me parallels the development of the I. Theories of the development of self-conceptions agree that as the person matures, his or her conception of the Me becomes more complex, differentiated, and integrated.

Part IV

Interpersonal Stories

Narrative Patterns in Human Lives

Chapter 11 Motivational Themes in Stories: The
    Legacy of Henry Murray
Chapter 12 Biography and the Life Course:
    Erikson, Adler, and the Seasons of Adulthood
Chapter 13 Life Scripts, Life Stories

Human lives are situated in time. To understand a person's life in time, even if that person is oneself, one must have a sense of beginning, middle, and ending, of how one thing "led to" the next over time, of how things might eventually "turn out." In other words, to know a life in time is to know the story of that life. Throughout human history, people have explained human lives in time by making and telling stories. This is because stories are the most natural and effective vehicle for expressing how actors strive to attain their most cherished goals and avoid their most dreaded fears over time. The ancient practice of storytelling has great relevance for contemporary personality psychology, as we see in Chapters 11–13. These chapters focus on approaches to persons that seek first and foremost to discern, discover, construct, and understand the interpersonal story that explains the single human life evolving over time.

In Chapter 11, we explore Henry Murray's contributions to the study of lives and the voluminous research that his work has stimulated. Murray developed a personological system that emphasized the time-binding nature of human life, as captured in his famous statement that "the history of the organism is the organism." Murray developed a rich assortment of concepts to characterize how lives change and remain the same over historical time. Especially influential were his concepts of need, press, and thema—concepts that could be employed to reveal a certain degree of thematic unity in a single life over time, even though that unity appeared against a backdrop of shifting perspectives and continuous change. Murray proposed a list of about 20 fundamental psychological needs and suggested that individual differences in needs might be assessed through content analysis of imaginative stories. In the last 40 years, a considerable body of research has employed Murray's narrative method, called the Thematic Apperception Test, to examine individual differences in the needs (motives) for achievement, power, and intimacy.

Chapter 12 considers the interpersonal stories that characterize human lives *in toto* as revealed in biography and autobiography. Erik Erikson provides a compelling theoretical perspective for comprehending a sequence of psychosocial chapters revealed in biographies of lives over time. While Erikson's contributions to personality psychology are usually seen from a psychoanalytic perspective, Chapter 12 suggests that Erikson has more to say about interpersonal stories than he does about intrapsychic mysteries, especially when he considers such complex, psychosocial concepts as ego identity and generativity. Similarly, the classic contributions of Alfred Adler, a follower and then rival of Freud, reveal an early appreciation for the storied nature of human lives in time, as evidenced in Adler's fascination with earliest memories (story beginnings) and with what he called the "fictional finalisms" of life (anticipated story endings). Finally, the work of Daniel Levinson and other psychological biographers seeks to discern predictable stages and consistent themes in the life histories of adults.

In Chapter 13, we entertain the proposition that people themselves create meaning and coherence in their own lives by constructing self-defining life stories and scripts. According to Silvan Tomkins, people reconstruct emotionally charged scenes from their past and organize them into life scripts. Scripts redefine the past and orient the person to the future. My own life-story model of identity suggests that beginning in late adolescence and young adulthood each of us fashions an internalized life story to provide our lives with a sense of unity and purpose, a story complete with setting, scene, character, plot, and theme. The recent narrative approaches of Hubert Hermans and Gary Gregg emphasize the multiplicity of selves and identity, how one's life in time becomes narrated by many different and conflicting storytellers. The theme of multiplicity in narrative runs throughout contemporary writings on the "post-modern self," suggesting that selves are made in narrative discourse, like shifting storied texts whose meanings can never fully be known.

Chapter 11

Motivational Themes in Stories
The Legacy of Henry Murray

Introduction

Icarus

The Personology of Henry A. Murray
Murray and the Harvard Psychological Clinic
Murray's System
Feature 11.A: Rising, Falling, Fantasy, and Sex
The Study of Lives
Personology After World War II
Science and the Single Case

Three Social Motives
The Thematic Apperception Test
Achievement Motivation
Measuring the Achievement Motive
Careers in Business
The Achieving Society
Power Motivation
Leadership
Love and Health
Intimacy Motivation
Feature 11.B: A Movie Is Like a TAT: The Case of Alfred Hitchcock
Motivation in Perspective

Summary

If you met Grope, you would be unimpressed. Picture a short, dark-haired, slightly disheveled young man, enrolled at Harvard College in the 1930s. Aside from his association with a prestigious university, he seems a rather unremarkable undergraduate—quiet, apathetic, uninvolved, and uninspired. By his own account, he is "a small frog in a big puddle," a "pretty nice guy." He is shy, and he speaks softly and rarely. He is a member of no extracurricular clubs or organizations. He dates no women and spends very little time studying. His withdrawal from so many instrumental and interpersonal activities enables him to "devote the maximum amount of time to sleep, relaxation, daydreaming, and playing bridge with a small clique" of buddies (Murray, 1955/1981, p. 544). Though you might call him lazy, there is nothing grossly wrong with Grope: he is not psychotic; he is not a psychopath; he has never committed a crime. We might be surprised to learn, therefore, that in his dreams, fantasies, and through the *story of his own life,* Grope longs to fly.

Icarus

In the ancient story of Icarus, a young boy fashions wings and flies toward the sun. As he soars higher and higher, the heat from the sun melts the wax in his wings, sending him plummeting to the sea below. The Icarus legend is a story about hot sun and cold sea, about fiery ambition ultimately quenched by watery defeat, about rising and falling. In a profound sense, the story of Icarus is the story of Grope's life. In a famous case study, Henry A. Murray (1955/1981) interpreted the life and the personality of this unassuming college student in terms of an ancient Greek story about a young boy who rises and then falls. According to Murray, Grope revealed a pervasive **Icarus complex.**

Grope was one of a number of students who volunteered to participate as subjects in a series of interviews, tests, and experiments conducted by Murray and his associates at the Harvard Psychological Clinic in the 1930s and 1940s (Murray, 1938). As a subject, Grope wrote a detailed autobiography that laid the groundwork for three subsequent 1-hour interviews. In addition, Grope was administered a series of questionnaires and rating scales and certain open-ended exercises such as the **Thematic Apperception Test (TAT)** in which a person is asked to create imaginative stories in response to pictures.

Some highlights from Grope's autobiography: Grope was the first of three children born to a college-educated couple. Grope's earliest memory was dumping his supper on the floor in a fit of revenge aimed at his mother. Grope wet his bed and his pants regularly until about the age of 11. By sixth grade, he had established himself as the premier student and athlete in his class. By seventh, he had started his self-described "fall" from supremacy after losing weight, failing to grow even an inch in the course of a year, and suffering repeated colds and bouts of sluggishness. Grope seemed to rebound slightly in high school, as he was elected treasurer of his sophomore class, chosen to serve on the student council and yearbook staff, and applauded as "Biggest Joker" in the senior class upon graduation. Attending Harvard, however, marked another fall into the mediocrity of the small frog in the big puddle. At the time of his first interview, Grope viewed himself as entering a behavioral and emotional limbo: "I am just biding my time and waiting for the day when my 'soul' will *ignite* and this inner *fire* will send me hurtling (two rungs at a time) *up* the ladder of success" (p. 543). Once his soul "ignited" and he began his ascent, Grope would be able to achieve what he saw as the ultimate values in life: "money, power, glory, and fame."

Murray tells us of a few of the stories Grope most liked to tell himself:

> His major recurrent fantasy was one of landing on a desert island in the Pacific with a band of followers, discovering an inexhaustible spring of fresh water and an abundant food supply, and then founding a new civilization with himself as king and lawgiver. He often dreamed and daydreamed of self-propelled flights and of jumping off a high place and floating gracefully and gently to the ground. But he was almost equally hospitable to less extravagant fantasies: he considered becoming a prize fighter, an actor, an army general, a millionaire, an inventor, a psychiatrist, and a teacher. "It would be a lot of fun working with kids, teaching them with a sense of humor, and having them think you are a 'good guy.'" He has imagined himself a famous tap dancer, a singer, and a movie comedian. He is attracted by the stage and has a tentative plan of enrolling in some school of the drama. His more immediate intention, however, is to enlist in the Air Corps and become a pilot. Although in his opinion world wars are preventable evils, he expects another one within fifteen years, which will destroy much or most of civilization. The two worst things that might happen to him are (a) to be maimed in the war and (b) to lose his self-confidence. Finally, he writes: "If I could remodel the world to my heart's content, I would establish a sound World Government and would like to be the dictator, a good dictator." He would be "most proud" of having his name "go down in history as a leader, or as an artist, or as a discoverer or inventor." (pp. 542–543)

The story of Icarus was reflected in Grope's images of who he was and who he had been, Grope's fantastical scripts foreshadowing who he might be and what he might do in the future, the critical scenes in Grope's past that stood out as turning points in his own life story, and the ideological underpinnings of the story that celebrated money, fame, and glory as the ultimate life values. Drawing mainly from Grope's autobiography, dreams, fantasies, and narrative responses on the TAT, Murray delineated a number of recurrent themes in Grope's life, summarized in Table 11.1, that converged to form the Icarus complex.

The first theme in the Icarus complex is *urethral erotism,* which means the thematic association of "hot" sexuality and "wet" urination. Images of urethral erotism concern the "cathection of fire, 'burning' ambition, exhibitionism, and voyeurism" (p. 548). Murray points to Grope's reported childhood belief that babies are made by urinating into a woman's rectum, the high incidence of fire imagery in Grope's imagination, a lifelong fascination with fire ("fire is a yellow-orange gas from outer space," Grope proclaimed as a precocious 6-year-old), and the persistent problem of enuresis (bed-wetting).

Murray argued that urethral erotism was fused, in the case of Grope, with a second theme of *ascensionism,* or sudden rising. Ascensionism assumed a variety of guises for Grope as he imagined himself riding through the air perched upon the buttocks of his childhood nurse (a significant night dream), shooting through space and landing on the planet Mars, hurtling up the ladder of success, and reaching dizzying heights of prestige and influence. Witness the merger of urethral erotism and ascensionism in this remarkable story Grope told in response to a TAT picture of a barn surrounded by snow and a winged horse flying across the sky:

> An old hermit went out into the woods and built himself a farm. After thirty years of living all by himself on the crops he produced, he got pretty tired of this humdrum existence, so he decided that he wanted to re-enter the competitive world, and try to sell, was planning on selling his crops, planning to build some sort of fortune. So he worked for a few years, couldn't seem to get very large crops, really good crops. They wouldn't grow. What he needed was more fertilizer, but he couldn't afford fertilizer in any quantity, so he was practically at his wit's end, and one night he decided to turn to religion; and as miracles will happen, the very next day Pegasus flew over and fertilized all his plants [assumedly by urinating on them]. Not only that, but the cow in the barn bore him a daughter [impregnated by Pegasus?!—urethral erotism]; something he had always wanted. In the picture here, he is squinting in his happiness; feeling that life has really been rewarding. So the picture is the spirit of happiness. (p. 549)

The third theme of the Icarus complex is *cynosural narcissism,* which denotes a craving for unsolicited attention and admiration. Grope's fantasies about who he might be in the future were populated by heroic images of self as the benevolent dictator, actor, prize fighter, inventor—all superstars acclaimed and venerated by millions. Murray commented on the significance of Grope's drawings for the Draw-A-Family Test in which he drew his own portrait twice the size of his father's and mother's, as well as his narrative response to a blank TAT card upon which he projected the image of a virtually naked, gigantic man

 **Table 11.1**

The Icarus Complex in the Case of Grope

Urethral Erotism

In short, sex was apperceived in urinary terms. Also he manifested, in high degree, every other concomitant of urethral erotism, as defined by Freud and his followers: cathection of fire, "burning" ambition, exhibitionism, and voyeurism. Remember Grope's bright saying: "Fire is a yellow-orange gas from outer space." Even today he "gets a thrill" by lighting wastepaper in his tin scrap basket and seeing it flare up. There is a high incidence of pertinent fire imagery in his projective protocols. Finally, there is the association of persistent enuresis and urethral erotism (dreams of urination accompanied by ejaculation) which we and others have found in a number of personalities. (p. 548)

Ascensionism

This is the name I have given to the wish to overcome gravity, to stand erect, to grow tall, to dance on tiptoe, to walk on water, to leap or swing in the air, to climb, to rise, to fly, or to float down gradually from on high and land without injury, not to speak of rising from the dead and ascending into heaven. There are also emotional and ideational forms of ascensionism—passionate enthusiasm, rapid elevations of confidence, flights of the imagination, exultation, inflation of spirits, ecstatic mystical up-reachings, poetical and religious—which are likely to be expressed in the imagery of physical ascensionism. (p. 548)

Cynosural Narcissism

This strikes me as a suitable term (more embracing than exhibitionism) to denote a craving for unsolicited attention and admiration, a desire to attract and enchant all eyes, like a star in the firmament. (p. 549)

Falling/Precipitation

"Falling" denotes an undesired or accidental descension of something (usually a human body or the status [reputation] of a person, but it may be feces, urine, or any cathected object). "Precipitation," on the other hand, means a consciously or subconsciously desired calamitous descension: the S allows himself to fall or leaps from a height (precipitative suicide), or he pushes another person over a cliff, throws something down, or purposely urinates or defecates on the floor. (p. 551)

Craving for Immortality

No doubt the narcissistic core in every man yearns for perpetual existence; but of all our subjects Grope is unexampled in giving Everlasting Life ("I might settle for 500 years") as one of his seven wishes for himself. (p. 553)

Table 11.1 continued

Table 11.1 continued

Depreciation and Enthrallment of Women, Bisexuality

> Grope spoke contemptuously of his mother, and cynically of women generally. Love was never a felt experience. But, as his projective protocols made plain, women were nonetheless important, if not indispensable, to him as glorifying agents: a female was (a) someone to be "swept off her feet," to be driven "sex-mad" by the mere sight of him; (b) someone to applaud his exploits; (c) someone of "wide hips" to bear him sons; and (d) someone to mourn his death. As one might expect in such a person, there were abundant evidences of a suffusing feminine component coupled with some degree of homosexuality. This is best illustrated by a story he told in the Tri-Dimensional Test. A king announces he will give half his kingdom to the person who creates the most beautiful thing in the world. The last contestant (hero of the story) comes forward and says, "I have created a replica of myself." Whereupon the king says, "*That* is the most beautiful thing in the world, therefore *you* are the most beautiful thing in the world. Will you be my queen?" The king takes the hero as his male queen and gives his androgynous beauty half his kingdom. (p. 554.)

From Murray (1955/1981).

surrounded by an adoring crowd. The man is the "most perfect physical specimen in all of Greece . . . a sensation . . . a wonderful box-office draw" (p. 550).

Finally, the fourth theme of *falling/precipitation* is linked to the first three themes in a series of ascension–decension cycles that Murray perceived at a number of different levels. In Grope's early memories, dreams, and TAT responses, as well as in his reconstruction of his own "falls" from prominence in seventh grade and upon entering Harvard, what goes up always comes down, and with a crash. (Indeed, Grope's supper falls crashing to the floor in his earliest memory.) In one grizzly story Grope told in response to a TAT picture, six people eventually die, four by falling into water. The "cold sea" quenched the flaming ambition of both the ancient Icarus and his modern counterpart. The images of fire and water, sun and sea, recall the first theme of urethral erotism.

In sum, Grope's Icarus complex constitutes a *biographical type,* a type centered on an ancient *story.* Evidence for the existence of this type comes mainly from the *stories* Grope tells—from his storied autobiographical account (a narrative about his own life) and from the imaginative stories he tells in response to TAT pictures. Presumably, there are other Gropes out there, other men (and perhaps some women) whose narrative renderings of their own lives and whose narrative imaginings might fit the same pattern we see in Grope. Presumably, there is a finite number of different narrative types, yielding a taxonomy of human stories. Ideally, each human life might be viewed as animating a central narrative form. For every life, there is a story that must be discovered. To know the story is to know the person. Rather than viewing personality from the standpoint of instincts, traits, situations, schemas, or selves, therefore, Murray suggested that stories were at the heart of things, that different personalities correspond to different story types (White, 1981). The emphasis on the *interpersonal stories* of personality distinguishes Murray's approach from all others we have encountered so far. As we will see, Murray's is a broadly eclectic system for personality that shares similarities with psychoanalytic, trait, interactionist, and cognitive approaches. But the emphasis on stories—stories as *methods* for investigating personality (the TAT) and stories as *metaphors* for human lives (the Icarus complex)—makes Murray very different, and makes his work deserving of our most careful attention.

The Personology of Henry A. Murray

Murray and the Harvard Psychological Clinic

In 1927 Harvard University hired a little-known physician with a Ph.D. in biochemistry to serve as an assistant to Morton Prince, a prominent psychologist at the Harvard Psychological Clinic. Although the 34-year-old Henry Murray had begun to distinguish himself in medical research, he was virtually untrained in psychology proper, having taken (and not enjoyed) only one undergraduate course in the subject 15 years before. Born of a wealthy family in New York City in 1893, Murray had travelled and studied widely in his 20s and 30s. He had been unable to find a fulfilling intellectual project for himself until he read, in 1923, Carl Jung's *Psychological Types* and, shortly thereafter, spent a vacation with Jung. Murray later wrote, Jung "provided [me] with an exemplar of genius that settled the question of [my] identity to come" (1967, p. 291). "We talked for hours, sailing down the lake and smoking before the hearth of his Faustian retreat. . . . Within a month a score of bi-horned problems were resolved, and I went off decided on depth psychology" (Murray, 1940, p. 153). At about the same time in Murray's life, a number of other influences appeared to work together to nudge him in the direction of psychology, including his reading of romantic authors such as Dostoyevsky and Melville and his growing professional and personal relationship with Christiana Morgan, who shared Murray's strong interest in human personality (Anderson, 1988; Murray, 1940, 1967; Robinson, 1992). Two years after Murray signed on at the Harvard clinic, Morton Prince died. Murray succeeded him as the director.

Prince had started the clinic as a place where undergraduates might be taught abnormal psychology with the aid of clinical demonstrations (Robinson, 1992; White, 1981). Known for his work on hysteria, multiple personality, and unconscious mental processes, Prince was able to draw upon his own intriguing case accounts to make abnormal psychology vivid for the students. Indeed, he was even able to bring patients into the classroom, so that they could display first-hand their often bizarre symptoms and strange abilities. While the method might sound like good pedagogy to us today, the Psychology Department at Harvard was not enthusiastic about Prince's showmanship, and they looked askance upon his enthusiasm for such unscientific-sounding phenomena. Thus, it was agreed that the clinic would be housed in a location far removed from the proper psychology laboratories, lest people get the wrong idea about what respectable psychology was supposed to be about. When Murray moved in to help, Prince's operation was moving along rather nicely. Classes were being taught and experiments were being undertaken in the domains of hypnotism and hysteria. A student at the clinic during this time, Robert White (1981) suggests in retrospect that if Prince had lived longer the clinic might have won some marginal respectability as a center for specialized research into rather peripheral human phenomena. Everything changed, however, when Murray took over:

> I was present as a graduate student during the year before and the year after Prince's death, then absent for the next three years in a teaching position. When I returned, it was to a wholly different world. Everyone was talking about needs, variables, and a mysterious process called thematic apperception. Strange people were wandering in and out, neither staff, patients, nor students, but simply personalities undergoing study. The ship had radically changed its course.
>
> When I recovered from my initial confusion I learned that certain important decisions had been made during the time I was away. First, because it was hard to interpret the results of an experiment when one knew nothing else about the subjects, the scheme had been adopted that all experimenters should use the same pool of subjects. Each worker could thus see his or her own findings in light of what the others had discovered. Second, the interpretations could be further enriched if one knew still more about the subjects, so it was decided to study them as individuals by means of interviews and tests. The third decision was the big one. If a lot of different workers were going to use each other's findings, there had to be a common language, a common scheme of variables, adequate to account for what was significant in personality. To accomplish such a purpose it was necessary to decide what really was significant, then work out a taxonomy to bring observation under orderly control. (White, 1981, p. 5)

Murray put the person at the center of inquiry. If the person is the center, then the investigator must become familiar with the person in many different contexts. Each person would be interviewed in depth and subjected to a wide assortment of data-gathering procedures. Different investigators should approach the person from different angles. The investigators should meet regularly to

Henry A. Murray

compare notes and synthesize their results on particular persons. Different investigators, therefore, made up what Murray called a *Diagnostic Council*. The diagnostic council entertained and synthesized information on the same person (subject) obtained from many different vantage points. So that different investigators would be able to communicate with each other, Murray devised an elaborate new nomenclature for personality processes. His comprehensive system provides a language for describing personality that remains highly influential today.

During the 1930s Murray headed a remarkable intellectual collaboration at the Harvard Psychological Clinic, bringing together scholars from academic psychology, psychoanalysis, anthropology, biology, and other disciplines to focus on personality study. Among the most noteworthy scholars who passed through the clinic in the years shortly before and after World War II were Robert White (Chapter 2 and this chapter), Donald MacKinnon, Jerome Frank, Saul Rosenzweig, R. Nevitt Sanford, Samuel Beck, M. Brewster Smith, Erik Erikson (Chapter 12),

Daniel Levinson (Chapter 12), Jerome Bruner (Chapter 13), and Silvan Tomkins (Chapter 13). The clinic became the setting for intensive, interdisciplinary, longitudinal studies of relatively normal college men. The overall aim of the research was to arrive at a complex understanding of the whole person. Murray's enterprise was especially remarkable in light of American psychology's commitment in the 1930s to the most rigorous and reductionistic methods and model of behavioral science. While American psychology glorified laboratory investigations of rats and pigeons, Murray sought to study real people in their natural habitats. While American psychology focused on the elementary laws of simple learning, Murray was fascinated with human motivation, especially as it functioned in complex and unconscious ways. While American psychology was decidedly suspicious of psychoanalysis, Jungian psychology, and anything smacking of nonorthodoxy, Murray invited scholars of all stripes, even some from the humanities, to partake in the heady intellectual discussions and analyses occurring at the clinic.

Murray himself looked to literature and mythology for inspiration in understanding human personality. He developed an abiding passion for the novels and short stories of Herman Melville, publishing in 1951 an enormously influential analysis of Melville's *Moby Dick* (Murray, 1951a). Drawing on Freud, Murray argues for an id/superego conflict between Captain Ahab and the mighty white whale. For Murray, Ahab represents the Devil and his forces of evil, psychologically transformed into the primitive forces of the id:

> [Melville] told [Nathaniel] Hawthorne that his book had been broiled in hell-fire and secretly baptized not in the name of God but in the name of the Devil. He named his tragic hero after the Old Testament ruler who "did more to provoke the Lord God of Israel to anger than all the Kings of Israel that were before him." King Ahab's accuser, the prophet Elijah, is also resurrected to play his original role, though very briefly, in Melville's testament. We are told that Captain Ahab is an "ungodly, god-like" man who is spiritually outside Christendom. He is a well of blasphemy and defiance, of scorn and mockery for the gods— "cricket-players and pugilists" in his eyes. Rumor has it that he once spat in the holy goblet on the altar of the Catholic Church at Santa. "I never saw him kneel," says Stubb. (Murray, 1951a, pp. 441–442)

And Moby Dick himself, the great white sperm whale, is an incarnation of the Protestant God, a mighty superego projected outward:

> Moby Dick is a veritable spouting, breaching, sounding whale, a whale who, because of his whiteness, his mighty bulk and beauty, and because of one instinctive act that happened to dismember his assailant, has received the projection of Captain Ahab's Presbyterian conscience, and so may be said to embody the Old

Murray was fascinated with the life and work of Herman Melville, author of *Moby Dick*. Here Gregory Peck is Captain Ahab in the movie version of Melville's classic.

Testament, Calvinistic conception of an affrighting Deity and his strict commandments, the derivative puritan ethic of nineteenth-century America, and the society that defended this ethic. Also, and most specifically, he symbolizes the zealous parents whose righteous sermonizings and corrections drove the prohibitions in so hard that a serious young man could hardly reach outside the barrier, except possibly far away among some tolerant, gracious Polynesian peoples. The emphasis should be placed upon that unconscious (and hence inscrutable) wall of inhibition which imprisoned the puritan's thrusting passions. "How can the prisoner reach outside," cries Ahab, "except by thrusting through the wall?" To me, the White Whale is that wall, shoved near to me. . . . I see in him outrageous strength, with an inscrutable malice sinewing it." As a symbol of a sounding, breaching, white-dark, unconquerable, New England conscience what could be better than a sounding, breaching, white-dark, unconquerable sperm whale? (Murray, 1951a, pp. 443–444)

The early work at the Harvard Psychological Clinic culminated in the publication of *Explorations in Personality* (Murray, 1938). In this landmark volume reporting the results of intensive studies of 50 college men, Murray and his colleagues envisioned a new agenda for what Murray came to call "personology." Murray defined personology as the scientific study of the whole person. Whereas psychologists of other persuasions studied discrete processes and functions of the human organism, the personologist was to operate on a more molar and synthetic level, casting his or her empirical eye upon the overall pattern of an individual's unique adaptation to the world. The personologist was to search for recurrent thematic constellations that characterized the individual as a whole. The molar approach to inquiry sacrifices a certain degree of precision and predictive power at the molecular level of particular behaviors and situations to achieve theoretical coherence at the level of the person.

Murray's System

A personological system must begin with a view of the person. What do you see when you see a person? Murray (1940) describes what *he* sees:

> Instead of seeing merely a groomed American in a business suit, travelling to and from his office like a rat in a maze, a predatory ambulating apparatus of reflexes, habits, stereotypes, and slogans, a bundle of consistencies, conformities and allegiances to this or that institution—a robot in other words—I visualize (just as I visualize the activity of his internal organs) a flow of powerful subjective life, conscious and unconscious; a whispering gallery in which voices echo from the distant past; a gulf stream of fantasies with floating memories of past events, currents of contending complexes, plots and counterplots, hopeful intimations and ideals. To a neurologist such perspectives are absurd, archaic, tender-minded; but in truth they are much closer to the actualities of inner life than are his own neat diagrams of reflex arcs and nerve anastomoses. A personality is a full Congress of orators and pressure groups, of children, demagogues, communists, isolationists, war-mongers, mugwumps, grafters, logrollers, lobbyists, Caesars and Christs, Machiavellis and Judases, Tories and Promethean revolutionists. And a psychologist who does not know this in himself, whose mind is locked against the flux of images and feelings, should be encouraged to make friends, by being psychoanalyzed, with the various members of his household. (1940, pp. 160–161)

Continued on p. 604

Rising, Falling, Fantasy, and Sex

Although he seemed like an ordinary guy when we first met him, Grope has turned out to be a pretty strange fellow, at least as far as his Icarian longings are concerned. We might suspect that, while he probably does not suffer from any serious pathology, this Harvard undergraduate is still a bit unusual, compared to most young men (and women). Clinical psychologist Robert May, however, would disagree. May (1980) maintains that the Icarian imagery manifested in Grope's fantasies, dreams, and autobiography are very common mythic features of the fantasies, dreams, and lives of *men* in general. Indeed, the theme of rising to glory and then falling into defeat may be a characteristically masculine pattern in narrative, and it can be contrasted to a characteristically feminine pattern in which falling *precedes* rising—a feminine pattern found in the myth of Persephone and Demeter.

Persephone and Hades

In the mythology of ancient Greece, Demeter is the goddess of fruit and fertility, and her beloved daughter is the innocent Persephone. While gathering flowers one day, Persephone is swallowed up by the earth and seized by Hades, lord of the underworld, who keeps her captive beneath the ground. Stricken with grief and rage, Demeter lashes out against the earth and causes a most dreadful and cruel famine. Zeus, king of the gods, eventually intervenes and forces Hades to return the lost daughter to her mother. Demeter and Persephone embrace in a joyful reunion. But Demeter soon learns that her daughter has made the mistake of tasting forbidden food while she was in captivity. Because of this, Persephone must return every year to the underworld, where she must live with Hades for about 4 months. These months, therefore, become the season of winter, during which Demeter mourns her lost daughter and the earth is barren and cold. But at the end of every winter, Persephone rises from the underworld, and the earth is blessed with the springtime abundance of fruit.

The stories of Icarus and Persephone are opposites in one fundamental way: Icarus goes up and then comes

Icarus

vation, sacrifice, and pain followed by enhancement, reward, and pleasure. Like Icarus, the man burns out early; like Persephone's return to Demeter, the woman's initial sacrifice is ultimately rewarded. It may even be the case, then, that men and women view the stories of their own lives in these two different ways.

May's notion is intriguing and thought-provoking. Indeed, one can imagine a number of different explanations for such a gender difference, if in fact it exists. For example, there may be something about the generally expected life course of males and females that engenders these different stories. Being a mother may be viewed, in part, as a self-sacrifice, a "going-down-under" that is eventually rewarded with freedom from child-rearing responsibilities when children grow up as well as the fulfillment of a "job (mothering) well-done." The prototypical life course for the man, on the other hand, may be seen as dominated by instrumental striving to "make it to the top," in many different senses, in the first half of life, followed by the realization, perhaps at midlife, that one is not going to make it. While these possibilities have been discussed by some observers of contemporary Western society (Giele, 1980; Jacques, 1965; Levinson, 1978; Sheehy, 1976), psychologist David Gutmann (1980) has suggested that such a sex difference may be even more striking in more traditional, non-Western societies. Gutmann suggests a cross-culturally valid pattern in which men

(crashing) down; Persephone goes down (to the underworld) and then comes back up. The Icarus myth is a story of enhancement followed by deprivation; the Persephone myth portrays deprivation followed by enhancement. May argues that this mythic distinction is reflected in different fantasies of men and women. In general, men construct imaginative narratives in which one first rises and is thus enriched, enhanced, or victorious and then falls and is finally impoverished, deprived, or defeated. By contrast, women construct narratives of depri-

Feature 11.A

rise to prominence in the first half of life but settle down into less active roles after midlife, while women rise to powerful positions in society only after midlife, once children have been raised.

Solid empirical evidence for May's claims, however, is not abundant, though there is some. May has developed a system for scoring TAT stories for patterns of Icarus and Persephone. Essentially, the system involves comparing the first half of a TAT story to the second half, with the expectation that men will show a generally positive first half followed by a negative second half and that women will show the opposite sequence. Research in support of May's claims about sex differences in TAT stories has been reported by Cramer and Carter (1978) and May (1966, 1975) with college students, and by Cramer and Hogan (1975) with older (age 11) but not younger (age 5) children. Other researchers, however, have failed to find meaningful sex differences on this TAT measure (Bernat, 1985; Fried, 1971; McClelland & Watt, 1968).

Continued from p. 601

There are many metaphors in this passage. Particularly powerful, however, is the metaphor of the personality as a "household" or "congress"—a collection of very different and often competing personages, like various *characters* in a narrative drama. To "know thyself," suggests Murray, is to become acquainted with the characters within oneself, to discern their disparate identities and the ways in which they interact with each other to produce the narrative of life. Thus, in Grope's life story a main character is Icarus. But there are doubtlessly many other characters in Grope's story, given that personality is extraordinarily complex and multifaceted. In the view of Elms (1987), Murray envisioned personality as a "fluid conglomerate" that is "constantly shifting, lacking a single stable core"; "individual combinations of components reign briefly and are then dethroned by new rulers" (pp. 3, 4). In other words, internal characters in the life story interact over time; certain protagonists capture center stage for a while, only to be replaced, eventually, by new heroes.

 A key idea in Murray's system is that *human lives are set in time.* The human being is "a time-binding organism," Murray wrote. Not merely a creature of the moment, the person can look beyond immediate stimuli in the environment and immediate urges within to act in accord with one's own view of the past or future:

> What he [the human being] does is related not only to the settled past but also to shadowy preconceptions of what lies ahead. Years in advance he makes preparations to observe an eclipse of the sun from a distant island in the South Pacific and, lo, when the

Do a behavior on this moment my mean nothing but over time...

moment comes he is there to record the event. With the same confidence another man prepares to meet his god. Man lives in an inner world of expected press (pessimistic or optimistic), and the psychologist must take cognizance of them if he wishes to understand his conduct or his moods, his buoyancies, disappointments, resignations. Time-binding makes for continuity of purpose. (Murray, 1938, p. 49)

The directedness of human lives becomes apparent over time. A given momentary behavior may seem meaningless in light of the current situation in which it is embedded. But with respect to the person's life over time, the behavior may be seen as part of a purposeful sequence of actions. Time is a defining feature of the person. Murray wrote that the "organism consists of an infinitely complex series of temporally related activities extending from birth to death" (1938, p. 39). The life cycle of the individual should, therefore, be the long unit of analysis for personology. While it is feasible to examine a person's life at a particular moment in time, one must never forget that such a venture represents an arbitrary selection of a part from the whole. One must never forget, therefore, that "the *history* of the organism *is* the organism" (p. 39). But what is a history? And how can an organism be a history? A history is a narrative reconstruction of how the past gave birth to the present, in light of an anticipated future. A *history* is a consensual interpretation of the past in light of what followed. It is a *story* about how events and changes *led up to* a subsequent state of affairs. Time, story, the person. Human beings are time-binding, story-telling creatures, whose lives themselves are situated in time, as time-binding narratives—past, present, future—to be interpreted by the personologist.

The smallest meaningful unit of time in human behavior is what Murray called the *proceeding*. A proceeding is a single episode of behavior abstracted from the temporal complexity of ongoing life. We may see it as a single instance of interaction between a person and his or her environment, an interaction long enough to initiate and complete "a dynamically significant pattern of behavior" (Murray, 1951b, p. 269). In that people may do more than one thing at a time, it is possible that at any given moment a person may be involved in more than one proceeding. For example, I may be talking to my mother on the phone while I am also flipping through a series of cards in my rolodex, searching for an address of one of my colleagues. I am involved in two proceedings at once. Murray argues that each proceeding is unique, and that a person's own uniqueness is a result in part of the cumulative effect of proceedings over time:

Every proceeding leaves behind it some trace of its occurrence—a new fact, the germ of an idea, a re-evaluation of something, a more affectionate attachment to some person, a slight improvement of a skill, a renewal of hope, another reason for despondency. Thus, slowly, by scarcely perceptible gradations—though sometimes suddenly by a leap forward or a slide backward—the person changes from day to day. Since his familiar associates also change, it can be said that every time he meets with one of them, both are different. In short, every proceeding is in some respects unique. (Murray & Kluckhohn, 1953, p. 10)

When you take all of the overlapping proceedings during a given period of time you have what Murray called a *durance*. Durances range from short scenes in a person's life (a visit to grandmother's house) to longer periods that may be viewed as "chapters" in one's evolving life story (living with grandmother between the ages of 3 and 5). A 30-year-old stockbroker, for example, may divide his life into four long durances: childhood, college years, early 20s while working at first job and living alone, and last four years while working for a large company and living with his wife. In this case, the transition to a new job and the marriage occurred around the same time in the man's life, marking a transition from the third to the fourth long durance or life chapter. A long durance may also be made up of what Murray called *serials*. A serial is a relatively long and directionally organized series of proceedings involving a particular life domain. Examples of serials are particular friendships, marriages, careers, etc. Each serial, therefore, organizes a sequence of life events having to do with a particular important area of personal investment. Serials may interact, such that the problems in, say, one's marriage may influence how well things go in one's career.

Remember that human beings are time-binding organisms. We act and interact in the present with views of the past and future in mind. As we survey the various serials in our lives, we evaluate our well-being and progress in each with respect to goals and aims for the future. Where is this relationship with my girlfriend going? Should I be taking more political science courses to prepare for law school? Do I need to lose some weight before I take that trip to Florida? We often develop particular programs for given serial domains, in order to meet future goals. Murray called these *serial programs*. A serial program is an orderly arrangement of subgoals stretching into the future for months or years such that achievement of the subgoals will assure progress toward some desired end state. Serial programs provide our strivings with direction and purpose. And they often connect up with fundamental psychological needs.

If the directional nature of human lives is to be known, then human behavior must be viewed in terms of proceedings, durances, serials, and serial programs organized in time. Time-binding provides lives with their characteristic direction and purpose. But what forces direct and select the ways in which human beings organize their lives and bind their time? Such forces, according to Murray, reside both within the organism and in the organism's environment. Within the organism are located the basic physiological and psychological **needs.** In the environment are located the various situational constraints and opportunities for need expression, or what Murray called **press** (plural = press). When a particular need repeatedly interacts with a particular press over an extended period of time, you have what Murray called a **thema.** Therefore, human motivation must be understood in terms of the interaction of needs and press to produce themas.

Murray defined a need as a

> construct (convenient fiction or hypothetical concept) which
> stands for a force (the physico-chemical nature of which is
> unknown) in the brain region, a force which organizes percep-
> tion, apperception, [interpreting perceptions], intellection
> [thinking], conation [striving], and action in such a way as to
> transform in a certain direction an existing unsatisfying situa-
> tion. (Murray, 1938, pp. 123–124)

Therefore, a need is the representation of a brain force that energizes, directs, selects, and organizes human perceiving, thinking, feeling, and striving. It operates to transform an unsatisfying situation into a more satisfying one. In this last regard, Murray's view of needs is similar to Freud's in that both held to the doctrine of *tension-reduction*. The tension for a particular need builds up over time and then is released through need-satisfying thought or behavior. However, Murray departed from Freud dramatically with respect to the kinds of human needs he identified. *Viscerogenic* needs are physiological wants and desires such as the need for air, water, and sentience (sleep). More relevant for personality, however, are the *psychogenic* needs, such as the needs for auton-omy, achievement, affiliation, dominance, play, order, and so on. Murray pro-posed 20 basic psychogenic needs, each of which exerts important effects on human behavior. Table 11.2 defines selected psychogenic needs from Murray's influential taxonomy.

At any given point in time, human behavior may be organized by a number of different viscerogenic and psychogenic needs operating simultaneously. But some needs are likely to be stronger or "prepotent" relative to others at a given time. Stronger or more urgent needs sometimes override weaker ones, as when a person's strong craving for dominance moves him to act in Machiavellian ways that violate his need for affiliation. In other instances, different needs may fuse, thereby working together to attain the same behavioral end. Playing softball with one's friends may, for example, satisfy the needs for affiliation, dominance, and play. Another important kind of relation among needs is *subsidiation*. A sub-sidiary need is one that operates in service of another. For example, a person may act in an aggressive way (revealing a strong aggressive need) in order to avoid pain (the need for harm avoidance). In this instance, the aggressive need serves the more encompassing need to avoid pain. The only reason the person desires to be aggressive is in order to remain safe.

Needs also interact with traits (Chapter 5). In general, the way in which a person achieves a goal may be partly determined by traits, such as extraversion-introversion. But the nature of the goal itself is more likely determined by needs. Traits and needs, therefore, fulfill different functions in the personality: needs establish goals; traits describe behavioral means whereby goals are met (McClel-land, 1981). In a sense, needs tell us *why* a person does what he does; traits tell us *how*.

 **Table 11.2**

Selected Psychogenic Needs From Murray (1938)

Need	Brief Definition
n Achievement	To accomplish something difficult. To master, manipulate, or organize physical objects, human beings, or ideas. To do this as rapidly and as independently as possible. To overcome obstacles and attain a high standard. To excel oneself. To rival and surpass others. To increase self-regard by the successful exercise of talent.
n Affiliation	To draw near and enjoyably cooperate or reciprocate with an allied other (an other who resembles the subject or who likes the subject). To please and win affection of a cathected object. To adhere and remain loyal to a friend.
n Aggression	To overcome opposition forcefully. To fight. To revenge an injury. To attack, injure, or kill another. To oppose forcefully or punish another.
n Autonomy	To get free, shake off restraint, break out of confinement. To resist coercion and restriction. To avoid or quit activities prescribed by domineering authorities. To be independent and free to act according to impulse. To be unattached, irresponsible. To defy convention.
n Dominance	To control one's human environment. To influence or direct the behavior of others by suggestion, seduction, persuasion, or command. To dissuade, restrain, or prohibit.
n Exhibition	To make an impression. To be seen and heard. To excite, amaze, fascinate, entertain, shock, intrigue, amuse, or entice others.
n Harmavoidance	To avoid pain, physical injury, illness, and death. To escape from a dangerous situation. To take precautionary measures.
n Nurturance	To give sympathy to and gratify the needs of a helpless object: an infant or any object that is weak, disabled, tired, inexperienced, infirm, defeated, humiliated, lonely, dejected, sick, mentally confused. To assist an object in danger. To feed, help, support, console, protect, comfort, nurse, heal.
n Order	To put things in order. To achieve cleanliness, arrangement, balance, neatness, tidiness, and precision.

Table 11.2 continued

Table 11.2 continued

Need	Brief Definition
n Play	To act for "fun" without further purpose. To like to laugh and make jokes. To seek enjoyable relaxation of stress. To participate in games, sports, dancing, drinking parties, cards.
n Sentience	To seek and enjoy sensuous impressions.
n Sex	To form and further an erotic relationship. To have sexual intercourse.
n Succorance	To have one's needs gratified by the sympathetic aid of an allied object. To be nursed, supported, sustained, surrounded, protected, loved, advised, guided, indulged, forgiven, consoled. To remain close to a devoted protector. To always have a supporter.
n Understanding	To ask or answer general questions. To be interested in theory. To speculate, formulate, analyze, and generalize.

Adapted from Murray (1938, pp. 152–226).

Just as the concept of "need" represents the significant determinants of behavior within the person so the concept of "press" represents the effective or significant determinants of behavior in the environmental situation. A press is a tendency in the environment to facilitate or obstruct the expression of a need. Wrote Murray, "the *press* of an object is what it can *do to the subject or for the subject*—the power that it has to affect the well-being of the subject in one way or another" (1938, p. 121). Such an "object" may indeed be a person or some feature of an interpersonal situation. Murray distinguished between *alpha* and *beta* press. An alpha press is made up of characteristics in the environment as they exist in reality or as objective inquiry discloses them. By contrast, a beta press is the person's subjective impression of those characteristics in the environment. Beta press, therefore, is always a matter of interpretation.

The full dynamics of human behavior are revealed in the interaction of needs and press, producing a thema. Imagine this example. A college student's strong need for order cannot be well expressed in her ceramics class, in which she is forced to work with materials that are sloppy and difficult to control. A thema develops whereby her inability to act in an orderly fashion initially produces a great deal of anxiety, which quickly gives way to an attitude of "don't worry about it, you don't have to be neat." The thema is the entire pattern of need/press interaction. In these kinds of unruly experiences (press), she experiences anxiety because her need for order cannot be expressed. But the anxiety eventually gives way to relaxation. Indeed, the relaxation response may be a function of the arousal of her need for play. Themas sometimes involve multiple needs and press.

Remember Murray's characterization of the person as a collection of "plots and counterplots." Between the lines of the plots and counterplots, certain relatively consistent motifs may be discerned *over time,* as the person's life unfolds in a narrative manner. These typically refer to recurrent desires, aims, and goals and the corresponding situations within which they are given expression. The operation of needs and press to produce themas over time provides direction and organization for the person's life. Needs, press, and thema come together so that the person can cut through the potential chaos of human existence, to produce and reveal subtle consistencies providing life with pattern and purpose.

Some lives are so dominated by a characteristic patterning of need, press, and thema that they may be said to exemplify a *unity-thema.* A unity-thema is a well-organized pattern of related needs and press that provides meaning to a large portion of the individual's life. Ultimately derived from infantile experience, a unity-thema may be viewed as the central, organizing motif of a person's life story. Grope's Icarus complex may qualify as one unity thema, though Murray preferred to call it a "complex." A unity-thema links the distant past with the present and anticipated future:

> A *unity-thema* is a compound of interrelated—collaborating or conflicting—dominant needs that are linked to press to which the individual was exposed on one or more particular occasions, gratifying or traumatic, in early childhood. The thema may stand for a primary infantile experience or a subsequent reaction formation to that experience. But, whatever its nature and genesis, it repeats itself in many forms during later life. (Murray, 1938, pp. 604–605)

The Study of Lives

Personology After World War II   The Second World War interrupted the program of research and theorizing at the Harvard Psychological Clinic as many researchers, including Murray himself, became involved in the war effort. Murray directed personality assessment programs for the Office of Strategic Services (OSS), a forerunner to the CIA. In order to choose the right men for sensitive positions in foreign espionage, Murray's staff designed a series of tests and assessment activities measuring a wide variety of abilities, competencies, traits, interests, opinions, and other personal characteristics assumed to predict human performance under oftentimes dangerous conditions. Reported in Murray's and the OSS Assessment Staff's (1948) *Assessment of Men*, the OSS assessment regimen was partly built on the principles of personology that Murray developed at the Harvard Psychological Clinic:

Assessment was "multiform," which is to say that the "whole person" was scrutinized in numerous and various settings. There were standardized tests of intelligence and mechanical comprehension; personal history forms and interviews; group problem-solving sessions, some of them "leaderless"; various measures of physical strength and endurance; stress tests, debating tests, even an indirect assessment of the candidates' need and tolerance for alcohol. Using a six-point rating scale, the staff rated the candidates on eleven variables (motivation for assignment, energy and zest, practical intelligence, emotional stability, and so on). Brief personality profiles were prepared for a culminating staff meeting at which final recommendations were hammered out. It was the [Harvard Psychological] Clinic in a nutshell, complete with ingenious procedures, an informal social setting, heavy staff involvement, an expanded Diagnostic Council, and a modified version of the concluding biographical narrative. (Robinson, 1992, p. 282)

After the war, Murray's brand of personology stimulated an interdisciplinary tradition of inquiry in the social sciences called *the study of lives*. The most prolific spokesman for this tradition has been Robert White (1948, 1952, 1963, 1972, 1981, 1987). You may remember from Chapter 2 that White (1959, 1960) exerted an important influence in psychoanalytic thinking about human motivation by introducing the concept of "competence." In books such as *The Study of Lives, Lives in Progress,* and *The Enterprise of Living,* White illustrated the value of Murray's program of personology by analyzing and bringing together intensive case studies of normal adults studied over time. Another important contributor to the study of lives was Donald MacKinnon (1962, 1963, 1965), who headed the Institute for Personality Assessment and Research (IPAR) at the University of California, Berkeley, and launched an influential series of studies of especially creative individuals.

Like Murray's original formulations for personology in the 1930s, the study of lives moved against the dominant tides in American academic psychology during the 1950s, 1960s, and 1970s. The study of lives requires a "generalist" approach to psychology whereby the investigator is able to draw from many different domains in order to construct a synthetic portrait of the human life in context. Yet American academic psychology became increasingly specialized after World War II and fewer and fewer psychologists cultivated a generalist perspective. Similarly, personality psychologists focused much of their energy after the war on the development and refinement of particular measures of carefully defined and specific constructs, such as particular personality traits. Psychology departments and research funding agencies tended to favor quantitative, construct-driven research over the more qualitative, person-driven approaches advocated by Murray, White, and other proponents of the study of lives. In the last 15 years, however, a number of trends in personality psychology and adjacent fields have come together to suggest that the study of lives is enjoying something of a renaissance. One small indication of this is the establishment of the Henry A. Murray Research Center for the Study of Lives, at Radcliffe College in 1979. Another is the founding of the Society for Personology in the early 1980s, a small organization dedicated to the principles of Murray's personology.

What are those principles? In organizing a collection of Murray's writings, Edwin Shneidman (1981) sets forth six general propositions that characterize Murray's personological approach and the tradition of studying lives that he and his followers developed.

1. *Personology (as well as the personologist) is shaped by numerous and various forces.* While many approaches to personality try to rule out competing explanations in order to arrive at the simplest and most consistent interpretation of an individual's behavior, Murray tended to welcome alternative formulations, suggesting that lives are shaped by a panoply of conflicting and inconsistent forces and factors. Recall his metaphor of the person as a "congress of orators and pressure groups." More than most other approaches, Murray challenges the psychologist to consider the person from many different standpoints, to consider forces existing in biology, society, culture, and history. This inclusive approach to inquiry is well illustrated in White's (1952, 1966, 1975) scrupulous analyses of the lives of three American adults—Hartley Hale, Joseph Kidd, and Joyce Kingsley. In each of these "lives in progress," White painstakingly documents the influence of biologically based drives and instincts, social motivations, constitutional endowments, learning patterns, psychosexual and psychosocial stages, values and beliefs, family dynamics, social structures, religion, and culture. Both Murray and White, furthermore, leave room for the extraordinary influence of random events and luck on the course of human life. In Murray's own life, a chance meeting with a fellow passenger on a ship directed Murray's attention to the writings of Melville, which piqued his curiosity about psychology and ultimately led him to personology. With so many forces to consider, therefore, it should not be surprising to learn that lives are difficult to understand and that behavior is sometimes impossible to predict.

2. *Personology is a complex, lifelong, never-ending enterprise.* As we have seen, a cardinal feature of Murray's approach is the emphasis on human lives situated *in time.* The history of the organism is the organism. In the terms of White (1952, 1972), lives are always "in progress"; living is a constantly evolving "enterprise." The personologist is likely to be frustrated in his or her attempts to get a final read on any given life in progress, in that personality continues to be constructed and reconstructed across the life-span. Any approach that attempts to fix the person in time—say, by focusing too closely on unchanging traits—fails to convey the dynamic quality of lives, in Murray's view.

3. *Personology focuses on the close examination of mental life—conscious and unconscious processes, including creativity.* Here Murray and the study of lives share affinities with psychoanalysis (Chapters 2 and 3), phenomenology (Chapter 8), and the cognitive movement in psychology (Chapters 9 and 10). Like

Freud and Jung, Murray wished to explore the deep gulf streams of the human unconscious. But like Sartre, he found human consciousness to be equally worthy of the psychologist's attention. For Murray, human lives are inherently creative, as people partially create themselves amidst the many forces and factors that shape that creation. But certain people are *more* creative than others. Either through the personalities they work to create or via their more tangible creative outpourings, individuals like Herman Melville reveal special gifts for transforming things and ideas into especially novel and useful combinations. In extraordinary creativity, boundaries between the conscious and unconscious are sometimes blurred. In some cases, a creative solution or configuration seems to spring forth spontaneously, like sea water shooting upward from the great whale's spout. One cannot fully control the creative urge. "The psyche is a *region* where creations may or may not flourish," but we cannot make them flourish, nor readily stop them from flourishing should they "wish" to flourish (Murray, 1959/1981, p. 322). One follows one's creative urges, even if this means that, like Melville, one sacrifices happiness and well-being along the way (Murray, 1959/1981; Robinson, 1992).

4. *Personology requires a multidisciplinary approach, as well as special strategies and techniques of investigation.* From the early days of the Harvard Psychological Clinic, through the OSS programs on assessing men, to the present-day interest among personologists in biography and narrative methods of analysis, psychologists who have followed Murray's agenda have tended to distrust the conventional methods of assessing personality dispositions, such as self-report questionnaires and rating scales. They have argued that personality must be examined instead from the standpoints of widely diverse methodologies, especially those that allow the subject to create imaginative responses. Murray's (1938) *Explorations* describes over twenty innovative methods of assessing personality, including the well-known Thematic Apperception Test (TAT), and measures of musical reverie, imaginal productivity, reactions to frustration, memories for failures, and autobiography. White's analyses of lives in progress employ interviews, autobiographical accounts, story responses to the TAT, intelligence tests, personality questionnaires, and many more. Murray suggested that a Diagnostic Council should synthesize the many different kinds of data on a single personality. Multiple researchers, therefore, might arrive at a coherent interpretation of a single case by pouring over a wide assortment of data and then discussing their different points of view.

5. *Personology studies living, historical, fictional, and mythological figures as well as special human "complexes."* As we saw in the case of Grope, Murray was not reluctant to borrow from ancient mythology to shed light on the shadowy workings of a contemporary life in progress. The "Icarus Complex" is one of a number of different portraits, inspired by literature and mythology, that have been composed by personologists in the Murray tradition. Murray (1962) himself described a malignantly narcissistic personality syndrome by detailing "The Personality and Career of Satan." McClelland (1963) delineated a "Harlequin Complex," to suggest that some women have historically held a strange fascination

with death—death viewed as a seducer. Drawing inspiration from the character of Ishmael in Melville's *Moby Dick,* Keniston (1963) painted a prophetic personological portrait of youthful alienation in the early 1960s. He wrote of a "prototypically alienated young man, separated partly by his own volition from the people, institutions, and beliefs which sustain most young men at his age in America; rejecting the forms by which most American men and women live; and condemned, like the Biblical Ishmael by his past and like Melville's Ishmael by his own temper, to live on the outskirts of society" (p. 42). For Murray, McClelland, Keniston, and others in this tradition, clues into the meanings of human lives may be found almost anywhere. Some of the richest sources are indeed outside science per se, in the great works of religion, mythology, and literature.

6.   *Personology encompasses a wide range of concerns, from specific practical issues to human values and urgent global problems.* Like Freud and Skinner, Murray held strong views on a wide range of issues inside and outside of psychology, and he translated some of those views into print. After World War II, he became increasingly convinced that the survival of humankind in a nuclear age depended on the establishment of a world democratic government and the universal adoption of an enlightened humanistic philosophy to augment impersonal science and replace authoritarian religious systems (Murray, 1960/1981). Although others who have followed in the tradition Murray began have been somewhat less vocal in their pronouncements about social policy, the study of lives has always endeavored to situate personality within the complex social and cultural forces of the day, implicitly examining how human lives are impacted by the social opportunities and constraints produced by national and international events and by social policies.

Murray's humanistic inclinations are also reflected in the metaphors and models for human growth and development that have come out of case research in the study of lives. For example, White (1975) describes five general growth trends in human personality, observable across different case studies of American men and women. In White's view, healthy personality development involves:

1.   *The stabilization of ego identity.* Over time, people should develop a clearer and more coherent understanding of who they are and how they fit into the adult world.
2.   *The freeing of personal relationships.* Traumatic and conflictual experiences from childhood may exert negative influences on relationships later on, but healthy development involves a freeing of the self from the negativities of the past and the positive engagement of others in mutual, collaborative, and intimate interpersonal relationships.
3.   *The deepening of interests.* Children and adolescents form short-term and superficial interests in many different areas, but as one moves into adulthood one should begin to focus interests and develop competence in those arenas of living that are deemed central to the self.

4. *The humanizing of values.* The direction of moral development is away from simple, authoritarian, and egocentric perspectives toward greater complexity in moral reasoning and greater tolerance for other points of view.

5. *The expansion of caring.* As people mature, their emotional investments in other people deepen considerably and they cultivate relationships of care and commitment for children, friends, lovers, spouses, and even casual acquaintances and fellow citizens of the world.

Science and the Single Case Since the time of Murray's *Explorations,* the study of lives has always been controversial because of its unswerving commitment to the psychology of the single case. While many personality psychologists would submit that "the whole person" is ideally the appropriate unit of analysis for personality studies, very few have taken this idea as literally as have Murray, White, and those other advocates of the study of lives who argue for "exploring personality the long way" (White, 1981, p. 3). To explore personality the long way, they maintain, one must focus inquiry on the single human life, examined over time through the **case study.** A case study is a "systematic presentation of information about the life of a single unit" (Runyan, 1982, p. 127). In personality psychology, the single unit is the individual life. But the case-study method has been used profitably, though sparingly, in many branches of psychology, from neurophysiology (Luria, 1972; Sacks, 1985) to social psychology (Festinger, Riecken, & Schachter, 1956; Janis, 1972). Outside of psychology proper, case studies have been extensively employed in anthropology (Agar, 1986; Kottak, 1979), sociology (Becker, 1970; Denzin, 1970; Thomas & Znaniecki, 1927), and political science (Allison, 1971; Redman, 1973). The "single unit" of analysis in an anthropological case study may be a particular culture or subculture; the sociologist may focus on a specific demographic group or organization; the political scientist may investigate a single political institution or event. In all of these instances, the scientist investigates in depth a single, specific phenomenon within its real-life context, synthesizing many different kinds of data drawn from multiple sources (Yin, 1984).

What is the proper role for the case study in personality psychology? Should it be the method of choice in personality research, as the study of lives suggests? Or is the case study too subjective and too limited by its focus on a single individual to be scientifically useful? The controversy over the case study in personality psychology has traditionally centered on the issues of (1) reliability, (2) internal coherence, (3) interpretive truth, (4) external validity, and (5) the problem of discovery versus justification in studying lives.

Critics of the study of lives have argued that the analysis of the single case is inherently unreliable. You cannot count on the results obtained, suggest many critics. A different observer of the case data could readily come up with a very different interpretation. The problem is particularly serious in psychoanalytic case studies, like Dora (Chapter 3), because of the many leaps in inference typically involved. Psychologists employing case studies often must analyze complex *qualitative data*—data that are not readily quantified (Kirk & Miller, 1986). The case-study researcher faces the triple task of (1) arriving at a high-level inference or interpretation about a critical aspect of the whole person's functioning by making sense of (2) an overabundance of unwieldy, qualitative data (3) in the absence of explicit rules for quantifying the data. The result, therefore, may be a highly *subjective* interpretation of the case with which another researcher, analyzing the same data in his or her own equally subjective way, may not agree.

The problem of low interjudge reliability in personality research is not limited to case studies, however. Scoring reliability tends to be a problem with qualitative data in general, such as interview conversations, reports of dreams, stories, and other open-ended response formats that are not readily quantified. In principle, a case study need not rely on qualitative data (Runyan, 1982) but can employ a wide range of data-gathering and data-interpreting methods, from the most quantifiable and reliable questionnaires and rating scales to the most qualitative and unreliable dream reports and interviews. Murray advocated a judicious blending of qualitative and quantitative measures, synthesized by a Diagnostic Council. Qualitative data, furthermore, may be translated into quantitative form through rigorous scoring rules and content-analysis systems (Krippendorff, 1980; Yin, 1984). Interviews may be videotaped and later subjected to objective content analysis to increase scoring reliability (Horowitz, 1979). To the extent that specific scoring rules for carefully recorded qualitative data are delineated and objectively employed, interjudge reliability will increase, and the personologist will be better able to count on the results and interpretations that are made. However, quantified scoring of qualitative data usually exacts a price, too. Important information can be lost because it cannot readily be translated into numbers.

A major criterion for judging the adequacy of a case study is the degree to which the psychologist's interpretation makes sense given the facts of the case. Does the analysis hang together? Is it consistent with what is known about the individual being studied? Is it *internally coherent?* A major problem with the criterion of internal coherence in evaluating case studies, however, is that many different explanations of a given case could conceivably be offered, each one equally internally coherent. As Campbell (1975) and others have pointed out, the human mind has an uncanny ability to make internal sense out of just about anything, even if that thing seems senseless at first. Thus, a given psychologist may have little trouble coming up with a coherent explanation for the facts in virtually any case study, after those facts have become known. Campbell warns that social scientists should beware of these *post hoc* explanations. He adds, however, that there is probably no way to get around them completely. Indeed, Campbell suggests that for certain questions about human behavior and experience, the case study may be "the only route to knowledge—noisy, fallible, and biased though it may be" (1975, p. 179). Therefore, personologists should evaluate carefully and critically their own interpretations of intensive case studies.

The personologist who seeks to formulate an internally coherent interpretation of an individual case usually proceeds according to an implicit **pattern-matching plan** (Bromley, 1986; Campbell, 1975; Runyan, 1982). Approaching the case data openly but with certain theoretical expectations that help orient his or her approach, the personologist looks for a *conceptual pattern* in the data that makes logical and psychological sense—the Icarus pattern, for example. The conceptual pattern that emerges gives rise to theoretical implications, which then function as a minitheory from which predictions can be generated and evaluated by looking at additional data in the case. Ideally, the personologist should function as a devil's advocate for his or her own interpretation, objectively testing the implications of that interpretation against the data of the case. The personologist should, in fact, invite alternative explanations of the same case from other investigators, and the scientific community should be able to evaluate rival interpretations of the same case against each other, in the way a judge or jury evaluates the cases made by opposing lawyers, to determine which one seems to be the best (Bromley, 1986; Campbell, 1975.)

What is a *true* interpretation in the study of the single life? While many people would say that truth means correspondence to the objective "facts" of the case, some investigators of human lives argue that, in addition to factual truth, case studies should be evaluated according to standards of *narrative truth* (Habermas, 1971; Schafer, 1981; Spence, 1982). Writes one scholar:

> Narrative truth can be defined as the criterion we use to decide when a certain experience has been captured to our satisfaction; it depends on continuity and closure and the extent to which the fit of the pieces takes on an aesthetic finality. Narrative truth is what we have in mind when we say that such and such is a good story, that a given explanation carries conviction, that *one* solution to a mystery must be true. Once a given construction has acquired narrative truth, it becomes just as real as any other kind of truth. (Spence, 1982, p. 31)

According to this view, the psychologist who seeks the true meaning of the single case must engage in **hermeneutics**—the art and science of interpreting texts (Ricoeur, 1970; Schafer, 1981; Steele, 1982). For centuries, hermeneutics was confined to sacred texts, such as the holy books of Christianity, Judaism, and Islam. In the last 150 years, however, certain social scientists such as Dilthey (1900) and Stern (in Allport, 1968) have brought hermeneutics into psychology and sociology, arguing that human lives and human societies are analogous to holy scriptures that hold within them many meanings. For Dilthey, hermeneutics involves a *dialogue* between investigator and text—be the "text" a holy book or another person—designed to decipher the many signs and symbols conveyed by the text. Through this highly subjective dialogue with the text emerge meaning and truth.

Interpreters of texts and single cases, therefore, often aim for narrative truth, argue Schafer and Spence. They evaluate their own interpretations according to the standards of "good story." A good story (1) is internally coherent, (2) makes for a continuous plot line in which early events "cause" or logically lead to later events, (3) embodies closure or a sense of things fitting into a final form, and

(4) is aesthetically pleasing (Spence, 1982). Yet, narrative truth is at best but one criterion of a "good" interpretation of a human life. Indeed, the interpretation of the single case can be profitably compared to the construction of scientific theories, as described in Chapter 1 of this book. Like a theory, an interpretation of a case study consists of a set of propositions designed to explain events. Scientists agree that, in principle, some theories are better than others, though they may disagree as to exactly which ones are better and worse. Scientists judge theories according to the criteria of (1) comprehensiveness, (2) parsimony, (3) coherence, (4) testability, (5) empirical validity, (6) usefulness, and (7) generativity (see Chapter 1). Similarly, in determining the "goodness" (rather than truth) of interpretations of the single case, the best that we can do may be to follow these same criteria. A good interpretation of the single case, therefore, may be one that (1) takes into consideration a comprehensive body of case information, (2) is simple and straightforward, (3) is internally coherent and consistent in the same way, perhaps, that a good story is, (4) provides hypotheses about human behavior that can be tested empirically, (5) is in accord with what empirical studies have documented to be valid, (6) is useful, and (7) generates new ideas.

But even if a personologist formulates an exceptionally illuminating interpretation of a single life in progress, what can the single case tell us about people in general? How can a single case be representative of any sample or population beyond itself? This is the problem of *external validity,* and because of this problem some psychologists dismiss case studies out of hand. They argue that experiments and large-scale correlation studies are more powerful research strategies because they allow the scientist to sample many different subjects drawn from a large population. These approaches also allow the researcher to compare and contrast different individuals, and "comparison is essential to science" (Carlsmith, Ellsworth, & Aronson, 1976, p. 39). The answer to poor external validity in the single case study, according to this view, is to sample many different individuals whose behavior and experience are studied in a more limited fashion, the general assumption being that many individuals together are more representative of a large population than is one.

In response to this criticism of case studies, some psychologists suggest that investigators collect multiple cases that can be compared and contrasted, gradually building up representative samples in given areas of investigation. Bromley (1986) maintains that personologists should eventually attempt to group and classify multiple cases, identifying key features of cases that distinguish them one from the other. In this way, certain exemplary cases could be chosen as prototypes that exhibit several distinguishing features of a given phenomenon. Other cases could then be compared and contrasted to the prototypes to determine the extent to which their features match those exhibited in the "ideal" or "pure" case.

Other proponents of the intensive study of the single case concede that single case studies can never be representative of large populations, but they counter that such cases need not be representative anyway. First of all, very few single experiments or correlation studies in personality psychology can truly claim to obtain fully representative samples. As we saw in Chapter 1, the scientist should strive to obtain the sample most appropriate for the given question to be addressed. The assumption that his or her sample is fully representative of a particularly robust population, however, may be based on the misguided belief that a single empirical study can establish truth once and for all, and for all time (Gergen, 1973).

Second, external validity refers to sampling of not only *subjects* but *situations* and *topics,* too (Brunswik, 1956; Dukes, 1965). Although a case study samples only one subject, it samples many different situations and topic areas in that subject's life. Conversely, an experiment or correlational study that samples many subjects probably samples only a few situations and a few areas of human functioning.

Third, generalization from a single case should be assessed in light of the soundness of the given analysis of that case rather than a prior notion about how "typical" a given case is. When a scientist makes a good interpretation of a case, he or she is justified in asserting that the analysis should hold for *comparable cases,* that is, cases of that sort (Mitchell, 1983). In case-study research, then, "the cases themselves come to define the population" (Bromley, 1986, p. 288). Grope, for example, might be an exemplar for the Icarus complex—a unity-thema to which a small number of other lives might also be assimilated. The extent to which Grope is a "prototypical" case against which psychologists could compare others may be determined by analyzing the entire family of cases within that genre.

Whatever one concludes about the external validity of any particular case study, certain general advantages of case studies over other research approaches that employ larger subject samples should be acknowledged. Unlike most other methods, "a case study allows an investigation to retain the holistic and meaningful characteristics of real-life events" (Yin, 1984, p. 14). A good case study may provide insight into a person's experience, clarifying what at first may have seemed incomprehensible; a good case study may effectively portray the person's social and historical milieu; and a good case study may deepen the reader's sympathy and empathy for the individual, while being vivid, evocative, and emotionally compelling to read (Runyan, 1982). (See Table 11.3)

Finally, in Chapter 1 we made an important distinction between two different ways of doing science. In the *context of discovery,* the scientist derives ideas, builds theories, and comes up with various hypotheses about a given phenomenon. In the *context of justification,* on the other hand, the scientist tests the validity of ideas, theories, and hypotheses that have already been derived. These two approaches to science build on each other as ideas are formulated, tested, and reformulated over time in a given area of scientific investigation. For which of these two contexts, then, is the single case appropriate? Should we derive (discover) theories through cases? Should we test (justify) theories though cases? Should we do neither? Should we do both?

A case study may be utilized to *disprove* a particular hypothesis that asserts that a given phenomenon is always true (Dukes, 1965). For instance, if scientists claim that event B always follows event A, then a single case in which B does not follow A would disprove the hypothesis. Unfortunately, there are very few such universal claims in personality psychology, and therefore this particular context-of-justification use of the case study is rare.

The prevailing view, then, is that cases are rarely useful in the context of justification, at least with respect to testing general propositions. Especially when

Table 11.3

Six Rules for Preparing a Psychological Case Study

1. The investigator must report truthfully on the person's life and circumstances and must be accurate in matters of detail.
2. The aims and objectives of the case study must be stated explicitly.
3. The case study should include an evaluation of the extent to which the stated aims and objectives have been achieved.
4. If the inquiry deals with material of deep emotional significance for the subject, then it must be carried out by someone trained and equipped to establish and manage a close, fairly long, and possibly difficult personal relationship.
5. The subject must be understood in the context of the specific historical, social, and symbolic world in which he or she lives.
6. The case report should be written in good plain English in a direct and objective way without, however, losing its human interest as a story. This can be done with sympathy and imagination and with due regard for high standards of evidence and argument.

From Bromley (1986, pp. 24–25).

it comes to justifying general cause-and-effect relationships, case studies are vastly inferior to experiments. As vehicles for discovery, however, case studies may be extremely useful, indeed much more useful than experiments, correlational designs, and most any other imaginable mode of investigation. As emphasized in Chapter 1, the context of discovery is a freewheeling realm in scientific inquiry. Ideas, hypotheses, and theories may be discovered in a multitude of ways, and among the most fruitful ways, as far as the personality psychologist is concerned, is the intensive study of the single case. Studies of lives in the tradition of Murray and White are gold mines for the derivation of ideas, hypotheses, and theories, which may then be put to the test via conventional scientific methodologies of justification.

Three Social Motives

The Thematic Apperception Test

Murray (1938) developed many methods for the study of personality, but the most popular and influential has probably been the Thematic Apperception, or TAT (Morgan & Murray, 1935; Murray, 1943). In the TAT, a person is presented with a series of ambiguous picture cues and is asked to compose, either verbally or in writing, a story in response to each. Like the Rorschach Inkblot Test (Chapter 3), the TAT is considered a "projective test," in that the person assumedly projects his or her own needs, wishes, conflicts, and so forth onto the ambiguous picture cue. But unlike the Rorschach, the TAT is less a test of perception—tapping into what the person "sees"—and more an exercise in imaginative *interpretation* of what one sees, or what Murray termed "apperception." The ambiguous picture cue is merely a stimulus designed to put into motion the process of constructing an imaginative narrative response (Lindzey, 1959). In Murray's view, such narrative responding reveals partially hidden themes of the personality, especially those concerning basic needs, conflicts, and complexes.

Murray (1943) provided rough guidelines for interpreting the stories told in response to TAT pictures. He believed that the psychologist should first identify the *hero* in the story—usually the main character or the character who most resembles the storywriter. Second, the psychologist should consider the hero's *motives, trends, and feelings*. Careful attention should be paid to story content that indicates psychogenic needs: a story in which the main character is trying to succeed in a difficult task would indicate a strong *n* Achievement; another story in which the character seeks friendship with others would suggest the affiliation motive. Third, the psychologist should note the *forces in the hero's environment* that impinge upon or provide opportunities for need-expression. Murray believed that a TAT story may reveal as much about how a person perceives the world as it does about internal needs. Fourth, the *outcomes* of stories may indicate the extent to which the storyteller believes that his or her own needs can be fulfilled in daily life. In this regard, Murray suggested that the psychologist keep track of the ratio of happy to unhappy story endings. Fifth, the psychologist should document the recurrent combinations of particular needs and particular environmental situations (what Murray termed *press*) across the stories. A need/press combination constitutes a simple *thema*. Sixth, *interests and sentiments* may appear in the story content. The psychologist may be able to obtain information on the storyteller's feelings about particular kinds of people (for example, authority figures, older women, children) or about particular aspects of the environment (such as politics, religion, the natural world). Regardless of how the psychologist interprets the TAT, however, Murray emphasized that "the conclusions that are reached by an analysis of TAT stories must be regarded as good 'leads' or working hypotheses to be verified by other methods, rather than as proved facts" (1943, p. 14).

Because there are so many ways of using and interpreting the TAT, it is virtually impossible to pass judgment on the measure's overall reliability and validity. While many clinicians express a great deal of faith in the TAT's clinical usefulness, some reviews of the test have provided mixed results (Eron, 1950; Holt, 1978; Rosenwald, 1968). Lindzey (1952) has cast doubt on some of the interpretive assumptions first laid out by Murray, such as the belief that the person projects needs onto a single hero in the story. Zubin, Eron, and Schumer (1965) suggest that TAT responses are more subject to conscious control than many clinicians suspect. As do most other investigators, these investigators caution against relying too heavily on the TAT for individual clinical diagnosis. On the other hand, they suggest that the measure is a useful indicator of general interests, motives, and areas of emotional disturbance, and can be used quite profitably in personality research.

The most profitable use of the TAT is to view it as an indicator of psychogenic needs, or **motives.** Three such motives have been studied in great detail: achievement, power, and intimacy. In considering each of these three motives, we will focus on the research tradition fathered by personality psychologist David C. McClelland. Reconceptualizing Murray's notion of "need," McClelland defines a motive as a recurrent preference or readiness for a particular quality of experience, which energizes, directs, and selects behavior in certain situations. The achievement motive, therefore, refers to the quality of human experience entailed in *doing better;* the power motive refers to *having impact;* and the intimacy motive denotes *feeling close.* McClelland (1980) argues that motives lie outside of a person's conscious awareness and cannot, therefore, be accurately assessed through conscious self-report. By sampling the everyday stream of imaginative thought, the TAT enables the researcher to find central themes that may indicate unconscious motives.

Achievement Motivation

My best friend, a research chemist who was my roommate in college, has a high **achievement motive.** He is strongly motivated to perform better—better in relation to other people and better in relation to personal standards of excellence—in all aspects of life. He strives with great persistence to be the best in his professional field. He is a fierce competitor on the basketball court. He even plays board games with a vengeance. More important, my friend's estimation of his own well-being depends strongly on the extent to which he is successful in different life realms. Although, like virtually all people, his mind covers diverse topics in a normal day, my friend spends more time than most thinking about achievement, often comprehending new events and environments as either opportunities for or obstacles to successful personal performance. A person whose achievement motivation is significantly lower than my friend's, on the other hand, is likely to be less preoccupied with achievement concerns. His or her conscious thought may run in different thematic directions, perhaps more in the direction of power, intimacy, or some other motive or goal.

Measuring the Achievement Motive   David McClelland and John Atkinson pioneered the use of the TAT to assess individual differences in achievement motivation (Atkinson, 1958; Atkinson & Birch, 1978; McClelland, Atkinson, Clark, & Lowell, 1953). The most important innovation of their approach was the derivation and validation of an objective, reliable, and quantitative system to score TAT stories for achievement motivation. In their original derivation studies, McClelland and Atkinson asked college students to write short TAT stories under various

David McClelland

laboratory conditions. In one condition, the students were first administered a series of cognitive tasks (such as unscrambling words) and then told that their performance on the tasks would be an indication of their general intelligence and leadership ability. It was assumed that such instructions would temporarily *arouse* achievement thoughts and feelings in these subjects, and that these thoughts and feelings would be projected onto the stories written on the TAT, administered immediately following the task. In another (neutral) condition, students were administered the same tasks but were told that the tasks were newly developed and not likely to be valid measures of much of anything. It was assumed that these subjects would be less aroused with respect to achievement strivings than the subjects in the first group.

McClelland and his colleagues detected a number of consistent content differences between the groups. Students in the arousal group tended to write more stories involving characters striving to do better, compared to students in the neutral group. Subsequent comparisons from different studies and various refinements produced a content scoring system for the TAT. The system is made up of the particular content themes that consistently differentiated between stories written under achievement arousal and under neutral conditions. The themes involve the story characters' behaviors, attitudes, and feelings about task performance (Table 11.4).

Table 11.4

Selected TAT Scoring Categories for Achievement Motivation

Category	Description	Examples
Achievement Imagery	A character in the story wants to perform better either by (1) outperforming someone else, (2) meeting an internal standard of excellence, (3) doing something unique, or (4) being involved in a long-term achievement project.	"Mary decided she would win first prize in the gymnastics competition." "Robert had spent 8 years practicing for tonight's performance."
Anticipating Success	Someone in the story thinks about or anticipates reaching the achievement goal.	"They feel certain they will be able to pull off the theft and become great thieves."
World Block	An obstacle in the environment blocks achievement.	"They will never be successful because they do not have the right equipment."
Negative Feelings	The person is discouraged when the achievement goal is not reached.	"Cindy failed the examination, and now she is very depressed."

Sources: McClelland et al. (1953) and McClelland & Steele (1972). These are 4 out of 11 categories in the achievement-motive scoring system. For each category, the scorer determines "presence" (score 1 point) or absence (0 points) in each story.

Although the achievement-motive scoring system was derived by examining group differences in narrative content, the system has proven extremely sensitive and valuable as an index of *individual differences* within groups. In a typical individual-differences study, a large number of people are administered the TAT under standardized *neutral* conditions. The subjects' TAT stories are then scored by trained coders according to the system referred to in Table 11.5. The results typically reveal a normal distribution in the sample, with achievement-motive scores ranging from high to low. It is assumed that each person's "natural" level of achievement motivation will be expressed in TAT stories written under such neutral, nonarousing conditions.

Table 11.5

Selected Correlates of High Achievement Motivation

High aspirations but moderate risk taking.
Preference for situations where personal responsibility can affect results.
Tendency to take personal credit for success but blame others or the situation for failures.
Cheating and/or bending the rules in order to reach a desired goal in an efficient and expeditious manner.
Penchant for travel.
Self-control, inhibition, and delay of gratification.
Preference for somber colors and formal fashion.
Extended future time perspective.
Upward social mobility and higher educational attainment.
Entrepreneurial activity and innovation.
Success in business.
Being raised in a family in which parents set high standards for performance.
Scheduled feeding during infancy and relatively stringent toilet training.

Note: Much of the research on achievement motivation has focused exclusively on men. While the relatively few studies investigating correlates of achievement motivation in women are generally consistent with results for men, there are some areas (such as entrepreneurship and risk taking) in which virtually no data on women have been obtained (Stewart & Chester, 1982).

Sources: McClelland (1985), Winter & Carlson (1988).

A substantial empirical literature suggests that people who score high on TAT achievement motivation behave in different ways than people who score low, supporting the construct validity (Chapter 5) of the TAT measure. For instance, people high in achievement motivation tend to prefer and show high performance in tasks of moderate challenge that provide immediate feedback concerning success and failure; they tend to be persistent and highly efficient in many kinds of performance, sometimes cutting corners or cheating in order to maximize productivity; they tend to exhibit high self-control and a future time perspective; and they tend to be restless, innovative, and drawn toward change and movement (Atkinson, 1957; Atkinson & Raynor, 1978; Crockett, 1962; Feather, 1961; Heckhausen, 1967; McClelland, 1961, 1985; Mischel, 1961; Mischel & Gilligan, 1964; Winter & Carlson, 1988). Some of the best-established findings in this regard are summarized in Table 11.5.

Careers in Business Young adults who are high in achievement motivation tend to be drawn to careers in business. In one study, college men with a high need for achievement manifested patterns of personal interests and values very similar to those expressed by stockbrokers, real estate agents, advertisers, merchandise buyers, and factory managers (McClelland, 1961). In another study, men with high achievement motivation in college tended to become employed in small businesses years later (McClelland, 1965). McClelland has argued that business is a good match for the achievement motive, because business requires that people take moderate risks, assume personal responsibility for their own performance, pay close attention to feedback in terms of costs and profits, and find innovative ways to make products or provide services. These hallmarks of **entrepreneurship** precisely characterize the behavior and attitudes of people high in achievement motivation (McClelland, 1985).

Among men, then, high achievement motivation is associated with a number of indexes of business success and productivity. Scoring high in the achievement motive, however, does *not* guarantee that one will reach the highest echelons of all large businesses and corporations. Andrews (1967) followed the careers of executives in a large company over 3 years and found that those with high achievement motivation received a larger number of promotions than those scoring low in achievement motivation. However, this was true only at an "achievement-oriented" firm, in which "doing well" was the major criterion of advancement. In another firm run by an authoritarian owner, achievement motivation was unrelated to promotions. McClelland and Boyatzis (1982) found that achievement motivation in managers at the time of their entry into the American Telephone and Telegraph (AT&T) Company was associated with promotion up to Level 3 in the company after 16 years, but not above that point. The managerial positions at Level 4 and above may have required skills and motives less associated with "doing better" and having more to do with "influencing people." McClelland has argued that, in large hierarchical organizations, high achievement motivation is likely to be instrumental in career advancement only up to a certain point. At the highest levels of prestige and influence, strong *power* motivation may prove more valuable.

Only a few studies have examined achievement motivation and career advancement in women (Stewart & Chester, 1982). Baruch (1967) and Stewart (1975) found that college women scoring high in achievement motivation tend to pursue challenging career patterns. Bloom (1971) showed that adolescent girls aiming to combine career and family are higher in achievement motivation than girls who do not plan to pursue a career. In a 14-year longitudinal study, Jenkins (1987) found that women with high achievement motivation in college tend to pursue careers in teaching, including college teaching. In Jenkins' study, professors and businesswomen showed larger increases in TAT achievement motivation over 14 years—the span from college through their mid-30s—than did women otherwise employed.

The Achieving Society   One of the more intriguing and controversial applications of McClelland's approach to achievement motivation is the analysis of *societal and historical differences*. McClelland (1961) has argued that entire societies and historical epochs differ in overall achievement motivation. While some societies actively promote achievement values and entrepreneurship, others appear less motivated to do so; in addition, a particular society's preoccupation with achievement may wax and wane over time. Such societal and historical differences should correspond to economic growth and ultimately to the rise and decline of entire states, regions, or peoples.

How might a personality psychologist measure societal differences in achievement motivation? McClelland answers that the procedure is virtually identical to that used with individuals: imaginative stories should be coded for achievement themes. Selected passages from a society's representative folk tales, myths, textbooks, or even its popular literature can be coded as if they were discrete TAT stories in order to provide a rough estimate of overall achievement motivation in a society at a particular time in history. McClelland assumes that these narrative expressions reflect pervasive cultural assumptions and values. Folk tales, literature, and societal myths are integral components of what we termed, in Chapter 7, a culture's *projective system.*

In his best-known book, *The Achieving Society,* McClelland (1961) reports a study in which he collected second- and fourth-grade readers (elementary school textbooks) published from 1920 to 1929 from 23 different countries and scored selected passages for achievement themes. McClelland found that achievement motive themes in children's readers in the 1920s were positively correlated with his index of economic growth, even when other societal factors, such as differences in natural resources, were taken into consideration. In other words, economic growth between 1929 and 1950 was much more pronounced in those countries showing a strong emphasis on achievement in children's readers in the 1920s (such as Turkey, Israel, and India) than in countries whose children's readers showed relatively few achievement themes (such as Italy, Belgium, and Algeria). The explanation for the linkage is presented in Figure 11.1. A society's books for children mirror prevalent

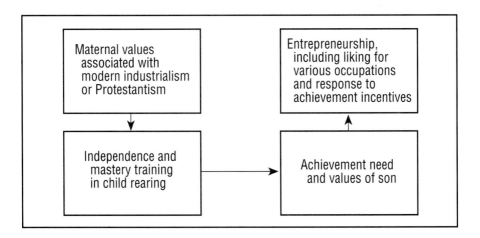

Figure 11.1

Relations Among Maternal Values, Child-Rearing Practices, Achievement Motivation, and Entrepreneurship in Society.

Adapted from McClelland, 1961, p. 58.

cultural values that are inculcated in children through various socialization processes, such as schooling and child training. Socialization for achievement encourages children to be masterful and independent, to plan for the future, to take moderate risks, and to value efficiency and gradual improvement or growth. Such training likely increases the achievement motivation of young boys and girls, who eventually develop a preference and proclivity for entrepreneurship as adults, which ultimately makes for greater economic growth.

Another index of a society's economic vitality is the proliferation of inventions and innovations. Figure 11.2 presents the rather striking findings from a

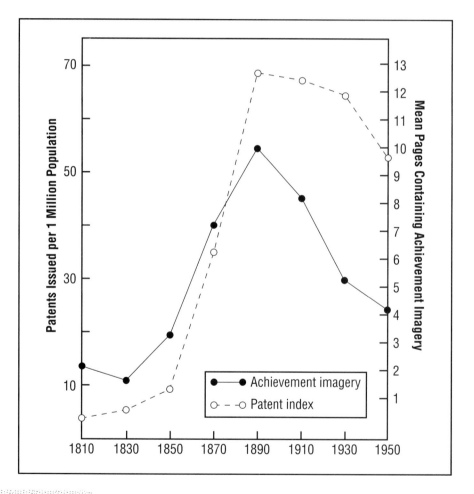

Figure 11.2

Relations Between Achievement Imagery in Children's Readers and Number of Patents Issued in the United States Between 1810 and 1950.

From de Charms & Moeller, 1962, p. 139.

study of the relationship between achievement motivation expressed in children's readers and the number of patents per capita issued to inventors over a period of 140 years in the United States (de Charms & Moeller, 1962). The rise and decline in the number of U.S. patents issued between the years 1810 and 1950 neatly parallels the rise and decline of achievement imagery in American children's readers. A similar relationship was discovered between achievement imagery in English popular literature and the amount of coal imported by England during the years 1550 to 1800. Again, changes in collective achievement motivation predict economic growth. A positive relation between achievement motivation and economic growth can be seen in non-Western, preliterate societies, as well. Among 39 preliterate tribes, 75% of those with high achievement content in their folktales were characterized as having at least some full-time entrepreneurs, as contrasted with only 38% of the tribes with less amounts of achievement imagery in their folktales.

McClelland's impressive findings on collective achievement motivation are not without their detractors. Some sociologists and historians object to McClelland's attempts to "reduce" complex societal phenomena to the workings of a single personality variable. Other critics have claimed that while McClelland's results are worthy of attention, they are not as statistically robust as his rather grand interpretations would suggest. In this regard, McClelland's more recent (1975, 1985) attempts to predict and explain social reform, civil unrest, and even war in terms of collective levels of achievement, power, and intimacy/affiliation motivation strike some readers as unconvincing. Finally, some critics have pointed to the mixed success that other researchers have had in replicating McClelland's findings, especially for more recent historical periods. While some studies support McClelland's claim for a strong positive linkage between collective achievement motivation and economic growth in nations since 1950 (Tekiner, 1980), others do not (Beit-Hallahmi, 1980).

Power Motivation

The **power motive** is a recurrent preference for having an impact on other people. People high in power motivation strive to wield power and to feel stronger, more masterful, more influential than others. Like the achievement motive, this recurrent desire for power energizes, selects, and directs human behavior in predictable ways. Also like achievement motivation, individual differences in the power motive are assessed through objective content analysis of TAT stories.

Veroff (1957) and Uleman (1966) designed early TAT scoring systems for the need for power, but the most popular system in recent research is the one developed and validated by David G. Winter (1973). Like McClelland and Atkinson on achievement, Winter derived the coding system for power motivation through comparing stories written by people under power-arousal and neutral conditions. Among the power-arousal conditions employed to derive the power-motive scoring system, Winter sampled TAT stories written by (1) candidates for student government office awaiting the results of voting, (2) subjects about to enact the powerful role of "psychological experimenter," (3) students who had seen a film of President John F. Kennedy's inauguration, and (4) students who had witnessed a multimedia presentation of inspirational speeches, such as Winston Churchill's speech on the evacuation of Dunkirk in World War II and excerpts from Shakespeare's *Henry V.* For "neutral" conditions, subjects wrote TAT stories in standard classroom settings. Table 11.6 describes a few thematic categories in Winter's (1973) scoring system for power motivation. Table 11.7 lists a few ways in which people high in power motivation differ from those scoring low on the motive.

 Table 11.6

Selected TAT Scoring Categories for Power Motivation

Category	Description	Examples
Power Imagery	A character in the story desires to have impact or to make an impression on others. This may be accomplished through strong, forceful actions (aggression), giving unsolicited help, or trying to control, persuade, or impress. Alternatively, a character may elicit strong emotions in others, or express concern about personal reputation.	"Barbara pushed the intruder aside and rescued the baby." "Bob tried to persuade the audience that he was right" "He is worried that his son will disgrace him."
Increased Prestige	The setting of the story or a character is described in ways that increase prestige or position.	"Ed was elected senator for the state of Maine."
Lower Prestige	The setting of the story or a character is described in ways that decrease prestige or position.	"He was a two-bit conman whom even the inmates scorned."
Effect	A power action produces a major, striking effect.	"The world was shocked by her bold words and brazen acts."

Sources: McClelland & Steele (1972), Winter (1973)

Table 11.7

Selected Correlates of High Power Motivation

Holding elected offices.

Liking for careers in which one directs the behavior of individuals in accordance with preconceived plans and with the use of positive and negative sanctions (careers such as executive, teacher, and psychologist).

Active, forceful, and influential in small groups.

Effective organizational leader.

Accumulation of prestige possessions, such as fancy cars and major credit cards.

Taking large risks in order to gain visibility.

Agentic, assertive style of friendship which emphasizes self-display and helping the other.

Getting into arguments.

Writing letters to the newspaper.

Somewhat negative self-image.

Prone to impulsive and aggressive behavior (men only).

Precocious and exploitative sexual activity (men only).

Instability in romantic relationships (men only).

Being raised in a family in which parents were relatively permissive concerning sexual behavior and aggression.

Sources: McAdams (1985 b), McClelland (1985), Stewart & Chester (1982), Winter (1973), Winter & Carlson (1988).

Leadership   Because people high in power motivation desire to have an impact on others, a number of researchers have explored the ways in which such impact is accomplished. Fodor and Smith (1982) investigated how students high in power motivation direct the behaviors of others in group decision making. Forty groups containing five students each met to discuss a business case study that concerned whether a company should market a new microwave oven. In each group, a leader was appointed. Based on a prior administration of the TAT, half the leaders scored extremely high on the power motive and half scored extremely low. In addition, half of the groups were given the opportunity to win a group reward for superior performance (in order to build "high group cohesiveness"), and half were offered no reward ("low group cohesiveness"). Each group member was given a fact sheet containing information that could be shared with the group during discussion.

Three major dependent variables were assessed in Fodor and Smith's study: (1) the number of *facts* from the sheet that each person shared with the group during discussion, (2) the number of alternative *proposals* for marketing the microwave considered by the group, and (3) the level of *moral concern* evidenced by the group, which was determined by a rating of the extent to which the group discussed such issues as the possible harmful effects of microwave radiation on people's health and the ethical propriety of various marketing strategies. Those groups in which the leader was high in power motivation tended to offer fewer facts and proposals and to show less moral concern, compared to groups headed by a low-power leader (Table 11.8). The level of group cohesiveness, on the other hand, did not influence the results. The authors interpreted these findings to mean that leaders high in power motivation encourage what Janis (1972) calls *group-think*—a form of hasty decision making characterized by diffusion of responsibility, failure to consider long-term ramifications, and the domination by a single strong leader whose opinion generally goes unchallenged.

 Table 11.8

Average Number of Facts and Proposals and Mean Moral Concern Ratings of Discussion Groups

| Level of *n* Power in President | Level of Group Cohesiveness | | | | | |
| | Low | | | High | | |
	Facts	Proposals	Moral Concern	Facts	Proposals	Moral Concern
Low	17.5	4.8	1.7	16.3	4.4	1.4
High	14.2	4.0	0.9	14.8	3.2	1.1

From Fodor & Smith (1982, p. 183)

A large number of studies have shown that people who perennially adopt strong leadership roles and/or rise to positions of high influence tend to score relatively high in power motivation (McAdams, Rothman, & Lichter, 1982; McClelland & Boyatzis, 1982; McClelland & Burnham, 1976; Winter, 1973). The most intriguing line of research in this regard is probably Winter's (1987; Donley & Winter, 1970) studies of American presidents. Winter has analyzed the published inaugural addresses of virtually all the American presidents, going back to George Washington, for achievement, power, and intimacy motivation. Winter has argued that, despite the help of speech-writers and the influences of various sociohistorical forces and events, the motivational imagery contained in these major speeches partially reflects the president's own personality.

Table 11.9 presents the standardized scores for the three motives for each inaugural address coded in Winter (1987). Presidents scoring particularly high in power motivation include Franklin D. Roosevelt (1933), Harry Truman (1949), John Kennedy (1961), and Ronald Reagan (1981). Especially low in power motivation are Warren Harding (1921) and Calvin Coolidge (1925). Richard Nixon (1969) and Jimmy Carter (1977) both score very high on achievement motivation. Winter correlated motive scores with various ratings of the presidents made by historians and political scientists. Power motivation was positively associated with ratings of "presidential greatness" ($r = +.40$) and number of historically significant decisions made ($r = +.51$). In other words, those presidents who have been rated as especially forceful and influential by political scholars tended to be the same ones whose inaugural addresses indicated especially high levels of power motivation. In addition, presidents high in power motivation were also more likely to lead the United States into war ($r = +.52$).

Love and Health   What about the personal lives of people high in power motivation? Some research suggests that *men* high in the need for power experience numerous difficulties in romantic relationships with women. Stewart and Rubin (1976) conducted a longitudinal study of 63 dating couples living in the Boston area. At the time of the initial testing, high power motivation in males was significantly associated with greater expressed dissatisfaction with the relationship on the part of both members of the couple and greater anticipation of future serious problems among the men. Two years later, 50% of the couples in which the man was high in power motivation had broken up and only 9% had married. In those couples in which the male was low in power motivation, only 15% had broken up and 52% had married over the 2-year span. Additionally, males high in power motivation were more likely to report that during the 2 years immediately preceding the start of this dating relationship, they had been seriously involved in a romantic relationship that eventually terminated. Stewart and Rubin concluded that men high in power motivation showed marked instability in romantic relationships, moving from one serious involvement to another in relatively rapid succession. Bolstering their claims are the findings of Winter (1973) in which power motivation among men was positively associated with the number of sexual partners and frequency of intercourse.

Table 11.9

Motive Imagery Scores of American Presidents' Inaugural Addresses, 1789–1981

President	Date	Standardized Motive Scores		
		Ach	**Int/Aff**[a]	**Pow**
Washington, George	1789	39	54	41
Adams, John	1797	39	49	42
Jefferson, Thomas	1801	49	51	51
Madison, James	1809	55	51	57
Monroe, James	1817	57	46	51
Adams, John Quincy	1825	48	51	37
Jackson, Andrew	1829	43	47	45
Van Buren, Martin	1837	42	48	40
Harrison, William Henry	1841	32	41	40
Polk, James	1845	33	41	50
Taylor, Zachary	1849	53	53	41
Pierce, Franklin	1853	49	44	50
Buchanan, James	1857	46	47	42
Lincoln, Abraham	1861	36	45	53
Grant, Ulysses	1869	56	47	36
Hayes, Rutherford	1877	51	48	48
Garfield, James	1881	46	35	49
Cleveland, Grover	1885	53	46	63

Table 11.9 continued

Table 11.9 continued

President	Date	Standardized Motive Scores		
		Ach	**Int/Aff[a]**	**Pow**
Harrison, Benjamin	1889	37	45	45
McKinley, William	1897	47	41	46
Roosevelt, Theodore	1905	62	38	38
Taft, William Howard	1909	44	38	58
Wilson, Woodrow	1913	66	49	53
Harding, Warren	1921	48	57	42
Coolidge, Calvin	1925	44	46	45
Hoover, Herbert	1929	68	45	48
Roosevelt, Franklin	1933	53	44	61
Truman, Harry	1949	56	65	78
Eisenhower, Dwight	1953	43	57	49
Kennedy, John	1961	50	85	77
Johnson, Lyndon	1965	55	59	49
Nixon, Richard	1969	66	76	53
Carter, Jimmy	1977	75	59	59
Reagan, Ronald	1981	60	51	63

[a]"Int/Aff" refers to intimacy/affiliation motivation. Although intimacy and affiliation are two separate motives with separate TAT scoring systems, they do overlap somewhat in that both refer to warm relationships. Intimacy motivation is the desire to share what is innermost with another in a warm and communicative relationship (McAdams, 1980); affiliation motivation is the desire to establish, maintain, or restore positive-affect relations (Atkinson, Heyns, & Veroff, 1954). In this particular study, Winter combined the two systems to assess motivational imagery concerning "warm relationships" in presidential speeches.

From Winter (1987, p. 198).

David Winter

Well-educated *women* high in power motivation tend to marry successful men (Winter, McClelland, & Stewart, 1981). Further, Veroff (1982) reports that power motivation in women is positively associated with marital *satisfaction*. While high-power women, therefore, tend to report happy marriages, men high in power motivation show a higher divorce rate (McClelland, Davis, Kalin, & Feld, 1972) and greater degree of marital *dissatisfaction* (Veroff & Feld, 1970). At the root of the high-power man's apparent dissatisfaction with and instability in romantic heterosexual relations may be a latent fear of women and the control they may exert. Slavin (1972) has shown that men high in power motivation express more themes of "feminine evil" in their fantasies than do men lower on the motive. These themes include females harming men through physical contact, females exploiting men, females rejecting men, females proving unfaithful in relationships, and females triumphing over men. In this regard, Winter and Stewart (1978) report that men high in power motivation, when asked to draw pictures of women, produce sometimes frightening and bizarre sketches with exaggerated sexual characteristics.

In the area of health, recent studies by McClelland and his colleagues suggest a possible association between power motivation and susceptibility to disease (McClelland, 1979; McClelland, Alexander, & Marks, 1982; McClelland, Davidson, Floor, & Saron, 1980; McClelland & Jemmott, 1980; McClelland, Ross, & Patel,

1985). The association, however, seems fairly complex. McClelland (1979) has argued that a strong need for power increases a person's vulnerability to illnesses of various sorts *if* the person's need for power is inhibited, challenged, or blocked. Especially vulnerable are individuals who show *all* of the following characteristics: (1) high power motivation, (2) low intimacy motivation, (3) high self-control (sometimes called "activity inhibition" and suggesting a tendency to "block" or "inhibit" one's own expression of power), and (4) high levels of power-related stresses (Jemmott, 1987).

Some evidence suggests that people high in power motivation are predisposed to show heightened activation of the sympathetic nervous system when faced with obstacles to or frustrations in the experience of having impact and feeling strong (Fodor, 1984, 1985; Steele, 1973). If power motivation is associated with heightened sympathetic activity, then one might expect it also to be associated with elevated blood pressure. In three different samples of German and American men, McClelland (1979) documented just such an association. In one sample followed longitudinally, 61% of the men scoring above average on a TAT index of power + self-control (taken when they were in their 30s) showed elevated diastolic blood pressure 20 years later, compared to only 23% of the men scoring below average on this index.

There is empirical evidence, albeit scattered, to suggest that high power motivation may be modestly associated with small deficits in the body's immune system. If this is true, one might expect high power motivation to be implicated indirectly in the breakdown of the body's defenses to sickness and disease. McClelland and Jemmot (1980) administered the TAT to 95 students and obtained self-report measures of health problems and life stresses. They classified each life stress identified by a subject as either a power/achievement event, an affiliation/intimacy event, or "other." Examples of power/achievement events included troubles with an employer, a substantial academic disappointment, and participating in a major sports event. The results of the study indicated that the students with (1) relatively high power motivation, (2) relatively high activity inhibition (self-control), and (3) an above-average number of power/achievement stresses over the past year reported more physical illnesses in the previous 6 months than did other students. In addition, the illnesses they reported were more severe. Thus, the highly controlled and highly power-oriented person may "bottle-up" his or her frustrations in such a way as to tax an internal physiological equilibrium. The result may be a greater number of colds, bouts of flu, and other maladies, especially during times of excessive power stress.

Intimacy Motivation

While our desires for achievement and power may motivate us to assert ourselves in effective and influential ways and to control, even master, our environments, our longings for close and warm relationships with other human beings pull us in

Continued on p. 640

Feature 11.B

A Movie Is Like a TAT
The Case of Alfred Hitchcock

If presidential speeches (Winter, 1987) and children's readers (McClelland, 1961) can be coded for motivational themes as if they were TAT stories, then other works of the imagination explicitly crafted as creative narratives should prove to be even richer and more illuminating sources for personological scrutiny. In his brilliant analysis of the life of film director Alfred Hitchcock, biographer Donald Spoto (1983) treats each of Hitchcock's movies as if it were a kind of projective test, through which the director plays out some of his most troubling conflicts in desire. Just as any person in a TAT research study is assumed to project certain dominant needs and issues into his or her imaginative stories, so Hitchcock revealed himself through the plots, characterizations, settings, themes, scenes, and techniques of such popular film classics as *North by Northwest* (1958), *Rear Window* (1954), and *Psycho* (1960).

One of Spoto's many insights into Hitchcock's troubled life and complex personality is the idea that the film director was obsessed, from early adulthood onward, with what seemed to be two very different sides of his own genius. On the one hand, he was the consummate perfectionist in the conception and realization of a film. A craftsman who was both bold and meticulous, Hitchcock made movies that were emotionally riveting while being revolutionary with respect to

Alfred Hitchcock

film-making technique. In this guise, Hitchcock was a brilliant, innovative, fastidious, suave, and sophisticated artist—a man of prodigious creative and financial means. On the other hand, he was a bumbling "fat boy" from a working-class neighborhood, a 300-pound glutton who was a physical slob and an emotional cripple. A cruel and alienated man who could not remember having a single playmate as a child, Hitchcock withdrew from interpersonal relationships to a world of macabre fantasy. He was incapable of experiencing intimacy with friends, acquaintances, and even his family. He

North by Northwest

films in which he sets up antagonistic *doubles.* Frequently, double characters and double scenes reflect opposite aspects of Hitchcock himself. The duality played itself out in Hitchcock's ambivalent treatment of women. His beautiful leading ladies, like Grace Kelly and Kim Novak, played roles as flawless paragons of feminine elegance and grace, worshiped and idealized by glamorous men. On the other hand, women were savagely raped, mutilated, and debased as we see in the famous shower scene in *Psycho,* in the last attack of Tippi Hedren in *The Birds,* and in numerous strangulations and slashings. Writes Spoto:

> Hitchcock's conflicting feelings about women were perhaps the single most dramatic and painful realization of a divided personality. On the one hand, Woman was an abstraction, almost a remote goddess in her purity and coolness. But—"in the back of a taxi," as he liked to say— what such a woman might do was really what he *wished* she would do. (p. 432)

behaved in grossly inappropriate ways in numerous social settings, threatening to slit his own throat at dinner parties and playing grotesque practical jokes on actors and actresses while they were on the set. And he lived "with inner demons of lust and possessiveness, of romantic, dark fantasies about killing, and of unfulfilled sexual daydreams" (Spoto, 1983, p. 275).

The two sides of Hitchcock are revealed in the many instances in his

Spoto argues that Hitchcock's dual nature was also projected onto his two favorite leading men—Cary Grant and Jimmy Stewart. Grant represented what Hitchcock wished to be: the suave and sophisticated man-of-the-world who always got the girl. Stewart, on the other hand, was closer to what Hitchcock saw as his own reality. Stewart was the theorist of murder in *Rope,* the chair-bound voyeur in *Rear Window,* and the obsessed and guilt-ridden pursuer of romance in *Vertigo.* While Grant personified the fastidious perfectionist who made his way in the world with style and grace, Stewart hinted at the darker underside of the brooding, inept fat boy. As Hitchcock got older, the fat boy became more dominant in both daily life and cine-matic fantasy, exploding onto center stage one climactic February afternoon in 1964 when the aging director made an overt sexual proposition to his lead-ing lady. Hitchcock's personal life appeared to deteriorate completely from this point onward, and the films he made in his last few years deterio-rated too into virtual pornography.

Continued from p. 637

a different direction, to the private life of intimate interpersonal communion (Bakan, 1966). Indeed, for some of us, the desire for intimacy is even grander and more compelling than our wishes for success, fame, and transcendence. As the novelist E. M. Forster wrote, "It is the private life that holds out the mirror to infinity; personal intercourse, and that alone, that ever hints at a personality beyond our daily vision" (1910, p. 78).

The desire for intimacy is a desire to share what is innermost with others. Ideally, the sharing is mutual; each person in an intimate encounter gives as well as receives. The intimate moment is intense and emotionally engaging; each per-son focuses unswervingly on the other, as if to suggest that during an intimate exchange virtually nothing else is important to the participants outside the process of relating to each other. The philosopher Martin Buber referred to this intense quality of interpersonal give-and-take as the *I–Thou* experience. He wrote:

> When I confront a human being as my Thou and speak the basic word I–Thou to him, then he is no thing among things nor does he consist of things. He is no longer He or She, a dot in the world grid of space and time, nor a condition to be experienced and described, a loose bundle of named qualities. Neighborless and seamless, he is Thou and fills the firmament. Not as if there were nothing but he; but everything else lives in his light. (1970, p. 59)

My own contribution to the scientific literature on human motivation con-cerns this quality of intimate experience described so lyrically by Martin Buber

(McAdams, 1980, 1982a). While all people doubtlessly desire to engage in close, warm, and communicative interaction with other people, some seem consistently more preoccupied with such intimate experience than others. **Intimacy motivation** is a recurrent preference for experiences of warm, close, and communicative interaction with others. Like the achievement and power motives, individual differences in intimacy motivation are assessed through content analysis of TAT stories. A few of the scoring categories for the intimacy motive are described in Table 11.10. These categories were derived and cross-validated in four different arousal experiments, wherein the stories written by people engaged in various kinds of intimate and friendly experiences were contrasted to stories written under neutral conditions (McAdams, 1980).

Table 11.10

Selected TAT Scoring Categories for Intimacy Motivation

Category	Description	Examples
Positive Affect	A relationship among characters promotes positive feelings, such as joy, excitement, love, liking, and happiness.	"She believes that she is in love with this strange man." "Sam and the boys are having a good time."
Dialogue	Characters in the story communicate with each other in a reciprocal and noninstrumental fashion.	"They talked all afternoon—about classes, music, the state of the world, and their feeling about each other."
Commitment or Concern	A character commits him- or herself to another or expresses humanitarian concern. The result is often a helping or self-sacrificial act.	"Dan had pity on the old woman and spent the next hour trying to cheer her up."
Surrender of Control	Characters in the story find themselves in a relationship that they cannot control; they give up any attempt to control and let events transpire spontaneously.	"She could not help herself; the sympathy she felt for the scoundrel made her stay and talk to him."

Source: McAdams (1984b)

A small but growing body of research supports the construct validity of the intimacy motive as assessed on the TAT. People high in intimacy motivation spend more time, over the course of a normal day, thinking about relationships with others than do people scoring lower in intimacy motivation (McAdams & Constantian, 1983). People high in intimacy motivation partake in a greater number of friendly conversations over the course of a normal day, and they laugh, smile, and make more eye contact when conversing, compared to people low in intimacy motivation (McAdams & Constantian, 1983; McAdams, Jackson, & Kirshnit, 1984). On the other hand, the person high in intimacy motivation may not be the "life of the party"; intimacy motivation is unrelated to extraversion–introversion. Instead, the high-intimacy person is likely to value close, one-on-one exchanges over boisterous group activities. When confronted with a large group, he or she is likely to promote group harmony and cohesiveness, viewing group activities as opportunities for everybody to get involved rather than for one or two people to dominate the action (McAdams & Powers, 1981). Partly for this reason, people high in intimacy motivation are rated by their friends and acquaintances as especially "sincere," "natural," "loving," "not dominant," and "not self-centered" (McAdams, 1980).

McAdams, Healy, and Krause (1984) investigated the relation between intimacy and power motivation on the one hand and patterns of friendship on the other. In this study, 105 college students wrote TAT stories, subsequently scored for intimacy and power motivation, and then described in some detail 10 friendship episodes that had occurred in their lives in the previous 2 weeks. A friendship episode was defined as any interaction with a friend that lasted at least 15–20 minutes. For each episode, the student provided information on how many friends were involved in the episode, what activity was undertaken, what the friends talked about, what role the person played in the episode, and what emotions were experienced.

Table 11.11 shows the main results of the study. Students high in intimacy motivation tended to report friendship episodes involving one-on-one interaction with a single other friend ("dyads") rather than "large-group" interactions (friendship episodes involving 5 or more people) and to describe conversations in which the participants in the episode disclosed personal information about themselves ("self-disclosure"). Therefore, when they got together with their friends, high-intimacy students were more likely than low-intimacy students to talk about, and listen to their friends talk about, their own fears, hopes, feelings, fantasies, and other highly intimate topics. Power motivation, on the other hand, was associated with large-group interactions and assertive friendship activities like making plans, initiating conversations, and helping others. In general, intimacy motivation is associated with a *communal* friendship style that places prime importance on *being* together and *sharing* secrets with others, while power motivation is associated with an *agentic* friendship style that emphasizes *doing* things and *helping* others (McAdams, 1984a, 1988a).

Because so many psychologists, novelists, and poets have told us that loving relationships with others are the key to happiness and well-being, we are certainly justified in asking if high intimacy motivation leads to health, happiness, and

Table 11.11

Correlations Between Motives and Friendship Patterns in College Students

| | Motive | |
| | Intimacy | Power |
Friendship Measure[a]		
Dyads (2 friends)	.20*	−.23*
Large groups (5 or more)	−.10	.21*
Listening role	.43***	−.15
Assertive role	−.04	.43***
Self-disclosure	.49***	−.16

Note: Total number of subjects was 105 (70 female and 35 male).
[a]These measures were based on students' descriptions of 10 friendship episodes that occurred in their lives in the previous 2 weeks.
*$p < .05$
**$p < .01$
***$p < .001$
Adapted from McAdams, Healy, & Krause (1984, p. 834).

overall life satisfaction. A few studies have examined the question directly. In one, McAdams and Vaillant (1982) found that high intimacy motivation at age 30 among male graduates of Harvard College significantly predicted overall psychosocial adjustment 17 years later, when the men were in their mid-40s. Men high in intimacy motivation in early adulthood reported greater marital satisfaction, job satisfaction, and even a marginally higher income at midlife compared to men scoring low in intimacy motivation.

In a second study, McAdams and Bryant (1987) drew upon a nationwide sample of over 1200 U.S. adults who were administered the TAT and a structured interview (Veroff, Douvan, & Kulka, 1981). The researchers found that, though intimacy motivation appears to bring certain benefits for both men and women, the benefits do not seem to be exactly the same for both sexes. High-intimacy women are relatively happy and satisfied, compared to low-intimacy women. On the other hand, high-intimacy men are *not* necessarily happier and more satisfied than low-intimacy men, but they do report less strain in life and less uncertainty.

Zeldow, Daugherty, and McAdams (1988) examined the relation between social motives assessed on the TAT and students' adjustment to medical school.

Students high in intimacy motivation and low in power motivation showed the highest levels of well-being. However, those high in intimacy motivation and *high* in power motivation were more depressed, neurotic, fatalistic, and self-doubting in their first two years of medical school, a relationship that was significant for both males and females. The authors suggested that the rigors of medical school make it extremely difficult for students with strong needs to feel close to others *and* to feel powerful and agentic to find satisfaction for their competing desires. By the time the students had finished their first two years and entered their clerkships, however, the negative effects of the high-intimacy/high-power pattern were no longer evident. A later study of this same cohort showed that those medical students high in intimacy motivation were more likely to choose pediatrics as a medical specialty than were students scoring low in intimacy motivation (Zeldow & Daugherty, 1991).

One other major sex difference has been found in research on intimacy motivation. Analysis of thousands of TAT stories, written mostly by college undergraduates in the United States, suggests that women tend to score higher than men on intimacy motivation (McAdams, Lester, Brand, McNamara, & Lensky, 1988). The difference is small but relatively consistent, and it is in keeping with the generally accepted view in American society that women tend to be more concerned with interpersonal relationships than are men (Bakan, 1966; Gilligan, 1982; Lewis, 1985). Even among fourth and sixth graders, girls score higher on intimacy motivation than boys (McAdams & Losoff, 1984). Interestingly, consistent sex differences in overall levels of achievement and power motivation have *not* been observed (Stewart & Chester, 1982).

A motive that bears some resemblance to intimacy motivation and that is also assessed via the TAT is the **affiliation motive** (Atkinson, Heyns, & Veroff, 1954; Boyatzis, 1973). Drawn from Murray's (1938) original list of psychogenic needs, affiliation motivation is the desire to establish, maintain, or restore positive-affect relations with others. TAT stories in which characters actively strive to improve or restore their relationships with others tend to score high on affiliation themes. McClelland (1975) has combined affiliation-motive scores with scores on achievement and power to yield interesting motivational profiles linked to behavior and attitudes. In general, however, the evidence for the construct validity of the affiliation motive is rather weak (Boyatzis, 1973), with many empirical studies yielding insignificant or contradictory results. Affiliation motivation tends to be positively correlated with intimacy motivation. To the extent that the two motive systems differ, the intimacy motive appears to emphasize the qualities of *being* in a warm and close relationship, whereas the affiliation motive emphasizes *doing*, or striving to achieve relationships.

Motivation in Perspective

The research employing the TAT to assess individual differences in motives of achievement, power, and intimacy rests on one crucial assumption, an assumption that Murray and McClelland share with Freud: people are not consciously aware of their motives. If motives were directly accessible to consciousness, psychologists would not need to use a projective measure like the TAT to tap motivational themes in narrative. Instead, people could simply report the strength of their motives on self-report questionnaires, like those used to assess personality traits (Chapter 5). Indeed, numerous self-report questionnaires have been developed to assess such constructs as achievement motivation (for example, Jackson, 1974). McClelland (1980) originally claimed that these self-report measures assess conscious "values" or "self-concepts" rather than "motives" per se. Recently, he and his colleagues have suggested that self-reports and TATs tap into two very different motivational systems that influence behavior in different ways (McClelland, Koestner, & Weinberger, 1989). Self-report questionnaires assess *self-attributed motives* whereas narrative measures like the TAT assess *implicit motives*. Self-attributed motives are primarily aroused by extrinsic, social factors whereas implicit motives are aroused by intrinsic factors in the task itself. Therefore, self-attributed achievement motivation should predict achieving behavior in situations that exert a strong social pressure to achieve. Implicit achievement motivation, by contrast, should predict achieving behavior that is perceived to be rewarding in and of itself. Implicit motives represent a more primitive motivational system derived from emotional experiences, whereas self-attributed motives are based on more cognitively elaborated and socially mediated constructs (Koestner, Weinberger, & McClelland, 1991). Measures of the two motives should not correlate with each other. A number of other arguments have been offered in support of the TAT as a measure of implicit motivational trends (Atkinson, Bongort, & Price, 1977; Reuman, Alwin, & Veroff, 1984). Despite these arguments, however, some critics still maintain that the TAT is a generally unreliable personality measure and that TAT scores of motives are probably not valid because they do not correlate highly with questionnaire measures of the same motives (Entwisle, 1972; Klinger, 1966).

Though the details of these controversies are beyond the scope of this book, there are two important points to make about the limitations of TAT assessments of human motives. First, despite its potential for revealing rich narrative data for personality, the TAT is a somewhat less reliable measure than a typical well-constructed personality questionnaire, all other things being equal. Under the best conditions, test–retest correlations for TAT motives are still lower (around $r = +.55$) than those for the best-established self-report traits (around $r = +.80$) (Lundy, 1985; Winter & Stewart, 1977). Ironically, this limitation stems directly from a cardinal TAT strength—the measure's exceptional *sensitivity*. Because the TAT is more sensitive to factors and influences in the person and in the situation than are most questionnaires assessing personality traits, a TAT assessment of motivation will naturally "reflect" a lot of extraneous and irrelevant material, like the subject's mood at the time of testing. There is no way to rid the TAT of this problem without undermining its essential sensitivity.

Second, the motives of achievement, power, and intimacy assessed on the TAT are probably less stable over time than are personality traits, such as extraversion and neuroticism, which are generally assessed on questionnaires. As we saw in Chapter 5, certain basic personality traits show marked longitudinal consistency. For instance, a highly extraverted person at age 16 is likely to be relatively extraverted at age 60. Part of the reason for this stability in certain traits over time may reside in their presumed biological or genetic basis, as in the case of extraversion. Although comparable TAT data do not exist, motives do not appear to be as stable over time as certain basic traits. Further, there is no evidence at present to suggest a genetic basis for motives.

The possibility that motives may change over time to a greater extent than basic traits reflects a fundamental distinction between motives and traits: motives deal with goals and desire; traits refer to basic behavioral style. Whereas it seems plausible to assume that a basic personality style is established early in life, perhaps partly as a function of biological temperament, and carried forward into adulthood as a stable set of personality traits, it appears equally reasonable to suggest that desires and goals may change markedly over the human life course. Motives for achievement, power, and intimacy may be similar to what Klinger (1977) has called *current concerns.* Motive scores indicate the major goal areas with which a person is concerned at a particular time in his or her life. For example, a person may experience high needs for intimacy and achievement in college, but these needs may subside somewhat in later years—in his or her 30s or 40s—to be "replaced" by high levels of power motivation. Less stable than traits but more enduring than temporary moods and states, motives appear to reflect major thematic goals, desires, and preoccupations during *a given period* of a particular person's life.

Another key difference between motives and traits concerns the close tie historically between the concepts of motivation and *narrative.* It is no accident that both Freud and Murray chose *stories* as the place where they should launch their explorations of motivation. Recall from Chapters 2 and 3 that Freud looked for the manifestations of unconscious motivation in the recurrent themes appearing in narrative accounts of dreams, and in the dreamer's free associations to those narrative accounts. Similarly, Murray and McClelland have argued that individual differences in social motives are best seen in the motivational themes that appear in TAT responses and other narrative accounts. By contrast, nobody has argued seriously that traits should be measured through stories. What is so special, then, about stories? And what is the nature of the connection between story and motive?

Jerome Bruner (1986) suggests that stories are fundamentally about "the vicissitudes of human intention" organized in time (p. 17). Stories organize human strivings, wants, and desires into a sequence of beginning, middle, and ending. As accounts of human intention, stories tell us what characters are *striving to do,* what they *want* and how they go about trying to get what they want over time. Put simply, motivation refers to the goals that people want and strive for over time. For example, power motivation refers to the goal of "having impact" on others and on one's world. A person with a strong power motive desires power intensely and acts *in the present* in such a way as to move toward the (*future*) goal of having impact, a goal that, when successfully met or achieved, brings with it the experience of strong positive emotion. We cannot think of goals outside the dimension of time, for any goal is always set in the future, even if the future is very short-term. Motivated behavior is goal-directed activity, and goal-directed activity is situated *in time*. According to Bruner, the story is the natural means of expression for goal-directed human activity. Stories are always about human motives of some kind. Without a character's striving to attain some sort of goal, there can be no story. Similarly, the major way that we as human beings can provide an account of our motivations is through stories. If you don't know my stories, then you cannot know my motives (McAdams, 1990, 1993).

In conclusion, we see that a major part of the legacy of Henry Murray and the study of lives is an implicit image of the person as a goal-directed and complexly motivated individual situated in time. Because human beings are time-binding organisms, they convey who they are and what they want in life through narrative, through the interpersonal stories they create in imaginative exercises like the TAT and in autobiographical accounts. Personological analyses of narrative accounts provide insights into the needs, press, and themes that explain the vicissitudes of human motivation. While individuals can be profitably compared and contrasted with respect to their relative rankings on such dimensions as achievement and power motivation, the personologist may also discover broader thematic patternings, as in the case of Grope's Icarus complex, in which we may see the workings of a central story or myth that guides, animates, and provides meaning for the individual life in progress.

Summary for Chapter 11

1. A vivid example of Henry Murray's interpersonal-stories approach to personality may be seen in the case of Grope, an undergraduate student whose erotic and narcissistic urges were organized in the imagery of rising and falling to create what Murray called an Icarus complex.

2. Murray developed a personological system that emphasized the time-binding nature of human life. Units of human time are conceived in terms of proceedings, durances, serials, and serial programs.

3. Human behavior is motivated by at least 20 different psychogenic needs, which interact with situational press to produce themes, or recurrent need-press relationships. Some human lives are dominated by a characteristic and deeply rooted patterning of need, press, and thema—what Murray called a unity thema.

4. Murray's personology gave birth to the interdisciplinary "study of lives" tradition in personality psychology, through which the individual lives of relatively normal adults were examined in depth and over time, with special emphasis on biography, fantasy, imagination, creativity, values, motivation, and myth.

5. The study of lives relied on case studies of individual persons. A controversial approach in personality psychology, the case-study method has been critiqued for problems in reliability and external validity.

6. Despite inherent limitations, case studies are especially valuable in the discovery and generation of new hypotheses in personality research and in the illustration of broad thematic patterns in lives.

7. Murray invented the Thematic Apperception Test (TAT) to assess individual differences in needs through the interpretation of imaginative story responses to picture cues.

8. Assessed through content analysis of TAT stories, the achievement motive (need for achievement) is a recurrent preference or readiness for experiences of "doing well."

9. The extent to which a society encourages achievement motivation can be estimated by scoring folk tales, children's readers, and popular literature for achievement themes, as research by David McClelland has shown.

10. Also assessed via the TAT, the power motive is a recurrent preference for experiences of "having impact" on others and feeling strong.

11. Intimacy motivation, assessed on the TAT, is a recurrent preference for experiences of "feeling close" through warm and communicative interaction with others.

12. Substantial evidence for the construct validity of TAT-based needs (motives) for achievement, power, and intimacy has been gathered in many research studies. These motives may be contrasted to personality traits, which are usually assessed via self-report questionnaires. Whereas traits seem to refer to basic behavioral styles laid down early in life, motives refer to unconscious desires and goals and are more likely to change over time. Motives are most naturally expressed through stories, which situate goal-directed (motivated) action in a narrative sequence of beginning, middle, and end.

Chapter 12

Biography and the Life Course
Erikson, Adler, and the Seasons of Adulthood

Introduction

Luther's Biography
Erikson's Theory of Psychosocial Development
Erikson and the Psychoanalytic Tradition
Stages as Chapters
The Early Stages
The Problem of Identity

Adolescence and Young Adulthood
Identity Statuses
Identity and Intimacy
Feature 12.A: The Feminine Social Clock Project

The Later Stages

A Model of Generativity
Stories of Generativity
Integrity

Story Beginnings and Endings: Alfred Adler
Alfred Adler and Individual Psychology
Beginnings: The Earliest Memory
Feature 12.B: Birth Order and the Family Saga
Endings: Fictional Finalism

Biography, Narrative, and Lives
Psychobiography
Feature 12.C: Why Did van Gogh Cut Off His Ear?
Life Histories
Seasons of Adult Life

Summary

Martin Luther was a Catholic monk in his early 20s when he suddenly fell raving to the ground one day and began roaring like a bull. According to three of Luther's contemporaries who witnessed the event, young Martin began screaming like one possessed by a demon after reading a passage in the New Testament about Christ's cure of a man who could not speak (Mark 9:17–27). In the midst of his fit, Martin was heard to exclaim *"Ich bin nit! Ich bin nit!"* ("I am not! I am not!"). Occurring during a period of profound religious doubt in Luther's life, his exclamation was a desperate cry of negation: "I am *not* this; I am *nothing;* I do *not* know who I am!"

Luther's emotional outburst took place some time around the year 1507 in the monastery choir, located in the German town of Erfurt. In psychological terms, the basic problem in young Luther's life at this time was that of *ego identity* (Erikson, 1958, 1959; McAdams, 1985b). In essence, young Luther was unable to formulate a coherent and convincing answer to the two fundamental questions of identity: "Who am I?" and "How do I fit into the adult world?" However, Luther soon made substantial headway in resolving his identity problem. By 1512, he had worked out an ideological solution. By 1517, he was translating the solution into radical public action. And by 1522, he had achieved the status of a religious and political celebrity destined to become one of the most influential men in the history of Western civilization. How did Luther do this? And what does his struggle tell us about identity and the adult life course today?

Luther's Biography

Martin Luther (1483–1546) is credited with starting the massive religious and cultural movement termed the Protestant Reformation, through which many Europeans severed their ties with the Roman Catholic Church and ultimately formed the various Protestant denominations of Christianity, such as the Lutherans, Methodists, Presbyterians, and Baptists. He is also credited with bringing the sacred writings of Christianity to the common people by providing the first authoritative translation of the Bible into German. He was a voluminous writer and a great preacher, and he wrote some of the most inspiring hymns in the Christian musical tradition. Outside the immediate domain of the church, Luther has been viewed as a monumental *political* figure in German history—one of the fathers of German nationalism and a hero for some revolutionaries. Of course, all of this would have been impossible to predict that day in the choir when young Martin fell raving to the ground. In 1507, Martin Luther was living out a rather conventional life story of the "good monk"—devoted to the Catholic Church and properly respectful of the authority of the Roman pope. The story changed radically, however, as Luther came to fashion a new kind of identity that provided him with a sense of unity and purpose.

One of the most provocative applications of personality theory to the life course of a single adult is Erik Erikson's (1958) psychobiographical analysis of Luther's identity formation, entitled *Young Man Luther*. Erikson begins his analysis with the "fit in the choir." In this critical life event, Luther expresses the utter terror and confusion of a young man who has come to deny the very assumptions upon which he has built his own sense of who he is and how he fits into the adult world. The fit in the choir symbolizes the low point of Luther's identity struggle—the point in his own life where he felt cut off from all that had previously provided his life with unity and purpose. In Luther's biography, this incident is sandwiched between two other key events.

The first event took place in the summer of 1505. At this point, Luther was following the career path sketched out for him by his father, a middle-class copper miner and early capitalist named Hans Luder. Hans wanted his son to be a lawyer. Entering the University of Erfurt in 1501, Martin appeared destined to fulfill his father's mandate. On one fateful summer evening, however, Martin was returning to the university by foot in a fierce thunderstorm when a bolt of lightning struck the ground near him, hurling him to the earth and sending him into what some biographers have claimed was a convulsion. Before he knew what was happening, the 18-year-old Martin screamed out, "Help me St. Anne . . . I want to be a monk!" On his safe return to Erfurt, he entered the monastery, telling his friends and eventually his father that his experience in the thunderstorm affirmed a commitment to the Catholic church.

This would-be-lawyer-turned-monk was no ordinary religious novice. He prayed more than the other monks. He tortured his body and his mind by denying himself even the simplest earthly comforts and ruminating obsessively, day and night, over the meaning of the tiniest nuances of scripture. Erikson suggests that Martin's initial love affair with the Catholic church and with the idea of being the most devout monk the church had ever seen was too intense, too passionate, and it provided a thin disguise for a deeper doubt and ambivalence:

> It makes psychiatric sense that under such conditions a young
> man with Martin's smoldering problems, but also with an honest

desire to avoid rebellion against an environment which took care of so many of his needs, would subdue his rebellious nature by gradually developing compulsive-obsessive states characterized by high ambivalence. His self-doubt thus would take the form of intensified self-observation in exaggerated obedience to the demands of the order; his doubt of authority would take the form of an intellectualized scrutiny of the authoritative books. This activity would, for a while longer, keep the devil in his place. (Erikson, 1958, p. 137)

But who was the Devil? And where was his "place"? As twentieth-century readers, it is difficult for most of us, regardless of our religious persuasion, to understand how literal a force Luther believed the Devil to be in his life. In the monastery at Erfurt, Luther struggled daily with the Devil, seeing him, fleeing him, fighting him, debating him, hating him, fearing him as a real person with superhuman power. Though many people of Luther's day believed, like Luther, that the Devil could be seen and tangibly experienced in daily life as if he were a flesh-and-blood person, few were as completely obsessed with the Devil's doings as was the troubled monk. In Luther's words, the Devil was "the old evil foe." In every human's raging war with the Devil, faith in God served as "the mighty fortress" and "sword and shield victorious." The battle cry was set to music in Luther's most famous hymn:

> A mighty fortress is our God,
> A sword and shield victorious;
> He breaks the cruel oppressor's rod
> And wins salvation glorious.
> The old satanic foe
> Has sworn to work us woe!
> With craft and dreadful might
> He arms himself to fight.
> On earth he has no equal.

More significant from a psychological standpoint, however, was Luther's *projection* of the Devil onto others. Throughout his life, Luther cast his enemies in the guise of the Devil, responding to them in the same way he daily responded to the old evil foe. The best example is the Catholic pope (and the church establishment he represented) who became for Luther and his life story the prototype of the Devil incarnate.

The seeds of Luther's discontent with the pope and the church were sown in the Erfurt monastery as he witnessed the enactment of corrupt church policies. Chief among these was the practice of selling "indulgences," through which a Christian could pay money to the church to purchase salvation for his or her dead relatives. The selling of indulgences was to become a rallying point for the entire Protestant Reformation as it came to represent both corruption in the church and the Catholic view of salvation as a commodity to be bought and sold.

By the time of his fit in the choir, then, Luther was renouncing his old identity as an obedient monk, identifying the Roman church as the enemy rather than the savior, and groping furiously for an alternative image of self with which to build a new identity. According to Luther's own account, his spiritual questioning and reformulation culminated in 1512 in a revelation of truth that took place, believe it or not, when visiting the monks' toilet in the Wittenberg tower. There, Luther was struck with a new insight into the meaning of the last sentence of Romans 1:17: "The just shall live by faith."

In the tower, Luther envisioned a new image of God more directly accessible to the common person than the distant God of the Catholic orthodoxy. According to Luther's radically new reading of this old passage, salvation was to be achieved by faith, not through good works or the sale of indulgences. God was not to be viewed as a distant force who waits for the day of judgment to decide if each man's and woman's earthly deeds merit entrance into the kingdom of heaven. Rather, men and women encounter God in the here and now—personally, rather than through the institutions of the church—through God's son Jesus; men and women need only accept Jesus—have faith that Jesus is the son of God—in order to be redeemed.

The course Luther's life followed after the revelation in the tower of Wittenberg is summarized in Table 12.1. These public events and developments marked the rise of Luther as a religious leader in Europe and the spread of his influence in the Protestant Reformation. On a psychological level, however, the story of Luther's identity formation and articulation is an extremely complex one that does not end with the revelation in the tower (Erikson, 1958; McAdams, 1985b). In the years before and after the incident in the tower, Luther fashioned his own unique *life story* that provided his life with unity and purpose. The ideological underpinnings of the story—what Luther finally believed to be true about God, faith, salvation, and the church—were established by 1512. But the heroic action or *plot* of the story had just begun. The main protagonists or *characters* in Luther's heroic life story were to include different images of Luther himself, different roles he played in the story: (1) Luther-the-*forceful-spokesman* of a new church, acting in the guise of a sixteenth-century Christ, (2) Luther-the-brooding-and-*defiant-son,* who repeatedly rebelled against his own father and against the pope ("father" of the Roman church), and (3) Luther-the-*authoritarian-father* of his own religious movement, treating others the way other "fathers" had treated him (McAdams, 1985b). Therefore, Luther's identity was not completely formed by 1512. But it had nevertheless come a long way since the days of the thunderstorm and the fit in the choir. He had come to a clearer understanding of who he was and how he might find a psychosocial place in the adult world.

Our brief excursion into Erikson's biographical study of Luther introduces six central themes around which this chapter is organized:

1.   Biographical analyses of lives reveal that personality development continues well beyond childhood and adolescence and through the adult life course. Adult lives over time may be divided into stages, chapters, seasons, and so on,

Table 12.1

Major Events in the Life of Martin Luther

1483	Born into a strict and pious mining family in Eisleben in eastern Germany.
1501	Became a student at Erfurt, then the best university in Germany.
1505	January: graduated from Erfurt. May: to please father, Luther took up law. July: the thunderstorm incident, in which he vowed to St. Anne to become a monk. He entered the Augustinian cloister at Erfurt without telling his family.
1507	Became a priest and celebrated his first mass at age of 23. Then fell into severe doubts, which may have precipitated the "fit in the choir."
1512	Became doctor of theology at age 28 and gave his first lectures on the Psalms at the University of Wittenberg, where he experienced the revelation "in the tower." Formulated the essential Protestant doctrine that human beings are saved by faith, not by good works. Despite having developed a revolutionary viewpoint, Luther still considered himself orthodox at this point.
1517	Emerged as a practical reformer by preaching against the system of indulgences. On October 31st, he nailed to door of Wittenberg Castle Church his 95 theses "For Elucidation of the Virtues of Indulgences." This event has traditionally been seen as the starting point of the Protestant Reformation.
1518	Luther was accused by many of heresy. He wrote to the pope in defense of his views.
1520	The pope publicly condemned Luther and his followers and gave him 60 days to retract his heretical views. Luther publicly burned the document of condemnation. Wrote major treatises on church reform.
1521	The pope moved to have Luther excommunicated (expelled) from the church. Luther went into hiding.
1522	Due to growing public support, Luther came out of hiding and resumed activity at Wittenberg. Published German translation of the New Testament and continued controversial writing. Composed hymns, including "A Mighty Fortress Is Our God." Luther's activities began to motivate radical evangelists and political movements in Germany.

Table 12.1 continued

Table 12.1 continued

1525	After expressing initial sympathy for the peasants' demands that serfdom be abolished, Luther sided instead with the lords and princes and called for the extermination of the "murdering hordes" of peasants. Luther married an ex-nun.
1526	First son, Hans, born. Hans was followed by 2 more sons and 2 daughters.
1526–1546	In these years, Luther was always active. He composed hymns, translated the Old Testament, issued many pamphlets, engaged in controversies with other reformers, and travelled extensively. He became the authoritarian father of the movement he had started.
1546	Died in Eisleben.

Major source: Osborne (1961).

suggesting both continuity and change as one moves through the story from beginning to middle to end.

2.   The key psychosocial question in the life course is "Who am I?"—the question of *identity*. In Western societies, identity first becomes a pressing psychosocial concern in late adolescence and young adulthood.

3.   In formulating an identity in adulthood, one of the most basic challenges is to consolidate a clear *ideological* position in life. The adult must decide what he or she believes in, what he or she values to be true and to be good.

4.   The life course is dramatically punctuated by particular events or incidents—the thunderstorm conversion, the fit in the choir, the revelation in the privy—that serve as high points, low points, turning points, beginning points, and ending points. Biographers and people themselves interpret, reconstruct, and anticipate these events in terms of their symbolic meaning and significance in an evolving life *story*.

5.   In ways both humble and grand, lives and life stories have an impact that goes beyond their own time. Through their actions and their reputations, adults influence the next generation and leave legacies of the self for the future.

6.   Even in the most momentous of lives, like Luther's, the formation of identity is never undertaken by the individual in isolation. Identity is a *psychosocial* achievement—jointly negotiated by the person and the society in which he or she lives. Furthermore, identity must be seen in the context of other psychosocial issues that arise first in infancy and childhood, such as trust, autonomy, and initiative.

Erikson's Theory of Psychosocial Development

Erik Homburger Erikson was born of Danish parents, in 1902, in Frankfurt, Germany. His father, a Protestant, abandoned the family prior to Erik's birth, and his Jewish mother subsequently married Dr. Theodor Homburger, a Jewish pediatrician. Growing up as Erik Homburger, the boy was a tall, fair-haired, and blue-eyed Jew of Scandinavian descent. To his Jewish peers, he did not look like a Jew. But he was not fully accepted by his non-Jewish peers, either. Thus, from an early age, Erikson cultivated an image of self as *outsider,* forced to define clearly how he was different from as well as similar to others in his environment.

An unexceptional student, Erik Homburger never earned a university degree of any kind. Dashing his adoptive father's hopes that he become a physician, he wandered around Europe in his early 20s, studying briefly at art schools and painting children's portraits. "I was an artist then," he later wrote, "which can be a European euphemism for a young man with some talent, but nowhere to go" (Erikson, 1964, p. 20). During this very difficult period, Homburger experienced a crisis in identity that brought with it excessive anxiety and even occasional panic. A major problem was the young artist's inability to work with discipline and regularity (Erikson, 1975). In 1927, he moved to Vienna and accepted a teaching position at a small school established for children of Freud's patients and friends. He was received warmly by a group of psychoanalysts who included Dorothy Burlingham and Anna Freud, and he eventually undertook training in psychoanalysis with and was psychoanalyzed by Anna Freud. In 1933, Homburger emigrated to the United States and settled in Boston, where he worked as a psychoanalyst for children and associated temporarily with Henry Murray at the Harvard Psychological Clinic. In 1939, he became a naturalized American citizen and officially adopted the surname of "Erikson," a highly symbolic event that marked the maturation of his own identity. Since then he has held various positions at Yale, the University of California at Berkeley, and Harvard, among other places. He has also continued his psychoanalytic practice. And he has written widely.

Erikson and the Psychoanalytic Tradition

One cannot deny Erikson's debt to Freud. Like Freud, Erikson delved into the intrapsychic mysteries of persons' lives, engaging in dream interpretation and utilizing free association to unearth the latent meanings of manifest behavior and thought (Chapters 2 and 3). Like Freud, he has couched early personality development in terms of stages that are linked to the libido. Because of his emphasis on the adaptive features of the human ego, furthermore, Erikson is often grouped as one of the preeminent ego psychologists, like Anna Freud herself (Chapter 2), whose main intellectual heritage is classical psychoanalysis.

Erik Erikson

On the other hand, there are profound differences in content and style between Erikson and much of the rest of the psychoanalytic tradition. One of the most important differences is that Erikson is generally *optimistic* about the human condition, whereas Freud and much of the psychoanalytic tradition appear far more pessimistic. The difference shows up clearly in the three basic tenets or assumptions of psychoanalysis, outlined in Chapter 2.

Recall that the first tenet of classic psychoanalytic theory is *determinism,* Freud's belief that all human behavior is determined by forces over which the individual has little control. Erikson's perspective on determinism is a bit different. He agrees wholeheartedly with Freud that all kinds of behavior and experience—especially such potentially rich manifestations as dreams, art, and play—can be interpreted as expressions of unconscious internal determinants rooted in childhood. To quote an oft-used expression, Erikson endorses Freud's view that "the child is father to the man." But, he also endorses the quintessentially anti-Freudian view that the "man can be father to the child." In other words, while early (childhood) events may determine later personality structure, *later personality structure can also feed back to determine past childhood events!* While Freud believed that the "early" (childhood) forever determines the "late" (adulthood), Erikson endorses the opposite view, that the late can determine the early. We are not simply what our childhoods have made us, Erikson firmly maintains: our childhoods are also what we, as adults, make them. This intriguing idea will become clearer when we look more closely at Erikson's concept of identity.

The second psychoanalytic tenet is *conflict:* human beings are in perpetual conflict, both with society and with themselves. Freud's tragic, romantic view of human nature dictated that the demands of society and the instinctual urges of the individual would forever clash, with society generally winning out. Further, Freud discerned conflict even at the core of the human instincts themselves, for all people are ultimately motivated by opposing life and death instincts. Because of conflict, people suffer anxiety; there is no way to escape conflict, and therefore anxiety is inevitable, even in the best of lives. According to the third tenet of psychoanalysis, furthermore, the sources of anxiety are generally *unconscious* to the individual. We do not know why we are miserable, so buried are the unconscious springs of human experience and action.

Erikson shares Freud's romanticism, but not his sense of inevitable tragedy. And while he would not deny the importance of the unconscious, Erikson also emphasizes such conscious shapers of personality as interpersonal relationships, social opportunities, and ideology. As Erikson views it, conflict may be a nemesis in many if not all lives, but there exist domains of living in which conflict is at a minimum, such as certain forms of play and art. More important, the individual need not be the pitiful loser in an unavoidable conflict with oppressive society. As active participants in—rather than helpless victims of—human societies, individuals can sometimes have as much impact on society as society has on them, as we see in the case of Luther. Further, most societies provide niches and opportunities for the expression of individuality—natural resources for the construction of identity. These resources include such abstractions as an economic order, specifications about adult roles, and value systems from which the individual can forge a personal ideology, as well as the more personal resources of role models, teachers, guides, and mentors. This is not to say that all societies at all times are equally beneficent. Erikson is keenly aware of the ways in which certain societies may pervert human development and ruin lives. Yet his view of social influence is much more charitable than Freud's, affirming a subtle and intricate dialectic between society and the individual.

The key to understanding the person, argues Erikson, is **triple bookkeeping** (Erikson, 1963). The person's life must be comprehended on three complementary levels: (1) the level of the *body* and all of the constitutional givens with which the individual is endowed, including sexual or libidinal dynamics; (2) the level of the *ego,* which refers to the person's unique ways of synthesizing experience to make sense of the world and cope with anxiety and conflict; and (3) the level of *family and society,* which refers both to the individual's developmental history within the family and the particular societal, cultural, and historical ethos that shapes, and in the cases of such extraordinary individuals as Luther, is shaped by the individual person. Erikson writes, "being unable to arrive at any simple sequence and causal chain with a clear location and a circumscribed beginning, only triple bookkeeping (or, if you wish, a systematic going around in circles) can gradually clarify the relevances and relatives of all the known data" (1963) p. 46).

In contrast to Freud, Erikson has made a theoretical commitment to the idea that personality development can only be understood in the context of the interpersonal–social–cultural–historical environment within which it occurs. While one cannot neglect the psychosexual dimensions of human development, the stages of the life cycle are more adequately seen as *psychosocial* in nature, the result of repeated transactions between the individual and society. Therefore, Erikson defines development in terms of particular psychosocial issues, rather than in terms of Freud's transformations of the libido. Whereas Freud suggests that personality development ends in early adolescence with attainment of genital maturity, Erikson proposes a *life-span model of development,* with eight psychosocial stages extending even into old age. At each of Erikson's eight stages, changes within the individual and within the individual's social world combine to create a central conflict that defines the stage. The conflict must be addressed, though not necessarily resolved, within the given stage, says Erikson, before the individual may move to the next stage. In a sense, the individual's experiences give rise to a unique question at each stage, which is typically "asked" and eventually "answered" through the individual's behavior. Though this question may not be consciously posed by the individual, the overall pattern of the individual's behavior within a given stage is structured as if the individual were asking a particular question. The stages, their corresponding questions, and other associated features are briefly outlined in Table 12.2.

A final difference between Erikson and Freud justifies Erikson's inclusion in this section on interpersonal stories. Though Erikson has not explicitly described himself as such, and though he has not generally been characterized in this way, Erikson is probably one of the most sophisticated *narrative psychologists* in personality psychology. Like Murray, and like Adler (later in this chapter), Erikson implies that understanding the person's life *in time* is achieved through stories and in terms of stories.

Like Murray, Erikson has made creative use of narrative methods for exploring human personality. In his examinations of child-rearing and personality in different cultures (Erikson, 1963) and in his biographical analyses of Luther (Erikson, 1958), Mahatma Gandhi (1969), and others (Erikson, 1959, 1978, 1980), Erikson has drawn on cultural folk tales, myths, legends, and even modern cinema to expose cultural and individual truths and to illuminate his theory of personality. In addition Erikson provides a generic psychosocial narrative for lives, complete with a "table of contents" containing the eight stages, which can be profitably viewed as eight psychosocial chapters of the expectable life story. As we have seen in Murray's scheme and as we will see with Adler, Levinson, and the narrative psychologists of Chapter 13, Erikson seeks first and foremost to make sense of the person's life as an evolving interpersonal pattern situated *in time.* Biography is at the heart of things because biography provides a storied account of a life over time. Lives in time make sense only as stories—as more-or-less coherent narratives complete with setting, scene, characters, plot, and theme, and structured to link beginning to middle to ending.

Table 12.2

Erikson's Eight Stages of Life

Age	Psychosexual Stage (Freud)	Psychosocial Issue	Central Question	Associated Virtue
1. Infancy	Oral	Trust *vs.* mistrust	How can I be secure?	Hope
2. Early Childhood	Anal	Autonomy *vs.* shame and doubt	How can I be independent?	Will
3. Childhood (play age)	Oedipal	Initiative *vs.* guilt	How can I be powerful?	Purpose
4. Childhood (school age)	Latency	Industry *vs.* inferiority	How can I be good?	Competence
5. Adolescence and Young Adulthood	Genital	Identity *vs.* role confusion	Who am I? How do I fit into the adult world?	Fidelity
6. Young Adulthood		Intimacy *vs.* isolation	How can I love?	Love
7. Mature Adulthood		Generativity *vs.* stagnation (or self-absorption)	How can I fashion a "gift"?	Care
8. Old Age		Ego integrity *vs.* despair	How can I receive a "gift"? (the "gift of life")	Wisdom

Stages as Chapters

We should begin by thinking of the eight stages summarized in Table 12.2 as eight chapters in a generic interpersonal story that people live out in one way or another as they develop from infancy through adulthood. Each chapter is defined by a central psychosocial challenge, such as "trust *versus* mistrust" for the first chapter. The challenge can also be posed as a fundamental experiential question in life, which for the first chapter is, "How can I be secure?" Much of personality development in the first chapter, therefore, can be understood in terms of how the infant negotiates with the environment to answer the basic question of how to be secure.

However, other things are also happening: other issues and topics are playing themselves out, though in minor and peripheral ways as secondary "subtexts" in the chapter. Thus, while the first chapter of the life course is dominated by the question "How can I be secure?" other questions are being set up, other lines of development are getting started, other life motifs are taking form at the same time. These other issues will emerge later in the life-span to dominate their own chapters: "autonomy *versus* shame and doubt" will dominate the second chapter of life, "initiative *versus* guilt" will dominate the third, and so on. As the life story unfolds, the concerns of early chapters fade into the subtexts of subsequent chapters. Therefore, the issue of "trust *versus* mistrust" never truly disappears in the later chapters. Instead, it fades from being of primary importance early on to secondary importance as new issues arise in the life-span. Psychosocial development, therefore, is the ebbing and flowing of particular life motifs in a storied sequence over the life-span.

The Early Stages

Erikson's first chapter parallels Freud's first stage of libidinal development, termed the oral stage. Erikson agrees with Freud that for the first year of life or so the libido is centered in the oral zone as sucking at the mother's breast or bottle becomes the starting point of sexual life. However, the expression of the libido through oral activity is only a part of a larger, multidimensional development of a series of interpersonal relationships in the first year of life. These relationships determine the extent to which the infant will experience basic **trust** or security on the one hand and basic **mistrust** or insecurity on the other. Most important, sucking forms a bond of love between the mother and the infant. More than anything else, this bond of love has the potential to provide the infant with a sense of trust and security in the first year, a feeling or understanding that the world is safe, the environment is predictable, and life is trustworthy. Experiences of mistrust or insecurity will inevitably arise in the first year of life. The infant must and will experience both trust and mistrust: healthy development is a function of the balance between the two.

Erikson's second stage of development—that concerned with the issue of **autonomy *versus* shame and doubt**—parallels Freud's second psychosexual stage, the anal stage. Again, Erikson agrees with Freud that, as far as psychosexuality in the toddler is concerned, the libido expresses itself through anal activity, as in the holding in and letting go of feces. For Erikson, however, the centerpiece of the 2- or 3-year-old's psychosocial experience is the struggle to attain a certain degree of autonomy, freedom, independence, and mastery of the self, and to avoid humiliation, shame, doubt, and other experiences in which the child's budding sense of self-sufficiency is threatened. Therefore, toilet training is important not so much as an expression of the libido but as an achievement of self-mastery and control.

Major advances in locomotion, language, and exploratory play in the second and third years of life provide unprecedented opportunities for attaining a certain degree of independence in the world. The child's environment must support his or her fledgling efforts to master the self and obtain a modicum of independence. As Erikson puts it, the "environment must back him [the child] up in his wish to 'stand on his own feet' lest he be overcome by that sense of having exposed himself prematurely and foolishly which we call shame, or that secondary mistrust, that looking back which we call doubt" (1963, p. 85). The overlapping psychosocial themes of the second chapter of life, therefore, are independence, self-mastery, self-control, and the avoidance of humiliation.

Simply being autonomous and independent, however, is not enough for the average 4-year-old. Unconsciously preoccupied with Freud's Oedipus complex, and confronting numerous challenges to efforts to move forward and to expand influence in the world, the naturally egocentric child in Erikson's third stage of the life cycle is preoccupied with questions of *power*. **Initiative *versus* guilt** is the basic psychosocial issue for the Oedipal boy or girl. At this time in the life cycle, children begin to take initiative in their daily lives—striving to master, divide, and conquer their worlds. They experience guilt when their aggressive attempts to make the world their own run afoul and as they, often unwittingly, threaten to hurt or damage others and their environment.

In keeping with Freud's view of the Oedipus complex, Erikson observes major sex differences in this third developmental chapter in the ways children carry out initiative and seek power. Boys tend to adopt a more **intrusive mode** of operation, which includes "the intrusion into other bodies by physical attack: the intrusion into other people's ears and minds by aggressive talking; the intrusion into space by vigorous locomotion; the intrusion into the unknown by consuming curiosity" (Erikson, 1963, p. 87). Girls tend to adopt a more **inclusive mode** of operation that can be "teasing, demanding, and grasping" (p. 88). Both boys and girls, however, are "on the make," to use Erikson's felicitous term. Though their styles may differ, both boys and girls at this stage in development strongly desire to make the world their own—to be king or queen, all-powerful and all-important, the center of everything.

Freud had little to say about the fourth chapter in the generic life story. The latency period following the resolution of the Oedipus complex and the establishment of the superego (Chapter 2 in this book) was viewed as a relatively peaceful and uneventful period in life wherein the libido simmers on a back burner. For Erikson, however, the elementary school child has begun a very important phase in which he or she will repeatedly face the challenges of **industry *versus* inferiority.** While internal changes such as the resolution of the Oedipus complex may help usher in this period, society overtly marks the transition with the virtually universal custom of beginning systematic instruction—schooling—of children at this time in their lives.

Beginning around age 6 or 7, children in most cultures undergo some form of systematic instruction outside the family. This schooling is designed to render the young boy or girl proficient in using the *tools* and assuming the *roles* of adulthood (Erikson, 1963). Tools include the basic implements of daily life in the society, ranging from bows and arrows to computers, which extend the powers of the human body and mind to promote the economic, technological, political, educational, and religious orders. Roles include those particular structured activities that adults perform with more or less skill as working members of society, such as the roles of teacher, parent, hunter, priest, and healer. Though children have been exposed to these tools and roles in previous stages, it is now time to learn them and learn about them in a systematic and societally scripted way.

The protagonist of the fourth chapter of Erikson's generic life story, there-fore, is the industrious schoolchild immersed in the "reading-'riting-'rithmetic" of his or her culture. The child learns the rudimentary skills required to become a productive member of society, as well as the proper modes and manners of con-duct expected outside the workplace. Erikson (1963) writes, "It is at this point that wider society becomes significant in its ways of admitting the child to an understanding of meaningful roles in its technology and economy" (p. 260). The elementary school child is learning how to be a good worker, a good citizen, and a good member of society.

Because this learning applies to matters that are both material and moral, economic and ethical, we may characterize the central psychosocial question of this stage as "How can I be good?" It is during this highly formative developmen-tal period that churches and schools deliver their most influential lessons on how to be a good boy or girl. And though we may be able to distinguish from an early age the subtle differences between being "good" by getting an "A" on a spelling test and being "good" by telling the truth (Nucci, 1981), both involve *being good* and thus converge on the central theme of experience for the schoolchild living Erikson's fourth chapter of the generic life story. In Erikson's essentially Freudian perspective on this particular point, the question of "How can I be good?" must await the resolution of the Oedipus complex, the establishment of a superego or internalized standard for goodness and badness, and the child's unconscious realization that the power he or she desired in the third chapter of life cannot yet be attained.

The Problem of Identity

The early stages are but a prelude to the main act of late adolescence and young adulthood. As we saw in the life of Luther, it is at this time in the life course that the person seriously addresses the question of *identity:* Who am I? The four stages of childhood leave the person with a unique pool of resources and handicaps, strengths and weaknesses that will be called upon in the making of an identity. In this sense, the past (the early) partly determines the future (the late). But to a cer-tain extent, the reverse is true, too. The adolescent or young adult looks back upon childhood now and comes to *decide what childhood meant.* In that this decision is made after childhood actually happened, there is a sense in which the late (that which follows childhood) partly determines the early (childhood itself). We cannot literally change what has happened already, but we can change its meaning. This new meaning thus becomes another part of and influence upon the making of identity. In addressing the issue of identity, we look back to the past in order to arrive at a plausible explanation—a story—that tells us how we came to be and where we may be going in the future. In *Young Man Luther,* Erikson writes:

> To be adult means among other things to see one's own life in continuous perspective, both in retrospect and prospect. By accepting some definition as to who he is, usually on the basis of a function in an economy, a place in the sequence of generations, and a status in the structure of society, the adult is able to selectively reconstruct his past in such a way that, step for step, it seems to have planned him, or better he seems to have planned it. In this sense, psychologically we *do* choose our parents, our family history, and the history of our kings, heroes, and gods. By making them our own, we maneuver ourselves into the inner position of proprietors, of creators. (Erikson, 1958, pp. 111–112)

Adolescence and Young Adulthood   In Freud's theory of psychosexual development, puberty marks the beginning of the libido's last stage—the genital stage—and the end of development. The physiological changes of puberty—such as the enlargement of the penis and testicles for boys, menstruation and the development of breasts for girls, changes in the distribution of body hair, changes in voice, the adolescent growth spurt—and the associated awakening of overt sexual longing in the teenage years signal the end of the libido's transformations. Erikson, too, views puberty as an ending and a transformation. It marks the end of childhood, thus closing the chapters of trust, autonomy, initiative, and industry. And it denotes the movement to a new stage/chapter that has momentous psychosocial consequences. For Erikson, physiological puberty combines with a number of other developments in the teenage years to usher in the psychosocial stage of **identity *versus* role confusion.**

Why do we confront the identity issue first in adolescence? There are many answers to this question, but they can be generally grouped into three categories: body, cognition, and society. First, as adolescents we find ourselves the unwitting inhabitants of new adultlike bodies—both wonderful and frightening—that seem qualitatively different from what we have known before. As you probably remember from your own experience, attaining physiological puberty is not simply a matter of getting bigger, as was the bodily transition from, say, age 6 to age 7. The emergence of primary and secondary sexual characteristics and the eruption of overt sexual longings at puberty tell us that, with respect to our bodies and our biologies, we are now truly different from what we used to be. Puberty, thus, may mark a turning point in the adolescent's perceived developmental course, as childhood comes to represent, in the adolescent's mind, a bygone era. In other

Adolescent girls.

words, the physical changes of puberty may help jog us into this sort of realization: "Hey, I'm not what I used to be; I'm not a kid anymore; I'm different from what I was before, but I am not sure what I am now."

Second, cognitive development may play a major role in launching the identity chapter of Erikson's generic life story. The developmental psychologist Jean Piaget (Inhelder & Piaget, 1958) has argued that in adolescence many people enter the cognitive stage of **formal operations.** According to Piaget, at this time in the life cycle we are first able to think about the world and about ourselves in highly abstract terms. In formal operations, one is able to reason about what is and what might be in terms of verbally stated and logically deduced hypotheses. Before adolescence, argues Piaget, we simply cannot do this. Therefore, the 10-year-old skillfully classifies and categorizes the world with wonderful accuracy and aplomb, but is cognitively bound to the concrete world of *what is* rather than the abstract world of *what might be.* Ask a smart American 10-year-old to recite the capitals of the 50 states of the United States and you should not be surprised if he or she rattles them off with 100% precision. However, if you ask that same prodigy to speculate as to what the capitals of the United States might be if there were only 10 states, he or she is likely to have more trouble. First, the child may argue that the proposition is inherently ridiculous because the United States *is* in fact made up of 50 states. Second, he or she may find it extremely difficult to devise a systematic plan for determining what the criteria of a capital should be in this hypothetical scenario. The 10-year-old is a slave to concrete facts: reality is everything. For the adolescent or adult blessed with formal operations, on the other hand, reality is understood as a *subset* of what might be. The real is one manifestation of the hypothetical, and viable and internally consistent alternative realities can also be imagined.

The serious questioning of the self—asking "Who am I?" and "How do I fit into the adult world?"—is catalyzed by the cognitive emergence of formal operations. The adolescent may look at the realities of the present and the past and contrast them with hypothetical possibilities concerning what might have been (in the past) and what might be (in the present and in the future). This introspective and abstract orientation to self and world may result in the formulation of hypothetical ideals: the ideal family, religion, society, life (Elkind, 1981). Adolescents begin to take seriously the possibilities of alternative lives and systems of living, motivating them in some cases to explore new and previously unthinkable ways of experiencing the world and to question those things learned in childhood that now seem "old." Furthermore, the adolescent may observe his or her own behavior and thought and come to question what the basic links are among the various different and conflicting ways in which he or she approaches the world: "Is there a real *me* behind all the different roles I play?" Such a cognitive problem is not likely to occur in the mind of the 10-year-old:

> During the early years, the child has different selves and is not bothered by inconsistencies between them, by his lack of unity or wholeness. He may be one person with his parents, another with his friends, and still another in his dreams. The limitations of [childhood thinking] permit such shifting about and contradictions. . . The idea of a unitary or whole self in which past memories of who one was, present experiences of who one is, and future expectations of who one will be, is the sort of abstraction that the child simply does not think about. . . With the emergence of formal operations in adolescence, wholeness, unity, and integration become introspectively real problems. Central to the idealism of adolescence is concern with an ideal self. Holden Caulfield's preoccupation with phoniness is a striking example of this concern. [Holden Caulfield is the teenaged hero of J.D. Salinger's well-known novel *The Catcher in the Rye*.] He, and many young people like him, become critical of those who only play at roles, who are one moment this and another moment that. This critical stance is taken toward themselves as well. Wholeness is, thus, an *ideal* conceived in late adolescence; a goal which may be pursued thereafter. (Breger, 1974, pp. 330–331)

Identity and intimacy: psychosocial issues of young adulthood.

But the physiological and cognitive changes of adolescence do not tell the whole story of identity's emergence at this time as the central psychosocial issue in the individual's life. A third factor is society. Paralleling the changes taking place within the individual are shifts in society's expectations about what the individual, who was a child but who is now almost an adult, should be doing, thinking, and feeling. Erikson (1959) writes, "It is of great relevance to the young individual's identity formation that he be responded to, and be given function and status as a person whose gradual growth and transformation make sense to those who begin to make sense to him" (p. 111). In general, Western societies "expect" their adolescents and young adults to examine the occupational, ideological, and interpersonal opportunities around them and to begin to make some decisions about what their lives as adults are to be about. This is to say that both society and the young person are ready for the young person's identity experiments and explorations by the time that he or she has in fact become a young person. As Erikson describes it:

The period can be viewed as a psychosocial moratorium during which the individual through free role experimentation may find a niche in some section of his society, a niche which is firmly defined and yet seems to be uniquely made for him. In finding it the young adult gains an assured sense of inner continuity and social sameness which will bridge what he was as a child and what he is about to become, and will reconcile his conception of himself and his community's recognition of him. (1959, p. 111)

There is, however, a tension in all of this. It is the tension between the "niche" carved out by society and the individual's desire to carve out his or her own niche. In constructing an identity that "fits" into society's roles and expectations, the young person should not blindly conform to what the family in particular or society in general wants him or her to do. In a sense, this is what Luther first did, in his initial decision to become a monk. But as we saw later, Luther eventually went beyond the niche carved out for him in the monastery to create a new and unique identity within his expanding and evolving world. Yet Luther did not—indeed could not—separate completely from society and its expectations. Even in the most revolutionary lives, Erikson maintains, *the individual and society create identity together.* The adolescent or adult should be neither victim nor master of his or her sociohistorical environment. Rather, the relationship between the self and society in the development of healthy identity is best characterized as one of dynamic tension.

Identity Statuses   One way to view identity is to focus on the *process* of formulating answers to the questions "Who am I?" and "How do I fit into the adult world?" during adolescence and young adulthood. According to this approach, the formation of identity in the adolescent and early adult years involves two related steps. In the first step, the young person breaks away from childhood beliefs and views, questions assumptions about the self and the world, and begins to investigate alternatives. During this first step of exploration, the person may challenge many of the viewpoints presented by parents, schools, churches, and other figures and institutions of authority. He or she may also come to question the past, wondering what might have been had things occurred differently in the earlier chapters of life—how life might be different now, for instance, if the person had been born into a different family, a different social class, a different ethnic group, a different society, a different period in history. Moving from what was and is to what might have been and what might be, the formal-operational thinker may begin to sample alternative beliefs, values, ideologies, behaviors, and life-styles, searching for that overall approach to life that seems to "fit." The exploration ends in the second step of identity formation in which the young person makes commitments to various roles and outlooks that define how the young person sees him- or herself fitting into the adult world. In the second step, the questions and doubts of the exploration phase are resolved, and identity ceases to be a pressing psychosocial concern.

James Marcia (1966, 1980) employs a semistructured interview to ask questions about exploration and commitment as they apply to the two areas of life that Erikson repeatedly suggests are at the heart of identity: (1) *occupation,* or what work role in society the person will occupy; and (2) *ideology,* or what the person's fundamental beliefs and values are, especially in the areas of religion and politics. Based on the responses to the interview, psychologists are able to classify young persons into one of four different **identity statuses,** displayed in Table 12.3. Each status may be viewed as a particular developmental position with respect to identity that the person holds at the current period in his or her life. Over time, people may move from one status to another, as identity is negotiated and reworked in different ways (Bourne, 1978; Waterman, 1982). Marcia's methodology and classification scheme have stimulated a large body of research over the last 25 years. Most of these studies have been done with college students, who as late adolescents and young adults are likely to be dealing, in one form or another, with the issue of "identity *versus* role confusion."

In terms of Erikson's theory, the most mature of the four identity statuses is **identity achievement.** Identity achievers have gone through a period of exploration and have come out of it having made commitments to well-articulated occupational and ideological goals and positions. They have successfully met the challenge of Erikson's fifth psychosocial stage and are now ready to begin the sixth. Identity achievers strive for internalized goals and rely on their own skills and capacities in meeting daily challenges. Less concerned with winning their parents' love than are young persons in some of the other identity statuses,

Table 12.3

Four Identity Statuses

Status	Process	
	Exploration, Crisis, Questioning	Commitment, Resolution
Identity Achievement	Yes	Yes
Moratorium	Yes	No
Foreclosure	No	Yes
Identity Diffusion	No	No

identity achievers may perceive their parents in balanced though somewhat ambivalent terms (Jordan, 1971; Josselson, 1973).

Several studies indicate that identity achievers are more academically inclined than persons in the other statuses. Cross and Allen (1970) showed that identity achievers received higher grades in college courses. Marcia and Friedman (1970) found that, among women, identity achievers chose more difficult college majors. Orlofsky (1978) found that identity achievers scored very high on the TAT measure of achievement motivation (Chapter 11). Other studies suggest that identity achievers make decisions, especially moral decisions, in an autonomous and principled fashion. They tend not to conform to peer pressure and social norms (Adams, Ryan, Hoffman, Dobson, & Nielson, 1984; Toder & Marcia, 1973). And they tend to base their moral decisions on abstract principles of justice and social contract rather than the conventional laws of societies and the egocentric needs of individuals (Podd, 1972).

The second identity status identified by Marcia is **moratorium.** People in moratorium are currently exploring identity issues but have not yet made commitments. You might say that these people do not know yet who they are and they know that they do not know. Uncertainty about the present and future may launch, as we saw with Luther in the monastery, a full-blown "identity crisis." But the moratoriums of the present should become the identity achievers of the near future as they pass from the sometimes anxiety-provoking period of exploration to stable commitment. Consequently, like identity achievers, moratoriums in college are usually viewed as relatively "mature" in Marcia's scheme, and many of the empirical findings for identity achievers also apply to individuals classified as moratorium.

Marked *ambivalence* is probably the best term to describe the characteristic relationship between the young person in moratorium and his or her parents. In moratorium, the individual may seek greater psychological distance from the family, rejecting old identifications and ingrained values and beliefs and setting up the parents or other authority figures as temporary **negative identities** (Erikson, 1959). These negative identities come to represent everything that the young person does *not* want to be. Therefore, parents may be cast into the unenviable role of "the enemy" in the adolescent's battle to discover what to believe and how to live as an adult. It is not surprising, then, that adolescents and young adults in moratorium often report stormy and contradictory feelings about their parents (Josselson, 1973; Marcia, 1980) as well as relatively high levels of general anxiety (Marcia, 1967; Oshman & Manosevitz, 1974). On the other hand, young adults in moratorium are often described as extremely friendly, likable, sensitive, and insightful (Josselson, 1973; Marcia, 1980).

In Erikson's terms, the person in the third status of **foreclosure** has failed to meet the identity challenge. In foreclosure, the young person fails to explore, but makes commitments to unquestioned positions taken from childhood. Rather than risk the uncertainty that might accompany a serious questioning of the past and of authority, the young person in foreclosure has opted for the security of childhood roles, beliefs, and expectations. With respect to occupation, the foreclosed individual "chooses" to do exactly what important authority persons have suggested, or perhaps insisted, he or she do. With respect to ideology, beliefs and values from childhood are transported into early adulthood intact and unsullied—rarely questioned and never reformulated. Not surprisingly, foreclosures report that they are very close to their parents, especially sons to fathers. They tend to describe their homes as loving and affectionate (Donovan, 1975).

Foreclosures appear the "best behaved" of the statuses (Marcia, 1980). College students in this status tend to study diligently, keep regular hours, and appear happy. The good behavior may be grounded in relatively traditional and conventional values adopted wholesale from authorities such as parents and the church. Indeed, a number of studies suggest that foreclosures adopt a more *authoritarian* outlook on the world than people in the other statuses (Marcia, 1966, 1967; Marcia & Friedman, 1970; Schenkel & Marcia, 1972). As we saw in Chapter 3, authoritarianism is a constellation of traits and attitudes centered around submission to and reverence for strong authority, conventional societal values, and rigid standards of right and wrong. Foreclosures tend to show rigid, authoritarian responses to moral dilemmas and tend to obey the dictates of powerful authority, even when the authority asks them to do things that seem wrong (Podd, 1972). With respect to other personality variables, foreclosures score extremely low on autonomy and anxiety, and they tend to show unrealistically high levels of aspiration (Marcia, 1966, 1967; Orlofsky, Marcia, & Lesser, 1973).

Marcia's fourth identity status, **identity diffusion,** is the most enigmatic. Like foreclosures, individuals in the diffusion status have yet to enter exploration, but, unlike foreclosures, they have yet to make commitments. With few strong allegiances to the past and few explicit commitments to a particular future, these young men and women appear to be afloat in a sea of ambiguity. The few studies that have obtained clear findings on diffusions suggest that they may be best characterized by the word *withdrawal.* Donovan (1975) found that diffusions tended to feel out of place and socially isolated. They saw their parents as distant and misunderstanding, and they approached new relationships with extreme caution. Josselson (1973) points to fantasy and withdrawal as favorite coping strategies for women of diffusion status. Summarizing the little available evidence, Marcia (1980) concludes that diffusions "seemed to sense little past to integrate, little future for which to plan; they were only what they felt in the present" (p. 176).

Identity and Intimacy   Erikson's stage model suggests that once an adult has arrived at some tentative answers to the question of Who am I? he or she is then psychosocially ready to begin the sixth chapter of the life course: **intimacy vs. isolation.** The relationship between these two stages, however, can be very complex. Many people seem to define themselves (identity) through intimate relationships with others. The proper sequence for the stages may indeed be reversed in many lives. Intimacy issues may arise before identity issues in many cases. Some have suggested that women's lives in American society have traditionally exemplified a merging of intimacy and identity issues, such that a woman's identity is intricately connected to her intimate relationships. The establishment of the adult self and the development of intimate relationships may be difficult to separate from each other. Nonetheless, Erikson seems to favor an idealized sequential scheme, suggesting that a person may be unable to be "truly" intimate with others until he or she has first made considerable progress in addressing the identity issue.

The closest thing to a definition that Erikson provides for intimacy is the following passage:

> Thus, the young adult, emerging from the search for and the insistence on identity, is eager and willing to fuse his identity with that of others. He is ready for intimacy, that is, the capacity to commit himself to concrete affiliations and partnerships and to develop the ethical strength to abide by such commitments, even thought they may call for significant sacrifices and compromises. Body and ego must now be masters of the organ modes and of the nuclear conflicts, in order to be able to face the fear of ego loss in situations which call for self-abandon: in the solidarity of close affiliations, in orgasms, and sexual unions, in close friendships and in physical combat, in experiences of inspiration by teachers and of intuition from the recesses of the self. The avoidance of such experiences because of a fear of ego loss may lead to a deep sense of isolation and consequent fear of self-absorption. (Erikson, 1963, pp. 263–264)

This difficult excerpt from *Childhood and Society* shows that Erikson holds to an extremely general and inclusive conceptualization of intimacy. Intimacy appears to involve a willingness to fuse one's identity with another, which results in love and strong commitment. It suggests a courageous willingness to lose the self in another—through close friendships, sexual unions, learning from teachers, and even (curiously) "physical combat." To be intimate is to be open and receptive to that "other" that is outside the ego, even remarkably when the "other" is "inside," that is, when the other is an internal part of one's own unconscious: "intuition from the recesses of the self." Exploring the recesses of the unconscious self—as in psychoanalysis—is a kind of intimacy, for Erikson, in that the individual is opening up to that which is alien, foreign, outside the ego (even though inside the psyche).

Most of the personality research that has addressed intimacy from an explicitly Eriksonian perspective has examined the relation between the resolution of identity and the quality of intimacy. Following Marcia's concept of identity status, Orlofsky, Marcia, and Lesser (1973) developed the parallel idea of **intimacy status.** These researchers devised a semistructured interview designed to determine the quality of intimacy in a person's life. Based on the respondent's answers to questions about dating, friendships, and interpersonal commitments, he or she may be classified as showing one of four intimacy statuses. Ranging from most intimate to least intimate, these are "intimate," "preintimate," "stereotyped relationships," and "isolate" (Table 12.4).

Table 12.4

Four Intimacy Statuses in Studies of College Students

Intimate	The person works at developing mutual personal relationships and has several close friends with whom he or she discusses personal matters. He or she is involved in a committed love relationship with a member of the opposite sex. This sexual relationship is mutually satisfactory, usually involving intercourse. The person is able to express both angry and affectionate feelings in the relationship. The person is generally interested in others.
Preintimate	The person has dated members of the opposite sex but is not involved in a committed love relationship. He or she is aware of the possibilities of relating intimately with a member of the opposite sex. The person has close friendships. The person has respect for the integrity of others, openness, responsibility, and mutuality. He or she feels conflicted about commitment, and love relationships may tend to be ambivalent.
Stereotyped	The person ranges from the moderately constricted and immature type of individual who has yet to go beyond superficial dating relationships to the playboy/playgirl type. Generally he or she has several friends; however, these relationships lack significant depth. He or she may date regularly but generally does not get involved.
Isolate	The isolated person lacks enduring personal relationships. Though he or she may have a few peer acquaintances seen infrequently, he or she rarely initiates social contact, and rarely dates members of the opposite sex. The anxiety accompanying close personal contact forces the person to withdraw into isolation. The person tends to be anxious and immature and generally lacking in assertiveness and social skills. The isolated individual may present him- or herself as bitter and mistrustful or smug and self-satisfied.

Source: Orlofsky, Marcia, & Lesser (1973).

Feature 12.A

The Feminine Social Clock Project

In 1958 and again in 1960, a representative two-thirds of the graduating class at a well-known women's college (a total of 141 women) participated in a study of personality characteristics and plans for the future. Born toward the end of the Great Depression and just before the onset of World War II, these women grew up in a period of relative prosperity in the United States. They were teenagers in the 1950s, and entered college at a time when American women were strongly encouraged to marry rather early and begin raising a family shortly thereafter. According to social expectations of the day, women were to organize their identities around the roles of wife, mother, and homemaker—a life pattern that was expected to remain intact until the death of the husband at a normative age. Indeed, virtually all of the women in this study expected a long-term marriage with children. Typically they wanted four children. And while women were being recruited into the labor force in increasing numbers in the late 1950s, most of the women in the study expected to work outside the home only until they were married and had children, with the chance of returning to the labor force only after the children were grown. These expectations about the timing of women's lives correspond to what psychologist Ravenna Helson has called the **feminine social clock project** (Helson, 1987; Helson, Mitchell, & Moane, 1984).

Helson has followed the lives of these women into their 40s, obtaining questionnaire information from most of them 5 years after college graduation and again in 1981. Helson's research reveals interesting individual differences in the extent to which the women have adhered to social clock patterns. A slight majority (53%) of the women had their first child before the age of 28, in accord with societal expectations. Helson classifies these women as FSC (feminine social clock). A smaller group (21%) had their first child after age 28, receiving the classification LA ("late adherent"). And 26% were classified as NFSC (never feminine social clock) because they never had children.

Adherence to the feminine social clock was related to personality traits manifested in the college years, before the women were married. Those who were destined to be "on time" with respect to marriage and family (FSCs) scored relatively high on the traits "achievement via conformance," "socialization," "intellectual efficiency," and "well-being," assessed on the California Psychological Inventory (CPI; see Chapter 5). In college, these women showed a relatively strong desire to do well and to have things structured and well-defined; they were highly responsive to social norms and expectations; they were confident, sensible, optimistic, and trusting. The CPI scores obtained at age 27 (after the FSCs had begun their families) showed that the transition to motherhood made for a relative increase in traits associated with responsibility, self-control, tolerance, and traditional femininity, and a decrease in scores on self-confidence and self-esteem and on sociability. Helson writes:

> Increased responsibility, tolerance, and nurturance can be seen as effective adaptations to the roles of wife and mother. The decrease in social participation may reflect absorption in family life rather than withdrawal or isolation. The increase in self-control, however, indicates a shift in the direction of suppression of impulse and spontaneity. In addition, the decline in self-confidence and self-esteem indicates a more negative self-image and decreased feelings of competence. These results confirm the hypothesis that for this cohort, at least, the FSC project demanded unique and difficult adjustments. (Helson, Mitchell, & Moane, 1984, p. 1085)

Very few of the women in college said that they aimed to establish careers. The world of work was considered a masculine domain, and there were many barriers that limited the progress women could make in a professional or business career. Yet a significant minority of the women did eventually enter career paths, adjusting their lives according to what Helson calls the **masculine occupational clock** (MOC). For the middle- and upper-middle class, the MOC "often was (and is) exceedingly articulated, with professional training at several different levels and with salary and status differentials that continued throughout one's work life. It is better to be 'ahead of time' than 'on time' by the MOC and bad to be interrupted" (Helson et al., 1984, p. 1082). The 24 women who were launched on the MOC by the age of 28 reported in college that they expected to marry later than the FSCs reported they would, and they scored lower than the FSCs on socialization, achievement via conformance, and communality. Of the 24, 15 showed continued upward mobility in their professional lives into midlife. These women exhibited very high levels of confidence, initiative, and intellectual independence.

Despite their adherence to very different kinds of social clocks, the FSCs and the MOCs shared many similarities when contrasted with those women who appeared to adhere to *neither* social clock. Helson writes that "because it is essential to the stability of a society to have large numbers of its members committed to social clock patterns, adherence is rewarded and those who do not conform to the schedules of their reference groups suffer from self-doubt and low self-esteem" (p. 1089). In this study, those women who never had children and who were not on the MOC at age 28 were less independent and self-accepting, "dwelling on a negative self-image, being at odds with themselves and others, feeling incompetent, wishing for the support and approval of others, and [seeing themselves] as self-indulgent— unable and unwilling to discipline themselves to sustain routine task performance" (p. 1089). In the adult years, failure to adhere to any social clock whatsoever—whether it be a traditionally masculine or feminine one— seems to exact great psychological costs. One midlife woman who had not raised children (NFSC) and who had not developed an MOC career path summed up the problems she saw for her future in this way:

My future is a giant question-mark. I keep thinking if I can settle down once and for all that I will be "safer." But I get restless with a remarkable degree of predictability. I am looking for a challenge, a life of real substance and meaning, yet I am lazy. I want excitement, but I want relaxation. I want to make plans, but I want freedom. . . . I am still single, but stubbornly hopeful, though I don't seem to be doing much about it. (Helson, Mitchell, & Moane, 1984, p. 1090)

The small body of research employing identity and intimacy status constructs shows a modest but significantly positive correlation between the two measures. Orlofsky, Marcia, and Lesser (1973) found that male college students who showed the relatively mature identity statuses of identity achievement and moratorium tended also to exhibit the more mature intimacy statuses of intimate and preintimate. Tesch and Whitbourne (1982) examined the relation between identity and intimacy in 48 men and 44 women in their mid-20s. The subjects were administered the standard identity-status and intimacy-status interviews. The authors added a fifth intimacy status, termed "merger," which designated relationships in which one partner dominated the other. Some of the results of the study are displayed in Table 12.5. Men and women who had successfully resolved identity questions (identity achievement) tended to show relatively high levels of intimacy (intimate status). Those showing the lowest levels of identity resolution (identity diffusion) tended also to score at low levels of intimacy (preintimate, stereotyped, isolate).

Kahn, Zimmerman, Csikszentmihalyi, and Getzels (1985) examined the relation between the extent to which a young adult resolves identity problems on the one hand, and the quality of married life—assessed 18 years later—on the

Table 12.5

Relationship Between Identity Status and Intimacy Status in a Study of Young Adults

Intimacy	Identity			
	Achievement	Foreclosure	Moratorium	Diffusion
	Males			
Intimate	8	2	0	2
Merger	2	3	0	0
Preintimate	4	1	0	4
Sterotyped	0	2	0	1
Isolate	0	0	0	3
	Females			
Intimate	7	4	0	1
Merger	0	2	0	1
Preintimate	3	1	3	1
Stereotyped	1	0	0	3
Isolate	0	0	0	0

Note: Numbers represent number of subjects (frequencies).
Adapted from Tesch & Whitbourne (1982, p. 1049).

other. They found that the degree of identity resolution in young adulthood predicted the establishment (for men) and the stability (for women) of marital relationships at midlife. Young men with high levels of identity resolution were more likely to marry, whereas those with low levels of identity tended to remain bachelors. Young women with high levels of identity were less likely to experience divorce and separation in their subsequent marriages compared to young women scoring low on identity.

The Later Stages

The last two stages/chapters in Erikson's model of lives in time correspond to middle and later adulthood. Middle adulthood focuses on caring for and leaving a legacy to benefit the next generation. In later adulthood, the person is concerned with looking back upon life and accepting it as good.

In Erikson's developmental scheme, **generativity vs. stagnation** is the seventh of eight sequential stages, generally identified with that long period in the life course after early adulthood but before "old age."

The prototype for generativity is raising children. By being good and caring parents, Erikson argues, many adults fulfill their basic "need to be needed" (Erikson, 1963) and directly promote the next generation. Yet there are many other ways to be generative, especially in one's occupational life, in creative activity, and through community involvements such as Girl Scouts, Little League, charitable contribution, church activities, and the like. In all of these endeavors, the generative adult acts on "the desire to invest one's substance in forms of life and work that will *outlive the self*" (Kotre, 1984, p. 10). The generative adult commits him- or herself to some activity that is larger than his or her own life, investing significant time and creative energy into an endeavor that will "live on." Kotre (1984) identifies four different ways in which adults may be generative: through biological, parental, technical, and cultural generativity (Table 12.6). Connecting all four are *acts of caring.* In his psychobiographical study of the life of Mahatma Gandhi, Erikson (1969) writes:

> A mature man of middle age has not only made up his mind as to what, in the various compartments of his life, he does and does not *care for,* he is also firm in his vision of what he *will* and *can* take *care of.* He takes as his baseline what he irreducibly is and reaches out for what only he can, and therefore, must *do.* (p. 255)

A Model of Generativity   Beyond Erikson, a number of theorists have written about the role of generativity in the adult life course (e.g., Browning, 1975; Gutmann, 1987; Kotre, 1984; Neugarten, 1968; Peterson & Stewart, 1990; Vaillant & Milofsky, 1980). Generativity has been variously described as a biological drive to reproduce oneself, an instinctual need to care for and be needed by others, a philosophical urge for transcendence and symbolic immortality, a developmental sign of maturity and mental health in adulthood, and a social demand to create a productive niche in society. It has been identified with behavior (such as raising children), with motives and values (concern for preserving what is good and making other things better), and with a general attitude about the world (having a broad perspective and understanding one's place in the sequence of generations).

In order to create an integrative framework to guide research on generativity, my students and I recently developed a model of generativity that brings together some of the best ideas on the concept and suggests specific ways to

Table 12.6

Four Types of Generativity

Type	Description
Biological	Begetting, bearing, and nursing offspring.
	Generative object: the infant.
Parental	Nurturing and disciplining offspring, initiating them into a family's traditions.
	Generative object: the child.
Technical	Teaching skills—the "body" of a culture—to successors, implicitly passing on the symbol system in which the skills are embedded.
	Generative objects: the apprentice, the skill.
Cultural	Creating, renovating, and conserving a symbol system—the "mind" of a culture—explicitly passing it on to successor.
	Generative objects: the disciple, the culture.

From Kotre (1984, p. 12).

measure different dimensions of generativity (McAdams, 1993; McAdams & de St. Aubin, 1992; McAdams, de St. Aubin, & Logan, 1993; McAdams, Foley, & Ruetzel, 1986; Van de Water & McAdams, 1989). The model suggests that generativity is a *configuration of seven psychosocial features,* all of which center on the personal and societal goal of *providing for the next generation.* To understand this model, you should think of generativity as something that exists both within the person and in the person's world. It is as much a quality of environments as it is a quality of people. In that generativity links the person and the social world, generativity can only "happen" in a psychosocial context, when certain variables within the person and in the person's world come together to provide for the next generation.

The model of generativity is presented in Figure 12.1. Starting on the far left, Boxes 1 and 2 in the model identify ultimate motivational sources for generativity. The first of these is (1) *cultural demand.* All human cultures demand that adults provide for the next generation. These demands are implicitly encoded in the societal expectations for age-appropriate behavior. In American society, we do

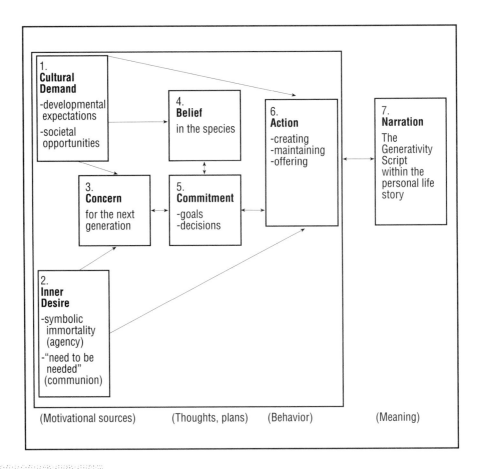

Figure 12.1

Seven Features of Generativity.

From McAdams & de St. Aubin, p. 1005.

not expect 10-year-old children to provide primary care for the next generation. We generally do not expect them to be thinking about the legacy they will leave after they die. But as people move into young- and middle-adulthood, we come to expect an increasing awareness of and commitment to their roles as providers. One of the reasons generativity emerges as a psychosocial issue in the adult years is that society comes to demand that adults take responsibility for the next generation, in their roles as parents, teachers, mentors, leaders, organizers, "creative ritualizers" (Browning, 1975), and "keepers of the meaning" (Vaillant & Milofsky, 1980). As adults move through their 30s and 40s, those who are unable or unwilling to contribute to and assume responsibility for the next generation, usually through family or work, are considered "off time" and at odds with the expected "social clock" (Neugarten & Hagestad, 1976).

But generativity doesn't happen only because society wants it to. Many theorists suggest that generativity springs as much from deeply rooted (2) *inner desire* as it does from cultural demand. Two sharply contrasting desires have typically been identified. The first is a desire for symbolic immortality. As Kotre (1984) and Becker (1973) suggest, adults desire to defy death in symbolic ways by constructing legacies that live on. In generativity, the adult creates, promotes, nurtures, or generates something or someone in "one's own image"—as an extension of the self. One's generative legacy can be as humble as a wise piece of advice offered to a coworker. It can be as grand as raising a large family, building a business, composing a song, painting a picture, leading a community, making a discovery, or even building a nation. Ideally, the product of one's generative efforts outlives the self, such that mature adults ultimately come to define themselves in terms of what they leave behind. In middle adulthood and beyond, writes Erikson, "I am what survives me" (1968, p. 141). The second desire is what Erikson terms the "need to be needed," the desire to nurture others, to be of use to those who are in need. While the desire for immortality suggests power and self-expansion, the need to be needed reveals generativity's soft and loving side. One of the most fascinating aspects of generativity is its conflictual essence—it celebrates the infinite expansion of the self and the surrender of the self at the same time. To be especially generative is to want to live forever and to want to give oneself up completely for the good of others, at the same paradoxical time.

Cultural demand and inner desire combine to promote in adulthood a conscious (3) *concern* for the next generation. Thus, developmental expectations about making a contribution to the next generation and inner desires for agential immortality and communal nurturance come together in adulthood to promote the extent to which the person cares for and about the development of the next generation. Along with concern, an adult may develop what Erikson (1963, p. 267) calls a (4) *"belief* in the species" (Van de Water & McAdams, 1989). This is a basic and general belief in the fundamental goodness and worthwhileness of human life specifically as envisioned for the future. To believe in the (human) species is to place hope in the advancement and betterment of human life in succeeding generations, even in the face of strong evidence of human destructiveness and deprivation. A strong belief in the species can help an adult translate his or her concern for the next generation into (5) generative *commitment,* taking responsibility for the next generation and making decisions to establish goals and strivings for generative behavior. When such a belief is lacking, however, the adult may find it difficult to make a strong generative commitment, because it may appear that a generative effort may not be very useful, anyway. Why commit yourself to promoting the next generation, some might say, if you think that the world is headed for disaster anyway and there is little you can do about it?

Guided by commitment, which itself is a product of demand, desire, concern, and belief, a person may act, may actually do something to provide for the next generation. Generative (6) *action* may be expressed in any of three loosely related guises: (a) creating, (b) maintaining, or (c) offering. First, generative action may involve giving birth to people, things, and outcomes, making, creating, generating, formulating, or discovering that which may be seen as "good." Second, generative action may involve passing on good things, preserving, conserving, maintaining, fostering, cultivating, nurturing that which is deemed worthy of such behavior, as in raising children, preserving good traditions, protecting the environment, and enacting rituals (in the school, home, or church) that link generations and assure continuity over time (Browning, 1975; Erikson, 1982). Third, generative action may involve the seemingly selfless offering up of that which has been created or maintained, passing something or someone on to the next generation as a gift, granting the gift its own autonomy and freedom (Becker, 1973; McAdams, 1985b). For example, the truly generative father is both a self-aggrandizing creator and a self-sacrificing giver. Biologically and socially, he creates a child in his own image, working hard and long to promote the development of the child and to nurture all that is good and desirable in the child. But he must eventually grant the child his or her own autonomy, letting go when the time is right, letting the child develop his or her own identity, make his or her own decisions and commitments, and ultimately create those offerings of generativity that will distinguish that child as someone who was "given birth to" in order to "give birth to."

Recent research has examined the relations among generative action, commitment, and concern and their relative salience at different points in the adult life course. In order to assess individual differences in an adult's conscious *concern* for the next generation, McAdams and de St. Aubin (1992) developed and validated the Loyola Generativity Scale (LGS), a 20-item self-report questionnaire. To assess *action,* they employed a behavior checklist that asks a person to endorse the number of times in the preceding two months that he or she had engaged in a number of different behavioral acts, many of which suggest generativity. Examples of possible generative acts are "taught somebody a skill," "served as a role model for a young person," and "performed a community service." Generative *commitments* were assessed by asking persons to describe ten "personal strivings" (Emmons, 1986; Chapter 9 in this book) or current goals that they were involved in, and then coding the responses for themes of generativity (McAdams, de St. Aubin, & Logan, 1993). The findings of two different studies show that generative concern and generative actions are significantly positively correlated. In other words, people who express a greater concern for the next generation on the LGS also tend to report a greater number of generative behaviors over the preceding two months. Concern and action are also positively associated with number of generative commitments. Finally, high scores on concern for the next generation are positively associated with self-ratings of life satisfaction and happiness. Being concerned about the next generation may be good for the next generation as well as for the self.

McAdams, de St. Aubin, and Logan (1993) administered measures of generativity to a community sample of 152 adults, divided into three age groups: young adults (ages 22–27), midlife adults (ages 37–42), and older adults (ages 67–72).

Controlling for educational and income differences among the three groups, the researchers found a significant effect of age/cohort on generativity. Overall, midlife adults tended to score higher than younger and older adults, as can be seen in Table 12.7. In keeping with Erikson's idea that generativity is an especially salient issue of middle adulthood, the researchers found that generative concern and action were higher among adults between the ages of 37 and 42 than they were among younger adults in their mid 20s and older adults around the age of 70. Of course, these differences could be due to cohorts. Because this was a cross-sectional study, we cannot determine if the differences observed are due to development per se or to possible historical differences between different generations of men and women growing up during different eras. In this study, the young adults were all born in the mid 1960s; the midlife adults were "baby-boomers" born in the early 1950s; and the older adults were from a generation who came of age during World War II.

Not all measures of generativity show the same age-related patterns. For example, older adults tended to score just as high as midlife adults on generative *commitments.* By contrast, young adults showed remarkably low scores on generative commitments. Adults between the ages of 22 and 27 years rarely reported that the things they were trying to do everyday (their personal strivings) involved such generative goals as becoming involved with younger people, caring for others, or making creative contributions to others. By way of illustration, consider the daily commitments reported by three women in the study—ages 26, 40, and 68 years, respectively. The young woman reports she is typically trying to "make my job more interesting than it really is," "be more open to others," "figure out what I want to do with my life," "be a good person," "enjoy life," "avoid uncomfortable situations," "keep up with current events," "be well-liked," "make my life more interesting and exciting," and "make others believe I am completely

Table 12.7

Mean Scores on Three Features of Generativity by Age/Cohort

	Ages 22–27	Ages 37–42	Ages 67–72
Generative Concern	40.14 (7.28)	41.82 (6.95)	38.26 (9.59)
Generative Commitments	1.62 (1.43)	3.28 (1.78)	3.39 (2.19)
Generative Action	26.63 (8.64)	31.55 (10.25)	28.16 (11.74)

Note: Numbers in parentheses are standard deviations.
From McAdams, de St. Aubin, & Logan (1993), p. 225.

Generativity: An older man tells stories to children.

confident and secure." Her strivings appear to revolve around social acceptance and the maintenance of daily well-being. There is no generative content, though she wishes to "be a good person." By contrast, the midlife woman describes four of her ten strivings in generative terms. She is trying to "be a positive role model for young people," "explain teenage experiences to my son and help him work through difficult situations," "provide for my mother to the best of my ability," and "be helpful to those who are in need of help." Similarly, the 68-year-old woman writes that she is trying to "counsel another who was recently let go from job due to cutbacks," "help another daughter with her sick child," "help as a volunteer at a nonprofit organization," "assist a candidate running for election," and "offer financial aid to someone close (friend or relative) if needed."

The final feature of the new model of generativity is (7) generative *narration*. Adults make sense of cultural demand, inner desire, concern for the next generation, belief in the species, generative commitment, and their own actions of creating, maintaining, and offering up in terms of their own narrative understanding of their life, evolving over time. Adults, therefore, consciously and unconsciously narrate for themselves and others, a *generativity script.* This is an inner story of the adult's own awareness of where efforts to be generative fit into his or her own personal history, into contemporary society and the social world he or she inhabits, and, in some extraordinary cases, into society's own encompassing history. In the context of a person's self-defining life story (a concept that we will explore in greater detail in Chapter 13), the generativity script provides the adult with an envisioned ending. As adults envision how their own life stories will end, they give birth to new people (children), new ideas, and new creations that ultimately "outlive the self." Although generativity is likely to be a major concern from early adulthood onwards, it may assume special prominence at midlife as the social clock suggests that the person begin the process of constructing endings, of figuring out how the story will eventually end. Of course, the literal end to life is a long way off, for most midlife adults. But their apprehension that they are now at the midway point orients them to endings, motivating them to make sense again of the past and present in terms of an envisioned future ending.

Stories of Generativity   The various ways in which adults construct their life stories to accommodate their generative concerns are poignantly portrayed in Kotre's (1984) book, *Outliving the Self.* Over a series of lengthy interviews, Kotre asked adults to tell in detail the stories of their own lives. For each case, Kotre created a dramatic narrative encapsulating what he believed to be the heart of the story and then analyzed the story in terms of two or three key themes of generativity. A major theme in a few of the stories concerns the ways in which our efforts to create legacies of the self and then offer them to others may encounter insurmountable and even tragic obstacles. Some people who desperately want to bear children, cannot. Some people who seek to be generative in artistic, political, scientific, literary, or social ways find their efforts stymied and their generated products rejected. Some people, by design or unwittingly, damage their own creations.

One of Kotre's most moving examples is the case of Dorothy Woodson, an African-American woman. Dorothy's account of her childhood and her adult years is pervaded by the issue of beauty *versus* ugliness. Growing up in a poor and abusive family, Dorothy believed that she was the ugliest girl in the world. "My mother was very beautiful, and I think she reacted to my ugliness." At 18, Dorothy married, and for a short time she felt that she had rid her life of ugliness. But then her first son was born:

> When my first son was born, he was very dark, and he was oh, so homely. He was just so little, you know, so withered. He was just three pounds, and he wasn't fully developed. I used to go up to the hospital every day to see him, and I'd think, "Why couldn't my first baby be more beautiful? He's ugly just like me. Why couldn't he have taken after his dad?" And sometimes I wonder, well, is that the reason he died? Did he sense that I didn't really

accept him because he wasn't a beautiful baby? Didn't he have the will to live because he sensed that? I used to think that way. I try not to entertain those thoughts anymore. (Kotre, 1984, p. 42)

Though the baby gained weight and Dorothy eventually took him home, her son died shortly thereafter, from complications associated with his premature birth. Dorothy's second child, Diana, was born about one year later. She was the beautiful child for whom Dorothy had longed. The baby thrived at home for a number of months. During this time, Dorothy's husband was working extremely long hours, and she was able to spend virtually no time with him. One evening she decided to meet him for dinner. She left Diana with a babysitter, who was 13 years old. Tragically, the baby suffered third-degree burns in a mysterious mishap at home and died. Her ugly blistered and swollen body is an image that haunts Dorothy to this day.

Life has been somewhat kinder in the years since the death of Diana. Dorothy has raised a healthy son, now an adolescent, with whom she seems to enjoy a positive relationship. Though she divorced her husband, she has become closer to her family of origin. She has been relatively successful in a number of different jobs. She has become heavily involved in a church, through which she is able to be generative. She has experienced a good deal of generativity, as well, through ballet, as she believes her beautiful dancing is a gift that she can offer others. Dorothy believes that the purpose of her life is to "undo" the damage she has unwittingly inflicted on her generative creations. She seeks to erase the ugliness of the past, to replace it with the beauty of her third child, her ballet, and her religious vision of being reunited someday with a restored and beautified Diana. Kotre elaborates on the theme of "generative damage" and Dorothy's attempt to "undo":

Recognizing that creations are flawed, knowing that one has in some way "slaughtered the innocents" under one's care can be devastating. Mirrorlike, progeny and works reflect their creator, misshapen ones saying that the creator's essence is deformed, for it grew and gave birth to this. From the subtle accusation lying in the product flows the urge to shatter or disown it, or, more commonly, to dim the recognition of damage. In the narratives I recorded, reactions to the recognition of damage varied from mild regret to extreme guilt, one of the most powerful emotions I encountered. Some realized that the destruction was a part of life, that one had both received it and dealt it out, and in neither case could it be undone. Some were silent about the harm they had done, while others alleviated their guilt by denying that harm existed, by blaming their victims, or by attributing their behavior to an uncontrollable disease that had afflicted them. A few rightly saw that their hand had been forced by external circumstances, and they were embittered; while they grieved, they retained their anger. The responsibility that Dorothy Woodson feels is almost beyond guilt, grief, or anger. No twisted defense mechanisms hide from her the fact of what happened. Her knowledge is tempered only by a belief in a resurrected life in which Diana will be "just as I saw her, but whole, not blistered." In this intuition of the future, the damage is emotionally undone. (pp. 60–61)

Integrity   The last stage of the life cycle, according to Erikson, is centered on the psychosocial issue of **ego integrity *versus* despair.** In old age, says Erikson, generativity fades as a major concern, and the adult becomes preoccupied with looking back and either accepting or rejecting one's own life as it was. In order to have integrity, the person must accept graciously his or her own life story as something that, for all its faults and foibles, "had to be and that, by necessity, permitted no substitutions" (Erikson, 1963, p. 268).

Erikson describes integrity as a postnarcissistic approach to life through which a person looks back, reviews, and critiques the one life story that has been produced. Butler (1975) agrees, suggesting that many elderly people undertake a **life review,** through which they reflect upon the past in order to "settle accounts." Ego integrity seems to involve attaining a certain distance on one's own biography. The elderly person who looks for integrity in life steps out of the life story he or she has been making and remaking since adolescence—steps away from identity, in a postnarcissistic fashion. Now it is time to look back at the story as it was—not as something to be revised yet again, but as something to accept, enjoy, even savor (McAdams, 1993). With this acceptance comes a new wisdom, writes Erikson, which exists as the final virtue of the human life cycle. On the other hand, when the person is unable to accept the life story as a gift, he or she experiences bitter despair.

Ego integrity and despair are probably the least examined of all of Erikson's ideas, the two most shrouded in conceptual mystery. One of the great mysteries concerns exactly *when* people encounter this final challenge of the life-span. "Old age" is a very imprecise term. Many Americans who have been employed retire around the age of 65 or 70. The years of retirement may be seen as a postgenerative period in some, if not many, lives. Though many adults in their 70s and 80s continue to be generative by being grandparents and making other contributions to the next generation, others (finances and health willing) disengage themselves from virtually all generative pursuits and devote themselves to relaxation, fun, and golf. Does the concept of ego integrity aptly capture what is going on at this time? How do we make psychological sense of this kind of postgenerative period of the life-span? Should it be seen as a kind of return to childhood? A reward for hard work? An escape? How does the older person make sense of this chapter in his or her life story in terms of those preceding it?

These are difficult questions that have generally not been addressed in personality theory and research. The healthy, postgenerative years that some American adults enjoy probably function in accord with a great many psychosocial demands that we do not yet clearly understand. To the extent that these years have anything to do with the urge to find ego integrity, they may be viewed as a movement away from seeing one's own life as a narrative in time. For some older adults, the "on-time" transition may, ironically, be a *transcendence* of time and the making sense of time through narrative. In other words, the postgenerative years of healthy retirement may be the right time for loosening time's grip on the self. Certain Eastern religions and mystical traditions speak of the "eternal moment" that people experience when they have attained true wisdom and enlightenment. The enlightened person no longer struggles to make sense of beginnings, middles, and endings—time's great demarcations—in terms of unifying stories about the self and the world. The person simply exists in the moment, embracing all time in the present twinkling of an eye. Perhaps, this is part of Erikson's message on ego integrity, and why its attainment in the human life cycle must necessarily await the end.

Story Beginnings and Endings: Alfred Adler

Alfred Adler and Individual Psychology

Alfred Adler (1870–1937) was an early disciple of Freud who eventually left the psychoanalytic fold to develop a new approach to personality called **individual psychology.** Because of his early association with psychoanalysis, Adler is often grouped with Freud, Jung, and other "depth psychologists" whose primary mission has always been, as we saw in Chapters 2–3 to unravel the intrapsychic mysteries of the unconscious mind. This grouping, however, is misleading, for it implies more similarity in theory than in fact exists between Freudians and Adlerians. Like Henry Murray and Erik Erikson, Adler presented a very eclectic and original theory of the person, which draws on, and has had a major influence on, a number of diverse approaches. Like Murray and Erikson, furthermore, Adler reveals a subtle but keen appreciation for the role of psychosocially constructed *narrative* in human lives organized in time.

Alfred Adler was born in Vienna in 1870 of a middle-class Jewish family. He was a second son, who, throughout his childhood, found himself continually trying to match the high achievements of his older brother. His family constellation included an envious younger brother and three other siblings. Sibling position and rivalry in the family are major themes of Adler's theory of personality development, as described in Feature 12.B. Adler received a degree in medicine from the University of Vienna in 1895 and began a private practice shortly thereafter. In 1897, he married Raissa Epstein, an ardent socialist whom he met at a political convention. Though he was not a militant activist, Adler espoused a decidedly socialist political philosophy throughout his life. Unlike Freud, Jung, and most of the other grand theorists of personality, Adler identified strongly with the working classes, giving many lectures to workers' groups in Europe and the United States in the 1920s and 1930s.

In 1902, Adler met Freud and immediately became active in psychoanalytic circles. He became the first president of the Viennese Psychoanalytic Society in 1910, but he cut his ties with Freud only a year later after a series of bitter disputes. As early as 1908, Adler had taken issue with Freud's insistence that sexuality was at the center of human instinctual life. Adler argued, instead, for a basic motive of aggression, an idea that Freud, ironically, accepted some 12 years later in his reformulation of human motivation to include both life and death instincts. At the time of Adler's proposal, however, such a departure from orthodox psychoanalytic theory was not welcomed. Adler formed his own group under the auspices of individual psychology, and he eventually attracted followers from all over the world. During World War I, Adler served as a physician in the Austrian army, and after the war he established the first child-guidance clinics in Vienna. Foreseeing the imminent Nazi menace, he left Europe in the early 1930s and settled in New York, where he continued his practice as a psychiatrist and his extensive lecturing and writing on individual psychology.

In contrast to Freud and Jung, Adler presents a very straightforward theory of the person. It is premised on a view of humankind that emphasizes conscious thought and the social determinants of personality. Like the social-learning theorists of Chapter 6, Adler suggests that personality is shaped by learning in a social environment. Like the cognitive approaches in Chapters 8–10, individual psychology argues that people are generally conscious of the reasons for their behavior and are capable of making rational life decisions with regard to conscious life goals and plans. Like the humanistic theories of Rogers and Maslow (Chapter 8), individual psychology paints a relatively optimistic picture of a developing and enhancing human organism, mastering the environment and creating the self over the human life course.

Beginnings: The Earliest Memory

Human beings are fascinated with beginnings. We want to know "how it all started," "where things come from," what the "origins" of a particular event or phenomenon are. We tend to believe that we can understand something fully only when we know its beginnings. Witness our fascination with creation myths, the theory of evolution, and scientists' speculations about the "Big Bang." Indeed, the very first verse of the first chapter of the Bible—the book of Genesis, whose name itself means "beginnings"—reads: "In the beginning God created the heaven and the earth." For Christians and Jews, this verse has traditionally served as the ultimate explanatory utterance.

When it comes to explaining our own lives and the lives of others, furthermore, we are just as strongly drawn to beginnings. From childhood onwards, we want to know "where we came from" and what our "roots" might be. In this vein,

Birth Order and the Family Saga

Does being the first child in a family have a special effect on the personality? Is the youngest child in the family predictably different from the others? Does your birth order have anything to do with your identity? Alfred Adler strongly believed that the answer to all three of these questions was "yes." Based on his own experience as a middle child, sandwiched between a dominant older brother and three younger siblings, and based on his own clinical cases, Adler maintained that ordinal position in the family was a major determinant of style of life. Over time, families appear to develop standard patterns and stories in which each "actor" plays a well-scripted role. These roles are internalized to become stable features of personality that the person reveals in many different settings outside the family domain.

According to Adler, the firstborn child is likely to adopt the views and attitudes of authority. Therefore, he or she should be relatively conservative and power-oriented, generally responsible, and predisposed toward leadership. Living in the shadow of the firstborn, the second child is likely to be especially competitive and rebellious. Secondborns should be much more skeptical of authority than firstborns and much more likely to identify with those who lack power and authority. The youngest child in the family—the last-born—is the one child most likely to be pampered and spoiled by the parents. Adopting the role of "baby in the family," the youngest should be especially dependent and inclined to view him- or herself as particularly special or unique. Only children—those from one-child families—should show characteristics of both oldest and youngest children. Therefore, they are likely to be both dependent and domineering, and they should be the most likely to show excessive self-centeredness.

Does research support these propositions? The research literature on birth order and personality is vast and difficult to comprehend as a whole (Forer, 1977; Sampson, 1962; Schooler, 1972). Many of the studies do not directly test Adlerian hypothe-

Adler accorded a great deal of significance to the person's earliest memory. What a person can consciously remember from the earliest years holds clues about that person's present and future identity (Adler, 1931, 1937). In Adler's view, the earliest memory reveals major themes in a person's **style of life,** that is, the person's unique mode of adjustment to life, most notably including the person's self-selected goals and means of achieving them. Adler believed that each life was patterned according to a unique style, the central features of which are outlined through early relationships in the person's family.

Although he did not couch his theory in explicitly narrative terms, Adler appeared to view the earliest memory as something like a personal creation myth

ses, and the results from those that do often seem contradictory. The consensus seems to be that birth order may have a small effect on personality, but the effect is mediated by such demographic factors as sex, social class, and ethnicity, and by a host of other variables that are more difficult to assess. Without intensive study of each family, it is difficult to know what a particular ordinal position means in a particular family constellation. A firstborn son in a large intact Catholic family living in a working-class section of Boston is likely to have a very different experience of family life than a firstborn daughter of a small but wealthy family where the parents are divorced and in which neither parent claims a religious affiliation, both parents travel extensively, and the daughter spends weekdays with Mom and weekends with Dad.

Despite numerous contradictions and ambiguities in the research, there do exist a small number of studies to support the idea that firstborns are *slightly* more achievement-oriented and conservative than persons of other ordinal positions. In addition, firstborns tend to score higher on intelligence tests (Zajonc, 1976). Kagan (1984) reports an interesting study by Sulloway (1972) in which firstborns were shown to be more reluctant in general than laterborns to endorse controversial new ideas. Sulloway examined the responses of eminent scientists in the nineteenth century to Darwin's highly controversial theory of evolution. He found a strong tendency for firstborn scientists to criticize the theory as untenable and for laterborns to endorse Darwin's revolutionary ideas. A similar result was found in a survey of reactions to the scientific discoveries of Copernicus, Bacon, and Freud. In keeping with Adler's suggestion that firstborns are more conservative and likely to adopt the views of authority, Sulloway's data suggest that firstborn scientists are less likely to endorse a controversial theory that puts them at odds with the majority view, compared to those scientists who are not firstborn.

or scene that implicitly foreshadows and symbolizes the overall tone of the person's subsequent life story. A number of his own examples are illuminating in this regard (Adler, 1927, 1929, 1931). Adler describes the case of a man whose first memory was that of being held in his mother's arms, only to be summarily deposited on the ground so that she could pick up his younger brother. His adult life involved persistent fears that others would be preferred to him, including extreme mistrust of his fiancée. Another man whose style of life emphasized fear and discouragement recalled falling out of his baby carriage. A woman who distrusted most people and feared that they would hold her back in her pursuits recalled that her parents prevented her from attending school until her younger

Alfred Adler

sister was old enough to accompany her. And a young man who was being treated for severe attacks of anxiety recalled an early scene in which he sat at a window and watched workmen build a house, while his mother knitted stockings. To Adler, this recollection indicated that the young man was probably pampered as a child and that he preferred to be a spectator who watches things happen rather than a participant who makes things happen. Adler believed that this interpretation was supported by the man's current situation, in that he perennially became anxious whenever he tried to take up a new vocation. In an effective piece of vocational counselling, Adler suggested to this patient that he find an occupation that involves looking and observing. He took Adler's advice and became a successful art dealer.

Although psychologists outside Adlerian circles have been slow to investigate the role of early memories in personality, a small flurry of recent research supports Adler's general insight that such memories illuminate current personality trends and strivings (Kihlstrom & Harackiewicz, 1982). Tying together early memories and Marcia's identity statuses described above, Orlofsky and Frank (1986) found that college students in identity achievement and moratorium expressed more mature developmental themes in their early memories compared to students in foreclosure and identity diffusion.

Table 12.8

Early Memories According to Feelings of Control Over the World

Category of Memory	Example From Student High on Control	Example From Student Low on Control
Achievement Mastery	I was playing with my dolls. I was teaching them spelling. Since I couldn't spell, I would write down random combinations of letters and take them to my mother. After many trials and errors I spelled "home"— the first word I ever wrote.	I remember sitting on the floor near my mother's feet and watching her iron. She was ironing a favorite outfit of mine. I remember stroking the skirt once or twice.
Punishment	When I wanted to put ketchup on my potatoes, my father said I would have to eat it even if I didn't like it. I poured a bottle of ketchup on the potatoes and was made to sit there until I ate every bite.	I wanted to prove that I was a "big boy" by going to the store alone. When I got home, my parents punished me for "running away from home."
Interpersonal Difficulty	One day a carpenter came to fix the bathroom. I locked him and my mother in the bathroom. Finally after an hour a neighbor let them out.	I was wrestling with an older boy. He pinned me down and sat on me for more than 10 minutes. It hurt like hell.

Note: Feelings of control were assessed through a self-report questionnaire.
From Bruhn and Schiffman (1982, pp. 389–390).

Bruhn and Schiffman (1982) analyzed early memories provided by over 200 college students. Each student recalled earliest memories and filled out a questionnaire designed to assess the extent to which the student believed that he or she exerted effective control in the world. The early memories were analyzed from the standpoint of (1) mastery, (2) punishment, and (3) interpersonal difficulties. Bruhn and Schiffman found that those students who felt they had control over their worlds described early memories in which (1) they actively mastered the environment, (2) punishment was contingent on their own behavior, and (3) they caused their own interpersonal difficulties. Those students whose questionnaire responses indicated that they felt little control over their worlds expressed opposite themes. They tended to describe early memories in which (1) they were passive rather than active, (2) punishment was unrelated to their behavior, and (3) they were victims rather than causes of interpersonal difficulties. Some examples of these responses can be seen in Table 12.8. In this study, we see that early memories reveal the beginnings of a general orientation toward life. For those students who believed they could control and master the world, early memories emphasized how they had exerted control in the past. For the other students, however, early memories hint at a very different kind of story: a story premised on the assumption that the world controls them, that they cannot control it.

Endings: Fictional Finalism

In Adler's earliest theorizing, he argued that a prime motive for human behavior was a striving to be aggressive. Later he replaced this motivational idea with a more general **will to power.** Adler believed that human beings want to feel strong and powerful in their interactions with the world and that they seek to avoid experiences in which they feel weak or inferior. Yet many children encounter repeated experiences of weakness and helplessness in the face of physical deficits and anomalies. Adler termed such deficits **organ inferiorities.** While these inferiorities can exert a debilitating effect on personality development, many people compensate for their own perceived inferiorities by working extra hard to strengthen what is weak. For example, a child who stutters may train him- or herself to be an exceptional speaker in adulthood. Or a child who is weak and sickly may undergo rigorous training to become a physical stalwart as an adult, as we saw in the case of Yukio Mishima in Chapter 1.

Adler eventually abandoned his concept of will to power in favor of an even more general motivational tendency termed **striving for superiority.** He described this universal, innate tendency as the "great upward drive" of human behavior and experience:

> I began to see clearly in every psychological phenomenon the striving for superiority. It runs parallel to physical growth and is an intrinsic necessity of life itself. It lies at the root of all solutions to life's problems and is manifested in the way in which we meet these problems. All our functions follow its direction. They strive for conquest, security, increase, either in the right or in the wrong direction. The impetus from minus to plus never ends. The urge from below to above never ceases. Whatever premises all our philosophers and psychologists dream of—self-preservation, pleasure principle, equalization—all these are but vague representations, attempts to express the great upward drive. (Adler, 1930, p. 398)

We see in this wonderful quotation that Adler meant something quite general and encompassing when he posited a universal striving for superiority. The striving aims toward superiority over the environment as well as perfection, completion, and wholeness. In the context of this general life force, Adler reconceptualized organ inferiority to refer more generally to any feeling of weakness that arises from a sense of incompletion or imperfection in any sphere of life. He also blended with his great upward drive the concept of **social interest,** or the person's innate sense of kinship with all humanity. According to Adler, the well-adjusted person strives for superiority and wholeness in his or her environment while expressing a true love for and communion with other people. An important individual difference in personality, therefore, is the prominence of social interest in the lives of different persons. In an attempt to operationalize this concept for research, Crandall (1980, 1984) has developed a short social-interest questionnaire. Supporting Adler's theoretical claims, Crandall has found that people with strong social interest score higher on various measures of psychological adjustment and report fewer negative results of stress in their lives, compared to people who are low in social interest.

Though all persons strive for completion and wholeness in their lives, each person strives in a different way and toward a different end. In the motivational terms of Chapter 11, behavior is energized by the great upward drive of superiority but it is given direction and guidance by the person's thoughts about the future. A major theme in Adlerian psychology is that people are more oriented to the subjectively expected and hoped-for future than they are bound to the objective past:

> Individual Psychology insists absolutely on the indispensability of finalism for the understanding of all psychological phenomena. Causes, powers, instincts, impulses, and the like cannot serve as explanatory principles. The final goal alone can explain man's behavior. Experiences, traumata, sexual development mechanisms cannot yield an explanation, but the perspective in which these are regarded, the individual way of seeing them, which subordinates all life to the final goal, can do so. (Adler, 1930, p. 400)

According to Adler, persons understand their lives in terms of *final goals,* and they organize their behavior and experience accordingly. Early experiences, traumata, and so on are not in and of themselves the determinants of behavior. Rather, like Erikson, Adler argues that early events are subjectively reorganized in light of the (later) final goals. The final goals envisioned by each person are subjective expectations about what might happen in the future. They are products of the imagination, not empirical or logical facts. Envisioned final goals are fictions, with respect to which we act *as if* they were true. According to Adler, then, human behavior and experience is guided, for better or worse, by **fictional finalisms.** What each of us perceives to be the final goal of our lives is a fiction that we create to give our lives direction and purpose. Though some fictions may be impossible to realize, they nonetheless function in our lives as supreme organizers for our strivings and ultimate explanations for our conduct. Adler was quick to point out that a wildly unrealistic fictional finalism may be the root cause of a neurotic's misery. Yet, all people create fictions about the future of one sort or another. The most adaptive fictional finalism incorporates realistic expectations into an imaginative narrative about the future, capable of sustaining and stimulating the person's strivings for superiority, wholeness, and completion.

Adler's concept of fictional finalism resembles Murray's "unity thema" and certain aspects of Erikson's "identity." Murray, Erikson, and Adler present us with theories of the person that assume that the individual's life is a patterned psychosocial totality that integrates past, present, and future, with beginnings, middles, and endings. People strive for narrative unity and purpose as their lives evolve over time.

Biography, Narrative, and Lives

How do we come to understand fully the life course of a single person? What is the most effective medium through which we may view the single life evolving over time so that we may discover what that whole life is all about? Like Murray, White, and those personologists dedicated to the "study of lives" (Chapter 11), Erikson and Adler suggested that a psychologically informed *biography* is probably the best means for capturing a human life situated in time. Erikson is particularly well known in this regard for his psychobiographies of Martin Luther (1958), Mahatma Gandhi (1969), and George Bernard Shaw (1959).

Yet, most personality psychologists have *not* historically viewed themselves as biographers (Elms, 1988). Despite the intuitively appealing claim that people may be best understood in their biographical contexts, biographical approaches to the person have traditionally occupied a controversial and ambiguous status in personality psychology (Anderson, 1981; Runyan, 1982, 1990). Critics have asserted that biographical methods of investigation are generally too unwieldy and subjective for clear and rigorous scientific study and that biographical examinations of the single case lack reliability and external validity, as discussed in Chapter 11. Biography's defenders counter that these critics hold an overly narrow view of science, that good biographical studies are highly illuminating, and that personologists are essentially shirking their intellectual responsibility to study the whole person if they dismiss biography out of hand. Nonetheless, the past 10 to 15 years have witnessed an upsurge of interest in and a growing acceptance of biographical and autobiographical approaches and frameworks among personality psychologists and other social scientists (Bertaux, 1981; McAdams & Ochberg, 1988; Moraitis & Pollack, 1987; Runyan, 1988; Wrightsman, 1981).

Early Christian saints: subjects of medieval hagiographies.

Psychobiography

Before the twentieth century, literary biographers rarely employed psychological concepts to interpret the lives of their subjects. During the Roman Empire, Plutarch (A.D. 46?–120?) wrote the *Lives of the Noble Greeks and Romans,* taking as subjects such famous men as Pericles (the Athenian statesman) and Julius Caesar. Essentially, Plutarch composed moral vignettes from history to illustrate exemplary character traits such as honesty and courage. In the Middle Ages, Christian scholars wrote **hagiographies** to venerate the saints. These biographical accounts of the lives of great Christians were written mainly to glorify God and to teach the reader about faith. Many followed a standard form, culminating in the saint's trial before a court of "unbelievers" and his or her sentencing and execution—mirroring the story of Christ's trial and crucifixion. These religious tales, however, were not penetrating explorations in personality. Instead, they functioned as moral and spiritual lessons.

In the seventeenth century, biography began to assume a more sophisticated form when biographers such as Izaak Walton, who wrote about the lives of high churchmen, and John Aubrey, who focused on more common folk, began to think of themselves as literary artists (Gittings, 1978). As artists, therefore, they sought to create narratives that were entertaining and artistically satisfying. The most artful and illuminating early biography—indeed, the most famous biography in Western literature—was published by James Boswell in 1791. In *The Life of Samuel Johnson,* Boswell wrote about Dr. Johnson (1709–1784), the prominent English author, critic, and lexicographer who traveled in the elite circles of European intellectual society. In striking contrast to his eminent subject, the younger Boswell was a loud-mouthed gossip and a heavy drinker, initially known

James Boswell (left) and the subject of his classic biography, Samuel Johnson (right).

more for his womanizing than his literary talents. At the age of 22, Boswell befriended Johnson (then age 54), and for years after they traveled together.

Boswell's study was a flesh-and-blood portrait that explored many facets of Johnson's life, from Johnson's sparkling conversations with the great men of the day to his persistent depression. Though Boswell clearly admired his subject, the central aim of his analysis was not to eulogize. Rather, he sought to explore the many dimensions of Johnson's character so as to illustrate the sweep and grandeur of one particular life. Boswell's biography was one of the first to entertain the problem of the biographer's own relationship to the subject of the study. Indeed, Johnson was something of a father-figure and a best friend for the younger Boswell. Yet their relationship was ambivalent and multilayered. As he moved in his text from one passage to the next, Boswell played the various roles of critic, fan, observer analyst, and participant in relation to Johnson's life.

In 1910, Freud wrote *Leonardo da Vinci and a Memory of his Childhood,* considered to be the first **psychobiography.** Much of Freud's interpretation rested on his analysis of a fantasy from Leonardo's childhood in which, "when I was still in the cradle, a vulture came down to me, opened my mouth with his tail and struck me many times with his tail against my lips" (Freud, 1916/1947, pp. 33–34). In a highly controversial and much disputed line of reasoning, Freud speculated that this particular fantasy symbolizes themes of homosexuality and infantile dependency. On one level, the vulture's tail is a phallic symbol, suggesting a male homosexual fantasy about fellatio. On another level, the vulture represents mother, an association for which Freud found some indirect evidence in

Leonardo da Vinci: a self-portrait from a sketch in his notebooks.

Egyptian mythology. In this case, the tail is the breast, and the fantasy an expression of Leonardo's longing to regress to the secure maternal world of oral dependency.

In order to preserve his mother as the sole love object in his life, Leonardo subsequently turned away from all gross sensual activities and dedicated himself to the life of the mind. The small portion of libido not exhausted in his relentless scientific and artistic work was transformed into an ideal love of boys, for boys offered no viable threat to his consuming love for mother. Thus, homosexuality served to protect his love of mother. During his early adult years, Leonardo's severe sexual inhibition carried over into his creative life, too. Despite his genius, Leonardo repeatedly failed to complete his artistic projects, producing many "unfinished masterpieces" with which he was never thoroughly satisfied. Around the age of 50, however, he was rejuvenated, Freud maintained, by reexperiencing the love of his mother through meeting and eventually painting the woman who has become known as the Mona Lisa.

Psychobiography may be defined as "the systematic use of psychological (especially personality) theory to transform a life into a coherent and illuminating story" (McAdams, 1988c, p. 2, italics omitted). In psychobiography, the life to be transformed is usually that of a famous, enigmatic, or paradigmatic figure. Most psychobiographies are more comprehensive than Freud's brief sketch of Leonardo. Many psychobiographical studies take the entire life, from birth to death, as their subject of study, aiming to discern, discover, or formulate the central story of the entire life, a story structured according to psychological theory.

In the case of Leonardo, Freud's theory of choice was, of course, psychoanalysis. Yet psychobiography need not employ a strictly psychoanalytic framework (Runyan, 1982). Many psychobiographies have drawn on the theories of Jung, Adler, Erikson, and the object-relations approaches to personality. Psychobiographies have also been written from the theoretical standpoints of social-learning theory (Mountjoy & Sundberg, 1981), humanistic psychology (Rogers, 1980), existential psychology (Sartre, 1981), McClelland's theory of motives (Winter & Carlson, 1988), and Tomkins' theory of scripts in Chapter 13 (Carlson, 1988). Furthermore, many contemporary biographies, written by nonpsychologists, draw liberally from personality theory. While some of these use theory naively or inappropriately, others have been celebrated as masterful and illuminating, such as Leon Edel's monumental study of the American author Henry James (Edel, 1985).

Since Freud's *Leonardo,* many psychobiographies have been written, and advances in understanding particular lives have been made. Still it is very difficult to write a *good* psychobiography. The best-intentioned psychobiographers face major constraints and obstacles that usually do not confront other kinds of researchers. For instance, the subjects of their studies are often dead, and thus cannot be interviewed, tested, or directly observed. The data for the analysis come in a troubling variety of forms—from unsubstantiated hearsay about the person being studied, to personal correspondence and other writings, to publicly documented facts about the person's life. The most reliable data (such as birthdate or number of siblings) may be the least illuminating. The most intriguing data (such as personal fantasies, reflections, or dreams) may be the least reliable and the most difficult to interpret in an intellectually responsible way. Indeed, one of the major problems facing some psychobiographers is the sheer amount of biographical data that they face. How does one choose which data to interpret?

Irving Alexander (1988) provides nine helpful guidelines by which the psychobiographer may reduce huge amounts of data to manageable quantities, by identifying which data are worthy of further consideration and which may be tossed aside for the time being. Alexander argues that the data may be evaluated in terms of primacy, frequency, uniqueness, negation, emphasis, omission, error, isolation, and incompletion (Table 12.10, p. 704). Each may be viewed as a rule for storymaking employed by the biographer who seeks to discern or create the central story of a life. Each gives the biographer a clue about what may be important in narrative. Thus, the guideline of *primacy* suggests that what comes first in stories is especially significant; *uniqueness* suggests that what stands out as odd and intriguing in a story may be of special consequence; *omission* suggests that what seems to be missing in the story may be revealing; *distortion* and *isolation*

Continued on p. 706

Table 12.9

Common Criticisms of Psychobiography

Critical-period fallacy | Some psychobiographers overemphasize the influence of one early "critical period" such as the first year of life or the Oedipal period while neglecting formative influences at later stages.

Eventism | Attempting to explain major trends in a human life solely in terms of one or two key or "traumatic" events is poor practice. While some events are obviously more important than others, the entire life must be viewed as a complex and multiple determined whole.

Inadquate evidence | Some psychobiographical interpretations rest on limited or erroneous evidence. The psychobiographer must synthesize many different kinds of data from multiple sources that converge on a particular interpretation. He or she must check and double-check historical and biographical sources.

Neglect of social and historical factors | Too many psychobiographies do not take into careful consideration the complex social and historical context within which the individual's life is or was embedded. A person's life is strongly shaped by culture. The biographer cannot understand the life if he or she does not attempt to understand the culture.

Originology | Many biographers attempt to trace everything about a person to its origins in childhood. Given that the issue of continuity and consistency in personality from childhood to adulthood is a controversial one in personality and developmental psychology, the biographer runs the risk of placing too much emphasis on childhood events as determinants of adult outcomes.

Overpathologizing | A good psychobiography should not aim to reduce an entire life to a particular psychiatric syndrome or neurotic tendency. A life must be evaluated in terms of both its weaknesses and strengths.

Reconstruction | The psychoanalytically oriented biographer may reconstruct unknown or unsubstantiated childhood events from known adult outcomes. For instance, a biographer may assume that an anally retentive and compulsive adult experienced severe toilet training as a toddler. In the absence of evidence from childhood, these kinds of reconstructions are usually unwarranted.

Sources: Anderson (1981); Runyan (1982).

Why Did Van Gogh Cut Off His Ear?

On the evening of December 23, 1888, Vincent van Gogh, then 35 years old, cut off the lower half of his left ear and took it to a brothel, where he requested to see a prostitute named Rachel. He handed her the ear and asked that she "keep this object carefully."

Van Gogh (1853–1890) is famous today for the many brilliant expressionist masterpieces he painted during his short and very troubled life. The Dutch artist developed a unique style of painting—using rough strokes and bold colors to portray scenes that are often haunting and ominous—a style that even the most untutored art observers immediately recognize. While millions of art lovers have enjoyed his paintings, psychologists and biographers have puzzled over his life. The incident with the ear stands out as the most memorable of all van Gogh's odd behaviors. We can't help but wonder, over and over: Why did van Gogh cut off his ear?

Psychologist William McKinley Runyan (1981, 1982) has surveyed the psychobiographical literature on van Gogh and identified at least 13 different psychological explanations for this bizarre incident in the artist's life. Here are a few of the more interesting ones:

1. He was frustrated by the failure to establish a working and friendly relationship with his fellow artist Paul Gauguin and turned his resultant aggressive feelings toward himself.

2. He felt conflict over his homosexual feelings toward Gauguin. The ear was a phallic symbol (the Dutch slang word for penis, *lul,* resembled the Dutch word for ear, *lel*), and the act was a symbolic self-castration.

3. He was imitating the actions of bullfighters, with whom he had been especially impressed in his visits to Arles. In such events, the matador receives the ear of the bull as an award, displays his prize to the crowd, and then gives the ear to the lady of his choice.

4. He was influenced by a number of newspaper reports concerning Jack the Ripper, who mutilated the bodies of prostitutes, sometimes cutting off their ears. Adopting the masochistic over the sadistic approach, van Gogh turned on himself.

5. He was reenacting a scene from the New Testament in which Simon Peter cuts off the ear of Malchus, a servant of the high priest, who had come to seize Christ. van Gogh had been thinking about this event recently and had tried to paint it.

6. He was experiencing auditory hallucinations and during a psychotic episode cut off his ear to silence the disturbing sounds.

What do we make of these different, competing interpretations? Are they all right, or wrong (in one way or another)? Are some better interpretations than others?

Runyan argues that competing psychobiographical interpretations can be reasonably compared and contrasted and evaluated according to clear standards. Different explanations may be judged according to standards such as:

(1) their logical soundness, (2) their comprehensiveness in accounting for a number of puzzling aspects of the events in question, (3) their survival of tests of attempted falsification, such as tests of derived predictions or retrodictions, (4) their consistency with the full range of available relevant evidence, (5) their support from above, or their consistency with more general knowledge about human functioning or about the person in question, and (6) their credibility relative to other explanatory hypotheses. (Runyan, 1982, p. 47)

Runyan maintains that there is room for more than one good explanation for any given biographical event. Indeed, events are highly overdetermined, and influences from many different levels may come to bear in producing a particular behavior in a particular situation.

Carefully weighing the various explanations for van Gogh's behavior, Runyan favors those interpretations that emphasize the role of the artist's brother, Theo. The ear-cutting incident and two later mental breakdowns coincide with Vincent's learning that Theo is to be married, Theo's wedding, and the birth of Theo's first child. Each of these events may have reinforced Vincent's fear that he was losing his brother's care and his financial support. In the past, van Gogh had exhibited masochistic responses to rejection. In 1881, he had visited the parents of Kee Voss, a woman whom he loved. When he learned that Kee had left the house to avoid seeing him, he thrust his hand into the flame of a lamp and vowed to keep it there until she returned. On one level at least, Vincent may have cut off his ear in response to the perceived loss of and rejection by his brother.

But, then, why did he mutilate himself in this way? Why the ear? And why did he give it to this particular prostitute? The Jack-the-Ripper explanation seems farfetched, for there is no evidence that van Gogh was familiar with or impressed by the exploits of this criminal. Runyan also finds little support for explanations emphasizing symbolic castration. Van Gogh had been impressed, however, by the bullfights. And he had pondered over the scene in the Garden of Gethsemane when Peter cut off Malchus' ear. Perhaps these latter two interpretations hold a grain of truth. Perhaps not. Without more definitive evidence from the life of the artist, at least a few plausible but competing interpretations will invariably remain.

Table 12.10

Nine Guidelines for Extracting Psychobiography Data

Primacy	That which comes *first*. "The association of 'first' with importance has a long-standing history in folklore and in human customs and mores. Certainly in psychology the idea is upheld in the importance assigned to early experience in the development of personality by both Freud and Adler and countless successors. The first as the 'foundation stone' upon which structures are built is also a common metaphor in language."
Frequency	That which appears *often*. "For the most part, we are tuned to frequency or repetition as increasing signs of certainty and of importance. The kind of importance a frequent message has, however, may be complex in terms of its value for the discovery of dynamic sequence. In many instances, frequency may be an expression of powerful conscious value schemas."
Uniqueness	That which is *singular,* odd. "A powerful example of this occurred in the autobiographical sketch of a paid student volunteer intensively studied in a graduate personality assessment course. The student recalled an incident from his first year in elementary school: At the end of a school day he returned home to find his mother hanging from a rope in her bedroom, a description that he followed only with a statement that he was sent off to a private school shortly afterward. Uniqueness in this instance is signaled not only by the event itself but by the kind of response to the event reported by the subject."
Negation	That which is denied, or turned into its *opposite*. "Imagine, for example, a therapeutic interview in which a dream about the father is mentioned, followed by the statement, 'Let's move on to something else. *It's not* that I think talking about father would drive me crazy, it usually leads to a feeling of helplessness.'"
Emphasis	That which is *underscored* or stressed. The biographer should be aware of that which seems either overemphasized or underemphasized. "Overemphasis can usually be detected when the hearer or reader begins to wonder why so much attention is focused on something considered to be so commonplace. 'I just could not get over the fact that this person, a native of the country, for whom I as a tourist had inquired about directions, took such pains to make sure I understood how to find my way. From that moment on I adored my visit to _____.' would be an example chosen by the criterion of overemphasis for retention in the reduced data pool. Its ultimate transformation might be, unexpected attention (kindness) when in distress ⟶ euphoria. This may be an analogue of the expectation that when one is in trouble, no help is expected."

Table 12.10 continued

Table 12.10 continued

Omission	That which is *missing*. "An illustrative example might be one in which the subject describes a memory of being punished by his mother after she had accused him of hostile behavior toward a sibling. The retelling goes on to include the subject's feelings as a result of the mother's actions but speaks not at all to whether he had in fact treated the other child in the manner suggested. What is omitted is attention to the subject's role in a sequence with a negative outcome which must be investigated for its possible repetitive properties."
Error, or Distortion	That which is a *mistake*. "In written exposition this is sometimes indicated by obvious undetected error by the subject in an otherwise error free or minimally error-prone sample. An example might be the statement, 'I came from a family of tall people, my father is 6'5", my brother is 6'4", my mother is 9'5", and I am the runt at 5'8". This not only calls attention to the possible importance of the size dimensions in the life of the subject but highlights (error signaled by incredibility) the overvaluing of mother on whatever dimension the size variable symbolizes, and by contrast the undervaluing of the writer who is described uniquely as a runt. Underlying these pointers there most likely exists a dynamic set of conditioned sequences constituting the subject's view of the family drama."
Isolation	That which is alone, or *doesn't fit*. "'I remember how we saved a touchdown by our opponents in a high school football game by something we learned from observing their game films. Oh! Did I remember to bank the fire in the fireplace before I left the house to come here? The films showed that the quarterback. . . .'"
Incompletion	That which is *not finished*. "'All through college I dated John. It started as a casual friendship, but within a short period of time we found that we enjoyed the same interests and people. By the time we reached senior year we were making plans for a future together. Marriage, while not an immediate prospect, was our ultimate goal. Three years later I married Fred Perkins, whom I had recently met, and moved to Pittsburgh where we have lived ever since.' This illustrates an uncompleted fragment or portion of a descriptive segment about courtship and marriage which in itself has an aura of

From Alexander (1988, pp. 269–278).

Continued from p. 700
suggest that when something in the story does not follow logically, the biographer should seek to straighten it out; and *incompletion* suggests that when stories do not end properly, the biographer should seek to understand why. The psychobiographer must be sensitive to the clues in the data suggesting how the story of a person's life is to be discovered, created, and told (Edel, 1984; McAdams, 1988c).

While Alexander's nine guidelines may assist the biographer in identifying the important data in a particular life, he or she is still faced with the task of using psychological theory to organize the data into an illuminating and coherent narrative. Psychological theory must be applied with flexibility and grace. Too many psychobiographers force life-history data into rigid theoretical categories, as if to prove that all aspects of a particular life fit perfectly in an existing theoretical scheme. Others apply theory in the most desultory and trite ways, relentlessly dragging a human life, say, through each of Erikson's eight psychosocial stages or Murray's 20 psychogenic needs. Still others fail to understand the single life within its particular social, cultural, and historical matrix, reducing complex behavior and experiences, for instance, to early problems in toilet training or single traumatic events. These kinds of psychobiographies are boring. Worse, they make straightjackets out of theories and caricatures out of lives. In a sophisticated psychobiography, the data and the theory relate to each other as equals, as if they were two speakers in a lively conversation. Each influences and is influenced by the other, and each respects the other's integrity. Therefore, the skilled psychobiographer uses theory in a subtle and nuanced manner, making sense out of what can be made sensible, struggling with complexity and contradiction, knowing when to back off from lofty theories and let the concrete, unique human life speak for itself.

Life Histories

While the psychobiographer concentrates energy on one particular life, social scientists who collect **life histories** adopt biographical methods to test hypotheses and examine relationships across many lives. In psychology, anthropology, and sociology, the life-history approach to scientific research has become increasingly popular in recent years (Bertaux, 1981; Craik, 1986). In life-history research, the scientist collects autobiographies—either written or told—from a sample of people who share some similarity, such as a particular ethnic lineage, occupation, social problem, or life-style choice. Typically, the investigator seeks to understand the particular group, society, or subculture of which the subjects are members, searching for common patterns. The focus is on similarities in different persons rather than the uniqueness of the single life (Rosenwald, 1988). In some cases, the investigator aims to expose hidden social problems and dilemmas "so that others [the readers] may more easily recognize them in their own experience" (Rosenwald, 1988, p. 261).

Beginning in the nineteenth century, anthropologists have traditionally collected oral life-histories and supplemented them with biographical information drawn from conversations. In the 1920s and 1930s, an influential group of sociologists championed life-history research to investigate such social problems as deviance (Shaw, 1930) and to illuminate the complex interaction of social systems and persons. Sociologist John Dollard—discussed in Chapter 6 for his learning-theory work with Neal Miller—argued that a biographical account must be carefully interpreted with respect to the ways in which the single life mirrors society and a cultural milieu (Dollard, 1935). For Dollard, a life history was not "a kind of fairy story built out of the imagination of the observer"; it was instead a "rigorously constructed map of a series of social events" (p. 7).

Two of the first psychologists to adopt life-history methods in research were Charlotte Bühler (1933) and Else Frenkel (1936). They examined life histories written by almost 400 European men and women in the 1930s, representing various nationalities, social classes, and vocations. Whenever possible, the written accounts were supplemented by letters, diaries, and other personal documents produced by the subjects. The content analysis of all the data "revealed rather sharply demarcated phases through which every person passed in the course of his life" (Frenkel, 1936, p. 2). Fifty years ago, Bühler and Frenkel proposed a surprisingly modern and detailed model of adult development complete with five well-articulated stages and numerous references to a kind of "midlife crisis" around the age of 40. More concerned with general principles in all lives than with the uniqueness of any single life, these researchers focused on three dimensions of the adult biography: (1) significant external events (such as economic and political changes, war), (2) internal reactions to these events (such as thoughts, feelings, wishes), and (3) specific accomplishments and creative contributions to life. Here are a few of their more interesting findings:

1.   During the first half of life, a person's subjective experience appears strongly influenced by bodily needs and short-term wishes, but the latter half is marked by a preoccupation with internalized duties that one "has set himself, or which have been set for him by society, or which have come from some code of values such as religion or science" (Frenkel, 1936, p. 15). Deviations from this general pattern were observed only in subjects who had been diagnosed by psychiatrists as neurotic.

2.   Lives in which the pursuit of sexual gratification takes precedence over work and child-rearing suffer "an unquestionable subjective decline in the second half" (p. 20).

3.   Experiences of loneliness and daydreaming peak in late adolescence and again in the midforties. The latter period is also occasioned by a transitory reexamination of one's past and, in many cases, a heightened interest in literature.

4.   The search for a "meaning in life" begins in late adolescence.

An interesting example of a more recent approach to life histories is the work of Csikszentmihalyi and Beattie (1979) on **life themes.** The researchers interviewed 15 professional and 15 blue-collar men between the ages of 36 and 75 years in order to elicit, in the subjects' own words, the major events and experiences that they considered formative in their own lives. For each life history, the researchers sought to identify the unique life theme that was "played out against a larger background of historical themes" and to trace its perceived origins and subsequent development (p. 45). A life theme is the "basis for an individual's fundamental interpretation of reality and his or her specific ways of coping with reality" (p. 45). The person's life theme appears to develop through four phases:

1. Recognition of existential stress.
2. Finding the problem.
3. Stating the problem in a form that will allow a solution.
4. Carrying out a method of solution.

Through their life-history interviewing, Csikszentmihalyi and Beattie found that life themes were reflected in men's understanding of their own career choices and their strivings for social mobility. Professional men differed markedly from blue-collar men in their integration of life themes within their own biographies. Professional men tended to understand their own existential crises as reflecting universal problems or issues that were embedded in human nature or the structure of society. They viewed their own lives as complexly integrated within a larger, encompassing social and cultural milieu. Blue-collar men, on the other hand, viewed existential problems in more personal and concrete terms. Although Csikszentmihalyi and Beattie interviewed only a small number of men, their findings are especially provocative in suggesting important individual differences in the extent to which adults link their own biographies to the larger stories of their culture and their world.

Seasons of Adult Life

In recent years, psychologists and popular writers have suggested that the adult years can be understood in terms of developmental "stages," "phases," or "seasons" (Gould, 1980; Sheehy, 1976; Vaillant, 1977). As the American baby-boom generation has grown up and entered middle age, a number of observers of adult development have proposed that people pass through predictable periods of transition and stability in their adult years. Developmental transformations are not limited to childhood, these observers suggest. Adults continue to grow and mature in a predictable, incremental fashion into and through middle age.

Daniel Levinson (1978, 1981) has formulated a detailed and influential model of the "seasons of a man's life," based in part on biographical interviews of 40 American men. Levinson and his colleagues interviewed men between the ages of 35 and 45 years who were employed in one of four occupational groups: biology professors, novelists, business executives, and hourly workers in industry. Each man was interviewed 6 to 10 times, each interview lasting between 1 and 2 hours. Subjects were asked to tell their life stories, concentrating mainly on the years from adolescence onwards. Although the interviewers did not follow a standardized format of questions and answers, they were guided by a number of general considerations for the investigations, such as these:

1.   We have to cover various "areas of living" such as family of origin, education, occupation, love relationships, marriage and family of procreation, leisure, bodily health and illness, ethnicity, religion, politics, and relation to self.
2.   Within each area, it is essential to trace the sequence over the adult years, being alert to major events, choices and turning points, as well as to the character of relatively stable periods.
3.   We must learn about the "interpretation" of the areas. Occupational and family life, for example, are often closely intertwined.
4.   As a series of interviews progresses, the interviewer gets a sense of different "chapters" in the life story: three years in military service; four to five years of relatively transient living; the years of starting a family and getting settled in a new city and job. It is important to apprehend the overall character of life within each of these chapters, as well as the kinds of changes that occurred within it. Here the emphasis is on the patterning among the many areas of living—the forms of integration as well as the contradictions, gaps, and fragments.
5.   In the lives of many persons, there are occasional periods, lasting a few months to a few years, that constitute dramatic "high points" or "rock bottom" periods. These times often mark the end of one life phase and the beginning of another. They must be examined from many vantage points.
6.   We are interested in the participant's view of his life as a whole, and of the interrelations among various parts and times within it. . . . [The past is] part of the present, and the biographer must so represent it. Likewise, the person's defined plans and more shadowy imaginings of the future shape and are shaped by the present. The future, too, forms a part of the present that the biographer must explore. (Levinson, 1981, pp. 61–62)

The central concept in Levinson's model is the individual **life structure,** which "refers to the patterning or design of the individual life at a given time" (Levinson, 1978, p. 99). One of the more encompassing concepts in personality theory, the individual life structure includes the individual's sociocultural world (class, religion, family, political systems, historical era), his participation in this world (relationships and roles with respect to significant people and institutions in his life), and various "aspects of the self," which may remain stable or may be transformed over time. Levinson views adult development as the evolution of the life structure. From adolescence through middle age, the life structure evolves through periods (seasons) of relative calm and periods of significant transition.

The first period in Levinson's scheme, Early Adult Transition (ages 17–22), roughly corresponds to the late-adolescent and early-adult period in which Erikson (1959) places the psychosocial crisis of identity *versus* role confusion (see Figure 12.2). The young man leaves home for college, the military, first employment, or some other living situation in which he begins to assume financial independence from his parents and achieves greater levels of autonomy. During the

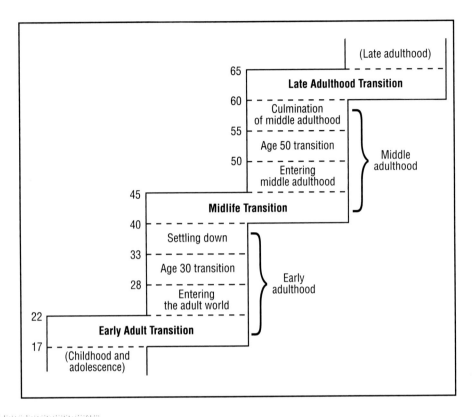

Figure 12.2

Levinson's Developmental Periods in Early and Middle Adulthood for Men.

From Levinson (1978, p. 57).

next phase, Entering the Adult World (ages 22–28), many young men explore adult roles and responsibilities and make provisional occupational commitments that link them to the wider society. In the late 20s, the man is likely to formulate a *dream* for the future. According to Levinson, the dream may include visions of occupational success and enhanced prestige, the development of a fulfilling family life, the establishment of certain kinds of relationships with friends and peers, and many other hopes and goals for the self, family, and significant others. Another significant aspect of development in the twenties, according to Levinson, is the establishment of a relationship with a *mentor*. The mentor is a man or woman who is usually somewhat older and more experienced than the young adult and therefore well positioned to shepherd the young adult through some of the difficult and challenging periods of the twenties. Mentors would appear to be most valuable and most common in the professional workplace. For example, a graduate student or junior professor heading for a career in college academia may find a mentor in his advisor. Through actions and advice, the adviser can teach the younger man how to make his way in the world of higher education, how to teach effectively, do good research, obtain governmental grants, get along with colleagues, and so on.

Around the age of 30, some men may encounter a significant transition period in which they feel the need to consolidate or rethink their tentative commitments from the 20s. The "Age 30 Transition" is followed by a period of Settling Down (early 30s). During Settling Down, the man is trying to carve a niche in the world and establish a timetable for advancement in his occupation, while simultaneously putting down roots in the sphere of his family. According to Levinson, the man in his early 30s is preoccupied both with "making it" and "building a nest," and he invests himself dearly in issues of order, stability, security, and control. By this time he has often generated a dream for the future, which will serve as a motivating vision of what he would like to accomplish and become.

With its emphasis on order and control, the Settling Down period of the 30s is oddly reminiscent of Erikson's second stage of psychosocial development: the toddler's period of autonomy *versus* shame and doubt. Like the toddler, the man in his early 30s seeks to control self and environment as an independent and autonomous agent. For the toddler, the next phase is Oedipal: Freud's universal ontogenetic tragedy of becoming the conquering king and then falling from power, captured in Erikson's third stage of initiative *versus* guilt. Levinson's next phase of the life structure—Becoming One's Own Man, or BOOM—likewise has a certain Oedipal ring to it:

> BOOM tends to occur in the middle to late 30s, typically in our sample around 35–39. It represents the high point of early adulthood and the beginning of what lies beyond. A key element in this period is the man's feeling that, no matter what he has accomplished to date, he is not sufficiently his own man. He feels overly dependent upon and constrained by persons or groups who have authority over him or who, for various reasons, exert great influence upon him. The writer comes to recognize that he is unduly intimidated by his publisher or too vulnerable to the evaluation of certain critics. The man who has successfully risen through the managerial ranks with the support and encouragement of his superiors now finds that they control too much and delegate too little, and he impatiently awaits the time when he will have the authority to make his own decisions and to get the enterprise really going. The untenured faculty member imagines that once he had tenure he will be free of all the restraints and demands he's been acquiescing to since graduate school days. (The illusions die hard!) (Levinson, Darrow, Klein, Levinson, & McKee, 1974, pp. 250–251)

BOOM sets the stage for the Midlife Transition. During this period (ages 40–45 years), 80% of the men Levinson interviewed encountered serious doubts concerning the directions of their lives. Taking stock of the various areas of commitment making up their life structures, many came to question the validity and worth of their hitherto most cherished goals and their plans for attaining them. For many, the Midlife Transition represented the bust following BOOM. Marital satisfaction, job performance, and enjoyment of outside pursuits declined. Confusion and despair became common as the sense of having established a home and a niche in the adult world, consolidated during Settling Down, gradually disintegrated, replaced by the nagging apprehension that one's life had been directed by and for the sake of illusions.

The Midlife Transition may be a very painful period in a man's life. Some of the men in Levinson's sample emerged from this period "cynical, estranged, unable to believe in anything" (Levinson, 1977, p. 108). Many others, however, benefitted from the searching reevaluation of life structure precipitated by the transition. Those who benefitted fashioned new life structures that opened up new opportunities and outlets for fulfillment in family, work, and friendships. Thus, the Midlife Transition may eventuate in a rejuvenated life structure in the second half of life—a restabilization around new plans and goals designed to maximize the individual's potential for fulfillment in many realms of life, especially the realms of intimacy and generativity.

Roberts and Newton (1987) describe four studies examining the life course of women, each of which employed Levinson's approach. Across the four studies, biographies from 39 contemporary women (ranging in age from 31 to 53, most middle-class and employed outside the home) were analyzed for the relevance and meaning of such Levinsonian concepts as (1) the dream, (2) the mentor, (3) the Age 30 Transition, and (4) the Midlife Transition. The authors conclude that these women passed through the same developmental seasons that Levinson sketched out for men. But a number of important differences were also noted. For example, women's dreams tended to be more complex and conflictual than men's, incorporating competing demands and hopes for family life and career success. Second, the women were much less likely than Levinson's men to report the existence of a satisfying mentoring relationship. Third, the women tended to place less emphasis than did Levinson's men on the importance of a Midlife Transition. However, they were more likely than the men to underscore the Age 30 transition as a period of accelerated and often dramatic personality change. This seemed to be especially true for women who by age 30 had not yet married or started a family. Some of these women began to feel a sense of urgency at this time. Soon it might be "too late" to become pregnant and bear children, some worried. Some of the women also began to question seriously the commitments they made in their 20s, and began to formulate a new life structure and a new dream to move them more rewardingly into their 30s. It would appear, therefore, that the Age 30 Transition *in women* could be somewhat analogous to the Midlife Transition *in men*. Both periods are described as having the potential for an urgent reexamination of the life structure because of the feeling that, in some sense or another, "time is running out."

The general idea that the adult life course may be viewed in terms of a sequence of periods or seasons is a controversial one today. Outside of in-depth biographical explorations like Levinson's, researchers have not found a great deal of support for a dramatic Midlife Transition in adult lives. For example, Costa and McCrae (1980a) developed a Midlife Crisis Scale to reflect the stresses of this portion of life identified by Levinson. No age differences were found on this scale in a large sample of men aged 33 to 79. Rossi (1980) and others have argued that the whole concept of an orderly life course in adulthood, complete with a progression of stages or seasons, does not accommodate well the lives of working-class adults and the lives of women. Levinson's stages may be descriptive of the lives of white, upper-middle class, professional men in America who entered midlife in the 1960s and 70s, but they may not generalize well to other samples.

On the other side of the coin, Helson and Wink (1992) find empirical support for some of Levinson's ideas in a longitudinal study of 101 women, followed between their early 40s and early 50s. The researchers document the existence of noteworthy developmental change around the age of 40, akin to a midlife transition, followed by increasing security, confidence, and decisiveness. Mercer, Nichols, and Doyle (1989) report data on women's lives that is both consistent with and different from Levinson's scheme. Overall, women in their study "tended to experience developmental periods at later ages and in sequences that were much more irregular" than those reported by Levinson (p. 180). However, something akin to a Midlife Transition manifested itself around the age of 40. The authors describe the age-40 time as a "Liberating Period" in many women's lives:

> For many women, the age-40 liberating period was the time of formulating a life dream. If they had rushed or were pushed into earlier choices such as marriage or had taken on a foreclosure identity, this was the time they focused on themselves. Earlier, their intense relationships with their husbands and children had had priority.

For many of the woman in this study, therefore, the Midlife Transition signalled "A time to be yourself" (Mercer, Nichols, & Doyle, 1989, p. 182).

Summary for Chapter 12

1. Erik Erikson's biographical study of Martin Luther illustrates how personality continues to develop in a complex psychosocial context in adulthood and how the problem of identity challenges adults to address again and again the central psychosocial question: Who am I?

2. Each of Erikson's eight stages of psychosocial development may be viewed as a chapter in a generic life story that all people live out as they progress from infancy and childhood through adolescence and adulthood.

3. The first four stages in Erikson's scheme—trust vs. mistrust, autonomy vs. shame and doubt, initiative vs. guilt, and industry vs. inferiority—present to the child and the child's world problems and issues concerning security, independence, power, and goodness, respectively.

4. Identity arises as a psychosocial problem in the fifth stage of development, according to Erikson, with the advent of puberty, formal-operational thinking, and changes in societal expectations.

5. Identity may be viewed as a process through which the young person first questions beliefs and values to explore new possibilities in defining the self and then makes provisional commitments to refashioned beliefs, values, roles, and images of the self.

6. Erikson's fifth and sixth stages—identity vs. role confusion and intimacy vs. isolation—may blend into each other in many lives, especially women's, when identity may be formulated through intimate interpersonal relationships.

7. Generativity vs. stagnation is Erikson's seventh chapter of the life course. In generativity an adult seeks to generate a legacy of the self that promotes the next generation. Through generativity, adults care for, nurture, guide, and shape children and those others who "follow" them. A new model of the concept describes generativity as a psychosocial constellation of seven features: cultural demand, inner desire for immortality and nurturance, concern for the next generation, belief in the goodness of the species, generative commitment, generative action (creating, maintaining, and offering), and generative narration.

8. The last stage of the life course centers on ego integrity vs. despair. When an adult reaches old age, says Erikson, he or she looks back to accept or reject the life story he or she has created.

9. Like Erikson, Alfred Adler presents a theory of personality that implies that people define themselves over time in terms of story. Adler argued that a person's overall style of life is presaged in his or her earliest memory.

10. From Adler's point of view, the well-adjusted person strives for superiority and wholeness while expressing strong social interest, defined as a sense of kinship with all humanity.

11. Shaping the way in which a person strives for superiority and wholeness is the fictional finalism, which is a person's imagined final goal (story ending) in life.

12. A psychobiography is the systematic use of personality theory to transform a life into a coherent and illuminating story. Freud's controversial study of Leonardo da Vinci is generally considered to be the first psychobiography.

13. Since Freud's study of Leonardo, psychobiographers have drawn on many different theoretical frameworks to interpret lives. The practice of psychobiography raises many difficult methodological and conceptual issues.

14. Related to psychobiography is the practice of collecting life histories on numerous individuals representing a particular social group.

15. Levinson collected life histories from 40 American men to develop his influential model of men's development in the early and middle adult years. The central concept in Levinson's life-course model is the life structure, defined as the

overall pattern or design of a person's life, encompassing the individual's socio-cultural world, significant relationships and roles, and aspects of the self.

16. Levinson's general idea that the adult life course can be portrayed as an orderly sequence of phases or seasons, containing dramatic turning points such as the Midlife Transition, is disputed by some scholars, especially as it applies to the lives of nonprofessional men and to the lives of women.

Chapter 13

Life Scripts, Life Stories

Introduction

The Meaning of Stories
The Narrating Mind
What Is a Story?
Healing and Integration
Feature 13.A. Time and Story in Bali

Feeling and Story: Tomkins' Script Theory
Affects
Scenes and Scripts
Basic Concepts
Types of Scripts

A Life-Story Model of Identity
Origins of the Story: Tone, Imagery, Theme
Characters in Narrative: The Imago
Storymaking in Midlife
Feature 13.B. When Did Identity Become a Problem?

Lives as Texts
Hermans' Dialogical Self
Music and Story: Gregg's Approach
The Postmodern Self

Summary

At the age of 35, Margaret Sands drove two thousand miles across country with her teenage daughter to break into an abandoned chapel and "rip the place apart" (from McAdams, 1993, Chpt. 1). The two of them scaled the cyclone fence surrounding the former Catholic boarding school for girls, and her daughter pried open a window, squeezed in, and ran around to the back to open a door so that Margaret could return to the scene of a childhood crime. It had been 25 years since Margaret left the California school. Upon her return everything looked so much smaller. But the smell was still there, a smell buried deep in her memory and associated forever with primitive loathing and fear. With brazen resolve, Margaret pushed her way behind the altar, where no women were ever allowed. She kicked the walls and punched the pulpit and the pews. She took her car keys and, on the great wooden doors at the chapel's entrance, carved out two rough inscriptions: "I hate nuns" and "They beat children." Then she calmly told her daughter, "Honey, we can leave now." They got back in the car and drove all the way home to Chicago.

Why would a law-abiding American woman in her mid-30s drive over 2000 miles to commit an act of petty vandalism? And why would she drag her teenaged daughter along? Does such a behavior indicate a "nervous breakdown," a reaction to "stress," a budding neurosis? Might we explain her seemingly bizarre actions in terms of an unresolved Oedipus complex, fixation at the oral stage, the working of the Jungian shadow, the result of a personality trait, a particular reinforcement schedule, a cognitive schema about churches, or even a striving for self-actualization? There are certainly a host of legitimate ways to analyze Margaret's long journey and her surprising crime. Let me tell you, though, how Margaret analyzes it. She makes sense of this event in terms of *the story of her life.* Ripping the chapel apart symbolizes a completion of a "chapter" in her own self-defining life narrative—the integrative story of the self she has crafted to provide her own life with unity, purpose, and coherence. Outside the context of her life story, the event makes no sense at all, she would claim. Margaret may not be a personality psychologist, but she expresses a keen insight about persons. Lives become sensible through the private making and the public telling of interpersonal stories and scripts—stories that integrate our reconstructed past, perceived present, and anticipated future into a meaningful whole.

Ten years after her break-in, Margaret tells me her story for a psychological interview. "I was born on July 21, 1941," she begins, "in San Diego, California, and today at age 45, I do not believe very strongly in my foundation as a human being." I learn that Margaret's is a story about foundations, weak and strong, about that which lies at the base of personal strivings, hidden beneath the ground as the indispensible support structure for the edifice of human life. In her life story, childhood failed to provide her with a foundation steadfast enough to sustain her growth and assure her happiness.

"The setting was set for stress before I was born," Margaret remarks. Beautiful, brilliant, and hopelessly naive, her mother was a writer and an actress when she married a heavy-drinking opera singer who was 19 years her senior. They hoped to achieve stardom in Hollywood, but they ended up divorced when Margaret was $4^1/_2$. At that crucial point, Margaret's mother decided to send her daughter to an elite Catholic boarding school, where Margaret stayed till she was ten. Thus began five horrendous years in Margaret's life, as she tells it, the key years that destroyed her foundation. While she received a good academic education, Margaret reports that she was regularly beaten, abused, and humiliated by the nuns. "I was imprisoned for five years; I was abandoned and left with pathetic old women; those years have haunted me ever since."

At the age of 10, her mother brought Margaret back to Chicago to live with her grandparents and enrolled her in a second boarding school. Margaret describes the second school as a "dumping ground for street people and incorrigible youth." "I was abused by the other kids. They stole my record collection. They stole all my things." After a year and a half at the new school, Margaret ran away. She ended up in downtown Chicago at a Walgreens drugstore where, after eating a bowl of chili at the lunch counter, she called her mother on the payphone and threatened that she would never come home again if she did not take her out of the boarding school at once. At the age of 12, "I blackmailed her," Margaret says. This was the first major showdown in Margaret's life, and she prevailed.

If her phone call from the drugstore is the first concrete indication of Margaret's defiant self, her confrontation with an adoption agency marks a second and even more significant watershed in the story. Unmarried, 21 years old, and pregnant, Margaret was pressured by her family and friends to give her baby up for adoption. Once the baby was born, she agreed that the baby would be housed in a private agency for two weeks, after which time she would sign the adoption papers. But when the time came, she could not sign them. The agency officials furiously tried to convince her to go through with the plan, but Margaret would not give in. She screamed at the authorities to give her baby back to her. They cursed her and tried to humiliate her, but they finally had to relent. Again, Margaret prevailed on her own. "This determined an awful lot of the rest of my life."

The rest of her life has revolved around her relationships with her daughter and her ailing mother. She has been a caregiver for both of them. Margaret has never married. Professionally, she has worked as a magazine editor, office manager, and a sales representative. Her political interests were galvanized by the women's movement in the 1970s, and she did a great deal of volunteer work for various women's organizations during that time. While she now fears that her future seems too hazy, she thinks she would like eventually to make a substantive contribution in the area of "women's health." This would require that she go back to college to obtain, at minimum, a bachelor's degree.

Up to now, Margaret has provided her life with unity and purpose by crafting a tragic personal story about her struggles to undo a horrific past through assertive action and gentle caring. The story contains many setbacks and failures, but at least two significant achievements seem to be recognized. She seems to have succeeded in providing her daughter with the foundation she never had. And she seems to have taken her symbolic revenge on the nuns. Ripping up the chapel may have been the first symbolic step in recasting her self-defining story in more self-fulfilling terms. Her childhood experience in the boarding school engendered an unresolved life plot that could reach its natural and satisfying resolution only when she carved her inscription in the chapel doors. Her crime pays the nuns back for their crime, 25 years later. Her daughter is there to bear witness to the revenge, and to learn a life lesson. "Don't get mad; get even," Margaret seems to be telling her. "If you want to survive in this world, you have to be tough, and you have to pay back your enemies in kind." Now that Margaret has reached some closure on this part of her story, what should she do next? How should she define herself now?

From the standpoint of her own psychosocial development, we might suggest that now may be the opportune time for Margaret to devote her considerable creative energies to the enterprise of rebuilding her own identity from the standpoint of someone who has helped build the identity of that which she has created—her daughter. Now that her daughter has moved away to college, Margaret may find that the time in her life is right to go back and try to repair her own foundation, this time from a position of relative strength. Her story shows that she can persevere now. She is not the fragile innocent that her mother was. She is a hardened survivor who has defied the odds. It appears, therefore, that she needs to reformulate the narrative of her life so that the story better recognizes her heroic achievements, enables her to reach a reconciliation with her tragic past, and propels her forward with energy and direction toward a future that she would be proud to create. I believe that Margaret's will always be a tragic life story. I believe that she will always be drawn to tragedy as a narrative form that makes her life meaningful. In tragedy great heroes, like Oedipus, fight valiantly against the overwhelming odds the world presents them. Yet some tragic stories have the power to inspire. It is possible that Margaret's story may inspire others, and indeed inspire Margaret herself, inspire her to find deeper satisfaction and broader fulfillment than she could have ever imagined that lonely afternoon at the Walgreens lunch counter, hunched pitifully over a bowl of chili, poised to take control of her fate for the very first time, at the age of 12.

The Meaning of Stories

In this chapter, we explore in more detail a theme introduced in the personality theories of Henry Murray (Chapter 11), Erik Erikson (Chapter 12), and Alfred

Adler (Chapter 12). This is the idea of *story*—how human lives may be viewed as interpersonal stories. In suggesting that "the history of the organism is the organism," Murray showed an early appreciation for the ways in which lives are situated in time as sequences of proceedings, durances, serials, and so on that may be revealed through stories. Human needs, such as the need for achievement, are expressed in time, as the actor strives in the present to attain a future goal. People express goal-directed action in time through the imaginative stories they tell, as we see in the Thematic Apperception Test. And people make sense of their lives as wholes through storied accounts, as we see in autobiography. Like Murray, Erikson and Adler explored personality "the long way," as lives evolving over time. Erikson organizes lives according to a generic psychosocial narrative—a grand story of birth, growth, decline, and death with eight chapters, described as stages. With his focus on the beginnings (earliest memories) and the anticiapted endings (fictional finalisms) of the life course, Adler understood people to be time-binding organisms, living today according to the stories they have constructed about how they came to be (in the past) and where they may be going (in the future).

The approaches to personality we will survey in this chapter push the metaphor of story further. Where Murray, Erikson, and Adler spoke of interpersonal stories in rather implicit ways, the approaches that follow are more explicit about the role of narrative in human lives. The modern narrative psychologists in this chapter begin with an image of the human being as a storytelling organism. The human mind is first and foremost a narrating mind—a mind that has evolved to create stories, even when stories are especially difficult to create. In some objective sense, human lives may be too disorganized and contingent to be structured like stories. But human beings strive to make lives into stories, anyway. Like Margaret Sands, we strive to transform the chaos of human existence into a story that makes sense. Such striving may be especially apparent in adulthood, especially in Western societies like ours in which people agree on no single, clear, and compelling portrait for what a good, mature, and well-functioning person should be. Where there is multiplicity, as in modern life, there is likely to be a tremendous flurry of life-storymaking effort (Gergen, 1992). If my world says that I can be many things, then I need to find the one thing that is right for me. I need to find, or create, the single story that makes my life make sense (McAdams, 1993).

The Narrating Mind

Human beings are storytellers by nature. In its many guises as folk tale, legend, myth, epic, history, pantomime, motion pictures, and even the evening news, that form of expression we call "the story" appears in every known human culture (Howard, 1991; Mink, 1978; Sarbin, 1986). The story is a natural package for organizing many different kinds of information. Storytelling appears to be a fundamental way of expressing ourselves and our worlds to others (Coles, 1989;

Howard, 1989; Linde, 1990; Vitz, 1990). Think of the last time you tried to explain something really important about yourself to another person. The chances are good that you accomplished this task by telling a story. Or think of an especially intimate conversation from your past. I suspect that what made the conversation good was the kind of stories that were told and the manner in which the stories were received. Indeed, much of what passes for everyday conversation between people is storytelling of one form or another. We are born to tell stories, some scholars suggest. This is part of what makes us so different from both the beasts and the computers.

Imagine our ancient ancestors, at day's end, in that ambiguous interlude between the victories and defeats of the daylight and the deep sleep of the dark. Home from the hunt, or resting at the end of a day's foraging for food, providing for the young, or defending the tribe, our primordial forebears sit down together and take stock. Before night falls, they tell stories of the day. They pass the time by making sense of past time. They tell of their experiences to entertain and enlighten each other, and perhaps, on occasion, just to stay awake. E. M. Forster (1954), the novelist and essayist, once wrote: [Primordial] "man listened to stories, if one may judge by the shape of his skull. The primitive audience was an audience of shock-heads, gaping round the campfire, fatigued with contending against the mammoth or the whooly rhinoceros, and only kept awake by suspense. What would happen next?"

The stories told at day's end created a shared history of people, linking them in time and event, as actors, tellers, and audience in an unfolding drama of life that was made more in the telling than in the actual events to be told. Stories are not like the secretary's minutes of the last meeting, written to report exactly what transpired at the meeting and at what time. Stories do not work to replay a video-taped past that can be objectively known and reviewed. Stories are less about facts and more about meanings. In the subjective and embellished telling of the past, the past is constructed—history is made. The history is judged to be true or false not solely with respect to its adherence to empirical fact. Rather history is judged with respect to such narrative criteria as "believability" and "coherence." There is a *narrative truth* in life that seems quite removed from logic, science, and empirical demonstration (Spence, 1982). It is the truth of a "good story." In the words of one writer, this is a form of truth with which our ancient ancestors were intimately familiar:

> No one in the world knew what truth was till someone had told a story. It was not there in the moment of lightning or the cry of the beast, but in the story of those things afterwards, making them part of human life. Our distant savage ancestor gloried as he told—or acted out or danced—the story of the great kill in the dark forest, and that story entered the life of the tribe and by it the tribe came to know itself. On such a day against the beast we fought and won, and here we live to tell the tale. A tale much embellished but truthful even so, for truth is not simply what

Expressing the self through storytelling: a !Kung bushman.

happened but how we felt about it when it was happening, and how we feel about it now. (Rouse, 1978)

Jerome Bruner (1986, 1990) argues that human beings understand the world in two very different ways. The first is what he terms the **paradigmatic mode** of thought. In the paradigmatic mode, we seek to comprehend our experience in terms of tightly reasoned analyses, logical proof, and empirical observation. We seek to order our world in terms of logical theories that explain events and help us predict and control reality. In the paradigmatic mode, we look for cause-and-effect relationships. When we understand how our car's engine works or how a water molecule is formed from the joining of two hydrogen atoms and one oxygen atom, then we are employing successfully our gifts of logical, causal reasoning. Much of our educational training reinforces the paradigmatic mode. Good logicians and scientists are especially well-trained in this general way of thinking.

By contrast, the **narrative mode** of thought concerns itself with stories, which themselves are about "the vicissitudes of human intention" organized in time (Bruner, 1986). In stories, events are not explained in terms of physical or logical causes. The narrative mode does not generally operate in the realm of automobile engines or molecular chemistry. Instead, it deals with human wants, needs, and goals. In the narrative mode, events are explained in terms of *human actors striving to do things over time.* If I am to tell a good story about anything, then I must present a believable narrative concerning the motivated actions and meaningful ends of human behavior, rendered in time, with beginning, middle, and end. Therefore, I may wish to explain a friend's unusual behavior this weekend in terms of my understanding of what the friend wants in life and why he has never been able to get it, going back in my account to frustrations he experienced three years ago with his wife. To understand him and his behavior, I say, you must know the story I am to tell. Similarly, to understand why one 35-year-old law-abiding woman drove 2,000 miles to desecrate an abandoned chapel we must understand *her* story of her childhood and the symbolic importance of the Catholic church in her life story. We must comprehend her storied account of her own intentions organized in time.

Good novelists and poets are masters of the narrative mode. These story-writers are especially effective when they, in Bruner's words, "mean more than they can say" (Cordes, 1986). In other words, a good story will generate many different meanings, functioning to trigger presuppositions in the reader. We have all had the experience of comparing what we "got out" of a good story—say, a movie, play, or novel—to the view of a friend, only to learn that the two of us have read or understood the same story in very different ways. This is part of the reason that stories are fun and valuable, for they give us many different ideas and opinions around which we can have friendly, and sometimes not-so-friendly, conversations and arguments. Good stories seem to *give birth* to many different meanings, generating "children" of meaning in their own image.

By contrast, masters of the paradigmatic mode try to "say no more than they mean" (Bruner, in Cordes, 1986). A good scientist or logician works for clarity and precision. Scientific and logical explanations are constructed in such a way as to block the triggering of presuppositions. These explanations do not create other explanations in their own image. They do not encourage differences of opinion. If they did, they would be accused of being vague or ambiguous, of generating too many different and competing interpretations for what demands a single objective truth. For all its power and precision, the paradigmatic mode is a strangely humbler form of thought than story making. While it seeks to untangle cause and effect and to explain the workings of the world in the clearest and most rational manner possible, it is not generally able to make much sense of human desire, goal, and social conduct. Moreover, unlike the story, it does not give birth.

What Is a Story?

My 6-year-old daughter knows what a story is. Of course, she cannot give me a formal definition that would pass muster in a literary journal. But she knows a story when she hears one. And she can tell the difference between a story and something else.

I might try this experiment with my daughter. Imagine that I were to read to her two different written passages, each about five-minutes long. Let us say that she has never heard either passage before. The first is a Portuguese folk tale about a young boy who tries to find a special fruit that gives off magical powers. The second is a set of instructions from a brand new game involving Barbie dolls. (It has to be *brand new* or else my daughter will have heard about it already.) Both accounts are written to be interesting and entertaining for children. After reading both, I ask my daughter which one is "a story." She will probably think the question odd, but I guarantee that if I press her to answer, she will say that the first one is a "story," even though she hasn't heard it before, and that the second is "something else" or "not as much a story." Like most 6-year-olds, my daughter knows what to expect in stories. She knows, for instance, that stories are about people, or peoplelike characters (Mickey Mouse, the three little pigs) trying to do things over time, that stories have beginnings, middles, and endings, that you need to know "how it's going to turn out" in a story. A set of instructions is different, no matter how well written or how beautiful the Barbie doll. There is no narrative tension in the instructions. We are not likely to await in eager anticipation the eventual victory or defeat of the protagonist, the resolution of the dramatic conflict, or the "happily ever after" ending. My daughter has an inner understanding of **story grammar** (Applebee, 1978; Mandler, 1984; Trabasso, Secco, & Van Den Broek, 1984). Like you and me, she knows a story when she hears one because she knows the implicit rules of story.

Here is what you, and I, and my 6-year-old daughter expect in a story. We first expect that a story will have a *setting* of some kind, and that we will learn what the setting is very early on. "'Twas the night before Christmas when all through the house. . . ." "Once upon a time in a faraway place. . . ." We need to know where and when the action of the story is situated. The story of Dasher, Prancer, and Vixen makes no sense if we fail to realize at the beginning that it's all happening on Christmas Eve. Even fairy tales require a setting: it is important to know that they happened long ago in faraway places, not yesterday in Rock Island, Illinois. Of course, not all stories are equal in the extent to which they develop a setting. Whereas some evoke vivid associations of particular times and places, others move briskly through the where's and when's to get to the action, leaving the setting as a taken-for-granted backdrop for the plot. In the rare instance in which a setting is unknown or highly ambiguous, a story may seem confusing and disconcerting, as we see in some absurdist fiction and drama. For example, Samuel Beckett's *Waiting for Godot* is both jarring and effective because, in part, we are provided with no setting, beyond a barren and bleak landscape that seems to be anytime and anyplace, or more likely no time and no place. But Beckett's play is rather unusual in providing virtually no context within which to place the events. It violates some of our assumptions about the structure of stories, experimenting with strange new story forms that my 6-year-old (and I suspect many of us) may not expect nor fully appreciate.

Second, we expect a story to have human or humanlike characters. At the beginning of the story, a character exists in a kind of neutral equilibrium. Noth-

A Native American storyteller.

ing has happened yet. Indeed, before anything happens, we may learn certain basic things about the character, such as what he or she looks like, how old he or she is, and so on. This information functions as a kind of "setting" for the character—a taken-for-granted background for the rest of the story. Eventually, however, something must happen. There must be an *initiating event*. The mother sends Little Red Riding Hood off to take cakes to her grandmother, and thus the action of the story begins. The initiating event motivates the character to make *the attempt*. The attempt is the character's effort to attain a certain goal. The character intends to reach the goal smoothly, but it is likely that a big, bad wolf, or its equivalent, will be waiting along the path. Tension builds when Little Red Riding Hood meets the wolf. "The plot thickens." In terms of story grammar, we see that the attempt leads in a narrative fashion to *the consequence*. The wolf is the consequence of Little Red Riding Hood's attempt to carry the cakes to her grandmother. Little Red Riding Hood reacts to the wolf. She divulges the location of the grandmother's cottage. We see, then, that *the reaction* complicates the plot further, for now her grandmother is also in danger and the story extends forward to future episodes in which the two main characters will face a showdown. Little Red Riding Hood intends to carry the cakes, but the wolf intends to eat her. Stories are about the vicissitudes of human intention, or in this case the intentions of humanlike wolves.

Each episode of a story may be seen as a sequence of the elements I have just described. You start with an initiating event that leads to the attempt. The consequence gives rise to the reaction. One episode follows another, each containing the same structural sequence (Mandler, 1984). Episodes mount and the story takes form. A great number of literary devices and conventions may enhance the buildup of tension in the story and enrich the ways in which different episodes relate to each other. The author may use flashbacks as when we learn half-way through the story that our middle-aged hero was abandoned by his parents shortly after birth. The author may shift perspectives, relating the same events from the competing points of view of different protagonists or observers. Trivial early events may foreshadow momentous later ones.

The buildup of tension within and across the many episodes of a story demands an eventual resolution. Aristotle proposed that the tension builds to a climax, a high point or turning point in the drama. What follows is the final unravelling or solution of the plot, what is called the *denouement*. Finally, the story reaches a conclusion. In Little Red Riding Hood, the tension builds as we move through the woods to grandmother's house, wherein awaits the wolf in granny's nightgown. The first-time listener feels *suspense* and *curiosity*—two indispensible emotions in a good story (Brewer & Lichtenstein, 1982). "What big teeth you have!" our heroine exclaims. "The better to eat you with," comes the falsetto reply. The wolf eats her, and then falls asleep. But the woodsman arrives. In the climactic scene, he chops open the wolf's stomach to rescue the little girl and her grandmother, neither one the worse for digestive wear. From here on, it's all denouement. Amazingly, the wolf is still sleeping. The woodsman fills his empty gut with boulders. When he awakes, the wolf falls down dead from the weight. Little Red Riding Hood returns home, and with her return the story ends. The story has taken us on a journey and then returned us to where we started, at home with Little Red Riding Hood. Things come around full circle. With the ending, we return to the beginning again, but we (and Little Red Riding Hood) have changed.

If you pay close attention to the kinds of things you hear and say in a normal day, you may be surprised to learn how much of your experience involves stories. When we watch television, for instance, we observe an endless series of stories presented in a multitude of forms. Situation comedies from "I Love Lucy" to "Roseanne" are structured as relatively simple stories, with well-defined settings, initiating events, attempts, consequences, and reactions. As comic tension builds, the observer becomes curious to see how it is all going to turn out. Climaxes are followed by rapid denouement. After a commercial break, a brief, upbeat conclusion brings the story "home" again. We are now prepared to watch another, or move to something else.

Game shows follow a similar structure as we watch each episode to see who, in the end, will win. Serials, like "All My Children" and "L.A. Law," consist of a series of overlapping and intersecting stories, each developing at its own pace. The writers of these shows do not want to resolve everything in one afternoon or evening. They keep you curious and in suspense from one week to the next by

Comedy in narrative: Roseanne and Dan in the popular television show.

building tension that cannot be resolved until future shows. Even the nightly news is structured, to a certain extent, like a story (Bird & Dardenne, 1988). Many news items are presented as mini-stories in their own right, each with a setting, characters, and goal-directed plot. Less obviously, the entire newscast itself seems to exemplify certain storylike qualities. The anchor men and women, the sportscaster, the weather expert take us on a narrative journey and then return us home, as safe and sound as Little Red Riding Hood, ending their newscasts with those upbeat human-interest stories or lighthearted commentaries and quips that, they hope, leave us smiling, resolved, and more likely than we were before to return to the set tomorrow night, same time and channel.

Healing and Integration

We are drawn to stories for many reasons. Stories entertain us, making us laugh and cry, keeping us in suspense until we learn how it is all going to turn out. Stories instruct. We learn how to act and live through stories; we learn about different people, settings, and ideas (Coles, 1989). Stories may teach us moral lessons, too. Aesop's fables and the parables of Jesus suggest lessons—some simple and

Continued on p. 730

Feature 13.A

Time and Story in Bali

The philosopher Paul Ricoeur (1984) writes that "time becomes human time to the extent it is organized after the manner of narrative; narrative in turn is meaningful to the extent it portrays the features of temporal existence" (p. 3). What Ricoeur means is that human beings tend to comprehend time in terms of story. Therefore, stories work well when they make good sense of time. When we comprehend our actions over time, we see what we do in terms of story. We see actions leading to reactions, goals attained, obstacles confronted, intentions realized and frustrated over time, tension building to climax, climax giving way to denouement, tension building again as we continue to move and change, moving forward from yesterday to today to tomorrow.

Imagine a society, however, in which human conduct is *not* situated in time as we understand it. The anthropologist Clifford Geertz (1973) describes just such a society among the people of Bali. Bali is an Indonesian island just east of Java. Its native inhabitants live within a culture that is radically different from ours in a great many ways. Three intriguing differences stand out in Geertz's account. These are differences in time, conduct, and identity.

First, Balinese life follows a complex and irregular calendar that seems neither to move forward nor in regular cycles. Time is classified by holidays. In Bali, today's "date" refers to how much time has elapsed since the last holiday and how much is left until the next one. Holidays fall irregularly on dates determined by overlapping cycles. As Geertz puts it, "the cycles and supercycles are endless, unanchored, unaccountable, and, as their internal order has no significance, without climax. They do not accumulate, they do not build, and they are not consumed. They don't tell you what time it is; they tell you what kind of time it is" (p. 393). For the Balinese, time is "punctual" rather than "durational." To know today's date is not to know time as we think of it; rather it is simply to know what kind of day today is. This is like calling today "Heavenday" and tomorrow "Baseball." In exactly a "week" from today (a "week" by our standards; the Balinese do not speak of weeks), we may have the day "Marshmallow." We do not know when the day "Heavenday" or "Marshmallow" will happen again, though of course each *will* happen again, some time. In this system, each day is punctuated like a discrete moment. It is not related to other days in a sequence of time.

Second, human conduct itself also seems to be punctual rather than durational. It is as if, Geertz maintains, the Balinese act and interact with each other in ways that themselves are outside of time. Each moment is discrete. Actions do not seem to build to climax and resolution the way we might expect they should. "Absence of climax," Geertz writes, is a remarkable quality of Balinese social behavior:

It amounts to the fact that social activities do not build, or are not permitted to build, toward definitive consummations. Quarrels appear and disappear, on occasion they even persist, but they hardly ever come to a head. Issues are not sharpened for decision, they are blunted and softened in the hope that the mere evolution of circumstances will resolve them, or better yet, that they will simply evaporate. Daily life consists of self-contained, monadic encounters in which something either happens or does not, intention is realized or it is not, a task is accomplished or not. (p. 403)

Geertz is suggesting that, in Bali, social life does not seem to be construed in storied terms. Each moment is a discrete performance, standing alone outside of time, rather than a connected episode in a time-organized plot. Social activities follow one another, but they do not march to some destination, gather toward some denouement. Both time and life are punctual, unstoried.

Third, as it goes for time and conduct in Bali, so it goes for a person's identity. Geertz observes that the Balinese go to great lengths to "depersonalize" each other so that everybody may be seen as a "stereotyped contemporary." This can be seen even in the giving of names. An adult in Bali does not have a distinct name that differentiates him or her from everybody else. Instead, he or she is named according to offspring. Thus, I might be called "Father of Ruth." Were Ruth to grow up and have a child named Paul, she would no longer be called "Ruth" but rather "Mother of Paul." At that time, my name would become "Grandfather of Paul" (which might also be the name of "Ruth's" father-in-law). And so on. The naming pulls one to the present moment and out of any kind of meaningful time duration. Ruth and I are now linked in identity by virtue of our joint cooperation in the production of Paul. Paul is like the present moment; in a sense, he is all that matters, and he defines who I and my daughter are. The implicit aim, says Geertz, is to create a society that collapses time to the discrete present and blurs distinctions between people.

We are all more or less the same in Bali. Even though things change, reality remains the same. No climaxes. No resolution of tension. No denouement. Balinese life does not conform to the kinds of stories we, as Westerners, know and tell. Indeed, it seems to defy our sense of what story is all about. Geertz's fascinating account should remind us that ours is not the only way to see time and story. In its sharp contrast, however, Geertz's portrait also brings into bold relief the extent to which most of us think about time as story, and story in terms of time. I suspect that few of us wish to exchange permanent places with one of the Balinese. Coming from a culture that stresses individual identity and the linear nature of time, we are not likely to feel comfortable in a society that seems to lie outside of time and personal identity. We may concede that their culture "works" for the Balinese, that perhaps it works so well as to make them quite happy and fulfilled.

Geertz does not compare them to us on these points. But the reasons the Balinese seem so strange to us is that we, unlike them, appear to live according to narrative assumptions about time and lives. Similarly, we, unlike them, appear to value strongly the individuality of our own life course. Take our stories of the past away from us and each of us would be forced to live as stereotyped contemporaries, out of time and out of self.

Continued from p. 727
some profound—about good and bad behavior, moral and immoral ways of conducting our lives, dilemmas concerning what is right and what is wrong. Beyond entertaining and edifying us, stories may also function to bring things together and to heal that which is sick or broken. Some scholars and scientists have suggested that *integration* and *healing* are two primary psychological functions of stories and storytelling. Stories may bring our lives together when we feel shattered, mend us when we are broken, heal us when we are sick, help us cope in times of stress, and even move us toward psychological fulfillment and maturity.

The psychoanalyst Bruno Bettelheim (1977) wrote eloquently about the psychological power of children's fairy stories. Bettelheim believed that such tales as "Jack and the Beanstalk" and "Cinderella" help children work through internal conflicts and crises. When a 4-year-old listens to the story of Cinderella, Bettelheim suggests, she may unconsciously identify with the heroine and vicariously experience Cinderella's frustration and sadness and her eventual triumph. Similarly, children may identify with such male heroes as Jack, who faces the menacing giant but eventually outwits him and escapes much the richer and wiser. The protagonists of these stories are unassuming children, like the listeners, and their deeply felt fears and concerns match closely the unconscious fears lurking in the hearts of children. In Bettelheim's view, the fairy tale speaks softly and subtly to the child, gently but steadily promoting psychological growth and adaptation. The fairy tale encourages the child to face the world with confidence and hope. Cinderella and Jack live happily ever after. Wicked stepsisters and ogres are punished in the end. Things have a way of working out, even when they look really scary.

As adults, we too may identify strongly with the protagonist of a story, experiencing vicariously what the character experiences and emerging from the narrative encounter happier, better adjusted, more enlightened, or improved in some way. In *When Bad Things Happen to Good People,* Rabbi Harold Kushner (1981) tells many true stories of pain and heartbreak from the lives of people he has known and, in some cases, loved. The book has been a great comfort to many people. Good friends whose baby was stillborn have told me that Kushner's book helped them deal with their grief. In this case, they identified strongly with the author himself, who was motivated to write the book after his own son died at an early age. By hearing a story with which they could relate intimately, my friends worked through an emotionally wrenching period in their own lives. Kushner reports that the stories helped *him,* too. By collecting and considering the tales of grief and suffering he had encountered in his years as a rabbi, Kushner reports, he was able to piece together parts of his own shattered life.

Simply writing or performing a story about oneself can prove to be an experience of healing and growth, as many who have written their own autobiographies will attest. A good autobiography puts life into story form, complete with setting, characters, initiating events, attempts, consequences, reactions, climaxes, denouement, recurrent themes and images, and the self-conscious reconstruction of human time through narrative. One of the first and most famous autobiographies in Western history was written by the Christian Saint Augustine (354–430 A.D.). His *Confessions* is a retrospective self-analysis written to regroup and recover from what he described as a "shattered" and "disordered" state of mind. By composing the story, Augustine was able to construct a unified view of himself and his place in God's creation and to orient to the envisioned future with direction and purpose (Jay, 1984).

Many men and women have tried to do what Augustine did, with varying degrees of success. There are many reasons to write an autobiography, but one commonly expressed is the desire to find some kind of personal integration—to put the pieces together into a meaningful whole. The writer may feel that the time in life has finally come to undertake this kind of synthesizing project. It may seem a natural time to look back. Or the writer may feel a great deal more urgency, like Augustine, looking to the story as a salvation for or solution to an impending crisis in life.

In his brief autobiography entitled *The Facts,* the novelist Philip Roth (1988) writes that he is seeking to "depathologize" his own life, to set things right after years of confusion and trouble. In Roth's case, the process of composing a life story involves distilling from his own complex past the stark truisms—"the facts"—concerning how he came to be a writer. Roth describes this process as a clearing away of the many layers of stories that he has created as a prolific novelist in order to arrive at a core of truth—shredding through the layers of superficial narrative in order to get at a single and simple tale to believe. The task is tricky and perhaps not well advised, as Roth seems to admit at the beginning and the end of the book when he engages in an imaginary conversation with Nathan Zuckerman, who is the fictional hero of a series of Roth's novels. Zuckerman tells Roth that he is a fool to strip away the stories in his fiction, for those are as much a part of Roth as anything else. Zuckerman seems to imply that he, Zuckerman, is more a part of Roth than is Roth himself—than is the Roth, that is, who functions as the central character in *The Facts*. Without me, Zuckerman seems to be saying, you (Roth) are a pretty boring and superficial fellow. "This is what you get in practically any artist without his imagination," Zuckerman says. "Your medium for the really merciless, self-evisceration, your medium for genuine self-confrontation, is me" (pp. 184–185).

Perhaps Roth actually agrees with Zuckerman, at least to a point. How else might we explain his choice of the most clichéd kind of chapter titles you could imagine for an autobiography? He gives his chapters titles like "Joe College," "Girl of My Dreams," and "All in the Family." Is Roth telling us that, when you strip away "the Roth" that he has projected onto his own fictional characters, like Zuckerman, all you are left with is cliché? Is he saying that without our imaginations, our lives reduce to simplistic platitudes and worn-out expressions? Is he saying that "the facts" are not enough? In Roth's case, autobiography turns ironic and self-mocking, as the storywriter comes to doubt the validity of the story he has composed. Yet the whole process seems to be enlightening, as well as entertaining. We feel that we *do* learn something important about Roth that we didn't know before. And we feel that he, too, has discovered something about himself, that he has made progress toward the goal of "depathologizing" his own life. Of course, we can never know for sure.

The healing power of story arises as a major theme in certain forms of psychotherapy, wherein the explicit goal of treatment is the depathologizing of life. For instance, some psychoanalysts maintain that the development of a coherent life story is a major goal in therapy. According to this view, psychoanalysis involves the coordination of successive narrations whereby the analyst and the client come to construct more adequate and vitalizing stories about the self (Schafer, 1981). Writes Marcus (1974), "human life is, ideally, a connected and coherent story, with all the details in explanatory place, and with everything (or as close to everything as is practically possible) accounted for, in its proper causal or other sequence." Similarly, "illness amounts at least in part to suffering from an incoherent story or an inadequate narrative account of oneself." The therapist and the client work together to produce a healing narrative of the self (Borden, 1992). Some psychological problems and a great deal of emotional suffering stem from our failures in making sense of our lives through story. Therapists help us rewrite and revise our stories of self. The process may produce a triumphant transformation, like that in the case of Saint Augustine. Or progress may be slower and less obvious, in therapeutic fits and starts, as Roth cautions in his own explorations in healing the self.

Researchers have begun to explore the extent to which life-storytelling can have positive effects on coping and mental health. Most notably, James Pennebaker (1988, 1989b, 1992) and his colleagues have conducted a series of studies on the salutary effects of disclosing narrative accounts of personal traumas. Volunteer participants in Pennebaker's studies receive instructions like these:

> Once you are seated in the experimental cubicle and the door is closed, I want you to write continuously about the most upset-

ting or traumatic experience of your entire life. Don't worry about the grammar, spelling, or sentence structure. In your writing I want you to discuss your deepest thoughts and feelings about the experience. You can write about anything you want, but whatever you choose, it should be something that has affected you very deeply. Ideally, it should be about something you have not talked with others about in detail. It is critical, however, that you let yourself go and touch those deepest emotions and thoughts that you have. I should warn you that many people find this study quite upsetting. Many people cry during the study and feel somewhat sad or depressed during and after it. (Pennebaker, 1989b, p. 215)

Many of the respondents in these studies are college students. Here are some representative sketches:

A female who has lived in fear for several weeks because of the physical and psychological harassment of a jealous woman who has apparently hired two thugs.

A male who, in his high school years, was repeatedly beaten by his stepfather. After attempting suicide with his stepfather's gun, the stepfather humiliated the subject by laughing at his failed attempt.

A female who, in a fit of rage at her father, accused him of marital infidelity in front of her mother. The accusation, which apparently was true and unknown to the mother, led to the separation and divorce of the parents and overwhelming guilt on the part of the daughter.

A female who, at the age of 10, was asked to clean up her room because of her grandmother who was to visit the home that evening. The girl did not do so. That night, the grandmother slipped on one of the girl's toys and broke her hip. The grandmother died a week later during a hip operation.

A man who, at age 9, was calmly told by his father that he was divorcing the boy's mother because their home life had been disrupted ever since the boy had been born. (Pennebaker, 1989b, p. 218)

As many as one quarter of the subjects in these studies cry during their disclosures, and many feel depressed for a time after the telling. Yet the respondents tend to rate the experience of disclosing the traumatic event to be especially valuable, and 98% of them say that they would do the experiment again. More important, the narrative act of translating personal trauma into words appears to have long-term health benefits. For example, Pennebaker and Beall (1986) required 46 healthy undergraduates to write about either the most traumatic and stressful experience of their lives or about a trivial assigned topic *for four consecutive days.* Of those assigned to write about traumatic events, one experimental group wrote about the facts surrounding the trauma but not their feelings about the trauma (trauma-factual condition), another about their feelings concerning the trauma but not the facts (trauma-emotion), and a third about both their feelings and the facts concerning the trauma (trauma-combination group). A six-month followup questionnaire revealed that the subjects who discolosed information about both the facts and their feelings in the traumatic event had better health during those six subsequent months than did the subjects in the other three groups. As Figure 13.1 shows, the trauma-combination group showed the lowest number of visits to the student health center during that period. The authors argued that the opportunity to tell the *full story* of a stressful experience

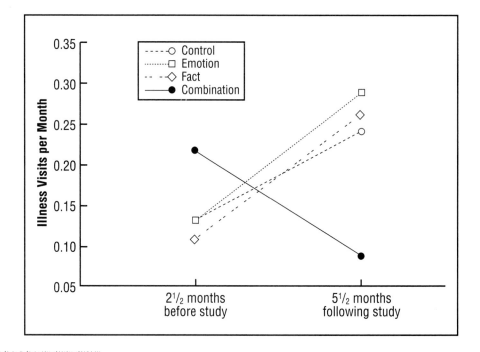

Figure 13.1

Number of Health Center Visits for Illness per Month as a Function of Writing Topic.

From Pennebaker & Beall, 1986.

from the past—providing both the facts and one's feelings about the facts—works to enhance one's health.

These findings are consistent with a small but growing number of studies showing how personal confession and disclosure of negative events can improve health and minimize unwanted thoughts about traumas. Pennebaker and O'Heeron (1984) surveyed people whose spouses had died in automobile accidents or suicides. They found that individuals who ruminated obsessively about the death of their spouse had more health problems during the year following the death. But those who talked with others about their spouses' deaths reported (1) fewer problems with unwanted ruminations and obsessive thoughts and (2) fewer health problems during the following year. Greenberg and Stone (1992) found a drop in physician visits for students who wrote about deeply traumatic events compared with subjects who either wrote about mild traumas or those who wrote about superficial topics. Francis and Pennebaker (1992) found that those who wrote about traumas once a week for four consecutive weeks had fewer absentee days and improved liver enzyme function in the two months after writing, compared to controls. Obtaining a series of blood samples on each subject, Pennebaker, Kiecolt-Glaser, and Glaser (1988) found that students who wrote about traumas over four consecutive days showed improved immune-system functioning by the fourth day, compared to those who wrote about trivial events.

Why does disclosure of traumatic events improve health? Pennebaker (1988) argues that the process of actively inhibiting feelings and thoughts about negative events requires excessive physiological work, as in higher heart rate, skin conductance, and blood pressure. Over the long haul, the effects of physiological arousal accumulate, leading to such stress-related illnesses as infections, ulcers, and so on. Furthermore, the more that a person tries to inhibit thoughts and emotions, the more he or she is likely to think about that which is being inhibited, leading to heightened anxiety and arousal (Wegner, Schneider, Carter, & White, 1987). But confiding and consciously confronting the perceptions and feelings associated with a traumatic event allow for the integration or cognitive reorganization of the event. The narrative disclosure of the event enables the person to "put it behind" him or her, to "close the book" on the problem. This leads to a reduction in physiological arousal, and it negates the need for further obsessing and inhibiting.

But what is it about disclosure itself that makes for the reduction in physiological arousal and obsessive thought? Recent research by Pennebaker (1992) suggests two important factors: (1) the degree of negative emotion expressed and (2) the extent to which a traumatic event is reconstructed as a *well-formed story*. Employing a computer content coding scheme to analyze accounts of traumatic events, Pennebaker discovered that subjects whose health improved the most following disclosure used significantly more negative emotion words and fewer positive emotion words compared to other subjects. In addition, subjects whose health improved evidenced overall higher levels of story organization and increasing degree of acceptance and optimism compared to those who failed to improve. Indeed, those who did not improve evidenced a gradual deterioration in their stories. They started their writing sessions with a clear story that, over time, fell apart. Pennebaker concludes that "both the disclosure of negative emotion and the building of a clear cognitive story are important components in healthy writing" (1992, p. 5). The movement over time toward a well-constructed story, then, is a desired outcome in writing and in some forms of therapy, and it appears to bring with it benefits for health.

Feeling and Story: Tomkins' Script Theory

The central role of story and storytelling in human lives is one defining feature of the broad perspective on personality offered by the late Silvan Tomkins (1911–1991). A drama student who wrote plays as a college undergraduate, Tomkins came to psychology as a storywriter. It was through dramatic narrative that Tomkins first wrestled with the question that has since driven his life's work: "What do human beings really want?" (Tomkins, 1981, p. 306). In search of an answer, Tomkins entered graduate school in psychology in 1930 but left a year later, disappointed with what he saw as psychology's failure to address adequately the question of motivation, or what people want. He then turned to philosophy to study logic and the theory of value, receiving a Ph.D. Tomkins eventually returned to psychology to work with Henry Murray and Robert White at the Harvard Psychological Clinic. Tomkins' early work reflected the influence of Murray and Harvard's personological tradition, as he published a book on the TAT (Tomkins, 1947) and devised a new projective test called the Tomkins–Horn Picture Arrangement Test (Tomkins & Miner, 1957).

Though Tomkins initially accepted Murray's belief that psychogenic needs were the main factors in human motivation, he soon departed from this view in favor of a theory emphasizing **affect,** or human emotion. As Tomkins tells it, two personal discoveries led directly to his own conviction that affects, not drives (Freud) or needs (Murray), are the primary motivators of human behavior.

The first discovery occurred in the late 1940s when Tomkins was struck by the sudden insight that such affects as excitement, joy, and anger are independent of drives, like hunger and sexuality, but *amplify* drives by providing them with motivational power. In Tomkins' view, for instance, the sex drive in and of itself is *not* generally a strong motivator of behavior. Rather, sex moves the person to act in a sexual manner when amplified (strengthened) by the affect of excitement. Tomkins' second discovery occurred when he became a father:

> The second critical discovery occurred when my son was born in 1955 while I was on sabbatical leave. Beginning shortly after his birth, I observed him daily, for hours on end. I was struck with the massiveness of the crying response. It included not only very

Silvan Tomkins

loud vocalization and facial muscular responses, but also large changes in blood flow to the face and engagement of all the striate musculature of the body. It was a massive total bodily response which, however, seemed to center on the face. Freud had suggested that the birth cry was the prototype of anxiety, but my son didn't seem anxious. What, then, was the facial response? I labelled it distress. Next, I was to observe intense excitement on his face when he labored after the first few months of his life to shape his mouth to try to imitate the speech he heard. He would struggle minutes on end and then give up, apparently exhausted and discouraged. I noted the intensity of the smiling response to his mother and to me, and again I became aware that nothing in psychoanalytic theory (and any other personality theory at that time) paid any attention to the specificity of enjoyment as contrasted with excitement. (Tomkins, 1981, p. 309)

In collaboration with psychologists Carroll Izard and Paul Ekman, Tomkins has articulated a broad theory of human emotion that proposes the existence of some 10 primary affects, each rooted in human biology and evolution (Ekman, 1972; Izard, 1977; Tomkins, 1962, 1963; Tomkins & Izard, 1965). Each affect is linked to characteristic movements of the muscles in the face. Thus, the face may be considered the organ of emotion. In recent years, Tomkins has expanded his theory to encompass the concepts of *scene* and *script,* providing a dramaturgical and narrative approach to personality that is reminiscent of his entry into psychology, over 50 years ago, as a writer of plays (Carlson, 1981; Tomkins, 1979, 1987). This new narrative perspective, *script theory,* was heralded in 1984 as "perhaps the most comprehensive and original theory of personality to emerge in the past twenty years" (Singer, 1984, p. 128).

Affects

When I worked in the steel mills in Gary, Indiana, I made friends with a man called "Tiny." I was a college student working summers; he was about 40 years old, married with three children, and he had never finished the sixth grade. Tiny's dream was to be a coal miner; by contrast, I could think of nothing more gruesome. I hated the steel mills; Tiny didn't mind the work, and he often tried to cheer me up when I was particularly fed-up and discouraged. I don't understand why we liked each other when we had so little in common. But I remember that we talked a lot, and I especially remember one conversation we had—I think the original topic was women and marriage—when Tiny cryptically observed, "Emotion is everything." In his own way, Tiny seemed to hit on the central point of human living in Tomkins' theory of personality. As Tomkins puts it:

> The primary function of affect is urgency via analogic and profile amplification to make one care by feeling. . . . Without affect amplification nothing else matters, and with its amplification anything can matter. (1981, p. 322)

According to Tomkins, natural selection has operated on humans to favor the evolution of a highly differentiated and specialized system of emotions. Therefore,

> the human being is equipped with innate affective responses which bias him to want to remain alive and to resist death, to want sexual experiences, to want to experience novelty and to resist boredom, to want to communicate, to be close to and in contact with others of his species and to resist the experience of head and face lowered in shame. (Tomkins, 1962, p. 27)

Those emotions most often identified as primary by Tomkins include interest/excitement, enjoyment, surprise, distress, anger, disgust, fear/anxiety, sadness, shame, and guilt. The first two are positive emotions; surprise can be positive, negative, or neither; and the last seven are negative emotions. In general, people seek to maximize experiences of positive emotions and minimize experiences of negative ones.

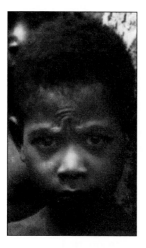

Universal facial expressions: anxiety, joy, disgust.

Each of the primary emotions can be distinguished on a number of different levels. First, each *feels* qualitatively different from all the others. For example, the phenomenology of surprise—the sudden increase in arousal in the wake of an unexpected event—is very different from the phenomenology of shame, joy, or sadness. Second, each emotion is innately linked to a specific *facial response*. As Darwin (1872/1965) believed over 100 years ago, human beings have evolved with particular facial expressions for showing particular emotions: enjoyment by the smile; surprise and interest/excitement by raised eyes and a focused, head-forward stance; sadness by a drooping mouth and slackening jaw muscles; disgust by tightened muscles beneath the nose and wrinkling of the nose; anger by clenched and exposed teeth and a flushed complexion; and fear by widened eyes. Each of these facial expressions sends sensory feedback from the face to the brain, and some psychologists believe that this feedback is instrumental in the experience of the emotion itself, especially in infancy. In one sense, then, the experience of joy is the result of the sensory information sent to the brain by the smiling face. In addition, facial expressions send social information to other persons who may observe the individual's smiles, frowns, or sneers.

Particular facial expressions, therefore, are thought to be natural manifestations of primary emotions. Evidence for this proposition comes from many sources. Cross-cultural research suggests that people from very different societies tend to agree on what facial responses "go with" what emotions. For instance, research by Izard (1971, 1977) and Ekman, Friesen, and Ellsworth (1972) showed that when subjects from 12 different countries were shown photographs selected to represent fundamental emotions, the percentage of agreement was very high. Mexicans, Brazilians, Germans, Japanese, Americans, and members of certain pre-literate tribes tend to agree about the meaning of different facial expressions. Even when there is no obvious change in facial expression, furthermore, the occurrence of certain emotions can be shown by measuring electrical activity in the face and brain. In one study, individuals were asked to imagine pleasant and unpleasant scenes while changes in the electrical muscular impulses in their faces were monitored (Schwartz, Fair, Greenberg, Freedman, & Klerman, 1974). The results indicated that electrical activity in the face matches the muscular movements that have been documented for various emotions. For example, during happy thoughts, the same facial muscles that produce a smile show increased electrical activity even though the facial expression appears blank.

While primary emotions appear to be biologically linked to specific facial expressions, different cultures establish different **display rules** that determine the appropriateness of expressing certain emotions through facial behavior in certain situations (Ekman, 1972). In American society, for example, it is generally considered more appropriate for women than men to cry when experiencing the emotion of sadness. While some societies sanction the full expression of many different affects in a wide variety of situations, other societies are more circumspect and may strongly discourage the public display of strong emotions.

A last way in which different emotions can be distinguished is in terms of their developmental course. As Izard (1978) has asserted, "emotions emerge as they become adaptive in the life of the infant" (p. 390). The cry of the newborn is generally a sign of *distress,* an extremely rudimentary emotion that signals that something is not quite right in the world. The distress cry motivates caregivers to attend to the infant and address the source of distress. The origins of *enjoyment* may reside in the early social smile and face-to-face interaction with the caregiver that is usually displayed by infants by 2 months of age. Out of early joyful interactions develop the caregiver–infant attachment bond and the first love relationship in the baby's life, as we saw in Chapter 4.

Interest/excitement can be traced back to at least the third and fourth months of life, when infants are engaged in what the developmental psychologist Jean Piaget (1952) viewed as attempts to "make interesting events last." The function of interest/excitement is to focus and maintain attention and to motivate exploratory activity. Interest is activated by novelty and change and serves as the basis for the infant's first self-initiated interactions with the world of objects. *Fear* and *sadness* may appear in the second half of the first year of life, especially in response to novelty, separation, and loss. It is quite common for 8-month-old infants to fear strangers and to cry when separated from their mothers and fathers. Finally, the emergence of *shame* and (later) *guilt* generally await the development of self-consciousness in the second year, following the child's consolidation of an initial sense of self-as-object, a sense of "me" (Chapter 10).

Scenes and Scripts

Basic Concepts   While affect is the supreme motivator in life, scenes and scripts are the great organizers. Tomkins views the person as a playwright who fashions his or her own personal drama from the earliest weeks of life. The basic compo-

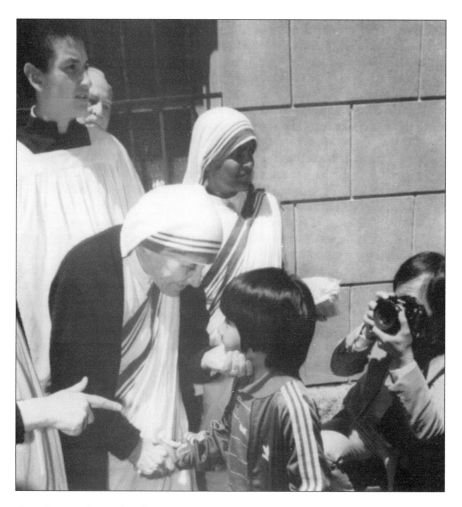

Commitment script: Mother Theresa.

nent of the drama is the **scene,** the memory of a specific happening or event in one's life that contains at least one affect and one object of that affect. Each scene is an "organized whole that includes persons, place, time, actions, and feelings" (Carlson, 1981, p. 502). We may each view our own lives, therefore, as a series of scenes, one after the other, extending from birth to the present. But certain kinds of scenes appear again and again, and certain typical groupings or families of scenes can be discerned. **Scripts** enable us to make sense of the relations among various scenes. A script is a set of rules for interpreting, creating, enhancing, or defending against a family of related scenes (Carlson, 1988). Each of us organizes the many scenes in our lives according to our own idiosyncratic scripts.

The *short-term* importance of any particular scene in a person's life is likely to be a function of the quality of the affect in the scene. In thinking back over yesterday's events, therefore, you may recall a particular happening that stands out because of the intense emotion you experienced during it. For instance, the lunchtime volleyball game you played with friends may have elicited strong feelings of joy, an argument with your mother may have brought forward feelings of anger, or the conversation you had with an attractive man or women may have elicited excitement—each of these scenes could conceivably stand out as special or important, for that given day. The *long-term* importance of a scene in the context of a person's entire life drama or narrative is likely to be a function of **psychological magnification,** which is the process of connecting related scenes into a meaningful pattern. To connect scenes into meaningful patterns, we must recognize basic similarities and differences among various scenes. For instance, an argument with your mother may remind you of a similar disagreement you had with a professor. In both cases, say, what began as a friendly exchange deteriorated into shouting over a petty difference of opinion. The two arguments appear to be *analogs* of each other. Psychological magnification often works by constructing such analogs—the detection of similarities in different experiences. When construing analogs in your life, you are likely to get that feeling of "here we go again," replaying the same scenario over and over. According to Tomkins, *negative*-affect scenes are often psychologically magnified through the formation of analogs. Therefore, in making sense of the many scenes of fear or sadness in your life, you are likely to discern the ways in which these scenes are essentially similar.

When, on the other hand, you focus on *differences* in organizing various life scenes, you are employing psychological magnification to construct *variants*. You are most likely to do this, argues Tomkins, in the magnification of *positive*-affect scenes. Therefore, in construing the many experiences of joy in your past, you are likely to focus on the ways in which the various scenes differ around a stable core. Consider joyful family gatherings. Last summer's family reunion, Thanksgiving dinner two years ago, and the day your mother brought your baby sister home from the hospital may all stand out in your life narrative as joyful scenes. While the various scenes are similar in some ways, you are likely to magnify them such that differences are accentuated. Therefore, the family reunion may stand out as "special" for the great conversation you had with your uncle who works for the FBI; the highlight of the Thanksgiving dinner may have been your sister's announcement that she and her boyfriend were planning to get married; and the day you saw your baby sister for the first time may stand out for the overwhelming feelings of tenderness and affection you felt.

Types of Scripts   While psychologists have been able to identify a finite number of basic human affects, the number of possible scenes and scripts in human life appears to be much larger. Therefore, no definitive list of scenes and scripts has been developed. However, Tomkins has identified at least two types of scripts that seem especially significant in human life and that help organize in powerful ways people's life narratives. These are commitment scripts and nuclear scripts (Carlson, 1988; Tomkins, 1987).

In a **commitment script,** the person binds him- or herself to a life program or goal that promises the reward of intense positive affect. A commitment script involves a long-term investment in "improving things." The person may have a vision of the ideal life or the ideal society and dedicate his or her life to realizing or accomplishing this vision. According to Tomkins, commitment scripts begin with an intensely positive early scene or series of scenes from childhood. This scene of enjoyment or excitement comes to represent an optimistic ideal of what might be—a Garden of Eden from the past that holds out the hope of a paradise in the future, the pursuit of which becomes one's life task.

In a commitment script, the person organizes scenes around a clearly defined and undisputed goal (Table 13.1). Therefore, commitment scripts are *not* likely to entail significant conflict between competing goals or troubling ambivalence about any single goal. The person whose life is organized around a strong commitment script strives, instead, to accomplish his or her desired paradise with singleness of purpose and steadfast dedication. Even in the face of great obstacles and repeated negative-affect experiences, such a person focuses steadily upon the object of commitment, laboring under the conviction that "bad things can be overcome" (Carlson, 1988).

In sharp contrast to commitment scripts are **nuclear scripts,** which are generally marked by ambivalence and confusion about one's life goals. In the terms of Miller and Dollard's conflict theory of Chapter 6, a nuclear script always

Table 13.1

Commitment Scripts *Versus* Nuclear Scripts

	Type of Script	
Script Feature	**Commitment**	**Nuclear**
Ratio of positive to negative affect	Positive greater than negative	Negative greater than positive
Affect Socialization	Intense, rewarding	Intense, ambivalent
Clarity of ideal scene	Clear, monistic	Confusing, pluralistic
Magnification of scenes via	Variants	Analogs
Sequences	"Bad things can be overcome"	"Good things turn bad"

Adapted from Carlson (1988, p. 111).

involves complex approach–avoidance conflicts. The person is irresistibly drawn toward and repelled by particularly conflictual scenes in his or her life narrative. The result is a life narrative that resembles the literary form of tragedy, as we see in such great Greek tragedies as *Oedipus Rex* and the *Oresteia,* and in the life of Margaret Sands.

A nuclear script begins with a **nuclear scene,** which is a positive childhood scene that eventually turns bad. As a good scene, it may involve the experience of enjoyment or excitement in the presence of others, especially those others who may provide the person with "stimulation, guidance, mutuality, support, comfort, and/or reassurance." The scene turns bad with the appearance of "an intimidation, or a contamination, or a confusion, or any combination of these which jeopardize the good scene" (Tomkins, 1987, p. 199). What begins, therefore, as joyful or exciting turns frightening, disgusting, contemptuous, shameful, or sad. A nuclear script is initially formed as an attempt to reverse the nuclear scene, to turn the bad scene into a good scene again. The attempt is only partially successful, however, as the person ultimately appears fated to repeat the nuclear scene continually through subsequent analog scenes.

Carlson (1981) describes a nuclear scene from the early childhood of one Jane W., a 37-year-old college professor:

> Four-year-old Janie is playing when she hears her mother cry for help. Running into the hall, she finds her mother lying on the floor in a heap of boxes, having fallen from a makeshift ladder to the attic. Mother asks Janie to call her father. Father arrives, helps mother to her feet, and supports her as they walk to the living room with Janie hovering nearby. Janie hears her father say "Sit here, honey" and promptly perches on the designated couch. Father angrily yells, "Get out of here!" and pushes Janie away so that her mother may lie down. Janie retreats in confusion, feeling deeply ashamed. (p. 504)

It turns out that Jane's mother was pregnant at the time of the fall and that this event probably caused her subsequent miscarriage. Further, when Jane's father said, "Sit here, honey," he was probably speaking to her mother, though of course the 4-year-old Janie assumed he was addressing her.

Carlson identifies five key features in this scene: (1) good things turn bad, (2) seduction and betrayal, (3) disorientation in space, (4) affects of shame and anger, and (5) withdrawal and inhibition. Each of these features was replayed in subsequent scenes in Jane's life, attesting to the power of the nuclear scene as the precipitating event in a nuclear script. Evidence for the psychological magnification of this scene through the formation of many analogs is evident in Jane's memories of her past, and in her dreams, fantasies, and interpersonal relationships. For example, she experienced many instances in her adult life in which she felt disoriented in space, in the same way she was disoriented in the nuclear scene when her father pushed her off the couch to make room for her mother.

Further, each of her 30 dream reports was characterized by repeated shifts in location. Shame, which was the dominant affect in the original scene, was abundantly evident as a recurrent emotional experience in both dreams and daily life. Inhibition and withdrawal were evident in autobiographical data suggesting that, despite her competence in many realms of life, Jane was often "frozen" at critical moments, especially when a difficult decision was to be made. Jane's inhibition was also evident in her repeated difficulties in mastering realms of physical activity, especially athletics and games.

Carlson suggests that at least two other scenes from Jane's childhood might be considered nuclear scenes, giving birth to nuclear scripts. The point of the analysis of the case of Jane, however, is not to show how any of these scenes actually *caused* subsequent events. Carlson does not contend that Jane is inhibited today *because* of the scene on the couch. Rather, the couch scene is a nuclear scene because it *organizes* the narrative of her life, giving meaning to many different experiences and serving as a template or pattern for other scenes in the story. As dramatists and storytellers of the self, human beings seek to discern a narrative order in their lives so that they may cast the many discordant events of the past into a meaningful and coherent life story. A major undercurrent in Jane's life story is a nuclear script about how good things can lead to disorientation, withdrawal, and shame.

A Life-Story Model of Identity

Consider again the case of Margaret Sands. In a lengthy biographical interview, Margaret gave me an account of the story of her life. She divided her life into chapters, and provided a name and plot summary for each. She described in detail a number of key events in her life, including the time she stood up to her mother at the drugstore payphone and when she travelled 2000 miles to rip the chapel apart. She sketched personality profiles of the most important people in her life, including her mother, her daughter, and a man she almost married. She told me of her fundamental beliefs and values concerning the nature of God and the universe, the meaning of life, what is good, true, evil. She gave me a sense of her hopes and dreams for the future, and what she fears the most. At the end of the interview, she reflected upon what might be the organizing theme and message of her entire life story.

What is the nature of the information that Margaret provided for me? How might I, a personologist, use this information? I must first concede that a 3-hour interview is not nearly sufficient to begin a full-fledged exploration of the intrapsychic mysteries buried deep in Margaret's unconscious. Therefore, the information I obtain is not likely to satisfy a Freudian or Jungian, except perhaps as a first step toward deeper analysis. And I must also admit that, compared to my life-story interview, there are surely more efficient and reliable ways to get good data on traits, motives, schemas, and the like. There are plenty of reliable and valid questionnaires around to measure these dimensions of personality. I might argue that the interview provides me with some factual information for her life, biographical data concerning what has really happened to her in the past, what kind of life she has had. These factual data might provide a context for interpreting more quantitative information I obtain on her personality dispositions. For example, I might be able to understand the way in which each of the Big Five traits (Chapter 5) manifests itself in her life. While the trait scales themselves would tell me where Margaret stands on fundamental dimensions of personality, the biographical information might provide insight into how her relative standings are expressed in thought and behavior over time.

It is certainly true, therefore, that Margaret's interview is likely to give me some more-or-less reliable, factual information about her past. But this is not why I do the interview. Facts are important, no doubt. But my main concern is meaning. What does Margaret's life *mean?* More specifically, what does it mean *to her?* Who does Margaret think that Margaret is? What is her *identity?*

As we saw in Chapter 12, Erikson employs the term identity to refer to an individual's attempt to answer the psychosocial question of "Who am I?" The question first poses itself in adolescence and young adulthood. The psychosocial process of addressing the question has been described in terms of exploring many options in life, especially those pertaining to ideology and occupation, and then making commitments to certain adult roles and positions (Marcia, 1980). Erikson describes the desired outcome of such a process as the construction of a *configuration,* the components of which include "constitutional givens, idiosyncratic libidinal needs, significant identifications, effective defenses, successful sublimations, and consistent roles" (1959, p. 116). The identity configuration works to integrate "all identifications with the vicissitudes of the libido, with the aptitudes developed out of endowment, and with the opportunities offered in social roles." The formulation of an identity configuration brings with it "the accrued confidence that the inner sameness and continuity prepared in the past are matched by the sameness and continuity of one's meaning for others" (Erikson, 1963, p. 261). I would submit that the configuration of Margaret's identity, and the configurations of yours and mine, *is a life story.* There are many aspects of personality that I cannot tap in my interview of Margaret. But the interview does enable me to focus sharply on that key part of personality that we call identity. This is because identity itself is structured like a story. I interview her because I want to get the internalized, integrative story—the **personal myth**—that she has constructed over time to provide her life with a sense of unity and purpose.

Like Tomkins' script theory, my own theoretical work on the meaning of human lives adopts a narrative approach, viewing the person as a storyteller who narrates life while living it (McAdams, 1984c, 1985b, 1985c, 1987, 1988b, 1990, 1993). But whereas Tomkins sketches a broad theory of personality connecting scenes and scripts to fundamental human affects, my own approach focuses somewhat more narrowly on the concept of identity. Identity is an internalized and evolving life story, or personal myth, that binds together the reconstructed past, perceived present, and anticipated future into a narrative configuration so as to confer upon the person's life what Erikson calls a sense of "inner sameness and continuity." As she lives and grows in a complex and multi-layered social world, Margaret Sands fashions and refashions a story about who she was, is, and will be. The story is based on facts for sure. But it is also a product of Margaret's narrative imagination, a myth that explains to Margaret and to her world how she came to be, where she may be going, and what her life means. Like the profound myths of religious and cultural traditions, Margaret's personal myth goes beyond facts to reveal the deeper truths she perceives in her own life (Feinstein & Krippner, 1988). Margaret's life story is not "made" in my interview with her. She has been making it all along. My interview is designed to get at some of what she has been making, to reveal the outlines of the story she has been working on for many years. In my interview, I know that not everything she tells me is important and that some of what she says may function to make her "look good" in my eyes. I also know that there is much that will remain untold, no matter how successful our interview and how intimate our rapport. Still, if I want the story, I have to ask her to tell it.

As Westerners living in a modern world, we seek to provide our lives with unity and purpose by constructing, consciously and unconsciously, integrative stories of the self. The storymaking begins in adolescence, when, as Erikson says, we first confront the question of Who am I? Able to entertain hypothetical realities through formal operational thought and motivated to reevaluate personal history and to explore new possibilities for the future, we begin to operate as both historians of the past and prophets for the future, seeking to cast our time-driven lives into narratives that work. Our first attempts to do this may seem naive and fantastical. Examining diaries and personal correspondence of adolescents, Elkind (1982) finds evidence for the construction of *personal fables*—fantastical stories about the self, underscoring the teenager's sense that he or she is unique in the world, destined for great goodness or badness, and forever misunderstood by others. For some adolescents, the personal fable may serve as a "rough first draft" of an evolving identity narrative, a story that will become more realistic and plausible in the years to come. Moving into young adulthood, Hankiss (1981) identifies *ontological strategies* that people adopt to explain how they came to be. For example, in a "dynastic" ontological strategy, a young adult fashions a story about how a very positive past life has now given birth to a very positive current life. By contrast, a "compensatory" strategy involves a story of how a bad past has given birth to a good present, as in the proverbial "rags to riches" life story celebrated by many Americans throughout our nation's history. (See Table 13.2)

Therefore, we begin to construct self-defining life stories in adolescence and young adulthood, when first confronted with the challenge of identity. But we do not begin our stories from scratch. And we do not quit working on our stories as we move beyond our early adult years. The origins of life stories can be traced back to infancy, and the process of life storymaking continues well into midlife and beyond (Cohler, 1982; McAdams, 1990, 1993). In infancy and childhood, we are implicitly "gathering material" for the story we will someday compose. When

 **Table 13.2**

Views From Six Different Scholars on the Relation Between Stories and Human Lives

Source	Concept	Description
Northrop Frye, literary scholar (1957)	Mythic archetypes	There exist four fundamental story forms which reflect four stages of human existence and the four seasons. *Comedy* highlights birth and spring; *romance* depicts the passion and adventure of youth and early adulthood, and the season of summer; *tragedy* suggests deterioration and eventual dying in later adulthood, and the season for autumn; *irony* depicts death and winter.
Lawrence Elsbree, literary scholar (1982)	Generic plots	There exist five basic plots in stories, each reflecting a fundamental human striving: (1) establishing a home; (2) fighting a battle; (3) taking a journey; (4) enduring suffering; and (5) pursuing consummation or completion.
Jean-Paul Sartre, philosopher (1964)	True novels	The essential form of the self is a retrospective story, or "true novel," that creates order out of the chaos of experience. Because contemporary religion and social institutions no longer provide people with sacred myths with which to identify, modern men and women are faced with seeking truth and meaning through creating their own myths about themselves. Ideally, a person's own true novel should reflect a central truth or dilemma about his or her historical epoch.
Alasdair MacIntyre, philosopher (1984)	Moral virtues	The "good" in human life must be understood in the context of narrative. What is good for a single person is what contributes to the completion of his or her life story. What is good for humankind must be derived from an analysis of the features that are common to all life stories.

Table 13.2 continued

Table 13.2 continued

Source	Concept	Description
David Elkind, developmental psychologist (1982)	Personal fable	In early adolescence, a person may construct a fantastical story about the self, underscoring the teenager's sense that he or she is unique in the world, destined for greater goodness or badness, and forever misunderstood by others. Elkind sees personal fable as a relatively normal phenomenon that is partly a result of the beginning of formal operational thinking. In terms of Erikson's theory of identity, personal fable may be a "rough draft" of an evolving narrative identity that will mature and become more realistic in later years.
Agnes Hankiss, sociologist (1981)	Ontological strategy	In early adulthood, people attempt to explain how they "came to be" (ontology) by "mythologically rearranging" the past and evaluating the present according to one of four different strategies: (1) dynastic (good past, good present), (2) antithetical (good past, bad present), (3) compensatory (bad past, good present), or (4) self-absolutory (bad past, bad present) strategy.

we arrive in adolescence ready to make sense of who we are, we are already bestowed with a wealth of experience that constitutes some of the most important "stuff" out of which our identities will be made. These are the biographical resources for our life stories. There is much that we can do with these resources, many possibilities that we can create. But in identity, as in life, we can never fully transcend our resources.

Origins of the Story: Tone, Imagery, Theme

Babies cannot tell stories. But the first two years of life provide infants with some of the most important material for the stories they will *someday* construct to make sense of their lives. As infants experience their first human relationship in attachment (Chapter 4) and develop a basic sense of self (Chapter 10), they are also learning their first lessons about story. The first two years of life leave people with a set of unconscious and nonverbal "attitudes" about self, other, and world, and about how the three relate to each other over time, in narrative. Before we understand what a story is, we have seen how human beings interact with each other and how they try to do things over time. We have known our own intentions. We have tried to do things in the world, and we have witnessed the results of our strivings. We have known trust and mistrust, times when "things work out in the end" and times when they don't. Recall Bruner's (1986) idea that stories are about "the vicissitudes of human intention" organized in time. The 2-year-old has experienced the vicissitudes of her own intentions, and she has begun to learn how they may be organized in time, from one moment to the next.

Erikson (1963) writes that the enduring legacy of infancy is *hope*. The infant who experiences the secure and trusting attachment bond with the caregiver moves through childhood and beyond with faith in the goodness of the world and hope for the future. Hope is "the enduring belief in the attainability of fervent wishes" (Erikson, 1963, p. 118). Before the infant is able to talk about "fervent wishes," he or she emerges from the first two years of life with an unconscious, pervasive, and "enduring belief" concerning the extent to which wishes, intentions, desires, and dreams are "attainable." A secure attachment bond with the caregiver (Chapter 4) reinforces an optimism about human strivings. It strengthens the unconscious belief that when people try to do things they will ultimately succeed. It proclaims that the world is trustworthy, that it is predictable, knowable, and ultimately good. By contrast, insecure attachment sends a less hopeful message. It suggests that human intentions may not be realized over time because the world is not altogether trustworthy. We do not get what we wish for. Things tend not to work out in the end.

The most fundamental relationship between the personal myths of adulthood and the first two years of life may be expressed in what I call *narrative tone* (McAdams, 1990, 1993). While some life stories exude optimism and hope, others are couched in the language of mistrust and resignation. Narrative tone refers, then, to a most basic sense of story—the sense in which the story speaks optimistically or pessimistically about human life. Adult life stories vary wildly in this regard, from the "happily ever after" varieties to the ones in which "they all die in the end." A hopeful, optimistic narrative tone or attitude suggests that human beings are indeed capable of attaining their most fervent wishes, that human intentions may be realized over time. The world is predictable and understandable. Things work out in the long run. Stories have happy endings. Positive tone is revealed in the narrative forms of "comedy" and "romance" (Frye, 1957; McAdams, 1985b; K. Murray, 1989). We may think of those joyful comedies from Shakespeare (e.g., *All's Well That Ends Well*) in which they all get married in the end, or of such movies as *When Harry Met Sally*. For romance, we may think of exciting adventure stories wherein the hero or heroine confronts one challenge after another, emerging victorious in the end: Homer's *Odyssey, Star Wars,*

The adventure story, an example of romance in narrative: Harrison Ford as Indiana Jones.

Raiders of the Lost Ark, the mysteries of Nancy Drew or the Hardy Boys. By contrast, a relatively pessimistic narrative tone or attitude suggests that human beings do not get what they wish for, that human intentions are repeatedly foiled over time. The world is capricious and unpredictable, narratives take unforeseen turns, things rarely work out over time, and stories are bound to have unhappy endings. In this regard, "tragedies" like *Oedipus Rex* tell of heroes and heroines struggling against an overpowering fate. Equally pessimistic are those many modern novels (stories from Kafka to Anne Beattie) that adopt the form of "irony," telling how main characters muddle through life's ambiguities, forever puzzled and engulfed by chaos, contradiction, and paradox.

Narrative tone is perhaps the most pervasive and identifiable feature of a life story in adulthood. It is a feature of identity that begins to reveal itself very early in the interview of Margaret Sands, as she gives a tragic account of what she calls "a wasted life." Narrative tone is conveyed both in story's plot and in the way the plot is interpreted. Therefore, an optimistic story can be optimistic because good things happen or it can be optimistic because even though bad things happen the person remains hopeful that things will improve. Similarly, a pessimistic story, like Margaret's, can be pessimistic because of the series of misfortunes and bad events the person describes or because good things are given a negative, pessimistic, or even cynical meaning.

Narrative tone speaks to the author's underlying faith in the possibilities of human intention and behavior. It reflects the extent to which a person dares to believe that the world can be good and that one's place can be more or less secure within it. This belief is prerational, prelogical. It is not something that people arrive at through conscious deliberation. Instead, it seems to be deeply ingrained in our minds from early childhood onwards. This is not to say that the belief, the faith, cannot change. Major life events and developmental change may certainly have an impact on the extent to which one adopts a relatively hopeful or hopeless perspective on life. But the first formative influences on narrative tone may be traced to the earliest years of life in which each person establishes a relatively secure or insecure attachment relationship and begins the process of consolidating a sense of self. Secure attachment, therefore, may provide a positively toned resource for subsequent identity formation. It may help provide lives with hope and trust and promote an unconscious belief in the attainability of fervent wishes. Insecure attachment may provide a negatively toned resource for identity. In the long run, it may work to color one's life story in more somber hues.

Moving from infancy to early childhood, we move in story from tone to *imagery*. The imagery of a story is determined by the word pictures, the sounds, even the smells and tastes the author creates, the metaphors, similes, and so on that provide certain kinds of stories with a distinctive "feel." Contrast, for example, the dark and frightening imagery of one of Edgar Allen Poe's short stories—say, "The Telltale Heart"—with the sunny and breezy imagery of many advertisements—themselves little stories—for the MacDonald's restaurants. In Poe, you are haunted by the relentlessly beating heart of a man who is supposed to be dead, by spooky rooms and creaking floors; you can see the cobwebs, smell the damp and decomposing floorboards in the ancient house. In the commercial for MacDonald's, by contrast, you see smiling faces, hear happy tunes, and you may even think you smell the familiar Big Mac or Bacon Cheeseburger Deluxe, with fries no less. Many MacDonald's ads on television suggest the imagery of youth, family, vigor, and good clean fun. For MacDonald's and Poe, you don't need to know the plot of the story to get a pretty good sense of what the imagery is all about. Pick up "The Telltale Heart" and turn to any page. Read a few sentences. You may not be able to figure out exactly what is going on, but you are likely to recognize the imagery of gloom and foreboding.

In the preschool years, children are cognitively predisposed to understand and appreciate the world from the standpoint of imagery. Preschoolers show what Piaget (1970) calls "preoperational" thinking. Preoperational thinking is fluid and magical, unrestrained by the dictates of logical reasoning. The child represents the world in symbols and images, but he or she does not insist that these representations remain true to logic or context. For the 4-year-old, Cinderella can be dead one minute and alive the next. She can perform actions that are completely at odds with her original narrative context. Although Cinderella is forever dutiful and sweet, preferring dancing to fighting in the fairy tale itself, the child may decide in her fantasy play that Cinderella should do battle one afternoon with the Wicked Witch of the West—with swords yet—and that the two of them should sit down afterwards to sip tea with Jesus. What appeals to many 4-year-olds about stories is their egocentric appropriation of image, the ways in which they can take the discrete images from a given story and make them do what they want them to do. This kind of fantasy-based egocentrism is a hallmark of preoperational thought.

The child's world of make-believe is populated with figures, symbols, pictures, and other idiosyncratic mental representations that are heavily loaded with affect. The major sources of these images are the family, peers, schools and churches, books, and increasingly the media. Fowler (1981) writes that religious traditions provide some of the most enduring images for stories. For example, children raised in Christian families develop rich imagery associated with such things as angels, devils, star, lamb, cross, etc. In Fowler's view, religious meaning is conveyed through imagery in the preoperational stage of cognitive development. A young child may believe that God is an old man with a white beard and Jesus is a soft baby.

People begin stockpiling emotionally charged images for identity in their preschool years. While much of this early imagery passes into oblivion as children grow up, some of the most significant images and representations may survive into adulthood and become magnified to assume prominent positions in people's life stories. Every life story has its own unique imagery. One stockbroker's personal myth is saturated with the imagery of mounting acceleration: Life moves faster and faster each day, people race to reach the top, but they never get there. A mother tells a life story filled with the verdant imagery of lush gardens, children blooming like flowers, lives reaching fruition in accord with nature's ways. Margaret Sands' story is filled with the ominous imagery of religious icons and cloistered classrooms, images connected to loathing and regret. While a person may find or create imagery for identity at virtually any point in the life cycle, emotionally charged images from early childhood often find their ways into the life stories of adults.

As children enter formal schooling and develop in the direction of increasingly logical and systematic thought, they come to appreciate stories as thematically organized wholes (Sutton-Smith, 1986). Older children implicitly understand that stories are about the "vicissitudes of human intention" organized in time (Bruner, 1986). Older children see stories as goal-oriented sequences, and they invest interest in the story's characters as a function of the desirability of the goals towards which the characters strive. As we move, then, from early to later childhood, we move in story from imagery to *theme* (McAdams, 1990, 1993). A theme is a recurrent goal-oriented sequence in narrative. As such, theme represents a more complex level of story than does imagery. An image exists in a moment, but a theme is articulated over time. An image is like a snapshot, or like a musical chord—frozen in time. By contrast, a theme is like a series of snapshots, strung together to form a motion picture, or like a musical melody, a sequence of notes forming a particular pattern over time.

Themes convey motivation—what characters want, desire, need, are trying to get. In many stories, what characters want and what they are often trying to get is some form of power or love, or both. David Bakan (1966) employs the terms **agency** and **communion** to refer to themes of power and love, respectively. Agency refers to separation of the individual from and mastery of the individual over the environment, subsuming such overlapping motifs as power, autonomy, achievement, control, and isolation. Agency denotes story material in which characters assert, expand, or protect themselves as autonomous and active *agents*. Communion refers to union of the individual with the environment and the surrender of individuality to a larger whole, covering such motifs as intimacy, love, reconciliation, caring, and merger. Life stories, therefore, may be compared and contrasted with respect to the degree to which the thematic lines of agency and communion dominate the text. In the motivational terms of Chapter 11, agentic life stories represent the personal translation of strong power (Winter, 1973) and achievement (McClelland, 1961) motivation into identity. Similarly, communal life stories show how strong intimacy motivation (McAdams, 1980) may be translated into an identity that celebrates love, caring, and concern for others. A person's motives, therefore, are readily expressed in identity through agentic and communal narrative themes.

As children move through elementary school, therefore, they begin to comprehend themselves in terms of their own recurrent wants and desires organized in time (Kegan, 1982). Unlike preschoolers, their thinking patterns seem to be dictated less by the impulses of the moment and more oriented to future goals and plans. The systematic and organized quality of what Piaget called "concrete operational thinking" in elementary school enables children to reason about the world in logical, cause-and-effect terms, expanding their understanding of how prior events lead to subsequent events over time. Thus, older children's understandings of themselves and of stories become couched in thematic, motivational terms. Their own recurrent desires and wants, furthermore, may become organized themselves into relatively stable motivational dispositions, such as achievement and power motivation. When they reach adolescence and adulthood, the organization of their characteristic desires will be reflected in the life stories they create. Reflecting her own strong intimacy motivation, Margaret Sands has constructed a personal myth that underscores caregiving and helping others. Yet she remains extremely ambivalent about establishing long-term relationships of intimacy with friends or lovers. She still feels that her "foundation" is not strong enough for that.

Characters in Narrative: The Imago

In the life-story model of identity, early experience does not determine the quality of identity. The tone, imagery, and themes of an adult's life story are not a direct result of experiences from infancy and childhood. Instead, early experience provides "raw materials" or "resources" for the making of identity in adolescence and adulthood. Other resources come from biology and culture. Many different forces and factors, some within the person and some in the person's environment, may help shape identity by providing raw materials for the making of the self. In adolescence, people begin to draw upon the resources at hand to *make their own identities.* Identities are always made in a psychosocial context, in relationships with others, in the midst of an interpersonal world. Our friends, families, teachers, pastors, and many others influence our identities. Still, identities are made; we author who we are. Therefore, we should not underestimate the power of the individual to shape his or her own destiny, to create a fulfilling life story even when the resources seem less than wonderful, and to create a dismal one even when one seems to be blessed with best and brightest of possibilities. While nobody can make a silk purse out of a sow's ear, we are all nonetheless active creators and synthesizers in the construction of our own life stories.

By the time we reach the teenage years, therefore, we have already internalized information and experiences that are likely to influence markedly the particular tone, images, and themes that our life story will eventually reveal. In adolescence, it is finally time to begin putting things together into narrative form. The adolescent may begin by consciously and unconsciously working through an *ideological setting* for the life story. An ideological setting is the backdrop of belief and value that situates the story within a particular ethical and religious location. A person's beliefs and values about truth, right versus wrong, God, and other ultimate concerns situate the action of the story in a particular ideological time and place. With the advent of formal-operational thinking, the adolescent may begin to search for answers to abstract philosophical, ethical, political, and religious questions. Indeed, the consolidation of an ideological setting may be the central task of identity formation for many adolescents (McAdams, Booth, & Selvik, 1981). It is very difficult to construct a meaningful life narrative before this setting of belief and value is firmly established, as we saw for example in the biography of Martin Luther (Chapter 12). Once established, however, the ideological setting generally does not change much. Like the geographical and historical settings of most stories, the ideological setting remains in the background, rarely questioned or examined by the person after adolescence and young adulthood and thus fairly resistant to change. Margaret Sands' hard-headed agnosticism provides an ideological setting for her life story. It remains today an unquestioned backdrop for the plot of her identity.

While the adolescent begins to formulate personalized beliefs and values, he or she is also likely to adopt, for the first time in the life cycle, an historical perspective on the self. Teenagers realize that childhood is now a thing of the past. For the first time in their lives, adolescents have a history. In their minds, they *were* something before, and now they *are* something else. They seek to understand the meaning of what they were in the context of what they are now and what they may become in the future. As a way, then, of gaining perspective on the past, adolescents begin to sort through their memories in order to highlight key events and major turning points in their perceived autobiography. I call this process the elaboration of *nuclear episodes.* Nuclear episodes are perceived high points, low points, beginning points, ending points, and turning points in one's past, each of which stands out in bold print in the evolving life story. What is important about nuclear episodes, like Margaret's visit to the chapel, is not so much what actually happened in the past but what the memory of the key event symbolizes in identity. As Erikson and Adler both maintained, we *choose* to remember the past in a particular way—in a way that affirms the personal myth we are beginning to formulate about the meaning of our own life (Charme, 1984).

Moving from adolescence into young adulthood, the central task in identity formation becomes the creation and refinement of "main characters" in the life story. All stories have main characters. In a life story, the main character is also the author—the person whose identity the story is. However, this main character may appear in a variety of forms. The various forms may be understood as main characters in their own right—semi-autonomous agents whose actions and interactions define the plot of the story. I call these **imagoes.** An imago is an idealized personification of the self that functions as a main character in the life story (McAdams, 1984c, 1985b, 1985c, 1993). Imagoes are one-dimensional, "stock" characters in the life story, and each integrates a host of different characteristics, roles, and experiences in the person's life. Imagoes are like little "me's" inside of me who act and think in highly personalized ways. The concept of imago resembles the idea of "possible selves" (Markus & Nurius, 1986) or "ideal" and "ought" selves (Higgins, 1987) described in Chapter 9. Imagoes also share conceptual space with certain psychoanalytic ideas such as "internalized objects" (Chapter 2) and inner "states" (Berne, 1964), "voices" (Watkins, 1986), and "personifications" (Sullivan, 1953). A person may see him- or herself as "the good boy (or girl) who never gets into trouble," "the sophisticated and intellectual professor," "the rough-around-the-edges working-class kid from the wrong side of town," "the corporate executive playing out the American dream," "the worldly traveller in search of all that is new and exotic," "the athlete," "the loyal friend," "the sage," "the soldier," "the teacher," "the clown," or "the peacemaker." Each of these capsule self-definitions might qualify as an imago. Each might exist within a particular life story as a carefully crafted part of the self that shows up as a main character in many different parts of the narrative. A person's life story is likely to contain more than one imago. Each of the imagoes lays claim to a particular set of identity resources.

In adulthood, imagoes may incorporate social roles. But imagoes are larger and more internal than social roles. The general features of a given role are defined by the society within which the role is operational. With respect to social roles, then, a mother is a woman who bears and/or raises children, providing care and counsel and endeavoring to promote her children's development in accord with her own values and society's demands. With respect to roles, a federal judge is a man or woman who presides over a courtroom trial, hears legal arguments, makes rulings about the admissability of evidence, renders judgments in accord with law, and so on. These roles are elaborately scripted by societal norms and expectations. And we are all very familiar with them.

If a role is to become an imago, however, the role must be *internalized and broadened* to function as a personally crafted aspect of the self that is applicable to a wide range of life activities. A person whose life story contains a strong *imago* of "the mother" acts, thinks, feels, and strives as a mother does in a wide variety of ways that go well beyond caring for her own biological or adopted children. She magnifies and personalizes the social role and appropriates it within her own self-defining life story in such a way as to make it a central identity character. Similarly, the woman who develops an imago of "the judge" may be concerned, as a judge would be, about issues of justice and fairness in many different realms of her life, acting and thinking as if she were a judge even in those situations in which, sociologically speaking, she isn't one, as when she is with her family and friends. This kind of judge is not merely enacting social roles. The script is as much her own as it is the one society handed her when she accepted the judicial appointment.

Imagoes may personify aspects of who you believe you are now, who you were, who you might be in the future, who you wish you were, or who you fear you might become. Any or all of these aspects of the self—the actual perceived self, the past self, the future self, the desired self, the undesired self—can be incorporated into the main characters of personal myths. Any or all of them can be given a distinctive characterization in narrative such that the resultant imago can come to dominate a particular chapter or personify a particular theme, idea, or value in the story. Any or all of them can serve to consolidate different social roles that one plays and internalize those roles in a self-defining manner.

As main characters in personal myths, imagoes provide a narrative mechanism for accommodating the diversity of modern life. In seeking pattern and organization for identity, the person in the early adult years (ages 20–40) may psychologically pull together social roles and other divergent aspects of the self to form integrative imagoes. Central conflicts or dynamics in one's life may be represented and played out as conflicting and interacting imagoes, as main characters in any story act and interact to push forward the plot. While modern life often insists that we be many different things to many different people, that we act in accord with a wide variety of roles (Gergen, 1992; Goffman, 1959), we are able to reduce the multiplicity by organizing our many roles and demands into a smaller and more manageable cast of life-story characters. As a modern adult who must find meaning at home, at work, and in all the other domains in my life, I cannot and do not want to be everything to everybody at every place and time. But I can be some important things in some important ways for some important people, at particular times and in particular places. Furthermore, I can be these things in a way that is unique to me, and in a way that is self-consistent, coherent, meaningful, purposeful, and gratifying. Creating a life story that contains a rich but finite source of characterization—a suitable cast of imagoes—enables me to resolve the problem of simultaneously playing many different roles but still being "myself" (Knowles & Sibicky, 1990).

Imagoes are partly scripted by culture, and they partly reflect the values to which a given culture aspires. The philosopher Alasdair MacIntyre (1984) writes, "*Characters* are the masks worn by moral philosophies" (p. 28). According to MacIntyre, all societies generate their own stock characters that personify those beliefs and standards that the society as a whole or a significant segment of society holds in greatest esteem. The character furnishes people at a given time and in a given place with a cultural and moral ideal, legitimating a particular mode of social existence. For example, Bellah and others (1990) suggest that "the independent citizen" served as a representative moral character type for early-nineteenth-century Americans. Reaching its culmination in the life of Abraham Lincoln, the independent citizen was the self-made, self-sufficient farmer or craftsman of small town America who held strongly to biblical religion and was fiercely devoted to the values of freedom and autonomy. The independent citizen captured the ideological spirit of the times, the moral exemplar of a young and idealistic nation.

The moral character types of which MacIntyre and Bellah speak are general models around which adults can pattern their own lives and articulate their own more personalized characterizations of self. Like moral character types at the societal level, furthermore, personal imagoes often speak a language of value and belief at the level of individual adult identity. Significant aspects of the adult's ideological setting may be clearly expressed in life-story imagoes. A fundamentalist Christian may develop an imago of "the evangelist," a character devoted to spreading the Christian gospel to all who have yet to accept it. A Christian with a slightly different perspective may create an imago of "the loyal friend," seeing in St. Paul's teachings on love and charity the ideological inspiration for his own life. Outside the realm of religion, imagoes may personify ethical, political, and aesthetic values. A prime function of imagoes in some personal myths is to be a mouthpiece or an exemplar for what a person holds to be right and to be true.

How many different kinds of imagoes are there? Because imagoes reflect, in part, a culture's values and possibilities and because people can be especially creative and imaginative in fashioning personifications of the self, there would appear to be a very large number of different kinds of imagoes that might be constructed by adults to serve as main characters in their life stories. In my studies of middle-class American adults, I have generated a taxonomy of general imago forms, into which many particular imagoes may be placed (McAdams, 1993). The taxonomy is presented in Figure 13.2. This classification system is organized along the twin thematic lines of agency and communion. Therefore, Class 1 imagoes are highly powerful and agentic characters such as "the warrior" and "the sage"; Class 3 imagoes are highly loving and communal such as "the friend" and "the caregiver"; Class 2 imagoes combine agency and communion to be both powerful and loving, and these include "the healer" and "the teacher"; finally, Class 4 imagoes express little agency or communion, such as "the survivor" and "the escapist." I have also labelled some of these forms (Classes 1 and 3) with names from the mythology of ancient Greece, in order to make them easier to remember. (Thus, the warrior is "Ares," and the caregiver is "Demeter.") In addition, the Greek labels draw on a comprehensive and timeless characterization of human diversity, for the deities of Mount Olympus represent projected personifications of what the ancient Greeks believed to be fundamental human qualities and propensities. Each imago category, moreover, should be seen as a type of *character in narrative,* not a type of person. A person's identity is not a single, simple imago. You are not "the sage," no matter how many of the qualities of Zeus your story suggests. You are more complex and multifaceted than any characterization com-

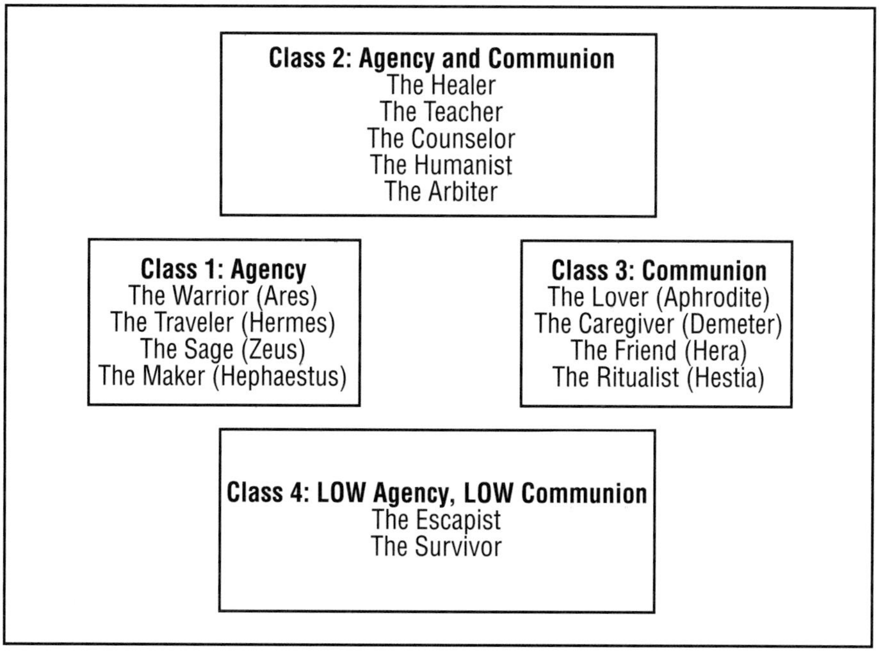

Figure 13.2

Imago Types: Some Main Characters in Life Stories.

Adapted from McAdams, 1985b, 1993.

ing from a Greek god, or from any other character type. A person's identity is *the story itself,* not any single character or part of the self in the story.

In a study of 50 men and women between the ages of 35 and 50, my colleagues and I attempted to identify and classify dominant imagoes in our subjects' life stories (McAdams, 1985b). Each of the adults in the study was asked to tell his or her life story. In addition, we administered a number of other personality measures, including the TAT. TAT responses were scored for power motivation and intimacy motivation, as described in Chapter 11. For each subject, we drew on an imago classification scheme similar to the one shown in Figure 13.2 and tried to discern the idealized personification that was most prominent in the story. As Table 13.3 shows, we found that those adults whose life stories displayed a highly agentic and powerful central imago (e.g., the warrior, the sage, the traveller, the maker) scored significantly higher on power motivation than other adults. Similarly, adults constructing life stories with a central communal imago (the lover, the friend, the caregiver, the ritualist) scored high on intimacy motivation. The results suggest an important connection between motivation and identity. People

Table 13.3

Motive Scores According to Predominant Imago

	Imago Class			
	1 (Agency)	2 (Agency + Communion)	3 (Communion)	4 (Lo/Lo)
Power Motivation	59.3	51.7	47.5	45.6
Intimacy Motivation	47.8	53.1	57.9	45.6
N (Women/Men)	11 (9/2)	7 (1/6)	12 (9/3)	20 (11/9)

Power and intimacy motivation are assessed via objective content analysis of imaginative stories written to six standard pictures on the Thematic Apperception Test (TAT). The mean differences among the four groups on power motivation are significant (F [3,46] = 6.16, $p < .01$), with Class 1 imagoes having significantly higher power motivation than Classes 3 and 4 combined ($p < .001$), and Classes 1 and 2 having higher power motivation than Classes 3 and 4 ($p < .01$).
The mean differences among the four groups on intimacy motivation are significant (F [3,46] = 5.31, $p < .01$), with Class 3 imagoes having significantly higher intimacy motivation than Classes 1 and 4 combined ($p < .001$), and Classes 2 and 3 imagoes having higher intimacy motivation than 1 and 4 combined ($p < .01$).
N = 50 adults between ages of 35 and 50 years.
From McAdams (1985b, pp. 192–196).

with a substantial need to feel strong and to have impact (high power motivation) construct self-defining life narratives with powerful and agentic protagonists. People with a strong need to feel close to others (high intimacy motivation) compose life stories whose central characters are caregivers, lovers, and loyal friends.

Storymaking in Midlife

In their 20s and 30s, many Western adults concentrate their identity work on the fashioning and refining of imagoes. As they enter the workplace, begin raising families, and become established in various sorts of communities, they make identity commitments to various social roles and they invest time and thought into making sense of their lives in terms of a delimited cast of main characters. They are figuring out what it means to be "the caregiver," "the healer," and so on; they are pushing these idealizations as far as possible, exploring the many ways in

Creativity before midlife: a painting by Francisco José de Goya at the age of 29.

which these characterizations of self can enrich their lives and help them forge that sense of "inner sameness and continuity" that Erikson describes as the heart of ego identity. As one approaches midlife, however, subtle shifts in storymaking may begin to appear.

In contemporary American society, midlife or middle age is considered to last from roughly age 40 to age 65. Certain biological changes play a role in demarcating this period of life, such as the end of the childbearing years. But for the most part, midlife is *socially* defined, based on the assumptions that most Americans have about the course of human life (Cohler, 1982). Midlife is situated in the temporal course of the human life cycle according to what Neugarten (1968) has called the **social clock.** The social clock is a set of expectations about age-appropriate transitions, setting the standards against which individuals evaluate the extent to which their lives are "on time" (Cohler & Boxer, 1984). Graduating from college in one's early 20s, raising a family in one's 20s and 30s, seeing the children leave home in one's 40s, witnessing parents' deaths in one's 50s and 60s, retiring at age 65 or 70—these are a few transitions in the life cycle that, in contemporary middle-class American society, are considered "on time." Many Americans expect to live well into their 70s and 80s. The midlife chunk of time is seen as comprising that period following early adulthood and preceding the retirement years.

As the adult enters midlife, he or she comes to realize that the life course is likely to be about half over and that there is now less time ahead in the future than behind in the past. Such a realization may lead to an increased concern with one's own mortality (Marshall, 1975; Sill, 1980), or what Neugarten and Datan (1972) call the "personalization of death." Experiences of loss become more salient—loss of others through death of parents and friends and through separation from children who have moved away, loss of vitality through changes in athletic and reproductive capacities, and loss of hopes and aspirations through the inevitable disappointments—both on-time and off-time—that accompany adult life (Jacques, 1965; Kernberg, 1980; Levinson, 1981).

Psychologists have observed a number of behavioral and attitudinal trends in midlife that may, on one level or another, be viewed as responses to one's growing, on-time concern about mortality. The middle years may bring an increase in the use of reminiscences in daily life (Livson & Peskin, 1980; Lowenthal, Thurnher, & Chiriboga, 1975), an enhanced appreciation for the internal world of thoughts and feelings, and somewhat less interest in establishing new interpersonal and instrumental engagements (Neugarten, 1979). According to Jung (1961), it is not until midlife that men are finally able to accept and integrate their suppressed femininity (the *anima*) and that women are able to express an inner masculinity (the *animus*), as we saw in Chapter 2. With the end of active parenting at midlife, Gutmann (1980) argues, women are likely to become more instrumental and executive in their approach to life, eschewing the dependent and self-effacing ways of their youth. Midlife men, on the other hand, are more likely to abandon the vigorous and aggressive manner of young adulthood in favor of more passive and contemplative roles.

Jacques (1965) has suggested that midlife may mark significant changes in the adult's efforts to be creative. Jacques examined biographical information and artistic productions for 310 painters, composers, poets, writers, and sculptors "of undoubted greatness or of genius" (p. 502). Included in his list were Mozart, Michelangelo, Bach, Gauguin, Raphael, and Shakespeare. Jacques found that before midlife the artists were more likely to produce masterpieces in a rapid and passionate fashion, as "hot-from-the-fire" productions. Their work tended to be highly optimistic and idealistic, laden with themes of pure desire and romance. After the age of about 40, however, the artists appeared to work in a more deliberate fashion, creating more refined and "sculpted" masterpieces. With the increasing concern over mortality at midlife, youthful idealism gave way to a more contemplative pessimism and a "recognition and acceptance that inherent goodness is accompanied by hate and destructive forces within" (Jacques, 1965, p. 505). Creative products speak a more philosophical and sober language during and after midlife—a result, says Jacques, of the artist's own confrontation with the prospect of death.

Though men and women may be at the prime of their lives in their middle years, the social clock suggests that the end of life is closer to the present than is

Creativity after midlife: a painting by Francisco José de Goya at the age of 69.

the beginning of life. It is likely, therefore, that midlife men and women should be especially concerned with *endings*. In their 40s and 50s, men and women in contemporary Western societies begin to consider in more detail and with greater urgency the problem of construing an appropriate ending for their self-defining life story. This does not mean that most middle-aged adults believe that at any moment they are going to die. Most middle-aged adults in American society are not morbidly obsessed with thoughts of their imminent demise. But they tend to be more cognizant of the sense of an ending in life and in their stories than they were in their early adult years. Their storymaking, consequently, tends to move in the direction of endings. Their identity task becomes the fashioning of an envisioned ending for the personal myth that will tie together the beginning and the middle to create a narrative affirming unity, purpose, and direction in life over time.

   Not just any kind of ending, however, will do. It is not enough that the envisioned ending of one's life story weaves together threads of continuity and purpose in life. It must also *produce new beginnings*. What we want in our identities as middle-aged men and women is to craft an ending for the personal myth that, paradoxically, suggests that the story *does not really end*. What we want is a narrative that enables us to attain a kind of symbolic immortality, generating a legacy of the self that will "live on" even after we are no longer living. As a result, we are challenged in middle adulthood to fashion what I call a *generativity script* (McAdams, 1985b; McAdams, Ruetzel, & Foley, 1986). As I suggested in Chapter 12, the generativity script is that part of the life story that concerns how the adult has and will continue to generate, create, nurture, or develop a *gift* of the self, to be offered to subsequent generations. The gift lives on; the ending gives birth to new beginnings; a legacy of the self is generated and offered up to others as the middle-aged adult comes to realize, in the words of Erikson, that "I am what survives me" (1968, p. 141).

As we saw in Chapter 12, people may be generative in a multitude of ways. Beyond our family life, generativity may be expressed in the realms of work, service, and even play. Writing a book, playing the piano, teaching a class, contributing to charity, donating blood, building a business, giving advice—these activities and many others with which adults are involved may be expressions of generativity. What determines the extent to which they are generative is partly the adult's attitude about them—an attitude of creating and presenting a gift. The generative adult commits him- or herself to some activity that is larger than his or her own life, investing significant time and creative energy into an endeavor that will "live on." As people approach and move through the midlife years of the 40s, 50s, and 60s, they may become increasingly concerned with their own mortality and with what they will be able to leave behind after they die. As integrated and responsible members of society, they begin to define themselves in terms of the gifts they create and offer. Generating gifts in their own image, they refashion their identities to accommodate their developing sense of an ending. They recast and revise their own life stories so that the past is seen as giving birth to the present and the future, so that beginning, middle, and ending make sense in terms of each other. In part, their identities become the stories of that which will survive them—how they were created so that *they* might create *it,* nurture it, and eventually let it go.

People are working on their life stories, consciously and unconsciously, throughout most of their adult years. At times the work is fast and furious, as during phases of exploration and moratorium. Periods of major identity change may follow significant life changes, such as getting married or divorced, having one's first child, changing jobs, changing residences, losing one's parents or one's spouse, menopause, retirement. They may also correspond to symbolic watersheds in the life course, such as hitting one's 40th birthday, the marriage of one's last child, the death of one's parents, retirement, or even getting those first gray hairs. During these periods, adults may call into question some of the assumptions they have lived by. They may recast their personal myths to embody new plots and characters and to emphasize different scenes from the past and different expectations for the future. They may set new goals. The sense of an ending may change substantially, and as the envisioned ending changes, the entire narrative may become oriented in a very different way. At other times, however, adults experience relative stability in identity. During these more tranquil periods, the story evolves slowly and in a very small ways. Adults may refine slightly their imagoes or tinker in minor ways with the sense of an ending. During these periods, major identity change may not seem to occur.

We see, therefore, that it is misleading to characterize the development of the life story in adulthood as either a smooth and continuous affair or a roller-coaster process of repeated change and growth. Rather, the development is both smooth and sudden, tranquil and tumultuous. Times of dramatic change and reformulation may be followed by long periods in which very little storymaking seems to occur. Every life is different in this regard, and every personal myth follows a unique course of development.

Nonetheless, certain developmental trends in storymaking may be observed as people move into and through midlife. There is a sense in which the development of identity in the midlife years should ideally move in the direction of *increasingly good narrative form* (McAdams, 1993, in press b). Six standards of good life-story form may be identified: (1) coherence, (2) openness, (3) credibility, (4) differentiation, (5) reconciliation, and (6) generative integration. The prototype of "the good story" in human identity—the personal myth that suggests considerable maturity in the search for unity and purpose in life—is one that receives high marks on these six narrative standards.

Coherence refers to the extent to which a given story makes sense on its own terms. Do the characters do things that make sense in the context of the story? Do the motivations for their behavior make sense in terms of what we know about how human beings generally act? Do events follow events in a causal manner? Do parts of the story contradict other parts? A story that lacks coherence is one that leaves the reader scratching his or her head, wondering why things turned out in such an inexplicable, puzzling way. Some stories, however, are almost too coherent. They hang together so neatly that they seem too consistent to be true. A personal myth need not make everything fit together in a person's life. We do not need perfect consistency in order to find unity and purpose in life. Indeed, a good life story is one that also shows considerable *openness* to change and tolerance for ambiguity. Such a story propels the person into the future by holding open a number of different alternatives for future action and thought. Life stories need to be flexible and resilient. They need to be able to change, grow, and develop as we ourselves change. Openness is, nonetheless, a difficult criterion to judge in personal myth, for there is always the danger that too much openness reflects lack of commitment and resolve.

A third standard is *credibility*. The good, mature, and adaptive personal myth cannot be based on gross distortions. Identity is not a fantasy. People create their identities, for sure. But they do not create them out of thin air, as one might a poem or a story of pure fiction. In identity, the good story should be accountable to the facts that can be known or found out. While identity is a creative work of the imagination, it is still grounded in the real world in which we all must live.

The good story is rich in characterization, plot, and theme. The reader is drawn into a complexly textured world in which full-bodied characters develop in intriguing ways over time, and their actions and interactions define compelling plots and subplots, as tension builds to climax and then resolution. In other

Continued on p. 768

Feature 13.B

When Did Identity Become a Problem?

The problem of identity may be a modern problem, most characteristic of middle-class Westerners living in industrial societies. In more agrarian and traditional societies and at earlier points in history, the problem of finding or creating the self in late adolescence and young adulthood may not have been as crucial. In societies in which sons are expected to grow up to do what their fathers do and daughters expected to follow directly in the footsteps of their mothers, identity is *conferred* upon the young person by a social structure. In such a context, ideology and occupation are received from established authorities, exploration of alternatives is minimal, and commitment to the status quo is a fait accompli.

Even among the intellectuals of Western societies, however, the notion that a person should find or create a unique self may be a relatively recent idea. In his book *Identity: Cultural Change and the Struggle for Self,* psychologist Roy Baumeister (1986) asks at what point in the history of Western civilization identity became a central concern. When did Westerners begin to report that they were experiencing identity "crises" in their own lives? As Baumeister views it, evidence of identity exploration and crisis may be gleaned from reports of two different kinds of problems in human living. The first is the problem of *continuity over time.* In this case, identity poses itself as a problem when the person begins to wonder or worry about the extent to which he or she is essentially the same kind of person over time: "Am I the same today as I was three years ago?" "Will I be the same ten years from now?" The second is the problem of *differentiation*. In this case, identity confronts the person with the task of determining how he or she is different from other people—others who, on the surface at least, seem quite similar to the self. In Baumeister's view, then, the person in the throes of an identity crisis is preoccupied with how he or she is essentially the same over time and how he or she is essentially different from other people.

Baumeister concludes that identity was not a major problem in Western societies before 1800, although many trends emerged before this time to prepare the way for it to become a problem. Medieval society in Europe operated on the basis of lineage, gender, home, and social class. A person's identity was assigned to him or her according to these external criteria. Even during the medieval era, however, certain strains of individualism emerged, including Christianity's emphasis on individual judgment and on individual participation in the church ritual. The Protestant Reformation split the ideological consensus of Europe and made religious belief a serious identity problem for many educated people. The rise of capitalism opened up economic opportunities and created an upwardly mobile middle class. Many people of the seventeenth and eighteenth centuries, therefore, confronted significant choices in their religious beliefs—whether to follow Rome or the Protestants, for instance—and enjoyed the prospect of enhancing one's material well-being in life through entrepreneurial activity in the marketplace. Other developments before 1800 that paved the way for identity's emergence as a central problem in human lives include a general rise in individualistic attitudes, increased desires for privacy, and the growing recognition that one's private self may be quite different from one's public self.

As Europe entered what has been termed the Romantic era in the last decade of the 1700s, the two great institutions of church and state were undergoing major transformation. While the Christian church's power and influence were waning rapidly, Europeans were also questioning the legitimacy of long-established political systems, as happened in the French Revolution. Men and women of the Romantic era substituted creativity, passion, and cultivation of the inner self for Christianity as new models for identity formation. If the self were not determined by God, then its construction was left to the individual. The Romantics also became increasingly dissatisfied with the relationship of the individual to society. This dissatisfaction was expressed as a concern with individual freedom, and it eventually gave birth to various Utopian movements as well as the rise of anarchism in the nineteenth century. In general, Europeans after 1800

believed that society's consensus about basic truths and ultimate values had been lost. The person was now to fashion a personal ideology as a foundation for identity.

In the twentieth century, the concern for identity has grown stronger as Westerners have witnessed a great proliferation of occupational and ideological choices. In addition, many social critics have lamented a growing alienation among twentieth-century adults who, more than ever before, feel cut off from and have lost faith in authoritative institutions (Lasch, 1979; Lifton, 1979; Sartre, 1965). In the Romantic literature of the nineteenth century, individual heroes struggled valiantly against societal constraints. In much of twentieth-century literature, on the other hand, the individual feels overwhelmed, even helpless, and more concerned than ever with finding continuity over time and establishing differentiation vis-à-vis other people.

Who am I? How do I fit into the adult world? In the wake of the industrial revolution, widespread urbanization, the decline of traditional religion, the rise of capitalism, the growing alienation of workers from their work, the demystification of life by science, the discovery of the unconscious, two world wars, and the atom bomb, these two questions appear more vexing today than ever before. As the literary critic Robert Langbaum (1982) puts it, identity may now be "*the* spiritual problem of our time" (p. 352).

Continued from p. 765

words, good story tends to be richly *differentiated*. Similarly, a personal myth should develop in the direction of increasing differentiation. As the adult matures and gathers new experiences, his or her personal myth takes on more and more facets and characterizations. It becomes richer, deeper, and more complex. As differentiation increases, however, the adult may seek *reconciliation* between and among conflicting forces in the story, harmony and resolution amidst the multiplicity of self. The good story raises tough issues and dynamic contradictions. And the good story provides narrative solutions that affirm the harmony and integrity of the self. Reconciliation is one of the most challenging tasks in the making of personal myth, especially in midlife and beyond.

The sixth standard for good story in identity is what I call *generative integration*. To understand well this last criterion, we must again remember that a personal myth is about a human life. It is not simply a story that one might read in *The New Yorker* magazine. It is a mythic rendering of a particular life of a real person living in a particular society at a particular point in history. The life story seeks coherence, credibility, and reconciliation to a greater extent than might some very good stories that are purely fiction. Similarly, the human life exists in a social and ethical context that does not generally apply, or apply in the same way, to other kinds of stories (Booth, 1988). In mature identity, the adult is able to function as a productive and contributing member of society. He or she is able to take on adult roles in the spheres of work and family. He or she is able and willing to promote, nurture, and guide the next generation, to contribute in some small or large way to the survival, enhancement, or progressive development of the human enterprise. Mature identity in adulthood requires a creative involvement in a social world that is larger and more enduring than the self. It is to that world, as well as to the self, that the story is to be oriented. Ideally, the storymaker's search for unity and purpose in life should benefit both the person fashioning the story and the society within which the story is fashioned.

Lives as Texts

Long before there were psychologists, human beings created and told stories about the problems and the possibilities in their lives. Poets, novelists, and film makers have continued to provide insights into human motivation and behavior through the stories they create, just as all of us—even as children—seek and find truths about ourselves and each other through making, hearing, and telling stories. In the last ten years, psychologists seem to have rediscovered the story. A growing number of developmental psychologists are now examining children's astute appreciation for stories and the ways in which they use stories in discourse (e.g., Lucariello, 1990; Mancuso, 1986; Pellegrini & Galda, 1990). Psychologists interested in education have begun to stress the powerful role of stories in teaching and learning, especially in education for values, and in moral development (Tappan, 1990; Tappan & Brown, 1989; Vitz, 1990). Social and personality psychologists have begun to explore the different kinds of narrative *accounts* that adults devise to cope with personal problems and explain puzzling or problematic life events (e.g., Baumeister, Stillwell, & Wotman, 1990; Harvey, Weber, Galvin, Huszti, & Garnick, 1986). Life-span theorists have begun to argue for the primacy of narrative in the understanding of adult lives. According to theorists such as Cohler (1982, 1990) and Whitbourne (1985), the adult life course should *not* be viewed as an orderly progression of developmental stages nor as a predictable expression of stable personality traits, but rather as an evolving narrative, situated in culture and history. As I have argued in the last three chapters, the outlines of a narrative perspective on the life course can be discerned even in the seminal writings of Murray, Erikson, and Adler. In more recent years, however, the narrative perspective has been developed in greater detail in Tomkins' script theory and my own life-story model of identity.

Three influential and articulate spokespersons for an emerging *narrative psychology* today are Theodore Sarbin (1986), Donald Polkinghorne (1988), and Jerome Bruner (1986, 1990). Sarbin (1986) argues that the narrative can serve as a **root metaphor** for contemporary psychology. According to Pepper (1942), a root metaphor is a basic analogy for understanding the world. The dominant root metaphor in Western civilization is *mechanism,* the basic analogy of the machine. "The kind of machine employed to provide imagery may be a clock, a dynamo, a computer, an internal combustion engine," or any other mechanism to which the workings of the human mind, human behavior, and human affairs may be compared (Sarbin, 1986, p. 6). Sarbin views the narrative as a liberating metaphor for psychology because narrative reveals part of what is distinctively human about human beings—humans, unlike machines, are by nature storytellers—and it provides for a nuanced understanding of how human lives are situated in social and historical context. Polkinghorne (1988) agrees. He argues that at the heart of the *human sciences*—the sciences concerned with human conduct—is *narrative knowing:*

> Our lives are ceaselessly intertwined with narrative, with the stories that we tell and hear told, with the stories that we dream or imagine or would like to tell. All these stories are reworked in the story of our own lives which we narrate to ourselves in an episodic, sometimes semiconscious, virtually uninterrupted monologue. We live immersed in narrative, recounting and reassessing the meanings of our past actions, anticipating the outcomes of our future projects, situating ourselves at the intersection of several stories not yet completed. We explain our actions in terms of plots, and often no other form of explanation can produce sensible statements. (p. 160)

As we have already seen, Bruner (1986, 1990) suggests that the narrative mode of human thought is especially amenable to the analysis of human intention and action, whereas the paradigmatic mode better addresses the demands for physical cause-and-effect explanations, like those required in the physical sciences. Bruner (1990) also points out that within the human sciences stories are especially useful in providing explanations for events that do not fit socially expectable patterns. He writes, "the function of the story is to find an intentional state that mitigates or at least makes comprehensible a deviation from a canonical cultural pattern" (1990, pp. 49–50). Similarly, Chafe (1990) writes that people devise stories when a particular event or phenomenon is "difficult to account for" (p. 83). If I wake up in the morning, brush my teeth, read the paper, and then get in my car to drive to work, as I do most days, I will not be very motivated to create a story to explain what I did. Nothing really needs to be accounted for, in that my morning routine fits what Bruner calls a "canonical cultural pattern." But if I wake up to find a baby lying in a basket on my doorstep, where the newspaper usually is, then there are stories to be learned and told, for events have transpired in a way that deviates from the expectable pattern. Where did this baby come from? Who abandoned her on my doorstep? What do I do now? As I rush the baby into the house, yell upstairs to my wife, and telephone the police, I am already creating narrations to explain what at the moment seems inexplicable.

If we extend this point to the field of personality psychology *in toto,* then we might suggest that each individual human life is analogous to an event or phenomenon that must be accounted for, because each individual life, in one way or another, deviates from what Bruner calls the "canonical cultural pattern." To put it another way, each person is unique. The uniqueness must be explained. It can best be explained through story. As we saw in Chapters 1 and 11, personality psychologists who have focused their attention on the uniqueness of the individual have tended to adopt what Allport called the *idiographic* approach to investigation, as with in-depth analyses of single cases. By contrast, those personality psychologists more interested in general laws and patterns across different individuals have traditionally adopted *nomothetic* approaches. How to put these two approaches together has been a perennial problem in personality psychology since the days of Allport.

Hermans' Dialogical Self

One contemporary personality psychologist who believes strongly that idiographic and nomothetic methods can be creatively combined in the study of lives is Hubert Hermans (1976, 1988, 1991, 1992a, 1992b, 1992c; Hermans & Bonarius, 1991; Hermans, Kempen, & van Loon, 1992). In a flurry of recent publications, Hermans has described his own narrative approach to understanding the self. It is an approach that draws upon both nomothetic and idiographic perspectives to make sense of how people make sense of themselves, through stories.

Hermans begins with the concept of **valuation.** A valuation is "anything that a person finds to be of importance when thinking about his or her life situation" (Hermans, 1988, p. 792). Valuations can include beloved persons in one's life as well as those whom one dislikes, disturbing dreams, difficult problems, cherished opportunities, memories of particularly important events from the past, plans or goals for the future, and so on. Each valuation is a unit of meaning in the person's life. Each valuation has either a positive, negative, or mixed (ambivalent) emotional quality. Through self-reflection, people organize their valuations into narratives that situate them in time and space.

From a nomothetic standpoint, Hermans suggests that different persons' valuations can be interpreted in terms of two primary motivational systems. Adapting Bakan's (1966) concepts of agency and communion (this chapter), Hermans distinguishes between agentic *S-motives* and communal *O-motives*. S-motives concern *s*elf-strivings for superiority, expansion, power, control, and so on. O-motives are *o*ther-oriented, longing for contact, union, intimacy, and so on, with others. These two motives give direction and organization to the wide variety of valuations in an individual's life story. A second dichotomy for organizing valuations is that between *positive* and *negative* affectivity. Different people may be compared and contrasted, then, with respect to the extent to which their valuation systems exhibit relatively high-to-low levels of S-motives, O-motives, positive affect, and negative affect.

Hermans has developed a *self-confrontation method* for collecting and assessing valuations. It is a method through which the research subject serves as a "co-investigator" rather than purely an object of investigation (Hermans & Bonarius, 1991). In other words, Hermans and his colleagues view the research enterprise as a matter of mutual cooperation between subjects and researchers. Data are obtained through dialogue, or conversation, between the researcher and the research participant. The philosophy of this approach assumes that subjects themselves are the "experts" when it comes to understanding their own lives. The researcher provides a series of questions to guide the conversation and to obtain a listing of the subject's most important valuations. Some of those questions are presented in Table 13.4.

The self-confrontation method typically yields between 20 and 40 discrete valuations for each participant. In the second phase of the research, the person goes back to each valuation and rates it, on 6-point scales, for each of 16 different emotion terms. Four of the terms refer to S-motives ("self-esteem," "strength," "self-confidence," and "pride"); four refer to O-motives ("caring," "love," "tenderness," and "intimacy"); four refer to positive affect only ("joy," "happiness," "enjoyment," and "inner calm"); and four refer to negative affect only ("worry," "unhappiness," "despondency," and "disappointment"). For each valuation, the researcher then calculates an S index by summing ratings on the four corresponding S-motive affects and comparable indexes for O (O-motives), P (positive affect), and N (negative affect). Other important indices include the "S minus O" score, to determine whether self or other motive ratings are stronger for a given valuation and the "P minus N" score to determine the relative strength of positive versus negative affect.

Table 13.4

Questions Used to Elicit Valuations in the Self-Confrontation Method

Set 1: The Past

—Was there something in your past that has been of major importance or significance for your life and which still plays an important part today?

—Was there, in the past, a person, an experience, or circumstances that greatly influenced your life and still appreciably affects your present existence?

You are free to go back into the past as far as you like.

Set 2: The Present

—Is there in your present life something that is of major importance for, or exerts a great influence on, your existence?

—Is there in your present life a person or circumstance which exerts a significant influence on you?

Set 3: The Future

—Do you foresee something that will be of great importance for, or of major influence on, your future life?

—Do you feel that a certain person or circumstance will exerts a great influence on your future life?

—Is there a goal or object that you expect to play an important role in your future life?

You are free to look as far ahead as you wish.

(From Hermans, 1991, p. 222).

In terms of nomothetic research, Hermans has explored how certain patterns of valuations characterize certain groups of people. For example, Hermans (1992b) identified an interesting group of psychotherapy clients whose valuations manifested "unhappy self-esteem." Whereas a considerable body of research suggests that ratings of happiness and self-esteem are positively correlated, certain people go against the grain, revealing valuations that score high on both S and N. Compared to other psychotherapy clients, these individuals have developed narratives of the self in which especially meaningful events and persons elicit in them a paradoxical mix of self-respect and strength on the one hand and unhappiness on the other. Hermans and van Gilst (1991) identified another group of psychotherapy clients whose valuations resembled the affective ratings made by 10 students of the ancient story of Narcissus (Feature 3.C in this book). When we think of "narcissism" and the story of Narcissus, we usually think of a person who is self-centered—high "S" in Hermans' scheme. However, the pattern of ratings that best captured the meaning of the Narcissus myth was *low* S, *high* O, low P, and high N. Therefore, the psychotherapy clients whose valuations most closely resembled the Narcissus myth seemed to be suffering more from a frustrated longing for union with others, rather than an overabundance of self-striving. Some of the valuations sampled in this study are shown in Table 13.5.

From the idiographic standpoint, Hermans suggests that the examination of valuations is a window into each person's uniquely positioned **dialogical self** (Hermans, Kempen, & van Loon, 1992). Following William James (Chapter 10), Hermans distinguishes between the senses of self as "I" and "Me." The I is the self as author of a life narrative, complete with the valuations that provide life with meaning. The Me is the self as actor in the life narrative, an actor who "moves" throughout the story to assume many different roles. But the I also moves, from one "I position" to another, making for multiple authors, multiple I's, for the same life story. Most views of the self with which we, as Westerners, are familiar are individualistic and rationalistic, viewing the I as a potentially rational and self-contained "thinker" or "knower." In Descartes' famous expression, "I think; therefore, I am." But Hermans rejects this prevailing view in favor of a dialogical self that is *multiple and embedded in dialogue.* As an author of its own life story, the I moves from one "I position" to another, adopting different perspectives from which to understand the self. The different I positions are in dialogue with each other. Hermans, Kempen, and van Loon (1992) write:

> We conceptualize the self in terms of a dynamic multiplicity of relatively autonomous *I* positions in an imaginal landscape. In its most concise form this conception can be formulated as follows. The *I* has the possibility to move, as in a space, from one position to the other in accordance with changes in situation and time. The *I* fluctuates among different and even opposed positions. The *I* has the capacity to imaginatively endow each position with a voice so that dialogical relations between positions can be established. The voices function like interacting characters in a story. Once a character is set in motion in a story, the character takes on a life of its own and thus assumes a certain narrative necessity. Each character has a story to tell about experiences from its own stance. As different voices, these characters exchange information about their respective *Mes* and their worlds, resulting in a complex, narratively structured self. (pp. 28–29)

This is a difficult idea to comprehend at first. We take for granted that the self is singular in some sense, that *I* create *my* life story. We may concede that the story may have many characters (or imagoes, as in McAdam's life-story model), but it is a single *I* who creates them. From Hermans' point of view, however, the I is really a host of storytellers; there is no single perspective for an author, but

Continued on p. 777

Table 13.5

Valuations With Highest Positive Correlation and Highest Negative Correlation With the Affective Pattern Derived From the Narcissus Myth

Valuation with highest positive correlation	S	O	P	N	r	Valuation with highest negative correlation	S	O	P	N	r
1. I think it's too bad that I couldn't remove some of my mother's loneliness when she was still alive with my cheerfulness	3	11	1	11	.90	People who listen to me and don't immediately pass judgment	13	2	10	0	-.84
2. I have guilt feelings when thinking about my father: He did his best for me, and I failed	1	18	0	19	.89	I want to start studying; I think it's very important that I build something up for myself, that I have something fun for myself.	19	0	16	0	-.86
3. About 4 years ago, I encountered Irma covered with (what I thought was) blood: I was confused and felt terribly stupid for having done that to her	2	15	0	19	.88	I enjoy my work: It gives me fulfillment, and I find it relaxing	12	8	14	2	-.75
4. All the attention, involvement, and hugging were drowning me; I wasn't allowed to see anyone else and I couldn't	4	17	1	20	.87	I dare to stand my own ground now	11	1	11	0	-.87

No.	Statement					Loading
5.	Dick's suicide: Failing to do anything for him; not being able to stop him; that I didn't see through it all	3	16	1	14	.82
6.	Death, retirement, nursing homes; the waning of good health	3	17	5	20	.80
7.	First, I meant everything to him. Now he means everything to me. The roles are now reversed	1	10	3	15	.79
8.	I think it's terrible that my sister and I can't communicate sensitively	3	13	2	14	.78
9.	I think it's sad that it's over with Jane [girlfriend]. I want to hold on to that feeling and not let the clichés get the upper hand; I think she's too valuable	6	16	0	14	.76
10.	I would like to share things in an equal, friendly way with my father but we both avoid it; we both hang onto our roles as father and child	1	12	0	20	.75

Statement					Loading
If I don't like someone, I now dare to vote against them	15	9	20	6	-.67
I'm a good teacher and I'm comfortable doing it	17	6	12	8	-.51
I was only my achievements; they were valued	18	5	14	0	-.64
I search for clarity and try to put that in words	18	7	15	4	-.78
I set myself goals, I strive to achieve them and live from peak to peak	16	7	17	5	-.52
The complete exploitation of my abilities fulfills me if I take my limitations into consideration	19	9	15	0	-.75

Table 13.5 continued

Table 13.5 continued

	Valuation with highest positive correlation	S	O	P	N	r	Valuation with highest negative correlation	S	O	P	N	r
11.	I'm gradually feeling just as confined as in my first relationship; that history is repeating itself even up to the bitter end and that I have to carry this all with me; once again, I've "used" a partner	4	15	1	14	.73	I enjoy tranquility	15	14	17	1	−.57
12.	The burned out, disappointed feeling since our first contact; trying to live up to my wife's expectations	2	6	0	17	.72	After the job change, I found that I could fulfill my job well, alone and independent: I could shape my work	15	9	16	5	−.75
13.	Thinking about the broken relationship	7	12	3	15	.71	I know the work context, I fall back on my knowledge and intelligence; I am less concerned about acceptance by others	12	0	6	1	−.66
14.	There are still a lot of things that bother me; I'm standing before a wall, which I have to get through	6	15	7	14	.68	My "Israel experience" gave me that feeling that I am somebody	12	8	12	5	−.75

Note: S = affect referring to self enhancement; O = affect referring to contact with the other; P = positive affect; N = negative affect; r = product-moment correlation between the affective patterns of the valuation and the Narcissus myth.

Continued from p. 773
rather many different positions from which the story is told. Each I position can establish itself as a more-or-less autonomous "voice." Drawing from the Russian literary critic M. M. Bakhtin (1973), Hermans conceives of the self as a *polyphonic novel*—a complex story with many voices. Each voice presents its own unified world, as in the great novels of Fyodor Dostoyevsky wherein different characters develop their own ideologies and world views, which in turn play off against each other:

> In Dostoyevsky's novels there is not one single author, Dostoyevsky himself, but several authors or thinkers (e.g., the characters Raskolnikov, Myshkin, Stavrogin, Ivan Karamazov, and the Grand Inquisitor). Each of these heroes has his own voice ventilating his own view, and each hero is authoritative and independent. A hero is not simply the object of Dostoyevsky's finalizing artistic vision but comes across as the author of its own ideology. According to Bakhtin, there is not a multitude of characters within a unified objective world, illuminated by Dostoyevksy's individual vision, but a plurality of perspectives and worlds: a polyphony of voices. As in a polyphonic composition, the several voices or instruments have different spatial positions and accompany and oppose each other in a dialogical relation. (Hermans, Kempen, & van Loon, 1992, p. 27)

In summary, Hermans offers a provocative new theory of the self in which persons provide their lives with meaning by organizing their valuations into life narratives. Rather than seeing the narrative as the product of a single author—a single storymaking "I"—Hermans argues that the I moves in imagination from one authorial position to another, as if it were a single *body* moving over a variegated landscape offering many different scenic views. Certain positions, or viewpoints, become especially important over time, and these are the positions from which the I develops a distinctive voice. Ultimately, a life story is the product of many different authors—many different I positions. The different authors may contradict each other, as different characters in a polyphonic novel offer their own unique and discordant world views. Instead of an individual, rational self, the person is endowed with multiple, storytelling selves, each in dialogue with the others.

Music and Story: Gregg's Approach

Another recent perspective on narrative that emphasizes the multiplicity of the self is offered by Gary Gregg (1991) in his stimulating book, *Self-Representation: Life Narrative Studies in Identity and Ideology.* Like Hermans, Gregg argues that the self is expressed through many different voices. For any given person, the different voices may seem to create a confusing cacophony; it may seem that there is little pattern, order, or organization to the different selves a person shows. However, closer examination of individual life stories convinces Gregg that beneath the phenotypic noise of clashing voices lies a genotypic piece of music, complexly patterned and meaningful, expressing endless variations on a small number of themes, like a fugue.

Music is the driving metaphor for Gregg's approach. Life stories reveal a musical structure of the self. The two primary axes of music are harmony (vertical) and melody (horizontal). Harmony is expressed in chords, as the musician plays different notes simultaneously to create an instantaneous blend. Melody is expressed as a sequence of notes, played over time. Harmony and melody are made possible by the structure of scales, such as the familiar diatonic scale of whole and half notes within an octave. (If you are having trouble following this, just sing "do, re, mi, fa, so, la, ti, do" to remind yourself of what a scale is. The range from the first "do" to the second "do" is called an octave.) How each note is heard in a musical piece is determined by the musical structures of the scales employed. For Gregg, personality is like a fugue, a musical form in which several voices play variations on a single theme. Typically, one voice introduces the theme (melody), and others answer it with variations, producing a dialogical form, a kind of musical conversation among the voices. In each voice, the theme can be expressed in a wide variety of ways. One voice may express the theme twice as quickly as another; another voice may change the rhythm of the theme; a third may invert the theme; and so on. Each voice is, therefore, both *the same as* and *different from* every other voice, in that each voice expresses the theme but is likely to express it in a very different way. And so it is in personality, argues Gregg. Among the many different voices of the self, one may discern an underlying "identity-in-difference" (p. 52).

Like Hermans and McAdams, Gregg suggests that the major themes of human identity concern power and love, or what Bakan (1966) calls agency and communion. People often invest the meanings associated with these themes into concrete images and objects in their worlds. For example, Gregg describes the case of "Sharon," a young woman whose major life themes are captured in the images of "tofu" and "junk food." When Gregg interviewed her in 1979, Sharon was one of two partners who had built a successful business that manufactures and distributes tofu and other health foods in the midwestern United States. For Sharon, tofu was more than just health food. It rather symbolized *for her* an entire "New Age" ideology celebrating diet, nutrition, exercise, good health, the simple life, and social renewal—a personal ideology that provided her life with a great deal of coherence. As an entrepreneur running a cooperative business, she could be an autonomous, healthy, and effective woman involved in improving the lives of those who worked in her company and those who consumed her products. Tofu also symbolized a number of personal habits and commitments connected with her New Age ideology. In addition to keeping a nondairy vegetarian diet, she studied T'ai Chi, practiced Yoga meditation, attended various self-fulfillment workshops, experimented with herbal medicines, campaigned against nuclear energy, and worked to sustain egalitarian community institutions.

By contrast, junk food symbolizes Sharon's past, growing up in Wisconsin, in a large family with an overweight mother, eating meat, dairy products, candy, and junk food. It was a "warm, cozy, still-in-the-womb type of existence," but it eventually proved too stifling and too indicative of what Sharon now views as an exceptionally unhealthy American life-style—eat lots of junk, get fat, have lots of kids, drive lots of cars, keep consuming, get lazier and lazier, die young. Junk food, therefore, symbolizes a way of living—a theme in her identity—that Sharon finds disgusting and wasteful. She never wants to be fat. She believes she is not ready to start a family. Yet, recently, she has felt a craving to have a baby. Pregnancy would make her "fat." The craving frightens her now, for it threatens to undermine the healthy, New Age existence she has created for herself. In a sense, junk food opposes tofu. In another sense, junk food and tofu are the same:

> To come to the theoretical point: Sharon craves love and nurturance in the form of dairylike foods. She differentiates this craving by symbolically differentiating its objects into natural and healthy foods, on the one hand, and chemicalized junk foods, on the other. Tofu and junk food thus stand in an essentially octave relation to each other: tofu is ice cream "raised" an octave, ice cream is tofu "lowered" an octave. The "raised" and "lowered" have moral, existential, and political meanings that are the essentials of "sublimation" and "regression," respectively. That is, tofu and ice cream encode the imperative she emphasizes in outlining her biography: to strive for autonomous self-nurturance against the recurrent beckoning of passive indulgence. They "work" by virtue of their "identity-in-difference." They are identical in some properties (their appearance, texture, and taste similarities make them interchangeable) and in the meanings these properties represent to her (nurturance, safety, and love). But at the same time they possess other properties that are different (origin, manufacturing, packaging, and preparation in particular) and so can represent antithetical meanings (natural versus artificial; healthy versus poisonous; industry versus lethargy). Logically represented: B = A and C = A, yet B ≠ C. The structural ambiguity of these symbols enables Sharon to establish an "octave" craving for nurturance via food into adult and autonomous versus infantile and dependent forms. (Gregg, 1991, p. 89)

What ultimately links and differentiates junk food and tofu, then, is their relation to each other as ends of an "octave." Each is like the "do" on the scale you sang to yourself a moment ago. But *tofu is the higher "do,"* the one an octave up. What makes it higher is its *moral significance.* Tofu connects to a New Age ideology within which Sharon finds a great deal that is good, right, and true. Tofu is the way people *should* live if the world is to be a better, happier, and healthier place. Junk food is lower because it connects to a slothful and wasteful life-style; it is bad, wrong, and false, in this sense. And yet there is another sense in which both tofu and junk food are good, in that both connote love and nurturance. Junk food is the easy love of her mother, cozy and warm. Tofu is a New Age kind of adult love, love for one's fellow woman or man, love between equals.

Tofu and junk food receive their moral significance from the culture in which Sharon lives. Her personal meanings for these symbols come ultimately from her experiences growing up in the 1950s and 60s in small-town Wisconsin and coming of age in the 1970s as a student at the University of Wisconsin. At the University, she was exposed to a wide variety of alternative life-styles, out of which she developed her current New Age viewpoints. An essential point in Gregg's approach to lives is his insistence that personal meanings derive ultimately from social, political, economic, and cultural realities. Following the sociologist Emile Durkheim, Gregg argues that social organization provides general categories of thought to the members of any particular society. Social organizations are not necessarily kind and gentle, and encouraging of healthy development, self-actualization, and the like. Rather, social organizations embody stratification and oppression, as revealed in class, ethnic, and gender inequalities. The life narratives that people create to provide their lives with the "identity-in-difference" that we find in the musical fugue reflect and even reinforce the social order in many cases. Gregg writes:

> I have insisted that a reality exists outside of the narratives: a reality of social/political inequality into which each individual is "thrown" and in which each individual constructs a self as an ideological tool with which to struggle for power and a semblance of personal dignity—typically denying equality and dignity to groups of Others in the process. I have argued that this reality is to be found not only outside the narrative as its efficient cause, but at its core, in the semantic/syntactic kernel that generates it: in [for example] Sharon's spiritual-dietary struggle for "New Age" self-sufficiency . . . (p. 199)

In conclusion, Gregg's approach to the self as both music and text underscores the multiplicity of voices with which the self speaks (or sings). It views the self as an orchestration of voices, each a variation on one of a small number of themes, that are similar to and different from each other by virtue of their formal relations within the music. The voices express a great deal of tension and conflict within the music, as well as peace and resolution. Voices and themes are often symbolized in complexly determined and emotionally charged images or objects, as we see in Sharon's appropriation of the images of tofu and junk food. Voices and themes express both personal and cultural meanings. Personal meanings are typically couched in cultural terms, reflecting the macrosocial order of the world within which the self is made.

The Postmodern Self

The 1980s and early 1990s have brought a good deal of discussion among some social scientists about the unique problems of making sense of the self in a *postmodern* world (e.g., Davies & Harre, 1990; Denzin, 1989; Gergen, 1992; Sampson, 1985, 1988, 1989a, 1989b; Shotter & Gergen, 1989). The term **postmodern** is used in many different ways to refer to an assortment of perceived trends in art, architecture, literature, the media, social organization, and human consciousness that seem to have come to the fore in Western thinking since the 1970s. It is difficult to characterize the idea of postmodernity in a few sentences, in part because it means different things in different arenas. At its heart, however, is a skeptical and playfully ironic attitude about grand systems, universal truths, and conventional ways of doing things (Harvey, 1990). In general, the postmodern attitude is to embrace, or at least "deal with," the ambiguity and multiplicity that follow a rejection of all universal claims. In a postmodern world, there ultimately are no large truths. Instead, there are various versions, accounts, narratives, and so on— "texts," all of them—each subjectively construed from a particular point of view. Texts change from one moment to the next. Nothing stays the same. "Postmodernism swims, even wallows, in the fragmentary and the chaotic currents of change as if that is all there is" (Harvey, 1990, p. 44). In general, we may celebrate postmodernity for its openness, tolerance, and dynamism. Yet at the same time, we may find the postmodern refusal to believe in anything for the long run, to count anything as holding intrinsic truth and goodness and value, to be discouraging and even frightening, especially since human beings seem always to have demanded that there be something enduring "to believe in."

The concept of narrative is especially appealing in considering the problems of the postmodern self. Lives are like texts, narratives that continue to be written and rewritten over time. But what are texts? They are nothing but patterns of words, pictures, signs, and other sorts of representations. There is nothing substantially "real" about them; nor is there any sense in which a text can be said to be really "true" or "good." In some ways, postmodernity dovetails with the influential literary movement of the 1970s and 1980s called *deconstructionism* (Derrida, 1972). Among the many claims of deconstructionism is the idea that literary texts have no inherent and stable meanings. Language is indeterminate. Every word is ambiguous in and of itself, and its particular meaning in a particular moment is dependent on its relation to other equally ambiguous words with which it is spoken or written.

If lives are like texts, then lives, too, have no inherent meanings (Denzin, 1989). People may think that they understand who they are, that their lives "stand for something" or "express something true." But they are mistaken, just as readers are mistaken when they think they have found a single meaning in a given novel or short story. The mistakes are to be expected, because "stories and texts are written 'as if' they do have centers. Thus, writers and readers presume and 'read into' texts real authors, real intentions, and real meanings" (Denzin, 1989,

p. 45). From the standpoint of deconstructionism, however, these readings are fallacies. A valid deconstructionist reading of a text, by contrast, exposes the many *inconsistencies* and *contradictions* in the text, and even reveals how authors of texts who think they are saying something true, or making a particular point, subtly "turn on themselves," proving themselves wrong in the texts themselves even when they don't realize it! Exhibiting a postmodern theme, a deconstructionist interpretation of a text may be "playfully ironic" in its revelation of texts as merely "language games" (Harre, 1989).

If lives are like texts, people construct selves in and through the sharing of texts in *discourse*. In other words, identities are made through talk, by uttering words and putting forth symbols in a social context. Shotter and Gergen (1989) write, "the primary medium within which identities are created and have their currency is not just linguistic but textual; persons are largely ascribed identities according to the manner of their embedding within a discourse—in their own or in the discourses of others" (p. ix). In a sense, each moment of discourse brings with it a new expression of the self. Over time, expressions are collected and patched together, much like a montage or collage.

The central problem of the postmodern self, then, is that of *unity*. Because all texts are indeterminate, no single life can really mean a single thing, no organizing pattern or identity can be validly discerned in any single human life. In his provocative book, *The Saturated Self*, Kenneth Gergen (1992) makes this point quite forcefully:

> The postmodern condition more generally is marked by a plurality of voices vying for the right to reality—to be accepted as legitimate expressions of the true and the good. As the voices expand in power and presence, all that seemed proper, right-minded, and well understood is subverted. In the post-modern world we become increasingly aware that the objects about which we speak are not so much "in the world" as they are products of perspective. Thus, processes such as emotion and reason cease to be real and significant essences of persons; rather, in the light of pluralism we perceive them to be impostors, the outcomes of our ways of conceptualizing them. Under postmodern conditions, persons exist in a state of continuous construction and reconstruction; it is a world where anything goes that can be negotiated. Each reality of self gives way to a reflexive questioning, irony, and ultimately the playful probing of yet another reality. The center fails to hold. (p. 7)

Drawing on deconstructionism and other postmodern themes, Edward Sampson (1989a, 1989b) argues that psychology needs to develop a new understanding of the person. Because postmodern life is so indeterminate and because technology and the global economy now link people together from all over the world, it no longer makes sense to think of persons as individuals. Indeed, thinking of persons as individuals has never made sense in many cultures. Geertz (1979) writes: "The Western conception of the person as a bounded, unique, more or less integrated motivational and cognitive universe, a dynamic center of awareness, emotion, judgment, and action, organized into a distinctive whole and set contrastively against other such wholes and against a social and natural background is, however incorrigible it may seem to us, a rather peculiar idea within the context of the world's cultures" (p. 229). The Western view of the person as a self-contained individual reached its zenith in the "modern" period of Western history, suggests Sampson, beginning in the 16th century and running into the 20th.

In Sampson's view, the person is a "location" of intersecting forces and interacting voices situated within a particular social community, and linked in the postmodern era to many other communities around the globe. It is difficult to know just how literally to interpret Sampson's argument, however. He surely is not suggesting that biologically distinct organisms are not in fact individual organisms. My body is not your body. Psychologically, however, what I consider to "my" self—that which is mine, that which I have authored—may not really be mine, Sampson suggests. "Persons become the *guardians* of particular assets, not their owners," Sampson writes (1992a, p. 919). Selves are "constitutive." "Persons are creatures whose very identities are constituted by their social locations" (Sampson, 1992a, p. 918). The stories of self are not inside the person, waiting to be told. Instead, the person seems to reside amidst the stories, which surround and define him or her. The self is as much "out there," in the swirl and confusion of the postmodern world, as it is "in the mind" of "the person."

Summary

1. Human beings are storytellers by nature. Stories appear to be a basic mechanism for conveying information about human behavior and intention in virtually every known society.

2. The narrative mode of thought, which involves storytelling, may be contrasted with the paradigmatic mode of logical analysis and systematic proof. In the narrative mode, stories explain how human actors strive to obtain desired goals over time.

3. A prime function of story is integration, or bringing diverse things together into a coherent whole. A second function may be healing, as shown in numerous anecdotal accounts and in recent research on how individuals cope with trauma.

4. An important narrative theory of the person is offered by Tomkins, which asserts that persons construct dramatic scripts out of their reconstructed life scenes in order to guide their actions and make sense of their lives.

5. Two important kinds of scripts in persons' lives are commitment scripts and nuclear scripts.

6. Scripts and scenes derive from affective experiences. Tomkins delineates 10 basic affects, each innately wired, he argues, into the central nervous system as a result of thousands of years of human evolution.

7. McAdams' life-story model of identity suggests that identity is an internalized and evolving narrative of the self, integrating one's reconstructed past, perceived present, and anticipated future. In adolescence and young adulthood, the person begins to construct a life story, or personal myth, to provide life with a sense of unity and purpose.

8. Early experiences in infancy and childhood provide narrative resources for the subsequent construction of a self-defining life story. The quality of infant attachment bonds may influence the development of a narrative tone; fantasy and pretend play in the preschool years may leave a legacy of emotional identity images; and goal-oriented experiences in later childhood may partly shape the kinds of motivational themes—agentic and communal—that will prevail in the adult life story.

9. In early and middle adulthood, story making may focus on the articulation and refinement of "imagoes," which are personified idealizations that serve as main characters in the life story. In midlife and beyond, the adult may seek a meaningful sense of an ending for the life story through the development of a generativity script.

10. According to the life-story model of identity, adult personality development may be construed as the psychosocial movement toward increasingly good narrative form, epitomized in a story that is coherent, open, credible, differentiated, harmonious, and integrated in a generative way within society.

11. A recent upsurge of interest in the role of narrative in human lives has led some to consider narrative to be a root metaphor for psychology.

12. Hermans' narrative theory focuses on the valuations that a person identifies as the units of meaning in his or her life. Valuations can be coded for the expression of positive and negative affect and for the relative salience of two basic motivations—agentic S-motives and communal O-motives.

13. Valuations are organized into narratives through the workings of a dialogical self. The dialogical self is a dynamic multiplicity of relatively autonomous I positions, each providing the person with a unique voice or standpoint.

14. Like Hermans, Gregg presents a narrative theory that emphasizes the multiplicity of the self and the self's involvement in dialogue. The driving metaphor in this theory, however, is that of music, each personality being akin to a musical fugue.

15. A number of writers have employed the idea of narrative in considering the problems and possibilities of the postmodern self. According to some, the contemporary self is deconstructed into a swirl of fleeting stories and postures, expressed in the ever-changing discourse of contemporary life and in the particular cultural contexts within which selves are constituted.

Epilogue

Chapter 14 Perspectives on the Person

Perspectives on the Person

Introduction

Four Conclusions About the Four Perspectives
No Single Perspective Is "The Best"
All Approaches Have Strengths and Weaknesses
Mixing and Matching Makes for a Muddle
Personologists Must Make a Choice

Ascendant Themes, Common Ground
Cognition and the Self
Affect
Interactionism
Biology

How are we to understand the person? I mean any person: a friend, a lover, a parent, a daughter, a patient, a client, a coworker, a classmate, a research subject, ourselves. What must we *know* to know a person well? What must we *do* to comprehend—to know in detail and as a whole—a person's life? How do we know when we know?

These are critical questions in personality psychology. And they are likely to be important questions in life, as well. While personality psychologists may puzzle over questions like these in the abstract, each of us confronts them in daily living, though we may not spend a lot of time consciously thinking about them. We deal with these questions at various concrete points in our lives, in real relationships with specific others. We resolve these questions to the best of our ability, implicitly formulating tentative half-answers that do their best to guide us through our most significant interpersonal relationships. But if pushed for a perfect, definitive, eternal, once-and-for-all answer to the question, "How do we understand the person?" we would probably have to admit that we don't know *the* "answer." If they are being honest, personality psychologists would probably have to admit the same thing.

Yet personality psychologists, like all of us, do the best they can with implicit and incomplete answers that, surprisingly enough, often lead to interesting discoveries. This book's thesis is that personality psychologists have traditionally offered four answers, partial and inadequate as they are, to the question "How do we understand the person?" The four answers correspond to the book's four main sections. To understand the person, one must focus either on (1) intrapsychic mysteries, (2) interaction episodes, (3) interpretive structures, or (4) interpersonal stories.

Personality psychologists of the first persuasion suggest that to know a person, one must delve into the unconscious secrets of that person's psyche—the mysteries about survival, sexuality, aggression, conflict, and the like that lurk beneath the conscious veneer of experience, both buried and disguised, linked ultimately to the biological reality of human life, be it instincts, archetypes, or the genetic mandates of natural selection. Sharing this perspective on the person are many psychoanalytic approaches, especially those of Freud and the object-relations theorists, and the analytical psychology of Carl Jung. Other approaches emphasizing evolution and instincts—sociobiological views, Hogan's socioanalytic theory, attachment theory—come into play here, too, though they also share similarities with approaches from one or two of the other three perspectives.

Personologists who adopt this general perspective of *intrapsychic mysteries* use many methods to investigate people's lives. Their favorites, however, tend to involve the interpretation of hidden or latent meanings in manifest "texts," as in dream interpretation. Thus, they tend to prefer rich, qualitative data, as we might glean from dreams and intensive interviews and in such assessment devices as the Rorschach Inkblot Test. Naturalistic observation is also a prominent mode of inquiry for biological instinct theories. All of the approaches to personality psychology that center on intrapsychic mysteries implicitly assume that understanding the person involves delving beneath the surface to expose the hidden instinctual truths.

From the second perspective, that of *interaction episodes,* the emphasis shifts from that which is hidden to that which is readily exposed, manifest, and observable. The most important goal here is to predict behavior. To know a person is to predict what that person will do in a particular episode of interaction with the world. Behavior is viewed as the product of persons endowed with certain personality traits or dispositions, as they interact with environments endowed with certain situational characteristics. Trait theorists such as Eysenck and Cattell focus on the internal dispositions, usually assessed through self-report personality questionnaires. Social-learning theorists such as Bandura emphasize the environment, relying more on experiments and controlled behavioral observation.

Nonetheless, these different approaches to personality agree that prediction of what a person will do in a particular situation is a *sine qua non* of understanding the person.

Within the perspective of interaction episodes, controversies stem from disagreement over what approach to take in maximizing predictive power. Mischel's (1968) critique of the field and the subsequent responses to his indictment; the rise of interactionism; the emphasis on aggregation; the template-matching approach; the act-frequency approach—are primarily concerned with analyzing and predicting what people will do when they interact with certain kinds of environments. Controversies over prediction have dominated the personality journals for the past 20 years. Most recently, however, the battles between trait theorists and situationists have died down somewhat, as many combatants in the fray have come to endorse, in one way or another, some version of "interactionism."

The third perspective on personality explicitly adopts the subjective perspective of the person him- or herself. According to Kelly, Rogers, Maslow, and many cognitive approaches to the person emphasizing schemas, prototypes, and the self, to know the person is to understand the *interpretive structures* by which the person makes sense of the world. While all four general perspectives on the person express some interest in human cognition and consciousness, it is within this third perspective that these aspects are more clearly emphasized and articulated. In the language of Chapter 10, to know the person is to know *how* the person knows (the I) and to know how the person is known by himself or herself (the Me). Therefore, the preferred methods of investigation are cognitive and phenomenological, like Kelly's Rep Test and self-descriptions, in which the person tells the psychologist how he or she interprets reality.

A fourth general perspective on the person can be seen in the writings of Murray, Erikson, Adler, Tomkins, and others who focus on the *interpersonal stories* through which humans organize their lives. From this general viewpoint, knowing a person means understanding the psychosocial pattern within which the person's life makes sense. The pattern is that of narrative—a dynamic and integrative story about the person, the person's emotions, and the interpersonal world within which the person lives. Though Murray, Erikson, and Adler are usually linked to other traditions and viewpoints—Erikson and Adler to psychoanalysis, Murray to trait theorists or "needs" approaches—they share a fundamental allegiance to the integrative power of stories in people's lives constructed over time. In methodological terms, people may be understood *through* stories—as in the personological methods that analyze early memories, TAT stories, and autobiographical accounts. In theoretical terms, people may be understood *in terms of* stories—as story makers who construct plots and then live according to these socially anchored narratives, myths, scripts, and dramas.

Four Conclusions About the Four Perspectives

No Single Perspective Is "The Best"

Personality psychology is often criticized for offering a smorgasbord of intriguing approaches but no single entree that everybody is willing to eat. Put another way, personality psychology has no single, dominant perspective. No particular theory commands the consensus that, say, Einstein's theory of relativity commands in physics or that Darwin's theory of evolution commands in biology. There is no single, agreed-upon *paradigm* in personality psychology from which and within which to organize all, or even a majority, of the theories, hypotheses, methodologies, and research findings that make up the discipline.

There is some irony in this. Personality psychology is well known for its "grand theories"—the integrative and systematic approaches offered by Freud, Adler, Jung, Erikson, Kelly, and others. Yet no single theory appears grand enough to encompass the whole person in a way satisfying to a majority of the scientific community. It seems naive, furthermore, to suppose that any of the currently popular theories will, in the foreseeable future, become grand enough. Many theories have promised to provide *the* encompassing integrative view. Psychoanalysis, behaviorism, social-learning theory, and information-processing approaches have all, at one time or another, been touted as integrative saviors for wayward personologists. None of these, however, has proven to be the messiah. Quite frankly, I do not think that any of them will ever assume that exalted status.

I do not say this is despair, nor even resignation. We should not apologize for the current diversity in personality psychology. We do not need to plead our case with statements such as "Give us time; we're a young science." We do not need to become disheartened, to feel inferior to those disciplines that seem to have a more organized point of view, especially those branches in the natural sciences that accumulate knowledge and make continual progress within a well-conceived paradigm. At this point in the development of personality psychology, diversity may be as much a sign of progress as it is of disagreement. Amidst the diversity, some bold and viable perspectives have been offered. All theories are not equal; all methodologies do not meet the same standards of excellence. But different theories and methods may be especially useful for different questions, different points of view.

I believe it is unfair to endorse any one of the four perspectives offered in this book—or any of the many theories organized within those perspectives—as *the* best one for all problems and issues. Each perspective is viable and generative in its own terms. And each fares less well when evaluated in terms of the other perspectives. For instance, psychoanalysis does not win many points for its ability to predict discrete behavior in particular situations. Trait theories and social-learning approaches tell us very little about the intrapsychic mysteries of life.

 **Table 14.1**

Some Common Criticisms of Prominent Approaches to Personality Psychology

Approach	Textbook Chapters	Criticisms
Freud's psychoanalysis	2–3	1. Theoretical concepts are ambiguous, poorly defined, and difficult to measure.
		2. Many hypotheses are impossible to test in research (context of justification).
		3. Empirical support for testable hypotheses is meager.
		4. Psychoanalytic interpretation is too subjective and idiosyncratic for science.
		5. Projective techniques, often used in research, are unreliable.
		6. The theory fails to appreciate how women are different from men.
Jung's analytic psychology	2–3	1. Many of the ideas are too "mystical" and ambiguous for scientific scrutiny.
		2. Few testable hypotheses are proposed.
		3. Jung's theory often contradicts itself; it is difficult to comprehend as a consistent whole.
		4. The concept of a "collective unconscious" does not seem credible.
Sociobiological viewpoints; instinct theories	4	1. These approaches reduce human beings to hapless victims of ruthless natural forces and to base instincts concerning survival and reproduction.
		2. Little mention is made of individual differences in personality.
		3. The person's unique adjustment to the social world is ignored or downplayed.

Approach	Textbook Chapters	Criticisms
Sociobiological viewpoints; instinct theories	4	4. Sociobiological approaches imply that what is "natural" is what is "right." 5. Diversity in learning and culture is badly deemphasized.
Trait theories (for example, Eysenck, Cattell, Costa & McCrae).	5	1. Traits don't explain why people do what they do; they merely label behavioral consistencies. 2. Trait theories are little more than lists of traits. 3. Self-report inventories are subject to many problems, including faking and response biases. 4. Little mention is made of personality development, growth, and change. 5. Trait approaches fail to take situations into account.
Social-learning theories	6	1. Theories are too narrow; they fail to consider individual differences in personality dispositions, organizations of the whole person, and personality development. 2. The strong emphasis on the environment and learning leaves the person without a strong and active contribution to his or her own development. 3. Recent cognitive additions to social-learning theory are limited, and fail to take into consideration unconscious processes. 4. Theories rely too heavily on contrived laboratory experiments.
Humanistic psychology: Rogers, Maslow	8	1. The theories are too blithely optimistic about human life.

Table 14.1 continued

Table 14.1 continued

Approach	Textbook Chapters	Criticisms
Humanistic psychology: Rogers, Maslow	8	2. Little research has been generated. 3. Concepts such as "self-actualization" are too general and vague for scientific scrutiny. 4. Individual differences are neglected. 5. Phenomenological methods are too subjective and unwieldly.
Kelly's construct theory	8	1. The model of "the person as scientist" is too extreme; people don't always act as scientists. 2. Many phenomena are neglected, such as emotions, the unconscious, and motivation. 3. Personality development is overlooked. 4. The Rep Test is too unwieldy for nomothetic research; other measurement devices are inadequate.
Cognitive and information-processing approaches	9–10	1. The computer metaphor is taken too far; people do not process information the way computers do. 2. Issues of affect and motivation are traditionally neglected. 3. No comprehensive personality theory based on this point of view has been developed yet. Instead, there are many "mini-theories." 4. Measurement strategies rely on simple self-reports.
Murray's and McClelland's approaches to motives	11	1. Motives are not organized into a comprehensive and coherent personality theory. 2. The assessment of motives relies on the TAT, which shows modest reliability. 3. TAT-based motives and self-report traits do not relate to each other in predictable ways.

Approach	Textbook Chapters	Criticisms
Murray's and McClelland's approaches to motives	11	4. Motives, like traits, do not explain behavior. 5. The development of motives over time remains a mystery.
Erikson's psychosocial theory	12	1. Like Freud, many concepts are ambiguous and difficult to measure. 2. Testable hypotheses are few. 3. The theory is so eclectic that it is sometimes difficult to pin down specific positions and viewpoints. 4. The psychosocial stages are too pat, too neat. Development is more complex.
Adler's individual psychology	13	1. The theory is very simple and offers relatively few constructs and hypotheses. 2. Some concepts, like "style of life," are too general and vague. 3. Adler's views on birth order have received only modest empirical support.
Tomkins' script theory	13	1. The cognitive and social dimensions of affect are neglected. 2. Concepts such as "scene" and "script" are not clearly defined. 3. Testable hypotheses have not yet been clearly delineated. 4. The theory's relation to other conventional personality theories is not known.

Note: These criticisms are matters of debate. Legitimate rebuttals have been offered to some of them. This table merely reports those critiques of well-known personality theories that are most often noted in the personality literature. You may wish to criticize some of the criticisms.

All Approaches Have Strengths and Weaknesses

For the most part, I have concentrated on the strengths of each of the four perspectives throughout this textbook. I have tried to present diverse viewpoints in the best possible light, without distorting the truth, and to acquaint you with what I consider to be the best and the most fruitful lines of research and assessment. Although I have often provided critiques and caveats, I have tended not to dwell on them. I believe that all of the theoretical approaches discussed in this book have much to offer. And I believe that most undergraduate students taking a course in personality psychology learn best when presented with material in an open-minded and affirmative manner. Further, I believe it presumptuous of any textbook author to insist that he or she has uncovered the "fatal flaws" of each approach.

Still, there *are* flaws in each approach. Some flaws are obvious, often stemming from a particular approach's inability to meet the standards set by an alternative approach. Behaviorists have traditionally criticized psychoanalysts for dealing with concepts that cannot be directly observed and precisely measured. Psychoanalysts have traditionally countered that behaviorists are mired in precise trivialities, that they will never be able to address the big questions about human life. Cognitive theorists have been criticized for failing to accommodate emotions and interpersonal relationships; motivational theories, like McClelland's and Murray's, have been criticized for failing to take cognition seriously enough. Maslow and Rogers are too optimistic, tending to overlook basic life conflicts. Freud is too pessimistic, dwelling too much on conflict and anxiety.

I do not mean to make light of criticisms of personality theory and research. Many extremely powerful and important critiques have been levied, against the field as a whole and against every particular approach therein. Table 14.1 lists some of the most common criticisms offered. I have mentioned some of them in earlier chapters. Others you have probably anticipated yourself. And some are likely to be new to you.

Mixing and Matching Makes for a Muddle

There is a line in the Book of Revelation about being hot, cold, or lukewarm:

> I know all about you: you are neither cold nor hot. I wish you were one or the other, but since you are neither, but only lukewarm, I will spit you out of my mouth. (Revelation 3:15–16)

The author of the Revelation had in mind things other than personality psychology, but the point, in my view, is still instructive. It is better to be hot or cold than lukewarm. It is better to embrace a coherent approach in personality psychology than to mix and match in search of a lukewarm eclecticism. Blend a bit of Freud with a little Bandura and add a dash of Kierkegaard and a pinch of cognitive-schema theory, and you will probably create a tepid and rather tasteless porridge. The reason is simple: to blend Freud, Bandura, Kierkegaard, and schema theory, you will probably have to disregard some of the most compelling aspects of each approach—the theoretical assumptions and points of view that give each theory its distinctive, tangy flavor. For example, you will probably have to throw out or disregard Freud's tenet of the unconscious, the existentialist view of bad faith, Bandura's commitment to observational learning, and schema theory's assumption that the self is multiple, in order to synthesize the four different approaches with any degree of harmony. This is essentially the problem that Miller and Dollard (Chapter 6) faced when they tried to integrate psychoanalysis and behaviorism. Too much of the good stuff was lost in the merger.

I do not mean to suggest that integration of different theoretical approaches is always a bad idea. Far from it. Many of the most creative advances in personality psychology result from a thoughtful eclecticism. For instance, Hogan's socioanalytic theory effectively sythesizes principles of evolutionary biology and the social role theories offered by Mead and Goffman. Erikson's theory of psychosocial development draws heavily from classic psychoanalysis while incorporating points of view from anthropology, sociology, and studies of child development. Higgins' self-discrepancy theory and Markus' conception of possible selves draw from many different approaches in personality and social psychology. Moreover, all personologists must be eclectic in the sense that they need to understand and know how to work with alternative points of view. A conscientious student of personality, therefore, should try to learn as much as possible about every standard perspective offered in the field.

Integrating different theoretical ideas into a coherent and illuminating whole, however, is not very easy. Most students cannot do it well right off the bat. Yet in their eagerness to adopt a consistent and comprehensive approach, they are quick to pick and choose what they like from disparate, even irreconcilable, perspectives and say that they have come up with an eclectic mixture that works for them. Almost every student I have ever interviewed for graduate school in psychology says that he or she is "eclectic" when it comes to theory. I want to say: "You can't be eclectic, at least not yet. You need to know more about each approach. You need to explore each perspective in great detail. Then, after you understand the uniqueness of each approach, you will be better prepared to appreciate some of the commonalities and points of intersection among the many rich and fascinating approaches that exist in the study of persons."

Personologists Must Make a Choice

I am not out to make you a died-in-the-wool Freudian, an implacable behaviorist, an unquestioning disciple of Henry A. Murray. But I do think that you ultimately have to make a choice. All the perspectives on the person discussed in this book offer viable theories and methods of inquiry. But no personologist can, in good faith, embrace them all. Science does not generally advance when scientists indiscriminantly pledge allegiance to all points of view. And our understanding of the person will generally not advance when we try to adopt all perspectives simultaneously. Instead, the personologist must fashion a particular viewpoint that incorporates certain aspects of contemporary theory and method and rejects others if he or she is to explore personality with coherence and depth. The viewpoint should be both stable and dynamic, seeking coherence and consistency but open to change and growth as well. The perspective should evolve, as the personologist learns more, reads more, experiences more.

Developing a perspective on the person is strikingly similar to the development of identity, in my view. As we saw in Chapter 12, identity development involves exploration and commitment. To fashion an integrative identity that binds together my past, present, and anticipated future, I must conscientiously explore various alternatives in ideology, life-style, personal relationships, and occupational fulfillment. Amid this confusing multiplicity and ambiguity, I must eventually make choices and become loyal, manifesting what Erikson (1964) calls "fidelity." I must commit myself to a particular vision of who I am, who I was, and who I will become. By contrast, in "identity diffusion," the person is unable to settle on a satisfactory view of the self. In a sense, identity diffusion means being lukewarm.

In this book, I have tried to encourage you to explore the alternatives to approaching the person offered by personality psychology. I have tried to "warm you up" to a number of different outlooks. I encourage you to explore all the perspectives presented in more detail before you begin to choose. But if you feel your "temperature rising" in response to one or a few particular views, you should explore them fully and with haste. Read the theorists in their original works. Begin exploring personality journals. Talk with your instructor. Start to articulate your own integrative and discriminating perspective on the person.

Ascendant Themes, Common Ground

It is hard to predict where personality psychology will go in the future, what theoretical frameworks will gain ascendancy, what methodologies for personality study will be developed, what important discoveries will be made in research. Each of the four perspectives discussed in this book holds the potential for significant growth and development. New perspectives are likely to rise to the fore. And certain themes that cut across perspectives may signal greater levels of integration in the discipline in years to come. From my admittedly subjective standpoint, I see at least four ascendant themes in personality psychology. Each offers a common ground wherein different perspectives may meet and engage in fruitful exchange.

Cognition and the Self

Personality psychology is still strongly influenced by the "cognitive revolution" in the social sciences. As we saw in Chapters 8–10, approaches to personality that emphasize the person's cognitive activity enjoy great popularity today and continue to stimulate a large amount of research. The cognitive revolution offers an image of the person that many find very congenial—the person as a complicated information system, making plans and formulating scripts, representing reality with symbols and images, operating according to well-articulated programs and strategies for dealing with challenges, and coping effectively with stress.

The cognitive "self" approaches described in Chapters 9 and 10 may prove to be especially influential in the future. Cognitive theories of self are becoming richer and more prominent with each passing year as a large number of creative theorists and researchers become more sophisticated in their employment of cognitive viewpoints. In addition, these theories appear to incorporate ideas from a wide range of perspectives outside cognitive psychology proper, opening up opportunities for thoughtful integrations across perspectives. The most fertile ground for integration may be that between perspectives emphasizing interpersonal stories and those emphasizing interpretive structures. A story itself may function as an interpretive structure for making sense of experience, a grand narrative "schema" for understanding the self, as my own work (Chapter 13) on a life-story model of identity suggests. It is quite likely that the new narrative approaches to personality, including those that emphasize the multiplicity of the "postmodern self," will command considerable attention in the next few years.

Affect

An increasing number of theorists and researchers are examining the role of human emotions and affects in personality. Tomkins' pioneering work on basic affects such as joy, excitement, and sadness has stimulated much research on the expression and experience of emotion, as we see in the work of Izard and Ekman (Chapter 13). Affects have replaced biological drives as predominant motivators for human behavior in a number of different viewpoints, from Tomkins' own script theory to Bowlby's theory of mother–infant attachment (Chapter 4). Attempts have also been made to integrate affect into basic cognitive and information-processing models of human behavior. This should become a major point of integration in personality psychology in the next 10 years. Cognitive perspectives on the person will need to incorporate affect in meaningful ways. Likewise, predominantly affective perspectives may evolve in such a way as to incorporate more cognitive dimensions of human experience.

Interactionism

In the wake of Mischel's (1968) critique and the person–situation debate (Chapter 7), many personality psychologists appear to have reaffirmed their commitment to interactionism. Behavior is a function of the interaction of person and environment. Traits and situations determine behavior together. Of course, this is easy to say. But what does it mean, for the development of personality theory and the enrichment of personality research? Personologists have been urged to study "real" interactions—reciprocal interchanges between people and environments, multidetermined and multidirectional transactions. The consensus on interactionism presents personologists with a difficult challenge. How are we to study interactions? This challenge promises to stimulate a wealth of personality research and theorizing in the near future.

Still disappointing, however, is the reluctance that many personality psychologists show to examine with any sophistication at all those environmental contexts that are larger and more encompassing that the single physical or social "situation." Interactionism will never fulfill its promises unless personologists take seriously the macrosocial contexts of human behavior—contexts such as social institutions, culture, and history.

Biology

In the last 15 years, approaches to the person that emphasize the biological bases of behavior appear to be on the rise. This can be seen in the recent attempts to understand personality from the standpoint of evolutionary theory (Chapter 4). It can also be seen in the proliferation of studies on the biological bases of traits, including research on infant temperament and studies of heritability (Chapter 5). These studies are partially responsible for the surge of interest in traits in general, including the emergence of the "Big Five" as a comprehensive taxonomy of trait dispositions. Personality psychologists appear to be more willing and able now than they were 20 years ago to explain personality differences in terms of neurophysiological, biochemical, and genetic differences. Learning and environmental influences on the development of personality (Chapter 6) tend increasingly to be qualified by and couched in terms of biology. A good example is the work of Eysenck and Gray which continues to gain prominence and influence.

Cognition and the self, affect, interactionism, and the biological bases of personality are four areas in personality psychology where considerable growth and development are likely to take place in the next few years. But other themes and emphases will surely also emerge. New viewpoints will be presented. New methodologies will rise to the fore. We are probably in store for a few surprises. As we move through the last decade of the twentieth century, the scientific study of the person is alive and well, flourishing in many different directions. The 1990s promise to be an exciting decade in personality psychology. I believe we are making notable progress in addressing that three-part question about persons with which we began this book: How is every person

1. like all other persons,
2. like some other persons, and
3. like no other person?

Glossary

A-babies insecurely attached infants who manifest a good deal of avoidant behavior in the presence of the caregiver. Contrast with *B-babies* and *C-babies*.

achievement motivation a recurrent preference or desire for experiences of doing well and being successful; also called the "need for achievement." Individual differences in achievement motivation may be assessed through the TAT.

act frequency Buss and Craik's approach to personality study whereby the researcher views personality dispositions as summary categories containing discrete and representative behavioral acts.

Adult Attachment Interview an interview for adults developed by Mary Main and colleagues and focused on the person's recollections of his or her own childhood attachments to parents. The interview yields four types of attachment: Secure/autonomous, Dismissing, Preoccupied, and Unresolved.

affect a term usually designating emotion.

affiliation motivation a recurrent preference or desire for establishing, maintaining, or restoring positive affective relationships; also called the "need for affiliation." Individual differences in affiliation motivation may be assessed through the TAT.

agency Bakan's general concept for the tendency to separate self from others, to master, dominate, and control the self and the environment. Contrast with *communion*.

agreeableness one of the Big Five traits, agreeableness encompasses personality descriptors having to do with interpersonal warmth, altruism, affection, empathy, cooperation, and other communal facets of personality.

aggregation the principle in psychological measurement that urges an investigator to collect many different samples of the same behavior across many different situations and/or over time in order to obtain a reliable estimate of personality and behavioral trends.

altruistic personality a personality type characterized by high ratings or scores on dimensions such as sympathy for others, social responsibility, and mature perspective taking.

anal-expulsive type according to Freud, one resultant cluster of personality characteristics associated with fixation at the anal stage. These characteristics include disorganization and disorderliness, explosiveness, and cruelty. Contrast with *anal-retentive type*.

anal-retentive type according to Freud, one resultant cluster of personality characteristics associated with fixation at the anal stage. These characteristics include stubbornness, stinginess, and an overly scheduled and compulsive life style. Contrast with *anal-expulsive type*.

anal stage the second stage of psychosexual development, according to Freud, wherein libidinal expression is concentrated in the anus, manifested in bowel movement, and shaped by toilet training.

analytical psychology Carl Jung's theory of personality.

Angst term from existentialist thought referring to anxiety about being and the prospects of nothingness.

anima the unconscious archetype of femininity in men (Jung).

animus the unconscious archetype of masculinity in women (Jung).

archetypes Jung's structural elements of the collective unconscious, referring to universal patterns or predispositions that influence how all humans consciously and unconsciously adapt to their world. Common archetypes include "the mother," "the child," "the hero," "the anima," "the animus," and "the shadow."

associationism the doctrine that various objects and ideas that are contiguous in time or space come to be connected, or associated, with each other into meaningful units.

associative network theory Bower's theory about emotions and memory which posits that an emotional state is an informational unit that is stored in memory and associated with other chunks of information that are also stored.

attachment a bond of love formed between two people, especially infant and caregiver, in which various behaviors are organized into an evolutionarily adaptive system designed to ensure close physical proximity of the two.

attachment behaviors in infancy, these include sucking, clinging, following, vocalizing, and smiling.

attachment styles three styles of approaching romantic relationships developed from research on adult romantic love. The three styles parallel Ainsworth's attachment types for infants: secure, avoidant, and resistant (anxious/ambivalent).

attitudes two general orientations to life: extraversion and introversion (Jung).

authoritarian personality a pattern of attitudes and traits suggesting an overly conventional, rigid, aggressive, hostile, and power-oriented kind of person.

autonomy *versus* shame and doubt the second stage in Erikson's scheme of psychosocial development, during which the toddler seeks to establish him- or herself as an independent and competent agent in the environment.

bad faith in existentialist thought, the failure to take responsibility for one's life and to seek to live an authentic life.

basic anxiety Horney's term for the feeling a child has of being isolated and helpless in a potentially hostile world.

B-babies securely attached infants, who use caregiver as a secure base from which to explore the world. Contrast with *A-babies* and *C-babies*.

behavioral approach system (BAS) In Gray's trait theory, one of two brain systems dealing with human emotionality. As the biological grounding for the trait "impulsivity," the BAS mediates positive affect and arouses a person to seek rewards. The BAS and impulsivity may be contrasted to the BIS (behavioral inhibition system) and anxiety.

behavioral inhibition system (BIS) in Gray's trait theory, one of two brain systems dealing with human emotionality. As the biological grounding for the trait "anxiety," the BIS mediates negative affect and motivates a person to inhibit goal-based behavior in order to avoid punishment. The BIS and anxiety may be contrasted to the BAS and impulsivity.

behaviorism an intellectual tradition in psychology emphasizing the rigorous and objective study of observable behavior shaped by learning and the environment.

being cognition Maslow's term for perceiving and understanding objects and events in terms of their wholeness.

being values in Maslow's theory, values that promote growth and the enrichment of experience.

belief in the species Erikson's term for the adult's hope for and faith in humankind, enabling him or her to be generative.

Big Five five broad personality traits assumed by some researchers to subsume the entire domain of possible traits. According to one formulation, the Big Five are extraversion—introversion, neuroticism, openness to experience, conscientiousness, and agreeableness.

bipolar self Kohut's term for the center of personality, made up of the opposite poles of ambitions and goals, which are connected via a tension arc of talents and skills.

California Psychological Inventory (CPI) a popular personality inventory for normal samples providing scores on 20 trait scales.

California Q-sort a standard assessment procedure in which psychologists sort 100 statements about personality into a distribution designed to explain many different facets of a single person.

case study an in-depth investigation of a single individual, sometimes conducted over a sub- stantial period of time.

castration anxiety the Oedipal boy's unconscious fear that his penis will be cut off, symbolizing a loss of power.

causal attributions the perceived causes of events.

C-babies insecurely attached infants who manifest a good deal of resistance and ambivalence in the presence of the caregiver. Contrast with *A-babies* and *B-babies*.

character structure in Hogan's socioanalytic theory, the person's characteristic ways of displaying the self to family members, especially parents. Contrast with *role structure*.

chum a special best friend that a preadolescent child is likely to have (Sullivan).

circumplex model of traits a circular arrangement of traits, proposed by Wiggins and others, in which trait terms are organized according to the two independent dimensions of strength (dominance *versus* submissiveness) and warmth (warm *versus* cold).

classical conditioning a form of simple learning whereby an unconditioned stimulus is repeatedly paired with a conditioned stimulus such that the conditioned stimulus, originally not likely to evoke a response, comes to be associated with the unconditioned stimulus so that it eventually does evoke a conditioned response.

client-centered therapy Rogers' brand of psychotherapy, emphasizing empathy, sincerity, warmth, acceptance, role playing, and respect for the dignity of the client.

cognition the activity of knowing: the acquisition, organization, and use of knowledge.

cognitive evaluation theory Deci and Ryan's theory of how rewards interact with intrinsic motivation, based on the assumption that people are self-determining beings.

cognitive/social learning/person variables Mischel's characteristic styles or strategies for approaching situations. Mischel lists five types of cognitive/social learning/person variables: competencies, encoding strategies, expectancies, subjective values, and self-regulatory systems and plans.

collective unconscious Jung's concept for an inherited storehouse of human potential that is a result of the evolution of the species, containing unconscious patterns and images called *archetypes*.

commitment script one kind of script identified by Tomkins, in which a person binds him- or herself to a life program or goal that promises the reward of intense positive affect.

communion Bakan's general concept for the tendency to merge or unite with others, to surrender the self as part of a larger whole. Contrast with *agency*.

competence Robert White's term for the ego's expanding ability to master the environment.

complex in Jung's theory, a clustering of emotionally charged ideas through which the psyche expresses itself.

condensation an aspect of Freud's concept of dream work whereby different latent elements are fused into a single manifest element.

conditioned generalized reinforcers in operant conditioning, reinforcers that acquire their power because of their associations with a large variety of other reinforcers.

conditions of worth in Rogers' theory, the belief that some aspects of one's experience are good or worthy and others are not worthy.

conflict-free sphere in neo-Freudian ego psychology, the sphere of ego functioning wherein the individual is free of the machinations of sexual and aggressive drives and intrapsychic conflict. According to Hartmann, the ego functions in the service of adaptation, rather than tension reduction, when operating in the conflict-free sphere.

conscientiousness one of the Big Five traits, conscientiousness encompasses personality descriptors denoting self-control, dependability, responsibility, persistence, and an achievement-oriented approach to life.

conservation of energy the nineteenth-century idea, adopted by Freud in his libido theory, that a system runs on a fixed amount of energy that cannot be created or destroyed.

construct approach to test construction an approach to designing a self-report questionnaire, or indeed any psychological measure, in which the investigator begins with a theory about the construct and then moves back and forth between theory and data to refine the evolving measure and the theory, following well-defined steps of test construction.

construct validity the extent to which a test measures the construct that it is theoretically intended to measure. Construct validity increases as empirical support is garnered for the various propositions contained in the construct's nomological net. Construct validity is the most basic and encompassing form of validity, and other forms of validity can be seen as derivatives from it.

content validity the degree to which the items of a test cover the entire content domain of a construct and are not confounded with other domains.

context of discovery the process of discovering new ideas and building theories in science. Contrast with *context of justification*.

context of justification the process of testing ideas derived from theory in science. Contrast with *context of discovery*.

continuous reinforcement reinforcement of a particular response after every occurrence. Contrast with *partial reinforcement*.

convergent validity the extent to which different measures of the same construct relate to each other. Contrast with *discriminant validity*.

coping strategies patterns of thought and behavior aimed at relieving anxiety and stress.

core conflictual relationship themes (CCRT) Luborsky's characterization of patterns of transference, observable in psychoanalytic psychotherapy. Employing his CCRT method, Luborsky codes accounts of the patient's interpersonal episodes in terms of the patient's main wish in the episode, the response of the other person in the episode, and the patient's response to the other person's response.

correlational design a methodology for research whereby the scientist examines the extent to which variables covary or relate to each other. Contrast with *experimental design*.

countertransference a term used in psychoanalytic therapy to refer to the therapist's tendency to relate to the patient in a way that unconsciously repeats or plays out his or her (the therapist's) own relationships with personally important people. Contrast with *transference*.

creative fidelity Marcel's term for finding authenticity in creative bonds of faithfulness to others.

criterion-key method of test construction a method of test construction, employed with the MMPI, in which items are chosen solely for their differential endorsement by subjects in different criterion groups.

criterion validity the extent to which a test is associated with external behaviors that it is designed to predict.

culture a tradition of rules and mores embraced by a particular society of people.

current concern Klinger's concept referring to the state of the organism between commitment to a goal and either attainment of the goal or disengagement from it.

Dasein an existentialist term, from Heidegger and Binswanger, translated as "being-in-the-world."

D-baby a recent classification category in attachment research, the D-baby suffers from disorganized or disoriented attachment patterns with the caregiver, appearing dazed and confused in the presence of the attachment object. This pattern is found among some victims of child abuse.

death instincts Freud's concept for a group of instinctual drives assumed to motivate the person toward behavior and experience promoting one's own death and destruction or aggression toward others. Contrast with *Eros* and *life instincts.*

declarative-episodic knowledge knowledge of experiences, thoughts, and actions of other people (person memory) and one's personal autobiographical record (autobiographical memory).

declarative-semantic knowledge abstract and categorical information that the person gleans over time concerning various phenomena.

deduction reasoning from the abstract and general to the concrete and particular. Contrast with *induction.*

defense mechanisms unconscious strategies of the ego (Freud) designed to distort reality in order to lessen anxiety.

deficiency motives in Maslow's theory, those needs based on lacks, absences, and tensions in the organism.

denial a primitive defense mechanism in which the person baldly refuses to acknowledge an anxiety-provoking event.

depersonalization the feeling or belief that one is not a whole and continuous person.

depressive schemata the overly negativistic frameworks for interpreting reality that depressed people often employ.

developmental lines Anna Freud's idea of trends in ego development during the childhood years through which the individual matures from complete dependency, passivity, and irrationality to rational independence and the active mastery of the environment.

dialectical humanism Fromm's view that the person's behavior is the complex and overdetermined product of internal needs manifesting themselves within the external social arrangements prescribed by a society at a particular moment in history.

dialectical reasoning reasoning through opposition.

dialogical self Hermans' concept of the self as a multiple narrator of experience. The dialogical self is a dynamic multiplicity of relatively autonomous I positions in an imaginal landscape. Each I position develops its own voice, or point of view.

difficult babies one of three temperament types identified by Thomas, Chess, and Birch, referring to babies with consistently negative moods, intense emotional reactions, and irregular sleeping and eating cycles. Contrast with *easy babies* and *slow-to-warm-up babies.*

discriminant validity the extent to which different measures of different constructs do *not* relate to each other.

displacement an aspect of Freud's concept of dream work whereby the dreamer unconsciously shifts the emphasis in a dream from an important but threatening source to a trivial but safer one, as when one displaces a powerful emotion from its intended object to a substitute.

display rules societal norms for the expression of different emotions.

dream work Freud's term for the processes utilized unconsciously by the dreamer as he or she creates a manifest dream from latent unconscious material. Aspects of dream work include condensation, displacement, symbolism, and secondary revision.

easy babies one of three temperament types identified by Thomas, Chess, and Birch, referring to babies with consistently positive mood, low-to-moderate intensity of emotional reactions, and regular sleeping and eating cycles. Contrast with *difficult babies* and *slow-to-warm-up babies.*

ego one of three divisions in Freud's structural model of the mind, serving as the mediator among the id, superego, and external reality, and operating according to the reality principle. According to Lovevinger, a person's overall framework of meaning, the master synthesizing I.

ego control the extent to which a person is able to reign in impulses, ranging from extreme undercontrol to overcontrol. One of two basic dimensions of personality in Jack Block's approach to personality typologies. See also *ego resiliency.*

ego integrity *versus* despair the eighth and last stage of psychosocial development in Erikson's scheme, associated with old age and the acceptance or re-

jection of one's own life as something that was.

ego psychology a modern derivative of Freudian theory emphasizing the adaptive and integrating power of the ego over and against the id and superego.

ego resiliency the capacity to modify one's typical level of ego control—toward either more control or less control of impulses—to adapt to demands of the situation. One of two basic dimensions of personality in Jack Block's approach to personality typologies. See also *ego control.*

Eigenwelt one of three features of the *Dasein*, according to existentialist thought, referring to the self-world of inner feelings and affections and including those experiences that people think of as being *within* their bodies. Contrast with *Mitwelt* and *Umwelt.*

Embedded Figures Test a test of field-independence/field-dependence in which a person attempts to find forms hidden in an embedding field.

empathy vicarious affective response to others, as when one person feels vicariously what another person feels directly.

empty-nest syndrome the supposed negative results for parents when their children attain adulthood and leave home.

entrepreneurship a collection of behavioral and attitudinal characteristics associated with high achievement motivation, including moderate risk taking, personal responsibility for performance, striving for productivity and innovative change, and careful attention to costs and profits.

erogenous zones bodily sites for libidinal expression, including the mouth, anus, and genitals.

Eros Freud's *life instincts.*

ethogram an extensive and detailed description of natural behavior observed over long periods of time.

ethology the study of the adaptive behavior of species in natural surroundings.

existential guilt Guilt over failing to fulfill the many possibilities and potentialities that life offers.

existentialism an intellectual movement beginning in Europe in the late nineteenth century and emphasizing consciousness, responsibility, becoming, and the individual's search for meaning in life.

expectancy in Rotter's and Mischel's social-learning theories, a subjectively held probability that a particular reinforcement will occur as the outcome of a specific behavior.

experience sampling method method of collecting samples of daily behavior, thought, and affect through the use of electronic pagers and other such devices.

experimental design a methodology for research whereby the scientist manipulates or alters one variable of interest (the independent variable) to observe its effect on another variable of interest (the dependent variable).

exploitative type Fromm's characterization of the aggressive and self-centered person, who exploits other people and the environment.

extraversion-introversion a broad personality trait, identified in many theories (including Eysenck's and Jung's), denoting a tendency to be outgoing, sociable, and impulsive on the one hand (extraversion) versus a tendency to be inwardly oriented, withdrawn, and deliberate on the other (introversion).

face validity the extent to which test items seem, in the eyes of the respondent, to measure what they are supposed to measure.

factor analysis a statistical procedure through which various items (as on a self-report questionnaire) are correlated with each other to determine the empirical clustering of the items.

feedback the self-regulation of a system through the repeated accumulation of information concerning the systems deviation from a particular set point or goal.

feedback hierarchy a system in which the output of one feedback loop becomes the reference value for the feedback loop that is subordinate to it.

feminine social clock project Helson's term for the conventional expectation about the timing of women's lives, involving getting married in one's 20s, having children shortly thereafter, and raising a family.

fictional finalism Adler's concept for an envisioned end or goal with respect to which the person orients his or her strivings. The goal is fictional in that it has not been realized and indeed may likely not be fully realized, but it still serves to energize and direct behavior.

field-independence/field-dependence a general dimension of cognitive style ranging from highly analytical and differentiated processing of information (field-independence) to highly contextual and global processing (field-dependence).

fixation Freud's concept for a problem, resulting from either overindulgence or deprivation, at a particular stage of psychosexual development. Fixations result in the development of particular personality characteristics in adulthood associated with earlier psychosexual stages.

fixed-action pattern a biologically programmed sequence of coordinated behaviors.

flashbulb memory an especially vivid memory of an important event from the past.

flow the subjective experience that a person feels when he or she is engaged in an intensely joyful and involving experience, characterized by a focused and ordered state of consciousness and an optimal ratio of skills to challenges.

folk concepts on the California Psychological Inventory (CPI), the name employed for the various trait scales to denote categories of personality that arise naturally out of human interactions in most, if not all, societies. Examples of the folk-concept scales include "responsibility," "socialization," and "flexibility."

foreclosure one of Marcia's four identity statuses, referring to the person who has not explored identity options but has rather made commitments to identity goals and outcomes that arose from childhood and remained unquestioned.

formal operations Piaget's term for abstract, hypothetico-deductive thinking, generally evidenced in adolescence and adulthood.

free association a procedure used in psychoanalytic therapy in which the patient lets his or her mind wander in response to a stimulus or event and reports all thoughts (associations) aloud to the therapist, spontaneous and uncensored.

frustration-aggression hypothesis Miller and Dollard's hypothesis that aggressive behavior is a socially molded behavior aimed at injuring another organism as a consequence of the frustration of goal-directed activity.

fully functioning person in Rogers' theory, the person who has attained maturity and actualization and is therefore consciously aware of the many different facets of his or her life and able to symbolize many seeming inconsistent aspects of experience and integrate them into a coherent whole.

functional analysis Skinner's term for the psychologist's attempt to measure the environmental causes and effects of behavior in precise and objective terms.

functions four ways in which persons make sense of reality: thinking, feeling, sensing, and intuiting (Jung).

fundamental attribution error a general tendency for people to overemphasize traits and underemphasize situations in explaining the causes of other people's behavior.

gender schema theory Bem's theory concerning the ways in which people differ with respect to their tendency to understand their life and the world in gender-related terms.

generalized other G. H. Mead's term for a person's conception of the generalized audience or observer for his or her behavior.

generativity *versus* stagnation the seventh stage of psychosocial development in Erikson's scheme, in which the adult seeks to guide the next generation and generate a legacy of the self.

genetic fitness an organism's overall potential to (1) survive longer, (2) reproduce more, and/or (3) enhance the survival and reproductive ability of biological kin relative to other organisms. Certain genetically transmitted characteristics increase genetic fitness, whereas others decrease genetic fitness.

genital stage Freud's fifth and last stage of psychosexual development, attained at puberty with full sexual maturation.

hagiographies biographical accounts of the lives of Christian saints written in the Middle Ages to venerate the Christian life.

hardiness a collection of personality dispositions—control, commitment, and challenge— thought to buffer the person from the ill effects of stress.

heritability quotient a numerical estimate of the proportion of variability in a given characteristic that can be attributed to genetic differences between people.

hermeneutics the art and science of interpreting texts.

higher-order conditioning the formation of complex associations in classical conditioning through which conditioned stimuli, which have obtained their eliciting power through associations with unconditioned stimuli, come to be associated with other neutral stimuli, which themselves become conditioned stimuli by virtue of the association.

hoarding type Fromm's characterization of the person who strives to accumulate possessions, power, and love, and to hold on to all that is accumulated.

hostile aggression aggression explicitly aimed at hurting or injuring the victim. Contrast with *instrumental aggression.*

humanistic psychology a general orientation in psychology that rose to prominence in the 1960s, emphasizing the creative, optimistic, and self-actualizing tendencies of human beings.

hysteria a form of psychopathology in which a person suffers from bodily symptoms, such as blindness or paralysis, that have no physical or biological cause.

Icarus complex Murray's concept for a cluster of themes in personality functioning, including urethral erotism, ascensionism, cynosural narcism, falling, craving for immortality, and depreciation and enthrallment of women—all modeled after the ancient Greek story of Icarus.

id one of three main divisions in Freud's structural model of the mind, serving as the home for instinctual impulses of sex and aggression and their unconscious derivative wishes, fantasies, and inclinations.

identification Freud's concept for the unconscious desire to "be" or to "be like" the other person. Contrast with *object choice.*

identity achievement one of Marcia's four identity statuses, referring to the person who has explored various identity options and successfully made commitments to realistic identity goals.

identity diffusion one of Marcia's four identity statuses, referring to the person who has not yet explored identity options and who has not made commitments.

identity status Marcia's concept referring to the extent to which a young person has explored and made commitments to different identity options, especially in the realms of occupation and ideology. The four statuses are identity achievement, moratorium, foreclosure, and identity diffusion.

identity *versus* role confusion the fifth stage in Erikson's scheme of psychosocial development, during which the adolescent strives to answer the questions "Who am I?" and "How do I fit into the adult world?"

ideological setting in the life-story model of identity, the background of a person's fundamental beliefs and values which provide the life story with a taken-for-granted setting.

idiographic Allport's term for an approach to personality study which focuses on the uniqueness of the individual case. Also called morphogenic. Contrast with *nomothetic.*

I–E Scale a popular self-report measure of locus of control, developed by Rotter.

illusion of control Langer's term for a person's mistaken belief that he or she is in control of events.

imago in the life-story model of identity, a personified and idealized image of self that functions as a main character in the life story.

implicit learning one of four related systems in what Kihlstrom calls the "psychological unconscious," implicit learning is the acquisition of knowledge in the absence of any reflective awareness of the knowledge itself.

implicit memory one of four related systems in Kihlstrom's "psychological unconscious," implicit memory is shown when a person's behavior is modified by the apprehension of a past event, though the event itself is not consciously remembered.

implicit perception one of four related systems in Kihlstrom's "psychological unconscious," implicit perception may be seen when the performance of a task changes as the result of some current event, but the current event is not consciously perceived.

implicit personality theory a person's own theory of human functioning, made up of intuitive knowledge concerning the causes of human behavior, population norms for various attributes of personality, and beliefs about how various personality attributes may relate to each other.

implicit thought one of four related systems in Kihlstrom's "psychological unconscious," implicit thought is problem-solving activity that occurs outside the problem solver's awareness.

imprinting very rapid learning during a particular sensitive period in development whereby the organism forms a lasting preference for a particular stimulus.

inclusive mode Erikson's concept for the young girl's characteristic approach to the world, involving "teasing, demanding, and grasping" in an attempt to "snare" others.

individual differences Characteristics of persons that can be said to differ with respect to amount or degree from one person to the next. Such concepts as personality "traits," "motives," "schemas," and "stages" are typically understood as aspects of individual differences in personality. These may be contrasted to *species-typical characteristics,* which are assumed to be more-or-less universal features of persons, that is, most all members of the human species.

individual psychology a term used to designate the personality theory developed by Alfred Adler.

individuation the full development of the self in Jungian theory, understood as a dynamic, complex, and life-long process whereby the person seeks to synthesize the various opposites in personality in order to become whole (Jung).

induction reasoning from the concrete and the particular to the abstract and general. Contrast with *deduction.*

industry *versus* inferiority the fourth stage in Erikson's scheme of psychosocial development, during which the schoolboy or schoolgirl receives systematic instruction from social institutions and begins to learn how to use the tools and adopt the characteristic roles of society.

initiative *versus* guilt the third stage in Erikson's scheme of psychosocial development, during which the young child experiences the Oedipus complex and becomes increasingly concerned with issues of power and taking initiative.

instinct for Freud, a mental representation of a physical or bodily need. Instincts are the ultimate motivators of behavior, providing the energy whereby action is driven and guided. In modern ethology, instincts are biologically rooted and adaptive motivational tendencies giving rise to particular urges, emotions, and behavioral plans that can be influenced, within limits, by the environment.

instrumental aggression aggression aimed at attaining a nonaggressive goal. Contrast with *hostile aggression.*

instrumental conditioning learning influenced by reinforcement and punishment. See *operant conditioning.*

integrative complexity the extent to which a person sees and interprets events in differentiated and integrated ways.

interactionism the general view that behavior is a function of the interaction of the person and the environment.

internalized objects internal representations of others with whom one has been involved in emotionally charged relationships, as discussed in object-relations theories.

interview a method of collecting data whereby the interviewer asks questions and engages the subject in a conversation with a purpose.

intimacy motivation a recurrent preference or desire for experiences of warm, close, and communicative interaction with others. Individual differences in intimacy motivation may be assessed through the TAT.

intimacy status parallel to Marcia's concept of *identity status,* referring to the characteristic quality of a person's interpersonal relationships and commitments at given point in time. At least four statuses have been identified: intimate, preintimate, stereotyped relationships, and isolate.

intimacy *versus* isolation the sixth stage of psychosocial development in Erikson's scheme, in which the young adult seeks to establish long-term affiliations with spouse, co-workers, friends, and so on.

intrinsic motivation motivation from within, rather than from external reinforcers and rewards.

intrusive mode Erikson's concept for the young boy's characteristically phallic and aggressive approach to the world.

item analysis a procedure in test construction whereby the investigator determines the relative contribution of each item to the total score on the test.

kin selection one sociobiological principle used to explain altruism, whereby an organism will engage in a helping or even self-sacrificial behavior that promotes the survival or reproductive success of kin.

latency Freud's fourth stage of psychosexual development, associated with elementary-school years, wherein the libido is rarely expressed in an overt manner.

libido Freud's concept for the sensual energy of sexual or life instincts.

life histories accounts of lives collected by social scientists, usually drawing on a wide variety of biographical data on the single individual.

life instincts Freud's concept for a group of instincts serving sexual reproduction and survival. Contrast with *death instincts.*

life review the process of taking stock of one's entire life, often evidenced in old age.

life-story model of identity the view that identity may be seen as a dynamic life story integrating a person's reconstructed past, present, and anticipated future into a coherent narrative whole that provides life with unity and purpose.

life structure Levinson's concept referring to the overall patterning or design of an individual's life at a given time.

life tasks the problems that individuals explicitly see themselves trying to solve at a particular time in their lives.

life themes an affective and cognitive representation of existential problems which a person wishes to resolve, as in the research of Csikszentmihalyi.

locus of control a personality dimension referring to individual differences in the extent to which a person believes that reinforcements are contingent on his or her behavior. A person who believes that behavior will lead to predictable reinforcements is said to have an *internal* locus of control; the person who believes that behavior and reinforcements tend to be unrelated—thus, assuming that external forces such as luck, fate, or powerful others determine reinforcement—is said to have an *external* locus of control.

logical learning theory Rychlak's theory of personality, emphasizing dialectical reasoning and the teleological nature of human behavior and experience.

looking glass self Cooley's term to designate the idea that the self is formed as the person comes to imagine how other people observe and understand him or her.

macrosystem Bronfenbrenner's term for an extremely broad and encompassing context within which behavior is organized, such as the macrosystems of race and social class.

maintenance system a culture's ecological, economic, and sociopolitical structure and the child-training or socialization practices accepted by the society as good and appropriate. Contrast with *projective system.*

mandala the ancient symbol of unity, representing individuation in Jungian psychology.

marketing type Fromm's characterization of the person who seeks to market him- or herself as a commodity to be bought and sold in the societal and interpersonal marketplace.

masculine occupational clock Helson's term for the standard expectation about the timing of men's lives, involving entering the job force in one's 20s and steadily moving up the occupational ladder for years to come.

mechanistic interactionism the procedure of partitioning the variance in behavior into that accounted for by the person, by the situation, and by the person-situation, interaction. Contrast with *reciprocal interactionism.*

metatrait the trait of having or not having a particular trait, which is conceptually independent of one's score on a trait scale. For a given trait, the behavior of "traited" people (those who "have" the trait) should be more predictable from trait scores than the behavior of "untraited" people (those who do not have the trait).

midlife crisis a period of profound personal questioning and reformulations reported by some men and women during their late 30s, 40s, or early 50s.

Minnesota Multiphasic Personality Inventory (MMPI) the most widely used personality inventory, containing 550 true-false statements and 10 different clinical scales.

Mitwelt one of three features of the *Dasein,* according to existentialist thought, referring to the world of interpersonal relations. Contrast with *Eigenwelt* and *Umwelt.*

moderator variables a variable that influences the relation of two other variables, such that the two other variables may be strongly related at certain levels of the moderator variable and only weakly related at other levels. In the wake of the situationist critique of the 1970s, some personality psychologists have successfully employed such moderator variables as self-reported "trait relevance" and "inner directedness" to improve the ability of trait scores to predict behavior.

mood-state-dependent memory the tendency for people to recall information congruent with their current mood.

moratorium one of Marcia's four identity statuses, referring to the person who is currently exploring various identity options but has not yet made commitments.

morphogenic see *idiographic.*

motive a term sometimes used synonymously with Murray's *need.* McClelland defines a motive as a recurrent preference or readiness for a particular quality of experience, which energizes, directs, and selects behavior in certain situations.

Myers–Briggs Type Indicator a self-report questionnaire measuring individual differences in Jungian personality types.

narcissism a preoccupation with the self, manifested in an apparent excess of self-love, grandiose sense of self-importance, and the need for constant attention and praise.

narrative mode one of two general modes of human thought, according to Jerome Bruner, referring to the human tendency to make sense of experience through stories. Stories are centrally concerned with the vicissitudes of human intention organized in time. Contrast to *paradigmatic mode.*

naturalistic observation a method of investigation in which the scientist observes behavior that occurs in natural habitats.

natural selection the process whereby those characteristics of organisms that promote survival and reproductive success come to predominate over less-adaptive characteristics in the course of evolution.

need in Murray's theory, a construct which stands for a force in the brain region which organizes perception, apperception, intellection, conation, and action in such a way as to transform in a certain direction an existing unsatisfying situation.

need hierarchy Maslow's ladder of needs, in which physiological needs provide a foundation for the successive emergence and satisfaction of safety needs, belongingness and love needs, esteem needs, and actualizing needs, respectively.

negative identities Erikson's term for representations, often embodied in other people, of everything that a person does *not* want to become.

neuroticism a broad personality trait, identified primarily with the theory of Eysenck, denoting a tendency to experience chronic anxiety, depression, emotional lability, nervousness, moodiness, hostility, vulnerability, self-consciousness, and hypochondriasis.

nomological network the interlocking system of propositions that constitute the theory of a given construct along with the empirical findings that support or fail to support those propositions.

nomothetic Allport's term for an approach to personality study which seeks to discover general laws for all persons. Contrast with *idiographic*.

nonadditive genetic variance the configural or interactive influence of genes on traits. Nonadditive genetic variance has been invoked to explain why the ratio of trait concordance for MZ twins and DZ twins is sometimes greater than 2.0, as in the case of recent studies on extraversion.

nuclear episode in the life-story model of identity, a particular scene that stands out in the story as especially important, often a high point, low point, or turning point in the story.

nuclear scene in Tomkins' script theory, a very good childhood scene that eventually turns very bad.

nuclear script one kind of script identified by Tomkins, marked by ambivalence and confusion about one's life goals.

object choice Freud's concept for the unconscious desire to "have" the other (another person) in a powerful and sensual way. In object choice, the person seeks to invest his or her libido, or sexual energy, in another. Contrast with *identification*.

object-relations theories a group of theories, owing varying intellectual debts to Freud, which center around the person's emotionally charged relationships with other people and the resultant development of representations of those people in the unconscious realms of the mind.

observational learning learning through observing an event and then imitating what is observed.

Oedipus complex Freud's concept denoting an unconscious struggle of power and sensuality experienced by boys and girls in the phallic stage of psychosexual development. In short, the child unconsciously desires to have the parent of the opposite sex in a powerful and sensual way but ultimately is forced to renounce that desire and settle for an unconscious identification with the same-sex parent.

openness to experience a broad personality trait, assessed by Costa and McCrae among others, designating a cluster of characteristics having to do with how reflective, imaginative, artistic, and refined a person is.

operant conditioning learning influenced by reinforcement and punishment through which behavior is modified by its consequences. In operant conditioning, freely emitted behaviors will increase when followed by positive consequences (reinforcement) or decrease when followed by negative consequences (punishment).

oral personality type according to Freud, the resultant pattern of personality characteristics associated with fixation at the oral stage. These characteristics cluster around either the *oral-passive* type, who is blithely cheerful and overly dependent, or the *oral-sadistic* type who is cynical, pessimistic, and bitingly sarcastic.

oral stage the first stage of psychosexual development, according to Freud, wherein the libido is expressed mainly through oral activities.

organ inferiorities Adler's concept for deficits and anomalies in the person with respect to which the person strives to compensate.

organismic valuing process in Rogers' theory, the fully functioning person's ability to view events and developments from the standpoint of his or her own growth and maturation.

overdetermination Freud's idea that the manifest content of dreams, symptoms, and certain other forms of behavior and experience are determined or caused by a vast amount of latent material, including unconscious wishes, impulses, and conflicts.

paradigmatic mode (of thought) one of two general modes of human thought, identified by Jerome Bruner, and referring to the human ability to understand reality through tightly reasoned analyses, propositional logic, and cause-and-effect relationships in the physico-chemical world. Contrast to *narrative mode*.

paratelic mode in Apter's reversal theory, the way of being characterized by activity-oriented as opposed to goal-oriented consciousness. See also *telic mode*.

partial reinforcement intermittent reinforcement of a particular response. Contrast with *continuous reinforcement*.

pattern-matching plan a procedure whereby an investigator seeks to find conceptual coherence in a case study according to certain preconceived theoretical assumptions or hypotheses.

peak experiences episodes in one's life filled with joy, excitement, wonder, and so on emphasized as signs of self-actualization in Maslow's humanistic theory.

peak performance performance above and beyond expectations, as in breaking an athletic record or putting on a

truly exceptional performance in the arts.

penis envy the Oedipal girl's unconscious disappointment concerning her lack of a penis, symbolizing a lack of power.

perceptual defense the unconscious monitoring of sensory perception by the censoring forces of repression within the person.

performance Goffman's term for all of the behavior produced by a person during a particular socially scripted interaction.

personal causation the extent to which a person feels that he or she is a causal agent in the environment.

personal construct Kelly's concept of a characteristic way of construing how some things are alike and some things are different from each other.

personal myth in McAdams' life-story model of identity, the particular life story that the adult creates as an internalized and integrative narrative of self designed to provide life with unity and purpose. Also called the "life story" or "life narrative."

personal unconscious in Jung's theory, the personal unconscious contains deeply buried memories, issues, conflicts, and so on from the individual's own developmental past. It corresponds to Freud's concept of the unconscious and stands in contrast to Jung's second realm of the unconscious, which he termed the "collective unconscious."

personality inventories self-report questionnaires containing many personality-trait scales.

personality psychology the scientific study of the whole person.

Personality Research Form (PRF) a personality inventory assessing individual differences in 20 of Murray's psychogenic needs.

Personal Orientation Inventory (POI) a self-report measure of dimensions of self-actualization.

personal projects activities with which a person is currently involved that are designed to achieve personal goals.

personal strivings characteristic goals that individuals try to achieve through their daily behavior.

personal work ethic a general interest and satisfaction in performing tasks industriously.

personification according to Sullivan, an image that an individual has of him- or herself or of another person.

personologist a psychologist who studies personality. The personologist considers the whole person in all of his or her complexity as the major unit of scientific study.

phallic stage the third stage of psychosexual development, according to Freud, wherein the libido is expressed through the genital region. The phallic stage is associated with ages 3–5 years and centers around the *Oedipus complex.*

phenomenal field Rogers' term for the entire panorama of a person's experience, and subjective apprehension of reality.

phenomenology the observation and description of immediate conscious experience.

pleasure principle the principle whereby the id operates, dictating that the individual seek immediate gratification of instinctual impulses and wishes. Contrast with *reality principle.*

positive reinforcement the presentation of a stimulus which increases the probability of the behavior it follows, commonly viewed as a reward.

possible selves a person's representations of what he or she would like to become, might become, or would be afraid to become.

postmodern referring to a diverse set of trends perceived in Western culture since the 1970s and emphasizing a skeptical and ironically playful attitude toward grand systems, universal truths, and authoritative conventions of virtually every kind.

power motivation a recurrent preference or desire for experiences of having an impact on others and on one's own environment; also called the "need for power." Individual differences in power motivation may be assessed through the TAT.

press in Murray's theory, a term denoting a determinant of behavior in the environment. A press can be seen as a situational opportunity or obstacle to the expression of a need in behavior.

primary process a very loose and irrational form of thinking driven by instinctual demands and associated with Freud's *id.* Contrast with *secondary process.*

private self-consciousness a tendency to introspect about the self.

procedural knowledge various competencies, strategies, and rules that enable the person to form impressions of others, make attributions, encode and retrieve memories, and predict social behaviors.

productive type Fromm's characterization of the most mature personality type, manifested in the person who fulfills his or her inner potential to become a creative worker and lover within a well-defined social identity.

projection a common defense mechanism in which the person attributes unacceptable internal states and qualities to external others.

projective system a culture's art, religion, folklore, and other expressive media. Contrast with *maintenance system.*

projective test a term designating a wide variety of tests, such as the Rorschach Inkblot Test and the Thematic Apperception Test, in which subjects give open-ended responses to various kinds of ambiguous stimuli, presumably "projecting" their wishes, conflicts, and motives onto the stimuli.

proprium Allport's concept for the self, or all aspects of personality that make for inward unity.

psychoanalysis a general term for the approach to psychology pioneered by Freud and others who tend to focus on the unconscious determinants of behavior, intrapsychic conflict, and instinctual drives concerning sexuality and aggression. The term also denotes the process of engaging in psychotherapy from a psychoanalytic standpoint.

psychobiography the systematic use of psychological (especially personality) theory to transform a life into a coherent and illuminating story.

psychodynamic activation method an experimental procedure whereby psychoanalytically relevant messages are transmitted subliminally to the subject, via a tachistoscope, in order to observe resultant changes in behavior or attitudes.

psychological androgyny the combination of masculine and feminine characteristics. A person who is highly androgynous sees him- or herself as possessing traits highly characteristic of both masculine and feminine sex-role stereotypes.

psychological magnification in Tomkin's script theory, the process of connecting related scenes into a meaningful pattern. Positive affect scenes are often magnified through the production of variants, or variations around a stable core. Negative affect scenes are often magnified through the production of analogs, or the detection of similarities in different scenes.

range of convenience Kelly's concept of the extent to which a given personal construct is likely to guide a person's interpretation of events and the behavior he or she is likely to show.

R data ratings of a person's behavior made by outside observers. Contrast with *S data* and *T data.*

reality principle the principle whereby the ego operates, pushing the individual toward behavior aimed at coping with conflicting demands, rationally weighing choices, and defending against various threats to the well-being of the person. Contrast with *pleasure principle.*

receptive type Fromm's characterization of the person who fulfills his or her needs by adopting a passive and dependent orientation in life, manifesting traits of cowardice, submissiveness, and sentimentality.

reciprocal altruism one sociobiological principle used to explain altruism, whereby an organism will aid another organism when such behavior is likely to result in reciprocation of the aid by the other organism at a later time.

reciprocal determinism in Bandura's social-learning theory, the idea that behavior is multiply determined by factors in the environment and in the person.

reciprocal interactionism the viewpoint suggesting that behavior, the person, and the environment influence each other through repeated and mutual transactions. Contrast with *mechanistic interactionism.*

reformulated learned-helplessness theory an attributional interpretation of depressive cognition, emphasizing the depressed person's tendency to explain negative events in his or her life as caused by internal, stable, and global factors.

regression in service of the ego the activity of employing primary-process thinking or other regressive strategies and behaviors in order to adapt to one's environment in a unique and highly creative way.

reinforcement value in Rotter's social-learning theory, the subjective attractiveness of a particular reinforcement.

reliability the consistency of a particular measure. Three forms of reliability are test-retest, split-half, and inter-scorer.

repression Freud's concept for the process of casting thoughts, memories, feelings, and conflicts out of consciousness, rendering them unremembered.

repressors as operationalized in recent research, individuals who show low levels of anxiety but high levels of defensiveness. Research suggests that repressors have less access than do other people to negative emotional memories about the self.

reversal theory Apter's theory of personality and motivation, which argues that human experience shifts over time between opposing metamotivational modes, such as the telic and the paratelic modes.

Role Construct Repertory (REP) Test Kelly's test designed to explore personal constructs in people's lives.

role structure in Hogan's socioanalytic theory, the person's characteristic ways of displaying self to one's colleagues, friends, peers, and children, and even to society at large.

Romanticism an intellectual movement in Western civilization (circa 1790–1850) rejecting classical teachings of reason, order, and the common good in favor of the celebration of the vigorous and passionate life of the individual.

root metaphor a basic analogy for understanding the world. Pepper has identified the following root metaphors: animism, mysticism, formism, mechanism, organicism, and contextualism.

Rorschach Inkblot Test a popular test in clinical work and in personality research in which the patient or subject looks at ambiguous inkblots and reports what he or she perceives.

scene a concept in Tomkins' script theory referring to a specific happening or event in one's life which contains at least one affect and one object of the affect.

schema an abstract knowledge structure.

script according to Tomkins, a set of rules for interpreting, creating, enhancing, or defending-against a family of related scenes. According to Abelson, encoded knowledge of stereotypic event sequences.

S data self-reports made by persons about their own behavior, as on well-validated personality scales. Contrast with *R data* and *T data.*

secondary process rational cognitive activity associated with the functioning of the ego (Freud). Contrast with *primary process.*

secondary revision an aspect of Freud's concept of dream work whereby the dreamer unconsciously smooths over the dream's rough spots, fills in gaps, clears up ambiguities, and edits the dream experience into a more-or-less coherent account.

seduction hypothesis Freud's early view that the origins of hysteria reside in the repressed affect associated with childhood sexual abuse. Freud eventually abandoned the seduction hypothesis in favor of the idea that most neurotics merely fantasize childhood sexual seduction.

self-actualization a term from humanistic psychology referring to the fundamental human striving toward fulfilling one's entire potential.

self as I following James's dichotomy, the self-as-subject, the I as actor and thinker. James believed that the self as I is but a moment in consciousness. Contrast with *self as Me.*

self as Me following James's dichotomy, the self-as-object, which refers to the self-concept. For James, the self as Me was composed of the material, social, and spiritual selves. Contrast with *self as I.*

self-discrepancy theory a theory put forth by Higgins focusing on the emotional outcomes of various discrepancies among actual, ideal, and ought selves.

self-efficacy Bandura's concept referring to a person's belief that he or she can successfully carry out courses of action required to deal with various challenging situations.

self-esteem a person's subjective, affective evaluation of the self.

self-monitoring the extent to which a person tends to modify his or her own behavior in response to shifting situational demands and contingencies.

self-objects in Kohut's theory, people who are so central to an individual's life that he or she feels that they are part of him or her.

self psychology a contemporary derivative of psychoanalytic theory, championed by Heinz Kohut, which is concerned with how people find unity and cohesiveness in life.

self-recognition the ability to recognize the self, especially in a mirror reflection as in studies with babies and toddlers.

self-regulation a general concept referring to many different abilities, such as the ability to comply with a request, to initiate and cease activities according to situational demands, to modulate the intensity, frequency, and duration of speech and behavior in various settings, to postpone acting upon a desired object or goal, and to generate socially approved behavior in the absence of external monitors.

self-schema an abstract knowledge structure about the self.

self-system according to Sullivan, a set of strategies designed to minimize the experience of anxiety.

self-understanding Damon's model of the self, involving the four features of the active, social, physical, and psychological selves, each developing through stages over time.

self-with-other a person's representation of his or her own characteristics as they are typically displayed in interaction with a particular other person. In Ogilvie and Ashmore's research, self-with-other representations exist in a complex configuration as basic units of the social Me.

sensation seeking the need for varied, novel, and complex sensations and experiences and the willingness to take physical and social risks for the sake of such experiences, measured on a scale developed by Zuckerman.

separation-individuation Mahler's term for the process of gaining independence from early symbiotic unions with caregivers and establishing a coherent sense of self and of others.

shadow the unconscious archetype representing a variety of socially unacceptable, even bestial, desires and impulses, inherited by virtue of humankind's evolution from lower forms (Jung).

shyness a personality trait defined as discomfort and inhibition in the presence of others.

sign stimulus a stimulus in the environment that naturally sets into motion a fixed action pattern.

situational prototypes an abstract set of features about a given class of situations.

situationism a general point of view, linked to social learning theory and the impact of experimental social psychology, that behavior is best explained and predicted by reference to the situation within which behavior occurs. The person-situation debate of the 1970s and early 1980s pitted situationism against trait perspectives in personality psychology.

situationist a personality psychologist who studies the environmental determinants of behavior to show the extent to which behavior is influenced by external factors in the situation. Contrast with *trait psychologist.*

slow-to-warm-up babies one of three temperament types identified by Thomas, Chess, and Birch, referring to babies with relatively negative moods, low intensity of emotional reactions, and the tendency to withdraw from new events at first but approach them later. Contrast with *easy babies* and *difficult babies.*

social clock a set of expectations about age-appropriate transitions, setting the standards against which individuals evaluate the extent to which their lives are "on time."

social desirability a term denoting the person's desire to present a favorable impression in responding to test items.

social intelligence each person's set of skills, abilities, and knowledge about social situations.

social interest Adler's concept for the person's innate sense of kinship with all humanity.

social-learning theories theories such as those proposed by Rotter, Mischel, and Bandura which adopt certain emphases of behaviorism but blend these with a greater emphasis on cognitive variables and social relationships.

Social Readjustment Rating Scale a measure of life stress in which the subject reports the number of life change events that have occurred in the recent past.

socioanalytic theory Hogan's theory of personality, emphasizing the evolutionary adaptiveness and ritualized social quality of patterns of human behavior.

sociobiology the study of the biological bases of social behavior, combining ethology, genetics, and ecology.

sociosexuality the extent to which an individual will (restricted sociosexuality) or will not (unrestricted sociosexuality) insist on closeness and commitment in an interpersonal relationship before engaging in sexual intercourse with the partner. Recent thinking in evolutionary personality psychology suggests that both restricted and unrestricted sociosexuality patterns may have proven adaptive (for both men and women) throughout evolution, in conjunction with various environmental constraints and selection pressures.

source traits Cattell's 16 basic factors underlying the many different surface traits that might be identified.

species-typical characteristics characteristics of persons that are believed to be nearly universal for the human species. They may be contrasted to *individual differences* in personality, which refer to characteristics ways in which persons can be said to differ from each other.

specification equation Cattell's approach to behavioral prediction whereby different trait scores for an individual are plugged into an equation and given differential weights according to the extent to which each is deemed to be relevant to the particular situation in which behavior is to occur.

split-half reliability the extent to which a test's results are consistent across different parts of the test, that is, the extent of internal consistency in the test.

state anxiety a relatively transitory emotional experience of fear and nervousness. Contrast with *trait anxiety*.

stimulus generalization the expansion of a conditioned response so that it is evoked in response to a wide variety of stimuli which resemble the conditioned stimulus in some way.

story grammar the implicit rules by which a story is structured. Most stories include a setting and characters, and action in the story proceeds in a sequence of initiating event, action attempt, consequence of attempt, reaction, and resolution.

Strange Situation an experimental procedure used to assess individual differences in the quality of caregiver–infant attachment, by subjecting the infant to brief separations from the caregiver and novel events.

striving for superiority Adler's concept for the "great upward drive" of human behavior, leading to perfection, completion, and wholeness.

style of life Adler's term for a person's unique mode of adjustment to life, most notably including the person's self-selected goals and means of achieving them.

subception Rogers' term for the detection of an experience before it enters awareness.

sublimation from Freud's theory, the channelling of instinctual energy into socially appropriate, productive, and even creative work. The higher achievements of humankind are a result of sublimating, or making more "sublime," sexual and aggressive instincts.

superego one of the three main divisions in Freud's structural model of the mind, serving as a primitive internalized representation of the norms and values of society as acquired through identification with the parents at the resolution of the Oedipus complex.

symbolism an aspect of Freud's concept of dream work whereby the dreamer conjures up concrete images and actions that convey hidden but common meanings.

system a general term referring to a highly differentiated and integrated totality, within which various components relate to and communicate with each other, each part affecting every other part and the whole.

TAT see *Thematic Apperception Test*.

T data observations and other information obtained from controlled laboratory situations and other contrived situations in which the person is maneuvered into behaving in one of a small number of ways. Contrast with *R data* and *S data*.

Telic Dominance Scale derived from Apter's reversal theory, a self-report scale assessing individual differences in the extent to which the telic and paratelic modes tend to characterize a person's experience over time.

telic mode in Apter's reversal theory, the way of being characterized by goal directedness and future-time orientation. See also *paratelic mode*.

telosponse Rychlak's term for a behavior that is produced for the sake of a *telos*, or goal.

temperament individual differences in basic behavioral style assumed to be present at birth in some form and, thus, largely biologically determined.

template matching an approach to personality study in which the researcher classifies situations according to the personality traits of the person who "fits" the situation in a particular way.

test–retest reliability the extent to which a test's results are consistent over time.

thema in Murray's theory, a particular behavioral unit represented as a need/press interaction.

Thematic Apperception Test (TAT) an assessment procedure, devised by Murray and Morgan, in which the subject writes or tells stories in response to a set of ambiguous picture cues.

theory a set of interrelated statements proposed to explain certain observations about reality.

thrownness a concept from existentialism referring to the natural and historical conditions into which a person is born. At birth, a person is "thrown" into a certain place and time, providing a multitude of constraints and potential opportunities, and he or she is ultimately responsible for creating meaning out of the thrownness.

topographical model Freud's model of the mind, which distinguishes among the conscious, preconscious, and unconscious regions. The conscious corresponds to everyday awareness; the preconscious contains the contents of ordinary memory, to which awareness may be directed at any time; and the unconscious contains wishes, feelings, memories, and so on that have been repressed because they threaten the well-being of the conscious self.

trait a general term in personality psychology referring to an individual-difference variable assumed to reflect an underlying, internal, and stable personality disposition. Traits are generally viewed to be linear and bipolar in nature, additive and independent, and suggestive of relatively broad individual differences in social and/or emotional functioning.

trait anxiety a relatively stable tendency to be fearful and nervous. Contrast with *state anxiety*.

trait psychologist a personality psychologist who studies measurable individual differences among persons with respect to internal and relatively stable dispositions, called *traits*. Contrast with *situationist*.

transcendent function Jung's concept of the guiding motivational force for individuation. The transcendent function is the developmental principle of personality for Jung, moving the individual in the direction of a full expression of all aspects of the self and an integration of opposites within a unique and harmonious whole.

transference a term used in psychoanalytic therapy to refer to the patient's tendency to relate to the therapist in a way that unconsciously repeats or plays out his or her relationships with other personally important people. Contrast with *counter-transference.*

triple bookkeeping Erikson's view that the person's life must be comprehended on the three levels of body, ego, and family/society.

trust *versus* mistrust the first stage in Erikson's scheme of psychosocial development, in which the infant seeks to establish a hopeful and trusting relation with the environment.

type a general term in personality psychology designating a coherent pattern of traits characteristic of particular individuals.

Type A constellation of overlapping characteristics including high ambitiousness, hostility, time-urgency, competitiveness, impatience, and irritability. The Type A person may be more susceptible to heart disease.

Umwelt one of three features of the *Dasein,* according to existentialist thought, referring to the "thrown" world of biology and the natural environment. Contrast with *Eigenwelt* and *Mitwelt.*

unconditional positive regard in Rogers' theory, love and acceptance provided in an uncritical and noncontingent manner.

unconscious the state of being outside of awareness. For Freud, the unconscious is a shadowy realm of the mind wherein reside repressed thoughts, feelings, memories, conflicts, and the like.

utilitarianism intellectual movement of the eighteenth and nineteenth centuries, associated with Bentham and Mill, arguing that the general good is defined in terms of the greatest good for the greatest number of people.

valuation in Hermans' theory of the self, anything that a person deems important in his or her life situation. Valuations are units of meaning in the life narrative. Each valuation is either positive, negative, or ambivalent in emotional tone.

Washington University Sentence Completion Test for Ego Development (WUSCTED) Loevinger's standardized assessment device for assessing stages of ego development: impulsive, self-protective, conformist, conformist/conscientious, conscientious, individualistic, autonomous, and integrated.

will to power in Adler's theory, the striving to feel strong and powerful in interactions with the world, later generalized by Adler to become a "striving for superiority."

working model in Bowlby's theory of attachment, a representation of the caregiver built up in the mind of the infant. A working model of the attachment object is an unconscious set of expectations about the caregiver's behavior and one's relation to the caregiver and serves as the earliest template for human love.

References

Abelson, R. (1981). Psychological status of the script concept. *American Psychologist, 36,* 715–729.

Abramson, L.Y., Seligman, M.E.P., & Teasdale, J.P. (1978). Learned helplessness in humans: Critique and reformulation. *Journal of Abnormal Psychology, 87,* 49–74.

Adams, G.R., Ryan, J.H., Hoffman, J.J., Dobson, W.R., & Nielson, E.C. (1984). Ego identity status, conformity behavior, and personality in late adolescence. *Journal of Personality and Social Psychology, 47,* 1091–1104.

Adler, A. (1927). *The practice and theory of individual psychology.* New York: Harcourt Brace World.

Adler, A. (1930). Individual psychology. In C. Murchison (Ed.), *Psychologies of 1930.* Worcester, MA: Clark University Press.

Adler, A. (1931). *What life should mean to you.* Boston: Little Brown.

Adorno, T.W., Frenkel-Brunswik, E., Levinson, D.J., & Sanford, R.N. (1950). *The authoritarian personality.* New York: Harper & Brothers.

Agar, M.H. (1986). *Speaking of ethnography.* Beverly Hills, CA: Sage.

Ainsworth, M.D.S. (1967). *Infancy in Uganda: Infant care and the growth of love.* Baltimore, MD: Johns Hopkins University Press.

Ainsworth, M.D.S. (1969). Object relations, dependency, and attachment: A theoretical review of the infant-mother relationship. *Child Development, 40,* 969–1025.

Ainsworth, M.D.S. (1989). Attachments beyond infancy. *American Psychologist, 44,* 709–716.

Ainsworth, M.D.S., Blehar, M.C., Waters, E., & Wall, T. (1978). *Patterns of attachment.* Hillsdale, NJ: Lawrence Erlbaum.

Ainsworth, M.D.S., & Bowlby, J. (1991). An ethological approach to personality development. *American Psychologist, 46,* 333–341.

Ainsworth, M.D.S., & Eichberg, C. (1991). Effects on infant-mother attachment of mother's unresolved loss of an attachment figure, or other traumatic experience. In C.M. Parkes, J. Stevenson-Hinde, and P. Marris (Eds.), *Attachment across the life cycle* (pp. 160–183). London: Tavistock/Routledge.

Akbar, N. (1991). The evolution of human psychology for African Americans. In R.L. Jones (Ed.), *Black psychology* (3rd Ed.) (pp. 99–124). Berkeley, CA: Cobb & Henry.

Alexander, I.E. (1988). Personality, psychological assessment, and psychobiography. *Journal of Personality, 56,* 265–294.

Albert, R.S. (1990). Identity, experiences, and career choice among the exceptionally gifted and eminent. In M.A. Runco and R.S. Albert (Eds.), *Theories of creativity* (pp. 13–34). Newbury Park, CA: Sage.

Alker, H.A. (1972). Is personality situationally specific or intrapsychically consistent? *Journal of Personality, 40,* 1–16.

Allison, G.T. (1971). *Essence of decision making: Explaining the Cuban missile crisis.* Boston: Little Brown.

Alloy, L.B., & Abramson, L.Y. (1979). Judgment of contingency in depressed and nondepressed college students: Sadder but wiser? *Journal of Experimental Psychology: General, 108,* 441–487.

Allport, G.W. (1937). *Personality: A psychological interpretation.* New York: Holt, Rinehart & Winston.

Allport, G.W. (1955). *Becoming: Basic considerations for a psychology of personality.* New Haven, CT: Yale University Press.

Allport, G.W. (1961). *Pattern and growth in personality.* New York: Holt, Rinehart & Winston.

Allport, G.W. (1965). *Letters from Jenny.* New York: Harcourt, Brace & World.

Allport, G.W. (1968). *The person in psychology: Selected Essays.* Boston: Beacon Press.

Allport, G.W., & Odbert, H.S. (1936). Trait-names, a psychological study. *Psychological Monographs, 47,* (1, Whole No. 211).

Allport, G.W., & Vernon, P.E. (1931). A test for personal values, *Journal of Abnormal and Social Psychology, 26,* 231–248.

Amabile, T.M., DeJong, W., & Lepper, M.R. (1976). Effects of externally imposed deadlines on subsequent intrinsic motivation. *Journal of Personality and Social Psychology, 34,* 92–98.

Amato, P.R., & Pearce, P. (1983). A cognitively-based taxonomy of helping. In M. Smithson, P.R. Amato, and P. Pearce (Eds.), *Dimensions of helping behavior* (pp. 22–36). Oxford: Pergamon.

Amelang, M., & Borkenau, P. (1986). The trait concept: Current theoretical considerations, empirical facts, and implications for personality inventory construction. In A. Angleitner and J.S. Wiggins (Eds.), *Personality assessment via questionnaires: Current issues in theory and measurement* (pp. 7–34). New York: Springer-Verlag.

American Psychiatric Association (1980). *Diagnostic and statistical manual of mental disorders: DSM-III.* Washington, D.C.: American Psychiatric Association.

Amsterdam, B.K. (1972). Mirror self-image reactions before age two. *Developmental Psychology, 5,* 297–305.

Anastasi, A. (1976). *Psychological testing* (4th Ed.). New York: Macmillan.

Anderson, J.W. (1981). Psychobiographical methodology: The case of William James. In L. Wheeler (Ed.), *Review of personality and social psychology* (Vol. 2, pp. 245–272). Beverly Hills, CA: Sage.

Anderson, J.W. (1988). Henry A. Murray's early career: A psychobiographical exploration. *Journal of Personality, 56,* 139–171.

Andrews, J.D.W. (1967). The achievement motive in two types of organizations. *Journal of Personality and Social Psychology, 6,* 163–168.

Angleitner, A., Ostendorf, F., & John, O.P. (1990). Towards a taxonomy of personality descriptors in German: A psycho-lexical study. *European Journal of Personality, 4.*

Anthony, E.J. (1970). The behavior disorders of childhood. In P.H. Mussen (Ed.), *Carmichael's handbook of child psychology,* (Vol. 1, pp. 667–764). New York: John Wiley & Sons.

Applebee, A.N. (1978). *The child's concept of story.* Chicago: University of Chicago Press.

Apter, M.J. (1982). *The experience of motivation: The theory of psychological reversals.* New York: Academic Press.

Apter, M.J. (1989). *Reversal theory: Motivation, emotion, and personality.* London: Routledge.

Archer, J. (1988). The sociobiology of bereavement: A reply to Littlefield and Rushton. *Journal of Personality and Social Psychology, 55,* 272–278.

Ardrey, R. (1970). *The social contract.* New York: Atheneum.

Arend, R., Gove, F.L., & Sroufe, L.A. (1979). Continuity of individual adaptation from infancy to kindergarten: A predictive study of ego-resiliency and curiosity in preschoolers. *Child Development, 50,* 950–959.

Arieti, S. (1976). *Creativity: The magic synthesis.* New York: Basic Books.

Argyle, M., & Little, B.R. (1972). Do personality traits apply to social behavior? *Journal for the Theory of Social Behavior, 2,* 1–35.

Ashmore, R.D., & Ogilvie, D.M. (1992). He's such a nice boy...when he's with grandma: Gender and evaluation in self-with-other representations. In T.M. Brinthaupt and R.P. Lipka (Eds.), *The self: Definitional and methodological issues* (pp. 236–289). Albany, NY: State University of New York Press.

Atkinson, J.W. (1957). Motivational determinants of risk-taking behavior. *Psychological Review, 64,* 359–372.

Atkinson, J.W. (Ed.). (1958). *Motives in fantasy, action, and society.* Princeton, NJ: D. Van Nostrand.

Atkinson, J.W., & Birch, D. (1978). *An introduction to motivation* (2nd ed.). New York: D. Van Nostrand.

Atkinson, J.W., Bongort, K., & Price, L.H. (1977). Explorations using computer simulation to comprehend TAT measurement of motivation. *Motivation and Emotion, 1,* 1–27.

Atkinson, J.W., Heyns, R.W., & Veroff, J. (1954). The effect of experimental arousal of the affiliation motive on thematic apperception. *Journal of Abnormal and Social Psychology, 49*, 405–410.

Atkinson, J.W., & Raynor, J.O. (Eds.). (1978). *Motivation and achievement* (2nd Ed.). Washington, DC: Winston.

Atkinson, R.C., & Shiffrin, R.M. (1968). Human memory: A proposed system and its control processes. In K.W. Spence and J.T. Spence (Eds.), *The psychology of learning and motivation* (Vol. 2, pp. 89–195). New York: Academic Press.

Auchincloss, L. (1986). *Diary of a yuppie*. Boston, MA: Houghton Mifflin.

Averill, J.R. (1984). The acquisition of emotions during adulthood. In C.Z. Malatesta and C.E. Izard (Eds.), *Emotion in adult development* (pp. 23–44). Beverly Hills, CA: Sage.

Avery, R.R., & Ryan, R.M. (in press). Object relations and ego development: Comparison and correlates in middle childhood. *Journal of Personality*.

Bakan, D. (1966). *The duality of human existence: Isolation and communion in Western man*. Boston: Beacon Press.

Bakan, D. (1971). *Slaughter of the innocents*. Boston: Beacon Press.

Bakhtin, M.M. (1973). *Problems of Dostoyevsky's poetics*. Ann Arbor, MI: Ardis. (Transl. by R.W. Rotsel). (Original work published 1929).

Baldwin, J.M. (1897). *Mental development in the child and the race*. New York: Macmillan.

Baley, J., & Shevrin, H. (1988). The subliminal psychodynamic activation method: A critical review. *American Psychologist, 43*, 161–174.

Ball, D.W. (1972). The definition of situation: Some theoretical and methodological consequences of taking W.I. Thomas seriously. *Journal for the Theory of Social Behaviour, 2*, 61–82.

Bandura, A. (1965). Influence of models' reinforcement contingencies on the acquisitions of imitative responses. *Journal of Personality and social Psychology, 1*, 589–595.

Bandura, A. (1971). *Social learning theory*. Morristown, NJ: General Learning Press.

Bandura, A. (1977). *Social learning theory* (2nd Ed.). Englewood Cliffs, NJ: Prentice-Hall.

Bandura, A. (1978). The self system in reciprocal determinism. *American Psychologist, 33*, 344–358.

Bandura, A. (1983). Temporal dynamics and decomposition of reciprocal determinism: A reply to Phillips and Orton. *Psychological Review, 90*, 166–170.

Bandura, A. (1988). Perceived self-efficacy: Exercise of control through self-belief. In J.P. Dauwalder, M. Perez, & V. Hobi (Eds.), *Annual series of European research in behavior therapy* (Vol. 2, pp.

27–59). Lisse, the Netherlands: Swets & Zeitlinger.

Bandura, A. (1989). Human agency in social cognitive theory. *American Psychologist, 44*, 1175–1184.

Bandura, A., Ross, D., & Ross, S.A. (1961). Transmission of aggression through imitation of aggressive models. *Journal of Abnormal and Social Psychology, 63*, 575–582.

Bandura, A., Ross, D., & Ross, S.A. (1963). Imitation of film-mediated aggressive models. *Journal of Abnormal and Social Psychology, 66*, 3–11.

Bandura, A., & Schunk, D.H. (1981). Cultivating competence, self-efficacy, and intrinsic interest through proximal self-motivation. *Journal of Personality and Social Psychology, 41*, 586–598.

Barash, D.P. (1977). *Sociobiology and behavior*. New York: Elsevier.

Barash, D.P. (1979). *The whisperings within: Evolution and the origin of human nature*. New York: Penguin.

Barash, D.P. (1986). *The hare and the tortoise: Culture, biology, and human nature*. New York: Penguin.

Barash, D.P. (1987). *The arms race and nuclear war*. Belmont, CA: Wadsworth Publishing.

Barrends, A., Westen, D., Leigh, J., Byers, S., & Silbert, D. (1990). Assessing affect-tone from TAT and interview data. *Psychological Assessment: A Journal of Consulting and Clinical Psychology, 2*, 329–332.

Barron, F. (1969). *Creative person and creative process*. New York: Holt, Rinehart & Winston.

Baruch, G.K. (1984). The psychological well-being of women in the middle years. In G.K. Baruch and J. Brooks-Gunn (Eds.), *Women in midlife* (pp. 161–180). New York: Plenum Press.

Baruch, R. (1967). The achievement motive in women: Implications for career development. *Journal of Personality and Social Psychology, 5*, 260–267.

Barry, H.H., Child, I.L., & Bacon, M.K. (1959). Relation of child rearing to subsistence economy. *American Anthropologist, 61*, 51–63.

Bateson, G. (1972). *Steps to an ecology of mind*. New York: Ballantine Books.

Bateson, M.C. (1984). *With a daughter's eye*. New York: Washington Square Press.

Batson, C.D., Dyck, J.L., Brandt, J.R., Batson, J.G., Powell, A.L., McMaster, M.R., & Griffit, C. (1988). Five studies testing two new egoistic alternatives to the empathy-altruism hypothesis. *Journal of Personality and Social Psychology, 55*, 52–77.

Battistich, V.A., & Thompson, E.G. (1980). Students' perceptions of the college milieu: A multidimensional scaling analysis. *Personality and Social Psychology Bulletin, 6*, 74–82.

Baumeister, R.F. (1986). *Identity: Cultural change and the struggle for self*. New York: Oxford University Press.

Baumeister, R.F. (1990). Suicide as escape from self. *Psychological Review, 97*, 90–113.

Baumeister, R.F., Stillwell, A., & Wotman, S.R. (1990). Victim and perpetrator accounts of interpersonal conflict: Autobiographical narratives about anger. *Journal of Personality and Social Psychology, 59*, 994–1005.

Baumeister, R.F., & Tice, D.M. (1988). Metatraits. *Journal of Personality, 56*, 571–598.

Baumgarten, F. (1933). Die Charaktereigenschaften. [The character traits.] In *Beiträge zur Charakter- und Persönlichkeitsforschung*. (Whole No. 1). Bern: A Francke.

Baumrind, D. (1971). Current patterns of parental authority. *Developmental Psychology Monograph, 4* (1, Pt. 2).

Beck, A.T. (1967). *Depression: Clinical, experimental, and theoretical aspects*. New York: Hoeber.

Beck, A.T. (1976). *Cognitive therapy and the emotional disorders*. New York: International Universities Press.

Becker, E. (1973). *The denial of death*. New York: The Free Press.

Becker, H.S. (1970). *Sociological work*. Chicago: Aldine.

Behrends, R.S., & Blatt, S.J. (1985). Internalization and psychological development throughout the life cycle. In A.J. Solnit, R.S. Eissler, and P.S. Neubauer (Eds.), *The psychoanalytic study of the child* (Vol. 40, pp. 11–39). New Haven, CT: Yale University Press.

Beit-Hallahmi, B. (1980). Achievement motivation and economic growth: A replication. *Personality and Social Psychology Bulletin, 6*, 210–215.

Bellah, R.N., Madsen, K., Sullivan, W.M., Sandler, A., & Tipton, S.M. (1985). *Habits of the heart*. Berkeley, CA: University of California Press.

Bellah, R.N., Madsen, R., Sullivan, W.M., Swidler, A., & Tipton, S.M. (1991). *The good society*. New York: Knopf.

Belsky, J., Steinberg, L., & Draper, P. (1991). Childhood experience, interpersonal development, and reproductive strategy: An evolutionary theory of socialization. *Child Development, 62*, 647–670.

Bem, D.J., & Allen, A. (1974). On predicting some of the people some of the time: The search for cross-situational consistencies in behavior. *Psychological Review, 81*, 506–520.

Bem, D.J., & Funder, D.C. (1978). Predicting more of the people more of the time: Assessing the personality of situations. *Psychological Review, 85*, 485–501.

Bem, S.L. (1974). The measurement of psychological androgyny. *Journal of Consulting and Clinical Psychology, 42*, 155–162.

Bem, S.L. (1974). Sex role adaptability: One consequence of psychological androgyny. *Journal of Personality and Social Psychology*, *31*, 634–643.

Bem, S.L. (1981). Gender schema theory: A cognitive account of sex typing. *Psychological Review*, *88*, 354–364.

Bem, S.L. (1987). Gender schema theory and the romantic tradition. In P. Shaver and C. Hendrick (Eds.), *Sex and gender: Review of personality and social psychology* (Vol. 7, pp. 251–271). Beverly Hills, Ca: Sage.

Bendig, A.W. (1963). The relation of temperament traits of social extraversion and emotionality to vocational interests. *Journal of General Psychology*, *69*, 311–318.

Benedict, R. (1946). *The chrysanthemum and the sword*. New York: Meridian World.

Berkowitz, J., & Powers, P.C. (1979). Effects of timing and justification of witnesses aggression on the observer's punitiveness. *Journal of Research in Personality*, *13*, 71–80.

Berkowitz, L. (1974). Some determinants of impulsive aggression: The role of mediated associations with reinforcements for aggression. *Psychological Review*, *81*, 165–176.

Berman, J.S., & Kenny, D.A. (1976). Correlational bias in observer ratings. *Journal of Personality and Social Psychology*, *34*, 263–273.

Bernat, E.F. (1985). *The relationship of gender and personality to fantasy patterns*. Unpublished Master's Thesis, Loyola University of Chicago.

Berne, E. (1964). *Games people play*. New York: Grove.

Bernstein, B.A. (1970). A sociolinguistic approach to socialization: With some reference to educability. In F. Williams (Ed.), *Language and poverty: Perspectives on a theme*. Chicago: Markham.

Berry, J.W. (1976). *Human ecology and cognitive style*. New York: Russell Sage.

Bertaux, D. (Ed.). (1981). *Biography and society: The life history approach in the social sciences*. Beverly Hills, CA: Sage.

Bertenthal, B.I., & Fischer, K.W. (1978). Development of self-recognition in the infant. *Developmental Psychology*, *14*, 44–50.

Bertini, M. Pizzamiglio, L., & Wapner, S. (Eds.). (1986). *Field dependence in psychological theory, research, and application*. Hillsdale, NJ: Lawrence Erlbaum.

Bertrand, S., & Masling, J. (1969). Oral imagery and alcoholism. *Journal of Abnormal Psychology*, *74*, 50–53.

Bettelheim, B. (1977). *The uses of enchantment: The meaning and importance of fairy tales*. New York: Vintage Books.

Bierhoff, H.W., Klein, R., & Kramp, P. (1991). Evidence for the altruistic personality from data on accident research. *Journal of Personality*, *59*, 263–280.

Biernat, M., & Wortman, C.B. (1991). Sharing of home responsibilities between professionally employed women and their husbands. *Journal of Personality and Social Psychology*, *60*, 844–860.

Binswanger, L. (1963). *Being-in-the-world*. New York: Basic Books.

Bird, S.E., & Dardenne, R.W. (1988). Myth, chronicle, and story: Exploring the narrative qualities of news. In J.W. Carey (Ed.), *Media, myths, and narratives: Television and the press* (pp. 67–86). Newbury Park, CA: Sage Publications.

Blake, R., Rosenbaum, M., & Duryea, R.A. (1955). Gift-giving as a function of group standards. *Human Relations*, *8*, 61–73.

Blaney, P.H. (1986). Affect and memory: A review. *Psychological Bulletin*, *99*, 229–246.

Blasi, A. (1988). Identity and the development of the self. In D.K. Lapsley and F.C. Power (Eds.), *Self, ego, and identity: Integrative approaches* (pp. 226–242). New York: Springer-Verlag.

Blass, J. (1984). Social psychology and personality: Toward a convergence. *Journal of Personality and Social Psychology*, *47*, 1013–1027.

Blatt, S.J., Brenneis, B., Schimek, J.G., & Glick, M. (1976). Normal development and psychopathological impairment of the concept of the object on the Rorschach. *Journal of Abnormal Psychology*, *85*, 364–373.

Blatt, S.J., & Lerner, H. (1983). Investigations in the psychoanalytic theory of object relations and object representations. In J. Masling (Ed.), *Empirical studies of psychoanalytical theories* (Vol. 1, pp. 189–250). New York: Analytic Press.

Blehar, M.C., Lieberman, A.F., & Ainsworth, M.D.S. (1977). Early face-to-face interaction and its relationship to later mother—infant attachment. *Child Development*, *48*, 182–194.

Bleuler, E. (1950). *Dementia praecox or the group of schizophrenias*. New York: International Universities Press.

Block, J. (1961). *The Q-sort method in personality assessment and psychiatric research*. Springfield, IL: Charles C. Thomas.

Block, J. (1971). *Lives through time*. Berkeley, CA: Bancroft Books.

Block, J. (1977). Advancing the psychology of personality: Paradigmatic shift or improving the quality of research? In D. Magnusson and N.S. Endler (Eds.), *Personality at the crossroads: Current issues in interactional psychology*. Hillsdale, NJ: Lawrence Erlbaum.

Block, J. (1981). Some enduring and consequential structures of personality. In A.I. Rabin, J. Aronoff, A.M. Barclay, and R.A. Zucker (Eds.), *Further explorations in personality* (pp. 27–43). New York: John Wiley & Sons.

Block, J. (1989). Critique of the act frequency approach to personality. *Journal of Personality and Social Psychology*, *56*, 234–245.

Block, J., Weiss, D.S., & Thorne, A. (1979). How relevant is a semantic similarity interpretation of personality ratings? *Journal of Personality and Social Psychology*, *37*, 1055–1074.

Block, J.H., & Block, J. (1980). The role of ego control and ego resiliency in the organization of behavior. In W.A. Collins (Ed.), *Development of cognition, affect, and social relations* (pp. 39–101). Hillsdale, NJ: Lawrence Erlbaum.

Bloom, A. (1987). *The closing of the American mind: How education has failed democracy and impoverished the souls of today's students*. New York: Simon & Schuster.

Bloom, A.R. (1971). *Achievement motivation and occupational choice: A study of adolescent girls*. Unpublished doctoral dissertation, Bryn Mawr College.

Blos, P. (1972). The epigenesis of the adult neurosis. In *The psychoanalytic study of the child* (Vol. 27). New York: Quadrangle.

Blos, P. (1979). *The adolescent passage*. New York: International Universities Press.

Bob, S. (1968). *An investigation of the relationship between identity status, cognitive style, and stress*. Unpublished doctoral dissertation, State University of New York at Binghampton.

Bolen, J.S. (1985). *Goddesses in everywoman: A new psychology of women*. New York: Harper & Row.

Bolen, J.S. (1989). *Gods in everyman: A new psychology of men's lives and loves*. New York: Harper & Row.

Bolger, N., & Schilling, E.A. (1991). Personality and the problems of everyday life: The role of neuroticism in exposure and reactivity to daily stressors. *Journal of Personality*, *59*, 355–386.

Booth, W.C. (1988). *The company we keep: An ethics of fiction*. Berkeley, CA: University of California Press.

Borden, W. (1992). Narrative perspectives in psychosocial intervention following adverse life events. *Social Work*, *37*(2), 135–141.

Borkovec, T.D., & Craighead, W.E. (1971). The comparison of the methods of assessing fear and avoidance behavior. *Behavior Research and Therapy*, *9*, 285–291.

Bornstein, R.F., & Masling, J. (1985). Orality and latency of volunteering to serve as experimental subjects: A replication. *Journal of Personality Assessment*, *49*, 306–310.

Bornstein, R.F. (1990). Subliminal mere exposure and psychodynamic activation effects: Implications for the psychoanalytic theory of conscious and unconscious mental processes. In J. Masling (Ed.), *Empirical studies of psychoanalytic theories* (Vol. 3, pp. 55–88). Hillsdale, NJ: The Analytic Press.

Boswell, T. (1904). *Life of Samuel Johnson L.L. D.* New York: Oxford University Press. (Originally published in 1791).

Bouchard, T.J., Jr., Lykken, D.T., McGue, M., Segal, N.L., & Tellegen, A. (1990). Sources of human psychological differences: The Minnesota Study of Twins Reared Apart. *Science, 250,* 223–228.

Bourne, E. (1977). Can we describe an individual's personality? Agreement on stereotype vs. individual attributes. *Journal of Personality and Social Psychology, 35,* 863–872.

Bourne, E. (1978). The state of research on ego identity: A review and appraisal (Part 1). *Journal of Youth and Adolescence, 7,* 223–255.

Bower, G.H. (1981). Mood and memory. *American Psychologist, 36,* 129–148.

Bowers, K.S. (1973). Situationism in psychology: An analysis and a critique. *Psychological Review, 80,* 307–336.

Bowers, K.S., & Meichenbaum, D. (Eds.). (1984). *The unconscious reconsidered.* New York: John Wiley & Sons.

Bowlby, J. (1969). *Attachment and loss. Vol. 1: Attachment.* New York: Basic Books.

Bowlby, J. (1973). *Attachment and loss Vol. 2: Separation.* New York: Basic Books.

Bowlby, J. (1980). *Attachment and loss. Vol. 3: Loss.* New York: Basic Books.

Bowlby, J. (1988). *A secure base.* New York: Basic Books.

Boyatzis, R.E. (1973). Affiliation motivation. In D.C. McClelland and R.S. Steele (Eds.), *Human motivation: A book of readings* (pp. 252–276). Morristown, NJ: General Learning Press.

Brazelton, T.B., Koslowski, B., & Main, M. (1974). The origins of reciprocity: The early mother–infant interaction. In M. Lewis and L.A. Rosenblum (Eds.), *The effect of the infant on the caregiver.* New York: John Wiley & Sons.

Breger, L. (1974). *From instinct to identity: The development of personality.* Englewood Cliffs, NJ: Prentice-Hall.

Breslow, R., Kocis, J., & Belkin, B. (1981). Contribution of the depressive perspective to memory function in depression. *American Journal of Psychiatry, 138,* 227–230.

Breuer, J., & Freud, S. (1893–1898). *Studies on hysteria.* In Vol. 2 of J. Strachey (Ed.), *The standard edition of the complete psychological works of Sigmund Freud.* London: Hogarth.

Brewer, W.F., & Lichtenstein, E.H. (1982). Stories are to entertain: A structural-affect theory of stories. *Journal of Pragmatics, 6,* 473–486.

Bridges, L.J., Connell, J.P., & Belsky, J. (1988). Similarities and differences in infant–mother and infant–father interaction in the strange situation: A component process analysis. *Developmental Psychology, 24,* 92–100.

Briggs, S.R. (1989). The optimal level of measurement for personality constructs. In D.M. Buss and N. Cantor (Eds.), *Personality psychology: Recent trends and emerging directions* (pp. 246–260). New York: Springer-Verlag.

Brittain, V. (1933/1970). *Testament of youth.* New York: Wideview Books.

Brody, N. (1970). Information theory, motivation, and personality. In H.M. Schroder and P. Suedfeld (Eds.), *Personality theory and information processing.* New York: Ronald Press.

Bromley, D.B. (1977). *Personality description in ordinary language.* Chichester, England: John Wiley & Sons.

Bromley, D.B. (1986). *The case-study method in psychology and related disciplines.* New York: John Wiley & Sons.

Bronfenbrenner, U. (1979). *The ecology of human development.* Cambridge, MA: Harvard University Press.

Broughton, J.M., & Zahaykevich, M.K. (1988). Ego and ideology: A critical review of Loevinger's theory. In D.K. Lapsley and F.C. Power (Eds.), *Self, ego, and identity: Integrative approaches* (pp. 179–208). New York: Springer-Verlag.

Brown, R, & Kulik, J. (1977). Flashbulb memories. *Cognition, 5,* 73–99.

Browning, D.S. (1975). *Generative man: Psychoanalytic perspectives.* New York: Dell.

Bruch, M.A., Gorsky, J.M., Collins, T.M., & Berger, P.A. (1989). Shyness and sociability reexamined: A multicomponent analysis. *Journal of Personality and Social Psychology, 57,* 904–915.

Bruhn, A.R. & Schiffman, H. (1982). Invalid assumptions and methodological difficulties in early memory research. *Journal of Personality Assessment, 46,* 265–267.

Bruner, J.S. (1986). *Actual minds, possible worlds.* Cambridge, MA: Harvard University Press.

Bruner, J.S. (1990). *Acts of meaning.* Cambridge, MA: Harvard University Press.

Bruner, J.S., & Tagiuri, R. (1954). The perception of people. In G. Lindzey (Ed.), *Handbook of social psychology* (Vol. 2). Reading, MA: Addison-Wesley.

Brunson, B.I., & Matthews, K.A. (1981). The Type A coronary prone behavior pattern and reactions to uncontrollable stress: An analysis of performance strategies, affect, and attributions during failure. *Journal of Personality and Social Psychology, 40,* 906–918.

Brunswik, E. (1956). *Perception and the representative design of psychological experiments.* Berkeley, CA: University of California Press.

Brunswik, E. (1957). Scope and aspects of the cognitive problem. In H. Gruber, R. Jessor, and K. Hammond (Eds.), *Cognition: The Colorado Symposium* (pp. 5–31). Cambridge, MA: Harvard University Press.

Buber, M. (1947). *Between man and man.* London: Routledge & Kegan Paul.

Buber, M. (1970). *I and Thou.* New York: Charles Scribner's Sons.

Bühler, C. (1933). *Der menschliche lebenslauf als psychologisches problem.* Leipzig: S. Hirzel Verlag.

Burisch, M. (1984). Approaches to personality inventory construction: A comparison of merits. *American Psychologist, 39,* 214–227.

Buss, A.H. (1986). Social rewards and personality. *Journal of Personality and Social Psychology, 44,* 553–563.

Buss, A.H. (1989). Personality as traits. *American Psychologist, 44,* 1378–1388.

Buss, A.H., & Finn, S.E. (1987). Classification of personality traits. *Journal of Personality and Social Psychology, 52,* 432–444.

Buss, A.H., & Plomin, R. (1975). *A temperament theory of personality.* New York: John Wiley & Sons.

Buss, A.H., & Plomin, R. (1984). *Temperament: Early developing personality traits.* Hillsdale, NJ: Lawrence Erlbaum.

Buss, D.M. (1984). Evolutionary biology and personality psychology: Toward a conception of human nature and individual differences. *American Psychologist, 39,* 1135–1147.

Buss, D.M. (1988). The evolution of human intrasexual competition: Tactics of mate attraction. *Journal of Personality and Social Psychology, 54,* 616–628.

Buss, D.M. (1989a). Sex differences in human mate preference: Evolutionary hypotheses tested in 37 cultures. *Brain and Behavior Sciences, 12,* 1–49.

Buss, D.M. (1989b). Conflict between the sexes: Strategic interference and the evocation of anger and upset. *Journal of Personality and Social Psychology, 56,* 735–747.

Buss, D.M. (1990). Toward a biologically informed psychology of personality. *Journal of Personality, 58,* 1–16.

Buss, D.M. (1991a). Evolutionary personality psychology. In M.R. Rosenzweig and L.W. Porter (Eds.), *Annual review of psychology* (pp. 459–491). Palo Alto, CA: Annual Reviews, Inc.

Buss, D.M. (1991b). Conflict in married couples: Personality predictors of anger and upset. *Journal of Personality, 59,* 663–688.

Buss, D.M., & Barnes, M. (1986). Preferences in human mate selection. *Journal of Personality and Social Psychology, 50,* 559–570.

Buss, D.M., & Cantor, N. (1989). Introduction. In D.M. Buss and N. Cantor

(Eds.), *Personality psychology: Recent trends and emerging directions* (pp. 1–12). New York: Springer-Verlag.

Buss, D.M., & Craik, K.H. (1983). Act prediction and the conceptual analysis of personality scales: Indices of act density, bipolarity, and extensity. *Journal of Personality and Social Psychology*, *45*, 1081–1095.

Buss, D.M., & Craik, K.H. (1984). Acts, dispositions, and personality. In B.A. Maher and W.B. Maher (Eds.), *Progress in experimental personality research* (Vol. 13, pp. 241–301). Orlando, FL: Academic Press.

Butler, R.N. (1975). *Why survive? Being old in America*. New York: Harper & Row.

Byrne, D., & Kelley, K. (1981). *An introduction to personality* (3rd Ed.). Englewood Cliffs, NJ: Prentice-Hall.

Cairns, R.B. (1979). Social interactional methods: An introduction. In R.B. Cairns (Ed.), *The analysis of social interaction: Methods, issues, and illustrations*. Hillsdale, NJ: Lawrence Erlbaum.

Calder, B.J., & Staw, B.M. (1975). The interaction of intrinsic and extrinsic motivation: Some methodological notes. *Journal of Personality and Social Psychology*; *31*, 76–80.

Campbell, A. (1975). The American way of mating: Marriage or children, only maybe. *Psychology Today*, May, 39–42.

Campbell, D.T. (1975). "Degrees of freedom" and the case study. *Comparative Political Studies*, *8*, 178–193.

Campbell, D.T., & Fiske, D.W. (1959). Convergent and discriminant validation by the multitrait–multimethod matrix. *Psychological Bulletin*, *56*, 81–105.

Campbell, J. (1949). *The hero with a thousand faces*. New York: Bollingen Foundation, Inc.

Cann, D.R., & Donderi, D.C. (1986). Jungian personality typology and the recall of everyday and archetypal dreams. *Journal of Personality and Social Psychology*, *50*, 1021–1030.

Cantor, N. (1990). From thought to behavior: "Having" and "doing" in the study of personality and cognition. *American Psychologist*, *45*, 735–750.

Cantor, N., Acker, M., & Cook-Flanagan, C. (1992). Conflict and preoccupation in the intimacy life task. *Journal of Personality and Social Psychology*, *63*, 644–655.

Cantor, N., & Kihlstrom, J.F. (1985). Social intelligence: The cognitive basis of personality. In P. Shaver (Ed.), *Self, situations, and social behavior* (pp. 15–34). Beverly Hills, CA: Sage.

Cantor, N., & Kihlstrom, J.F. (1987). *Personality and social intelligence*. Englewood Cliffs, NJ: Prentice-Hall.

Cantor, N., & Kihlstrom, J.F. (1989). Social intelligence and cognitive assessments of personality. In R.S. Wyer, Jr., and T.K. Srull (Eds.), *Advances in so-cial cognition: Vol. II. Social intelligence and cognitive assessments of personality* (pp. 1–59). Hillsdale, NJ: Lawrence Erlbaum.

Cantor, N., & Mischel, W. (1979). Prototypes in person perception. In L. Berkowitz (Ed.), *Advances in experimental social psychology* (Vol. 12). New York: Academic Press.

Cantor, N., Mischel, W., & Schwartz, J.C. (1982). A prototype analysis of psychological situations. *Cognitive Psychology*, *14*, 45–77.

Cantor, N., Norem, J.K., Niedenthal, P.M., Langston, C.A., & Brower, A.M. (1987). Life tasks, self-concept ideals, and cognitive strategies in a life transition. *Journal of Personality and Social Psychology*, *53*, 1178–1191.

Cantor, N., & Zirkel, S. (1990). Personality, cognition, and purposive behavior. In L. Pervin (Ed.), *Handbook of personality theory and research* (pp. 135–164). New York: Guilford Press.

Cantor, N.F. (1971). *Western civilization, its genesis and destiny: The modern heritage. From 1500 to the present*. Glenview, IL: Scott, Foresman and Company.

Carlo, G., Eisenberg, N., Troyer, D., Switzer, G., & Speer, A.L. (1991). The altruistic personality: In what contexts is it apparent? *Journal of Personality and Social Psychology*, *61*, 450–458.

Carlsmith, J.M., Ellsworth, P.C., & Aronson, E. (1976). *Methods of research in social psychology*. Reading, MA: Addison-Wesley.

Carlson, R. (1971). Where is the person in personality research? *Psychological Bulletin*, *75*, 203–219.

Carlson, R. (1980). Studies of Jungian typology: II. Representations of the personal world. *Journal of Personality and Social Psychology*, *38*, 801–810.

Carlson, R. (1981). Studies in script theory: I. Adult analogs of a childhood nuclear scene. *Journal of Personality and Social Psychology*, *40*, 501–510.

Carlson, R. (1984). What's social about social psychology? Where's the person in personality research? *Journal of Personality and Social Psychology*, *47*, 1304–1309.

Carlson, R. (1988). Exemplary lives: The uses of psychobiography for theory development. *Journal of Personality*, *56*, 105–138.

Carlson V., Cicchetti, D., Barnett, D., & Braunwald, K. (1989). Disorganized/disoriented attachment behaviors in maltreated infants. *Developmental Psychology*, *25*, 525–531.

Carment, D.W., Miles, G.G., & Cervin, V.B. (1965). Persuasiveness and persuasability as related to intelligence and extraversion. *British Journal of Social and Clinical Psychology*, *4*, 1–7.

Carver, C.S. (1975). Physical aggression as a function of objective self-awareness and attitudes towards punishment. *Journal of Experimental Social Psychology*, *11*, 510–519.

Carver, C.S., & Scheier, M.F. (1981). A control systems approach to behavioral self-regulation. In L. Wheeler (Ed.), *Review of personality and social psychology* (Vol. 2, pp. 107–140). Beverly Hills, CA: Sage.

Carver, C.S. & Scheier, M.F. (1992). *Perspectives on personality*. 2nd Ed Boston, MA: Allyn & Bacon.

Caspi, A., Bem, D.J., & Elder, G.H., Jr. (1989). Continuities and consequences of interactional style across the life course. *Journal of Personality*, *57*, 375–406.

Caspi, A., Elder, G.H., Jr., & Bem, D.J. (1988). Moving away from the world: Life-course patterns of shy children. *Developmental Psychology*, *24*, 824–831.

Caspi, A., & Moffitt, T.E. (in press). When do individual differences matter? A paradoxical theory of personality coherence. *Psychological Inquiry*.

Cattell, R.B. (1943). The description of personality: Basic traits resolved into clusters. *Journal of Abnormal and Social Psychology*, *38*, 476–506.

Cattell, R.B. (1965). *The scientific analysis of personality*. Baltimore, MD: Penguin.

Cattell, R.B. (1990). Advances in Cattellian personality theory. In L.A. Pervin (Ed.), *Handbook of personality theory and research* (pp. 101–110). New York: Guilford Press.

Chafe, W. (1990). Some things that narratives tell us about the mind. In B.K. Britton and A.D. Pellegrini (Eds.), *Narrative thought and narrative language* (pp. 79–98). Hillsdale, NJ: Lawrence Erlbaum.

Chaikin, A.L., Derlega, V.J., Bayma, B., & Shaw, J. (1975). Neuroticism and disclosure reciprocity. *Journal of Consulting and Clinical Psychology*, *43*, 13–19.

Chaplin, W.F. (1991). The next generation of moderator research in personality psychology. *Journal of Personality*, *59*, 143–178.

Chaplin, W.F., & Goldberg, L.R. (1984). A failure to replicate the Bem and Allen study of individual differences in cross-situational consistency. *Journal of Personality and Social Psychology*, *47*, 1074–1090.

Charme, S.T. (1984). *Meaning and myth in the study of lives: A Sartrean perspective*. Philadelphia: University of Pennsylvania Press.

Chassan, J.D. (1967). *Research designs in clinical psychology and psychiatry*. New York: Appleton-Century-Crofts.

Cheek, J.M. (1982). Aggregation, moderator variables, and the validity of personality tests: A peer-rating study. *Journal of Personality and Social Psychology*, *43*, 1254–1269.

Cheek, J.M., & Buss, A.H. (1981). Shyness and sociability. *Journal of Personality and Social Psychology*, *41*, 330–339.

Chodorow, N. (1978). *The reproduction

of mothering: Psychoanalysis and the sociology of gender. Berkeley, CA: University of California Press.

Christie, R., & Jahoda, M. (Eds.). (1954). Studies in the scope and method of "The Authoritarian Personality." Glencoe, IL: Free Press.

Church, A.T., & Katigbak, M.S. (1989). Internal, external, and self-report structure of personality in a non-Western culture: An investigation of cross-language and cross-cultural generalizability. Journal of Personality and Social Psychology, 57, 857–872.

Cialdini, P.B., Schaller, M., Fultz, J., & Beaman, A.L. (1987). Empathy based helping: Is it selflessly or selfishly motivated? Journal of Personality and Social Psychology, 52, 749–758.

Clarke-Stewart, K.A. (1989). Infant day care: Maligned or malignant? American Psychologist, 44, 266–273.

Cochran, S.D., & Hammen, C.L. (1985). Perceptions of stressful life events and depression: A test of attributional models. Journal of Personality and Social Psychology, 48, 1562–1571.

Cohen, R. (1977). The effects of four subliminally introduced merging stimuli on the psychopathology of schizophrenic women. Unpublished doctoral dissertation, Columbia University.

Cohler, B.J. (1982). Personal narrative and the life course. In P. Baltes & O.G. Brim, Jr. (Eds.), Life span development and behavior (Vol. 4, pp. 205–241). New York: Academic Press.

Cohler, B.J. (1990). The life-story and the study of resilience and response to adversity. New England Symposium on Narrative Studies, Clark University.

Cohler, B.J., & Boxer, A.M. (1984). Personal adjustment, well-being, and life events. In C.Z. Malatesta and C.E. Izard (Eds.), Emotion in adult development (pp. 85–100). Beverly Hills, CA: Sage.

Cole, J. (1970). Culture: Negro, black, and nigger. Black Scholar, 1, 341–350.

Coles, R. (1989). The call of stories: Teaching and the moral imagination. Boston: Houghton Mifflin.

Conger, J.J., & Petersen, A.C. (1984). Adolescence and youth: Psychological development in a changing world (3rd ed.). New York: Harper & Row.

Conley, J.J. (1985a). A personality theory of adulthood and aging. In R. Hogan and W.H. Jones (Eds.), Perspectives in personality (Vol. 1, pp. 81–116). Greenwich, CT: JAI Press.

Conley, J.J. (1985b). Longitudinal stability of personality traits: A multitrait-multimethod-multioccasion analysis. Journal of Personality and Social Psychology, 49, 1266–1282.

Constantinople, A. (1973). Masculinity—femininity: An exception to a famous dictum. Psychological Bulletin, 80, 389–407.

Cooley, C.H. (1902). Human nature and the social order. New York: Scribners.

Cooper, J., & Scalise, C.J. (1974). Dissonance produced by deviations from life-styles: The interaction of Jungian typology and conformity. Journal of Personality and Social Psychology, 29, 566–571.

Coopersmith, S. (1967). The antecedents of self-esteem. San Francisco: W.H. Freeman.

Cordes, C. (1986). Narrative thought neglected. Interview with Jerome Bruner in the APA Monitor (monthly newspaper of the American Psychological Association).

Coser, L.A. (1977). Masters of sociological thought (2nd ed.). New York: Harcourt Brace Jovanovich.

Costa, P.T., Jr., & McCrae, R.R. (1978). Objective personality assessments. In M. Storandt, I.C. Siegler, and M.F. Elias (Eds.), The clinical psychology of aging. New York: Plenum.

Costa, P.T., Jr., & McCrae, R.R. (1980a). Influence of extraversion and neuroticism on subjective well-being: Happy and unhappy people. Journal of Personality and Social psychology, 38, 668–678.

Costa, P.T., Jr., & McCrae, R.R. (1980b). Somatic complaints in males as a function of age and neuroticism: A longitudinal analysis. Journal of Behavioral Medicine, 3, 245–257.

Costa, P.T., Jr., & McCrae, R.R. (1984). Personality as a lifelong determinant of well-being. In C.Z. Malatesta and C.E. Izard (Eds.), Emotion in adult development (pp. 141–158). Beverly Hills, CA: Sage.

Costa, P.T., Jr., & McCrae, R.R. (1985). The NEO Personality Inventory. Odessa, FL: Psychological Assessment Resources.

Costa, P.T., Jr., & McCrae, R.R. (1988). From catalog to classification: Murray's needs and the five-factor model. Journal of Personality and Social Psychology, 55, 258–265.

Costa, P.T., Jr., McCrae, R.R. & Arenberg, P. (1980). Enduring dispositions in adult males. Journal of Personality and Social Psychology, 38, 793–800.

Costa, P.T., Jr., McCrae, R.R., Zonderman, A.B., Barbano, H.E., Lebowitz, B., & Larson, D.M. (1986). Cross-sectional studies of personality in a national sample: 2. Stability in neuroticism, extraversion, and openness. Psychology and Aging, 1, 144–149.

Coyne, J.C., & Gotlib, I.H. (1983). The role of cognition in depression: A critical appraisal. Psychological Bulletin, 94, 472–505.

Cramer, P. (1987). The development of defense mechanisms. Journal of Personality, 55, 597–614.

Cramer, P. (1988). The Defense Mechanism Inventory: A review of research and discussion of the scales. Journal of Personality Assessment, 52, 142–164.

Cramer, P. (1991). The development of defense mechanisms. New York: Springer-Verlag.

Cramer, P., & Carter, T. (1978). The relationship between sexual identification and the use of defense mechanisms. Journal of Personality Assessment, 42, 63–73.

Cramer, P., & Hogan, K. (1975). Sex differences in verbal and play fantasy. Developmental Psychology, 11, 145–154.

Crandall, J.E. (1980). Adler's concept of social interest: Theory, measurement and implications for adjustment. Journal of Personality and Social Psychology, 39, 481–495.

Crandall, J.E. (1984). Social interest as a moderator of life stress. Journal of Personality and Social Psychology, 47, 164–174.

Crockett, H.J., Jr. (1962). The achievement motive and differential occupational mobility in the United States. American Sociological Review, 27, 191–204.

Crockett, W.H. (1965). Cognitive complexity and impression formation. In B.A. Maher (Ed.), Progress in experimental personality research (Vol. 1, pp. 47–90). New York: Academic Press.

Cronbach, L.J. (1975). Beyond the two disciplines of scientific psychology. American Psychologist, 30, 116–127.

Cronbach, L.J., & Meehl, P.E. (1955). Construct validity in psychological tests. Psychological Bulletin, 52, 281–302.

Cross, H., & Allen, J. (1970). Ego identity status, adjustment, and academic achievement. Journal of Consulting and Clinical Psychology, 34, 288.

Crowne, D.P., & Marlowe, D. (1960). A new scale of social desirability independent of psychopathology. Journal of Consulting Psychology, 24, 349–354.

Crowne, D.P., & Marlowe, D. (1964). The approval motive: Studies in evaluative dependence. New York: Wiley.

Csikszentmihalyi, M. (1977). Beyond boredom and anxiety. San Francisco: Jossey-Bass.

Csikszentmihalyi, M. (1982). Toward a psychology of optimal experience. In L. Wheeler (Ed.), Review of personality and social psychology (Vol. 3, pp. 13–36). Beverly Hills, CA: Sage.

Csikszentmihalyi, M. (1990a). Flow: The psychology of optimal experience. New York: Harper & Row.

Csikszentmihalyi, M. (1990b). The domains of creativity. In M.A. Runco and R.S. Albert (Eds.), Theories of creativity (pp. 190–212). Newbury Park, CA: Sage.

Csikszentmihalyi, M., & Beattie, O.V. (1979). Life themes: A theoretical and empirical exploration of their origins and effects. Journal of Humanistic Psychology, 19(1), 45–63.

Cummings, E.E. (1973). Complete poems (Vol. 1). Bristol, England: McGibbon & Kee.

Cunningham, M.R. (1981). Sociobiology as a supplementary paradigm for social psychological research. In L. Wheeler

(Ed.), *Review of personality and social psychology* (Vol. 2, pp. 69–106). Beverly Hills, CA: Sage.

Cunningham, M.R. (1985). Measuring the physical in physical attractiveness: Quasi-experiments on the sociobiology of female facial beauty. *Journal of Personality and Social Psychology, 50,* 925–935.

Cunningham, M.R., Barbee, A.P., & Pike, C.L. (1990). What do women want? Facialmetric assessment of multiple motives in the perception of male facial physical attractiveness. *Journal of Personality and Social Psychology, 59,* 61–72.

Curran, J.P., & Gilbert, F.S. (1975). A test of the relative effectiveness of a systematic desensitization program and an interpersonal skills training program with date anxious subjects. *Behavior Therapy, 6,* 510–522.

Dabbs, J.M., Jr., Frady, R.L., Carr, T.S., & Besch, N.F. (1987). Salivary testosterone and criminal violence in young adult prison inmates. *Psychosomatic Medicine, 49,* 174–182.

Dabbs, J.M., Jr., de LaRue, D., & Williams, P.M. (1990). Testosterone and occupational choice: Actors, ministers, and other men. *Journal of Personality and Social Psychology, 59,* 1261–1265.

Dabbs, J.M., Jr., & Morris, R. (1990). Testosterone, social class, and antisocial behavior in a sample of 4,462 men. *Psychological Science, 1,* 209–211.

Dabbs, J.M., Jr., Ruback, R.B., Frady, R.L., Hopper, C.H., & Sgoutas, D.S. (1988). Saliva testosterone and criminal violence among women. *Personality and Individual Differences, 9,* 269–275.

Damon, W. (1983). *Social and personality development.* New York: W.W. Norton.

Damon, W., & Hart, D. (1982). The development of self-understanding from infancy through adolescence. *Child Development, 53,* 841–864.

Darwin, C. (1859). *On the origin of species by means of natural selection.* New York: Appleton.

Darwin, C. (1872/1965). *The expression of the emotions in man and animals.* Chicago: University of Chicago Press.

Dauber, R.M. (1984). Subliminal psychodynamic activation in depression: On the role of autonomy issues in depressed college women. *Journal of Abnormal Psychology, 93,* 9–18.

Davidson, R.J., & Tomarken, A.J. (1989). Laterality and emotion: An electrophysiological approach. In F. Boller and J. Grafman (Eds.), *Handbook of neuropsychology* (pp. 419–441). Amsterdam: Elsevier.

Davies, B., & Harre, R. (1990). Positioning: The discursive production of selves. *Journal for the Theory of Social Behavior, 20,* 43–63.

Davis, P.J. (1987). Repression and the inaccessibility of affective memories. *Journal of Personality and Social Psychology, 53,* 585–593.

Davis, P.J., & Schwartz, G.E. (1987). Repression and the inaccessibility of affective memories. *Journal of Personality and Social Psychology, 52,* 155–162.

Dawkins, R. (1976). *The selfish gene.* New York: Oxford University Press.

Deary, I.J., Ramsay, H., Wilson, J.A., & Raid, M. (1988). Stimulated salivation: Correlations with personality and time of day effects. *Personality and Individual Differences, 9,* 903–909.

Deaux, K., Kite, M.E., & Lewis, L. (1985). Clustering and gender schema: An uncertain link. *Personality and Social Psychology Bulletin, 11,* 387–397.

de Charms, R. (1968). *Personal causation: The internal affective determinants of behavior.* New York: Academic Press.

de Charms, R., & Moeller, G.H. (1962). Values expressed in American children's readers: 1800–1950. *Journal of Abnormal and Social Psychology, 64,* 136–142.

Deci, E.L. (1971). Effects of externally mediated rewards on intrinsic motivation. *Journal of Personality and Social Psychology, 18,* 105–115.

Deci, E.L. (1975). *Intrinsic motivation.* New York: Plenum.

Deci, E.L., & Ryan, R.M. (1980). The empirical exploration of intrinsic motivational processes. In L. Berkowitz (Ed.), *Advances in experimental social psychology* (Vol.13,pp. 39–80). New York: Academic Press.

Deci, E.L., & Ryan, R.M. (1985). *Intrinsic motivation and self-determination in human behavior.* New York: Plenum.

Deci, E.L., & Ryan, R.M. (1991). A motivational approach to self: Integration in personality. In R. Dienstbier and R.M. Ryan (Eds.), *Nebraska symposium on motivation: 1990* (pp. 237–288). Lincoln, NE: University of Nebraska Press.

Dentan, R.N. (1968). *The Semai: A nonviolent people of Malaysia.* New York: Holt, Rinehart & Winston.

Denzin, N.K. (Ed.). (1970). *Sociological methods.* Chicago: Aldine.

Denzin, N.K. (1989). *Interpretive biography.* Newbury Park, CA: Sage.

DePaulo, B.M., Kenny, D.A., Hoover, C., Webb, W., & Oliver, P.V. (1987). Accuracy of person perception: Do people know what kinds of impressions they convey? *Journal of Personality and Social Psychology, 52,* 303–315.

DeRaad, B., Mulder, E., Kloosterman, K., & Hofstee, W.K. (1988). Personality-descriptive verbs. *European Journal of Personality, 2,* 81–96.

deReincourt, A. (1974). *Sex and power in history.* New York: David McKay.

Derrida, J. (1972). *Positions.* Chicago: University of Chicago Press.

Derry, P.A., & Kuiper, N.A. (1981). Schematic processing and self-reference in clinical depression. *Journal of Abnormal Psychology, 90,* 286–297.

Deutsch, F.A. (1957). A footnote to Freud's "Fragment of an analysis of a case of hysteria." *Psychoanalytic Quarterly, 26,* 159–167.

Dewsbury, D.A. (1978). *Comparative animal behavior.* New York: McGraw-Hill.

Diener, E., Colvin, C.R., Pavot, W.G., & Allman, A. (1991). The psychic costs of intense positive affect. *Journal of Personality and Social Psychology, 61,* 492–503.

Diener, E., Larsen, R.J., & Emmons, R.A. (1984). Person– situation interactions: Choice of situations and congruence response models. *Journal of Personality and Social Psychology, 47,* 580–592.

Digman, J.M. (1989). Five robust trait dimensions: Development, stability, and utility. *Journal of Personality, 57,* 195–214.

Digman, J.M. (1990). Personality structure: Emergence of the five-factor model. In M.R. Rosenzweig and L.W. Porter (Eds.), *Annual review of psychology* (Vol. 41, pp. 417–440). Palo Alto, CA: Annual Reviews, Inc.

Digman, J.M., & Inouye, J. (1986). Further specification of the five robust factors of personality. *Journal of Personality and Social Psychology, 50,* 116–123.

Digman, J.M., & Takemoto-Chock, N.K. (1981). Factors in the natural language of personality: Reanalysis, comparison, and interpretation of six major studies. *Multivariate Behavioral Research, 16,* 149–170.

Dillehay, R.C. (1978). Authoritarianism. In H. London and J.E. Exner (Eds.), *Dimensions of personality* (pp. 85–128). New York: John Wiley & Sons.

Dilthey, W. (1976). The development of hermeneutics. In H.P. Rickman (Ed.), *W. Dilthey: Selected writings.* Cambridge: Cambridge University Press. (Originally published in 1900).

Dixon, T.M., & Baumeister, R.F. (1991). Escaping the self: The moderating effect of self-complexity. *Personality and Social Psychology Bulletin, 17,* 363–368.

Dixon, V.J. (1976). World views and research methodology. In L. King, V.J. Dixon, and W. Nobles (Eds.), *African philosophy: Assumptions and paradigms for research on black persons.* Los Angeles: Fanon Center Publication.

Dohrenwend, B.J., & Dohrenwend, B.P. (1974). *Stressful life events: Their nature and effects.* New York: John Wiley & Sons.

Doherty, W.J., & Baldwin, C. (1985). Shifts and stability in locus of control during the 1970s: Divergence of the sexes. *Journal of Personality and Social Psychology, 48,* 1048–1053.

Dollard, J. (1935). *Criteria for the life history.* New Haven: Yale University Press.

Dollard, J., Doob, L.W., Miller, N.E., Mowrer, O.H., & Sears, R.R. (1939). *Frustration and aggression.* New Haven, CT: Yale University Press.

Dollard, J., & Miller, N.E. (1950). *Personality and psychotherapy*. New York: McGraw-Hill.

Dollinger, S.J., & Cramer, P. (1990). Children's defensive responses and emotional upset following a disaster: A projective assessment. *Journal of Personality Assessment, 54*, 116–127.

Donley, R.E., & Winter, D.G. (1970). Measuring the motives of public officials at a distance: An exploratory study of American presidents. *Behavioral Science, 15*, 227–236.

Donnerstein, E. (1980). Aggressive erotica and violence toward women. *Journal of Personality and Social Psychology, 39*, 269–277.

Donovan, J.M. (1975). Identity status and interpersonal style. *Journal of Youth and Adolescence, 4*, 37–55.

Dostoyevsky, F. (1960). *Notes from underground and The grand inquisitor*. New York: Dutton (Transl. by Ralph E. Matlaw). (*Notes from Underground* was written in 1864).

Doty, R.M., Peterson, B.E., & Winter, D.G. (1991). Threat and authoritarianism in the United States, 1978–1987. *Journal of Personality and Social Psychology, 61*, 629–640.

Duck, S.W. (1973). *Personal relationships and personal constructs: A study of friendship formation*. London: John Wiley & Sons.

Duck, S.W. (1979). The personal and interpersonal in construct theory: Social and individual aspects of relationships. In P. Stringer and D. Bannister (Eds.), *Constructs of sociality and individuality* (pp. 279–297). London: Academic Press.

Duck, S.W., & Craig, G. (1978). Personality similarity and the development of friendship: A longitudinal study. *British Journal of Social and Clinical Psychology, 17*, 237–242.

Duck, S.W., & Spencer, C. (1972). Personal constructs, and friendship formation. *Journal of Personality and Social Psychology, 23*, 40–45.

Duke, M.P. (1986). Personality science: A proposal. *Journal of Personality and Social Psychology, 50*, 382–385.

Dukes, W.F. (1965). *N* =1. *Psychological Bulletin, 64*, 74–79.

Dunn, J., & Plomin, R. (1990). *Separate lives: Why siblings are so different*. New York: Basic Books.

Dworkin, R.H. & Goldfinger, S.H. (1985). Processing bias: Individual differences in the cognition of situations. *Journal of Personality, 53*, 480–501.

Eagle, M.N. (1984). *Recent developments in psychoanalysis: A critical evaluation*. New York: McGraw-Hill.

Edel, L. (1984). *Writing lives: Principia biographica*. New York: W.W. Norton.

Edel, L. (1985). *Henry James: A life*. New York: Harper & Row.

Edwards, A.L. (1957). *The Edwards Personal Preference Schedule*. New York: The Psychological Corporation.

Edwards, C.P., & Whiting, B.B. (1980). Differential socialization of girls and boys in light of cross-cultural research. In C.M. Super and S. Harkness (Eds.), *Anthropological perspectives on child development*. San Francisco: Jossey-Bass.

Edwards, V.J., & Spence, J.T. (1987). Gender-related traits, stereotypes, and schemata. *Journal of Personality and Social Psychology, 53*, 146–154.

Egeland, B., & Farber, E.A. (1984). Infant–mother attachment: Factors related to its development and change over time. *Child Development, 57*, 753–771.

Egeland, B., & Sroufe, L.A. (1981). Attachment and early maltreatment. *Child Development, 52*, 44–52.

Eibl-Eibesfeldt, I. (1977). *Ethology: The biology of behavior* (2nd ed.). New York: Holt, Rinehart & Winston.

Eisenberg, N., & Miller, P.A. (1987). The relation of empathy to prosocial and related behaviors. *Psychological Bulletin, 101*, 91–119.

Eisenberger, R., & Andornetto, M. (1986). Generalized self-control of delay and effort. *Journal of Personality and Social Psychology, 51*, 1020–1031.

Eisenberger, R., & Shank, D.M. (1985). Personal work ethic and effort training affect cheating. *Journal of Personality and Social Psychology, 49*, 520–528.

Ekehammer, B. (1974). Interactionism in personality from an historical perspective. *Psychological Bulletin, 81*, 1026–1048.

Ekman, P. (1972). Universal and cultural differences in facial expression of emotion. In J.R. Cole (Ed.), *Nebraska symposium on motivation* (Vol. 26). Lincoln, NE: University of Nebraska Press.

Ekman, P., Friesen, W.V., & Ellsworth, P.C. (1972). *Emotion in the human face: Guidelines for research and an integration of findings*. New York: Pergamon.

Elder, G.H., Jr. (1986). Military times and turning points in men's lives. *Developmental Psychology, 22*, 233–245.

Elkind, D. (1981). *Children and adolescents*. (3rd ed.). New York: Oxford University Press.

Ellenberger, H. (1970). *The discovery of the unconscious*. New York: Basic Books.

Elms, A.C. (1987). The personalities of Henry A. Murray. In R. Hogan and W.H. Jones (Eds.), *Perspectives in personality* (Vol. 2, pp. 1–14). Greenwich, CT: JAI Press.

Elms, A.C. (1988). Freud as Leonardo: Why the first psychobiography went wrong. *Journal of Personality, 56*, 19–40.

Elsbree, L. (1982). *The rituals of life: Patterns in narratives*. Port Washington, NY: Kennikat Press.

Emmons, R.A. (1984). Factor analysis and construct validity of the Narcissistic Personality Inventory. *Journal of Personality Assessment, 48*, 291–300.

Emmons, R.A. (1986). Personal strivings: An approach to personality and subjective well-being. *Journal of Personality and Social Psychology, 51*, 1058–1068.

Emmons, R.A. (1987). Narcissism: Theory and measurement. *Journal of Personality and Social Psychology, 52*, 11–17.

Emmons, R.A. (1989). The personal striving approach to personality. In L.A. Pervin (Ed.), *Goal concepts in personality and social psychology* (pp. 87–126). Hillsdale, NJ: Lawrence Erlbaum.

Emmons, R.A. (1992). Abstract versus concrete goals: Personal striving level, physical illness, and psychological well-being. *Journal of Personality and Social Psychology, 62*, 292–300.

Emmons, R.A., & Diener, E. (1985). Personality correlates of subjective well-being. *Personality and Social Psychology Bulletin, 11*, 89–97.

Emmons, R.A., & Diener, E. (1986a). Influence of impulsivity and sociability on subjective well-being. *Journal of Personality and Social Psychology, 50*, 1211–1215.

Emmons, R.A., & Diener, E. (1986b). An interactional approach to the study of personality and emotion. *Journal of Personality, 54*, 371–384.

Emmons, R.A., Diener, E., & Larsen, R.J. (1986). Choice and avoidance of everyday situations and affect congruence: Two models of reciprocal interactionism. *Journal of Personality and Social Psychology, 51*, 815–826.

Emmons, R.A., & King, L.A. (1988). Conflict among personal strivings: Immediate and long-term implications for psychological and physical well-being. *Journal of Personality and Social Psychology, 54*, 1040–1048.

Emmons, R.A., & McAdams, D.P. (1991). Personal strivings and motive dispositions: Exploring the links. *Personality and Social Psychology Bulletin, 17*, 648–654.

Endler, N.S. (1975). A person–situation interaction model for anxiety. In C.P. Spielberger and I.G. Sarason (Eds.), *Stress and anxiety* Vol. 1. Washington, DC: Hemisphere.

Endler, N.S. (1981). Persons, situations, and their interactions. In A.I. Rabin, J. Aronoff, A.M. Barclay, and R.A. Zucker (Eds.), *Further explorations in personality*, (pp. 114–151). New York: John Wiley & Sons.

Endler, N.S. (1983). Interactionism: A personality model, but not yet a theory. In M.M. Page (Ed.), *Personality: Current theory and research* (pp. 155–200). Lincoln, NB: University of Nebraska Press.

Endler, N.S., & Magnusson, D. (1976). Toward an interactional psychology of personality. *Psychological Bulletin, 83*, 956–974.

Endler, N.S., & Okada, M. (1975). A multidimensional measure of trait anxiety: The S—R Inventory of General Trait Anxiousness. *Journal of Consulting and Clinical Psychology, 43*, 319–329.

Endler, N.S., Parker, D.A., Bagby, R.M., & Cox, B.J. (1991). Multidimensionality of state and trait anxiety: Factor structure of the Endler Multidimensional Anxiety Scales. *Journal of Personality and Social Psychology, 60,* 919–926.

Entwisle, D.R. (1972). To dispel fantasies about fantasy-based measures of achievement motivation. *Psychological Bulletin, 77,* 377–391.

Epstein, S. (1973). The self-concept revisited: Or a theory of a theory. *American Psychologist, 28,* 404–416.

Epstein, S. (1979). The stability of behavior: 1. On predicting most of the people much of the time. *Journal of Personality and Social Psychology, 37,* 1097–1126.

Epstein, S. (1984). The stability of behavior across time and situations. In R.A. Zucker, J. Aronoff, and A.I. Rabin (Eds.), *Personality and the prediction of behavior* (pp. 209–268). New York: Academic Press.

Epstein, S. (1986). Does aggregation produce spuriously high estimates of behavior stability? *Journal of Personality and Social Psychology, 50,* 1199–1210.

Erdelyi, M.H. (1974). A new look at the new look: Perceptual defense and vigilance. *Psychological Review, 81,* 1–25.

Erdelyi, M.H. (1985). *Psychoanalysis: Freud's cognitive psychology.* New York: Freeman.

Erdelyi, M.H., & Goldberg, B. (1979). Let's not sweep repression under the rug: Toward a cognitive psychology of repression. In J.F. Kihlstrom and F.J. Evans (Eds.), *Functional disorders of memory* (pp. 355–402). Hillsdale, NJ: Lawrence Erlbaum.

Erikson, E.H. (1958). *Young man Luther: A study in psychoanalysis and history.* New York: W.W. Norton.

Erikson, E.H. (1959). Identity and the life cycle: Selected papers. *Psychological Issues, 1*(1), 5–165.

Erikson, E.H. (1963). *Childhood and society* (2nd ed.). New York: W.W. Norton.

Erikson, E.H. (1964). *Insight and responsibility.* New York: W.W. Norton.

Erikson, E.H. (1968). *Identity: Youth and crisis.* New York: W.W. Norton.

Erikson, E.H. (1969). *Gandhi's truth: On the origins of militant nonviolence.* New York: W.W. Norton.

Erikson, E.H. (1975). *Life history and the historical moment.* New York: W.W. Norton.

Erikson, E.H. (1978). Reflections on Dr. Borg's life cycle. In E.H. Erikson (Ed.), *Adulthood* (pp. 1–31). New York: W.W. Norton.

Erikson, E.H. (1980). Themes of adulthood in the Freud-Jung correspondence. In N.J. Smelser and E.H. Erikson (Eds.), *Themes of work and love in adulthood* (pp. 43–74). Cambridge, MA: Harvard University Press.

Erikson, E.H. (1982). *The life cycle completed: A review.* New York: W.W. Norton.

Eron, L.D. (1950). A normative study of the Thematic Apperception Test. *Psychological Monographs, 64* (315).

Eron, L.D. (1982). Parent–child interaction, television, violence, and aggression of children. *American Psychologist, 37,* 197–211.

Eron, L.D. (1987). The development of aggressive behavior from the perspective of a developing behaviorism. *American Psychologist, 42,* 435–442.

Eron, L.D., & Huesmann, L.R. (1984). The relation of prosocial behavior to the development of aggression and psychopathology. *Aggressive Behavior, 10,* 243–253.

Eron, L.D., Huesmann, L.K., Lefkowitz, M.M., & Walder, L.O. (1972). Does television violence cause aggression? *American Psychologist, 27,* 253–263.

Eron, L.D., Laulicht, J.H., Walder, L.O., Farber, I.E., & Spiegel, J.P. (1961). Application of role and learning theories to the study of the development of aggression in children. *Psychological Reports, 9,* 291–334.

Evans, I.M. (1983). Behavioral assessment. In C.E. Walker (Ed.), *The handbook of clinical psychology* (Vol. 1) (pp. 391–419). Homewood, IL: Dow Jones-Irwin.

Eysenck, H.J. (1952). *The scientific study of personality.* London: Routledge & Kegan Paul.

Eysenck, H.J. (1967). *The biological basis of personality.* Springfield, IL: Thomas.

Eysenck, H.J. (1973). *Eysenck on extraversion.* New York: John Wiley & Sons.

Eysenck, H.J. (1980). Hans Jurgen Eysenck. In G. Lindzey (Ed.), *A history of psychology in autobiography* (Vol. 7, pp. 153–187). San Francisco: W.H. Freeman.

Eysenck, H.J. (1990). Biological dimensions of personality. In L. Pervin (Ed.), *Handbook of personality theory and research* (pp. 244–276). New York: Guilford Press.

Eysenck, H.J., & Eysenck, S.B.G. (1964). *Manual of the Eysenck Personality Inventory.* London: University of London Press.

Eysenck, H.J., & Wilson, G.D. (1976). *Know your personality.* New York: Penguin.

Fairbairn, W.R.D. (1952). *Psychoanalytic studies of the personality: The object relation theory of personality.* London: Routledge & Kegan Paul.

Farkas, G.M., Evans, I.M., Sine, L.F., Eifert, G., Wittleib, E., & Vogelmann-Sine, S. (1979). Reliability and validity of the mercury-in-rubber strain gauge measure of penile circumference. *Behavior Therapy, 10,* 555–561.

Feather, N.T. (1961). The relationship of persistence at a task to expectation of success and achievement-related motives. *Journal of Abnormal and Social Psychology, 63,* 552–561.

Feather, N.T. (1975). *Values in education and society.* New York: The Free Press.

Feather, N.T. (1980). Values in adolescence. In J. Adelson (Ed.), *Handbook of adolescent psychology* (pp. 247–294). New York: John Wiley & Sons.

Feather, N.T. (1984). Masculinity, femininity, psychological androgyny, and the structure of values. *Journal of Personality and Social Psychology, 47,* 604–620.

Feeney, J.A., & Noller, P. (1990). Attachment style as a predictor of adult romantic relationships. *Journal of Personality and Social Psycholog, 58,* 281–291.

Feinstein, D., & Krippner, S. (1988). *Personal mythology: The psychology of your evolving self.* Los Angeles: Jeremy P. Tarcher.

Feldman, P. (1978). *Body type, oral imagery, and group behavior.* Unpublished doctoral dissertation, State University of New York at Buffalo.

Fenigstein, A., Scheier, M.F., & Buss, A.H. (1975). Public and private self-consciousness: Assessment and theory. *Journal of Consulting and Clinical Psychology, 43,* 522–527.

Feshbach, N.D., & Feshbach, S. (1969). The relationship between empathy and aggression in two age groups. *Developmental Psychology, 1,* 102–107.

Feshbach, S. (1974). The development and regulation of aggression: Some research gaps and a proposed cognitive approach. In W.W. Hartup and J. De Wit (Eds.), *Determinants and origins of aggressive behavior.* The Hague: Morton.

Feshbach, S., & Weiner, B. (1986). *Personality* (2nd ed.). Lexington, MA: D.C. Heath.

Festinger, L., Riecken, H., & Schachter, J. (1956). *When prophecy fails.* Minneapolis, MN: University of Minnesota Press.

Fineberg, H.V. (1989). The social dimension of AIDS. In *The science of AIDS: Readings from Scientific American* (pp. 111–121). New York: W.H. Freeman.

Fingarette, H. (1969). *Self-deception.* London: Routledge & Kegan Paul.

Fischer, R.E., & Juni, J. (1982). The anal personality: Self-disclosure, negativism, self-esteem, and superego severity. *Journal of Personality Assessment, 46,* 50–58.

Fischman, J. (1987). Type A on trial. *Psychology Today,* February, 42–50.

Fisher, J., & Greenberg, R.P. (1977). *The scientific credibility of Freud's theories and therapy.* New York: Basic Books.

Fiske, D.W. (1949). Consistency of the factorial structures of personality ratings from different sources. *Journal of Abnormal and Social Psychology, 44,* 329–344.

Fiske, D.W. (1974). The limits of the conventional science of personality. *Journal of Personality, 42,* 1–11.

Fiske, S.T., & Taylor, S.E. (1984). *Social cognition.* Reading, MA: Addison-Wesley.

Floderus-Myrhed, B., Pedersen, N., & Rasmuson, I. (1980). Assessment of heritability for personality, based on a short form of the Eysenck Personality Inventory: A study of 12,898 twin pairs. *Behavior Genetics, 10*, 153–162.

Fodor, E.M. (1984). The power motive and reactivity to power stresses. *Journal of Personality and Social Psychology, 47*, 853–859.

Fodor, E.M. (1985). The power motive, group conflict, and physiological arousal. *Journal of Personality and Social Psychology, 49*, 1408–1415.

Fodor, E.M., & Smith, T. (1982). The power motive as an influence on group decision making. *Journal of Personality and Social Psychology, 42*, 178–185.

Folkman, S., & Lazarus, R.J. (1980). An analysis of coping in a middle-aged community sample. *Journal of Health and Social Behavior, 21*, 219–239.

Folkman, S., & Lazarus, R.J. (1985). If it changes it must be a process: Study of emotion and coping during three stages of college examination. *Journal of Personality and Social Psychology, 48*, 150–170.

Folkman, S., Lazarus, R.S., Gruen, R.J., & DeLongis, A. (1986). Appraisal, coping, health status, and psychological symptoms. *Journal of Personality and Social Psychology, 50*, 571–579.

Fonagy, P., Steele, H., & Steele, M. (1991). Maternal representations of attachment during pregnancy predict the organization of infant–mother attachment at one year of age. *Child Development, 62*, 891–905.

Forer, L.K. (1977). Bibliography of birth order literature in the '70's. *Journal of Individual Psychology, 33*, 122–141.

Forgas, J.P. (1978). Social episodes and social structure in an academic setting: The social environment of an intact group. *Journal of Experimental Social Psychology, 14*, 434–448.

Forgas, J.P. (1983). Episode cognition and personality: A multidimensional analysis. *Journal of Personality, 51*, 34–48.

Forgas, J.P., Brown, L.B., & Menyhart, J. (1980). Dimensions of aggression: The perception of aggressive episodes. *British Journal of Social and Clinical Psychology, 19*, 215–227.

Forster, E.M. (1910). *Howards end.* Hammondsworth, Middlesex: Penguin.

Forster, E.M. (1954). *Aspects of the novel.* San Diego, CA: Harcourt Brace Jovanovich.

Forsyth, D.R. (1980). A taxonomy of ethical ideologies. *Journal of Personality and Social Psychology, 39*, 175–184.

Forsyth, D.R. (1985). Individual differences in information processing during moral judgment. *Journal of Personality and Social Psychology, 49*, 264–273.

Fowler, J.W. (1981). *Stages of faith: The psychology of human development and the quest for meaning.* New York: Harper & Row.

Fox, N.A., Kimmerly, N.L., & Schafer, W.D. (1991). Attachment to mother/attachment to father: A meta-analysis. *Child Development, 62*, 210–225.

Frable, D.E.S., & Bem, S.L. (1985). If you're gender schematic, all members of the opposite sex look alike. *Journal of Personality and Social Psychology, 49*, 459–468.

Francis, M.E., & Pennebaker, J.W. (1992). Putting stress into words: The impact of writing on physiological, absentee, and self-reported emotional well-being measures. *American Journal of Health Promotion, 6*, 280–287.

Frank, B.M., & Noble, J.P. (1985). Field independence–dependence and cognitive restructuring. *Journal of Personality and Social Psychology, 47*, 1129–1135.

Frank, S., & Quinlain, D. (1976). Ego developmental aspects of female delinquency. *Journal of Abnormal Psychology, 85*, 505–510.

Frankl, V. (1965). *The doctor and the soul: From psychotherapy to logotherapy.* New York: Alfred A. Knopf.

Frauman, D.C., Lynn, S.J., Hardaway, R., & Molteni, A. (1984). Effect of subliminal symbiotic activation on hypnotic rapport and susceptibility. *Journal of Abnormal Psychology, 93*, 481–483.

Frenkel, E. (1936). Studies in biographical psychology. *Character and Personality, 5*, 1–35.

Freud, A. (1946). *The ego and the mechanisms of defense.* New York: International Universities Press.

Freud, A. (1965). *Normality and pathology in childhood.* In Vol. 6 of *The writings of Anna Freud.* New York: International Universities Press.

Freud, E.L. (1960). (Ed.). *The letters of Sigmund Freud.* New York: Basic Books.

Freud, S. (1898/1962). Sexuality in the aetiology of the neuroses. In Vol. 3 of *The standard edition.* London: Hogarth.

Freud, S. (1900/1953). *The interpretation of dreams.* In Vols. 4 and 5 of *The standard edition.* London: Hogarth.

Freud, S. (1901/1960). *The psychopathology of everyday life.* In Vol. 6 of *The standard edition.* London: Hogarth.

Freud, S. (1905/1953). Three essays on the theory of sexuality. In Vol. 7 of *The standard edition.* London: Hogarth.

Freud, S. (1905/1960). Jokes and their relation to the unconscious. In Vol. 8 of *The standard edition.* London: Hogarth.

Freud, S. (1905/1963). *Dora: An analysis of a case of hysteria.* (With an Introduction by P. Rieff). New York: Macmillan.

Freud, S. (1909/1955). Analysis of a phobia in a five-year-old boy. In Vol. 10 of *The standard edition.* London: Hogarth.

Freud, S. (1909/1963). Notes upon a case of obsessional neurosis. In S. Freud, *Three case histories* (pp. 15–102). New York: Collier Books.

Freud, S. (1910/1957). *Five lectures on psychoanalysis.* In Vol. 11 of *The standard edition.* London: Hogarth.

Freud, S. (1910/1957). Leonardo da Vinci and a memory of his childhood. In Vol. 11 of *The standard edition.* London: Hogarth.

Freud, S. (1913/1958). *Totem and taboo.* In Vol. 13 of *The standard edition.* London: Hogarth.

Freud, S. (1914/1957). On narcissism: An introduction. In Vol. 14 of *The standard edition.* London: Hogarth.

Freud, S. (1915/1957). Repression. In Vol. 14 of *The standard edition.* London: Hogarth.

Freud, S. (1916/1947). *Leonardo da Vinci: A study in psychosexuality.* New York: Vintage Books. (Transl. by A.A. Brill).

Freud, S. (1916/1961). *Introductory lectures on psychoanalysis.* In Vols. 15 and 16 of *The standard edition.* London: Hogarth.

Freud, S. (1917/1957). Mourning and melancholia. In Vol. 14 of *The standard edition.* London: Hogarth.

Freud, S. (1920/1955). *Beyond the pleasure principle.* In Vol. 18 of *The standard edition.* London: Hogarth.

Freud, S. (1921/1955). Group psychology and the analysis of the ego. In Vol. 18 of *The standard edition.* London: Hogarth.

Freud, S. (1923/1961). *The ego and the id.* In Vol. 19 of *The standard edition.* London: Hogarth.

Freud, S. (1926/1959). *Inhibitions, symptoms, and anxiety.* In Vol. 20 of *The standard edition.* London: Hogarth.

Freud, S. (1927/1961). *The future of an illusion.* In Vol. 22 of *The standard edition.* London: Hogarth.

Freud, S. (1930/1961). *Civilization and its discontents.* In Vol. 21 of *The standard edition.* London: Hogarth.

Freud, S. (1933/1964). *New introductory lectures.* In Vol. 21 of *The standard edition.* London: Hogarth.

Freud, S. (1936/1964). A disturbance of memory on the Acropolis. In Vol. 22 of *The standard edition.* London: Hogarth.

Freud, S. (1940/1964). *An outline of psychoanalysis.* In Vol. 23 of *The standard edition.* London: Hogarth.

Freud, S. (1954). *The origins of psychoanalysis: Letters to Wilhelm Fliess, drafts and notes, 1897–1902.* M. Bonaparte, A Freud, and E. Kris (Eds.). New York: Basic Books.

Fried, C. (1971). Icarianism, masochism, and sex differences in fantasy. *Journal of Personality Assessment, 35*, 38–55.

Friedman, H.S., Hall, J.A., & Harris, M.J. (1985). Type A behavior, nonverbal expressive style, and health. *Journal of Personality and Social Psychology, 48*, 1299–1315.

Friedrich-Cofer, L., & Houston, A.C. (1986). Television violence and aggression: The debate continues. *Psychological Bulletin, 100*, 364–371.

Fromm, E. (1941). *Escape from freedom.* New York: Farrar & Rinehart.

Fromm, E. (1947). *Man for himself.* Greenwich, CT: Fawcett.

Fromm, E. (1955). *The sane society.* Greenwich, CT: Fawcett.

Fromm, E. (1962). *Sigmund Freud's mission: An analysis of his personality and influence.* New York: Simon & Schuster.

Fromm, E. (1973). *The anatomy of human destructiveness.* New York: Holt, Rinehart and Winston.

Frye, N. (1957). *Anatomy of criticism.* Princeton, NJ: Princeton University Press.

Fujita, F., Diener, E., & Sandvik, E. (1991). Gender differences in negative affect and well-being: The case for emotional intensity. *Journal of Personality and Social Psychology, 61,* 427–434.

Funder, D.C., & Block, J. (1989). The role of ego-control, ego-resiliency, and IQ in delay of gratification in adolescence. *Journal of Personality and Social Psychology, 57,* 1041–1050.

Funder, D.C., Block, J.H., & Block, J. (1983). Delay of gratification: Some longitudinal personality correlates. *Journal of Personality and Social Psychology, 44,* 1198–1213.

Funder, D.C., & Colvin, C.R. (1991). Explorations in behavioral consistency: Properties of persons, situations, and behaviors. *Journal of Personality and Social Psychology, 60,* 773–794.

Funder, D.C., & Ozer, D.J. (1983). Behavior as a function of the situation. *Journal of Personality and Social Psychology, 44,* 107–112.

Gadlin, H., & Rubin, S.H. (1979). Interactionism: A nonresolution of the person–situation controversy. In A.R. Buss (Ed.), *Psychology in social context* (pp. 213–238). New York: Irvington.

Gaertner, S.L., & Dovidio, J.F. (1977). The subtlety of white racism, arousal, and helping behavior. *Journal of Personality and Social Psychology, 35,* 691–707.

Gambrill, E.D., & Richey, C.A. (1975). An assertion inventory for use in assessment and research. *Behavior Therapy, 6,* 550–561.

Ganellen, R.J., & Blaney, P.H. (1984). Hardiness and social support as moderators of the effects of life stress. *Journal of Personality and Social Psychology, 47,* 156–163.

Gangestad, S.W. (1989). The evolutionary history of genetic variation: An emerging issue in the behavioral genetic study of personality. In D.M. Buss and N. Cantor (Eds.), *Personality psychology: Recent trends and emerging directions* (pp. 320–332). New York: Springer-Verlag.

Gangestad, S.W., & Simpson, J.A. (1990). Toward an evolutionary history of female sociosexual variation. *Journal of Personality, 58,* 69–96.

Gardner, R.W. (1951). Impulsivity as indicated by Rorschach test factors. *Journal of Consulting Psychology, 15,* 464–468.

Garnett, A.C. (1928). *Instinct and personality.* New York: Dodd, Mead & Company.

Gatchel, R.J., & Mears, F.G. (1982). *Personality: Theory, assessment, and research.* New York: St. Martin's Press.

Gay, P. (1984). *The bourgeois experience: Victoria to Freud.* Volume 1. *The education of the senses.* New York: Oxford University Press.

Gay, P. (1986). *The bourgeois experience: Victoria to Freud,* Volume 2. *The tender passion.* New York: Oxford University Press.

Geen, R.A. (1984). Preferred stimulation levels in introverts and extraverts: Effects on arousal and performance. *Journal of Personality and Social Psychology, 46,* 1303–1312.

Geen, R.A., & Thomas, S.L. (1986). The mediated effects of media violence on behavior. *Journal of Social Issues, 42*(3), 7–28.

Geertz, C. (1973). *The interpretation of cultures.* New York: Basic Books.

Geertz, C. (1979). From the native's point of view: On the nature of anthropological understanding. In P. Rabinow and W.M. Sullivan (Eds.), *Interpretive social science* (pp. 225–241). Berkeley, CA: University of California Press.

George, C., Kaplan, N., & Main, M. (1985). An adult attachment interview: Interview protocol. Unpublished manuscript, University of California at Berkeley.

Gergen, K.J. (1973). Social psychology as history. *Journal of Personality and Social Psychology, 26,* 309–320.

Gergen, K.J. (1982). *Toward transformation in social knowledge.* New York: Springer-Verlag.

Gergen, K.J. (1992). *The saturated self: Dilemmas of identity in contemporary life.* New York: Basic Books.

Ghiselli, E.E. (1956). Differentiation of individuals in terms of their predictability. *Journal of Applied Psychology, 40,* 374–377.

Giele, J.Z. (1980). Adulthood as transcendence of age and sex. In N.J. Smelser and E.H. Erikson (Eds.), *Themes of work and love in adulthood* (pp. 151–173). Cambridge, MA: Harvard University Press.

Giese, H., & Schmidt, S. (1968). *Studenten sexualität.* Hamburg: Rowohlt.

Gilligan, C.A. (1982). *In a different voice: Psychological theory and women's development.* Cambridge, MA: Harvard University Press.

Gittings, R. (1978). *The nature of biography.* Seattle, WA: University of Washington Press.

Glaser, B.G., & Strauss, A.L. (1967). *The discovery of grounded theory.* Chicago: Aldine.

Glass, D.C. (1977). *Behavior patterns, stress, and coronary disease.* Hillsdale, NJ: Lawrence Erlbaum.

Gleser, G.C., & Ihilevich, D. (1969). An objective instrument for measuring defense mechanisms. *Journal of Con-* *sulting and Clinical Psychology, 33,* 51–60.

Glisky, M.L., Tataryn, D.J., Tobias, B.A., Kihlstrom, J.F., & McConkey, K.M. (1991). Absorption, openness to experience, and hypnotizability. *Journal of Personality and Social Psychology, 60,* 263–272.

Goffman, E. (1959). *The presentation of self in everyday life.* Garden City, NY: Doubleday.

Gold, S.N. (1980). Relations between level of ego development and adjustment patterns in adolescents. *Journal of Personality Assessment, 44,* 630–638.

Goldberg, L.R. (1981). Language and individual differences: The search for universals in personality lexicons. In L. Wheeler (Ed.), *Review of personality and social psychology* (Vol. 2, pp. 141–166). Beverly Hills, CA: Sage.

Goldberg, L.R. (1990). An alternative "description of personality": The Big-Five factor structure. *Journal of Personality and Social Psychology, 59,* 1216–1229.

Goldfried, M.R., & Kent, R.N. (1972). Traditional vs. behavioral personality assessment: A comparison of methodological and theoretical issues. *Psychological Bulletin, 77,* 409–420.

Golding, W. (1962). *Lord of the flies.* New York: Coward-McCann.

Goleman, D. (1985). *Vital lies, simple truths: The psychology of self-deception.* New York: Simon & Schuster.

Gong-Guy, E., & Hammen, C.L. (1980). Causal perceptions of stressful live events in depressed and nondepressed outpatients. *Journal of Abnormal Psychology, 89,* 662–669.

Goodenough, D.R. (1978). Field dependence. In H. London and J.E. Exner (Eds.), *Dimensions of personality* (pp. 165–216). New York: John Wiley & Sons.

Goosens, F.A. (1987). Maternal employment and day care: Effects on attachment. In L.W.C. Tavecchio and M.H. van Ijzendoorn (Eds.), *Attachment in social networks* (pp. 135–183). Amsterdam: Elsevier.

Gorham, D. (1985). *Vera Brittain and The Great War.* Unpublished manuscript, Carleton University.

Gough, H.G. (1952). *The Adjective Checklist.* Palo Alto, CA: Consulting Psychologists Press.

Gough, H.G. (1957). *California Psychological Inventory: Manual.* Palo Alto, CA: Consulting Psychologists Press.

Gough, H.G. (1987). *California Psychological Inventory: Administrator's guide.* Palo Alto, CA: Consulting Psychologists Press.

Gough, H.G., & Bradley, P. (1992). Delinquent and criminal behavior as assessed by the revised California Psychological Inventory. *Journal of Clinical Psychology, 48,* 298–308.

Gould, R.L. (1980). Transformations during early and middle adult years. In N.J. Smelser and E.H. Erikson (Eds.),

Themes of work and love in adulthood (pp. 213–237). Cambridge, MA: Harvard University Press.

Gould, S.J. (1981). *The mismeasure of man*. New York: Norton.

Gray, J.A. (1982). *The neuropsychology of anxiety: An enquiry into the functions of the septo-hippocampal system*. New York: Oxford University Press.

Gray, J.A. (1987). Perspectives on anxiety and impulsivity: A commentary. *Journal of Research in Personality*, 21, 493–509.

Graziano, W.G., Feldesman, A.B., & Rahe, D.F. (1985). Extraversion, social cognition, and the salience of aversiveness in social encounters. *Journal of Personality and Social Psychology*, 49, 971–980.

Graziano, W.G., & Ward, D. (1992). Probing the Big Five in adolescence: Personality and adjustment during a developmental transition. *Journal of Personality*, 60, 425–439.

Green, R.C. (1981). Behavioral and physiological reactions to observed violence: Effects of prior exposure to aggressive stimuli. *Journal of Personality and Social Psychology*, 40, 868–875.

Greenberg, M.A., & Stone, A.A. (1992). Writing about disclosed versus undisclosed traumas: Immediate and long-term effects on mood and health. *Journal of Personality and Social Psychology*, 63, 75–84.

Greene, L.R. (1973). *Effects of field independence, physical proximity, and evaluative feedback on affective reactions and compliance in a dyadic interaction*. Unpublished doctoral dissertation, Yale University.

Gregg, G.S. (1991). *Self-representation: Life narrative studies in identity and ideology*. New York: Greenwood Press.

Grossmann, K.E., & Grossmann, K. (1991). Attachment quality as an organizer of emotional and behavioral responses in a longitudinal perspective. In C.M. Parkes, J. Stevenson-Hinde, and P. Marris (Eds.), *Attachment across the life cycle* (pp. 93–114). London: Tavistock/Routledge.

Groth-Marnat, G. (1984). *Handbook of psychological assessment*. New York: Van Nostrand Reinhold.

Gruber, H.E. (1989). The evolving systems approach to creative work. In D.B. Wallace and H.E. Gruber (Eds.), *Creative people at work* (pp. 3–24). New York: Oxford University Press.

Gruber, H.E., & Davis, S.N. (1988). Inching our way up Mount Olympus: The evolving-systems approach to creative thinking. In R.J. Sternberg (Ed.), *The nature of creativity: Contemporary psychological perspectives* (pp. 243–270). New York: Cambridge University Press.

Grunbaum, A. (1984). *The foundations of psychoanalysis: A philosophical critique*. Berkeley: University of California Press.

Guilford, J.P. (1959). *Personality*. New York: McGraw-Hill.

Guilford, J.P., & Zimmerman, W.S. (1949). *The Guilford-Zimmerman temperament survey*. Beverly Hills, CA: Sheridan Supply Company.

Gurtman, M.B. (1991). Evaluating the interpersonalness of personality scales. *Personality and Social Psychology Bulletin*, 17, 670–677.

Gurtman, M.B. (1992). Construct validity of interpersonal personality measures: The interpersonal circumplex as a nomological net. *Journal of Personality and Social Psychology*, 63, 105–118.

Gutmann, D. (1987). *Reclaimed powers: Toward a new psychology of men and women in later life*. New York: Basic Books.

Habermas, J. (1971). *Knowledge and human interests*. Boston: Beacon.

Hale, H.D., & Goldberg, L.R. (1967). Comparative validity of different strategies of constructing personality inventory scales. *Psychological Bulletin*, 67, 231–248.

Hales, S. (1979). *Developmental processes of self-esteem*. Paper presented at the Society for Research in Child Development, San Francisco.

Haley, J. (1980). *Leaving home: The therapy of disturbed young people*. New York: McGraw-Hill.

Hall, C.S. (1953). *The meaning of dreams*. New York: Harper & Row.

Hall, J.A., & Taylor, M.C. (1985). Psychological androgyny and the masculinity–femininity interactions. *Journal of Personality and Social Psychology*, 49, 429–435.

Hall, M.H. (1968). A conversation with Abraham H. Maslow. *Psychology Today*, 2(92), 35–37, 54–57.

Hallaq, J.H. (1977). Scaling and factor analyzing peak experiences. *Journal of Clinical Psychology*, 33, 77–82.

Hammen, C., & Cochran, S. (1981). Cognitive correlates of life stress and depression in college students. *Journal of Abnormal Psychology*, 90, 23–27.

Hampson, S.E., John, O.P., & Goldberg, L.R. (1986). Category breadth and hierarchical structure in personality: Studies of asymmetries in judgments of trait implications. *Journal of Personality and Social Psychology*, 51, 37–54.

Hankiss, A. (1981). On the mythological rearranging of one's life history. In D. Bertaux (Ed.), *Biography and society: The life history approach in the social sciences* (pp. 203–209). Beverly Hills, CA: Sage.

Hansen, R.D., & Hansen, C.H. (1988). Repression of emotionally tagged memories: The architecture of less complex emotions. *Journal of Personality and Social Psychology*, 55, 811–818.

Hanson, N.R. (1972). *Patterns of discovery: An inquiry into the conceptual foundations of science*. Cambridge: Cambridge University Press.

Hardaway, R.A. (1990). Subliminally activated symbiotic fantasies: Facts and artifacts. *Psychological Bulletin*, 107, 177–195.

Harre, R. (1989). Language games and the texts of identity. In J. Shotter and K.J. Gergen (Eds.), *Texts of identity* (pp. 20–35). London: Sage.

Hart, D. (1988). The adolescent self-concept in social context. In D.K. Lapsley and F.C. Power (Eds.), *Self, ego, and identity: Integrative approaches* (pp. 71–90). New York: Springer-Verlag.

Harter, S. (1983). Development perspectives on the self-system. In P.H. Mussen (Ed.), *Handbook of child psychology (4th ed.): Vol. 4. Socialization, personality, and social development* (pp. 275–386). New York: John Wiley & Sons.

Hartmann, H. (1939). *Ego psychology and the problem of adaptation*. New York: International Universities Press.

Hartmann, H. (1964). *Essays on ego psychology: Selected problems in psychoanalytic theory*. New York: International Universities Press.

Hartshorne, H., & May, M.A. (1928). *Studies in the nature of character*. Vol. 1. *Studies in deceit*. New York: Macmillan.

Hartup, W.W. (1974). Aggression in childhood: Developmental perspectives. *American Psychologist*, 29, 336–341.

Harvey, D. (1990). *The condition of postmodernity: An enquiry into the origins of cultural change*. Cambridge: Basil Blackwell.

Harvey, J.H., Weber, A.L., Galvin, K.S., Huszti, H.C., & Garnick, N.N. (1986). Attribution in the termination of close relationships: A special focus on the account. In R. Gilmour and S. Duck (Eds.), *The emerging field of personal relationships* (pp. 189–201). Hillsdale, NJ: Lawrence Erlbaum.

Haspel, K.C., & Harris, R.S. (1982). Effect of tachistoscopic stimulation of subconscious Oedipal wishes on competitive performance: A failure to replicate. *Journal of Abnormal Psychology*, 91, 437–443.

Hastie, R., Park, B., & Weber, R. (1984). Social memory. In R. Wyer and T.K. Srull (Eds.), *Handbook of social cognition* (Vol. 2). Hillsdale, NJ: Lawrence Erlbaum.

Hauser, S.T. (1976). Loevinger's model and measure of ego development: A critical review. *Psychological Bulletin*, 80, 928–955.

Hazan, C., & Shaver, P. (1987). Romantic love conceptualized as an attachment process. *Journal of Personality and Social Psychology*, 52, 511–524.

Hazan, C., & Shaver, P. (1990). Love and work: An attachment-theoretical perspective. *Journal of Personality and Social Psychology*, 59, 270–280.

Hazen, N.L., & Durrett, M.E. (1982). Relationship of security of attachment to exploration and cognitive mapping abilities in 2-year-olds. *Development Psychology*, 18, 751–759.

Heaven, P.C.L. (1985). Construction and validation of a measure of authoritarian personality. *Journal of Personality Assessment, 49*, 545–555.

Heckhausen, H. (1967). *The anatomy of achievement motivation*. New York: Academic Press.

Heilbrun, A.B. (1981). *Human sex-role behavior*. New York: Pergamon.

Heilbrun, A.B., Jr., Palchanis, N., & Friedberg, E. (1986). Self-report measurement of Type A behavior: Toward refinement and improved prediction. *Journal of Personality Assessment, 50*, 525–539.

Heilbrun, K.S. (1980). Silverman's subliminal psychodynamic activation: A failure to replicate. *Journal of Abnormal Psychology, 89*, 560–566.

Helson, R. (1976). Women and creativity. In A. Rothenberg and C.R. Hausman (Eds.), *The creativity question* (pp. 242–250). Durham, NC: Duke University Press.

Helson, R. (1987). Which of those young women with creative potential became productive? II. From college to midlife. In R. Hogan and W.H. Jones (Eds.), *Perspectives in personality* (Vol. 2, pp. 51–92). Greenwich, CT: JAI Press.

Helson, R. (1990). Creativity in women: Outer and inner views over time. In M.A. Runco and R.S. Albert (Eds.), *Theories of creativity* (pp. 46–58). Newbury Park, CA: Sage.

Helson, R., Mitchell, V., & Moane, G. (1984). Personality and patterns of adherence and nonadherence to the social clock. *Journal of Personality and Social Psychology, 46*, 1079–1096.

Helson, R., & Wink, P. (1992). Personality change in women from early 40s to the early 50s. *Psychology and Aging, 7*, 46–55.

Hermans, H.J.M. (1976). *Value areas and their development: Theory and method of self-confrontation*. Amsterdam: Swets & Zeitlinger.

Hermans, H.J.M. (1988). On the integration of nomothetic and idiographic research methods in the study of personal meaning. *Journal of Personality, 56*, 785–812.

Hermans, H.J.M. (1991). The person as co-investigator in self-research: Valuation theory. *European Journal of Personality, 5*, 217–234.

Hermans, H.J.M. (1992a). The narrative approach in personality psychology. Sixth Conference of the European Association for Personality Psychology, Groningen, the Netherlands.

Hermans, H.J.M. (1992b). Unhappy self-esteem: A meaningful exception to the rule. *Journal of Psychology, 126*, 555–570.

Hermans, H.J.M. (1992c). Telling and retelling one's self-narrative: A contextual approach to life-span development. *Human Development, 35*, 361–375.

Hermans, H.J.M., & Bonarius, H. (1991). The person as co-investigator in personality research. *European Journal of Personality, 5*, 199–216.

Hermans, H.J.M., Kempen, H.J.G., & van Loon, R.J.P. (1992). The dialogical self: Beyond individualism and rationalism. *American Psychologist, 47*, 23–33.

Hermans, H.J.M., & van Gilst, W. (1991). Self-narrative and collective myth: An analysis of the Narcissus story. *Canadian Journal of Behavioural Science, 23*, 423–440.

Herrnstein, R.J., & Boring, E.G. (1965). (Eds.). *A sourcebook in the history of psychology*. Cambridge, MA: Harvard University Press.

Hess, R.D., & Shipman, V.C. (1965). Early experience and the socialization of cognitive modes in children. *Child Development, 34*, 869–886.

Hewitt, J.K. (1984). Normal components of personality variation. *Journal of Personality and Social Psychology, 47*, 671–675.

Higgins, E.T. (1987). Self-discrepancy: A theory relating self and affect. *Psychological Review, 94*, 319–340.

Hill, G.J. (1989). An unwillingness to act: Behavioral appropriateness, situational constraint, and self-efficacy in shyness. *Journal of Personality, 57*, 872–890.

Hill, T., & Lewicki, P. (1991). The unconscious. In V.J. Derlega, B.A. Winstead, and W.H. Jones (Eds.), *Personality: Contemporary theory and research* (pp. 207–229). Chicago: Nelson-Hall.

Hillman, J. (1979). *The dream and the underworld*. New York: Harper & Row.

Hoffman, M.L. (1981). Is altruism part of human nature? *Journal of Personality and Social Psychology, 40*, 121–137.

Hofstee, W.K.B., deRaad, B., & Goldberg, L.R. (1992). Integration of the Big Five and the circumplex approaches to trait structure. *Journal of Personality and Social Psychology, 63*, 146–163.

Hogan, R. (1973). Moral conduct and moral character: A psychological perspective. *Psychological Bulletin, 79*, 217–232.

Hogan, R. (1976). *Personality theory: The personological tradition*. Englewood Cliffs, NJ: Prentice-Hall.

Hogan, R. (1982). A socioanalytic theory of personality. In M. Page (Ed.), *Nebraska symposium on motivation* (pp. 55–89). Lincoln, NE: University of Nebraska Press.

Hogan, R. (1986). *Hogan Personality Inventory manual*. Minneapolis, MN: National Computer Systems.

Hogan, R. (1987). Personality psychology: Back to basics. In J. Aronoff, A.I. Rabin, and R.A. Zucker (Eds.), *The emergence of personality* (pp. 79–104). New York: Springer.

Hogan, R., DeSoto, C.B., & Solano, C. (1977). Traits, tests, and personality research. *American Psychologist, 32*, 255–264.

Hogan, R., Jones, W.H., & Cheek, J.M. (1985). Socioanalytic theory: An alternative to armadillo psychology. In B.R. Schlenker (Ed.), *The self and social life* (pp. 175–198). New York: McGraw-Hill.

Holmes, D.S. (1967). Pupillary response, conditioning and personality. *Journal of Personality and Social Psychology, 5*, 98–103.

Holmes, D.S. (1974). Investigations of repression: Differential recall of material experimentally or naturally associated with ego threat. *Psychological Bulletin, 81*, 632–653.

Holmes, D.S. (1978). Projection as a defense mechanism. *Psychological Bulletin, 85*, 677–688.

Holmes, D.S., McGilley, B.M., & Houston, B.K. (1984). Task-related arousal of Type A and Type B persons: Level of challenge and response speciality. *Journal of Personality and Social Psychology, 46*, 1322–1327.

Holmes, T.H., & Rahe, R.H. (1967). The Social Readjustment Rating Scale. *Journal of Psychosomatic Research, 11*, 213–218.

Holt, R.R. (1962). Individuality and generalization in the psychology of personality: An evaluation. *Journal of Personality, 30*, 377–402.

Holt, R.R. (1978). *Methods in clinical psychology. Vol. 1: Projective assessment*. New York: Plenum.

Holt, R.R. (1980). Loevinger's measure of ego development: Reliability and national norms for male and female short forms. *Journal of Personality and Social Psychology, 39*, 909–920.

Holt, R.R. (1985). The current status of psychoanalytic theory. *Psychoanalytic Psychology, 2*, 289–315.

Hoppe, C. (1972). *Ego development and conformity behavior*. Unpublished doctoral dissertation, Washington University in St. Louis.

Horney, K. (1939). *New ways in psychoanalysis*. New York: Norton.

Horney, K. (1945). *Our inner conflicts*. New York: Norton.

Horney, K. (1950). *Neurosis and human growth*. New York: Norton.

Hornstein, H.A., Fisch, E., & Holmes, M. (1968). Influence of a model's feeling about his behavior and his relevance as a comparison other on observers' helping behavior. *Journal of Personality and Social Psychology, 10*, 222–226.

Horowitz, M.J. (1979). *States of mind: Analysis of change in psychotherapy*. New York: Plenum.

Houts, A.C., Cook, T.D., & Shadish, W.R., Jr. (1986). The person-situation debate: A critical multiplist perspective. *Journal of Personality, 54*, 52–105.

Howard, G.S. (1989). *A tale of two stories: Excursions into a narrative psychology*. Notre Dame, IN: University of Notre Dame Press.

Howard, G.S. (1991). Culture tales: A narrative approach to thinking, cross-cultural psychology, and psychotherapy. *American Psychologist, 46*, 187–197.

Howard, J. (1984). *Margaret Mead: A life*. New York: Simon & Schuster.

Howard, J.H., Cunningham, D.A., &

Rechnitzer, P.A. (1977). Work patterns associated with Type A behavior: A managerial population. *Human Relations*, *30*, 825–836.

Huesmann, L.R., & Malamuth, N.M. (1986). Media violence and antisocial behavior. *Journal of Social Issues*, *42*(3), 1–6.

Hull, C. (1943). *Principles of behavior*. New York: Appleton-Century-Crofts.

Hull, J.G., Van Treuren, R.R., & Virnellis, S. (1987). Hardiness and health: A critique and alternative approach. *Journal of Personality and Social Psychology*, *53*, 518–530.

Hyland, M.E. (1988). Motivational control theory: An integrative framework. *Journal of Personality and Social Psychology*, *55*, 642–651.

Ingram, R.E. (1984). Toward an information-processing analysis of depression. *Cognitive Therapy and Research*, *8*, 443–478.

Ingram, R.E., Smith, T.W., & Brehm, S.S. (1983). Depression and information processing: Self-schemata and the encoding of self-referent information. *Journal of Personality and Social Psychology*, *45*, 412–420.

Inhelder, B., & Piaget, J. (1958). *The growth of logical thinking from childhood to adolescence*. New York: Basic Books.

Isabella, R.A., Belsky, J., & von Eye, A. (1989). Origins of infant–mother attachment: An examination of interactional synchrony during the infant's first year. *Developmental Psychology*, *25*, 12–21.

Izard, C.E. (1971). *The face of emotion*. New York: Appleton-Century-Crofts.

Izard, C.E. (1977). *Human emotions*. New York: Plenum.

Izard, C.E. (1978). On the ontogenesis of emotions and emotion—cognition relationships in infancy. In M. Lewis and L.A. Rosenblum (Eds.), *The development of affect* (pp. 389–413). New York: Plenum.

Jackson, D.N. (1971). The dynamics of structured personality tasks. *Psychological Review*, *78*, 229–248.

Jackson, D.N. (1974). *The Personality Research Form*. Port Huron, MI: Research Psychologists Press.

Jackson, D.N., & Messick, S. (1958). Content and style in personality assessment. *Psychological Bulletin*, *55*, 243–252.

Jackson, D.N., & Paunonen, S.V. (1980). Personality structure and assessment. In M.R. Rosenzweig and L.W. Porter (Eds.), *Annual review of psychology: 31* (pp. 503–552). Palo Alto, CA: Annual Reviews, Inc.

Jackson, J. (1981). *The effects of fantasies of oneness with mother and father on the ego functioning of male and female schizophrenics*. Unpublished doctoral dissertation. New York University.

Jacques, E. (1965). Death and the midlife crisis. *International Journal of Psychoanalysis*, *46*, 502–514.

James, W. (1892/1963). *Psychology*. Greenwich, CT: Fawcett.

Janis, I.L. (1972). *Victims of group think*. Boston: Houghton Miflin.

Janoff-Bulman, R., & Brickman, P. (1980). Expectations and what people learn from failure. In N.T. Feather (Ed.), *Expectancy, incentive, and failure*. Hillesdale, NJ: Lawrence Erlbaum.

Jay, P. (1984). *Being in the text: Self-representation from Wordworth to Roland Barthes*. Ithaca, NY: Cornell University Press.

Jemmott, J.B., III. (1987). Social motives and susceptibility to disease: Stalking individual differences in health risks. *Journal of Personality*, *55*, 267–298.

Jenkins, C.D., Zyzanski, S.J., & Rosenman, R.H. (1976). Risk of new myocardial infarction in middle-age men with manifest coronary heart disease. *Circulation*, *53*, 342–347.

Jenkins, S.R. (1987). Need for achievement and women's careers over 14 years: Evidence for occupational structure effects. *Journal of Personality and Social Psychology*, *53*, 922–932.

Jennings, J.L. (1986). Husserl revisited: The forgotten distinction between psychology and phenomenology. *American Psychologist*, *41*, 1231–1240.

John, O.P. (1989). Towards a taxonomy of personality descriptors. In D.M. Buss and N. Cantor (Eds.), *Personality psychology: Recent trends and emerging directions* (pp. 261–271). New York: Springer-Verlag.

John, O.P. (1990). The "Big Five" factor taxonomy: Dimensions of personality in the natural language and in questionnaires. In L. Pervin (Ed.), *Handbook of personality theory and research* (pp. 66–100). New York: Guilford Press.

Johnson, J.E., Petzel, T.P., Hartney, L.M., & Morgan, L.M. (1983). Recall and importance ratings of completed and uncompleted tasks as a function of depression. *Cognitive Therapy and Research*, *7*, 51–56.

Johnson, R.N. (1972). *Aggression in man and animals*. Philadelphia: W.B. Saunders.

Jones, A., & Crandall, R. (1986). Validation of a short index of self-actualization. *Personality and Social Psychology Bulletin*, *12*, 63–73.

Jones, E. (1961). *The life and work of Sigmund Freud*. New York: Basic Books.

Jones, E.E., Kanouse, D.E., Kelley, H.H., Nisbett, R.E., Valins, S., & Weiner, B. (1971). *Attribution: Perceiving the causes of behavior*. Morristown, NJ: General Learning Press.

Jones, E. E., & Nisbett, R.E. (1972). The actor and the observer: Divergent perceptions of the causes of behavior. In E.E. Jones, D.E. Kanouse, H.H. Kelley, R.E. Nisbett, S. Valins, and B. Weiner (Eds.), *Attribution: Perceiving the causes of behavior* (pp. 79–94). Morristown, NJ: General Learning Press.

Jones, J.M. (1983). The concept of race in social psychology: From color to culture. In L. Wheeler and P. Shaver (Eds.), *Review of personality and social psychology* (Vol. 4, pp. 117–150). Beverly Hills, CA: Sage.

Jones, R.R., Reid, J.B., & Patterson, G.R. (1975). Naturalistic observation in clinical assessment. In P. McReynolds (Ed.), *Advances in psychological assessment* (Vol. 3, pp. 42–95). San Francisco: Jossey-Bass.

Jones, W.H., Briggs, S.R., & Smith, T.G. (1986). Shyness: Conceptualization and measurement. *Journal of Personality and Social Psychology*, *51*, 629–639.

Jones, W.H., & Russell, D. (1982). The social reticence scale: An objective measure of shyness. *Journal of Personality Assessment*, *46*, 629–631.

Jordan, D. (1971). *Parental antecedents and personality characteristics of ego identity statuses*. Unpublished doctoral dissertation, State University of New York at Binghampton.

Josselson, R.L. (1973). Psychodynamic aspects of identity formation in college women. *Journal of Youth and Adolescence*, *2*, 3–52.

Josselson, R.L. (1988). The embedded self: I and Thou revisited. In D.K. Lapsley and F.C. Power (Eds.), *Self, ego, and identity: Integrative approaches* (pp. 91–106). New York: Springer-Verlag.

Judson, H.F. (1980). The rage to know. *Atlantic Monthly*.

Jung, C.G. (1936/1969). *The archetypes and the collective unconscious*. In Vol. 9 of *The collected works of C.G. Jung*. Princeton, NJ: Princeton University Press.

Jung, C.G. (1961). *Memories, dreams, reflections*. New York: Vintage.

Jung, C.G., von Franz, M.-L., Henderson, J.L., Jacobi, J., & Jaffe, A. (1964). *Man and his symbols*. Garden City, NY: Doubleday.

Juni, S., Masling, J., & Brannon, R. (1979). Interpersonal touching and orality. *Journal of Personality Assessment*, *43*, 235–237.

Juni, S., & Rubenstein, V. (1982). Anality and routine. *Journal of Personality Assessment*, *46*, 142.

Justice, M.T. (1969). *Field dependency, intimacy of topic and interpersonal distance*. Unpublished doctoral dissertation, University of Florida.

Kagan, J. (1984). *The nature of the child*. New York: Basic Books.

Kagan, J. (1989). Temperamental Contributions to Social behavior. *American Psychologist*, *44*, 668–674.

Kagan, J., & Moss, H.A. (1962). *Birth to maturity*. New York: John Wiley & Sons.

Kahane, C. (1985). Introduction: Why Dora now? In C. Bernheimer and C. Kahane (Eds.), *In Dora's case: Freud-hysteria-feminism* (pp. 19–31). New York: Columbia University Press.

Kahn, S., Zimmerman, G., Csikszentmihalyi, M., & Getzels, J.W. (1985). Relations between identity in young adulthood and intimacy at midlife. *Journal of Personality and Social Psychology, 49*, 1316–1322.

Kahneman, D., & Tversky, A. (1984). Choices, values, and frames. *American Psychologist, 39*, 341–350.

Kanfer, F.H., & Saslow, G. (1969). Behavioral diagnosis. In C.M. Franks (Ed.), *Behavior therapy: Appraisal and status*. New York: McGraw-Hill.

Kegan, R. (1982). *The evolving self: Problem and process in human development*. Cambridge, MA: Harvard University Press.

Kelley, H.H., & Michela, J.L. (1980). Attribution theory and research. In M.R. Rosenzweig and L.W. Porter (Eds.), *Annual review of psychology* (Vol. 31, pp. 457–502). Palo Alto, CA: Annual Reviews, Inc.

Kelly, E.L., & Conley, J.J. (1987). Personality and compatibility: A prospective analysis of marital stability and marital satisfaction. *Journal of Personality and Social Psychology, 52*, 27–40.

Kelly, G. (1955). *The psychology of personal constructs*. New York: W.W. Norton.

Kelly, K.E., & Houston, B.K. (1985). Type A behavior in employed women: Relation to work, marital and leisure variables, social support, stress, tension, and health. *Journal of Personality and Social Psychology, 48*, 1067–1079.

Keniston, K. (1963). Inburn: An American Ishmael. In R.W. White (Ed.), *The study of lives* (pp. 40–70). New York: Holt, Rinehart & Winston.

Kenrick, D.T. (1989). A biosocial perspective on mates and traits: Reuniting personality and social psychology. In D.M. Buss and N. Cantor (Eds.), *Personality psychology: Recent trends and emerging directions* (pp. 308–319). New York: Springer-Verlag.

Kenrick, D.T., & Funder, D.C. (1988). Profiting from controversy: Lessons from the person-situation debate. *American Psychologist, 43*, 23–34.

Kenrick, D.T., Montello, D.R. & McFarlane, S. (1985). Personality: Social learning, social cognition, or sociobiology? In R. Hogan and W.H. Jones (Eds.), *Perspectives in personality* (Vol. 1, pp. 201–234). Greenwich, CT: JAI Press.

Kenrick, D.T., & Stringfield, D.O. (1980). Personality traits and the eye of the beholder: Crossing some traditional philosophical boundaries in the search for consistency in all the people. *Psychological Review, 87*, 88–104.

Kernberg, O. (1975). *Borderline conditions and pathological narcissism*. New York: Jason Aronson.

Kernberg, O. (1980). *Internal world and external reality*. New York: Jason Aronson.

Kierkegaard, S. (1843/1941). Fear and trembling. In W. Lowrie (Transl.), *Fear and trembling and sickness unto death*. Princeton, NJ: Princeton University Press.

Kiesler, D.J. (1982). The 1982 interpersonal circle: A taxonomy of complementarity in human transactions. *Psychological Review, 90*, 185–214.

Kihlstrom, J.F. (1981). On personality and memory. In N. Cantor and J.F. Kihlstrom (Eds.), *Personality, cognition, and social interaction* (pp. 123–179). Hillsdale, NJ: Lawrence Erlbaum.

Kihlstrom, J.F. (1984). Conscious, subconscious, unconscious: A cognitive perspective. In K.S. Bowers and D. Meichenbaum (Eds.), *The unconscious reconsidered* (pp. 149–211).

Kihlstrom, J.F. (1990). The psychological unconscious. In L. Pervin (Ed.), *Handbook of personality theory and research* (pp. 445–464). New York: Guilford Press.

Kihlstrom, J.F., & Harackiewicz, J.M. (1982). The earliest recollection: A new survey. *Journal of Personality, 50*, 134–148.

King, G.A., & Sorrentino, R.M. (1983). Psychological dimensions of goal-oriented interpersonal situations. *Journal of Personality and Social Psychology, 44*, 140–162.

Kirk, J., & Miller, M.L. (1986). *Reliability and validity in qualitative research*. Beverly Hills, CA: Sage.

Kirkpatrick, L.A. (1992). An attachment-theory approach to the psychology of religion. *The International Journal for the Psychology of Religion, 2*, 3–28.

Kirkpatrick, L.A., & Shaver, P. (1992). An attachment-theoretical approach to romantic love and religious belief. *Personality and Social Psychology Bulletin, 18*, 266–275.

Klages, L. (1926/1932). *The science of character*. London: George Allen & Unwin.

Klavetter, R.E., & Mogar, R.E. (1967). Peak experiences: Investigation of their relationship to psychedelic therapy and self-actualization. *Journal of Humanistic Psychology, 7*, 171–177.

Kline, P. (1972). *Fact and fantasy in Freudian theory*. London: Methuen.

Klinger, E. (1966). Fantasy need achievement as a motivational construct. *Psychological Bulletin, 66*, 291–308.

Klinger, E. (1977). *Meaning and void*. Minneapolis, MN: University of Minnesota Press.

Kluckhohn, C., & Murray, H.A. (1953). Personality formation: The determinants. In C. Kluckhohn, H.A. Murray, and D.M. Schneider (Eds.), *Personality in nature, society, and culture* (pp. 53–67). New York: Alfred A. Knopf.

Knowles, E.S., & Sibicky, M.E. (1990). Continuity and diversity in the stream of selves: Metaphorical resolutions of William James's one-in-many-selves paradox. *Personality and Social Psychology Bulletin, 16*, 676–687.

Kobak, R.R., & Hazan, C. (1991). Attachment in marriage: Effects of security and accuracy of working models. *Journal of Personality and Social Psychology, 60*, 861–869.

Kobasa, S.C. (1979). Stressful life events, personality, and health: An inquiry into hardiness. *Journal of Personality and Social Psychology, 37*, 1–12.

Kobasa, S.C. (1982). Commitment and coping in stress resistance among lawyers. *Journal of Personality and Social Psychology, 42*, 707–717.

Kobasa, S.C. (1985). Personality and health: Specifying and strengthening and conceptual links. In P. Shaver (Ed.), *Review of personality and social psychology* (Vol. 6, pp. 291–311). Beverly Hills, CA: Sage.

Kobasa, S.C., Maddi, S.R., & Kahn, S. (1982). Hardiness and health: A prospective study. *Journal of Personality and Social Psychology, 42*, 168–177.

Kobasa, S.C., & Pucetti, M.C. (1983). Personality and social resources in stress resistance. *Journal of Personality and Social Psychology, 45*, 839–850.

Kock, S.W. (1965). *Management and motivation*. Unpublished doctoral dissertation, Swedish School of Economics.

Koestner, R., Bernieri, F., & Zuckerman, M. (1989). Trait-specific versus person-specific moderators of cross-situational consistency. *Journal of Personality, 57*, 1–16.

Koestner, R., Weinberger, J., & McClelland, D.C. (1991). Task-intrinsic and social-extrinsic sources of arousal for motives assessed in fantasy and self-report. *Journal of Personality, 59*, 57–82.

Koestner, R., Zuckerman, M., & Koestner, J. (1987). Praise, involvement, and intrinsic motivation. *Journal of Personality and Social Psychology, 53*, 383–390.

Kohlberg, L. (1969). Stage and sequence: The cognitive-developmental approach to socialization. In D.A. Goslin (Ed.), *Handbook of socialization theory and research* (pp. 347–480). Skokie, IL: Rand McNally.

Kohlberg, L. (1981). *The philosophy of moral development: Moral stages and the idea of justice* (Vol. 1). *Essays on moral development*. New York: Harper & Row.

Kohut, H. (1971). *The analysis of the self*. New York: International Universities Press.

Kohut, H. (1977). *The restoration of the self*. New York: International Universities Press.

Kohut, H. (1984). *How does analysis cure?* Chicago: University of Chicago Press.

Konner, M. (1983). *The tangled wing: Biological constraints on the human spirit*. New York: Harper & Row.

Kopp, C.G. (1982). Antecedents of self-regulation: A developmental perspective. *Developmental Psychology, 18*, 199–214.

Kotre, J. (1984). *Outliving the self: Generativity and the interpretation of lives. Baltimore, MD: Johns Hopkins University Press.

Kottak, C.P. (1979). Cultural anthropology (2nd ed.). New York: Random House.

Krahe, B. (1992). Personality and social psychology: Toward a synthesis. London: Sage.

Krebs, D.L. (1975). Empathy and altruism. Journal of Personality and Social Psychology, 32, 1124–1146.

Kreuz, I.E., & Rose, R.M. (1972). Assessment of aggressive behavior and plasma testosterone in a young criminal population. Psychosomatic Medicine, 34, 321–332.

Krippendorff, K. (1980). Content analysis: An introduction to its methodology. Beverly Hill, CA: Sage.

Kris, E. (1952). Psychoanalytic explorations in art. New York: International Universities Press.

Kris, E. (1954). Editor's introduction. In M. Bonaparte, E. Kris, and A. Freud (Eds.), The origins of psychoanalysis: Letters of Sigmund Freud to Wilhelm Fliess, drafts and notes, 1897–1902. New York: Basic Books.

Kuhn, T.S. (1962). The structure of scientific revolutions. Chicago: University of Chicago Press.

Kunce, J.T., & Anderson, W.P. (1984). Perspectives on uses of the MMPI in nonpsychiatric settings. In P. McReynolds and G.J. Chelune (Eds.), Advances in psychological assessment (Vol. 6, pp. 41–76). San Francisco: Jossey-Bass.

Kurdek, L.A., & Schmitt, J.P. (1986). Interaction of sex role self-concept with relationship quality and relationship belief, in married, heterosexual cohabiting, gay, and lesbian couples. Journal of Personality and Social Psychology, 51, 365–370.

Kushner, H. (1981). When bad things happen to good people. New York: Avon.

Labov, W. (1972). Language in the inner city. Philadelphia: University of Pennsylvania Press.

Lachman, M.E. (1986). Locus of control in aging research: A case for multi-dimensional and domain-specific assessment. Psychology and Aging, 1, 34–40.

Lachman, R., Lachman, J.L., & Butterfield, E.C. (1979). Cognitive psychology and human information processing. Hillsdale, NJ: Lawrence Erlbaum.

LaFreniere, P.J., & Sroufe, L.A. (1985). Profiles of peer competence in the preschool: Interrelations between measures, influence of social ecology, and relation to attachment history. Developmental Psychology, 21, 56–69.

Lamb, M.E. (1976). The role of the father in child development. New York: John Wiley & Sons.

Lamiell, J.T. (1981). Toward an idiothetic psychology of personality. American Psychologist, 36, 276–289.

Lando, H.A., & Donnerstein, E.I. (1978). The effects of a model's success or failure on subsequent aggressive behavior. Journal of Research in Personality, 12, 225–234.

Langbaum, R. (1982). The mysteries of identity: A theme in modern literature. Chicago: University of Chicago Press.

Langer, E.J. (1975). The illusion of control. Journal of Personality and Social Psychology, 32, 311–328.

Langer, E.J. (1981). Old age: An artifact? In J. McGaugh and S. Kiesler (Eds.), Aging: Biology and behavior. New York: Academic Press.

Langer, E.J., & Rodin, J. (1976). The effects of choice and enhanced personal responsibility for the aged: A field experiment in an institutional setting. Journal of Personality and Social Psychology, 34, 191–198.

Lanyon, R.I. (1984). Personality assessment. In M.R. Rosenzweig and L.W. Porter (Eds.), Annual review of psychology (Vol. 35, pp. 667–701). Palo Alto, CA: Annual Reviews, Inc.

Lapsley, D.K., & Power, F.C. (Eds.). (1988). Self, ego, and identity: Integrative approaches. New York: Springer-Verlag.

Lapsley, D.K., & Rice, K. (1988). The "new look" at the imaginary audience and personal fable: Toward a general model of adolescent ego development. In D.K. Lapsley and F.C. Power (Eds.), Self, ego, and identity: Integrative approaches (pp. 109–129). New York: Springer-Verlag.

Larsen, R.J., & Diener, E. (1987). Affect intensity as an individual difference characteristic: A review. Journal of Research in Personality, 21, 1–39.

Larsen, R.J., & Kasimatis, M. (1991). Day-to-day symptoms: Individual differences in the occurrence, duration, and emotional concomitants of minor daily illnesses. Journal of Personality, 59, 387–423.

Lasch, C. (1979). The culture of narcissism: American life in an age of diminishing expectations. New York: W.W. Norton.

Lazarus, R.J. (1982). Thoughts on the selection between emotion and cognition. American Psychologist, 37, 1019–1024.

Lazarus, R.J. (1984). On the primacy of cognition. American Psychologist, 39, 124–129.

Leak, G.K., & Christopher, S.B. (1982). Freudian psychoanalysis and sociobiology: A synthesis. American Psychologist, 37, 313–322.

Leary, T. (1957). Interpersonal diagnosis of personality. New York: Ronald Press.

Lee, L., & Snarey, J. (1988). The relationship between ego and moral development: A theoretical review and empirical analysis. In D.K. Lapsley and F.C. Power (Eds.), Self, ego, and identity: integrative approaches (pp. 151–178). New York: Springer-Verlag.

Lefcourt, H.M., Martin, R.A., Fick, C.M., & Salch, W.E. (1985). Locus of control for affiliation and behavior in social interactions. Journal of Personality and Social Psychology, 48, 755–759.

Leigh, L., Westen, D., Barrends, A., & Mendel, M. (in press). Assessing complexity of representations of people from TAT and interview data. Journal of Personality.

Lepper, M.R., & Greene, D. (1978). The hidden costs of reward: New perspectives on the psychology of human motivation. New York: Halsted.

Lepper, M.R., Greene, D. & Nisbett, R.E. (1973). Undermining children's intrinsic interest with extrinsic rewards: A test of the "overjustification" hypothesis. Journal of Personality and Social Psychology, 28, 129–137.

Lerner, H., & St. Peter, S. (1984). The Rorschach H response and object relations. Journal of Personality Assessment, 48, 345–350.

Levine, L.E., & Hoffman, M.L. (1975). Empathy and cooperation in 4-year-olds. Developmental Psychology, 11, 533–534.

LeVine, R.A. (1982). Culture, behavior, and personality. (2nd ed.). New York: Aldine.

Levinson, D.J. (1978). The seasons of a man's life. New York: Alfred A. Knopf.

Levinson, D.J. (1981). Explorations in biography: Evolution of the individual life structure in adulthood. In A.I. Rabin, J. Aronoff, A.M. Barclay, and R.A. Zucker (Eds.). Further explorations in personality (pp. 44–79). New York: John Wiley & Sons.

Levinson, D.J., Darrow, C.M., Klein, E.B., Levinson, M.H., & McKee, B. (1974). The psychosocial development of men in early adulthood and the mid-life transition. In D. Ricks, A. Thomas, and M. Roff (Eds.), Life history research in psychopathology (Vol. 3). Minneapolis, MN: University of Minnesota Press.

Lewicki, P. (1984). Self-schemata and social information processing. Journal of Personality and Social Psychology, 47, 1177–1190.

Lewicki, P. (1986). Nonconscious social information processing. New York: Academic Press.

Lewin, K. (1935). A dynamic theory of personality. New York: McGraw-Hill.

Lewinsohn, P.M., & Libet, T. (1972). Pleasant events, activity schedules, and depression. Journal of Abnormal Psychology, 79, 291–295.

Lewis, H.B. (1971). Shame and guilt in neurosis. New York: International Universities Press.

Lewis, H.B. (1985). Depression vs. paranoia: Why are there sex differences in mental illness? Journal of Personality, 53, 150–178.

Lewis, M. (1990). Self-knowledge and social development in early life. In L. Pervin (Ed.), Handbook of personality theory and research (pp. 277–300). New York: Guilford Press.

Lewis, M., & Brooks-Gunn, J. (1979). Social cognition and the acquisition of self. New York: Plenum.

Lewontin, R.C., Rose, S., & Kamin, L.J. (1985). Not in our genes: Biology, ideology, and human nature. New York: Pantheon Books.

Liebert, R.M., & Baron, R.A. (1972). Short-term effects of televised aggression on children's aggressive behavior. In J.P. Murray, E.A. Rubinstein, and G.A. Comstock (Eds.), Television and social behavior: II. Television and social learning. Washington, DC: U.S. Government Printing Office.

Liebert, R.M., & Spiegler, M.D. (1978). Personality: Strategies and issues. (3rd ed.). Homewood, IL: Dorsey Press.

Lifton, R.J. (1979). The broken connection: On death and the continuity of life. New York: Simon & Schuster.

Linde, C. (1990). Life-stories: The creation of coherence. Palo Alto, CA: Institute for Research on Learning Monograph No. IRL90-0001.

Lindzey, G. (1952). Thematic Apperception Test: Interpretive assumptions and related empirical evidence. Psychological Bulletin, 49, 1–25.

Lindzey, G. (1959). On the classification of projective techniques. Psychological Bulletin, 56, 158–168.

Lindzey, G. (1961). Projective techniques and cross-cultural research. New York: Appleton-Century-Crofts.

Linville, P.W. (1987). Self-complexity as a cognitive buffer against stress-related illness and depression. Journal of Personality and Social Psychology, 52, 663–676.

Lishman, W.A. (1972). Selective factors in memory. Part I: Age, sex, and personality attributes. Psychological Medicine, 2, 121–138.

Little, B.R. (1989). Personal projects analysis: Trivial pursuits, magnificent obsessions, and the search for coherence. In D.M. Buss and N. Cantor (Eds.), Personality psychology: Recent trends and emerging directions (pp.15–31). New York: Springer-Verlag.

Littlefield, C.H., & Rushton, J.P. (1986). When a child dies: The sociobiology of bereavement. Journal of Personality and Social Psychology, 51, 797–802.

Littlefield, C.H., & Rushton, J.P. (1988). Levels of explanation in sociobiology and psychology: A rejoinder to Archer. Journal of Personality and Social Psychology, 56, 625–628.

Livson, N., & Peskin, H. (1980). Perspectives on adolescence from longitudinal research. In J. Adelson (Ed.), Handbook of adolescent psychology (pp. 47–98). New York: John Wiley & Sons.

Lloyd, G.G., & Lishman, W.A. (1975). Effect of depression on the speed of recall of pleasant and unpleasant experiences. Psychological Medicine, 5, 173–180.

Locke, J. (1690). An essay concerning human understanding. Excerpted in R.J. Herrnstein and E. G. Boring (Eds.). (1965), A source book in the history of psychology (pp. 584–586).

Cambridge, MA: Harvard University Press.

Loehlin, J.C. (1989). Partitioning environmental and genetic contributions to behavioral development. American Psychologist, 44, 1285–1292.

Loehlin, J.C. (1992). Genes and environment in personality development. Newbury Park, CA: Sage.

Loehlin, J.C., & Nichols, R.C. (1976). Heredity, environment, and personality: A study of 850 sets of twins. Austin, TX: Texas University Press.

Loehlin, J.C., Willerman, L., & Horn, J.M. (1987). Personality resemblance in adoptive families: A 10-year follow-up. Journal of Personality and Social Psychology, 53, 961–969.

Loevinger, J. (1957). Objective tests as instruments of psychological theory. Psychological Reports, 3, 635–694.

Loevinger, J. (1969). Theories of ego development. In L. Breger (Ed.), Clinical-cognitive psychology: Models and integrations. Englewood Cliffs, NJ: Prentice-Hall.

Loevinger, J. (1976). Ego development. San Francisco: Jossey-Bass.

Loevinger, J. (1979). Construct validity of the sentence-completion test of ego development. Applied Psychological Measurement, 3, 281–311.

Loevinger, J. (1983). On ego development and the structure of personality. Developmental Review, 3, 339–350.

Loevinger, J. (1984). On the self and predicting behavior. In R.A. Zucker, J. Aronoff, and A.I. Rabin (Eds.), Personality and the prediction of behavior (pp. 43–68). New York: Academic Press.

Loevinger, J. (1987). Paradigms of personality. New York: W.H. Freeman.

Loevinger, J. (1992). Has psychology lost its conscience? Henry Murray Award Address, American Psychological Association, Washington DC.

Loevinger, J., Cohn, L.D., Bonneville, L.P., Redmore, C., Streich, D.D., & Sargent, M. (1985). Ego development in college. Journal of Personality and Social Psychology, 48, 947–962.

Loevinger, J., & Wessler, R. (1970). Measuring ego development 1. Construction and use of a sentence-completion test. San Francisco: Jossey-Bass.

Loevinger, J., Wessler, R., & Redmore, C. (1970). Measuring ego development 2. Scoring manual for women and girls. San Francisco: Jossey-Bass.

London, P. (1970). The rescuers: Motivational hypotheses about Christians who saved Jews from the Nazis. In J.R. Macaulay and L. Berkowitz (Eds.), Altruism and helping behavior. New York: Academic Press.

Lorenz, K. (1950). The comparative method in studying innate behavior patterns. Symposium of the Society of Experimental Biology, 4, 211–268.

Lorenz, K. (1969). On aggression. New York: Harcourt, Brace & World.

Lowenthal, M.F., Thurnher, M., Chiriboga, D., & Associates. (1975). Four

stages of life: A comparative study of men and women facing transitions. San Francisco, CA: Jossey-Bass.

Luborsky, L., & Crits-Christoph, P. (1991). Understanding transference: The core conflictual relationship theme method. New York: Basic Books.

Luborsky, L., Crits-Christoph, P., & Mellon, J. (1986). Advent of objective measures of the transference concept. Journal of Consulting and Clinical Psychology, 54, 39–47.

Lucariello, J. (1990). Canonicality and consciousness in child narrative. In B.K. Britton and A.D. Pellegrini (Eds.), Narrative thought and narrative language (pp. 131–150). Hillsdale, NJ: Lawrence Erlbaum.

Luria, A.R. (1972). The man with a shattered world. New York: Basic Books. (Transl. by L. Solotaroff).

Lundy, A. (1985). The reliability of the Thematic Apperception Test. Journal of Personality Assessment, 49, 141–145.

Lütkenhaus, P., Grossmann, K.E., & Grossmann, K. (1985). Infant-mother attachment at twelve months and style of interaction with stranger at the age of three years. Child Development, 56, 1538–1542.

Lykken, D.T., McGue, M., Tellegen, A., & Bouchard, Jr., T.J. (1992). Emergenesis: Genetic traits that may not run in families. American Psychologist, 47, 1565–1577.

Lyons-Ruth, K., Connell, D.B., Zoll, D., & Stahl, J. (1987). Infants at social risk: Relations among infant maltreatment, maternal behavior, and infant attachment behavior. Developmental Psychology, 23, 223–232.

Maccoby, E.E. (1991). Different reproductive strategies in males and females. Child Development, 62, 676–681.

Maccoby, E.E., & Jacklin, C.N. (1974). The psychology of sex differences. Stanford, CA: Stanford University Press.

Maccoby, E.E., & Martin, J.A. (1983). Socialization in the context of the family: Parent–child interaction. In P.H. Mussen (Ed.), Handbook of child psychology, (4th ed.), Vol. 4 (pp. 1–102). New York: John Wiley & Sons.

MacIntyre, A. (1984). After virtue. Notre Dame, IN: University of Notre Dame Press.

Mackenzie-Mohr, D., & Zanna, M.P. (1990). Treating women as sexual objects: Look to the (gender schematic) male who has viewed pornography. Personality and Social Psychology Bulletin, 16, 296–308.

MacKinnon, D.W. (1962). The nature and nurture of creative talent. American Psychologist, 17, 484–495.

MacKinnon, D.W. (1963). Creativity and images of the self. In R.W. White (Ed.), The study of lives (pp. 250–279). New York: Prentice-Hall.

MacKinnon, D.W. (1965). Personality

and the realization of creative potential. *American Psychologist, 20,* 273–281.

MacPhillamy, D.J., & Lewinsohn, P.M. (1974). Depression as a function of levels of desired and obtained pleasures. *Journal of Abnormal Psychology, 83,* 651–657.

Maddi, S.R. (1980). *Personality theories: A comparative analysis* (4th ed.). Homewood, IL: The Dorsey Press.

Maddi, S.R. (1984). Personology for the 1980s. In R.A. Zucker, J. Aronoff, and A.I. Rabin (Eds.), *Personality and the prediction of behavior* (pp. 7–41). New York: Academic Press.

Maddi, S.R., Kobasa, S.C., & Hoover, M. (1979). An alienation test. *Journal of Humanistic Psychology, 19*(4), 73–76.

Magnusson, D., & Endler, N.S. (1977). *Personality at the crossroads: Current issues in interactional psychology.* New York: John Wiley & Sons.

Maher, B. (1969). (Ed.). *Clinical psychology and personality: The selected papers of George Kelly.* New York: John Wiley & Sons.

Mahler, M.S. (1968). *On human symbiosis and the vicissitudes of individuation: Infantile psychosis.* New York: International Universities.

Mahler, M.S., Pine, F., & Bergman, A. (1975). *The psychological birth of the human infant.* New York: Basic Books.

Mahoney, M.J., & Arnkoff, D.B. (1979). Self-management. In O.F. Pomerleau and J.P. Brady (Eds.), *Behavioral medicine: Theory and practice.* Baltimore, MD: Williams & Wilkins.

Main, M. (1981). Avoidance in the service of attachment: A working paper. In K. Immelmann, G. Barlow, L. Petrinovich, and M. Main (Eds.), *Behavioral development: The Bielefeld interdisciplinary project.* New York: Cambridge University Press.

Main, M. (1983). Exploration, play, and cognitive functioning related to mother–infant attachment. *Infant Behavior and Development, 6,* 167–174.

Main, M. (1991). Metacognitive knowledge, metacognitive monitoring, and singular (coherent) vs. multiple (incoherent) model of attachment. In C.M. Parkes, J. Stevenson-Hinde, and P. Marris (Eds.), *Attachment across the life cycle* (pp. 127–159). London: Tavistock/Routledge.

Main, M., & Cassidy, J. (1988). Categories of response to reunion with the parent at age 6: Predictable from infant attachment classifications and stable over a 1-month period. *Developmental Psychology, 24,* 415–426.

Main, M., Kaplan, N., & Cassidy, J. (1985). Security in infancy, childhood, and adulthood: A move to the level of representation. *Monographs of the Society for Research in Child Development, 50* (1 & 2), 66–104.

Main, M., & Weston, D. (1981). Security of attachment to mother and father: Related to conflict behavior and the readiness to establish new relationships. *Child Development, 52,* 932–940.

Malamuth, N.M., & Briere, J. (1986). Sexual violence in the media: Indirect effects on aggression against women. *Journal of Social Issues, 42*(3), 75–92.

Mancuso, J.C. (1986). The acquisition and use of narrative grammar structure. In T.R. Sarbin (Ed.), *Narrative psychology: The storied nature of human conduct* (pp. 91–110). New York: Praeger.

Mandel, N.M., & Shrauger, J.S. (1980). The effects of self-evaluation statements on heterosocial approach in shy and nonshy males. *Cognitive Therapy and Research, 4,* 369–381.

Mandler, J.M. (1984). *Stories, scripts, and scenes: Aspects of schema theory.* Hillsdale, NJ: Lawrence Erlbaum.

Manning, M.M., & Wright, T.L. (1983). Self-efficacy expectancies and the persistence of pain control in childbirth. *Journal of Personality and Social Psychology, 45,* 421–431.

Marcel, G. (1964). *Creative fidelity.* New York: Farrar, Straus & Giroux.

Marcia, J.E. (1966). Development and validation of ego identity status. *Journal of Personality and Social Psychology, 3,* 551–558.

Marcia, J.E. (1967). Ego identity status: Relationships to change in self-esteem, "general maladjustment," and authoritarianism. *Journal of Personality, 35,* 119–133.

Marcia, J.E. (1980). Identity in adolescence. In J. Adelson (Ed.), *Handbook of adolescent psychology* (pp. 159–187). New York: John Wiley & Sons.

Marcia, J.E., & Friedman, M.L. (1970). Ego identity status in college women. *Journal of Personality, 38,* 249–263.

Marcus, S. (1977). Freud and Dora: Story, history, case history. In T. Shapiro (Ed.), *Psychoanalysis and contemporary science* (pp. 389–442). New York: International Universities Press.

Markus, H. (1977). Self-schemata and processing information about the self. *Journal of Personality and Social Psychology, 35,* 63–78.

Markus, H. (1983). Self-knowledge: An expanded view. *Journal of Personality, 51,* 543–565.

Markus, H., Crane, M., Bernstein, S., & Saladi, M. (1982). Self-schemas and gender. *Journal of Personality and Social Psychology, 42,* 38–50.

Markus, H., & Cross, S. (1990). The interpersonal self. In L. Pervin (Ed.), *Handbook of personality theory and research* (pp. 576–608). New York: Guilford Press.

Markus, H., & Nurius, P. (1986). Possible selves. *American Psychologist, 41,* 954–969.

Markus, H., & Sentis, K. (1982). The self in social information processing. In J. Suls (Ed.), *Psychological perspectives on the self* (Vol. 1, pp. 41–70). Hillsdale, NJ: Lawrence Erlbaum.

Markus, H., & Smith, J. (1981). The influence of self-schema on the perception of others. In N. Cantor and J.F. Kihlstrom (Eds.), *Personality, cognition, and social interaction* (pp. 233–262). Hillsdale, NJ: Lawrence Erlbaum.

Marsh, H.W., Antill, J.K., & Cunningham, J.P. (1987). Masculinity, femininity, and androgyny: Relations of self-esteem and social desirability. *Journal of Personality, 55,* 661–685.

Marshall, V. (1975). Age and awareness of finitude in developmental gerontology. *Omega, 6,* 113–129.

Martin, J.A. (1981). A longitudinal study of the consequence of early mother-infant interaction: A microanalytic approach. *Monographs of the Society for Research in Child Development, 46* (3, Serial No. 190).

Martindale, C. (1989). Personality, situation, and creativity. In J.A. Golver, R.R. Ronning, and C.R. Reynolds (Eds.), *Handbook of creativity* (pp. 211–232). New York: Plenum.

Masling, J. (1986). Orality, pathology, and interpersonal behavior. In J. Masling (Ed.), *Empirical studies of psychoanalytic theories* (Vol. 2, pp. 73–106). New York: Analytic Press.

Masling, J., Johnson, C., & Saturansky, C. (1974). Oral imagery, accuracy of perceiving others, and performance in Peace Corps training. *Journal of Personality and Social Psychology, 30,* 414–419.

Masling, J., O'Neill, R, & Jayne, C. (1981). Orality and latency of volunteering to serve as experimental subjects. *Journal of Personality Assessment, 45,* 20–22.

Masling, J., O'Neill, R., & Katkin, E.S. (1982). Autonomic arousal, interpersonal climate, and orality. *Journal of Personality and Social Psychology, 42,* 529–534.

Maslow, A.H. (1954). *Motivation and personality.* New York: Harper & Row.

Maslow, A.H. (1968). *Toward a psychology of being* (2nd ed.). New York: D. Van Nostrand.

Maslow, A.H. (1976). Creativity in self-actualizing people. In A. Rothenberg and C.R. Hausman (Eds.), *The creativity question* (pp. 86–92). Durham, NC: Duke University Press.

Masson, J.M. (1984a). Freud and the seduction theory. *Atlantic Monthly,* February, 33–60.

Masson, J.M. (1984b). *The assault on truth: Freud's suppression of the seduction theory.* New York: Farrar, Straus & Giroux.

Matarazzo, J.D. (1965). The interview. In B. Wolman (Ed.), *Handbook of clinical psychology.* New York: McGraw-Hill.

Matas, L., Arend, R., & Sroufe, L.A. (1978). Continuity of adaptation in the second year: The relationship between quality of attachment and later competence. *Child Development, 49,* 547–556.

Matthews, K.A. (1978). Assessment and

developmental antecedents of the coronary-prone behavior pattern in children. In T.M. Dembroski, S.M. Weiss, J.L. Sheilds, S.G. Haynes, and M. Feinleib (Eds.), *Coronary prone behavior* (pp. 207–217). New York: Springer-Verlag.

Matthews, K.A. (1982). Psychological perspectives on the Type A behavior pattern. *Psychological Bulletin, 91,* 293–323.

Matthews, K.A., Krantz, D.S., Dembroski, T.M., & MacDougall, J.M. (1982). Unique and common variance in structured interview and Jenkins Activity Survey measures of the Type A behavior pattern. *Journal of Personality and Social Psychology, 42,* 303–313.

May, R. (1958). The origins and significance of the existential movement in psychology. In R. May, E. Angel, and H.F. Ellenberger (Eds.), *Existence* (pp. 3–36). New York: Simon & Schuster.

May, R. (1966). Sex differences in fantasy patterns. *Journal of Projective Techniques and Personality Assessment, 30,* 576–586.

May, R. (1975). Further studies on deprivation/enhancement patterns. *Journal of Personality Assessment, 39,* 116–122.

May, R. (1980). *Sex and fantasy: Patterns of male and female development.* New York: W.W. Norton.

McAdams, D.P. (1980). A thematic coding system for the intimacy motive. *Journal of Research in Personality, 14,* 413–432.

McAdams, D.P. (1982a). Intimacy motivation. In A.J. Stewart (Ed.), *Motivation and Society* (pp. 133–171). San Francisco: Jossey-Bass.

McAdams, D.P. (1982b). Experiences of intimacy and power: Relationships between social motives and autobiographical memory. *Journal of Personality and Social Psychology, 42,* 292–302.

McAdams, D.P. (1984a). Human motives and personal relationships. In V. Derlega (Ed.), *Communication, intimacy, and close relationships* (pp. 41–70). New York: Academic Press.

McAdams, D.P. (1984b). Scoring manual for the intimacy motive. *Psychological Documents, 14,* No. 2613, p. 7.

McAdams, D.P. (1984c). Love, power, and images of the self. In C.Z. Malatesta and C.E. Izard (Eds.), *Emotion in adult development* (pp. 159–174). Beverly Hills, CA: Sage.

McAdams, D.P. (1985a). Fantasy and reality in the death of Yukio Mishima. *Biography: An Interdisciplinary Quarterly, 8,* 292–317.

McAdams, D.P. (1985b). *Power, intimacy, and the life story: Personological inquiries into identity.* New York: The Guilford Press.

McAdams, D.P. (1985c). The "imago": A key narrative component of identity. In P. Shaver (Ed.), *Review of personality and social psychology* (Vol. 6, pp. 115–141). Beverly Hills, CA: Sage.

McAdams, D.P. (1987). A life-story model of identity. In R. Hogan and W.H. Jones (Eds.), *Perspectives in personality* (Vol. 2, pp. 15–50). Greenwich, CT: JAI Press.

McAdams, D.P. (1988a). Personal needs and personal relationships. In S.W. Duck (Ed.), *Handbook of personal relationships* (pp. 7–22). London: John Wiley & Sons.

McAdams, D.P. (1988b). Self and story. In A.J. Stewart, J.M. Healy, and D.J. Ozer (Eds.), *Perspectives in personality: Approaches to understanding lives.* London: Jessica Kingsley

McAdams, D.P. (1988c). Biography, narrative, and lives: An introduction. *Journal of Personality, 56,* 1–18.

McAdams, D.P. (1989). *Intimacy: The need to be close.* New York: Doubleday.

McAdams, D.P. (1990). Unity and purpose in human lives: The emergence of identity as a life story. In A.I. Rabin, R.A. Zucker, R.A. Emmons, and S. Frank (Eds.), *Studying persons and lives* (pp. 148–200). New York: Springer.

McAdams, D.P. (1992a). How the I and the Me come to be: Attachment vs. intimacy. Invited address, Sixth International Conference of the Society for the Study of Personal Relationships, Orono, Maine.

McAdams, D.P. (1992b). The five-factor model *in* personality: A critical appraisal. *Journal of Personality, 60,* 329–361.

McAdams, D.P. (1993). *The stories we live by: Personal myths and the making of the self.* New York: William Morrow.

McAdams, D.P. (in press a). Image, theme, and character in the life story of Karen Horney. In C. Franz and A.J. Stewart (Eds.), *Women creating lives.* Boulder, CO: Westview Press.

McAdams, D.P. (in press b). Can personality change? Levels of stability and growth in personality across the lifespan. In T. Heatherton and J. Weinberger (Eds.), *Can personality change?* Washington, DC: American Psychological Association.

McAdams, D.P., Booth, L., & Selvik, R. (1981). Religious identity among students at a private college: Social motives, ego stage, and development. *Merrill-Palmer Quarterly, 27,* 219–239.

McAdams, D.P., & Bryant, F. (1987). Intimacy motivation and subjective mental health in a nationwide sample. *Journal of Personality, 55,* 395–413.

McAdams, D.P., & Constantian, C.A. (1983). Intimacy and affiliation motives in daily living: An experience sampling analysis. *Journal of Personality and Social Psychology, 45,* 851–861.

McAdams, D.P., & de St. Aubin, E. (1992). A theory of generativity and its assessment through self-report, behavioral acts, and narrative themes in au-

tobiography. *Journal of Personality and Social Psychology, 62,* 1003–1015.

McAdams, D.P., de St. Aubin, E., & Logan, R.L. (1993). Generativity among young, midlife, and older adults. *Psychology and Aging, 8,* 221–230.

McAdams, D.P., Healy, S., & Krause, S. (1984). Social motives and patterns of friendship. *Journal of Personality and Social Psychology, 47,* 828–838.

McAdams, D.P., Jackson, R.J., & Kirshnit, C. (1984). Looking, laughing, and smiling in dyads as a function of intimacy motivation and reciprocity. *Journal of Personality, 52,* 261–273.

McAdams, D.P., Lensky, D.B., Daple, S.A., & Allen, J. (1988). Depression and the organization of autobiographical memory. *Journal of Social and Clinical Psychology, 7,* 332–349.

McAdams, D.P., Lester, R., Brand, P., McNamara, W., & Lensky, D.B. (1988). Sex and the TAT: Are women more intimate than men? Do men fear intimacy? *Journal of Personality Assessment, 52,* 397–409.

McAdams, D.P., & Losoff, M. (1984). Friendship motivation in fourth and sixth graders: A thematic analysis. *Journal of Social and Personal Relationships, 1,* 11–27.

McAdams, D.P., & Ochberg, R.L. (Eds.). (1988). *Psychobiography and life narratives.* Durham, NC: Duke University Press.

McAdams, D.P., & Powers, J. (1981). Themes of intimacy in behavior and thought. *Journal of Personality and Social Psychology, 40,* 573–587.

McAdams, D.P., Rothman, S., & Lichter, S.R. (1982). Motivational profiles: A study of former political radicals and politically moderate adults. *Personality and Social Psychology Bulletin, 8,* 593–603.

McAdams, D.P., Ruetzel, K., & Foley, J.M. (1986). Complexity and generativity at mid-life: Relations among social motives, ego development, and adults' plans for the future. *Journal of Personality and Social Psychology, 50,* 800–807.

McAdams, D.P., & Vaillant, G.E. (1982). Intimacy motivation and psychosocial adjustment: A longitudinal study. *Journal of Personality Assessment, 46,* 586–593.

McClelland, D.C. (1951). *Personality.* New York: Holt, Rinehart & Winston.

McClelland, D.C. (1961). *The achieving society.* New York: D. Van Nostrand.

McClelland, D.C. (1963). The Harlequin complex. In R.W. White (Ed.), *The study of lives* (pp. 94–119). New York: Holt, Rinehart & Winston.

McClelland, D.C. (1965). *N* achievement and entrepreneurship: A longitudinal study. *Journal of Personality and Social Psychology, 1,* 389–392.

McClelland, D.C. (1975). *Power: The inner experience.* New York: Irvington.

McClelland, D.C. (1979). Inhibited power

motivation and high blood pressure in men. *Journal of Abnormal Psychology, 88*, 182–190.

McClelland, D.C. (1980). Motive dispositions: The merits of operant and respondent measures. In L. Wheeler (Ed.), *Review of personality and social psychology* (Vol. 1, pp. 10–41). Beverly Hills, CA: Sage.

McClelland, D.C. (1981). Is personality consistent? In A.I. Rabin, J. Aronoff, A.M. Barclay, & R.A. Zucker (Eds.), *Further explorations in personality* (pp. 87–113). New York: John Wiley & Sons.

McClelland, D.C. (1985). *Human motivation*. Glenview, IL: Scott, Foresman.

McClelland, D.C., Alexander, C., & Marks, E. (1982). The need for power, stress, immune function, and illness among male prisoners. *Journal of Abnormal Psychology, 91*, 61–70.

McClelland, D.C., Atkinson, J.W., Clark, R.A., & Lowell, E.L. (1953). *The achievement motive*. New York: Appleton-Century-Crofts.

McClelland, D.C., & Boyatzis, R.E. (1982). The leadership motive pattern and long term success in management. *Journal of Applied Psychology, 67*, 737–743.

McClelland, D.C., & Burnham, D.H. (1976). Power is the great motivator. *Harvard Business Review*, March-April, 100–110, 159–166.

McClelland, D.C., Davidson, R.J., Floor, E., & Saron, C. (1980). Stressed power motivation, sympathetic activation, immune function, and illness. *Journal of Human Stress, 6* (2), 11–19.

McClelland, D.C., Davis, W.N., Kalin, R., & Wanner, E. (1972). *The drinking man: Alcohol and human motivation*. New York: The Free Press.

McClelland, D.C., & Jemmott, J.B., III (1980). Power motivation, stress, and physical illness. *Journal of Human Stress, 6*(4), 6–15.

McClelland, D.C., Koestner, R., & Weinberger, J. (1989). How do self-attributed and implicit motives differ? *Psychological Review, 96*, 690–702.

McClelland, D.C., Ross, G., & Patel, V. (1985). The effect of an academic examination on salivary norepinephrine and immunoglobulin levels. *Journal of Human Stress, 11*(2), 52–59.

McClelland, D.C. & Steele, R.S. (1972). *Motivation workshops*. New York: General Learning Press.

McClelland, D.C., & Watt, N. (1968). Sex-role alienation in schizophrenia. *Journal of Abnormal Psychology, 73*, 226–239.

McClelland, J.L., Rummelhart, D.E., & the PDP Research Group. (1986). *Parallel distributed processing: Explorations in the microstructure of cognition. Vol. 2. Psychological and biological models*. Cambridge, MA: MIT Press.

McCrae, R.R., & Costa, P.T., Jr. (1980). Openness to experience and ego level in Loevinger's Sentence Completion Test: Dispositional contributions to developmental models of personality. *Journal of Personality and Social Psychology, 39*, 1179–1190.

McCrae, R.R., & Costa, P.T., Jr. (1984). Personality is transcontextual: A reply to Veroff. *Personality and Social Psychology Bulletin, 10*, 175-179.

McCrae, R.R., & Costa, P.T., Jr. (1985). Updating Norman's "adequate taxonomy": Intelligence and personality dimensions in natural language and in questionnaires. *Journal of Personality and Social Psychology, 49*, 710–721.

McCrae, R.R., & Costa, P.T. Jr. (1985b). Openness to experience. In R. Hogan and W.H. Jones (Ed.), *Perspectives in personality* (Vol. 1, pp. 145–172).

McCrae, R.R., & Costa, P.T., Jr. (1986). Personality, coping, and coping effectiveness in an adult sample. *Journal of Personality, 54*, 385–405.

McCrae, R.R., & Costa, P.T., Jr. (1987). Validation of the five-factor model of personality across instruments and observers. *Journal of Personality and Social Psychology, 52*, 81–90.

McCrae, R.R., & Costa, P.T., Jr. (1989). The structure of interpersonal traits: Wiggins' circumplex and the five-factor model. *Journal of Personality and Social Psychology, 56*, 586–595.

McCrae, R.R., & Costa, P.T., Jr. (1990). *Personality in adulthood*. New York: Guilford Press.

McCrae, R.R., & Costa, P.T., Jr. (1991). Adding *Liebe und Arbeit:* The full five-factor model and well-being. *Personality and Social Psychology Bulletin, 17*, 227–232.

McCrae, R.R., & John, O.P. (1992). An introduction to the five-factor model and its applications. *Journal of Personality, 60*, 175–215.

McCranie, E.W., & Simpson, M.E. (1987). Parental childrearing antecedents of Type A behavior. *Personality and Social Psychology Bulletin, 12*, 493–501.

McDowall, J. (1984). Recall of pleasant and unpleasant words in depressed subjects. *Journal of Abnormal Psychology, 93*, 401–407.

McGinnies, E. (1949). Emotionality and perceptual defense. *Psychological Review, 56*, 244–251.

McGue, M., Bacon, S., & Lykken, D.T. (1993). Personality stability and change in early adulthood: A behavioral genetic analysis. *Developmental Psychology, 29*, 96–109.

McInerney, J. (1984). *Bright lights, big city*. New York: Random House.

McKenna, F.P. (1984). Measures of field dependence: Cognitive style or cognitive ability? *Journal of Personality and Social Psychology, 47*, 593–603.

Mead, G.H. (1934). *Mind, self, and society*. Chicago: University of Chicago Press.

Mead, M. (1972). *Blackberry winter: My earlier years*. New York: Washington Square Press.

Meehl, P.E., & Dahlstrom, W.G. (1960). Objective configural rules for discriminating psychotic from neurotic MMPI profiles. *Journal of Consulting Psychology, 24*, 375–387.

Mercer, R.T., Nichols, E.G., & Doyle, G.C. (1989). *Transitions in a woman's life: Major life events in developmental context*. New York: Springer.

Mettlin, C. (1976). Occupational careers and the prevention of coronary-prone behavior. *Social Science and Medicine, 10*, 367–372.

Meyer, G.J., & Shack, J.R. (1989). Structural convergence of mood and personality: Evidence for old and new directions. *Journal of Personality and Social Psychology, 57*, 691–706.

Mikulincer, M., & Nachson, O. (1991). Attachment styles and patterns of self-disclosure. *Journal of Personality and Social Psychology, 61*, 321–331.

Miller, G.A., Galanter, E., & Pribram, K.H. (1960). *Plans and the structure of behavior*. New York: Holt, Rinehart & Winston.

Miller, J.G. (1984). Culture and the development of everyday social explanation. *Journal of Personality and Social Psychology, 46*, 961–978.

Miller, N.E., & Dollard, J. (1941). *Social learning and imitation*. New Haven, CT: Yale University Press.

Miller, P.C., Lefcourt, H.M., Holmes, J.G., Ware, E.E., & Saleh, W.E. (1986). Marital locus of control and marital problem solving. *Journal of Personality and Social Psychology, 51*, 161–169.

Millon, T. (1973). (Ed.). *Theories of psychopathology and personality* (2nd ed.). Philadelphia: W.B. Saunders.

Mink, L.O. (1978). Narrative form as a cognitive instrument. In R.H. Canary and H. Kozicki (Eds.), *Literary form and historical understanding* (pp. 129–149). Madison, WI: University of Wisconsin Press.

Minuchin, S. (1974). *Families and family therapy*. Cambridge, MA: Harvard University Press.

Mischel, W. (1961). Delay of gratification, need for achievement, and acquiescence in another culture. *Journal of Abnormal and Social Psychology, 62*, 543–552.

Mischel, W. (1966). Theory and research on the antecedents of self-imposed delay of reward. In B.A. Maher (Ed.), *Progress in experimental personality research* (Vol. 3, pp. 85–132). New York: Academic Press.

Mischel, W. (1968). *Personality and assessment*. New York: John Wiley & Sons.

Mischel, W. (1973). Toward a cognitive social learning reconceptualization of personality. *Psychological Review, 80*, 252–283.

Mischel, W. (1977). On the future of personality measurement. *American Psychologist, 32*, 246–254.

Mischel, W. (1979). On the interface of cognition and personality: Beyond the person–situation debate. *American Psychologist, 34*, 740–754.

Mischel, W. (1983). Delay of gratification as process and as person variable in development. In D. Magnusson and V.P. Allen (Eds.), *Interactions in human development* (pp. 149–165). New York: Academic Press.

Mischel, W. (1986). *Introduction to personality* (4th ed.). New York: Holt, Rinehart & Winston.

Mischel, W., & Ebbesen, E.B. (1970). Attention in delay of gratification. *Journal of Personality and Social Psychology, 16*, 329–337.

Mischel, W., & Gilligan, C. (1964). Delay of gratification, motivation for the prohibited gratification, and response to temptation. *Journal of Abnormal and Social Psychology, 69*, 411–417.

Mischel, W., & Peake, P.K. (1982). Beyond déjà vu in the search for cross-situational consistency. *Psychological Review, 89*, 730–755.

Mishima, Y. (1958). *Confessions of a mask*. New York: New Directions Books.

Mishima, Y. (1970). *Sun and steel*. New York: Grove Press.

Mitchell, J.C. (1983). Case and situation analysis. *The Sociological Review, 31*, 187–211.

Moi, T. (1981). Representation of patriarchy: Sexuality and epistemology in Freud's Dora. *Feminist Review, 9*, 60–73.

Monte, C.F. (1987) *Beneath the mask: An introduction to theories of personality*. (3rd ed.) New York: Holt, Rinehart & Winston.

Moos, R.H. (1973). Conceptualizations of human environments. *American Psychologist, 28*, 652–665.

Moos, R.H. (1974). Systems for the assessment and classifications of human environments: An overview. In R.H. Moos and P.M. Insel (Eds.), *Issues in social ecology* (pp. 5–28). Palo Alto, CA: National Press Books.

Moos, R.H. (1976). *The human context: Environmental determinants of behavior*. New York: John Wiley & Sons.

Moraitis, G., & Pollack, G.H. (Eds.). (1987). *Psychoanalytic studies of biography*. Madison, CT: International Universities Press.

Morawski, J. G (1986). The troubled quest for masculinity, femininity, and androgyny. In P. Shaver and C. Hendrick (Eds.), *Sex and gender: Review of personality and social psychology* (Vol. 7, pp. 44–69). Beverly Hills, CA: Sage.

Morris, C.W. (1956). *Varieties of human value*. Chicago, IL: University of Chicago Press.

Morris, D. (1967). *The naked ape*. New York: McGraw-Hill.

Moser, K. (1989). The act-frequency approach: A conceptual critique. *Personality and Social Psychology Bulletin, 15*, 73–83.

Moskowitz, D.S. (1982). Coherence and cross-situational generality in personality: A new analysis of old problems. *Journal of Personality and Social Psychology, 43*, 754–768.

Moskowitz, D.S. (1990). Convergence of self-reports and independent observers: Dominance and friendliness. *Journal of Personality and Social Psychology, 58*, 1096–1106.

Mountjoy, P.J., & Sundberg, M.L. (1981). Ben Franklin the protobehaviorist I: Self-management of behavior. *The Psychological Record, 31*, 13–24.

Mumford, M., Stokes, G.S., & Owens, W.A. (1990). *Patterns of life history: The ecology of human individuality*. Hillsdale, NJ: Lawrence Erlbaum.

Murray, H.A. (1938). *Explorations in personality*. New York: Oxford University Press.

Murray, H.A. (1940). What should psychologists do about psychoanalysis? *Journal of Abnormal and Social Psychology, 35*, 150–175.

Murray, H.A. (1943). *The Thematic Apperception Test: Manual*. Cambridge, MA: Harvard University Press.

Murray, H.A. (1949). Introduction. In H. Melville, *Pierre, or the ambiguities* (pp. xiii–ciii). New York: Farar Straus.

Murray, H.A. (1951b). Some basic psychological assumptions and conceptions. *Dialectica, 5*, 266–292.

Murray, H.A. (1955/1981). American Icarus. In E.S. Shneidman (Ed.), *Endeavors in psychology: Selections from the personology of Henry A. Murray* (pp. 535–556). New York: Harper & Row.

Murray, H.A. (1959). Preparations for the scaffold of a comprehensive system. In S. Koch (Ed.), *Psychology: A study of a science*. New York: McGraw-Hill.

Murray, H.A. (1959/1981). Vicissitudes of creativity. In E.S. Shneidman (Ed.), *Endeavors in psychology: Selections from the personology of Henry A. Murray* (pp. 312–330). New York: Random House.

Murray, H.A. (1960/1981). Two versions of man. In E. Shneidman (Ed.), *Endeavors in psychology: Selections from the personology of Henry A. Murray* (pp. 581–604). New York: Harper & Row.

Murray, H.A. (1962). The personality and career of Satan. *Journal of Social Issues, 28*, 36–54.

Murray, H.A. (1966). Bartleby and I. In H.P. Vincent (Ed.), *Bartleby the scrivener* (pp. 3–24). Ohio: Kent State University Press.

Murray, H.A. (1967). The case of Murr. In E.G. Boring and G. Lindzey (Eds.), *A history of psychology in autobiography* (Vol. 5, pp. 285–310). New York: Appleton-Century-Crofts.

Murray, H.A. (1967). Dead to the world: Or the passions of Herman Melville. In E.J. Shneidman (Ed.), *Essays in self-destruction*. New York: Science House.

Murray, H.A., & Kluckhohn, C. (1953). Outline of a conception of personality. In C. Kluckhohn, H.A. Murray, and D. Schneider (Eds.), *Personality in nature, society, and culture* (2nd ed.) (pp. 3–52). New York: Knopf.

Murray, H.A. with staff. (1948). *Assessment of men*. New York: Rinehart & Co.

Murray, H.A. (1951a). *In nomine diaboli. New England Quarterly, 24*, 435–452.

Murray, K. (1989). The construction of identity in the narratives of romance and comedy. In J. Shotter and K.J. Gergen (Eds.), *Texts of identity* (pp. 176–205). London: Sage.

Muslin, H., & Gill, M. (1978). Transference in the Dora case. *Journal of the American Psychoanalytic Association, 26*, 311–328.

Myers, I. (1962). *The Myers–Briggs Type Indicator*. Princeton, NJ: Educational Testing Service.

Myers, I.B., & McCaulley, M.H. (1985). *Manual: A guide to the development and use of the Myers–Briggs Type Indicator*. Palo Alto, CA: Consulting Psychologists Press.

Nasby, W. (1985). Private self-consciousness, articulation of the self-schema, and the recognition memory of trait adjectives. *Journal of Personality and Social Psychology, 49*, 704–709.

Nathan, J. (1974). *Mishima: A biography*. Boston: Little, Brown.

National Institute of Mental Health. (1982). *Television and behavior: Ten years of scientific progress and implications for the eighties* (Vol. 1). Washington, DC: U.S. Department of Health and Human Services.

Neisser, U. (1976). *Cognition and reality: Principles and implications of cognitive psychology*. San Francisco, CA: W.H. Freeman.

Neisser, U. (1982). *Memory observed: Remembering in natural contexts*. San Francisco, CA: W.H. Freeman.

Nemiah, J.C. (1984). The unconscious and psychopathology. In K.J. Bowers and D. Meichenbaum (Eds.), *The unconscious reconsidered* (pp. 49–87). New York: John Wiley & Sons.

Neugarten, B.L. (Ed.). (1968). *Middle age and aging*. Chicago: University of Chicago Press.

Neugarten, B.L. (1979). Time, age, and the life cycle. *American Journal of Psychiatry, 136*, 887–894.

Neugarten, B.L., & Datan, N. (1974). The middle years. In S. Arieti (Ed.), *American handbook of psychiatry* (Vol. 1). New York: Basic Books.

Nichols, S.L., & Newman, J.P. (1986). Effects of punishment on response latency in extraverts. *Journal of Personality and Social Psychology, 50*, 624–630.

Nisbett, R.E., & Ross, L.D. (1980). *Human inference: Strategies and shortcomings of social judgment*. Englewood Cliffs, NJ: Prentice Hall.

Norem, J.K. (1989). Cognitive strategies as personality: Effectiveness, specificity, flexibility, and change. In D.M. Buss and N. Cantor (Eds.), *Personality psychology: Recent trends and emerging directions* (pp. 45–60). New York: Springer-Verlag.

Norem, J.K. & Cantor, N. (1986). Defensive pessimism: Harnessing anxiety as motivation. *Journal of Personality and Social Psychology, 51*, 1208–1217.

Norman, R.M.G., & Watson, L.D. (1976). Extraversion and reactions to cognitive inconsistency. *Journal of Research in Personality, 10*, 446–456.

Norman, W.T. (1963). Toward an adequate taxonomy of personality attributes: Replicated factor structure in peer nomination personality ratings. *Journal of Abnormal and Social Psychology, 66*, 574–583.

Noy, P. (1979). Form creation in art: An ego-psychological approach to creativity. *Psychoanalytic Quarterly, 48*, 229–257.

Nucci, L. (1981). Conceptions of personal issues: A domain distinct from moral or societal concepts. *Child Development, 52*, 114–121.

O'Brien, R., & Dukore, B.F. (1969). *Tragedy: Ten major plays* (Sophocles' *Oedipus Rex*.) New York: Bantom Books.

Ogilvie, D.M. (1987). The undesired self: A neglected variable in personality research. *Journal of Personality and social Psychology, 52*, 379–385.

Ogilvie, D.M., & Ashmore, R.D. (1991). Self-with-other representation as unit of analysis in self-concept research. In R.A. Curtis (Ed.), *The relational self: Theoretical convergences in psychoanalysis and social psychology* (pp. 282–314). New York: Guilford Press.

Oliver, J.M., & Burkham, R. (1982). Subliminal psychodynamic activation in depression: A failure to replicate. *Journal of Abnormal Psychology, 91*, 337–342.

Olson, D.H. (1985). Struggling with congruence across theoretical models and methods. *Family Process, 24*.

Olweus, D. (1977). Aggression and peer acceptance in adolescent boys: Two short-term longitudinal studies of ratings. *Child Development, 48*, 1301–1313.

Olweus, D. (1979). Stability and aggressive reaction patterns in males: A review. *Psychological Bulletin, 86*, 852–875.

Olweus, D., Mattson, A., Schalling, D., & Low, H. (1980). Testosterone, aggression, physical and personality dimensions on normal adolescent males. *Psychosomatic Medicine, 42*, 253–269.

Omoto, A.M., & Snyder, M. (1990). Basic research in action: Volunteerism and society's response to AIDS. *Personality and Social Psychology Bulletin, 16*, 152–165.

Omoto, A.M., Snyder, M., & Berghuis, J.P. (in press). The psychology of volunteerism: A conceptual analysis and a program of action research. In J.B. Pryor and G.D. Reeder (Eds.), *The social psychology of HIV infection*. Hillsdale, NJ: Lawrence Erlbaum.

Orlofsky, J.L. (1978). Identity formation, achievements, and fear of success in college men and women. *Journal of Youth and Adolescence, 7*, 49–62.

Orlofsky, J.L., & Frank, M. (1986). Personality structure as viewed through early memories and identity status in college men and women. *Journal of Personality and Social Psychology, 50*, 580–586.

Orlofsky, J.L., Marcia, J.E., & Lesser, I.M. (1973). Ego identity status and the intimacy versus isolation crisis of young adulthood. *Journal of Personality and Social Psychology, 27*, 211–219.

Orlofsky, J.L., & O'Heron, C.A. (1987). Stereotypes and nonstereotypic sex role trait and behavior orientations: Implications for personal adjustment. *Journal of Personality and Social Psychology, 52*, 1024–1042.

Ormel, J., & Wohlfarth, T. (1991). How neuroticism, long-term difficulties, and life situation changes influence psychological distress: A longitudinal model. *Journal of Personality and Social Psychology, 60*, 744–755.

Ortega, D.F., & Pipal, J.E. (1984). Challenge seeking and the Type A coronary-prone behavior pattern. *Journal of Personality and Social Psychology, 46*, 1328–1334.

Osborne, J. (1961). *Luther*. New York: Criterion Books.

Oshman, H., & Manosevitz, M. (1974). The impact of the identity crisis on the adjustment of late adolescent males. *Journal of Youth and Adolescence, 3*, 207–216.

Ovcharchyn, C.A., Johnson, H.H., & Petzel, T.P. (1981). Type A behavior, academic aspirations, and academic success. *Journal of Personality, 49*, 248–256.

Ozer, D.J. (1986). *Consistency in personality: A methodological framework*. New York: Springer-Verlag.

Ozer, D.J., & Gjerde, P.F. (1989). Patterns of personality consistency and change from childhood through adolescence. *Journal of Personality, 57*, 483–507.

Ozer, E.M., & Bandura, A. (1990). Mechanisms governing empowering effects: A self-efficacy analysis. *Journal of Personality and Social Psychology, 58*, 472–486.

Pachter, M. (Ed.). (1979). *Telling lives: The biographer's art*. Washington, DC: New Republic Books.

Palys, T.S., & Little, B.R. (1983). Perceived life satisfaction and the organization of personal project systems. *Journal of Personality and Social Psychology, 44*, 1221–1230.

Parke, R.D., & Slaby, R.G. (1983). The development of aggression. In P.H. Mussen (Ed.), *Handbook of child psychology*. (4th ed.). Vol. 4: *Socialization, personality, and social development* (pp. 547–642). New York: John Wiley & Sons.

Parke, R.D., & Walters, R.H. (1967). Some factors influencing the efficacy of punishment training for inducing response inhibitions. *Monographs of the Society for Research in Child Development, 32*, (1, Serial No. 109).

Parkison, S.C. (1982). Family therapy. In C.E. Walker (Ed.), *Handbook of clinical psychology* (Vol. 2, pp. 1009–1027. Homewood, IL: Dorsey Press.

Passini, F.T., & Norman, W.T. (1966). A universal conception of personality structure? *Journal of Personality and Social Psychology, 4*, 44–49.

Patterson, C.M., Kosson, D.J., & Newman, J.P. (1987). Reaction to punishment, reflectivity, and passive avoidance learning in extraverts. *Journal of Personality and Social Psychology, 52*, 565–575.

Paulhus, D.L., & Martin, C.L. (1987). The structure of personality capabilities. *Journal of Personality and Social Psychology, 52*, 354–365.

Paunonen, S.V., Jackson, D.N., & Keinonen, M. (1990). The structured nonverbal assessment of personality. *Journal of Personality, 58*, 481–502.

Paunonen, S.V., Jackson, D.N., Trzebinski, J., & Forsterling, F. (1992). Personality structure across cultures: A multi-method evaluation. *Journal of Personality and Social Psychology, 62*, 447–456.

Paykel, E.S., Emms, E.M., Fletcher, J., & Rassaby, E.S. (1980). Life events and social support in puerperal depression. *British Journal of Psychiatry, 136*, 339–346.

Payne, T.J., Connor, J.M., & Colletti, G. (1987). Gender-based schematic processing: An empirical investigation and reevaluation. *Journal of Personality and Social Psychology, 52*, 937–945.

Peabody, D. (1966). Authoritarianism scales and response bias. *Psychological Bulletin, 65*, 11–23.

Peabody, D. (1987). Selecting representative trait adjectives. *Journal of Personality and Social Psychology, 52*, 59–71.

Peabody, D., & Goldberg, L.R. (1989). Some determinants of factor structures from personality-trait descriptors. *Journal of Personality and Social Psychology, 57*, 552–567.

Pearce-McCall, D., & Newman, J.P. (1986). Expectation of success following noncontingent punishment in introverts and extraverts. *Journal of Personality and Social Psychology, 50*, 439–446.

Pearson, C.S. (1986). *The hero within: Sex archetypes we live by*. New York: Harper & Row.

Pederson, D.R., Moran, G., Sitko, C., Campbell, K., Ghesquire, K., & Acton, H. (1990). Maternal sensitivity and the security of infant–mother attachment: A Q-sort study. *Child Development, 61*, 1974–1983.

Pekala, R.J., Wenger, C.F., & Levine, R.L. (1985). Individual differences in phenomenological experience: States of consciousness as a function of absorption. *Journal of Personality and Social Psychology, 48*, 125–132.

Pellegrini, A.D., & Galda, L. (1990). The joint construction of stories by preschool children and an experimenter. In B.K. Britten and A.D. Pellegrini (Eds.), *Narrative thought and narrative language* (pp. 113–130). Hillsdale, NJ: Lawrence Erlbaum.

Pennebaker, J.W. (1988). Confiding traumatic experiences and health. In S. Fisher and J. Reason (Eds.), *Handbook of life stress, cognition, and health* (pp. 669–682). New York: Wiley.

Pennebaker, J.W. (1989a). Stream of consciousness and stress: Levels of thinking. In J.S. Uleman and J.A. Bargh (Eds.), *Unintended thought* (pp. 327–349). New York: Guilford Press.

Pennebaker, J.W. (1989b). Confession, inhibition, and disease. In L. Berkowitz (Ed.), *Advances in experimental social psychology* (Vol.22, pp. 211–244). New York: Academic Press.

Pennebaker, J.W. (1992). Putting stress into words: Health, linguistic, and therapeutic implications. Paper presented at the American Psychological Association Convention, Washington, DC.

Pennebaker, J.W., & Beall, S.K. (1986). Confronting a traumatic event: Toward an understanding of inhibition and disease. *Journal of Abnormal Psychology, 95,* 274–281.

Pennebaker, J.W., Kiecolt-Glaser, J.K., & Glaser, R. (1988). Disclosure of traumas and immune function: Health implications for psychotherapy. *Journal of Consulting and Clinical Psychology, 56,* 239–245.

Pennebaker, J.W., & O'Heeron, R.C. (1984). Confiding in others and illness rate among spouses of suicide and accidental death victims. *Journal of Abnormal Psychology, 93,* 473–476.

Pepper, S. (1942). *World hypotheses.* Berkeley, CA: University of California Press.

Perry, W.C. (1970). *Forms of intellectual and ethical development in the college years.* New York: Holt, Rinehart & Winston.

Persky, H., Smith, K.D., & Basu, G.K. (1971). Relation of psychological measures of aggression and hostility to testosterone production in men. *Psychosomatic Medicine, 33,* 265–277.

Pervin, L.A. (1989). (Ed.). *Goal concepts in personality and social psychology.* Hillsdale, NJ: Lawrence Erlbaum.

Peterson, B.E., & Stewart, A.J. (1990). Using personal and fictional documents to assess psychosocial development: The case study of Vera Brittain's generativity. *Psychology and Aging, 5,* 400–411.

Peterson, C., Luborsky, L., & Seligman, M.E.P. (1983). Attributions and depressive mood shifts: A case study using the symptom–context method. *Journal of Abnormal Psychology, 92,* 96–103.

Peterson, C., & Seligman, M.E.P. (1984). Causal explanations as a risk factor for depression: Theory and evidence. *Psychological Review, 91,* 347–374.

Peterson, C., Villanova, P., & Raps, C.S. (1985). Depression and attributions:

Factors responsible for inconsistent results in the published literature. *Journal of Abnormal Psychology, 94,* 165–168.

Phares, E.J. (1957). Expectancy changes in skill and chance situations. *Journal of Abnormal and Social Psychology, 54,* 339–342.

Phares, E.J. (1978). Locus of control. In H. London and J.E. Exner, Jr. (Eds.), *Dimensions of personality* (pp. 263–304). New York: John Wiley & Sons.

Phares, E.J. (1984). *Introduction to personality.* Glenview, IL: Scott, Foresman and Company.

Phares, E.J. (1988). *Introduction to personality* (2nd ed.). Glenview, IL: Scott, Foresman and Company.

Piaget, J. (1952). *The origins of intelligence in children.* New York: International Universities Press.

Piaget, J. (1965). *The moral judgment of the child.* New York: The Free Press.

Piaget, J. (1970). *Genetic epistemology.* New York: Columbia University Press.

Pilkonis, P.A. (1977). The behavioral consequences of shyness. *Journal of Personality, 45,* 596–611.

Plomin, R., Chipuer, H.M., & Loehlin, J.C. (1990). Behavioral genetics and personality. In L. Pervin (Ed.), *Handbook of personality theory and research* (pp. 225–243). New York: Guilford Press.

Plomin, R., DeFries, J.C., & McClearn, G.E. (1980). *Behavior genetics: A primer.* San Francisco: Freeman.

Plomin, R., Lichtenstein, P., Pederson, N.L., McClearn, G.E., & Nesselroade, J.R. (1990). Genetic influence on life events during the last half of the life span. *Psychology and Aging, 5,* 25–30.

Podd, M.H. (1972). Ego identity status and morality: The relationship between two developmental constructs. *Developmental Psychology, 6,* 497–507.

Polkinghorne, D. (1988). *Narrative knowing and the human sciences.* Albany, NY: State University of New York Press.

Pollak, J.M. (1979). Obsessive-compulsive personality: A review. *Psychological Bulletin, 86,* 225–241.

Popper, K. (1959). *The logic of scientific discovery.* New York: Basic Books.

Porter, C.A., & Suedfeld, P. (1981). Integrative complexity in the correspondence of literary figures: Effects of personal and societal stress. *Journal of Personality and Social Psychology, 40,* 321–330.

Porterfield, A.L., & Golding, S.L. (1985). Failure to find an effect of subliminal psychodynamic activation upon cognitive measures of pathology in schizophrenia. *Journal of Abnormal Psychology, 94,* 630–639.

Postman, L., Bruner, J.S., & McGinnies, E. (1948). Personal values as selective factors in perception. *Journal of Abnormal and Social Psychology, 32,* 142–154.

Powers, W.T. (1973). Feedback: Beyond behaviorism. *Science, 179,* 351–356.

Price, V.A. (1982). *Type A behavior pattern: A model for research and practice.* New York: Academic Press.

Privette, G. (1983). Peak experience, peak performance, and flow: A comparative analysis of positive human experiences. *Journal of Personality and Social Psychology, 45,* 1361–1368.

Privette, G., & Landsman, T. (1983). Factor analysis of peak performance: The full use of potential. *Journal of Personality and Social Psychology, 44,* 195–200.

Proust, M. (1923/1934). *Remembrance of things past.* New York: Random House.

Purifoy, F.E., & Koopmans, L.H. (1979). Androstenedione, testosterone, and free testosterone concentration in women of various occupations. *Social Biology, 26,* 179–188.

Quinn, S. (1987). *A mind of her own: The life of Karen Horney.* Reading, MA: Addison-Wesley.

Radke-Yarrow, M., Zahn-Waxler, C., & Chapman, M. (1983). Children's prosocial dispositions and behavior. In P.H. Mussen (Ed.), *Handbook of child psychology.* (4th ed.) Vol. 4: *Socialization, personality, and social development* (pp. 469–546). New York: John Wiley & Sons.

Rank, O. (1936). *Truth and reality.* New York: W.W. Norton.

Rank, O. (1968). *Art and artist: Creative urge and personality development.* New York: Agathon Press.

Rapaport, D. (1959). A historical survey of psychoanalytical ego psychology. *Psychological Issues, Vol. 1.* New York: International Universities Press.

Raskin, R.N., & Hall, C.J. (1979). A narcissistic personality inventory. *Psychological Reports, 45,* 590.

Raskin, R.N., & Hall, C.J. (1981). The Narcissistic Personality Inventory: Alternate form reliability and further evidence of construct validity. *Journal of Personality Assessment, 45,* 159–162.

Raskin, R.N., & Shaw, R. (1988). Narcissism and the use of personal pronouns. *Journal of Personality, 56,* 393–404.

Redman, E. (1973). *The dance of legislation.* New York: Simon & Schuster.

Redmore, C., Loevinger, J., & Tamashiro, R. (1978). *Measuring ego development: Scoring manual for men and boys.* Unpublished manuscript.

Redmore, C., & Waldman, K. (1975). Reliability of a sentence completion measure of ego development. *Journal of Personality Assessment, 39,* 236–243.

Reichenbach, H. (1938). *Experience and prediction.* Chicago, IL: University of Chicago Press.

Reid, J.B. (1978). *A social-learning approach to family intervention: Observation in home settings* (Vol. 2). Eugene, OR: Castalia Publishing.

Reinisch, J.M. (1981). Prenatal exposure to synthetic progestins increases potential for aggression in humans. *Science, 211,* 1171–1173.

Repetti, R.L. (1987). Individual and common components of the social environment at work and psychological well-being. *Journal of Personality and Social Psychology. 52,* 710–720.

Rescorla, R.A. (1987). A Pavlovian analysis of goal-directed behavior. *American Psychologist, 42,* 119–129.

Rescorla, R.A. (1988). Pavlovian conditioning: It's not what you think it is. *American Psychologist, 43,* 151–160.

Reuman, D.A., Alwin, D.F., & Veroff, J. (1984). Assessing the validity of the achievement motive in the presence of random measurement error. *Journal of Personality and Social Psychology, 47,* 1347–1362.

Ricoeur, P. (1970). *Freud and philosophy: An essay on interpretation.* New Haven, CT: Yale University Press.

Ricoeur, P. (1984). *Time and narrative* (Vol. 1). Chicago: University of Chicago Press. (Translated by Kathleen McGlaughlin and David Pellauer.).

Rieff, P. (1959). *Freud: The mind of the moralist.* Chicago: University of Chicago Press.

Ritzler, B., Zambianco, D., Harder, D., & Kaskey, M. (1980). Psychotic patterns of the concept of the object on the Rorschach test. *Journal of Abnormal Psychology, 89,* 46–55.

Rizzo, R., & Vinacke, E. (1975). Self-actualization and the meaning of critical experiences. *Journal of Humanistic Psychology, 15,* 19–30.

Roberts, P., & Newton, P.M. (1987). Levinsonian studies of women's adult development. *Psychology and Aging, 2,* 154–163.

Robins, C.J. (1988). Attributions and depression: Why is the literature so inconsistent? *Journal of Personality and Social Psychology, 54,* 880–889.

Robinson, D.N. (1981). *An intellectual history of psychology.* New York: Macmillan.

Robinson, F.G. (1992). *Love's story told: A life of Henry A. Murray.* Cambridge, MA: Harvard University Press.

Robinson, J.A. (1976). Sampling autobiographical memory. *Cognitive Psychology, 8,* 578–595.

Roche, S.M., & McConkey, K.M. (1990). Absorption: Nature, assessment, and correlates. *Journal of Personality and Social Psychology, 59,* 91–101.

Rodin, J., & Langer, E.J. (1977). Long-term effects of a control-relevant intervention with the institutionalized aged. *Journal of Personality and Social Psychology, 35,* 897–902.

Rodriguez, M.L., Mischel, W., & Shoda, Y. (1989). Cognitive person variables in the delay of gratification of older children at risk. *Journal of Personality and Social Psychology, 57,* 358–367.

Rogers, C.R. (1951). *Client-centered therapy.* Boston: Houghton-Mifflin.

Rogers, C.R. (1959). A theory of therapy, personality, and interpersonal relationships, as developed in the client-centered framework. In S. Koch (Ed.), *Psychology: A Study of a Science* (Vol. 3). New York: McGraw-Hill.

Rogers, C.R. (1976). Toward a theory of creativity. In A. Rothenberg and C.R. Hausman (Eds.), *The creativity question* (pp. 296–305). Durham, NC: Duke University Press.

Rogers, C.R. (1980). Ellen West and loneliness. In C.R. Rogers, *A way of being.* Boston: Houghton-Mifflin.

Rogow, A.A. (1978). A further footnote to Freud's "Fragment of an analysis of a case of hysteria." *Journal of the American Psychoanalytic Association, 26,* 331–356.

Rokeach, M. (1973). *The nature of human values.* New York: The Free Press.

Romer, D., Gruder, C.L., & Lizzadro, T. (1986). A person–situation approach to altrustic behavior. *Journal of Personality and Social Psychology, 51,* 1001–1012.

Roos, P.E., & Cohen, L.H. (1987). Sex roles and social support as moderators of life stress adjustment. *Journal of Personality and Social Psychology, 52,* 576–585.

Rootes, M.D., Moras, K., & Gordon, R. (1980). Ego development and sociometrically evaluated maturity: An investigation of the validity of the Washington University Sentence-Completion Test of Ego Development. *Journal of Personality Assessment, 44,* 613–620.

Rorschach, H. (1921). *Psychodiagnostik.* Bern: Bircher.

Rosch, E. (1975). Cognitive reference points. *Cognitive Psychology, 1,* 532–543.

Rosenberg, M. (1979). *Conceiving the self.* New York: Basic Books.

Rosenberg, S. (1976). New approaches to the analysis of personal constructs in person perception. In A.W. Landfield (Ed.), *Nebraska symposium motivation* (Vol. 23). Lincoln, NE: University of Nebraska Press.

Rosenhahn, D.L. (1969). Some origins of concern for others. In P.H. Mussen, J. Langer, and M. Covington (Eds.), *Trends and issues in developmental psychology.* New York: Holt, Rinehart & Winston.

Rosenman, R.H., Brand, R.J., Jenkins, C.D., Friedman, M., Straus, R., & Wurm, M. (1975). Coronary heart disease in the Western collaborative group study: Final follow-up experience of $8^{1}/2$ years. *Journal of the American Medical Association, 233,* 872–877.

Rosenwald, G.C. (1968). The Thematic Apperception Test (TAT). In A.I. Rabin (Ed.), *Projective techniques in personality assessment* (pp. 172–221). New York: Springer.

Rosenwald, G.C. (1988). A theory of multiple-case research. *Journal of Personality, 56,* 239–264.

Ross, L.D. (1977). The intuitive psychologist and his shortcomings: Distortions in the attribution process. In L. Berkowitz (Ed.), *Advances in Experimental Social Psychology* (Vol. 10). New York: Academic Press.

Rossi, A.S. (1980). Life-span theories and women's lives. *Signs, 6*(1), 4–32.

Rosznafszky, J. (1981). The relationship of level of ego development to Q-sort personality ratings. *Journal of Personality and Social Psychology, 41,* 99–120.

Roth, P. (1988). *The facts: A novelist's autobiography.* London: Penguin.

Rothbart, M.K. (1986). Longitudinal observation of infant temperament. *Developmental Psychology, 22,* 356–365.

Rothman, S., & Lichter, S.R. (1982). *Roots of radicalism: Jews, Christians, and the New Left.* New York: Oxford University Press.

Rotter, J.B. (1954). *Social learning and clinical psychology.* Englewood Cliffs, NJ: Prentice-Hall.

Rotter, J.B. (1966). Generalized expectancies for internal versus external control of reinforcement. *Psychological Monographs, 80* (1, Whole No. 609).

Rotter, J.B. (1972). *Applications of a social learning theory of personality.* New York: Holt.

Rotter, J.B. (1975). Some problems and misconceptions related to the construct of internal versus external reinforcement. *Journal of Consulting and Clinical Psychology, 43,* 56–67.

Rouse, J. (1978). *The completed gesture: Myth, character, and education.* New Jersey: Skyline Books.

Rowe, D. (1982). *The construction of life and death.* New York: John Wiley & Sons.

Royko, M. (1986). Modified Cub rule says bet the Mets. *Chicago Tribune,* October 17.

Ruehlman, L.S., West, S.G., & Pasahow, R.J. (1985). Depression and evaluative schemata. *Journal of Personality, 53,* 46–92.

Runyan, W.M. (1981). Why did Van Gogh cut off his ear? The problem of alternative explanations in psychobiography. *Journal of Personality and Social Psychology, 40,* 1070–1077.

Runyan, W.M. (1982). *Life histories and psychobiography: Explorations in theory and method.* New York: Oxford University Press.

Runyan, W.M. (1990). Individual lives and the structure of personality psychology. In A.I. Rabin, R.A. Zucker, R.A. Emmons, and S. Frank (Eds), *Studying persons and lives* (pp. 10–40). New York: Springer.

Rusbult, C. E. (1987). Responses to dissatisfaction in close relationships: The exit-voice-loyalty neglect model. In D. Perlman and S.W. Duck (Eds.), *Intimate relationships: Development, dynamics, and deterioration* (pp. 209–237). Newbury Park, CA: Sage.

Rushton, J.P. (1980). *Altruism, social-*

ization, and society. Englewood Cliffs, NJ: Prentice-Hall.

Rushton, J.P. (1990). Sir Francis Galton, epigenetic rules, genetic similarity theory, and human life history analysis. *Journal of Personality*, *58*, 117–140.

Rushton, J.P., Brainerd, C.J., & Presley, M. (1983). Behavioral development and construct validity: The principle of aggregation. *Psychological Bulletin*, *94*, 18–38.

Rushton, J.P., Fulker, D.W., Neale, M.C., Nias, D.K., & Eysenck, H.J. (1986). Altruism and aggression: The heritability of individual differences. *Journal of Personality and Social Psychology*, *50*, 1192–1198.

Russell, B. (1945). *A history of Western philosophy*. New York: Simon & Schuster.

Rutter, D.R., Morley, I.E., & Graham, J.C. (1972). Visual interaction in a group of introverts and extraverts. *European Journal of Social Psychology*, *2*, 371–384.

Ryan, R.M. (1991). The nature of the self in autonomy and relatedness. In J. Strauss and G.R. Goethals (Eds.), *The self: Interdisciplinary approaches* (pp. 208–238). New York: Springer-Verlag.

Ryan, R.M., & Grolnick, W.J. (1986). Origins and pawns in the classroom: Self-report and projective assessments of individual differences in children's perceptions. *Journal of Personality and Social Psychology*, *50*, 550–558.

Rychlak, J.F. (1977). *The psychology of rigorous humanism*. New York: John Wiley & Sons.

Rychlak, J.F. (1981). Logical learning theory: Propositions, corollaries, and research evidence. *Journal of Personality and Social Psychology*, *40*, 731–749.

Rychlak, J.F. (1986). Logical learning theory: A teleological alternative in the field of personality. *Journal of Personality*, *54*, 734–762.

Sackheim, H.A. (1983). Self-deception, self-esteem, and depression: The adaptive value of lying to oneself. In J. Masling (Ed.), *Empirical studies of psychoanalytical theories* (Vol. 1, pp. 101–158). New York: The Analytic Press.

Sacks, O. (1985). *The man who mistook his wife for a hat, and other clinical tales*. New York: Summit Books.

Sales, S.M. (1973). Threat as a factor in authoritarianism: An analysis of archival data. *Journal of Personality and Social Psychology*, *28*, 44–57.

Sampson, E.E. (1962). Birth order, need achievement, and conformity. *Journal of Abnormal and Social Psychology*, *64*, 155–159.

Sampson, E.E. (1985). The decentralization of identity: Toward a revised concept of personal and social order. *American Psychologist*, *40*, 1203–1211.

Sampson, E.E. (1988). The debate on individualism: Indigenous psychologies of the individual and their role in personal and societal functioning. *American Psychologist*, *43*, 15–22.

Sampson, E.E. (1989a). The challenge of social change for psychology: Globalization and psychology's theory of the person. *American Psychologist*, *44*, 914–921.

Sampson, E.E. (1989b). The deconstruction of the self. In J. Shotter and K.J. Gergen (Eds.), *Texts of identity* (pp. 1–19). London: Sage.

Sander, L.W. (1975). Infant and caretaking environment: Investigation and conceptualization of adaptive behavior in a system of increasing complexity. In J. Anthony (Ed.), *Explorations in child psychiatry* (pp. 129–165). New York: Plenum.

Sarason, I.G., Smith, R.E., & Diener, E. (1975). Personality research: Components of variance attributed to the person and the situation. *Journal of Personality and Social Psychology*, *32*, 199–204.

Sarbin, T.R. (1986). The narrative as a root metaphor for psychology. In T.R. Sarbin (Ed.), *Narrative psychology: The storied nature of human conduct* (pp. 3–21). New York: Praeger.

Sartre, J.-P. (1965). *Essays in existentialism*. Secaucus, NJ: The Citadel Press.

Sartre, J.-P. (1981). *The family idiot: Gustave Flaubert, 1821–1857* (Vol. 1). Chicago: University of Chicago Press (Transl. by C. Cosman.).

Scaramella, T.C., & Brown, W.A. (1978). Serum testosterone and aggressiveness in hockey players. *Psychosomatic Medicine*, *40*, 262–265.

Scarr, J., Webber, P.L., Weinberg, R.A., & Wittig, M.A. (1981). Personality resemblance among adolescents and their parents in biologically related and adoptive families. *Journal of Personality and Social Psychology*, *40*, 885–898.

Scarr, S., & Grajek, S. (1982). Similarities and differences among siblings. In M.E. Lamb and B. Sutton-Smith (Eds.), *Sibling relationships: Their nature and significance across the lifespan* (pp. 357–382). Hillsdale, NJ: Lawrence Erlbaum.

Scarr, S., & McCartney, K. (1983). How people make their own environments: A theory of genotype → environment effects. *Child Development*, *54*, 424–435.

Schafer, R. (1968). *Aspects of internalization*. New York: International Universities Press.

Schafer, R. (1981). Narration in the psychoanalytic dialogue. In W.J.J. Mitchell (Ed.), *On narrative* (pp. 25–49). Chicago: University of Chicago Press.

Schank, R.C., & Abelson, R.P. (1977). *Scripts, plans, goals, and understanding*. Hillsdale, NJ: Lawrence Erlbaum.

Scheibe, K.E. (1985). Historical perspectives on the presented self. In B.R. Schlenker (Ed.), *The self and social life* (pp. 33–64). New York: McGraw-Hill.

Scheier, M.F., & Carver, C.J. (1981). Private and public aspects of self. In L. Wheeler (Ed.), *Review of personality and social psychology* (Vol. 2, pp. 189–216). Beverly Hills, CA: Sage.

Scheier, M.F., & Carver, C.S. (1987). Dispositional optimism and physical well-being: The influence of generalized outcome expectancies on health. *Journal of Personality*, *55*, 169–210.

Schenkel, S., & Marcia, J.E. (1972). Attitudes toward premarital intercourse in determining ego identity status in college women. *Journal of Personality*, *40*, 472–482.

Schindler, G.L. (1979). Testosterone concentration, personality patterns, and occupational choice among women. *Dissertations Abstracts International*, *40*, 1411A.

Schmied, L.A., & Lawler, K.A. (1986). Hardiness, Type A behavior, and the stress-illness relation in working women. *Journal of Personality and Social psychology*, *51*, 1218–1223.

Schooler, C. (1972). Birth order effects: Not here, not now! *Psychological Bulletin*, *78*, 161–175.

Schroder, H.M., Driver, M.J., & Streufert, S. (1967). *Human information processing*. New York: Holt, Rinehart & Winston.

Schur, M. (1972). *Freud, living and dying*. New York: International Universities Press.

Schutte, N.S., Kenrick, D.T., & Sadalla, E.K. (1985). The search for predictable settings: Situational prototypes, constraint, and behavioral variation. *Journal of Personality and Social Psychology*, *49*, 121–128.

Schwartz, D.P., Burish, T.G., O'Rourke, D.F., & Holmes, D.S. (1986). Influence of personal and universal failure on the subsequent performance of persons with Type A and Type B behavior patterns. *Journal of Personality and Social Psychology*, *51*, 459–462.

Schwartz, G.E., Fair, P.L., Greenberg, P.S., Freedman, M., & Klerman, J.L. (1974). Facial electromyography in the assessment of emotion. *Psychophysiology*, *11*, 237.

Scott-Stokes, H. (1974). *The life and death of Yukio Mishima*. New York: Farrar, Straus & Giroux.

Sears, R.R., Maccoby, E.E., & Levin, H. (1957). *Patterns of child rearing*. Evanston, IL: Row Peterson.

Seligman, M.E.P. (1975). *Helplessness: On depression, development, and death*. San Francisco: W.H. Freeman.

Seligman, M.E.P., & Maier, S.F. (1967). Failure to escape traumatic shock. *Journal of Experimental Psychology*, *74*, 1–9.

Selman, R.L. (1976). Social-cognitive understanding: A guide to educational and clinical practice. In T. Lickona (Ed.), *Moral development and behavior: Theory, research and social issues*. New York: Holt, Rinehart & Winston.

Selman, R.L. (1980). *The growth of interpersonal understanding*. New York: Academic Press.

Selva, P.C.D., & Dusek, J.B. (1984). Sex role orientation and resolution of Eriksonian crises during the late adolescent years. *Journal of Personality and Social Psychology, 47,* 204–212.

Semmer, N., & Frese, M. (1985). Action theory in clinical psychology. In M. Frese and J. Sabini (Eds.), *Goal directed behavior: The concept of action in psychology* (pp. 503–549). Hillsdale, NJ: Lawrence Erlbaum.

Shaver, P.R., & Brennan, K.A. (1992). Attachment styles and the "Big Five" personality traits: Their connections with each other and with romantic relationship outcomes. *Personality and Social Psychology Bulletin, 18,* 536–545.

Shaver, P., & Rubenstein, C. (1980). Childhood attachment experience and adult loneliness. In L. Wheeler (Ed.), *Review of personality and social psychology* (Vol. 1, pp. 42–73). Beverly Hills, CA: Sage.

Shaw, C. (1930). *The jackroller: A delinquent boy's own story*. Chicago: University of Chicago Press.

Shaw, J.S. (1982). Psychological androgyny and stressful life events. *Journal of Personality and Social Psychology, 43,* 145–153.

Sheehy, G. (1976). *Passages: Predictable crises of adult life*. New York: E.P. Dutton.

Shevrin, H., & Dickman, S. (1980). The psychological unconscious: A necessary assumption for all psychological theory? *American Psychologist, 35,* 421–434.

Shils, E.A. (1954). Authoritarianism: Right and left. In R. Christie and M. Jahoda (Eds.), *Studies in the scope and method of "The Authoritarian Personality."* Glencoe, IL: Free Press.

Shneidman, E.S. (1981). (Ed.). *Endeavors in psychology: Selections from the personology of Henry A. Murray*. New York: Harper & Row.

Shostrom, E. (1965). An inventory for the measurement of self-actualization. *Educational and Psychological Measurement, 24,* 207–218.

Shostrom, E. (1966). *Manual for the Personal Orientation Inventory (POI): An inventory for the measurement of self-actualization*. San Diego, CA: Educational and Industrial Testing Service.

Shotter, J. (1970). Men, and man-makers: George Kelly and the psychology of personal constructs. In D. Bannister (Ed.), *Perspectives in personal construct theory*. New York: Academic Press.

Shotter, J., & Gergen, K.J. (1989). Preface and Introduction. In J. Shotter and K.J. Gergen (Eds.), *Texts of identity* (pp. ix–xi). London: Sage.

Shweder, R.A. (1975). How relevant is an individual difference theory of personality? *Journal of Personality, 43,* 455–484.

Shweder, R.A., & D'Andrade, R.G. (1979). Accurate reflection or systematic distortion? A reply to Block, Weiss, and Thorne. *Journal of Personality and Social Psychology, 37,* 1075–1084.

Sill, J. (1980). Disengagement reconsidered: Awareness of finitude. *Gerontologist, 20,* 457–462.

Silverman, L.H. (1976). Psychoanalytic theory: The reports of my death are greatly exaggerated. *American Psychologist, 31,* 621–637.

Silverman, L.H. (1983). The subliminal psychodynamic activation method: Overview and comprehensive listing of studies. In J. Masling (Ed.), *Empirical studies of psychoanalytical theories* (Vol. 1, pp. 69–100). New York: The Analytic Press.

Silverman, L.H. (1985). Comments on three recent subliminal psychodynamic activation investigations. *Journal of Abnormal Psychology, 94,* 640–643.

Silverman, L.H., & Fishel, A.K. (1981). The Oedipus complex: Studies in adult male behavior. In L. Wheeler (Ed.), *Review of personality and social psychology* (Vol. 2, pp. 43–67). Beverly Hills, CA: Sage.

Silverman, L.H., Lachmann, F.M., & Milich, R.H. (1982). *The search for oneness*. New York: International Universities Press.

Silverstein, L.B. (1991). Transforming the debate about child care and maternal employment. *American Psychologist, 46,* 1025–1032.

Simonton, D.K. (1986). Presidential personality: Biographical use of the Gough Adjective Check List. *Journal of Personality and Social Psychology, 51,* 149–160.

Simpson, J.A. (1990). Influence of attachment styles on romantic relationships. *Journal of Personality and Social Psychology, 59,* 971–980.

Simpson, J.A., & Gangestad, S.W. (1991). Individual differences in sociosexuality: Evidence for convergent and discriminant validity. *Journal of Personality and Social Psychology, 60,* 870–883.

Simpson, J.A., & Gangestad, S.W. (1992). Sociosexuality and romantic partner choice. *Journal of Personality, 60,* 31–51.

Singer, J.A., & Singer, J.L. (1990). Transference in psychotherapy and daily life: Implications of current memory and social cognition research. Unpublished manuscript, Connecticut College and Yale University.

Singer, J.L. (1984). *The human personality*. San Diego, CA: Harcourt Brace Jovanovich.

Singer, J.L. (1987). Private experience and public action: The study of ongoing conscious thought. In J. Aronoff, A.I. Rabin, and R.A. Zucker (Eds.), *The emergence of personality* (pp. 105–146). New York: Springer.

Singh, S. (1978). Achievement motivation and entrepreneurial success: A

follow-up study. *Journal of Research in Personality, 12,* 500–503.

Skinner, B.F. (1938). *Behavior of organisms*. New York: Appleton-Century-Crofts.

Skinner, B.F. (1948/1962). *Walden two*. New York: Macmillan.

Skinner, B.F. (1966). Operant behavior. In W.K. Honig (Ed.), *Operant behavior: Areas of research and application* (pp. 12–32). New York: Appleton-Century-Crofts.

Skinner, B.F. (1971). *Beyond freedom and dignity*. New York: Alfred A. Knopf.

Skinner, B.F. (1979). *The shaping of a behaviorist*. New York: Alfred A. Knopf.

Skinner, B.F. (1987). *Upon further reflection*. Englewood Cliffs, NJ: Prentice-Hall.

Slade, A. (1987). Quality of attachment and early symbolic play. *Developmental Psychology, 23,* 78–85.

Slavin, M.O. (1972). *The theme of feminine evil: The image of women in male fantasy and its effects on attitudes and behavior*. Unpublished doctoral dissertation. Harvard University.

Slife, B.D., & Rychlak, J.F. (1982). Role of affective assessment in modelling aggressive behavior. *Journal of Personality and Social Psychology, 43,* 861–868.

Smith, K.D., Keating, J.P., & Stotland, E. (1989). Altruism reconsidered: The effect of denying feedback on a victim's status to empathic witnesses. *Journal of Personality and Social Psychology, 57,* 641–650.

Smith, T.W., & Anderson, N.B. (1986). Models of personality and disease: An interactional approach to Type A behavior and cardiovascular risk. *Journal of Personality and Social Psychology, 50,* 1166–1173.

Snowdon, C.T. (1983). Ethology, comparative psychology, and animal behavior. In M.R. Rosenzweig and L.W. Porter (Eds.), *Annual review of psychology* (Vol. 34, pp. 63–94). Palo Alto, CA: Annual Reviews, Inc.

Snyder, M. (1974). The self-monitoring of expressive behavior. *Journal of Personality and Social Psychology, 30,* 526–537.

Snyder, M. (1979). Self-monitoring processes. In L. Berkowitz (Ed.), *Advances in experimental social psychology* (Vol. 12). New York: Academic Press.

Snyder, M. (1983). The influence of individuals on situations: Implications for understanding the links between personality and social behavior. *Journal of Personality, 51,* 497–516.

Snyder, M., & Gangestad, S. (1986). On the nature of self-monitoring: Matters of assessment, matters of validity. *Journal of Personality and Social Psychology, 51,* 125–139.

Snyder, M., & Omoto, A.M. (1992). Who helps and why? The psychology of AIDS volunteerism. In S. Spacapan and S. Oskamp (Eds.), *Helping and being helped: Naturalistic studies* (pp. 213–239). London: Sage.

Spear, W.E., & Lapidus, L.B. (1981). Qualitative differences in manifest object representations: Implications for a multi-dimensional model of psychological functioning. *Journal of Abnormal Psychology, 90,* 157–167.

Spence, D.P. (1982). *Narrative truth and historical truth: Meaning and interpretation in psychoanalysis.* New York: Norton.

Spence, J.T., Helmreich, R., & Stapp, J. (1975). Ratings of self and peers on sex role attributes and their relation to self-esteem and conceptions of masculinity and femininity. *Journal of Personality and Social Psychology, 32,* 29–39.

Spieker, S.J., & Booth, C.L. (1988). Maternal antecedents of attachment quality. In J. Belsky and T. Nezworksi (Eds.), *Clinical implications of attachment* (pp. 95–135). Hillsdale, NJ: Lawrence Erlbaum.

Spielberger, C.D. (1966). The effects of anxiety on complex learning and academic achievement. In C.D. Spielberger (Ed.), *Anxiety and behavior.* New York: Academic Press.

Spoto, D. (1983). *The darker side of genius: The life of Alfred Hitchcock.* New York: Ballatine.

Sroufe, L.A. (1983). Infant-caregiver attachment and patterns of adaptation in the preschool: The roots of maladaptation and competence. In M. Perlmutter (Ed.), *Minnesota symposium on child psychology* (Vol. 16,pp. 41–83). Minneapolis, MN: University of Minnesota Press.

Sroufe, L.A. (1985). Attachment classification from the perspective of infant–caregiver relationships and infant temperament. *Child Develop- ment, 56,* 1–14.

Sroufe, L.A. (1988). The role of infant–caregiver attachment in development. In J. Belsky and T. Nezworksi (Eds.), *Clinical implications of attachment* (pp. 18–38). Hillsdale, NJ: Lawrence Erlbaum.

Sroufe, L.A., & Waters, E. (1977). Attachment as an organizational construct. *Child Development, 48,* 1184–1199.

Steele, R.S. (1977). Power motivation, activation, and inspirational speeches. *Journal of Personality, 45,* 53–64.

Steele, R.S. (1982). *Freud and Jung: Conflicts of interpretation.* London: Routledge & Kegan Paul.

Stelmack, R.M. (1990). Biological bases of extraversion: Psychophysiological evidence. *Journal of Personality, 58,* 293–311.

Stern, D.N. (1985). *The interpersonal world of the infant: A view from psychoanalysis and developmental psychology.* New York: Basic Books.

Steuer, F.B., Applefield, J.M., & Smith, R. (1971). Televised aggression and the interpersonal aggression of preschool children. *Journal of Experimental Child Psychology, 11,* 442–447.

Steven, P.J. (1976). *C.G. Jung: The haunted prophet.* New York: Braziller.

Stevens, A. (1983). *Archetypes.* New York: Quill.

Stewart, A.J. (1975). *Longitudinal prediction from personality to life outcomes among college educated women.* Unpublished doctoral dissertation, Harvard University.

Stewart, A.J. (1982). The course of individual adaptation to life changes. *Journal of Personality and Social Psychology, 42,* 1100–1113.

Stewart, A.J., & Chester, N.L. (1982). Sex differences in human social motives. In A.J. Stewart (Ed.), *Motivation and society* (pp. 172–218). San Francisco, CA: Jossey-Bass.

Stewart, A.J., Franz, C., & Layton, L. (1988). The changing self: Using personal documents to study lives. *Journal of Personality, 56,* 41–74.

Stewart, A.J., & Healy, J.M., Jr. (1985). Personality and adaptation to change. In R. Hogan and W.H. Jones (Eds.), *Perspectives in personality* (Vol. 1, pp. 117–144). Greenwich, CT:JAI Press.

Stewart, A.J., & Healy, J.M., Jr. (1986). The role of personality development and experience in shaping political commitment: An illustrative case. *Journal of Social Issues, 42*(2), 11–32.

Stewart, A.J., & Rubin, Z. (1976). Power motivation in the dating couple. *Journal of Personality and Social Psychology, 34,* 305–309.

Stewart, A.J., Sokol, M., Healy, J.M., Jr., & Chester, N.L. (1986). Longitudinal studies of psychological consequences of life changes in children and adults. *Journal of Personality and Social Psychology, 50,* 143–151.

Stewart, A.J., Sokol, M., Healy, J.M., Jr., Chester, N.L., & Weinstock-Savoy, D. (1982). Adaptation to life changes in children and adults: Cross-sectional studies. *Journal of Personality and Social Psychology, 43,* 1270–1281.

Stolorow, R.D., & Atwood, G.E. (1979). *Faces in a cloud: Subjectivity in personality theory.* New York: Aronson.

Strube, M.J. (1985). Attributional style and the Type A coronary-prone behavior pattern. *Journal of Personality and social Psychology, 49,* 500–509.

Strube, M.J., Berry, J.M., Goza, B.K. & Fennimore, D. (1985). Type A behavior, age, and psychological well-being. *Journal of Personality and Social Psychology, 49,* 203–218.

Strube, M.J., & Boland, S.M. (1986). Postperformance attributions and task persistence among Type A and B individuals: A clarification. *Journal of Personality and Social Psychology, 50,* 413–420.

Strube, M.J., Lott, C.L., Heilizer, R., & Gregg, B. (1986). Type A behavior pattern and the judgment of control. *Journal of Personality and Social Psychology, 50,* 403–412.

Strube, M.J., & Ota, J. (1982). Type A coronary-prone behavior pattern: Re-

lationship to birth order and family size. *Personality and Social Psychology Bulletin, 8,* 317–323.

Strube, M.J., & Werner, C. (1985). Relinquishment of control and the Type A behavior pattern. *Journal of Personality and Social Psychology, 48,* 688–701.

Suedfeld, P. (1985). APA Presidential addresses: The relation of integrative complexity to historical, professional, and personal factors. *Journal of Personality and Social Psychology, 49,* 1643–1651.

Suedfeld, P., & Piedrahita, L.E. (1984). Intimations of mortality: Integrative simplification as a precursor of death. *Journal of Personality and Social Psychology, 47,* 848–852.

Sullivan, H.S. (1953). *The interpersonal theory of psychiatry.* New York: W.W. Norton.

Sulloway, F.J. (1972). Family constellations, sibling rivalry, and scientific revolutions. Unpublished manuscript.

Sulloway, F.J. (1979). *Freud: Biologist of the mind.* New York: Basic Books.

Suls, J., & Rittenhouse, J.D. (1987). Personality and physical health: An introduction. *Journal of Personality, 55,* 155–167.

Sutton-Smith, B. (1986). Children's fiction making. In T.R. Sarbin (Ed.), *Narrative psychology: The storied nature of human conduct* (pp. 67–90). New York: Praeger.

Tappan, M. (1990). Hermeneutics and moral development: Implementing narrative representation of moral experience. *Developmental Review, 10,* 239–265.

Tappan, M., & Brown, L. (1989). Stories told and lessons learned: Toward a narrative approach to moral development and moral education. *Harvard Educational Review, 59,* 182–205.

Taylor, M.C., & Hall, J.A. (1982). Psychological androgyny: Theories, methods, and conclusions. *Psychological Bulletin, 92,* 347–366.

Taylor, S.E. (1983). Adjustment to threatening events: A theory of cognitive adaptation. *American Psychologist, 38,* 1161–1173.

Taylor, S.E., & Brown, J.D. (1988). Illusion and well-being: A social psychological perspective on mental health. *Psychological Bulletin, 103,* 193–210.

Tekiner, A.C. (1980). Need achievement and international differences in income growth: 1950–1960. *Economic Development and Cultural Change,* 293–320.

Tellegen, A. (1982). *Brief manual for the Differential Personality Questionnaire.* Unpublished manuscript, University of Minnesota.

Tellegen, A. (1985). Structures of mood and personality and their relevance to assessing anxiety, with an emphasis on self-report. In A.H. Tuma and J.D. Masser (Eds.), *Anxiety and the anxiety disorders* (pp. 681–716). Hillsdale, NJ: Lawrence Erlbaum.

Tellegen, A., & Atkinson, G. (1974). Openness to absorbing and self-altering experiences ("absorption"), a trait related to hypnotic susceptibility. *Journal of Abnormal Psychology, 83,* 268–277.

Tellegen, A., Lykken, D.J., Bouchard, T.J., Jr., Wilcox, K.J., Segal, N.L., & Rich, S. (1988). Personality similarity in twins reared apart and together. *Journal of Personality and Social Psychology, 54,* 1031–1039.

Tesch, S.A., & Whitbourne, S.K. (1982). Intimacy and identity status in young adults. *Journal of Personality and Social Psychology, 43,* 1041–1051.

Tetlock, P.E. (1981a). Pre- to post-election shifts in presidential rhetoric: Impression management or cognitive adjustment? *Journal of Personality and Social Psychology, 41,* 207–212.

Tetlock, P.E. (1981b). Personality and isolationism: Content analysis of senatorial speeches. *Journal of Personality and Social Psychology, 41,* 737–743.

Tetlock, P.E. (1984). Cognitive style and political belief systems in the British House of Commons. *Journal of Personality and Social Psychology, 46,* 365–375.

Tetlock, P.E., Bernzweig, J., & Gallant, J.L. (1985). Supreme Court decision making: Cognitive style as a predictor of ideological consistency of voting. *Journal of Personality and Social Psychology, 48,* 1227–1239.

Tetlock, P.E., Hannum, K., & Micheletti, P. (1984). Stability and change in the complexity of senatorial rhetoric: Testing the cognitive versus rhetorical style hypotheses. *Journal of Personality and Social Psychology, 46,* 979–990.

Thomas, A., & Chess, S. (1977). *Temperament and development.* New York: Bruner/Mazel.

Thomas, A., Chess, S., & Birch, H.G. (1970). The origin of personality. *Scientific American, 223,* 102–109.

Thomas, W.I., & Znaniecki, F. (1927). *The Polish Peasant in Europe and America.* New York: Alfred A. Knopf.

Thompson, C. (1942). Cultural pressures in the psychology of women. *Psychiatry, 5,* 331–339.

Thompson, S.C., Sobolew-Shubin, A., Galbraith, M.E., Schwankovsky, L., & Cruzen, D. (1993). Maintaining perceptions of control: Finding perceived control in low-control circumstances. *Journal of Personality and Social Psychology, 64,* 293–304.

Thorne, A. (1989). Conditional patterns, transference, and the coherence of personality across time. In D.M. Buss and N. Cantor (Eds.), *Personality psychology: Recent trends and emerging directions* (pp. 149–159). New York: Springer-Verlag.

Thorne, A., & Gough, H. (1991). *Portraits of type: An MBTI research compendium.* Palo Alto, CA: Consulting Psychologists Press.

Thorndike, R.L. (1959). Review of the California Psychological Inventory. In O.K. Buros (Ed.), *Fifth mental measurements yearbook.* Highland Park, NJ: Gryphon Press.

Tice, D.M. (1989). Metatraits: Interitem variance as personality assessment. In D.M. Buss and N. Cantor (Eds.), *Personality psychology: Recent trends and emerging directions* (pp. 194–200). New York: Springer-Verlag.

Tinbergen, N. (1951). *The study of instinct.* London: Oxford University Press.

Titus, H.E., & Hollander, E.P. (1957). The California F scale in psychological research: 1950–1955. *Psychological Bulletin, 54,* 45–64.

Toder, N., & Marcia, J.E. (1973). Ego identity status and response to conformity pressure in college women. *Journal of Personality and Social Psychology, 26,* 287–294.

Tolman, E.C. (1948). Cognitive maps in rats and men. *Psychological Review, 55,* 189–208.

Tomkins, S.S. (1947). *The Thematic Apperception Test.* New York: Grune & Stratton.

Tomkins, S.S. (1962). *Affect, imagery, consciousness* (Vol. 1). New York: Springer.

Tomkins, S.S. (1963). *Affect, imagery, consciousness* (Vol. 2). New York: Springer.

Tomkins, S.S. (1979). Script theory. In H.E. Howe, Jr., and R.A. Dienstbier (Eds.), *Nebraska symposium on motivation* (Vol. 26, pp. 201–236). Lincoln, NE: University of Nebraska Press.

Tomkins, S.S. (1981). The quest for primary motives: Biography and autobiography of an idea. *Journal of Personality and Social Psychology, 41,* 306–329.

Tomkins, S.S. (1987). Script theory. In J. Aronoff, A.I. Rabin, and R.A. Zucker (Eds.), *The emergence of personality* (pp. 147–216). New York: Springer.

Tomkins, S.S., & Izard, C.E. (1965). *Affects, cognition, and personality.* New York: Springer.

Tomkins, S.S., & Miner, J.R. (1957). *The Tomkins—Horn picture arrangement test.* New York: Springer.

Tooby, J., & Cosmides, L. (1990). On the universality of human nature and the uniqueness of the individual: The role of genetics and adaptation. *Journal of Personality, 58,* 17–67.

Trabasso, T., Secco, T., & Van Den Broek, P. (1984). Causal cohesion and story coherence. In H. Mandl, N.L. Stein, and T. Trabasso (Eds.), *Learning and comprehension of text.* Hillsdale, NJ: Lawrence Erlbaum.

Trapnell, P.D., & Wiggins, J.S. (1990). Extension of the Interpersonal Adjective Scales to include the Big Five dimensions of personality. *Journal of Personality and Social Psychology, 59,* 781–790.

Trivers, R.L. (1971). The evolution of reciprocal altruism. *Quarterly Review of Biology, 46,* 35–57.

Tulving, E. (1972). Episodic and semantic memory. In B. Tulving and W. Donaldson (Eds.), *Organization and memory.* New York: Academic Press.

Tupes, E.C., & Christal, R.C. (1961). *Recurrent personality factors based on trait ratings.* (Tech. Rep. No. ASD-TR-61-97). Lackland Air Force Base, TX: U.S. Air Force.

Turner, P.J. (1991). Relations between attachment, gender, and behavior with peers in preschool. *Child Development, 62,* 1475–1488.

Uleman, J.S. (1966). *A new TAT measure of the need for power.* Unpublished doctoral dissertation, Harvard University.

Underwood, B., & Moore, B.J. (1981). Sources of behavioral consistency. *Journal of Personality and Social Psychology, 40,* 780–785.

Urist, J. (1977). The Rorschach test and the assessment of object relations. *Journal of Personality Assessment, 41,* 3–9.

Vaillant, G.E. (1971). Theoretical hierarchy of adaptive ego mechanisms. *Archives of General Psychiatry, 24,* 107–118.

Vaillant, G.E. (1977). *Adaptation to life.* Boston: Little, Brown.

Vaillant, G.E., & Drake, R.E. (1985). Maturity of ego defense in relation to DSM III Axis II personality disorder. *Archives of General Psychiatry, 42,* 597–601.

Vaillant, G.E., & Milofsky, E. (1980). The natural history of male psychological health: IX. Empirical evidence for Erikson's model of the life cycle. *American Journal of Psychiatry, 137,* 1349–1359.

Vallacher, R.R., & Wegner, D.M. (1987). What do people think they're doing? Action identification and human behavior. *Psychological Review, 94,* 3–15.

Van de Water, D., & McAdams, D.P. (1989). Generativity and Erikson's "belief in the species." *Journal of Research in Personality, 23,* 435–449.

Veroff, J. (1957). Development and validation of a projective measure of power motivation. *Journal of Abnormal and Social Psychology, 54,* 1–8.

Veroff, J. (1982). Assertive motivation: Achievement versus power. In A.J. Stewart (Ed.), *Motivation and society* (pp. 99–132). San Francisco: Jossey-Bass.

Veroff, J. (1983). Contextual determinants of personality. *Personality and Social Psychology Bulletin, 9,* 331–343.

Veroff, J., Douvan, E., & Kulka, R. (1981). *The inner American.* New York: Basic Books.

Veroff, J., & Feld, S.C. (1970). *Marriage and work in America.* New York: Van Nostrand Reinhold.

Vitz, P.C. (1990). The use of stories in moral development: New psychological reasons for an old education method. *American Psychologist, 45,* 709–720.

Wainer, H.A., & Rubin, I.M. (1969). Motivation of research and development entrepreneurs. *Journal of Applied Psychology, 53,* 178–184.

Wallace, D.B., & Gruber, H.E. (Eds.). (1989). *Creative people at work.* New York: Oxford University Press.

Wallston, K.A., & Wallston, B.S. (1981). Health locus of control scales. In H.M. Lefcourt (Ed.), *Research with the locus of control construct: Assessment methods* (Vol. 1, pp. 189–243). New York: Academic Press.

Walster, E.H., & Walster, G.W. (1978). *A new look at love.* Reading, MA: Addison-Wesley.

Washburn, S.L., & Lancaster, C.J. (1973). The evolution of hunting. In C.L. Brace and J. Motress (Eds.), Man in evolutionary perspective. New York: John Wiley & Sons.

Waterman, A.S. (1982). Identity development from adolescence to adulthood: An extension of theory and a review of research. *Developmental Psychology, 18,* 341–358.

Watkins, M. (1986). *Invisible guests: The development of imaginal dialogues.* Hillsdale, NJ: Analytic Press.

Watson, D., & Clark, L.A. (1984). Negative affectivity: The disposition to experience aversive emotional states. *Psychological Bulletin, 96,* 465–490.

Watson, D., & Clark, L.A. (1992). Affects separable and inseparable: On the hierarchical arrangement of the negative affects. *Journal of Personality and Social Psychology, 62,* 489–505.

Watson, D., Clark, L.A., McIntyre, C.W., & Hamaker, S. (1992). Affect, personality, and social activity. *Journal of Personality and Social Psychology, 63,* 1011–1025.

Watson, D., & Tellegen, A. (1985). Toward a consensual structure of mood. *Psychological Bulletin, 98,* 219–235.

Watson, J.B. (1913). Psychology as the behaviorist views it. *Psychological Review, 20,* 158–177.

Watson, J.B. (1924). *Behaviorism.* Chicago: University of Chicago Press.

Watson, J.B., & Raynor, R. (1920). Conditional emotional reactions. *Journal of Experimental Psychology, 3,* 1–14.

Watson, P.J., Grisham, S.O., Trotter, M.V., & Biderman, M.D. (1984). Narcissism and empathy: Validity evidence for the Narcissistic Personality Inventory. *Journal of Personality Assessment, 48,* 301–305.

Weakland, J. (1976). Communication theory and clinical change. In P.G. Guerin (Ed.), *Family therapy* (pp. 111–128). New York: Gardner Press.

Wegner, D.M., Schneider, D.J., Carter, S.R., & White, T.L. (1987). Paradoxical effects of thought suppression. *Journal of Personality and Social Psychology, 53,* 5–13.

Weinberger, D.A., Schwartz, G.E., & Davidson, R.J. (1979). Low-anxious, high-anxious, and repressive coping styles: Psychometric patterns and behavioral and physiological responses to stress. *Journal of Abnormal Psychology, 88,* 369–380.

Weiner, B. (1979). A theory of motivation for some classroom experiences. *Journal of Educational Psychology, 71,* 3–25.

Weiner, B. (1980). *Human motivation.* New York: Holt, Rinehart & Winston.

Weiner, B. (1990). Attribution in personality psychology. In L. Pervin (Ed.), *Handbook of personality theory and research* (pp. 465–485). New York: Guilford Press.

Weisen, A. (1965). *Differential reinforcing effects of onset and offset of stimulation on the operant behavior of normals, neurotics, and psychopaths.* Unpublished doctoral dissertation, University of Florida.

Weiss, L., & Masling, J. (1970). Further validation of a Rorschach measure of oral imagery: A study of six clinical groups. *Journal of Abnormal Psychology, 76,* 83–87.

Weiss, L.R. (1969). Effects of subject, experimenter, and task variables on compliance with the experimenter's expectation. *Journal of Projective Techniques and Personality Assessment, 33,* 247–256.

Werner, H. (1957). The concept of development from a comparative and an organismic point of view. In D. Harris (Ed.), *The concept of development.* Minneapolis, MN: University of Minnesota Press.

West, S.G. (1983). Personality and prediction: An introduction. *Journal of Personality, 51,* 275–285.

Westen, D. (1990). Psychoanalytic approaches to personality. In L. Pervin (Ed.), *Handbook of personality theory and research* (pp. 21–65). New York: Guilford Press.

Westen, D. (1991a). Social cognition and object relations. *Psychological Bulletin, 109,* 429–455.

Westen, D. (1991b). Clinical assessment of object relations using the TAT. *Journal of Personality Assessment, 56,* 56–74.

Westen, D., Klepfer, J., Ruffins, S., Silverman, M., Lifton, N., & Boekamp, J. (in press). Object relations in childhood and adolescence: The development of working representations. *Journal of Consulting and Clinical Psychology.*

Westen, D., Lohr, N.E., Silk, K., Gold, L., & Gerber, K. (1990). Object relations and social cognition in borderlines, major depressives, and normals: A thematic apperception test analysis. *Psychological Assessment: A Journal of Consulting and Clinical Psychology, 2,* 355–364.

Westen, D., Ludolph, P. Silk, K., Kellam, A., Gold, L., & Lohr, N.E. (1990). Object relations in borderline adolescents and adults: Developmental differences. *Adolescent Psychiatry, 17,* 360–384.

Whitbourne, S.K. (1985). The psychological construction of the life span. In J.E. Birren and K.W. Schaie (Eds.), *Handbook of the psychology of aging* (2nd ed.) (pp. 594–618). New York: Van Nostrand Reinhold.

Whitbourne, S.K. (1986). Openness to experience, identity flexibility, and life changes in adults. *Journal of Personality and Social Psychology, 50,* 163–168.

White, J.L., & Parham, T.A. (1990). *The psychology of blacks: An African-American perspective.* Englewood Cliffs, NJ: Prentice-Hall.

White, R.W. (1948). *The abnormal personality.* New York: Ronald Press.

White, R.W. (1952). *Lives in progress* (1st ed.). New York: Holt, Rinehart & Winston.

White, R.W. (1959). Motivation reconsidered: The concept of competence. *Psychological Review, 66,* 297–333.

White, R.W. (1960). Competence and the psychosexual stages of development. In M.R. Jones (Ed.), *Nebraska symposium on motivation* (Vol. 8). Lincoln, NE: University of Nebraska Press.

White, R.W. (1963). Sense of interpersonal competence: Two case studies and some reflections on origins. In R.W. White (Ed.), *The study of lives* (pp. 72–93). New York: Prentice-Hall.

White, R.W. (1963). (Ed.). *The study of lives: Essays on personality in honor of Henry A. Murray.* New York: Prentice-Hall.

White, R.W. (1966). *Lives in progress* (2nd ed.). New York: Holt, Rinehart & Winston.

White, R.W. (1972). *The enterprise of living: A view of personal growth.* New York: Holt, Rinehart & Winston.

White, R.W. (1975). *Lives in progress* (3rd ed.). New York: Holt, Rinehart & Winston.

White, R.W. (1981). Exploring personality the long way: The study of lives. In A.I. Rabin, J. Aronoff, A.M. Barclay, and R.A. Zucker (Eds.), *Further explorations in personality* (pp. 3–19). New York: John Wiley & Sons.

White, R.W. (1987). *Seeking the shape of personality: A memoir.* Marlborough, NH: The Homestead Press.

Whiting, J.W.M., & Child, I.L. (1953). *Child training and personality: A cross-cultural study.* New Haven, CT: Yale University Press.

Whitley, B.E., Jr. (1983). Sex role orientation and self esteem: A critical meta-analytic review. *Journal of Personality and Social Psychology, 44,* 765–778.

Whitson, E.R. (1983). *Oral, obsessive, and hysterical personality and cigarette-smoking behaviors.* Unpublished doctoral dissertation, State University of New York at Buffalo.

Wicklund, R.A., & Duvall, J. (1971). Opinion change and performance facilitation as a result of objective self-awareness. *Journal of Experimental Social Psychology, 7,* 319–342.

Wiebe, D.J., & McCallum, D.M. (1986). Health practices and hardiness as mediators in the stress-illness relationship. *Health Psychology, 5,* 425–438.

Wiedenfeld, S.A., O'Leary, A., Bandura, A., Brown, S., Levine, S., & Raska, K. (1990). Impact of perceived self-efficacy in coping with stressors on components of the immune system. *Journal of Personality and Social Psychology, 59,* 1082–1094.

Wiggins, J.S. (1973). *Personality and prediction: Principles of personality assessment.* Reading, MA: Addison-Wesley.

Wiggins, J.S. (1979). A psychological taxonomy of trait-descriptive terms: The interpersonal domain. *Journal of Personality and Social Psychology, 37,* 395–412.

Wiggins, J.S. (1982). Circumplex models of interpersonal behavior in clinical psychology. In P.C. Kendall and J.N. Butcher (Eds.), *Handbook of research methods in clinical psychology* (pp. 183–221). New York: Wiley.

Wiggins, J.S. (1992). Have model, will travel. *Journal of Personality, 60,* 527–532.

Wiggins, J.S., & Broughton, R. (1985). The interpersonal circle: A structural model for the integration of personality research. In R. Hogan & W.H. Jones (Eds.), *Perspectives in personality* (Vol. 1, pp. 1–47). Greenwich, CT: JAI Press.

Willerman, L. (1979). *The psychology of individual and group differences.* San Francisco, CA: W.H. Freeman.

Wilson, E.O. (1975). *Sociobiology: The new synthesis.* Cambridge, MA: Harvard University Press.

Wilson, E.O. (1978). *On human nature.* Cambridge, MA: Harvard University Press.

Wilson, G.D. (1978). Introversion-extroversion. In H. London and J.E. Exner, Jr. (Eds.), *Dimensions of personality* (pp. 217–261). New York: John Wiley & Sons.

Wilson, G.D., & Nias, D.K.B. (1975). Sexual types. *New Behaviour, 2,* 330–332.

Wincze, J.P., & Lange, J.D. (1981). Assessment of sexual behavior. In D. Barlow (Ed.), *Behavioral assessment of adult disorders.* New York: Guilford Press.

Wink, P. (1991). Two faces of narcissism. *Journal of Personality and Social Psychology, 61,* 590–597.

Wink, P. (1992a). Three types of narcissism in women from college to midlife. *Journal of Personality, 60,* 7–30.

Wink, P. (1992b). Three narcissism scales for the California Q-set. *Journal of Personality Assessment, 58,* 51–66.

Winnicott, D.W. (1965). *The naturational processes and the facilitating environment.* New York: International Universities Press.

Winter, D.G. (1973). *The power motive.* New York: The Free Press.

Winter, D.G. (1987). Leader appeal, leader performance, and the motive profiles of leaders and followers: A study of American Presidents and elections. *Journal of Personality and Social Psychology, 52,* 196–202.

Winter, D.G., & Carlson, L.A. (1988). Using motive scores in the psychobiographical study of an individual: The case of Richard Nixon. *Journal of Personality, 56,* 75–103.

Winter, D.G., McClelland, D.C., & Stewart, A.J. (1981). A new case for the liberal arts: Assessing institutional goals and student development. San Francisco, CA: Jossey-Bass.

Winter, D.G., & Stewart, A.J. (1977). Power motive reliability as a function of retest instructions. *Journal of Consulting and Clinical Psychology, 45,* 436–440.

Winter, D.G., & Stewart, A.J. (1978). The power motive. In H. London and J.E. Exner (Eds.), *Dimensions of personality* (pp. 391–447). New York: John Wiley & Sons.

Wish, M., Deutsch, M., & Kaplan, S.J. (1976). Perceived dimensions of interpersonal relations. *Journal of Personality and Social Psychology, 33,* 409–420.

Witkin, H.A. (1949). Perception of body position and of the position of the visual field. *Psychological Monographs, 63,* (7 Whole No. 302).

Witkin, H.A. (1950). Individual differences in ease of perception of embedded figures. *Journal of Personality, 19,* 1–15.

Witkin, H.A., & Berry, J. (1975). Psychological differentiation in cross-cultural perspective. *Journal of Cross-Cultural Psychology, 6,* 4–87.

Witkin, H.A., Goodenough, D.R., & Oltmann, P.K. (1979). Psychological differentiation: Current status. *Journal of Personality and Social Psychology, 37,* 1127–1145.

Wolf, E.S. (1982). Comments on Heinz Kohut's conceptualization of a bipolar self. In B. Lee (Ed.), *Psychosocial theories of the self* (pp. 23–42). New York: Plenum.

Wolpe, J. (1973). *The practice of behavior therapy* (2nd ed.) New York: Pergamon Press.

Wolpe, J., & Lazarus, A.A. (1966). *Behavior therapy techniques: A guide to the treatment of neuroses.* Oxford: Pergamon Press.

Wright, J.C., & Mischel, W. (1987). A conditional approach to dispositional constructs: The local predictability of social behavior. *Journal of Personality, 53,* 1159–1177.

Wrightsman, L.S. (1981). Personal documents as data in conceptualizing adult personality development. *Personality and Social Psychology Bulletin, 7,* 367–385.

Wyer, R.S., Jr., & Srull, T.K. (1989). (Eds.). *Advances in social cognition: Vol. II: Social intelligence and cognitive assessments of personality.* Hillsdale, NJ: Lawrence Erlbaum.

Wylie, R. (1979). *The self-concept,* Vol. 2. *Theory and research on selected topics.* Lincoln, NE: University of Nebraska Press.

Wymer, W.E., & Penner, L.A. (1985).

Moderator variables and different types of predictability: Do you have a match? *Journal of Personality and Social Psychology, 49,* 1002–1015.

Wynne-Edwards, V.C. (1963/1978). Intergroup selection in the evolution of social systems. In T.H. Clutton-Brock and P.H. Harvey (Eds.), *Readings in sociobiology* (pp. 10–19). San Francisco, CA: Freeman.

Yin, R.K. (1984). *Case study research: Design and methods.* Beverly Hills, CA: Sage.

York, K.L., & John, O.P. (1992). The four faces of Eve: A typological analysis of women's personality at midlife. *Journal of Personality and Social Psychology, 63,* 494–508.

Zajonc, R.B. (1976). Family configuration and intelligence: Variations in scholastic aptitude scores parallel trends in family size and the spacing of children. *Science, 192* (4236), 227–236.

Zajonc, R.B. (1980). Feeling and thinking: Preferences need no inferences. *American Psychologist, 35,* 151–175.

Zajonc, R.B. (1984). On the primacy of affect. *American Psychologist, 39,* 117–123.

Zeldow, P.B., Clark, D.C., & Daugherty, S.R. (1985). Personality indicators of psychosocial adjustment in first-year medical students. *Social Science Medicine, 20,* 95–100.

Zeldow, P.B., Daugherty, S.R., & Clark, D.C. (1987). Masculinity, femininity, and psychosocial adjustment in medical students: Two-year follow-up. *Journal of Personality Assessment, 51,* 3–14.

Zeldow, P.B., & Daugherty, S.R. (1991). Personality profiles and specialty choices of students from two medical school classes. *Academic Medicine, 66,* 283–287.

Zeldow, P.B., Daugherty, S.R., & McAdams, D.P. (1988). Intimacy, power, and psychological well-being in medical students. *The Journal of Nervous and Mental Disease, 176,* 182–187.

Zimbardo, P.G. (1977). *Shyness: What it is, what to do about it.* Reading, MA: Addison-Wesley.

Zinbarg, R., & Revelle, W. (1989). Personality and conditioning: A test of four models. *Journal of Personality and Social Psychology, 57,* 301–314.

Zubin, J., Eron, L.D., & Schumer, F. (1965). *An experimental approach to projective techniques.* New York: John Wiley.

Zuckerman, M. (1960). The development of an affective adjective check list for the measurement of anxiety. *Journal of Consulting and Clinical Psychology, 24,* 457–462.

Zuckerman, M. (1978). Sensation seeking. In H. London and J.E. Exner (Eds.), *Dimensions of personality* (pp. 487–560). New York: John Wiley & Sons.

Zuckerman, M. (1979). *Sensation seek-*

ing: Beyond the optimal level of arousal. Hillsdale, NJ: Lawrence Erlbaum.

Zuckerman, M., Bernieri, F., Koestner, R., & Rosenthal, R. (1989). To predict some of the people some of the time: In search of moderators. Journal of Personality and Social Psychology, 57, 279–298.

Zuckerman, M., Miyake, K., Koestner, R., Baldwin, C.H., & Osborne, J.W. (1991). Uniqueness as a moderator of self-peer agreement. Personality and Social Psychology Bulletin, 17, 385–391.

Zukav, G. (1979). The dancing Wu Li masters: An overview of the new physics. New York: William Morrow & Company.

Zuroff, D.C. (1986). Was Gordon Allport a trait theorist? Journal of Personality and Social Psychology, 51, 993–1000.

Name Index

Abelson, R., 487, 490, 519
Abraham, K., 65, 89
Abramson, L. Y., 435, 507
Acker, M., 513
Acton, H., 225
Adams, G. R., 670
Adams, J., 634
Adams, J. Q., 634
Adler, A., 19, 29, 37–38, 44, 53, 65, 86, 87, 291, 293, 455, 469, 473, 588, 659, 688–696, 700, 704, 719–720, 756, 769, 788, 789, 794
Adorno, T. W., 162
Agar, M. H., 615
Ainsworth, M. D. S., 50, 218, 219, 220, 223, 225, 229, 235, 236, 291
Akbar, N., 407
Albert, R. S., 27
Alexander, C., 636
Alexander, I. E., 700, 705
Alker, H. A., 363
Allen, A., 366, 372
Allen, J., 506, 670
Allison, G. T., 615
Allman, A., 282
Alloy, L. B., 435
Allport, G. W., 44, 45, 250–251, 252, 264, 296, 353, 358, 368, 410, 455, 469, 473, 530, 540–541, 548, 617, 770
Alwin, D. F., 645
Amabile, T. M., 441
Amato, P. R., 393
Amelang, M., 372
American Psychiatric Association, 173
Amsterdam, B. K., 549
Anastasi, A., 259
Anderson, J. W., 596, 696, 701
Anderson, N. B., 387
Anderson, W. P., 259
Andornetto, M., 344
Andrews, J. D. W., 626
Angleitner, A., 265
Anthony, E. J., 152
Antill, J. K., 501
Applebee, A. N., 724
Applefield, J. M., 347
Apter, M. J., 451–455
Archer, J., 202
Ardrey, R., 179
Arenberg, P., 272
Arend, R., 226, 227
Argyle, M., 363
Arieti, S., 22
Aristotle, 315, 726
Arnkoff, D. B., 338
Aronson, E., 618
Asch, S., 522
Ashmore, R. D., 577–578, 579, 582
Atkinson, G., 286
Atkinson, J. W., 622, 625, 629, 635, 644, 645
Atkinson, R. C., 143
Atwood, G. E., 58
Aubrey, J., 697
Auchincloss, L., 172

Averill, J. R., 508, 509
Avery, R. R., 562

Bach, J. S., 762
Bacon, F., 691
Bacon, S., 306
Bagby, R. M., 398
Bakan, D., 131, 293, 294, 308, 640, 644, 753, 771, 778
Bakhtin, M. M., 777
Baldwin, C. H., 372
Baldwin, J. M., 543, 564
Baley, J., 151
Ball, D. W., 391
Bandura, A., 16, 28, 242, 323, 330–336, 346, 347, 357, 364, 400, 444, 787, 790, 795
Banks, E., 332
Barash, D. P., 186, 188, 191–192, 213
Barbano, H. E., 274
Barbee, A. P., 199
Barlow, D. H., 34
Barnes, M., 193, 199
Barnett, D., 230
Baron, R. A., 347
Barrends, A., 167
Barron, F., 22
Baruch, R., 626
Basu, G. K., 211
Bateson, G., 9, 403
Bateson, M. C., 7, 9
Batson, C. D., 214
Batson, J. G., 214
Battistich, V. A., 393
Baumeister, R. F., 56, 69, 371, 497, 521, 766, 769
Baumgarten, F., 264
Baumrind, D., 356
Bayma, B., 278, 279
Beall, S. K., 734
Beaman, A. L., 214
Beattie, A., 751
Beattie, O. V., 707–708
Beck, A. T., 505, 506
Beck, S., 598
Becker, E., 428–430, 681, 682
Becker, H. S., 615
Beckett, S., 724
Behrends, R. S., 96
Beier, J., 145
Beit-Hallahmi, B., 629
Belkin, J., 505
Bellah, R. N., 172, 409–410, 758
Belsky, J., 226, 231, 232–234
Bem, D. J., 205, 366, 372, 394, 395, 401, 788
Bem, S. L., 498, 499, 500, 501, 502, 503, 504
Bendig, A. W., 267
Benedict, R., 19
Bennett, A., 532
Bentham, J., 316, 531
Berger, P. A., 205
Berghuis, J. P., 216
Bergman, A., 98
Berkowitz, J., 347
Berkowitz, L., 351

Berler, R., 298–299
Berman, J. S., 363
Bernat, E. F., 604
Bernays, M., 60
Berne, E., 756
Bernieri, F., 371, 372
Bernstein, B. A., 405
Bernstein, S., 504
Bernzweig, J., 529
Berry, J., 527
Berry, J. M., 388
Berry, J. W., 408
Bertaux, D., 696, 706
Bertenthal, B. I., 549
Bertini, M., 523
Bertrand, S., 157
Besch, N. F., 211
Bettelheim, B., 730
Biderman, M. D., 173
Bierhoff, H. W., 215
Biernat, M., 78
Binswanger, L., 424, 431, 456, 541
Birch, D., 622
Birch, H. G., 296
Bird, S. E., 727
Blake, R., 353
Blaney, P. H., 449, 508
Blasi, A., 539, 540, 549
Blass, J., 45, 396
Blatt, S. J., 96, 166, 167
Blehar, M. C., 218, 219, 225
Bleuler, E., 3, 101
Block, J., 28, 264, 344, 356, 363, 365, 370, 377- 382, 384, 386, 394, 411, 788
Block, J. H., 344, 379
Bloom, A., 409
Bloom, A. R., 626
Blos, P., 125, 153, 557
Boekamp, J., 167
Boland, S. M., 387
Bolen, J. S., 110–111
Bolger, N., 277
Bonarius, H., 770, 771
Bongort, K., 645
Bonneville, L. P., 562
Booth, C. L., 229
Booth, L., 755
Booth, W. C., 768
Borden, W., 732
Boring, E. G., 314
Borkenau, P., 372
Borkovec, T. D., 338
Bornstein, R. F., 149, 158
Boss, M., 424, 431
Boswell, J., 697–698
Bouchard, T. J., Jr., 300, 301, 303
Bourne, E., 411, 669
Bower, G. H., 508–509
Bowers, K. S., 397
Bowlby, J., 28, 50, 182, 218–219, 221, 222, 228, 235, 237, 291, 797
Boxer, A. M., 761
Boyatzis, R. E., 626, 633, 644
Bradley, P., 259
Brainerd, C. J., 375
Brand, P., 644
Brand, R. J., 387

Brandt, J. R., 214
Brannon, R., 157
Braunwald, K., 230
Brazelton, T. B., 226
Breger, L., 182, 666
Brehm, S. S., 506, 507
Brennan, K. A., 291, 292
Brenneis, B., 166
Breslow, R., 505
Breuer, J., 60–61, 63, 129, 130
Brewer, W. F., 726
Brickman, P., 440
Bridges, L. J., 231
Briere, J., 348
Briggs, S. R., 204, 413
Brill, A. A., 67
Brittain, V., 57, 245–249, 251
Brody, N., 487
Bromley, D. B., 616, 617, 618, 619, 620
Bronfenbrenner, U., 389, 404
Brooks-Gunn, J., 549
Brosnan, J., 299
Broughton, J. M., 559
Broughton, R., 293
Brower, A. M., 493
Brown, J. D., 435, 436
Brown, L., 769
Brown, N. O., 54
Brown, R., 483, 484
Brown, S., 335
Brown, W. A., 212
Browning, D. S., 678, 680, 682
Bruch, M. A., 205
Brucke, E., 59–60, 66
Bruhn, A. R., 693
Bruner, J. S., 145, 363, 599, 646, 647, 722–723, 750, 753, 769, 770
Brunson, B. I., 387
Brunswik, E., 400, 401, 619
Bryant, F., 643
Buber, M., 424, 427, 463, 466, 640
Buchanan, J., 634
Buckner, B., 299
Bühler, C., 707
Burisch, M., 249, 257
Burish, T. G., 387
Burkham, R., 151
Burlingham, D., 656
Burnham, D. H., 633
Buss, A. H., 204, 205, 297, 300, 322, 323, 411, 413, 497
Buss, D. M., 4, 188–191, 193, 199, 200, 234, 368–369, 370, 512
Butler, R. N., 687
Butterfield, E. C., 485
Byers, S., 167
Byrne, D., 42, 163
Byron, G. G., 54

Caesar, J., 697
Cairns, R. B., 180
Calder, B. J., 441
Campbell, D. T., 255, 616, 617
Campbell, J., 111–112
Campbell, K., 225
Cann, D. R., 171

Cantor, N., 392, 416, 486, 487, 488, 488–493, 491, 493, 512, 513
Cantor, N. F., 54, 56, 57
Carlo, G., 215
Carlsmith, J. M., 618
Carlson, L. A., 625, 631, 700
Carlson, R., 42, 171, 174, 386, 700, 738, 741, 742, 743, 744–745
Carlson, V., 230
Carment, D. W., 267
Carr, T. S., 211
Carter, J., 633, 635
Carter, S. R., 735
Carter, T., 152, 604
Carver, C. J., 517
Carver, C. S., 62, 436, 486, 511, 516, 517, 518, 519, 520
Caspi, A., 205, 401–402
Cassidy, J., 218, 228, 235
Catlin, G., 246, 247
Cattell, R. B., 247, 249, 250, 251–253, 263, 264, 365, 472, 473, 787, 792
Cervin, V. B., 267
Chafe, W., 770
Chaikin, A. L., 278, 279
Chamberlain, W., 191
Chaplin, W. F., 371, 372
Chapman, M., 215, 352
Charcot, J. M., 60, 69
Charme, S. T., 756
Cheek, J. M., 202, 204, 205, 366
Chess, S., 296
Chester, N. L., 159, 160, 164, 625, 626, 631, 644
Child, I. L., 408
Chipuer, H. M., 302, 303, 306
Chiriboga, D., 762
Chodorow, N., 77, 78–80
Christal, R. C., 264, 265
Christie, R., 163
Christopher, S. B., 188
Church, A. T., 265
Churchill, W., 630
Cialdini, R. B., 214
Cicchetti, D., 230
Clark, D. C., 501
Clark, L. A., 267, 274, 277
Clark, R. A., 622
Clarke-Stewart, K. A., 230
Cleveland, G., 634
Cochran, S. D., 511
Cohen, L. H., 500
Cohen, R., 151
Cohler, B. J., 747, 761, 769
Cohn, L. D., 562
Cohn, M., 273
Cole, J., 407
Coleridge, S. T., 54
Coles, R., 720, 727
Colletti, G., 504
Collins, T. M., 205
Colvin, C. R., 282, 365, 411
Conger, J. J., 557
Conley, J. J., 249, 272, 277, 412
Connell, D. B., 230
Connell, J. P., 231
Conner, J. M., 504

Constantian, C. A., 642
Constantinople, A., 500
Cook, T. D., 365
Cook-Flannagan, C., 513
Cooley, C. H., 564
Coolidge, C., 633, 635
Cooper, J., 269
Coopersmith, S., 580, 581
Copernicus, N., 691
Cordes, C., 723
Coser, L. A., 568
Cosmides, L., 190
Costa, P. T., Jr., 264, 265, 266, 267, 272, 274, 277, 284, 285, 286, 287, 288, 289, 291, 292, 294, 412, 414, 562, 713, 792
Cowen, D., 145
Cox, B. J., 398
Coyne, J. C., 510
Craig, G., 480
Craighead, W. E., 338
Craik, K. H., 368–369, 370
Cramer, P., 152, 153, 154, 155, 159, 604
Crandall, J. E., 695
Crandall, R., 464–465
Crane, M., 504
Cressman, L., 8
Crits-Christoph, P., 127
Crockett, H J., Jr., 625
Crockett, W. H., 479
Cronbach, L. J., 255
Cross, H., 670
Cross, S., 539, 571
Crowne, D. P., 146
Cruzen, D., 438
Csikszentmihalyi, M., 24, 465–466, 467, 676, 707–708
Cummings, E. E., 510
Cunningham, D. A., 388
Cunningham, J. P., 501
Cunningham, M. R., 188, 192, 199, 220
Curran, J. P., 338, 339

Da Vinci, L., 22–23, 24, 698–700
Dabbs, J. M., Jr., 211, 212
Dahlstrom, W. G., 259
Dali, S., 83
Damon, W., 409, 557, 583, 585
D'Andrade, R. G., 363, 411
Daple, S. A., 506
Dardenne, R. W., 727
Darrow, C. M., 711
Darwin, C., 26, 76, 182–183, 190, 200, 691, 739
Datan, N., 762
Dauber, R. M., 151
Daugherty, S. R., 501, 643, 644
Davidson, R. J., 146, 275, 636–637
Davies, B., 781
Davis, B., 636
Davis, P. J., 146
Davis, S. N., 26
Dawkins, R., 212
de Charms, R., 433, 628, 629
de LaRue, D., 212
De Paulo, B. M., 204
deReincourt, A., 429
de St. Aubin, E., 679, 680, 682, 683

Deary, I. J., 271
Deaux, K., 504
Deci, E. L., 440–441, 442–445
DeFries, J. C., 302
DeJong, W., 441
Dembroski, T. M., 389
Dentan, R. N., 208
Denzin, N. K., 615, 781
DeRaad, B., 265, 295
Derlega, V. J., 278, 279
Derrida, J., 781
Derry, P. A., 505
Descartes, R., 563
DeSoto, C. B., 363
Deutsch, F. A., 124–125
Dewsbury, D. A., 182
Dickens, C., 532
Dickman, S., 142
Diener, E., 267, 268, 277, 282, 283, 397, 400, 401
Diener, R., 282
Digman, J. M., 264, 265, 290
Dillehay, R. C., 163
Dilthey, W., 617
Dixon, T. M., 497
Dixon, V. J., 407
Dobson, W. R., 670
Dohrenwend, B. J., 445
Dohrenwend, B. P., 445
Dollard, J., 326–328, 331, 345, 473, 707, 743, 795
Dollinger, S. J., 153, 155
Donderi, D. C., 171
Donley, R. E., 633
Donnerstein, E. I., 347, 348
Donovan, J. M., 671
Doob, L. W., 326
Dostoyevsky, F., 145, 596, 777
Doty, R. M., 164
Douvan, E., 643
Dovidio, J. F., 215
Doyle, G. C., 713
Drake, R. E., 156
Draper, P., 232–234
Driver, M. J., 528
Duck, S. W., 480
Duke, M. P., 43
Dukes, W. F., 619
Dukore, B. F., 74
Dunn, J., 304, 305, 306
Durkheim, E., 780
Durrett, M. E., 226, 227
Duryea, R. A., 353
Dusek, J. B., 500
Duvall, J., 518
Dworkin, R. H., 391
Dyck, J. L., 214

Eagle, M. N., 96
Ebbesen, E. B., 341, 342
Edel, L., 700, 706
Edwards, A. L., 257
Edwards, C. P., 409
Edwards, V. J., 504
Egeland, B., 225, 230, 356
Eibl-Eibesfeldt, I., 181, 220
Eichberg, C., 229

Eifert, G., 338
Eisenberg, N., 215
Eisenberger, R., 344, 345
Eisenhower, D., 635
Ekman, P., 737, 739, 740, 797
Elder, G. H., Jr., 205, 401
Eliot, G., 532
Elkind, D., 666, 747, 749
Ellenberger, H., 69
Ellsworth, P. C., 618, 739
Elms, A. C., 604, 696
Elsbree, L., 748
Emmons, R. A., 173, 267, 268, 277, 400, 401, 416, 514, 515, 516, 517, 522, 682
Endler, N. S., 390, 396, 397, 398–400
Entwisle, D. R., 645
Epictetus, 423
Epicurus, 315–316, 331
Epstein, R., 688
Epstein, S., 35, 372–375, 412, 539
Erdelyi, M. H., 142, 143, 145
Erikson, E. H., 19, 20–21, 29, 31, 37, 53, 87, 94, 96, 99, 125, 222, 361, 541, 545, 548, 557, 559, 588, 598, 650, 651–652, 653, 656–673, 678, 681, 682, 683, 687–688, 695, 696, 700, 706, 709, 711, 719–720, 746, 747, 749, 750, 756, 761, 764, 769, 788, 789, 794, 795, 796
Eron, L. D., 347, 348, 348–351, 352, 621
Evans, I. M., 336, 338, 339
Eysenck, H. J., 14, 15, 16, 28, 264, 265, 267, 269, 270–271, 272, 274, 275, 276, 280–283, 295, 296, 303, 313, 358, 368, 414, 464, 473, 787, 792, 798
Eysenck, S. B. G., 15, 267

Fair, P. L., 740
Fairbairn, W. R. D., 50, 87, 96, 99
Farber, E. A., 225
Farber, I. E., 348
Farkas, G. M., 338
Feather, N. T., 530, 531, 625
Feeney, J. A., 237
Feinstein, D., 747
Feld, S. C., 636
Feldesman, A. B., 268
Feldman, P., 157
Fenigstein, A., 497
Fennimore, D., 388
Ferenczi, S., 65, 67
Feshbach, N. D., 215
Feshbach, S., 182, 215
Festinger, L., 615
Fick, C. M., 440
Fineberg, H. V., 217
Fisch, E., 353
Fischer, K. W., 549
Fischer, R. E., 157
Fischman, J., 389
Fishel, A. K., 149, 151
Fisher, J., 116
Fiske, D. W., 255, 264, 265, 363
Fiske, S. T., 494
Fliess, W., 61–62, 117
Floderus-Myrhed, B., 302–303
Floor, E., 636–637
Fodor, E. M., 631, 632, 637

Foley, J. M., 679, 764
Fonagy, P., 235
Forer, L. K., 690
Forgas, J. P., 392, 393
Forster, E. M., 640, 721
Forsterling, F., 265
Forsyth, D. R., 531
Fowler, J. W., 753
Fox, N. A., 231
Frable, D. E. S., 499, 502, 503
Frady, R. L., 211, 212
Francis, M. E., 735
Frank, B. M., 523
Frank, J., 598
Frank, M., 692
Frank, S., 562
Frankl, V., 424, 431, 456
Franz, C., 245
Freedman, M., 740
Frenkel, E., 707
Frenkel-Brunswik, E., 162
Frese, M., 515
Freud, Alexander, 59
Freud, Amalie, 57–58
Freud, Anna, 11, 50, 53, 65, 86, 88, 152, 656
Freud, E. L., 60
Freud, J., 58–59
Freud, S., 11–12, 13, 22–24, 25, 28, 34, 44, 50, 52–89, 91, 93, 94, 95, 96–97, 99, 101–102, 103, 107, 116, 117–138, 141, 145, 149–150, 152, 156–157, 159, 161, 165, 179, 180, 183, 190, 202, 218, 237, 245, 288, 293, 295, 313, 326–328, 358, 365, 423, 425, 428, 457, 458, 469, 473, 506, 508, 512, 539, 541, 545, 548, 599, 607, 613, 614, 645, 646, 656–659, 660, 661, 662, 664, 688, 689, 691, 698–700, 704, 711, 736, 737, 787, 789, 790, 791, 794, 795
Fried, C., 604
Friedberg, E., 389
Friedman, H. S., 389
Friedman, M., 386, 387
Friedman, M. L., 670, 671
Friedrich-Cofer, L., 347
Friesen, W. V., 739
Fromm, E., 50, 53, 87, 92–96, 101, 116, 136, 162, 455
Frye, N., 748, 750
Fujita, F., 283
Fultz, J., 214
Funder, D. C., 344, 365, 382, 394, 395, 411, 412, 413

Gadlin, H., 402
Gaertner, S. L., 215
Galanter, E., 487
Galbraith, M. E., 438
Galda, L., 769
Galen, C., 275
Gallant, J. L., 529
Galvin, K. S., 769
Gambrill, E. D., 338
Gandhi, M., 659, 678, 696
Ganellen, R. J., 449
Gangestad, S., 569

Gangestad, S. W., 194, 194–197, 197, 234
Garfield, J., 634
Garnett, A. C., 44
Garnick, N. N., 769
Gatchel, R. J., 251
Gauguin, P., 702, 762
Gay, P., 56, 69
Geen, R. A., 271, 347
Geertz, C., 728–730, 783
George, C., 235
Gerber, K., 167
Gergen, K. J., 25, 35, 36, 42, 388, 619, 720, 757, 781, 782
Getzels, J. W., 676
Ghesquire, K., 225
Ghiselli, E. E., 366
Giele, J. Z., 603
Giese, H., 267
Gilbert, F. S., 338, 339
Gill, M., 125
Gilligan, C., 625
Gilligan, C. A., 80, 644
Gittings, R., 697
Gjerde, P. F., 384
Glaser, B. G., 34
Glaser, R., 735
Glass, D. C., 387
Glenn, J., 483
Gleser, G. C., 152
Glick, M., 166
Glisky, M. L., 288
Goethe, J. W. von, 54, 57, 60
Goffman, E., 203, 566–568, 570, 757, 795
Gold, L., 167
Gold, S. N., 562
Goldberg, L. R., 247, 249, 264, 265, 267, 289, 290, 295, 372, 414
Goldfinger, S. H., 391
Goldfried, M. R., 336
Golding, S. L., 151
Golding, W., 179
Gong-Guy, E., 511
Goodenough, D. R., 523, 524, 525
Goosens, F. A., 230
Gordon, R., 562
Gorham, D., 248
Gorsky, J. M., 205
Gotlib, I. H., 510
Gough, H. G., 170, 171, 175, 176, 259, 261, 262, 264
Gould, R. L., 708
Gould, S. J., 186, 187
Gove, F. L., 227
Goya, F. J. de, 135, 761, 763
Goza, B. K., 388
Graham, J. C., 267
Graik, 706
Grajek, S., 306
Grant, C., 639–640
Grant, U., 634
Gray, J. A., 280–283, 414, 798
Graziano, W. G., 268, 290
Greenberg, M. A., 735
Greenberg, P. S., 740
Greenberg, R. P., 116

Greene, D., 440, 441
Greene, L. R., 525
Greenwald, A., 539, 583
Gregg, B., 387
Gregg, G. S., 589, 777–780
Griffit, C., 214
Grinstein, S., 133
Grisham, S. O., 173
Grolnick, W. J., 433, 434
Grossmann, K., 226–227, 228
Grossmann, K. E., 226–227, 228
Gruber, H. E., 26, 26–27
Gruder, C. L., 396, 397
Grunbaum, A., 116
Guilford, J. P., 263
Gur, D., 145
Gurtman, M. B., 293, 294
Gutmann, D., 603, 678, 762

Haan, N., 152, 382
Habermas, J., 617
Hagestad, G. O., 681
Hales, S., 581
Haley, J., 403
Hall, C. J., 44, 102, 173
Hall, C. S., 133
Hall, G. S., 65, 67
Hall, J. A., 389, 501
Hall, M. H., 460
Hallaq, J. H., 465
Hamaker, S., 267
Hammen, C. L., 511
Hankiss, A., 747, 749
Hannum, K., 529
Hansen, C. H., 147, 148–149
Hansen, R. D., 147, 148–149
Hanson, N. R., 32, 33
Harackiewicz, J. M., 692
Hardaway, R. A., 151
Harder, D., 167
Harding, W., 633, 635
Harlow, H., 459
Harre, R., 781, 782
Harris, M. J., 389
Harris, R. S., 151
Harrison, B., 635
Harrison, W. H., 634
Hart, D., 540, 557, 571, 583, 584, 585
Harter, S., 548, 550, 560, 581, 583
Hartmann, H., 50, 53, 86, 87, 88
Hartney, L. M., 506
Hartshorne, H., 362, 375
Hartup, W. W., 206
Harvey, D., 781
Harvey, J. H., 769
Hase, 249
Haspel, K. C., 151
Hastie, R., 490
Hathaway, S., 258
Hauser, S. T., 560
Hawthorne, N., 130, 599
Hayes, R., 634
Hazan, C., 218, 235, 236, 237
Hazen, N. L., 226, 227
Healy, J. M., Jr., 159, 160, 164, 246, 247
Healy, S., 642, 643

Heaven, P. C. L., 163
Heckhausen, H., 625
Hegel, G. W. F., 424
Heidegger, M., 424, 425
Heilbrun, A. B., 500
Heilbrun, A. B., Jr., 389
Heilbrun, K. S., 151
Heilizer, R., 387
Helmholtz, H., 144
Helmreich, R., 500
Helson, R., 24–25, 674–676, 713
Henderson, J. L., 137
Hepburn, A., 216
Hermans, H. J. M., 589, 770–777, 778
Herrnstein, R. J., 314
Hersen, M., 34
Hess, R. D., 405
Heyns, R. W., 635, 644
Higgins, E. T., 573, 575, 576, 756, 795
Hill, G. J., 205
Hill, T., 142
Hitchcock, A., 638–640
Hoffman, J. J., 670
Hoffman, M. L., 214, 215
Hofstee, W. K. B., 265, 295
Hogan, K., 604
Hogan, R., 28, 50, 76, 202–204, 203, 205, 265, 363, 473, 531, 564, 787, 795
Hollander, E. P., 163
Holmes, D. S., 142, 152, 271, 387
Holmes, J. G., 440
Holmes, M., 353
Holmes, T. H., 445
Holt, R. R., 45, 116, 562, 621
Holtby, W., 247
Homburger, T., 656
Homer, 750
Hoover, C., 204
Hoover, H., 635
Hoppe, C., 562
Hopper, C. H., 212
Horn, J. M., 304
Horney, K., 50, 53, 77, 87, 89–92, 101, 116, 136
Hornstein, H. A., 353
Horowitz, M. J., 616
Houston, B. K., 387
Houts, A. C., 365
Howard, G. S., 720, 721
Howard, J., 7, 8–9, 10, 16
Howard, J. H., 388
Huesmann, L. K., 348
Huesmann, L. R., 347, 348, 352
Hull, C., 313, 326, 331, 353, 358
Hull, J. G., 450
Husserl, E., 425, 463
Huston, A. C., 347
Huszti, H. C., 769
Hyland, M. E., 516

Ibsen, H., 128
Ihilevich, D., 152
Ingram, R. E., 506, 507
Inhelder, B., 543, 665
Isabella, R. A., 226
Izard, C. E., 737, 739, 740, 797

Jacklin, C. N., 210
Jackson, A., 634
Jackson, D. N., 249, 253, 257, 262, 263, 265, 290, 645
Jackson, J., 151
Jackson, R. J., 642
Jacobi, J., 137
Jacques, E., 603, 762
Jaffe, A., 137
Jahoda, M., 163
James, H., 128, 700
James, W., 420, 473, 536–538, 539, 541, 564, 570–571, 580, 773
Janis, I. L., 615, 632
Janoff-Bulman, R., 440
Jaspers, K., 424
Jay, P., 54, 731
Jayne, C., 157
Jefferson, T., 634
Jemmott, J. B., III, 637
Jenkins, C. D., 387
Jenkins, S. R., 626
Jennings, J. L., 425, 432
John, O. P., 264, 265, 290, 382–384, 385
Johnson, C., 158
Johnson, H. H., 387
Johnson, J. E., 506
Johnson, L., 635
Johnson, R. N., 207
Johnson, S., 697–698
Jones, A., 464–465
Jones, E., 54, 57, 61, 67
Jones, E. de E., 362
Jones, E. E., 492
Jones, J. M., 405–407
Jones, R. R., 338
Jones, W. H., 202, 204
Jordan, D., 670
Josselson, R. L., 559, 670, 671
Joyce, J., 128, 130
Judson, H. F., 32, 34–35
Jung, C. G., 11, 28, 44, 50, 53, 65, 67, 86, 95, 101–113, 116, 136–141, 170–176, 190, 265, 313, 358, 423, 469, 473, 512, 539, 558, 596, 613, 688, 689, 700, 762, 787, 789, 791
Jung, E., 101
Jung, P., 101
Juni, J., 157
Juni, S., 157
Justice, M. T., 525

Kafka, F., 751
Kagan, J., 205–206, 210, 296, 300, 354, 404–405, 691
Kahane, C., 125
Kahn, S., 449, 676
Kalin, 636
Kamin, L. J., 187
Kanfer, F. H., 340
Kanouse, D. E., 492
Kant, I., 249, 253, 424, 531
Kaplan, N., 218, 235
Kasimatis, M., 277
Kaskey, M., 167
Katigbak, M. S., 265

Katkin, E. S., 158
Keating, J. P., 214
Kegan, R., 293, 545–548, 555, 556, 557, 558, 559, 563, 754
Keillor, G., 205
Keinonen, M., 262, 263
Kekule, F., 34–35
Kellam, A., 167
Kelley, H. H., 492
Kelley, K., 42, 163
Kelly, E. L., 277
Kelly, G., 17, 18, 29, 420, 455, 469, 472–480, 474, 486, 494, 512, 523, 545, 788, 789, 793
Kelly, K. E., 387
Kempen, H. J. G., 770, 773, 777
Keniston, K., 614
Kennedy, J. F., 483, 484, 630, 633, 635
Kenny, D. A., 204, 363
Kenrick, D. T., 184, 192, 366, 367, 372, 392, 395, 412
Kent, R. N., 336
Kernberg, O., 99, 172, 173, 762
Kiecolt–Glaser, J. K., 735
Kierkegaard, S., 424, 428, 430, 431, 456, 790, 795
Kiesler, D. J., 293
Kihlstrom, J. F., 142, 143, 144–145, 288, 488–493, 513, 692
Kimmerly, N. L., 231
King, G. A., 393
King, L. A., 514, 515
Kinsey, A., 197
Kirk, J., 615
Kirkpatrick, L. A., 218
Kirshnit, C., 642
Kite, M. E., 504
Klages, L., 264
Klavetter, R. E., 465
Klein, E. B., 711
Klein, R., 215
Kleinmutz, R., 259
Klepfer, J., 167
Klerman, J. L., 740
Kline, P., 116
Klinger, E., 645, 646
Kloosterman, K., 265
Kluckhohn, C., 3, 606
Knowles, E. S., 757
Kobak, R. R., 237
Kobasa, S. C., 445, 448, 449, 450
Kocis, J., 505
Koestner, J., 441, 442
Koestner, R., 371, 372, 441, 442, 645
Kohlberg, L., 522, 543, 545, 556, 559
Kohut, H., 50, 53, 87, 99–101, 116, 172, 539
Konner, M., 208, 209, 210, 219
Koopmans, L. H., 212
Kopp, C. G., 340
Koslowski, B., 226
Kosson, D. J., 269
Kotre, J., 678, 679, 681, 685–687
Kottak, C. P., 186, 615
Krahe, B., 364, 390, 391, 393, 395–396
Kramp, P., 215

Krantz, D. S., 389
Krause, S., 642, 643
Krebs, D. L., 215
Kreuz, I. E., 211
Krippendorff, K., 616
Krippner, S., 747
Kris, E., 24, 87
Kuhn, T. S., 182
Kuiper, N. A., 505
Kulik, J., 483, 484
Kulka, R., 643
Kunce, J. T., 259
Kurdek, L. A., 501
Kushner, H., 731

Labov, W., 405
Lachman, J. L., 485
Lachman, M. E., 439, 440
Lachman, R., 485, 486
Lachmann, F. M., 149
LaFreniere, P. J., 227, 228
Lamb, M. E., 231
Lamiell, J. T., 369
Lancaster, C. J., 184
Lando, H. A., 347
Landsman, T., 467
Langbaum, R., 54, 767
Lange, J. D., 338
Langer, E. J., 435, 506
Langston, C. A., 493
Lanyon, R. I., 258
Lapidus, L. B., 517
Lapsley, D. K., 539, 557
Larsen, R. J., 277, 282, 400, 401
Larson, D. M., 274
Lasch, C., 172, 762
Laulicht, J. H., 348
Lawler, K. A., 450
Layton, L., 245
Lazarus, A. A., 338
Lazarus, R. J., 145, 508, 509–510
Leak, G. K., 188
Leary, T., 293
Lebowitz, B., 274
Lee, L., 545, 560, 562
Lefcourt, H. M., 440
Lefkowitz, M. M., 348
Leigh, J., 167
Leigh, L., 167
Leighton, R., 245
Lensky, D. B., 506, 644
Lepper, M. R., 440, 441
Lerner, H., 166, 167
Lesnik-Oberstein, 273
Lesser, I. M., 671, 672, 673, 676
Lester, R., 644
Levin, H., 357
Levine, L. E., 215
LeVine, R. A., 408
Levine, R. L., 288
Levine, S., 335
Levinson, D. J., 29, 162, 588, 599, 603, 659, 708–713, 762
Levinson, M. H., 711
Lewicki, P., 142, 495
Lewin, K., 364

Lewinsohn, P. M., 339
Lewis, H. B., 523, 526, 644
Lewis, L., 504
Lewis, M., 549
Lewontin, R. C., 187
Libet, T., 339
Lichtenstein, E. H., 726
Lichtenstein, P., 307
Lichter, S. R., 163, 633
Lieberman, A. F., 225
Liebert, R. M., 347
Lifton, N., 167
Lifton, R. J., 767
Lincoln, A., 634
Linde, C., 721
Lindzey, G., 44, 102, 621
Linville, P. W., 497, 522
Lippold, R., 140
Lishman, W. A., 269, 505
Little, B. R., 363, 416, 513
Littlefield, C. H., 201, 202
Livson, N., 762
Lizzadro, T., 396, 397
Lloyd, G. G., 505
Locke, J., 314–315, 315, 316, 354
Loehlin, J. C., 302, 303, 304, 306
Loevinger, J., 29, 249, 254, 386, 421,
    542–545, 545, 555, 556, 557, 558, 559,
    560, 561, 562, 563
Logan, R. L., 679, 682, 683
Lohr, N. E., 167
London, P., 352
Lorenz, K., 180, 181, 182, 208, 221
Losoff, M., 644
Lott, C. L., 387
Low, H., 212
Lowell, E. L., 622
Lowenthal, M. F., 762
Luborsky, L., 127, 128, 511
Lucariello, J., 769
Luder, H., 651
Ludolph, P., 167
Lundy, A., 645
Luria, A. R., 615
Luther, M., 650–655, 658, 659, 663, 668,
    670, 696, 755
Lütkenhaus, P., 226–227
Lykken, D. J., 303
Lykken, D. T., 300, 301, 304, 306
Lyons-Ruth, K., 230

Maccoby, E. E., 210, 234, 355, 356, 357
MacDougall, J. M., 389
MacIntyre, A., 748, 757, 758
Mackenzie-Mohr, D., 502, 504
MacKinnon, D. W., 598, 611
MacPhillamy, D. J., 339
Maddi, S. R., 4, 142, 364, 449, 464
Madison, J., 634
Madsen, R., 172
Magnusson, D., 390, 391, 393, 397, 399
Maher, B., 472
Mahler, M. S., 11, 50, 53, 87, 98, 99, 313,
    539, 548, 549, 552
Mahoney, M. J., 338
Maier, S. F., 507
Main, M., 218, 225, 226, 228, 231, 235, 236

Malamuth, N. M., 347, 348
Mancuso, J. C., 769
Mandel, N. M., 205
Mandler, J. M., 724, 726
Manning, M. M., 334
Manosevitz, M., 670
Marcel, G., 424, 427
Marcia, J. E., 669, 670, 671, 672, 673,
    676, 692, 746
Marcus, S., 125, 732
Marks, E., 636
Markus, H., 494, 495, 496, 504, 539,
    571–572, 756, 795
Marlowe, D., 146
Marsh, H. W., 501
Marshall, V., 762
Martin, 490
Martin, J. A., 355, 356
Martin, R. A., 440
Martindale, C., 24
Marx, K., 93, 94, 95
Masling, J., 157, 158
Maslow, A. H., 17, 25–26, 29, 96, 420,
    455, 456, 459–463, 465, 467, 470, 473,
    512, 539, 541, 545, 558, 559, 560, 689,
    788, 790, 792
Masson, J. M., 62, 65
Matas, L., 226
Matthews, K. A., 387, 388, 389
Mattson, A., 212
May, M. A., 362, 375
May, R., 9, 424, 456, 602–604
McAdams, D. P., 11, 21, 89, 238, 291,
    293, 413, 465, 506, 514, 631, 633, 635,
    640, 641, 642, 643, 644, 647, 650, 653,
    679, 680, 681, 682, 683, 687, 696, 700,
    706, 717, 720, 746, 747, 750, 753, 754,
    755, 756, 758, 759, 760, 764, 765, 773,
    778
McCallum, D. M., 449
McCartney, K., 306
McCaulley, M. H., 170
McClearey, N., 145
McClearn, G. E., 302, 307
McClelland, D. C., 29, 94, 249, 256, 365,
    473, 604, 607, 613, 614, 622, 623, 624,
    625, 626, 627, 629, 630, 631, 633,
    636–637, 638, 644, 645, 646, 700, 754,
    790, 793
McClelland, J. L., 143
McConkey, K. M., 286, 288
McCrae, R. R., 264, 265, 266, 267, 272,
    274, 277, 284, 285, 286, 287, 288, 289,
    291, 292, 294, 412, 414, 562, 713, 792
McCranie, E. W., 388
McDowall, J., 505
McFarlane, S., 184
McGilley, B. M., 387
McGinnies, E., 145
McGue, M., 300, 301, 306
McInerney, J., 172
McIntyre, C. W., 267
McKee, B., 711
McKenna, F. P., 528
McKinley, J. C., 258
McKinley, W., 635
McMaster, M. R., 214

McNamara, W., 644
Mead, G. H., 202–203, 564, 795
Mead, M., 7–10, 13–14, 16–17, 19–22,
    24, 27, 267
Mears, F. G., 251
Meehl, P. E., 255, 259
Mellon, J., 127
Melville, H., 130, 596, 599, 600, 613,
    614
Mendel, M., 167
Mercer, R. T., 713
Meredith, G., 532
Messick, S., 257
Mettlin, C., 387
Meyer, G. J., 277
Michela, J. L., 492
Michelangelo, 762
Micheletti, P., 529
Mikulincer, M., 237
Miles, G. G., 267
Milich, R. H., 149
Mill, J. S., 316, 531
Miller, G. A., 487
Miller, J. G., 409
Miller, M. L., 615
Miller, N. E., 326–328, 331, 345, 473,
    743, 795
Miller, P. A., 215
Miller, P. C., 440
Millon, T., 35
Milofsky, E., 678, 680
Mink, L. O., 720
Minuchin, S., 403
Mischel, W., 28, 42, 142, 242, 268, 323,
    324–325, 329, 330, 340–341, 342, 343,
    357, 361–364, 366, 369, 370, 372, 374,
    375, 376, 377, 385, 388, 392, 395, 398,
    410, 411, 412, 414, 416, 473, 487, 625,
    788, 798
Mishima, Y., 4–7, 10–13, 17–19, 22,
    23–24, 26, 27, 76–77, 97
Mitchell, J. C., 619
Mitchell, V., 674–676
Miyake, K., 372
Moane, G., 674–676
Moeller, G. H., 628, 629
Moffitt, T. E., 401
Mogar, R. E., 465
Moi, T., 125
Monroe, J., 634
Monte, C. F., 60, 62, 64, 65
Montello, D. R., 184
Moore, B. J., 366
Moos, R. H., 390, 391, 404
Moraitis, G., 696
Moran, G., 225
Morawski, J. G., 501
Morgan, 620
Morgan, C., 596
Morgan, L. M., 506
Morley, T. E., 267
Morris, C. W., 530
Morris, D., 179
Morris, R., 212
Moser, K., 370
Moskowitz, D. S., 375, 376, 377, 412

Moss, H. A., 210
Mother Theresa, 741
Mountjoy, P. J., 700
Mowrer, O. H., 326
Mozart, W. A., 762
Mulder, E., 265
Mumford, M., 384
Murray, H. A., 3, 4, 19, 29, 262, 358, 457,
    469, 473, 588, 591–592, 593, 595–620,
    621, 622, 644, 645, 646, 647, 656, 659,
    688, 696, 706, 719–720, 736, 769, 788,
    790, 793
Murray, K., 750
Muslin, H., 125
Myers, I. B., 170

Nachson, O., 237
Napoleon I, 54, 57, 60
Nasby, W., 497
Nathan, J., 6, 19
National Institute of Mental Health, 347
Neale, M. C., 303
Neisser, U., 484, 486, 494
Nesselroade, J. R., 307
Neugarten, B. L., 678, 681, 761, 762
Newman, J. P., 269, 270
Newton, I., 32
Newton, P. M., 712
Nias, D. K. B., 267, 303
Nichols, E. G., 713
Nichols, R. C., 303
Nichols, S. L., 269
Niedenthal, P. M., 493
Nielson, E. C., 670
Nietzsche, F., 69, 424
Nisbett, R. E., 362, 411, 441, 492
Nixon, R., 483, 633, 635
Noble, J. P., 523
Noller, P., 237
Norem, J. K., 416, 493
Norman, R. M. G., 269
Norman, W. T., 247, 264, 265, 284,
    363
Nucci, L., 663
Nurius, P., 571–572, 756

O'Brien, R., 74
Ochberg, R. L., 696
Odbert, H. S., 264
Ogilvie, D. M., 576–579, 582
O'Heeron, R. C., 735
O'Heron, C. A., 501
Okada, M., 399, 400
O'Leary, A., 335
Oliver, J. M., 151
Oliver, P. V., 204
Olson, D. H., 404
Oltmann, P. K., 523
Olweus, D., 210, 211, 212
Omoto, A. M., 216, 216–217, 218
O'Neill, R., 157, 158
Orlofsky, J. L., 501, 670, 671, 672, 673,
    676, 692
Ormel, J., 277
O'Rourke, D. F., 387
Ortega, D. F., 387
Osborne, J., 655

Osborne, J. W., 372
Oshman, H., 670
OSS Assessment Staff, 610
Ostendorf, F., 265
Ota, J., 388
Ovcharchyn, C. A., 387
Owens, W. A., 384
Ozer, D. J., 384, 396, 400, 413
Ozer, E. M., 334, 335

Palchanis, N., 389
Palys, T. S., 416, 513
Parham, T. A., 407
Park, B., 490
Parke, R. D., 206, 210, 333
Parker, D. A., 398
Parkison, S. C., 403
Pasahow, R. J., 506
Passini, F. T., 363
Patel, V., 637
Patterson, C. M., 269
Patterson, G. R., 338
Paunonen, S. V., 249, 257, 262, 263,
    265
Pavlov, I. P., 316, 317, 358
Pavot, W. G., 282
Payne, T. J., 504
PDP Research Group, 143
Peabody, D., 163, 264
Peake, P. K., 376
Pearce, P., 393
Pearce-McCall, D., 269, 270
Pearson, C. S., 111–113
Pedersen, N., 302–303
Pederson, D. R., 225
Pederson, N. L., 307
Pekala, R. J., 288
Pellegrini, A. D., 769
Pennebaker, J. W., 515, 732–736
Penner, L. A., 367, 371
Pepper, S., 769
Pericles, 697
Perry, W. C., 543
Persky, H., 211
Pervin, L. A., 512
Peskin, H., 762
Petersen, A. C., 557
Peterson, B. E., 164, 678
Peterson, C., 507, 510, 511
Petzel, T. P., 387, 506
Phares, E. J., 323, 330, 438, 439, 440
Piaget, J., 34, 522, 542, 543, 545, 665,
    740, 752, 754
Piedrahita, L. E., 532
Pierce, F., 634
Pike, C. L., 199
Pilkonis, P. A., 205
Pine, F., 98
Pipal, J. E., 387
Pizzamiglio, L., 523
Plato, 312, 508
Plomin, R., 297, 300, 302, 303, 304, 305,
    306, 307
Plutarch, 697
Podd, M. H., 670, 671
Poe, E. A., 752
Polk, J., 634

Polkinghorne, D., 769
Pollack, G. H., 696
Pollack, J. M., 157
Popper, K., 37
Porter, C. A., 528, 532, 533
Porterfield, A. L., 151
Postman, L., 145
Powell, A. L., 214
Power, F. C., 539
Powers, J., 642
Powers, P. C., 347
Powers, W. T., 519
Presley, M., 375
Pribram, K. H., 487
Price, L. H., 645
Price, V. A., 388
Prince, M., 596
Privette, G., 467, 468
Proust, M., 128
Puccetti, M. C., 449, 450
Purifoy, F. E., 212

Quinlain, D., 562
Quinn, S., 89–90

Radke-Yarrow, M., 215, 352
Rahe, D. F., 268
Rahe, R. H., 445
Raid, M., 271
Ramsay, H., 271
Rank, O., 65, 428, 429, 430
Rapaport, D., 87
Raphael, 762
Raps, C. S., 510
Raska, K., 335
Raskin, R. N., 173
Rasmuson, I., 302–303
Raynor, J. O., 625
Raynor, R., 316
Reagan, R., 633, 635
Rechnitzer, P. A., 388
Redman, E., 615
Redmore, C., 560, 561, 562
Reichenbach, H., 33, 36
Reid, J. B., 338
Reinisch, J. M., 212
Repetti, R. L., 404
Rescorla, R. A., 318
Reuman, D. A., 645
Revelle, W., 282
Rice, K., 557
Rich, S., 303
Richey, C. A., 338
Ricoeur, P., 132, 617, 728
Riecken, H., 615
Rieff, P., 56, 125
Rittenhouse, J. D., 436
Ritzler, B., 167
Rizzo, R., 465
Roberts, P., 712
Robins, C. J., 510, 511
Robinson, D. N., 44, 56
Robinson, F. G., 596, 611, 613
Robinson, J. A., 490
Roche, S. M., 286
Rodin, J., 435
Rodriguez, M. L., 343

Rogers, C. R., 25–26, 29, 99, 420, 455, 456–459, 463–464, 465, 472, 473, 512, 539, 541, 689, 700, 788, 790, 792
Rogow, A. A., 125
Rokeach, M., 529, 530
Romer, D., 396, 397
Roos, P. E., 500
Roosevelt, F. D., 633, 635
Roosevelt, T., 635
Rootes, M. D., 562
Rorschach, H., 157
Rosch, E., 368
Rose, R. M., 211
Rose, S., 187
Rosenbaum, M., 353
Rosenberg, M., 581
Rosenberg, S., 490
Rosenhahn, D. L., 352
Rosenman, R. H., 386, 387
Rosenthal, R., 372
Rosenwald, G. C., 621, 706
Rosenzweig, S., 598
Ross, D., 332, 346, 347
Ross, G., 637
Ross, L. D., 362, 411
Ross, S. A., 332, 346, 347
Rossi, A. S., 713
Rosznafszky, J., 562
Roth, P., 731–732
Rothbart, M. K., 296
Rothman, S., 163, 633
Rotter, J. B., 28, 323–324, 325, 329, 330, 438, 439, 440, 473, 486
Rouse, J., 722
Royko, M., 298–299
Ruback, R. B., 212
Rubenstein, C., 222
Rubenstein, V., 157
Rubin, S. H., 402
Rubin, Z., 633
Ruehlman, L. S., 506
Ruetzel, K., 679, 764
Ruffins, S., 167
Rummelhart, D. E., 143
Runyan, W. M., 416, 615, 616, 619, 696, 700, 701, 702–703
Rusbult, C. d E., 501
Rushton, J. P., 188, 201, 202, 215, 303, 375
Russell, B., 54, 316
Russell, D., 204
Rutter, D. R., 267
Ryan, J. H., 670
Ryan, R. M., 433, 434, 442, 442–445, 562
Rychlak, J. F., 347, 470–472, 473

Sackheim, R., 145
Sacks, O., 615
Sadalla, E. K., 392
Sagi, M., 214
Saint Augustine, 731, 732
St. Peter, S., 167
Saladi, M., 504
Saleh, W. E., 440
Sales, S. M., 163
Salinger, J. D., 666

Sampson, E. E., 501, 690, 781, 782, 783
Sander, L. W., 549
Sandvik, E., 283
Sanford, R. N., 162, 598
Sarason, I. G., 397
Sarbin, T. R., 720, 769
Sargent, M., 562
Saron, C., 636–637
Sartre, J.-P., 424–425, 426, 427, 428, 431, 456, 541, 559, 613, 700, 748, 767
Saslow, G., 340
Saturansky, C., 158
Scalise, C. J., 269
Scaramella, T. C., 212
Scarr, J., 304
Scarr, S., 306
Schachter, J., 615
Schafer, R., 152, 617, 732
Schafer, W. D., 231
Schaller, M., 214
Schalling, D., 212
Schank, R. C., 490
Scheibe, K. E., 539, 564
Scheier, M. F., 62, 436, 486, 511, 516, 517, 518, 519, 520
Schenkel, S., 671
Schiffman, H., 693
Schiller, J. C. F. von, 54
Schilling, E. A., 277
Schimek, J. G., 166
Schindler, G. L., 212
Schmidt, S., 267
Schmied, L. A., 450
Schmitt, J. P., 501
Schneider, D. J., 735
Schoenrade, 214
Schooler, C., 690
Schopenhauer, A., 69
Schroder, H. M., 528
Schumer, F., 621
Schunk, D. H., 333
Schur, M., 59
Schutte, N. S., 392
Schwankovsky, L., 438
Schwartz, D. P., 387
Schwartz, G. E., 146, 740
Schwartz, J. C., 392
Scott-Stokes, H., 6
Sears, R. R., 326, 357
Secco, T., 724
Segal, N. L., 300, 303
Seligman, M. E. P., 507, 510, 511
Selman, R. L., 543, 565, 566, 583
Selva, P. C. D., 500
Selvik, R., 755
Semmer, N., 515
Sentis, K., 494
Sgoutas, D. S., 212
Shack, J. R., 277
Shadish, W. R., Jr., 365
Shakespeare, W., 630, 750, 762
Shank, D. M., 344, 345
Shaver, P. R., 218, 222, 235, 236, 237, 291, 292
Shaw, C., 707
Shaw, G. B., 696

Shaw, J., 278, 279
Shaw, J. S., 500
Shaw, R., 173
Sheehy, G., 603, 708
Sheier, M. F., 497
Sherwood, D., 152
Shevrin, H., 142, 151
Shiffrin, R. M., 143
Shils, E. A., 163
Shipman, V. C., 405
Shneidman, E., 612
Shoda, Y., 343
Shostrom, E., 464
Shotter, J., 473, 781, 782
Shrauger, J. S., 205
Shweder, R. A., 363, 411
Sibicky, M. E., 757
Silbert, D., 167
Silk, K., 167
Sill, J., 762
Silverman, L. H., 149, 150–151
Silverman, M., 167
Silverstein, L. B., 229, 230
Simpson, J. A., 194–197, 234, 237
Simpson, M. E., 388
Sine, L. F., 338
Singer, J. A., 128
Singer, J. L., 42, 128, 523, 524, 738
Sitko, C., 225
Skinner, B. F., 310–313, 314, 315, 319, 325, 331, 334, 340, 342–343, 353, 358, 362, 614
Slaby, R. G., 206, 210
Slade, A., 226
Slavin, M. O., 636
Slife, B. D., 347
Smith, J., 495, 496
Smith, K. D., 211, 214
Smith, M. B., 598
Smith, R., 347
Smith, R. E., 397
Smith, T., 631, 632
Smith, T. G., 204
Smith, T. W., 387, 506, 507
Snarey, J., 545, 560, 562
Snowdon, C. T., 182, 193
Snyder, M., 216–217, 218, 568, 569
Sobolew-Shubin, A., 438
Sokol, M., 159, 160, 164
Solano, C., 363
Sophocles, 73
Sorrentino, R. M., 393
Spear, W. E., 167
Speer, A. L., 215
Spence, D. P., 617, 618, 721
Spence, J. T., 500, 504
Spence, K., 330
Spencer, C., 480
Spiegel, J. P., 348
Spieker, S. J., 229
Spielberger, C. D., 399
Spoto, D., 638–639
Spranger, E., 250
Sroufe, L. A., 221, 222, 225, 226, 227, 228, 230, 356
Srull, T. K., 486

Stahl, J., 230
Stapp, J., 500
Staw, B. M., 441
Steele, H., 235
Steele, M., 235
Steele, R. S., 59, 60, 61, 125, 617, 624, 630, 637
Steinberg, L., 232–234
Stelmack, R. M., 272
Stern, D. N., 102, 226, 549, 552–555, 617
Stern, W., 250
Steuer, F. B., 347
Stevens, A., 103
Stewart, A. J., 159, 160, 161, 164, 245, 246, 247, 625, 626, 631, 633, 636, 644, 645, 678
Stewart, J., 639–640
Stillwell, A., 769
Stokes, G. S., 384
Stolorow, R. D., 58
Stone, A. A., 735
Stotland, E., 214
Strachey, J., 64
Straus, R., 387
Strauss, A. L., 34
Streich, D. D., 562
Streufert, S., 528
Stringfield, D. O., 366, 367, 372
Strube, M. J., 387, 388
Suedfeld, P., 528, 532, 533
Sugiyama, Y., 6
Sullivan, H. S., 541–542, 548, 556, 756
Sullivan, W. M., 172
Sulloway, F. J., 691
Sulloway, J. J., 54, 61, 123, 183
Suls, J., 436
Sundberg, N. L., 339, 700
Sutton-Smith, B., 753
Swidler, A., 172
Swift, J., 428
Switzer, G., 215

Taft, W. H., 635
Tagiuri, R., 363
Takemoto-Chock, N. K., 264
Tamashiro, R., 560
Tappan, M., 769
Tataryn, D. J., 288
Taylor, E., 146
Taylor, M. C., 501
Taylor, S. E., 435–436, 437, 494, 506
Taylor, Z., 634
Teasdale, J. P., 507
Tekiner, A. C., 629
Tellegen, A., 267, 286, 300, 301, 303
Tesch, S. A., 676, 677
Tetlock, P. E., 528, 529, 532
Thomas, A., 296
Thomas, S. L., 347
Thomas, W. I., 615
Thompson, C., 77
Thompson, E. G., 393
Thompson, S. C., 438
Thoreau, H. D., 311
Thorndike, R. L., 259, 358

Thorne, A., 128, 170, 171, 175, 176, 411, 415–416
Thurnher, M., 762
Tice, D. M., 371
Tinbergen, N., 180, 181, 182
Tipton, S. M., 172
Titus, H. E., 163
Tobias, B. A., 288
Toder, N., 670
Tolman, E. C., 313
Tomarken, A. J., 275
Tomkins, S. S., 29, 473, 588, 599, 700, 736–745, 788, 794, 797
Tooby, J., 190
Trabasso, T., 724
Trapnell, P. D., 294
Trivers, R. L., 201, 213
Trotter, M. V., 173
Troyer, D., 215
Truman, H., 633, 635
Trzebinski, J., 265
Tulving, E., 487
Tupes, E. C., 264, 265
Turner, J. M. W., 55
Turner, P. J., 227

Uleman, J. S., 629
Underwood, B., 366
Urist, J., 166

Vaillant, G. E., 156, 643, 678, 680, 708
Valins, S., 492
Vallacher, R. R., 516, 520, 522
Van Buren, M., 634
Van de Water, D., 679, 681
Van Den Broek, P., 724
van Gilst, W., 772
Van Gogh, T., 703
Van Gogh, V., 702–703
van Loon, R. J. P., 770, 773, 777
Van Treuren, R. R., 450
Vernon, P. E., 530
Veroff, J., 388, 629, 635, 636, 643, 644, 645
Victoria, Queen of Great Britain, 55
Villanova, P., 510
Vinacke, E., 465
Virnellis, S., 450
Vitz, P. C., 721, 769
Vogelmann-Sine, S., 338
von Eye, A., 226
von Franz, M.-L., 137
Voss, K., 703

Walder, L. O., 348
Waldman, K., 560
Wall, T., 218, 219
Wallace, D. B., 26
Wallston, B. S., 440
Wallston, K. A., 440
Walters, R. H., 333
Walton, I., 697
Wapner, S., 523
Ward, D., 290
Ware, E. E., 440
Washburn, S. L., 184
Washington, G., 633, 634

Waterman, A. S., 669
Waters, E., 218, 219, 221, 222
Watkins, M., 756
Watson, D., 267, 274, 277
Watson, J. B., 313, 315, 316, 323, 325, 353, 358, 362
Watson, L. D., 269
Watson, P. J., 173
Watt, N., 604
Weakland, J., 403
Webb, W., 204
Webber, P. L., 304
Weber, A. L., 769
Weber, M., 531
Weber, R., 490
Wegner, D. M., 516, 520, 522, 735
Weinberger, D. A., 146
Weinberger, J., 645
Weiner, B., 182, 492
Weinstock-Savoy, D., 159
Weisen, A., 271
Weiss, D. S., 411
Weiss, L. R., 157
Wenger, C. F., 288
Werner, C., 387
Werner, H., 543
Wessler, R., 560, 561
West, S. G., 364, 506
Westen, D., 53, 116, 142, 145, 165–166, 167, 169, 170
Weston, D., 231
Whitbourne, S. K., 286, 676, 677, 769
White, J. L., 407
White, R. W., 27, 30–31, 86, 88–89, 334, 444, 455, 596, 597, 598, 611, 612, 613, 614, 615, 620, 696, 736
White, T. L., 735
Whiting, B. B., 409
Whiting, J. W. M., 408
Whitley, B. E., Jr., 501
Whitson, E. R., 157
Wicklund, R. A., 518
Wiebe, D. J., 449
Wiedenfeld, S. A., 335
Wiggins, J. S., 249, 254, 293, 294
Wilcox, K. J., 303
Willerman, L., 296, 304
Williams, P. M., 212
Wilson, E. O., 15, 184, 185, 186, 192–193, 206, 213, 214, 267, 270
Wilson, G. D., 15, 267
Wilson, J. A., 271
Wilson, W., 635
Wincze, J. P., 338
Wink, P., 173, 713
Winnicott, D. W., 96
Winter, D. G., 164, 625, 629, 630, 631, 633, 635, 636, 638, 645, 700, 754
Wish, M., 393
Witkin, H. A., 522, 523, 524, 527, 528
Wittig, M. A., 304
Wittlieb, E., 338
Wohlfarth, T., 277
Wolf, E. S., 100, 101
Wolpe, J., 338
Woodson, D., 685–687

Woolf, V., 532
Wordsworth, W., 26, 54
Wortman, C. B., 78
Wotman, S. R., 769
Wright, J. C., 416
Wright, T. L., 334
Wrightsman, L. S., 696
Wurm, M., 387
Wyer, R. S., Jr., 486, 490
Wylie, R., 580, 581
Wymer, W. E., 367, 371
Wynne-Edwards, V. C., 208

Yin, R. K., 34, 615, 616, 619
York, K. L., 382–384, 385

Zahaykevich, M. K., 559
Zahn-Waxler, C., 215, 352
Zajonc, R. B., 510, 691
Zambianco, D., 167
Zanna, M. P., 502, 504
Zeldow, P. B., 501, 643, 644
Zimbardo, P. G., 204
Zimmerman, G., 676
Zimmerman, W. S., 263

Zinbarg, R., 282
Zirkel, S., 486, 488, 493, 512, 513
Znaniecki, F., 615
Zoll, D., 230
Zonderman, A. B., 274
Zubin, J., 621
Zuckerman, M., 272, 273, 371, 372, 398, 441, 442
Zukav, G., 33
Zuroff, D. C., 416
Zyzanski, S. J., 387

Subject Index

A-babies, 223–225
Absolutism, 531
Absorption, 286, 288
Absurd, 428–430
Achievement motive
    careers in business, 625–626
    correlates of high achievement
        motivation, 625
    definition of, 622
    measurement of, 622–625
    societal and historical differences in,
        626–629
Achieving Society, The (McClelland), 627
ACL. *See* Adjective Check List (ACL)
Act-frequency approach, to personality
    traits, 368–370
Action identification theory, 520–521
Adjective Check List (ACL), 264
Adolescence
    adaptation in, following life
        transition, 164
    aggression in adolescent males,
        210–211
    defense mechanisms in, 153
    Erikson's identity vs. role confusion
        in, 663–671
    and S. Freud's stages of
        psychosexual development, 80–81
    Kegan's evolving self and, 546,
        547–548
    life-story model of, 754–756
    perspective taking in, 565, 566
    self as I during, 557–558
    self as Me during, 585
    self-understanding in, 584–585
    Sullivan's self-system and, 542
Adult Attachment Interview, 235–236
Adult attachments, 235–238, 291–292
Adult I, 558–560
Adult life, seasons of, 708–713
Affect. *See also* Emotion
    definition of, 736
    in personality psychology, 797–798
    Tomkins' script theory and, 736–740
Affect congruence model, of reciprocal
    interactionism, 401
Affect intensity, 282–283
Affective attunement, 555
Affective rewards, 322, 323
Affiliation motive, 644
African Americans, 405–408, 581
Agape, 458
Age 30 Transition, 711, 712
Aggregation, 365, 372–377, 412
Aggression
    of animals, 207–208
    Bandura and bobo doll, 346–347
    definition of, 206
    evolutionary perspectives on,
        179–180, 206–212
    examples of, 207
    Freud on, 179, 180
    hostile aggression, 206–207
    instrumental aggression, 206–207
    longitudinal stability of, 210–212
    in the Semai of Malaysia, 208–210
    social-learning theories on, 345–352

television violence and, 347–351
    testosterone levels and, 211–212
Agreeableness, 288–293
AIDS volunteerism, 216–217
All's Well That Ends Well (Shakespeare),
    750
Altruism
    in animals, 213
    compensation and, 396–397
    empathy and, 214–215
    evolutionary perspectives on,
        212–218
    reciprocal altruism, 213
    social-learning theories and,
        352–353
Altruistic motivation, 214
Altruistic personality, 215
Ambivalence, 97
Anal-expulsive personality, 73
Anal-retentive personality, 72–73, 157
Anal stage, 72–73
Analytical psychology
    and basic nature of human beings,
        102–106
    criticisms of, 790
    goddesses and heroes in, 109–113
    and Jung's life story, 101–102
    myth and symbol in, 136–141
    overview of, 101–102
    personality types and personality
        development in, 106–109,
        170–176
    research on, 170–176
Androgyny, 500–501
Anima, 104, 105–106, 762
Animals
    adaptations favoring physical
        survival, 190
    aggression of, 207–208
    altruism in, 213
    attachment in infant rgesys
        monkeys, 219–220
    characteristics promoting
        reproductive success, 200
    imprinting in, 220–221
    instinctive behavior of, 180–182
Animus, 105–106, 762
Anna O. case, 60, 129
Anxiety
    basic anxiety, 91
    Freud on, 68
    interactional model of, 398–400
    Kelly on, 476
    moral anxiety, 68
    neurotic anxiety, 68
    as personality trait, 280–283
    realistic anxiety, 68
    self-discrepancies and, 575–576
    state anxiety, 399–400
    Sullivan on, 541–542
    trait anxiety, 399–400
Approach-approach conflict, 328
Approach-avoidance conflict, 98, 328
Archetypes, 103–106, 110–113, 170, 748
Arousal
    Apter on, 452–453
    extraversion and, 269–273

Arousal-avoidance mode, 452
Arousal-seeking mode, 452
Art and Artist (Rank), 430
Artist, 429–430
Ascensionism, 593, 594
Assertion Inventory, 338
Assessment. *See* Measurement
Assessment of Men (Murray and OSS
    Assessment Staff), 610–611
Associative network theory, 508–509
Attachment
    adult attachments, 235–238,
        291–292
    in animals, 219–221
    Bowlby on, 218–219
    day care and, 230
    definition of, 219
    fathers and, 231
    in infancy, 219–222, 750
    secure and insecure attachments,
        223–234
Attachment behaviors, 221
Attachment objects, 221
Attachment styles, 236–237
Attitudes, and Jung's personality types,
    106–107
Authoritarian personality, 162–164
Authoritarian Personality, The (Adorno
    et al.), 162–163
Authoritarian style of parenting, 356
Authoritative-reciprocal style of
    parenting, 355–356
Autism, normal, 98
Autobiographical memory, 490–491
Autobiography, 731–732
Autonomous self, 100
Autonomous stage, of ego development,
    559
Autonomy support, 444
Autonomy vs. shame and doubt, 660,
    661–662
Autotelic activities, 465–466
Average person, 429
Avoidance-avoidance conflict, 328
Avoidant behavior, in babies, 225

B-babies, 223–225
B-cognition, 463
B-values, 461–462
Babies. *See* Infancy
Bad faith, 430–431
Balinese time and story, 728–730
BAS. *See* Behavioral approach system
    (BAS)
Basic anxiety, 91
Becoming, 457
Becoming One's Own Man (BOOM),
    711–712
Bedwetting, 123, 123n
Behavior
    biological bases of, 798
    complexity of, 364–385
    context of, 385, 388–410
    family-systems perspective on,
        402–404
    Goffman on social behavior,
        566–568

Behavior *(cont.)*
  hierarchical control of, 516–517
  macrocontexts of, 402–410
  regulation of, in cognitive
    psychology, 516–521
Behavior therapy, 339–340
Behavioral approach system (BAS), 280
Behavioral assessment, 336–340
Behavioral Avoidance Test, 338
Behavioral inhibition, 296
Behavioral inhibition system (BIS), 280
Behavioral modification, 339–340
Behaviorism. *See also* Social-learning
  theories
  definition of, 312–313
  environmentalism and, 314–315
  fictional account of, 310–312
  integration with Freudian
    psychoanalysis, 326–328
  learning and, 315–323
  observation and, 313
  personality and, 353, 357–358
Being cognition (B-cognition), 463
Being values (B-values), 461–462
Beyond Boredom and Anxiety
  (Csikszentmihalyi), 465–466
Beyond the Pleasure Principle (Freud),
  64
Big Five, 265, 266, 413–416
Biographical type, 595–596
Biography. *See also* Life stories
  Adler and individual psychology,
    688–696
  Adler's fictional finalism and,
    694–696
  Erikson and psyhoanalytic tradition,
    656–659
  Erikson's biographies, 651–652, 659,
    664
  Erikson's psychosocial development
    theory, 656–688
  Freud's psychobiography of
    Leonardo da Vinci, 698–700
  historical developments in, 697–699
  of Leonardo da Vinci, 698–700
  life histories, 706–708
  of Luther, 650–655, 664
  psychobiography, 697–706
  seasons of adult life, 708–713
  of Van Gogh, 702–703
Biology. *See* Evolution
Bipolar self, 100
Birds, The, 639
Birth order, 690–691
BIS. *See* Behavioral inhibition system
  (BIS)
Blacks, 405–408, 581
Bodily self, 540–541
Body image, differentiation of, 98
BOOM. *See* Becoming One's Own Man
  (BOOM)
Business careers, 625–626

C-babies, 223–225
California Psychological Inventory (CPI),
  259–261, 674

California Q-Sort, 264, 377–379
Cancer, 435–438
Case studies
  in behaviorism, 316–317
  and context of discovery versus
    justification, 619–620
  criterion for judging adequacy of,
    616
  criticisms of, 615–616
  definition of, 34, 615
  external validity of, 618, 619
  hermeneutics and, 617
  interpretation of, 617–518
  pattern-matching plan for, 616–617
  personology and, 615–620
  in psychoanalysis, 60, 117–128,
    129–130, 134–135, 138, 615
  reliability of, 615–616
  rules for preparation of, 620
Castration anxiety, 76
Catcher in the Rye, The (Salinger), 666
Causal attributions, 492–493
Causation, personal, 433–438
CCRT. *See* Core conflictual relationship
  themes (CCRT)
Character and Personality, 44
Character structure, 203
Child-God, as Jungian archetype, 104
Child rearing. *See* Parenting
Child sexual abuse, 61–62, 118–119
Childhood. *See also* Infancy
  achievement motive in, 627–629
  adaptation in, following life
    transition, 164
  and Adler on earliest memory,
    689–694
  aggression in, 346–351
  Allport's proprium and, 540–541
  birth order and, 690–691
  day care in, 230
  defense mechanisms in, 153–156
  delay of gratification in, 340–343
  Erikson's psychosocial development
    theory and, 660, 661–663
  A. Freud's developmental lines, 88
  and S. Freud's stages of
    psychosexual development, 72–80
  Horney's basic anxiety of, 91
  individual differences and personal
    work ethic in, 343–345
  Kegan's evolving self and, 545–547
  Kohut's self psychology on, 100–101
  life-story model of, 749–754
  Mahler's object relations perspective
    on, 98–99
  nuclear scene in, 744–745
  Oedipus complex for boys and girls,
    73–80
  parenting styles and, 354–356,
    404–405
  perception of classroom climate
    during, 433–434
  perspective taking in, 565, 566
  secure and insecure attachments in,
    223–234
  self as I during, 554–556

  self as Me during, 583
  self-esteem during, 581
  self-understanding in, 584–585
  separation anxiety in, 221–222
  stranger anxiety in, 221–222
  Sullivan's self-system and, 541–542
  television violence and, 347–351
  and values of competition versus
    cooperation, 409–410
Childhood and Society (Erikson), 672
Choice of situations model, of reciprocal
  interactionism, 401
Choleric type of person, 276
Chum, 542
Circumplex model of traits, 293–295
Civilization and Its Discontents (Freud),
  64, 68
Classical conditioning, 316–318
Client-centered therapy, 456–459
Client-Centered Therapy (Rogers), 456
Cognition
  interpretive structures and, 17
  self and, 797
  unconscious information
    processing, 142–145
Cognitive complexity, Rep Test and,
  479–480
Cognitive deconstruction, 521
Cognitive developmental paradigm,
  542–543
Cognitive personology, 488
Cognitive psychology
  basic concepts of, 486–488
  computers and robots as metaphors
    in, 486, 511–512
  criticisms of, 792
  definition of, 485–486
  depressive schemata, 504–507,
    510–511
  differentiation and integration,
    522–533
  field independence-dependence,
    522–527
  gender schemata, 497–504
  integrative complexity, 528–533
  Kelly as bridge from humanistic
    psychology to, 469, 472–480
  middle-level units and purposive
    behavior, 512–516
  mood-state-dependent memory,
    508–510
  regulation of behavior, 516–521
  self-schemata, 494–497
  social intelligence, 488–494
Collective unconscious, 103, 139–140
Commitment, 445, 681, 683
Commitment script, 743
Competence, 88–89, 444
Competencies, Mischel on, 325, 329
Competitive infanticide, 208
Complexes, 103
Concepts, and social intelligence, 490
Concrete operational thinking, 754
Condensation, in dream work, 133
Conditioned generalized reinforcers, 323
Conditioned response, 316

Conditioned stimulus, 316
Conditioning
    classical conditioning, 316–318
    higher-order conditioning, 317
    instrumental conditioning, 319–323
    operant conditioning, 319–323
Conditions of worth, 458
Confessions (Augustine), 731
Conflict
    with approach and avoidance
        characteristics, 328
    Erikson on, 658
    Freud on, 68, 85–86, 658
    Horney on neurotic conflicts, 91–92
    Rogers on, 458–459
Conflict-free sphere, 88
Conformist stage, of ego development,
    556
Conscientious stage, of ego
    development, 558
Conscientious/conformist stage, of ego
    development, 557–558
Conscientiousness, 288–293
Consciousness
    Freud on, 69
    humanistic personality theories and,
        424–425
    interpretive structures and, 17
Consolidation of individuality, 98–99
Construct approach, 249
Construct similarity, and Rep Test, 480
Construct validity, 255–256
Constructs, definition of, 255
Context of discovery, 33, 619–620
Context of justification, 36, 619–629
Continuous reinforcement, 321–322
Control
    cancer and, 435–438
    and early memories, 693–694
    illusion of control, 435
    locus of control, 438–440, 449
    personal causation and, 433–438
Coping strategies, 287, 288
Core conflictual relationship themes
    (CCRT), 127–128
Core self, 553
Correlation coefficient, 39–41
Correlational design, of research, 39–41
Correspondence rules, in science, 35
Countertransference, 125
CPI. *See* California Psychological
    Inventory (CPI)
Creative deceit, 136
Creative fidelity, 427
Creativity, 22–27
Criterion-key method, 258
Cubness, 298–299
Cues, 326
Culture
    definition of, 408
    field independence-dependence and,
        527
    individualism and, 409–410
    maintenance system of, 408
    projective system of, 408–409
Cynosural narcissism, 593–595

D-babies, 230
Dasein, 425
Day care, 230
Death instincts, 66–68
Declarative-episodic knowledge,
    490–491
Declarative-semantic knowledge, 490
Deconstructionism, 781–782
Defense mechanisms
    Freud on, 83–85
    research on, 152–156
Defensive pessimism, 493–494
Deficiency motives, 461
Delay of gratification, 340–343
Demeter and Persephone myth, 602–604
Denial, 152–153, 154
Denial of Death, The (Becker), 428
Dependent variable, 41
Depersonalization, 3
Depression
    depressive schemata, 504–507,
        510–511
    self-discrepancies and, 575–576
Despair vs. integrity, 687–688
Determinism, 66–68, 657–658
Developmental lines, 88
Developmental stages
    of adolescent I, 557–558
    of adult I, 558–561
    Allport's proprium, 540–541
    of child I, 554–556
    Erikson's psychosocial development
        theory, 660–688
    A. Freud's developmental lines, 88
    Freud's psychosexual stages, 70–81,
        156–159
    of infant I, 548–555
    Jung on, 107–108
    Kegan's evolving self, 545–548
    Levinson's seasons of adult life,
        708–713
    Loevinger's stages of ego
        development, 544–545, 556,
        557–559
    Mahler's stages of childhood, 98–99
    Pearson on the hero myth, 111–113
    personology and, 614–615
    of perspective-taking, 565, 566
    research on, 156–165
    of self as I, 540–548
    of self-understanding, 584–585
Diagnostic council, 598
Dialectical humanism, 93–94
Dialectical reasoning, 470–472
Dialogical self, 770–777
Differentiation, 522
Differentiation of body image, 98
Difficult babies, 296
Discourse, 782
Discriminant stimuli, 319
Disorganized attachment pattern, 230
Displacement, 84, 119–120, 133
Display rules, 740
Dizygotic twins, 300–307
Dora case, 117–128, 134–135, 138
Double approach-avoidance conflict, 328

Doubt vs. autonomy, 660, 661–662
Downward social comparison, 346
Dream analysis, 131–132, 138–139
Dream work, 132–133
Dreams
    Dora's dream of jewel-case,
        120–124, 138
    Freud on, 131–133, 136, 137
    Jung on, 136–141
    and Jungian personality types, 171
    manifest versus latent content of,
        131–133
    overdetermined content of, 131
Drive reduction, 327
Drives, 181–182, 326
Durances, 606

EASI Temperament Survey, 296, 297
Easy babies, 296
Ego. *See also* headings beginning with
    Self
    defense mechanisms of, 83–85,
        152–156
    ego psychologists on, 87–89
    S. Freud on, 82–85, 87
    A. Freud on, 88
    Hartmann on, 88
    Loevinger on, 542–545
    White on, 88–89
Ego and Mechanisms of Defense, The (A.
    Freud), 88
Ego and the Id, The (Freud), 64
Ego control, 379, 382
Ego identity, 20. *See also* Identity
Ego psychologists, 86–89
Ego resiliency, 382
Egoistic motivation, 214
Eigenwelt, 425
Embedded Figures Test, 523
Emergent self, 552
Emotion. *See also* specific emotions
    during infancy, 740
    facial expressions and, 739–740
    mood-state-dependent memory,
        508–510
    in personality psychology, 797–798
    self-discrepancies and agitation-
        related emotions, 573–577
    thinking and, 508–510
    Tomkins' script theory and, 736–740
Empathy, and altruism, 214–215
Empirical study, 37–39
Encoding, 329, 487
Energy sources, 181
Enterprise of Living, The (White), 611
Environmentalism, and behaviorism,
    314–315
Environmentally labile, 182
Environmentally stable, 182
Episodes, and social intelligence,
    490–491
Episodic memory, 487
Equality, 530–532
Equivalence, principle of, 102
Erikson's developmental stages. *See*
    Psychosocial development theory

Erogenous zones, 70–71
Ethic of conscience, 531
Ethic of responsibility, 531
Ethograms, 180
Ethology, 180
Evolution
    aggression and, 206–212
    altruism and, 212–218
    animals' instinctive behavior and,
        180–182
    attachment theory and, 218–238
    evolutionary personality psychology,
        188–191
    huma evolution, 182–184
    instinct and, 180–206
    of love, 218–238
    mating and, 191–202
    socioanalytic theory and shyness,
        202–206
    sociobiology and, 184–188
    survival and reproductive problems
        for humans, 190–191
Evolutionary personality psychology,
    188–191
Exceptionalism, 531
Existential guilt, 431
Existentialism, 424–431, 456. *See also*
    Humanistic themes
Expectancies, 323–324, 329
Experimental design, of research, 41–43
Exploitative character type, 95
Explorations of Personality (Murray),
    601, 615
Extinction, 320
Extraversion
    arousal and, 269–273
    coping strategies associated with,
        287, 288
    description of, 265, 267–274
    Eysenck on, 14, 16
    feeling good and, 267–269
    Jung on, 106–107
    on Myers-Briggs Type Indicator,
        170–171, 174–176
    questionnaire measuring, 14–16
    stability and change in, 272, 274

F Scale, 163
Faces
    attractiveness of women's and men's
        faces, 199–200
    emotions and facial response,
        739–740
Factor analysis, 254
Facts, The (Roth), 731–732
Fairy tales, 724–726, 730
Falsifiable, 37
Family-systems perspective, 402–404
Fantasy, 61–62, 65, 81–82
FAP. *See* Fixed-action pattern (FAP)
Fathers. *See also* Parenting
    attachment and, 231
    of Freud, 58–59
    as idealizing self-object, 100
    Kohut on, 100
    Oedipus complex and, 76–77, 80
Fear and Trembling (Kierkegaard), 431

Fear Survey Schedule, 338, 339
Feedback hierarchy, 519–520
Feedback loop, 487
Feeling. *See* Emotion; and specific
    feelings
Females. *See* Gender
Feminine social clock project, 674–675
Femininity, 500–501. *See also* Gender
Fictional finalism, 694–696
Field dependence, 522–527
Field independence, 522–527
Final goals, 695
Fixations, 71
Fixed-action pattern (FAP), 180–182
Flashbulb memory, 483–485
Flow, 465–467
Flow (Csikszentmihalyi), 465
Folk concepts, 259
Foreclosure, 669, 670–671
Formal operations, 665–666
Fragmenting self, 100
Frau Emmy von N. case, 129
Free association, 119
Freedom, 530–532
Freudian slip, 133
Freudian theory. *See* Psychoanalysis
Friendship, 642–643
Front, 567
Frustration-aggression hypothesis,
    326–328
FSC. *See* Feminine social clock (FSC)
    project
Fully functioning person, 458
Functional analysis, 340
Functions, and Jung's personality types,
    106–107
Fundamental attribution error, 362–363
Fuzzy sets, 369

Gender
    affect intensity and, 283
    attractiveness of women's and men's
        faces, 199–200
    and Erikson's initiative vs. guilt, 662
    feminine social clock project,
        674–675
    field independence-dependence and,
        527
    gender schema theory, 497–504
    grief and, 201–202
    imagoes in life stories, 759–760
    intimacy motivation and, 643–644
    intrusive versus inclusive mode, 662
    masculine occupational clock
        (MOC), 675–676
    masculinity, femininity, and
        androgyny, 500–501
    mating and, 192–202
    myths of Icarus versus Demeter and
        Persephone, 602–604
    Oedipus complex, 76–80
    personality types, 380–383
    power motive and, 633, 636–637
    reproductive strategies and,
        192–193
    in seasons of adult life, 708–713
    self-esteem and, 581

sex differences in reproduction, 201
sex-role stereotypes, 500–501
    and values of competition versus
        cooperation, 409–410
    women with cancer, 435–438
    women's responses to Washington
        University Sentence Completion
        Test for Ego Development
        (WUSCTED), 561
Gender schema theory, 497–504
Generalization, 319
Generalized expectancies, 324
Generative integration, 768
Generativity
    age differences in, 682–684
    Erikson's generativity vs. stagnation,
        96, 660, 678–687
    model of, 678–685
    stories of, 685–687
    types of, 679
Generativity script, 685, 764
Generativity vs. stagnation, 660,
    678–687
Genes, 183–185
Genetic fitness, 185
Genetics
    heritability studies of twins and
        personality traits, 300–307
    infant temperament and, 295–300
    personality traits and, 295–307
Genital stage, 80–81
Goddesses, 109–111, 602–604
Goddesses in Everywoman (Bolen),
    110–111
Gratification delay, 340–343
Grieving, 201–202, 731
Guilford-Zimmerman Temperament
    Survey (GZTS), 263
Guilt
    existential guilt, 431
    field independence and, 526–527
    Kelly on, 476
Guilt vs. initiative, 660, 662
GZTS. *See* Guilford-Zimmerman
    Temperament Survey (GZTS)

Hagiographies, 697
Hallucinatory wish fulfillment, 82
Hardy personality, 445–450
Hare and the Tortoise, The (Barash),
    188
Harlequin Complex, 613–614
Harvard Psychological Clinic, 596–601,
    610
Healing, and stories, 727–736
Health. *See* Illness
Helping. *See* Altruism
Heritability quotient, 302
Heritability studies, and personality
    traits, 300–307
Hermeneutics, 617
Hero Within, The (Pearson), 111–113
Heroes, 104, 111–113
Hierarchical control of behavior,
    516–517
High-level strivers, 515–516
Higher-order conditioning, 317

History, 408–410, 605, 721
Hoarding character type, 95
Hostile aggression, 206–207
Humanistic psychology
    criticisms of, 791
    definition of, 455
    examples of humanistic research,
        463–468
    Maslow's psychology of being,
        459–463
    Rogers' theory of, 456–459
Humanistic themes
    absurd and, 428–430
    consciousness as primary in,
        424–425
    control, 433–440
    creation of self, 425–427
    examples of humanistic research,
        463–468
    existentialism, 424–431
    freedom, control, and challenge,
        431–455
    hardy personality, 445–450
    humanistic psychology, 455–468
    introduction to, 423
    Kelly as bridge to cognitive
        psychology, 469, 472–480
    Kelly's personal constructs, 473–480
    Maslow's psychology of being, 17,
        459–463
    personal causation and control,
        433–438
    phenomenology, 425
    responsibility for personal
        development, 430–431
    reversal theory, 450–455
    Rogers' theory, 456–459
    Role Construct Repertory Test (Rep
        Test), 477–480
    Rychlak's logical learning theory,
        470–472
    self-determination theory, 440–445
Hypotheses, 35, 37
Hysteria
    Anna O. case, 60, 129
    Breuer's work on, 60–61
    Charcot's study of, 60
    Dora case, 117–128, 134–135
    Freud on, 60–61

I. *See* Self as I
I-E Scale, 439–440
I-Thou encounter, 427, 463, 640
Icarus complex, 591–596, 602–604, 613
Id, 81–82, 88
Identification, 11–12, 153, 154
Identity
    Erikson on, 548, 557, 655, 696, 746
    Erikson's stage of identity vs. role
        confusion, 663–671, 709–711
    historical perspectives on, 766–767
    intimacy and, 671–677
    life story model of, 745–768
    statuses of, 668–671, 677
*Identity: Cultural Change and the
    Struggle for Self* (Baumeister), 766
Identity achievement, 669–670

Identity diffusion, 669, 671
Identity statuses, 668–671, 677
Identity vs. role confusion, 663–671,
    709–711
Idiographic approach, 45, 770, 773
Illness, 435–438, 448, 449, 515–516,
    636–637
Illusion of control, 435
Imagery, 752–753
Imagoes, 754–760
Implicit learning, 143, 144
Implicit memory, 143, 144
Implicit motives, 645
Implicit perception, 143, 144
Implicit personality theory, 363, 490
Implicit thought, 143, 144
Impression management, 203, 567–568
Imprinting, 220–221
Impulsive stage, of ego development,
    555–556
Impulsivity, 280–283
Incentives, 572
Inclusive mode, 662
Independent variable, 41
Individual differences, 4
Individual psychology
    Adler on, 688–689
    Adler's fictional finalism, 694–696
    criticisms of, 793
    earliest memory and, 689–694
Individualism, 409–410
Individualistic stage, of ego
    development, 559
Individuation, 107
Induction, 33–34
Indulgent-permissive style of parenting,
    356
Industry vs. inferiority, 660, 662–663
Infancy
    A-babies, 223–225
    Allport's proprium and, 540–541
    attachment in, 219–222
    B-babies, 223–225
    C-babies, 223–225
    D-babies, 230
    difficult babies, 296
    easy babies, 296
    emotions during, 740
    empathy in, 214–215
    Erikson's stage of, 660, 661
    and S. Freud's stages of
        psychosexual development, 71
    Kegan's evolving self and, 545, 546
    Mahler's object relations perspective
        on, 98
    self as I during, 548–555
    self-determination in, 443
    separation anxiety in, 221–222
    slow-to-warm-up babies, 296
    stranger anxiety in, 221–222
    Sullivan's self-system and, 541–542
    temperament in, 282, 295–297, 300
Infanticide, 208
Inferiority vs. industry, 660, 662–663
Information, 487
Information processing, unconscious,
    142–145

Initiative vs. guilt, 660, 662
Insecure attachment, 223–234
Instincts. *See also* Sexual instinct
    animals' instinctive behavior,
        180–182
    death instincts, 66–68
    definition of, 182
    evolution and, 180–206
    Freud on, 59–60, 66–68
    life instincts, 66
Instrumental aggression, 206–207
Instrumental conditioning, 319–323
Instrumental values, 530
Integrated stage, of ego development, 559
Integration
    definition of, in cognitive
        psychology, 522
    generative integration, 768
    stories and, 727–736
Integrative complexity, 528–533
Integrity vs. despair, 687–688
Interaction episodes. *See also*
    Personality traits; Social learning
    creativity and, 24–25
    as perspective on person, 13–17, 28,
        788
Interaction of person and environment
    aggregating behaviors, 372–377
    comlexity of behavior, 364–385
    contextual nature of behavior,
        388–410
    current thinking on, 410–416
    macrocontexts, 402–410
    Mischel's critique, 361–364
    modern interactionism, 395–402
    and nature of situation, 390–395
    patterns of traits over time,
        377–385
    and prediction of behavior, 366–372
Interactional continuity, 401–402
Interactional synchrony, 226
Interactionism
    anxiety and, 398–400
    mechanistic interactionism, 396
    modern interactionism, 395–402
    in personality psychology, 798
    persons versus situations versus
        interactions, 396–398
    reciprocal interactionism, 400–402
Internalized objects, 96–98, 165–170
Interpersonal circumplex, 293–295
Interpersonal stories. *See also*
    Biography; Life stories; Motivation
    creativity and, 26–27
    as perspective on person, 19–22,
        28–29, 788
Interpretation of Dreams, The (Freud),
    63
Interpretive structures. *See also*
    Cognitive psychology; Humanistic
    themes; Self, creativity and, 25–26 as
    perspective on person, 17–19, 28–29,
    788
Intimacy. *See also* Love
    Erikson's intimacy vs. isolation,
        671–677
    identity and, 671–677

Intimacy motivation, 637, 640–644
Intimacy status, 672–673, 677
Intimacy vs. isolation, 671–677
Intrapsychic mysteries. *See also*
  Evolution; Psychoanalysis
    creativity and, 22–24
    definition of, 50
    as perspective on person, 10–13, 28,
      787
Intrinsic motivation, 440–443
Introversion
  compared with extraversion, 14,
    267–274
  Jung on, 106–107
  on Myers-Briggs Type Indicator,
    170–171, 174–176
Intrusive mode, 662
Involvement, 444
Isolation vs. intimacy, 671–677
Item analysis, 254

JAS. *See* Jenkins Activity Survey (JAS)
Jenkins Activity Survey (JAS), 387
Journal of Personality, 44
Jungian psychology. *See* Analytical
  psychology

Kin selection, 213

Laboratory observation, 180, 338
Latency, 80
Latent level, in psychoanalytic
  interpretation, 131–136
Leadership, 631–633
Learned-helplessness theory,
  reformulated, 507, 510
Learning. *See also* Social-learning
  theories
    behaviorism and, 315–323
    classical conditioning, 316–318
    implicit learning, 143, 144
    instrumental conditioning, 319–323
    observational learning, 330–333
    Rychlak's logical learning theory,
      470–472
Letters from Jenny (Allport), 251
Libido, 66–67, 68, 102–103
Life histories, 706–708
Life instincts, 66
Life scripts
  concepts pertaining to, 740–742
  criticisms of Tomkins' script theory,
    793
  scenes in, 741–742
  scripts in, 741–742
  Tomkins' script theory, 736–745,
    793
  types of scripts, 742–745
Life situations, 390
Life stories. *See also* Biography
  affects and, 738–740
  characters in, 754–760
  example of, 717–719
  Gregg's approach using music and
    story, 777–780
  and healing and integration,
    727–736

Hermans' dialogical self, 770–777
  imagery of, 752–753
  imagoes in, 754–760
  lives as texts, 768–783
  meaning of stories, 719–736
  in midlife, 760–765, 768
  model of identity from, 745–768
  narrative mind and, 720–723
  nature of stories, 723–727
  postmodern self and, 781–783
  relation between stories and human
    lives, 748–749
  themes of, 753–754
  Tomkins' script theory, 736–745
  tone of, 749–752
Life-story-making process, 557
Life structure, 709
Life tasks, 493, 513
Life themes, 707–708
Literature, 532, 533, 599–601, 614–615,
  666, 723, 724–726, 730, 748–749, 777,
  781. *See also* Myths
Little Albert case, 316–317
Little Hans case, 129
Lives in Progress (White), 611
Lives of the Noble Greeks and Romans
  (Plutarch), 697
Locus of control, 438–440, 449
Logical learning theory, 470–472
Logotherapy, 431–432
Looking glass self, 564
Lord of the Flies (Golding), 179
Love. *See also* headings beginning with
  Intimacy
    adult attachments and, 235–238
    attachment theory, 218–238,
      291–293
    Big Five personality traits and,
      291–293
    intimacy motivation, 637, 640–644
    power motive and, 633, 636–637
Low-level strivers, 515–516

Macrocontexts, of behavior, 402–410
Macrosystems, 404
Maintenance system, of culture, 408
Males. *See* Gender
Mandala, 109
Manifest level, in psychoanalytic
  interpretation, 131–136
Marketing character type, 95
Masculine occupational clock (MOC),
  675–676
Masculinity, 500–501. *See also* Gender
Masturbation, 123, 123n
Material Me, 537
Mating
  evolution and, 191–202
  gender differences in, 192–202
  sociosexuality and, 194–197
  tactics of mate attraction, 200–201
MBTI. *See* Myers-Briggs Type Indicator
  (MBTI)
Me. *See* Self as Me
Measurement
  of achievement motive, 622–625
  behavioral assessment, 336–340

construction of trait measure,
  249–249, 252–255
criteria of good trait measure,
  255–258
personality inventories, 258–263
of personality traits, 248–263
of self as I, 560–562
Mechanistic interactionism, 396
Melancholic type of person, 276
Memory
  autobiographical memory, 490–491
  earliest memory, 689–694
  episodic memory, 487
  flashbulb memory, 483–485
  implicit memory, 143, 144
  long-term memory, 487
  mood-state-dependent memory,
    508–510
  person memory, 490
  semantic memory, 487
  short-term memory, 487
Men. *See* Gender
Mentor, 710–711
Metatraits, 371–372
Middle-level units, 512–513
Midlife, 712–713, 760–765, 768
Midlife Crisis Scale, 713
Midlife Transition, 712–713
Mind, Freud's structural model of, 81–86
Minnesota Multiphasic Personality
  Inventory (MMPI), 258–259
Mistrust vs. trust, 660, 661
Mitwelt, 425
MMPI. *See* Minnesota Multiphasic
  Personality Inventory (MMPI)
Moby Dick (Melville), 599–601, 614
MOC. *See* Masculine occupational clock
  (MOC)
Model, in science, 35
Modeling, of aggression, 346–347, 351
Moderator variables, 365, 366–367, 371
Modern interactionism, 395–402
Monozygotic twins, 300–307
Mood-state-dependent memory, 508–510
Moody Problem Checklist, 338
Moral anxiety, 68
Moratorium, 669, 670
Mothers. *See also* Parenting
  and attachment in infancy, 219–222
  of Freud, 57–58
  Horney on motherhood, 89–90
  as idealizing self-object, 100
  as Jungian archetype, 103, 104, 105
  Kohut on, 100
  mirroring relationship with, 100
  Oedipus complex and, 76–80
  and secure and insecure
    attachments, 223–234
Motivation
  achievement motivation, 622–629
  affiliation motive, 644
  altruistic motivation, 214
  criticisms of Murray's and
    McClelland's approaches to, 792
  egoistic motivation, 214
  historical perspectives on study of,
    44

Icarus complex and, 591–596
implicit motives, 645
intimacy motivation, 637, 640–644
intrinsic motivation, 440443
Kelly on, 473, 512
and Murray's personology, 596–620, 792
perspectives on, 644–647
power motive, 629–637
reversal theory of, 450–455
self-attributed motives, 645
Thematic Apperception Test (TAT) and, 620–622
Motivational tendencies, 182
"Mourning and Melancholia" (Freud), 96–97
Movies, 638–640
MPQ. *See* Multidimensional Personality Questionnaire (MPQ)
Multidimensional Personality Questionnaire (MPQ), 286
Music, 777–780
Myers-Briggs Type Indicator (MBTI), 170–171, 174–176
Myths
compared with human lives, 748
Demeter and Persephone, 602–604
Icarus complex, 591–596, 602–604
Jugian meanings of, 109–113, 136–141
personal myth, 747

Naked Ape, The (Morris), 179
Narcissism, 67, 99–101, 172–174, 593–595, 772–776
Narrative knowing, 769
Narrative mode, 722–723
Narrative psychology, 659, 769
Narrative tone, 749–752
Narrative truth, 617, 721
Natural attitude, 425
Natural selection, 183
Naturalistic observation, 180, 338
Need hierarchy, 460
Needs
Freud on, 607
Fromm on, 94
Maslow's need hierarchy, 460
Murray on, 606–609
Negative affect, 277, 282–283
Negative correlation, 39
Negative identities, 669, 670
Negative reinforcement, 320
Neglecting style of parenting, 356
Neurotic anxiety, 68
Neuroticism
coping strategies associated with, 287, 288
description of, 274–279
Freud on neurosis, 119
Horney on neurotic conflicts, 91–92
Nomological network, 256
Nomothetic approach, 45, 770, 772–773
Nonadditive genetic variance, 304–305
Nonbeing, 426
Nonconscious social information processing, 142–143

North by Northwest, 638
Notes from Underground (Dostoyevsky), 145
Nuclear episodes, 755–756
Nuclear scene, 744–745
Nuclear script, 743–744

O-motives, 771
Object choice, 11–12, 67
Object relations
description of, 87, 96–99
five levels of, 167, 168–169
internalized objects, 165–170
research on, 165–170
Objects, 96
Observation
behaviorism and, 313
laboratory observation, 180, 338
naturalistic observation, 180, 338
in science, 32–34
Observational learning, 330–333
Obsession neurosis, 130
Odyssey (Homer), 750
Oedipus complex
compared with Erikson's stages, 662
definition of, 59
Freud on, 73, 76–77, 80
in Freud's life, 58–59
gender and, 76–80, 123–125
Horney on, 91
Oedipus Rex (Sophocles), 73–76, 744
Office of Strategic Services (OSS), 610
On the Origin of the Species (Darwin), 182–183
Ontological strategies, 747, 749
Openness to experience, 284–288
Operant conditioning, 319–323
Optimism, 493–494
Oral-passive personality, 71, 157
Oral personality, 71, 157–159
Oral-sadistic personality, 71
Oral stage, 71
Oresteia, 744
Organ inferiorities, 694
Organismic enhancement, 457
Organismic integration, 444
Organismic valuing process, 458
OSS. *See* Office of Strategic Services (OSS)
Other
generalized other, 564, 566
self and, 564–566
Outliving the Self (Kotre), 685–687
Overburdened self, 101
Overdetermined content of dream, 131
Overstimulated self, 100

Paradigm, 182, 789
Paradigmatic mode, 722
Parallel distributed processing (PDP), 143
Parenting. *See also* Fathers; Mothers
authoritarian style of, 356
authoritative-reciprocal style of, 355–356
indulgent-permissive style of, 356
neglecting style of, 356

self-esteem and, 581
social class differences in, 404–405
styles of, 354–356
and values of competition versus cooperation, 409–410
Partial reinforcement, 321–322
Pattern-matching plan, 616–617
Pavlovian conditioning. *See* Classical conditioning
PDP. *See* Parallel distributed processing (PDP)
Peak experiences, 462–463, 465–468
Peak performance, 468
Penis envy, 77
Perception
implicit perception, 143, 144
of situations, 391–393
Perceptual defense, 145
Performance, 567
Persephone and Demeter myth, 602–604
Person. *See also* Identity; Personality psychology; Self
creativity and, 22–27
definition of, 3
as integrated totality, 3
interaction episodes as perspective on, 13–17, 28, 787–788
interpersonal stories as perspective on, 19–22, 28–29, 788
interpretive structures as perspective on, 17–19, 28–29, 788
intrapsychic mysteries as perspective on, 10–13, 28, 787
M. Mead as example of, 7–10, 13–14, 16–17, 19–22
Y. Mishima as example of, 4–7, 10–13, 17–19
no single best perspective on, 789
questions of personality psychology, 786–787
scientific study of, 27, 29–43
similarities and differences among different persons, 3–4, 799
White's study of ordinary American adults, 30–31
Person memory, 490
Persona, 105
Personal causation, and control, 433–438
Personal construct psychology, 17
Personal constructs
definition of, 18, 475
Kelly's psychology of, 473–476
Role Construct Repertory Test (Rep Test), 477–480
Personal fables, 747, 749
Personal myth, 746
Personal Orientation Inventory (POI), 464
Personal projects, 513–514
Personal strivings, 514–516
Personal unconscious, 103
Personal work ethic, 345
Personality: A Psychological Interpretation (Allport), 44
Personality and Assessment (Mischel), 361

Personality inventories, 258–263
Personality psychology. *See also*
  Biography; Cognitive psychology;
  Developmental stages; Humanistic
  psychology; Individual psychology;
  Life stories; Psychoanalysis;
  Psychosocial development theory;
  Social-learning theories
  choice of perspective on, 794–796
  definition of, 4
  emphases of, 43, 45–46
  evolutionary personality psychology,
    188–191
  history of, 44–46
  interaction episodes as perspective
    in, 13–17, 28, 787–788
  interpersonal stories as perspective
    in, 19–22, 28–29, 788
  interpretive structures as
    perspective on, 17–19, 28–29, 788
  intrapsychic mysteries as
    perspective in, 10–13, 28, 787
  no single best perspective on, 789
  nomothetic versus idiographic
    approach to, 45
  questions in, 786–787
  strengths and weaknesses of
    different perspectives, 790–794
  themes in, 796–799
Personality Research Form (PRF),
  262–263, 265
Personality traits
  act-frequency approach to, 368–370
  aggregating behaviors and, 372–377,
    412
  agreeableness, 288–293
  Allport on, 250–251, 264, 368, 410
  anxiety, 280–283
  basic traits, 263–295
  Big Five, 265, 266, 413–416
  Cattell on, 249, 251–253
  and complexity of behavior, 364–385
  conscientiousness, 288–293
  construction of trait measure,
    249–249, 252–255
  criteria of good measure for,
    255–258
  criticisms of, 791
  critique of, 410–416
  definition of, 248–249
  environmental influences on,
    305–306
  example of, 245–248
  extraversion, 265, 267–274
  Eysenck on, 274–276, 281–283
  genetics and, 295–307
  Gray's approach on impulsivity and
    anxiety, 280–283
  heritability studies and, 300–307
  impulsivity, 280–283
  in infancy, 282, 295–300
  interpersonal circumplex, 293–295
  longitudinal consistency of, 412
  measurement of, 248–263
  for men and women, 380–383
  metatraits, 371–372
  Mischel on, 361–364, 410–411

motives compared with, 645–646
  Murray on, 607
  neuroticism, 274–279
  openness to experience, 284–288
  patterns of, over time, 377–385
  personality inventories, 258–263
  and prediction of behavior, 366–372
Personality types
  anal personality, 72–73
  authoritarian personality, 162–164
  Eysenck on, 274–276, 281–283
  Fromm on, 95–96
  Galen on, 275–276
  Jung on, 106–107, 170–176
  for men and women, 380–383
  oral personality, 71, 157–159
  psychosexual types, 71, 72–73,
    157–161, 164–165
  Stewart's system, 159–161, 164–165
  Type A/B personality, 386–389
Personifications, 542
Personologists, 4
Personology
  after World War II, 610–615
  case study and, 615–620
  during World War II, 610–611
  growth trends in human personality,
    614–615
  Murray and Harvard Psychological
    Clinic, 596–601
  Murray on, 596–620
  Murray's system of, 601, 604–610
  principles of, 612–614
  study of lives, 610–620
Phallic stage, 73–77, 80
Phenomenal field, 456–457
Phenomenology, 425, 456. *See also*
  Humanistic themes
Phlegmatic type of person, 275
Plan, definition of, 487
Pleasant Events Schedule, 339
Pleasure principle, 81
POI. *See* Personal Orientation Inventory
  (POI)
Polygyny, 192–193
Polyphonic novel, 777
Pornography, 502–504
Portraits of Type (Thorne and Gough), 171
Positive affect, 267–269, 282–283
Positive correlation, 39
Positive reinforcement, 311–312, 320
Possible selves, 571–573
Postmodern self, 781–783
Power hierarchy, in family system, 403
Power motive
  correlates of high power motivation,
    631
  definition of, 629
  health and, 636–637
  leadership, 631–633
  love and, 633, 636
  TAT categories for, 629–630
Practicing, 98
Preconscious, 69–70
Preoperational thinking, 752–753
*Presentation of Self in Everyday Life,
  The* (Goffman), 567

Press, 609
PRF. *See* Personality Research Form
  (PRF)
Primary-process thought, 81–82
Principle of equivalence, 102
Private self-consciousness, 497
Problem checklists, 338
Procedural knowledge, 491–492
Proceeding, 605–606
Productive character type, 96
Projection, 83, 84, 85, 153, 154
Projective system, of culture, 408–409,
  627
Projective test, 157, 621
Propriate strivings, 541
Proprium, 540–541
Prosocial behavior, 352–353. *See also*
  Altruism
Protective stage, of ego development, 556
Prototype, 487
Prototypicality gradient hypothesis, 369
Psycho, 638, 639
Psychoanalysis
  after Freud, 65, 86–113
  anal stage in, 72–73
  Anna O. case, 60, 129
  behaviorism integrated with,
    326–328
  conflict in, 68
  criticisms of, 790
  determinism in, 66–68
  developmental stages of sexual
    instinct, 70–77, 80–81, 156–159
  Dora case, 117–128, 134–135, 138
  dream analysis in, 131–132
  dream work in, 132–133
  ego in, 82–85
  ego psychology and, 86–89
  Erikson and psychoanalytic tradition,
    656–659
  European setting affecting, 53–57
  feminist reinterpretations of, 77–80
  Frau Emmy von N. case, 129
  S. Freud on, 65–77, 80–86
  A. Freud on, 88
  and S. Freud's life story, 53–62, 65
  S. Freud's writings on, 63–64
  Fromm on, 92–96
  genital stage in, 80–81
  Hartmann on, 88
  Horney on, 89–92
  id in, 81–82
  internalized objects in, 165–170
  Jung's analytical psychology,
    101–113, 136–141, 170–176
  Kohut on, 99–101
  latency in, 80
  Little Hans case, 129
  Mahler on, 98–99
  main tenets of, 65–70
  manifest and latent level in
    psychoanalytic interpretation,
    131–133
  myth and symbol in Jungian
    psychology, 136–141
  object relations and, 87, 96–99,
    165–170

oral stage in, 71
phallic stage in, 73–77, 80
Rat Man case, 130
and research on developmental
    stages, 156–165
Romanticism and, 54–55
science, reason, morality and, 55–56
self psychology and, 87, 99–101
significance of, 52–53
social-psychological theories and,
    87, 89–96
structural model of the mind, 81–86
superego in, 85–86
symptoms and everyday life in,
    133–136
text and treaty in psychoanalytic
    interpretation, 130–131
unconscious in, 69–70, 141–152
White on, 88–89
World War I and, 57
Psychobiography, 697–706
Psychodynamic Activation Method,
    149–151
Psychogenic needs, 607, 608–609
Psychological androgyny, 500–501
Psychological magnification, 742
Psychological Types (Jung), 596
Psychology of Personal Constructs
    (Kelly), 469, 472, 473
Psychopathology of Everyday Life, The
    (Freud), 63, 136
Psychophyiological measures, 338
Psychosexual stages. *See* Sexual instinct
Psychosocial development theory
    autonomy versus shame and doubt,
        660, 661–662
    criticisms of, 793
    generativity vs. stagnation, 660,
        678–687
    identity vs. role confusion, 663–671
    industry vs. inferiority, 660,
        662–663
    initiative vs. guilt, 660, 662
    integrity vs. despair, 687–688
    intimacy vs. isolation, 671–677
    psychoanalytic tradition and,
        656–659
    stages of, 660–688
    trust vs. mistrust, 660, 661
Punishment, in operant conditioning,
    319, 320

R data, 377, 378
Race, 405–408, 581
Raiders of the Lost Ark, 751
Range of convenience, 475–476
Rapprochement, 98
RAS. *See* Reticular activating system
    (RAS)
Rat Man case, 130
Rating scales, 249
Rationalization, 84
Reaction formation, 84
Realistic anxiety, 68
Reality principle, 82–83
Rear Window, 638, 640
Receptive character type, 95

Reciprocal altruism, 213
Reciprocal determinism, 335–336
Reciprocal interactionism, 400–402
Reformulated learned-helplessness
    theory, 507, 510
Regression, 84
Reinforcement
    conditioned generalized reinforcers,
        323
    continuous reinforcement, 321–322
    drive reduction and, 327
    negative reinforcement, 320
    in operant conditioning, 319–323
    partial reinforcement, 321–322
    positive reinforcement, 311–312,
        320
Reinforcement value, 324
Reliability
    in case studies, 615–616
    in personality testing, 256
Religion, 186–187
Rep Test, 477–480
Representations of Interactions that
    have been Generalized (RIGS), 553
Repression, 68, 84, 141–142, 145–149
Repressive personality style, 515–516
Repressors, 146–149
Reproduction, sex differences in, 201
Reproduction of Mothering, The
    (Chodorow), 78–80
Research. *See* Science
Resistant behavior, in babies, 225
Response, 316, 326
Reticular activating system (RAS), 269
Reversal of affect, 119
Reversal theory, 450–455
Rewards, 322, 323, 440–441
RIGS. *See* Representations of
    Interactions that have been
    Generalized (RIGS)
Rogerian psychology. *See* Humanistic
    psychology
Rokeach Value Survey, 530–531
Role confusion vs. identity, 663–671,
    709–711
Role Construct Repertory Test (Rep
    Test), 477–480
Role playing, 203
Role structure, 203
Romanticism, 54–55
Root metaphor, 769
Rope, 640
Rorschach Inkblot Test, 157, 167,
    336–337, 621
Routine, definition of, 567
Rules, and social intelligence, 491–492

S data, 377, 378
S-motives, 771
"S-R Inventory of General Trait
    Anxiousness," 399
Sanguine type of person, 275
Satan, personality and career of, 613
Saturated Self, The (Gergen), 782
Scenes, 741
Schema-irrelevant, 496
Schema-relevant, 496

Schemata
    definition of, 487, 494
    depressive schemata, 504–507,
        510–511
    gender schemata, 497–504
    self as Me as, 571
    self-schemata, 494–497
Schizophrenia, 3
Science
    case study and, 615–620
    correlational design, 39–41
    empirical study, 37–39
    evaluation of propositions in, 36–43
    experimental design, 41–43
    Freud's view of, 59–60
    perspective of, 28–29, 32
    psychoanalysis and, 55–56
    steps in, 32–43
    theory building in, 34–36
    unsystematic observation as step in,
        32–34
Scripts, 17, 487, 490, 519–520, 741–745
Seasons of adult life, 708–713
Secondary-process thought, 82–83
Secure attachment, 223–234
Seduction hypothesis, 61–62
Self. *See also* Ego
    bipolar self, 100
    cognition and, 797
    core self, 553
    dialogical self, 770–777
    discrepancies among selves,
        573–577
    emergent self, 552
    Freud on, 539
    interpretive structures and, 17
    Jung on, 539
    Kohut on, 99–101, 539
    looking glass self, 564
    Maslow on, 539
    object-relations theorists on, 539
    and other, 564–566
    possible selves, 571–573
    postmodern self, 781–783
    Rogers on, 539
    self-creation of, 425–427
    social intelligence and, 490
    subjective self, 553, 555
    verbal self, 555
Self as I
    adolescent I, 557–558
    adult I, 558–560
    Allport's proprium, 540–541
    assessment of, 560–562
    characteristics of, 539–540
    child I, 554–556
    description of, 562–563
    development of, 540–548
    infant I, 548–555
    James on, 536, 538–539
    Kegan's evolving self, 545–548
    Loevinger's ego, 542–545
    Sullivan's self-system, 541–542
Self as Me
    development of, 583–585
    discrepancies among selves,
        573–577

Self as Me *(cont.)*
    Goffman on, 566–568, 570
    James on, 536–539, 564, 570–571
    material Me, 537
    multiplicity of the Me, 570–583
    possible selves, 571–573
    self and other, 564–566
    self-with-other, 577–579, 582–583
    Selman's stages of perspective-
      taking, 565, 566
    social Me, 537–538
    social nature of, 566–569
    spiritual Me, 538
Self-actualization, 96, 460, 461, 462,
    464–468
Self-as-knower, 541
Self-attributed motives, 645
Self-confrontation method, 771–772
Self-consciousness, private, 497
Self-determination theory, 440–445
Self-discrepancy theory, 573–577
Self-efficacy, 333–335
Self-esteem, 541, 580–581
Self-evaluation, 572
Self-extension, 541
Self-identity, 541
Self-involvement, 443
Self-monitoring, 338, 568–569
Self-objects, 100
Self psychology, 87, 99–101
Self-recognition, 549–551
Self-regard, 458
Self-regulation
    in cognitive psychology, 517–519
    definition of, 340
    delay of gratification, 340–343
    individual differences and personal
      work ethic, 343–345
    Mischel on, 329
Self-report questionnaires, 249
Self-Representation (Gregg), 777
Self-schemata, 494–497
Self-system, 541–542
Self-understanding, 583–585
Self-with-other, 577–579, 582–583
Semai of Malaysia, 208–210
Semantic memory, 487
Sensation seeking, 272, 273
Separation anxiety, 221–222
Separation-individuation, 98
Seppuku, 4–7, 10–13, 18–19
Serial programs, 606
Serials, 606
Sex differences. *See* Gender
Sex-role stereotypes, 500–501
Sexual abuse of children, 61–62,
    118–119
Sexual instinct
    anal stage of, 72–73, 156–157
    Freud on, 70–77, 80–81
    genital stage of, 80–81, 156–157
    latency in, 80, 156
    oral stage of, 71, 156–157
    phallic stage of, 73–77, 80, 156
Shadow, 105–106
Shame, and field dependence, 526–527
Shame vs. autonomy, 660, 661–662
Shaping, 321

Short-term memory, 487
Shyness, 202–206, 204–206, 296
Sign stimulus, 181
Situational events, 390
Situational prototypes, 392
Situational stimuli, 390
Situational variables, 413
Situationism, 363–364, 531
Situationist critique, 357
Situationists, definition of, 14
Situations
    nature of, 390–395
    traits and, 410–416
Slow-to-warm-up babies, 296
Social class, as macrosystem, 404–405
Social clock, 674–676, 761–763
Social Contract, The (Ardrey), 179
Social desirability, 257–258
Social ecology, 389–390
Social intelligence, 488–494
Social interest, 695
Social-learning theories
    aggression and, 345–352
    altruism, prosocial behavior and,
      352–353
    of Bandura, 330–336
    criticisms of, 791
    definition of, 323
    Mischel on cognitive/social
      learning/person variables,
      324–325, 329
    observational learning, 330–333
    personality and, 353, 357–358
    reciprocal determinism, 335–336
    Rotter on expectancies and values,
      323–324
    self-efficacy and, 333–335
    self-regulation, 340–345
    situationist critique in, 357
Social-psychological theories, 87, 89–96
Social Readjustment Rating Scale,
    445–447
Socioanalytic theory
    definition of, 202
    description of, 202–203
    shyness and, 204–206
Sociobiology
    aggression and, 206–212
    altruism and, 212–218
    criticisms of, 790
    definition of, 184
    description of, 184–188
    of mating, 191–202
Sociobiology: A New Synthesis (Wilson),
    184
Sociosexuality, 194–197
Species-typical characteristics, 4
Spiritual Me, 538
Split-half reliability, 256
Stagnation vs. generativity, 660,
    678–687
Star Wars, 750
State anxiety, 399–400
Stimulation rewards, 322, 323
Stimulus, 316
Stimulus barrier, 98
Stimulus generalization, 317
Stimulus hunger, 14

Stories. *See also* Biography;
    Interpersonal stories; Life stories;
    Motivation
    in Bali, 728–730
    characteristics of, 723–727
    and healing and integration,
      727–736
    narrating mind and, 720–723
    relation with human lives, 748–749
Story grammar, 724
Storytelling, 720–723
Strange Situation, 223–225
Stranger anxiety, 221–222
Stress, 445, 448–450
Striving for superiority, 694–695
Studies in Hysteria (Breuer and Freud),
    61, 63
Study of lives, 610–620
Study of Lives, The (White), 611
Style of life, 690
Subception, 459
Subject-object balance, 545
Subjective self, 553, 555
Subjective values, Mischel on, 329
Subjectivism, 531
Sublimation, 24, 84
Subsidiation, 607
Suicide, 4–7, 10–13, 18–19, 521
Superego, 76, 77, 85–86
Superiority, striving for, 694–695
Survey of Ethical Attitudes, 531
Symbiosis, 552
Symbiosis, normal, 98
Symbols
    definition of, 137
    in dream work, 133
    Jungian meanings of, 136–141
Synchrony, 226

T data, 377, 378
Tabula rasa doctrine, 314–315
TAS. *See* Tellegen Absorption Scale
    (TAS)
TAT. *See* Thematic Apperception Test
    (TAT)
Television violence, 347–351
Telic Dominance Scale, 454
Tellegen Absorption Scale (TAS), 286
Telosponse, 470–472
Temperament
    definition of, 296
    of infants, 282, 295–297, 300
Template-matching approach, 394–395
Tension-reduction, 607
Terminal drop, 532
Terminal values, 530
Testable hypotheses, 37
Testosterone, and aggression, 211–212
Test-retest reliability, 256
Text. *See also* Life stories
    Gregg's approach using music and
      story, 777–780
    Hermans' dialogical self, 770–777
    lives as texts, 768–783
    postmodern self and, 781–783
    in psychoanalytic interpretation,
      130–131
Themes, 606, 609–610

Thematic Apperception Test (TAT), 159, 167, 170, 591, 604, 620–625, 629–630, 641–646
Theory, 34–36
Thought, implicit, 143, 144. *See also* Cognitive psychology
Three Essays on the Theory of Sexuality (Freud), 63
Thrownness, 425–426
Topographical model, of human functioning, 69–70
Total situation, 390
Totem and Taboo (Freud), 63–64, 76
Trait anxiety, 399–400
Trait psychologists
    criticisms of, 791
    definition of, 14
Traits. *See* Personality traits
Transcendent function, 108, 560, 688
Transference, 125–128
Treaty, in psychoanalytic interpretation, 130–131
Trickster, 104
Triple bookkeeping, 658
Trust vs. mistrust, 660, 661
Twin studies, and personality traits, 300–307
Type A personality, 386–389
Type B personality, 387–389

Umwelt, 425
Unconditional positive regard, 458
Unconditioned response, 316
Unconditioned stimulus, 316

Unconscious
    activation of, 149–152
    cognitive aspects of, 143, 144
    collective unconscious, 103, 139–140
    definition of, 69
    Erikson on, 658
    Freud on, 69–70, 658
    intrapsychic mysteries as, 11
    Jung on, 103
    Kelly on, 476
    personal unconscious, 103
    repression studies and, 145–149
    research on, 141–152
    unconscious information processing, 142–145
Unconscious information processing, 142–145
Understimulated self, 100
Unity-thema, 610, 696
Upset rating, 153, 155–156
Urethral erotism, 593, 594
Utilitarianism, 316

Vacuum behavior, 181
Validity
    construct validity, 255–256
    external validity of case studies, 618, 619
    in personality testing, 275
Valuation, 771
Value plurality, 529–532
Values
    cognitive psychology and, 530–531

    instrumental values, 530
    terminal values, 530
Variables
    moderator variables, 365, 366–367, 371
    in research, 41–42
    situational variables, 413
Verbal self, 555
Vertigo, 640
Violence. *See* Aggression
Viscerogenic needs, 607
Volunteerism, 216–218

Waiting for Godot (Beckett), 724
Walden Two (Skinner), 310–312, 342–343, 362
Washington University Sentence Completion Test for Ego Development (WUSCTED), 560–562
When Bad Things Happen to Good People (Kushner), 731
When Harry Met Sally, 750
Will to meaning, 436
Will to power, 694
Wise Old Man, 104
Withdrawal, 671
Women. *See* Gender
Working model, 222
WUSCTED. *See* Washington University Sentence Completion Test for Ego Development (WUSCTED)

Young Man Luther (Erikson), 651–652

Photo Credits

Copyrights and Acknowledgments

Text and Tables

Figures